HANDBOOK OF RESEARCH ON COMPARATIVE HUMAN RESOURCE MANAGEMENT

T0314093

Handbook of Research on Comparative Human Resource Management

Second Edition

Edited by

Chris Brewster

Henley Business School, University of Reading, UK

Wolfgang Mayrhofer

WU Vienna, Austria

Elaine Farndale

School of Labor and Employment Relations, The Pennsylvania State University, USA and Tilburg University, the Netherlands

 Edward Elgar
PUBLISHING

Cheltenham, UK • Northampton, MA, USA

Published by
Edward Elgar Publishing Limited
The Lypiatts
15 Lansdown Road
Cheltenham
Glos GL50 2JA
UK

Edward Elgar Publishing, Inc.
William Pratt House
9 Dewey Court
Northampton
Massachusetts 01060
USA

Paperback edition 2019

A catalogue record for this book
is available from the British Library

Library of Congress Control Number: 2017959498

This book is available electronically in the **Elgar**online
Business subject collection
DOI 10.4337/9781784711139

ISBN 978 1 78471 112 2 (cased)
ISBN 978 1 78471 113 9 (eBook)
ISBN 978 1 78471 136 8 (paperback)

Typeset by Servis Filmsetting Ltd, Stockport, Cheshire
Printed and bound by CPI Group (UK) Ltd, Croydon, CR0 4YY

Contents

Contributors

Ina Aust, Louvain School of Management, Belgium.

Hugh Bainbridge, University of New South Wales, Australia.

Christine Bischoff, University of the Witwatersrand, South Africa.

Tanya Bondarouk, University of Twente, The Netherlands.

Paul Boselie, Utrecht University, The Netherlands.

Anna Bos-Nehles, University of Twente, The Netherlands.

Peter Boxall, University of Auckland, New Zealand.

Julia Brandl, University of Innsbruck, Austria.

Mary Yoko Brannen, University of Victoria, Canada / Copenhagen Business School, Denmark.

Chris Brewster, University of Reading, UK.

Jon Briscoe, Northern Illinois University, USA.

Pawan Budhwar, Aston University, UK.

Heejung Chung, University of Kent, UK.

David G. Collings, Dublin City University, Ireland.

Ngan Collins, RMIT University, Australia.

Gwendolyn Combs, University of Nebraska-Lincoln, USA.

Anabella Davila, Tecnologico de Monterrey, Mexico.

Philippe Debroux, Soka University, Japan.

Michael Dickmann, Cranfield School of Management, UK.

Peter J. Dowling, La Trobe University, Australia.

Marta M. Elvira, IESE Business School, Spain.

Allen D. Engle Sr, Eastern Kentucky University, USA.

Elaine Farndale, The Pennsylvania State University, USA / Tilburg University, The Netherlands.

Marion Festing, ESCP Europe Business School Berlin, Germany.

Stephen Frenkel, University of New South Wales, Australia.

Barry Gerhart, University of Wisconsin-Madison, USA.

Lonnie Golden, The Pennsylvania State University, USA.

Douglas T. (Tim) Hall, Boston University, USA.

Rana Haq, Laurentian University, Canada.

Wes Harry, Cass Business School, UK.

Shigeaki Hayashi, Tokyo Institute of Technology, Japan.

Noreen Heraty, University of Limerick, Ireland.

Michel Hermans, IAE Business School – Universidad Austral, Argentina.

Manjusha Hirekhan, Staffordshire University, UK.

Heh Jason Huang, National Sun Yat-sen University, Taiwan.

Keith Jackson, SOAS, University of London, UK / Doshisha University, Japan.

Susan E. Jackson, Rutgers University, USA.

Andrea Kim, Sungkyunkwan University, South Korea.

Toru Kiyomiya, Seinan Gakuin University, Japan.

Alain Klarsfeld, Toulouse Business School, France.

Mila Lazarova, Simon Fraser University, Canada.

Yih-teen Lee, IESE Business School, Spain.

Paul E.M. Ligthart, Radboud University Nijmegen, The Netherlands.

Jessica A. Los Baños, Universitas Pelita Harapan, Indonesia.

Sergio M. Madero-Gómez, Tecnologico de Monterrey, Mexico.

Wolfgang Mayrhofer, Vienna University of Economics and Business, Austria.

Kamel Mellahi, University of Warwick, UK.

Elham Kamal Metwally, The American University in Cairo, Egypt.

Snejina Michailova, University of Auckland, New Zealand.

Dana Minbaeva, Copenhagen Business School, Denmark.

Fiona Moore, Royal Holloway, University of London, UK.

Michael J. Morley, University of Limerick, Ireland.

Michael Muller-Camen, Vienna University of Economics and Business, Austria.

Werner Nienhüser, University of Duisburg-Essen, Germany.

Irene Nikandrou, Athens University of Economics and Business, Greece.

Miguel R. Olivas-Luján, Clarion University, USA.

Jaap Paauwe, Tilburg University, The Netherlands.

Leda Panayotopoulou, Athens University of Economics and Business, Greece.

Emma Parry, Cranfield School of Management, UK.

Tuomo Peltonen, Turku School of Economics, University of Turku, Finland.

Andrew Pendleton, University of Durham, UK.

Erik Poutsma, Radboud University Nijmegen, The Netherlands.

Alexandros Psychogios, Birmingham City Business School, UK.

Javier Quintanilla, IESE Business School, Spain.

B. Sebastian Reiche, IESE Business School, Spain.

Huub J.M. Ruël, Hotelschool/Hospitality Business School The Hague, The Netherlands.

Ihar Sahakiants, Cologne Business School, Germany.

Randall S. Schuler, Rutgers University, USA.

Paul Sparrow, Lancaster University Management School, UK.

Esperanza Suarez, UPV, Polytechnic University of Valencia, Spain.

Vivien T. Supangco, University of the Philippines, The Philippines.

Lourdes Susaeta, Complutense University of Madrid, Spain.

Stephen Sweet, Ithaca College, USA.

Leslie T. Szamosi, International Faculty of the University of Sheffield, CITY College, Greece.

Tarek Tantoush, Libyan Academy of Graduate Studies, Libya.

Olga Tregaskis, University of East Anglia, UK.

Eero Vaara, Aalto University School of Business, Finland.

Arup Varma, Loyola University Chicago, USA.

Chris Warhurst, University of Warwick, UK.

Malcolm Warner, University of Cambridge, UK.

Ingo Weller, LMU Munich, Germany.

Geoffrey Wood, University of Essex, UK.

Ying Zhu, University of South Australia, Australia.

David B. Zoogah, Xavier University, USA.

Acknowledgements

The first edition of the *Handbook of Research on Comparative Human Resource Management* was a significant accomplishment, bringing together experts from across the globe to showcase the field of comparative human resource management. It reached so many people that the publisher invited us to update, revise and enlarge. Therefore, bringing in a third editor with great expertise and reputation as well as unfailing collegiality was clearly required. The work on this second edition has been equally interesting and challenging to bring to fruition, now including 84 authors from 24 countries worldwide. We are extremely grateful for the collegiality and responsiveness of all authors and the collaborative atmosphere in which we were able to complete this task.

Of course, when editing such a volume, there is also a great deal of work that takes place behind the scenes. We wish here to thank those who aided us in this editorial role, particularly Renate Gellner-Bächer and Gisela Ullrich-Rosner at the Vienna University of Economics and Business in Austria, without whose help the task would likely still be continuing today. Likewise, the unwavering support of the team at Edward Elgar Publishing, in particular Francine O'Sullivan and Ellen Pearce, was a great encouragement for us academics always having these nagging doubts about the worth of their work at the back of their mind.

In summary, we send our thanks to all family, friends and colleagues who have helped us in publishing this second edition of the *Handbook*, as well as to you for reading this book. We are very much obliged to you all.

Chris Brewster, Wolfgang Mayrhofer and Elaine Farndale
London, UK / Vienna, Austria / University Park, USA
August 2017

1. The meaning and value of comparative human resource management: an introduction

Elaine Farndale, Wolfgang Mayrhofer, and Chris Brewster

WHY COMPARATIVE HRM?

The 2012 edition of this *Handbook* was the first to bring together, systematically, expert researchers studying comparative human resource management (HRM). The need at that time for a comparative book was manifest as the subject was increasingly being researched and taught, as part of a general HRM or international HRM course. Since then, the demand for a comparative perspective has grown, as scholars and practitioners alike become more aware of the need to understand the relationship between national or regional context and HRM, which lies at the core of this new edition. This second edition of the *Handbook on Comparative Human Resource Management* draws on the work of many of the world's leading researchers in this area to present the current state of the art to scholars, students, and practitioners. Building on the solid base of the first edition, this latest edition of the *Handbook* provides an extended focus on the theoretical underpinnings of comparative HRM (CHRM), includes additional studies in comparative areas of HRM practice, and covers a broader set of countries and regions.

HRM as a subject for study and teaching was identified and popularised in the United States of America (USA) in the late 1970s and early 1980s, encapsulated in two famous textbooks (Beer et al., 1985; Fombrun et al., 1984). The two books took different approaches, but both differentiated HRM from personnel management as the administration of employment. They argued that the latter involved running, monitoring, and controlling the employment systems within the organisation, whereas HRM involved more integration of personnel policies across functions and with the corporate strategy (with HRM being the downstream function); a greater role for line managers; a shift from collective to individual relationships; and an accent on enhancing company performance. In HRM, workers are a resource 'to be obtained cheaply, used sparingly and developed and exploited as fully as possible' (Sparrow & Hiltrop, 1994: 7) in the interests of the organisation.

Managing people in a systematic and consistent way with the intention of ensuring their effective contribution to the success of the organisation – one definition of human resource management – utilises the same processes in every case: a workforce has to be recruited, deployed, and assessed, trained, paid, and all of this within conditions that allow motivation to develop and be sustained. Some argue, therefore, that HRM is a-contextual, in other words, findings related to HRM practices are applicable to all settings because context is not part of the discussion (Christensen Hughes, 2002). Others, the authors here included, counter that HRM is contextual, and that HRM findings can predominantly be explained by contextual, in particular cultural (Reiche et al., 2012) or institutional (Wood et al., 2012), theorising. CHRM relies on this perspective, emphasising that we cannot understand the adoption or effectiveness of HRM without understanding – or at least taking into account – the context in which it is being applied. This constitutes the fundamental premise behind our *Handbook*.

One of the major aspects of context is the country in which organisations operate. Because most studies of HRM take place within a single national context, commentators have long been aware of the differences in HRM policies and practices in different sizes of organisation and the sector (or sectors) in which they operate (e.g., Brewster et al., 2014; Goergen et al., 2013). Largely, perhaps, owing to the spread of HRM research across the world, HRM scholars have become aware of the differences between countries and have argued that this is a matter not only of differences in practice but also of differences in the way that the subject is thought about: its meaning and its purpose. Even if we accept that the purpose of HRM should be to improve the performance of the firm (that is, be profit-centric; Kaufman, 2016), Gerhart (2005: 178) has argued: 'it seems unlikely that one set of HRM practices will work equally well no matter what the context'. The focus of HRM as having a profit motive is also brought into question in different contexts, where some note that a primary outcome of HRM should be employee well-being (Guest, 2002).

Much of the new thinking and innovation in HRM has historically come from the USA, where it originated. Concepts and ideas about HRM have followed the 'Gulf Stream . . . drifting in from the USA and hitting the UK [United Kingdom] first, then crossing the Benelux countries . . . and Germany and France and proceeding finally to southern Europe' (DeFidelto & Slater, 2001: 281), and then, usually later, on to the rest of the world. The hegemony of the United States (US) model is such that many universities and business schools as well as consultancies around the world use US teaching materials, US teaching methods, and US textbooks and case studies, more or less ignoring HRM in the local context despite the availability of more locally focused teaching materials and cases (for example, the various editions of the *Global Human Resource Management Casebook*: Hayton et al., 2012; Christiansen et al., 2017). Like many others, we believe that this is an error. HRM does not operate the same way in every country. The idea that HRM varies around the world is by no means new, but much HRM commentary either ignores that fact or assumes that countries that do HRM differently are 'lagging behind'. 'Best-practice' HRM may not even be that common in the USA, but it certainly looks and feels very different elsewhere in the world.

Against a backdrop of contextual differences and a more dynamic view of changes over time, CHRM is concerned with understanding and explaining differences between contexts as constituted by countries or clusters of countries, and analysing how much changes over time, in particular through the process of globalisation, are or are not leading to a harmonisation of HRM across the world, and how far countries retain their distinctive national flavour.

This chapter introduces both the subject of comparative HRM and this *Handbook*. We attempt to identify the establishment of the subject and its boundaries; we discuss the role of context in HRM; we address the issue of whether globalisation is making such analysis increasingly irrelevant as societies seem to converge; and we explore levels and units of analysis of comparative HRM. We then outline the shape and content of the *Handbook*, which includes theoretical and empirical issues in comparative HRM, the way that these affect particular elements of HRM, and the way that different countries and regions think about the topic.

THE DEVELOPMENT OF THE STUDY OF COMPARATIVE HRM

The classic texts marking the origin of HRM identified, respectively, four (employee influence, human resource flow, reward systems, and work systems; Beer et al., 1985) or five (selection, performance, appraisal, rewards, and development; Fombrun et al., 1984) areas that can be used to analyse HRM. The unstated implication was that these areas can be used in any organisation, anywhere in the world. Most universities and business schools across the world tend to teach a very similar version of HRM to that outlined in these books.

In reality there has been little agreement about the meaning of the term 'human resource management'. We are not the first to note the confusion surrounding the concept (see, as early examples, Boxall, 1992; Guest, 1990; Goss, 1994; Storey, 1992). Conceptually, a range of definitions of HRM is possible: from an almost etymological analysis at one end to a clearly normative perspective at the other. Within this range two broad categories can be discerned:

- HRM as a subject area: exploring processes by which an organisation deals with the labour it needs to perform its functions and encompassing, therefore, traditional definitions of personnel management (including manpower planning, resourcing, training and development, and industrial relations) and also subcontracting, out-sourcing, and similar arrangements for utilising human resources even when not employed within the organisation.
- HRM as a programme: contributing to organisational (usually business) effectiveness. In many cases this usage has defined itself as strategic HRM (see, for early examples, Armstrong, 2008; Boxall & Purcell, 2007; Hendry & Pettigrew, 1990; Schuler, 1992).

Whereas the first kind of focus concentrates upon identifying and studying either the whole relationship between people at work and their organisations or a particular aspect of it, the second category is focused on the activities of management and the practices that management can adopt to improve organisational or firm efficiency and effectiveness. Arguably, a contributory reason for these different approaches to the topic is similar to the basic argument of comparative HRM: it is perhaps little wonder that researchers, based in a different institutional and cultural context, with different historical antecedents of research perspectives and different practical problems to explain, have different views of what is central to the topic.

The still developing stream of work in CHRM leans towards interpreting HRM as a subject area. Partly, this is due to its roots in different traditions: the industrial relations tradition, the growth of international business as a subject of study, and the equally fast-growing topic of international HRM (Stahl et al., 2012). We describe each of these traditions in relation to CHRM further.

In Europe and Australasia, particularly, many of the earlier researchers and teachers in HRM moved into the field from industrial relations studies. Industrial relations vary markedly from country to country and this has traditionally been an area of study much concerned with nationally comparative issues, such as for example why union membership is so much higher in some countries than in others, why different consultation structures apply in different countries, and whether the embeddedness of industrial relations in its national context was a given. Therefore, it was obvious for the specialists who moved across from that field to take a more comparative view of the closely linked subject of HRM.

The growth of the study of international business has also identified the need for a better understanding of how the management of workforces varies across national boundaries. Multinational corporations (MNCs) have struggled to find an appropriate balance between the efficiencies of a globally standardised approach to HRM and the effectiveness of adapting HRM practice to local contexts. Born out of these struggles is the field of strategic international HRM (SIHRM), which focuses on corporate HRM as practiced by MNCs, and how practices or people are transferred between headquarters and subsidiary locations (Stahl et al., 2012). This relies on the exploration of complex interactions between external (home and host country) and internal (strategy, structure, and relationships) factors (Brewster et al., 2016b). CHRM, in contrast, has as its objective to observe and explain commonalities and differences between countries or regions or clusters of countries (Brewster et al., 2016b; Kaufman, 2016).

CHRM now has a firmly established place within the HRM discipline (see, for example, the contributions on comparative HRM in overview works on HRM and international HRM such as Harzing & Pinnington, 2015; Parry et al., 2013; Collings & Wood, 2009; Sparrow, 2009). Starting in the 1990s, early works described the differences between countries and explored the theoretical foundations of the subject (e.g., Brewster & Tyson, 1991; Begin, 1992; Hegewisch & Brewster, 1993; Boxall, 1995). Since then the balance of the discussion has changed from a primarily descriptive perspective to a more explanatory angle looking into 'why' and 'how'; that is, the reasons for and the processes leading to commonalities and differences in HRM between different countries, cultures, and institutional settings. The major theoretical underpinnings and conceptual approaches to the topic are summarised in Part I of this *Handbook*.

THE ROLE OF CONTEXT

The core issue underlying the study of CHRM is the importance of context. Jackson and Schuler (1995) describe how a range of theories can be applied to understand the context–HRM relationship, arguing that there is a need to shift from 'treating organisational settings as sources of error variance, to attending as closely as we have traditionally attended to individual characteristics'. In developing their 'integrative framework of HRM in context', they highlight the importance of internal factors such as technology, structure, size, life cycle stage, and business strategy, as well as external factors such as the legal, social, and political environment, unionisation, labour market conditions, industry characteristics, and national culture.

Other commentators have also raised concerns about assumptions being made that theories developed in one national context might be universally applicable, without this actually being tested (Brewster et al., 2016a). Beer et al. (2015) make a plea for a renewed push to develop a more contextual view of HRM in order to make a stronger connection with human and societal outcomes. Similarly, questions have been raised as to whether the Anglo-Saxon models of HRM such as Fombrun et al.'s (1984) matching model or Schuler's (1992) 5-P model are applicable worldwide (Budhwar & Debrah, 2001).

Watson (2004) calls for a more critical perspective on how and why HRM systems emerge in different organisational contexts, contending that HRM 'strategies specifically are outcomes of human interpretations, conflicts, confusions, guesses, and rationalisations . . . The adoption of particular HR[M] strategies and practices is inevitably the result of decisions made by human actors'. Here, the emphasis is more on the role of actors in organisations, rather than internal or external institutional or cultural factors, placing greater emphasis on the role of power and politics in organisations. Critically, actors mediate the relationship between context and the HRM system, which in turn has a resultant effect on the context (Paauwe & Farndale, 2016).

CONVERGENCE AND DIVERGENCE

As well as context, another striking feature of the CHRM literature is its interest in time, that is, whether observed commonalities or differences are persistent or subject to change (Brewster et al., 2016b). This gives rise to the convergence/divergence debate within the field, which explores the role of context (national or supranational-level explanatory mechanisms) in creating patterns of HRM worldwide over time.

The SIHRM literature pays some attention to change over time, but here the emphasis is largely on standardisation, particularly on how MNCs might be creating global standards of HRM practice, especially in transferring practices deemed superior from advanced to emerging economies. In this scenario, context is seen more as a constraint to standardisation. However, CHRM scholars generally argue that context, particularly in the form of institutional factors, may be more strongly determinant of HRM practice adoption than the standardisation attempts of MNCs: it is not just a question of whether a practice is feasible, but also whether it is desirable (Al Ariss & Sidani, 2016a). Context, in the CHRM literature, is the variable of interest as different solutions to similar problems emerge. A problem in both SIHRM and CHRM is creating understanding of what lies behind the process of (or lack of) standardisation or convergence, rather than mere observation of patterns of HRM practices; a problem that this *Handbook* is designed, in part, to address.

A popular meaning of 'globalisation', related perhaps most closely to marketing, argues that the spread of international awareness and international business has led to, for example, young people in Beijing wearing American blue jeans, enjoying American Cola drinks, and listening to European pop groups. In other words, countries are losing their national distinctiveness and becoming more alike. A more scholarly interpretation (Meyer et al., 2011; Rugman & Verbeke, 2001) notes these consumer possibilities but also notes that in terms of providing goods and services countries may find most advantage in differentiating themselves and concentrating upon the things they are good at.

Hidden in much of this popular and scholarly literature is the notion that globalisation is an unstoppable force; that the experience of ever-increasing integration of national markets, economies, and businesses will inevitably continue into the future. History warns us to be wary of any assumptions of inevitability. The global slowdown that followed the economic crisis that started in 2008 led to a stalling in the number of MNCs and international mergers and acquisitions, and a decrease in global trade that, as we write in August 2017, is only gradually recovering to former levels. Further, the victories of the Brexit campaign in the United Kingdom in 2016, leading to the separation of the UK, the fifth-largest economy in the world, from one of the world's largest free trading areas and, in the same year, of the avowedly anti-globalisation Donald Trump campaign for the US Presidency, remind us of the need for caution in such assumptions. Interestingly, as we write, stock markets in the UK and the USA are reaching record highs, indicating that investors at least believe that the fears accompanying these events in some quarters may be worse than the eventual outcomes.

How does globalisation apply to HRM? Are countries in fact becoming more alike in the way that they think about and practice HRM, so that the differences between them will be of diminishing importance? Are they retaining consistent differences? Of course, no country's social systems remain exactly the same so, more sensibly, what is the direction of movement? Or are different units of analysis (aspects of HRM, for example, or policy and practice) heading in different directions? Are countries, in short, becoming more or less alike in the way that people are managed? Contributions to answering these questions – often labelled within the frame of convergence and divergence – arise from theoretical, methodological, and empirical perspectives.

Theoretical Perspectives

Over many decades, the arguments over convergence and divergence swept back and forth, with different importance being given to convergence one moment and divergence the next. Arguably, early contributions in this debate emphasised convergent tendencies. Given that before the industrial revolution much of the production of wealth in a country depended on the primary sector, it is hardly surprising that the new emerging technology and the developments in its wake led commentators to assume strong convergent developments. Early voices include Marx's (1844 [2002]) ideas of capitalist accumulation, Veblen's (1904) proposition that the consequence of countries modernising is their inevitable convergence with regard to organisational structures and value systems, Weber's (1921 [1980]) analysis of bureaucracy and rationalisation processes, and Durkheim's (1933 [1967]) argument for a shift from mechanical to organic solidarity. Since then, the upper hand between advocates of convergence and divergence has changed regularly. Here, we constrain ourselves to outlining the basic positions that have become relevant for organisation studies in general, and comparative HRM in particular (see also Brewster & Mayrhofer, 2012).

One stream of voices favouring convergence relates to rational actor models of the firm (see the classic texts, Simon, 1955; Coleman, 1990). They argue that firms pursue economic success by implementing, under conditions of bounded rationality, practices that contribute to economic goals. Given that capitalism is a global phenomenon, some of its central tenets – rationality, cost-effectiveness, flexibility, and best-practice models – support the global emergence of reasonably similar organisational structures and processes. At the organisational level, and perhaps most pointedly, tendencies towards similarity are claimed by transaction cost economics: 'Most transaction cost theorists argue that there is one best organisational form for firms that have similar or identical transaction costs' (Hollingsworth & Boyer, 1997: 34).

Arguably, the most elaborate theoretical view comes from the world polity approach within sociological neo-institutionalism (see Meyer & Rowan, 1977; DiMaggio & Powell, 1983). It argues that, especially since 1945, Western cultural patterns and institutions dominate global developments so that core individual and collective actors, including organisations and nation states, are subject to isomorphic pressures to follow the 'Western model' of rationalisation (Drori et al., 2006b). Underlying these considerations is the assumption that the role of the nation states will further decrease (Ohmae, 1995) and that a world system (Wallerstein, 1974; Frank & Gills, 1993) or a world society (Krücken & Drori, 2009) emerges, which is the primary locus of rationalisation. We will see, it is argued, a systematisation of social life on the basis of standardised schemes and rules requiring the reconstruction of all social organisation (Jepperson, 2002). Succinctly put:

> We see three particular features of globalization as fuelling the modern pattern of expanded organisation: (a) the rise of the global as the relevant social horizon, (b) rationalization and standardization processes, reinforced through the expanding globalized institutions of science and expertise, and (c) a culture of actorhood and empowerment, carried by the rapidly expanding and globalized educational institutions. These dimensions of globalization, we argue, create a real or imagined society on a world scale. (Drori et al., 2006c: 13)

Hence, 'it is clearly the modern world society that is the institutional core, setting the model of the culture of rationality' (Drori et al., 2006a: 209f.). Rational bases, required for collective and cooperative action, 'are understood to have a universalistic character. They are objectively true, and true everywhere, so that it is possible to prescribe rational organisational forms even in unfamiliar or distant contexts' (Meyer et al., 2006: 26).

Of course, this does not mean complete uniformity. There is room for local variation and distinctiveness. However, this is legitimate only as long as it is consistent with homogeneity in the primary dimensions of the emerging world society (Meyer, 2000). Research interested in the translation of various business and political practices across cultural and national borders emphasises that both freedom for social action as well as isomorphic pressure coexist (see, for example, the work of Boxenbaum, 2006; Czarniawska & Sevón, 2005; Sahlin-Andersson & Engwall, 2002). As practices travel across the globe and become institutionalised, they are edited and customised to specific contextual settings.

Opposition to the convergence thesis is often characterised as arguing for divergence, perhaps because it sounds nice as an opposite. Few of those who oppose the convergence thesis, however, would actually argue that countries are getting more dissimilar. What they usually mean is that countries are not getting more similar to any significant extent. Although several core HRM debates, such as those concerning the importance of HRM for organisational performance, implicitly or explicitly assume a convergent, one-best-way solution (see, e.g., Pfeffer, 1998; Wright et al., 2001), human resources are difficult to standardise, and it has been argued that HRM is the aspect of management most likely to reflect local circumstances (Rosenzweig & Nohria, 1994).

The leading naysayers to the convergence thesis come from both the cultural and the institutional camp. As we have two chapters on these respective angles (see Chapters 2 and 3), we can be brief here. The literature on cultural differences argues that culture is 'one of those terms that defy a single all-purpose definition and there are almost as many meanings of culture as people using the term' (Ajiferuke & Boddewyn, 1970: 154). Subsequent years and studies have added further complexity, rather than clarifying the issue. Fundamental to this literature is the notion that where there is change, it happens very slowly, so that the underlying differences in values between societies tend to remain the same for decades (Beugelsdijk et al., 2015).

From an institutional angle, too, there are also significant doubts about converging tendencies. Theories of comparative capitalism (e.g., Amable, 2003; Hall & Soskice, 2001; Whitley, 1999) argue that institutional arrangements at the national level show considerable inertia, so that it is hard to see how existing differences between systems of economic organisation will disappear. Whitley (1999) points out that '[n]ation states constitute the prevalent arena in which social and political competition is decided in industrial capitalist societies'. This emphasises differences, the slow nature of institutional change (Djelic & Quack, 2003) and the limits of globalisation (Guillén, 2001). Institutional perspectives concentrate on the institutions within a society as being the environmental structures that keep them distinctive. Institutions are likely to shape the social construction of the nature of organisations and will certainly structure policies and practices within them. The institutional perspective (Meyer & Rowan, 1977; DiMaggio & Powell, 1983) argues that isomorphism between organisations is determined less by cultural differences than by institutions. Adding in a cross-national element has led some institutionalists to argue that it is the economic, social, and legal arrangements of societies that keep the nations distinctive (Hollingsworth & Boyer, 1997; Whitley, 1999).

Methodological Perspectives

What convergence and divergence actually mean and how they are conceptualised is by no means clear. The literature shows a broad variety of interpretations. Arguably most questionable, or to say the least, hardly helpful, are single point in time studies that have equated convergence with similarity, as is done by some HRM studies claiming to find convergence in a cross-sectional study (e.g., Bae et al., 1998; Chen et al., 2005; Pudelko, 2005). Most commentators would argue that the notion of convergence – and, for that matter, divergence and stasis – requires a more dynamic view and looking at developments over time where the phenomena of interest become more or less similar at different points. Taking a closer look at the way these terms have been used suggests that one can differentiate between at least two different variants of 'convergence' (Mayrhofer et al., 2002).

First, there is final convergence. Over time the differences between the variables analysed decrease and ultimately tend towards a common end point; even if they never actually reach that point, the differences between them become smaller. Based on a classical article on convergence (Hotelling, 1933), Friedman (1992: 2129) suggests that the 'real test of a tendency to convergence would be in showing a consistent diminution of variance . . . among individual [countries]' Figure 1.1 illustrates the basic idea by showing three country pairs where developments in, for example, the use of a specific HRM practice vary in their directions, but still converge towards some point in time.

Second, there is directional convergence. This occurs when the analysed variables point in the same direction, that is, when similar trends appear. Such a development does not depend on a specific initial starting level or the relative distance of these levels at the end. All it requires is a change of variables in the same direction over time. For example, while membership of trade unions has been declining in most countries over the last 25 years, the relative differences between countries regarding levels of union membership have remained relatively constant (Scheuer, 2011; Schmitt & Mitukiewicz, 2012). This indicates

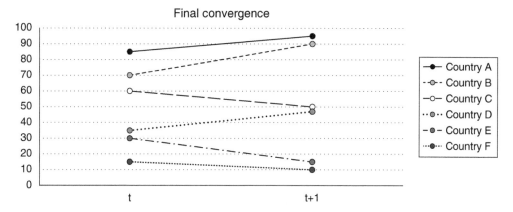

Figure 1.1   Examples of final convergence

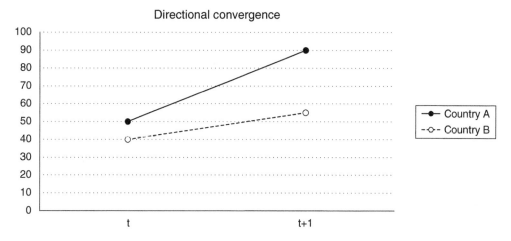

Figure 1.2   Example of directional convergence

directional convergence, but not final convergence. Hence, seeing similar trends does not justify diagnosing final convergence. Figure 1.2 shows the basic idea. In both countries the trend goes in the same direction; for example, the use of a certain HRM practice in each country increases. Nevertheless, there is no common end point, that is, no final convergence, and also the frequency of use of the practice is different.

Empirical Perspectives

Unlike in some adjacent fields such as industrial relations (e.g., Bamber et al., 2016), hard evidence of long-term development in HRM is scarce. What is available comes from two different angles: analyses of the role of MNCs in diffusing HRM globally; and studies following the development of a single HRM practice or a broader set of HRM policies, practices, and characteristics across countries, regions, or market economies.

MNCs play an important role both for economic development globally as well as in specific regions and countries (e.g., Dunning, 1992; Chandler & Mazlish, 2005; Meyer, 2008; Dunning & Lundan, 2008; Elfstrom, 1991; Haley, 2001; Wettstein, 2009). HRM is no exception here. There is substantial work on the relationship between MNC head-quarters and subsidiaries and the various ways in which MNCs from different countries undertake HRM around the globe. MNCs may strongly influence local HRM practices and policies, particularly so in some areas of HRM and in some countries. Sophisticated global policies and practices rolled out and policed by a central HRM function have an impact on MNCs' subsidiaries (e.g., Björkman et al., 2007; Gamble, 2003). Beyond that, in many countries MNCs also serve as role models that are sometimes seen as sources for good practice.

To be sure, this does not happen through simple transfer and homogenisation. Rather, HRM practices and policies are translated – that is, reshaped, resisted, and redeployed – in the local environment due to the various social processes that govern the local situa-tion (D'Aunno et al., 2000; Ferner, 1997; Ferner & Quintanilla, 1998). One can argue that foreign as well as indigenous MNCs handle their human resources differently from organisations operating solely in their home country. However, country of location rather than country of origin is the most important factor when it comes to explaining differ-ences in HRM (Brewster et al., 2008; Farndale et al., 2008). In this sense, MNCs bring in new forms of HRM, adapt to local ones, and develop hybrid forms.

When looking at HRM policies and practices at the broader level of countries and regions, the available empirical evidence is most detailed for Europe. This is partly due to the existence of a large HRM dataset collected by Cranet (www.cranet.org), a research network that has been conducting a trend study about developments in HRM in public and private organisations since 1989, and has conducted nine survey rounds in currently more than 40 countries worldwide (see Brewster & Hegewisch, 1994; Brewster et al., 2000; Brewster et al., 2004; Parry et al., 2013).

Results (e.g., Mayrhofer et al., 2011) show that in Europe many aspects of HRM show directional convergence, that is, the trends are the same. Thus, there are increases in most countries most of the time in such issues as the professionalisation of the HRM function, the use of more sophisticated recruitment and selection systems, the use of contingent rewards, and the extent of communication with employees. However, contrary to the received wisdom in the universalistic texts, there is no sign of common trends in the size of the HRM department (Brewster et al., 2006), nor in training and development, which is given high priority in many countries but seems to remain the first area for cuts when finances become tight.

The evidence is summarised as follows: 'from a directional convergence point of view, there seems to be a positive indication of convergence. However, when one looks at the question from a final convergence point of view, the answer is no longer a clear positive. None of the HRM practices converge' (Mayrhofer et al., 2004: 432). While the exist-ence of clear directional convergence 'acknowledges the capacity for HRM in European countries to be influenced by supranational drivers from the global and European level' (Mayrhofer et al., 2011: 60), the absence of any form of final convergence 'is testimony to the enduring effects of national institutional contexts, particularly in Europe, and espe-cially apparent in HRM configuration and practices which previously have been identified as prone to the influence of the national environment' (ibid.).

Outside of Europe and at the global level, there is no comparable empirical insight regarding HRM and it is therefore not possible to develop an understanding or explanation on any sound empirical basis. However, at a theoretical level we suggest that there are some parallels to the European situation. Of course, Europe is unique in the sense that there is no other world region with such a strong central actor as the European Union (EU) covering the same number of nation states. Arguably, however, other world regions are also covered by supranational forces. Examples include efforts to create common economic and partly political areas such as the Eurasian Economic Union (EEU), the Sistema de la Integración Centroamericana (SICA, the Central American Integration System), or the Southern African Development Community (SADC). At a more general level, drivers such as globalisation, rationalisation, or efficiency constitute major driving forces. At the same time, there are substantial contextual idiosyncrasies. Nation states – despite premature announcements of their death (Ohmae, 1995) – seem to be alive and well, and constitute unique contexts for HRM. Neither institutions nor cultures change quickly; and rarely in ways that are the same as in other counties. In addition, nation states are affected by path-dependency and locked-in effects which make quick and radical change rare.

It seems far from overstated, then, that the evidence supports those who would argue, for various reasons, that globalisation might not be taking place in the clear, straightforward way of 'making things more similar'. As Al Ariss and Sidani (2016b) succinctly put it: 'we maintain that the case for total or dominant convergence can now be laid to rest'. Hence, the broader issue of factors explaining similarities and differences between HRM in different countries and their development becomes crucial, and constitutes a core element of CHRM: 'Rather than trying to identify one winning side, a better route is to identify situations, at the micro, meso, and macro levels, that cause relative convergence in some instances and divergence in others' (Al Ariss & Sidani, 2016b: 283).

The exploration of convergence in the CHRM literature, although extensive, still has its limitations. Often, convergence is studied across advanced economies (North American and European), with less exploration of emerging economies (Al Ariss & Sidani, 2016a; Horwitz & Budhwar, 2015), leaving us with a gap in our knowledge. Kaufman (2016) also argues that we are not necessarily measuring convergence appropriately, advocating for a more economic-driven view, considering the extent of difference between countries by observing both means and degrees of dispersion of HRM practice adoption. He argues furthermore that economic theories of comparative advantage, trade and location suggest divergence of HRM, compared with the common convergence theme of strategy theories such as the resource based view of the firm.

LEVELS/UNITS OF ANALYSIS

CHRM research usually focuses on individual and collective actors as well as the respective structures and processes linked with these actors, all of them in different countries, cultures or regions (Brewster & Mayrhofer, 2009). The degree of social complexity constitutes a useful main differentiation criterion in order to group these actors according to different analytical levels. Actors are characterised by low social complexity if the emerging social relationships between these actors are either non-existent as in the case of individuals or have comparatively little complexity, for example, in face-to-face groups. However, collective actors such as countries or supranational units show high social complexity. A complex fabric of social relationships constitutes their internal environment.

Looking back to the early 1990s, an analysis of published CHRM research reveals that country, organisation, and individual-level analyses dominate the scene. Reflecting the view of Clark et al. (1999) ten years earlier, a review of peer-reviewed articles published in the years from 1990 to 2005 (Mayrhofer & Reichel, 2009) shows that comparative HRM was typically empirical rather than conceptual; focused on the country, organisation, or individual as the primary unit of analysis; used cross-sectional 'snapshot' rather than longitudinal, that is, panel or trend study designs; and focused on comparison of one or more sets of HRM practices, for example, recruitment procedures, and/or HRM configuration such as strategic orientation or size of the HRM department rather than the link between HRM and some kind of output like satisfaction, performance, or commitment. Overall, early comparative HRM research placed an emphasis on actors and respective processes and structures at a low to medium level of social complexity. Typical blind spots were networks of organisations and supranational actors. Moreover the research tended to be focused on a very limited number of countries and regions of the world. More recent work has attempted to address some of these issues, as we note.

When looking at HRM from a comparative angle, a key question concerns the levels of analysis (Kochan et al., 1992; Locke et al., 1995). This implies decisions about how to conceive of the differences in HRM systems and approaches and then how to choose an appropriate perspective. A telescope analogy has been proposed as useful in this context (Brewster, 1995). Changing the focus on a telescope provides the viewer with ever more detail and the ability to distinguish ever finer differences within the big picture than can be seen with the naked eye. None of the chosen perspectives are wrong or inaccurate, but some are more useful for some purposes than for others. HRM can be conceived of in this way. In HRM, as we have argued, there are universals, for example the need for organisations to attract, deploy, assess, train, and pay workers; but we have also argued that there are some things that are shared within regions; some that are distinctive for certain nations; some that are unique to certain sectors; some that fit a particular organisation or even a section of an organisation; and there are some factors that are unique to each individual manager and employee. Each perspective sharpens the focus on some aspects but, inevitably, blurs others. The many (within-country) studies that (accurately) find differences between sectors within a country, for example, have been extended to studies of particular sectors across countries with the implicit (but inaccurate) assumption that there will be more differences between the sectors than between the countries. Hence, when discussing comparative HRM it is important to take into account the chosen perspective and to be aware of the missing complexity. Many commentators either state, or imply by omission, that their analysis is universal. CHRM challenges that view.

To date the CHRM field has included multiple different levels of analysis on which to observe comparisons, including individual, organisational, national, and supranational (Mayrhofer & Reichel, 2009). We provide examples of each of these in turn here. First, comparisons of HRM practices between countries can be explained through individual-level variables: through, for example, typical employee expectations or desires related to HRM in a given national context (Lowe et al., 2002); or through employee ability to deal with exposure to cultural diversity, which in turn influences employee behaviour (Strauss & Connerley, 2003).

Second, comparisons can also be explained through organisation-level variables: the Japanese organisational preference for on-the-job training and knowledge sharing produces 'specialist' engineers, compared to the preference of UK organisations to rely on 'professional' engineers, who receive a more general education before joining the firm (Lam, 1994); organisational size and sector combine to explain clusters of complementarities that make for patterns of HRM practice adoption (Goergen et al., 2012); organisation-level influence of unionism, which varies both between and within countries, has been found to increase the extent of strategic integration of the HRM function (Vernon & Brewster, 2013); organisation size, which also varies both between and within countries, impacts upon the adoption of employee direct involvement practices (Brewster et al., 2014) as well as the assignment of HRM to line managers (Brewster et al., 2015a).

Third, comparisons based on national institutional and cultural factors are most common in the CHRM field, and make up much of the content of this *Handbook*. Some examples include facilitating the understanding of the relative strength of workers and managers from the perspective of different corporate governance regimes (Goergen et al., 2009); linking transitional economies to the modernisation of HRM (Poor et al., 2011); the relative propensity of firms to lay people off based on national political structures (Goergen et al., 2013); and the adoption of contingent employment practices (Tregaskis & Brewster, 2006).

Finally, at the supranational level, there are frequent comparisons of HRM across market economies. The comparative capitalisms literature argues that there is a limited range of institutional factors that shape the choices of rational actors, creating path dependency (Goergen et al., 2012), and that these institutional factors, such as law and political systems, interact with each other to have a combined effect on HRM (Psychogios & Wood, 2010). Empirical examples include the use of non-standard working time across market economies (Richbell et al., 2011), levels of voluntary and involuntary employee turnover (Croucher et al., 2012), use of a broad range of HRM practices (Farndale et al., 2008), and extent of union recognition (Brewster et al., 2015b). The notion of complementarities is again key here, whereby complex patterns of institutional factors combine to create similar HRM outcomes (Croucher et al., 2012; Walker et al., 2014).

Many of the seminal management and HRM texts are written as if the analysis applies at all levels, something one can call 'false universalism' (Rose, 1991). The cultural hegemony of US teaching and publishing, particularly in the leading US 'international' journals, means that these texts are often utilised by readers and students in other countries. US-based literature searches – now all done on computer, of course – tend to privilege texts in English, texts in the US-based journals, and texts in the universalist tradition (Brewster, 1999a, 1999b). For analysts and practitioners elsewhere with interests in different sectors, countries, and so on, many of these descriptions and prescriptions fail to meet their reality and a more context-sensitive analysis is necessary.

CHRM strives to provide such analyses. In its simplest form, HRM in two different countries is compared and contrasted at a merely descriptive level. In a broader sense the criteria for comparison, derived from theoretical reasoning or closely linked to observable phenomena, go far beyond that:

Examples include groups of countries formed by criteria such as geographical distance, cultural similarity, economic output, political power or historical bonds; regions cutting across nation states, for example, geographically neighbouring areas in the Mediterranean or in central Europe as well as dislocated regions such as those with highest-level subsidies within the EU; areas with similarities in terms of demography or political activity, for example, population growing vs. shrinking areas; regions with similar infra-structure [*sic*] characteristics, for example, in terms of highway and railway quality and density, access to the internet or administrative quality of government; or organisational characteristics such as sector and size. (Mayrhofer, 2007: 191)

This book adopts a mid-level position, concentrating upon CHRM at the country and country cluster level. As with the telescope metaphor, this picture is no more or less accurate than the others: it just helps us to understand some things more clearly.

THE FUTURE OF CHRM

The comparative study of HRM is thus complex, with competing debates around globalisation, convergence, and divergence, with multiple units and levels of analysis, and above all significant challenges in collecting empirical data that can counter the limitations of cross-sectional studies across a limited number of 'popular' countries and regions. Nevertheless, progress continues, and as this *Handbook* demonstrates, our knowledge of HRM in different countries and regions of the world is increasing. Perhaps even more importantly, however, we are now gaining more insight into 'why' HRM practices differ or are the same across borders, rather than just acknowledging that differences exist, and we are also learning about how these different HRM patterns result in various individual and organisational outcomes.

We hope that after reading the following chapters, scholars from around the world will feel inspired to continue to address the gaps in our knowledge, particularly those in lessstudied emerging economies, so that we can continue to develop the CHRM field. There is much still to do. To date, we have seen progress in three areas: understanding the theoretical and methodological frameworks that can be applied to comparative HRM; exploring different tasks and themes in HRM from a comparative viewpoint; and describing countries and regions in terms of the way in which they understand and practice HRM. These three areas form the main sections of this book.

OUTLINE OF THE BOOK

Part I of the *Handbook* consists of five chapters underpinning comparative HRM as a field by presenting the underlying theories and methodologies that can help us to understand HRM in context. Part II is devoted to different activities or themes of HRM practice, with each chapter reflecting on pertinent extant comparative research. Part III then switches the emphasis from areas of HRM practice to regions of the world, with each chapter commenting on what typical HRM in that region might look like, and what differences and similarities exist between countries within the region. The *Handbook* concludes in Part IV with a reflection on the evidence presented, summarising some of the themes and ideas to emerge, and adding to the HRM convergence/divergence debate. All chapters have been thoroughly updated since the first edition of this *Handbook*, and new chapters have been added to broaden the range of methodologies, topics, and regions covered.

Opening Part I, Chapter 2, 'Comparative institutional analysis and comparative HRM' (Wood, Psychogios, Szamosi, and Collings), develops our understanding of how context influences HRM. Exploring relevant institutional factors, the complementarities of regulatory features of an organisation's environment are discussed. The authors highlight some of the most influential institutional approaches to understanding variations in HRM policy and practice, and draw out the implications of recent theoretical developments. The authors define the institutional context, particularly highlighting how this affects employee rights.

Chapter 3, 'Cultural perspectives on comparative HRM' (Reiche, Lee, and Quintanilla), focuses on national cultural explanations of variation in HRM practice. Presenting multiple frameworks of national culture, the authors demonstrate how managerial choices across HRM practices are shaped by cultural values and norms, and consider what this means for MNCs and the transfer of practices across national borders. The chapter reflects critically on the limitations of the cultural perspectives on comparative HRM, and discusses directions for future research.

Chapter 4, 'Critical approaches to comparative HRM' (Peltonen and Vaara), draws from critical theories and methodologies largely related to globalisation (global labour process theory, postcolonial analysis, and transnational feminism) to demonstrate how the boundaries of comparative HRM research might be expanded. The chapter suggest directions for future research in this field, particularly reflecting on the critical approach to suggest avenues for positive change.

Chapter 5, 'Methodological challenges for quantitative research in comparative HRM' (Weller and Gerhart), discusses methodological challenges in doing empirical quantitative research on HRM and effectiveness in the field of comparative HRM. In particular, attention is paid to the challenges of adopting an appropriate level of analysis and of inferring causality in studying the HRM–effectiveness link. The authors provide examples of how to handle methodological problems when working with quantitative data, including advice on fixed-effects models and conducting quasi-experiments in comparative HRM studies.

Chapter 6, 'The anthropological comparative method as a means of analysing and solving pressing issues in comparative HRM' (Moore and Brannen), provides insight into qualitative approaches to comparative HRM studies, focusing in particular on the anthropological comparative method. The authors present a detailed international case study to demonstrate how international HRM might usefully adopt the comparative method as a means of analysis, drawing useful conclusions from data that do not easily lend themselves to generalisation.

Part II, shifting our attention to specific areas of HRM practice, opens with Chapter 7, 'Recruitment and selection in context' (Farndale, Nikandrou, and Panayotopoulou), which highlights commonalities within nations, but differences between nations, to present a cross-national comparison of recruitment and selection practices. The authors examine how these practices relate to, interact with, and are influenced by the national institutional and cultural context. The chapter reflects on recruitment and selection practice variation between nations.

Chapter 8, 'Comparative total rewards policies and practices' (Sahakiants, Festing,

Engle, and Dowling), explores the effect of national context on monetary and non-monetary (total) rewards. The authors consider the potential for total rewards policies and practices to converge across the globe, discussing whether they can be standardized in MNCs. The chapter provides insights into comparative reward packages for managers across countries, raising important questions around the social acceptability of executive pay.

Chapter 9, 'Comparing performance management across contexts' (Boselie, Farndale, and Paauwe), defines performance management from an international perspective, and presents an overview of the most important developments over time, comparing performance management in different contexts using both case study data from large MNCs and national survey data. Focusing on country-level data, the chapter explores the balance between the need to standardise or localise performance management practice in different types of organisation across the globe.

Chapter 10, 'Human resource development: national embeddedness' (Tregaskis and Heraty), examines the organisational logic underpinning investment in human resource knowledge and skills, and compares national systems as the fulcrum upon which variation in HRD systems and practices turns. The authors explore globalisation pressures and what these mean for the significance of national institutions in shaping firm-level behaviour in HRD. The chapter focuses on labour market change, discussing the impact of technological advances, changes in migration patterns, and age demographics on skill and knowledge bases.

Chapter 11, 'Comparative employment relations: definitional, disciplinary, and development issues' (Nienhüser and Warhurst), outlines how employment relations are understood and how they are said to be changing. Following a detailed definition of 'employment relations', the authors present the different theoretical underpinnings of this field of study and how each might be more or less relevant in different country academic traditions. A detailed presentation is made of the convergence debate within the comparative employment relations field, exploring how things might be changing over time across countries. Consequently, this chapter includes a discussion of the 'Uberisation' of employment relations, when employment itself disappears.

Chapter 12, 'The psychological contract within the international and comparative HRM literature' (Sparrow), explores comparative and international HRM traditions associated with psychological contract research. Emphasis is placed on comparing a micro individual-level approach to understanding psychological contracts with a macro national-level approach, making a strong case for cultural embeddedness.

Chapter 13, 'Positive and negative application of flexible working time arrangements: comparing the United States of America and the EU countries' (Golden, Sweet, and Chung), explores flexible work schedule practices as they vary among individuals, organisations, and nations, and explains reasons for the observed variations. The authors argue that depending on the metric used, flexibility can be seen as widely available, or as seriously constrained or limited. They also consider the connection between flexible working and work–family harmonisation. Concluding, the chapter notes that, particularly among European nations, the industrial relations context – such as collective bargaining institutions – and prevalence of service and public sectors, influence the diffusion of working time flexibility practices across organisations and countries.

Chapter 14, 'Comparative career studies: conceptual issues and empirical results'

(Lazarova, Mayrhofer, Briscoe, Dickmann, Hall, and Parry), explores the emergent field of study of comparative careers. The authors point to examples that illustrate relevant current research, providing definitions of key concepts and examples of comparative analyses in studies of individual careers and organisational career management. Survey results from two leading-edge career-related research studies are presented to illustrate current trends in the field.

Chapter 15, 'Financial participation: the nature and causes of national variation' (Ligthart, Pendleton, and Poutsma), questions why legislation has been more forthcoming in some countries than others, given that the availability of fiscal benefits to companies and employees is an extremely important influence on the use of financial participation schemes. The authors discuss the main forms of financial participation, presenting survey evidence on the incidence of financial participation in Europe and further afield. They conclude with a reflection on the reasons for differences between countries in the character and incidence of financial participation. Country profiles of financial participation practices are presented.

Chapter 16, 'Comparative perspectives on diversity and equality: the challenges of gender, sexual orientation, race, ethnicity, and religion' (Combs, Haq, Klarsfeld, Susaeta, and Suarez), discusses the emergence of diversity management and how international comparisons can inform our understanding of and perspectives regarding the general shift from equality to diversity and associated human resource policy. The chapter takes a more focused perspective on four specific diversity strands (gender, sexual orientation, race/ethnicity/immigration, and religion) where important developments have been unfolding in recent years, sometimes amidst extreme conditions. The authors reveal important disparity in legal protections between and within the various diversity strands and cultural contexts.

Chapter 17, 'Organising HRM in a comparative perspective' (Brandl, Bos-Nehles, and Aust), presents a state-of-the-art review of research on cross-national variation in organising HRM work based on open systems theorizing of organisations. The authors suggest that practical efforts for organising HRM are based on three alternative models (classic, neo-classic, and modern), and identify the major theoretical traditions that have guided research in this field. Based on the inclusion of empirical studies, the chapter includes a new section on research in the tradition of new institutional theory as well as key issues and future research directions.

Chapter 18, 'The intersection between information technology and human resource management from a cross-national perspective: towards a research model' (Ruël and Bondarouk), develops a model for future comparative qualitative and quantitative e-HRM research in an international context, based on a constructivist view of the relationship between technology and organisations. The authors present a picture of what is known about e-HRM in different national contexts, and a discussion linked to the convergence/divergence debate.

Chapter 19, 'Sustainable HRM: a comparative and international perspective' (Aust, Muller-Camen, and Poutsma), brings a comparative and institutional perspective to the emergent concept of sustainable HRM, which links corporate social responsibility (CSR) and HRM. Sustainable HRM is defined as the adoption of HRM strategies and practices that enable the achievement of financial, social, and ecological goals, with an impact inside and outside of the organisation and over a long-term time horizon, while controlling for unintended side effects and negative feedback. The authors suggest that there may not be a universal version of sustainable HRM, but that different national institutional environments lead to the emergence of different models. Some of these are more conducive to develop sustainability in HRM, whereas others mean it is more challenging for the HRM function to achieve environmental, social, and human sustainability.

Part III of the *Handbook* spans the globe in regions, moving from North to South America, across Western and Central and Eastern Europe and the former Soviet Union, through the Middle East to Africa, across Asia through the Indian subcontinent, East and South East Asia, finally coming to a conclusion in Australasia.

Chapter 20, 'HRM practice and scholarship in North America' (Jackson, Kim, and Schuler), presents the current state of North American HRM practice and scholarship in larger public and private sector organisations, paying particular attention to three issues: the burgeoning freelance economy; achieving gender balance among the managerial tier of organisations; and heightened corporate transparency. Additionally, the authors reflect on the rising awareness of the long-term implications of climate change and environmental degradation and their relationship to HRM. The North American approach to HRM reflects the liberal market economies found in the USA and Canada, with a strong interest in the strategic role of effective HRM.

Chapter 21, 'Revisiting the Latin American HRM model' (Davila and Elvira), identifies the key (silent) stakeholders involved in employment relationships, determining how HRM systems have been configured. The authors develop arguments supporting the three pillars on which this stakeholder HRM model is built. They also present a systematic analysis of ten Latin American multinational corporations' annual and sustainability reports to identify how organisations promote employee involvement with the local community, and the HRM practices that link employees with their proximal community to foster social inclusion.

Chapter 22, 'HRM in Mexico, Central America, and the Caribbean' (Madero-Gómez and Olivas-Luján), focuses on HRM in the Central America region. In a systematic review of extant literature, the authors describe how national (economic, linguistic, historical, and cultural) characteristics have so far fostered research in certain HRM areas. The authors identify research gaps and make a plea for more systematic documentation of this under-researched region of the world.

Chapter 23, 'Comparative HRM research in South America: a call for comparative institutional approaches' (Hermans), argues that extant insights into South American HRM derived from cross-cultural approaches could be enhanced by integrating comparative institutional perspectives. This insightful chapter lays out opportunities and challenges for integrating comparative institutional approaches into HRM research in South America. A primary contribution is an identification of five core issues common to comparative institutional approaches and that are particularly relevant to HRM research in the South American context.

Chapter 24, 'HRM in Western Europe: differences without, differences within' (Brewster, Mayrhofer, and Sparrow), examines the ways in which Western Europe is different from other regions in the world, identifying particularly differences in approaches to stakeholders, the role of government, and employee involvement as crucial. The authors discuss differences within Europe and the various cultural and institutional clusters that have been proposed. The chapter sets this within developments in globalisation but notes that the economic crisis that began in 2008, the UK's 'Brexit' vote, and the election of

President Donald Trump in the USA, have all raised questions about the 'inevitability' of globalisation. The authors conclude that HRM in Europe is likely to remain different from that in the other parts of the world, and the regions within Europe are unlikely to become more standardised in their approach to HRM.

Chapter 25, 'The transition states of Central and Eastern Europe and the former Soviet Union' (Morley, Minbaeva, and Michailova), explores the many countries that have pursued aggressive development trajectories since the early 1990s with varying economic, political, and HRM outcomes. Arising from a review of nomothetic and idiographic studies on HRM in these countries, the authors landscape some key idiosyncratic features at play in the region and chart core aspects of the development of HRM. They question the extent to which 'Western' theories and 'best practices' can be applied to the territory, or whether there is evidence of a unique or hybrid approach to HRM emerging. They conclude that knowledge of HRM in the region remains exploratory at best, and encourage future empirical research.

Chapter 26, 'HRM in the Middle East' (Budhwar and Mellahi) considers the impact on HRM of the major socio-political, economic, and security-related developments that have taken place in the region and which are still unfolding. Particular attention is paid to the dominance of the Arab culture and of Islam in the region, whereby HRM systems are strongly governed by these principles. The authors contend that due to significant differences between the Middle East and other parts of the world (the 'West', in particular), foreign elements of management tend to be, at best, not conducive to the development of sound HRM practices in the region. They also caution that apparent similarities across the region are masking deep-set differences between nations.

Chapter 27, 'HRM in Northern Africa' (Zoogah, Metwally, and Tantoush), reviews historical, institutional, governance, business environment, competitiveness, human development, and demographic factors influencing human resource management (HRM) in Algeria, Egypt, Libya, and Tunisia. Based in case studies, examples are provided of how reactions to similar contexts can produce very different strategic HRM outcomes. The authors conclude with a discussion of the implications and challenges of HRM research in northern Africa, given the paucity of research in the region.

Chapter 28, 'HRM in sub-Saharan Africa: comparative perspectives' (Bischoff and Wood), draws from a small but growing body of HRM research in Africa. Increasing attention is being paid to contextual circumstances, with attention shifting to the relationship between institutions and HRM practice, particularly drawing on the literature on comparative capitalisms and rational hierarchical accounts. This chapter further extends reflections on cultural and institutional factors influencing HRM in the sub-Saharan Africa region, including an exploration of the emerging body of research on Chinese MNCs in Africa.

Chapter 29, 'HRM in the Indian subcontinent' (Budhwar, Varma, and Hirekhan), presents the geographical and socio-economic context of the Indian subcontinent and discusses how relevant factors influence HRM practice in India, Pakistan, Bangladesh, Sri Lanka, Nepal, and Bhutan (including updated insights on each of these countries). The review of extant research emphasises the scarcity of HRM research across the region, and in particular a reliance on exploring the applicability of Western practice rather than understanding indigenous practice. Given the political and economic instability across much of this region, the authors note that this gives rise to major challenges for rapidly evolving HRM systems, where strategic HRM has yet to be recognised as a source of value for organisations.

Chapter 30, 'HRM and Asian socialist economies in transition: China, Vietnam, and North Korea' (Collins, Zhu, and Warner), examines the relationship between economic reform and changes in the employment relationship in three Asian socialist economies: China and Vietnam, both in a 'transitional' stage; and North Korea, which has yet to open itself up to the forces of globalisation. The authors explore the comparable and contrasting experiences of each country, examining the employment relations and HRM systems. This chapter includes data about the recent changes regarding managing the 'new generation' of employees and developing a new status quo in people management at both societal and firm levels.

Chapter 31, 'Japan, South Korea, and Taiwan: issues and trends in HRM' (Debroux, Harry, Hayashi, Huang, Jackson, and Kiyomiya), explores HRM in three countries that share common geographic (East Asia) and economic (embracing capitalism) features despite considerable differences in their ethnic and cultural make-up. The chapter presents reviews of each country's typical approach to HRM explained by the increasingly (financially and politically) challenging contextual settings, including a new discussion on workplace diversity (and discrimination) management.

Chapter 32, 'Comparative HRM research in Indonesia, Malaysia, and the Philippines' (Supangco and Los Baños), reviews both qualitative and quantitative studies including Indonesia, Malaysia, or the Philippines, leading the authors to conclude that there is a substantial research gap in understanding these economies, and to call for new studies to complement other more widely studied Asian economies. The three countries have a shared history and ethnic lineage, but also have in common that we, as yet, know little about how HRM is conducted here.

Chapter 33, 'Styles of HRM in Australia and New Zealand' (Boxall, Bainbridge, and Frenkel), concludes the review of HRM in regions across the world, comparing and contrasting HRM models in Australia and New Zealand. The authors discuss how, despite both being liberal market economies, the differences between the countries in size (geographically and economically) result in variance in HRM practice. In particular, the review emphasizes the importance of small business and informal characteristics of HRM in New Zealand, compared to the typically larger Australian organisations.

Finally, in Part IV, Chapter 34 (Mayrhofer, Brewster, and Farndale) brings this *Handbook* to a conclusion, drawing together common themes from across all chapters, mapping the field of CHRM. We conclude with a reflection of the challenges that remain for comparative analyses, commenting on how the field might continue to develop in the future. Calls are made for a greater range of countries and country clusters to be covered by comparative analyses (which this *Handbook* has already started to address), as well as demanding greater clarity in the HRM phenomena that we are comparing. By adopting more rigorous methodologies and stronger theorizing for comparisons, this will improve our ability to explain rather than just describe the differences and similarities observed across different contexts.

REFERENCES

Ajiferuke, M., & Boddewyn, J. 1970. 'Culture' and other explanatory variables in comparative management studies. *Academy of Management Journal*, 13: 153–163.

Al Ariss, A., & Sidani, Y. 2016a. Comparative international human resource management: Future research directions. *Human Resource Management Review*, 26(4): 352–358.

Al Ariss, A., & Sidani, Y. 2016b. Divergence, convergence, or crossvergence in international human resource management. *Human Resource Management Review*, 26(4): 283–284.

Amable, B. 2003. *The Diversity of Modern Capitalism*. Oxford: Oxford University Press.

Armstrong, M. 2008. *Strategic Human Resource Management: A Guide to Action*. London: Kogan Page.

Bae, J., Chen, S.-J., & Lawler, J.J. 1998. Variations in human resource management in Asian countries: MNC home-country and host-country effects. *International Journal of Human Resource Management*, 9(4): 653–670.

Bamber, G.J., Lansbury, R.D., Wailes, N., & Wright, C.F. (eds). 2016. *International and Comparative Employment Relations* (6th edn). Melbourne: Allen & Unwin.

Beer, M., Boselie, P., & Brewster, C. 2015. Back to the future: Implications for the field of HRM of the multi-stakeholder perspective proposed 30 years ago. *Human Resource Management*, 54(3): 427–438.

Beer, M., Spector, B., Lawrence, P.R., Mills, D.Q., & Walton, R.E. 1985. *Human Resource Management*. New York, USA and London, UK: Free Press.

Begin, J.P. 1992. Comparative human resource management (HRM): A systems perspective. *International Journal of Human Resource Management*, 3: 379–408.

Beugelsdijk, S., Maseland, R., & Hoorn, A. 2015. Are scores on Hofstede's dimensions of national culture stable over time? A cohort analysis. *Global Strategy Journal*, 5(3): 223–240.

Björkman, I., Fey, C.F., & Park, H.J. 2007. Institutional theory and MNC subsidiary HRM practices: evidence from a three-country study. *Journal of International Business Studies*, 38(3): 430–446.

Boxall, P.F. 1992. Strategic human resource management: Beginnings of a new theoretical sophistication?. *Human Resource Management Journal*, 2(3): 60–79.

Boxall, P.F. 1995. Building the theory of comparative HRM. *Human Resource Management Journal*, 5(5): 5–17.

Boxall, P., & Purcell, J. 2007. *Strategy and Human Resource Management*. Management, Work and Organisations series. Basingstoke: Palgrave Macmillan.

Boxenbaum, E. 2006. Lost in translation: The making of Danish diversity management. *American Behavioral Scientist*, 49: 939–948.

Brewster, C. 1995. Towards a 'European' model of human resource management. *Journal of International Business Studies*, 26(1): 1–21.

Brewster, C. 1999a. Different paradigms in strategic HRM: Questions raised by comparative research. In P. Wright, L. Dyer, J. Boudreau, and G. Milkovich (eds), *Research in Personnel and HRM*: 213–238. Greenwich, CT: JAI Press.

Brewster, C. 1999b. Strategic human resource management: The value of different paradigms. *Management International Review*, 39(9): 45–64.

Brewster, C., Brookes, M., & Gollan, P.J. 2015a. The institutional antecedents of the assignment of HRM responsibilities to line managers. *Human Resource Management*, 54(4): 577–597.

Brewster, C., Brookes, M., Johnson, P., & Wood, G. 2014. Direct involvement, partnership and setting: A study in bounded diversity. *International Journal of Human Resource Management*, 25(6): 795–809.

Brewster, C., Gooderham, P.N., & Mayrhofer, W. 2016a. Human resource management: The promise, the performance, the consequences. *Journal of Organizational Effectiveness: People and Performance*, 3(2): 181–190.

Brewster, C., & Hegewisch, A. (eds). 1994. *Policy and Practice in European Human Resource Management. The Price Waterhouse Cranfield Survey*. London, UK and New York, USA: Routledge.

Brewster, C., & Mayrhofer, W. 2009. Comparative human resource management policies and practices. In D.G. Collings and G. Wood (eds), *Human Resource Management: A Critical Approach*: 353–366. London, UK and New York, USA: Routledge.

Brewster, C., & Mayrhofer, W. 2012. Comparative human resource management: An introduction. In C. Brewster and W. Mayrhofer (eds), *Handbook of Research on Comparative Human Resource Management*: 1–23. Cheltenham, UK and Northampton, MA, USA: Edward Elgar Publishing.

Brewster, C., Mayrhofer, W., & Morley, M. (eds). 2000. *New Challenges in European Human Resource Management*. London: Macmillan.

Brewster, C., Mayrhofer, W., & Morley, M. (eds). 2004. *Human Resource Management in Europe: Evidence of Convergence?*. Oxford: Elsevier/Butterworth-Heinemann.

Brewster, C., Mayrhofer, W., & Smale, A. 2016b. Crossing the streams: HRM in multinational enterprises and comparative HRM. *Human Resource Management Review*, 26(4): 285–297.

Brewster, C., & Tyson, S. (eds). 1991. *International Comparisons in Human Resource Management*. London: Pitman.

Brewster, C., Wood, G., & Brookes, M. 2008. Similarity, isomorphism and duality? Recent survey evidence on the HRM Policies of MNCs. *British Journal of Management*, 19(4): 320–342.

Brewster, C., Wood, G., Brookes, M., & van Ommeren, J. 2006. What determines the size of the HR function? A cross-national analysis. *Human Resource Management*, 45(1): 3–21.

Brewster, C., Wood, G., & Goergen, M. 2015b. Institutions, unionization and voice: The relative impact of context and actors on firm level practice. *Economic and Industrial Democracy*, 36(2): 195–214.

Budhwar, P.S., & Debrah, Y. 2001. Rethinking comparative and cross-national human resource management research. *International Journal of Human Resource Management*, 12(3): 497–515.

Chandler, A.D., & Mazlish, B. (eds). 2005. *Leviathans: Multinational Corporations and the New Global History*. Cambridge: Cambridge University Press.

Chen, S.-J., Lawler, J.J., & Bae, J. 2005. Convergence in human resource systems: A comparison of locally owned and MNC subsidiaries in Taiwan. *Human Resource Management*, 44(3): 237–256.

Christiansen, L.C., Kuvaas, B., Biron, M., & Farndale, E. (eds). 2017. *Global Human Resource Management Casebook* (2nd edn). New York, USA and Abingdon, UK: Routledge.

Christensen Hughes, J.M. 2002. HRM and universalism: Is there one best way?. *International Journal of Contemporary Hospitality Management*, 14(5): 221–228.

Clark, T., Gospel, H., & Montgomery, J. 1999. Running on the spot? A review of twenty years of research on the management of human resource in comparative and international perspective. *International Journal of Human Resource Management*, 10(3): 520–544.

Coleman, J.S. 1990. *Foundations of Social Theory*. Cambridge, MA: Harvard University Press.

Collings, D.G., & Wood, G. (eds). 2009. *Human Resource Management: A Critical Approach*. London, UK and New York, USA: Routledge.

Croucher, R., Wood, G., Brewster, C., & Brookes, M. 2012. Employee turnover, HRM and institutional contexts. *Economic and Industrial Democracy*, 33(4): 605–620.

Czarniawska, B., & Sevón, G. (eds). 2005. *Global Ideas: How Ideas, Objects and Practices Travel in the Global Economy*. Copenhagen: Liber, Copenhagen Business School Press.

D'Aunno, T., Succi, M., & Alexander, J. 2000. The role of institutional and market forces in divergent organisational change. *Administrative Science Quarterly*, 45: 679–703.

DeFidelto, C., & Slater, I. 2001. Web-based HR in an international setting. In A.J. Walker (ed.), *Web-Based Human Resources: The Technologies that are Transforming HRL*: 277–294. London: McGraw-Hill.

DiMaggio, P.J., & Powell, W.W. 1983. The iron cage revisited: Institutional isomorphism and collective rationality in organizational fields. *American Sociological Review*, 48: 147–160.

Djelic, M.-L., & Quack, S. (eds). 2003. *Globalization and Institutions: Redefining the Rules of the Economic Game*. Cheltenham, UK and Northampton, MA, USA: Edward Elgar Publishing.

Drori, G.S., Jang, Y.S., & Meyer, J.W. 2006a. Sources of rationalized governance: Cross-national longitudinal analyses 1985–2002. *Administrative Science Quarterly*, 51: 205–229.

Drori, G.S., Meyer, J.W., & Hwang, H. (eds). 2006b. *Globalization and Organization: World Society and Organizational Change*. Oxford: Oxford University Press.

Drori, G.S., Meyer, J.W., & Hwang, H. 2006c. Introduction. In G.S. Drori, J.W. Meyer, and H. Hwang (eds), *Globalization and Organization: World Society and Organizational Change*: 1–22. Oxford: Oxford University Press.

Dunning, J.H. 1992. *Multinational Enterprises and the Global Economy*. Wokingham: Addison-Wesley.

Dunning, J.H., & Lundan, S.M. 2008. *Multinational Enterprises and the Global Economy* (2nd edn). Cheltenham, UK and Northampton, MA, USA: Edward Elgar Publishing.

Durkheim, É. 1933 [1967]. *De la division du travail social*. Paris: Presses Univ. de France.

Elfstrom, G. 1991. *Moral Issues and Multinational Corporations*. New York: St Martin's Press.

Farndale, E., Brewster, C., & Poutsma, E. 2008. Coordinated vs. liberal market HRM: The impact of institutionalization on multinational firms. *International Journal of Human Resource Management*, 19(11): 2004–2023.

Ferner, A. 1997. Country of origin effects and HRM in multinational companies. *Human Resource Management Journal*, 7(1): 19–38.

Ferner, A., & Quintanilla, J. 1998. Multinationals, national business systems and HRM: The enduring influence of national identity or a process of 'Anglo-Saxonisation'. *International Journal of Human Resource Management*, 9(4): 710–731.

Fombrun, C.J., Tichy, N., & Devanna, M.A. 1984. *Strategic Human Resource Management*. New York: Wiley.

Frank, A.G., & Gills, B.K. (eds). 1993. *The World System: Five Hundred Years or Five Thousand?*. London: Routledge.

Friedman, M. 1992. Do old fallacies ever die?. *Journal of Economic Literature*, 30: 2129–2132.

Gamble, J. 2003. Transferring human resource practices from the United Kingdom to China: The limits and potential for convergence. *International Journal of Human Resource Management*, 14(3): 369–387.

Gerhart, B. 2005. Human resources and business performance: Findings, unanswered questions and an alternative approach. *Management Revue*, 16: 174–185.

Goergen, M., Brewster, C., & Wood, G. 2009. Corporate governance regimes and employment relations in Europe. *Relations industrielles/Industrial Relations*, 64(4): 620–640.

Goergen, M., Brewster, C., Wood, G., & Wilkinson, A. 2012. Varieties of capitalism and investments in human capital. *Industrial Relations*, 51(2): 501–527.

Goergen, M., Brewster, C., & Wood, G.T. 2013. The effects of the national setting on employment practice: The case of downsizing. *International Business Review*, 22(6): 620–640.

Goss, D. 1994. *Principles of Human Resource Management*. London: Routledge.

Guest, D. 1990. Human resource management and the American dream. *Journal of Management Studies*, 27(4): 377–397.

Guest, D. 2002. Human resource management, corporate performance and employee wellbeing: Building the worker into HRM. *Journal of Industrial Relations*, 44(3): 335–358.

Guillén, M.F. 2001. *The Limits of Convergence: Globalization and Organizational Change in Argentina, South Korea and Spain*. Princeton, NJ, USA and Oxford, UK: Princeton University Press.

Haley, U.C.V. 2001. *Multinational Corporations in Political Environments: Ethics, Values and Strategies*. River Edge, NJ: World Scientific.

Hall, P.A., & Soskice, D. (eds). 2001. *Varieties of Capitalism: The Institutional Foundations of Comparative Advantage*. Oxford: Oxford University Press.

Harzing, A.-W., & Pinnington, A. (eds). 2015. *International Human Resource Management* (4th edn). London: SAGE.

Hayton, J.C., Kuvaas, B., Castro Christiansen, L., & Biron, M. (eds). 2012. *Global Human Resource Management Casebook*. London: Routledge.

Hegewisch, A., & Brewster, C. (eds). 1993. *European Developments in Human Resouurce Management*. London: Kogan Page.

Hendry, C., & Pettigrew, A. 1990. Human resource management: An agenda for the 1990s. *International Journal of Human Resource Management*, 1(1): 17–44.

Hollingsworth, J.R., & Boyer, R. 1997. Coordination of economic actors and social systems of production. In J.R. Hollingsworth and R. Boyer (eds), *Contemporary Capitalism*: 1–47. Cambridge: Cambridge University Press.

Horwitz, F., & Budhwar, P. (eds). 2015. *Handbook of Human Resource Management in Emerging Markets*. Cheltenham, UK and Northampton, MA, USA: Edward Elgar Publishing.

Hotelling, H. 1933. Review of *The Triumph of Mediocrity in Business* by Horace Secrist. *Journal of the American Statistical Association*, 28: 463–465.

Jackson, S.E., & Schuler, R.S. 1995. Understanding human resource management in the context of organizations and their environments. *Annual Review of Psychology*, 46: 237–264.

Jepperson, R. 2002. The development and application of sociological neoinstitutionalism. In J. Berger and M. Zelditch (eds), *New Directions in Contemporary Sociological Theory*: 229–266. Lanham, MD: Rowman & Littlefield Publishers.

Kaufman, B.E. 2016. Globalization and convergence–divergence of HRM across nations: New measures, explanatory theory, and non-standard predictions from bringing in economics. *Human Resource Management Review*, 26(4): 338–351.

Kochan, T.A., Dyer, L., & Batt, R. 1992. International human resource management studies: a framework for future research. In D. Lewin, O.S. Mitchell, and P.D. Sherer (eds), *Research Frontiers in Industrial Relations and Human Resources*: 309–337. Madison, WI: IRRA.

Krücken, G., & Drori, G.S. 2009. *World Society: The Writings of John W. Meyer*. Oxford: Oxford University Press.

Lam, A. 1994. The utilisation of human resources: A comparative study of British and Japanese engineers in electronics industries. *Human Resource Management Journal*, 4(3): 22–40.

Locke, R., Piore, M., & Kochan, T. 1995. Introduction. In R. Locke, T. Kochan, and M. Piore (eds), *Employment Relations in a Changing World Economy*: i–xviii. Cambridge, MA: MIT Press.

Lowe, K.B., Milliman, J., Cieri, H., & Dowling, P.J. 2002. International compensation practices: A ten-country comparative analysis. *Human Resource Management*, 41(1): 45–66.

Marx, K. 1844 [2002]. Ökonomisch-philosophische Manuskripte aus dem Jahre 1844 – Kap. 4. Die Akkumulation der Kapitalien und die Konkurrenz unter den Kapitalisten, *MEW Bd.* 40: 465–589.

Mayrhofer, W. 2007. European comparative management research: Towards a research agenda. *European Journal of International Management*, 1(3): 191–205.

Mayrhofer, W., Brewster, C., Morley, M., & Ledolter, J. 2011. Hearing a different drummer? Convergence of human resource management in Europe: A longitudinal analysis. *Human Resource Management Review*, 21(1): 50–67.

Mayrhofer, W., Morley, M., & Brewster, C. 2004. Convergence, stasis, or divergence?. In C. Brewster, W. Mayrhofer, and M. Morley (eds), *Human Resource Management in Europe: Evidence of Convergence?*: 417–436. London: Elsevier/Butterworth-Heinemann.

Mayrhofer, W., Müller-Camen, M., Ledolter, J., et al. 2002. The diffusion of management concepts in Europe: Conceptual considerations and longitudinal analysis. *Journal of Cross-Cultural Competence and Management*, 3: 315–349.

Mayrhofer, W., & Reichel, A. 2009. Comparative analysis of HR. In P.R. Sparrow (ed.), *Handbook of*

International Human Resource Management: Integrating People, Process, and Context: 41–62. Chichester: Wiley.

Meyer, J.W. 2000. Globalization: Sources and effects on national states and societies. *International Sociology*, 15: 233–248.

Meyer, J.W., Drori, G.S., & Hwang, H. 2006. World society and the proliferation of formal organization. In G.S. Drori, J.W. Meyer, and H. Hwang (eds), *Globalization and Organization: World Society and Organizational Change*: 25–49. Oxford: Oxford University Press.

Meyer, J.W., & Rowan, E. 1977. Institutionalized organizations: Formal structure as myth and ceremony. *American Journal of Sociology*, 83: 340–363.

Meyer, K.E. (ed.). 2008. *Multinational Enterprises and Host Economies*. Cheltenham, UK and Northampton, MA, USA: Edward Elgar Publishing.

Meyer, K.E., Mudambi, R., & Narula, R. 2011. Multinational enterprises and local contexts: The opportunities and challenges of multiple embeddedness. *Journal of Management Studies*, 48(2): 235–252.

Ohmae, K. 1995. *The End of the Nation State: The Rise of Regional Economies*. New York: Free Press.

Paauwe, J., & Farndale, E. 2016. Modelling the SHRM–performance relationship: The contextual SHRM model. Paper presented at 10th Human Resource Management Workshop, Cadiz, Spain: University of Cadiz, October 28.

Parry, E., Stavrou, E., & Lazarova, M.B. (eds). 2013. *Global Trends in Human Resource Management*. Houndsmills, UK and New York, USA: Palgrave Macmillan.

Pfeffer, J. 1998. *Putting People First*. Boston, MA: Harvard Business School Press.

Poor, J., Karoliny, Z., Alas, R., & Vatchkova, E.K. 2011. Comparative international human resource management (CIHRM) in the light of the Cranet Regional Research Survey in Transitional Economies. *Employee Relations*, 33(4): 428–443.

Psychogios, A., & Wood, G.T. 2010. Human resource management in comparative perspective: Alternative institutional perspectives and empirical reality. *International Journal of Human Resource Management*, 21(4): 2614–2630.

Pudelko, M. 2005. Cross-national learning from best practice and the convergence–divergence debate in HRM. *International Journal of Human Resource Management*, 16(11): 2045–2074.

Reiche, B.S., Lee, Y.-T., & Quintanilla, J. 2012. Cultural perspectives on comparative HRM. In C. Brewster and W. Mayrhofer (eds), *Handbook of Research on Comparative Human Resource Management*: 51–68. Cheltenham, UK and Northampton, MA, USA: Edward Elgar Publishing.

Richbell, S., Brookes, M., Brewster, C., & Wood, G. 2011. Non-standard working time: An international and comparative analysis. *International Journal of Human Resource Management*, 22(4): 945–962.

Rose, M.J. 1991. Comparing forms of comparative analysis. *Political Studies*, 39: 446–462.

Rosenzweig, P.M., & Nohria, N. 1994. Influences on human resource development practices in multinational corporations. *Journal of International Business Studies*, 25(1): 229–251.

Rugman, A., & Verbeke, A. 2001. Subsidiary specific advantages in multinational enterprises. *Strategic Management Journal*, 22(3): 237–250.

Sahlin-Andersson, K., & Engwall, L. 2002. Carriers, flows, and sources of management knowledge. In K. Sahlin-Andersson and L. Engwall (eds), *The Expansion of Management Knowledge: Carriers, Flows, and Sources*: 3–32. Stanford, CA: Stanford University Press.

Scheuer, S. 2011. Union membership variation in Europe: A ten-country comparative study. *European Journal of Industrial Relations*, 17(1): 57–73.

Schmitt, J., & Mitukiewicz, A. 2012. Politics matter: Changes in unionisation rates in rich countries, 1960–2010. *Industrial Relations Journal*, 43(3): 260–280.

Schuler, R.S. 1992. Strategic human resource management: Linking the people with the strategic needs of the business. *Organizational Dynamics*, 21(1): 18–32.

Simon, H.A. 1955. A behavioral model of rational choice. *Quarterly Journal of Economics*, 69(1): 99–118.

Sparrow, P.R. (ed.). 2009. *Handbook of International Human Resource Management: Integrating People, Process, and Context*. Chichester: Wiley.

Sparrow, P., & Hiltrop, J.M. 1994. *European Human Resource Management in Transition*. Hempel Hempstead: Prentice Hall.

Stahl, G., Björkman, I., & Morris, S. (eds). 2012. *Handbook of Research in International Human Resource Management* (2nd edn). Cheltenham, UK and Northampton, MA, USA: Edward Elgar Publishing.

Storey, J. 1992. *Developments in the Management of Human Resources: An Analytical Review*. Oxford: Blackwell Publishers.

Strauss, J.P., & Connerley, M.L. 2003. Demographics, personality, contact, and universal-diverse orientation: An exploratory analysis. *Human Resource Management*, 42(2): 159–174.

Tregaskis, O., & Brewster, C. 2006. Converging or diverging? A comparative analysis of trends in contingent employment practice in Europe over a decade. *Journal of International Business Studies*, 37(1): 111–126.

Veblen, T. 1904. *The Theory of Business Enterprise*. New York: Charles Scribner's Sons.

Vernon, G., & Brewster, C. 2013. Structural spoilers or structural supports? Unions and the strategic integration of HR functions. *International Journal of Human Resource Management*, 24(6): 1113–1129.

Walker, J.T., Brewster, C., & Wood, G. 2014. Diversity between and within varieties of capitalism: Transnational survey evidence. *Industrial and Corporate Change*, 23(2): 493–533.

Wallerstein, I.M. 1974. *The Modern World-System*. New York: Academic Press.

Watson, T. 2004. HRM and critical social science analysis. *Journal of Management Studies*, 41(3): 447–467.

Weber, M. 1921 [1980]. *Wirtschaft und Gesellschaft* (5th edn). Tübingen: Mohr.

Wettstein, F. 2009. *Multinational Corporations and Global Justice: Human Rights Obligations of a Quasi-Governmental Institution*. Stanford, CA: Stanford Business Books.

Whitley, R. 1999. *Divergent Capitalisms: The Social Structuring and Change of Business Systems*. Oxford: Oxford University Press.

Wood, G., Psychogios, A., Szamosi, L.T., & Collings, D.G. 2012. Institutional approaches to comparative HRM. In C. Brewster and W. Mayrhofer (eds), *Handbook of Research on Comparative Human Resource Management*: 27–50. Cheltenham, UK and Northampton, MA, USA: Edward Elgar Publishing.

Wright, P.M., Dunford, B.B., & Snell, S.A. 2001. Human resources and the resource based view of the firm. *Journal of Management*, 27: 701–722.

PART I

THEORETICAL, CONCEPTUAL, AND EMPIRICAL ISSUES IN COMPARATIVE HRM

2. Comparative institutional analysis and comparative HRM

Geoffrey Wood, Alexandros Psychogios, Leslie T. Szamosi, and David G. Collings

INTRODUCTION

There has been an increasing interest in institutional approaches to understanding people management. What such approaches have in common is a recognition that the choices made by individual and collective actors are moulded by context. A fundamental distinction between different strands of institutionalist thinking, however, centres on the relative desirability of regulatory features that enhance employee rights and constrain the extent to which the firm should be purely a vehicle for the advancement of shareholder value. A further distinction is between those that accord a primary focus to institutional processes – most notably the sociological tradition – and those that seek to draw links between specific types of regulation, and the types of organisational practice that emerge and persist.

Dominant in the economics and finance literature is the view that the primary function of institutions should be the protection of private property rights, to secure the maximisation of shareholder value (North, 1990; Shleifer & Vishny, 1997). Such approaches hold that contextual features that encourage empowerment of employees and codetermination are inherently undesirable, in that they result in a misdirection of what rightly belongs to owners, ultimately making for wasteful and uncompetitive firms. In contrast, socioeconomic perspectives suggest the possibility of complementarities, that is, sets of rules and practices that can work together to produce better results than a single regulatory dimension on its own might yield (Hall & Soskice, 2001b). In turn, this means that other national recipes than the liberal market shareholder value-centred model are potentially at least equally viable. In turn, this would suggest that in more coordinated institutional settings, human resource management (HRM) policies and practices characterised by co-determination may yield superior results, even if they dilute shareholder rights (Whitley, 1999; Hall & Soskice, 2001b).

In this chapter, we highlight some of the most influential approaches to understanding variations in HRM policy and practice, and draw out the implications of recent theoretical developments. Although the different comparative approaches vary in the relative attention they accord to the specific details of HRM practice, they all make broad predictions as to the impact of context on the relative attention accorded to a firm's employees and whether they are treated primarily in instrumental cost–benefit terms.

Sociological Accounts

Although sociological new institutionalism has many faces and indeed has taken on a number of guises, its central tenets remain consistent (see Scott, 1987). The underlying thesis of the approach is that advances in technology and communications are creating a less differentiated world order, where differences in management practices which had been perpetuated by geographic isolation of businesses are superseded by the logic of technology. Hence it predicts convergence in management practices globally (Kidger, 1991). Organisations have a tendency to copy what is done elsewhere in an attempt to gain legitimacy or the support of external agencies within a society (Strauss & Hanson, 1997). Thus it emphasises the influence of the societal or cultural environment on organisations (DiMaggio & Powell, 1983; Meyer & Rowan, 1977).

Institutionalisation has been defined as the 'process by which social processes, obligations, or actualities come to take on a rule-like status in social thought and action' (Meyer & Rowan, 1977: 341). What this means in practical terms is that, whilst existing in an institutional context, the firm may itself be subject to institutionalisation, developing its own specific – albeit context aligned – embedded patterns and rules of behaviour (Phillips et al., 2004). However, a primary concern with the latter process and with the forces securing homogenisation across national settings has meant that only limited attention is accorded to the specific nature of commonalities in HRM practice within them. Again, a focus on institutionalisation processes has meant that there has been a relative neglect of the commonalities and differences between different national institutional frameworks, and what really sets different types of national institution apart.

In order to ensure their survival, organisations must respond to expectations and cultural pressures emanating from their environment, and duly fit in through aligning themselves with widely expected management practices and associated organisational structures (Meyer & Rowan, 1977). Thus, firms operating in the same regulatory environment will adopt similar HRM practices, a process referred to as 'isomorphism' (Kostova & Roth, 2002). This isomorphic process may be mimetic (firms copy practices associated with success), coercive (firms are forced to do certain things), or normative (firms do what is considered to be the 'right thing' to do in a particular environment (DiMaggio & Powell, 1983). At earlier stages of adaptation functional or technical criteria may be key determinants of adoptions of innovations; the importance of these determinants, however, become weaker over time (Tolbert & Zucker, 1983). The decision to conform to a set of institutionalised practices is premised on the expectation that organisations are rewarded for doing so through increased legitimacy, resources, or survival capabilities rather than simply because they are taken for granted or 'constitute reality' (Meyer & Rowan, 1977). In other words, there are some external incentives which inform the organisation's decision to adopt the practices.

In theorising how a process becomes institutionalised, Tolbert and Zucker (1996) identify a three-stage process of institutionalisation. Initially, in the pre-institutionalised stage, there is limited knowledge of a process and few adaptors of it. As diffusion of the practice increases and it begins to gain normative acceptance, it becomes semi-institutionalised. Finally, in the last stage, full institutionalisation, the practice becomes 'taken for granted by members of a social group as efficacious and necessary' (Tolbert and Zucker, 1996: 179). A further distinction relates to the extent to which policies are internalised (Kostova & Roth, 2002) vis-à-vis mere 'ceremonial adoption' reflecting a lack of belief or commitment to practices or structures, resulting in loose coupling between the practices and day-to-day activity. Internalisation is hypothesised to be a function of the belief that the practice is valuable, whereas when actors do not perceive the practice to be valuable ceremonial adoption is more likely. However, as noted above, it is largely left to other accounts to identify commonalities and differences between specific national institutional frameworks, and the types of HRM practices likely to occur in those sharing broadly similar features.

INSTITUTIONS, WORK, AND EMPLOYMENT: RATIONAL HIERARCHICAL APPROACHES

Economics and Finance Approaches

There are a range of different ways in which the impact of institutions on the practice of HRM (and vice versa) may be understood. Whilst the rational choice approach focuses on the actions of rational profit-seeking individuals which, it is assumed, will operate most effectively in the absence of regulatory restraints, developments of this tradition have taken on board the possible effects of institutions. In a classic study, North (1990) argued that embedded property rights would make for more optimal economic outcomes; they would encourage rational actors to make the 'right decisions', focusing on the optimal utilisation of resources, which would be conducive to higher organisational returns and overall economic growth (ibid.).

A substantive component of the literature in this tradition has retained North's (1990) preoccupation with property rights and sought to extend it to draw conclusions as to the optimal relationship between a firm and its employees. For example, Shleifer and Vishny (1997) argue that, as only shareholders have sunk funds into the organisation, its objectives should primarily be the maximisation of returns. Indeed, it has been argued that improving the terms and conditions of employment dilutes managerial accountability to shareholders: as employees gain more rights, this restrains the ability of managers to act autonomously, and hence to act as effective agents of owners (Djankov et al., 2003).

Within this approach, a particularly influential view is that it is the legal tradition that will mould corporate governance and, hence, HRM practice. La Porta et al. (1997) argue that common law countries – for example, the United States of America (USA) and the United Kingdom (UK) – are associated with stronger rights for owners but weaker rights for employees. On the one hand, a long tradition of legal precedents has made for clearly defined owner rights and effective mechanisms to ensure that companies are governed in a manner that is in the owner's interest. In contrast, in civil law countries, employer rights are weaker. Given weaker investor protection, there will be a lower degree of formal separation of ownership from control (La Porta et al., 1997, 1998). In addition, employee rights are likely to be stronger in such contexts (Djankov et al., 2003). In civil law countries, labour legislation tends to be more comprehensive, making individual employees and unions more confident of their rights. In common law countries, labour legislation tends to be of the broad brushstroke variety, which is fleshed out by case law. In practice, this means that individual employees will have to make greater use of litigation, a highly risky process with uncertain outcomes, with the firm having a much greater pool of resources (that is, capital and legal expertise) at its disposal during a dispute. In terms of practical work and employment relations, this means that firms in civil law countries will find it much more difficult to shed labour; from a neoliberal perspective, this may generate greater 'inefficiencies'. Again, firms will face greater constraints on their ability to deploy labour power, resulting in a greater degree of codetermination.

La Porta et al. (1997, 1998) see the relationship between employer and employee rights as a zero-sum game: if one side has more rights (and is more powerful), the other side will necessarily have fewer rights (Djankov et al., 2003). This viewpoint can be contrasted with more optimistic strands of the HRM literature which suggest that employers and employees can mutually benefit from a situation that combines a focus on the 'bottom line' (that is, shareholder value), with cooperative paradigms in the workplace (Kochan & Ostermann, 1994).

In practical terms, what this amounts to is that shareholder-dominant contexts will be associated with instrumentalist HRM policies and practices, designed to closely align employees with the shareholder value maximisation agenda. These would include contingent pay systems, particularly linking reward to share prices; a high emphasis on numerical flexibility and contingent employment; and an effort to shift the costs of training and development onto the individual employee (Brewster et al., 2012). A further feature is an emphasis on keeping staffing to a bare minimum, in order not to unnecessarily tie up resources (Goergen et al., 2013). It is argued that any system that accords voice to employees, or accords them more pay than the minimum the external labour market will bear, is a misdirection of shareholder value, and reflects an ability for managers to conspire with employees in the interests of empire building (Djankov et al., 2003).

A central drawback with this approach is that it assumes that such techniques, and – more broadly speaking – strong owner rights, are more efficient, whilst the evidence is rather more mixed. Countries that have been particularly successful in incrementally innovative high value-added manufacturing are associated with high levels of employee rights, making for an environment conducive to mutual trust and effective human capital development. It is worth noting that, whilst commonly dismissed by neoliberals as an uncompetitive basket case throughout the 1990s, Germany remained the world's biggest exporter (even larger than China), and recovered from the 2008 economic crisis quite rapidly. Again, a close scrutiny of Organisation for Economic Co-operation and Development (OECD) data from 1980 to 2014 reveals that many countries with strong levels of employee rights (for example, across Scandinavia) have outperformed deregulated liberal markets such as the USA and the UK (OECD, 2015). Finally, a recent study by Johnson et al. (2017) highlighted the limitations of La Porta's usage of country taxonomies. Firstly, Scandinavia cannot, as suggested by La Porta et al., be considered as simply a diluted version of civil law with strong common law features; rather, the system works to secure even stronger levels of employee countervailing power than encountered in France, the archetypical civil law case. Secondly, civil law countries impart many beneficial features in their own right, which can include greater levels of overall well-being; institutions cannot simply be considered as a blunt instrument to serve economic ends.

Political Science Approaches

Roe (2003) suggests that, above all, it is government ideology that will determine the relative position of employees vis-à-vis owners. In countries with right-wing governments, owner rights are likely to be stronger and worker rights weaker; this will allow managers to act more effectively in the interests of owners. However, this process should be qualified: there is a degree of path dependence, which can be traced back to the underlying structures of the national economy at a formative stage, in addition to formal rules and regulations which may be adjusted according to the government of the day (Bebchuk & Roe, 1999). Path dependency also represents a product of the manner in which vested interests operate; Bebchuk and Roe (1999) suggest that, for example, if employee rights are stronger, employees will resist deregulation even if this may result in greater efficiency.

What does this translate to in practical HRM terms? Roe (2003) suggests that managers and workers, if not subject to the control of shareholders, have a vested interest in retaining and expanding job provision; the managers, as with legal origin tradition, for reasons of empire building, and workers for security. Similarly, wage rates are likely to be inflated under such circumstances. In contrast, where owner rights are stronger, human resources can be deployed instrumentally: surplus labour can readily be shed, wages are restrained, and what is commonly termed 'hard' HRM techniques (for example, focused performance appraisals, narrowly defined performance-based pay) can be deployed.

Another strand of the rational hierarchical literature that explores the relationship between institutions, politics, and workplace practice looks at the effects of electoral systems. Pagano and Volpin (2005) argue that employees will have weaker rights and employers stronger rights in first-past-the-post electoral systems, such as found in the USA and the UK. The reason is that such systems result in clear governing majorities (even if the electoral verdict was more mixed), allowing governments to concentrate on promoting shareholder value (and, hence, a particular trajectory of economic growth), unhampered by pressures posed by interest groupings. In contrast, in proportional representation countries (such as continental Europe), coalition governments are more common, giving interest groupings (such as unions) more influence. In practical workplace terms, this may result in unions having stronger legal rights, forcing firms to adopt more pluralist employment relations policies, centring on the collective representation of employees via collective bargaining or works councils.

There appears to be some evidence to support these arguments: it is worth noting that New Zealand, which formerly had a first-past-the-post electoral system, gradually drifted away from extremist neoliberalism following the adoption of a German-style proportional representation system. Again, whilst a first-past-the-post system, the need to modify policies to appease Québécois potential separatist voters and effective regulations against gerrymandering have meant that Canadian governments have, whatever their inclination, been unable to implement more extremist neoliberal policies without facing electoral defeat. Hence, worker rights are stronger, and union density greater in Canada, than is the case in liberal markets without such checks and balances.

Summarising Rational Hierarchical Approaches

Rational hierarchical economic and political science approaches assume that the relationship between owner and worker rights is a zero-sum game. Where owner rights are stronger, this will make for HRM policies that are more 'bottom line' orientated, characterised by individually orientated performance evaluation and reward systems, and low security of tenure. Where owner rights are weaker, worker (and union) rights will invariably be stronger: this will make for stronger job security (and hence lower staff turnover rates) which, from a neoliberal perspective, will make firms less numerically flexible. At

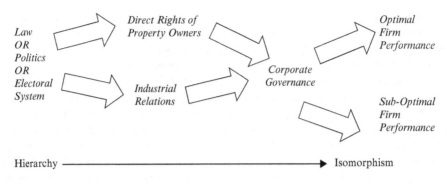

Source: Boyer (2006).

Figure 2.1   Rational choice accounts of institutional setting, property owners, and outcomes

the same time, managerial (and owner) power will be diluted through co-determinist structures for employee representation in the workplace, which could encompass both collective bargaining and works councils. Figure 2.1 summarises this process.

Although it could be assumed that light regulation in other areas would make for 'diffuse diversity', rational hierarchical approaches suggest that uniformities in practices are likely to emerge and persist even in heavily deregulated liberal markets, reflecting both the existence of efficient best practices and an isomorphic process imposing commonalities based on practical efficiencies and shared rules (Boyer, 2006). Table 2.1 further illustrates differences and similarities.

Recent developments and extensions of the finance literature have examined the issue of complementarity. For Gordon and Roe (2004: 16), complementarity is where practices fit together, mutually increasing the overall system benefits; this means that practices that are objectively 'inferior' may persist if they can generate overall benefits. Hence, a problem with systemic change may be that existing complementarities may be jettisoned, with no assurances that better complementarities may replace them. This is an important departure from the mainstream neoliberal economic tradition, in that it concedes that liberalisation may not be uniformly possible or desirable; it also means that institutional orders where property rights are mediated are not necessarily inferior.

The Literature on Comparative Capitalism

The 'relationship' approaches within the varieties of capitalism (VoC) literature do not see owner dominance as necessarily resulting in superior organisational and macroeconomic outcomes, given that the inputs of other social actors contribute to the emergence and persistence of combinations of complementarities that may be beneficial to a large component of society (see Figure 2.2). Nor is the relationship a linear one, with hierarchy making for isomorphism: no single institutional feature is necessarily the most important or dominant one (Boyer, 2006).

If a number of different institutions and practices are found clustered together, this

Table 2.1   Variations in rational hierarchical approaches

Theory characteristic	Political science	Political science	Economic
Key theorists	Roe	Pagano & Volpin	La Porta et al.
Determines strength of non-owner stakeholders	Government policy and ideology	Electoral system	Legal system
Measure	Left- or right-wing governments	Proportional representation (PR) or first-past-the-post	Common or civil law
Path dependence	Only one optimal trajectory possible	Limited number of alternatives; electoral systems rarely changed	Path dependence
Predictions: shareholder rights	Property owners stronger under right-wing governments	Property owners stronger under majoritarian systems	Property owners stronger under common law
Predictions: employee rights	Right-wing governments are likely to make for weaker employee rights, and hence, fewer constraints on corporate governance	First-past-the-post electoral systems are likely to make for weaker employee rights, and hence, fewer constraints on corporate governance	Common law systems are likely to make for weaker employee rights, and hence, fewer constraints on corporate governance
Number of optimal arrangements	One	Onc	One

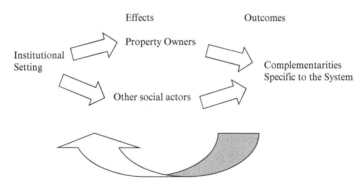

Figure 2.2   Alternative accounts of institutional setting, social outcomes and outcomes: a complementarity perspective

would suggest coherence and complementarity (Boyer, 2006). Proponents of the shareholder model focus on a single hierarchical set of relations; those who question the superiority of the shareholder model would argue that alternative sets of relationships may make for alternative complementarities (Boyer, 2006). In other words, even if owners are weaker, firms and/or other stakeholders – and indeed, the economy at large – may do equally as well (if not better) than when owner rights are stronger.

A further question is the issue of sustainability. Rational choice incentives approaches suggest that systemic inertia, imposed by non-rational social relations – superstitions and their modern counterparts (for example, worker rights) – may lock a system onto a suboptimal path (see North, 1990). The VoC literature suggests that, whilst institutional arrangements are subject to development and adjustment over time, there is a similar degree of path dependence, but that this is often positive: social actors know how the system works, lowering transaction costs, and making the retention of the existing order viable, even if it is operating suboptimally (see Marsden, 1999; Whitley, 1999).

To summarise, firstly, particular institutional designs may be seen as encouraging owners and managers to make optimal choices: a particular hierarchy imposes isomorphism (Boyer, 2006). Alternatively, it can be argued that there is no single set of optimal choices; rather, rules and practices may be combined in different ways to bring about different types of complementarity. In other words, one system may work nearly (or equally) as well as another; there is no single 'best' way of doing things, as would be suggested by the rational choice model. Finally, institutions may evolve in a linear path-dependent way, or be prone to periodic restructuring and redesign in response to ad hoc systemic crises.

The Varieties of Capitalism Approach

Possibly the most influential strand of the literature on comparative capitalism is the varieties of capitalism approach. The ascendancy of right-wing governments into power in both the UK and the USA in the 1980s led to increasingly confident neoliberal questioning of the viability of more regulated economies in continental Western Europe and Japan. The fact that such economies continued to outperform liberal markets economies such as the UK and USA through much of the 1980s did little to deter them. These attacks intensified when, during the late 1990s and the early 2000s, liberal markets outperformed Germany and Japan. The fact that more regulated Scandinavian countries performed even better than liberal markets during these years, and Germany and Japan not very much worse (OECD, 2007), did little to deter these attacks.

It was partially in reaction to this that the influential VoC literature emerged (Lincoln & Kalleberg, 1990; Dore, 2000; Hall & Soskice, 2001b). This literature draws on both the structuralist sociology of Talcott Parsons (1951) and the political economy of Karl Polanyi (1957). In his classic account of institutions, firms, and practice, Dunlop (1975) argued that what firms did reflected their wider social context. Formal political frameworks, and the nature of socialisation, located economic transactions in the context of rights and obligations; within the firm, this means that industrial relations (and HRM) will tend to follow certain patterns in specific contexts which are ever developing (Wood et al., 2015). This could aid in generating greater levels of predictability and trust, allowing for better outcomes for individual actors than were this not the case. Similarly, Bendix (1956) argued that, rather than through autocratic owner power, firms may work better through softer, more cooperative ways of doing things, promoted by wider institutional realities.

Central to the varieties of capitalism is a distinction between the above-mentioned liberal market economies (LMEs) and the coordinated market economies (CMEs) of continental North-Western Europe ('Rhineland' and Scandinavia) and the Far East

(Japan and Korea). Within the former, shareholders are more powerful, and within the latter they share power with other stakeholders (Dore, 2000). Whilst this may not sound that much different from rational-hierarchical approaches, a defining feature of the VoC literature is that it saw LMEs as no 'better' in terms of organisational performance and macroeconomic outcomes than CMEs; implicit, however, is that they were worse in terms of securing sustainable growth and stakeholder well-being (cf. Dore, 2000; Lincoln & Kalleberg, 1990).

This difference reflects the VoC literature's conception of institutions themselves, the nature of complementarity and of path dependence. The rational-hierarchical literature primarily views institutions as providers of incentives and disincentives to rational actors. In contrast, the VoC literature saw them as webs of relationships, linking together social actors: in short, in any context, 'economic man' is bounded and constrained. Whilst institutions are concentrated at the state level, reflected in formal law and societal conventions, they enmesh and bind together economic and non-economic associations and individuals.

Institutions are likely to persist if complementarities are present: that is, if one works better through the presence of another (Hall & Soskice, 2001a: 18). For example, banking regulations and the operation of financial markets may encourage more 'patient' investor behaviour. This may be complementary to labour market institutions characterised by a high degree of protection of employment rights. This might mean in turn that owners are not only under less short-term pressure to maximise profits, but also cannot easily make workers redundant in the event of a downturn. This should encourage human capital development, which is likely to be good for both employees and the long-term future of the firm. In such contexts, firms will have a workforce with a high degree of organisation-specific skills, and the knowledge base of the firm will be preserved; this will be particularly good for incrementally innovative areas of economic activity, such as high value-added manufacturing (Thelen, 2001). Here, two institutional features working together yield greater benefits than they might have had on their own (cf. Boyer, 2006). Social compromises are likely to take place and continue through the operation of complementarities: trade-offs and concessions are likely to occur if they will result in a disproportionately 'good' pay-off (see Figure 2.3).

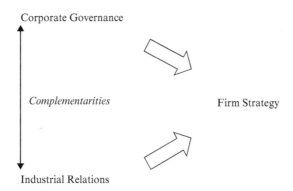

Source: Jackson (2005: 378).

Figure 2.3   Corporate governance and HR: a complementarity perspective

There is little doubt that such an approach adds much to our understanding of why national economies are, and remain, different: specific configurations encourage firms to take on ways of doing things in a wide range of areas that are likely to harness systemic complementarities (Hall & Soskice, 2001a: 18). Clusters of practices are, hence, likely to emerge and persist within individual national regulatory contexts. Rational hierarchical approaches argue that, as deregulated economies are more efficient, they would be more likely to supplant others. In contrast, the VoC literature holds that distinct national developmental paths will develop and emerge; hence, path dependence, with national systems evolving but remaining distinct.

There are two major criticisms that can be levelled against the VoC approach. The first is that some critics have suggested that the VoC literature is overly functionalist (Streeck, 2005). In other words, it assumes that institutional features work together in such a way as to make for overall systemic functionality, and that new institutional features will be introduced to strengthen and broaden existing complementarities, making for even evolution. However, it can be argued that complementarities need not always be the product of functioning institutional components; rather, complementarities may compensate for institutional weaknesses (Crouch, 2005). For example, Crouch argues that the German vocational training system provides industry-specific skills, allowing individual employees to move within a particular industry. Not all complementarities are about synergies (Deeg, 2005); indeed, some may flow from dysfunctional systemic features, such as the operation of a military–industrial complex in the USA, which has nonetheless had some positive spin-offs in the high-technology sector. The range of permutations in the operation of complementarities are summarised in Figure 2.4.

A further criticism levelled against the early VoC literature was a perceived lack of attention to institutional change. If institutions had attained a certain level of maturity, it was assumed that strong benefits would accrue to key players, which would then be strongly committed to maintaining the status quo (Hall & Soskice, 2001b). In short, this would suggest that systems evolve in a linear and orderly fashion towards a particular optimal state. However, as Hollingsworth (2006) argues, the process of institutional building and redesign is uneven and episodic; again, what works at one specific time will not necessarily work in another. In response to this, proponents of the VoC approach have conceded that institutional arrangements are conditional and contingent, and key actors will constantly seek to test the boundaries, in order to see if they can enhance their returns through modifying the system (Wilkinson et al., 2014). Again, it could be argued that whatever the shortfalls of the VoC approach, it does point to a persistent truth: liberal and coordinated markets are associated with fundamental differences in dominant approaches to people management, which has been verified by repeated firm-level survey evidence (Brewster et al., 2014).

Business Systems Theory

A variation of the VoC literature is the business systems approach. Business systems are: 'distinctive patterns of economic organisation that vary in their degree and mode of authoritative co-ordination of economic activities, and in the organisation of, and interconnections between, owners, managers, experts and other employees' (Whitley, 1999: 33).

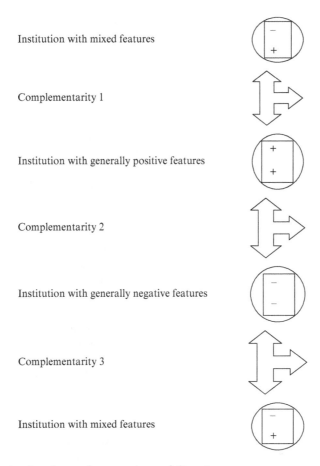

Institution with mixed features

Complementarity 1

Institution with generally positive features

Complementarity 2

Institution with generally negative features

Complementarity 3

Institution with mixed features

Figure 2.4   Institutional complementarity and diversity

Hence, business systems represent ways of regulating market relations, making possible everyday economic exchange relationships through imitation, administrative structures, and social and network ties (Pedersen & Thomsen, 1999). Business systems approaches share the VoC literature's central concern with the nature of complementarity. From a business systems perspective, complementarities result not only from economic experimentation, but also from innovations by organisations constantly seeking new advantages; similarly, old complementarities are likely to be subject to constant modification and renewal (Morgan, 2007). In contrast to the VoC literature, business systems theory places the firm at the centre of this web of relationships. In practical terms, this means that more explicit attention is accorded to the HRM effects of institutions.

The degree to which managers are autonomous (vis-à-vis capital markets, owners, and providers of credit), the power of unions, and the extent to which employees can impact upon what firms do reflects the degree to which, in a particular context, managers and workers can have common interests and establish particular work and employment relations practices (Whitley, 1999). The latter can be divided into two broad categories. Firstly, there is the degree of employer–employee interdependence (ibid.). This can be defined as both a product of security of tenure, and the extent to which each side has committed resources to continuing the relationship. From the point of view of employees, this would include developing their organisation-specific skills; while from the firm's point of view the focus is on the degree of spending on training, particularly focused on long-term skills and capability development. Secondly, there is the degree of delegation to employees. This may range from advanced forms of delegation (for example, via collective bargaining; here managers agree to share through negotiation, to a greater or lesser degree, decision-making regarding the nature of the employment contract) and works councils, to weaker, more consultative forms of delegation (for example, through quality circles).

Empirical research by Brewster et al. (2007) has confirmed the strong relationship between national context and variations in both the degree of delegation and interdependence. In liberal markets, both employer–employee interdependence will be lower (weaker job security and less emphasis on long-term human capital development), as will be delegation to employees (collective representation of employees will be similarly weaker than in more cooperative varieties of capitalism) (Whitley, 1999; Brewster et al., 2007).

If the first major difference between the VoC literature and business systems theory is the fact that the latter is more firm-orientated, the second major difference is the number of systemic archetypes. Whitley (1999) has identified six archetypical business systems; Table 2.2 summarises their key features.

Wood and Frynas (2006) identify a seventh business systems archetype – the segmented business system – which can be found in tropical Africa. Within such systems, unions are likely to be weak, and only encountered in a few pockets of relatively stable employment; a large proportion of jobs are in the informal sector, where there is little prospect of unionism. Moreover, a tradition of patriarchal management is further likely to mitigate against meaningful delegation. Given intense cost-based competition from abroad, firms are likely to be under pressure to cut short-term costs, leading to weak job security. Whilst extensive labour legislation may be in place, enforcement is likely to be poor. Finally, national skills training systems are likely to face crises of funding, leading to poor skills bases, and a large pool of poorly skilled job seekers. Again, this makes for very low levels of employer–employee interdependence; labour is in a poor bargaining position, and very easily shed (Wood & Frynas, 2006).

REGULATION APPROACHES

Drawing on the radical political economy tradition, regulation theory explores the role of institutions in stabilising and providing the basis for periods of economic growth, always on a spatially and temporarily confined basis (Jessop, 2001). Central to regulationist thinking, it is the role of institutions to provide both rules and informal norms that encourage firms and other social actors to behave in a particular way. Regulationist thinking assumes that, in turn, social actors will impact on institutions, and on each other; institutional interaction is a similar dynamic process. This situation is summarised in Figure 2.5.

Thus, regulation theory begins from a very different starting point to both the VoC literature and business systems theory. Rather than being path dependent, institutional innovations and experiments have foreseen and unforeseen consequences in relation to

Table 2.2 National business system archetypes

Type Form	Fragmented	Co-ord. industrial district	Compartmentalised	State organised	Collaborative	Highly coordinated
Examples	Hong Kong	Italy	USA, UK, NewZealand, Australia	Post-war South Korea	Sweden, Austria, Norway	Japan
Ownership coordination, owner control	Direct	Direct	Market	Direct	Alliance	Alliance
Ownership integration of production chains or sectors	Low	Low	High	Some to high	High/limited	Some/limited
Non-ownership coordination alliance coordination of production chains or sectors	Low	Limited/low	Low	Low	Limited/low	High/some
Collaboration between competing firms	Low	Some	Low	Low	High	High
Work and employment relations delegation to employees	Low	Some	Low	Low	Some	High
Interdependence between managers and workers	Low	Some	Low	Low	High	Considerable

Source: Brookes et al. (2005), based on Whitley (1999: 41–44).

Industrial Relations

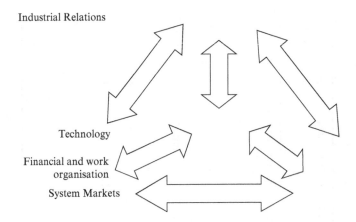

Technology

Financial and work
organisation

System Markets

Figure 2.5   Industrial relations, markets and the financial system

firm-level behaviour; this may or may not result in a period of strong firm and macro-economic performance (Boyer, 2006). Hence, national evolution is non-linear, uneven, and episodic: systems will not function in an optimal manner for more than a few decades, followed by a period of crisis, innovation, and experimentation that, in turn, may provide the foundations for a new period of growth (Jessop, 2001; Hollingsworth, 2006).

Furthermore, whilst sharing the VoC and business systems theory's emphasis on national variations in institutional configurations, contemporary regulationist thinking suggests that institutions are nested at regional, industrial, national, and supranational levels; the fact that institutions may be particularly concentrated at the national level does not detract from the importance of concentrations of institutions at other levels (Boyer & Hollingsworth, 1997). For example, the European Union has encouraged not only the opening of markets, but also the adoption of common labour practices in a range of areas. The latter range from anti-discriminatory measures to the introduction of consultative mechanisms (for example, European Works Councils in pan-European firms). Likewise, national and regional governments, and clusters of local firms, may work together (or even in opposition) in promoting specific regional development initiatives, which may reinforce sub-national particularism (Hudson, 2006). For example, rising imbalances between the north and the south led to specific regional development policies being promoted in North-Eastern England.

Regional specificity may not necessarily be the only result of governmental interventions. Firms may seek to exploit the opportunities provided by local markets to produce specialised goods and services, resulting in sub-national modes of organisation coexisting with what happens nationwide (Collinge, 2001). Given the tendency for different segments of capital to band together, it might seem that there will be a greater diversity within liberal market economies (Collinge, 2001: 183). Divergent parcels of interests may coalesce on sectoral lines, particularly in relatively diverse social systems: there will always be industries with approaches towards the deployment of technology and to work and employment relations that will differ along national norms (Hollingsworth & Boyer, 1997: 270).

Regulationist accounts link the dominance of specific forms of work organisation with particular modes of regulation; for example, in the Fordist era, national governments promoted policies aimed at supporting mass production and consumption. The crisis of this model in the 1970s led to a number of alternative regulatory experiments (Jessop, 2001). In practical organisational terms, this translated into a broad range of alternative production paradigms, distinguished by variations in employee rights and responsibilities, and differences in the development and deployment of skills and technologies.

Reflecting its progressive origins, regulationist thinking suggests that the mediation of owner power provided the basis of the golden age of economic growth in the 1950s and 1960s and that a similar – or even greater – degree of mediation may be necessary to ensure future prosperity. This would suggest paradigms for work and employment relations that formally entrench worker rights on a collective basis, and the use of technology in a manner that promotes efficiency and imparts a dignity to working life. This does not mean that regulation theory is utopian: it recognises that there are strong pressures in the opposite direction. For example, an emphasis on short-term returns in shareholder dominant models will enrich a few key actors, entrenching such approaches, even if they are proven to be dysfunctional in the long term. Likewise, waves of opportunistic experiments may do little to promote long-term growth (or more inclusive work and employment relations), but may assist in further directing resources to the economically powerful (Wolfson, 2003).

SOCIAL ACTION, DIVERSITY AND INSTITUTIONS

Whatever their provenance, a persistent critique of institutional approaches is a perceived lack of attention accorded to the impact of social action; much more attention is accorded to how institutions mould individual and group behaviour than vice versa. Over the years there have been numerous attempts to combine institutional theories with those of social action, most notably those of Norbert Elias (1984), and the somewhat simplified and flashier version of his basic arguments developed by Anthony Giddens (1991). Central to the latter's arguments is that the relationship between action and structure is characterised by 'structuration', the ongoing and dynamic process by which each reshapes the other. From the mid-2000s onwards, theories of comparative institutional analysis have sought to more explicitly take account of social action, although they have tended to focus more on actual mechanisms than the broad-sweep and intellectually light approach associated with structuration theory.

From a historical perspective, Sorge (2005) argues that institutions are bound together by social actions. At the same time, social actions break down the partitions that define these same institutions. Hence, social actions both sustain the present order and change it (Sorge, 2005: 55). At the level of the firm, social actors have considerable room to innovate in a manner that may be independent of national government policy, even if the key actors are broadly supportive of it (ibid.: 188). Hence, institutions are both rigid and fluid, and national contexts diverse (ibid.: 55). New areas of activity may emerge and old ones be reconfigured. This will make for not only dominant HRM paradigms within national contexts, but also the existence of a wide range of alternatives. Even clearly definable sets of HRM practices (for example, high-involvement practices organised on collective lines) may vary greatly in both form and effect. Whilst a highly insightful account, a limitation of Sorge's (2005) analysis is the difficulties it poses in terms of effectively analysing and comparing work and employment practices across national boundaries; and, indeed, in clearly defining what really situates HRM at the firm level. Recent historical institutionalist debates have been dominated by the work of writers such as Thelen (2012, 2014) and Streeck (2013, 2014). Whilst both are preoccupied with the long legacies of institutional solutions developed in response to grave systemic crisis, Streeck's (2013, 2014) conclusions are profoundly pessimistic. It is argued that institutionally embedded social compromises will ultimately unwind; all societies are presently liberalizing, albeit at uneven rates, a process that leaves workers very much worse off, with little sign of a new counter-movement in the offing (ibid.). In contrast, Thelen (2014) argues that, even as some institutional features of coordinated markets may be dismantled, others have persisted or even become strengthened; capitalist diversity is a great deal more durable than is commonly assumed.

An alternative view is provided by Wood (Wood, 2013; Wood & Lane, 2012), who links the present condition to a long energy transition. A feature of the contemporary global capitalist system is the relative empowerment of owners of highly fungible assets (rentiers and sovereign wealth funds), leaving more patient investors and workers very much worse off (Wood, 2013). As with the economic crisis of the first half of the early twentieth century (when oil and gas ousted coal as the primary energy sources), the present time is one where a significant energy transition is unfolding (oil and gas have been declining as a percentage of the global energy mix for over a decade); again, volatile and shifting energy prices challenge those with capital tied up in industries and processes, and favour those who can readily redeploy their investments (Wood, 2013). Not only has this led to the oil and gas industry becoming highly financialised (notoriously, the fracking industry appears to have found debt leverage very much more lucrative than anything that might be extracted from the ground) but unpredictable and increasing input and distribution costs place pressures for cost cutting elsewhere, most notably by squeezing labour (Wood, 2013). However, whilst highly mobile investors have become much more powerful, this has not eroded differences between different capitalist archetypes; indeed, many prominent coordinated markets have made significant progress in moving beyond oil and gas, whilst the USA and the UK remain doggedly committed to a primarily hydrocarbon-based future. The former process has high initial but more predictable long-term costs. This is likely to have significant implications for both different categories of investor and workers.

A further concern of the recent literature has been the issue of internal diversity within different institutional settings. As Wood and Lane (2012) note, institutions are never perfectly coupled, and national institutional arrangements might support a number of quite different production regimes. Many firms may, through a process of experimentation, devise their own solutions, which may involve not only building on systemically imparted strengths, but also compensating for weaknesses. This makes the process of regulatory reform challenging, in that efforts to promote competitiveness in one area may undermine another. Again, HRM solutions that are appropriate in one region or sector may be less than appropriate in another. For example, there remain substantial differences in Germany between large conglomerates and their smaller or middle-sized counterparts; together they constitute a highly effective export-orientated production system, but the HRM policies and practices in the former need to be adjusted to suit the resource constraints under which the latter operate (Wilkinson et al., 2014).

CONCLUSION

Although there has been a tendency in the less cerebral areas of the literature to lump different types of institutional analysis together, there are many fundamental differences between strands of institutional theory. Above all, a core distinguishing feature is how they view a firm's employees, and the optimal mechanism by which they should be managed. A frequent critique of the neoliberal analysis is that it 'knows the price of everything and the value of nothing'; broadly, neoliberal rational hierarchical approaches fall into this trap in their analysis of labour. This is treated largely in cost terms, and not in terms of the accumulated value of a firm's human capital both individually and collectively, and the circumstances under which their capabilities may be nurtured. Whilst the literature on comparative capitalism devotes more attention to the latter issue, it has been argued that it adopts a somewhat static approach, with a restricted view as to what constitutes complementarity. These are shortfalls that have been highlighted and at least partially corrected in later accounts.

REFERENCES

Bebchuk, L.A., & Roe, M.J. 1999. A theory of path dependence in corporate ownership and governance. *Stanford Law Review*, 52: 127–170.

Bendix, R. 1956. *Work and Authority in Industry*. New York: John Wiley.

Boyer, R. 2006. How do institutions cohere and change?. In G. Wood and P. James (eds), *Institutions and Working Life*. Oxford: Oxford University Press.

Boyer, R., & Hollingsworth, J.R. 1997. From national embeddedness to spatial and institutional nestedness. In J.R. Hollingsworth and R. Boyer (eds), *Contemporary Capitalism: The Embeddedness of Institutions*. Cambridge: Cambridge University Press.

Brewster, C., Croucher, R., Wood, G., & Brookes, M. 2007. Collective and individual voice: Convergence in Europe?. *International Journal of Human Resource Management*, 18(7): 1246–1262.

Brewster, C., Goergen, M., & Wood, G. 2014. Ownership rights and employment relations. In A. Wilkinson, G. Wood, and R. Deeg (eds), *Oxford Handbook of Employment Relations: Comparative Employment Systems*. Oxford: Oxford University Press.

Brewster, C., Goergen, M., Wood, G., & Wilkinson, A. 2012. Varieties of capitalism and investments in human capital. *Industrial Relations*, 51: 501–527.

Brookes, M., Brewster, C., & Wood, G. 2005. Social relations, firms and societies: A study of institutional embeddedness. *International Sociology*, 20(4): 403–426.

Collinge, C. 2001. Self organisation of society by scale. In B. Jessop (ed.), *Regulation Theory and the Crisis of Capitalism. Volume 4: Development and Extensions*. Cheltenham, UK and Northampton, MA, USA: Edward Elgar Publishing.

Crouch, C. 2005. Models of capitalism. *New Political Economy*, 10(4): 439–456.

Deeg, R. 2005. Complementary and institutional change: How useful a concept. 21. Social Science Research Centre, Vol. Discussion Paper SP II. Berlin.

DiMaggio, P., & Powell, W. 1983. The iron cage revisited: Institutional isomorphism and collective rationality in organizational fields. *American Sociological Review*, 48(2): 147–160.

Djankov, S., Glaeser, E., La Porta, R., Lopez-de-Silanes, F., & Shleifer, A. 2003. The new comparative economics. *Journal of Comparative Economics*, 31(4): 595–619.

Dore, R. 2000. *Stock Market Capitalism: Welfare Capitalism*. Cambridge: Cambridge University Press.

Dunlop, J. 1975. Political systems and industrial relations. In B. Barrett, E. Rhodes, and J. Beishon (eds), *Industrial Relations and Wider Society*. London: Collier Macmillan.

Elias, N. 1984. *What is sociology?*. New York: Columbia University Press.

Giddens, A. 1991. *Modernity and Self-Identity: Self and Society in the Late Modern Age*. Cambridge: Polity Press.

Goergen, M., Brewster, C., & Wood, G. 2013. The effects of the national setting on employment practice: The case of downsizing. *International Business Review*, 22(6): 1051–1067.

Gordon, J., & Roe, M. 2004. Introduction. In J. Gordon and M. Roe (eds), *Convergence and Persistence in Corporate Governance*. Cambridge: Cambridge University Press.

Hall, P., & Soskice, D. 2001a. An introduction to varieties of capitalism. In P. Hall and D. Soskice (eds), *Varieties of Capitalism: The Institutional Foundations of Competitive Advantage*. Oxford: Oxford University Press.

Hall, P., & Soskice, D. 2001b. *Varieties of Capitalism: The Institutional Foundation of Comparative Advantage*. Oxford: Oxford University Press.

Hollingsworth, J.R. 2006. Advancing our understanding of capitalism with Niels Bohr's thinking about complementarity. In G.T. Wood and P. James (eds), *Institutions, Production and Working Life*. Oxford: Oxford University Press.

Hollingsworth, J.R., & Boyer, R. 1997. Coordination of economic actors and social systems of production. In J.R. Hollingsworth and R. Boyer (eds), *Contemporary Capitalism: The Embeddedness of Institutions*. Cambridge: Cambridge University Press.

Hudson, R. 2006. The production of institutional complementarity? The case of North East England. In G. Wood and P. James (eds), *Institutions and Working Life*. Oxford: Oxford University Press.

Jackson, G. 2005. *Reforming Stakeholder Models: Comparing Germany and Japan*. London: DTI Eco.

Jessop, B. 2001. Series preface. In B. Jessop (ed.), *The Parisian Regulation School. Regulation Theory and the Crisis of Capitalism Volume 1*: ix–xxiii. Cheltenham, UK and Northampton, MA, USA: Edward Elgar Publishing.

Johnson, P., Brookes, M., Wood, G., & Brewster, C. 2017. Legal origin and social solidarity: The continued relevance of Durkheim to comparative institutional analysis. *Sociology*, 51(3), 646–665.

Kidger, P.J. 1991. The emergence of international human resource management. *International Journal of Human Resource Management*, 2(2): 149–163.

Kochan, T., & Ostermann, P. 1994. *The Mutual Gain Enterprise*. Boston, MA: Harvard Business School Press.

Kostova, T., & Roth, K. 2002. Adoption of an organizational practice by subsidiaries of multinational corporations: Institutional and relational effects. *Academy of Management Journal*, 45(1): 215–233.

La Porta, R., Lopez-de-Silanes, F., Shleifer, A., & Vishny, R. 1997. Legal determinants of finance. *Journal of Finance*, 52(3): 1131–1150.

La Porta, R., Lopez-de-Silanes, F., Shleifer, A., & Vishny, R. 1998. Law and finance. *Journal of Political Economy*, 106(6): 1113–1155.

Lincoln, J., & Kalleberg, A. 1990. *Culture, Control and Commitment: A Study of Work Organization in the United States and Japan*. Cambridge: Cambridge University Press.

Marsden, D. 1999. *A Theory of Employment Systems*. Oxford: Oxford University Press.

Meyer, J.W., & Rowan, B. 1977. Institutionalized organizations: Formal structure as myth and ceremony. *American Journal of Sociology*, 83(2): 340–363.

Morgan, G. 2007. National business systems research: Progress and prospects. *Scandinavian Journal of Management*, 23(2): 127–145.

North, D.C. 1990. *Institutions, Institutional Change and Economic Performance*. Cambridge: Cambridge University Press.

OECD. 2007. *Country Statistical Profiles*. Paris: OECD.

OECD. 2015. *Country Statistical Profiles*. Paris: OECD.

Pagano, M., & Volpin, P.F. 2005. The political economy of corporate governance. *American Economic Review*, 95(4): 1005–1030.

Parsons, T. 1951. *The Social System*. Glencoe: Free Press.

Pedersen, T., & Thomsen, S. 1999. Business systems and corporate governance. *International Studies of Management and Organisation*, 29(2): 42–59.

Phillips, N., Lawrence, T.B., & Hardy, C. 2004. Discourse and institutions. *Academy of Management Review*, 29(4): 635–652.

Polanyi, K. 1957. *The Great Transformation*. Boston, MA: Beacon Press.

Roe, M. 2003. *Political Determinants of Corporate Governance*. Oxford: Oxford University Press.

Scott, W.R. 1987. The adolescence of institutional theory. *Administrative Science Quarterly*, 32(4): 493–511.

Shleifer, A., & Vishny, R.W. 1997. A survey of corporate governance. *Journal of Finance*, 52(2): 737–783.

Sorge, A. 2005. *The Global and the Local: Understanding the Dialectics of Business Systems*. Oxford: Oxford University Press.

Strauss, G., & Hanson, M. 1997. Review article. American anti-management theories of organization: A critique of paradigm proliferation. *Human Relations*, 50(9): 1426–1429.

Streeck, W. 2005. Rejoinder: On terminology, functionalism, (historical) institutionalism and liberalization. *Socio-Economic Review*, 5(3): 577–587.

Streeck, W. 2013. *Gekaufte Zeit: Die vertagte Krise des demokratischen Kapitalismus*. Berlin: Suhrkamp Verlag.

Streeck, W. 2014. How will capitalism end?. *New Left Review*, 87: 35–64.

Thelen, K. 2001. Varieties of labor politics in the developed democracies. In P.A. Hall and D. Soskice (eds),

Varieties of Capitalism: The Institutional Foundations of Comparative Advantage. Oxford: Oxford University Press.

Thelen, K. 2012. Varieties of capitalism: Trajectories of liberalization and the new politics of social solidarity. *Annual Review of Political Science*, 15: 137–159.

Thelen, K. 2014. *Varieties of Liberalization and the New Politics of Social Solidarity*. Cambridge: Cambridge University Press.

Tolbert, P.S., & Zucker, L.G. 1983. Institutional sources of change in the formal structure of organizations: The diffusion of civil service reform, 1880–1935. *Administrative Science Quarterly*, 28(1): 22–39.

Tolbert, P.S., & Zucker, L.G. 1996. The institutionalisation of institutional theory. In S. Clegg, C. Hardy, and W.R. Nord (eds), *Handbook of Organisation Studies*. London: SAGE.

Whitley, R. 1999. *Divergent Capitalisms: The Social Structuring and Change of Business Systems*. Oxford: Oxford University Press.

Wilkinson, A., Wood, G., & Deeg, R. 2014. *Oxford Handbook of Employment Relations: Comparative Employment Systems*. Oxford: Oxford University Press.

Wolfson, M. 2003. Neoliberalism and the social structure of accumulation. *Review of Radical Political Economics*, 35(3): 255–263.

Wood, G. 2013. Institutional diversity: Current contestations and emerging issues. *Journal of Comparative Economic Studies*, 8: 7–20.

Wood, G., & Frynas, J.G. 2006. The institutional basis of economic failure: Anatomy of the segmented business system. *Socio-Economic Review*, 4(2): 239–277.

Wood, G., & Lane, C. 2012. Institutions, change and diversity. In C. Lane and G. Wood (eds), *Capitalist Diversity and Diversity within Capitalism*. London: Routledge.

Wood, G., Szamosi, L.T., Psychogios, A., Sarvanidis, S., & Fotopoulou, D. 2015. Rethinking Greek capitalism through the lens of industrial relations reform: A view until the 2015 referendum. *Relations Industrielles/ Industrial Relations Quarterly Review*, 70(4): 698–717.

3. Cultural perspectives on comparative HRM
B. Sebastian Reiche, Yih-teen Lee, and Javier Quintanilla

INTRODUCTION

Over the past few decades, increased globalization of business transactions, the emergence of new markets such as the BRIC countries (Brazil, Russia, India and China), as well as more intense competition among organizations at the domestic and international level alike, have been associated with an increased interest in and need for comparative human resource management (HRM) studies (Budhwar & Sparrow, 2002a). As a result, a growing number of conceptual (Aycan, 2005; Edwards & Kuruvilla, 2005) and empirical studies (Bae et al., 1998; Budhwar & Sparrow, 2002b; Easterby-Smith et al., 1995) have addressed the configuration of HRM in different national contexts.

The literature has developed different frameworks to analyse and explain how historical evolution, social institutions, and different national cultures can influence firm behaviour in general and HRM in particular. One line of inquiry builds on path dependency arguments and claims that a firm's historical development shapes its extant organizational features such as the configuration of assets and capabilities, the dispersal of responsibilities, the prevailing management style and organizational values (Bartlett & Ghoshal, 1998). This administrative heritage leads an organization to adopt specific structures and behaviours. A second strand of literature takes an institutional perspective and investigates the social and institutional determinants that underlie the logic of organizing business enterprises and their competitive behaviour in different national contexts (see Chapter 2, this volume). A systematic emphasis for understanding the permanent interaction between firms and markets on the one hand, and other social-economic institutions on the other, has been conceptualised in terms of national industrial orders (Lane, 1994) and national business systems (Whitley, 1991, 1992).

In contrast, the cultural perspective has concentrated its attention on the cultural distinctiveness of practices, beliefs, and values shared by a community. Culture and values are associated with the national culture of a country as boundaries that allow interaction and socialization within them. Scholars have analysed the influence of these national cultural values, attitudes, and behaviours on business and management styles (Hofstede, 1980; House et al., 2004; Laurent, 1986; Trompenaars & Hampden-Turner, 1997). At the same time, the movement of people across national borders and the preservation of particular groups with specific idiosyncratic customs, together with differences in social and economic experiences, highlights that subcultures can coexist in many countries.

In this chapter, we focus on the cultural approaches to comparative HRM, examining how cultural values and norms shape managerial choices across national contexts and how these may, in turn, explain differences in HRM. In a first step, we review conceptualizations of culture and consider the main cultural frameworks applied in comparative research on HRM. We also explain the sources for these national effects and describe mechanisms through which culture influences the design of HRM. In a second step, we review specific areas of HRM that are subject to the influence of culture, placing a particular focus on four key HRM functions. In a third step, we concentrate on multinational companies (MNCs) as carriers of culture that promote the flow and adaptation of culturally imbued HRM practices. Finally, we reflect critically on the limitations of the cultural perspectives on comparative HRM, and we conclude with directions for future research.

THE ROLE OF CULTURE IN HUMAN RESOURCE MANAGEMENT

The study of the effect of culture on the design, implementation, and experience of HRM policies and practices is not only limited to national cultural differences but also encompasses individual (Stone et al., 2007) and organizational (Aycan et al., 2000) cultural variation. However, in this chapter we will focus on the role of national cultural differences to reflect the primary focus that previous comparative HRM research has taken. In the following sections, we first define the concept of culture and review major cultural frameworks that have been adopted to examine national cultural differences in HRM. Subsequently, we discuss sources and mechanisms through which culture is thought to impact on the design and implementation of HRM policies and practices.

Defining Culture

Implicit to the concept of cultural effect is the notion that societies are considered to vary in terms of the arrangements which their institutions and organizations are composed of, and that these variations reflect their distinctive traditions, values, attitudes, and historical experiences. In this regard, culture can be defined as the 'crystallization of history in the thinking, feeling and acting of the present generation' (Hofstede, 1993: 5). Bartlett and Ghoshal (1998) also suggest that the history, infrastructure, resources, and culture of a nation state permeate all aspects of life within a given country, including the behaviour of managers. Accordingly, traditional national cultural values are thought to affect managerial processes and organizational behaviours, which in turn affect economic performance. It has been common to conceptualize and measure culture through various value dimensions (Hofstede, 1980; House et al., 2004; Schwartz, 1994; Trompenaars & Hampden-Turner, 1997). Although reducing the concept of culture to a limited number of value dimensions is not without criticism (d'Iribarne, 1991; McSweeney, 2002; Morris et al., 2015), this approach allows for comparability across cultural studies and offers valid measures for what is a highly elusive construct.

Cultural Frameworks in Comparative HRM

An important strand of the cultural perspective is based on Hofstede's (1980) conceptualization of four distinct cultural value dimensions. The four dimensions he postulates in his examination of dominant value patterns across countries are power distance, uncertainty avoidance, individualism/collectivism, and masculinity/femininity. Hofstede suggests that cultural patterns are rooted in the value systems of substantial groupings of the population and that they stabilize over long periods in history. These notions are useful in analysing and understanding managerial behaviour and reactions. Specifically, as cultural differences are embedded in managers' frames of reference and ways of thinking they reinforce particular values and guide managerial actions and choices. In short, all national cultural factors can be regarded as potential influences on how managers make decisions and perform their roles. Nevertheless, Hofstede has been criticized (d'Iribarne, 1991; McSweeney, 2002) not only for the limited number of dimensions, which fail to capture the richness of national environments, and his insistence that national cultural features persist over time, but also because his dimensions essentially are statistical constructs based on clusters of responses without in-depth understanding of the underlying processes.

Another important contribution to the understanding of cultural differences concerns the difference between low context and high context societies (Hall, 1976). Hall describes context as the information that surrounds an event. In high context societies, the situation, the external environment, and non-verbal cues are crucial in the communication process. Examples of high context cultures are Japan as well as Arab and Southern European societies, where the meaning of communication is mainly derived from paralanguage, facial expressions, setting, and timing (Boyacigiller & Adler, 1991). Low context cultures, in contrast, appreciate clearer, more explicit, and written forms of communication. Northern European countries and the United States are examples of low context societies. The implications of these different cultural contexts for managerial attitudes and organizational behaviour are evident. However, this approach fits much better with a generic concept of culture, in the sense of a broad cultural community such as Arabs, Latins, or Chinese, than with the constrained boundaries of a nation state, where individual and organizational diversity allows for a pluralistic coexistence of both low and high context.

The work of Kluckhohn and Strodtbeck (1961) offers another useful framework to understand cultural differences. Viewing culture as a set of assumptions and deep-level values regarding relationships among humans and between humans and their environments, Kluckhohn and Strodtbeck proposed five basic value orientations, which can be further divided into subdimensions to capture the complex cultural variations across societies. The major orientations in their model are human nature (evil, mixed, good), man–nature relationship (subjugation, harmony, dominant), social relation with people (hierarchical, collateral, individual), human activity (being, becoming, doing), and time sense (past, present, future). The cultural orientation framework has been adopted by researchers to explain variations of HRM practices across countries (e.g., Aycan et al., 2007; Nyambegera et al., 2000; Sparrow & Wu, 1998). However, this framework has been applied less frequently to comparative HRM research than that of Hofstede, due to its complexity and the existence of certain overlaps between the two models.

Building on the framework of Hofstede (1980) and Kluckhohn and Strodtbeck (1961), the more recent development of the GLOBE project (House et al., 2004; House et al., 2014) offers a rather comprehensive nine-dimension framework to explain cultural similarities and differences. The nine cultural dimensions reflect both previously identified values (for example, power distance, uncertainty avoidance, and individualism/collectivism) and new ones (for example, gender egalitarianism, performance orientation, and humane orientation). In addition, GLOBE differentiates between individualism/collectivism at the societal and organizational levels. Moreover, by further differentiating each value into 'as it is' and 'as it should be', this framework allows researchers to investigate cultural variations and their impacts on managerial practices in a more refined way. As this framework has started to be integrated into research practice and establishes an accumulated body of knowledge, its future application in cross-cultural research promises to shed additional light on exploring differences and similarities in HRM across countries.

Finally, mainly drawing on the work of Parsons and Shils (1951), Trompenaars and Hampden-Turner's (1997) framework of value dilemmas also enjoys a high level of popularity in the teaching of cultural differences. Based on data collected in over 40 countries, Trompenaars identified seven cultural dimensions, five of which focus on relationships between people (for example, the relative importance of applying universal and standardized rules, and the extent to which people are free to express their emotions in public), while the remaining two concern time management and a culture's relationship with nature. However, its adaptation in scientific research remains limited due to concerns over conceptual and methodological ambiguities.

More recent research has added additional cultural dimensions for studying the effect of culture on the design and implementation of HRM policies and practices. For example, the dimension of paternalism concerns the extent to which a society encourages and accepts that individuals with authority provide care, guidance, and protection to their subordinates (Aycan et al., 2000; Aycan et al., 1999). Subordinates in paternalistic societies, in turn, are expected to show loyalty and deference to their superiors. In contrast, fatalism refers to the belief of societal members that the outcomes of their actions are not fully controllable.

The concept of tightness/looseness has been introduced to measure the relative strength of a relevant cultural context (Gelfand et al., 2011). Tight cultures such as India and Korea possess strong norms that determine behaviour in everyday situations, and low tolerance for deviations from them; whereas loose cultures such as Ukraine and the Netherlands have weaker social norms and higher tolerance of deviant behaviour. In tight cultures, organizations – and by extension their practices – are likely to have greater order, precision, cohesion, and efficiency, and can be expected to be more stable, less flexible, and more resistant to change (Gelfand et al., 2006).

Sources and Mechanisms of Cultural Influences on HRM

In the process of understanding how national cultural features influence organizations in general and HRM in particular, scholars highlight the fact that the cultural environment is not external to organizations but rather permeates them. Crozier (1963: 307), for example, argues that the mechanisms of social control 'are closely related to the values and patterns of social relations', as manifested within organizations. Similarly, Scott (1983: 16) points out that 'the beliefs, norms, rules and understandings are not just "out there" but additionally "in here". Participants, clients, constituents all participate in and are carriers of the culture'. This means that organizations and environmental culture interpenetrate. This process of interpenetration highlights several sources of cultural influences on the design and implementation of HRM policies and practices.

First, national culture is thought to shape its members' basic assumptions (Hofstede, 1983; Kluckhohn & Strodtbeck, 1961). Individuals who take on managerial positions in a particular culture are thus socialized along similar values and beliefs (Van Maanen &

Schein, 1979) and will form similar views about the managerial role itself as well as the relevance of and choice between alternative organizational practices.

Second, the enduring character of culture helps to continuously socialize new generations of members and reinforce the predominant cultural values and norms (Child & Kieser, 1979) which, in turn, influence the preference individuals have for particular HRM policies and practices (Sparrow & Wu, 1998), and the degree to which these policies and practices will function effectively within a given cultural system. Accordingly, while the 'what' aspects of HRM (which instruments to adopt in order to achieve HRM outcomes) may be universal across cultures, the 'how' question that determines the particular configuration and design of a specific instrument and the extent to which a desired outcome is reached will be culture-specific (Tayeb, 1995).

Third, according to social cognition theory, individual cognition is strongly influenced by one's cultural background (Abramson et al., 1996; Bandura, 2001). Specifically, culture may influence the way in which individuals 'scan, select, interpret and validate information from the environment in order to identify, prioritize and categorize issues' (Budhwar & Sparrow, 2002b: 603). According to the constructivist perspective, culture influences behaviour (and subsequently HRM practices) through the schemas or cognitive lens that cultural members use to make sense of information (Leung & Morris, 2015). In other words, culture is a powerful determinant in how human performance problems are perceived and how their solutions in the form of employee development interventions are created, implemented, and evaluated. As a lens, cultural frames colour both the design and implementation of HRM in that specific socio-cultural context. In particular, cultural values and norms will shape the way in which people assess justice rules and criteria (Fischer, 2008; Morris et al., 1999). Because ensuring fairness or justice is one of the key concerns of HRM, the culture-bounded appreciation of justice will, in turn, influence how key HRM practices such as recruitment, appraisal, compensation, and promotion are designed and implemented in a specific society.

Fourth, culture is considered to influence the creation of social institutions, which subsequently provide value frameworks for individuals in these socio-cultural settings to learn which behaviours and opinions are rewarded and which are punished. In other words, culture may influence behaviours and HRM practices through members' intersubjective interpretation of social norms that define adequate or acceptable behaviours in a given situation (Leung & Morris, 2015). For example, cultures may encompass idiosyncratic social elites or pressure groups (Keesing, 1974). The existence of such groups may make the implementation of specific HRM policies and practices politically and socially unacceptable (Budhwar & Sparrow, 2002a). Although it is generally recognized that the relationship between culture and institutions is reciprocal, and that no clear consensus has been reached about which should precede which (Vaiman & Brewster, 2015), the influence of culture on HRM through its impact on institutions is also considered to be an important mechanism.

Existing research has also considered the level at which HRM is affected by culture. In general, scholars agree that whereas HRM philosophies may entail culturally universal traits, it is the specific HRM practices that are culture-bound and thus show variation across cultures (Teagarden & Von Glinow, 1997). For example, in their study of United Kingdom (UK) and Indian firms Budhwar and Sparrow (2002b) show that even despite a convergence in the desire among Indian and British HR managers to integrate HRM with business strategy, they differ in the underlying logic of implementing this integration. In the following section, we therefore examine the implementation of different HRM policies and practices across cultures in more detail.

CULTURAL DIFFERENCES IN NATIONAL HRM PRACTICES

Scholars have studied the design and implementation of HRM policies and practices across a wide range of cultural contexts, including China (Smale et al., 2013; Warner, 2008), Korea (Bae & Lawler, 2000; Horak, 2017), Singapore (Barnard & Rodgers, 2000), Hong Kong (Ngo et al., 1998), Vietnam (Zhu & Verstraeten, 2013), Latin America (Bonache et al., 2012), Kenya (Nyambegera et al., 2000), and the Middle East (Afiouni et al., 2013; Darwish et al., 2016). In addition, existing studies have compared HRM practices and systems across different cultural contexts such as the United States of America (USA), Canada, and the Philippines (Galang, 2004), the USA, Japan, and Germany (Pudelko, 2006), East Asia (Zhu et al., 2007), Australia, Indonesia, Malaysia, and Hong Kong (Mamman et al., 1996), the United Kingdom (UK) and China (Easterby-Smith et al., 1995), Turkey, Germany, and Spain (Özçelik & Aydinli, 2006), China and the Netherlands (Verburg et al., 1999), China, Japan, and South Korea (Rowley et al., 2004), China, Germany, and the USA (Festing & Knappert, 2014), China, India, Germany, and Hungary (Baum & Kabst, 2013), the UK and India (Budhwar & Khatri, 2001; Budhwar & Sparrow, 2002b), and China and Taiwan (Warner & Zhu, 2002). Despite the multitude of cultural contexts that are examined, the studies generally focus on similar dimensions of HRM. Our following discussion is framed along cultural differences in HRM with regard to four key HRM practices: recruitment and selection, compensation and benefits, performance appraisal, and training and development.

Recruitment and Selection

Existing research has shown recruitment, selection, and retention practices to be culture-bound. First, the scope and strength of underlying selection criteria have been found to differ across cultures. Based on a review of extant literature, Aycan (2005) suggests that recruitment and selection in cultures high on performance orientation or universalism are based on hard criteria such as job-related knowledge and technical skills; whereas cultures that are low on performance orientation, oriented towards ascribed status, or particularistic tend to favour soft criteria such as relational skills or social class affiliation. Other research has found cultural differences in prioritizing applicant attributes, suggesting that members from collectivistic societies require higher levels of the attributes most associated with different jobs than members from individualistic societies, who prefer more well-rounded candidates for each job (Wee et al., 2014).

Second, there is also evidence that the recruitment and selection strategy differs across cultures. For example, collectivist cultures seem to prefer the use of internal labour markets in order to promote loyalty to the firm (Budhwar & Khatri, 2001). In collectivist societies it is also often difficult for externally recruited candidates to enter the strong social networks within the organization and to cope with resistance following their appointment, especially in cases where an internal candidate has been supported (Björkman & Lu, 1999).

Third, selection methods are likely to be culture-bound. Evidence suggests that cultures high on uncertainty avoidance tend to use more types of selection tests, use them more extensively, conduct more interviews, and monitor their processes in more detail, thus suggesting a greater desire to collect objective data for making selection decisions (Ryan et al., 1999). Cultures high on performance orientation or universalism will also employ more standardized and job-specific selection methods (Aycan, 2005). Practices concerning the retention of staff in short-term oriented cultures tend to focus on transactional employment relationships and to be more responsive in nature. In contrast, retention practices in long-term oriented cultures entail a more preventive character and centre on relational employment needs (Reiche, 2008). At the same time, research also suggests important similarities in selection instruments across cultures. For example, based on data from 1199 individuals across 21 countries, Ryan et al. (2009) investigated the role of two cultural values (independent and interdependent self-construals, achievement and ascription orientations) in perceptions of eight selection tools, and found evidence for convergence in individuals' perceptions. Research has also demonstrated that selection methods such as situational judgement tests appear to be culturally transferable (Lievens et al., 2015).

Compensation and Benefits

Evidence also suggests that compensation and benefit schemes need to be tailored to different cultural settings. A key dimension refers to the basis upon which employees are compensated. Specifically, the literature differentiates between job-based and skill- or person-based pay systems (Lawler, 1994). In this vein, performance-oriented or universalistic cultures are likely to devise compensation systems that are based on formal, objective, and systematic assessments of the relative value of a job within the organization. In contrast, in high power-distance or particularistic cultures, pay systems will be influenced by subjective decisions from top management and will focus on the person rather than the job itself (Aycan, 2005). There is also evidence for cultural variation concerning the accepted level of performance-based rewards. For example, high power distance and fatalistic cultures tend to have lower performance-reward contingencies (Aycan et al., 2000). In addition, Schuler and Rogovsky (Schuler & Rogovsky, 1998) showed that high uncertainty-avoidance cultures prefer seniority- and skill-based reward systems given their inherent predictability; whereas low uncertainty-avoidance cultures place a stronger focus on individual performance-based pay. Similarly, they found that employee share options and stock ownership plans are more widespread in low power-distance cultures.

Compensation systems also differ considerably between individualist and collectivist cultures. While pay-for-performance schemes are very common in individualist cultures, collectivist societies tend to use group-based reward allocation and reveal lower overall pay dispersion (Easterby-Smith et al., 1995; Schuler & Rogovsky, 1998). Finally, there are also different cultural preferences for indirect pay components. Huo and Von Glinow (1995) discovered a relatively greater use of flexible benefit plans, workplace childcare practices, maternity leave programmes, and career break schemes in the collectivist context of China; while Schuler and Rogovsky (1998) found these practices to be less important in masculine cultures.

Performance Appraisal

The process of evaluating employee performance usually comprises three distinct stages: (1) preparation for the appraisal process, which concerns the performance criteria and goals to be assessed; (2) the appraisal method or process; and (3) the content of the performance evaluation (Milliman et al., 1998). Concerning the preparation stage, evidence suggests that individualistic societies tend to emphasize personal achievement in the appraisal, whereas collectivist cultures highlight group-based achievement (Miller et al., 2001). In a study on performance appraisal in Hungary, Kovach (1994) showed that fatalistic cultures, in which individuals perceive work outcomes to be beyond their influence, tend to accept performance below expectations as long as the focal individual displays effort and willingness. Furthermore, low power-distance and universalistic cultures are also more likely to stress task-related competencies and outcomes (Aycan, 2005).

There is support for the notion that culture also has a bearing on the process of conducting performance appraisal. For example, evidence suggests that feedback quality and relational quality between supervisor and subordinate tend to be higher for matched collectivist–collective and individualist–individual dyadic relationships than for mismatched dyads (Van De Vliert et al., 2004). In general, researchers emphasize that evaluation based on direct feedback is more prevalent in individualist cultures, whereas collectivist societies focus on indirect, subtle, relationship-oriented, and personal forms of feedback (Hofstede, 1998). Similarly, direct, explicit, and formal processes of appraisal are more widespread in low context cultures (Milliman et al., 1998). Moreover, low power-distance cultures appear to use more participative and egalitarian forms of performance appraisal, whereas members of high power-distance cultures tolerate autocratic assessment styles that do not require them to openly express their perspectives in the appraisal review (Snape et al., 1998). Research has also shown power distance to negatively correlate with the number of rating sources employed in appraisals (Peretz & Fried, 2012). Other research found that French employees focused relatively more on the performance criteria and the evaluation process, while German employees seemed to be more concerned about appraisal outcomes (Bacouel-Jentjens & Brandl, 2015).

Finally, there is some indication that the topics and issues discussed during the performance appraisal are also likely to vary across cultures. Individualistic cultures are considered to place a stronger focus on discussing employees' potential for future promotion based on task performance, whereas collectivist societies concentrate on seniority-based promotion decisions (Milliman et al., 1998). However, empirical evidence supporting this notion is inconsistent. For example, Snape et al. (1998) found that the content of performance appraisal in Hong Kong companies was more strongly geared towards reward and punishment, and less towards training and development, compared to UK firms. This suggests that other factors may play a role and that cultural dimensions are likely to interact in influencing the design and implementation of HRM practices in different cultural contexts.

Training and Development

A last set of HRM policies and practices concerns training and development. Cultural variation exists both with regard to the importance of training and development as well as with regard to the content and methods of training. First, there is evidence that fatalistic cultures perceive training and development as less relevant for organizations, given the prevalent assumption that employees have limited abilities that cannot easily be enhanced (Aycan et al., 2000). Similarly, research suggests that because high power-distance cultures value inequalities, managers or organizations in these societies are less likely to invest in training that improves employees' skills and, hence, may decrease a superior's competitive advantage (Peretz & Rosenblatt, 2011). Second, individual learning styles are inherently culture-bound (see Harvey, 1997; Yamazaki, 2005) and therefore call for a different design and delivery of training across cultures. For example, high power-distance cultures generally prefer one-way over participative delivery of training and education courses, in which the instructor is perceived to possess sufficient authority. In these cultures, organizations tend to employ senior managers rather than external trainers as instructors in order to ensure a high level of credibility and trust (Wright et al., 2002). Furthermore, it is found that cultural values such as high uncertainty avoidance and low assertiveness drive managers to pursue internal, systematic, and long-term orientations in personnel development (Reichel et al., 2009).

Existing research on cultural variations in the design and implementation of other HRM practices such as HR planning and job analysis has attracted very little attention (Aycan, 2005). One recent exception is a study challenging the assumption that work practices that involve employees are necessarily less effective in high power-distance cultures (Jiang et al., 2015). Specifically, the scholars found that while the symbolic impact of high involvement work practices is more pronounced in egalitarian cultures, their instrumental impact is more pronounced in hierarchical cultures. Research has also started to examine the role of national culture for the performance effects of bundles of HRM practices (e.g., Rabl et al., 2014). Overall, it has to be acknowledged that not all HRM practices possess the same level of culture-specificity. Indeed, practices such as recruitment and selection or training are likely to be less culture-bound than practices such as career development, performance appraisal, and reward allocation, since the latter deal with interpersonal relationships rather than technology (Evans & Lorange, 1990; Verburg et al., 1999) and are thus more embedded within the cultural fabric of the local context.

MULTINATIONALS AS INTER-CULTURAL AGENTS

One of the most relevant implications of comparative HRM research is to provide managers, particularly those working in MNCs, with specific guidelines concerning how to design and implement an effective HRM system when their business operation enters into different cultural contexts. This notion has generated controversial yet critical topics of discussion in comparative HRM, such as the debate on localization versus standardization, and the process of transferring HRM policies and practices across nations.

Localization versus Standardization Debate

In the presence of cultural differences, one critical challenge that HR managers in MNCs face is how to maintain a consistent global HRM system while, at the same time, responding sensitively to local cultural norms. Implicit in this standardization versus localization (or integration versus responsiveness) debate is the more fundamental assumption about whether a set of universally valid best practices can be identified, irrespective of the cultural context (also known as the convergence versus divergence debate; see Pudelko & Harzing, 2007). If best practices exist, it makes sense to identify them and transfer them to different parts of the world. Whereas various authors have proclaimed the existence of international HRM best practices (e.g., Von Glinow et al., 2002), other scholars refute this idea and argue that practices need to be closely adapted to the local context in order to be effective (e.g., Marchington & Grugulis, 2000; Newman & Nollen, 1996). From the latter perspective, the congruence between management practices and national culture is so critical that local responsiveness may become an inevitable task.

In fact, Brewster et al. (2008) found that while indigenous firms demonstrate clear national differences in how they manage people, such differences are less significant for their multinational counterparts. In other words, MNCs tend to manage their human resources in ways that are distinct from those of their host country. Based on these findings, Brewster et al. (2008) suggest that duality theories may offer the best lens to understand the localization versus standardization debate, because such theories emphasize the conflicting pressures towards global integration and local adaptation (Evans et al., 2002; Kostova & Roth, 2002), and incorporate factors such as regulatory issues, organizational size, structure, market conditions, and/or the strategic choices made by managers to account for the final result of such tension. MNCs may hence consciously manage such duality and buffer the local versus global tension in their design and implementation of HRM practices.

Transfer of HRM Practices

In general, there is a strong temptation for MNCs to transfer their HRM policies and practices to various other countries, either from the headquarters (that is, country-of-origin effect) or from a third country which has set the standard of global best practices (that is, dominance effect; Pudelko & Harzing, 2007). Scholars subscribing to the culturalist approach maintain that it could be very difficult, if not impossible, to transfer HRM practices between two countries with different national cultures (Beechler & Yang, 1994). For instance, implementing an individualistic HRM system (for example, merit-based promotion) in a collectivist culture may encounter difficulties (Ramamoorthy & Carroll, 1998). In the same vein, national cultural distance has been considered as an indicator to predict the transferability of HRM systems across countries (Kogut & Singh, 1988; Liu, 2004; Shenkar, 2001).

Despite the existence of fierce debates about the cross-cultural transfer of HRM practices, scholars generally agree that: (1) it is necessary to distinguish between HRM policies and HRM practices; and (2) although some HRM policies may be similar across MNC subsidiaries, the actual practices are more prone to respond to local norms and display differences across cultures (Khilji, 2003; Tayeb, 1998).

LIMITATIONS OF THE CULTURAL PERSPECTIVE

While an increasing number of studies have investigated the role of national culture in shaping local HRM policies and practices, this perspective is not without criticism on both conceptual and empirical fronts. An important risk of culturalist approaches is the tendency to oversimplify national cultures and construct cross-cultural comparative analysis based on exaggerated cultural stereotypes. As Child and Kieser (1979: 269) have indicated, a methodological problem of using cultural variables is that these have not been incorporated into 'a model which systematically links together the analytical levels of context, structure, role and behaviour'.

Often, it is also difficult to distinguish clearly between cultural values and institutional arrangements. Traditionally, scholars have tried to blend and probe the relationship between them. Dore (1973) points out how institutions are created or perpetuated by powerful actors following their interests and cultural orientations. Likewise, Hofstede (1980, 1993) argues that institutions reflect culture. Whitley (1992) also acknowledges strong cultural features within his dominant contingency institutional perspective, arguing that institutions include cultural attitudes. He identified two main groups of major institutions – background and proximate – which constrain and guide the behaviour of organizations. Whereas background institutions entail trust relations, collective loyalties, individualism, and authority relations, proximate institutions comprise the political, financial, and labour systems, and so on. As Whitley (1992: 269) points out, 'background institutions may be conceived as predominantly "cultural"'. More recently, scholars have also examined the different degrees of latitude that culturalist and institutionalist approaches offer for the design of HRM practices (Vaiman & Brewster, 2015). According to this line of argument, organizations tend to have relatively more influence over the effect of cultural as opposed to institutional factors, for example by recruiting and selecting local employees that are culturally untypical of the wider local environment and, in fact, share cultural values with those of the organization, or through systematic induction and socialization programmes. By comparison, cultural differences may be most significant for the design of HRM practices in areas where institutional requirements are less restrictive, such as in training and communication, personnel selection, and talent management.

Another weakness of the culturalist approach is the lack of a priori theorizing in existing research (Schaffer & Riordan, 2003). Rather than explicitly incorporating culture into their underlying theoretical framework, researchers frequently explain observed differences only *ex post*. With few exceptions (e.g., Aycan et al., 1999) studies do not sufficiently explain how and why – that is, through which sources and mechanisms – culture affects the design and implementation of HRM. Similarly, by using the nation state as a proxy for culture, research runs the risk of not capturing all relevant sub-cultural differences that may influence HRM (Ryan et al., 1999). For example, the calculated cultural distance between Hofstede and Hofstede's (2005) cultural scores of the Czech Republic and Slovakia, which shared the same national flag for a long time, is higher than for many other cultural pairs. The case of the literature on entry-mode choice suggests that an almost blind reliance on an overly simplistic measure of national cultural distance not only may lead to inconsistent results but also overlooks more subtle cultural factors that may play a role (Harzing, 2004). We would encourage more research to account for within-culture variation when studying cultural preferences for HRM policies and practices (e.g., Aycan et al., 2007) and examine how such variation affects the design and perception of HRM policies and practices.

Comparative cross-cultural research is plagued by a variety of methodological problems (Tsui et al., 2007; Harzing et al., 2013) that may reduce the researcher's ability to draw valid conclusions about relevant differences in the design, implementation, and in particular, the perception of HRM policies and practices across cultures. As Galang (2004) points out, comparative HRM studies not only need to ensure functional and conceptual invariance of the underlying practices of interest but must also pay attention to the metric and linguistic equivalence of their measures. Moreover, there is a lack of studies applying multilevel models in investigating culture's impacts on HRM policies and practices. For example, Minbaeva (2016) calls for more careful theorizing about the differences between intended, implemented, and perceived HRM practices in MNCs, and suggests that these differences may be influenced by factors located at varying levels of analysis. Scholars should strive to include a larger number of countries in their study to insure that a full range of the predictor variable distribution (that is, cultural values) is covered (Milliman et al., 1998), which in turn would allow researchers to attribute the variations in HRM systems found across countries to cultural differences in a more convincing way.

By over-relying on the dimensional models of culture (e.g., Hofstede, 1980), studies adopting a culturalist approach also suffer from the weaknesses inherited in those models, particularly when culture is not directly measured but scores of cultural dimensions reported in the cultural models are applied. In other words, if the cultural scores are flawed in the first place, the analyses using these scores may also be contaminated, thus rendering the conclusions suspicious. Related criticism concerns the categorical and static assumptions underlying traditional cultural frameworks. For example, psychologists have pointed out that individuals' relationships to cultures are likely partial and plural, and that individuals take influences from multiple cultures, thereby becoming conduits through which cultures can influence each other (Morris et al., 2015). This notion further limits the usefulness of examining the effect of stable cultural value dimensions on the design of HRM practices. Furthermore, the coverage of culture in comparative HRM may also be constrained by the original cultural models. Therefore, while there are abundant cases studying the USA and Western European countries, accompanied by Japan and some emerging economies in Asia and Latin America, the African, Middle East, and Arabic worlds are still largely absent in the current body of literature.

Finally, even if culture is actually measured in the studies, a huge risk of confusion of levels still persists. It is not rare that researchers fail to align their level of theory, measurement, and analysis, thus committing various types of multilevel fallacies (Klein et al., 1994; Vijver et al., 2008). For example, scholars may measure values at the individual level and test their hypotheses at this level accordingly. However, this approach constitutes an ecological fallacy by assuming that all individuals share the group attribute. Further, it is an atomistic fallacy to conclude that the results obtained at the individual level are valid at the societal level. Consequently, some of the results reported by this culturalist line of research should be considered with caution. We would urge researchers who are interested in examining cross-national differences in individual outcomes to develop cross-level models, and to avoid theorizing and conducting the research at only the individual or the national level.

CONCLUSION

In this chapter, we have discussed how cultural values and norms shape managerial choices across national contexts and how these may, in turn, explain differences in HRM.

While this approach certainly deserves merit, as shown by the growing number of empirical studies and conceptual debate, it is clear that national cultural factors can serve as only one among several determinants that influence the design and implementation of HRM policies and practices across different contexts. Subsequent research would greatly benefit from expanding the scope of the cultural perspective to entail additional factors. In this vein, our review serves as a modest starting point to organize a future research agenda.

REFERENCES

Abramson, N., Keating, R., & Lane, H.W. 1996. Cross-national cognitive process differences: A comparison of Canadian, American and Japanese managers. *Management International Review*, 36(2): 123–147.

Afiouni, F., Karam, C.M., & El-Hajj, H. 2013. The HR value proposition model in the Arab Middle East: Identifying the contours of an Arab Middle Eastern HR model. *International Journal of Human Resource Management*, 24(10): 1895–1932.

Aycan, Z. 2005. The interplay between cultural and institutional/structural contingencies in human resource management practices. *International Journal of Human Resource Management*, 16(7): 1083–1119.

Aycan, Z., Al-Hamadi, A.B., Davis, A., & Budhwar, P.S. 2007. Cultural orientations and preferences for HRM policies and practices: The case of Oman. *International Journal of Human Resource Management*, 18(1): 11–32.

Aycan, Z., Kanungo, R.N., Mendonca, M., et al. 2000. Impact of culture on human resource management practices: A 10-country comparison. *Applied Psychology*, 49(1): 192–221.

Aycan, Z., Kanungo, R.N., & Sinha, J.B.P. 1999. Organizational culture and human resource management practices: The model of culture fit. *Journal of Cross-Cultural Psychology*, 30(4): 501–526.

Bacouel-Jentjens, S., & Brandl, J. 2015. Cross-cultural responses to performance appraisals in Germany and France: A refinement of the picture. *International Journal of Cross Cultural Management*, 15(3): 285–304.

Bae, J., Chen, S.-J., & Lawler, J.J. 1998. Variations in human resource management in Asian countries: MNC home-country and host-country effects. *International Journal of Human Resource Management*, 9(4): 653–670.

Bae, J., & Lawler, J.J. 2000. Organizational and HRM strategies in Korea: Impact on firm performance in an emerging economy. *Academy of Management Journal*, 43(3): 502–517.

Bandura, A. 2001. Social cognitive theory: An agentic perspective. *Annual Review of Psychology*, 52(1): 1–26.

Barnard, M.E., & Rodgers, R.A. 2000. How are internally oriented HRM policies related to high-performance work practices? Evidence from Singapore. *International Journal of Human Resource Management*, 11(6): 1017–1046.

Bartlett, C.A., & Ghoshal, S. 1998. *Managing across Borders: The Transnational Solution* (2nd edn). Boston, MA: Harvard Business School Press.

Baum, M., & Kabst, R. 2013. How to attract applicants in the Atlantic versus the Asia-Pacific region? A cross-national analysis on China, India, Germany, and Hungary. *Journal of World Business*, 48(2): 175–185.

Beechler, S., & Yang, J.Z. 1994. The transfer of Japanese-style management to American subsidiaries: Contingencies, constraints, and competencies. *Journal of International Business Studies*, 25(3): 467–491.

Björkman, I., & Lu, Y. 1999. The management of human resources in Chinese–Western joint ventures. *Journal of World Business*, 34(3): 306–324.

Bonache, J., Trullen, J., & Sanchez, J.I. 2012. Managing cross-cultural differences: Testing human resource models in Latin America. *Journal of Business Research*, 65(12): 1773–1781.

Boyacigiller, N.A., & Adler, N.J. 1991. The parochial dinosaur: Organizational science in a global context. *Academy of Management Review*, 16(2): 262–290.

Brewster, C., Wood, G., & Brookes, M. 2008. Similarity, isomorphism or duality? Recent survey evidence on the human resource management policies of multinational corporations. *British Journal of Management*, 19(4): 320–342.

Budhwar, P.S., & Khatri, N. 2001. A comparative study of HR practices in Britain and India. *International Journal of Human Resource Management*, 12(5): 800–826.

Budhwar, P.S., & Sparrow, P.R. 2002a. An integrative framework for understanding cross-national human resource management practices. *Human Resource Management Review*, 12(3): 377–403.

Budhwar, P.S., & Sparrow, P.R. 2002b. Strategic HRM through the cultural looking glass: Mapping the cognition of British and Indian managers. *Organization Studies*, 23(4): 599–638.

Child, J., & Kieser, A. 1979. Organization and managerial roles in British and West German companies: An examination of the culture-free thesis. In J. Cornelis and D. Hickson (eds), *Organizations Alike and Unlike:*

International and Inter-institutional Studies in the Sociology of Organizations: 251–271. London: Routledge & Kegan Paul.

Crozier, M. 1963. *The Bureaucratic Phenomenon*. Chicago, IL: University of Chicago.

D'Iribarne, P. 1991. The usefulness of an ethnographic approach to international comparisons of the functioning of organizations. Paper presented at the EGOS Colloquium, Vienna, July 15–17.

Darwish, T.K., Singh, S., & Wood, G. 2016. The impact of human resource practices on actual and perceived organizational performance in a Middle Eastern emerging market. *Human Resource Management*, 55(2): 261–281.

Dore, R. 1973. *British Factory, Japanese Factory: The Origins of National Diversity in Industrial Relations*. Los Angeles, CA: University of California Press.

Easterby-Smith, M., Malina, D., & Yuan, L. 1995. How culture-sensitive is HRM? A comparative analysis of practice in Chinese and UK companies. *International Journal of Human Resource Management*, 6(1): 31–59.

Edwards, T., & Kuruvilla, S. 2005. International HRM: National business systems, organizational politics and the international division of labour in MNCs. *International Journal of Human Resource Management*, 16(1): 1–21.

Evans, P., & Lorange, P. 1990. The two logics behind human resource management. In Y.D. Evans and A. Laurent (eds), *Human Resource Management in International Firms*: 144–161. New York: St Martins Press.

Evans, P., Pucik, V., & Barsoux, J.-L. 2002. *The Global Challenge*. New York: McGraw-Hill Publishing Company.

Festing, M., & Knappert, L. 2014. Country-specific profiles of performance management in China, Germany, and the United States: An empirical test. *Thunderbird International Business Review*, 56(4): 331–351.

Fischer, R. 2008. Organizational justice and reward allocation. In P.B. Smith, M.F. Peterson, and D.C. Thomas (eds), *The Handbook of Cross-Cultural Management*: 135–150. London: SAGE.

Galang, M.C. 2004. The transferability question: Comparing HRM practices in the Philippines with the US and Canada. *International Journal of Human Resource Management*, 15(7): 1207–1233.

Gelfand, M.J., Nishii, L.H., & Raver, J.L. 2006. On the nature and importance of cultural tightness–looseness. *Journal of Applied Psychology*, 91(6): 1225–1244.

Gelfand, M.J., Raver, J.L., Nishii, L.H., et al. 2011. Differences between tight and loose cultures: A 33-nation study. *Science*, 332(6033): 1100–1104.

Hall, E.T. 1976. *Beyond Culture*. New York: Anchor Press/Doubleday.

Harvey, M. 1997. 'Inpatriation' training: The next challenge for international human resource management. *International Journal of Intercultural Relations*, 21(3): 393–428.

Harzing, A.-W. 2004. The role of culture in entry-mode studies: From neglect to myopia?. In J.L.C. Cheng and M.A. Hitt (eds), *Advances in International Management*, Vol. 15: 75–127. Oxford: Elsevier JAI.

Harzing, A.-W., Reiche, B.S., & Pudelko, M. 2013. Challenges in international survey research: A review with illustrations and suggested solutions for best practice. *European Journal of International Management*, 7(1): 112–134.

Hofstede, G. 1980. *Culture's Consequences: International Differences in Work-Related Values*. Beverly Hills, CA: SAGE.

Hofstede, G. 1983. The cultural relativity of organizational practices and theories. *Journal of International Business Studies*, 14(2): 75–89.

Hofstede, G. 1993. Intercultural conflict and synergy in Europe: Management in Western Europe. In D.J. Hickson (ed.), *Society, Culture and Organization in Twelve Nations*: 1–8. New York: de Gruyter.

Hofstede, G. 1998. Think locally, act globally: Cultural constraints in personnel management. *Management International Review*, 38(Special Issue 2): 7–26.

Hofstede, G., & Hofstede, G.J. 2005. *Cultures and Organizations: Software of the Mind* (2nd edn). New York: McGraw-Hill.

Horak, S. 2017. The informal dimension of human resource management in Korea: *Yongo*, recruiting practices and career progression. *International Journal of Human Resource Management*, 28(10): 1409–1432.

House, R.J., Dorfman, P.W., Javidan, M., et al. 2014. *Strategic Leadership across Cultures: The GLOBE Study of CEO Leadership Behavior and Effectiveness in 24 Countries*. Thousand Oaks, CA: SAGE.

House, R.J., Hanges, P.J., Javidan, M., et al. 2004. *Culture, Leadership, and Organizations: The GLOBE Study of 62 Societies*. London: SAGE.

Huo, Y.P., & Von Glinow, M.A. 1995. On transplanting human resource practices to China: A culture-driven approach. *International Journal of Manpower*, 16(9): 3–15.

Jiang, Y., Colakoglu, S., Lepak, D.P., et al. 2015. Involvement work systems and operational effectiveness: Exploring the moderating effect of national power distance. *Journal of International Business Studies*, 46(3): 332–354.

Keesing, R.M. 1974. Theories of culture. *Annual Review of Anthropology*, 3: 73–97.

Khilji, S.E. 2003. 'To adapt or not to adapt': Exploring the role of national culture in HRM – a study of Pakistan. *International Journal of Cross Cultural Management*, 3(1): 109–132.

Klein, K.J., Dansereau, F., & Hall, R.J. 1994. Levels issues in theory development, data collection, and analysis. *Academy of Management Review*, 19(2): 195–229.

Kluckhohn, F., & Strodtbeck, F. 1961. *Variations in Value Orientations*. Evanston: Row-Peterson.

Kogut, B., & Singh, H. 1988. The effect of national culture on the choice of entry mode. *Journal of International Business Studies*, 19(3): 411–432.

Kostova, T., & Roth, K. 2002. Adoption of an organizational practice by subsidiaries of multinational corporations: Institutional and relational effects. *Academy of Management Journal*, 45(1): 215–233.

Kovach Jr, R.C. 1994. Matching assumptions to environment in the transfer of management practices: Performance appraisal in Hungary. *International Studies of Management and Organization*, 24(4): 83–99.

Lane, C. 1994. Industrial order and the transformation of industrial relations: Britain, Germany and France compared. In R. Hyman and A. Ferner (eds), *New Frontiers in European Industrial Relations*: 167–196. Oxford: Blackwell.

Laurent, A. 1986. The cross-cultural puzzle of international human resource management. *Human Resource Management*, 25(1): 91–102.

Lawler, E.E. 1994. From job-based to competency-based organizations. *Journal of Organizational Behavior*, 15(1): 3–15.

Leung, K., & Morris, M.W. 2015. Values, schemas, and norms in the culture–behavior nexus: A situated dynamics framework. *Journal of International Business Studies*, 46(9): 1028–1050.

Lievens, F., Corstjens, J., Sorrel, M.A., et al. 2015. The cross-cultural transportability of situational judgment tests: How does a US-based integrity situational judgment test fare in Spain?. *International Journal of Selection and Assessment*, 23(4): 361–372.

Liu, W. 2004. The cross-national transfer of HRM practices in MNCs: An integrative research model. *International Journal of Manpower*, 25(6): 500–517.

Mamman, A., Sulaiman, M., & Fadel, A. 1996. Attitudes to pay systems: An exploratory study within and across cultures. *International Journal of Human Resource Management*, 7(1): 101–121.

Marchington, M., & Grugulis, I. 2000. 'Best practice' human resource management: Perfect opportunity or dangerous illusion?. *International Journal of Human Resource Management*, 11(6): 1104–1124.

McSweeney, B. 2002. Hofstede's model of national cultural differences and their consequences: A triumph of faith – a failure of analysis. *Human Relations*, 55(1): 89–118.

Miller, J.S., Hom, P.W., & Gomez-Mejia, L.R. 2001. The high cost of low wages: Does Maquiladora compensation reduce turnover?. *Journal of International Business Studies*, 32(3): 585–595.

Milliman, J., Nason, S.W., Gallagher, E., et al. 1998. The impact of national culture on HRM practices: The case of performance appraisal. In J.L. Cheng and R.B. Peterson (eds), *Advances in International Comparative Management*, Vol. 12: 157–183. Greenwich, CT: JAI Press.

Minbaeva, D. 2016. Contextualising the individual in international management research: Black boxes, comfort zones and a future research agenda. *European Journal of International Management*, 10(1): 95–104.

Morris, M.W., Chiu, C.-Y., & Liu, Z. 2015. Polycultural psychology. *Annual Review of Psychology*, 66: 631–659.

Morris, M.W., Leung, K., Ames, D., & Lickel, B. 1999. Views from inside and outside: Integrating emic and etic insights about culture and justice judgment. *Academy of Management Review*, 24(4): 781–796.

Newman, K.L., & Nollen, S.D. 1996. Culture and congruence: The fit between management practices and national culture. *Journal of International Business Studies*, 27(4): 753–779.

Ngo, H.-Y., Turban, D., Lau, C.-M., & Lui, S.-y. 1998. Human resource practices and firm performance of multinational corporations: Influences of country origin. *International Journal of Human Resource Management*, 9(4): 632–652.

Nyambegera, S.M., Sparrow, P.R., & Daniels, K. 2000. The impact of cultural value orientations on individual HRM preferences in developing countries: Lessons from Kenyan organizations. *International Journal of Human Resource Management*, 11(4): 639–663.

Özçelik, A.O., & Aydinli, F. 2006. Strategic role of HRM in Turkey: A three-country comparative analysis. *Journal of European Industrial Training*, 30(4): 310–327.

Parsons, T., & Shils, E.A. 1951. *Toward a General Theory of Action*. Cambridge, MA: Harvard University Press.

Peretz, H., & Fried, Y. 2012. A cross culture examination of performance appraisal and organizational performance. *Journal of Applied Psychology*, 97(2): 448–459.

Peretz, H., & Rosenblatt, Z. 2011. The role of societal cultural practices in organizational investment in training: A comparative study in 21 countries. *Journal of Cross-Cultural Psychology*, 42(5): 817–831.

Pudelko, M. 2006. A comparison of HRM systems in the USA, Japan and Germany in their socio-economic context. *Human Resource Management Journal*, 16(2): 123–153.

Pudelko, M., & Harzing, A.-W. 2007. Country-of-origin, localization, or dominance effect? An empirical investigation of HRM practices in foreign subsidiaries. *Human Resource Management*, 46(4): 535–559.

Rabl, T., Jayasinghe, M., Gerhart, B., & Kühlmann, T.M. 2014. A meta-analysis of country differences in the high-performance work system–business performance relationship: The roles of national culture and managerial discretion. *Journal of Applied Psychology*, 99(6): 1011–1041.

Ramamoorthy, N., & Carroll, S. 1998. Individualism/collectivism orientations and reactions toward alternative human resource management practices. *Human Relations*, 51(5): 571–588.

Reiche, B.S. 2008. The configuration of employee retention practices in multinational corporations' foreign subsidiaries. *International Business Review*, 17(6): 676–687.

Reichel, A., Mayrhofer, W., & Chudzikowski, K. 2009. Human resource development in Austria: A cultural perspective of management development. In C.D. Hansen and Y.-T. Lee (eds), *The Cultural Context of Human Resource Development*: 90–107. Basingstoke: Palgrave Macmillan.

Rowley, C., Benson, J., & Warner, M. 2004. Towards an Asian model of human resource management? A comparative analysis of China, Japan and South Korea. *International Journal of Human Resource Management*, 15(4/5): 917–933.

Ryan, A.M., Boyce, A.S., Ghumman, S., et al. 2009. Going global: Cultural values and perceptions of selection procedures. *Applied Psychology: An International Review*, 58(4): 520–556.

Ryan, A.M., McFarland, L., Baron, H., & Page, R. 1999. An international look at selection practices: Nation and culture as explanations for variability in practice. *Personnel Psychology*, 52(2): 359–392.

Schaffer, B.S., & Riordan, C.M. 2003. A review of cross-cultural methodologies for organizational research: A best-practices approach. *Organizational Research Methods*, 6(2): 169–215.

Schuler, R.S., & Rogovsky, N. 1998. Understanding compensation practice variations across firms: The impact of national culture. *Journal of International Business Studies*, 29(1): 159–177.

Schwartz, S.H. 1994. Beyond individualism/collectivism: New cultural dimensions of values. In K. Uichol, C. Kagitcibasi, H.C. Triandis, and G. Yoon (eds), *Individualism and Collectivism: Theory, Method, and Applications*: 85–119. Thousands Oaks, CA: SAGE.

Scott, W.R. 1983. The organizations of environments: Network, cultural, and historical elements. In J.W. Meyer and W.R. Scott (eds), *Organizational environments: Ritual and Rationality*: 155–175. Beverly Hills, CA: SAGE.

Shenkar, O. 2001. Cultural distance revisited: Towards a more rigorous conceptualization and measurement of cultural differences. *Journal of International Business Studies*, 32(3): 519–535.

Smale, A., Björkman, I., & Sumelius, J. 2013. Examining the differential use of global integration mechanisms across HRM practices: Evidence from China. *Journal of World Business*, 48(2): 232–240.

Snape, E., Thompson, D., Yan, F.K.-C., & Redman, T. 1998. Performance appraisal and culture: practice and attitudes in Hong Kong and Great Britain. *International Journal of Human Resource Management*, 9(5): 841–861.

Sparrow, P.R., & Wu, P.-C. 1998. Does national culture really matter? Predicting HRM preferences of Taiwanese employees. *Employee Relations*, 20(1): 26–56.

Stone, D.L., Stone-Romero, E.F., & Lukaszewski, K.M. 2007. The impact of cultural values on the acceptance and effectiveness of human resource management policies and practices. *Human Resource Management Review*, 17(2): 152–165.

Tayeb, M. 1995. The competitive advantage of nations: The role of HRM and its socio-cultural context. *International Journal of Human Resource Management*, 6(3): 588–605.

Tayeb, M. 1998. Transfer of HRM practices across cultures: An American company in Scotland. *International Journal of Human Resource Management*, 9(2): 332–358.

Teagarden, M.B., & Von Glinow, M.A. 1997. Human resource management in cross-cultural contexts: Emic practices versus etic philosophies. *Management International Review*, 37(Special Issue 1): 7–20.

Trompenaars, F., & Hampden-Turner, C. 1997. *Riding the Waves of Culture: Understanding Cultural Diversity in Business* (2nd edn). London: McGraw-Hill.

Tsui, A.S., Nifadkar, S.S., & Ou, A.Y. 2007. Cross-national, cross-cultural organizational behavior research: Advances, gaps, and recommendations. *Journal of Management*, 33(3): 426–478.

Vaiman, V., & Brewster, C. 2015. How far do cultural differences explain the differences between nations? Implications for HRM. *International Journal of Human Resource Management*, 26(2): 151–164.

Van De Vliert, E., Shi, K., Sanders, K., et al. 2004. Chinese and Dutch interpretations of supervisory feedback. *Journal of Cross-Cultural Psychology*, 35(4): 417–435.

Van Maanen, J., & Schein, E.H. 1979. Toward a theory of organizational socialization. In B.M. Staw (ed.), *Research in Organizational Behavior*, Vol. 1: 209–264. Greenwich, CT: JAI Press.

Verburg, R.M., Drenth, P.J.D., Koopman, P.L., et al. 1999. Managing human resources across cultures: A comparative analysis of practices in industrial enterprises in China and The Netherlands. *International Journal of Human Resource Management*, 10(3): 391–410.

Vijver, F.J.R., Hemert, D.A., & Poortinga, Y.H. 2008. Conceptual issues in multilevel models. In F.J.R. Vijver, D.A. Hemert, and Y.H. Poortinga (eds), *Multilevel Analysis of Individuals and Cultures*: 3–26. New York: Erlbaum.

Von Glinow, M.A., Drost, E.A., & Teagarden, M.B. 2002. Converging on IHRM best practices: Lessons learned from a globally distributed consortium on theory and practice. *Human Resource Management*, 41(1): 123–140.

Warner, M. 2008. Reassessing human resource management 'with Chinese characteristics': An overview. *International Journal of Human Resource Management*, 19(5): 771–801.

Warner, M., & Zhu, Y. 2002. Human resource management 'with Chinese characteristics': A comparative study of the People's Republic of China and Taiwan. *Asia Pacific Business Review*, 9(2): 21–42.

Wee, S., Jonason, P.K., & Li, N.P. 2014. Cultural differences in prioritizing applicant attributes when assessing employment suitability. *European Journal of Work and Organizational Psychology*, 23(6): 946–956.

Whitley, R. 1991. The social construction of business systems in East Asia. *Organization Studies*, 12(1): 1–28.

Whitley, R. 1992. Societies, firms and markets: The social structuring of business systems. In R. Whitley (ed.), *European Business Systems: Firms and Markets in their National Contexts*: 5–45. London: SAGE.

Wright, P., Szeto, W.F., & Cheng, L.T.W. 2002. Guanxi and professional conduct in China: A management development perspective. *International Journal of Human Resource Management*, 13(1): 156–182.

Yamazaki, Y. 2005. Learning styles and typologies of cultural differences: A theoretical and empirical comparison. *International Journal of Intercultural Relations*, 29(5): 521–548.

Zhu, Y., & Verstraeten, M. 2013. Human resource management practices with Vietnamese characteristics: A study of managers' responses. *Asia Pacific Journal of Human Resources*, 51(2): 152–174.

Zhu, Y., Warner, M., & Rowley, C. 2007. Human resource management with 'Asian' characteristics: A hybrid people-management system in East Asia. *International Journal of Human Resource Management*, 18(5): 745–768.

4. Critical approaches to comparative HRM
Tuomo Peltonen and Eero Vaara

INTRODUCTION

Comparative HRM occupies an important position in the scholarship of international human resource management (IHRM) (Brewster, 1999; Brewster & Hegewisch, 1994; Brewster et al., 2004; Clark & Pugh, 2000; Dickmann et al., 2008). This is because it adopts a broader view of the human resource practices and strategies than the mainstream approaches in IHRM research (Greenwood, 2013; Keating & Thompson, 2004). By 'broader' we mean that it takes seriously the recent calls for more societally embedded organizational research as evidenced by the widespread use of neo-institutional theory (Drori et al., 2006; Granovetter, 1985; Scott, 2001), national business systems approach (Morgan et al., 2001; Quack et al., 2000; Whitley, 2002; Whitley & Kristensen, 1996), and cross-cultural perspectives in management studies in general (Hall & Soskice, 2001; Maurice & Sorge, 2000). Thus, comparative research is prone to look into the wider societal issues and problems in its description and explanation of organizational and working life phenomena.

The comparative stance has demonstrated the limits of the HRM theories and models derived from the institutional realities of the North American context. The individualized approach to employment relations and people management has its roots in the United States (US) institutional environment where the unions are relatively weak and where there is a strong belief in the potency of the free markets in the organization of labour relations. In contrast, the continental European system has traditionally been organized along corporatist lines, with strong trade union membership and a tradition of collective bargaining. The European system, with its more regulative and representative character, has put more weight on the societal-level agreements and on the active role of the government. At the same time, it is important to note that the HRM environments in developing countries tend to lack the well-established institutional frameworks that are taken for granted in the mainstream HRM literature (cf. Jackson, 2004). For example, despite market liberalization, independent trade unions are still non-existent in Asian countries such as, for example, China (Chan & Hui, 2014; Friedman & Kuruvilla, 2015); whereas in Africa one can find societies where the informal or grey job market dominates the whole economy, as is the case, for example, in South Africa (Neves & du Toit, 2012). With these kinds of insights, comparative HRM research has successfully demonstrated that what we take as the universal model of HRM is in reality a local North American approach transferred into the rest of the world as 'best practice' (Gooderham & Nordhaug, 2011; Janssens & Steyaert, 2012; Mayrhofer et al., 2011). Given the debates on the ethical shortcomings and societal irrelevance of Americanized management practices and theories (Dore, 2000; Ghoshal, 2005; Mintzberg, 2004; Pfeffer & Fong, 2005), this is a timely message.

Whilst we acknowledge the advances made in comparative studies, we want to push this approach even further in terms of its ability to connect with and apply critical perspectives.

We draw from the critical theories and methodologies that have been put forward by the critical management studies movement. In particular, we offer global labour process theory, postcolonial analysis, and transnational feminism as perspectives that can further advance the comparative approach to IHRM. Although some scholars have already used and developed such ideas, a great deal can and needs to be done to map out and examine the various problematic aspects of IHRM in our globalizing world.

The next section provides an overview of comparative HRM research and its contributions. This is followed by a look at the globalization of employment management as a manifestation of neoliberal economic and societal policies and practices. The fourth section discusses critical management studies as a fruitful approach to organizations and organizational research. The fifth section focuses on global labour process theory, postcolonial analysis, and transnational feminism, which are presented as useful approaches that can shed more light on the problems and challenges of HRM in contemporary society and thus advance critical comparative HRM research. We then reflect upon the possibility of change from a critical perspective. A brief concluding section wraps up our argument and suggests some avenues for further research.

COMPARATIVE HRM AS A 'BROADER' VIEW ON THE HUMAN RESOURCE MANAGEMENT PHENOMENA

Comparative HRM as a field of study focuses on the national-institutional differences in human resource management practices, strategies, and systems. Originally contained within the emerging study of IHRM, it has in recent years developed into an independent area in its own right. According to Brewster (1999, 2007), comparative HRM relies on a distinct research paradigm that sets it apart from the mainstream US human resource management discipline. The US scholars tend to view HRM from a universalist perspective, treating HRM as a general phenomenon that exists irrespective of the institutional environment where it is practiced. Comparative HRM, instead, insists that human resource management practices are best understood as societal phenomena, shaped by the institutional, cultural, and political contexts of their occurrence. Brewster (2007) argues that a contextualist paradigm in comparative HRM makes a crucial difference in many respects. These include a more critical stance towards the 'goodness' of the North American conception of HRM as manipulation of individual employees and employment contracts, incorporation of industrial relations issues and trade union topics into the conception of HRM, and a willingness to look at HRM from a national, European Union, or even global world systems level of analysis. The different realities of contexts such as the European welfare states as well as the Asian and African developing economies all need to be accounted for in search of a more accurate picture of human resource management worldwide (Jackson, 2004).

Comparative HRM also differs from the mainstream human resource study in terms of methodological preferences (Brewster, 1999, 2007). Comparative HRM seeks to understand individual national contexts and the way in which HRM is organized in each particular country. It is not interested in the discovery of general laws and causal mechanisms in HRM, but in gaining sensitivity for the locally contingent circumstances surrounding the particular forms and approaches to labour management. The focus on the particular is also reflected in the tendency to rely on the insights of empirical data in theory development. Comparative HRM seeks to develop new theories and understandings of the HRM outcomes without a strong commitment to a priori models and theories of human resource management. It is inductive rather than deductive in its methodology. Empirical data used in comparative HRM are often a combination of quantitative and qualitative materials, used heuristically to reach a deeper understanding of the different forms of HRM and how they are shaped in various institutional national contexts (Keating & Thompson, 2004). Overall, comparative HRM has tried to set itself apart from the positivist deductive methodology that has dominated HRM research in the North American field, with an interest in developing a non-managerialist theory of HRM as embedded in the variety of institutional and socio-political contexts and relations.

However, comparative HRM has not made explicit its standing vis-à-vis the various theoretical issues that preoccupy organization and management studies as a branch of social science. Using the classical outline of organizational theoretical paradigms by Burrell and Morgan (1979), it is not clear whether comparative HRM is committed to consensus sociology characterized by a unitarist conception of work organizations, to conflict theories that approach organizations as sites of structural contradictions and tensions, or to some other position. At times it seems to agree with the neo-Marxist and other radical views on the continuing presence of a power asymmetry between managers and workers, but this is not systematically noted, nor made explicit. Comparative HRM also seems to hesitate between objective and interpretative positions with regard to epistemology and methods. While it is keen to stress the use of qualitative data in making sense of organizing HRM, it tends to resort to quantitative survey studies of national forms of HRM (for example, the Cranet survey; see Brewster et al., 2004; Parry et al., 2013). Given the broad range of different epistemological alternatives to objectivist approaches to methodology (Morgan & Smircich, 1980), comparative HRM still tends to represent a fairly conventional area within organizational inquiry. These limitations become apparent if we take a closer look at the globalization of HRM as a manifestation of the spread of neoliberal capitalism to new areas around the world.

GLOBALIZATION AND NEOLIBERAL CAPITALISM

The spread of the individualized, market-based employment systems is one of the key interests in comparative HRM. The rise of contingent work, flexible working patterns, and new organizational forms are manifestations of what Sennett (2006) calls the 'culture of new capitalism'. According to Sennett (1998, 2006), late modern capitalism is characterized by a shift from bureaucratic organizations and stable careers to flexible networks and contingent employment. The assumption that an employee is committed to one corporation for the whole of their working life is no longer valid; instead workers are left largely to rely on their own devices as free agents seeking jobs in the constantly changing economic situations. Employees are treated as entrepreneurs, who are responsible for their own employment. As Bauman (2000) has noted, ours is the era of 'liquid modernity' in which capital is globally mobile and seeks to guarantee the best possible returns, at the same time as labour continues to stay tied to its local communal contexts. The global economic crisis starting in 2008/09 has shown (again) that unregulated international financial markets can create major economic crises. The promise of the finance-driven economy to bring prosperity to all through continuous growth has turned out to be a one-sided and ethically questionable arrangement. The continuously shifting organizational and economic contexts had already made it difficult to build coherent working lives before the financial crisis. Now, as the economic problems have spread from banking to other sectors, it is the workers who have to carry the burden of unsuccessful policies in the form of lay-offs.

At the same time, however, organizational control has intensified its grip over the empowered employees. The market model of employment relations has not displaced managerial control in organizations. The emerging organizational model is akin to a rationally controlled network, envisioned as a lean, managerially diluted, and dispersed network of individual employees. Kunda and Ailon-Suday (2005) (cf. Barley & Kunda, 1992) call this the market rationalist ideology, which has connections to the classical Taylorist and Fordist techniques of managerial control. Employees constitute minuscule 'business units' that are analysed, measured, and managed just like any other economic entities. Rational managerial techniques developed for financial accounting are applicable to human individuals, a development that has made work in large organizations highly competitive, short-term oriented, and instrumental.

Global capitalism has institutionalized uncertainty to an extent that it can be regarded as one of the most acute problems facing working life today. While HRM scholars have noted this change, they have been unable to fully describe the human and social consequences of market-based human resource strategies. The notions of boundaryless careers (Arthur, 1994) and transactional psychological contracts (Rousseau, 1995) refer to transformations in the world of work, but they have not been sufficient to illuminate the full scale of human experiences brought about by the 'HRM-ist' employment models. In a similar way, studies examining the global convergence or divergence of HRM practices have tended to look at the surface patterns and structural manifestations of contingent labour, instead of elucidating the social meanings and lived experiences of workers, professionals, and managers worldwide (Hassard et al., 2007).

Let us exemplify this with a reference to our own immediate working environment as Finnish academic employees. Finland is typically portrayed in the comparative studies as following the Nordic model of HRM (Lilja, 1998; Lindeberg et al., 2004). This includes a high trade union organization rate, comparatively strong government presence in business regulation, and the tradition of collective bargaining processes. Yet recent changes in private and public organizations suggest a rapid 'Anglo-Americanization' of economic systems and industrial relations (Tainio & Lilja, 2002). Collective bargaining is in crisis, and precarious employment is on the rise. In the public sector, traditional bureaucratic careers are being demolished in favour of flexible arrangements typical of the New Economy.

Yet it is fair to note that while we see Finnish development as an example of a profound change in working life, people in other countries often suffer from more acute problems. The core human rights such as the freedom to join trade unions are not within the reach of employees in many emerging economies. Without the social safety net, employees in those countries are much more vulnerable to external changes: for example the current global economic crisis seems to hit hardest the poorest nations and their citizens. To make better sense of these types of global shifts, and their human and social consequences for the employees, it is useful to take a closer look at the insights offered by critical management studies.

CRITICAL MANAGEMENT STUDIES

Critical management studies (CMS) has become a legitimate approach within management and organization studies. Following openings such as the paradigm analysis of organizational studies by Burrell and Morgan (1979), CMS has expanded during the last 25 years in the form of special conferences (International Critical Management Studies Conference), interest groups (the CMS Division at the American Academy of Management), and scholarly outlets. The roots of CMS lay in three discussions: labour process theory (LPT), critical theory (CT), and also some forms of postmodernist or poststructuralist theorizing. Labour process theory is a more materialist approach to the structuring of organizational hierarchies under the forces of late modern capitalism. Its main argument, the so-called deskilling thesis, was originally formulated by Braverman (1974). According to Braverman, the advances in modern people management techniques have not delivered autonomy and self-fulfilment for the employees of the modern corporation, but instead have intensified the clash between the capitalist interests and the working conditions of organizational labour. Modern management strategies strip away individual creativity and dignity, providing the employees with monotonous tasks that are detached from their own personal aspirations. According to Braverman's deskilling thesis, work is degraded under monopoly capitalism because of an inexorable tendency for the conception or planning of work to be separated from its execution. Conception is concentrated in an ever-smaller section of the workforce, while most workers are reduced to executing tasks conceived by others. In the LPT view, this Taylorist division of labour makes work meaningless for the majority of organizational employees.

Critical theory is a more humanistic stream of radical theorizing. Its roots lay in the so-called Frankfurt School and the work of scholars such as Adorno, Marcuse and Habermas. Critical theory is interested in the one-dimensionality of our cultural beliefs and in the ways in which ideological constructions serve the interests of the powerful, or capital. The work of Habermas (1972, 1984) has been pivotal in guiding the research on organizational culture and communication towards a critical agenda. According to Habermas (1984), the realm of work has been estranged from its self-realizing and dialogic potentials, and has instead transformed into dispassionate activity with no connection to the deeper social and communicative needs of the employees. Organizational life takes on an instrumental outlook as the members resort to external motivations and markers of personal attachment. Also, communication is restricted to ideologically acceptable discourses, and the free flow of debate is blocked by the accumulation of power and authority into the hands of the few, such as professional managers. Disciplines and scientific articulations of organizational management such as those contained within human resource management can be seen as manifestations of the broader ideological milieu where prevailing forms of understanding are shaped by the structures of power (Alvesson & Willmott, 1996). All this takes place in a world of conflicting interests between the privileged and those excluded from the benefits of contemporary capitalism. In addition, CT is keen to restore some of the emancipatory potential of the alienated employees and organizations in order to help them to better address their own interests and how they could be articulated in the corporate decision-making and communication (Alvesson & Deetz, 2006).

The CMS movement has also been inspired by various postmodernist and poststructuralist theories and methodologies, especially by the work of Foucault, Deleuze and Derrida. Foucault's discourse analysis has been particularly influential, as it has provided means to examine and elucidate how managerial and organizational phenomena are structured and governed by specific discourses (Alvesson & Karreman, 2000). His ideas have also been very useful in highlighting how subjectivities and identities are constructed in contemporary organizations (Knights & Morgan, 1991). Foucauldian analysis of institutional practices aims to uncover the techniques and relations of power implicit in the constitution of organizational objects and subjects (Foucault, 1977, 1978). HRM appears in this theoretical landscape as a central set of seemingly neutral practices (recruitment, performance appraisal, employee development, and so on) that gives rise to various sorts of power relations in organizations. This perspective has been reflected in a stream of critical analyses of HRM practices and discourses as modalities of social power (Barratt, 2003; Legge, 1989; McKinlay & Starkey, 1998; Townley, 1993).

In an attempt to develop a generalized research agenda for the CMS community, Alvesson and Willmott (2003) introduce five general themes that define the theoretical and epistemological approach taken by critical management scholars:

1. Developing a non-objective view of management techniques and processes: management techniques such as those practiced in HRM (for example, selection, assessment, career development) are not merely technical procedures as they are deeply implicated in constructing the social realities and relations in the workplaces. Formal techniques are subjective or reality-constituting in the same way as informal social practices.
2. Exposing asymmetrical power relations: organizations are microcosms that enact and reproduce wider power structures. Critical inquiry is motivated to expose and challenge the privileged position of corporate elites such as top managerial classes. Ideas such as the division of labour between the strategic apex and the rest of the organization are seen as political constellations that sustain inequality between different occupational or social groups.
3. Counteracting discursive closure: rational management practices are often taken for granted and not openly debated. Critical management studies aims to break up the communicative closures and to prompt democratic dialogue between the various stakeholders.
4. Revealing the partiality of shared interests: organizational goals and corporate decisions are often legitimized as being in the interest of the whole organization or economy. However, a critical perspective reveals that shared interests often represent the aspirations of a limited clique (top managers, economic elite, state elite) instead of being declarations of negotiated intentions of a wider set of viewpoints.
5. Appreciating the centrality of language and communicative action: language is a socio-historical realm that carries, reproduces and transforms social realities and relations in and around organizations. Linguistic or discursive focus serves as a bridge between the issues related to power, class, and ideology and the local construction of social meanings in organizational life.

We subscribe to these ideas, and wish to present specific critical perspectives as fruitful avenues to further these interests in the context of comparative HRM.

CRITICAL PERSPECTIVES ON COMPARATIVE HRM

Having introduced a critical approach to management studies, we turn our attention back to comparative HRM. As noted, there is a need to account for and analyse the spread of new employment practices and organizational forms, associated with the emerging hegemony of neoliberal policies across countries and regions. We argue that this type of critical agenda can be informed and further developed by three theoretical and methodological approaches: global labour process theory, postcolonial discourse analysis, and transnational feminism (Table 4.1).

Global Labour Process Theory

Global labour process theory (GLPT) is an application of the main tenets of labour process theory to the globalizing economy and working life. Whereas the traditional labour process theory (LPT) research has tended to focus on nation states and their organization and management of work, GLPT takes a more explicitly global or transnational look. The aim is to analyse how deskilling and related phenomena appear in contexts other than those researched in the US and United Kingdom (UK) studies of labour processes and management. With multinational corporations extending their operations to non-Western countries, and the Anglo-American liberal market economy occupying a dominant role in the worldwide structuring of societies and organizations, it is of interest to test the deskilling hypothesis in new national and cultural environments. The GLPT research is particularly interested in analysing whether there is an emerging convergence of employment management practices and organizational forms. The focus is on the adoption of neo-Fordist and neo-Taylorist HRM practices that manifest the intensification of managerial control. Unlike the more inductive convergence/divergence debates, GLPT takes as its starting point the deskilling hypothesis originally introduced by Braverman and subsequently empirically studied and theoretically elaborated by a number of organizational scholars. However, GLPT is more attuned to the contemporary theorizing that takes into account the role of agency and subjectivity in the organizing of social relations at work (Knights & Willmott, 1989). In this regard it departs from the 'orthodox' LPT and its structuralistic assumptions about social and organizational life that have tended to neglect the role of subjective experiences and interpretations. This can be seen also in the methodology: GLPT uses qualitative methods such as field studies and organizational cases to complement the more broad-brush approaches such as surveys. At the same time, however, GLPT is inclined to adopt a more realist stance on epistemology than some of the alternative interpretative and poststructuralist perspectives.

Global LPT is to our mind perhaps best exemplified by the studies of the UK team of Hassard, Morris and McCann. Their empirical research (e.g., McCann et al., 2004) has studied the changing work and organization patterns in a variety of national contexts, including the United Kingdom (UK), the United States of America (USA), Germany, Japan, and China. The empirical data for the research programme have been drawn

Table 4.1   Three critical perspectives on comparative human resource management

	Global labour process theory	Postcolonial discourse analysis	Transnational feminism
Background influences	Labour process theory: Braverman (1974) Reconstructed labour process theory: Knights & Willmott (1989)	Discourse analysis: Foucault (1977, 1978) Postcolonial theory: Said (1978), Bhabha (1994), Spivak (1987), Young (2001)	Feminist theories Postcolonial theory: Spivak (1987) Transnational feminism: Mohanty (2004)
Focus	Global convergence of management of work	Institutional-cultural differences between West and non-West (as constructed in practices and discourses)	Divisions of labour and social relations between men and women in globalizing world, and differences between them
Research questions	How does global convergence link to the spread of capitalist principles and practices? Is there a trend towards deskilling around the world? Are emerging economies adapting neo-Fordist or neo-Taylorist management methods? Are there national variations in the adoption of neo-Fordist techniques? How are employees across the world experiencing new organizational forms and management practices?	What are the underlying assumptions about West and non-West in comparative HRM? How are West and non-West represented in discourses of comparative management research and practice? What are the implications of the identities of the West and the non-West to the structuring of power? What kinds of practices are being legitimized with reference to colonial identities and rhetoric?	How are workplace and social relations organized between men and women in global capitalism in different locations? How do Western conceptions of women in emerging economies reproduce domination and subjugation? Are there alternative discourses that allow one to go beyond simplified categories of 'gender' and 'Third World'? What role do HRM practices and discourses play in reproducing particular identities and subjectivities?
Epistemology	Objectivist/realist	Subjectivist/ constructionist	Subjectivist/constructionist
Ontology	Structural	Relational	Structural and relational
Methods	Field work, organizational case studies National comparisons	Discourse analysis Critical reading of canonical texts Case studies	Discourse analysis Activism
Exemplar studies	Morris et al. (2006)	Westwood (2001) Vaara et al. (2005)	Mohanty (2004)

from organizational case studies of large and mid-sized companies undergoing major restructurings. Qualitative material includes interviews with senior and HRM management, as well as with employees from a variety of levels. In some cases, field studies are complemented with macro-data from surveys and economic statistics. Methodologically, Hassard et al. advocate a middle-of-the-road position, which tries to get closer to the lived experiences and personal meanings of the employees without losing sight of the contextual and political structures affecting the organization of working life in modern companies. Their approach can be seen as a response to the critiques of traditional structural theories in that they ignore the role of subjectivity in the actualization and reproduction of social structures (Giddens, 1979, 1984; Knights & Willmott, 1989). In short, the aim is to provide a counterweight to the undersocialized accounts of the mainstream international and comparative management research, while at the same time arguing for a realist reading of the employee informants' narratives.

Recent studies have revealed the structuring of work and human resource management against the continuing capitalist accumulation of surplus value in the globalized modernity. The work of Hassard, McCann and Morris on Japanese middle managers provides an illuminating example (Hassard et al., 2012; McCann et al., 2004; Morris et al., 2006). In their study of Japanese middle managers, Morris et al. (2006) find that the Japanese management culture, famous for its focus on lifetime employment, strong corporate culture, and seniority-based hierarchy, shows signs of moving towards an Anglo-American model of individualized employment terms and flatter hierarchies. Management layers have been reduced in many companies to comply with the post-bureaucratic ideal celebrated in the market ideologies of the new organizational forms, although elements of the more stable hierarchies have remained. Similarly, companies have been forced to abandon the tradition of lifetime employment as restructurings have led to redundancies and early-retirement arrangements. Career moves and reward system have become more individualized and competitive instead of following the traditional Japanese emphasis on seniority and collective unity.

In comparison, the middle managers in a number of UK corporations seem to have experienced a more direct transformation. McCann et al. (2008) report that the middle managers interviewed all reported increasing workloads and pace of change. Many companies have cut their workforces, including middle management, and the remaining employees have faced longer working hours, intensifying monitoring of their performance, as well as tightening competition over the shrinking vacancies at the top management level. To some extent, the restructurings have meant constant reskilling of the individual competencies of the employees, but this has come at the price of having to lead ever more dispersed and fragmented teams and projects. Recent changes have often led to serious cases of stress and even deep burnout among middle managers continuing in their jobs after downsizings and restructurings.

The main argument from these studies is that although the changes among the UK and Japanese middle managers are not structurally similar, there is a remarkable similarity in the way recent work and HRM-related transformations are experienced at the employee level. Hassard and his colleagues refer to the influence of the neoliberal ideology that has led to organizational arrangements such as the demolition of the internal labour market, rise of performance-related pay, reduced job security, and increased work hours; all implemented in the name of international competitiveness. Although the factual statistical labour data do not always support the argument that the changes they identify are wide-spread, the subjective experiences and the way middle managers and other employees interpret their situations give rise to global convergence. Insofar as employees in a variety of national-institutional contexts construct their own organizational environment as highly individualized, competitive, and uncertain, the global convergence of employment management becomes produced as an enduring reality.

This comparative study of middle managers in the UK and Japan is an interesting extension and modification of the traditional labour process theory. The work of Hassard et al. contains an underlying assumption that global capitalism is intimately connected to the intensification of the labour process, manifested as increased workloads and the introduction of neo-Taylorist techniques such as the close surveillance of individual performance and the installing of individualistic reward systems. This process touches not only the rich industrial countries but also the less developed economies: although the empirical studies mainly focus on developed industrial nations, a similar type of approach could be applied for researching the effects of the new ideologies on the working conditions and experiences of the employees in developed countries. The hypothesis of the globally intensifying labour process is then explored through case studies of different organizations across a variety of national-institutional contexts. While there are national-institutional variations in the way in which the labour process is transformed, the overall trend is towards intensified control and exploitation of the worker input, including also middle managers.

Postcolonial Discourse Analysis

Postcolonial discourse analysis (PCDA) is an interpretative form of critical inquiry. It has its roots in the pioneering work of Edward Said. Said's study on *Orientalism* (Said, 1978) opened new avenues for analysing the relations between West and non-West, which has led to an emergence of postcolonial analysis as a theory in its own right (Bhabha, 1994; Spivak, 1987; Young, 2001). According to Said, the 'Orient' – or, more generally, non-West – is a Western construction. Analysing the discursive production of West and non-West is influenced by the ideas of critical theory where ideological beliefs about various social groups are seen as manifestations of dominance and hegemony. Said's approach was partly inspired by the work of Foucault, especially in regard to how the non-West, or the Other, is constructed in various linguistic and institutional practices. Foucault's (1977, 1978) ideas have helped postcolonial theory to study both non-West and West as mutually sustaining subject positions that are ideologically imposed but at the same time empower those who adapt them as bases of identity and agency. This hybrid theoretical background has given rise to a vivid research programme, also applied to organization and management studies (e.g., Prasad, 1997a, 2003; Westwood, 2001, 2004, 2006; Westwood & Jack, 2006, 2007).

While there are numerous potential objects of inquiry, perhaps the most interesting stream of research has focused on the way in which differences between West and non-West are constructed in the theory and practice of international management. Following Said and other postcolonial writers, organizational studies have concentrated on the production and consumption of ideas about cultural identity in discursive and institutional practices. The main questions have been: 'How are West and non-West represented and constructed in discourses of comparative management', and 'What are the implications of colonial identities to the structuring of power in West-non-West relations?'. The research programme is epistemologically constructionist or relativist, meaning that it is mainly interested in the linguistic and textual articulations of identities and social relations, acknowledging that its own truth claims are also rhetorical accomplishments that have no external reference point outside of the discussion in which they participate. Constructionist epistemology is complemented with a relational ontology that assumes that the social world is composed of emerging and evolving relations of actors and identities. In terms of methodology, PCDA leans toward discourse analytical approaches, which implies a close reading of selected disciplinary, institutional, and media texts in order to reveal the tacit privileges and hierarchies inscribed to the meaning constructions of literary and oral representations of cultural difference.

Postcolonial discourse analysis looks at the discursive processes of producing identities and relations between West and non-West. Essentially, PCDA aims to reveal the implicit Western perspective in the allegedly 'neutral' descriptions and representations of non-West, West, and the relations between them. As such, its empirical scope is somewhat broader than that of GLPT, encompassing a wealth of scientific, disciplinary, and institutional (for example, media) texts engaging with international relations and business management.

This has led scholars to inquire about the underlying assumptions of authoritative texts such as the academic writings on cross-cultural management (Kwek, 2003) and stereotypical notions that are reproduced in textbooks on international management (Tipton, 2008). Westwood (2001, 2006) has provided insightful analyses that criticize the very conceptions that characterize comparative international management. The point is that the Other (non-West) is always represented as underdeveloped, dangerous, exotic, or mystical; while the West is seen as developed, modern, rational, and normal. Although these analyses have not only focused on IHRM practices, the conclusion is clear: both the problems (HRM and other management issues) and the solutions (specific HRM practices) that are usually considered in this field echo this colonial mindset. Thus, postcolonial analysis can bring another critical perspective to comparative IHRM by deepening our understanding of the fundamental reasons of what is seen as normal and natural and what is not, as well as the implications of such assumptions.

Another important aspect of postcolonial analysis is its linkage to neocolonialism (Banerjee & Linstead, 2001, 2004). In this view, neocolonial means a new form of colonialism linked with contemporary globalization. Corporate-driven globalization can be interpreted as implying cultural homogenization and even North American hegemony. While this is a relevant point for most areas of international management research, IHRM is a case in point here. As illustrated by the recent writings in comparative HRM (Brewster, 2007), American dominance is evident in the assumptions that the specific practices originating from US corporations would be universal, normal, or transferable to all places on the globe. This kind of neocolonialism is not, however, normal or natural, and such assumptions bring with them cultural insensitivity, stereotypical thinking, and prejudice; in the worst cases, something that comes close to xenophobia. Furthermore, such thinking is ideological in the sense of reproducing neoliberal ideals and Anglo-American hegemony.

Although postcolonial analysis is often thought to apply mainly to classic cases of colonial (Western powers) and colonized (the non-West), or to the relationships of more developed and developing countries, constructions of postcolonial relationships can be found elsewhere, too. A revealing example is provided by Vaara et al. (2005), who have studied mergers and acquisitions in the Nordic financial services sector. They focused on language skills and policies in a Finnish–Swedish merger, which led to the choice of Swedish as the official language. Their analysis shows how language skills served as empowering or disempowering resources in organizational communication, how language skills became associated with professional competence, and how this led to the creation of new social networks that favoured Swedish-speakers. The case also illustrates how language can be regarded as an essential element in the construction of international confrontation, how this policy led to a construction of superiority (Swedes) and inferiority (Finns), and also reproduced postcolonial identities in the merging bank (Swedes as the colonial power). Finally, they also pointed out how such policies ultimately led to the reification of postcolonial and neocolonial structures of domination in this setting. Thus, the reconstruction of international power relations has concrete implications on HRM issues such as career mobility (Itani et al., 2015).

Future research could apply postcolonial discourse analysis to better understand a variety of topics such as the meanings and implications of 'competence', 'mobility', 'talent management', 'career advancement', or 'boundarylessness' across various cultural and political contexts. It is also important to note that the economic and societal development and China, India and other BRICS (Brazil, Russia, India, China, South Africa) countries may also partially subvert traditional power relations or create new discourses and practices with novel implications on the construction of power relations and identities in international contexts.

Transnational Feminism

Feminism provides an array of critical perspectives that can be useful in comparative HRM. This, however, requires a broad conception of HRM and the key issues at play. One of the key points of feminist organization and management studies has been to extend organization analysis to issues such as civil rights, well-being, equal opportunities, work–life balance, family, and sexuality. These issues are not usually seen as the immediate concerns of management in general or HRM in particular; however, the feminist argument is that they should be. In fact, in addition to bringing up marginalized or silenced issues, or giving voice to those who are under-represented or in a less privileged position, feminism emphasizes societal and corporate responsibility for such issues.

Feminism has a great deal to offer to contemporary analyses of globalization from the point of view of linking the global division of labour to social relations between women and men and gendered social practices in and around organizations. For example, Calás and Smircich (1993) show how a discourse that emphasizes women's specific qualities in management is appropriated by management writers. They demonstrate how this discourse serves to legitimate the gendered status quo where men occupy the central positions in the international arena while women 'keep the home fires burning'. Such observations have clear linkages to (I)HRM, especially in terms of explaining why inequality still prevails at top echelons in global corporations.

However, there is not one form of feminism, but many. For example, Calás and

Smircich (2006) distinguish liberal, radical, psychoanalytic, socialist, poststructuralist and postmodern, and transnational and (post)colonial feminism. We will here focus attention on transnational feminism because of its potential for opening up new avenues for critical analysis in comparative HRM. The key characteristic of transnational feminism is that while it continues to probe into central questions of inequality from a feminist angle, it also problematizes key assumptions of Western feminism. This is the case especially with how dominant Western feminist discourses tend to construct the women in the emerging economies. In this sense, transnational feminism is linked with postcolonial analysis. For instance, Mohanty (1997, 2004) has made the point that Western discourses of 'Third World women' construct them as oppressed, underdeveloped, and lacking essential qualities that they 'should have'. This picture is problematic precisely in the sense that, again, Western models and ideologies are naturalized, and the multiple and different cultural issues and values that are relevant are disregarded. As a result, the constructions of 'normal' or preferred careers, responsibilities at work and at home, equal opportunities, and related HRM practices remain one-sided and ideologically laden. Moreover, even the well-intended feminist analyses easily portray women in emerging economies as victims and passive recipients of knowledge and aid, thus reducing their agency and subjectivity.

Some forms of transnational feminism also question the usefulness of 'gender' as a sufficient category to be applied across cultures. It is less clear what the alternative is, but the implication is that future analyses of (I)HRM would do well to map out various complex linkages between gender, race, religion, nationality, education, career, and sexuality without assuming that the solutions that appear the most natural or progressive from the Western point of view would be that for other cultures, religious settings, forms of family, and so on.

Mohanty (1997) provides an analysis that advances such understanding. Her critical starting point is that exploitation in its various kinds is linked with the political economy of globalization in its material and discursive forms. She has chosen to speak of 'One-Third' and 'Two-Thirds' worlds instead of the common notion of the 'Third World'. Through such discursive choices, she has focused attention on commonly held and naturalized conceptions that deal with the legitimacy of Western consumerism and its ideals set for women – as well as men – in different parts of the world. As a way to improve the state of affairs, she has called for transnational solidarity building and struggle against harmful forms of globalization (Mohanty, 2004).

Such reflections may at first appear remote for comparative HRM, but we maintain that they are not, if we wish to pursue broad understanding of the issues that HRM can or should be dealing with, and a critical attitude toward the universalist 'best practices' and other solutions provided. The fact remains, however, that to date we lack studies that would spell out the full-fledged implications of transnational feminism on IHRM and comparative HRM. This is a major challenge for future research.

THE CRITICAL APPROACH AND THE POSSIBILITY OF POSITIVE CHANGE

While critical approaches are particularly adept in valorizing the ways in which power and control operate through taken-for-granted discourses and administrative arrangements, a critical position on international management makes it possible to suggest avenues for positive change. Traditionally, the critical or Marxist thinking has seen organizations and societies as historical phenomena that are evolving from more coercive forms towards liberated and humanly more fulfilling alternatives. In Marx's thought (e.g., Lukács, 1971), this social transformation was to take place through the conscious actions of the oppressed classes, most notably the proletariat. In the later version of critical theories, such as in the writings of the Frankfurt School (Marcuse, 1964) and Habermas (1984), the attention turned from the revolutionary consciousness of the underclass to the potential for more gradual change within the everyday life of cultural meanings and social interaction patterns. In critical management studies, the programme of initiating positive change has been discussed under labels such as 'micro-emancipation' (Alvesson & Willmott, 1996) and 'critical performativity' (Spicer et al., 2009), and other writers such as Kelemen and Rumens (2008) have introduced methods derived from the application of American pragmatism and action research.

At the same time, the turn to poststructural theorizing within critical management studies has opened a new kind of position regarding the relationship between critical analysis and the practice of positive or transformative change. For poststructuralists, the analysis of relations of power and ideological closure is not performed outside of the domain of the immanent structures and cultural discourses, but as a deconstructive and disruptive reading of the contemporary conditions within the prevailing cultural and philosophical contexts (Hoy, 1998; Ingram, 1994). Adopting this type of post-metaphysical stance, Derridean–Foucauldian analysis does not offer exterior motives or normative grounds for practices that would help us out of the labyrinth of modern Western structures and their power effects. Instead, it tends to warn about the easy solutions that may seemingly offer an alternative to the prevailing hegemony, but that may eventually just bind us ever more deeply into the subtle ideologies playing themselves out beneath the more overt structures of domination and colonization.

Critical management studies in general, and critical approaches to international management in particular, have inherited this complex understanding of power and positive change. In Said's (1978, 1983) postcolonial theory, this duality comes out clearly as he complements a Derridean–Foucauldian critique of the subtle workings of the institutionalized colonial discourse within our sense of the West and the East, whilst at the same time calling for the critical scholars to adopt an oppositional stance to the hegemonic articulations, thus providing voice to the silenced non-Westerners in the construction of cultural and institutional meanings. Essentially, this would involve presenting the non-West with its own, alternative history, philosophy, language, and identity (Chakrabarty, 1992; Prasad, 1997b).

However, from a poststructuralist perspective, there is no easy escape from the Eurocentric project of modern thinking (cf. Chomsky & Foucault, 2006). We are all Europeans, in the sense of being fundamentally moulded by our participation in the modern ideas and values such as reason, progress, human rights, and economic development. Instead of trying to craft oppositional movements aiming at contradicting or challenging the power of Western ideologies, poststructuralists believe that deconstructive analysis coupled with a conception of human creativity constitutes the best way forward (Connolly, 1998). Alongside the critical interrogations into the power effects of modern structures and ideologies such as discourse of comparative human resource management, a careful nurturing of one's own existential consciousness in the form of 'stylization' and 'aestheticization' of life may provide resources for positive change (Barratt, 2008). It is thus in the realm of identity fashioning that poststructuralists such as Foucault find hope for overcoming the impasse of prevailing discourses and regimes of Eurocentric truth. That these higher virtues are reminiscent of artistic and even aristocratic ways of life (Nietzsche, 1994) may be disappointing for those embracing traditional ideals such as democracy and equality in their search for alternatives for the modern 'iron cage' of instrumental reason. And yet, pursuing a noble life could be considered a timely effort in the late modern attempts to escape the flattening effects of Eurocentric discourses without falling back to the matrix of humanist metaphysics. Ironically, the kind of self-stylization suggested by Foucault and others had its early incarnation in ancient Greece, where the journey of deeper personal transformation was called *theoria* (Nightingale, 2004; Peltonen, 2016). This was the original meaning of 'theory'. Contemplative theoretical practices of the Greek could still be viewed as a prototype of the kind of transformative practice towards higher forms of existence to which scholars and practitioners could resort in their pursuit of a more creative and thoughtful style of intellectual and organizational life (Hadot, 1995).

CONCLUSION

The starting point for this chapter was a need to spell out ways in which we could advance critical analysis in comparative HRM. We think that comparative HRM – more than other approaches or emergent subfields in HRM – can precisely lead to better understanding of broader social and societal issues in and around globalizing organizations. For this purpose, we have argued that comparative HRM should be linked with critical management studies; at least in the sense that comparative HRM could make use of theoretical and methodological approaches that have already proven useful in other areas, and have particular potential in view of the issues that IHRM can and should deal with. Hence, we have proposed global labour process theory, postcolonial analysis, and transnational feminism as examples of perspectives that can further advance the comparative approach to HRM. As our discussion has illustrated, there are seminal studies that at least implicitly already deal with key issues of HRM in globalizing organizations and economy. However, it is equally clear that a great deal can and should be done to further our understanding in these important and fascinating areas. It is also important to note that our discussion of the three critical perspectives is in no way meant as an exhaustive presentation of the available critical perspectives on comparative human resource management. Rather, we would like to invite a multitude of different theoretical programmes to enrich and challenge the current state of the art in this developing area of management studies scholarship.

REFERENCES

Alvesson, M., & Deetz, S. 2006. Critical theory and postmodernism approaches to organizational studies. In S. Clegg, C. Hardy, B. Lawrence, and W.R. Nord (eds), *The Sage Handbook of Organization Studies*: 255–283. London: SAGE.

Alvesson, M., & Karreman, D. 2000. Varieties of discourse: On the study of organizations through discourse analysis. *Human Relations*, 53(9): 1125–1149.

Alvesson, M., & Willmott, H. 1996. *Making Sense of Management: A Critical Introduction*. London: SAGE.

Alvesson, M., & Willmott, H. 2003. *Studying Management Critically*. London: SAGE.

Arthur, M.B. 1994. The boundaryless career: A new perspective for organizational inquiry. *Journal of Organizational Behavior*, 15(4): 295–306.

Banerjee, S.B., & Linstead, S. 2001. Globalization, multiculturalism and other fictions: Colonialism for the new millennium?. *Organization*, 8(4): 683–722.

Banerjee, S.B., & Linstead, S. 2004. Masking subversion: Neocolonial embeddedness in anthropological accounts of indigenous management. *Human Relations*, 57(2): 221–247.

Barley, S., & Kunda, G. 1992. Design and devotion: surges of rational and normative ideologies of control in managerial discourse. *Administrative Science Quarterly*, 47(3): 363–399.

Barratt, E. 2003. Foucault, HRM and the ethos of the critical management scholar. *Journal of Management Studies*, 40(5): 1069–1087.

Barratt, E. 2008. The later Foucault in organization and management studies. *Human Relations*, 61(4): 515–537.

Bauman, Z. 2000. *Liquid Modernity*. Cambridge: Polity.

Bhabha, H.K. 1994. *The Location of Culture*. London: Routledge.

Braverman, H. 1974. *Labor and Monopoly Capital: The Degradation of Work in the Twentieth Century*. New York: Monthly Review Press.

Brewster, C. 1999. Strategic human resource management: The value of different paradigms. In M. Festing (ed.), *Management International Review: Strategic Issues in International Human Resource Management*: 45–64. Wiesbaden: Gabler Verlag.

Brewster, C. 2007. Comparative HRM: European views and perspectives. *International Journal of Human Resource Management*, 18(5): 769–787.

Brewster, C., & Hegewisch, A. 1994. *Policy and Practice in European Human Resource Management: The Price Waterhouse Cranfield Survey*. London: Routledge.

Brewster, C., Mayrhofer, W., & Morley, M. 2004. *Human Resource Management in Europe: Evidence of Convergence?*. London: Butterworth-Heinemann.

Burrell, G., & Morgan, G. 1979. *Sociological Paradigms and Organizational Analysis*. London: Heinemann.

Calás, M.B., & Smircich, L. 1993. Dangerous liaisons: The 'feminine-in-management' meets 'globalization'. *Business Horizons*, 36(2): 71–81.

Calás, M.B., & Smircich, L. 2006. From the 'woman's point of view' ten years later: Towards a feminist organization studies. In S. Clegg, C. Hardy, and W.R. Nord (eds), *The SAGE Handbook of Organization Studies* (2nd edn): 284–346. London: SAGE Publications.

Chakrabarty, D. 1992. Provincializing Europe: Postcoloniality and the critique of history. *Cultural Studies*, 6(3): 337–357.

Chan, C.K., & Hui, E.S. 2014. The development of collective bargaining in China: From 'collective bargaining by riot' to 'party state-led wage bargaining'. *China Quarterly*, 217: 221–242.

Chomsky, N., & Foucault, M. 2006. *The Chomsky–Foucault Debate: On Human Nature*. New York: New Press.

Clark, T., & Pugh, D. 2000. Similarities and differences in European conceptions of human resource management. *International Studies of Management and Organization*, 29(4): 84–100.

Connolly, W. 1998. Beyond good and evil: The ethical sensibility of Michel Foucault. In J. Moss (ed.), *The Later Foucault: Politics and Philosophy*: 108–128. London: SAGE.

Dickmann, M., Brewster, C., & Sparrow, P.R. 2008. *International Human Resource Management: A European Perspective*. London: Routledge.

Dore, R.P. 2000. *Stock Market Capitalism: Welfare Capitalism: Japan and Germany versus the Anglo-Saxons*. New York, USA and Oxford, UK: Oxford University Press.

Drori, G., Meyer, J.W., & Hwang, H. 2006. *Globalization and Organization: World Society and Organizational Change*. Oxford: Oxford University Press.

Foucault, M. 1977. *Discipline and Punish*. New York: Random House.

Foucault, M. 1978. *History of Sexuality*. New York: Vintage.

Friedman, E., & Kuruvilla, S. 2015. Experimentation and decentralization in China's labor relations. *Human Relations*, 68(2): 181–195.

Ghoshal, S. 2005. Bad management theories are destroying good management practices. *Academy of Management Learning and Education*, 4(1): 75–91.

Giddens, A. 1979. *Central Problems in Social Theory*. London: Macmillan.

Giddens, A. 1984. *The Constitution of Society*. Cambridge: Polity.

Gooderham, P., & Nordhaug, O. 2011. One European model of HRM? Cranet empirical contributions. *Human Resource Management Review*, 21(1): 27–36.

Granovetter, M. 1985. Economic action and social structure: The problem of embeddedness. *American Sociology Review*, 91(3): 481–510.

Greenwood, M.R. 2013. Ethical analyses of HRM: A review and research agenda. *Journal of Business Ethics*, 114(2): 355–366.

Habermas, J. 1972. *Knowledge and Human Interests*. London: Heinemann.

Habermas, J. 1984. *The Theory of Communicative Action*. London: Heinemann.

Hadot, P. 1995. *Philosophy as a Way of Life: Spiritual Exercises from Socrates to Foucault*. Oxford: Blackwell.

Hall, P., & Soskice, D. 2001. *Varieties of Capitalism: The Institutional Foundations of Comparative Advantage*. New York: Oxford University Press.

Hassard, J., McCann, L., & Morris, J. 2007. At the sharp end of new organizational ideologies: Ethnography and the study of multinationals. *Ethnography*, 8(3): 324–344.

Hassard, J., Morris, J., & McCann, L. 2012. 'My brilliant career'? New organizational forms and changing managerial careers in Japan, the UK, and USA. *Journal of Management Studies*, 49(3): 571–599.

Hoy, D.C. 1998. Foucault and critical theory. In J. Moss (ed.), *The Later Foucault: Politics and Philosophy*: 8–32. London: SAGE.

Ingram, D. 1994. Foucault and Habermas on the subject of reason. In G. Gutting (ed.), *The Cambridge Companion to Foucault*: 215–261. Cambridge: Cambridge University Press.

Itani, S., Järlström, M., & Piekkari, R. 2015. The meaning of language skills for career mobility in the new career landscape. *Journal of World Business*, 50(2): 368–378.

Jackson, T. 2004. HRM in developing countries. In A.-W. Harzing and J. v. Ruysseveldt (eds), *International Human Resource Management* (2nd edn): 221–248. London: SAGE.

Janssens, M., & Steyaert, C. 2012. Towards an ethical research agenda for international HRM: The possibilities of a plural cosmopolitan framework. *Journal of Business Ethics*, 111(1): 61–72.

Keating, M., & Thompson, K. 2004. International human resource management: Overcoming disciplinary sectarianism. *Employee Relations*, 26(6): 595–612.

Kelemen, M.L., & Rumens, N. 2008. *An Introduction to Critical Management Research*. London: SAGE.

Knights, D., & Morgan, G. 1991. Corporate strategy, organizations, and subjectivity: A critique. *Organization Studies*, 12(2): 251–273.

Knights, D., & Willmott, H. 1989. Power and subjectivity at work: From degradation to subjugation in social relations. *Sociology*, 23(4): 535–558.

Kunda, G., & Ailon-Suday, G. 2005. Managers, markets and ideologies: Design and devotion revisited. In S. Ackroyd, R. Batt, P. Thompson, and P.S. Tolbert (eds), *The Oxford Handbook of Work and Organization*: 200–219. Oxford: Oxford University Press.

Kwek, D. 2003. Decolonizing and re-presenting culture's consequences: A postcolonial critique of cross-cultural studies in management. In A. Prasad (ed.), *Postcolonial Theory and Organizational Analysis: A Critical Engagement*: 121–147. New York: Palgrave Macmillan.

Legge, K. 1989. Human resource management: A critical analysis. In J. Storey (ed.), *New Perspectives on Human Resource Management*: 19–40. London: Routledge.

Lilja, K. 1998. Finland. In A. Ferner & R. Hyman (eds), *Changing Industrial Relations in Europe*. Oxford: Blackwell.

Lindeberg, T., Manson, B., & Vanhala, S. 2004. Sweden and Finland: Small countries with large companies. In C. Brewster, W. Mayrhofer, and M. Morley (eds), *Human Resource Management in Europe: Evidence of Convergence?*: 279–312. London: Butterworth-Heinemann.

Lukács, G. 1971. *History and Class Consciousness: Studies in Marxist dialectics*, Vol. 215. Cambridge, MA: MIT Press.

Marcuse, H. 1964. *One-Dimensional Man*. London: Routledge.

Maurice, M., & Sorge, A. 2000. *Embedding Organizations: Societal Analysis of Actors, Organizations and Socio-Economic Context*. Amsterdam: John Benjamins.

Mayrhofer, W., Brewster, C., Morley, M., & Ledolter, J. 2011. Hearing a different drummer? Convergence of human resource management in Europe – a longitudinal analysis. *Human Resource Management Review*, 21(1): 50–67.

McCann, L., Hassard, J., & Morris, J. 2004. Middle managers, the new organizational ideology and corporate restructuring: Comparing Japanese and Anglo-American management systems. *Competition and Change*, 8(1): 27–44.

McCann, L., Morris, J., & Hassard, J. 2008. Normalized intensity: The new labour process of middle management. *Journal of Management Studies*, 45(2): 343–371.

McKinlay, A., & Starkey, K.P. 1998. *Foucault, Management and Organization Theory: From Panopticon to Technologies of Self*. London: SAGE.

Mintzberg, H. 2004. *Managers, not MBAs*. San Francisco, CA: Berrett-Koehler Publishers.

Mohanty, C.T. 1997. Women workers and capitalist scripts: Ideologies of domination, common interests, and the politics of solidarity. In J. Alexander and C.T. Mohanty (eds), *Feminist Genealogies, Colonial Legacies, Democratic Futures*: 3–29. New York: Routledge.

Mohanty, C.T. 2004. *Feminism Without Borders*. Durham, NC, USA and London, UK: Duke University Press.

Morgan, G., Kristensen, P.H., & Whitley, R. 2001. *The Multinational Firm: Organizing across Institutional and National Divides*. Oxford: Oxford University Press.

Morgan, G., & Smircich, L. 1980. The case for qualitative research. *Academy of Management Review*, 5(4): 491–500.

Morris, J., Hassard, J., & McCann, L. 2006. New organizational forms, human resource management and structural convergence? A study of Japanese organizations. *Organization Studies*, 27(10): 1485–1511.

Neves, D., & du Toit, A. 2012. Money and sociality in South Africa's informal economy. *Africa*, 82(1): 131–149.

Nietzsche, F. 1994. *On the Genealogy of Morality*, Trans. K. Ansell-Pearson and C. Diethe. Cambridge Texts in the History of Political Thought. New York: Cambridge University Press.

Nightingale, A.W. 2004. *Spectacles of Truth in Classical Greek Philosophy: Theoria in its Cultural Context*. Cambridge: Cambridge University Press.

Parry, E., Stavrou, E., & Lazarova, M.B. 2013. *Global Trends in Human Resource Management*. Houndsmills, UK and New York, USA: Palgrave Macmillan.

Peltonen, T. 2016. *Organization Theory: Critical and Philosophical Engagements*. Bingley: Emerald.

Pfeffer, J., & Fong, C.T. 2005. The business school 'business': Some lessons from the US experience. *Journal of Management Studies*, 41(8): 1501–1520.

Prasad, A. 1997a. The colonizing consciousness and representations of the other. In P. Prasad (ed.), *Managing the Organizational Melting Pot*: 285–311. Thousand Oaks, CA, USA; London, UK; New Delhi, India: SAGE.

Prasad, A. 1997b. Provincializing Europe: Towards a post-colonial reconstruction: a critique of Baconian science as the last stand of imperialism. *Studies in Cultures, Organizations and Societies*, 3(1): 91–117.

Prasad, A. 2003. *Postcolonial Theory and Organizational Analysis*. New York: Palgrave Macmillan.

Quack, S., Morgan, G., & Whitley, R. 2000. *National Capitalisms, Global Competition, and Economic Performance*. Amsterdam: John Benjamins Publishing.

Rousseau, D. 1995. *Psychological Contracts in Organizations: Understanding Written and Unwritten Agreements*. Thousand Oaks, CA, USA; London, UK; New Delhi, India: SAGE.

Said, E. 1978. *Orientalism*. New York: Vintage Books.

Said, E. 1983. *The World, the Text and the Critic*. Cambridge, MA: Harvard University Press.

Scott, R. 2001. *Institutions and Organizations* (2nd edn). Thousand Oaks, CA, USA; London, UK; New Delhi, India: SAGE.

Sennett, R. 1998. *The Corrosion of Character: The Personal Consequences of Work in the New Capitalism*. London: W.W. Norton.

Sennett, R. 2006. *The Culture of the New Capitalism*. New Haven, CT: Yale University Press.

Spicer, A., Alvesson, M., & Karreman, D. 2009. Critical performativity: The unfinished business of critical management studies. *Human Relations*, 62(4): 537–560.

Spivak, G.C. 1987. *In Other Worlds: Essays in Cultural Politics*. New York: Methuen.

Tainio, R., & Lilja, K. 2002. The Finnish business system in transition: Outcomes, actors, and their influence. In B. Czaniawska and G. Sevon (eds), *The Northern Lights: Organisation Theory in Scandinavia*: 69–90. Malmö: Liber.

Tipton, F.B. 2008. Thumbs-up is a rude gesture in Australia: The presentation of culture in international business textbooks. *Critical Perspectives on International Business*, 4(1): 7–24.

Townley, B. 1993. Foucault, power/knowledge, and its relevance for human resource management. *Academy of Management Review*, 18(3): 519–545.

Vaara, E., Tienari, J., Piekkari, R., & Säntti, R. 2005. Language and the circuits of power in a merging multinational corporation. *Journal of Management Studies*, 42(3): 595–623.

Westwood, R. 2001. Appropriating the other in the discourses of comparative management. In R. Westwood and S. Linstead (eds), *The Language of Organization*: 241–282. London: SAGE.

Westwood, R. 2004. Towards a postcolonial research paradigm in international business and comparative management. In R. Marschan-Piekkari and C. Welch (eds), *Handbook of Qualitative Research Methods in International Business*: 56–83. Cheltenham, UK and Northampton, MA, USA: Edward Elgar Publishing.

Westwood, R. 2006. International business and management studies as an orientalist discourse: A postcolonial critique. *Critical Perspectives on International Business*, 2(2): 91–113.

Westwood, R., & Jack, G. 2006. Postcolonialism and the politics of qualitative research in international business. *Management International Review*, 46(4): 481–501.

Westwood, R., & Jack, G. 2007. Manifesto for a post-colonial international business and management studies: A provocation. *Critical Perspectives on International Business*, 3(3): 246–265.

Whitley, R. 2002. *Competing Capitalisms: Institutions and Economies*, Vols 1 and 2. Cheltenham, UK and Northampton, MA, USA: Edward Elgar Publishing.

Whitley, R., & Kristensen, P.H. 1996. *The Changing European Firm*. London: Routledge.

Young, R. 2001. *Postcolonialism: An Historical Introduction*. Oxford: Blackwell.

5. Methodological challenges for quantitative research in comparative HRM

Ingo Weller and Barry Gerhart

INTRODUCTION

Human resource management (HRM) is about the policies, practices, and processes that influence organisational effectiveness by affecting employees' behaviour, attitudes, and performance. Thereby, HRM shapes and influences the human capital of the organisation (Noe et al., 2015). Its ultimate goal is to provide business value through the management of people (Barney & Wright, 1998; Becker & Gerhart, 1996; Boxall & Purcell, 2015; Paauwe, 2004; Ployhart & Hale, 2014). Successful strategy execution depends on the HRM system effectively attracting and selecting, developing, and motivating its human capital and making sure that structures and processes permit it to be put to productive use. In this chapter we discuss methodological challenges in doing empirical research on HRM and effectiveness in the field of comparative HRM. Some methodological issues we discuss here will be specific to comparative HRM research, while others apply to HRM research in both single-nation and comparative contexts. Moreover, we take a quantitative approach in that we focus on basic and applied statistical methods and issues. We refer readers to recent overviews of how to conceptualise and conduct cross-cultural studies (see Chapter 3 in this *Handbook*; and Cascio, 2012; Spector et al., 2015) or how to integrate qualitative and quantitative methodologies in comparative research (Allardt, 1990; Hantrais, 2014), but do not discuss these important issues in this chapter.

It is widely recognised that cross-country differences are important for the management of people in organisations. As highlighted by new institutionalists (see Chapter 2 in this *Handbook*), countries differ in regulations, institutions, and culture (Brewster, 1999; Brewster et al., 2004; Dowling et al., 2008; Evans et al., 2002; Hofstede, 1980, 2001; Kostova, 1999). While new institutionalism covers a range of fairly heterogeneous approaches, the basic premise is that advances in technology and communications lead to less diversification within particular bounded contexts (see Chapter 2), a process called isomorphism (Kostova & Roth, 2002). Thus, the institutionalist approach stresses the tendency of organisations to respond to their environment in ways that signal conformity and enhance legitimacy (DiMaggio & Powell, 1983; Meyer & Rowan, 1977). To the degree that 'final convergence' (Mayrhofer & Brewster, 2005; Tregaskis & Brewster, 2006) is limited by national regulations, institutions, and culture, institutionalists would expect that the managerial discretion of multinational firms is constrained by the respective national settings in which they are operating. Following this line of thought, some of the key questions of comparative HRM research are: (1) How much do countries differ in their use of particular HRM practices and systems? (2) What specific country characteristics account for such country differences? (3) To what degree do certain HRM practices and systems fit certain countries and show misfit in others, as evidenced by effectiveness outcomes? and (4) To what degree are differences in either use or effectiveness of HRM practices and systems stable versus changing over time?

A common explanation for country differences is national culture (Kirkman et al., 2006). In thinking about the four key questions raised above, it is clear that one theme is an interest in understanding the degree to which organisations are constrained by country differences such as national culture in choosing which HRM practices and systems to use. To the degree that organisations are constrained, it suggests the need for them to localise HRM to fit different country contexts, rather than standardise across countries towards a global version of HRM (Dowling et al., 2008). In the case of national culture, the constraint argument has been made frequently (e.g., Adler, 2002; Early & Erez, 1997; Hofstede, 1983, 1993, 2001; House et al., 2004; Laurent, 1983; Trompenaars & Hampden-Turner, 2000). In other words, the answer from this perspective to the four questions above would be that HRM practices differ significantly between countries, have differential effectiveness across countries, and remain stable over time. National culture would be seen as the key reason for these country effects. The implication for organisations then is that they need to localise (rather than standardise) HRM to a considerable degree to fit different national cultures.

However, the support for these conclusions, upon close examination of the empirical evidence, is less compelling than might be expected (Gerhart & Fang, 2005; Gerhart, 2009b, 2009a; Kirkman et al., 2006). For example, Gerhart and Fang (2005) re-examined Hofstede's results and found that about 4 per cent of the variance in individual cultural values was explained by country membership. This relation is nicely expressed by the intraclass correlation coefficient, ICC. Specifically, the ICC(1) is defined as the level 2 (in this example: between-country) variance divided by total variance (we return to ICC analysis below). Given that Hofstede's study was conducted with a single firm (IBM), one can easily conclude that the results are indicative of strong self-selection tendencies of individuals into certain organisations, and that organisations have quite some discretion in 'exporting' their organisational cultures (Bloom & Milkovich, 1999; Gerhart, 2009a). In addition, there is more evidence that organisations show varying degrees of consistency across countries in HRM and other organisation practices. In another example, Beck et al. (2009) – analysing a sample of 14 European countries from the CRANET project (Brewster et al., 2004) – found headquarters influence on subsidiary management practices when headquarters and subsidiaries operated in different countries and systems of vocational education and training. In light of their findings, they suggested considerable potential for managerial agency above and beyond local cultural influences. Other research has also documented headquarters effects on HRM (Ferner & Quintanilla, 1998; Quintanilla & Ferner, 2003) and/or organisation practices (Kostova & Roth, 2002), again suggesting that organisations have some discretion and do not necessarily find the need to localise all aspect of HRM fully.

Finally, Rabl et al. (2014), in a meta-analysis of the correlation between use of high-performance work systems (HPWSs) and business performance across countries, found that the mean correlation relationship was positive overall (corrected $r = 0.28$) and positive in every country (and statistically significant in all but three countries). Conventional wisdom based on the national culture literature regarding where HPWSs would have the largest positive effect size (that is, 'work best') was not supported. In fact, there was some evidence that effect sizes were larger in countries where HPWSs might be seen as having a relatively poor fit to the national culture. Rabl et al. (2014) suggested that in a global economy, even an organisation that wishes to conform to the norms of other organisations in choosing HRM strategies and practices may be faced with the complication that norms in the domestic economy may differ from those in the global economy (e.g., Kostova et al., 2008).

Certainly, there are both constraints and room for discretion (Brewster, 1999; Dowling et al., 2008; Gerhart, 2009b). Our objective here is not to provide a comprehensive review of the literature in an attempt to conclusively say what their relative importance is. Instead, we wish to caution against focusing only on constraints, and to map out some ideas and methods that should be useful in understanding the relative role of constraints and discretion. For interesting substantive work on the constraints versus discretion debate, in addition to that discussed above, we also refer the reader to research by Brewster et al. (2004), Edwards et al. (2013), Pudelko et al. (2006), and Pudelko and Harzing (2007).

Our discussion of quantitative methods in comparative HRM research focuses on two major conceptual and technical challenges that comparative HRM researchers (and also single-country HRM researchers) must deal with: (1) level of analysis; and (2) inferring causality in studying the HRM–effectiveness link. The two challenges are also reflected in the structure of this chapter.

Comparative HRM research is necessarily a multilevel endeavour. For example, country effects (based on national cultures, institutions and legal regulations, industrial and competitive forces, and so on) may vary across organisations in the degree to which they constrain versus enable managerial agency in managing HRM (Gerhart, 2009b, 2009a; Gerhart & Fang, 2005). Staffing practices may differ across countries (for example, because of country legislation) and organisations (for example, because of firm histories; Dierickx & Cool, 1989), and attract workers with specific knowledge stocks, skills, and abilities that they anticipate will fit the organisation (Bloom & Milkovich, 1999; Ployhart, 2006; Schneider, 1987). As such, there are three basic levels to consider: individuals, firms, and firm environment (which may be local area, region, industry, country, and so on). For reasons of simplicity, we assume that individuals are nested in firms which in turn are nested in countries, but as mentioned above, there may be more relevant environmental dimensions than country. In comparative HRM research, we need to determine at which level of analysis the main source of variation (and explanatory power) resides.

The ultimate goal of the HRM function is to create business value, which is important for multiple stakeholders, including, of course, shareholders and employees. To understand whether and to what degree HRM influences firm effectiveness, it is desirable to use research designs (for example, longitudinal studies and natural experiments that may occur when national legislations change) that permit stronger causal inferences, and to be aware of specification challenges that may arise, as well as the statistical methods available that can potentially deal with these challenges. It is also important to be as specific as possible regarding the magnitude of HRM effects (that is, report relevant effect size estimates). These considerations are important in both single-country and comparative HRM research. To give policy advice, we need to be as confident as possible of what HRM's effects really are.

This chapter is organised as follows: in the next section we provide a short outline of the multilevel structure of comparative HRM research with a focus on culture research; we explain the potential pitfalls in the analysis of multilevel data, and provide recommendations on how to analyse such data. Specifically, we introduce multilevel or HLM (hierarchical linear modelling) techniques to solve some of the problems frequently encountered in comparative HRM research. The chapter then deals with the HRM–performance link and, in particular, highlights specification errors in HRM–firm performance regression models. Among others, we explain the endogeneity problem and its potential consequences, and outline a few common solutions.

MULTIPLE LEVELS OF ANALYSIS IN COMPARATIVE HRM RESEARCH

A fundamental issue in addressing the four central comparative HRM questions is how to deal most effectively with the multilevel nature of comparative HRM conceptual models and data. We illustrate how multilevel or hierarchical linear modelling (e.g., Raudenbush & Bryk, 2002) can be used to address some of these questions. However, given the central role of concepts such as national culture and HRM practices in such comparative research, we begin with a brief treatment of issues in defining and measuring these constructs, before addressing the four substantive comparative HRM questions.

National Culture

Hofstede (1980: 19) has called national culture the 'collective programming of the mind'. His focus was on cultural values, which he defined as a 'broad tendency to prefer certain states of affairs over others' (see also Spector et al., 2015). Hofstede (1980: 19) saw cultural values as 'an attribute of individuals as well as of collectivities' though he stated that 'culture presupposes a collectivity'. Thus, Hofstede's definition of national culture also includes the shared aspect and, likewise, implies that within-country variance (where values are shared) should be considerably less (given 'broad tendency' differences) than between-country variance (Gerhart, 2009a). National culture means are more likely to be effective in explaining country effects to the degree that individual cultural values vary greatly between countries and vary little within countries, consistent with Hofstede's definition.

Consider a hypothetical example where we have data on 1000 respondents or individuals (which could, for example, be persons, plants, or firms) in ten countries. (For some applications, $K = 10$ level 2 (country) observations is not considered a sufficient sample size. We use $K = 10$ here to simplify the presentation.) The fact that individuals are nested within countries implies that the individual-level observations are not independent. Rather, if country matters, they are clustered by country such that respondents are more homogenous within countries than across. A common solution to deal with this kind of data non-independence is employing fixed-effects. An often used form of fixed-effects is the construction of dummy variables. Dummies are dichotomous indicator variables that separate the individual-level effects from the country effects in the model. Fixed-effects or dummy estimations identify each country's effect on the outcome (that is, the country fixed-effect), and they control for all unobserved heterogeneity that strictly operates on the country level. However, under certain conditions they become unwieldy, for example when the number of countries is very large, when country main effects and/or interactions between country and organisation- or individual-level variables are theoretically interesting, or when the countries are a true random sample from the population of all countries (Wooldridge, 2013). Also, a fixed-effects model trades off efficiency and statistical power to correct for bias. To the degree such bias is small, fixed-effects estimates become less helpful. In such cases, random-effects methods may be superior techniques. We return to the fixed-effects model later in this chapter.

We can also use multilevel modelling to address this question. In this example, we start with a two-level HLM model, thus accounting for the two structural levels represented in the data, respondents (level 1) and countries (level 2), with respondents nested in countries. In HLM analysis (Hox, 2002; Raudenbush & Bryk, 2002; Snijders & Bosker, 1999), one typically begins with a 'null model' (that is, with no independent variables other than intercepts), which is called a 'random intercepts' model. At level 1, the model is:

$$ICV_{ij} = \beta_{0j} + r_{ij}$$

with ICV as the individual cultural values of individual i in country j, β_{0j} as a country specific intercept, and r_{ij} as an idiosyncratic error term. Specific level 1 predictors of ICV (for example, demographics, education, etc.) could also be added to this model. The country specific intercept is then specified on 'level 2', the macro level, as

$$\beta_{0j} = \gamma_{00} + u_{0j}$$

where γ_{00} is the 'grand mean', and u_{0j} is a country specific error term (a so-called 'random-effect'). Again, this is a random intercepts model, to which could be added specific level 2 explanatory variables. The ten country intercepts of our example (that is, the β_{0j} terms) will have a certain distribution around the grand mean γ_{00} (note that the grand mean equals the mean of country intercepts only if all of the subgroups have the same size). Around the country means, individual observations will also follow a certain (within-country) distribution. The closer the individual observations are centred around the country intercept (that is, the smaller the within-country variance), the more reliable is the country intercept. The closer the country means are centred around the grand mean, the less variance in individual cultural values is explained by country variance relative to individual variance. This relation is expressed by the ICC(1), which is defined as the level 2 variance divided by total variance, that is:

$$ICC(1) = \tau_{00} / (\tau_{00} + \sigma^2)$$

where τ_{00} is the level 2 variance, $\tau_{00} = Var(u_{0j})$, and σ^2 is the level 1 variance, $\sigma^2 = Var(r_{ij})$.[1] ICC(1) (Bliese, 2000), also known as ICC(1,1) (Shrout & Fleiss, 1979), tells us how much

---

[1]   This regression-based equation for ICC(1) refers to the HLM-case. Here the formula for ICC(1) equals Eta-squared (η^2): $ICC(1) = \eta^2 = SS_{between} / SS_{total}$, that is, between variance divided by total variance. If estimated from a one-way random-effects ANOVA model, the ICC(1) is defined as $ICC(1) = (MSB - MSW) / [MSB + (k-1)MSW]$, where MSB is the mean square between, MSW is the mean square within, and k is group size (Shrout & Fleiss, 1979). In the ANOVA case, η^2 asymptotically approaches ICC(1) as group size increases. When group sizes are small (or only few groups exist, or gross outliers dominate the distribution), η^2 values are likely to be inflated and need to be corrected. Bliese and Halverson (1998) provide solutions and recommendations for applied organisational research.

of the variance in individual responses (individual cultural values) can be predicted by country membership. If all of the individual variance is attributable to country, ICC(1) = 1, all individual responses equal the country means, and σ^2 is zero. If individual variance is completely idiosyncratic, ICC(1) = 0, the country means coincide with the grand mean, and τ_{00} is zero. In most cases, of course, the estimate falls somewhere in between.

As we saw in the case of Hofstede's (1980, 2001) data, however, Gerhart and Fang (2005) found an ICC(1) of less than 0.05. There are other studies, most notably the GLOBE study (House et al., 2004) that find much larger country effects (that is, larger ICCs). In the GLOBE case, there are two important likely reasons (Gerhart, 2009a). First, GLOBE respondents were asked to describe not their own personal cultural values (as in Hofstede, 1980; Hofstede et al., 1990), but rather those of their country and of their organisation. Works by McCrae et al. (2005) and Terracciano et al. (2005) suggest the possibility that a methodology like that used in GLOBE can result in responses that may be national stereotypes having very limited accuracy. A second likely reason for the higher country effects found by GLOBE is that they excluded from their study any multinational companies headquartered outside the country being studied. By doing so, they may have excluded multinationals that may standardise employment practices across countries. Such an exclusion would increase between-country differences and decrease within-country differences, thus increasing the country effect size/ICC.

In addition to examining the magnitude of the ICC(1) estimate, the statistical significance of the variances should be interpreted. On a different but related note, we can also use HLM strategies to estimate average group-mean reliability. Inferences drawn from small, few, or unevenly sized subsamples may be unreliable. An ICC-based coefficient of group-mean reliability is the ICC(2) (Bliese, 2000), or ICC(1,k) (Shrout & Fleiss, 1979).[2]

As a recommendation, researchers should estimate both effect sizes and significance levels to determine the impact of macro-level variables (for example, country) on individual-level attributes such as cultural values. Moreover, researchers should report means and standard deviations of the variables of interest for the total sample and for each country (or macro unit) separately. They should realise that low group-mean reliability (low ICC(2) values) may limit the potential to interpret results. However, as noted above, a high ICC(2) does not necessarily imply high predictive power. Reliability, of course, is a necessary but not sufficient condition for this. In a similar vein, a considerable degree of within-country variation relative to between-country variation (low ICC(1) values) indicates significant potential for managerial agency.

HRM Practices

There are many issues regarding what concepts are most central to the functioning of HRM, and how to measure them. Examples of relevant concepts are HRM philosophies, policies, practices, and processes (Jackson et al., 2014). A conceptual framework

---

[2]   The ICC(2) can be constructed from a one-way random-effects analysis of variance (ANOVA) model, and is then defined as ICC(2) = $(MSB - MSW) / MSB$, with MSB as the between-country mean square, and MSW as the within-country mean square. ICC(2) is thus a function of group size and the ICC(1) via the Spearman–Brown correction formula (compare Bliese, 2000). As an estimate of reliability, ICC(2) values >0.70 indicate acceptable stability of the group means. Note that both ICC(1) and ICC(2) are omnibus tests. In particular, ICC(2) does not inform us if some of the groups are unreliable; rather, it gives us an overall estimate.

that has received increasing attention is the AMO model, which suggests that HRM practices increase organisational effectiveness to the degree that they increase employees' ability, motivation, and opportunity to contribute (Appelbaum et al., 2000; Boxall & Purcell, 2015; Gerhart, 2007; Jiang et al., 2012). Our focus here, however, is on a level of analysis issue that arises in some research intended to examine the effect of HRM. Specifically, one often sees studies that measure HRM practices and assess their impact at the individual level of analysis. Yet, the source of true variance in HRM practices is almost never individual-level, idiosyncratic differences in perceptions of HRM practices, but rather the variance in perceptions of HRM practices that is shared by multiple respondents. We would argue that any study of HRM practices must be conducted at the level of analysis where true variance in HRM practices takes place. In a design with one employee per organisation or unit, it is not possible to compute an ICC. That is a strong indicator that the design is not adequate for studying HRM practices.[3] In other cases, a researcher may have multiple employee respondents from each organisation or unit. There are, in fact, three different options in analysing such data (Raudenbush & Bryk, 2002):

1. Individual level: N = # employees.
2. Aggregate level: N = # employing units (units within a single organisation, units across multiple organisations, organisations, or even countries).
3. HLM.

Option 1, the individual level analysis, may not make sense conceptually and may not be supported by the ICC(1). Think of a single organisation study with employees from multiple units. If there is institutional evidence (for example, a stated policy) that HRM practices are permitted to vary within the organisation, the ICC(1) is likely to be non-trivial, and the individual level design is not likely to be adequate. That is because observations nested within a unit or organisation are dependent to a degree (as indicated by a non-zero ICC(1)), thus violating a key assumption of ordinary least squares (OLS).[4] The consequence would be standard errors that are too small, thus increasing the probability of Type I error (that is, rejecting the null hypothesis when it is true).

Option 2, the aggregate level, averages employee responses (by unit or organisation). The drawback here is that degrees of freedom are lost, compromising statistical power (relative to the HLM option), making Type II errors (failure to reject the null hypothesis when false) more likely. Option 3, multilevel analysis, avoids inflating Type I errors (as in Option 1, individual-level analysis) and also has more statistical power than Option 2, the aggregate-level analysis.

---

[3]   The issue here is somewhat different than that debated in *Personnel Psychology* (Gerhart et al., 2000a, 2000b; Huselid & Becker, 2000). That debate concerned the reliability and validity of responses from one HRM manager or executive per organisation. However, there was no debate over level of analysis. These respondents are in a better position than the typical employee respondent to describe HRM practices at the organisation level.

[4]   One can use dummy variables to control for higher-level unit effects, as explained above. However, the approach is easily complicated and becomes unwieldy when many higher-level units need to be controlled for, or when interactions are interesting. In the latter case, cross-level interactions of the explaining variables with all of the dummy variables (that is, country indicators) are necessary. HLM provides random-effects methodologies which can better account for this complexity. We return to such methods below.

KEY COMPARATIVE HRM QUESTIONS AND HLM ANALYSIS

In this section we elaborate on the four key comparative HRM questions outlined in the introduction to this chapter.

Question 1: How much do Countries Differ in their Use of Particular HRM Practices and Systems?

We begin by specifying a level 1 random intercepts model, but this time at the organisational level, i. The dependent variable could be organisation culture or it could be use of one or more HRM practices, the example we use.

$$\text{HRM}_{ij} = \beta_{0j} + r_{ij}$$

The model could be expanded to include explanatory variables such as firm size, industry, employee characteristics, and other factors thought to influence HRM practices within countries. Next, we specify a level 2 random intercepts only model that specifies the intercepts from the level 1 model as a function of country, j:

$$\beta_{0j} = \gamma_{00} + u_{0j}$$

As before, we can compute the ICC(1) to estimate the overall effect of the level 2 variable, in this case country, on the use of certain HRM practices.

Question 2: What Specific Country Characteristics (for example, National Culture) Account for Country Effects?

Researchers often mistakenly equate country effects to national culture effects. For example, Bhagat and McQuaid (1982: 653–685) observed that 'culture has often served simply as a synonym for nation . . . [and] national differences found in the characteristics of organisations or their members have been interpreted as cultural differences'. In a more recent review article, Yeganeh and Su (2006: 364) similarly state that 'most researchers, especially during the last decade, adhere to a culture-bound perspective', and that this has led to 'overemphasising the importance of culture to the detriment of other social, economic, or contextual variables' and that 'many cross cultural researchers simply [compare] some aspects of organisational behaviour and then, in the absence of other explanations for these differences, attribute them to culture' (see also Schaffer & Riordan, 2003; Sawang et al., 2006).

Clearly, there is a need to distinguish between country and national culture effects. As the comparative HRM literature recognises, national culture effects are just one of a multitude of contextual effects which may influence HRM use and effectiveness across countries. Employment laws and regulations, industry structure and competition, and other institutional factors (for example, labour unions) all play some role as well. Thus, researchers need to specify carefully their conceptual model and then take care to ensure that their measures correspond to the theoretical constructs accordingly. Once that is done, HLM is well suited to decomposing the overall country effect into specific country characteristics, including culture.

To estimate the culture effect, we add national culture scores (and/or other explanatory variables that may explain country effects, such as unions, labour market characteristics, and so on) to the level 2 random intercepts model specified above:

$$\beta_{0j} = \gamma_{00} + \gamma_{01} NC_j + u_{0j}$$

where NC_j is the national culture score. The ICC(1) estimate obtained from this last model is called a 'conditional ICC' (Raudenbush & Bryk, 2002), which will be the same size (maximum) or smaller than the ICC(1) from the intercepts only model. To estimate the percentage of the overall country effect explained specifically by national culture (that is, the proportion of variance explained in β_{0j} by national culture), we need to compute the variance of the intercepts (τ_{00}) with and without national culture in the model and use the following formula:

$$[\tau_{00} \text{ (intercepts only)} - \tau_{00} \text{ (national culture)}] / \tau_{00} \text{ (intercepts only)}$$

For example, if τ_{00} (intercepts only) = 100 and τ_{00} (national culture) = 80, then we would have (100–80)/100 = 0.20, or 20 percent of the country effect of HRM explained by national culture.

Question 3: To what Degree do Certain HRM Practices and Systems Fit Certain Countries and Show Misfit in Others, as Evidenced by Effectiveness Outcomes?

We again use a two-level HLM model, here with effectiveness as the dependent variable and HRM as the independent variable. We then introduce cross-level interactions (estimated using slopes-as-intercepts models) to determine whether HRM effects vary by country:

$$\text{Effectiveness}_{ij} = \beta_{0j} + \beta_{1j} \text{HRM}_{ij} + r_{ij}$$
$$\beta_{0j} = \gamma_{00} + u_{0j}$$
$$\beta_{1j} = \gamma_{10} + u_{1j}$$

In the model, the country effect is accounted for with random effects, and the interaction with HRM becomes more obvious when we plug the level 2 equations into the level 1 equation:[5]

$$\text{Effectiveness}_{ij} = [\gamma_{00} + u_{0j}] + [\gamma_{10} \text{HRM}_{ij} + u_{1j} \text{HRM}_{ij}] + r_{ij}$$

We can further expand the model and check if the effectiveness of HRM practices differs by country and also national cultures:

$$\text{Effectiveness}_{ij} = \beta_{0j} + \beta_{1j} \text{HRM}_{ij} + r_{ij}$$

---

[5] From the single equation it becomes obvious that the HLM approach explicitly models potential heteroskedasticity with a random term.

$$\beta_{0j} = \gamma_{00} + \gamma_{01} NC_j + u_{0j}$$
$$\beta_{1j} = \gamma_{10} + \gamma_{11} NC_j + u_{1j}$$

In general, when testing for interaction, all lower-order effects must also be included in the model. In HLM analysis, it is thus necessary to expand the level 2 equations. Most statistical packages will provide significance tests for the random components of the models. If statistically significant random variation remains after macro-level variables are controlled for (that is, u_{0j} and/ or u_{1j} remain significant in the culture model), this tells us that there is unobserved heterogeneity at the country level which is not sufficiently described by national culture. HLM analysis may thus provide an exploratory basis for further theorising on the determinants of HRM practice effectiveness across countries.

Question 4: To what Degree are Differences in either Use or Effectiveness of HRM Practices and Systems Stable versus Changing over Time?

To address this question, one would use the same models as above, but those two-level models would need to become three-level models because time (for example, year) would need to be added as a level 3 variable. Thus, organisations are at level 1, countries are at level 2, and years are at level 3. One would address the preceding three comparative HRM questions in the same way as above, except now there would be tests of whether findings regarding country effects on HRM practices and differential effectiveness of HRM practices are stable over years. Likewise, it would be possible to compare the ability of national culture to explain any such country effects at different points in time, using the same general approach as described earlier.

So far we have focused on the advantages of HLM analysis for comparative HRM research. A positive issue is that ICC analysis is readily incorporated in HLM. Further, HLM can be used to determine the amount of variance at different levels of analysis. However, HLM analysis is best suited to datasets that contain a sufficiently large number of higher-level units (for example, countries or organisations). The reason is that the reliability of the grand mean estimate increases with the number of groups, and likewise the Bayesian HLM estimators increase in precision. Since HLM analysis has large-sample or asymptotic properties (that is, it uses Bayesian estimators and full or restricted maximum likelihood algorithms; Hox, 2002), OLS regression with fixed-effects is superior if there are only a few higher-level units.

In addition, it is important to note that HLM is not the only means for obtaining correct standard error estimates with multilevel data. OLS regression with robust and clustered (or cluster-adjusted) standard errors also provides correct standard errors when observations are nested within some otherwise not controlled for higher-level units (Steenbergen & Jones, 2002). Clustered standard errors are available for various regression models and econometric packages such as STATA (Lin & Wei, 1989; Rogers, 1994). However, single-level regression does not account for ICC analysis, and fit between conceptual and empirical models is hard to determine and may be hard to achieve.

HRM–PERFORMANCE LINKS AND MODEL ENDOGENEITY

Now we turn to the causal link between HRM practices and firm performance. The analysis of the management–performance link is frequently subject to concerns of model misspecification. Take a study that finds a positive effect of the use of contingent reward systems (for example, merit pay) on firm performance.[6] One may argue that successful firms can afford contingent reward systems, and thus the use of contingent reward systems is not exogenous, but rather endogenous to firm performance. In somewhat more technical terms, endogeneity can be defined more broadly to include any situation where the independent variable in a regression model is correlated with the error term, $\text{cov}(x_i, r_i) \neq 0$. If endogeneity exists, the expected value of the residual is no longer zero, $E(r_i \mid x_{1i}, x_{2i}, \ldots, x_{ki}) \neq 0$, and OLS estimates are biased and inconsistent (Wooldridge, 2013). We note that the term 'endogeneity' can be used in one of two ways. It can be used to refer specifically to simultaneity bias (as in the brief example above) or it can be used to refer more broadly, as just stated, to any situation where the error term is not independent of one or more so-called exogenous or independent variables.

Using the broad definition of endogeneity means that a number of different specification errors can be subsumed under that general heading (Hamilton & Nickerson, 2003; Shaver, 1998; Wooldridge, 2013). Specification errors that cause endogeneity comprise omitted variables (unobserved heterogeneity), measurement error, and simultaneity (that is, reciprocal or non-recursive causation). While these problem have distinct features and precursors, they have in common that they result in non-zero covariance between the exogenous variables and the residual, and thus change in the variable of interest originates partly within the model under study (and thus, this change is endogenous rather than exogenous).

Omitted Variables Bias

Omitted variables bias occurs if some unmeasured causes ('unobserved heterogeneity') are correlated with the exogenous variables of the model. In the above example, prior performance is likely to be correlated with the use of contingent reward systems. Prior performance is unmeasured, however, and thus captured by the error term. As a consequence the error term is correlated with the reward system measure. More generally, the HRM–performance link may be estimated with a fully (that is, 'correctly') specified regression model (cf. Kmenta, 1971: 392–393):

$$\text{Perf}_i = \delta_0 + \delta_1 \, \text{HRM}_i + \delta_2 \, \text{Control}_i + e_i$$

where Perf is firm performance of firm i, HRM is the practice (for example, a contingent reward system), and Control is a control variable of interest. If we omit the control variable we estimate instead:

$$\text{Perf}_i = \beta_0 + \beta_1 \, \text{HRM}_i + r_i$$

---

[6] For the following discussion it is of no regard whether the HRM–performance relationship is subject to cross-country differences. The HLM view makes the relationship more complex in terms of a cross-level interaction; the focal question (HRM–performance linkage) remains the same, however.

The control variable effect is now contained in the error term ($r_i = \delta_2$ Control$_i + e_i$) which is thus correlated with HRM if the control variable was correlated with HRM.[7] There may be many reasons why a control variable is omitted: for example, theory is incomplete, or data are unavailable. In any case, β_1 will be different from δ_1:

$$\beta_1 = \delta_1 + \delta_2\,\pi_1$$

where π_1 is the coefficient from an auxiliary regression of the control on HRM:

$$\text{Control}_i = \pi_0 + \pi_1\,\text{HRM}_i + u_i$$

The bias in the reduced HRM model on performance (without the control) grows more severe as δ_2 and π_1 deviate more from zero. Beck et al. (2008) provide compelling evidence that omitted variable bias can be substantial in organisational research (see also Huselid & Becker, 2000). Several approaches exist to lessen concerns about endogeneity from omitted variables. One is the randomised experiment (Cook & Campbell, 1979). Under random assignment, cov(HRM$_i$, r_i) is zero by definition.[8] Of course, random assignment in studying HRM-effectiveness relationships is often not a practical option.

An alternative that is more often possible is making use of a 'natural experiment'. Natural experiments are so-called 'quasi-experiments' because the respondents (or organisations, and so on) are not randomly assigned to the treatment, but belong to a social unit which experiences (but does not actively initiate) the treatment. For example, if labour market legislation changes in one country but not in others, then the countries may be compared prior and after the event, and under some conditions the 'diff-in-diff' estimate of the legislation change can approximate the average treatment effect on the treated (ATT) from a true experiment. The term 'diff-in-diff' stands for a group of so-called 'difference-in-difference estimators' which have in common that they subtract the pre-treatment values of a treatment group from its post-treatment values, and compare the difference to the same difference from the non-treated group. Many variations of diff-in-diff estimators exist, and many of them are highly relevant for comparative studies. An important reason is that they do not necessarily need before-and-after comparisons on the individual level, but under some conditions may produce unbiased estimates if group dummies (for example, country dummies) are used. Lechner (2010) provides a short but comprehensive discussion of the diff-in-diff methodology.

The lack of random assignment in such designs means, however, that there is no assurance that the treatment group and comparison group(s) are equivalent. This sort of design

---

[7]   As Gerhart (2007) points out, it is the partial correlation of the control variable and the dependent variable (δ_2) times the partial correlation of the independent and the omitted variable (as expressed below by π_1) that determines whether omitted variables bias is serious or negligible. As such, the correlation between the independent and the omitted variable may be high and still produce little bias in the OLS estimates.

[8]   We wish to note that survey plans, data structures, estimation techniques, and biases in estimates go hand in hand. Real experiments (survey plan) may be one-shot (that is, produce a cross-sectional observation of the treated and non-treated groups) and use cross-sectional regression or simple comparison of mean techniques without producing bias because the random assignment condition allows the researcher to draw causal inference from such data. A general recommendation is to better improve the data collection process than to employ sophisticated methodologies *ex post* to rule out biases ('design trumps analysis'). The reason is that more sophisticated methods usually have stronger assumptions that either cannot be tested or do not hold with field data.

is referred to by Cook and Campbell (1979: 103) as 'the untreated control group design with pretest and posttest', and they discuss the 'threats to validity' (challenges in drawing causal inferences) in such designs. Diff-in-diff designs can be strengthened by using statistical methods such as analysis of covariance, propensity scores (see below), and so forth to help make the treatment and comparison groups(s) more equivalent. Such a design is also stronger to the extent confounding events (for example, a change in labour market conditions happening at the same time that new legislation is passed and implemented) appear not to have occurred.

Natural experiments have huge potential, in particular in the international or comparative HRM setting, but as of yet this potential has not been fully exploited by comparative HRM scholars. While natural experiments lend themselves well to studies of institutional change across countries, a drawback is that culture change does not follow the logic of occurring events, but develops slowly and endogenously instead. Natural experiments should thus be identified and used more often for comparative HRM research, but they are constrained in answering the key cultural questions asked above.

Two further approaches, which may have greater practical application are: (1) propensity scores and selection models; and (2) fixed-effects methodologies. Propensity scores (Harder et al., 2010; Heckman et al., 1999; Li, 2013; Rosenbaum & Rubin, 1983) are, loosely speaking, a more sophisticated case of the better-known matching procedures. For example, Fulmer et al. (2003) used a matching approach to compare the '100 Best Companies to Work For' with a set of companies matched on industry, size, and previous financial performance. Matching can become unwieldy, though, as the number of boundary conditions (that is, relevant controls like industry, firm size, age, and so on) increases. In terms of experimental research, a propensity score is the probability of receiving a treatment, conditional on a set of observables. The score can be derived by regressing participation in the treatment (for example, by using a binary logit or probit model) on a set of covariates, and can then be used as a covariate in the final model. The idea lies in the so-called counterfactual approach to causality (also called Rubin's model). That is, to infer how a company reacts (for example, in terms of performance) to a certain treatment (for example, implementation of the reward system), we need to know how it would have reacted in the absence of the treatment. While facts are never counterfactual, we can compare two sets of companies that are identical except for the treatment. It can be shown then that, in large samples, 'if treatment and control groups have the same distribution of propensity scores, they have the same distribution of all observed covariates, just like in a randomised experiment' (Rubin, 2001: 171).

While the propensity score approach has many positive features, it comes at some cost (Gerhart, 2007; Li, 2013): unlike random assignment, which when it is implemented successfully requires no knowledge of which specific covariates must be included to control for non-equivalence of groups or heterogeneity, propensity scores require one to have sufficient knowledge to identify the relevant covariates (e.g., Steiner et al., 2010) that could otherwise act as omitted variables, as well as sufficient ability and resources to measure and include them. Thus, omitted variable bias may still persist. Other issues are that non-response is assumed to be random (e.g., Heinsman & Shadish, 1996); assignment to the treatment needs to be exogenous to the outcome variable; and responses in one treatment group must not be affected by the treatment received by another group (that is, stable unit treatment value assumption, SUTVA; Rosenbaum & Rubin, 1983; Lechner, 2010). The latter case occurs, for example, when groups compete for resources. In comparative HRM research this may be the rule, though, and not an exception: companies that implement a contingent rewards practice are likely to attract a certain workforce, and this workforce is thus unavailable to other companies with similar practices. Another problem is that propensity score groups (treatment/no treatment) can more easily be established if relatively few companies in the sample receive the treatment. In sum, propensity score methods are currently receiving some attention in the methodological literature; because the method requires some strict assumptions to be met, however, there appear to be few (or virtually no) applications in the management and in the comparative HRM literature as of yet. Alternative approaches to propensity scores for addressing the omitted variable problem are standard analysis of covariance, Heckman's Heckit estimator, and instrumental variables (e.g., DeMaris, 2014; Wooldridge, 2013).

Sampling issues are also important to consider. In comparative HRM research, one rarely if ever encounters the use of random samples of the respective country populations. Failure to generate random samples is a widespread phenomenon in applied research. Short et al. (2002: 379), for example, found that less than 20 per cent of the studies in strategic management research on performance used a random sample, and that the 'size and direction of the association [among strategy and performance] is partly a function of sampling procedures'. They also noted that 'past sampling practices have rarely been in accordance with established methodological guidelines' and that an 'improvement in future sampling practices will help the field . . . to achieve its objective of explaining the determinants of performance' (ibid.: 382). Given that most samples in comparative HRM research are not random either, alternative methods should be used if possible.

Closely related to the propensity score methodology and developed in the context of concerns about sampling are selection models. Sample selection bias occurs if observations above or below a certain threshold on the dependent or endogenous variable (for example, firm success or financial performance) are not observed. For example, firms with less effective HRM practices may be less successful and thus less likely to survive than those with more effective strategies (Gerhart et al., 1996). The issue is, in essence, an omitted variable problem: firms have an inherent and unmeasured probability to survive, and thus different probabilities to be sampled (Beck et al., 2008). The consequence of observing only survivors (that is, the more successful firms) is a downward bias in the estimate of the HRM–performance relation. The Heckman two-step correction procedure (Heckman, 1979) estimates a selection equation and a substantive equation. From the selection equation the inverse Mills ratio is calculated and then added as an additional variable to the substantive equation. The success of this 'correction' depends, however, on the specific characteristics of the data (Stolzenberg & Relies, 1997). Thus, whenever a Heckman correction is used, the full selection equation (variables, coefficients, and fit) must be reported.

Finally, a different approach to omitted variables and endogeneity is the panel (or cross-sectional time-series) fixed-effects methodology. As a requirement for the fixed-effects model, one needs multiple measurements of the same variables from the same subjects (that is, panel data), and sufficient variation in between the measurements. Basically, in panel models the residual term is split into two components: a time-constant term and a time-varying term. Corresponding to our earlier example, and using the error components model, firm performance can be modelled as:

$$\text{Perf}_{it} = \beta_0 + \beta_1 \text{HRM}_{it} + v_i + r_{it}$$

where Perf is performance of firm i at time t, HRM is the practice of firm i at t, v_i is the time-constant error component ('unit-fixed-effect'), and r_{it} is the time-varying idiosyncratic error. Essentially, the fixed-effects model predicts changes in the dependent variable from changes in the independent variable (within-estimation), and thus differences away all time-constant residual variation across panel waves:

$$\text{Perf}_{it} = (\beta_0 + \delta_0) + \beta_1 \text{HRM}_{it} + v_i + r_{it}$$
$$\text{Perf}_{it-1} = \beta_0 + \beta_1 \text{HRM}_{it-1} + v_i + r_{it-1}$$

with δ_0 as a time dummy (Wooldridge, 2013). The fixed-effects (FE) model then specifies

$$(\text{Perf}_{it} - \text{Perf}_{it-1}) = \delta_0 + \beta_1 (\text{HRM}_{it} - \text{HRM}_{it-1}) + (r_{it} - r_{it-1})$$

In this last equation the time-constant error has disappeared.[9] As a consequence, the fixed-effects model controls for all unobserved heterogeneity on the subject level that is time-invariant. Typical examples include industry, within-industry competition, and country membership (if firm is the level of observation). As such, unmeasured national country components which are stable over time can be controlled for by fixed-effects models. This may even include national culture, given that it does not alter quickly over time. In this case, though, culture is controlled for but its generic influence on the variable of interest is not estimated. This drawback can be attenuated when culture (or any other time-invariant characteristic) is interacted with time-varying measures. In sum, the FE-estimator has many favourable properties (Beck et al., 2008; Wooldridge, 2010, 2013), and its use is highly recommended to the degree that unobserved time-invariant omitted variables would otherwise significantly bias parameter estimates. However, it has costs as well: measurement error may be exacerbated by using difference scores (as the FE-estimator does) (Cronbach & Furby, 1970; Huselid & Becker, 1996); and degrees of freedom are lost from the denominator which decreases efficiency.

In general, panel models are suspect for non-spherical error terms; that is, the disturbances are supposed to be heteroskedastic (errors have unstable variances conditional on the values of the exogenous variables), autocorrelated (errors of the same unit are correlated over time), or contemporaneously correlated (errors of different units are correlated at one point of time). All these problems are serious issues in comparative HRM research. For example, the same type of measurement error might appear across all panel waves in each unit (for example, organisation) if the same single respondent is the source of information. Many advanced econometric programmes such as STATA allow the estimation of heteroskedasticity robust standard errors for fixed-effects models, and have special procedures for AR(1) regressions which control for autocorrelation. As a general

---

[9] More specifically, we have presented the first-difference estimator here (Wooldridge, 2013). The first-difference estimator equals the fixed-effects estimator only if there are exactly two panel waves to be differenced. With more than two panel waves the first-difference estimator will yield different results. The fixed-effects estimator works very similarly, though, since it time-demeans the data instead of differencing them. See Wooldridge (2013) for an introduction.

recommendation, one should always use time dummies with panel regression models of any kind.[10]

A related question is whether fixed-effects models are to be preferred over a random-effects model. While the fixed-effects model is similar to a dummy approach, in the random-effects model v_i is drawn from a random population (Wooldridge, 2013). Whether to use fixed- or random-effects depends in part on the question whether the exogenous variables are correlated with v_i or not. The random-effects model assumes that $cov(X_i, v_i) = 0$; the fixed-effects model allows the correlation. In comparative HRM research the fixed-effects model will be adequate in most instances for two reasons. First, we seldom have a real random sample, which would argue in favour of the random-effects model.[11] Second, HRM practices are likely to be correlated with the governance mechanisms with which the practices are implemented and enforced (for example, control systems, labour relations, and so on). Such governance mechanisms are usually fairly stable over time (in between panel waves), and in most cases remain unobserved; random-effects estimates will be biased then.

In many cases, multilevel issues are neglected with panel data. If there are only a few higher-level units in the data, cross-level interactions between the level 2 constructs (for example, country dummies, national culture scores) and the level 1 explanatory variables can be introduced to the FE-panel model. With many countries and substantial intra-country correlations (that is, a non-trivial ICC(1)) the dummy approach becomes unwieldy. Generalised estimating equations (GEE) may then be used to model both the longitudinal data structure and intra-cluster correlations introduced by country membership (Ballinger, 2004; Ghisletta & Spini, 2004).

From the above discussion it appears that the choice of the 'best' model is difficult for many reasons. The first step should always be to develop strong theory, and then to evaluate how assumptions and predictions can be modelled statistically. One might think, for example, that including more control variables will reduce omitted variable bias. However, arbitrarily adding control variables will primarily reduce efficiency, and the F-statistic or an equivalent indicator (like the deviance statistic) will show the loss in statistical power. To stress the importance of theory and model building prior to model fitting, Gerhart (2007) employs an example where a mediator is incorrectly modelled as a simple control:

$$\text{Perf}_i = \beta_0 + \beta_1 \, \text{HRM}_i + \beta_2 \, \text{AMO}_i + r_i$$

---

[10]   As Certo and Semadeni (2006) report, contemporaneous correlation has not received as much attention, and causes problems for fixed-effects, random-effects, and general least squares (GLS) estimators alike (in particular if the errors are also heteroskedastic). The problem is decidedly lessened when time dummies are used. Specific panel models such as panel corrected standard errors (PCSE) which control for heteroskedasticity, autocorrelation, and contemporaneous correlation (Beck & Katz, 1995), are not recommended in the context of typical HRM data which are cross-sectionally dominated (that is, the number of units is substantially larger than the number of repeated measurements: $N > T$). The same applies for GLS estimators (Certo & Semadeni, 2006).

[11]   Wooldridge (2013) suggests to use the fixed-effects estimator if all members of a known population are sampled (for example, '100 Best Companies to Work For'), or if few members with distinctive (that is, fixed) rather than random features are observed; to the contrary, the random-effects estimator should be used if a true random sample is drawn from the population (for example, a random sample of 5000 individuals from all residents of a country). In most applied cases, the fixed-effects estimator will be the better choice, since the assumption of strict exogeneity is at risk even with large random samples (for example, because of systematic non-response).

where AMO is a composite of human capital ability, motivation, and opportunity to contribute. Using a hypothetical but realistic correlation matrix of the variables, Gerhart (2007) demonstrates that the effect of HRM on performance differs by a factor of four, depending on whether AMO is considered as a control or as a mediator of the HRM–performance relation (that is, in the mediator case the indirect effect also contributes to the total effect).[12] In other words, it is primarily a theoretical question of which model is adequate for the question of interest.

Measurement Error and Construct Validity

Measurement error may be introduced through various sources. In comparative HRM research studies are frequently conducted at the firm level (as, for example, in the Cranet project). In the standard design of such studies, HRM practices are measured as the percentage of employees covered by the practice. Also, rating scales are sometimes applied to measure the strength, importance, or use of the practices. Depending on whether the scores of the HRM practices are modelled as reflective measures (as compared to formative measures; see Diamantopoulos & Winklhofer, 2001; Edwards & Bagozzi, 2000), internal consistency is the typical standard of reliability (estimated with a coefficient such as Cronbach's alpha, or with more sophisticated methodologies such as LISREL; Jöreskog & Sörbom, 1999). Recent evidence suggests, however, that measurement error due to the sampling of raters may be much more substantial. Gerhart and colleagues (Gerhart et al., 2000b, 2000a; Wright et al., 2001) reported in their first study that inter-rater reliability in studies at the firm level was 0.30 at best, and probably as low as 0.20. Basically, this means that the obtained scores reflect the idiosyncratic perceptions of informants rather than valid reflections of the practices in the firms. As such, in research on HRM and performance where multiple sources of measurement error exist (in both items and raters), estimation of a generalisability coefficient is recommended (Cronbach et al., 1972; Gerhart et al., 2000a).

Another and also a very promising approach is to use multiple respondents from different perspectives. For example, Fulmer et al. (2003) used the employees' views in organisations to construct their index of employee relations, which they hypothesised to predict performance. Süß et al. (8) created organisation-level variables from employee responses to estimate HRM level and consensus effects on customer satisfaction in a service environment. Moreover, they combined fixed-effects analyses (by using a four-wave panel design) and multiple groups of respondents (matched employee and customer data) to attenuate a potential common variance bias. Similarly, Ostroff et al. (2002) created organisational level variables from individual responses, and used different subsamples in each organisation to create the different variables, thus eliminating within-person correlations between measures. The multiple respondent approach, while undoubtedly more

---

[12] Statistical testing for mediation may be intricate. In Gerhart's (2007) illustrative example, the indirect effect of HRM on performance equals the difference in the HRM coefficients from a full and a reduced model (that is, with and without AMO in the model). Statistically, this idea follows Baron and Kenny's (1986) approach, which has been very influential in psychological research. However, their approach does not offer a coherent significance test for the indirect path. MacKinnon et al. (2002) discuss such tests and compare them to alternative procedures such as products-of-coefficients tests (e.g., Sobel, 1982). A recent overview that highlights mediation procedures for panel data and multilevel data is provided by Preacher (2015).

demanding than the standard single respondent approach, is also useful to eliminate common method bias (Doty & Glick, 1998; Podsakoff et al., 2003, 2012), which occurs if the independent and dependent variables are all reported by the same source (for example, a single informant). Strategies to control for common methods bias include the multi-trait, multi-method (MTMM) matrix (Campbell & Fiske, 1959), which is particularly promising if assessed with confirmatory methods (Widaman, 1985).[13] Another suggestion is the use of a marker variable (Lindell & Whitney, 2001). Design (for example, separating data collection stages in time) can also help to reduce common method variance. The fixed-effects approach presented earlier can also be used to eliminate time-invariant measurement error (for example, bias from a single respondent with consistently positive or negative response errors across scales and time).

Simultaneity (Reciprocal Causality)

In a recursive model, causation runs in one direction. In a non-recursive model causation is reciprocal, that is, there is simultaneity (Duncan, 1975). The following example was adapted from Duncan (1975: Ch. 5; see also Gerhart, 2007). Take a simple model of performance and HRM, where both variables predict each other (that is, both are exogenous and endogenous):

$$\text{Perf}_i = \beta_0 + \beta_1 X_{1i} + \beta_2 \text{HRM}_i + u_i$$
$$\text{HRM}_i = \delta_0 + \delta_1 X_{1i} + \delta_2 \text{Perf}_i + e_i$$

In the joint model, HRM practices predict performance, and performance predicts HRM. OLS estimates will be biased because the right-hand-side variables are correlated with the errors. For example, if performance predicts HRM, then u_i, the error in the performance equation, will be correlated with HRM. Duncan (1975) demonstrates that (as applied here) the OLS estimate of β_2 will be biased and equal instead:

$$\beta_2^{\text{OLS}} = \beta_2 + r(\text{HRM}_i, u_i) / [1 - r^2(\text{HRM}_i, X_1)]$$

The second part of the additive equation is usually referred to as simultaneity bias. To correct for endogeneity from simultaneity several solutions have been suggested. We will briefly refer to instrumental variables (IV) methods, and simultaneous equation modelling such as LISREL.

First, to establish a causal relation of HRM practices and performance, time precedence of cause and effect is a necessary condition (Cook & Campbell, 1979). The question of time and temporally informed theory is arguably one of the most urgent question in organisational research (see, for example, the contributions to the Special Issue on 'Time

---

[13]   We should note, however, that the assessment of MTMM matrices with confirmatory methods such as LISREL is sometimes problematic. In Widaman's (1985) suggestion, nested models are formulated which allow for the evaluation of overall fit across models (that is, the evaluation of how many traits and methods are represented in the data). Such nested models are often hard to estimate, and in particular, local underidentification frequently causes problems. Marsh (1989) and Eid (2000) have developed Widaman's (1985) strategy further and suggested some solutions.

in Organisations' of the *Academy of Management Review*, 26(4); Goodman et al., 2001). In particular, we need stronger theory about when a cause is likely to occur in the time frame of the study window, how much time elapses before the cause shows an effect, and about when and how the relation among cause and effect changes over the time of the study. Interestingly, a recent review finds that the condition of time precedence is only seldom met in the HRM–performance literature; even worse, HRM practices are often measured after performance (Wright et al., 2005).

If only cross-sectional data are available (this is the more common case in comparative HRM research), instrumental variables (IV) methods may help to reduce endogeneity concerns.[14] In principle, in IV estimation the endogenous explanatory variable is replaced by an estimate of that variable, which is not correlated with the error term. Think again of an HRM practice which we suspect to be endogenous in the prediction of firm performance (because of a non-recursive relationship):

$$\text{Perf}_i = \beta_0 + \beta_1 X_{1i} + \beta_2 \text{HRM}_i + u_i$$

A special case of IV methods is the so-called two-stage least squares (2SLS) estimator. In 2SLS, the first stage is to estimate the HRM practice from the full set of exogenous variables from the performance model, plus at least one additional exogenous variable Z (we use two Z's in the example below):

$$\text{HRM}_i = \pi_0 + \pi_1 X_{1i} + \pi_2 Z_{1i} + \pi_3 Z_{2i} + e_i$$

Based on some econometric assumptions (cf. Wooldridge, 2010, 2013) we know that the best 'instrumental variable' for HRM (that is, a predictor of performance that is not correlated with u_i) is the estimate of HRM:

$$\text{HRM}_i^* = \pi_0 + \pi_1 X_{1i} + \pi_2 Z_{1i} + \pi_3 Z_{2i}$$

For HRM* not to be a perfect linear combination of X_1, a necessary condition is that either π_2 or π_3 are different from zero (identification assumption): if the effects of Z_1 and Z_2 are not jointly significant in the HRM equation, 'we are wasting our time with IV estimation' (Wooldridge, 2013: 529). In the second stage of 2SLS we can then use the predicted values of HRM (as empirical counterparts to the population model HRM*) in the estimation of performance. The reason is that HRM consists of two components: HRM* which is not correlated with u_i, and e_i which is potentially correlated with u_i. Thus, 2SLS first 'purges [HRM] of its correlation with u_i before doing the OLS [performance] regression' (Wooldridge, 2013: 529).

The IV and 2SLS estimators may differ substantially from OLS estimates. Moreover, they are consistent rather than unbiased (that is, they have favourable large sample properties but may be unreliable in smaller samples). Most statistical packages such as STATA have commands for 2SLS or IV estimation. While the two stages can be separately performed by OLS, one should avoid doing the second stage manually because the

---

[14]   Note, however, that reducing endogeneity (through a technical procedure such as IV estimation) does not remedy the substantial problem (time precedence needed to establish a causal relation).

standard errors and test statistics are not valid. The reason is that if we plug HRM = HRM* + e_i into the performance equation, the error term $(u_i + \beta_2\, e_i)$ includes e_i, but the standard errors are based on u_i only (Wooldridge, 2013). Finally, the success of IV or 2SLS estimation is based on the credibility of the assumptions that the instruments are exogenous to performance, $\operatorname{cov}(Z_i, u_i) = 0$, and that the partial R^2 between the Z's and the endogenous explanatory variable is sufficiently large. Given these restrictions, researchers need to provide a convincing rationale for the instruments. Second, statistical tests such as the Hausman (1978) test should be used to evaluate the potential for endogeneity in the given data. Third, the full results of the equation used to obtain the predicted variable values must be reported (Bound et al., 1995; Staiger & Stock, 1997). While simultaneity is clearly an issue, there are only a few examples of IV or 2SLS in the HRM–performance literature. Gerhart (2007) summarises the existing evidence and gives some further recommendations.

A structural equations modelling (SEM) approach such as LISREL can also be used to estimate parameters from a non-recursive model. LISREL is most useful when there are measurement error issues, simultaneity issues, or where a full-information estimator (for example, maximum-likelihood) is useful to either increase efficiency or to provide a goodness of fit test for a system of equations. If none of these conditions hold, then LISREL may be unnecessary and more parsimonious methods should be preferred. In addition, econometricians have long relied more heavily on limited information estimators such as 2SLS as compared to full-information estimators such as maximum-likelihood because the latter assume multivariate normality, while having superior large-sample properties, may not perform as well in finite samples, which empirical research uses, and allow a specification error in one equation (for example, an incorrectly specified zero path) to bias parameter estimates for other equations (Bollen, 1996; Curran et al., 1996; Kennedy, 1992).

SUMMARY

Our goal was to give a review of primarily quantitative methodological issues in the comparative HRM literature, and to provide some recommendations and solutions for these issues. To sum up:

1. Stronger and more substantive theory is needed. Such theory needs to specify cause-and-effect relations, when causes are supposed to influence the outcome, how long the reaction will take, and how and when relations will change over time. Measurement error can be reduced and construct validity enhanced if theory explicitly states the boundary conditions of effects and the domains of the constructs of interest.
2. Sampling issues are salient problems in comparative HRM research. To enhance comparability across nations (or organisations) we need more studies of random samples from different countries and organisations. The analysis of pooled cross-sectional data from random samples can enhance our understanding of HRM policy effects (Wooldridge, 2013). Better, however, are panel data from random samples that allow for advanced causal modelling strategies that have the potential to advance the field.
3. HLM methods (including ICC analysis) should be used to estimate the within and

between portions of variance in multilevel data, and to determine the influence of macro-level constructs (for example, national cultures) on micro-level units (for example, individuals or organisations). ICC analysis should also be used to determine country (or group) mean reliability, and to decide how much macro variance is attributable to specific macro-level constructs such as culture, institutions, regulations, and competition.

4. The analysis of the HRM–performance link is often limited by endogeneity concerns. Omitted variables, measurement error, and simultaneity are major issues in this respect. Strong theory and the collection of longitudinal data are the best advice to overcome such limitations. In the absence of panel data, propensity score techniques, selection models, and IV estimation may help to reduce endogeneity concerns. With panel data the fixed-effects approach is useful. Combinations of panel and HLM methodologies are particularly promising.

5. There is no universal or general 'best modelling strategy'. Rather, the question of interest, the theory used, and the data collected determine which model is the most adequate. If doubts remain, Blossfeld and Rohwer (2002: 277) are probably right: 'In summary, specification bias is pervasive in empirical social research. What can be recommended in such a situation . . .? First . . . try to find better data that allow for representation of the important factors in the model', and, 'the most sensible strategy is to estimate and compare a variety of different models and to find out to what degree the estimation results are robust (that is, do not depend on the selected model)' (ibid.: 276).

REFERENCES

Adler, N.J. 2002. *International Dimensions of Organizational Behaviour* (4th edn). Cincinnati, OH: South-Western.

Allardt, E. 1990. Challenges for comparative social research. *Acta Sociologica*, 33(3): 183–193.

Appelbaum, E., Bailey, T., Berg, P., & Kalleberg, A. 2000. *Manufacturing Advantage: Why High Performance Work Systems Pay Off*. Ithaca, NY: Cornell University Press.

Ballinger, G.A. 2004. Using generalized estimating equations for longitudinal data analysis. *Organizational Research Methods*, 7(2): 127–150.

Barney, J.B., & Wright, P.M. 1998. On becoming a strategic partner: The role of human resources in gaining competitive advantage. *Human Resource Management*, 37(1): 31–46.

Baron, R.M., & Kenny, D.A. 1986. The moderator–mediator variable distinction in social psychological research: Conceptual, strategic, and statistical considerations. *Journal of Personality and Social Psychology*, 51(6): 1173–1182.

Beck, N., Brüderl, J., & Woywode, M. 2008. Momentum or deceleration? Theoretical and methodological reflections on the analysis of organizational change. *Academy of Management Journal*, 51(3): 413–435.

Beck, N., Kabst, R., & Walgenbach, P. 2009. The cultural dependence of vocational training. *Journal of International Business Studies*, 40(8): 1374–1395.

Beck, N., & Katz, J.N. 1995. What to do (and not to do) with time-series cross-section data. *American Political Science Review*, 89(3): 634–647.

Becker, B., & Gerhart, B. 1996. The impact of human resource management on organizational performance: Progress and prospects. *Academy of Management Journal*, 39(1): 779–801.

Bhagat, R.S., & McQuaid, S.J. 1982. Role of subjective culture in organizations: A review and directions for future research. *Journal of Applied Psychology*, 67(5): 653–685.

Bliese, P.D. 2000. Within-group agreement, non-independence, and reliability: implications for data aggregation and analysis. In K.J. Klein and S.W.J. Kozlowski (eds), *Multilevel Theory, Research, and Methods in Organizations*: 349–381. San Francisco, CA: Jossey-Bass.

Bliese, P.D., & Halverson, R.R. 1998. Group size and measures of group-level properties: An examination of eta-squared and ICC values. *Journal of Management*, 24(2): 157–172.

Bloom, M., & Milkovich, G.T. 1999. A strategic human resource management perspective on international compensation and rewards. In G.R. Ferris (ed.), *Research in Personnel and Human Resource Management* (Suppl. 4): 283–304. Greenwich, CT: JAI Press.

Blossfeld, H.P., & Rohwer, G. 2002. *Techniques of Event History Modeling: New Approaches to Causal Analysis* (2nd edn). Mahwah, NJ: Lawrence Erlbaum Associates.

Bollen, K.A. 1996. An alternative two stage least squares (2SLS) estimator for latent variable equations. *Psychometrika*, 61(1): 109–121.

Bound, J., Jaeger, D.A., & Baker, R.M. 1995. Problems with instrumental variables estimation when the correlation between the instruments and the endogenous explanatory variable is weak. *Journal of the American Statistical Association*, 90(430): 443–450.

Boxall, P., & Purcell, J. 2015. *Strategy and Human Resource Management* (4th edn). Basingstoke: Palgrave Macmillan.

Brewster, C. 1999. Different paradigms in strategic HRM: Questions raised by comparative research. *Research in Personnel and Human Resources Management*, 4: 213–238.

Brewster, C., Mayrhofer, W., & Morley, M. 2004. *Human Resource Management in Europe: Evidence of Convergence?*. London: Butterworth-Heinemann.

Campbell, D.T., & Fiske, D.W. 1959. Convergent and discriminant validation by the multitrait-multimethod matrix. *Psychological Bulletin*, 56(2): 81–105.

Cascio, W. F. 2012. Methodological issues in international HR management research. *International Journal of Human Resource Management*, 23(12): 2532–2545.

Certo, S.T., & Semadeni, M. 2006. Strategy research and panel data: Evidence and implications. *Journal of Management*, 32(3): 449–471.

Cook, T.D., & Campbell, D. 1979. *Quasi-Experimentation: Design of Analysis Issues for Field Settings*. Chicago, IL: Rand Mc Nally College Publishing.

Cronbach, L.J., & Furby, L. 1970. How we should measure change – or should we?. *Psychological Bulletin*, 74(1): 68–80.

Cronbach, L.J., Gleser, G.C., Nanda, H., & Rajaratnam, N. 1972. *The Dependability of Behavioral Measurements: Theory of Generalizability of Scores and Profiles*. New York: John Wiley.

Curran, P.J., West, S.G., & Finch, J.F. 1996. The robustness of test statistics to nonnormality and specification error in confirmatory factor analysis. *Psychological Methods*, 1(1): 16–29.

DeMaris, A. 2014. Combating unmeasured confounding in cross-sectional studies: Evaluating instrumental-variable and Heckman selection models. *Psychological Methods*, 19(3): 380.

Diamantopoulos, A., & Winklhofer, H.M. 2001. Index construction with formative indicators: An alternative to scale development. *Journal of Marketing Research*, 38(2): 269–277.

Diericks, I., & Cool, K. 1989. Asset stock accumulation and sustainability of competitive advantage. *Management Science*, 35(12): 1504–1511.

DiMaggio, P.J., & Powell, W.W. 1983. The iron cage revisited: Institutional isomorphism and collective rationality in organizational fields. *American Sociological Review*, 48(2): 147–160.

Doty, D.H., & Glick, W.H. 1998. Common methods bias: Does common methods variance really bias results?. *Organizational Research Methods*, 1(4): 374–406.

Dowling, P.J., Festing, M., & Engle, A.D.S. 2008. *International Human Resource Management* (5th edn). London: Thomson Learning.

Duncan, O.D. 1975. *Introduction to Structural Equation Models*. New York,: Academic Press.

Early, P.C., & Erez, M. 1997. *The Transplanted Executive: Why You Need to Understand How Workers in Other Countries See the World Differently*. New York: Oxford University Press.

Edwards, J.R., & Bagozzi, R.P. 2000. On the nature and direction of relationships between constructs and measures. *Psychological Methods*, 5(2): 155–174.

Edwards, T., Marginson, P., & Ferner, A. 2013. Multinational companies in cross-national context: Integration, differentiation, and the interactions between MNCS and nation states. *Industrial and Labor Relations Review*, 66(3): 547–587.

Eid, M. 2000. A multitrait-multimethod model with minimal assumptions. *Psychometrika*, 65(2): 241–261.

Evans, P., Pucik, V., & Barsoux, J.L. 2002. *The Global Challenge: Frameworks for International Human Resource Management*. New York: McGraw-Hill/Irwin.

Ferner, A., & Quintanilla, J. 1998. Multinationals, national business systems and HRM: The enduring influence of national identity or a process of 'Anglo-Saxonization'. *International Journal of Human Resource Management*, 9(4): 710–731.

Fulmer, I.S., Gerhart, B., & Scott, K.S. 2003. Are the 100 best better? An empirical investigation of the relationship between being a 'great place to work' and firm performance. *Personnel Psychology*, 56(4): 965–993.

Gerhart, B. 2007. Modeling HRM and performance linkages. In P. Boxall, J. Purcell, and P. Wright (eds), *The Oxford Handbook of Human Resource Management*: 552–580. Oxford, UK and New York, USA: Oxford University Press.

Gerhart, B. 2009a. Does national culture constrain organization culture and human resource strategy? The role of individual level mechanisms and implications for employee selection. *Research in Personnel and Human Resources Management*, 28: 1–48.

Gerhart, B. 2009b. How much does national culture constrain organizational culture?. *Management and Organization Review*, 5(2): 241–259.

Gerhart, B., & Fang, M. 2005. National culture and human resource management: Assumptions and evidence. *International Journal of Human Resource Management*, 16(6): 971–986.

Gerhart, B., Trevor, C.O., & Graham, M. 1996. New directions in employee compensation research: Synergies, risk and survival. In G.R. Ferris (ed.), *Research in Personnel and Human Resources Management*, Vol. 14: 143–203. Greenwich, CT: JAI Press

Gerhart, B., Wright, P.M., & McMahan, G.C. 2000a. Measurement error in research on human resources and firm performance: How much error is there and how does it influence effect size estimates?. *Personnel Psychology*, 53(4): 803–834.

Gerhart, B., Wright, P.M., & McMahan, G.C. 2000b. Measurement error in research on the human resources and firm performance relationship: further evidence and analysis. *Personnel Psychology*, 53: 855–872.

Ghisletta, P., & Spini, D. 2004. An introduction to generalized estimating equations and an application to assess selectivity effects in a longitudinal study on very old individuals. *Journal of Educational and Behavioral Statistics*, 29(4): 421–437.

Goodman, P.S., Ancona, D., Lawrence, B., & Tushman, M. 2001. Introduction. *Academy of Management Review*, 26(4): 507–511.

Hamilton, B.H., & Nickerson, J.A. 2003. Correcting for endogeneity in strategic management research. *Strategic Organization*, 1(1): 51–78.

Hantrais, L. 2014. Methodological pluralism in international comparative research. *International Journal of Social Research Methodology*, 17(2): 133–145.

Harder, V.S., Stuart, E.A., & Anthony, J.C. 2010. Propensity score techniques and the assessment of measured covariate balance to test causal associations in psychological research. *Psychological Methods*, 15(3): 234–249.

Hausman, J.A. 1978. Specification tests in econometrics. *Econometrica: Journal of the Econometric Society*, 46(6): 1251–1271.

Heckman, J. 1979. Sample selection bias as a specification error. *Econometrica*, 47(1): 153–161.

Heckman, J.J., LaLonde, R.J., & Smith, J.A. 1999. The economics and econometrics of active labor market programs. In O. Ashenfelter and D. Card (eds), *Handbook of Labor Economics*: 1865–2097. Amsterdam: Elsevier.

Heinsman, D.T., & Shadish, W.R. 1996. Assignment methods in experimentation: When do nonrandomized experiments approximate answers from randomized experiments?. *Psychological Methods*, 1(2): 154–169.

Hofstede, G. 1980. *Culture's Consequences: International Differences in Work-Related Values*. Beverly Hills, CA: SAGE.

Hofstede, G. 1983. The cultural relativity of organizational practices and theories. *Journal of International Business Studies*, 14(2): 75–89.

Hofstede, G. 1993. Cultural constraints in management theories. *Academy of Management Executive*, 7(1): 81–94.

Hofstede, G. 2001. *Culture's Consequences: Comparing Values, Behaviors, Institutions, and Organizations Across Nations*. Thousand Oaks, CA: SAGE.

Hofstede, G., Neuijen, B., Ohayv, D.D., & Sanders, G. 1990. Measuring organizational cultures: A qualitative and quantitative study across twenty cases. *Administrative Science Quarterly*, 35(2): 286–316.

House, R.J., Hanges, P.J., Javidan, M., et al. 2004. *Culture, Leadership, and Organizations: The GLOBE Study of 62 Societies*. Thousand Oaks, CA: SAGE Publications.

Hox, J. 2002. *Multilevel Analysis: Techniques and Applications*. London: Lawrence Erlbaum Associates.

Huselid, M.A., & Becker, B.E. 1996. Methodological issues in cross-sectional and panel estimates of the human resource–firm performance link. *Industrial Relations: A Journal of Economy and Society*, 35(3): 400–422.

Huselid, M.A., & Becker, B.E. 2000. Comment on 'Measurement error in research on human resources and firm performance: how much error is there and how does it influence effect size estimates?' by Gerhart, Wright, McMahan, and Snell. *Personnel Psychology*, 53: 835–854.

Jackson, S.E., Schuler, R.S., & Jiang, K. 2014. An aspirational framework for strategic human resource management. *Academy of Management Annals*, 8(1): 1–56.

Jiang, K., Lepak, D.P., Hu, J., & Baer, J.C. 2012. How does human resource management influence organizational outcomes? A meta-analytic investigation of mediating mechanisms. *Academy of Management Journal*, 55(6): 1264–1294.

Jöreskog, K.G., & Sörbom, D. 1999. *LISREL 8: Structural Equation Modeling with the SIMPLIS Command Language*. Lincolnwood, IL: Scientific Software International.

Kennedy, P. 1992. *A Guide to Econometrics* (3rd edn). Cambridge, MA: MIT Press.

Kirkman, B.L., Lowe, K.B., & Gibson, C.B. 2006. A quarter century of culture's consequences: A review of empirical research incorporating Hofstede's cultural values framework. *Journal of International Business Studies*, 37(3): 285–320.

Kmenta, J. 1971. *Elements of Econometrics*. New York: Macmillan.

Kostova, T. 1999. Transnational transfer of strategic organizational practices: A contextual perspective. *Academy of Management Review*, 24(2): 308–324.

Kostova, T., & Roth, K. 2002. Adoption of an organizational practice by subsidiaries of multinational corporations: Institutional and relational effects. *Academy of Management Journal*, 45(1): 215–233.

Kostova, T., Roth, K., & Dacin, M.T. 2008. Institutional theory in the study of multinational corporations: A critique and new directions. *Academy of Management Review*, 33(4): 994–1006.

Laurent, A. 1983. The cultural diversity of western conceptions of management. *International Studies of Management and Organization*, 13(1/2): 75–96.

Lechner, M. 2010. The estimation of causal effects by difference-in-difference methods. *Foundations and Trends in Econometrics*, 4(3): 165–224.

Li, M. 2013. Using the propensity score method to estimate causal effects: A review and practical guide. *Organizational Research Methods*, 16(2): 188–226.

Lin, D.Y., & Wei, L.-J. 1989. The robust inference for the Cox proportional hazards model. *Journal of the American Statistical Association*, 84(408): 1074–1078.

Lindell, M.K., & Whitney, D.J. 2001. Accounting for common method variance in cross-sectional research designs. *Journal of Applied Psychology*, 86(1): 114–121.

MacKinnon, D.P., Lockwood, C.M., Hoffman, J.M., West, S.G., & Sheets, V. 2002. A comparison of methods to test mediation and other intervening variable effects. *Psychological Methods*, 7(1): 83–104.

Marsh, H.W. 1989. Confirmatory factor analyses of multitrait-multimethod data: Many problems and a few solutions. *Applied Psychological Measurement*, 13(4): 335–361.

Mayrhofer, W., & Brewster, C. 2005. European human resource management: researching developments over time. *Management Revue*, 16(1): 36–62.

McCrae, R.R., Terracciano, A., & 79 members of the Personality Profiles of Cultures Project. 2005. Personality profiles of cultures: Aggregate personality traits. *Journal of Personality and Social Psychology*, 89(3): 407–425.

Meyer, J.W., & Rowan, B. 1977. Institutionalized organizations: Formal structure as myth and ceremony. *American Journal of Sociology*, 83(2): 340–363.

Noe, R.A., Hollenbeck, J.R., Gerhart, B., & Wright, P. 2015. *Human Resource Management: Gaining a Competitive Advantage* (9th edn). Boston, MA: McGraw-Hill/Irvin.

Ostroff, C., Kinicki, A.J., & Clark, M.A. 2002. Substantive and operational issues of response bias across levels of analysis: An example of climate–satisfaction relationships. *Journal of Applied Psychology*, 87(2): 355–368.

Paauwe, J. 2004. *HRM and Performance: Achieving Long-Term Viability*. New York: Oxford University Press.

Ployhart, R.E. 2006. Staffing in the 21st century: New challenges and strategic opportunities. *Journal of Management*, 32(6): 868–897.

Ployhart, R.E., & Hale Jr, D. 2014. The fascinating psychological microfoundations of strategy and competitive advantage. *Annual Review of Organizational Psychology and Organizational Behavior*, 1(1): 145–172.

Podsakoff, P.M., MacKenzie, S.B., Lee, J.-Y., & Podsakoff, N.P. 2003. Common method biases in behavioral research: A critical review of the literature and recommended remedies. *Journal of Applied Psychology*, 88(5): 879.

Podsakoff, P.M., MacKenzie, S.B., & Podsakoff, N.P. 2012. Sources of method bias in social science research and recommendations on how to control it. *Annual Review of Psychology*, 63: 539–569.

Preacher, K.J. 2015. Advances in mediation analysis: A survey and synthesis of new developments. *Annual Review of Psychology*, 66: 825–852.

Pudelko, M., Fink, G., Carr, C., & Wentges, P. 2006. The convergence concept in cross cultural management research. *International Journal of Cross Cultural Management*, 6: 15–18.

Pudelko, M., & Harzing, A.W. 2007. Country-of-origin, localization, or dominance effect? An empirical investigation of HRM practices in foreign subsidiaries. *Human Resource Management*, 46(4): 535–559.

Quintanilla, J., & Ferner, A. 2003. Multinationals and human resource management: Between global convergence and national identity. *International Journal of Human Resource Management*, 14(3): 363–368.

Rabl, T., Jayasinghe, M., Gerhart, B., & Kühlmann, T.M. 2014. A meta-analysis of country differences in the high-performance work system–business performance relationship: The roles of national culture and managerial discretion. *Journal of Applied Psychology*, 99(6): 1011–1041.

Raudenbush, S.W., & Bryk, A.S. 2002. *Hierarchical Linear Models: Applications and Data Analysis Methods*. London: SAGE.

Rogers, W. 1994. Regression standard errors in clustered samples. *Stata Technical Bulletin*, 3(13): 19–23.

Rosenbaum, P.R., & Rubin, D.B. 1983. The central role of the propensity score in observational studies for causal effects. *Biometrika*, 70(1): 41–55.

Rubin, D.B. 2001. Using propensity scores to help design observational studies: Application to the tobacco litigation. *Health Services and Outcomes Research Methodology*, 2(3/4): 169–188.

Sawang, S., Oei, T.P., & Goh, Y.W. 2006. Are country and culture values interchangeable? A case example using occupational stress and coping. *International Journal of Cross Cultural Management*, 6(2): 205–219.

Schaffer, B.S., & Riordan, C.M. 2003. A review of cross-cultural methodologies for organizational research: A best-practices approach. *Organizational Research Methods*, 6(2): 169–215.

Schneider, B. 1987. The people make the place. *Personnel Psychology*, 40(3): 437–453.

Shaver, J.M. 1998. Accounting for endogeneity when assessing strategy performance: Does entry mode choice affect FDI survival?. *Management Science*, 44(4): 571–585.

Short, J.C., Ketchen, D.J., & Palmer, T.B. 2002. The role of sampling in strategic management research on performance: A two-study analysis. *Journal of Management*, 28(3): 363–385.

Shrout, P.E., & Fleiss, J.L. 1979. Intraclass correlations: Uses in assessing rater reliability. *Psychological Bulletin*, 86(2): 420–428.

Snijders, T.A.B., & Bosker, R.J. 1999. *Multilevel Analysis: An Introduction to Basic and Advanced Multilevel Modeling*. London, UK: Sage.

Sobel, M.E. 1982. Asymptotic confidence intervals for indirect effects in structural equation models. *Sociological Methodology*, 13: 290–312.

Spector, P.E., Liu, C., & Sanchez, J.I. 2015. Methodological and substantive issues in conducting multinational and cross-cultural research. *Annual Review of Organizational Psychology and Organizational Behavior*, 2(1): 101–131.

Staiger, D., & Stock, J.H. 1997. Instrumental variables regression with weak instruments. *Econometrica*, 65(3): 557–586.

Steenbergen, M.R., & Jones, B.S. 2002. Modeling multilevel data structures. *American Journal of Political Science*, 46(1): 218–237.

Steiner, P.M., Cook, T.D., Shadish, W.R., & Clark, M.H. 2010. The importance of covariate selection in controlling for selection bias in observational studies. *Psychological Methods*, 15(3): 250–267.

Stolzenberg, R.M., & Relies, D.A. 1997. Tools for intuition about sample selection bias and its correction. *American Sociological Review*, 62(3): 494–507.

Süß, J., Weller, I., Evanschitzky, H., & Wangenheim, F. 2018. Transformational leadership, high performance work system consensus, and customer satisfaction. Unpublished manuscript, LMU Munich.

Terracciano, A., Abdel-Khalek, A.M., Adám, N., et al. 2005. National character does not reflect mean personality trait levels in 49 cultures. *Science*, (310): 96–100.

Tregaskis, O., & Brewster, C. 2006. Converging or diverging? A comparative analysis of trends in contingent employment practice in Europe over a decade. *Journal of International Business Studies*, 37(1): 111–126.

Trompenaars, F., & Hampden-Turner, C. 2000. *Riding the Waves of Culture: Understanding Cultural Diversity in Business*. London: Nicholas Breazley.

Widaman, K.F. 1985. Hierarchically nested covariance structure models for multitrait-multimethod data. *Applied Psychological Measurement*, 9(1): 1–26.

Wooldridge, J.M. 2010. *Econometric Analysis of Cross Section and Panel Data*. Cambridge, MA: MIT Press.

Wooldridge, J.M. 2013. *Introductory Econometrics: A Modern Approach* (5th edn). Mason, OH: South-Western Cengage Learning.

Wright, P.M., Gardner, T.M., Moynihan, L.M., & Allen, M.R. 2005. The relationship between HR practices and firm performance: Examining causal order. *Personnel Psychology*, 58(2): 409–446.

Wright, P.M., Gardner, T.M., Moynihan, L.M., et al. 2001. Measurement error in research on human resources and firm performance: Additional data and suggestions for future research. *Personnel Psychology*, 54(4): 875–901.

Yeganeh, H., & Su, Z. 2006. Conceptual foundations of cultural management research. *International Journal of Cross Cultural Management*, 6(3): 361–376.

6. The anthropological comparative method as a means of analysing and solving pressing issues in comparative HRM

Fiona Moore and Mary Yoko Brannen

INTRODUCTION

While many in business and management studies see the value of using qualitative data, quantitative studies nonetheless dominate both disciplines, and qualitative methods are often conservatively used. Moreover, as Piekkari et al.'s (2009) study indicates, interviews dominate the literature at the expense of other qualitative methods such as participant-observation, discourse analysis, narrative studies and others. One barrier to the uptake of qualitative research methods in business and management studies appears to be the lack of generalisability (see Ghauri & Grønhaug, 2005: 201–211): while rich data about the lived experiences of individuals in organisations may provide valuable insights for human resource managers, it is difficult, if not impossible, to determine whether these insights are universally true, or whether they relate solely to people and organisations in a particular time and place (or indeed whether they may be unique). However, in many disciplines, the scientific value of data is not limited to whether or not it can be generalised. In anthropology, for instance, the focus on ethnographic method is toward the primary goal of generating deep descriptive insights for comparison, rather than generalisability.

In this chapter, we consider the comparative method in anthropology and, using an international case study, will explore how international human resource management (HRM) can usefully adopt the comparative method as a means of analysing, and drawing useful conclusions from, data which do not easily lend themselves to generalisation; focusing on, but not limited to, qualitative or mixed-method studies.

THE COMPARATIVE METHOD

Comparative analysis dominated science and the social sciences in the nineteenth and early twentieth centuries. Scholars compared institutions and practices across different societies to construct evolutionary histories of civilisation, culture, and society from whence to generate a progressive logic of social forms through distinct and developmental stages (Holý, 1987). Others used the comparative method to infer relationships among cultures, institutions, and languages to advance the notion of a process of transmission. As one example, the Australian anatomist Grafton Elliot Smith's comparison of Mayan pyramids, Japanese pagodas, and American Indian burial mounds with elements of earlier Egyptian culture led to his inferential history that these were inspired from Egyptian prototypes (Smith, 1928). As it was hard to determine whether similarities across units of comparison arose from a common history or independently from functions, one response was that scholarship in sociology and anthropology adopted a more scientific approach. Durkheim (1895 [1938]) rejected lay interpretations of reality, but recognised that they may serve as suggestions and guides for analysis. Comparison was, therefore, viewed as necessary to establish relations of causality between events. This led to a shift to more controlled comparisons, such as were adopted in studies of kinship in anthropology (Evans-Pritchard, 1963; Radcliffe-Brown, 1951). In a similar vein, albeit less positivist, was Max Weber's (1968) use of the comparative method to formulate ideal types, which he used to compare and contrast societal and organisational forms and their distinct attributes. Whether driven to understand a progressive logic, search for diffused practices, or look for relations of causality, in each case significant organisational learning was facilitated by means of comparison.

Over the past 60 years, anthropologists have focused on the systematic comparison of contemporary cultures as a means of gaining insights into human thought, behaviour, and social activity. Radcliffe-Brown, a pioneering social anthropologist and one of the originators of the structuralist school of anthropology, argued, in his 1951 essay 'The comparative method in social anthropology', that anthropology should be based on the systematic comparison of present-day cultures, as opposed to the historical method, which he deemed to be the aim of his predecessors, to reconstruct an evolutionary sequence of the development of humankind through effectively ranking present cultures.

Radcliffe-Brown's aim, in line with the dominant functionalist project of anthropology at the time, was to uncover the underlying similarities of all cultures and, thus, to ascertain the essence of what it is to be human (Peel, 1987). The process was initially aimed at generalisation: determining the essence of humanity through considering what all cultures have in common, identifying shared traits such as binary classification systems (Needham, 1973), the presence of kinship systems (Barnes, 1987), religion, and others (Holý, 1987). However, in doing so, the complexities and diversity of these different concepts between cultures became a focus for exploration. While comparison may be used for the purposes of attempted generalisation (Holý, 1987: 3), its value to anthropology is that it is not limited to this, but can also be used to establish functional correlations, facilitate description, and to develop inter- and intra-cultural comparisons (Holý, 1987: 9–12).

Furthermore, as anthropology began what Chapman (1997: 5) refers to as the shift 'from function to meaning'; that is to say, when anthropology ceased to be a functionalist discipline that aimed at being an objective study of human behaviour, and instead focused on analysing the meanings that people attribute to various practices, some other form of developing scientific value had to be found. As structuralism developed, the value of finding the underlying similarities between all cultures began to be questioned (Peel, 1987), and comparison was increasingly used more as a tool for finding contrasts between cultures. This is exemplified in Lévi-Strauss's (1969) classic argument that the phenomena that Radcliffe-Brown and his contemporaries had lumped together under the rubric of 'totemism' were in fact diverse phenomena that often bore only a slight resemblance to each other.

Later, the post-structuralist movements of the 1970s and 1980s challenged the development of overarching theory as being a 'grand narrative', arguing that to focus on the idea of human universals is to ignore the context in which the definition of such concepts takes place (see Holý, 1987: 15ff). Comparison, for them, emerges in the concept of reflexivity, of acknowledging that the ethnographer is, subconsciously, comparing the group under study both to their own society and to others they may have encountered, personally or in literature, and considering how this comparison plays out. The comparative method can thus take another commonly raised issue with qualitative data – the fact that it is inherently subjective – and turn it into a strength, by allowing the analysis of the researcher's own perspective.

The comparative method in contemporary social anthropology is, therefore, a search for both similarity and contrast – usually at the same time, even if one aspect may dominate. The problem with generalizing in such an analytical environment is that it is of limited utility, becoming effectively meaningless or analytically useless. While it is possible to say, for instance, that all human societies have 'religion' or 'kinship systems', the differences in the ways in which these universals are expressed are such that the analytical value lies more in considering the patterns of similarity and difference in how these ideas are expressed or developed. Anthropologists thus do not simply compare, but actively use comparison as a means of analysing results.

COMPARISON IN INTERNATIONAL HRM

The possible utility of anthropological comparison as a means of analysing qualitative data should be of particular concern to researchers and practitioners in areas relating to human resource management. International and comparative HRM is arguably better positioned than most subfields of international business studies to benefit from ways of extracting value from qualitative data, given that many issues in HRM revolve around the lived experiences of individuals and the cultures of locations and organisations; for instance: training and development, managing expatriate failure, health and safety, recruitment and selection, culture at the national and organisational levels, and post-acquisition integration. All of these, and many others, are issues that benefit from study based either wholly or partly on qualitative methods, and could thus be usefully analysed using the comparative method.

There are also wider theoretical issues that the comparative method could address. The comparative method could be used to simultaneously determine the essence, or basic elements, of international or shared practices, and also to identify where the differences lie, so that HRM managers can successfully transfer practices without attempting to impose a one-size-fits-all solution across a diverse international operation (see, e.g., Brannen et al., 1999). It might also be used to investigate 'culture' in a way that incorporates the complexities and nuances of the idea (see, e.g., Brannen, 1994; Brannen, 1998; Sackmann & Phillips, 2004) without sacrificing a wider perspective. Finally, it can be used to link comparative HRM into wider research on transnationalism, culture, and organisations, through incorporating perspectives from history, sociology, anthropology, and others.

Comparison, as a research tool, is widely used in the study of HRM policy and practice; a literature search of the *International Journal of Human Resource Management* yields more than 2000 results for the keyword 'comparison'. Indeed, some studies approach anthropological uses of the comparative method, although its potential as a tool for analysis is seldom highlighted. Much international HRM involves the comparison of two or more national contexts, for instance Murakami (1998) and Beekun et al. (2003); the comparison of different HRM systems (Pieper, 1990); or the study of individuals who span different contexts, for instance Brannen and Thomas (2010) and Furusawa and Brewster (2015).

It might, therefore, be instructive to consider a few indicative works in international HRM, and how comparison is employed. Templer et al. (1997) use a survey-based comparison of HRM professionals in Canada, South Africa, and Zimbabwe, attempting to determine whether different countries do, in fact, have different ideas of what constitutes excellence in HRM, as a challenge to the assumption of convergence under globalisation. While the nominal focus is quantitative, the country background is extensively considered for all three sites, making this a study with elements of rich data. The project does consider similarities and differences between the three countries; however, it is primarily inductive research, and ultimately focuses on supporting the idea that there remain national differences in HRM priorities despite the influence of globalisation. Comparison is thus employed to consider similarities and differences between groups; however, the analysis is ultimately lacking in complexity.

Schaaper et al. (2013), although their material is much more qualitative (being primarily interview-based), employ a more deductive and positivistic approach to comparison. Their aim is to compare and contrast the expatriation strategies of French and Japanese multinational enterprises (MNEs), but there is little consideration of the French and Japanese cultural backgrounds. However, the use of comparison is appropriate for the subject in that it is able to explore what is, generally, a fairly individualised process, and sheds light on the lived experiences of expatriates and the HRM managers tasked with organising their assignments. The results also go against some of the received wisdom about the HRM practices of Japanese companies, and explore the wider context in highlighting the extent to which foreign direct investment depends on expatriates. A study of this kind is thus more useful to practitioners and researchers than one attempting to generalise about HRM policy and practice.

Kim et al. (2013), by contrast, state that their focus is on different companies of a single national origin (in this case, South Korea), to try to determine patterns in the ways in which HRM systems have adapted to the financial crisis (although there is also a comparison with United States companies included). The study is based on two surveys of the same companies before and after the financial crisis. Although the paper appears to generalise in that it identifies two types of HRM systems that Korean companies favour, it also tries to identify patterns within this, for instance exploring whether larger and smaller firms take different strategies and how different firms change in light of the crisis. While comparison is here primarily used as a means of generalising, it nonetheless can include the acknowledgement, and exploration, of complexity.

Finally, Shen et al. (2015) is a good example of how something like the anthropological comparative method might prove useful in comparative HRM studies. The project is a qualitative study, based mainly on in-depth interviews, though also involving reflexive work with teams, and a highly diverse array of research assistants involved with data-gathering and analysis. Like Templer et al. (1997), the paper is aimed at examining the issue of convergence, and the extent to which HRM practices remain rooted in locality, and is also primarily inductive research. The significant thing in this case is that the researchers use comparison to develop a complex analysis, which does not attempt to identify similarity or difference as a primary goal, or to generalise about particular nations or regions, but instead explores the subtleties and nuances involved in HRM practices, acknowledging that similarities and differences can occur within the same group. This can be seen in their summary of the study's contributions:

> First, we provide a better basis for HRM policies and practices in MNEs regarding how to handle careers of their workforce in different countries and institutional contexts. Second, we add a cross-cultural perspective to the discussion about agentic careers. Finally, we inform the universalist versus contextualist debate in HRM by adding a career management perspective. (Shen et al., 2015: 1754)

Perhaps crucially, one of the study's main aims is to obtain data and analysis that goes beyond so-called WEIRD (Western, educated, industrialised, rich, and democratic) perspectives (Henrich et al., 2010), thus approaching the anthropological interest in the small-scale and developing world. While the reflexivity element arguably gets somewhat lost in the analysis, this study thus uses comparison to note similarities and differences along a variety of different criteria, and uses this to consider the relative importance of contextual factors, and in doing so, approaches the anthropological use of comparison.

An exploration of the comparative method in anthropology and a consideration of how comparison is used in analysing issues relevant to HRM, therefore, suggests that it can be meaningfully used as a means of analysing data which are difficult or impossible to generalise, where generalisation is not a useful aim, where non-Western perspectives must be considered, or where a degree of complexity is required to add nuance to an otherwise generalisation-focused analysis. Comparison, in anthropology, seeks not to generalise meaninglessly but to contextualise experiences and consider the contextual factors underlying similarities and differences; in HRM, comparison appears to be particularly useful in cases where the aim is not to correlate specific factors with specific outcomes, but to analyse the lived experiences of managers with a view to learning from them. The HRM example also indicates that comparison can be used with a variety of different kinds of data; while it would seem particularly pertinent to qualitative research methods, as above, it can also be used to provide a more nuanced analysis of quantitative methods, and thus is of wider utility. The value of anthropological comparison is thus the ability to deal with large amounts of rich data, particularly qualitative and experiential, and to analyse this data meaningfully without spurious generation. We now consider a case in which comparison was usefully employed to solve HRM-related pressing issues in global management.

CASE STUDY: SURFACING AND LEVERAGING COMPARATIVE INSIGHTS FROM SUBSIDIARY MANAGERS AT TESCO PLC FOR GLOBAL IDENTITY INTEGRATION AND ORGANISATIONAL RENEWAL

Background

In the spring of 2010, Tesco Plc, at the time Britain's number one private sector employer and the world's third-largest food retailer, with stores in 14 countries across Asia, Europe, and North America, began to lose its competitiveness in its United Kingdom (UK) home base (Tesco, 2012), though still maintaining substantial profit growth worldwide, led by its

Asian subsidiaries located, at the time, in Japan, Korea, China, Malaysia, Thailand, and India. Tesco's international operations were diverse, including joint ventures with local partners (for example, Samsung-Tesco Home Plus in South Korea, and Tesco Lotus in Thailand), reflecting Tesco's strategy of being locally responsive to host country market opportunities, culture, and policies.

The challenge for Tesco lay in first identifying what constitutes the essence of Tesco's organisational identity, comparing and contrasting this with that of its Asian subsidiaries, identifying best practices (what Brannen, 2004: 612, terms 'positive recontextualisations'), and finally, integrating these across its global footprint. Tesco chose to answer this challenge by means of an innovative project led by Tesco's chief executive officer (CEO) Asia, David Potts, and based on the anthropological method, in which a multicultural team of nine Asian managers (subsequently called the 'Project Team') were trained to become in-house ethnographers of Tesco UK for a three-month period studying 52 stores. This was fundamentally a comparative exercise, with dual objectives for the Asian management team to help Tesco: (1) understand and evaluate the core practices that comprised the essence of Tesco's home country advantage; and (2) to identify sources of learning from Tesco's foreign subsidiaries to aid in reinvigorating its core in light of increasing competition in its home market. The potential for a comparative approach to reveal the fundamentals of the heart of the organisational culture is thus clear from the set-up of the Tesco project.

Research Design

The research design of this study, which was termed 'The Essence of Tesco', comprised three main phases. As surfacing contextually based implicit (and often tacit) knowledge is difficult to do from within one's own context, and because Tesco's global performance was being led by strong positive performance by its Asian subsidiaries with perhaps the most to offer the home base in terms of learning, the study began with the formation of a global team of nine managers chosen from Tesco's Asian operations in China, Japan, Korea, Malaysia, India, and Thailand to come to the UK, where they would be based for six months.

In the first phase, the academic research team of four scholars skilled in organisational and strategic field-based analysis trained the project team in ethnographic, cultural analysis, and grounded theorising techniques. Training sessions were held on topics including observation skills, note-taking methods, analysis of media and documentation, interviewing techniques, and on organising and making sense of data through techniques of content analysis, coding, triangulation, and, significantly, the comparative method.

In the second phase of the study, the project team conducted fieldwork across the five principal grocery retail formats developed and operationalised in the UK: Tesco Express, Tesco Metro, Tesco Extra, Tesco Direct, and Tesco Bank. During this phase, the academic team provided ongoing guidance and feedback to the project team as they conducted their fieldwork. Our emphasis during this phase was on the quality of, and routines for, note-taking, and on initial and focused coding of data.

The final phase of the project comprised data analysis and recommendations. This began with the project team coding their own field notes and interview transcriptions and, through comparison and contrast, surfacing the major themes that emerged as the underlying practices that were the essence of Tesco in its UK context. The full research team then met in order to triangulate across the individually collected data to check for inter-rater reliability, shared understanding of the codes, consolidate related codes as sub-codes, and surface the main themes common across the data collected by the nine project team members. Ten core themes emerged that were salient, robust, and common across the individual project team members' data. The ten themes were then coded using Schein's corporate culture diagnostic (Schein, 1985) to ascertain whether they were robust and congruent across the artefact, value, and assumption levels of analysis. This was done in the following way. The team colour-coded each of the ten thematic sets of consolidated field notes, marking phrases and quotes that were indicative of the theme as: an arte-fact – an explicit manifestation of the theme; a value – an espoused manifestation; or an assumption – a tacit expectation. We then looked at the frequency of artefacts, values, and assumptions for each theme. A comparative approach was thus inherent in the analysis.

Some of the themes were heavy on assumptions and values and lean on artefacts, thus indicating that Tesco does not deliver in these areas. For example, for the theme 'oppor-tunity to get on', employees thought that if they joined Tesco, they would have an oppor-tunity to move up the job levels; however, in fact many employees complained that they were not given this option. Others were heavy on artefacts but lean on espoused values and basic assumptions, thus indicating that Tesco needs to question whether there is a shared understanding of the purpose and meaning behind these protocols, rituals, and behaviours. For example, for the theme 'customer is at the heart of everything', whereas there were many slogans, signs, and so on stating that this was so, there were in fact con-tradictions at the value and assumption levels where employees felt they were walking a tightrope, having to meet key performance indicators (KPIs) at the expense of customer needs.

This project therefore represented an opportunity for academics to work with an in-house mixed global team, as they identified the 'Essence of Tesco' through their applica-tion of ethnographic fieldwork techniques, to use the comparative method to highlight similarities and differences between their subsidiary organisational context and the UK home context, with a view to developing an understanding of the organisation's fundamental values without sacrificing complexity and nuance.

Findings

Fieldwork: performance in note-taking, coding, and analysis using Schein's model

The design of the project generally, and the training that comprised its first phase, was driven by the expressed desired outcomes of Tesco plc. In the training phase, all the project team members had difficulty with the absorption of the nature of ethnographic practice, the techniques of observation and judicious participation, and the painstak-ing technique of note-taking. Whilst some of these uncertainties were eased when the academic team accompanied the project team members on pilot sessions in local stores, some key uncertainties persisted, such as the border between 'objective' and 'subjective' phenomena and the way in which they should be recorded. In order to help the project team focus their participant observation, we offered a simple rubric of focus on three questions: What is familiar? What is surprising? What do I want to learn more about? We termed these the F, S, and Ms, and asked team members to mark these in their field notes.

Some of the project team members were concerned about how they would be received in the stores, and worried about being viewed as 'Asian spies'. Fortunately, Tesco already had a policy wherein all store managers and Tesco executives must spend one week per year working in the stores so as not to lose touch with the customer. We therefore counselled the project team to use this practice, termed 'Tesco Week in Stores' or TWIST, as a way of helping the Tesco UK store employees understand their presence in the stores and to explain that this was just a new global 'twist' on this standard routine.

Some of the managers also struggled with the discipline of writing up field notes, and took more time to construct the personal routine required. Others required remedial sessions to help with decision-making and weaknesses with their English. In order to facilitate this, we devised a template for field note-taking and a daily checklist. This included a left-hand column for subjective reflections, a right-hand column for objective notes, and check boxes for F, S, and M's. The team members then sent their weekly field notes to two of the academic advisors, who regularly gave feedback and encouraged them to register their subjective opinions regarding their observations as much as possible. This latter point was very important for the project because in order for Tesco to learn from insider–outsider eyes, the project team members needed to register and communicate differences between how things were done in their home context versus in the UK. These differences, termed 'recontextualisations' (Brannen, 2004), can be sources of innovation and continuous sustainable improvement for Tesco plc that could distinguish it from its competitors.

Coding posed even more problems for the group. Whilst content that they were, in almost all cases, assembling sufficient field notes, they found it very difficult to stand back from their work and analyse, identify, and highlight relevant sections of text, and apply the comparative method. Again, remedial sessions gave the group confidence to work systematically on their burgeoning file of notes as they gradually covered the majority of the UK, visiting stores and offices.

An important dimension of the project, which represented a particular challenge, was that of language. Although all the project team members came from Asia, they had differing native languages. Mandarin, Thai, Hindi, Japanese, and several others all figured in the profile of the group, and alongside their language identity each manager had a strong cultural belonging to an individual nation, that was further nourished by a strong desire to see Tesco in their country excel within the Asian context. In addition, the level of proficiency in English of the project team members was by no means even. In spoken English, four stood out as having more ability than the others because of residence, study, or work experience in English-speaking countries. Three project team members were noticeably weaker than the rest in spoken English and one of them had never before visited an English-speaking country. Our knowledge of their respective abilities in writing, reading, and listening was to be discovered in the course of the induction, training, and fieldwork, and the gap between the more and less able turned out to be smaller in writing than in speaking. While these issues of language proficiency and use and its relationship with ethnographic skills is not the focus of this chapter, it is relevant at this stage to point out some of these key issues as they pertain to performance generally, and more specifically to competence in understanding what they heard and read, and their ability to conduct interviews and gather data directly from Tesco employees in a variety of scenarios. Note-taking and analysing data were of course also key tasks in the project, which relied on a good command of English.

'The Essence of Tesco': identification of themes

The aim of the project, as far as the company and multicultural management team were concerned, was to ascertain, through ethnographic data and the comparative method, what was the 'essence' of Tesco, what part of that essence might lend itself to global integration, and what was more vulnerable to local recontextualisation (Brannen, 2004), and hence provide an opportunity for learning and reinvigorating Tesco UK. In addition to this overarching aim, we were asked to focus on the following three areas: (1) people and culture; (2) brand management; and (3) operational excellence. The identification of key themes that made up the essence of Tesco UK was achieved by adapting traditional ethnographic coding techniques to a team process. This was not an easy feat, given the diverse cultural and linguistic challenges posed by a multicultural team of this sort. Each of the nine project team members were asked to code their own field notes first by using open coding, considering their data in minute detail while developing initial categories, then to surface recurring themes by using selective coding around core concepts. We then pooled all of the themes that were surfaced by the nine team members. This came to an initial 34 themes, which we then discussed, defined, and sorted; integrating themes and sub-themes until we refined the list into ten overall themes: (1) customer at the heart of everything; (2) leadership DNA; (3) opportunity to get on; (4) teamwork and collaboration (intangibles); (5) work environment (tangibles); (6) embracing and implementing change; (7) 'it's my business'; (8) operational efficiency; (9) trusted brand; and (10) respect for facts and insights.

On the surface, these themes might appear to be quite generic strategic initiatives for any business. Rather, out of a plethora of initiatives generated by Tesco management, these are the ones that surfaced from the project team's field notes as being relevant and present on the shop floor. This is an important aspect of the methodology that distinguishes itself from the rather more superficial readings of organisations generated by consulting firms that are unable to leverage insider perspectives on the phenomena under study. These ten themes were derived from complex, deep bodies of *in vivo* text generated by a bottom-up inductive process, rather than having been given to the project team members in a top-down communication from Tesco executives. Taken in isolation by their titles, the themes do not convey the full depth and meaning that the project team members were able to understand through their research. For example, the theme 'opportunity to get on' may appear to be a key theme in any company, but in the retail sector, especially in the UK, one of Tesco's competitive advantages in recruiting and developing staff is seen by employees as a key differentiator from other shops on the high street.

Further, after initially identifying each theme, the project team members carefully and collectively defined and clarified what comprised their essence, using *in vivo* quotes. For instance, the following was the descriptive essence of the theme, 'opportunity to get on':

- variety of jobs and levels for everybody;
- staff morale (also pay);
- an interesting job;
- career development and personal development;
- talking about how to develop people in a fair way;
- long-term service – employees working at Tesco for a long time (lifetime);
- personal development as well as career development;

- powerful message around people development;
- leadership by coaching and inclusivity;
- the company's ability to change lives.

The process of developing these themes was significant to the subsequent analysis. When listening to induction speeches by Tesco UK management, and in subsequent follow-up interviews with various UK managers, during the initial training period, the project team developed an idea of the official version of the company's values and identity. However, they also often noted that the UK managers seemed to rely heavily upon Tesco's tools and rhetoric without actually engaging their teams or enacting effective people-management skills. The reflexive skills that the project team members had learned to employ in their roles as strategic ethnographers enabled them to go beyond considering the corporate values unproblematically, to further analyse, triangulate, and critique them. They were thus able to consider how their reactions to the different Tesco UK managers' presentations affected how they received their opinions: for example, that they would pay more attention to the presenters with whom they felt a rapport because of a shared functional identity or point of view, and thus prioritised these managers' version of events. The process of coming up with the themes was also subject to power relations internal to the project team, as some wanted to see the corporate values reflected in the themes, while others, having formulated different opinions during the training process, were more ambivalent. This process of discussion and debate made for a more complex image of corporate culture and, more importantly, one incorporating contradictory discourses, as the research team compared and contrasted different messages and practices within the group. Furthermore, they were able to consider the managers' views in another context: how these values were experienced at the shop level. For instance, one project team member critiqued the concept of efficiency by saying: 'I began putting some labels on products, as I wanted to experience the process for myself. The system was slow for the time given to change the labels and it can be quite frustrating when you do not find the product to match the label.'

The project team members thus did not simply develop a managerial image of Tesco, but were able to conduct holistic ethnography (see Moore, 2011) to obtain perspectives on the firm from different levels of the organisation. The use of comparison to analyse their data also provided the team with new insights into the culture of the organisation.

Ethnography, culture, and nuance: analysing the themes through comparison
One significant outcome of the methodological choice was that in identifying the themes, the project team members were able to incorporate critiques, even outright contradictions, of the themes in their analysis. For instance, under 'opportunity to get on', the project team members noted that the examples cited to them were generally of people who had risen in the company through taking their own initiative, rather than people who had been helped by the company to success. Therefore, while it was certainly true that the company was seen as a place where people could 'get on' in their careers, and that the opportunity was provided, the company generally did not help employees to meet this goal.

The project team thus, via the comparative method, identified a gap between Tesco's espoused values and practices. For instance, they noted that Tesco has an official value of being a 'great place to work', and yet also noted employees saying, 'What's special about

Tesco? Nothing much. They pay me and that's all'. One of the focal espoused values of Tesco, and indeed one of their overall themes, is 'customers at the heart of everything we do', meaning that the company tries to manage effectively the conflict between KPIs and customer needs. An analysis of the ethnographers' field notes demonstrates that this essence is, indeed, robust at all three of Schein's levels. However, with 453 affirmative and 263 contradictory field observations, the analysis also indicates that Tesco currently has conflicting values in place around trying to achieve KPIs, such as sales targets, while concurrently keeping customers at the heart of the organisation. In the process of placing heavy emphasis upon trying to meet and exceed performance goals, at the store level, managers and front-line staff have forgotten what it means to truly place customers first. Consider the following: 'I could not believe they would have a staff meeting on the shopping floor. Although it is a wide corridor, it is disturbing for customers. It is a huge store and they should find another place to meet.'

By exploring the espoused values, and the lived experience of being members of the company, through comparing their assumed norms and values in Asia, their observations at different Tesco stores, and each other's experiences, the project team members were able to acknowledge the company's self-identification, but also embrace the ambivalences, contradictions, and variations embodied in these themes, rather than taking the statements as a simple, objective, and unproblematic truth about the company. The use of the ethnographic method thus allowed for a complex and dynamic analysis and understanding of the firm's culture by its managers.

Reflexivity and comparison: the analytic process
Another significant factor in the process of generating and analysing the data was the diversity of the team. Tesco's international operations are diverse, including joint ventures with local partners, reflecting Tesco's strategy of being locally responsive to host country market opportunities and policies, and the project team members therefore came not just from different countries, but from firms that had a quite different relationship to the parent company. Some of the participants were employees of companies that were joint ventures between Tesco and a failing or weak local partner; whereas in other cases, for instance the South Korean operation, the power balance between Tesco and the local partner was more equal, leading to power struggles over whose values would dominate. As ethnography is inevitably a comparative act (see Ellis & Bochner, 2000), implicitly if not explicitly, there was always an element of comparison with the project team members' home situation; for instance, one observer critiqued a store's front-of-house display by saying that it is not what she would have expected in her home country, leading her to reflect on why the differences were present. Again, the diverse backgrounds and power relations of the project team members conducting the study led, through comparison, to a dynamic view of the corporations' culture.

For the academic team, there was also a substantial opportunity for reflexivity in regards to both the research process around training and working with insider ethnographers, as well as theory development regarding the evolution of corporate culture in global organisations. The academic team was charged to facilitate the Asian project team to carry out a number of tasks, including observing the operations and behaviour of people in a selection of Tesco stores across the UK, interviewing store staff, office staff and suppliers, and reviewing past reports conducted in-house or by consultancies, but not to conduct the actual in-store ethnographic research ourselves, providing opportunities to reflect on our own research practice and its strengths and weaknesses. The process did certainly, as noted, generate a more complex image of corporate culture, and one that could include the ambivalences and contradictions found in organisations (as noted in Martin, 1992). However, as Burawoy (2013) notes in his critique of ethnographic methodology, it is also the case that researchers can miss important things that they are not looking for; the British class system, for instance, appeared not to be very significant to the team of managerial researchers, yet this subject would feature prominently in most lectures or courses on the subject of organisations in British life.

This study also had to overcome numerous challenges to both the academic and business viability of the project posed by language differences between headquarters and the Asian project team, and indeed within the project team itself. Traditional expectations are that if the working language is English and everyone is speaking it, non-native speakers will usually be competent and motivated enough to get the job done despite native English speakers often being unaware of the difficulties they are encountering (CILT, 2005). Other research (Neeley, 2013) has indicated that fluency in the *lingua franca* of the organisation does not necessarily determine status or performance. This project gave rise to findings that rather expand our understanding of this important language dynamic in multicultural teamwork. In fact, language competence does matter, but not necessarily as expected. In this project team, the three best performers (as assessed by the academic co-leads and triangulated by the project team lead from Tesco Asia) over the entire project on all levels were the ones who had the weakest spoken English, yet had the longest tenure in Tesco in their native country. This indicates that familiarity with company language and identification with the organisation is a key component of communicative efficacy in global organisations. We also uncovered a significant lack of correlation between ability in spoken English and written English across the whole team, with several project team members producing field notes of much higher quality than expected based on their speaking ability. A significant attenuating factor here may be the language 'strategy' of Tesco as a company, which holds that simplicity and clarity with the needs of the customer (and the interlocutor) are key elements of development and behaviour at all levels of the organisation.

These findings draw into question some key tenets of internationally distributed research projects that do not build in control mechanisms to combat these unreliable assumptions about language competence, which Kubota (2011) labels under the term 'linguistic instrumentalism'. The findings also suggest that international companies which adopt a developmental approach to language in all its forms and functions may as a result obtain advantage through better, deeper communication and the production of more unifying codes which work across borders. Language policy consists of much more than selection and imposition of a *lingua franca* (Harzing et al., 2011). The reflexive aspects of the project therefore also show the utility of the comparative method for analysing organisational culture, identifying common themes while not sacrificing complexity, and allowing researchers to understand and take into account the role of language and of ethnographer experience in conducting qualitative or mixed-method studies of organisations.

Contributions of the Study

The utility of ethnographic techniques and analytical methods beyond research
This study's first main contribution is in developing the uses of ethnographic techniques and analytical methods (including, but not limited to, the comparative method) in international business beyond their established role as a means by which academics and others can study organisations. In this case, ethnographic methods were essential to obtaining a complex picture of the organisations. The need for research methods that facilitate the understanding of complex, micro-level cultural phenomena is especially essential in international business research, where the research settings are rife with multilevel cultural interactions based on diverging organisational and national cultural assumptions brought together in real time by the merging of various national cultural groups across distance and differentiated contexts.

Another, equally important reason why ethnographic methodology is particularly useful to international business research is that much of the organisational phenomena under study are emergent and relatively new. The domain of international business is characterised by the ongoing evolution of institutional contexts, country borders, organisational forms, and even workplace demographics; witness the surge of biculturals and people of mixed cultural identities entering the global workplace (Brannen & Thomas, 2010). New techniques are needed, such as those that have been shown in other fields to be crucial to understanding identity-based and complex phenomena. As ethnography has been shown to be useful in studying transnational phenomena such as diaspora (Cohen, 1997) and identity construction (Eriksen, 1993), so it can be useful for understanding emergent phenomena in international business.

Crucially, the ethnography was enacted by the company's own managers: traditionally the objects of study rather than its agents. As such, the study was able to obtain complex emic as well as etic perspectives, and also to add value to the study for the organisation by enabling its managers to develop critical, reflexive views of the organisation. Furthermore, the experience encouraged the academic ethnographers to reflect critically on their own role in the development of corporate identity and native categories in business (as advised in Buckley & Chapman, 1997); academic work does not take place in a vacuum, but as part of an ongoing process.

The contributions of the comparative method
In the Tesco case, the comparative method was crucial to the success of the project. The most visible role of comparison was, as discussed, to determine the essence of the company's international and shared practices, which the research team was able to achieve through observing, and critically comparing their observations to their expectations and to the norms at the different Tesco subsidiaries across Asia and with the firm's domestic operations. In doing so, however, the company was also able to consider where the differences lie, with a view to creating an organisation that was simultaneously globally integrated in terms of its shared values, but responsive to local needs between subsidiaries embedded in quite different cultural contexts. The company thus not only has a plan for developing cohesion, but also an understanding of how policy and practice can be successfully transferred across borders without creating unnecessary conflict.

On another level, this method allowed the research team to incorporate and acknowledge the contradictions and complexities within the culture; to allow the company to be united in terms of its basic values, and yet to allow strong differences in how these values are understood and expressed across different branches. This has a clear basis in the structuralist anthropological project to simultaneously understand the underlying similarities between, and the differences in expression within, different human cultures (Holý, 1987). In doing so, the research team was able to achieve an analysis of the sort of complexity that normally requires intensive, longitudinal study by trained academic researchers (e.g., Martin, 1992). The Tesco case thus allows an academic theory of culture to be successfully reapplied in a business environment.

By teaching the research team how to reflect critically on themselves and their observations, the academic team has also ensured that the comparative method can be built into normal international management practice. Managers can understand their organisation better on its local and global levels, and make their decisions and formulate their policies based on this understanding. Furthermore, the implications of this fact are wider than the Tesco case: the basic principle could be implemented by any organisation seeking to develop itself, and to any number of cross-cultural issues, such as post-merger integration (as in Moore, 2011), or the development of a successful expatriate programme which takes the needs of both parent and subsidiary into account, thereby ensuring that conflict and misunderstandings are kept to a minimum.

Furthermore, from a research perspective, the use of the comparative method has linked a practical problem in international HRM into wider research on transnationalism, culture, and organisations. The results of the study have provided greater insight into how a company such as Tesco is able to expand successfully across borders, and what happens to its culture during this process, contributing to the literature on cross-cultural management, integration, and branch–headquarters relations (e.g., Kristensen & Zeitlin, 2004), as well as the literature on the use of language in organisations (e.g., Piekkari & Zander, 2005). The use of the comparative method thus contributes to long-standing theoretical debates in international HRM.

Finally, from a more general research perspective, the comparative method provides a means for researchers to make greater use of qualitative methodologies, due to the fact that it does not focus exclusively on generalisability as an indicator of the value of the results. This can also be seen in the comparative studies discussed, such as Shen et al. (2015) and Beekun et al. (2003). Tesco's experience can be understood not as something that can be generalised out wholesale to all MNEs, but as a narrative which, through comparison and contrast, can allow us to understand the processes through which MNEs expand across borders in both general and specific terms, taking into account the unique nature of the organisation as well as the common experiences of its managers. Further studies seeking a means of developing useful conclusions from qualitative data might be encouraged to consider the comparative method.

CONCLUSIONS

In sum, the Tesco case study demonstrates not only that the anthropological comparative method can be applied successfully to a problem in comparative HRM, but also that doing so provides a number of useful insights for managers, as well as ways for researchers to make better use of qualitative data in research. Comparative HRM can thus improve its theoretical and practical success through adopting an interdisciplinary approach, and considering how techniques from other social sciences can best be applied to issues of managing people and organisations across borders.

REFERENCES

Barnes, R. 1987. Anthropological comparison. In L. Holý (ed.), *Comparative Anthropology*: 119–134. Oxford: Basil Blackwell.
Beekun, R.I., Stedham, Y., Yamamura, J.H., & Barghouti, J.A. 2003. Comparing business ethics in Russia and the US. *International Journal of Human Resource Management*, 14(8): 1333–1349.
Brannen, M.Y. 1994. Your next boss is Japanese: Negotiating cultural change at a Western Massachusetts paper plant. Unpublished doctoral dissertation, University of Massachusetts, Amherst.
Brannen, M.Y. 1998. Negotiated culture in binational contexts: A model of culture change based on a Japanese/ American organizational experience. *Anthropology of Work Review*, 18(2/3), 6–17.
Brannen, M.Y. 2004. When Mickey loses face: Recontextualization, semantic fit, and the semiotics of foreignness. *Academy of Management Review*, 29(4): 593–616.
Brannen, M.Y., Liker, J.K., & Fruin, W.M. 1999. *Recontextualization and Factory-to-Factory Knowledge Transfer from Japan to the United States*. New York: Oxford University Press.
Brannen, M.Y., & Thomas, D.C. 2010. Bicultural individuals in organizations implications and opportunity. *International Journal of Cross Cultural Management*, 10(1): 5–16.
Buckley, P.J., & Chapman, M. 1997. The use of native categories in management research. *British Journal of Management*, 8(4): 283–299.
Burawoy, M. 2013. Ethnographic fallacies: Reflections on labour studies in the era of market fundamentalism. *Work, Employment and Society*, 27(3): 526–536.
Chapman, M. 1997. Social anthropology, business studies, and cultural issues: Preface. *International Studies of Management and Organization*, 26(4): 3–29.
Centre for Information on Language Teaching (CILT). (2005). *Talking to the World*. London: CILT.
Cohen, R. 1997. *Global Diasporas: An Introduction*. Seattle, WA: University of Washington Press.
Durkheim, E., Solovay, S.A., Mueller, J.H., & Catlin, S.G.E.G. 1895 [1938]. *The Rules of Sociological Method – Translated by Sarah A. Solovay and John H. Mueller and Edited by George EG Catlin*. Glencoe, IL and New York, NY: Free Press.
Ellis, C.S., & Bochner, A. 2000. Autoethnography, personal narrative, reflexivity: Researcher as subject. In N.K. Denzin, and Y.S. Lincoln (eds), *Handbook of Qualitative Research* (2nd edn): 733–768. Thousand Oaks, CA: SAGE.
Eriksen, T.H. 1993. *Ethnicity and Nationalism: Anthropological Perspectives*. London: Pluto Press.
Evans-Pritchard, E.E. (1963). *The Comparative Method in Social Anthropology*, Vol. 33. London: Athlone Press.
Furusawa, M., & Brewster, C. 2015. The bi-cultural option for global talent management: The Japanese/ Brazilian 'Nikkeijin' example. *Journal of World Business*, 50(1): 133–143.
Ghauri, P.N., & Grønhaug, K. 2005. *Research Methods in Business Studies: A Practical Guide*. London: Pearson Education.
Harzing, A.-W., Köster, K., & Magner, U. 2011. Babel in business: The language barrier and its solutions in the HQ–subsidiary relationship. *Journal of World Business*, 46(3): 279–287.
Henrich, J., Heine, S.J., & Norenzayan, A. 2010. The weirdest people in the world?. *Behaviour and Brain Sciences*, 33(2/3): 61–83.
Holý, L. 1987. Introduction. Description, generalization and comparison: Two paradigms. In L. Holý (ed.), *Comparative Anthropology*: 1–21. Oxford: Basil Blackwell.
Kim, Y., Bae, J., & Yu, G.-C. 2013. Patterns and determinants of human resource management change in Korean venture firms after the financial crisis. *International Journal of Human Resource Management*, 24(5): 1006–1028.
Kristensen, P.H., & Zeitlin, J. 2004. *Local Players in Global Games: The Strategic Constitution of a Multinational Corporation*. Oxford: Oxford University Press.
Kubota, R. 2011. Questioning linguistic instrumentalism: English, neoliberalism, and language tests in Japan. *Linguistics and Education*, 22(3): 248–260.
Lévi-Strauss, C. 1969. *The Elementary Structures of Kinship*. Translated from the French by James Harle Bell, John Richard Von Sturmer, and Rodney Needham. New York: Beacon Press.
Martin, J. 1992. *Cultures in Organizations: Three Perspectives*. Oxford: Oxford University Press.

Moore, F. 2011. Holistic ethnography: Studying the impact of multiple national identities on post-acquisition organizations. *Journal of International Business Studies*, 42(5): 654–671.

Murakami, T. 1998. The formation of teams: A British and German comparison. *International Journal of Human Resource Management*, 9(5): 800–817.

Needham, R. 1973. Introduction. In R. Needham (ed.), *Right and Left: Essays on Dual Symbolic Classification*: i–xxxvii. Chicago, IL: University of Chicago Press.

Neeley, T.B. 2013. Language matters: Status loss and achieved status distinctions in global organizations. *Organization Science*, 24(2): 476–497.

Peel, J.D. 1987. History, culture and the comparative method: A West African puzzle. In L. Holy (ed.), *Comparative Anthropology*: 88–118. Oxford: Basil Blackwell.

Piekkari, R., Welch, C., & Paavilainen, E. 2009. The case study as disciplinary convention: Evidence from international business journals. *Organizational Research Methods*, 12: 567–589.

Piekkari, R., & Zander, L. 2005. Preface: Language and communication in international management. *International Studies of Management and Organization*, 35(1): 3–9.

Pieper, R. 1990. *Human Resource Management: An International Comparison*. New York: Walter de Gruyter.

Radcliffe-Brown, A.R. 1951. The comparative method in social anthropology. *Journal of the Royal Anthropological Institute*, 81, 15–22.

Sackmann, S.A., & Phillips, M.E. (2004). Contextual influences on culture research: shifting assumptions for new workplace realities. *International Journal of Cross Cultural Management*, 4(3), 370–390.

Schaaper, J., Amann, B., Jaussaud, J., et al. 2013. Human resource management in Asian subsidiaries: Comparison of French and Japanese MNCs. *International Journal of Human Resource Management*, 24(7): 1454–1470.

Schein, E.H. 1985. *Organisational Culture and Leadership: A Dynamic View*. San Francisco, CA: Jossey-Bass.

Shen, Y., Demel, B., Unite, J., et al. 2015. Career success across 11 countries: Implications for international human resource management. *International Journal of Human Resource Management*, 26(13): 1753–1778.

Smith, G.E. 1928. *In the Beginning: The Origin of Civilization*. New York: William Morrow & Company.

Templer, A.J., Hofmeyr, K.B., & Rall, J.J. 1997. An international comparison of human resource management objectives and activities. *International Journal of Human Resource Management*, 8(4): 550–562.

Tesco. 2012. Annual Review. www.tescoplc.com, accessed August 2015.

Weber, M. 1968. *Economy and Society*. Edited by Guenther Roth and Claus Wittich. New York: Bedminster.

PART II

HRM TASKS AND THEMES

7. Recruitment and selection in context
Elaine Farndale, Irene Nikandrou, and
Leda Panayotopoulou

INTRODUCTION

The process of recruitment and selection is a crucial one, as ensuring the right people to join the workforce helps the organisation to meet its short- and long-term objectives. Indeed, both human resource and line managers around the world agree that selecting the right person to fill a job vacancy is an important factor contributing to organisational effectiveness. For the organisation, recruitment and selection imply long-term commitment to a decision that may have a considerable impact on its operations.

The context in which organisations operate, however, is changing the role and process of recruitment and selection. Demographic changes and growing globalisation have led to changes in labour markets characterised by a diversified workforce, raising issues of fairness and equal opportunities in the selection process (Cohen-Charash & Spector, 2001). Moreover, the demand for a more flexible, multiskilled labour force and the emphasis on teamwork has led to the adoption of a 'social process' or 'exchange' model that emphasises the fit of the person with 'the team or organisation' (Newell, 2005).

In brief, recruitment and selection is a two-way decision-making process. The organisation seeks, assesses, and decides to make an offer of employment to the candidate, while at the same time the candidate decides whether to apply and enter into an employment relationship with the organisation. Thus, the whole process involves issues of power, politics, ethics, diversity, and equal opportunity, as well as knowledge and skills (Iles, 2007).

In this chapter, we focus on highlighting commonalities within nations to present a cross-national comparison of recruitment and selection practices. It is worth emphasising, however, that differences exist among organisations in the same countries, reinforcing the importance of managerial choice and the impact of organisational fit decisions. For example, a significant difference has been noted between the manufacturing and service sectors in India: the former relying on more direct applicants, recruitment agencies, and interviews; and the latter using advertisements, websites, and selection tests (Kundu et al., 2012). Within the Indian manufacturing sector there are also differences between public and private sector organisations, with public sector firms more likely to use formal rather than informal recruitment methods (Absar, 2012). Across the globe, differences can be found in recruitment and selection practices within the same organisation for employees at different levels, or between core and peripheral workforce members. Similarly, it is unlikely that small organisations will have the same range of resources available for recruitment and selection activities as large multinational corporations (MNCs).

In this chapter, we review extant literature on recruitment and selection practices, examining how they relate, interact, and are influenced by their context. Intense competition, changing demands, speed, flexibility, and adaptability, all combined with cost, are forces that demand a deep understanding in order to define and implement adequate recruitment and selection strategies and practices. Both institutional factors and cultural contingencies affect the why and the how of recruitment and selection (Aycan, 2005). In exploring contextual determinants of recruitment and selection, we focus our attention particularly on these national-level factors.

RECRUITMENT AND SELECTION METHODS AND CRITERIA

With increasing emphasis on human capital as an important source of competitive advantage (Hatch & Dyer, 2004), organisations have developed systematic approaches to recruitment and selection. We will explore some of these approaches in detail here. However, before we do so, it is important to acknowledge that although many organisations (particularly those that are large) are implementing these rigorous systems, perhaps the majority of organisations worldwide actually rely on very loose mechanisms to bring in individuals. Word-of-mouth or employee referrals are quick, cost-effective, and relatively easy mechanisms for recruitment when compared with complex assessment centre or psychological testing approaches. We discuss the advantages and disadvantages of some of these informal mechanisms, alongside the more formalised approaches to recruitment and selection, below.

To start this discussion, we first need to clarify definitions, as 'recruitment' and 'selection' are terms that are often (incorrectly) used interchangeably. Recruitment focuses on using various mechanisms to communicate with and attract appropriate people to fill vacancies, while selection entails the process of applying relevant assessment criteria to decide who to actually appoint. Prior to these two stages, organisations adopting a systematic approach have probably been through a process of deciding the type of vacancy that exists, and the competencies that will be required for it to be filled successfully. Finally, there comes the decision of who is to be involved in the process and the level of centralisation of decision-making.

Recruitment Methods

Some of the most common methods used for recruitment include informal personal contacts, advertisements, electronic recruitment via websites, formal personal contacts (such as careers fairs and open days), and external assistance (such as employment agencies and head hunters). Recruitment methods can be distinguished along two dimensions: (1) level of formality; and (2) internal versus external orientation. Research has established that recruitment methods are related to turnover and employee morale (e.g., Earnest et al., 2011). Informal recruitment through existing employees can reduce both voluntary and involuntary turnover due to the fact that candidates have more realistic information about the job and the organisation. Moreover, even though organisations may use a variety of recruitment methods for different employee levels, internal recruitment appears to be preferred, as it is cost-effective and contributes to the improvement of the quality of the internal labour market (DeVaro & Morita, 2013). Increased career opportunities, skills updating and recognition through promotion create a positive organisational climate and improved morale with motivated employees.

Table 7.1   Percentage of organisations across a selection of countries using a range of recruitment methods (Cranet, 2009/10)

	Denmark	France	Germany	Greece	Sweden	UK	Japan	USA
Recruiting managers:								
Internal	66.7	67.9	69.5	77.0	48.9	92.8	96.3	91.9
Recruitment agency	56.4	60.3	70.7	61.2	51.8	80.9	28.1	69.7
Word of mouth	27.8	20.5	27.1	44.1	17.4	63.9	13.2	86.7
Own website	45.9	35.9	46.4	40.4	45.7	74.3	17.8	83.0
Commercial website	41.2	48.1	30.7	45.3	21.3	66.3	12.4	75.9
Speculative applications	9.6	43.6	24.1	25.0	1.1	29.9	16.3	19.5
Recruiting professionals:								
Internal	47.7	66.7	54.8	56.2	27.3	90.8	86.8	90.7
Recruitment agency	40.6	36.1	38.6	28.1	20.2	83.4	51.8	61.0
Word of mouth	43.0	17.0	44.9	54.4	18.4	67.3	28.6	90.5
Own website	64.9	38.1	82.5	44.2	55.7	78.0	66.1	88.3
Commercial website	55.8	46.3	57.3	54.7	29.4	71.1	50.3	81.8
Speculative applications	25.4	55.1	60.9	41.7	9.9	38.6	50.7	32.4
Recruiting manual staff:								
Internal	28.1	76.7	30.8	29.8	30.1	76.1	78.8	68.6
Recruitment agency	8.5	54.0	1.6	5.8	2.1	49.2	27.2	15.8
Word of mouth	55.8	47.1	50.3	52.8	28.0	71.5	31.4	75.1
Own website	47.4	53.3	38.3	24.5	41.8	66.4	55.4	71.2
Commercial website	37.7	51.2	19.7	26.3	11.0	50.8	45.2	47.5
Speculative applications	39.8	91.4	45.6	44.0	27.3	57.1	51.5	54.3

Based on data collected through the Cranet project (involving academic institutions worldwide, gathering data on human resource management policies and practices at country level: see Parry et al., 2013), Table 7.1 illustrates the percentage of organisations per country using the various recruitment methods for different grades of employee.

As Table 7.1 demonstrates, there is considerable variation between countries and across grades of employee in the different methods used to attract talent. Internal recruitment shows evidence of being a preferred approach, particularly for managerial grades, although Sweden is an exception among the countries studied here, as less than half (48.9 per cent) of organisations there use this practice. Informal word-of-mouth practices are used particularly in the United Kingdom (UK) (92.8 per cent, 90.8 per cent, 76.1 per cent) and United States of America (USA) (91.9 per cent, 90.7 per cent, 68.6 per cent) for all grades of employee (managerial, professional, manual, respectively). Speculative applications appear to be most popular in France for manual staff (91.4 per cent of organisations) and in Germany for professionals (60.9 per cent); whereas in Sweden, for example, only 1.1 per cent of organisations use speculative applications for managerial positions.

Selection Methods

Selection processes often involve a combination of several methods determined by a number of factors: the available time to fill the position, cost, custom and practice, accuracy, acceptability and appropriateness of the methods, the abilities that human resource management (HRM) and the line managers involved bring to the process, criteria for the position to be filled, and level of vacancy. The question this raises is whether some selection practices are more commonly used in given contexts than in others.

A popular method across contexts is interviewing, closely followed by the use of application forms for gathering standard information. Other practices, such as references from former employers, work sampling, and graphology, are used more specifically only in certain country contexts. Across the range of available methods, a distinction can be made between 'subjective' and 'objective' selection. Objective selection methods – that is, those that are claimed to be replicable due to their use of data upon which to base judgements (Schmidt & Hunter, 2004) – such as the use of psychometric testing as a selection tool, are generally growing, especially for managerial employees, as they become more readily available (Torrington et al., 2002). Such tests claim to help to identify and match the 'right' people to the 'right' jobs, stressing the importance of 'person–job' fit through objective measures. More subjective measures are those associated with an increased potential level of bias due to the more personal level of assessment, such as interviews (particularly one-on-one) and references (Purkiss et al., 2006).

Based on Cranet project data (2009/10), Table 7.2 illustrates how the proportion of organisations in different countries varies for the use of a range of selection methods.

Table 7.2   *Percentage of organisations across a selection of countries using a range of selection methods (Cranet, 2009/10)*

	Denmark	France	Germany	Greece	Sweden	UK	Japan	USA
Selecting managers:								
Interview panels	83.9	17.6	77.1	62.9	48.9	88.1	8.6	80.4
One-on-one interviews	39.5	98.7	72.0	82.5	80.5	71.1	69.9	92.9
Application forms	21.3	61.4	32.5	41.6	40.4	67.6	61.4	88.6
Psychometric tests	70.5	14.4	14.0	25.9	64.9	60.0	20.3	14.6
Assessment centres	9.4	7.8	41.1	16.3	13.1	32.5	6.9	14.3
References	81.9	52.3	68.8	67.5	90.1	91.3	12.0	98.4
Selecting professionals:								
Interview panels	78.2	7.6	69.8	53.1	33.3	86.6	20.9	76.4
One-on-one interviews	44.4	97.9	73.2	80.4	78.0	74.4	88.3	91.0
Application forms	21.9	59.3	41.4	48.5	39.4	76.7	85.7	91.0
Psychometric tests	54.3	9.0	10.4	24.6	30.9	48.4	32.5	13.6
Assessment centres	4.1	2.1	31.6	15.5	3.5	31.1	9.1	12.2
References	71.2	42.8	51.3	62.6	85.5	89.1	11.6	96.8
Selecting manual staff:								
Interview panels	45.6	15.0	18.3	14.4	11.7	52.8	27.8	33.9
One-on-one interviews	50.9	99.1	46.4	60.1	69.1	66.1	84.5	75.7
Application forms	31.6	72.6	39.7	52.6	35.8	81.2	81.4	84.5
Psychometric tests	14.0	21.4	1.2	4.6	2.5	14.8	29.4	6.0
Assessment centres	0.6	2.6	1.9	2.6	0.4	9.5	6.2	7.7
References	41.8	60.4	17.5	42.8	63.1	80.6	7.9	78.9

Looking across the different countries, large variations in the use of each practice for the different employees can be observed. For selecting managers, 17.6 per cent of organisations in France use interview panels, whereas 88.1 per cent or organisations in the UK use this method. Similarly, application forms are used by 21.3 per cent of organisations in Denmark, compared to 88.6 per cent in the USA. References are barely used for any grade of employee in Japan (7.9 to 12.0 per cent of organisations report using this practice), whereas they are used by almost all organisations in the USA for managerial and professional appointments in particular. There is also some commonality across countries, such as the low use of assessment centres for manual staff (0.4 per cent of organisations in Sweden, to 9.5 per cent in the UK reporting using this practice), probably due to cost considerations. Assessment centres are primarily used for managerial or professional staff, respectively, particularly in Germany (41.1 per cent, 31.6 per cent) and the UK (32.5 per cent, 31.1 per cent).

Selection Criteria

Hiring criteria should be closely aligned with job requirements, while being consistent with long-term organisational goals and strategies of the firm to ensure person–organisation fit (Werbel & DeMarie, 2005). The question is whether there are some universally desirable selection criteria that can be used for recruiting new employees in any organisational setting.

A first distinction can be made between 'hard' and 'soft' criteria (Aycan, 2005). Hard criteria include such aspects as technical competence, job-related knowledge, and cognitive skills. The evaluation of technical skills has two aspects: ability and potential (Huo et al., 2002). In other words, are job candidates able to do the job, or do they have the potential to meet the technical requirements? This question reflects, in part, the difference between 'jobs' and 'careers'. The former assumes that jobs can be clearly defined and that specific skills exist to fit them, while the latter points at the unpredictability of the nature of the person's career in the future (Schneider, 1988). Soft criteria are human relational, social, and interpersonal skills. Huo et al. (2002) make a further distinction of the job candidate's social calibre on the basis of interpersonal or inter-organisational skills. The former is assessed by the person's ability to get along with other organisational members, and their level of fit with the company's values and culture. The latter refers to the candidate's connections to internal or external constituencies.

A second distinction, relevant to the nature of the skills acquired by the national educational system, is that between 'specialists' and 'generalists' (Segalla et al., 2001). Specialists are individuals with highly technical, narrowly focused skills that make functional mobility more difficult; while generalists may have received a broader educational base.

Finally, there is the distinction between 'doing' and 'being', or 'active' versus 'passive' (Schneider, 1988). This means that selection can be based either on achievement and concrete results, or on who the person is or knows, based on characteristics such as socio-economic background, ascribed status, family ties, school, and birthplace (Aycan, 2005).

The relevance of these distinctions becomes clear as we explore selection activities in different organisational contexts. Organisations in one context are perhaps more likely to support a soft criteria, generalist, passive approach; whereas others in a different context may find a hard criteria, specialist, active approach more effective for selecting the right candidate.

CONTEXT

As Chapter 1 in this volume has highlighted, the contextualist paradigm argues that an understanding of the contextual factors contributing to a distinctive form of HRM is essential when comparing one country with another (Gooderham & Nordhaug, 2011). The concept of fit, when applied to recruitment and selection practices, assumes that their effectiveness will be context-specific. In other words, in order for recruitment and selection to be effective, organisations need to implement practices that are considered legitimate in their operating environment, aligning with socio-cultural values and institutional factors, such as education systems, labour markets, legal environments, and industry, sector, or stakeholder interests such as unions, professional bodies, and work councils (Ignjatović & Svetlik, 2003).

There are four types of 'fit' related to HRM that can be applied to recruitment and selection practices. First is horizontal or internal fit (Becker & Gerhart, 1996): within the HRM system, the various practices should complement each other to promote the same outcomes (Wright, 1998). Second is vertical or strategic fit: for HRM to be effective, it must add value to the organisation's key resource – that is, the human factor – by aligning employee perceptions and behaviours to business strategy (Boxall & Purcell, 2011). Third is organisational fit (Wood, 1999): this emphasises how HRM practices support other organisational systems (operations, finance, marketing, and so on). This has been referred to as organisational fit. Finally is 'environmental fit' (Wood, 1999): this is the fit between HRM and the organisation's external institutional environment, and is particularly relevant in cross-national comparisons of HRM. We relate these four types of fit to HRM systems in organisations, with a particular emphasis on recruitment and selection activities.

Horizontal Fit

By examining the internal fit among the HRM practices one can understand the logic of the HRM system. The unique bundles of HRM practices that an organisation possesses contribute to the creation of a sustainable competitive advantage (Paauwe & Boselie, 2005). The selection of the right people to join the organisation, the accumulation and the development of the human capital, can be a basis for creating a largely inimitable competitive advantage (Campbell et al., 2012).

A well-known distinction in HRM philosophy concerns the 'buy' or 'make' orientation (Miles & Snow, 1978) that incorporates the notion of HRM bundles, pointing to the need for consistency between all HRM practices. Organisations adopting the 'buy' orientation turn to the external labour market as a source of employees, generally compensate them on a performance basis, and provide minimum attention or commitment to training and career development. Wages, benefits, and labour fluctuation are determined by market pressures. On the other hand, the ideal-type 'make' orientation uses external recruitment only at the entry level, emphasises training and career development, and assesses and rewards performance based on internal rather than market criteria. Behaviour and process are important, and employees are expected to show loyalty and remain with the organisation for a long time. These are, of course, ideal types and most organisations will in practice use different orientations for different groups within their employment.

Sonnenfeld and Peiperl (1988) proposed a typology of career systems based on resourcing and assignment flow. They argue that organisations may focus either on the internal or the external market to identify the right people. Those organisations that rely on the internal market view people as assets with long-term development value. On the other hand, organisations may allocate new tasks based either on the individual contribution to performance or on group contribution. Organisations that reward individual contribution expect individuals to add value on a continuous basis, whereas those that emphasise group contribution view employees as having extrinsic value.

A typical example of horizontal fit that starts from critical recruitment and selection practices, is lifetime employment, a distinct feature of the twentieth-century Japanese HRM system. Lifetime employment is not a contract, but a particular way of thinking that makes employees devote themselves to the organisation and stay there until their retirement. Equally, the firm does not terminate the employment lightly. It provides a long socialisation process, continuous training, skills updating in cases of restructuring, internal career paths, seniority-based promotions, and skill-grade pay assisted by broadly designed job classifications that encourage long-term learning (Koen, 2005). Therefore, an important selection criterion used by Japanese firms is 'trainability', the ability to learn, rather than the ability to execute duties (Huo et al., 2002).

Vertical Fit

HRM is a source of organisational competence and competitive advantage (Hatch & Dyer, 2004), and thus needs to be fully integrated into corporate strategy (Buller & McEvoy, 2012). The rationale for this linkage was first developed by Schuler and Jackson (1987), arguing that, in order to perform a specific task, employees need certain technical knowledge, skills, and abilities, but also certain role behaviours stemming from the social environment in which they work. There are likely to be major differences in these required role behaviours across different corporate strategies, as they require different necessary organisational conditions for their implementation. In addition, resourcing should consider what skills, aptitudes, and behavioural styles are most compatible with future organisational objectives and directions (Olian & Rynes, 1984).

Schuler and Jackson's (1987) seminal work developed six HRM practice 'menus' that concern different aspects of HRM and together define how HRM practices link with strategy. Each menu runs along a continuum, and different choices stimulate and reinforce different role behaviours. The recruitment and selection – or staffing choice, as they name it – involves selecting between internal or external recruitment sources, narrow or broad paths, single or multiple ladders, explicit or implicit criteria, limited or extensive socialisation, and closed or open procedures. The authors, however, now acknowledge that this 'menu' view of HRM was too simple, and in reality the link between staffing practices (as well as other areas of HRM) and strategy involves many more contextual factors, both internal and external to the organisation (Schuler & Jackson, 2014).

One study in particular (Bowen et al., 2002) emphasises this importance of context, focusing on the relevance of national context to vertical fit. This research revealed slight geographical differences across ten countries. More specifically, the authors studied three types of organisational strategy and their links to various HRM practices, including selection criteria. They found HRM practices to be strongly linked to cost leadership strategy in Korea and China; to differentiation strategy in China, Japan, and Indonesia; and to organisational capability in the Anglo-Saxon countries (Australia, Canada, USA). These results imply a cultural effect on vertical fit.

Organisational Fit

The organisational level of analysis emphasises how HRM practices support other organisational systems (Wood, 1999). For example, recruitment and selection practices vary according to the life cycle stage of the organisation, whereby recruitment is most problematic in no-growth firms, whereas low-growth firms do not report recruitment as a challenge (Rutherford et al., 2003).

Size also matters: the larger the organisation, the more complex its management, and the greater the need for rules and formalised procedures (McEvoy & Buller, 2013). Large organisations are most likely to have structured HRM departments that emphasise formal and objective recruitment and selection methods. In small organisations, HRM departments may not even exist, and informal and subjective channels and methods of recruitment and selection may be used. Moreover, the financial position and constraints of an organisation will influence both the number and quality of recruitment and selection methods available for use (Beardwell et al., 2004: 201). In countries with a high percentage of small and medium-sized enterprises (SMEs), such as Greece and Cyprus, there is a major impact of the founder or owner of the firm in recruitment and selection decision-making, leading recruitment to rely to a large extent on family, friends, and personal referrals (Stavrou-Costea & Manson, 2006). Similarly, Spanish managers indicate that having the qualities to handle SMEs is the second most important criterion when hiring international managers (Segalla et al., 2001).

Trade unions may not affect the way firms recruit and select employees directly, but they can affect choices about staffing practices and the extent of use of specific recruitment and selection methods. Although there are limited studies examining the impact of unionism on recruitment and selection practices, Gill and Meyer (2013) highlight reduced costs of recruitment when unions are present, due to lower levels of employee withdrawal. In particular, they highlight that unions facilitate the introduction of high-performance work practices, especially when employee relations in the organisation are positive.

Such thinking is based on the arguments of Freeman and Medoff (1983), that it is the economic effects of unionism that affect organisational recruitment and selection practices through wage effects and voice effects. They argue that as unions push for higher wages, higher-quality applicants are attracted. This, in turn, pushes companies to identify superior workers to offset the effect of higher wages through productivity gains. Moreover, unions provide employees with a voice mechanism to express their dissatisfaction and concerns while, at the same time, demanding more job security and better working conditions from companies, which leads to reduced turnover and increased tenure. In addition, unionism requires management to 'share' authority with non-management employees. Thus, the union voice effect impacts upon hiring practices by making dismissal more costly. At the same time, HRM specialists need to adopt more sophisticated selection methods to identify superior applicants, as it is more difficult and expensive to dismiss less-satisfactory employees once they are hired. For example, in a study conducted in the USA, Koch and Hundley (1997) found that there is strong evidence that unionisation is associated with decreased use of recruitment sources. As unionism contributes to higher wages, jobs become more attractive, thus increasing the supply of applicants and reducing the need for costly recruitment methods. Of course, when examining the effect of unionism on recruitment and selection practices, for comparative purposes, we need to examine the structure and the nature of employee relations in each country and how they affect wages and working conditions.

Environmental Fit

National culture
National culture is the set of collective beliefs and values that distinguish people of one nationality from those of another (Hofstede, 1991; House et al., 2004), and is considered an important factor in the differentiation of HRM across countries (see, e.g. Stone & Stone-Romero, 2012; see also Chapter 3 in this volume). National culture is incorporated in various HRM models as affecting the formation of HRM practices (Lawler et al., 2008). Some authors argue that national culture affects some aspects of organisational practices more than others, for example those aspects of management practices that involve human interactions with one another (Tayeb, 1998). Tayeb (1995) also suggests that while the 'what' question in HRM might be universal, the 'how' question is culture-specific. For instance, as a practice, employee recruitment might be universal, but the degree of reliance on e-recruitment versus more traditional recruitment methods is very likely to be attributable at least in part to national culture.

National culture influences multiple aspects of the recruitment and selection process (Aycan, 2005; Huo et al., 2002). First, it affects the criteria used for selecting employees. Interpersonal criteria are more relevant in cultures that are collectivistic, low on performance orientation and high on femininity; while 'hard' criteria such as knowledge, skills, and abilities are more common in cultures that are high on performance orientation (Aycan, 2005). For example, selection criteria widely adopted in the USA (high performance orientation) include a person's ability to perform the technical requirements of a job, and proven work experience in a similar job (Huo et al., 2002). In Japan and Taiwan (high collectivism societies), getting along with others is extremely important (Huo et al., 2002). Budhwar and Khatri (2001) suggest that collectivistic and high power distance countries, such as India, tend to place greater importance on criteria such as ascribed status and socio-political connections. With regard to 'generalists' and 'specialists', the match between a specialised position and the capacities of a specialised person is valued in the USA and Germany (Koen, 2005); whereas the Italians, the British, and the French tend to choose candidates with a generalist educational background (Segalla et al., 2001); and the Dutch assess a mix of generalist and specialist characteristics (Koen, 2005).

Second, national culture affects the choice of methods used for both recruitment and selection. Internal recruitment is preferred in cultures with high uncertainty avoidance, as they tend to maintain the status quo (Aycan, 2005). Also, in collectivistic cultures, the limited use of external recruitment sources is due to the fact that it is difficult for externally recruited candidates to become part of strong social networks and cope with the resistance following their appointment, especially in cases where an internal candidate is supported (Björkman & Lu, 1999). In highly collectivistic cultures, employees are highly committed to their organisation, and ready to make personal sacrifices to fulfil their obligations, while organisations take responsibility for employee welfare (Gelfand et al., 2004). Thus, internal recruitment methods are more likely to be employed. Past studies have shown positive relationships between in-group collectivism and word-of-mouth recruitment (Lee, 1999), especially since this method of recruitment is believed to increase commitment and loyalty (Bian & Ang, 1997). Budhwar and Khatri (2001) argue that internal recruitment promotes loyalty to the organisation. Moreover, in highly human-oriented societies the need for belonging and affiliation motivates people, which promotes internal recruitment (Kabasakal & Bodur, 2004).

Cultures that are collectivistic, uncertainty-avoidant and oriented toward ascribed status tend to adopt informal and network-based recruitment channels and methods; whereas in cultures high on universalism or performance orientation, recruitment is more formal, structured, and widespread (Aycan, 2005). Thus, in low performance-oriented cultures where societal and family relationships are valued, it is more common for organisations to adopt informal recruitment methods (Javidan, 2004). Societies that are high on uncertainty avoidance tend to rely on formalised policies and procedures and thus adopt more formal recruitment methods (ibid.).

Regarding selection, different methods are used to varying degrees across countries, which can be partly attributed to differences in national culture. For example, there is a higher use of interview panels in cultures that are high on future orientation, performance orientation, or uncertainty avoidance (Papalexandris & Panayotopoulou, 2004). In Korea, the participation of several executives in the interview process is a means of assessing the applicant's potential for working in harmony and becoming part of a team (Lee, 1999). Psychometric testing is avoided in some cultures such as France, as it can be considered offensive in violating the candidate's privacy (Steiner & Gilliland, 1996). France previously had the particularity of using graphology as a selection tool to a larger extent than any other European country (Buyens et al., 2004), though this has reduced sharply in recent years. The assessment centre as a selection technique has varying cross-cultural validity and utility because cultural context determines what constitutes good performance (Briscoe, 1997). So, while very popular in North America, assessment centres are rarely used in Denmark, Finland, Norway, and Sweden (Lindeberg & Vanhala, 2004; Rogaczewska et al., 2004). In general, according to Aycan (2005), in cultures that are high on performance orientation or universalism, selection methods are standardised and job-specific; whereas they are more broad-ranging and rely on face-to-face interactions in cultures high on particularism or femininity.

Institutional factors

Complementing the focus on national values and beliefs, the employment infrastructure within different countries can also affect the recruitment and selection process. Socio-economic factors such as unemployment rates can determine the extent to which candidates are motivated to be offered a new position. From the applicant's perspective, the extent to which self-presentational conduct is necessary – that is, presenting oneself in a favourable light in order to create a good impression – has been found to be much lower in some European countries than in the USA, for example (König et al., 2011).

When organisations turn to the external labour market for recruitment, they need to be aware of factors such as the competency, age, and gender profiles existing in the market. Unemployment rates influence the availability of competencies and increase the number of potential recruits. In former socialist countries, the state system provided for full employment, which created problems of high unemployment during the transition to more competitive market conditions. Recruitment and selection is therefore a mechanism for meeting societal as well as economic needs. Svetlik and Alas (2006) report that new European Union (EU) countries, such as Bulgaria, Cyprus, the Czech Republic, and Estonia, use more informal channels for recruiting managers than longer-term EU countries. They offer three possible reasons to explain this. First, the organisational culture in the majority of new EU countries favours informality; second, the labour market mechanisms are less developed in these countries; and third, the relatively small size of these countries allows informal networks to have a greater role in shaping the labour market.

Some countries have very specific local recruitment traditions related to internal and external labour markets. For example, *blat* (the practice of recruitment via personal social networks rather than through formal procedures) is very popular in the Central and Eastern European transition economies, whereas such activities are conceived as nepotism in other cultures (Onoshchenko & Williams, 2014). In particular, smaller organisations prefer these informal, word-of-mouth recruitment methods compared with larger organisations (Zaharie & Osoian, 2013). Similar processes known as *guanxi* in China, *wasta* in the Middle East, *vartan bhanji* in Pakistan, and *sociolismo* in Cuba (Saher & Mayrhofer, 2014) are used, relying heavily on personal connections to find candidates (Aladwan et al., 2014). These methods generally result in smaller applicant pools, but more detailed candidate information. Challenges of such informal recruitment processes, however, have been noted: in Italy, those employees recruited informally receive lower wages, and have a greater disparity between actual skills and those required for the job (Meliciani & Radicchia, 2011). Nevertheless, organisations in China, for example, are keen proponents of the use of network-based recruiting processes, which is perceived as quick and resulting in high-quality candidates (Han & Han, 2009).

The availability of required skills in the labour market is influenced by national education systems. Ashton et al. (2000) suggest that to understand the process of skill formation one has to study the underlying relationships between the state, in the form of the political elite; the apparatus of state, the education and training systems that deliver skills; capital in the form of employers through which the demand for skills arise; and workers in the form of employees and their organisations that influence the supply of skills. These educational systems have been found to influence the choice of recruitment methods. For example, in France the educational elite system of the *grandes écoles* provides organisations with a prestigious source of new managerial blood, thus limiting the use of internal recruitment for junior managers (Buyens et al., 2004). The educational systems also influence the selection criteria applied. In some contexts it is more important to evaluate the candidates' potential to do a good job rather than their technical skills. In Japan the state focuses on the provision of academic education, leading organisations to recruit talented generalists and to invest in training them for a wide array of responsibilities (Huo et al., 2002). Likewise, the German system of initial vocational training is standardised, rendering it less important for organisations to test the technical knowledge of employees holding such qualifications (Koen, 2005).

Countries also vary in the extent to which their education system is more focused on vocational or academic programmes. Germany is a typical example of a country with a strong vocational education system, where preferred job candidates are those who have received practical training whilst completing their advanced vocational degrees (Hippach-Schneider et al., 2013). In Japan, there is a similar focus on ensuring students can successfully enter the workplace when they graduate, with a preference for professional over academic skills (Pilz et al., 2015). Japan also has a preference for hiring college graduates rather than mid-career professionals, while US firms place greater emphasis on work experience than education status (Huo et al., 2002).

The level of dynamism in the environment influences the degree of formalisation of selection criteria, with organisations operating in a stable environment often clearly articulating the types and levels of qualifications required of job applicants, as opposed to firms operating in a more dynamic environment (Olian & Rynes, 1984). Moreover, innovation, dynamism, and the need for multi-experiences may force organisations to emphasise external recruitment to fill their vacancies (Heraty & Morley, 1998). Atterbury et al. (2004) note a trend towards the use of external sources in the UK and Ireland which, they argue, may reflect the growing pressures for innovation which push organisations to attract 'new' people externally. Related to innovation, the internet and advances in technology are affecting the type of labour demanded, while at the same time providing a new channel for recruitment and selection. Huo et al. (2002) argue that the spread of the internet has contributed to an accelerated convergence in recruiting practices. Furthermore, e-recruitment is increasingly popular, largely driven by the social pressures of the labour market (Holm, 2014).

Another aspect of external context likely to influence the level of formality is market growth. Market growth increases competitive intensity, which forces organisations to give greater emphasis to creating sustained competitive advantage. Market growth has been found to be related to the degree to which organisations define higher levels of formalisation and systematisation of corporate strategies (Cunha et al., 2003), whereby organisations that operate in growing markets are expected to emphasise the systematic analysis of the labour market and formalisation of recruitment methods.

National-level legislation plays a significant role in the recruitment and selection process by creating boundaries within which organisations must operate, even though they are free to choose the people they want to recruit. In many countries, legislation provides the framework for protecting employees against discrimination on grounds of gender, race, or disability (see also Chapter 16 in this volume). These rules vary between countries, however, so that the rules governing non-discrimination in the USA in relation to affirmative action might be illegal in Europe, which requires that each selection decision must be non-discriminatory in its own right.

Finally, there is the impact of MNCs on the adoption of recruitment and selection practices, which reveals evidence of home country practices being exported to host countries. For example, Pudelko and Harzing (2007) found that US MNC subsidiaries are localising their HRM practices in Japan and Germany, although this localisation seems set to decrease in the future; subsidiaries of Japanese MNCs tend to abandon traditional Japanese HRM practices and move toward US practices; German subsidiaries tend to adopt US practices, while they are unwilling to adapt to the Japanese host practices. In less-developed nations, Western MNCs have been found to apply more rigorous recruitment and selection processes (including less discrimination and nepotism) than domestic firms, preferring to focus on the external labour market (Daspro, 2009; Forstenlechner et al., 2012; Mohamed et al., 2013). This may result over time in domestic firms copying

MNC practices, shifting the focus of local priorities. Ultimately, however, isomorphic behaviour is reliant on the skills of local practitioners to carry out potentially more advanced practices. Organisations in the Czech Republic and Bulgaria, for example, have been found not to use modern selection methods due to inadequate competence and professional capacity in recruitment and selection (Koubek & Vatchkova, 2004).

CONCLUSIONS

The analysis presented here has important implications for both practitioners and academics. We have identified context-specific factors affecting recruitment and selection across nations. Across all countries, however, cost considerations are extremely important to organisations when deciding on appropriate recruitment and selection activities. Many organisations prefer to use low-cost options, and take the risk of using less valid techniques with potentially higher costs incurred over the longer term (Zaharie & Osoian, 2013). In some professions, however, investment in more reliable processes is preferred. In nursing in the UK, for example, hospitals are keen to guarantee high-quality hires, and thus make more use of expensive combined evaluation tools and assessment centres (Newton et al., 2015).

As highlighted in the introduction, our emphasis here has been on generalising within countries in order to make cross-national comparisons. This limits the focus on differences within countries, especially between organisations of different size or operating in different sectors, but highlights the importance of 'fit'. Future research should continue to study both the differences and similarities found within and between organisations and nations in terms of recruitment and selection activities. In doing so, research should take into account the multiple levels of fit to understand better the recruitment and selection process. In particular, future research could benefit greatly from multilevel studies, exploring factors at both organisational and national levels simultaneously.

REFERENCES

Absar, M.M.N. 2012. Recruitment and selection practices in manufacturing firms in Bangladesh. *Indian Journal of Industrial Relations*, 47(3): 436–449.

Aladwan, K., Bhanugopan, R., & Fish, A. 2014. Managing human resources in Jordanian organizations: Challenges and prospects. *International Journal of Islamic and Middle Eastern Finance and Management*, 7(1): 126–138.

Ashton, D., Sung, J., & Turbin, J. 2000. Towards a framework for the comparative analysis of national systems of skill formation. *International Journal of Training and Development*, 4(1): 8–25.

Atterbury, S., Brewster, C., Communal, C., et al. 2004. The UK and Ireland: Traditions and transitions in HRM. In C. Brewster, W. Mayrhofer, and M. Morley (eds), *Human Resource Management in Europe: Evidence of Convergence?*: 29–72. Oxford: Elsevier Butterworth-Heinemann.

Aycan, Z. 2005. The interplay between cultural and institutional/structural contingencies in human resource management practices. *International Journal of Human Resource Management*, 16(7): 1083–1119.

Beardwell, I., Holden, L., & Claydon, T. 2004. *Human Resource Management: A Contemporary Approach* (4th edn). Harlow: Prentice Hall.

Becker, B.E., & Gerhart, B. 1996. The impact of human resource management on organizational performance: Progress and prospects. *Academy of Management Journal*, 39(4): 779–801.

Bian, Y., & Ang, S. 1997. Guanxi networks and job mobility in China and Singapore. *Social Forces*, 75(3): 981–1005.

Björkman, I., & Lu, Y. 1999. The management of human resources in Chinese–Western joint ventures. *Journal of World Business*, 34(3): 306–324.

Bowen, D., Galang, C., & Pillai, R. 2002. The role of human resource management: An exploratory study of cross-country variance. *Asia Pacific Journal of Human Resources*, 40(1): 123–145.

Boxall, P., & Purcell, J. 2011. *Strategy and Human Resource Management* (3rd edn). New York: Palgrave Macmillan.

Briscoe, D.R. 1997. Assessment centers: Cross-cultural and cross-national issues. *Journal of Social Behavior and Personality*, 12(5): 261–270.

Budhwar, P.S., & Khatri, N. 2001. A comparative study of HR practices in Britain and India. *International Journal of Human Resource Management*, 12(5): 800–826.

Buller, P.F., & McEvoy, G.M. 2012. Strategy, human resource management and performance: Sharpening line of sight. *Human Resource Management Review*, 22(1): 43–56.

Buyens, D., Dany, F., Dewettinck, K., & Quinodon, B. 2004. France and Belgium: Language, culture and differences in human resource practices. In C. Brewster, W. Mayrhofer, and M. Moorley (eds), *Human Resource Management in Europe: Evidence of Convergence?*: 123–159. Oxford: Elsevier Butterworth-Heinemann.

Campbell, B.A., Coff, R., & Kryscynski, D. 2012. Rethinking sustained competitive advantage from human capital. *Academy of Management Review*, 37(3): 376–395.

Cohen-Charash, Y., & Spector, P.E. 2001. The role of justice in organizations: A meta-analysis. *Organizational Behavior and Human Decision Processes*, 86(2): 278–321.

Cunha, R., Cunha, M., Morgado, A., & Brewster, C. 2003. Market forces, strategic management, HRM practices and organizational performance: A model based in a European sample. *Management Research*, 1(1): 79–91.

Daspro, E. 2009. An analysis of US multinationals' recruitment practices in Mexico. *Journal of Business Ethics*, 87(1): 221–232.

DeVaro, J., & Morita, H. 2013. Internal promotion and external recruitment: A theoretical and empirical analysis. *Journal of Labor Economics*, 31(2): 227–269.

Earnest, D.R., Allen, D.G., & Landis, R.S. 2011. Mechanisms linking realistic job previews with turnover: A meta-analytic path analysis. *Personnel Psychology*, 64(4): 865–897.

Forstenlechner, I., Madi, M.T., Selim, H.M., & Rutledge, E.J. 2012. Emiratisation: Determining the factors that influence the recruitment decisions of employers in the UAE. *International Journal of Human Resource Management*, 23(2): 406–421.

Freeman, R.B., & Medoff, J.L. 1983. The impact of collective bargaining: Can the new facts be explained by monopoly unionism?. In J.D. Reid (ed.), *Supplement 2 of Research in Labor Economics*: 3–26. Greenwich, CT: JAI Press.

Gelfand, M.J., Bhawuk, D.P.S., Nishii, L.H., & Bechtold, D.J. 2004. Individualism and collectivism. In R.J. House, P.J. Hanges, M. Javidan, P.W. Dorfman, and V. Gupta (eds), *Culture, Leadership and Organizations: The GLOBE Study of 62 Societies*: 437–512. Thousand Oaks, CA: SAGE.

Gill, C., & Meyer, D. 2013. Union presence, employee relations and high performance work practices. *Personnel Review*, 42(5): 508–528.

Gooderham, P., & Nordhaug, O. 2011. One European model of HRM? Cranet empirical contributions. *Human Resource Management Review*, 21(1): 27–36.

Han, J., & Han, J. 2009. Network-based recruiting and applicant attraction in China: Insights from both organizational and individual perspectives. *International Journal of Human Resource Management*, 20(11): 2228–2249.

Hatch, N.W., & Dyer, J.H. 2004. Human capital and learning as a source of sustainable competitive advantage. *Strategic Management Journal*, 25(12): 1155–1178.

Heraty, N., & Morley, M. 1998. In search of good fit: Policy and practice in recruitment and selection in Ireland. *Journal of Management Development*, 17(9): 662–685.

Hippach-Schneider, U., Weigel, T., Brown, A., & Gonon, P. 2013. Are graduates preferred to those completing initial vocational education and training? Case studies on company recruitment strategies in Germany, England and Switzerland. *Journal of Vocational Education & Training*, 65(1): 1–17.

Hofstede, G. 1991. *Cultures and Organizations*. London: Harper Collins Business.

Holm, A.B. 2014. Institutional context and e-recruitment practices of Danish organizations. *Employee Relations*, 36(4): 432–455.

House, R.J., Hanges, P.J., Javidan, M., et al. 2004. *Culture, Leadership, and Organizations: The GLOBE Study of 62 Societies*. Thousand Oaks, CA: SAGE.

Huo, Y.P., Huang, H.J., & Napier, N.K. 2002. Divergence or convergence: A cross-national comparison of personnel selection practices. *Human Resource Management*, 41(1): 31–44.

Ignjatović, M., & Svetlik, I. 2003. European HRM clusters. *EBS Review*, 17(Fall): 25–39.

Iles, P. 2007. Employee resourcing and talent management. In J. Storey (ed.), *Human Resource Management: A Critical Text* (3rd edn): 97–114. London: Thomson.

Javidan, M. 2004. Performance orientation. In R.J. House, P.J. Hanges, M. Javidan, et al. (eds), *Culture, Leadership and Organizations: The GLOBE Study of 62 Societies*: 239–281. Thousand Oaks, CA: SAGE.

Kabasakal, H., & Bodur, M. 2004. Humane orientation in societies, organizations, and leader attributes. In R.J. House, P.J. Hanges, M. Javidan, P.W. Dorfman, and V. Gupta (eds), *Culture, Leadership and Organizations: the GLOBE Study of 62 Societies*: 564–601. Thousand Oaks, CA: SAGE.

Koch, M.J., & Hundley, G. 1997. The effects of unionism on recruitment and selection methods. *Industrial Relations*, 36(3): 349–370.

Koen, C. 2005. *Comparative International Management*. London: McGraw-Hill.

König, C.J., Hafsteinsson, L.G., Jansen, A., & Stadelmann, E.H. 2011. Applicants' self-presentational behavior across cultures: Less self-presentation in Switzerland and Iceland than in the United States. *International Journal of Selection and Assessment*, 19(4): 331–339.

Koubek, J., & Vatchkova, E. 2004. Bulgaria and Czech Republic: Countries in transition. In C. Brewster, W. Mayrhofer, and M. Morley (eds), *Human Resource Management in Europe: Evidence of Convergence?*: 313–351. Oxford: Elsevier Butterworth-Heinemann.

Kundu, S.C., Rattan, D., Sheera, V.P., & Gahlawat, N. 2012. Recruitment and selection techniques in manufacturing and service organizations operating in India. *Journal of Strategic Human Resource Management*, 1(3): 9–19.

Lawler, J.J., Walumbwa, F.O., & Bai, B. 2008. National culture and cultural effects. In M.M. Harris (ed.), *Handbook of Research in International Human Resource Management*: 5–28. New York: Taylor & Francis Group/Lawrence Erlbaum Associates.

Lee, H.-C. 1999. Transformation of employment practices in Korean businesses. *International Studies of Management and Organization*, 28(4): 26–39.

Lindeberg, T., & Vanhala, S. 2004. Sweden and Finland: Small countries with large companies. In C. Brewster, W. Mayrhofer, and M. Morley (eds), *Human Resource Management in Europe: Evidence of Convergence?*: 279–312. Oxford: Elsevier Butterworth-Heinemann.

McEvoy, G.M., & Buller, P.F. 2013. Human resource management practices in mid-sized enterprises. *American Journal of Business*, 28(1): 86–105.

Meliciani, V., & Radicchia, D. 2011. The informal recruitment channel and the quality of job-worker matches: An analysis on Italian survey data. *Industrial and Corporate Change*, 20(2): 511.

Miles, R.E., & Snow, S.S. 1978. *Organizational Strategy, Structure, and Process*. New York: McGraw-Hill.

Mohamed, A.F., Singh, S., Irani, Z., & Darwish, T.K. 2013. An analysis of recruitment, training and retention practices in domestic and multinational enterprises in the country of Brunei Darussalam. *International Journal of Human Resource Management*, 24(10): 2054–2081.

Newell, S. 2005. Recruitment and selection. In S. Bach (ed.), *Managing Human Resources* (4th edn). Oxford: Blackwell.

Newton, P., Chandler, V., Morris-Thomson, T., Sayer, J., & Burke, L. 2015. Exploring selection and recruitment processes for newly qualified nurses: A sequential-explanatory mixed-method study. *Journal of Advanced Nursing*, 71(1): 54–64.

Olian, J., & Rynes, S. 1984. Organizational staffing: Integrating practice with strategy. *Industrial Relations*, 23(2): 170–183.

Onoshchenko, O., & Williams, C. 2014. Evaluating the role of *blat* in finding graduate employment in post-Soviet Ukraine. *Employee Relations*, 36(3): 254–265.

Paauwe, J., & Boselie, P. 2005. HRM and performance: What next?. *Human Resource Management Journal*, 15(4): 68–83.

Papalexandris, N., & Panayotopoulou, L. 2004. Exploring the mutual interaction of societal culture and human resource management practices: Evidence from 19 countries. *Employee Relations*, 26(5): 495–509.

Parry, E., Stavrou, E., & Lazarova, M. 2013. *Global Trends in Human Resource Management*. Basingstoke: Palgrave Macmillan.

Pilz, M., Schmidt-Altmann, K., & Eswein, M. 2015. Problematic transitions from school to employment: Freeters and NEETs in Japan and Germany. *Compare: A Journal of Comparative and International Education*, 45(1): 70–93.

Pudelko, M., & Harzing, A.W. 2007. Country-of-origin, localization, or dominance effect? An empirical investigation of HRM practices in foreign subsidiaries. *Human Resource Management*, 46(4): 535–559.

Purkiss, S.L.S., Perrewé, P.L., Gillespie, T.L., et al. 2006. Implicit sources of bias in employment interview judgments and decisions. *Organizational Behavior and Human Decision Processes*, 101(2): 152–167.

Rogaczewska, A.P., Holt Larsen, H., Nordhaug, O., et al. 2004. Denmark and Norway: Siblings or cousins? In C. Brewster, W. Mayrhofer, and M. Morley (eds), *Human Resource Management in Europe: Evidence of Convergence?*: 231–277. Oxford: Elsevier Butterworth-Heinemann.

Rutherford, M.W., Buller, P.F., & McMullen, P.R. 2003. Human resource management problems over the life cycle of small to medium-sized firms. *Human Resource Management*, 42(4): 321–335.

Saher, N., & Mayrhofer, W. 2014. The role of *Vartan Bhanji* in implementing HRM practices in Pakistan. *International Journal of Human Resource Management*, 25(13): 1881–1903.

Schmidt, F.L., & Hunter, J. 2004. General mental ability in the world of work: Occupational attainment and job performance. *Journal of Personality and Social Psychology*, 86(1): 162–173.

Schneider, S.C. 1988. National versus corporate culture: Implications for human resource management. *Human Resource Management*, 27(2): 231–246.

Schuler, R.S., & Jackson, S.E. 1987. Linking competitive strategies with HRM practices. *Academy of Management Executive*, 1(3): 207–219.

Schuler, R.S., & Jackson, S.E. 2014. Human resource management and organizational effectiveness: Yesterday and today. *Journal of Organizational Effectiveness: People and Performance*, 1(1): 35–55.

Segalla, M., Sauquet, A., & Turati, C. 2001. Symbolic versus functional recruitment: Cultural influences on employee recruitment policy. *European Management Journal*, 19(1): 32–43.

Sonnenfeld, J.A., & Peiperl, M.A. 1988. Staffing policy as a strategic response: A typology of career systems. *Academy of Management Review*, 13(4): 588–600.

Stavrou-Costea, E., & Manson, B. 2006. HRM in small and medium enterprises: Typical, but typically ignored. In H.H. Larsen, and W. Mayrhofer (eds), *Managing Human Resources in Europe*: 107–130. London: Routledge.

Steiner, D., & Gilliland, S. 1996. Fairness reactions to personnel selection techniques in France and the United States. *Journal of Applied Psychology*, 81(2): 134–142.

Stone, D.L., & Stone-Romero, E.F. 2012. *The Influence of Culture on Human Resource Management Processes and Practices* (2nd edn). New York: Taylor & Francis Group/Lawrence Erlbaum Associates.

Svetlik, I., & Alas, R. 2006. The European Union and HRM: Impact on present and future members. In H.H. Larsen, and W. Mayrhofer (eds), *Managing Human Resources in Europe*: 21–43. London: Routledge.

Tayeb, M. 1995. The competitive advantage of nations: The role of HRM and its socio-cultural context. *International Journal of Human Resource Management*, 6(3): 588–605.

Tayeb, M. 1998. Transfer of HRM practices across cultures: An American company in Scotland. *International Journal of Human Resource Management*, 9(2): 332–358.

Torrington, D., Hall, L., & Taylor, S. 2002. *Human Resource Management* (5th edn). Harlow: Prentice Hall.

Werbel, J.D., & DeMarie, S.M. 2005. Aligning strategic human resource management and person–environment fit. *Human Resource Management Review*, 15(4): 247–262.

Wood, S. 1999. Human resource management and performance. *International Journal of Management Reviews*, 1(4): 367-413.

Wright, P.M. 1998. HR fit: Does it really matter?. *Human Resource Planning*, 21(4): 56–57.

Zaharie, M., & Osoian, C. 2013. Job recruitment and selection practices in small and medium organizations. *Studia Universitatis Babes-Bolyai*, 58(2): 86–94.

8. Comparative total rewards policies and practices

Ihar Sahakiants, Marion Festing, Allen D. Engle Sr, and Peter J. Dowling

INTRODUCTION

Rewards are crucial for both employers and employees. They are an important source of motivation and an instrument for attracting and retaining staff (Newman et al., 2017), but at the same time they represent a significant part of the production costs of a firm. Most of the research in the respective field focuses on monetary elements of pay, which makes the analysis incomplete. Therefore, this chapter takes a broader perspective by focusing on the total rewards concept – including, in addition to monetary elements, non-monetary rewards – which has been used increasingly in recent work to provide an international comparison of national compensation data.

Despite the importance of the field of compensation, the topic of comparative rewards is still an underdeveloped area. It is part of comparative management research, the major objective of which is to 'identify aspects of organizations which are similar and aspects which are different in cultures around the world' (Adler, 1984: 32). The academic work in this field either takes a macroeconomic approach, focusing on labour cost and productivity indicators, or follows a human resource management perspective. In the latter case, variables such as the impact of institutional or cultural environments on the choice of pay elements and attitudes are at the centre of consideration. The complexity involved in considering the variety of influencing factors on comparative total rewards explains the research deficit in this field and the limited amount of suggested practical implications for designing total rewards in an international context.

However, there has been a growing interest in the topic of comparative rewards over the last few decades, which can be explained in the first place by the growing internationalization of national economies, or to use Perlmutter's (1969) terminology, by the shift from an ethnocentric to a geocentric mentality in many cases. At the same time, research interests have shifted from a focus on expatriate compensation (e.g., Reynolds, 1986) to a more all-encompassing view of international compensation, ranging from cross-national compensation studies (Lowe et al., 2002) and transnational remuneration practices (Festing et al., 2007), to emerging global compensation structures (Baranski, 1999; Dwyer, 1999; Festing & Perkins, 2008; Gross & Wingerup, 1999; Milkovich & Bloom, 1998; White, 2005).

The objective of this contribution is to build on this knowledge and to draw a holistic picture of comparative total rewards by considering various practices, the most prevalent theoretical explanations and methodological approaches, as well as the limited amount of empirical evidence. The main research questions are as follows. What are the differences in approaches to total rewards in international contexts? How can these differences be explained, and what are the limits for international best practices in certain national contexts? Finally, what are the possibilities for the global standardization of total rewards?

For a descriptive analysis illustrating our arguments we will use selected data generously provided by AON Hewitt.

In this chapter, we first introduce the total rewards concept and present a literature review, including comparative perspectives. We provide empirical data on comparative total rewards and discuss these in the context of possible influencing factors accounting for international differences. The conclusion draws implications for the possibilities and limits of converging or diverging total rewards across the globe, before it moves on to discuss whether the respective practices can be standardized in multinational enterprises. Finally, the implications of this approach for future research are discussed.

UNDERSTANDING TOTAL REWARDS

Over the last few decades, there has been increased attention on the total rewards approach in both the academic (Newman et al., 2017) and the practitioner literature (Festing et al., 2015; Hewitt Associates, 1991; White, 2005). Manas and Graham (2003: 1) define total rewards as including 'all types of rewards – indirect as well as direct, and intrinsic as well as extrinsic', such as base pay, short- and long-term variable compensation, benefits, perquisites, and other non-cash rewards. The importance of the total rewards concept has also been emphasized with respect to designing pay programmes in the international context (Milkovich & Bloom, 1998), including international assignments (Kroeck & Von Glinow, 2015).

The importance of non-monetary reward elements in national and international contexts can be presented in light of their relative weight in the total remuneration package. For example, according to a recent assessment made by the Cologne Institute for Economic Research (Schröder, 2015), pay for hours worked in the manufacturing sector in Germany accounts for about 75 per cent of the total cash compensation package. Table 8.1 shows that compensation for time not worked accounts for nearly 17 per cent of total pay.

A strong argument in favour of using the total rewards approach for international comparisons of pay structures is the substitutive effect between the monetary (wages/salaries and incentives) and non-monetary (benefits and perquisites) elements of pay, which may vary significantly between different countries and cultures. A study by Zhou and Martocchio (2001), focusing on compensation award decisions and mainly looking at the determination of bonus amounts and non-monetary recognition by Chinese and American managers, underlines the importance of looking at these dimensions simultaneously. The results of this study show that, compared with their American counterparts, Chinese managers: (1) place less emphasis on work performance when making bonus decisions; (2) place more emphasis on relationships with co-workers when making non-monetary decisions; (3) place more emphasis on relationships with managers when making non-monetary award decisions; and (4) place more emphasis on personal needs when making bonus decisions (Zhou and Martocchio, 2001: 115). Thus, this broader conceptualization of total rewards ensures more objective comparisons of compensation packages; for example, in multinational enterprises (MNEs) it can be used as an important concept to benchmark pay systems around the globe, either to install external competitiveness or to promote internal consistency. Furthermore, the total rewards approach can be instru-

Table 8.1   Labour costs in Germany: manufacturing sector, as a percentage of gross wages and salaries[a]

Remuneration elements	2012	2014
Compensation for hours worked (direct pay)[b,c]	75.4	75.4
+ Pay for time not worked[d]	17.1	17.2
+ Bonuses	7.6	7.4
= Total remuneration	100.0	100.0
+ Employer's social security contributions	18.1	17.7
+ Company pension plan	4.0	3.9
+ Other additional personnel expenses[e]	5.1	5.0
= Total labour costs	127.2	126.7

Notes:
a   Compensation for hours worked, pay for time not worked and bonus payments (excluding benefits in kind).
b   Including additional payments for performance.
c   Calendar adjusted.
d   Including vacations, paid sick leave, paid days off.
e   less refunds.

Source: Adapted from Schröder (2015: 89).

mental in ensuring the strategic flexibility necessary to operate in multiple institutional environments (Gross & Wingerup, 1999; Milkovich & Bloom, 1998; White, 2005).

THE NATIONAL CONTEXT AS A MAJOR DETERMINANT OF TOTAL REWARDS

Research on the determinants of rewards is rich and varied. Here, three levels of analysis, featuring individual (employee), organizational, and environmental (economic and institutional) factors, can be identified. Table 8.2 presents examples of the parameters included in each level. While we will briefly discuss how individual and organizational factors influence compensation decisions, the focus is clearly on the impact of environmental factors, as these matter the most in comparative rewards.

The first level of analysis deals with individual preferences and expectations of employees that influence compensation decisions. According to Dittrich and Carrell (1976), negative perceptions of pay-related organizational fairness result in absenteeism and employee turnover. This points to the relative nature of the justice perception of pay (Newman et al., 2017), whereby pay levels and structures are compared to those of the social referents chosen by an individual. For instance, Kulik and Ambrose (1992) identify a variety of personal characteristics that determine the process of referent selection: gender, race, age, position, and professionalism. This means that any international comparison and measurement of specific national attitudes and values should control for these variables in order to achieve valid results. Furthermore, situational factors such as job facet comparison, changes in allocation procedures, and physical proximity (Kulik & Ambrose, 1992) may deliver additional insights into the perception of justice in the international context.

Table 8.2   Factors influencing compensation decisions

Levels of analysis	Factors
Individual	Age
	Job tenure
	Marital status
	Family size
	Education
	(Churchill et al., 1979; Huddleston et al., 2002)
Organizational	Stage in the product life cycle
	Size of the firm
	Industry traits
	Ownership structure
	Organizational culture
	Profitability
	(Balkin & Gomez-Mejia, 1987)
Environmental	Employer federations
	Trade unions
	Social contract
	Culture/politics
	Competitive dynamics/markets
	Taxes
	(Newman et al., 2017)

In a globalized economy supported by sophisticated information and communication devices, individuals are basically in a situation where they can compare their pay conditions with anyone around the globe with the same demographic features and holding comparable positions, albeit in most cases the limits of physical proximity seem to hamper the selection of referents beyond national borders. Moreover, individual differences have an impact not only on the selection of referents, but also on pay preferences themselves, including elements of monetary and non-monetary rewards. Frey (1997) presents empirical studies from Europe and the United States of America (USA) supporting the contention that extrinsic rewards 'crowd out' intrinsic rewards across a wide range of employee groups. Newman et al. (2017) report preferences for pension plans among older workers and preferences for health insurance among employees with dependants.

The second level of analysis presented in Table 8.2 concerns the impact of organizational features on compensation decisions. Here, an important influence factor is corporate strategy (Boudreau & Ramstad, 2007). In the case of remuneration, this was confirmed by an early empirical study by Balkin and Gomez-Mejia (1987); however, especially in large international and diversified corporations, other contingencies such as the functional area matter as well. For instance, in their analysis of factors influencing compensation strategies in foreign subsidiaries in Finland, Björkman and Furu (2000) note a higher incidence of pay-for-performance (PfP) schemes in sales companies than in production and research and development (R&D) units. Similar results are presented by Hannon et al. (1990), who find that organizations adopting research and development-intensive strategies differ from other firms in the pattern of their pay practices. The impact of ownership structure on both chief executive officer (CEO) compensation and the pay of all employees (Werner et al., 2005) is another example of the influence of the respective contingencies. In international comparisons these factors become crucial, due to significant variations in ownership and control schemes around the globe (Whitley, 1999).

The third level of analysis deals with external contextual factors which, according to Hofer (1975), include economic conditions, demographic and socio-cultural trends, political, legal, and other environmental factors. The explicit consideration of environmental factors in the study of comparative human resource management (HRM) reflects a contextual rather than a universalistic paradigm (Brewster, 2007). This points to two major explanations for the variation of HRM practices including compensation (for a discussion, see Sahakiants et al., 2016): the institutional approach (DiMaggio & Powell, 1983; Whitley, 1992) and the cultural perspective (Sánchez Marín, 2008a, 2008b; Sparrow, 2009). The institutional approach highlights the importance of exogenous factors and recognizes that contextual institutional pressures may be powerful influences on pay strategy (De Cieri & Dowling, 1999; Sánchez Marín, 2008a, 2008b; Wächter et al., 2003). Whitley (1992) noted that differences in business practices and organizational structures around the globe are important features of distinctive business systems, which are linked to the institutional environments in which they develop and emphasize the contextual nature of firms as economic agents.

These environmental factors become of primary importance especially for MNEs that operate in multiple institutional contexts and are confronted with the need to promote internal consistency and at the same time face local isomorphic pressures (Festing et al., 2007; Festing & Sahakiants, 2013; Rosenzweig & Nohria, 1994). Empirical studies have confirmed the impact of institutional factors on compensation design (see, e.g., Wächter et al., 2003); for instance, trade unions, which are part of the national institutional environment, play an important role in the collective determination of wages and salaries in many countries (Parboteeah & Cullen, 2003; Traxler et al., 2008) and may oppose the diffusion of compensation practices (Kurdelbusch, 2002). However, according to Brewster et al. (2007), the empirically tested correlation between union density and the incidence of pay-for-performance practices is far from obvious, and the key focus of both trade unions and legislators often seems to concern working hours. For example, according to the Organisation for Economic Co-operation and Development's Economic Policy Reforms Report (OECD, 2008a), high union density accounts for lower hours actually worked by men and higher hours actually worked by women. Nonetheless, no other reward elements seem to be as much affected by national institutions as benefits, largely due to the influence of taxation laws, as confirmed by Festing et al. (2015) in their survey of reward management practices. As Brewster et al. (2007: 122) point out, 'in China, but also in Japan and Korea, employees value benefits increases and bonuses above basic pay increases, partly because tax is levied on basic pay'. The same is true in the USA.

Contextual paradigm researchers have also extensively explored the impact of cultural variables on national compensation design (Gomez-Mejia & Welbourne, 1991; Newman & Nollen, 1996; Schuler & Rogovsky, 1998; Tosi & Greckhamer, 2004; Townsend et al., 1990), either by applying Hofstede's (1980) dimensions directly or using similar cultural factors such as 'individualism/collectivism' as reference points (Lowe et al., 2002). Following the national culture approach means that 'national culture can play a significant part in the evolution of pay systems and the effectiveness of compensation strategies' (Gomez-Mejia & Welbourne, 1991: 39). Since Hofstede's research, many other scholars have recognized the importance of culture and its impacts on human resource and compensation issues (Gerhart, 2008; Rogovsky et al., 2000; Sparrow, 2004). Tosi and Greckhamer (2004), for instance, present evidence that cultural dimensions may influence CEO pay practices more powerfully, compared to overall firm practices, due to the 'symbolic' attention socially ascribed to more public and visible executive pay practices.

However, some researchers have pointed out deficiencies in cultural typologies and their application to the comparative studies of remuneration design (Milkovich & Bloom, 1998; Newman et al., 2017). Vernon (2006: 225), for example, states that '[a]ssertions about the nature of a particular nation's culture are sometimes ill-based and simplistic, evidence of a particular pay system is sketchy, and the claim that there is some link between the two is left unsubstantiated by any contrast with the situation in other nations'. To conclude the discussion on the influence of national contexts on compensation decisions, it should be mentioned that even though arguments based on the institutional point of view seem to be more robust, the importance of research based on the cultural perspective should not be underestimated. Thus, some researchers call for a richer theoretical framework which would allow for the explicit inclusion and further development of cultural and institutional arguments (see, e.g., Brewster, 2004; Sánchez Marín, 2008a, 2008b; Sorge, 2004).

It should be borne in mind that due to the large number of contingency factors affecting compensation strategy (Balkin & Gomez-Mejia, 1987), and the large choice of benefit programmes that could potentially be offered to employees, even a nationwide comparison of total rewards can be problematic. An international comparison of total rewards is even more complex (for an attempt, see Festing et al., 2015) in view of different regulatory environments with respect to taxation, social security systems, and work time regulations. However, a number of features that may characterize each country or region can be identified with respect to the elements and structure of pay, as analysed in the next section.

EMPIRICAL EVIDENCE FOR NATION-BASED DIFFERENCES IN TOTAL PAY: ANALYSING ELEMENTS OF TOTAL REWARDS

There are considerable pay level and pay mix variations across nations (Dowling et al., 2017, based on Dowling et al., 2005). First of all, compensation levels differ due to varying economic conditions in low- and high-pay countries. This is confirmed by macro-economic indicators such as gross domestic product (GDP) per capita levels calculated by purchasing power parity (UNDP, 2014). These variations have been studied extensively by a number of national and international organizations that carry out regular surveys on international pay (for example, the OECD and the European Foundation for the Improvement of Living and Working Conditions). The information provided by these agencies, along with data from national or supranational organizations such as the Bureau of Labor Statistics of the US Department of Labor or the International Labor Organization, are rich but sometimes limited in their comparability, due to aggregation problems. Besides evidence on pay levels, evidence on the pay mix is collected by most of the leading international HRM consulting firms.

Evidence on Working Hours and Paid Leave

Working hours and paid leave provide important additional information when analysing pay level in a comparative way, because these two elements provide data on how the institutional context influences total rewards packages. However, while the comparison of statutory minimum vacation can provide an accurate picture of the differences in some regulatory environments around the globe, there are substantial differences in some countries between the mandatory minimum and customary length of paid time off. For instance, the statutory minimum vacation in Germany is 24 working days for employees working six days per week, and it is 20 working days for those working five days per week (Germany Trade and Invest, 2015; International Labour Organization, 2012). This is less than the average collectively agreed vacation period of 30 days (Eurofound, 2015), which is the result of the influence of trade unions that stipulate in collective agreements the duration of the paid time off, which normally exceeds the statutory minimum. Even though nearly 70 per cent of German enterprises were not bound by any collective agreement in 2013, a significant number of these companies (30 per cent) used collective agreements as a guide to arrange employment conditions (Institut der deutschen Wirtschaft, 2015).

A second way to compare working time internationally is to measure the hours worked per year in different countries. Differences in working arrangements can be shown by comparing collectively agreed working hours. Figure 8.1 presents graphs of data on collectively agreed working conditions with regard to weekly hours and annual working hours in Europe.

Thus, a focus on the base pay rate alone does not make compensation at different locations comparable. International comparative data on vacations is an underrated but important issue for MNEs. For example, agreements on vacation time for international transferees have become an indispensable part of transfer planning (Poe, 2001). Employees on international assignments may have a choice between a longer vacation or the monetary equivalent. For instance, according to Oechsler et al. (2011), BASF, one of the world's largest MNEs in the chemical industry, offers its transferees a choice between taking a vacation according to German home country regulations or an additional allowance to compensate for the shorter annual leave in the host country. Even more emphasis on the issue of working time has been exerted by a recent ruling of the European Court of Justice, according to which mobile workers without a fixed workplace have to be paid for their commuting time to work (Deschenaux, 2015).

Total Cash Compensation

The data presented in this and the subsequent two subsections of the chapter (provided courtesy of AON Hewitt) allow us to go into further detail with respect to specific positions within organizations, thereby providing greater comparability than publicly available aggregated data. These results are based on the total compensation survey for 2014 and compensation and benefits databases. The data for each country were initially recorded in local currencies but were subsequently converted to euros, based on the annual average exchange rates of the European Central Bank (Deutsche Bundesbank, 2015) or, in the case of Argentina, by using the annual average exchange rate based on the rates provided by the country's Central Bank (Banco Central de la República Argentina, 2015). The data in Figure 8.2 are based on median values for the positions

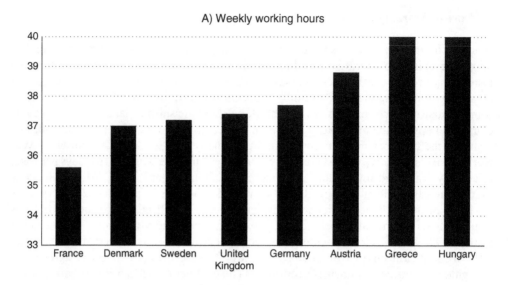

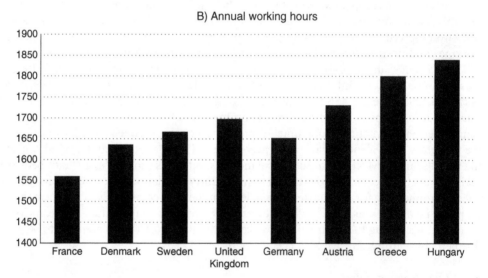

Source: Eurofound (2015).

Figure 8.1   Average collectively agreed normal working hours, 2014

'country manager' and 'head of human resource management', and show target total cash compensation levels, including base pay and short-term variable compensation. The data for all countries, except for Germany, are based on total samples, whereas the total cash compensation data for respective positions in Germany are limited to companies with an annual turnover of up to €200 million. The reason for this is the fact that, overall, German companies in our sample have much higher median turnover than companies in the remaining countries. By taking this approach we ensure data comparability across

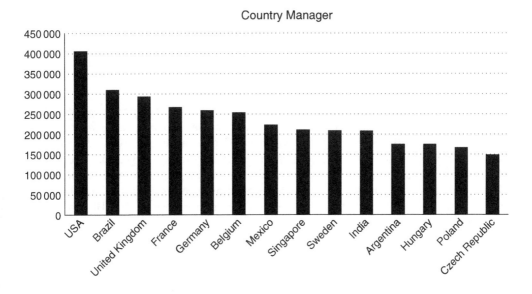

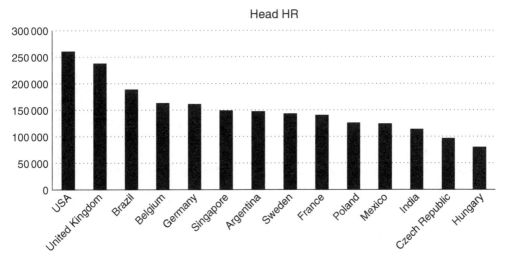

Source: Aon Hewitt (2014).

Figure 8.2 International comparison of median target total cash compensation levels in euros, 2014

countries. The comparison of total cash compensation levels for these positions shows the following patterns:

- Levels of total executive cash compensation in the USA significantly exceed levels in other countries, which has been confirmed by various studies on global executive compensation (e.g., Berrone & Otten, 2008). The next-highest level of total cash compensation for country managers in our sample is seen in Brazil, as confirmed in local surveys and reports (*The Economist*, 2011).

● With respect to target total compensation pay for heads of the human resource (HR) management function, the highest levels of respective rewards are again offered in the USA, followed by the United Kingdom and Brazil.

The data presented in Figure 8.2 also demonstrate one more important aspect characterizing national compensation systems, namely the pay differentials between the pay levels typical of different managerial positions. For instance, the levels of total cash compensation provided to heads of HR in countries such as Argentina, the United Kingdom, or Poland, taken as a proportion of the respective rewards allocated to country managers, are higher than in all the remaining countries in the sample, which could be seen as indirect evidence of the increased importance of the HR function in those countries.

Share of Target Short-Term Variable Pay

An analysis of the median target share of short-term variable compensation, as a percentage of base pay, allows us to observe further differences between the countries surveyed with respect to the pay mix:

● Figure 8.3 shows that high shares of short-term variable compensation for country heads are offered to executives in countries such as the USA and Singapore.
● The proportion of PfP provided to heads of HR in the United Kingdom is even higher than that of country heads in the same locations, which could be seen as an indicator of the increased emphasis on rewarding positive outcomes with respect to HRM in the British companies.

With respect to the ratio of variable pay to total pay, Tosi and Greckhamer (2004) reported in their study on cultural influences on CEO compensation that this ratio is influenced by cultural concepts such as Hofstede's (1980) individualism dimension. The data in Figure 8.3 may in fact show the complex interaction between a pattern of cultural values and assumptions interacting with historically derived – yet dynamic institutional and contextual – artefacts codified into laws and operating on a national level. The difficulty is that all national pay systems probably result from a complex web of cultural-historical-institutional and regulatory elements (Balkin, 2008; Berrone et al., 2008; Festing & Sahakiants, 2010, 2013; Greene, 2008). Recent institutional concerns over the dysfunctional consequences of executive pay programmes may yet result in even more explicit and transparent systems in North America (Makri & Gomez-Mejia, 2007; Thompson, 2006). The extent to which culture interacts with other contextual variables to influence reward preferences clearly warrants future research (Chiang, 2005).

Increased applications of more formalized performance management systems as 'best practice' across cultures may provide a more standardized, explicit platform for justifying PfP practices for a range of employee groups (DeNisi et al., 2008). At the same time, an adequate conceptualization of a performance management system that 'travels well' across cultures continues to elude practitioners and researchers alike

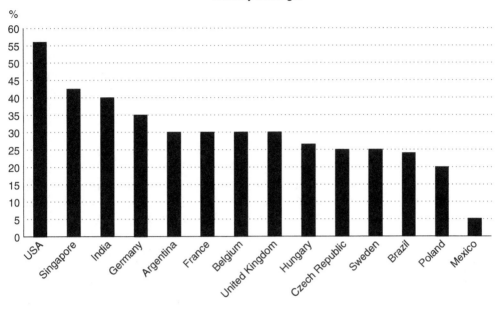

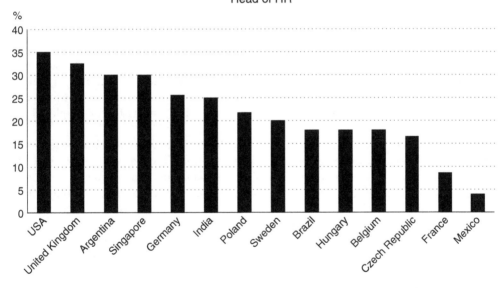

Source: Aon Hewitt (2014).

Figure 8.3   Median share of target variable pay as a percentage of base salary, 2014

(Brody et al., 2006; Engle et al., 2008). In the absence of a compelling, flexible performance management system, it is likely that local and regional compensation traditions will continue to operate. It is also the case that the exact nature of the targets and systems operationalized as triggers for performance-based payouts vary significantly amongst firms that emphasize variable pay (Hope & Fraser, 2003). Wide variations in some combinations of internal and external measures of performance, combined with latitude in weights placed on these measures and the timing of these combinations of triggers, provide ample opportunity for 'gamesmanship' by actors within these PfP systems (Ellig, 2008).

Other Elements of Total Rewards

An international comparison of other elements of total rewards represents an even more difficult challenge (see also Chapter 15 in this volume). Varying local social security and taxation laws, as well as the specifics of local financial markets, make national comparisons of long-term incentives, benefits, and perquisites a very problematic area. A comparison of the prevalence of certain compensation elements can give an idea of differences with respect to total pay structures across the globe. For instance, significant differences in the provision of equity-based pay related to management positions have been reported in the results of international comparative studies such as the Cranet survey (Brewster et al., 2007). Pendleton et al. (2002) examined the extent of financial participation in the European Union and reported that the incidence of profit sharing and share ownership differed considerably among member states, and was greatly influenced by the degree of national legislative and fiscal support for these practices. Festing et al. (1999) reported similar results and noted that legal complexity and a formalized German workplace industrial relations system are the main reasons why financial participation schemes are not common in Germany. In summary, country-level factors strongly influence the incidence of financial participation in Europe, and their impact exceeds the importance of many internal influencing factors in global pay systems.

As discussed above, a focus on non-monetary elements of rewards such as benefits and perquisites contributes to higher precision in international comparisons of pay systems. Figure 8.4 shows the prevalence of providing company cars as a perquisite to country managers and heads of HR across a range of countries. However, while the comparative data in this respect deliver important information in relation to pay benchmarking and differences among countries, it is impossible to compare the monetary values of this perquisite consistently with the total remuneration approach. There are numerous schemes to acquire a car, ranging from direct purchase to leasing, and employees are often required to pay contributions for the private use of company-owned vehicles from their net income. This, however, does not diminish the primary impact of national tax environments on decisions with respect to perquisites in general, and corporate cars in particular. A similar conclusion can be drawn with regard to the comparison of total cash compensation levels across countries: there are significant differences in taxation and social security regulations among countries, as well as significant variations in costs of living, that account for differences with respect to real compensation levels.

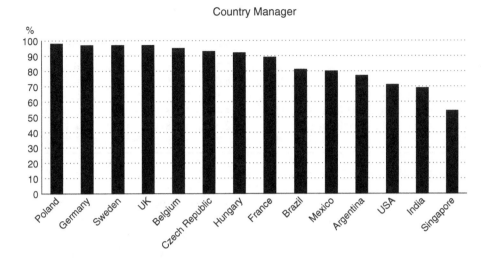

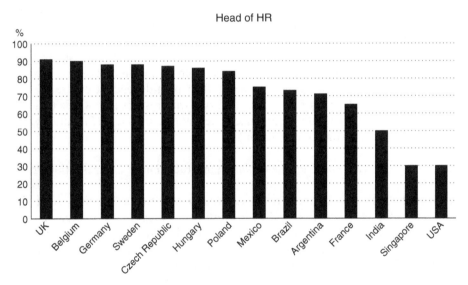

Source: Aon Hewitt (2015).

Figure 8.4   Eligibility for company cars, in percentage terms, 2015

CONCLUSION

Convergence and Divergence in International Pay Systems

Fay (2008) reviewed the theoretical arguments for and against converging compensation practices. He pointed out the limits of such convergence at the international level, due to considerable variations in compensation levels and practices within and across nations.

Table 8.3   Average annual real wage growth by region, 2006–2011

Regions	2006	2007	2008	2009	2010	2011
Africa	2.7	1.3	2.6	0.5	6.2	2.1
Asia	6.7	6.6	3.9	5.7	6.3	5.0
Developed economies	0.9	1.1	−0.3	0.8	0.6	−0.5
Eastern Europe and Central Asia	11.7	14.4	8.3	−3.5	5.5	5.2
Latin America and the Caribbean	3.5	2.9	0.8	1.6	1.4	2.2
Middle East	1.2	1.9	−2.9	−1.5	−1.2	−0.2

Source: International Labour Organization (2013: 8–9).

While there is multiple evidence for convergence of pay structures across the globe (Abe, 2007; Newman et al., 2017; White, 2005), an equalization of pay levels between developing and developed economies in the foreseeable future is unlikely. Although, as Table 8.3 shows, the real wage growth levels in Asia, Eastern Europe, and Central Asia significantly exceed respective wage increases in developed countries, the economic analysis still highlights that 'absolute differences in wage levels across countries and regions remain considerable' (International Labour Organization, 2013: 10).

Moreover, beyond mere differences in wage levels and standards of living between countries and institutional environments, factors such as traditions, the historical development of compensation practices, and hence their path-dependent nature (Festing & Sahakiants, 2010, 2013), variations in social norms with respect to rewards (Sahakiants & Festing, 2014) and corporate governance systems (Sahakiants, 2015) build significant barriers to converging rewards internationally.

Implications for MNEs: Space for the Global Standardization of Compensation Practices

Morgan et al. (2003: 389) underscore the fact that unlike 'the nationally based firm, the multinational does not exist in a unified institutional context that reinforces and reproduces particular practices'. MNEs react to this situation by trying to install a 'transnational social space . . . [by means of creating] common policies and procedures and the application of formal means of monitoring and accounting for performance' (Morgan et al., 2003: 389). Lowe et al. (2002: 46) note that 'the traditional factors of production (capital, technology, raw materials and information) are increasingly fungible, with employee quality the only sustainable source of competitive advantage to developed country multinationals'. A way to maintain this competitive advantage is to promote internal consistency by means of standardized HRM practices, including rewards. The topic of the international standardization of compensation practices has been increasingly discussed both in the academic (Festing et al., 2007; Festing & Perkins, 2008) and practitioner literature (Baranski, 1999; Dwyer, 1999; Gross & Wingerup, 1999; Milkovich & Bloom, 1998; White, 2005).

Based on the results of their survey of reward management practices in MNEs, Festing et al. (2015) found that the major reasons for centralizing reward management are corporate strategy and culture, while legal and cultural environments and local industrial relations systems constitute the most important reasons for decentralizing the respective decisions. The authors also identified the importance of the country-of-origin effect, with MNEs with headquarters in the USA promoting centralized rewards management. In addition, they noted that centralization occurs to a larger extent for the rewards of senior managers than for those of middle managers and operational employees.

Due to significant variations in economic conditions among countries, pay practices could be standardized by introducing global compensation elements, including non-monetary rewards, and salary level determination systems (Abosch et al., 2008; Festing & Sahakiants, 2013). For example, employees at a specified job grade could be eligible for a base salary on a certain market level (for example, 50th or 75th percentile); a specified percentage of variable pay based on individual, organizational unit, or global performance; stock options and perquisites (for example, a company car).

However, as noted above, such standardization strategies can be significantly hampered by national social, political, and legal institutions, especially employment regulations in the form of statutory minimums with respect to pay or benefits. While there is evidence that the wages and salaries offered to the employees of MNEs – as a rule – exceed average country levels (OECD, 2008b), regulations or collectively agreed practices such as paid time off considerably hinder the implementation of a universal strategy. Local institutions can also significantly influence the transfer of PfP schemes; for example, all companies in France with more than 50 employees must implement a statutory profit-sharing (partici-pation) plan (Schulze-Marmeling, 2014). Fakhfakh and Perotin (2000) noted the positive impact of voluntary profit-sharing schemes on factor productivity in French companies, notwithstanding the reported limited motivational effects of such legally required finan-cial participation programmes (Hewitt Associates, 1991).

Trends and Directions for Future Research

The research literature on international compensation has increasingly concentrated on the incidence of pay elements, notably PfP schemes, including short-term and long-term incentives (Antoni et al., 2005; Kurdelbusch, 2002; Pendleton et al., 2001). However, there is a dearth of comparative research on non-monetary rewards such as paid time off, pension plans, and medical insurance. There is also insufficient research on the impact of universal healthcare provided by the national governments of many developed economies (for example, in the European Union, Canada, Australia, and New Zealand) compared to the USA, where employers have traditionally funded much of the cost of health insur-ance for both employees and retirees, a situation dramatically illustrated by the current difficulties of the major US auto manufacturers that are carrying very large pension and health insurance liabilities for their retirees. A comprehensive measurement of the value of benefits for employees in different countries would support international total rewards comparisons.

Additional areas where further research is needed include:

- The future direction of hierarchical pay patterns in executive compensation (particularly in the USA and the United Kingdom) in light of the consequences of the 2008 global economic crisis and an apparent disconnect between executive pay and long-term firm performance. The recent global economic and financial crisis revealed many deficiencies in current long-term compensation schemes which – albeit to a different extent internationally – represent failures of the respective corporate governance models with respect to executive pay (Sahakiants, 2015). These deficiencies have been sharply criticized recently (Bebchuk & Fried, 2006, 2010). However, still more work is necessary to develop the link between social norms and executive rewards, or the socially responsible character of CEO pay (Sahakiants, 2017). Such research has the potential to contribute to an increased social acceptance of executive compensation approaches across the globe.

- The need to expand the scope of research on cross-national pay and practice. Current empirical research and publications have a clear North American bias in terms of the number of articles published and the subject matter and firms surveyed. Much of the data we have are from US-based researchers, consulting firms or samples. Recent activities by the academic Cranet consortium and more globally focused consulting firms have partially alleviated this challenge, but significant concerns remain in terms of the over-weighted North American samples in cross-national reward research. There is a clear paucity of research in Latin America and the emerging economies outside of China and India.
- A comprehensive analysis of total rewards practices in international enterprises with respect to comparable contingency factors among employees with comparable demographic features, in order to allow further insights into a number of topics, including comparative analysis of preferences for and the motivational effect of elements of pay, variations in distributive and procedural justice perceptions across the nations, and the convergence of pay practices.

In an initial step toward building a vocabulary with which to pursue cross-cultural reward studies more effectively, we present two models. Milkovich and Bloom (1998) outline a three-part model of global compensation strategy from the firm perspective (see Figure 8.5). In the first element, core pay practices are standardized across all the regions and cultures in which the firm operates; next, a crafted set of pay practices is customized to local and regional contexts and markets; and finally, individual employees are given a choice of pay practices, along the lines of flexible benefits. It is this combination of these three elements that provides the global firm with a combination of systematic logic and responsiveness to local and individual interests.

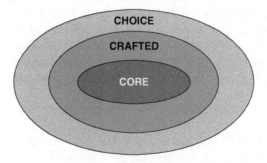

Source: Adapted from Milkovich and Bloom (1998: 22).

Figure 8.5   Elements of global pay

Figure 8.6   Institutional, cultural and strategic discretion in pay

We propose an approach to comparative or cross-cultural management based on a similar composite model (see Figure 8.6). In the outer oval we present externally influenced, institutionally mandated pay elements, required by legislation as well as industrial regulation. In the middle oval we present culturally influenced norms and values, practices influenced by historical context, local and regional supply and demand aspects, and the need for competitive responsiveness. Finally, the centre oval represents strategically linked practices dependent on more internally based decisions on business intent and executive practice (for more on the theoretical origins supporting internal as opposed to external foci for pay systems, see Dowling et al., 2005).

Given this framework, researchers can distinguish between 'demanding contexts' characterized by prescribed legislation and/or strongly held values and preferences affecting major reward system decisions, and more 'permissive contexts' characterized by limited legislative or institutional frameworks and/or more indifferent social norms or values related to employment exchange and rewards. More demanding social or institutional contexts are associated with pay systems that emphasize local customization and an external focus on the rewards system, whereas more permissive contexts are thought to be associated with global (or firm-level) standardization and an internal focus on the reward system. How these two roughly outlined contexts relate to specific pay practices (for example, base cash, short-term variable, long-term variable, benefits, perquisites, and other non-cash rewards) is a starting point for a more systematic approach to examining a very complex topic area. Distinguishing between when a given pay practice is an independent variable varying over a wide range; an independent variable ranging over a narrower or prescribed range; or is a constant, prescribed and given, is a critical first step in this challenging and complex subject area.

REFERENCES

Abe, M. 2007. Why companies in Japan are introducing performance-based treatment and reward systems: The background, merits, and demerits. *Japan Labor Review*, 14(2): 7–36.
Abosch, K., Schermerhorn, J., & Wisper, L. 2008. Broad-based variable pay goes global. *Workspan*, 5(8): 56–62.
Adler, N.J. 1984. Understanding the ways of understanding: Cross-cultural management methodology reviewed. In R.N. Farmer (ed.), *Advances in International Comparative Management*, 1: 37–67. Greenwich, CT: JAI Press.
Antoni, C.H., Berger, A., Baeten, X., et al. 2005. *Wages and Working Conditions in the European Union*. Dublin: European Foundation for the Improvement of Living and Working Conditions.

Aon Hewitt. 2014. TCM™ cash and prevalence reports. Aon Hewitt database.

Aon Hewitt. 2015. Company car eligibility. Aon Hewitt database.

Balkin, D.B. 2008. Explaining high US CEO pay in a global context: An institutional perspective. In L. Gomez-Mejia and S. Werner (eds), *Global Compensation. Foundations and Perspectives*: 192–205. London, UK and New York, USA: Routledge.

Balkin, D.B., & Gomez-Mejia, L.R. 1987. Toward a contingency theory of compensation strategy. *Strategic Management Journal*, 8(2): 169–182.

Banco Central de la República Argentina. 2015. Statistics: Foreign exchange variables: Rates by date. Retrieved 24 August 2015, from http://www.bcra.gob.ar/Estadisticas/estforeing050501.asp.

Baranski, M. 1999. Think globally, pay locally: Finding the right mix. *Compensation and Benefits Review*, 31(4): 15–24.

Bebchuk, L.A., & Fried, J.M. 2006. Pay without performance: Overview of the issues. *Academy of Management Perspectives*, 20(1): 5-24.

Bebchuk, L.A., & Fried, J.M. 2010. Paying for long-term performance. *University of Pennsylvania Law Review*, 158(7): 1915–1959.

Berrone, P., Makri, M., & Gomez-Mejia, L.R. 2008. Executive compensation in North American high-technology firms: A contextual approach. *International Journal of Human Resource Management*, 19(8): 1534–1552.

Berrone, P., & Otten, J. 2008. A global perspective on executive compensation. In L.R. Gomez-Mejia and S. Werner (eds), *Global Compensation. Foundations and Perspectives*: 206–218. London, UK and New York, USA: Routledge.

Björkman, I., & Furu, P. 2000. Determinants of variable pay for top managers of foreign subsidiaries in Finland. *International Journal of Human Resource Management*, 11(4): 698–713.

Boudreau, J., & Ramstad, P. 2007. *Beyond HR: The New Science of Human Capital*. Boston, MA: Harvard Business School Press.

Brewster, C. 2004. European perspectives on human resource management. *Human Resource Management Review*, 14(4): 365–403.

Brewster, C. 2007. Comparative HRM: European views and perspectives. *International Journal of Human Resource Management*, 18(5): 769–787.

Brewster, C., Sparrow, P., & Vernon, G. 2007. Comparative HRM: Reward. In C. Brewster, P. Sparrow, and G. Vernon (eds), *International Human Resource Management* (2nd edn): 121–147. London: Chartered Institute of Personnel and Development.

Brody, R.G., Lin, S., & Salter, S.B. 2006. Merit pay, responsibility, and national values: A US–Taiwan comparison. *Journal of International Accounting Research*, 5(2): 63–79.

Chiang, F. 2005. A critical examination of Hofstede's thesis and its application to international reward management. *International Journal of Human Resource Management*, 16(9): 1545–1563.

Churchill, G.A., Ford, N.M., & Walker, O.C. 1979. Personal characteristics of salespeople and the attractiveness of alternative rewards. *Journal of Business Research*, 7(1): 25–50.

De Cieri, H., & Dowling, P.J. 1999. Strategic human resource management in multinational enterprises: Theoretical and empirical developments. In P.M. Wright, L. Dyer, J.W. Boudreau, and G.T. Milkovich (eds), *Research in Personnel and Human Resource Management, Supplement 4*: 305–327. Stamford, CT, USA and London, UK: JAI Press.

DeNisi, A.S., Varma, A., & Budhwar, P.S. 2008. Performance management around the globe: What have we learned? In A.S. DeNisi, A. Varma, and P.S. Budhwar (eds), *Performance Management System: A Global Perspective*: 254–261. Abingdon: Routledge.

Deschenaux, J. 2015. European workers must be paid for travel time. Retrieved 10 October 2015, from http://www.shrm.org/hrdisciplines/global/articles/pages/travel-time-in-eu.aspx?utm_source=SHRM%20Global%20HR%20_%20PublishThis%20%282%29&utm_medium=email&utm_content=October%2020,%202015&MID=00193416&LN=Engle&spMailingID=23785365&spUserID=ODM1OTIzOTEyNzkS1&spJobID=661975052&spReportId=NjYxOTc1MDUyS0.

Deutsche Bundesbank. 2015. Euro-Referenzkurse der Europäischen Zentralbank: Jahresendstände und -durchschnitte. Retrieved 24 August 2015, from https://www.bundesbank.de/Redaktion/DE/Downloads/Statistiken/Aussenwirtschaft/Devisen_Euro_Referenzkurs/stat_eurorefj.pdf?__blob=publicationFile.

DiMaggio, P.J., & Powell, W.W. 1983. The iron cage revisited: Institutional isomorphism and collective rationality in organizational fields. *American Sociological Review*, 48(2): 147–160.

Dittrich, J.E., & Carrell, M.R. 1976. Dimensions of organizational fairness as predictors of job satisfaction, absence, and turnover. *Academy of Management Proceedings*: 79–83.

Dowling, P.J., Engle, A., Festing, M., & Müller, B. 2005. Complexity in global pay – a meta-framework. Paper presented at the 8th Conference on International Human Resource Management, Cairns, Australia.

Dowling, P.J., Festing, M., & Engle, A. 2017. *International Human Resource Management* (7th edn). Andover: Cengage Learning EMEA.

Dwyer, T.D. 1999. Trends in global compensation. *Compensation and Benefits Review*, 31(4): 48–53.

The Economist. 2011. Top whack. Executive pay in Brazil: Big country, big pay cheques. Retrieved 10 September 2015, from http://www.economist.com/node/18010831.

Ellig, B. 2008. What pay for performance should measure. *World at Work Journal*, 17(2): 64–75.

Engle, A., Dowling, P.J., & Festing, M. 2008. State of origin: Research in global performance management, a proposed research domain and emerging implications. *European Journal of International Management*, 2(2): 153–169.

Eurofound. 2015. *Developments in Collectively Agreed Working Time 2014*. Dublin: European Foundation for the Improvement of Living and Working Conditions.

Fakhfakh, F., & Perotin, V. 2000. The effects of profit-sharing schemes on enterprise performance in France. *Economic Analysis*, 3(2): 93–111.

Fay, C.H. 2008. The global convergence of compensation practices. In L.R.R. Gomez-Mejia and S. Werner (eds), *Global Compensation*: 131–141. Abingdon: Routledge.

Festing, M., Eidems, J., & Royer, S. 2007. Strategic issues and local constraints in transnational compensation strategies: An analysis of cultural, institutional and political influences. *European Management Journal*, 25(2): 118–131.

Festing, M., Groening, Y., Kabst, R., & Weber, W. 1999. Financial participation in Europe: Determinants and outcomes. *Economic and Industrial Democracy*, 20(2): 295–329.

Festing, M., & Perkins, S. 2008. Rewards for internationally mobile employees. In P. Sparrow, M. Dickmann, and C. Brewster (eds), *International HRM: A European Perspective* (2nd edn): 150–173. London: Routledge.

Festing, M., & Sahakiants, I. 2010. Compensation practices in Central and Eastern European EU Member States: An analytical framework based on institutional perspectives, path dependencies, and efficiency considerations. *Thunderbird International Business Review*, 52(3): 203–216.

Festing, M., & Sahakiants, I. 2013. Path-dependent evolution of compensation systems in Central and Eastern Europe: A case study of multinational corporation subsidiaries in the Czech Republic, Poland and Hungary. *European Management Journal*, 31(4): 373–389.

Festing, M., Tekieli, M., & Aleweld, T. 2015. *European Reward Governance Survey 2015*. Munich: AON.

Frey, B. 1997. *Not Just for the Money: An Economic Theory of Personal Motivation*. Cheltenham, UK and Brookfield, VT, USA: Edward Elgar Publishing.

Gerhart, B. 2008. Compensation and national culture. In L.R. Gomez-Mejia and S. Werner (eds), *Global Compensation. Foundations and Perspectives*: 142–157. London, UK and New York, USA: Routledge.

Germany Trade and Invest. 2015. Terms of Employment. Retrieved 21 August 2015, from http://www.gtai.de/GTAI/Navigation/EN/Invest/Investment-guide/Employees-and-social-security/terms-of-employment,t=working-times,did=6782.html.

Gomez-Mejia, L.R., & Welbourne, T. 1991. Compensation strategies in a global context. *Human Resource Planning*, 14(1): 29–41.

Greene, R.J. 2008. Reward management in multinational enterprises: Global principles; local strategies. *WorldatWork Journal*, 17(3): 45–54.

Gross, S.E., & Wingerup, P.L. 1999. Global pay? Maybe not yet! *Compensation and Benefits Review*, 31(4): 25–34.

Hannon, J., Milkovich, G.T., Gerhart, B., & Friedrich, T. 1990. The effects of research and development intensity on managerial compensation in large organizations. *Academy of Management Best Paper Proceedings*: 279–283.

Hewitt Associates. 1991. *Total Compensation Management: Reward Management Strategies for the 1990s*. Oxford: Blackwell.

Hofer, C.W. 1975. Toward a contingency theory of business strategy. *Academy of Management Journal*, 18(4): 784–810.

Hofstede, G. 1980. *Culture's Consequences: International Differences in Work Related Values*. Beverly Hills, CA: SAGE.

Hope, J., & Fraser, R. 2003. New ways of setting rewards: The beyond budgeting model. *California Management Review*, 45(4): 104–119.

Huddleston, P., Good, L., & Frazier, B. 2002. The influence of firm characteristics and demographic variables on Russian retail workers' work motivation and job attitudes. *International Review of Retail, Distribution and Consumer Research*, 12(4): 395–421.

Institut der deutschen Wirtschaft. 2015. Deutschland in Zahlen [Database]. Retrieved 21 August 2015, from http://www.deutschlandinzahlen.de/.

International Labour Organization. 2012. Germany – working time. Retrieved 21 August 2015, from http://www.ilo.org/dyn/travail/travmain.sectionReport1?p_lang=en&p_countries=DE&p_sc_id=1001&p_year=2012&p_structure=2.

International Labour Organization. 2013. *Global Wage Report 2012/2013: Wages and Equitable Growth*. Geneva: International Labour Office.

Kroeck, K.G., & Von Glinow, M.A. 2015. Total rewards in the international context. In A.-W. Harzing and A.H. Pinnington (eds), *International Human Resource Management* (4th edn): 429–467. London: SAGE.

Kulik, C.T., & Ambrose, M.L. 1992. Personal and situational determinants of referent choice. *Academy of Management Review*, 17(2): 212–237.

Kurdelbusch, A. 2002. Multinationals and the rise of variable pay in Germany. *European Journal of Industrial Relations*, 8(3): 325–349.

Lowe, K.B., Milliman, J., De Cieri, H., & Dowling, P.J. 2002. International compensation practices: A ten-country comparative analysis. *Human Resource Management*, 41(1): 45–66.

Makri, M., & Gomez-Mejia, L.R. 2007. Executive compensation: Something old, something new. In S. Werner (ed.), *Managing Human Resources in North America*: 158–171. London: Routledge.

Manas, T.M., & Graham, M.D. 2003. *Creating a Total Rewards Strategy: A Toolkit for Designing Business-Based Plans*. New York: AMACOM.

Milkovich, G.T., & Bloom, M. 1998. Rethinking international compensation. *Compensation and Benefits Review*, 30(1): 15–23.

Morgan, G., Kelly, B., Sharpe, D., & Whitley, R. 2003. Global managers and Japanese multinationals: internationalization and management in Japanese financial institutions. *International Journal of Human Resource Management*, 14(3): 389–407.

Newman, J.M., Gerhart, B., & Milkovich, G.T. 2017. *Compensation* (12th edn). New York: McGraw-Hill.

Newman, K.L., & Nollen, S.D. 1996. Culture and congruence: The fit between management practices and national culture. *Journal of International Business Studies*, 27(4): 753–779.

OECD. 2008a. *Economic Policy Reforms: Going for Growth*. Paris: OECD Publishing.

OECD. 2008b. *Employment Outlook*. Paris: OECD Publishing.

Oechsler, W.A., Trautwein, G., & Schwab, M. 2011. Auslandsdelegation bei der BASF SE. In J. Zentes, B. Swoboda, and D. Morschett (eds), *Fallstudien zum Internationalen Management: Grundlagen – Praxiserfahrungen – Perspektiven* (4th edn): 751–767. Wiesbaden: Gabler.

Parboteeah, K.P., & Cullen, J.B. 2003. Social institutions and work centrality: Explorations beyond national culture. *Organization Science*, 14(2): 137–148.

Pendleton, A., Poutsma, E., Brewster, C., & van Ommeren, J. 2002. Employee share ownership and profit sharing in the European Union: Incidence, company characteristics and union representation. *Transfer*, 8(1): 47–62.

Pendleton, A., Poutsma, E., van Ommeren, J., & Brewster, C. 2001. *Employee Share Ownership and Profit Sharing in the European Union*. Luxembourg: Office for Official Publications of the European Communities.

Perlmutter, H.V. 1969. The tortuous evolution of the multinational corporation. *Columbia Journal of World Business*, 4(1): 9–18.

Poe, A.C. 2001. When in Rome ... determining vacation time for international transferees. Retrieved 2 September 2008, from http://www.shrm.org.

Reynolds, C. 1986. Compensation of overseas personnel. In J.J. Famularo (ed.), *Handbook of Human Resource Administration*: 47–61. New York: McGraw-Hill.

Rogovsky, N., Schuler, R.S., & Reynolds, C. 2000. How can national culture affect compensation practices of MNCs? *Global Focus*, 12(4): 35–42.

Rosenzweig, P.M., & Nohria, N. 1994. Influences on human resource management practices in multinational corporations. *Journal of International Business Studies*, 25(2): 229–251.

Sahakiants, I. 2015. Corporate governance failures: An international perspective. In M. Aluchna and G. Aras (eds), *Transforming Governance: New Values, New Systems in the New Business Environment*: 41–58. Farnham: Gower.

Sahakiants, I. 2017. Investigating the Concept of Socially Responsible Executive Pay. In M. Aluchna and S. Idowu (eds), *Responsible Corporate Governance: Towards Sustainable and Effective Governance Structures*: 207–222. New York: Springer.

Sahakiants, I., & Festing, M. 2014. The Minder initiative and executive pay narratives in Germany and Russia: Cases of path dependence? ESCP Europe Working Paper No. 64. Berlin: ESCP Europe.

Sahakiants, I., Festing, M., & Perkins, S. 2016. Pay-for-performance in Europe. In M. Dickmann, C. Brewster, and P. Sparrow (eds), *International Human Resource Management: Contemporary Human Resource Issues in Europe* (3rd edn): 354–374. New York, USA and London, UK: Routledge.

Sánchez Marín, G. 2008a. The influence of institutional and cultural factors on compensation practices around the world. In L.R. Gomez-Mejia and S. Werner (eds), *Global Compensation. Foundations and Perspectives*: 3–17. London, UK and New York, USA: Routledge.

Sánchez Marín, G. 2008b. National differences in compensation: The influence of the institutional and cultural context. In L.R. Gomez-Mejia and S. Werner (eds), *Global Compensation. Foundations and Perspectives*: 18–28. London, UK and New York, USA: Routledge.

Schröder, C. 2015. Die Struktur der Arbeitskosten in der deutschen Wirtschaft. *IW-Trends*, 2: 79–95.

Schuler, R.S., & Rogovsky, N. 1998. Understanding compensation practice variations across firms: The impact of national culture. *Journal of International Business Studies*, 29(1): 159–177.

Schulze-Marmeling, S. 2014. France: Study finds bonus payments have no effect on total employee remuneration.

Retrieved 10 September 2015, from http://www.eurofound.europa.eu/observatories/eurwork/articles/working-conditions-industrial-relations/france-study-finds-bonus-payments-have-no-effect-on-total-employee-remune ration.

Sorge, A. 2004. Cross-national differences in human resources and organization. In A.-W. Harzing and J.V. Ruysseveldt (eds), *International Human Resource Management* (2nd edn): 117–140. London: SAGE Publications.

Sparrow, P. 2004. International rewards systems: To converge or not to converge? In C. Brewster and H. Harris (eds), *International HRM: Contemporary Issues in Europe*: 102–119. London: Routledge.

Sparrow, P. 2009. International reward management. In G. White and J. Drucker (eds), *Reward Management: A Critical Text* (2nd edn): 233–257. London, UK and New York, USA: Routledge.

Thompson, M.A. 2006. Investors call for better disclosure of executive compensation in Canada. *Focus: Workspan*, 2(6): 5–6.

Tosi, H.L., & Greckhamer, T. 2004. Culture and CEO compensation. *Organization Science*, 15(6): 657–670.

Townsend, A.M., Scott, K.D., & Markham, S.E. 1990. An examination of country and culture-based differences in compensation practices. *Journal of International Business Studies*, 21(4): 667–678.

Traxler, F., Arrowsmith, J., Nergaard, K., & López-Rodó, J.M.M. 2008. Variable pay and collective bargaining: A cross-national comparison of the banking sector. *Economic and Industrial Democracy*, 29(3): 406–431.

UNDP. 2014. *Human Development Report 2014. Sustaining Human Process: Reducing Vulnerabilities and Building Resilience*. New York: United Nations Development Programme.

Vernon, G. 2006. International pay and reward. In T. Edwards and C. Rees (eds), *International Human Resource Management*: 217–241. London: FT/Prentice Hall.

Wächter, H., Peters, R., Tempel, A., & Müller-Camen, M. 2003. *The 'Country-of-Origin Effect' in the Cross-National Management of Human Resources*. Munich and Mering: Rainer Hampp Verlag.

Werner, S., Tosi, H.L., & Gomez-Mejia, L. 2005. Organizational governance and employee pay: How ownership structure affects the firm's compensation strategy. *Strategic Management Journal*, 26(4): 377–384.

White, R. 2005. A strategic approach to building a consistent global rewards program. *Compensation and Benefits Review*, 37(4): 23–40.

Whitley, R. 1992. Societies, firms and markets: The social structuring of business systems. In R. Whitley (ed.), *European Business Systems: Firms and Markets in their National Contexts*: 5–45. London, UK; Newbury Park, CA, USA; New Delhi, India: SAGE Publications.

Whitley, R. 1999. *Divergent Capitalisms. The Social Structuring and Change of Business Systems*. New York: Oxford University Press.

Zhou, J., & Martocchio, J.J. 2001. Chinese and American managers' compensation award decisions: A comparative policy-capturing study. *Personnel Psychology*, 54(1): 115–145.

9. Comparing performance management across contexts
Paul Boselie, Elaine Farndale, and Jaap Paauwe

INTRODUCTION

Performance management (PM) is one of the key human resource management (HRM) issues facing contemporary organizations, picked up by both private sector and public sector organizations (Moynihan & Pandey, 2010). The process of measuring and subsequently actively managing organization and employee performance in order to improve effectiveness is critical to organizations' development and survival (Den Hartog et al., 2004), but is also linked to employee outcomes such as employee engagement (Gruman & Saks, 2011), trust, and perceived justice (Farndale et al., 2011). Performance management today encompasses a whole range of HRM activities beyond what we might traditionally assume to have been limited to annual performance appraisals, such as goal setting, feedback, consequences for training and development, and remuneration. Having said this it is relevant to notice two developments. First, the importance of PM is emphasized in the academic literature as possibly affecting the HRM and PM rhetoric at the board room level of large organizations in both the private and public sector. We are not sure whether this is affecting small and medium-sized organizations. And we know little about the actual implementation of PM in organizations, linking this issue in a way to Legge's (1995) classic 'rhetorics and realities' debate on HRM. Second, lately several large multinational companies such as Deloitte, Accenture, Microsoft, and GE have explicitly abandoned the more classic performance management system (in particular, the annual performance appraisal) and have instead started looking for alternatives, among which are emphasizing the importance of a continuous dialogue between direct supervisor and employee on employee motivation, targets, and support.

The attention to performance management over the last decades is clear for all to see. A special issue of the *European Journal of International Management* (2008) emphasized this. The discussions presented suggest that performance management issues include:

- a global tendency towards performance management through culture management;
- aligning corporate goals with individual employee goals;
- using PM for talent management and leadership development;
- using PM as a mechanism for distinguishing good performers from bad performers;
- linking PM and 360-degree feedback systems;
- integrating PM and information technology systems;
- emphasizing self-appraisal and appraisals by peers;
- linking PM to specific employee outcomes such as engagement, trust, perceived justice (both distributive and procedural), and job performance;
- performance management in the public sector as part of an increasing efficiency

focus, and new public management developments in these specific contexts (for example in local governments, schools, and health care organizations); and

- PM as a tool for general employee development purposes.

Performance management is seen as the key to maximizing the return on investment in human capital and hence creating corporate competitive advantage. These are some of the findings of the Global Human Resource Research Alliance (GHRRA), based on extensive case study research within leading multinational corporations (MNCs) including Shell, Unilever, IKEA, Siemens, Procter & Gamble, and IBM. Another particularly informative piece of research which explores international developments in HRM practices is the Cranet survey. Such quantitative data are a rich source of information on how the use of different performance management systems in different countries has changed (or remained the same) over the last decade. We will return to these studies shortly, as they provide us with a unique opportunity to study contemporary performance management in different organizations and in different countries around the world.

The aim of this chapter is to define performance management, giving an overview of the most important developments over time, and comparing performance management in different contexts using both case study data from large multinationals and country survey data. We start by exploring what performance management means, especially in an international context.

DEFINITIONS OF PERFORMANCE MANAGEMENT

Performance management can be seen as a broad range of activities which creates a bridge between managing employee performance and enhancing overall firm performance. Performance management thus 'deals with the challenge organisations face in defining, measuring, and stimulating employee performance with the ultimate goal of improving organisational performance' (Den Hartog et al., 2004: 556). This view is upheld by DeNisi (2000), who maintains that performance management refers to the range of activities engaged in by an organization to enhance the performance of a target person or group, with the ultimate purpose of improving organizational effectiveness.

Baron and Armstrong (1998: 38), examining the position in the United Kingdom (UK), emphasize the strategic and integrated nature of performance management, which in their view focuses on 'increasing the effectiveness of organizations by improving the performance of the people who work in them and by developing the capabilities of teams and individual contributors'. However, they go further and start to describe more about the process and characteristics of performance management. They see it as a continuous process involving performance reviews focusing on the future rather than the past. In their empirical research among British practitioners they find that the key characteristics of performance management (those identified by more than half of the respondents) are goal setting and evaluation (85 per cent of respondents), annual appraisal (83 per cent), and personal development programmes (68 per cent). Less frequently mentioned items include self-evaluation (45 per cent of respondents), pay for performance (43 per cent), coaching and mentorship (39 per cent), career management (32 per cent), competence management (24 per cent), and 180-degree feedback systems (20 per cent). In summary, goal setting, employee monitoring, and modification through employee development are the central characteristics. However, these data are more than a decade old and changes might have taken place in the performance management arena. The empirical results of more recent studies (GHRRA and Cranet) will shed light on performance management characteristics in contemporary settings.

One core part of the performance management process is undoubtedly the (annual) appraisal meeting. This is 'the system whereby an organization assigns some "score" to indicate the level of performance of a target person or group' (DeNisi, 2000: 121). This may or may not then be linked to an employee's rewards. Performance appraisal (PA) is often considered to be performance management, and the other way around; while in our definition of PM, building on PM literature, annual performance appraisal is just one part of performance management. A second core feature is the focus on competence development (through training, coaching, and feedback) and individual career planning (Fletcher, 2001; Roberts, 2001). Thirdly, there is the important task of goal setting: the setting of corporate, departmental, team, and individual objectives (sometimes labelled 'policy deployment'; the cascading down of strategic objectives to a meaningful set of targets for every individual involved) (Roberts, 2001). The line manager or direct supervisor plays an important role as the enactor of performance management in practice. Thus, performance management involves day-to-day management, as well as the support and development of people.

Alongside the variation in content of a PM system, according to Baron & Kreps (1999), performance management can also have different purposes, including:

- an extensive evaluation to improve job matching;
- communication of corporate values and objectives;
- providing information for self-improvement, training, and development, and career development;
- linking pay to individual and/or team performance;
- collecting information for hiring strategies;
- validating HRM practices including appraisal and rewards, retention, and reductions in the workforce; and
- input for legal defences (for example, when an organization is trying to fire an employee because of poor job performance).

However, how does an organization know what elements to include in a PM system in order to achieve the desired outcomes? Baron and Kreps (1999) summarize the important and relevant aspects of different performance evaluation systems that need to be taken into account when designing a performance management system:

1. Who or what is to be evaluated? One can look at an individual's attitudes, behaviours or cognitive abilities, but one can also look at team performance or subunit outcomes.
2. Who performs the evaluation? Traditionally, the direct supervisor plays an important role in being the evaluator. However, more recently we have seen developments towards self-evaluations, evaluations by peers, and even including evaluations by customers.
3. What is the time frame? Traditionally, appraisals took place on an annual basis. Nowadays we can see illustrations in practice of employee monitoring on a monthly, weekly, and even daily basis.
4. Should we be using objective or subjective evaluations? Objective evaluations include

hard data, for example productivity and service quality outcomes; while subjective data are mainly collected using questionnaires ranking the candidate on the basis of multiple criteria, for example with respect to the candidate's individual job performance, employee development, and general attitude towards the job and colleagues.

5. Do we apply relative or absolute performance indicators? Relative performance indicators represent an individual's score in comparison to another person or the general average score. Absolute performance indicators focus on the real score.

6. Should we use a forced distribution? In a forced distribution approach, individual employees are ranked and the evaluator is forced to classify the candidates into different groups ranging from poor performers to high performers. Forced distribution is often introduced to create variance in scores, otherwise the organization runs the risk of ending up with 80 per cent relatively good performers, 10 per cent excellent performers and only 10 per cent poor performers.

7. How many performance indicators should be used? The evaluation might include multiple outcome variables rather than a single one. However, using multiple performance indicators raises questions about the weights of the indicators and the technique for calculating the overall score.

In addition, Biron et al. (2011) propose a framework, based on input from 16 world-leading firms, including four performance management system facilitators, which cover: (1) taking a broad view of performance management that includes both strategic and tactical elements; (2) involving senior managers in the process; (3) clearly communicating performance expectations; and (4) formally training performance raters.

There is thus a considerable range of considerations regarding the design and implementation of performance management systems, especially when, in addition to the points raised above, we start to add the complexity of multiple country contexts. First, however, we start our comparative assessment by considering how performance management has developed over time.

PERFORMANCE MANAGEMENT DEVELOPMENTS OVER TIME

Performance management has its roots in the early 1900s with special attention for this practice in the US and British military for evaluating officers (Den Hartog et al., 2004). Drucker's (1954) concept of 'management by objectives', being part of a new school of thought (business administration and management), played an important role in linking appraisal to goal setting and people management. Bach (2000) argues that 'assessment of performance has become a pervasive feature of modern life', identifying three main reasons for the growing popularity of performance management in the 1980s:

1. Globalization resulted in increased competition and therefore a growing performance focus and more attention to achieving organizational goals by good people management.

2. Everybody, including HRM professionals, line managers, and employees, was dissatisfied with the administrative nature of the classic performance appraisals, mainly perceived as annual administrative obligations.

3. HRM professionals saw in PM an instrument for showing the added value of HRM in an organization.

Guest and Conway (1998) argued that performance management before 1990 was focused primarily on the content and the system, with an emphasis on the direct supervisor as the evaluator. They also point out that performance management before 1990 was typically top-down, being the property of the HRM department, and with a strong link to performance-related pay. After 1990, performance management changed fundamentally to include more attention to the underlying process, a joint evaluation (employee and supervisor), 360-degree feedback instead of top-down evaluation, performance management being the property of line management, and finally, a strong focus on employee development instead of performance-related pay (Guest & Conway, 1998).

More recently, performance management has attracted a lot of attention within public sector organizations, given governmental budget constraints, new public management (NPM) trends, and general cost cutting as a direct result of the global financial crisis (van Dooren et al., 2015). Ter Bogt and Scapens (2012), for example, claim the increased measurement of research and teaching performance in higher education is driven by the rise of NPM. This is supported by the study of Decramer et al. (2012), who note that the budgets for higher education and research have come under pressure since 2008.

In summary, in recent times there has been quite a marked shift in performance management from content to process, from supervisor evaluation to joint evaluation, from top-down to 360-degree, from performance-related pay to development, and from performance management being the property of the HRM department to it being owned by line management (see Figure 9.1). In addition, PM has received significant attention within

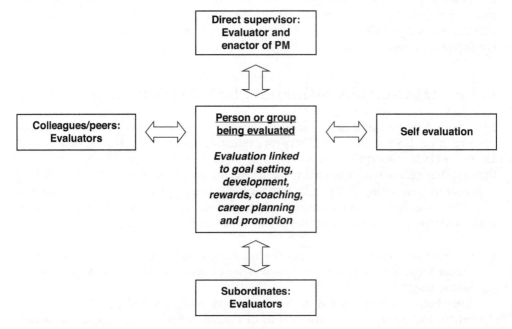

Figure 9.1   Performance management

the public sector context. As performance management has been expanding in these new directions, what does this mean for its linkage with other aspects of the HRM system?

PERFORMANCE MANAGEMENT AND HRM

Performance management is often seen as a microcosm of HRM, transferring the broader debate around the added value of human resource management to the performance management arena (Bach, 2000; Dewettinck, 2008). Special attention in both areas (HRM and performance management) is paid to alignment with the overall business strategy (strategic fit), alignment of practices towards a high-performance work system (horizontal or internal fit), line management involvement in the enactment of the practices, soft versus hard approaches (stressing the employee developmental side versus the individual performance side), and special attention to the search for interventions to increase firm performance. An ideal performance management system of practices is actually a sort of mini high-performance work system focused on goal setting, monitoring, appraising, developing, and rewarding employees in order to increase employee performance and to achieve organizational goals.

However, this performance management system can take on many guises. Several authors emphasize the relevance of different contextual factors that affect the ideal system for an organization (Dewettinck, 2008; Haines III & St-Onge, 2012; van Dooren et al., 2015). These contextual factors may include industry characteristics, firm size, degree of unionization, the history of the organization, and private versus public sector organization factors. Most importantly here, they may also include potential country and national institutional and cultural differences affecting performance management in an organization in a specific geographical location.

Claus and Briscoe (2008) present an overview of 64 articles published between 1985 and 2005 on employee performance management from an international perspective. The authors conclude that the academic literature on cross-border performance management is relatively atheoretical and exploratory in nature. They also conclude that the design and the substance of the empirical studies are weak. The majority of the empirical articles identified are focused upon or based upon performance management in multinational companies (e.g., Lam et al., 2002). Overall, Claus and Briscoe (2008) summarize the following major themes and findings from their literature review:

- Performance ratings of expatriates are influenced by the nationality of raters and ratees; the type of rater (self-evaluation, front line manager, or peer); personality characteristics of the raters and ratees; and by contextual factors including company size, international nature of the company, organizational structure, position and task of the expatriate, and geographical location.
- Context is important in performance management. Contextual factors that affect performance management include cultural factors affecting leadership styles and communication.
- The international literature focuses almost exclusively on the performance appraisal process rather than on the broader issue of the performance management system. In other words, it is important to understand more about the full system, rather than purely the evaluation process, for us to extend our international understanding.

- The convergence/divergence of performance management practices debate is mainly focused on the transferability of Western performance management practices to Asian countries, in particular China. Most empirical studies indicated a trend towards convergence. The convergence in this context refers to the tendency of applying universalistic performance management practices or best practices, such as 360-degree feedback mechanisms, irrespective of the country.

We observe an increasing number of empirical studies on performance management

Building on this work by Claus and Briscoe (2008), we now have an opportunity to study performance management in an international comparative setting using two distinct datasets: (1) comparative interview data from large, high-performing multinational companies (Global HR Research Alliance); and (2) comparative survey data from a range of organization in different countries (Cranet). The following sections describe how the data were gathered and the findings which emerged.

METHODS

Global HR Research Alliance

This study was designed to explore what MNCs themselves described as HRM excellence, and was carried out as part of a collaborative project together with Cambridge University (UK), Cornell University (USA), Insead (Singapore), and Erasmus University Rotterdam/Tilburg University (The Netherlands). Companies were selected for inclusion based on superior business performance and reputation as an employer based on 2004 Fortune and similar listings. Results from 16 companies (ABB, BAE Systems, BT, EDF, IBM, IKEA, Infosys, Matsushita, Oracle, Procter & Gamble, Rolls-Royce, Samsung Electronics, Shell, Siemens, TCL, Unilever) are discussed here.

In 2004–05, interviews were held with 248 interviewees (153 HRM professionals and 95 representatives of senior management, line managers, and employee representatives) in the 16 multinationals based in 19 countries (Belgium, Brazil, China, Dubai, France, Germany, India, Italy, Japan, Korea, Malaysia, Netherlands, Norway, Singapore, Spain, Switzerland, Sweden, UK, USA). These interviews were carried out at corporate headquarters, regional or country-level offices, or at division or site level within a specific business. The questions asked covered the whole range of HRM practices in these MNCs to try to uncover what they considered to be examples of best practice.

Case studies of each company describing their best practices in HRM were then drawn up and are analysed further here. The first step in the analysis was to group the companies at a regional level to try to observe patterns in performance management activities. This resulted in six Anglo-American MNCs, six continental European MNCs, and four Asian MNCs.

Cranet Survey

The Cranet data are collected through a standardized questionnaire that is sent to HRM directors at organizational level, and on average around 70 per cent of respondents fit this description. It covers the major areas of HRM. The survey gathers figures or requests

Table 9.1 Number of responses per country per survey round

Country	1999/2000	2004/05	2009/10
Austria	230	270	203
Belgium	282	230	240
Bulgaria	150	157	267
Czech Republic	188	72	54
Denmark	520	516	362
Finland	290	293	136
France	400	140	157
Germany	743	347	420
Greece	136	180	214
Italy	79	117	157
Netherlands	234	397	116
Norway	391	303	98
United Kingdom	1091	1101	218

'yes/no' answers to factual questions rather than asking for opinions. Only organizations with at least 200 employees are included in the study presented here. Data are used here from survey rounds in 1999/2000, 2004/05 and 2009/10 to show how HRM practice use might have changed over this decade. Due to slight changes in questions posed per data collection round, not all years can be reported for each question analysed. Although this is not intended to be a detailed trend analysis, it is indicative of some of the patterns we see in the use of the appraisal practices. Twelve countries from across Europe were selected from the full dataset for discussion (see Table 9.1).

The three core questions included in the survey that relate to performance management are analysed further here:

- Who is appraised: management, professional, clerical, manual staff?
- Who contributes to the appraisal: next-level manager, the employee themselves, subordinate?
- What are the outcomes of the appraisal system: training, HRM planning, career development, pay decisions?

RESULTS

In this section, we describe the findings from the two studies in turn, starting with the GHRRA study.

Comparative Analysis I: Performance Management in High-Performing Multinationals (GHRRA Study)

The first stage of the analysis was to look at what was common across this group of high-performing MNCs in terms of performance management. The findings can be divided into multiple dimensions, such as content, aims, and design criteria as described above.

However, more nuanced thinking behind the performance management systems also emerged.

First, these MNCs were talking about the strategic aims of performance management. More specifically, the emphasis was on creating alignment within the company, for example to create a high-performance culture, and performance management was seen as a tool to achieve this. In addition to alignment, another strategic goal was the development of individuals for the future, linked to talent management and succession planning processes. Thus, performance management is being used as a tool to support forward thinking and planning in these firms.

Second, interviewees talked about the performance management process in terms of the actual outcomes. Three key foci emerged here:

1. Career planning: facilitating succession planning, identifying high potentials and promotion opportunities.
2. Development: creating personal development plans.
3. Reward: determining performance-related pay, employee benefits and bonuses.

The third issue that interviewees raised was the criteria used in performance evaluation. Here there was a clear dichotomy between a desire to assess current performance at an individual or team level. The focus on technical skills and behavioural aspects was another issue raised by the interviewees. Firms were also using performance management as a means to assess potential performance (future performance). For this, they were taking capability or competency approaches, considering a person's current skill set against desired competency models of different job profiles.

The actual performance management tools and processes themselves can be divided into two categories. A first set contains tools designed to provide feedback, such as twice-annual appraisal meetings, two-way feedback, 360-degree appraisals, and benchmarking. The second set of tools were designed more as supporting frameworks: defining competency frameworks for specific roles in the organization, producing scorecards to enable discussion about performance, applying forced ranking or distribution systems, and clear goal setting.

One striking finding from the case studies is the extent to which information technologies (ITs) are playing a leading role in these performance management developments. IT enables standardization of systems. This means that it is easier to have a single performance management system for all employees across the globe, and to benchmark internally on employee performance. The IT systems also enable online support and resources, creating a broader toolkit for managers undertaking the performance evaluation and recording process.

Having reached these broad conclusions about what these high-performing MNCs from across the world have in common regarding PM, the case study data was then, as a next step, explored for any differences between MNCs in Anglo-American contexts (the United States of America and the United Kingdom), continental European contexts (Sweden, Switzerland, France, Germany, and the Netherlands) and Asian contexts (China and Singapore). This part of the analysis, perhaps surprisingly, raised very few results. Perhaps the nature of these globally operating firms means that they are benchmarking against each other, and hence are adopting very similar practices. Indeed, true

Table 9.2   *Percentage of firms with an appraisal system in operation for management, professional, clerical, manual staff grades (1999/2000 and 2009/10)*

	Management		Professional		Clerical		Manual	
	1999/2000	2009/10	1999/2000	2009/10	1999/2000	2009/10	1999/2000	2009/10
Austria	66.5	58.6	60.4	50.5	55.6	41.0	47.8	27.2
Belgium	79.5	83.8	86.0	82.9	78.4	82.9	71.4	42.5
Bulgaria	40.0	34.1	58.3	44.1	52.2	40.6	62.8	40.7
Czech Republic	59.0	80.4	60.0	79.6	48.6	79.6	38.6	52.3
Denmark	51.7	59.6	46.4	42.4	44.7	41.8	31.2	30.9
Finland	47.8	52.0	52.3	60.2	50.7	62.5	42.2	59.2
France	86.8	68.6	84.7	60.3	76.5	55.8	68.9	34.6
Germany	55.8	78.9	59.7	77.7	54.2	74.7	46.6	58.2
Greece	76.2	80.0	65.8	80.0	66.7	81.1	54.6	59.4
Netherlands	84.1	62.9	82.9	75.9	83.6	76.7	83.0	61.2
Norway	49.1	53.7	36.4	44.0	27.4	40.9	27.5	42.0
United Kingdom	91.2	85.5	90.1	84.9	85.5	83.1	68.5	63.1

patterns of difference in the data hardly emerged; however, some underlying trends were discernable. For example, there appeared to be the strongest talk of linking performance management to corporate-level activity (goal setting and culture) within the Anglo-American firms. In the Asian firms, there appeared to be slightly more focus on measuring current performance rather than potential performance (which perhaps is surprising, given the traditionally longer-term approach to the employment relationship within such firms). The continental Europe sample could be said to be paying the most attention to employee development issues emerging from the performance management process, with a clear separation (for example, in the Netherlands) between assessment for the purpose of determining reward, and assessment for development purposes. The survey data in the following analysis may shed further light on potential differences at country level.

Comparative Analysis II: Comparing Performance Management in Different Countries using Cranet Data

Because the data are collected from a range of different types of organizations (with a dominance of domestic organizations rather than the purely MNC sample presented above), we can gain a clearer picture at country level of performance management practices. Tables 9.2, 9.3 and 9.4 demonstrate different patterns of performance management practices, and how they change over time in multiple countries.

Table 9.2 shows a somewhat mixed result over time (1999/2000 compared to 2009/10), with organizations in seven countries reporting an increase in the use of appraisal systems for management, but five countries reporting a decrease in use. The opposite figures are true for appraisal systems for professional and manual grades. For clerical grades, there are six countries reporting an increase, and six reporting a decrease. In short, levels of appraisal use appear to be shifting, but not evenly across countries. The general pattern

Table 9.3   *Percentage of firms where the following people contribute formally to the appraisal process*

	Next level manager		Employee self		Subordinate	
	1999/2000	2004/05	1999/2000	2004/05	1999/2000	2004/05
Austria	48.3	64.7	37.2	76.3	12.2	23.1
Belgium	66.3	75.6	80.6	85.9	7.0	14.5
Bulgaria	67.0	81.2	24.5	43.5	13.2	21.1
Czech Republic	40.3	53.2	36.3	75.9	7.3	13.2
Denmark	36.0	59.4	76.3	96.2	16.3	19.6
Finland	40.7	62.9	79.1	90.5	26.0	35.9
France	38.2	62.4	71.9	92.7	5.3	11.0
Germany	56.7	68.7	32.2	68.9	7.1	19.5
Greece	83.2	90.7	51.4	75.5	9.3	17.9
Netherlands	62.9	62.0	83.4	82.9	8.8	16.3
Norway	42.3	42.6	65.3	66.7	13.1	13.5
United Kingdom	60.4	80.2	93.9	98.6	11.9	22.1

within countries is that the more senior you are, the more likely you are to be appraised. Exceptions to this include the Netherlands and Finland, where organizations are more likely to use appraisal for professional and clerical grades than they are for managerial grades. Bulgarian and Greek organizations report similar levels of use of appraisal for management, professional, and clerical grades. What is consistent across a large majority of countries is that appraisal is used least for manual staff.

Table 9.3 presents who contributes to evaluating employees as part of the appraisal process, comparing 1999/ 2000 with 2004/05 data. Here, we can see almost all increases in the contribution of managers who are the next level above direct supervisors, employees themselves, and subordinates who are being given the opportunity to contribute to the appraisal process. This 360-degree approach of asking for feedback from multiple stakeholders linked to the employee appears to be increasing in popularity across countries in Europe. The results are consistent in showing that subordinates are still by far the least likely group to be consulted.

Finland stands out here as the country in which organizations are most likely to involve subordinates in the appraisal process. Similarly, in the GHRRA research reported here, one company is already using an HRM 'dashboard' with information about the leadership capabilities of all the front-line managers from their subordinates. Red 'warning lights' against a front-line manager indicate poor evaluations by subordinates and a reason to take action. These actions might involve developmental interventions, but can also result in the replacement of the manager.

The final aspect of performance management considered here is the purpose of the appraisal process. Four options were given to respondents: identification of training needs, HRM planning (for example, promotion), career development, and pay determination. On average, identification of training needs remains the most popular outcome of the appraisal process (particularly in the Nordic countries of Norway, Finland, and Denmark, as well as Belgium). However, career planning and pay determination have increased in popularity as an outcome of the appraisal process over this ten-year period (1999/2000 to 2004/05 to 2009/10). HRM planning as an outcome is used least, on average, although many organizations in France and the Czech Republic continue to rely on this practice. If we look more closely at Table 9.4 there appears to be an interesting pattern for identification of training needs and career development. For these two themes a majority of countries in the dataset first show an increase when comparing the 1999/2000 data with the 2004/05 data, and then a decrease in the 2009/10 dataset. Given the nature of training and career development (long-term HRM investment related) this might be a direct result of the global financial crisis (GFC) that started in 2008. Participating organizations might have been confronted with economic crisis and forced to focus on short-term issues and decrease long-term efforts such as employee training and development. Unfortunately we do not have additional data to support these findings, and additional research is required. These findings might also have different causes, given the fact that the impact of external developments such as the GFC might take more than two years to observe in the empirical data (lag effects).

So What Do All These Empirical Data Tell Us?

Looking first at the case study data, these suggest that Guest and Conway's (1998) observed shift from content to process attention, from appraisal by the direct supervisor to joint evaluation (including employees' direct supervisors, peers, and clients), from top-down evaluation to 360-degree feedback mechanisms, from a strong emphasis on performance-related pay to a strong focus on employee development, and from performance management being the property of the HRM department to being the property of line management, is still relevant and being confirmed by our case studies in contemporary multinational companies. However, based on the results, we observe an extension of Guest and Conway's (1998) observations within the MNCs:

- First, there is a global tendency to use performance management to support corporate values and to align the corporate goals with individual employee goals. Performance management has become a vehicle for culture management in many multinational companies, which may explain why we are witnessing a great degree of similarity in this area of practice.
- Second, there is an increasing tendency among MNCs to apply performance management for identifying, developing, and rewarding talent (high potential). Performance management is often integrated with or part of the talent management programmes of an organization.
- Third, performance management is used for leadership development; for example, reflected in performance management as part of succession planning or the search and development of the future leaders of an organization.
- Fourth, there is increasing attention to applying performance management to distinguish good performers and bad performers.
- Fifth, the criteria used in the evaluation are linked to past performance, present performance, and potential performance, the last of these often measured through competency frameworks. Competency management and performance management often go hand in hand in the MNCs in this study.

Table 9.4   Percentage of firms where the appraisal system is used to determine the following outcomes

	1999/2000				2004/05				2009/10			
	Training	HR planning	Career	Pay	Training	HR planning	Career	Pay	Training	HR planning	Career	Pay
Austria	72.7	44.8	45.3	43.0	89.3	52.8	89.6	73.7	82.0	54.8	78.9	76.3
Belgium	87.6	68.2	63.2	66.7	92.5	52.7	87.2	78.5	83.3	35.8	78.8	70.8
Bulgaria	34.9	31.1	23.6	53.8	89.7	70.0	64.5	94.6	71.3	45.5	54.3	88.1
Czech Republic	66.1	63.7	53.2	71.0	97.0	78.1	93.9	77.8	89.6	78.3	86.4	76.6
Denmark	85.1	46.8	51.3	41.5	85.6	54.5	70.6	61.9	90.2	62.3	88.4	77.2
Finland	83.1	23.7	29.9	46.9	85.5	65.4	68.6	83.7	69.4	60.4	53.1	82.2
France	94.4	74.9	74.9	61.6	97.6	57.0	93.5	65.8	87.0	79.5	89.2	65.6
Germany	61.5	58.6	43.1	58.2	85.5	45.8	86.6	72.6	88.1	40.4	78.8	67.9
Greece	69.2	83.2	66.4	69.2	87.4	72.4	83.0	81.6	83.4	59.9	88.2	69.5
Netherlands	72.8	49.8	54.9	54.5	53.4	29.3	56.1	63.8	73.3	37.1	72.4	66.4
Norway	98.2	48.4	53.7	41.5	79.3	50.6	66.1	86.5	88.1	49.1	76.4	84.7
United Kingdom	72.7	44.8	45.3	43.0	89.3	52.8	89.6	73.7	84.6	53.3	73.7	55.8

- Sixth, performance management and 360-degree feedback mechanisms are often quite time-consuming and expensive. However, when applied, the outcomes can serve as input for benchmarks and scorecards reflecting the relative position of an individual employee, a specific department, a business unit, and/or an organization.
- Finally, performance management and new technology in terms of hardware, software, and networks are interwoven. There is a strong tendency towards corporate standardization and central control using new technology (for example, embedded in information and communication technology systems and used through shared service centres) affecting how performance is managed in MNCs.

In summary, performance management has developed further since Guest and Conway's (1998) observations, with a stronger strategic linkage to areas of culture management, talent management, leadership development, competency management, and technology.

The results of the Cranet survey support some of these case study findings, as well as expanding our understanding of how appraisal systems are implemented in multiple countries. First, the data show that organizations in different countries might be increasing or decreasing the use of appraisal systems, with little consistency in the pattern observed. Manual staff, however, remain least likely to be included in an appraisal system.

Second, the data show an increase in appraisal participation by people other than the direct supervisor. Other evaluators can be next-level managers, the individual employees themselves, and subordinates, although the use of subordinates in the evaluation system remains least used. These results are in line with the case study findings, supporting the notion that including multiple raters in the appraisal system increases the validity and reliability of the actual evaluation (Den Hartog et al., 2004). For example, including the next-level manager or other raters in the appraisal process potentially helps to eliminate bias that may occur if only the direct supervisor is involved.

The reported Cranet data focus on the 'use' or 'application' of performance appraisal. Wright et al. (2008) present survey data on appraisal practices that highlight both the use of a practice and its effectiveness. Their findings suggest that simply reporting that a practice is present is not the full picture: the effectiveness of these practices is regularly rated low, indicating the importance of the actual implementation process.

Finally, the survey data show an increase in the application of appraisal systems aimed at determining the training and development needs of employees, career development, and pay determination. It is interesting to note that training and development purposes have the highest scores. In other words, employee development is one of the most important elements of contemporary performance management. The GFC that started in 2008, however, might have affected the training and career component negatively in 2009/10 as a result of, for example, cost-cutting and 'short-termism' (focus on short-term actions that lead to short-term results). This does not hold for all countries in the dataset, and not for the components planning and pay.

Summary Conclusions

The Global HR Research Alliance case study data and the Cranet survey data show some interesting findings with respect to performance management in contemporary organizations. First, performance management is linked to or embedded in relevant areas of interest in practice such as culture management, talent management, leadership development (succession planning), competency management, and new technology.

Second, appraisal systems continue to be popular, in particular for more senior employee grades. There is also a shift towards 360-degree feedback systems with an emphasis on self-evaluation and feedback from next-level supervisors. The appraisal system is in place to determine career development and pay; however, most emphasis is on training and development.

Third, although there are few differences between regions in the case studies (probably because of their multinational nature), the Cranet data did highlight both some general patterns of appraisal system features that were common across countries, but also differences between countries. In particular, the use of appraisal systems in general showed a mix of some countries increasing whilst others are decreasing their use. The data taken together may be considered indicative of increasing standardization of performance management practices across the globe. If we look in more detail, however, there are contextual differences that may affect performance management in different countries. The main driver of these differences between countries appears to be associated to cultural differences reflected in variance in leadership, communication, and self-evaluation. In other words, the leadership styles, the nature of communication and information sharing, and the role of the individual in the appraisal procedure, differ between countries when looking through the lens of performance management.

With these conclusions, we enter into the debate around the extent to which HRM practices can be standardized across different countries, or whether the national context has an overriding effect. Guest and Hoque (1996: 50) start with the premise that 'even in an increasingly global economy, where transnationals compete in similar markets, we find persistent variations in the approaches to the management of human resources'. Indeed there is substantial evidence for this statement. For example, national-level characteristics (in this case, levels of spending on education and some aspects of national culture) have been found to affect the link between training and development practices and firm performance (Nikandrou et al., 2008). Equally, Parry et al. (2008) found evidence of certain HRM practices being more common within a specific type of market economy: firms in liberal market economies are more likely to use sophisticated selection techniques and have diversity programmes, whilst those in coordinated market economies are more likely to have trade union recognition and collective bargaining rights in place. This said, there is also some support for a more universalistic approach: Gooderham et al. (2008) argue that there is evidence of a link between calculative HRM practices (for example, individual performance-related pay and individual bonuses) and firm performance in multiple countries, but that these practices need to be embedded at organization level in a firm's strategic processes. However, none of the studies reported here are specific to performance management practices, about which recent research is scarcer.

Perhaps the debate can be clarified somewhat if we consider the type of organization we are looking at. Focusing on the difference between MNCs and domestic firms, there is clear evidence that these two types of operations adopt different approaches to HRM within the same country setting (Farndale et al., 2008). This gives some support to our findings that, in the case of performance management, it may well be that multinational firms are managing to implement standardized practices in many different country contexts, whilst the activities of domestic firms are more country-specific. The distinction between the 'best practices' and the 'best fit' schools of thought in the HRM field (Boxall & Purcell, 2008) can be applied to this MNC debate. Brewster et al. (2000) make a distinction between two paradigms: the universalist and the contextual. They argue that the universalist paradigm assumes the existence of best practices in HRM:

> careful and extensive systems for recruitment, selection and training; formal systems for sharing information with the individuals who work in the organization; clear job design; local level participation procedures; monitoring of attitudes; performance appraisals; properly functioning grievance procedures; and promotion and compensation schemes that provide for the recognition and financial rewarding of high performing members of the workforce. (Brewster et al., 2000: 11)

And that these can be successfully applied by multinational companies worldwide. In Europe, in particular, the contextual paradigm is more widespread (Brewster et al., 2000), building on the notion that there might be some general best principles in HRM (Boxall & Purcell, 2008), but the organizational context in the end determines the nature of the specific human resource practice. An illustration of the contextual paradigm in an international HRM perspective is the typical recruitment and selection of employees in much of Southern Europe through networks of family and friends (Brewster et al., 2000). The debate may then shift to the level of implementation: the empirical field is still lacking in research which explores the extent to which a global HRM policy from headquarters is implemented as intended in all the different subsidiaries, or whether differences at national and individual manager levels mean that the practice is implemented substantially differently in each location. We explore this point further below.

Finally, even if we start to look at an even broader range of countries than presented here, we start to reach some similar conclusions. Performance management in the United States of America (USA) is based strongly on the individualist culture and focuses primarily on linking individual performance to rewards. Performance management processes are also seen as organizational tools to avoid legal problems such as those covered by equal opportunities legislation (Pulakos et al., 2008). This US model of performance management was adopted in Mexico in the 1970s; however, a different culture and a lack of training of managers to carry out the systems, led to little progress in the development of sophisticated systems: the problems of implementing systems means they remain in an 'infancy' stage of progress (Davilla & Elvira, 2008). Similar slow progress is being seen in Turkey: there is evidence of wide use of performance management systems, but also evidence of these systems still being highly ineffective (Aycan & Yavuz, 2008).

Looking to Asia, in India there is substantial variation in the degree of sophistication of performance management practices between companies. The notion of performance evaluation is also difficult in this culture where the line manager often takes on a paternalistic role, raising issues of how objective feedback can be (Sharma et al., 2008). Finally, looking at China, this country has a long history of performance management, initially being a mechanism for monitoring attendance and skills. It has been harder to introduce a more Western approach to evaluation due to the values ascribed to age and seniority in this context (Cooke, 2008); nevertheless, there is evidence of merit-based performance appraisal systems emerging here too. In summary, this broader global picture still points to a certain degree of convergence in performance management practices, as concluded also by DeNisi et al. (2008: 258): 'as a country becomes more economically mature, [performance management systems] tend to move more closely towards the type of systems we find in the US and Western Europe'. In addition we have identified patterns of decrease related to PM, training and careers that are potentially the result of the global financial crisis, highlighting the potential impact of external economic factors on the shaping of PM in organizations.

Implications for Future Research

The findings in this chapter provide input for a future research agenda in performance management. First, there is little attention currently being paid to the enactment of performance management by line management, as suggested by Den Hartog et al. (2004). An exception is the study by Farndale and Kelliher (2013), which explores the important role that line managers play in creating employee experiences of the appraisal process. Other scholars emphasize the relevance of strategy implementation for creating organizational success (Becker & Huselid, 2006). One of the issues related to enactment is the role of the direct supervisor in the performance management process. HRM practices including internal promotion opportunities, employee development opportunities and pay increases are often closely linked to performance appraisal with a central role of the direct supervisor of the employee being evaluated. In general, the role of the front-line manager is neglected in HRM, and this is also the case in performance management.

Second, justice literature shows that part of the performance management success is a result of employee involvement in the design of a performance management system (Colquitt et al., 2001). Future research could focus on other potential critical success factors. These factors might include top management support, good communication, appropriate training, and the right IT infrastructure in terms of hardware and software available to support the performance management system.

Third, several authors have suggested that performance management and HRM show several commonalities (Bach, 2000; Dewettinck, 2008), including the alignment of individual practices (human resource practices or performance management practices) into coherent and consistent bundles. Future research could focus on ideal performance management bundles targeted at achieving internal fit within these bundles, and the linkage between the bundle as a whole to the organizational context (organizational fit).

Fourth, more attention could be paid in future research to the role of technology in controlling and standardizing performance management systems. Management information systems (MIS) and HR information systems (HRIS) play a crucial role in the underlying performance management processes, for example with respect to data collection, storage, access, analysis, and reporting. The development of the promising field of HRM analytics and Big Data approaches using advanced computer programs for analysing performance management data across a range of years is interesting and relevant.

Finally, our empirical findings showed very little variance in general between multinationals in their performance management practices, irrespective of their country of origin. It is possible that these MNCs pay more attention to their own organizational culture than to the impact of national cultures of local subsidiary operations. Future comparative research should therefore make a distinction between performance management practices in MNCs and performance management practices in domestic companies, the latter potentially being more subject to the national context than the MNCs which impose their own organizational culture across national borders. The increased attention for PM in public sector organizations also opens a whole new range of research areas both local and global. Large international governmental organizations such as the United Nations and European Union have shown an increased interest in performance management practices in recent years, partly caused by the global financial crisis (Boselie et al., 2013).

Implications for Practitioners and Practice

Contemporary performance management is a potentially powerful instrument that can be used to help solve organizational challenges including strategy implementation, talent management (attraction and retention of valuable employees), leadership development, and culture management aimed at creating a high-performance culture based on strong corporate values. Performance management has become a vehicle for culture management in many multinational companies by emphasizing the mission, goals, and values of the corporation in the competencies and criteria which are being used in the performance appraisal and management process. In this respect it is important to note that performance management includes (or should) all employees (clerical workers, manual workers, management, and professionals), and that it is a way to set organizational goals linked to individual goals.

It is also worthwhile noting that the alignment of individual practices (for example, appraisal, development, promotion, career development, and reward) into a coherent and consistent performance management system will be more likely to be successful than the application of single performance management practices without linking these together. A coherent and aligned performance management system will unequivocally send consistent messages to all employees concerning relevant and effective behaviours for realizing the stated goals at every level in the organization.

Some large and leading companies have recently decided to abandon (classic) performance appraisal and performance management systems, replacing them with a more continuous system of providing feedback and stimulating learning. This development will no doubt in the near future become more prominent due to the availability of digital data (HRM-Analytics) on a wide range of performance indicators on an almost continuous base.

Finally, it may be important to take into account international cultural differences (Brewster et al., 2004) that might affect the leadership style, the type of communication, the nature of rewards, and the use of self-evaluation in the performance management approach. The differences between Japan (large power distance, strong hierarchy) and Sweden (small power distance, emphasis upon employee empowerment and participation) are illustrative in this respect and determine the (im)possibilities for feedback vis-à-vis leaders and the involvement of employees in that process. However, due to the influence of so-called best practices, as being promoted by the large MNCs and management consultancy firms, we expect that for the years to come performance management will continue in the direction of increased inclusion of subordinates in the appraisal system. Mobilizing subordinates will then act as an important device for ensuring managers receive feedback on the different aspects of their leadership behaviour, which is indispensable for facilitating their learning process. In this respect it is interesting to note that line management's focus on and involvement with employee development is one of the most important elements of contemporary performance appraisal and performance management.

REFERENCES

Aycan, Z., & Yavuz, S. (2008). Performance management in Turkey. In A. Varma, P.S. Budhwar, and A.S. DeNisi (eds), *Performance Management Systems: A Global Perspective*: 168–179. London, UK and New York, USA: Routledge.

Bach, S. (2000). From performance appraisal to performance management. In S. Bach and K. Sisson (eds), *Personnel Management* (3rd edn): 341–263. Oxford: Blackwell.

Baron, A., & Armstrong, M. (1998). *Performance Management: The New Realities*. London: CIPD.

Baron, J.N., & Kreps, D.M. (1999). *Strategic Human Resources: Frameworks for General Managers*. Danvers, MA: John Wiley & Sons.

Becker, B.E., & Huselid, M.A. (2006). Strategic human resource management: Where do we go from here?. *Journal of Management*, 32(6), 898–925.

Biron, M., Farndale, E., & Paauwe, J. (2011). Performance management effectiveness: Lessons from world-leading firms. *International Journal of Human Resource Management*, 22(6), 1294–1311.

Boselie, P., Brewster, C., & Vos, E. (2013). *The Impact of the Global Crisis on the HRM of International Organizations*. Geneva: Association of HRM in International Organizations.

Boxall, P., & Purcell, J. (2008). *Strategy and Human Resource Management* (2nd edn). New York: Palgrave Macmillan.

Brewster, C., Mayrhofer, W., & Morley, M. (eds). (2000). *New Challenges for European Human Resource Management*. Oxford: Macmillan Press.

Brewster, C., Mayrhofer, W., & Morley, M. (2004). *Human Resource Management in Europe: Evidence of Convergence?*. London: Butterworth-Heinemann.

Claus, L., & Briscoe, D.B. (2008). Employee performance management across borders: A review of relevant academic literature. *International Journal of Management Reviews*, 10(2), 1–22.

Colquitt, J.A., Conlon, D.E., Wesson, M.J., et al. (2001). Justice at the millennium: A meta-analytic review of 25 years of organizational justice research. *Journal of Applied Psychology*, 86(3), 425–445.

Cooke, F.L. (2008). Performance management in China. In A. Varma, P.S. Budhwar, and A.S. DeNisi (eds), *Performance Management Systems: A Global Perspective*: 193–209. London, UK and New York, USA: Routledge.

Davilla, A., & Elvira, M.M. (2008). Performance management in Mexico. In A. Varma, P.S. Budhwar, and A.S. DeNisi (eds), *Performance Management Systems: A Global Perspective*: 115–130. London, UK and New York, USA: Routledge.

Decramer, A., Smolders, C., Vanderstraeten, A., & Christiaens, J. (2012). The impact of institutional pressures on employee performance management systems in higher education in the Low Countries. *British Journal of Management*, 23(1), 88–103.

Den Hartog, D.N., Boselie, P., & Paauwe, J. (2004). Performance management: A model and research agenda. *Applied Psychology: An International Review*, 53(4), 556–569.

DeNisi, A. (2000). Performance appraisal and performance management: A multilevel analysis. In S.W.J. Kozlowski and K.J. Klein (eds), *Multilevel Theory, Research, and Methods in Organizations: Foundations, Extensions, and New Directions*: 121–156. San Francisco, CA: Jossey-Bass.

DeNisi, A., Varma, A., & Budhwar, P.S. (2008). Performance management around the globe: What have we learned?. In A. Varma, P.S. Budhwar, and A. DeNisi (eds), *Performance Management Systems: A Global Perspective*: 254–262. London, UK and New York, USA: Routledge.

Dewettinck, K. (2008). Employee performance management systems in Belgian organisations: Purpose, contextual dependence and effectiveness. *European Journal of International Management*, 2(2), 192–207.

Drucker, P. (1954). *The Practice of Management*. New York: Harper & Snow.

European Journal of International Management. (2008). Special Issue on Global Performance Management. 2(2). Guest editors L. Claus and D. Briscoe.

Farndale, E., Brewster, C., & Poutsma, E. (2008). Coordinated vs. liberal market HRM: The impact of institutionalization on multinational firms. *International Journal of Human Resource Management*, 19(11), 2004–2023.

Farndale, E., Hope-Hailey, V., & Kelliher, C. (2011). High commitment performance management: The roles of justice and trust. *Personnel Review*, 40(1), 5–23.

Farndale, E., & Kelliher, C. (2013). Implementing performance appraisal: Exploring the employee experience. *Human Resource Management*, 52(6), 879–897.

Fletcher, C. (2001). Performance appraisal and management: The developing research agenda. *Journal of Occupational and Organizational Psychology*, 74(4), 473–487.

Gooderham, P., Parry, E., & Ringdal, K. (2008). The impact of bundles of strategic human resource management practices on the performance of European firms. *International Journal of Human Resource Management*, 19(11), 2041–2056.

Gruman, J.A., & Saks, A.M. (2011). Performance management and employee engagement. *Human Resource Management Review*, 21(2), 123–136.

Guest, D.E., & Conway, N. (1998). *Fairness at Work and the Psychological Contract*. London: CIPD.

Guest, D.E., & Hoque, K. (1996). National ownership and HR practices in UK greenfield sites. *Human Resource Management Journal*, 6(4), 50–74.

Haines III, V.Y., & St-Onge, S. (2012). Performance management effectiveness: Practices or context?. *International Journal of Human Resource Management*, 23(6), 1158–1175.

Lam, S.S.K., Chen, X.P., & Schaubroeck, J. (2002). Participative decision making and employee performance in different cultures: The moderating effects of allocentrism/idiocentrism and efficacy. *Academy of Management Journal*, 45(5), 905–914.

Legge, K. (1995). *Human Resource Management: Rhetorics and Realities*. London: Macmillan Business.

Moynihan, D.P., & Pandey, S.K. (2010). The big question for performance management: Why do managers use performance information?. *Journal of Public Administration Research and Theory*, 20(4), 849–866.

Nikandrou, I., Apospori, E., Panayotopoulou, L., Stavrou, E.T., & Papalexandris, N. (2008). Training and firm performance in Europe: The impact of national and organizational characteristics. *International Journal of Human Resource Management*, 19(11), 2057–2078.

Parry, E., Dickmann, M., & Morley, M. (2008). North American MNCs and their HR policies in liberal and coordinated market economies. *International Journal of Human Resource Management*, 19(11), 2024–2040.

Pulakos, E.D., Mueller-Hanson, R.A., & O'Leary, R.S. (2008). Performance management in the United States. In A. Varma, P.S. Budhwar, and A. DeNisi (eds), *Performance Management Systems: A Global Perspective*: 97–114. London, UK and New York, USA: Routledge.

Roberts, I. (2001). Reward and performance management. In J. Beardwell and T. Claydon (eds), *Human Resource Management: A Contemporary Approach* (3rd edn): 506–558. Edinburgh: Pearson.

Sharma, T., Budhwar, P.S., & Varma, A. (2008). Performance management in India. In A. Varma, P.S. Budhwar, and A.S. DeNisi (eds), *Performance Management Systems: A Global Perspective*: 180–192. London, UK and New York, USA: Routledge.

Ter Bogt, H.J., & Scapens, R.W. (2012). Performance management in universities: Effects of the transition to more quantitative measurement systems. *European Accounting Review*, 21(3), 451–497.

van Dooren, W., Bouckaert, G., & Halligan, J. (2015). *Performance Management in the Public Sector* (2nd edn). London: Routledge.

Wright, P.M., Holwerda, J.A., Stiles, P., et al. (2008). Sanyo Global HR Research Consortium: Global Survey of MNC HR Practices. Technical report.

10. Human resource development: national embeddedness
Olga Tregaskis and Noreen Heraty

INTRODUCTION

In a commentary on education across Europe, the Organisation for Economic Co-operation and Development (OECD) acknowledged human capital as a major factor driving economic growth, both in the world's most advanced economies and in those experiencing rapid development. This reflects a widely accepted recognition that an organisation's ability to create and share knowledge is a critical determinant of competitive functioning and organisational capabilities around the world today. The landscape of national skills markets across developed countries (OECD, 2011) is evolving in response to a range of pressures arising from technological advances, migration patterns, and national demographic change. In recognition of the scale of these changes, and the potential effects for the skills and knowledge base of labour markets, we scrutinise the debates and evidence in this chapter, updated from the first edition of this volume. Specifically, the chapter identifies the firm and institutional logics that have shaped human capital development within nations, but adds to this through a focus on changes in labour markets and the challenges these raise for individuals, firms, and policy-makers.

We begin with a brief examination of the organisational logic underpinning investment in human resource knowledge and skills, and use this as the foundation for exploring variation in national or geographic approaches to skills development. Beyond the organisational level, we review wider national systems as the fulcrum upon which variation in human resource development (HRD) systems and practices might be understood. Drawing upon the European institutional tradition where institutions are defined as the building blocks for social order, both to govern and to legitimise behaviour (Bosch et al., 2007: 253; Streeck & Thelen, 2005), we review both the national business systems literature and the more specialised literature on national innovations systems to demonstrate their influence on the nature of firm-level skills and learning. The chapter concludes with an examination of globalisation pressures and what these mean for the significance of national institutions in shaping firm-level behaviour.

HUMAN RESOURCE DEVELOPMENT AND FIRM LOGIC

The development of national competitive capability is strongly predicated upon an appropriate organisational base that places developed organisational learning processes as the vehicle for organisational knowledge and skill development. Kang et al. (2007) highlight knowledge as the most distinctive and inimitable resource available to firms that enables them to effectively employ, manipulate, and transform various organisational resources.

This notion of employees as representing the source of prime sustainable competitive advantage is largely attributable to the early work of Barney (1991) and Prahalad and Hamel (1990) on both the resource-based view of the firm and the development of core competencies, and, for the purposes of this chapter, has spawned a well-established literature on, among others, organisational learning (Senge, 1990; Pedler et al., 1994; Nonaka, 1991; Prahalad & Hamel, 1990; Watkins & Marsick, 1996) and human capital accumulation (Hitt et al., 2001; Carmeli & Schaubroeck, 2005; Antonacopoulou & FitzGerald, 1996; Huselid, 1995). Here, human capital is conceptualised as the levels and types of education, knowledge, skills, ideas, and experience available to the organisation, and is, according to Luthans & Youssef (2004), accumulated only through time, tenure, and organisational-specific developmental efforts. An organisation's absorptive capacity (Cohen & Levinthal, 1990), which reflects the stock of knowledge accumulated within the firm that is embodied in skilled human resources and accrued through in-house learning efforts, is seen as a critical enabler of competitive functioning, and as organisations struggle with competitiveness issues we have witnessed renewed interest in exploring the value and nature of work-based learning and HRD.

Garavan & McCarthy (2008) note that organisational learning is generally defined as a process enhancing the actions of organisations through better knowledge and understanding (Lundberg, 1995; Korth, 2000), and is conceptualised as an iterative process that involves action and reflection, change, and the creation of new knowledge and insight (Gond & Herrbach, 2006). It is also recognised as having a strong collective identity (Adler & Cole, 1993; Cook & Yanow, 1993; Huber, 1991). Kogut & Zander (1992: 385) underscored this presumption that organisational knowledge be understood as socially constructed, and pointed to the importance of the manner in which human resources are organised as a means of developing new knowledge. Drucker (1992) similarly depicted organisations as knowledge communities where knowledge is created, shared, and stored, thus compelling organisations to build continuous learning into their operating systems. The point was echoed by both Adler et al. (1999), who suggested that the main task of management involves the creation of an environment of knowledge interaction between individuals and the organisation; and Ulrich et al. (1993), who called for learning to become part of the organisation's normal functioning. Indeed Applebaum & Reichart (1998) cautioned that how well or badly the organisation learns will depend on the policies, structures, and processes that characterise the organisation.

However, notwithstanding the broad acceptance of the value and utility of well-developed and appropriate HRD efforts, here we echo Garrick (1999) in cautioning that any true understanding of HRD in organisations must necessarily be predicated by an awareness of the range of influences that affect it, including personal, political, and institutional features. This embedded nature of HRD is taken up in the following sections of this chapter, and we argue that the nature of an organisation's HRD effort is inexorably shaped and moulded by the national institutional and regulatory systems within which it operates. Learning embeddedness, as originally depicted by Polanyi (1962), acknowledges that all forms of exchange are inherently rooted in social relationships; here we argue that an organisation's HRD efforts are embedded in the social and institutional environment within which it is situated.

NATIONAL INSTITUTIONS AND HUMAN RESOURCE DEVELOPMENT

While a range of institutional perspectives exist, the one we focus on here is the varieties of capitalism perspective offered by Hall and Soskice (2001), which has been extensively applied to the consideration of human resource development in organisations (e.g., Estevez-Abe et al., 2001; Lam, 2003; Tregaskis et al., 2010). The comparative capitalisms literature is explored in detail in Chapter 2 of this volume. For our purposes here it is sufficient to note that these two market trajectories signpost different perspectives on competence creation through education, training, and development. In liberal market economies (LMEs), for example, employment conditions can become a critical bargaining tool for organisations which often engage in poaching to attract and retain scarce and valuable skill and knowledge resources. Here, employees are encouraged to invest in transferable skills and to use their investment in skills as a route to employability; while, in turn, firm strategy is adaptive and reinforces the skills available in the labour market. Coordinated market economies (CMEs), by contrast, support career trajectories which evolve around firm-specific skills to a greater degree. Moreover, education and training systems tend to be tailored to the needs of flexible labour markets, in that they provide certification and qualification of general skills as opposed to specialised skills. In this way, labour market skills are more transferable and therefore the mobility of the labour market is protected. In LMEs general education is provided by educational institutions through a combination of state and individual funding. Firms therefore focus on specific skills, but these are generally not sufficiently in-depth to lead to certification or qualification. In contrast, CMEs tend to emphasise specialisation in skill development, some of which is conducted through strong academic–industry partnerships. For example, apprenticeships can play an important role in the development of organisational or industry-specific skills. Such divergent approaches arguably lead to labour markets in LMEs which are rich in general transferable skills and thus promote greater labour mobility; while in CMEs there is likely to be a stronger reliance on specialised internal labour markets that result from the close tying of skills development to the needs of the firm or industry. Given the considerable employer costs associated with the development of specialised skills and developed internal labour markets, human resource management strategies are likely then to be heavily geared toward retention of, and maximising the contributions from, this internal labour market. Beyond the level of the individual firm, an educational system that promotes in-depth industry or firm-specific skills also facilitates the development of a common knowledge base, thus making inter-firm collaboration and knowledge transfer feasible.

Estevez-Abe et al. (2001) examined in more detail how different national approaches to skill formation shape organisational radical or incremental innovation strategies by examining the role of employment and unemployment protection. In a comparison of 18 OECD countries, they identified particular country clusters with identifying characteristics as follows:

- Weak employment and unemployment protection and a focus on the development of general skills represented by the Anglo-Saxon countries including the United States of America (USA), the United Kingdom (UK), Australia, New Zealand, Canada, and Ireland.

- Strong employment and/or unemployment protection and firm, industry, and occupational-specific skills. This includes the continental European countries, along with Japan. Within this cluster were countries such as Japan and Italy that had a particularly strong focus on firm-specific skills and employment protection; while Denmark, Switzerland, and the Netherlands focused on industry-specific skills and legal and fiscal protections against unemployment.

Estevez-Abe et al. suggest that the linkages between social protection and the emphasis on general or specialised skill formation puts certain countries in a stronger position to pursue business strategies more or less reliant on radical or incremental innovation. Economies where labour flexibility at the lowest cost to employers is coupled with transferable general skills, as exemplified in the Anglo-Saxon countries, allow organisations to be responsive and to change direction to pursue new business opportunities. However, where firm or industry-specific skills are dominant, this makes it more difficult for organisations to change business direction rapidly. This, coupled with high costs associated with labour skills, results in them being more vulnerable to the risks associated with failed exploration into new areas. This is offset, however, by the fact that firms in these countries can better maximise the returns on current products via their ongoing improvement and development due to the in-depth skills profile of their internal labour markets.

Using an index of scientific citation rates and low-wage employment, Estevez-Abe et al. found empirical support for the proposed relationship between skills and social protection on the one hand, and incremental or innovation strategy on the other. Specifically, the Anglo-Saxon countries were found to have much higher scientific citation rates, which were taken as a proxy for radical innovation, compared to continental European countries and Japan. Firms that have high skills and stronger social protection were much less likely to penetrate markets that relied on low-tech product markets.

In a related line of enquiry Hanushek et al. (2011) have examined the relative merits of apprenticeship-based compared to general education-based national systems of competence creation in terms of the effects on the economic health of the individual. On the one hand it is argued that vocational-based systems, being job-focused, represent a highly beneficial mechanism to enable the transition of young people from school into employment. However, it is also argued that the specificity of such technical and job-focused training makes it more difficult for individuals and firms to adapt to dynamic business environments or the rapid changes associated with, for example, technological change. Research examining the impact of vocation or general education credentials on employment across an individual's life-span indicates that: (1) earnings for those with general skills outstrips those with vocational skills; and (2) while vocational education appears to ease the transition from school to work, employability later in life is lower than for those with general education. There is some evidence to suggest, however, that vocational education is somewhat less effective in equipping individuals with the necessary skills to adapt to changes in the knowledge base arising from industry upgrading and technological change (Hanushek et al., 2011).

There is a more specific body of work that has examined the institutional arrangements associated with technical innovation (Patel & Pavitt, 1997; Pavitt, 1999) and, arguably, it brings the organisation and sector into greater focus (Lundvall, 2007;

Guerreri & Tylecote, 1997) in that it provides a useful analytical tool for examining human resource development in a comparative context. Comparing across OECD countries we see divergent patterns in research and development (R&D) expenditure across different sectors (Table 10.1). For example, the USA has traditionally concentrated on R&D in defence and health and is still by far the greatest investor in health-related R&D, accounting for three-quarters of that of the OECD countries (OECD, 2007). In proportionate terms, health-related R&D was just over 0.22 per cent of gross domestic product (GDP) in the USA in 2006; the UK was the second-largest investor at 0.11 per cent; and France invested 0.06 per cent; which compares with 0.03 per cent for both Japan and Germany. In contrast, Japan focused more on energy R&D and Germany on industrial R&D. It is argued that this pattern of R&D investment also explains the emphasis within the USA, UK, and France on radical innovation strategies which are science-intensive and where the primary motivation for effort and funding is linked to finding the next new technology or scientific breakthrough. The types of industries that R&D activity and investment focused on in the USA, the UK, and France tend to be what are referred to as technology-intensive, that is, aerospace, instruments, pharmaceuticals, office machinery and computers, electrical machinery, electronic equipment, and components.

These divergent national trends in industrial specialisation illustrate the interdependencies between competence creation approaches (that is, general versus apprenticeship systems), and the role of external labour markets in meeting firm-level competitive strategies. For example, close relationships between universities and private industry in the USA are argued to be central to the innovation capability of the USA, enabling organisational flexibility. US universities are also the main destination for students overseas to study for graduate and PhD programmes (OECD, 2007). US universities are viewed as undertaking a significant proportion of world-class research that, since it is funded by industry, is therefore easily accessible to industry. External labour markets and employee mobility provide the means through which skills and knowledge are shared (Lam, 2003). Professional networks across science communities or communities of practice (Brown & Duguid, 1991) are also arguably significant in this context as a means through which employees can update their skills and knowledge base. As competition is high among R&D-intensive industries, collaboration is minimal. This places a high price on specific skills, which makes individual knowledge and skills a valuable commodity. In this way, providing demand for these skills remains, there is an incentive for individuals to invest in their own skill development, and for the employer in return to provide high financial rewards or the opportunity for skill enhancement.

By contrast, the German innovation system is seen as supportive of incremental innovation, whereby technological change is aided by adaptation and its primary focus is the diffusion of innovation as opposed to the pursuit of a specific mission. German R&D activity also focuses on supporting medium-technology-intensive industries such as industrial chemicals and motor vehicles (see Table 10.1). The dual system of vocational education is often seen as one of the primary institutional structures reinforcing this innovation system. An apprenticeship system which combines quality academic study and practical experience has yielded a skilled labour force, allowing skills to be updated through the process of work and influencing how work is organised. The implication for human resource development in firms within this type of innovation system is quite

Table 10.1   Share of business R&D in the manufacturing sector by technology intensity

	High-technology	Medium-high-technology	Medium-low- and low-technology
Finland	66.4	19.5	14.0
Canada	64.3	16.3	19.4
United States (2003)	63.6	26.3	10.1
Ireland	62.7	22.3	15.0
United Kingdom	62.5	28.2	9.20
Korea	60.2	29.6	10.1
Sweden (2003)	58.5	34.1	7.40
Denmark	57.9	26.5	15.5
OECD (2003)	53.0	35.4	11.7
France (2003)	51.8	34.8	13.5
Netherlands	50.9	36.9	12.2
Belgium	49.5	29.9	20.5
EU (2003)	46.7	42.2	11.2
Italy	46.5	41.0	12.5
Japan (2003)	42.8	43.8	13.4
Spain	35.9	39.1	25.0
Germany	33.5	58.6	7.80
Norway	31.6	32.5	36.0
Poland	30.5	48.2	21.3
Australia (2003)	26.5	39.2	34.2
Czech Republic	18.8	66.6	14.6

Source: OECD (2007).

different from those associated with the US, discussed above. For example, the dual system places considerable emphasis on the firm to support skill creation and its ongoing development. Skills and knowledge are of less value as an individual commodity, and more value to the firm. This is because more of the labour market share similar skill sets, and wage protection for skilled employees restricts employers' ability to use financial incentives to poach skilled staff. In addition, the value of skills to the employer comes into play when skilled employees, who require less supervision than their counterparts in the UK or the USA, are able to problem-solve and innovate to improve performance as an integral dimension of work organisation. This capability is obviously critical to sustaining an innovation strategy based on incremental adaption, as opposed to radical innovation.

The dynamic nature of the interplay between institutions and organisation is clear, although much of the institutionalist theorisation has been criticised for its failure to adequately capture the change mechanisms at play (Bosch et al., 2007). Future work needs to unpick the nature of the interaction between actors within the institutional systems as a means of understanding how both organisations and institutions are changing. Further, there has been an emphasis on matching organisational and institutional responses to maximise innovation and learning. But as we shall argue below, the dynamics of national and international labour markets raise issues with respect to consequences for the economic, social, and psychological well-being of employees that may well be key drivers of institutional and organisational change.

LABOUR MARKET CHANGE: IMPLICATIONS FOR HRD CREATION AND UTILISATION

Here we consider how technological advances, and changes in migration patterns and the age demography of the labour force, impact upon the skills and knowledge base inherent in labour markets and the implications these have for competence creation and utilisation.

Technological Advances

Technological advances in developed economies are reducing demand for unskilled labour in traditional trades, whilst emergent technologies and industries are pushing toward cross-disciplinary skills hybridisation, leaving a skills vacuum as formal training lags behind R&D advances. Expansion of international outsourcing also brings changes to national labour market skill structures. As firms in developed countries outsource lower-skilled activities to developing or lower-wage-based economies, it reduces the demand for low skills in those home countries. At the same time, high-skilled technology remains robust in the developed countries, thus creating a shift in the labour market skill structure in developed countries (Hijzen et al., 2005).

Technological advances create industrial upgrading in the sense that they allow some firms to integrate high-tech solutions within their production, R&D, and service processes. Industrial upgrading can demand changes in product architectures such as lean production systems whereby in order to shorten the time from product development to market, firms in automotive or machine tool industries require inter-functional work designs between product developers and the shopfloor. As a result the competences required by employees shift (Jürgens & Krzywdzinski, 2015) and we see the relevance of problem-solving skills and general education competence come to the fore. International comparative research has examined lean production in Japanese firms, US firms, and European – most notably UK and German – firms (Lazonick, 1990; Barton & Delbridge, 2004). This work has demonstrated barriers to effective lean production arising from employee cooperative competence. Communication, cooperation, and problem-solving across functional areas of expertise is critical to meet the productive demands of firms in contemporary business contexts (Collins & Smith, 2006; Jürgens, 2000; Fujimoto, 2000; Lazonick, 2005). When we consider earlier debates around the relative merits of general and apprenticeship-based competence creation systems, the challenges arising from technological advances would indicate the need for very different organisational HRD responses across countries.

Migration and Skills

In the HRM literature the term 'migrant' appears to be used as an umbrella term that captures those who move geographical locations, cross national borders, and change their main country of residence. To better understand the resources this group bring to national labour markets, and the effective utilisation of migrant skill resources, the need to define and identify the heterogeneity amongst this broad group is critical. Al Ariss (2010) noted four differentiating features: the national origin of these individuals, voluntary or forced nature of their migration, time away from their home nation, and the host nation's symbolic treatment of this group. For example, migrants from the USA, Australia, and Western Europe are often referred to as expatriates whilst those from developing or transitioning countries may be referred to as migrants or immigrants (Al Ariss & Crowley-Henry, 2013). Further, the degree of heterogeneity within this group is vast and thus presents different opportunities and challenges for both firms and nations. Understanding the heterogeneity and the implications this may have for skill utilisation nationally and at firm level is only beginning to be evidenced (Dietz, 2010; Doherty, 2013; Kofman, 2000; Suutari & Brewster, 2001).

Western labour markets have witnessed an increasing reliance on migrants (Al Ariss & Syed, 2011; Zikic et al., 2010). However, the evidence base suggests that migrants face specific issues in terms of their skills being undervalued, sometimes referred to as 'skill discounting' (Li et al., 2006). The migrant labour market is often treated as a homogenous group and as such has given rise to an underutilisation of skilled resources. Evidence indicates that the qualification and experience of skilled migrants is often devalued. For example, evidence from analysis of Canadian labour force data indicated that unskilled migrants were as likely to gain employment as locals. But skilled migrants were significantly less likely to gain employment than locals (Dietz et al., 2015). These results may in part be explained with reference to employment protection, which usually indicates that international applicants can only be used to fill positions in the absence of equivalent local skills. However, employers raise ongoing concerns about skill shortages across national labour markets. The devaluation of skilled migrant human capital and their potential underemployment warrants closer understanding. Skill discounting can include a devaluing of foreign academic qualification or education, foreign work experience, or competence development activities. This often leads to underemployment of migrants, with jobs being filled by those who are vastly overqualified for the role, or a migrant working in a job that has no relationship to the profession or vocation for which the individual has invested (e.g., Salaff et al., 2002; Dietz et al., 2015).

Research has explored explanations for this devaluation, suggesting that there are a number of explanations. First, the employers often do not see the value of international experience or qualifications, and this is a situation that can apply as much to a local as a migrant. Thus, unless international competences relates to the specifics of a firm's strategic goals, and unless there is familiarity with such competence, there is a general perception that this is of less relevance. Second, skilled migrants are particularly vulnerable to their skills being devalued as a result of their skills being perceived as a threat to local careers (Dietz et al., 2015). Equally, research evidence suggests that where firms emphasise inclusiveness or a fit between international competence and strategic needs, then devaluation of migrant skill is less likely (Dietz et al., 2015). Effective utilisation of migrant skill from labour markets would seem to be tightly tied to the firm's capability in mastering their approach to diversity and understanding the business case for diversity.

At an institutional level the regulatory framework and policy on migration can have a profound impact on the types of migrant resources in national labour markets. Administration around work permits and visa restrictions makes some countries more or less attractive to skilled migrants choosing to move (Rodriguez & Mearns, 2012).

Guo and Al Ariss (2015) highlight the gap in our evidence base on gender and migration despite the fact that women constitute half the total numbers worldwide (OECD, 2013) and dominate professions such as nursing (Kofman, 2000). The UK National Health Service (NHS) is highly reliant on skilled migrant nurses, and in many of these instances family migration has been led by the female in the household and not the male. Thus the evidence base is revealing migration as a gendered experience. For women, career opportunities abroad that are not available at home are particularly important antecedents of migration.

Skilled international migrants offer employers a means of addressing local labour market skill shortages. However, the evidence base suggests that to be able to effectively tap into this potential resource, employers need to be more mindful of developing inclusive resource strategies and considering the strategic value these resources bring. Institutional barriers in some countries may also mean that employers in some country contexts may need to be cognisant of the additional support required by prospective talent. If individual migrants have to absorb the costs or navigate complex institutional systems, the likely result is that this labour resource will be diverted to other countries that are seen to be less complex to access. Parallels here can be drawn with the efforts governments make to attract multinationals, and the concomitant support they create to help firms navigate resources and opportunities locally (Almond et al., 2015). Further, the focus on how people management practices might impact upon employee or organisational well-being (Purcell & Hutchinson, 2007; Tregaskis et al., 2013) becomes potentially magnified when we consider migrant labour. The reason for this is that migrant workers may be exposed to more precarious forms of employment contract, face challenges arising from the need to adjust to different cultural and national work norms, and face particular financial burdens arising from the institutional structures around country migration policy and skill and education recognition. As a result, firms may need to look to how their HRM processes can support migrant workers as they navigate regulatory conditions, but also in adjusting to work performance expectations, work relationships, and community norms (Bahn, 2015).

Age and Skills

Described by Chand and Tung (2014) as a seismic demographic transformation, the ageing of the world's population is at the forefront of most developed economies' policy agendas. In her Foreword to the European Commission (2014) report on *Population Ageing in Europe*, the Commissioner for Research, Innovation and Science, Máire Geoghean-Quinn noted that longevity is one of the biggest achievements of modern societies and one that will likely bring about significant changes to the structure of European society, particularly since, by 2020, a quarter of Europeans will be over 60 years of age. Concomitant to stagnant replacement rates in these ageing economics is population growth in several developing economies, thus pointing to polarisation in global populations, and linking with altering patterns of global migration as discussed above. This 'greying' of the population in developed economies is of particular interest to labour market analysts and firms' management alike. For the first time, there are four distinct generations employed in the workplace, with suggestions that these distinct generational cohorts have somewhat different values and knowledge expectations, which may give rise to more individualistically tailored approaches to career and skills development. Ageing labour forces pose a range of challenges at national as well as firm level since, in the West at least, dominant stereotypes of 'older', and older workers in particular, tend overall to be more negative than positive, and to attribute mostly negative job-related characteristics to this group which, in this context here, include lower job performance, more resistant to change, less able to learn, and less economically beneficial than are younger workers. The salience of the issue is evidenced in the number of age discrimination cases across the world, where in spite of increasingly protective employment legislation workers perceive that they have been discriminated against in organisations because they are older. Whilst acknowledging some growth in positive attitudes toward older workers, and the likely existence of simultaneous negative and positive attitudes (Parry & Tyson, 2009), the persistence of negative age stereotypes remains and impacts upon access to employment, access to opportunities and development during employment, and selection for exit from employment. As life expectancy increases around the globe, and people may expect to live for up to 20 years post-retirement, we are more likely to see people remaining within the workforce for longer, or seeking alternative forms of phased retirement bridge employment, or some other variant, in order to ensure greater financial security into their older years. Donaldson et al. (2010) argue that organisations are now giving increased consideration to how older workers are deployed in the workplace, while Topa et al. (2009) suggest that we explore alternatives to our current models of utilising older workers, and revisit our career trajectories to ensure greater generativity and knowledge sharing at the level of the firm. Thus national and local systems of knowledge and skill deployment and development will be affected by increasing longevity, and the different pressure points that can be identified at different stages in the employment life cycle.

GLOBALISATION AND THE EMBEDDEDNESS OF HRD

Globalisation on many levels, including the internationalisation of businesses, financial markets, consumer markets, and technology, has had a significant impact on the interconnectedness of economic activity across countries and regions of the world. Here we consider the globalising effect of multinationals, supranational institutions, and sub-national institutions, and the potential consequences for human resource development approaches.

First, the multinational is seen as one of the lead drivers of globalisation (see Held et al., 1999 for an overview) or global dominance effects. As multinationals expand their global reach, it is argued that they attempt to increase their control of overseas operations to minimise costs and maximise efficiencies. This has the effect of promoting greater standardisation across the supply chain of firms captured within the multinational corporation (MNC) network, pressing for integration across activities on multiple levels such as cross-border investment, production, and intra-organisational trade. In contrast, the network models of MNC organisation suggest that the strength of the multinational lies in its ability to leverage the local competitive advantage which is embedded within the local communities and combine this with knowledge from other local sites to create global innovation (e.g., Hedlund, 1999; Ghoshal & Bartlett, 1990). In this way national comparative advantage remains important to the MNC, as actions that undermine this could have knock-on effects for the global capabilities of the firm. The evidence, perhaps not surprisingly, demonstrates that the globalising impact of the MNC is mixed and quite contradictory (see, e.g., Kristensen & Zeitlin, 2006). While the evidence is well debated in Chapter 2 in this volume, it is worth reiterating here that different priorities with respect to global learning, coupled with strategic cost management models that can result in the loss of recently developed skill sets, do have appreciable effects on the globalisation of the HRD effort.

In an examination of the influence of MNC country of origin on the diffusion of human resource practices across national borders, Ferner and Varul (2000) argue that firms may assimilate practices from other countries into their own models of operating, such that 'a distinctive national business system may learn to adapt to the demands of internationalized operation while retaining and even consolidating its distinctiveness'. Indeed, survey data on foreign- and home-owned MNCs operating in the UK (Edwards et al., 2007), and in Ireland (Lavelle et al., 2009), attest to the continuing significance of country of origin in explaining the diversity of MNC practice. One stream of analysis from this work examined the presence of intra-organisational learning structures (that is, expatriate assignment, international project groups) in the UK operations of home- and foreign-owned firms. These structures were argued to be key elements supporting global learning in multinationals in that, for example, they allowed for new knowledge to be created through identifying synergies, or for best practices to be diffused. The results suggested that the extent to which such global learning structures were adopted depended, in part, on the country of origin of the parent. Specifically, it was argued that the way in which skills and knowledge were created differs in Japanese firms compared to US, German, and other European firms because of their embeddedness in institutions affecting career progression, international mobility, internal labour utilisation, and the strategic business function of subsidiaries (Tregaskis et al., 2010). Similarly Lam (2003) argued that the distinctive national institutions in Japan related to firm-specific skill development meant that Japanese firms were less able to create systems to support the development of knowledge and skills in international learning spaces, compared with US MNCs. In sum, the evidence suggests that while MNCs may be seen as sources of innovation on global practices, this has not necessarily led to standardisation across MNCs or a weakening of the impact of national business systems. Instead firms appear to be more or less able to absorb elements of global practice and assimilate them within their norms of practice, creating an adjustment but not necessarily a fundamental shift in the assumption of organisation.

Second, globalisation is argued to have brought into play the importance of supranational institutions and their role in shaping organisational behaviour and skill acquisition at the national and firm levels. As discussed in Chapter 2 in this volume, while globalisation has initiated institutional changes at the supranational level that have affected a wide variety of organisational behaviours, there is less evidence that national models are becoming obsolete. Indeed it may be the case that we are likely to see greater variation across countries. For example, Bosch et al. (2007: 262) argued that while the institutional structures around skill acquisition may have prevented UK manufacturing moving away from a low-skills base dependent on mass production, in parallel there has been the growth of its 'specialisation in tradable as well as more domestically-orientated services'. As a consequence, the low-skills base in manufacturing may be of less salience than heretofore because the nature of productive activity is changing. They also showed that the supranational governance structures which have led to deregulation of product markets (that is, the move toward privatisation of transport, energy, and telecommunications) has led to greater variety in national employment models, rather than greater homogeneity. This is largely explained by the extent to which product markets and employment market regulation are intertwined. In Scandinavian countries such as Sweden and Denmark, labour standards are statutorily based and collectively agreed. Therefore multinationals attempting to provide services in industries protected by these agreements must conform to national pay levels and agreements. In Germany, however, the privatisation of telecommunications and establishment of call centres by foreign firms which were not bound by collective agreements has led to a fragmentation of collective bargaining and low wages. This has implications for the sustainability of high investment skills models in labour-intensive industries embedded within a high-protection employment model.

Finally, institutions at the sub-national regional level are becoming recognised as potentially powerful players in interpreting local responses to globalisation pressure (Ferner et al., 2006; Cantwell & Piscitello, 2002). Here the evidence suggests that regions within countries have organised as competitive clusters, whereby businesses are attracted to certain regions because of the availability of specific skills and knowledge resources. The types of actors that are important here include, for example, trade unions, economic development agencies, those involved in skill provision, research bodies, and employers' groups. Sub-national governance structures have been identified as particularly pertinent in debates on the supply and demand for high and low skills (Fuller et al., 2002; Keep et al., 2006). The dynamic engagement between firm and local institutional actors indicates relational processes at work that enable a degree of adaptation between firms and state resources (Almond et al., 2015), and the potential for positive and reciprocal synergies within the interaction (Monaghan et al., 2014; Tregaskis and Almond, 2018). These are issues that come to the fore when you consider, for example, countries where institutional arrangements at the sub-national level vary significantly, as in the case of eastern and western Germany, or Spain where autonomous regional governments exist, or Canada and the USA which are organised as federal states. Crouch (2005) argues that the role of sub-national actors is important to consider as they can potentially work to create specific local advantages that are aimed at encouraging business to locate to a local region, and to remain there, and which can shape the nature of labour market skills in those local areas. He refers to this as 'institutional entrepreneurship', and makes the important point that such action may be contradictory to the national business model. However, the role of these sub-national players and how they interact with local or global business and supranational institutions and their impact on learning and skills is largely under-researched.

CONCLUSION

In this chapter we have considered the strategic logic underpinning management models of human resource development in firms. While these models allude to the embeddedness of the organisation in local and international environments, there is scant evidence of conceptualisation of how this embeddedness operates and influences the manner in which practices are incorporated into firms' management regimes. In an effort to extend this conceptualisation, we have drawn on the institutional literature to demonstrate how national and sub-national institutions can shape labour market skills acquisition and firm behaviour. The national business systems literature demonstrated the importance of the interaction between national approaches to skill development focused on general or specific skills, and the mobility of these skills, on the one hand; and on the other hand, firm strategies with regard to incremental or radical innovation. We also considered how technological changes, migrant workers' skills, and indeed the changing age demographic, impact on the structure of national labour markets. Firms require, and can access, work skills that have been created from within foreign national systems of education and training. This offers opportunities for firms to more efficiently attenuate skill shortages at local and national levels. Similarly, the age diversity of labour markets brings with it specific challenges in terms of how resources are utilised and deployed at the level of the firm. Attitudes towards different cohorts of workers can have appreciable effects on the decision-making process at the local level, and may require more careful monitoring to avoid polarisation effects into the future. The research evidence suggests that greater learning and adaptation may be required at both the firm and institutional levels to enhance understanding, amongst the range of skills stakeholders of how best to value and tap into these resources. When looking at globalisation debates and the influence of multinationals on national models of employment and skills acquisition, we suggest that there is growing evidence of the reciprocal evolution in firm strategy and institutional arrangements. The relational bridges built between different stakeholders involved in employment and skills ecosystems is a critical causal mechanism explaining change (Tregaskis and Almond, 2018), but more work is required in this area.

Global changes in technology and labour market structures are impacting on the nature of work and the skills required by individuals, and businesses. The attraction of foreign investment to developed countries and the development of an agile and sustainable skills arena at the national level has led to calls by policy-makers for partnerships between the beneficiaries of skills (OECD, 2011). It is argued that such a response is needed to better apportion some of the costs of skills development to governments; to stimulate a demand-led skills market; and to create flexible (content, mode, and cost) delivery mechanisms in order to widen participation and thus improve the well-being (financial, wealth, and health) of the individual and society. Skills partnerships require the capacity at the institutional, organisational, and individual level for cross-boundary working and innovations in skills models that enable a more dynamic skills response. Differences in motivation, incentives, and social identity between stakeholders can create barriers to effective partnership. Further, spatial disparities between economic growth within countries – argued as preferable by some (Cheshire et al., 2014; World Bank, 2009) and not by others (Gardiner et al., 2010; OECD, 2012) – raises important questions with respect to the role of social partners and individual actors in how skills partnership are enacted in practice, outside of the large conglomerations or in contexts that proactively promote spatial rebalancing. It also requires comparative research that can explore the complexity of interactions through multi-method and multivariate models to aid in teasing out the casual mechanisms at play and to identify where and how changes occur.

REFERENCES

Adler, P.S., & Cole, R.E. 1993. Designed for learning: A tale of two auto plants. *Sloan Management Review*, 34(3): 85–94.

Adler, P.S., Goldoftas, B., & Levine, D.I. 1999. Flexibility versus efficiency? A case study of model changeovers in the Toyota production system. *Organization Science*, 10(1): 43–68.

Al Ariss, A. 2010. Modes of engagement: Migration, self-initiated expatriation, and career development. *Career Development International*, 15(4): 338–358.

Al Ariss, A., & Crowley-Henry, M. 2013. Self-initiated expatriation and migration in the management literature: Present theorizations and future research directions. *Career Development International*, 18(1): 78–96.

Al Ariss, A., & Syed, J. 2011. Capital mobilization of skilled migrants: A relational perspective. *British Journal of Management*, 22(2): 286–304.

Almond, P., Ferner, A., & Tregaskis, O. 2015. The changing context of regional governance of FDI in England. *European Urban and Regional Studies*, 22(1): 61–76.

Antonacopoulou, E.P., & FitzGerald, L. 1996. Reframing competency in management development. *Human Resource Management Journal*, 6(1): 27–48.

Appelbaum, S.H., & Reichart, W. 1998. How to measure an organization's learning ability: The facilitating factors – Part II. *Journal of Workplace Learning*, 10(1): 15–28.

Bahn, S. 2015. Managing the well-being of temporary skilled migrants. *International Journal of Human Resource Management*, 26(16): 2102–2120.

Barney, J. 1991. Firm resources and sustained competitive advantage. *Journal of Management*, 17(1): 99–120.

Barton, H., & Delbridge, R. 2004. HRM in support of the learning factory: Evidence from the US and UK automotive components industries. *International Journal of Human Resource Management*, 15(2): 331–345.

Bosch, G., Rubery, J., & Lehndorff, S. 2007. European employment models under pressure to change. *International Labour Review*, 146(3/4): 253–277.

Brown, J.S., & Duguid, P. 1991. Organizational learning and communities-of-practice: Toward a unified view of working, learning, and innovation. *Organization Science*, 2(1): 40–57.

Cantwell, J., & Piscitello, L. 2002. The location of technological activities of MNCs in European regions: The role of spillovers and local competencies. *Journal of International Management*, 8(1): 69–96.

Carmeli, A., & Schaubroeck, J. 2005. How leveraging human resource capital with its competitive distinctiveness enhances the performance of commercial and public organizations. *Human Resource Management*, 44(4): 391–412.

Chand, M., & Tung, R.L. 2014. The aging of the world's population and its effects on global business. *Academy of Management Perspectives*, 28(4): 409–429.

Cheshire, P., Nathan, M., & Overman, H.O. 2014. *Urban Economics and Urban Policy: Challenging Conventional Policy Wisdom*. Cheltenham, UK and Northampton, MA, USA: Edward Elgar Publishing.

Cohen, W.M., & Levinthal, D.A. 1990. Absorptive capacity: A new perspective on learning and innovation. *Administrative Science Quarterly*, 35(1): 128–152.

Collins, C.J., & Smith, K.G. 2006. Knowledge exchange and combination: The role of human resource practices in the performance of high-technology firms. *Academy of Management Journal*, 49(3): 544–560.

Cook, S.D., & Yanow, D. 1993. Culture and organizational learning. *Journal of Management Enquiry*, 2(4): 373–390.

Crouch, C. 2005. *Capitalist Diversity and Change: Recombinant Governance and Institutional Entrepreneurs*. Oxford, UK and New York, USA: Oxford University Press.

Dietz, J. 2010. Introduction to the special issue on employment discrimination against immigrants. *Journal of Managerial Psychology*, 25(2): 104–112.

Dietz, J., Joshi, C., Esses, V.M., Hamilton, L.K., & Gabarrot, F. 2015. The skill paradox: explaining and reducing employment discrimination against skilled immigrants. *International Journal of Human Resource Management*, 26(10): 1318–1334.

Doherty, N. 2013. Understanding the self-initiated expatriate: A review and directions for future research. *International Journal of Management Review*, 15(4): 447–469.

Donaldson, T., Earl, J.K., & Muratore, A.M. 2010. Exploring the influence of mastery, planning and conditions of workforce exit on retirement adjustment. *Journal of Vocational Behavior*, 77(2): 279–289.

Drucker, P. 1992. *Managing for the Future*. Oxford: Butterworth-Heinemann.

Edwards, T., Tregaskis, O., Edwards, P., et al. 2007. Charting the contours of MNCs in Britain: Methodological challenges in survey research. Jointly published by DMU's Occasional Paper Series and Warwick Business School's School's Warwick Papers in Industrial Relations.

Estevez-Abe, M., Iversen, T., & Soskice, D. 2001. Social protection and the formation of skills: A reinterpretation of the welfare state. In P. Hall and D. Soskice (eds), *Varieties of Capitalism: The Institutional Foundations of Comparative Advantage*: 145–183. Oxford: Oxford University Press.

European Commission. 2014. *Population Ageing in Europe*. Directorate General for Research and Innovation. Brussels: European Commission.

Ferner, A., Quintanilla, J., & Sánchez-Runde, C. 2006. *Multinationals, Institutions and the Construction of Transnational Practices: Convergence and Diversity in the Global Economy*. Basingstoke: Palgrave.

Ferner, A., & Varul, M. 2000. 'Vanguard' subsidiaries and the diffusion of new practices: A case study of German multinationals. *British Journal of Industrial Relations*, 38(1): 115–140.

Fujimoto, T. 2000. Shortening lead time through early problem-solving: A new round of capability-building competition in the auto industry. In U. Jürgens (ed.), *New Product Development and Production Networks*: 23–53. Berlin: Springer.

Fuller, C., Bennett, R., & Ramsden, M. 2002. The economic development role of English RDAs: The need for greater discretionary power. *Regional Studies*, 36(4): 421–428.

Garavan, T.N., & McCarthy, A. 2008. Collective learning processes and human resource development. *Advances in Developing Human Resources*, 10(4): 451–471.

Gardiner, B., Martin, R., & Tyler, P. 2010. Does spatial agglomeration increase national growth? Some evidence from Europe. *Journal of Economic Geography*, 11(6): 1–28.

Garrick, J. 1999. *Understanding Learning at Work*. London: Routledge.

Ghoshal, S., & Bartlett, C.A. 1990. The multinational corporation as an interorganizational network. *Academy of Management Review*, 15(4): 603–626.

Gond, J.-P., & Herrbach, O. 2006. Social reporting as an organisational learning tool? A theoretical framework. *Journal of Business Ethics*, 65(4): 359–371.

Guerreri, P., & Tylecote, A. 1997. Interindustry differences in technical change and national patterns of technological accumulation. In C. Edquist (ed.), *Systems of Innovation: Technologies, Institutions and Organisations*: 107–129. London: Pinter.

Guo, C., & Al Ariss, A. 2015. Human resource management of international migrants: Current theories and future research. *International Journal of Human Resource Management*, 26(10): 1287–1297.

Hall, P., & Soskice, D. 2001. *Varieties of Capitalism: The Institutional Foundation of Comparative Advantage*. Oxford: Oxford University Press.

Hanushek, E., Woessmann, L., & Zhang, L. 2011. General education, vocational education, and labor-market outcomes over the life-cycle. NBER Working Paper 17504, National Bureau of Economic Research, October.

Hedlund, G. 1999. The intensity and extensity of knowledge and the multinational corporation as a nearly recomposable system (NRS). *Management International Review*, 1(1): 5–44.

Held, D., McGrew, A., Goldblatt, D., & Perraton, J. 1999. *Global Transformations: Politics, Economics and Culture*. CA: Stanford University Press.

Hijzen, A., Görg, H., & Hine, R.C. 2005. International outsourcing and the skill structure of labour demand in the United Kingdom. *Economic Journal*, 115: 860–878.

Hitt, M.A., Biermant, L., Shimizu, K., & Kochhar, R. 2001. Direct and moderating effects of human capital on strategy and performance in professional service firms: A resource-based perspective. *Academy of Management Journal*, 44(1): 13–28.

Huber, G.P. 1991. Organizational learning: The contributing processes and the literatures. *Organization Science*, 2(1): 88–115.

Huselid, M.A. 1995. The impact of human resource management practices on turnover, productivity, and corporate financial performance. *Academy of Management Journal*, 38(3): 635–672.

Jürgens, U. 2000. Communication and cooperation in the new product and process development networks – an international comparison of country- and industry-specific patterns. In U. Jürgens (ed.), *New Product Development and Production Networks*: 107–147. Berlin: Springer.

Jürgens, U., & Krzywdzinski, M. 2015. Competence development on the shop floor and industrial upgrading: case studies of auto makers in China. *International Journal of Human Resource Management*, 26(9): 1204–1225.

Kang, S.-C., Morris, S.S., & Snell, S.A. 2007. Relational archetypes, organizational learning, and value creation: Extending the human resource architecture. *Academy of Management Review*, 32(1): 236–256.

Keep, E., Mayhew, K., & Payne, J. 2006. From skills revolution to productivity miracle: Not as easy as it sounds? *Oxford Review of Economic Policy*, 22(4): 539–559.

Kofman, E. 2000. The invisibility of skilled female migrants and gender relations in studies of skilled migration in Europe. *International Journal of Population Geography*, 6(1): 45–59.

Kogut, B., & Zander, U. 1992. Knowledge of the firm, combinative capabilities and the replication of technology. *Organization Science*, 3(3): 383–397.

Korth, S.J. 2000. Single and double-loop learning: Exploring potential influence of cognitive style. *Organization Development Journal*, 18(3): 87–98.

Kristensen, P.H., & Zeitlin, J. 2006. *Local Players in Global Games*. Oxford: Oxford University Press.

Lam, A. 2003. Organizational learning in multinationals: R&D networks of Japanese and US MNEs in the UK. *Journal of Management Studies*, 40(3): 673–703.

Lavelle, J., McDonnell, A., & Gunnigle, P. 2009. *Human Resource Practices in Multinational Companies in Ireland: A Contemporary Analysis*. Government Publications. Dublin: Stationery Office.

Lazonick, W. 1990. *Competitive Advantage on the Shop Floor*. Cambridge, MA: Harvard University Press.

Lazonick, W. 2005. The innovative firm. In J. Fagerberg, D. Mowery, and R. Nelson (eds), *The Oxford Handbook of Innovation*: 29–55. Oxford: Oxford University Press.

Li, C., Gervais, G., & Duval, A. 2006. The dynamics of overqualification: Canada's underemployed university graduates. Statistics Canada, Income Statistics Division.

Lundberg, C.C. 1995. Learning in and by organizations: Three conceptual issues. *International Journal of Organizational Analysis*, 3(1): 353–360.

Lundvall, B.Å. 2007. National innovation systems: analytical concept and development tool. *Industry and Innovation*, 14(1): 95–119.

Luthans, F., & Youssef, C.M. 2004. Human, social, and now positive psychological capital management: Investing in people for competitive advantage. *Organizational Dynamics*, 33(2): 143–160.

Monaghan, S., Gunnigle, P., & Lavelle, J. 2014. Courting the multinational: Subnational institutional capacity and foreign market insidership. *Journal of International Business Studies*, 45(2): 131–150.

Nonaka, I. 1991. The knowledge-creating company. *Harvard Business Review*, 69: 96–104.

OECD. 2007. Science, technology and industry scoreboard. Paris: OECD.

OECD. 2011. Towards an OECD skill strategy. Paris: OECD.

OECD. 2012. Promoting growth in all regions. Paris: OECD.

OECD. 2013. World migration in figures. Paris: OECD.

Parry, E., & Tyson, S. 2009. *Managing an Age-Diverse Workforce*. London: Palgrave Macmillan.

Patel, P., & Pavitt, K. 1997. The technological competencies of the world's largest firms: complex and path-dependent, but not much variety. *Research Policy*, 26(2): 533–546.

Pavitt, K. 1999. *Technology, Management and Systems of Innovation*. Cheltenham, UK and Northampton, MA, USA: Edward Elgar Publishing.

Pedler, M., Boydell, T., & Burgoyne, J. 1994. *A Manager's Guide to Self-Development*. London: McGraw-Hill.

Polanyi, M. 1962. *Personal Knowledge*. Chicago, IL: University of Chicago Press.

Prahalad, C., & Hamel, G. 1990. The competence of the corporation. *Harvard Business Review*, 68(3): 79–93.

Purcell, J., & Hutchinson, S. 2007. Front-line managers as agents in the HRM–performance causal chain: theory, analysis and evidence. *Human Resource Management Journal*, 17(1): 3–20.

Rodriguez, J.K., & Mearns, L. 2012. Problematising the interplay between employment relations, migration and mobility. *Employee Relations*, 34(6): 580–593.

Salaff, J., Greve, A., & Ping, L.X.L. 2002. Paths into the economy: Structural barriers and the job hunt for skilled PRC migrants in Canada. *International Journal of Human Resource Management*, 13(3): 450–464.

Senge, P. 1990. *The Fifth Discipline*. New York: Doubleday.

Streeck, W., & Thelen, K. 2005. *Beyond Continuity: Institutional Change in Advanced Political Economies*. Oxford: Oxford University Press.

Suutari, V., & Brewster, C. 2001. Making their own way: International experience through self-initiated foreign assignments. *Journal of World Business*, 35(4): 417–436.

Topa, G., Moriano, J.A., Depolo, M., et al. 2009. Antecedents and consequences of retirement planning and decision-making: A meta-analysis and model. *Journal of Vocational Behavior*, 75(1): 38–55.

Tregaskis, O., & Almond, P. 2018. Multinationals and skills policy networks: HRM as a player in economic and social concerns. *British Journal of Management*. DOI: 10.1111/1467-8551.

Tregaskis, O., Daniels, K., Glover, L., et al. 2013. High performance work practices and firm performance: A longitudinal case study. *British Journal of Management*, 24(2): 225–244.

Tregaskis, O., Edwards, T., Edwards, P., et al. 2010. Transnational learning structures in multinational firms: Organizational context and national embeddedness. *Human Relations*, 63(4): 471–499.

Ulrich, D., Jick, T., & Von Glinow, M.A. 1993. High-impact learning: Building and diffusing learning capability. *Organizational Dynamics*, 22(2): 52–66.

Watkins, K.E., & Marsick, V.J. 1996. *In Action: Creating the Learning Organization*. Alexandria, VA: American Society for Training and Development.

World Bank. 2009. *World Development Report: Reshaping Economic Geography*. Washington, DC: World Bank.

Zikic, J., Bonache, J., & Cerdin, J.L. 2010. Crossing national boundaries: A typology of qualified immigrants' career orientations. *Journal of Organizational Behavior*, 31(5): 667–686.

11. Comparative employment relations: definitional, disciplinary, and development issues
*Werner Nienhüser and Chris Warhurst**

INTRODUCTION

In the United States of America (USA), the hotel industry is regarded as a 'classic' low-wage industry (Bernhardt et al., 2003). Concerned about the perilous low level of wages in the US industry, a multinational team of US-led researchers turned their attention to Europe, anticipating that similar jobs in the European hotel industry would be better. 'In fact', the researchers discovered, 'things don't seem that much better on the other side of the Atlantic' (Vanselow et al., 2010: 270). Jobs in the European countries' hotels were also low-skilled, and work intensification was likewise common. As in the USA, low pay was endemic but, strikingly, the relative level of that low pay varied amongst the countries. Moreover, some aspects of hotel jobs in Germany were coming to resemble those in the USA. The initial expectations of an enlightened European hotel industry were thus confounded: there were as many differences amongst the countries of Europe as there were between those countries and the USA, and even then, jobs in Europe were changing. These findings were replicated across a number of other service and manufacturing industries included in the study, and 'there is no simple one-dimensional US-versus-Europe story. There is variation within Europe too', Solow and Wanner (2010) noted. Whilst this research was overtly concerned with job quality, as Solow and Warner note, defining job quality is difficult, even pointless they say; in practice, the focus was on employment relations within each country, how those employment relations are constructed, and how they are developing or might be developed.

This example neatly captures how the term 'employment relations' envelops both practice and a field of study: both a set of material practices and a way of looking at those practices. It also highlights how employment relations are dynamic: that the practices and the ways of looking at them develop. In this respect, a key debate in an era of putative 'globalisation' centres on not just what shapes employment relations, but also the extent to which employment relations in different countries are converging or remain different.

This chapter maps out and engages with these debates and developments. It has two main objectives: first, to outline how employment relations are understood; and second, to highlight how employment relations are said to be changing. Given our opening comments, the starting point to understanding comparative employment relations has to be an explication of those relations; more precisely, what characterises and shapes employment relations as practice. This explication is the focus of the next section of this chapter. The chapter then outlines the differing disciplinary lenses through which employment rela-

---

* Within this chapter when Britain is referred to this excludes Northern Ireland; when the UK is referred to this includes Northern Ireland.

tions are typically studied and explained. These two discussions are used in the chapter's fourth section to frame an exposition of what is happening to employment relations; or rather, the claims that are being made about what is happening to employment relations, with an illustration from a key debate about 'Japanisation'. The concluding section of the chapter offers some suggestions about the future agenda for employment relations in terms of practice and field of study.

CHARACTERISING EMPLOYMENT RELATIONS: SIMILAR TERM, DIFFERENT MEANINGS/SAME MEANING, DIFFERENT TERMS

It would be useful to be able to start with a clear definition of 'employment relations'. Unfortunately, providing this definition is no easy task. There are competing proprietorial claims to employment relations both as practice and field of study, and which also reflect their development over the last half century. The two key claimants are industrial relations and, more recently, human resource management. Whilst historically sequential and nominally different, the two terms are useful analytical springboards for they indicate a common concern through which employment relations can start to be characterised and its features identified.

For historical reasons, the starting point is industrial relations. It is within the field of industrial relations that what is now termed employment relations were framed for most of the second half of the twentieth century. According to Bamber et al. (2016: 3), industrial relations focuses 'on the formal and informal institutions of job regulation, including collective bargaining, unions, employers' associations and labour tribunals'. The primary concern is with trade unions and management's negotiations with those unions over pay, the terms and conditions of employment, and employee voice, for example; sometimes with the state acting as third-party convenor or mediator, sometimes with the state aligning with one side in those negotiations. Indeed, the key actors shaping industrial relations are employers, trade unions, and the state. Bi- and trilateral arrangements between these actors are sometimes referred to as 'corporatism', which itself has a number of forms in different countries (Panitch, 1981). As such, the individual country – or, less often, a sector within a country – is the primary level of analysis for industrial relations.

It is interesting to note that some texts claiming to offer comparative industrial or employment relations are often little more than a collection of national country studies, albeit sometimes very good collections (e.g., Ferner & Hyman, 1998; Bamber et al., 2016). It is only recently that publications have appeared offering comparisons of two or more selected countries (e.g., Barry & Wilkinson, 2011; Frege & Kelly, 2013a; Wilkinson et al., 2014). It is also unfortunately true that industrial relations has become synonymous not just with collective action but also, in attempting to deal with the putative 'labour problem', with conflict; and so associated with confrontation, strikes, and disruption (Bray et al., 2009; Kochan, 1998). Some interests in some countries, for example employer associations such as the Business Council of Australia and the Howard governments in Australia over the turn of the twenty-first century, have used these unhelpful connotations to attack and undermine trade unions (Bray et al., 2009: 5). Whilst the attack upon trade unions in Australia was overt, similar outcomes have occurred in other countries, with trade union density, coverage, and power having declined in most of the advanced economies over the last decades of the twentieth century (Kelly, 2015). As a consequence, the capacity and willingness of employers (and the state) to countenance trade unions has also declined (Kelly, 1994; Upchurch et al., 2009).

In this respect, human resource management (HRM) is sometimes claimed to have superseded industrial relations, and has now become the main claimant on employment relations. It is concerned with 'all those activities associated with the management of the employment relationship' (Boxall & Purcell, 2003: 1[1]). Within this approach, staff in organisations dealing with personnel issues no longer sit down around a table with trade union officials to hammer out collectively agreed terms and conditions of employment, but instead are tasked with aligning the organisations' human resource needs (read: labour power) with the needs of individual employees, and so are more concerned with planning and development issues (Schein, 1988) and, in its harder US version, the 'auditing' of human resources to better match organisational supply and demand (Legge, 1995). However, although supposedly shifting away from the 'labour problem', the (now recast) management of performance is still 'the dominant research issue', according to Guest (1997: 263). Indeed, generating high-performance work systems has become the Holy Grail of human resource management. Of course, delivery remains elusive. As a consequence, as it faces a crisis of legitimacy, human resource management has attempted to become more 'strategic' (Kochan, 2007). The attempt by human resource professionals to better manage the relationship with individual employees has become distilled into the more individualised 'employee relations'. With its 'milder tone' (McKenna & Beech, 2002: 255), employee relations is an HRM approach that seeks direct communication with employees at the level of the individual employee. Now, though, human resource professionals themselves need to possess the right 'skills and competencies' to elicit 'performance benefits' from employees (CIPD, 2009). Again however, the 'roots' of employee relations are to be found in the organisational provision of social welfare as a means of social control to address the 'labour question' (Blyton & Turnbull, 1998).

What the shift over the last 50 years from industrial relations to HRM, with its variant employee relations, reveals is that whilst terminology and (some) practices change, the concerns remain the same. Whether cast as performance management or the 'labour question', the need to elicit efficacious labour from employees is the key issue. It is not surprising therefore that, despite the different terminology, it is often difficult to disentangle industrial relations and human resource management in terms of purpose; and the same is true of the turn to employment relations.

The attempt to align employer and employee interests again features in the broad definition of employment relations offered by Rollinson and Dundon (2007: 5); they state that, as a field of study, it 'embraces the potentially wide range of interactions and processes by which parties to the relationship adjust to the needs, wants and expectations of each other in the employment situation'. This bland definition masks a number of complex issues and also the crux of the 'relationship'. As Edwards (1995: 47) makes clear:

---

[1]   In the third edition Boxall and Purcell define HRM as 'management of work and people in organisations' (Boxall & Purcell, 2015: 1).

the subject of employment relations has developed a focus on the organisation and control of the employment relationship: the processes through which employers and employees – who are tied together in relations of mutual dependence underlain by exploitation – negotiate the performance of work tasks, together with the laws, rules, agreements and customs that shape these processes.

As with HRM, the decision to use the term 'employment relations' rather than 'industrial relations' is often simply a matter of choice, framed by the shift from collectivism to individualism in the workplace (e.g., Rose, 2004) and, with this shift, the need for practitioners (and some academics) to maintain their utility (see Blyton & Turnbull, 1998; Edwards, 2003; Bamber et al., 2016; Frege & Kelly, 2013a). It is as if employment relations is for researchers of industrial relations who 'dare not speak its name', given its bad press through association with (declining) trade unions, and who feel uncomfortable with the more managerialist human resource management. Occasionally the mask slips to reveal the overlaps, as McKenna and Beech (2002: 255) illustrate: 'Prior to the advent of HRM, employee relations was often called industrial relations' (see also CIPD, 2009). Of course, the approach to dealing with the labour–performance 'problem' or 'question' often but not always differs (Blyton & Turnbull, 1998; Legge, 1995); but at its most basic, employment relations, as with industrial relations, human resource management, and employee relations, is concerned with the employment relationship and what is a reward–effort (or wage–effort) bargain. At the centre of this bargain is a labour contract: a legal artefact in which one party (the employer) agrees to exchange money (pay) for what becomes the employee's labour (effort and time, usually) (Kaufman, 2004a).

The employment relationship has a number of complexities. First, although it is contract-based, what is being exchanged in that contract – labour – is not like other commodities in that it is intangible; what is bought by employers is potential, not actual, labour. It only becomes actual labour in its execution. This complexity is often called the indeterminacy of labour. Through the employment relationship employers seek to overcome this indeterminacy not just by signing a contract but, in the workplace, having the right to direct, monitor, evaluate, and even discipline employee performance – within reasonable limits (Kaufman, 2004b). As a consequence, the employment relationship is continuous, not a one-off exchange (Blyton & Turnbull, 1998), and is often contested because what is exchanged can at times be scarce or abundant, and employer profits can be high or low, which decreases or increases pressure on employee performance (usually expressed as 'productivity') (Edwards, 1979; Rollinson & Dundon, 2007).

The second complexity arises from the various – and usually said to be differing – interests and objectives brought to the employment relationship by the key actors concerned with it: employers, employees, and the state. In the workplace the interests of employers (and their proxies: managers) and employees can be conflictual, cooperative, or harmonious, as Fox (1974) long ago noted in what remains an important exposition of the ideologies informing industrial relations. The interests of employers and employees are in general conflictual regarding the appropriation and distribution of surplus value arising from expended labour. At the same time, employers and employees have a mutually common interest: to maintain the organisation, and its profitability if in the private sector (Cressey & MacInnes, 1980). As a consequence, some form of compromise, or at least acquiescence, is usually achieved. If acquiescence occurs it is because an asymmetry of power exists within the employment relationship, usually in favour of employers; which is why collective action through trade unions often provides more power for employees.

A third complexity arises out of the embeddedness of the employment relationship within countries and, as a consequence, how these interests and objectives can be mediated by the laws, rules, regulations, and norms of each country. These country differences are sometimes expressed as 'business systems' (Whitley, 1992), 'production regimes' (Gallie, 2007) or, more popularly amongst researchers, 'varieties of capitalism' (Hall & Soskice, 2001b). The legal context of countries is particularly important here because it defines the content of the labour contract – for example, regulations for ending the contract – and the basic rights and obligations of the exchange parties. Other important influences are the industrial structure and labour market of each country, both of which can be dynamic; each country has sunset and sunrise industries, and rising and falling levels of unemployment, both of which affect the bargaining power of the parties. Union density too within countries influences the voice or exit options for employees within the employment relationship (Hirschman, 1970).

Referring to both a field of study and material practices, the analytical core of employment relations is thus the employment relationship and the exchange between employer and employee centred on the reward–effort bargain. This relationship is complex, contextual, and dynamic. This characterisation provides some clarity, although it belies a number of underpinning theoretical considerations that usefully signal the importance of recognising the range of disciplines that seek to explain the *gestalt* of employment relations, and to which we now turn.

THE DIFFERENT DISCIPLINARY LENSES ON EMPLOYMENT RELATIONS

It should be noted that employment relations is not a discipline but a field of study upon which different disciplinary lenses focus, as Table 11.1 illustrates. The key disciplines concerned with employment relations are economics, sociology, political science, and social psychology. Within each discipline there are core assumptions (for example, efficiency and cost minimisation, power and conflict, need satisficing) about employment relations drawn, first, from particular theoretical approaches (transaction cost theory, labour process theory, institutional theory and the psychological contract); and second, pitched at particular levels of analysis (individual, firm, or national level). We now briefly review these different approaches, showing how they conceptually capture and present employment relations. It should be noted that theories can be used cross-disciplinarily, becoming decoupled from their disciplinary origin. Transaction cost theory, for instance, has become influential in sociology and the political sciences; likewise, the varieties of capitalism approach has crossed over from political economy and political sciences into sociology and economics.

Within economics, transaction cost theory seeks to explain what type of employment relations occurs under which circumstances (Williamson, 1984, 1985). The theory assumes that transactions in general, and the effort–reward bargain in particular, are characterised by incomplete information and the possibility of opportunistic behaviour. Because of these uncertainties, individuals and firms safeguard against negative conse-

Table 11.1   Different approaches to employment relations (ER)

Discipline	Typical theories	Core assumption on mechanism explaining differences in ER	Employment relations are mainly seen as . . .	Typical level of analysis
Economics	Transaction cost theory	Cost-minimising behaviour (of the employer)	Cost-minimising institutions regarding the effort–reward bargain	Firm
Sociology	Labour process theory	Power-maximising behaviour (of the employer)	Means of power and exploitation	Country, historical analysis
Political economy/ political sciences	Institutional theory (varieties of capitalism)	Adaption to the institutional context	Institutional context securing the supply of an adequately skilled and motivated workforce at reasonable wages	Country
Social psychology	Psychological contract	Need (of the employee) for a balanced, equitable psychological contract	(Implicit) contract between employer and employee	Individual (firm)

quences by means of specific institutional arrangements. The institutionalisation and operation of the employment relationship and the resulting nature of employment relations are understood as institutional arrangements that reduce the uncertainties in the exchange between employee and employer (Williamson, 1984; Williamson et al., 1975). The employer attempts to secure income from investments in human capital and to ensure control of productivity. In contrast to classical and neoclassical economics, transaction costs as well as production costs (wages) are important. Transaction costs include the costs of procuring information about the employee, the costs of the possible *ex post* negotiation performance of the employee, and other conflicts between the employer and employee (Williamson, 1984).

The central hypothesis of transaction cost theory regarding employment relations and its core, the employment relationship, can be summarised as follows: the harder the monitoring (or 'metering' in the language of Williamson, 1984) of the productivity of an employee, and the more the employer needs firm-specific qualifications, the more a long-term employment relationship is effective and the less effective is a market-oriented, short-term relationship (spot market). Long-term employment helps to prevent the migration of specific human capital. Examples of jobs for which such an exchange system would be efficient could include consulting activities by bank employees when granting loans or in the real estate business. An example of jobs for which employees can be hired and fired without incurring costs would be migrant workers in (Californian) agriculture (Williamson, 1984).[2] Transaction cost theory thus attempts to answer the question why there are differences in firm strategies: different forms of employment relations are seen as institutional arrangements for regulating the transactions within the employment relationship; and differences in employment relations depend on the need for firm-specific human capital and the extent of control problems. A key assumption of transaction cost theory is that the claims of employers and employees cannot be completely specified and claims must therefore be enforced within the work process – within the exchange itself – and cannot be adequately addressed externally. Hence, the typical level of analysis of transaction cost theory is the firm.

Sociology-orientated, labour process theory also takes the indeterminacy of labour (that is, that the employer purchases potential, not actual, labour) as its explicit starting point but, unlike transaction cost theory, posits that an asymmetry of power exists in the employer's favour in the exchange with the employee (Marginson, 1993). Nevertheless, a transformation problem exists for the employer: the transformation of potential labour power into actual labour through work (Müller-Jentsch, 2004). Following Marx, Braverman (1974) argued that labour organisations and the type of employment relations provide capitalists with a solution to their problems. Braverman assumes that employers not only have to solve the problem of surplus value production but also have to deal with the problem of surplus value appropriation. In order to solve both problems employers have to exert control; which means, in practice, having to manage their workers (Nienhüser, 2004; Warhurst, 1997). For Braverman, scientific management or Taylorism was the means of control and with it came a specific form of employment relations. Scientific management involved the creation of managers as agents of capitalist owners who have conceptual responsibility for organising work, leaving workers only the execution of managerial defined tasks, which were subdivided, standardised, and simplified. The result is a loss of control over work by employees and work that is deskilled, with employees to be incentivised by piece-rate payments (Taylor, 1911 [2006]).

Braverman's deskilling thesis has been criticised as too simplistic. More diverse typologies of control take into account that employees can resist managerial imposition, and that excessive Taylorism can have effects on employees (alienation, demotivation, learned helplessness) that can also be negative for management. Other types of control give employment relations (starting at the firm level) other forms. Simple control is based on personal supervision and sanctioning of employees by their immediate superiors. Technical control is exercised through a technical arrangement of the labour process, for instance in the form of assembly-line work or, as is currently emerging, through use of information and communication (ITC)-based algorithms (Knight, 2015). With bureaucratic control, behaviour is governed by (mostly written) rules and regulations. With responsible autonomy, management transfers some task responsibility to employees and increases loyalty to the organisation through benefits (Edwards, 1979; Friedman, 1977). For labour process theorists this last type represents a 'sophisticated' solution to the problem of transformation and appropriation (Thompson & Smith, 2010).

From the perspective of labour process theory, the employment relationship and

---

[2]   Williamson (1984: 93) differentiates two other forms of employment relations – primitive team and obligational market – analytically located between the two extreme constellations of spot market and relational teams.

employment relations are means of solving or reducing the problem of control for the employer. The transformation problem results from the indeterminacy of the employment contract. Over time, as markets, technology, and workers' political organisation changes, so too must the means of control. Thus whilst the form of employment relations changes on the surface, the deeper structural issue remains: with the exchange, a transformation problem characterised by capitalist exploitation and managerial control. This foregrounding of political economy was an important development in understanding employment relations, but it too tended to push into the background national variations in the forms of control, at least initially (Warhurst, 1997).

Political economy – an amalgamation of political science and economics, which understands the economy as mediated by politics – brings another disciplinary lens to the study of employment relations. Formerly a critique of neoclassical economics, institutional theory (see also Chapter 2 in this volume), posits that economic activity is a political rather than a utilitarian outcome. Through institutional theory, the central impact of country-specific institutions, rules, norms, and values become important because it is recognised that each nation state has a distinct legal framework, financial and banking regulations, training and education policies, industrial relations systems, and familial arrangements, for example. Organisations are embedded within configurations of these institutions, which are external and are superior to the firm (Zucker, 1987). Economic actors within firms adopt organisational forms that are legitimate within the normative order of the institutional configurations within which they are embedded.

The latest, and very influential, development from within the political economy perspective, sometimes called the 'new institutionalists' (Frege & Kelly, 2013b; see also Chapter 2 in this volume), is the 'varieties of capitalism' approach of Hall and Soskice (2001a). This approach examines how firms and other actors, such as government and producer groups, solve coordination problems through either market or non-market institutions. The spheres over which the coordination problems range include, on the one hand, industrial relations and bargaining over wages and working conditions, and relations with employees such as information sharing and work effort incentives; and on the other hand, the adequate supply of financial resources, raw materials, and so forth as well as a stable demand for products and services. The first category of problems refers to employment relations. This approach quickly gained purchase amongst researchers of employment relations, even spawning 'varieties of unionism' (Frege & Kelly, 2004).

The review of the varieties of capitalism approaches in Chapter 2 discusses the distinction Hall and Soskice (2001b) make between liberal market economies (LMEs) and coordinated market economies (CMEs). Such different arrangements also cover employment relations. The political economy of a country can be understood as offering opportunities for, and constraints on, how firms structure work and the wage–effort bargain, resulting in different forms of employment relationships and employment relations. It is implied that firms in LMEs and CMEs respond differently to similar changes in their environment, for example to globalisation, with its increasing wage competition. In LMEs, for instance, there is an expectation of stronger and faster wage reductions; in CMEs there is more decentralised bargaining and a stronger trend toward reduced union influence (Thelen, 2001).

Although the varieties of capitalism literature provides a currently popular approach to studying comparative employment relations – and it at least delivers comparative analysis – the approach is not without its critics (see Chapter 2). They have argued that national ideal types may not be applicable to all sectors within a country; that the approach implicitly seeks to defend the German model; or that it simply elucidates category difference and, in reality, a dualist opposition (Allen, 2004; Crouch, 2009; Kenworthy, 2009). What is clear, as Crouch (2009: 79) suggests, is that varieties of capitalism has become 'the emblematic citation for all studies of diversity in capitalist economies'.

Psychology research on employment relations often draws on the idea of a 'psychological contract' between employer and employee (Rousseau, 1995; Coyle-Shapiro & Conway, 2004; see also Chapter 12 in this volume) and it is a theory that has been gaining traction in HRM as a field of study. In stark contrast to theories within the political economy approach, its level of analysis is the individual. The core of employment relations is conceptualised as an informal psychological contract between employer and employee. The construct of the psychological contract as used currently was provided by Rousseau (1995) but it has a long history going back to the work of Argyris (1960) and Blau (1964). Also, Fox's (1974) seminal work on industrial relations included a very similar concept drawing on Gouldner's construct of a 'norm of reciprocity' (Gouldner, 1960; Guest, 2004: 545). The psychological contract seeks to achieve both high performance and high employee satisfaction (Guest, 2007), drawing as it does on psychological theories about individual needs, cognitions, and values (compare different contributions in Coyle-Shapiro & Conway, 2004). Guest rightly argues that the psychological contract now provides an 'analytical framework for the analysis of employment relations' (Guest, 2004: 545).

The contract centres on promises and obligations, for example over pay for performance, working hours, and employers' accommodation of employees' domestic responsibilities (Guest, 2007). These contracts can be transactional and thus explicit and formal, or relational and thus implicit and informal, but trust and fairness are important: 'whether the promises and obligations have been met, whether they are fair and their implications for trust' (Guest, 2004: 549), in short, whether or not employees and employers each deliver their side of the 'deal'. Two issues then arise: what are the determinants and consequences of the psychological contract? Guest suggests a kind of causal chain: the state of the contract is influenced by human resource policies and practices, which are in turn determined by contextual factors such as sector, firm size, ownership, business strategy, and union recognition (Guest, 2004). The consequences centre on attitudinal outcomes such as commitment, work satisfaction, motivation, or stress; and also behavioural outcomes such as work attendance, intention to quit, job performance, and 'organisational citizenship behaviour'. An important debate in this approach is over whether or not the nature of the psychological contract has changed, with Herriot and Pemberton (1995) framing the change in terms of 'old' and 'new' deals. In the old deal, secure, long-term, upwardly mobile careers within tall organisational hierarchies were offered by employers in exchange for employee loyalty and commitment. Now, with flatter organisations, employers can no longer offer such careers and workers face employment insecurity, must provide for their own 'employability' (Bridges, 1995), and accept 'boundaryless careers' (Arthur & Rousseau, 1995). As Guest (2007) notes, this change creates problems for employers: contract violation can be frequent, workers' expectations difficult to discern and thereby meet, and contracts more bespoke than generic.

Although analyses of the consequences of the breaking of the psychological contract include employee (dis)satisfaction, it is employee performance that is again the driving concern. With the individual as the level of analysis, most empirical studies concentrate on the consequences of the subjectively perceived failure of the employer to meet the psychological contract. As such, Guest (2004: 545f.) explicitly criticises the psychological contract for having 'typically been studied from the individual worker's perspective', and points out that there is too little research on the perceptions of the employer within the contract. Nevertheless outcomes for workers are still studied in relation to an employer perspective, with issues in the interests of employers at the heart of analyses. Moreover, because of the level of analysis, institutions other than the firm and the psychological contract's connectedness to – and embeddedness within – the societal level are too often ignored.

Although the different disciplines offer a number of theories with varying core assumptions and are pitched at different levels of analysis, the key concern throughout is still with employee performance, no matter how that performance is framed. It is noteworthy, however, that different disciplinary approaches dominate the study of employment relations in different countries. For example, theories centred on the individual (mainly economic but also psychological) tend to dominant in the USA, and sociological and contextually informed psychological theories in the United Kingdom (UK), whilst in Germany sociological theories still prevail but economic theories are gaining ground (see also Frege, 2005; Keller, 2005). Thus, there remains a conceptual coherence to the study of employment relations, but also a need for different disciplinary inputs (with expertise often centred in different countries) if a rounded understanding is to be generated.

THE DEVELOPMENT OF EMPLOYMENT RELATIONS

Some of these theories underpin attempts to explain what is happening to employment relations, to which this section of the chapter now turns. Basically, there are two camps in the debate about the future of employment relations. Echoing wider debates about globalisation (Warhurst & Nickson, 2001; Barry & Wilkinson, 2011), these two camps argue polemically for, on the one hand, convergence or, on the other, continued diversity in employment relations. Both camps have an inherent interest in comparative analysis, for comparative analysis allows for the identification of developmental trajectories. For example, and to return to the hotel industry example at the start of this chapter, one interesting possibility to emerge from the research findings about employment relations in German hotels is that they are becoming more like those in the Anglo-Saxon countries such as the USA or the UK (Vanselow et al., 2010). However, as this example once again illustrates, the issue is not just one of difference but also, implicitly and sometimes explicitly, perceived superiority and the transfer, through adoption or adaption, of types of employment relations.

Discerning this possibility requires points of analysis – descriptively the past and current characterisation of each country's employment relations – and also sometimes, based on the dynamic between these two points, prescriptive articulation of a third point, the future point of arrival for these countries' employment relations. At the start of the latter half of the twentieth century there was a common assumption that a 'one best way', usually the putative US model, was the future of employment relations and all other industrialised countries would adopt this model, including, as it did, scientific management (Thompson, 1989; Warhurst & Nickson, 2001). As Lawrence (1988) has noted, that differences might exist in employment was only really appreciated in the late 1970s and early 1980s when studies began to emerge that highlighted 'national-cultural'-based industrial organisation, and as a consequence attention turned to comparative analysis; in Lawrence's case, of management styles in a range of different countries (e.g., Lawrence, 1980). It is an approach that remains popular, as the best-selling edited collections on industrial relations (more recently retitled 'employment relations') by Bamber et al. (1987), Bamber et al. (2004), Bamber et al. (2016), Morley et al. (2006), Frege and Kelly (2013a), and Barry and Wilkinson (2011) illustrate. If researchers in management, industrial, and employment relations discovered the importance of comparative analysis from the late 1970s onwards, it was a key feature of organisational sociology from the 1950s, prompted by the seminal work on bureaucracy by Stinchcombe (1959). Comparative analysis is a field of research rather than a discipline, though it does draw upon the disciplines that we identified earlier: sociology, economics, and psychology. Its purpose is to classify types and then discern and explain the identified similarities and differences between these types. Of course, what to compare and how to compare then become salient issues.

In this respect, one of the key problems in comparative analysis is the 'incommensurability of concepts' (Sztompka, 1990: 47). At its most basic, there can be different terms for the same instruments: for example, in the UK the 'collective agreement', in the USA the 'labour contract', and in Australia the 'industrial award'. Language, Hofstede (1995) has noted, is the most clearly recognisable part of a culture and so affects the study of employment relations; as Crompton and Lynette (2006) discovered in their research on Portugal and the UK. Portugal has strong labour market protection and the deregulation of employment has been resisted by employees because of the benefits that accrue with job tenure. By contrast, the UK labour market is lightly regulated and employment relations are increasing individualistic. When the researchers asked respondents in a survey about the importance of 'moving up the job ladder at work', the Portuguese answers were puzzling. It turned out that the translation by the Portuguese team of the English wording was correct, but that the meaning of the phrase varied between employees of the two countries: 'In Portugal, "moving up the job ladder" means progression through an ordered hierarchy, whereas in Britain, "moving up the job ladder" has come to mean "putting oneself forward for individual enhancement"' (Crompton & Lyonette, 2006: 408). Contextualisation is therefore important in comparative analysis. Unfortunately, too often, that contextualisation is too readily ignored. The outcome is poor research, even if it produces headline-grabbing claims, as we will see in our example of Japanisation below.

The convergence thesis too emerged out of an academic headline-grabbing futuristic account by economist Clark Kerr and his colleagues (Kerr et al., 1960) of the consequences of industrialism as it spread throughout the world in the latter half of the twentieth century. They argued that the logic of industrialism dictated that industrialising countries required and adopted certain characteristics: the use of particular technologies; an ideological consensus centred on pluralism, urbanisation, and big government; an increasingly higher skilled and more educated workforce; and a rule-bound industrial relations system. 'Industrial systems', the authors argued, 'tend to become more alike . . . The process of convergence moves sometimes faster sometimes slower . . . but it is a long-run development' (Kerr et al., 1960: 296). Some critics argued that Kerr and his colleagues were masking US values and imperialism, and decried the US ethnocentrism of the logic being asserted. Others questioned the deterministic assumptions underpinning the logic, and whether industrialism did generate convergence. They pointed out that different countries exhibited different solutions to the same industrial relations problems, or that some but not all aspects of employment converged such that national regulatory regimes mediated industrialism (for a short overview, see Wailes et al., 2016).

These criticisms did not stop more radical sociologists countering with their own logic of convergence. Braverman's (1974) kick-starting analysis of labour process through deskilling was a challenge to optimistic accounts, such as those of Kerr and his colleagues, that workers were now being employed in more skilled jobs. Braverman stated that Taylorism represented 'nothing less than the explicit verbalisation of the capitalist mode of production' (ibid.: 86). Braverman, however, also had his critics, even from those broadly sympathetic to his 'It's capitalism, stupid!' position, for his tendency to substitute one universal claim – job amelioration – with another: the degradation of work; and one form of determinism – technology – with another: mode of production. The pervasiveness of Taylorism, assumed by Braverman, was challenged by comparative analyses that show a variety of forms of control and the uneven application and extent of Taylorism where it was introduced (Lane, 1987). Friedman (1977) and Litter (1982) demonstrated the differences between Japanese and British labour processes resulting from different national political and cultural trajectories. Different forms of employee resistance also exist and develop historically (Edwards, 1979). The second wave of labour process analysis post-Braverman therefore concluded that labour process analysis 'must be supplemented by reference to "cultural" factors resting on distinctive national and historical traditions' (Thompson, 1989: 216). As such, the possibility of continued divergence needed to be recognised and a conceptual framework provided for its study. Unfortunately, as Nichols (1994) pointed out, labour process theory accepted the first point but failed to deliver the conceptual framework of the second, though attempts have been made subsequently (Warhurst, 1997).

In a still influential article, Lane (1987) had already taken up this challenge of providing a conceptual framework, and sought to show how labour process analysis needed to be supplemented by analyses that are sensitive to culture, comprising national institutional histories and social values and attitudes (see also Smith & Meiksins, 1995; Warhurst, 1997). Unfortunately, at the time, her approach was overshadowed by work that became paradigm-setting in the study of cross-national management and organisation – Hofstede's (1980) *Culture's Consequences* (see also Chapter 3 in this volume). Hofstede argued that cultural dimensions exemplified the 'collective mental programming' (Hofstede, 1995: 142) by which individual countries' workplace practices were shaped. The UK, for example, was characterised as low on power distance and uncertainty avoidance, and high on individualism, and somewhat high on masculinity. As a consequence, the British workplace is like 'a village market; no decisive hierarchy, flexible rules, and a resolution of problems by negotiating' (ibid.: 155). Moreover, the diffusion of management practices is limited, he insisted, constrained by this programming: countries can only successfully adopt other countries' management models, theories, and practices if those nations were culturally close; even then, 'convergence . . . will never come', he claimed (ibid.: 157). Hofstede's dimensions, or variants of them, are still very influential in research of cross-cultural management, as Trompenaars and Turner (1997) exemplify.

Brewster (1995: 215) gave lukewarm support for Hofstede's culturalist approach: 'it is the best we have' he stated, and at least 'makes us aware of cultural differences and the challenges that exist'. Others (Baskerville, 2003) made more detailed and explicit challenges.

What was required was a more systematic approach to discerning national differences, and this approach seemed to be provided with sociologist Marc Maurice et al.'s (1979, 1980) identification of 'societal effects' to explain differences in the organisation of manufacturing in France, Germany and, later, Britain. Intending to avoid 'vaguely specified cultural variables' and utilising 'closely matched-pair comparisons', the research sought to examine 'the interaction of people at work, work characteristics of jobs, systems of recruitment, education, training, remuneration and industrial relations' (Maurice et al., 1980: 61). In the first study comparing France and Germany, the researchers found that the span of control between supervisors and employees was greater in France than in Germany; that in France the dispersion of salary levels was also longer; and that qualification levels were highest amongst German employees, both blue- and white-collar. These findings seemed to be explicable only by reference to factors external to the firm; the 'societal effects' and the historical interconnectedness of manufacturing, industrial relations, education, and training, for example. The upshot, according to Rose (1985: 74), is that 'employment relationships are . . . societally specific'. Unfortunately Rose, in his critical overview of the research of the 'Aix group' as it became known, claims that the research falls short of its aim, failing to make the bridge between the particular cases and general theorisation. The 'text never settles down into a sustained exposition of the concepts and procedures of the societal approach . . . nowhere are the numerous explanatory asides, passing comments, and definite claims for it threaded together to show with clarity and precision what it does involve', he says (Rose, 1985: 76).

It did pave the way, though, for the mainstreaming of economics-based institutional theory into comparative analysis. For these theorists organisational forms are symbolic rather than technically superior, and organisational isomorphism occurs so that firms come to resemble each other with common structures, practices, and strategies that facilitate their aggregate distinctiveness. Embeddedness does not mean that reproduction is mechanically determined but rather, and echoing Maurice et al., that the rational actions of management are informed by the institutions of business education, for example (Fores et al., 1992). The past therefore shapes the present. The approach has been criticised for being too static: good at identifying the process of reproduction but unable to explain innovation and so how structures, practices, and strategies change. Indeed, 'path dependency' has emerged as a subfield within this approach (Liebowitz & Margolis, 1995).

Neo-institutionalism attempts to deal with this problem by recognising that a plurality of organisational forms is possible, shaped not only by embeddedness but also – and now foregrounding choice and not just constraint – the conscious enactment of that embeddedness by economic actors (DiMaggio, 1990; Granovetter, 1985; Whitley, 1992). However, difference rather than commonality remains the key focus and forces that might create pressures for commonality are downplayed. As Smith and Meiksins (1995) observe, 'systems effects', not only societal effects, exist that reflect the political economy of modes of production and comprise distinct social relations, and which also affect the social organisation of economic activity regardless of within which national state that activity occurs. Thus the institutional arrangements of states within capitalism are more similar to each other than they are to those within the former state socialist countries, because as different modes of production they have different political economies (for a short discussion, see Warhurst, 1998). It should be noted that most of the 'new institutionalists' (the phrase is Kelly and Frege's, 2004: 182) who have taken up the 'varieties of capitalism' approach of Hall and Soskice (2001b), 'body swerve' this criticism by only focusing on capitalist countries.

Such debates, whether arguing for convergence or diversity, have at their heart three concerns: difference, superiority, and transfer – the later involving either adoption or adaption. Focusing on employment relations specifically, these concerns coalesced and are starkly highlighted in research on Japanisation. Long before the twenty-first century was being described as China's 'red dawn' (Harris, 2010), the new century was being hailed as Japan's century. In the 1980s and into the 1990s there was a welter of books and articles proclaiming Japan as the new superpower from which other countries had to learn (e.g., Horsley & Buckley, 1990). In particular, a social and physical technology, 'lean production', was feted; as prominent MIT-based eulogists Womack et al. (1990: 12) proclaimed, 'lean production . . . will change everything in almost every industry – choices for consumers, the nature of work, the fortune of companies, the fate of nations'. Of course, Japan's economy nosedived in the 1990s and interest shifted elsewhere. By then, however, there had been a raft of studies that examined Japanese employment relations, drawing upon some of the approaches outlined above and which produced widely differing findings, as Table 11.2 illustrates.

Table 11.2 does not depict the debate chronologically, but rather its claims and approaches; and it is not a comprehensive review of the Japanisation debate: instead it identifies some of the key positions in that debate. The starting point was Womack et al.'s (1990) claim that classic lean production was to be found at auto manufacturer Toyota, but there was general consensus about the Japanese model of employment relations

Table 11.2   Understanding the Japanese model of employment relations

Claim	Approach	Example
Superior and can be universalised through transfer and adoption; provides convergence	Technologically determinist, within a broad definition of technology*	Womack et al. (1990)
Rooted in and specific to country-of-origin/host country adoption problems; questions transferability and convergence	Variations in national institutional arrangements matter, variously influenced by culturalism, societal effects, and labour process theory	Wilkinson and Oliver (1990)
No comprehensive form but disaggregated by production chain and country	Focus on business strategy, influenced by labour process theory	Dedoussis and Littler (1994)
Not superior but is different; lack of understanding of residual country-specific differences	Critical accounting, echoing institutional theory	Williams et al. (1994)

Note: * See Friedman (1990).

inherent to this technology: quality-orientated and 'just-in-time' work, seniority-based wages, lifetime employment, company welfarism, enterprise unionism. Using 'half the human effort' (ibid.: 13) and yet being 'twice as productive' (ibid.: 81), Womack et al. argued that lean production was superior and would become 'the standard global production system' (ibid.: 278), supplanting Fordist mass production and any residual craft production. Indeed, through Japanisation these practices were transferred into Europe, the USA, and elsewhere through the inward investment of Japanese firms or through their adoption by European and US firms in their home territories (Elger & Smith, 1994; Kirkland, 1990; Thompson & McHugh, 1990; Womack et al., 1990). The Japanese model was therefore different, but its transfer was not only possible but an imperative.

And yet some practices did not travel: lifetime employment and seniority-based wages, for example (Thompson & McHugh, 1990). Indeed, it was argued that there were obstacles to Japanisation. These obstacles arose because of differences between country-of-origin and host countries. This argument had two dimensions: first, that the Japanese model was a product of particular, historical institutional arrangements between capital, the state, and labour in Japan; and second, that different institutional environments and cultures existed in host countries such as the UK – as the infamous banner, 'We're Brits not Nips', held up by striking British Ford workers protesting about the Japanisation of the company, hammered home (Thompson, 1988; see also Morris & Wilkinson, 1995; Wilkinson & Oliver, 1990). Further research revealed this limited transfer to be an outcome not just of 'cultural constraint' but also of firm strategy. Japanese firms investing overseas tended to target geographical locales with low wage costs and acquiescent labour (Elger & Smith, 1994). Examining the management practices of Japanese firms in Australia, and working within the labour process tradition, Dedoussis and Littler (1994) argued that a 'peripheral model of Japanese management' had been established, whereby the parent companies sought cost minimisation with overseas workforces, 'hiving off labour intensive activities to subsidiaries and subcontracting firms' (ibid.: 176). 'Human resource management practices . . . in overseas Japanese firms differ significantly compared with human resource management practices . . . in parent companies' Dedoussis and Littler (ibid.: 177) conclude. Even more damning, far from heralding a new form of production, Japanese transplants continued 'conventional Taylorised mass production techniques', according to Danford (1998: 41) in his empirical research of Japanese firms in Wales. In other words, transfer was neither desired nor intended by the Japanese parent firms. Instead these firms relied upon and exploited national differences in order to maximise profitability. Finally, Williams et al. (1994) challenged not the feasibility and desirably of transferred Japanisation, but its very claim to be superior. Revisiting the calculations used by Womack et al. (1990) as the basis for the claim of higher Japanese performance, Williams et al. (1994) discovered serious flaws in the measurements. Productivity studies, they state, tend to focus only on the bottom line and not on how that bottom line is calculated. Applying a consistent form of calculation across Japanese, US, and European auto manufacturers reveals Toyota to be no more productive – even, less productive – than many of its competitors. Indeed the reputation of US manufacturers is 'rehabilitated', with Ford 'captur[ing] the title of most productive assembler from Toyota' (Williams et al., 1994: 257). Too many researchers in Europe and the USA failed to identify and appreciate that productivity and performance measurement is done differently in Japan. Whilst productivity and performance measurement may seem technical and boring, Williams et al. comment, if done properly it raises important political issues which, in the case of Japanisation, were being used to destabilise existing capital, state, and labour settlements in the USA, Europe, and elsewhere.

What the research on Japanisation highlights more generally are the competing claims about the development of employment relations and the factors that influence that development. Different approaches do not just claim different futures; they also foreground different issues. No single approach has a monopoly on understanding. As with globalisation, any perceived developmental trajectory in employment relations – whether convergent or divergent – can continue or be checked, or simply be contested. The future is a matter of empirical investigation and, as the Japanisation debate indicates, research on employment relations past, present, and future benefits greatly from comparative research.

CONCLUDING REMARKS ON THE FUTURE OF EMPLOYMENT RELATIONS

This chapter has sought to outline how employment relations are understood and how they are changing, doing so by distinguishing between employment relations as practice and as field of study. At the heart of employment relations, as we demonstrated, are common concerns that centre on what is variously cast as the 'labour problem', the 'labour question' or, more recently, 'performance management'. These differing terms, though, do not emerge from a vacuum but align with competing proprietorial claims over employment relations as practice and field of study: what was once industrial relations is now human resource management, most obviously. Often the use of the terms 'industrial relations', 'human resource management', and 'employment relations' is simply a matter of choice, reflecting the shift from collectivism to individualism in the workplace (e.g., Rose, 2004) and, with this shift, the need for practitioners (and some academics) to maintain their utility (see Blyton & Turnbull, 1998).

The key actors shaping employment relations as practice are employers, trade unions, and the state, and their interests. The balance of power between these three actors is dynamic temporally, and varied spatially, most obviously by country. If employment relations is centred on the labour problem, understanding that labour problem requires more than just the study of work: it requires appreciation and analysis of the contextual factors that influence how that work, and the transformational problem, is shaped; for example embeddedness within the political economy narrowly defined as the nation state and more widely conceived as related to mode of production (Warhurst, 1997).[3] In this respect, the differing disciplinary lenses that we noted do not simply mark out the interests of researchers in different countries (e.g., Frege, 2005) but highlight the range of issues that need to be taken into account in the study of employment relations.

Any discussion of the future of employment relations needs to encompass developments in the practice and the field of study. The question as to what model of employment relations practice will dominate in the future is of course not easy to answer. In the 1990s it was quite usual to map out the future as one of competing practice between Japanese,

---

[3]   There are yet other influences such as gender regimes that we have not discussed in this chapter, but which are no less important (for a discussion, see Rubery, 2009).

German, and Anglo-Saxon models (e.g., Kelly, 1994). What is included within the scope of discussion is linked, as we noted, to notions of perceived superiority. In this respect, whilst the latter two models are still benchmarks – as the job quality research cited at the start of this chapter highlights – the Japanese model has vanished from the debate, to be replaced by concern with China, with the state-led marketisation of its economy, and its economic dynamism and growing political influence. Moreover, as with Japan before it, there is now significant investment by Chinese firms in overseas countries and firms. If Japan was once cited as the model for the future, Halper (2010) raises the possibility of China now being that model. However, as with Japan before it, such prescriptions have often fallen at the hurdle of evidence (or unforeseen economic problems). Whether China provides that model will be determined by empirical investigation as the evidence base begins to emerge (e.g., Friedman & Kuruvilla, 2015; Liu & Smith, 2016). What is clear is that employment relations remain dynamic both as practice and as field of study.

In the meantime most debate still centres on the battle of practice between the German and Anglo-Saxon models. The German model, with its long-term employment, highly qualified employees with general skills, strong co-determination and trade unions, multi-employer bargaining, and an extensive welfare system, is often held up as best practice, with advocates amongst UK economic commentators such as Hutton (1995) arguing for its adoption in the Anglo-Saxon countries. Even US business professors such Pfeffer (1998) advocate this model because it aligns well with the workplace Holy Grail of HRM – the elusive high-performance work system – and offers positive economic performance and social benefits. Nevertheless, the German model's adoption by other countries is not evident, and indeed it is regularly claimed to be under threat (Lane, 1987; Grahl & Teague, 2004; Behrens, 2015), as the research into employment relations in German hotels indicates (Vanselow, 2008). The model has also come under fire from advocates of the Anglo-Saxon model, that is characterised by the individualisation of employee interests and representation, and flexible forms of employment (Bosch et al., 2009). Some argue that a US or Anglo-Saxon model of employment relations will become more widespread, so that if a new convergence is to emergence, it will be one driven by the Anglo-Saxon variety of capitalism (e.g., Stanford, 2008). This potential development needs to be understood, recognising that models of employment relations are also normative and some forms of employment relations can have an advantage in 'system competition'. Thus, a model (in the sense of an ideal type) has a 'competitive advantage' if it accords with the productive forces. The Anglo-Saxon model fits better with neoliberalism, and advantage accrues for those models of employment relations that align with that neoliberalism. Even if President Trump decries globalisation, he still wants to reassert US superiority.

Explicitly or implicitly, such debates still centre on the two developments or trends that have dominated studies of comparative employment relations, and around which we have framed this chapter: the convergence and divergence of practice. There is a third empirical possibility: that employment itself disappears. Not to be confused with the death of (human) work through robotisation and automation (see Ford, 2015), this other possibility arises out of what is cast as 'digital disruption', by which workers are no longer employed by a company but are paid by individual buyers to perform a single task: assemble flat-pack furniture or provide a ride in a car, for example. The buying and selling of these tasks is brokered by platform companies which, for a fee, claim to provide nothing more than the connecting app. Although Uber is the topical example of such companies, there are many others internationally, and for different types of tasks: for example, TaskRabbit, clickworker, and cloudfactory. The key innovation of this business model is that workers become freelancers, no longer involved in an employment relationship exchanging labour for wages with an employer bound by an employment contract. The extent of this development has yet to be reliably ascertained. However, what is interesting at the moment is the way that this technology-driven 'Uberisation', as it is sometimes called, is (again) playing out differently depending on national contexts, as different countries' law courts, trade unions, and employer organisations variously demand its incorporation within existing business systems, outright banning, or argue for the development of new legal forms of employment (e.g., Adam et al., 2016; Warhurst et al., 2017).

It should also be appreciated that, as we noted above, claims about trends in employment practice disappear as often as they appear; what seems likely today, sometimes seems laughable tomorrow. What actually happens has to be the subject of empirical longitudinal, or at least repeated, cross-sectional studies, informed by appropriate theoretical frameworks, if the fashions of time are to be unravelled.

The question of how the future of the study of employment relations will develop is more difficult to answer. Certainly, as HRM struggles to assert its legitimacy it is possible that it too will wither as a way of framing analysis of and practice within the employment relationship. Thus, as industrial relations was displaced, so too might HRM. It is instructive to note that the use of the term 'employment relations' is becoming more in vogue (e.g., Bamber et al., 2016; Bray et al., 2009; Frege & Kelly, 2013a; Rose, 2004), and it is possible that those academic departments once called 'industrial relations', but which by the 1990s had been renamed 'human resource management', might soon undergo another name change. Certainly 'employment relations' appears less loaded normatively than HRM and so is potentially more palatable to researchers who look fondly on industrial relations.

Given our comments in this chapter, it is easier to say what kind of research is desirable: longitudinal, international, multilevel research that has at its analytical core the employment relationship. Being comparative, such research would be able to establish essentiality, difference, and developments (cf. Stinchcombe, 1959). It should be remembered, however, that the analytical tools used in this research will develop as much as the practice that they examine. There is an emerging trend to draw more upon theoretical perspectives from the economics and psychology disciplines such as transaction costs and the psychological contract. Rightly focusing on the exchange relationship between employer and employee, these approaches have advantages but also shortcomings in ignoring the embeddedness of the employment relationship beyond that of the individual or at best the firm level. Such approaches run the risk of being blind to social and economic inequalities, power differences, and domination structures.

These disciplinary approaches, however, are also subject to the very influences that bear upon employment relations as practice, with research on employment relations also varying between countries. Drawing on an analysis of 1300 articles in industrial relations journals, Frege (2005) found distinctive US, UK, and German 'research patterns'.[4] In the USA, where researchers are primarily trained as economists, the analysis of labour

---

[4]   The findings refer to industrial relations but can – with caution – be applied to the study of employment relations (see also Frege, 2013).

markets and pay is more prevalent than in the UK or Germany; research is also mainly quantitative and draws more on large-scale datasets, and the level of analysis tends to be the micro (individual) level. Contrasting with the USA, research in the UK is dominated by sociologists, with research focusing much more on trade unions, using more small-scale samples, most obviously case studies, and is pitched at the firm level more than the individual level. In Germany, sociologists in particular undertake less empirical research, offering 'think pieces' and 'essays' focused on the firm level. Frege concludes that even if (industrial) employment relations in the advanced economies converge and international communication between research communities increases, there is still a 'distinctive national research pattern' (Frege, 2005: 203) that shows no sign of convergence. Context clearly still matters: how employment relations are studied still differs in the three countries and is an outcome of 'long-standing intellectual traditions' (Frege, 2005: 204; see also Keller, 2005). These findings underpin our argument that not only must explanations of differences in employment relations take context into account, but we need to be aware that the theories used to explain these differences can also be context-influenced. Of course, name changes and disciplinary demarcations cannot be allowed to mask the common concern: the labour problem. This concern will remain so long as paid employment exists. Understanding how the field of study and practice of employment relations develop temporally and spatially is the reason why comparative analysis is so important.

REFERENCES

Adam, D., Bremerman, M., Durna, J., et al. 2016. *Digitalisation and Working Life*. Dublin: Eurofound.
Allen, M. 2004. The varieties of capitalism paradigm: Not enough variety?. *Socio-Economic Review*, 2(1): 87–108.
Argyris, C. 1960. *Understanding Organisational Behaviour*. Homewood, IL: Dorsey Press.
Arthur, M., & Rousseau, D. 1995. *The Boundaryless Career*. Oxford: Oxford University Press.
Bamber, G., & Lansbury, R. 1987. *International and Comparative Industrial Relations*. London: SAGE Publications.
Bamber, G., Lansbury, R.D., & Wailes, N. 2004. Introduction. In G.J. Bamber, R.D. Lansbury, and N. Wailes (eds), *International and Comparative Employment Relations*: 1–35. London: SAGE.
Bamber, G.J., Lansbury, R.D., Wailes, N., & Wright, C.F. 2016. *International and Comparative Employment Relations: National Regulation, Global Changes*. Los Angeles, CA: SAGE.
Barry, M., & Wilkinson, A. 2011. *Research Handbook of Comparative Employment Relations*. Cheltenham, UK and Northampton, MA, USA: Edward Elgar Publishing.
Baskerville, R.F. 2003. Hofstede never studied culture. *Accounting, Organizations and Society*, 28(1): 1–14.
Behrens, M. 2015. Weakening structures, strong commitment: The future of German employment relations. In B. Unger (ed.), *The German Model: Seen by Its Neighbours*: 135–145: SE Publishing.
Bernhardt, A., Dresser, L., & Hatton, E. 2003. The Coffee Pot Wars: Unions and firm restructuring in the hotel industry. In E. Appelbaum, A. Bernhardt, and R.J. Murnane (eds), *Low Wage America*: 33–76. New York: Russell Sage Foundation.
Blau, P.M. 1964. *Exchange and Power in Social Life*. New York: John Wiley & Sons.
Blyton, P., & Turnbull, P. 1998. *The Dynamics of Employment Relations*. London: Macmillan.
Bosch, G., Lehndorff, S., & Rubery, J. 2009. *European Employment Models in Flux*. Basingstoke: Palgrave Macmillan.
Boxall, P., & Purcell, J. 2003. *Strategy and Human Resource Management*. London: Palgrave.
Boxall, P., & Purcell, J. 2015. *Strategy and Human Resource Management* (3rd edn). London: Palgrave.
Braverman, H. 1974. *Labor and Monopoly Capital*. New York: Monthly Review Press.
Bray, M., Waring, P., & Cooper, R. 2009. *Employment Relations: Theory and Practice*. Sydney: McGraw-Hill.
Brewster, C. 1995. National cultures and international management. In S. Tyson (ed.), *Strategic Prospects for HRM*: 206–228. London: Institute of Personnel and Development.
Bridges, W. 1995. *Job Shift*. London: Nicolas Brearly.

CIPD. 2009. Chartered Institute of Personnel and Development Employee relations: An overview. Available at: http://www.cipd.co.uk/subjects/empreltns/general/emprelsovr.htm.

Coyle-Shapiro, J.A.M., & Conway, N. 2004. The employment relationship through the lens of social exchange. In J.A.M. Coyle-Shapiro, L.M. Shore, M.S. Taylor, and L.E. Tetrick (eds), *The Employment Relationship*: 5–28. Oxford: Oxford University Press.

Cressey, P., & MacInnes, J. 1980. Voting for Ford: Industrial democracy and the control of labour. *Capital and Class*, 4(2): 5–33.

Crompton, R., & Lyonette, C. 2006. Some issues in cross-national comparative research methods: A comparison of attitudes to promotion, and women's employment, in Britain and Portugal. *Work, Employment and Society*, 20(2): 403–440.

Crouch, C. 2009. Typologies of capitalism. In B. Hanké (ed.), *Debating Varieties of Capitalism*: 75–94. Oxford: Oxford University Press.

Danford, A. 1998. Work organisation inside Japanese firms in South Wales: A break from Taylorism?. In P. Thompson and C. Warhurst (eds), *Workplaces of the Future*: 40–64. London: Macmillan.

Dedoussis, V., & Littler, C.R. 1994. Understanding the transfer of Japanese management practices: The Australian case. In T. Elger and C. Smith (eds), *Global Japanisation?*: 175–194. London: Routledge.

DiMaggio, P.J. 1990. Cultural aspects of economic action and organisation. In R. Friedland and A.F. Robertson (eds), *Beyond the Marketplace*: 113–136. New York: Aldine de Gruyter.

Edwards, P. 1995. From industrial relations to the employment relationship. *Relations Industrielles*, 50: 39–65.

Edwards, P. 2003. The employment relationship and the field of industrial relations. In P. Edwards (ed.), *Industrial Relations: Theory and Practice*: 1–35. Malden, MA: Blackwell.

Edwards, R.C. 1979. *Contested Terrain*. New York: Basic Books.

Elger, T., & Smith, C. 1994. Global Japanisation? Convergence and competition in the organisation of the labour processes. In T. Elger and C. Smith (eds), *Global Japanisation*: 31–59. London: Routledge.

Ferner, A., & Hyman, R. 1998. *Changing Industrial Relations in Europe*. Oxford: Blackwell.

Ford, M. 2015. *Rise of the Robots*. New York: Basic Books.

Fores, M., Glover, I., & Lawrence, P. 1992. Management thought, the American identity and the future of European labour processes. Paper presented at the UMIST Conference on the Labour Process, Aston University.

Fox, A. 1974. *Beyond Contract: Work, Power and Trust Relations*. London: Faber & Faber.

Frege, C. 2005. Varieties of industrial relations research: Take-over, convergence or divergence?. *British Journal of Industrial Relations*, 43(2): 179–207.

Frege, C. 2013. Comparative perspectives in employment relations research. *Industrielle Beziehungen / The German Journal of Industrial Relations*, 20(4): 285–303.

Frege, C., & Kelly, J. 2004. *Varieties of Unionism*. Oxford: Oxford University Press.

Frege, C., & Kelly, J. 2013a. *Comparative Employment Relations in the Global Economy*. London: Routledge.

Frege, C., & Kelly, J. 2013b. Theoretical perspectives on comparative employment relations. In C. Frege and J. Kelly (eds), *Comparative Employment Relations in the Global Economy*: 8–26. London: Routledge.

Friedman, A. 1977. *Industry and Labour*. London: Macmillan.

Friedman, A. 1990. Managerial strategies, activities, techniques and technology: Towards a complex theory of the labour process. In D. Knights and H. Willmott (eds), *Labour Process Theory*: 177–208. Basingstoke: Macmillan.

Friedman, E., & Kuruvilla, S. 2015. Experimentation and decentralization in China's labor relations. *Human Relations*, 68(2): 181–195.

Gallie, D. 2007. Production regimes and the quality of employment in Europe. *Annual Review of Sociology*, 33: 85–104.

Gouldner, A.W. 1960. The norm of reciprocity: A preliminary statement. *American Sociological Review*, 25: 161–178.

Grahl, J., & Teague, P. 2004. The German model in danger. *Industrial Relations Journal*, 35(6): 557–573.

Granovetter, M. 1985. Economic action and social structure: The problem of embeddedness. *American Journal of Sociology*, 91(3): 481–510.

Guest, D.E. 1997. Human resource management and performance: A review and research agenda. *International Journal of Human Resource Management*, 8(3): 263–276.

Guest, D.E. 2004. The psychology of the employment relationship: An analysis based on the psychological contract. *Applied Psychology*, 53(4): 541–555.

Guest, D.E. 2007. HRM: Towards a new psychological contract. In P. Boxall, J. Purcell, and P.M. Wright (eds), *The Oxford Handbook of Human Resource Management*: 128–146. Oxford: Oxford University Press.

Hall, P.A., & Soskice, D. 2001a. An introduction to varieties of capitalism. In P.A. Hall, & D. Soskice (eds), *Varieties of Capitalism*: 1–68. Oxford: Oxford University Press.

Hall, P.A., & Soskice, D. 2001b. *Varieties of Capitalism*. Oxford: Oxford University Press.

Halper, S. 2010. *The Beijing Consensus*. London: Basic Books.

Harris, P. 2010. Hollywood Finds a New Enemy to Fight – China. *Observer*: 12.

Herriot, P., & Pemberton, C. 1995. *New Deals*. Chichester: Wiley.

Hirschman, A.O. 1970. *Exit, Voice, and Loyalty: Response to Decline in Firms, Organizations, and States*. Cambridge, MA: Harvard University Press.

Hofstede, G. 1980. *Culture's Consequences*. London: SAGE Publications.

Hofstede, G. 1995. The cultural relativity of organisational practices and theories. In J. Drew (ed.), *Readings in International Enterprise*: 141–158. London: Routledge.

Horsley, W., & Buckley, R. 1990. *Nippon: New Superpower*. London: BBC Books.

Hutton, W. 1995. *The State We're*. London: Cape.

Kaufman, B.E. 2004a. Employment relations and the employment relations system: A guide to theorizing. In B.E. Kaufman (ed.), *Theoretical Perspectives on Work and the Employment Relationship*: 41–75. Champaign, IL: Industrial Relations Research Association.

Kaufman, B.E. 2004b. Towards an integrative theory of human resource management. In B.E. Kaufman (ed.), *Theoretical Perspectives on Work and the Employment Relationship*: 321–366. Champaign, IL: Industrial Relations Research Association.

Keller, B. 2005. The industrial relations field in Germany: An empirical and comparative analysis. *Advances in Industrial and Labor Relations*, 14: 239–277.

Kelly, J. 1994. *Does the Field of Industrial Relations Have a Future?*. Oxford: British Universities Industrial Relations Association.

Kelly, J. 2015. Trade union membership and power in comparative perspective. *Economic and Labour Relations Review*, 26(4): 526–544.

Kelly, J., & Frege, C. 2004. Conclusions: varieties of unionism. In C.M. Frege and J. Kelly (eds), *Varieties of Unionism*: 181–196. Oxford: Oxford University Press.

Kenworthy, L. 2009. Institutional coherence and macroeconomic performance. In B. Hanké (ed.), *Debating Varieties of Capitalism*: 180–199. Oxford: Oxford University Press.

Kerr, C., Dunlop, J.T., Harbison, F.H., & Meyers, C.A. 1960. *Industrialism and Industrial Man*. Cambridge, MA: Harvard University Press.

Kirkland, R.I. 1990. The big Japanese push into Europe. *Fortune*, 2 July: 26–32.

Knight, S. 2015. How Uber conquered London. *Guardian*, 27 April: 12.

Kochan, T.A. 1998. What is distinctive about industrial relations research. In K. Whitfield and G. Strauss (eds), *Researching the World of Work*: 31–50. Ithaca, NY: Cornell University Press.

Kochan, T.A. 2007. Social legitimacy of the human resource management profession: A US perspective. In P. Boxall, J. Purcell, and P.M. Wright (eds), *The Oxford Handbook of Human Resource Management*: 599–619. Oxford: Oxford University Press.

Lane, C. 1987. Capitalism or culture? A comparative analysis of the position in the labour process and labour market of lower white-collar workers in the financial services sector of Britain and the Federal Republic of Germany. *Work, Employment and Society*, 1(1): 57–83.

Lawrence, P. 1980. *Managers and Management in Germany*. London: Croome Helm.

Lawrence, P. 1988. In another country. In A. Bryman (ed.), *Research Methods and Organisation Studies*: 96–107. London: Unwin Hyman.

Legge, K. 1995. *Human Resource Management*. Houndmills: Macmillan.

Liebowitz, S.J., & Margolis, S.E. 1995. Path dependence, lock-in, and history. *Journal of Law, Economics and Organization*, 11(1): 205–226.

Litter, C. 1982. *The Development of the Labour Process in Capitalist Societies*. London: Heinemann.

Liu, M., & Smith, C. 2016. *China at Work*. London: Palgrave.

Marginson, P. 1993. Power and efficiency in the firm: Understanding the employment relation. In C. Pitelis (ed.), *Transaction Costs, Markets and Hierarchies*: 133–165. Oxford: Oxford University Press.

Maurice, M., & Sellier, F. 1979. Societal analysis of industrial relations: A comparison between France and West Germany. *British Journal of Industrial Relations*, 17(3): 322–336.

Maurice, M., Sorge, A., & Warner, M. 1980. Societal differences in organizing manufacturing units: A comparison of France, West Germany, and Great Britain. *Organization Studies*, 1(1): 59–86.

McKenna, E., & Beech, N. 2002. *Human Resource Management*. London: FT Prentice Hall.

Morley, M., Heraty, N., & Collings, D. 2006. *International Human Resource Management and International Assignments*. London: Palgrave Macmillan.

Morris, J., & Wilkinson, B. 1995. The transfer of Japanese management to alien institutional environments. *Journal of Management Studies*, 32(6): 719–730.

Müller-Jentsch, W. 2004. Theoretical approaches to industrial relations. In B.E. Kaufman (ed.), *Theoretical Perspectives on Work and the Employment Relationship*: 1–40. Champaign, IL: Industrial Relations Research Association.

Nichols, T. 1994. Theoretical perspectives in industrial sociology and the labour process debate. Paper presented at the Work, Organisation and Social Structure Conference, University of Durham.

Nienhüser, W. 2004. Political (personnel) economy: A political economy perspective to explain different forms of human resource management strategies. *Management Revue*, 15(2): 228–248.

Panitch, L. 1981. Trade unions and the capital state. *New Left Review*, (125): 21–43.

Pfeffer, J. 1998. *Human Equation*. Boston, MA: Harvard Business School Press.

Rollinson, D., & Dundon, T. 2007. *Understanding Employment Relations*. London: McGraw-Hill Higher Education.

Rose, E. 2004. *Employment Relations*. London: Prentice Hall/Financial Times.

Rose, M. 1985. Universalism, culturalism and the Aix group: Promise and problems of a societal approach to economic institutions. *European Sociological Review*, 1(1): 65–83.

Rousseau, D. 1995. *Psychological Contracts in Organizations: Understanding Written and Unwritten Agreements*. Thousand Oaks, CA, USA; London, UK; New Delhi, India: SAGE.

Rubery, J. 2009. How gendering the varieties of capitalism requires a wider lens. *Social Politics*, 16(2): 192–203.

Schein, E.H. 1988. *Organizational Psychology*. Upper Saddle River, NJ: Pearson Education.

Smith, C., & Meiksins, P. 1995. System, society and dominance effects in cross-national organisational analysis. *Work, Employment and Society*, 9(2): 241–267.

Solow, B., & Wanner, E. 2010. Foreword. In J. Gautié and J. Schmitt (eds), *Low-Wage Work in the Wealthy World*: xv–xx. New York: Russell Sage Foundation.

Stanford, J. 2008. *Economics for Everyone: A Short Guide to the Economics of Capitalism*. London: Pluto Press.

Stinchcombe, A.L. 1959. Bureaucratic and craft administration of production: A comparative study. *Administrative Science Quarterly*, 4: 168–187.

Sztompka, P. 1990. Conceptual frameworks in comparative enquiry divergence or convergent. In M. Albrow and E. King (eds), *Globalisation, Knowledge and Society*: 47–61. London: SAGE Publications.

Taylor, F.W. 2006. *The Principles of Scientific Management*. New York: Cosimo.

Thelen, K. 2001. Varieties of labor politics in the developed democracies. In P.A. Hall and D. Soskice (eds), *Varieties of Capitalism*: 71–104. Oxford: Oxford University Press.

Thompson, P. 1988. Japanisation? Threat or myth?. *International Labour Reports*, 27–28.

Thompson, P. 1989. *The Nature of Work*. Houndmills: Macmillan.

Thompson, P., & McHugh, D. 1990. *Work Organisations*. Houndmills: Macmillan.

Thompson, P., & Smith, C. 2010. *Working Life*. London: Palgrave.

Trompenaars, F., & Turner, C.H. 1997. *Riding the Waves of Culture: Understanding Cultural Diversity in Business*. New York: McGraw-Hill.

Upchurch, M., Taylor, G., & Mathers, A. 2009. *The Crisis of Social Democratic Trade Unionism in Western Europe*. Aldershot: Ashgate.

Vanselow, A. 2008. Still lost and forgotten? The work of hotel room attendants in Germany. In G. Bosch and C. Weinkopf (eds), *Low-Wage Work in Germany*: 214–252. New York: Russell Sage Foundation.

Vanselow, A., Warhurst, C., Bernhardt, A., & Dresser, L. 2010. Working at the wage floor: Hotel room attendants and labor market institutions in Europe and the US. In J. Gautié and J. Schmitt (eds), *Low-Wage Work in the Wealthy World*: 269–318. New York: Russell Sage Foundation.

Wailes, N., Wright, C.F., Bamber, G.J., & Lansbury, R.D. 2016. Introduction: An internationally comparative approach to employment relations. In G.J. Bamber, R.D. Lansbury, N. Wailes, & C.F. Wright (eds), *International and Comparative Employment Relations*: 1–19. Los Angeles, CA: SAGE.

Warhurst, C. 1997. Political economy and the social organisation of economic activity: A synthesis of neo-institutional and labour process analyses. *Competition and Change*, 2(2): 213–246.

Warhurst, C. 1998. Recognizing the possible: The organization and control of a socialist labor process. *Administrative Science Quarterly*, 43(2): 470–497.

Warhurst, C., Mathieu, C., & Wright, S. 2017. Workplace innovation and the quality of working life in an age of Uberisation. In P. Oeij, F. Pot, and D. Rus (eds), *Workplace Innovation*. Berlin: Springer.

Warhurst, C., & Nickson, D. 2001. From globalisation to internationalisation to Americanisation: The example of 'Little Americas' in the hotel sector. In M.B. Taggart, and M. McDermott (eds), *Multinationals in a New Era*: 207–225. London: Palgrave.

Whitley, R. 1992. The social construction of organisations and markets: The comparative analysis of business recipes. In M. Reed and M. Hughes (eds), *Rethinking Organisation*: 120–143. London: SAGE Publications.

Wilkinson, A., Wood, G., & Deeg, R. 2014. *The Oxford Handbook of Employment Relations*. Oxford: Oxford University Press.

Wilkinson, B., & Oliver, N. 1990. Obstacles to Japanisation: The case of Ford UK. *Employee Relations*, 12(1): 17–21.

Williams, K., Haslam, C., Williams, J., & Johal, S. 1994. Deconstructing car assembler productivity. *International Journal of Production Economics*, 34(3): 253–265.

Williamson, O.E. 1984. Efficient labour organization. In F.H. Stephen (ed.), *Firms, Organization and Labour*: 87–118. London: Macmillan.

Williamson, O.E. 1985. *The Economic Institutions of Capitalism.* New York: Simon & Schuster.
Williamson, O.E., Wachter, M.L., & Harris, J.E. 1975. Understanding the employment relation: The analysis of idiosyncratic exchange. *Bell Journal of Economics,* 6: 250–278.
Womack, J.P., Jones, D.T., & Roos, D. 1990. *The Machine that Changed the World.* New York: Macmillan.
Zucker, L.G. 1987. Institutional theories of organization. *Annual Review of Sociology,* 13(1): 443–464.

12. The psychological contract within the international and comparative HRM literature
Paul Sparrow

INTRODUCTION

In the 2012 edition of the *Handbook* this chapter focused on the comparative analysis of employment contracts. It began with an exploration of the issues associated with a comparative understanding of the implicit, or psychological, contract and then gave attention to the formal employment contract in the context of the broader employment relationship, from both a cultural and an institutional perspective. It examined what an employment contract actually was, the nature of its terms, and how the rights and obligations – codified or implied – of the formal contract were in turn embedded in highly nationalistic legal systems and frameworks. Since this time, there has been a very significant increase within the international human resource management (IHRM) literature in attention given to the first topic: the implicit or psychological contract.

This chapter, for the first time, captures this new area of investigation. Although the new research on the psychological contract has been conducted from within two traditions, an international organisation HRM perspective and a cross-cultural or cross-national HRM perspective, it is, in keeping with the nature of this book, the second one which we focus on here. The chapter shows how the cross-cultural or cross-country perspective has adopted either a micro or a macro level of analysis. The micro-level studies have examined the specific psychological dynamics involved in the implicit employment relationship, being conducted in previously under-researched national contexts, and questioning whether the dynamics observed may be generic, and acultural, or whether there is some imprint of culture even within the core psychological contract of an employee. The macro-level studies have shifted the broad meaning of a psychological contract, and have used it as a metaphor to capture shifts in the employment relationship at country level that might be expected to result in new behaviours and management challenges. Finally, the chapter considers some of the main conclusions that we can derive from this work.

PSYCHOLOGICAL CONTRACT THEORY

When researchers co-opt a theoretical construct and begin to apply it to new domains, it is important to remind ourselves of some of the fundamentals of the original theory. Briefly, these are as follows. Study of the psychological contract explores the open-ended agreements concerning the social and emotional aspects of exchange between an employer and employee: the unwritten and reciprocal expectations that act as deep drivers of employee behaviour. The original and mainstream definition of a psychological contract comes from the work of Rousseau (1989, 1990, 1995). She portrayed it as a subjective perception of mutual obligations (a commitment to some future action) regarding the reciprocal exchange relationship between an employee and organisation:

> an individual's belief in the terms and conditions of a reciprocal exchange agreement between the focal person and another party. A psychological contract emerges when one party believes that a promise of future returns has been made, a contribution has been given, and thus, an obligation has been created to provide future benefits. (Rousseau, 1989: 123)

Hattori (2015) observes from a comparative perspective that this definition triggers four key areas for research: individual beliefs, level of agreement (implicitly, relative power of employees and organisations), the terms of the exchange, and the implicitness of obligations.

Contracting theory, at the heart of the psychological contract, is based around four important principles. First, organisations do not have psychological contracts per se. Rather, their agents do. The contract is therefore established during the initial phase of employment, conveyed by a number of organisational agents. For there to be an implicit contract, the relationship has to be underwritten by trust that the other party will fairly discharge their obligations, and a judgement that the exchange partners in the relationship will strive for balance, and attempt to restore balance if an imbalance occurs.

Second, the psychological contract is seen as having a mental representation, as we gradually develop a schema (a schema is a cognitive pattern of thought that individuals use to organise categories of information and the relationships between them) from past experience, which subsequently guides the manner in which information is processed. Once we form such a schema, we tend to maintain it, with new information being interpreted in light of the early schema, but within a short time, as employees become socialised into an organisational setting, their psychological contract evolves from the perception of a series of discrete obligations, into an elaborately organised schema.

Third, psychological contracts can be categorised as either transactional or relational (Coyle-Shapiro & Conway, 2005; Rousseau, 1995). Transactional contracts are based on the principle of economic exchange and more short-term exchanges. As such they are structured with emphasis on material rewards that have a short-term duration and are relatively narrow in scope. The terms of exchange can often be given a monetary value, are specific, and exist for a limited duration of time. The essence of the transactional component of psychological contract can be expressed as 'a fair day's work for a fair day's pay' (Rousseau & Wade-Benzoni, 1994); or as the 'effort exchange–effort bargain', that is, the reciprocal process of exchanging effort for reward.

Relational contracts reflect mutual obligations between employees and the organisation that support each other's interests (Guzzo et al., 1994). They contain terms that may not be easily monetisable, and broadly concern open-ended relationships. These have a significant duration, often without an implied end-date, and are subject to the individual parties' beliefs. As such they involve considerable investments by employees and employers and are structured around intangible rewards.

Fourth, an important distinction exists between breach and violation of the psychological contract. Breach is a perceived underfulfilment of the contract. It occurs when an employee perceives that their organisation has failed to follow through on obligations that were expected by the individual. Breach is a significant enough perception to have an impact on many important attitudes and behaviours, such as job satisfaction, organisational commitment, work engagement, turnover intentions, organisational citizenship behaviours, and well-being (Agarwal & Bhargava, 2014). Given the level of change in many employment relationships around the world, it is now considered to have become a common and inevitable occurrence (Restubog et al., 2013; Zagenczyk et al., 2009). Psychological contract violation, in contrast, is an emotionally charged feeling of anger or frustration, triggered by the perceived betrayal created by a significant breach of a psychological contract (Robinson & Morrison, 2000).

To clarify the relationship between the psychological contract and other ways in which we think about contracts within the employment relationship, Rousseau (1995) went on to identify four levels of analysis:

- individual-level psychological contracts;
- contracts implied by third parties;
- normative contracts shared across groups at unit, work process, or organisational level; and
- shared social contracts that reflect the broad beliefs about obligations associated with a society's culture.

In summary, the psychological contract has always been seen as a micro perspective on the employee–organisation relationship, standing alongside more macro perspectives such as transactional cost theory or agency theory from economics, and macro approaches to human resource management (Coyle-Shapiro & Shore, 2007). Human resource management (HRM) practices are presented as serving an important role within this micro relationship, and the psychological contract is presented as one of several important 'mediating' mechanisms that sit between HRM practices and performance outcomes (Bal et al., 2013; Guest, 2007; Guest & Conway, 2002; Katou et al., 2014; Raeder et al., 2012; Sonnenberg et al., 2011).

An effective psychological contract is therefore considered to be an intermediate factor that helps to transfer HRM practices into organisational performance. The type of HRM practices determines the nature of the psychological contract, which may be considered as transactional or relational in nature, but in either instance there are direct connections between HRM practices and the state of the contract (Aggarwal & Bhargava, 2009; Ostroff & Bowen, 2016; Suazo et al., 2009).

THE PSYCHOLOGICAL CONTRACT IN COMPARATIVE CONTEXT

The general literature on psychological contracts has moved in recent years into topics such as the psychological contracts of various forms of casual labour, the link between corporate social responsibility and psychological contracts, overall assessments of (un) fairness and psychological contract breach, the role of employer branding in establishing a psychological contract, and psychological contract breach and emotional well-being. This work has extended our general understanding of psychological contracts by:

- examining in greater detail the potential antecedents to the contract;
- understanding the range of situational and contextual factors that influence its

operation (with the study of international differences in the contract or its operation falling within this category);
- extending the range of outcomes and behaviours that it might explain;
- better understanding the processes through which various aspects of the contract
  (such as contract breach) lead to work performance;
- linking the use of the psychological contract research lens to other more mainstream strategic HRM debates.

We note here that in addition to, but separate from, this there has also been a discernible
strand of literature that has applied the concept of psychological contracts to traditional
HRM areas of research within multinational enterprises, principally because there is
potential for cross-cultural differences to be found in how psychological contracts mediate
the relationship between HRM practices and performance.

The Theoretical Arguments as to Why Psychological Contracts might be Culturally Embedded

Reflecting this, early discussion debated how cross-cultural differences in the employer–
employee relationship might impact upon the contract process (Rousseau & Schalk,
2000; Schalk & Soeters, 2008; Sparrow, 1998; Thomas et al., 2003; Thomas et al., 2010).
Sparrow (1998), in asking whether the literature on psychological contracting was transferable across countries, identified a series of cross-cultural and psychological dynamics
that should be considered when we attempt to understand contractual behaviour in a
comparative context:

- Evidence from the field of comparative HRM suggests that distinctive patterns of
  HRM policy and practice are likely to send very different structural signals about
  the nature of the psychological contract.
- The work of organisational sociologists and political economists showed that
  national business systems were subject to distinctive policy trajectories, creating
  unique institutional contexts within which the formal/informal contract trade-off
  takes place.
- Evidence from cross-cultural research suggests several mechanisms through which
  national culture might impact upon the internal motivational schema that employees have, and the external social cues that they will respond to.
- Evidence from social psychologists and sociologists suggests a number of ways in
  which societal and institutional processes feed directly into the trade-off between
  the formal and informal aspects of the contract.

For Thomas et al. (2003), national culture influences the psychological contract
through the zone of negotiability that is deemed acceptable: 'every society . . . sets a zone
of negotiability through its own set of constraints and guarantees . . . between societies
the zone of negotiability is shaped by societal tolerance for unequal outcomes and . . .
societal regulation of employment' (Thomas et al., 2003: 286). Researchers therefore
need to interpret two things: (1) the contractual and behavioural signals that are sent by
the general nature of HRM in a country setting; and (2) the mechanisms through which

cross-cultural differences in the psychological contracting process might be created. There has been some research in the first area, though very little research in the second.

Examining Micro-Level Processes in Different Cultural Contexts: Are There Generic or Culture-Specific Mechanisms?

Raeder et al. (2012) noted that the notion of the psychological contract has been used as an explanatory framework to understand the employment relationship in IHRM research at either a macro or a micro level. The micro researchers view the psychological contract as a cognitive sense-making process through which employees attempt to attach meaning to events. However, beginning around the year 2000, it was becoming clear that the vast majority of research on the psychological contract had been conducted in highly industrialised and developed countries. China has received significant attention (see Bao et al., 2011; Liu et al., 2012; Jing et al., 2014; Lu et al., 2015). Studies have also recently looked at Malaysia (Arshad & Sparrow, 2010) and India (Agarwal & Bhargava, 2014). In Europe, attention has been given to Belgium (Bernhard-Oettel et al., 2011) and Greece (Tomprou et al., 2012; Giannikis & Nikandrou, 2013). In Latin America, attention has been given to Columbia (Roman-Calderon et al., 2015).

The majority of these studies have been what would be classed as construct validation studies; that is, applying propositions from psychological contract theory in new (geographical) samples, but with the assumption that the generic propositions will also hold in this new setting. The reasons for conducting the studies might have a local element, in that local labour market conditions or changes in the employment relationship would suggest that the psychological contract of employees might be impacted upon, but there is no intent to challenge the basic tenets of psychological contract theory.

These researchers have all examined the micro-level processes involved in the psychological contract, the processes through which employees respond to changes in the employment relationship, in order to understand whether the dynamics linked to organisational phenomena may differ from one cultural context to another. In short, they form a narrative seeking to establish whether there are generic (acultural) or culture-specific reactions to important organisational events. However, given the nature of academic publishing, these studies have faced a dual challenge: (1) to examine whether the concept of the psychological contract has relevance to other geographic and industrial settings; whilst (2) simultaneously advancing our generic understanding of how contracts actually work.

In Malaysia, Arshad and Sparrow (2010) invoked the notion of psychological contract when they examined employee reactions to downsizing in organisations, arguing that the traditional justice and fairness perspective might be influenced by important attitudes and behaviours implicit within the psychological contract. Whilst the study was used to lay out in more detail the psychological reactions triggered by the downsizings at a micro level, what they found was that these psychological reactions could be considered to be generic, that is, culture-free. There was little direct overlay that might be attributed to cultural differences.

In Belgium, Bernhard-Oettel et al. (2011), building on earlier work by De Cuyper et al. (2005) and De Cuyper and De Witte (2006), used the notion of psychological contract to examine the effects of job insecurity on employees, and how perceptions of job insecurity and fairness were associated with individual job satisfaction, and general health and organisational attitudes such as organisational commitment and turnover intention. Again, their study was used to help refine understanding of some of the psychological dynamics at play, but always assumed and argued for generic impacts.

Two studies have been conducted in Greece. Tomprou et al. (2012) examined the dynamics of how the psychological contract operated amongst a sample of 236 bank employees; specifically, how psychological contract violation moderated the relationship between contract breach and attitudinal outcomes. They found, as would be predicted, that violated feelings intervened between perceptions of contract breach and attitudinal outcomes of job satisfaction and organisational commitment. Trust also partially mediated the relationship of perceived contract breach with organisational commitment and an employee's job satisfaction. Again, however, the micro-dynamics of the process of breach and violation were considered to be acultural. Similarly, Giannikis and Nikandrou (2013), in a sample of 424 employees from four organisations in the manufacturing sector, used social exchange theory to examine whether the psychological contract acted as an important mediator for the relationship between two aspects of innovative organisations (corporate entrepreneurship and high-performance work systems) and subsequent employee job attitudes of satisfaction and commitment. The selection of Greece as a site of study was because it faced turbulent times, and the study could assess how employees respond to innovative work environments. The findings showed that, as would be expected, psychological contract breach did serve as an important mediator.

In India, Agarwal and Bhargava (2014) examined elements of the psychological contract amongst 1302 managers. The authors legitimised the study in an Indian context by drawing attention to macro changes in the employment relationship context (intensified organisational competition post-liberalisation; a withdrawal of many benefits such as job security, retirement provisions, and time-based career growth; altered employee expectations such as work–life balance; and new employee segments such as the presence of women in professional roles), and the potential impact of cultural differences (individualism versus collectivism, and power distance). They used the cultural context to argue for the study of two important contextual antecedents (that is, organisation and supervisor relationship quality and trust) noting the greater associative and nurturing needs and importance of superior–subordinate relationships paralleling parent–child relationships in a collectivist culture. In addition to bringing in these two antecedents, and looking at traditional outcomes of affective commitment and intention to quit, they also brought in a new outcome of innovative work behaviour, also of particular relevance to the Indian context. However, they were looking at generic micro-processes, and argued that the insights have generic application across countries and cultures: 'Similar findings in both Indian and Western countries suggest the effects of psychological contract breach can be generalised to culturally diverse regions' (Agarwal & Bhargava, 2014).

In Columbia, Roman-Calderon et al. (2015) used psychological contract theory to examine the relationship between the ideological components of the employee–employer relationship and resultant positive attitudes and cooperative organisational behaviours in a sample of 218 employees working in a hybrid (for-profit, socially oriented) Colombian organisation. The results were as would be expected based on current generic theory.

In China, Jing et al. (2014), in a survey of 228 employees in a Chinese telecoms organisation, conducted a validation study in which propositions grounded in psychological contract literature were applied to the Chinese context and assumed to be generic, that is, acultural. They examined the relationship between the type of psychological contract and the perceptions that employees had for the reasons for change, and the resultant levels of organisational commitment and the impacts these then had on well-being, exit, or aggressive voice. As would be expected, a transactional contract was not related to affective, continuance, or normative commitments to change, but the strength of a relational contract was positively related to the level of normative commitment to change. A relational contract was, however, negatively related to continuance commitment.

Set against these studies that generally support the proposition that at a micro level the psychological contract operates in an acultural way, there is some evidence that there might be indirect effects of national culture on these micro-dynamics. In China, although the Jing et al. (2014) study assumes an acultural operation of the psychological contract, three other studies on micro-aspects of the psychological contract in a Chinese context argue for some imprint of national culture and institutional context (Bao et al., 2011; Liu et al., 2012; Lu et al., 2015).

Bao et al. (2011) positioned their study of 200 Chinese executives as both extending the study of contracts to an untested employee segment (more senior employees: that is, chief executive officers, executive vice-presidents, and general managers) and determining whether employees, embedded in the Chinese national culture, developed psychological contracts and, if so, whether contract violations had similar impacts on Chinese employees as on their Western counterparts. They argued that the Chinese culture means that employees rely more heavily on interpersonal and social exchange relationships than on legal contracts in employee–employer relationships, due to the underdevelopment of employment contracts, and that there is an emphasis on the in-group. While still recognising the importance of submitting to authority, hierarchical status often requires favours from subordinates, such that the perceived 'reciprocity' of the relationship may require uncomfortable behaviour on the part of those within the network:

> as formal HR rules exist to ensure fair treatment, employees engaged in work places with less emphasis on formal rules would likely be keen to monitor the employee–employer exchange relationship to ensure the materialisation of perceived promises from their employer. An absence of laws concerning severance packages and job security would induce executives to keenly monitor their working relationship within the firm. Therefore, we argue that the development of psychological contracts would be very pronounced in certain countries such as China. (Bao et al., 2011: 3375)

They examined the interaction effects of psychological contract violation and a series of job- and person-related constructs, looking at the potential moderating role of job satisfaction, job involvement, job demand, hope, and locus of control, all seen as important factors in the employment relationship of more senior staff, and all potentially capable of moderating (lessening) the negative impacts of contract violation. The study found, as expected from a contracting theory perspective, that violations of psychological contracts decreased affective organisational commitment, and that job satisfaction, job involvement, and hope all provided a buffer to the negative effects that a violated psychological contract had on organisational commitment. It also claimed that the correlation between violation of psychological contracts and affective organisational commitment was sufficiently large enough for the contract to be seen as particularly important in a Chinese context (though we do not yet have any meta-analysis studies that might allow us to establish comparative national effects). Again, therefore, the study attempts to serve two masters: using the cultural context to legitimise the micro-level variables under study, whilst attempting to generalise the more detailed moderating relationships that are exposed to the broader literature.

Similarly, Liu et al. (2012) examined how employer and employee psychological contract fulfilment influenced employee turnover, alongside what they called the influence of the boundary conditional role of Chinese traditional values on the process. Their results suggested that at a broad level Chinese employees behave similarly to those in Western cultures in terms of turnover behaviour, but that individual value orientations (that can be traced to national culture traits) did serve to moderate some of the generic relationships. They argued that 'traditionality' – defined as an indigenous Chinese construct signifying the extent to which an individual endorses the traditional hierarchical role relationships prescribed by Confucian social ethics – should be expected to impact upon turnover behaviour. They found that the reciprocation of employee and employer contract fulfilment did not lower turnover as expected, but that discrepancies between the two parties' fulfilment did activate employee turnover. From a cultural perspective, the construct of traditionality moderated this fulfilment–turnover linkage. Compared to non-traditional employees, traditional employees were more likely to leave their organisations when as an individual they felt they had failed to fulfil their promised obligations to their employers. However, traditionality weakened an employee's negative reactions to their employer's lack of contract fulfilment. They also found that that the less traditional employees reacted more strongly than more traditional employees to the situation where employees fulfilled their contracts but employers failed to fulfil their obligations.

Finally, Lu et al. (2015) examined the moderating role that leader–member exchange has on the relationship between psychological contract breach and employee outcomes in China. They found that psychological contract breach, as expected, influences an employee's turnover intention, organisational identification, and organisational citizenship behaviours. Leader–member exchange can act as a mediating variable between psychological contract breach and organisational identification and organisational citizenship behaviour, but it does not affect the relationship between psychological contract breach and turnover intentions in Chinese firms. Again, the researchers made no assumption that these dynamics were different because of the cultural context.

Examining Macro-Level Processes in Different Cultural Contexts: The Use of Psychological Contract as a Metaphor for Labour Market Change

Despite the evidence for a generally culture-free operation of the psychological contract at a micro level, we are seeing the emergence of a macro perspective on psychological contracts. Macro-level researchers have switched to a macro national or organisational level of analysis, generally investigating the psychological contract as a set of reciprocal obligations held by a broader set of actors within a national labour market, such as co-workers, supervisors, and managers (e.g., Dabos & Rousseau, 2004; Tekleab & Taylor, 2003; Westwood et al., 2001). Here, the notion of psychological contract is being used as a broad metaphor to capture changes taking place within an employment relationship, and in labour markets, within a particular national economy.

There seems to be continued relevance in using the lens of psychological contract to examine macro issues in Western contexts. For example, a recent study in the UK by Conway et al. (2014), examined the impact of the twin pressures of austerity and recession following the 2007–08 global financial crisis using longitudinal data in a sample of 340 employees from a range of public sector organisations. They tested whether these organisational changes breached the psychological contract of employees (they did); whether employee reactions to any such psychological contract breach varied across different foci, that is, the organisation (contributions to it were negatively impacted upon), co-workers and public service users (contributions to them was not impacted upon); and whether these relationships were moderated by job insecurity or public sector commitment (they were).

However, this perspective has become more widely adopted in a number of country studies. In Japan, Hattori (2015) examined the evolving nature of the employee relationship in a Japanese company using the lens of the psychological contract (and organisational commitment) based on data from 3789 employees of a large Japanese pharmaceutical company. Again, macro changes in the employment relationship were used to legitimise the use of a contracting lens. Confronted with the low productivity of white-collar employees and Japan's low economic growth, many Japanese organisations have been forced to introduce their own employment relationship, moving away from a national model. With externalisation of employment increasing at a considerable rate, more firms have adopted pay-for-performance schemes for their middle and senior managers and introduced demotion systems. The study found patterns of response that matched other (non-Japanese) studies, with for example the pattern of transactional and relational elements of the contract reflecting a theoretically expected structure. However, some of the findings were given a cultural interpretation (unfortunately, cross-sectional data are of limited value in arguing for any degree of contract change, let alone imposing a cultural overlay to the pattern of change). So, the finding that as tenure of Japanese employees increased, their perceived obligations incrementally decreased (that is, as time passes, employees gradually no longer intentionally seek information, and become less concerned about their employer's and their own obligations, and attention only increased when the employees experience discontinuous changes in the relationship) was used to argue that general changes in the Japanese employment context will have negative impacts on individual-level outcomes, especially on high-tenure (established) employees.

A Swiss macro-level study (Raeder et al., 2012) examined the attitudes of 92 Swiss HRM managers, finding that for them, whilst high-involvement HRM practices were considered to lead to their organisation generally fulfilling the psychological contract of its employees, and whilst some individual HRM practices were linked to contract fulfilment, overall there was no evidence for 'a mediation effect for the psychological contract nor an association with organisational performance' (ibid.: 3178).

In the Western literature, the notion of an old and a new psychological contract has been used to portray changes in the employment relationship, with the old contract being stereotyped as an offer of a reasonably secure job in exchange for loyalty (Millward & Brewerton, 2000). This notion of an old psychological contract as a metaphor is now being used to capture the complex situation which faces individuals and institutions in a number of emerging markets, to capture threatened or forthcoming new psychological contracts, and to hypothesise what the new challenges might therefore be. In some of the emerging economies, echoing earlier work in Europe (Millward & Brewerton,

2000; Schalk et al., 1995; Turnley & Feldman, 1999), the impact of globalisation along with more evolutionary developments are characterised as creating rapid change in the employment relationship. As with the European research, the psychological contract has become a metaphor to describe and to understand the employer–employee relationship and to predict potential organisational implications.

Two Indian studies fall into this category (Agarwal, 2011; Tyagi & Agrawal, 2010). Tyagi and Agrawal (2010: 383) argue that the psychological contract 'offers a metaphor, or representation, of what goes on in the workplace and highlights important but often neglected features'. Using a review of fundamental theoretical concepts, such hidden exchanges, contract breach and violation, they attribute presumed changes in the psychological contract within India to be a result of 'rapid changes and new dimensions in business space [that] are constantly created, while some are destroyed . . . Forces such as technological breakthroughs, economic growth, market evolution, and shifts in customer tastes, social changes, and political events . . . [mean] the nature of the employment relationship is undergoing fundamental changes' (Tyagi & Agrawal, 2010: 381).

Another cross-sectional study has examined 140 employees in the Indian information technology sector (Agarwal, 2011), a sector in which organisations are under pressure to make rapid and continual changes in the employment relationship, and the psychological contracts that underlie it. Again, the uniqueness of the Indian cultural setting was proffered as a reason to test the relationships, but the findings of relationships between type of contract, contract items, and commitment were ones that might generally be expected.

The changing labour market conditions in the Middle East have been examined using the frame of psychological contracts. Forstenlechner and Baruch (2013) use the metaphor of psychological contract breach to contrast Western notions of careers with the realities of emerging labour markets in a traditional society: that of the emerging Arabian Gulf economy. Government and other public sector organisations are already changing old traditions and norms, with the native citizens of the United Arab Emirates (UAE) being a minority of 12 per cent in their own country, with an estimated share of around 4 per cent of overall employment, falling to around 1 per cent of the private sector workforce. The social protection that exists in many developed countries does not operate the same way in the Gulf region. This has resulted in macro-level descriptions of the psychological contract at the national level (Al Gergawi, 2008). The old contract is seen as having strong collectivist characteristics, and being influenced by the use of personal connections for personal gain. The Arabic concept of *wasta* means 'connections' or 'pull', understood as the use of infrastructures of belief, family, kinship, or obligation. The old psychological contract has therefore been portrayed as one based on citizens finding ample job opportunities in the public sector, with a degree of welfare support, providing salaries well above the market rate, with demands well below market demands; that is, with 'employees benefitting from the sponsorship systems, soft loans and ample public sector employment opportunities with little performance control – or demands – of the principal over its agents' (Forstenlechner & Baruch, 2013: 631).

This old psychological contract has now been breached, and the UAE cannot keep offering similar jobs to the growing number of young people entering the labour market. The new contract, it is argued, is now embedded in the competition for private sector employment and the need to engage with the notion of a career. Aldossari and Robertson (2016) specifically addressed some cultural influences on the psychological contracts of expatriates. They examined the way in which *wasta* served to breach the psychological contract of repatriates in a Saudi organisation, and impacted upon the way in which psychological contracts were formed and changed.

Summarising the above studies, there is of course a methodological criticism that can be made of the existing micro and macro studies. For the micro studies, as noted, their purpose is usually mixed. They are attempting to use (often novel) geographical samples (for understandable reasons of access, or to meet calls for generalisability) to conduct studies that are simultaneously being used to advance generic theory. So, the refinement to our understanding that is being argued for, and claimed to be generic, probably is generic – but cannot always be assumed to be so. What we lack are detailed multi-country studies that test for standardised micro-dynamics across the (otherwise controlled-for) national samples. Perhaps such studies might soon start to emerge. For the macro studies, the existing research has to be seen as exploratory. It is of course again a rather unreasonable 'ask', but methodologically we cannot assert, say, that Chinese employees are more sensitised to contract breaches in the informal contract, unless we simultaneously make the same tests in other national samples. As yet, again, we have no such evidence. Perhaps, both at the micro and the macro levels, in the future we shall see the conduct of truly comparative studies. For now, however, researchers are testing the boundaries around the potential generalisability of psychological contract theory, or the use of it to address interesting macro-developments in employment relationships.

CONCLUSIONS

Comparative HRM specialists and HRM researchers examining multinational enterprises have long given attention to the type of HRM practices in a cultural and country context. This chapter shows, however, that whilst there has been some research on the contractual and behavioural signals that are sent by the general nature of HRM in a country setting, surprisingly there has been very little research on the mechanisms through which cross-cultural or cross-national differences in the psychological contracting process might be created. We have two different sets of researchers using the notion of psychological contracts within the comparative and cross-national tradition. The micro-process researchers have sought evidence for a generally culture-free operation of the psychological contract. In the main, the findings support such a notion, although it should be noted that studies designed to test generic relationships, by design, do not seek to explore variations in process. The studies have been aimed at advancing generic contracting theory, using national labour market context as a justification for study, not as the focus of the study. Whilst we can safely assume the generalisability of contract processes, we seem to have lost track of the original expectation that, from a comparative perspective, we need to explain how individual beliefs, levels of agreement (relative levels of power of employees and organisations), the terms of the exchange, and the implicitness of obligations, operate and serve to influence subsequent behaviour.

There has been much wider application of the construct of psychological contract by macro-level researchers. In switching to a macro, national – or organisational – level of analysis, the notion of psychological contract is being used as a broad metaphor to capture changes taking place within an employment relationship, in labour markets, or within a particular national economy. Again, we need to have some caution. Whilst using the contract more broadly as a metaphor for changes in the employment relationship can be useful for signalling important areas to research, as original contracting theory always argued, we need to differentiate the psychological relationship from the shared social contracts that exist at country level, and that reflect the broad beliefs about obligations associated with a society's culture. We should never assume that all nationals of a country operate to or share this social contract. They do not.

As this research becomes more common and mainstream, we shall likely see calls for further methodological refinement. For example, theory reminds us that organisations do not have psychological contracts per se. Rather, their agents do. It is important to be clear about which people act as agents, sending promissory signals, and what assumptions and expectations are made about the fair discharge of obligations. Given that the agents are also many, the question arises as to which agents have the most importance in the relationship (and this will not always be the HRM department). Psychological contracts will always contain both transactional and relational elements, and it is the relational elements that are most important. We also need to understand how the psychological contract evolves from the perception of a series of discrete obligations into more elaborate schema, and what becomes important in this evolution of a contract in terms of shaping behaviour. We need to be very clear about the distinction between breach and violation: the deal may be breached numerous times and at many points in the day by some agents, but it is the more consequential violation that serves to influence behaviour. Whilst career theory gives us some important clues as to likely different contracts across various categories of employee, the highly subjective nature of perceived promises means that the psychological contract could differ between individuals, and change over time within the individual as the relationship between an employer and employee also changes. As McNulty et al. (2013: 211) note: 'psychological contracts can change over time as [employees] re-negotiate and re-evaluate their employment contracts, content items of a psychological contract may also change'.

Finally, we shall likely see continued efforts to reconcile a number of related literatures. Although it has not been the focus of this chapter (which has looked principally at the use of the psychological contract in the comparative literature), the psychological contract has also been used increasingly within the IHRM literature, in particular in the context of expatriates and other forms of international mobility. In the expatriate management literature at the moment, we see early bridges being forged between the talent management and expatriate management literatures, and also between expatriation and careers research. This research will have implications for the comparative literature, however, because it signals the topics that should form the focus of future comparative analysis.

As a final comment, as this chapter has hopefully made clear, we might still be making assumptions about the nature of change in the psychological contract, based on what is still only a limited set of country analyses, case studies, surveys, and interviews. We should in future expect to see a broadened range of studies, moving away from broadly Western organisations to a wider range of geographies and important employee segments within these geographies.

REFERENCES

Agarwal, P. 2011. Relationship between psychological contract and organizational commitment in Indian IT industry. *Indian Journal of Industrial Relations*, 47(2): 290–305.

Aggarwal, U., & Bhargava, S. 2009. Reviewing the relationship between human resource practices and psychological contract and their impact on employee attitude and behaviours: A conceptual model. *Journal of European Industrial Training*, 33(1): 4–31.

Agarwal, U.A., & Bhargava, S. 2014. The role of social exchange on work outcomes: A study of Indian managers. *International Journal of Human Resource Management*, 25(10): 1484–1504.

Al Gergawi, M. 2008. *Emiratisation and the Curse of Entitlement*. Dubai: The National.

Aldossari, M., & Robertson, M. 2016. The role of wasta in repatriates' perceptions of a breach to the psychological contract: A Saudi Arabian case study. *International Journal of Human Resource Management*, 27(16): 1854–1873.

Arshad, R., & Sparrow, P. 2010. Downsizing and survivor reactions in Malaysia: Modelling antecedents and outcomes of psychological contract violation. *International Journal of Human Resource Management*, 21(11): 1793–1815.

Bal, P.M., Kooij, D.T., & De Jong, S.B. 2013. How do developmental and accommodative HRM enhance employee engagement and commitment? The role of psychological contract and SOC strategies. *Journal of Management Studies*, 50(4): 545–572.

Bao, Y., Olson, B., Parayitam, S., & Zhao, S. 2011. The effects of psychological contract violation on Chinese executives. *International Journal of Human Resource Management*, 22(16): 3373–3392.

Bernhard-Oettel, C., De Cuyper, N., Schreurs, B., & De Witte, H. 2011. Linking job insecurity to well-being and organizational attitudes in Belgian workers: The role of security expectations and fairness. *International Journal of Human Resource Management*, 22(9): 1866–1886.

Conway, N., Kiefer, T., Hartley, J., & Briner, R.B. 2014. Doing more with less? Employee reactions to psychological contract breach via target similarity or spillover during public sector organizational change. *British Journal of Management*, 25(4): 737–754.

Coyle-Shapiro, J.A., & Conway, N. 2005. Exchange relationships: examining psychological contracts and perceived organizational support. *Journal of Applied Psychology*, 90(4): 774–781.

Coyle-Shapiro, J.A., & Shore, L.M. 2007. The employee–organization relationship: Where do we go from here?. *Human Resource Management Review*, 17(2): 166–179.

Dabos, G.E., & Rousseau, D.M. 2004. Mutuality and reciprocity in the psychological contracts of employees and employers. *Journal of Applied Psychology*, 89(1): 52–72.

De Cuyper, N., & De Witte, H. 2006. The impact of job insecurity and contract type on attitudes, well-being and behavioural reports: A psychological contract perspective. *Journal of Occupational and Organizational Psychology*, 79(3): 395–409.

De Cuyper, N., Isaksson, K., & De Witte, H. 2005. *Employment Contracts and Well-Being among European Workers*. Aldershot: Ashgate.

Forstenlechner, I., & Baruch, Y. 2013. Contemporary career concepts and their fit for the Arabian Gulf context: A sector level analysis of psychological contract breach. *Career Development International*, 18(6): 629–648.

Giannikis, S., & Nikandrou, I. 2013. The impact of corporate entrepreneurship and high-performance work systems on employees' job attitudes: Empirical evidence from Greece during the economic downturn. *International Journal of Human Resource Management*, 24(19): 3644–3666.

Guest, D.E. 2007. HRM and the worker: Towards a new psychological contract?. In P. Boxall, J. Purcell, and P. Wright (eds), *Oxford Handbook of Human Resource Management*: 128–146. New York: Oxford University Press.

Guest, D.E., & Conway, N. 2002. Communicating the psychological contract: An employer perspective. *Human Resource Management Journal*, 12(2): 22–38.

Guzzo, R.A., Noonan, K.A., & Elron, E. 1994. Expatriate managers and the psychological contract. *Journal of Applied Psychology*, 79(4): 617–626.

Hattori, Y. 2015. Impact of career change on employee–organization relationship: A case of Japanese company. *Journal of International Business Research*, 14(2): 75–89.

Jing, R., Lin Xie, J., & Ning, J. 2014. Commitment to organizational change in a Chinese context. *Journal of Managerial Psychology*, 29(8): 1098–1114.

Katou, A.A., Budhwar, P.S., & Patel, C. 2014. Content vs. process in the HRM–performance relationship: An empirical examination. *Human Resource Management*, 53(4): 527–544.

Liu, J., Hui, C., Lee, C., & Chen, Z.X. 2012. Fulfilling obligations: Why Chinese employees stay. *International Journal of Human Resource Management*, 23(1): 35–51.

Lu, Y., Shen, Y., & Zhao, L. 2015. Linking psychological contract breach and employee outcomes in China: Does leader–member exchange make a difference?. *Chinese Economy*, 48(4): 297–308.

McNulty, Y., De Cieri, H., & Hutchings, K. 2013. Expatriate return on investment in the Asia Pacific: An empirical study of individual ROI versus corporate ROI. *Journal of World Business*, 48: 209–221.

Millward, L.J., & Brewerton, P.M. 2000. Psychological contracts: Employee relations for the twenty-first century?. *International Review of Industrial and Organizational Psychology*, 15: 1–62.

Ostroff, C., & Bowen, D.E. 2016. Reflections on the 2014 decade award: Is there strength in the construct of HR system strength?. *Academy of Management Review*, 41(2): 196–214.

Raeder, S., Knorr, U., & Hilb, M. 2012. Human resource management practices and psychological contracts in Swiss firms: An employer perspective. *International Journal of Human Resource Management*, 23(15): 3178–3195.

Restubog, S.L.D., Zagenczyk, T.J., Bordia, P., & Tang, R.L. 2013. When employees behave badly: The roles of contract importance and workplace familism in predicting negative reactions to psychological contract breach. *Journal of Applied Social Psychology*, 43(3): 673–686.

Robinson, S.L., & Morrison, E.W. 2000. The development of psychological contract breach and violation: A longitudinal study. *Journal of Organizational Behavior*, 21: 525–546.

Roman-Calderon, J.P., Odoardi, C., & Battistelli, A. 2015. Cause-fit, positive attitudes and behaviors within hybrid Columbian organizations. *Revista de Administração de Empresas*, 55(4): 408–417.

Rousseau, D.M. 1989. Psychological and implied contracts in organizations. *Employee Responsibilities and Rights Journal*, 2(2): 121–139.

Rousseau, D.M. 1990. New hire perceptions of their own and their employer's obligations: A study of psychological contracts. *Journal of Organizational Behavior*, 11(5): 389–400.

Rousseau, D.M. 1995. *Psychological Contracts in Organizations: Understanding Written and Unwritten Agreements*. London: SAGE.

Rousseau, D.M., & Schalk, R. 2000 *Psychological Contracts in Employment: Cross-National Perspectives*. Thousand Oaks, CA: SAGE.

Rousseau, D.M., & Wade-Benzoni, K.A. 1994. Linking strategy and human resource practices: How employee and customer contracts are created. *Human Resource Management*, 33(3): 463–489.

Schalk, R., Freese, L., & Van den Bosch, J. 1995. The psychological contract of part-time and full-time employees: An investigation into the expectations of employees about the reciprocal obligations between the organization and the employee in the employment situation. *Gedrag en Organisatie (Behavior and Organization)*, 8(5): 307–I307.

Schalk, R., & Soeters, J. 2008. Psychological contracts around the globe: Cultural agreements and disagreements. In P.B. Smith, M.F. Peterson, and D.C. Thomas (eds), *Handbook of Cross-Cultural Management Research*: 117–133. Thousand Oaks, CA: SAGE.

Sonnenberg, M., Koene, B., & Paauwe, J. 2011. Balancing HRM. The psychological contract of employees: A multi-level study. *Personnel Review*, 40(6): 664–683.

Sparrow, P.R. 1998. Reappraising psychological contracting: Lessons for the field of human-resource development from cross-cultural and occupational psychology research. *International Studies of Management and Organization*, 28(1): 30–63.

Suazo, M.M., Martínez, P.G., & Sandoval, R. 2009. Creating psychological and legal contracts through human resource practices: A signaling theory perspective. *Human Resource Management Review*, 19(2): 154–166.

Tekleab, A.G., & Taylor, M.S. 2003. Aren't there two parties in an employment relationship? Antecedents and consequences of organization–employee agreement on contract obligations and violations. *Journal of Organizational Behavior*, 24(5): 585–608.

Thomas, D.C., Au, K., & Ravlin, E.C. 2003. Cultural variation and the psychological contract. *Journal of Organizational Behavior*, 24(5): 451–471.

Thomas, D.C., Fitzsimmons, S.R., Ravlin, E.C., et al. 2010. Psychological contracts across cultures. *Organization Studies*, 31(11): 1437–1458.

Tomprou, M., Nikolaou, I., & Vakola, M. 2012. Experiencing organizational change in Greece: The framework of psychological contract. *International Journal of Human Resource Management*, 23(2): 385–405.

Turnley, W.H., & Feldman, D.C. 1999. The impact of psychological contract violations on exit, voice, loyalty, and neglect. *Human Relations*, 52(7): 895–922.

Tyagi, A., & Agrawal, R.K. 2010. Emerging employment relationships: Issues and concerns in psychological contract. *Indian Journal of Industrial Relations*, 45(3): 381–395.

Westwood, R., Sparrow, P., & Leung, A. 2001. Challenges to the psychological contract in Hong Kong. *International Journal of Human Resource Management*, 12(4): 621–651.

Zagenczyk, T.J., Gibney, R., Kiewitz, C., & Restubog, S.L.D. 2009. Mentors, supervisors and role models: Do they reduce the effects of psychological contract breach?. *Human Resource Management Journal*, 19(3): 237–259.

13. Positive and negative application of flexible working time arrangements: comparing the United States of America and the EU countries
Lonnie Golden, Stephen Sweet, and Heejung Chung

INTRODUCTION

This chapter focuses on flexible working time arrangements and presents flexible work schedule practices as they vary among individuals, organisations, and nations, explaining reasons for observed variations. It highlights the need to focus on specific types of flexible work options; distinctions between availability, access, and use; as well as formal and informal use practices. We show that, depending on the metric used, flexibility can be seen as widely available, or as seriously constrained or limited. If structured as employee-centred, flexible work arrangements can improve work–family harmonisation. Creating contexts with flexible work options that can enhance employee well-being requires attention at the organisational level, with cultural contexts that support both formal and informal implementation, as well as national-level policies that regulate the terms under which work hours can be, and should be, open to adjustment by employees.

DEFINITIONS AND DISTINCTIONS

A typology of flexible work arrangements (FWAs) identifies configurations that deviate from prevailing standards, options that would enable employees to alter the amount or timing of work. We highlight distinctions that shape use and availability, considering the type of work time flexibility, formality of provision, and perception of usability. It is possible for one type of flexibility to be available (for example, arriving at work later than is customary) while other types are absent (for example, reducing hours to part-time). It is also possible for companies to have some flexible work options 'on the books' as well as informal and often idiosyncratic or periodic arrangements that vary from employee to employee, or from work unit to work unit. FWAs that are intended to be 'employee-centred' are commonly or ostensibly adopted to enhance work–non-work family time harmonisation (including work–family or work–life balance, facilitation, or integration). Sometimes, however, employees find such options provided by their employers to be in reality out of reach, unusable, or even resulting in some form of penalisation. Lastly, we introduce the distinction between positive flexibility: arrangements that enhance prospects for work–family harmonisation; and negative flexibility: arrangements that introduce unpredictability and instability in employee lives. The focus of this chapter is on the positive, employee-centred type of flexibility, which may occur by coincidence with the employer-centred type, but more often may not.

MAIN FORMS OF WORKING TIME FLEXIBILITY

Four different categories of working time flexibility are: daily work schedule flexibility (flexitime or taking time off during the workday), flexhours (accumulated, banked for time off in the future at employees' discretion), reduced workweeks (temporary, voluntary part-time, or refusable extra hours), and options that allow for relatively short-term, temporary cessation of work (Chung & Tijdens, 2013; Sweet et al., 2014). Flexible working time arrangements might be combined (for example, an employee who has shifted to reduced hours as well as more flexible start and end times), and may also be combined with flexible work location (although beyond the scope of this chapter, that would include work at home, remotely, or an off-site workplace, in which employees save on commuting time while employers save money on building, leasing, or maintaining office or shop space).

It is common for many types of flexible work to be ostensibly available, and provided to at least some employees, but far less often are such options widely available, meaning that they are often not extended to all or even most employees within organisations. As a consequence, accessibility rates among employees can be far lower than is commonly assumed (Cooper & Baird, 2015). Furthermore, even if a given FWA is implemented and considered accessible by the employer, certain employees might not perceive FWA use to be viable, given the environment of informal support extended by supervisors and/or fellow co-workers, or as a consequence of long-term career risks that result from use. It is additionally important to recognise the tremendous variation that exists between and even within industries, as well as between and within nations (Stavrou et al., 2015; Chung, 2009, 2014).

To employees, 'flexible work hours' often connotes an opportunity to custom fit work responsibilities with non-work commitments, which can include not only care-giving obligations, but also personal interests. The flexibility afforded workers to adjust their working hours is often a matter of degree, and the impact on work–life harmonisation is shaped by employer objectives. While the range of flexibility certainly occurs along a continuum, we identify three discrete degrees along that spectrum. Worker well-being is likely to increase with any amount of discretion to influence both the timing and number of work hours across the workday, workweek, or year. Moreover, the well-being gain from an FWA may rise not only with its use, but even with availability. A zero marker would be fixed shift lengths and fixed daily schedule timing, such as 'nine to five'. However, contingent on this framing is the assumption that flexibility is designed, ostensibly, to enhance workers' control, whereas employers often post schedules or shifts at short notice. Thus, on this continuum, zero represents a standard, rigid schedule; positive scores above zero represent flexibilities that enhance employee well-being via control extended to the employee; and scores below zero represent flexibilities that undermine employee well-being by removing control and predictability.

THREE DEGREES OF POSITIVE FLEXIBILITY

'First-degree' positive flexibility exists when employees can make marginal adjustments in their work schedule, at least periodically. For example, a workplace might rely on set daily work schedules, but also occasionally allow employees to start and leave somewhat earlier or later than the usual fixed daily schedule. First-degree flexibility is found in most flexitime practices, representing a formal workplace programme that permits employees to vary their starting times around a range in a 'band' of required 'core' hours. This could be starting a typical full-time shift any time between 7 am and 10 am and leaving between 3 pm and 6 pm. It may also reflect more informal flexible schedule arrangements, when a supervisor or co-workers facilitate an employee desire to shift the start or end times of work.

'Second-degree' positive flexibility goes a step further. It provides employees with discretion, either at the onset or during the course of the employment relationship, to continuously adjust their workday to their preferred timing, such that it is no longer reliant on a standard shift as a reference point. For example, this might provide licence to leave the workplace for a few hours to attend to an unexpected non-work responsibility, and finishing the work either later that day or even that week. If there were no everyday core hours at all, this offers workers the option to compress the required workweek over a worker's preferred days around a core set of days (for example, taking Friday off). Second-degree flexibility can also be achieved with 'shift swapping' among employees, where a worker exchanges a shift directly with another employee, often with permission granted first, in ways that are 'Pareto-enhancing', that is, improving the matching for one individual without harming the matching for the other. This flexibility likely improves welfare potentially more than first-degree flexibility. The welfare gain does not depend on whether a schedule is flexible because of a formal workplace programme or an informal arrangement; the latter is actually more common among those with flexible daily schedules (Golden, 2009; Ortega, 2009). Nevertheless, crucial for assessing whether a practice facilitates better work–life balance is its perceived usability (Hayman, 2009) and also the extent to which flexibility or even having control results in longer average working hours or greater work intensity (Golden, 2009; Kelliher & Anderson, 2010; White et al., 2003).

'Third-degree' positive flexibility allows employees to adjust not only the timing, but also the duration of their working hours across a week, month, or year. In contrast, the first and second degrees both involve providing a given volume of daily or weekly work. Third-degree flexibility could mean working not more than standard hours when overtime is required; or for a spell, going to shorter workdays, fewer workdays, or part-time job status when less work is preferred (all presumably with some commensurate reduction in compensation). It might also enable workers to pursue overtime work at their discretion. This kind of autonomy or control of working time is likely valued the most, and is the most welfare-enhancing. Moreover, having only periodic, marginal control over work schedules, such as basic flexitime, is not necessarily universally welfare-improving in all cases. Some workers prefer the impermeable boundaries and borders in their work–life integration efforts provided by fixed daily and weekly schedules (Kossek et al., 2004; Schieman & Young, 2010), since a work–life border permeability heightens demands and responsibility. Third-degree positive flexibilities enable the creation of truly customised schedules, tailored to one's preferences to cope with expected and unexpected time conflicts. Such control is almost certainly welfare-enhancing (Berg et al., 2004; Golden et al., 2013; Lyness et al., 2012).

THREE DEGREES OF NEGATIVE FLEXIBILITY

Front-line managers in a wide variety of industries are commonly pressed into scheduling practices that vary the number of hours of employees and the distribution of those hours across a week or even a day. While the organisation gains more labour flexibility, and some protected employees gain stability, this may come at the expense of instability for others (Lambert, 2008), particularly those in part-time positions (Henly & Lambert, 2014). In some circumstances the language of 'flexibility' has been used to expand prospects of dismantling secure and predictable employment, and partly for that reason organised labour has often opposed the expansion of FWAs (Pollert, 1988). Thus, there is a negative end to the spectrum of degrees of flexibility, which actually falls below zero.

First-degree negative flexibility would be occasional minor variations in schedules, initiated by the employer, in ways that could be disruptive to employee lives. Second-degree negative flexibility operates by employers imposing consistently unpredictable work schedule assignments. More often than not, these unpredictable schedules are accompanied with prospects for third-degree negative flexibility, which involves penalisation that further escalates the negative impact of erratic scheduling practices, such as curtailing working hours if the employee does not abide by the schedule shifts imposed, or by forcing even more excessive overtime demands.

These employer-sided flexibilities introduce uncertainties in workers' lives, such as in the case of the fast-food worker who sees hours fluctuate unpredictably from week to week with only a day or two advance notice (Lambert et al., 2012). Thus, the flip side of positive flexibility, individual discretion or autonomy, is not just inflexibility or rigidity, but rather uncontrolled variability of work schedules and hours, set according to the employer's momentary needs, with no advance notice of changes and no predictability of upcoming changes, accompanied by work schedules or work location penalties for failing to abide by these arrangements. The variability introduced by unpredictable or involuntary work, including overtime, is particularly detrimental to work–life outcomes and economic security, given its association with both greater work–family conflict and fatigue (Clawson & Gerstel, 2014; Henly et al., 2006; Lambert, 2009a). Thus, schedule rigidity is not always comparatively bad, as lower variability can enhance life quality as compared to more chaotic schedules (Costa et al., 2006).

WORKING TIME FLEXIBILITY IN THE UNITED STATES OF AMERICA

One way to study FWA availability is to focus on organisations. Below is a list of common FWAs within the United States of America (USA), in which working time flexibilities are provided, within the overarching categories. Especially notable in the case of the USA is a near complete lack of statutory regulations that provide rights to flexible work. Percentages indicate how frequently specific types of arrangements are offered by employers in the USA. The data come from Boston College's 2015 Talent Management Study (N = 224 private sector employers). These data reflect reports from high-level human resource officers or company presidents in response to questions that asked whether a given FWA option is available to none (0 per cent), some (1–50 per cent), most (51–85 per cent), or all/nearly all (86–100 per cent) employees. Percentages reported below indicate, respectively, reports of 'some', and of 'most' and 'all/nearly all' employees. Note that most companies can be simultaneously classified as having a wide range of FWA options, while simultaneously offering these options only to constrained sets of employees. Additionally, note that schedule flexibility is most widely available, but less so are options to reduce or temporarily stop work.

Schedule Flexibility

- Labour in a schedule that varies from the typical schedule at worksite (85.2 per cent / 29.6 per cent).
- Change starting and quitting times for an extended duration (91.5 per cent / 37.1 per cent).
- Change in starting and quitting times on a day-to-day basis (52.7 per cent / 8.1 per cent).
- Compress the work week, longer hours for fewer days (56.7 per cent / 12.0 per cent).
- Opportunity to select and change shifts times (56.9 per cent / 15.3 per cent).

Work Reduction Flexibility

- Reduce work hours to a part-time basis while remaining in the same position or level (48.9 per cent / 8.5 per cent).
- Job share where both persons receive proportional compensation (21.0 per cent / 3.1 per cent).
- Phase into retirement by working reduced hours prior to full retirement (54.5 per cent / 8.5 per cent).
- Transfer to jobs with reduced pay and responsibilities (71.3 per cent / 19.9 per cent).

Work Cessation Flexibility

- Work part year (28.6 per cent / 4.0 per cent).
- Take sabbaticals or career breaks (18.5 per cent / 6.8 per cent).
- Take paid or unpaid time away from work for education or training to improve job skills (55.4 per cent / 23.9 per cent).

It is important to note that these figures, based on reports gathered by the authors in 2015 from human resource executives, provide no more than one window on formal availability. They do not offer entirely reliable information to properly gauge the extent of informal availability, usability perceived by employees themselves, or actual use. To gain further insight on these concerns we turn to employee-level data, examining the USA's General Social Survey (GSS) Quality of Work Life (QWL) module. It contains 76 items for a sample of some 1800 employed per year, pooled for the years 2002, 2006, and 2010. Included in this instrument are three questions that pertain directly to flexibility in working time:

- 'How often are you allowed to change your starting and quitting times on a daily basis?'

- 'How hard is it to take time off during [. . .] work to take care of personal or family matters?'
- 'When you work overtime, is it mandatory (required by your employer)?' (This is asked of workers who responded with one or more days to the question, 'How many days in a month during the last year did you work beyond your usual schedule?')

Using the pooled data from 2002, 2006, and 2010, the following represent the mean of all responses (see Table 13.1). First, 'how often [is a worker] allowed to change [his or her] starting and quitting times on a daily basis?' (4 = often, 3 = sometimes, 2 = rarely, and 1 = never). The responses show significant disparity by type of job status: salaried, hourly, and other. Next, how difficult is it 'to take time off during your work to take care

Table 13.1   Percentages of workers reporting access, ease of use, and mandatory overtime: United States, 2002, 2006, 2010, combined years

	All workers	Salaried workers	Hourly workers
General Social Survey, Quality of Worklife, 2002, 2006, 2010			
Time off during day (%)			
very hard	10.2	8.8	10.7
somewhat hard	16.5	17.3	16.3
not too hard	31.6	31.7	32.7
not at all hard	41.7	42.1	40.3
Change start/end time (%)			
never	31.6	23.3	40.6
rarely	15.6	12.9	19.1
sometimes	20.3	21.5	21
often	32.4	42.3	19.3
Observations	2982	1583	1132
W-F Community Nexus Survey, 2006			
Difficult to take time off			
always true	11.8		
often true	9.1		
sometimes true	27.6		
never true	51.5		
Can set own regular work schedule			
at no cost	47.9		
with small cost	9.0		
with high cost	1.0		
not available	42.2		
Can take day off without permission			
at no cost	31.9		
with small cost	12.0		
with high cost	6.1		
not available	50.0		
Observations	2668		

of personal or family matters?' (4 = not at all hard, 3 = not too hard, 2 = somewhat, 1 = very hard), and finally, when workers 'work extra hours [on your main job], is it mandatory (required by your employer)'? The latter two questions display almost none of the disparity observed in the first question by hourly or salaried type of job. Table 13.1 shows that almost a third of all workers can often change the daily start and end times of their workday. Just over half of all workers find it at least not too hard to do so. There are significant differences, however, by job status. Six out of ten hourly-paid workers find it at least somewhat hard – including four out of ten finding it very hard – to change start and end times. In contrast, among salaried workers, less than 10 per cent find it very hard, and almost three-quarters of salaried workers find it at least not too hard to take time off. Finally, about four out of ten hourly workers can take off time during the day, without much difficulty. Thus, in contrast to start and end time schedule flexibility, hourly workers have almost as much flexibility when it comes to taking time off during the workday.

The Work–Family Community Nexus Survey (a nationally representative survey of American adults aged 18–69) polled workers in 2005–06 regarding 'how true' they perceived that the following were available at their workplace: the ability to adjust one's start or stop time if the need arises; difficulty to take time off; ability to take a day off work (or parts of days) without asking permission; ability to set one's own regular schedule; and ability to move from full-time to part-time and back while remaining in the same position. The survey measures not only the availability of each policy or practice, but the worker's perceived (current and future) 'cost' of utilising them. Respondents rated the extent to which a practice was available at their workplace, and then assessed the personal cost to themselves of taking this benefit (at their workplace): (1) 'at no cost'; (2) 'with a small cost or penalty' (for example, supervisor is unhappy with me); or (3) 'with a large cost or penalty' (for example, sacrifices future promotion).

As shown in the second part of Table 13.1, not dissimilarly to the GSS, about half the workers find no difficulty taking days or parts of days off, while 21 per cent find it quite difficult. Thus, half find it at least sometimes difficult to take time off. In addition, 42 per cent feel as if setting their own schedule is not an option. This percentage is quite consistent with findings from a similar question in the International Social Survey Program's Work Orientations module in 2005–06, which asked whether workers or their employers set their work schedule. Moreover, at least half the workers did not have the option to take off a day without permission. Finally, 53 per cent of the workforce feel they cannot move between part-time and full-time hours. This suggests that a majority of workers do not feel that second-degree flexibility is available at their job or workplace. Thus, availability is to be distinguished not only from the actual application or implementation of FWAs, but also from its use by employees.

Even in organisations that have FWAs formally available, or in situations where informal availability exists, employees may forgo use, for fear of reprisal from managers or co-workers, incompatible workload demands, and negative impacts on long-term career prospects (Eaton, 2003). In sum, at least about 15 per cent considered that there would be some sort of cost or penalty to using an available work–life flexibility practice or policy at their workplace, about 10 per cent feel some sort of backlash from setting their own schedule, 15 per cent suspect such a cost of moving to part-time (and/or back), and almost 20 per cent anticipate costs were they to take a day off without permission.

FLEXIBLE WORKING ARRANGEMENTS AND WORK–LIFE FIT OUTCOMES

In ideal situations, FWAs facilitate work-family harmonisation or work–life balance by enabling workers to have input into decisions on when or where work is to be performed so as to enhance 'work–life fit' (James et al., 2015). When FWAs are applied in the interests of attaining work–life fit, the corpus of existing research provides compelling evidence that employee family lives benefit, especially by enhancing capacity to provide care to children or ageing parents (Sweet, 2014). Additionally, FWAs can contribute to other dimensions of employee lives, such as enhancing healthy lifestyles and buffering stress (Grzywacz & Butler, 2008; Grzywacz & Tucker, 2008; Moen et al., 2011b). However, there are circumstances where FWAs can complicate employee lives by blurring boundaries that keep work and family obligations distinct or segmented (Golden, 2001; Moen et al., 2013). Evidence suggests that not all employees respond to FWAs in the same way or have the same work-style preferences, and not all types of work–family situations are equally suited to FWAs (Kossek & Lautsch, 2012). For example, one employee might thrive with a flexible schedule that allows use of a home office, whereas another employee may prefer times that would keep home and workspace separate. While it is commonly assumed that workers seek flexibility to reduce work hours, sometimes they do so to increase opportunities to engage in more work or more intensive work.

There are compelling reasons to believe that some employers should anticipate positive outcomes resulting from FWA use. Norms of reciprocity, for example, might lead employees to feel grateful for FWA access and respond with increased dedication and loyalty. Past studies indicate that FWA use tends to increase individual performance, affective commitment, and proactive behaviours (Liu et al., 2013; Muse et al., 2008; Yang & Zheng, 2011; Yasbek, 2004). Workplace experiments show that employee schedule control enhances employee retention (Moen et al., 2011a). Conversely, when FWAs are limited or removed, this can lead employees to feel deprived and in turn drive team morale downwards (Sweet et al., forthcoming). To our knowledge, no study has effectively determined whether FWAs offer a positive return on investment from a strict cost–benefit standpoint, in part because such determinations are exceedingly difficult to establish (Kelly et al., 2008).

Of the studies that affirm positive consequences on individual and team performance, the strength of relationships tend to be modest. However, few organisations have implemented wide-scale access to diverse arrays of FWAs (Sweet et al., 2014), and as a consequence researchers have had scarce opportunity to track the full potential impact of alternate work arrangements (Kossek et al., 2010). It has been suggested that when managers and organisations become more familiar with the use of FWAs, a 'cycle of affirmation' will be activated, such that positive outcomes of FWA use will be witnessed, which in turn will affirm subsequent expansion of FWAs (Putnam et al., 2013). Studies testing this proposition suggest that this cycle might exist (Sweet et al., 2015; Sweet et al., forthcoming). Current evidence does not support contrary assumptions regarding negative outcomes, such as prospects for a decline in worker commitment resulting from FWA use.

It is probably reasonable to assume that lower work–life conflict has the potential to enhance efficacy in both work and family domains. Table 13.2, generated from the GSS, QWL, 2002 and 2006 shows the reported levels of work interference with family associated with its two main measures of working time flexibility. Those with frequent daily

Table 13.2 *Working hours flexibility use and job interference with family life, USA, 2002, 2006, pooled (% of organisations)*

	Frequency that work interferes with family								
	Often	Significance	Sometimes	Significance	Rarely		Never	Significance	N
Frequency of altering start and end times									
often/sometimes	10.9		34.5	**	31.0		23.4	**	895
rarely/never	10.3		28.2	**	29.4		32.1	**	774
Difficulty in taking time off									
not hard/not too hard	6.6	**	28.8	**	33.0	**	31.6	**	1228
somewhat hard/very hard	22.0	**	39.2	**	23.4	**	15.4	**	441
Mandatory overtime									
yes	18.9	**	38.2		24.6		30.1		341
no	10.8	**	38.0		30.1		20.7		766

Note: ** difference in proportions is statistically significant at p<.05.

schedule flexibility appear to be likely never to experience work-to-family interference. Those with less difficulty taking time off report much lower frequency of experiencing work–family conflict. Similarly, those lacking the flexibility to refuse overtime hours (that is, the inflexibility to have to work overtime), clearly have higher frequency of work–family conflict, vis-à-vis those working overtime hours but without it being considered 'required' by the employer, and those working no overtime at all.

SOURCES OF VARIATION IN POSITIVE AND NEGATIVE FWAS

Comparing Occupations and Industries

Clearly specific types of FWAs options are not suited to all forms of employment and this may explain, in part, why specific types of FWAs vary by occupation and industry (den Dulk & de Ruijter, 2008; Chung, 2009, 2014). How FWAs play out in practice varies remarkably. For example, work in the accommodation and food services sector as well as in the retail sector can be viewed as having flexibility, but not necessarily the type of flexibility that facilitates work–life fit. Often the challenge for these workers is locating predictable work and sufficient work. Thus flexibility in those industries might be more commonly the type that is negative for employees (Lambert, 2009b; Lambert et al., 2012). Manufacturing and construction sectors tend to have relatively lower rates of FWA availability of employee-centred types of flexible work arrangements compared to work located in other industry sectors (Golden, 2009; Ortega, 2009). In contrast, employers in the healthcare sector and in the professional, scientific, and technical services sector tend to offer a diverse array of options and to make those options more widely available (Sweet et al., 2014).

One explanation for these types of variations is the inherent demands of the job, such as assembly line manufacturing or construction site building trades work. In contrast, an institutional perspective (Meyer & Rowan, 1977) focuses on normative pressures and customary expectations in the workplace. This perspective questions why, for example, schedule flexibility remains rarely available in the manufacturing sector, as there are a variety of approaches that are currently used in the healthcare sector that could map onto the manufacturing sector, but are not being implemented by management. This suggests that industries operate within sealed reference frameworks, such that each industry establishes its own normative ways of organising work, and often tends not to look beyond its boundaries for examples of how to arrange work in alternative ways. Likely, both explanations hold sway in determining the types of flexibilities made available and the motivations for doing so.

ROLE OF LABOUR UNIONS

Institutions such as labour unions, historically, sought to standardise the workday and workweek, as a means to protect and enhance the interests of a typical worker from employer-centred (negative) types of FWAs. In addition, unions tend to increase the take-up rate of the positive, family-friendly practices or negotiated contract provisions. Unions appear to be assisting workers with better information and leverage (Budd & Mumford, 2004; Gerstel & Clawson, 2001). Indeed, some unions are actively involved in organising (campaigns) and bargaining around work–life balance issues, particularly in the public sector, but within severe constraints imposed by employers (Gregory & Milner, 2009). Examining Germany and the United Kingdom (UK), Seeleib-Kaiser and Fleckenstein (2009) note that organised labour within the establishment might allow for the introduction of family policies that managers otherwise would not have adopted. In North America, union membership or contract coverage has a negative effect on the odds of having access to daily flexibility in start and end times of work, as demonstrated in Canada (Zeytinoglu et al., 2009). In the USA, labour union workers have only a slightly reduced likelihood of having access to formal flexitime, but a far more pronounced reduced access to the less formal type of scheduling flexibility (Golden, 2009). Similarly, in Europe, having an employee representative on site does not necessarily result in increasing worker access to flexitime (Chung, 2014). Organised labour, which has not always embraced positive flexibility, has recently mounted campaigns against negative flexibility (Luce, 2014).

Comparing the USA with European Union Countries

The USA stands apart from other societies with respect to the limited number of statutes that provide employee rights that enable use of alternative work arrangements and paid leave of absence (Hegewisch & Gornick, 2008; Kelly, 2006; Sweet & Meiksins, 2017). Variation in national policy presents one of the most significant challenges for multinational corporations (MNCs) in establishing FWA policies, because what might be permissible in one society (such as banking of work hours for future time off) may not be permissible in other societies (Muse, 2011). In the USA, the 2015 Schedules That Work Act is designed to create monetary disincentives against the use and spread of employer-dominated scheduling practices that lead to negative flexibility. It also contains provisions that would generate the kind of individualised 'right to request' hours and scheduling adjustments that have existed for at least a decade in many European countries.

When examining the institutions that govern the use of flexible working arrangements in the European Union (EU), it is important to look first at the EU Working Time Directive (2003/88/EC). This sets out the maximum weekly working hours (48 hours), along with regulations on daily and weekly rest periods, annual leave, and protection mechanisms regarding working during unusual hours: weekends, and evening and night shifts. Although such policies govern employee working hours, there are no directives directly governing policies on flexible working schedules. However, several countries, including the UK, the Netherlands, Germany, Finland, and Norway, have developed regulations that allow workers access to flexible working (Hegewisch, 2009).

The Dutch Working Hours Adjustment Act (Wet Aanpassing Arbeidsduur, WAA) was introduced in 2000 and allows employees to request changes in their working hours after one year of employment (Visser, 2003). This regulation allows both reduction and extension, and thus can be reversed after a period of time (Yerkes, 2009). Employers have to provide justifications for rejecting this request, demonstrating serious repercussions to the business. The Dutch WAA changed in 2016 to become the Flexible Working Act (Wet Flexiebel Werken), which provides rights to make requests not only about working hours but also for the times or schedules to be adjusted, as well as requesting the possibility to work from home. The new regulations also extended the right to those who have been in the job for less than one year, and they have reduced the time a worker needs to wait before submitting a new request once rejected.

In the UK the right to request flexible working was introduced in 2003. This right was initially applied only to parents of preschool-aged children but was extended to carers of adults in 2007, and to all parents with children below the age of 17 in 2009. Finally, in 2014 the right was extended to cover all workers who have been in employment for at least six months, regardless of their caring responsibility. The 'right to request' allows workers to request flexible working patterns including the reduction of hours (part-time work), condensed working weeks, flexitime (flexible scheduling of hours), job sharing, and term-time working. Employers can reject this request based on various business grounds including the burden of additional costs.

Figure 13.1 examines the take-up of flexible work arrangements via the European Company Survey of 2013. The chart shows that 66 per cent of all companies across the 27 EU member countries provide flexitime, for at least one of their employees, making it the most commonly available positive type of FWA apart from part-time working. Northern European countries such as Finland, Denmark, and Sweden, alongside Austria, had the highest likelihood of companies providing flexitime in 2013, while some Eastern and Southern European countries such as Bulgaria, Cyprus, Greece, Poland, and Romania had the lowest likelihood. Furthermore, in Northern Europe, once flexitime is provided in a company, a larger proportion of workers are covered by the scheme, and it is used flexibly: that is, allowing employees to work longer on some days and to compensate this later by working less on other days, and/or accumulating hours to take full days off. In

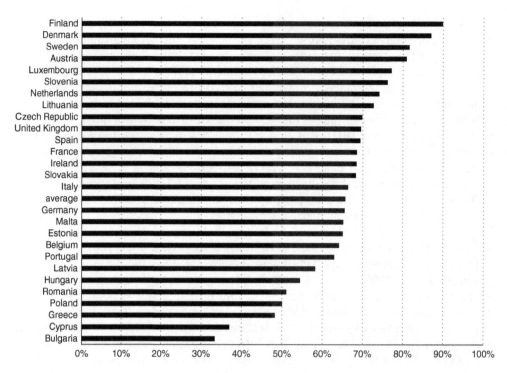

Source: Author's own calculation based on European Company Survey 2013 (establishment weighted).

Figure 13.1   Percentage of companies providing flexitime for at least one of their employees, 2013

Bulgaria, Hungary, Portugal, Cyprus, and Malta, amongst others, a smaller proportion of workers are covered by flexitime provision, and when it is used, it is restrictive in terms of the accumulations of hours.

Flexitime provision made at the company level may not be what workers perceive as real access, since organisational policies may not be implemented equally for all workers in the company, and there may be gaps in the policy or practice (Blair-Loy & Wharton, 2002; Cooper & Baird, 2015). The proportion of individual workers reporting access to flexitime is much lower than we see via the company data. Similar to what was found through the company-level data, the Northern European countries are where workers are most likely to gain access to flexitime. The Southern and Eastern European countries are again those where workers are not able to gain much access to flexitime. In all countries, the levels provided by the managers are much higher than workers' perceptions of access, especially in the UK.

Approximately 5 per cent of all workers have full working time autonomy. As Figure 13.2 highlights, autonomy is most prevalent in Sweden, Denmark, and the Netherlands. In comparison, in Finland working time autonomy is not as frequently provided. Austria, Germany, and France are also countries where there are a large number of workers with more freedom concerning their working hours.

In sum, in general, in Northern European countries, flexitime is more widely provided and it covers a wider group of employees. On the other hand, Southern European coun-

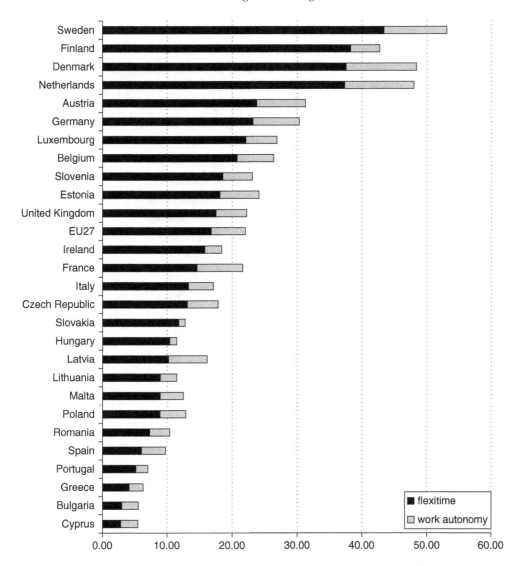

Source: Authors' own calculations based on the European Working Condition's Survey of 2010.

Figure 13.2 *Access to working time autonomy and flexitime for employees across 27 European Union countries, 2010*

tries do not use flexitime as much and are more restrictive as to how it is used by employees, even once they allow for its use.

Lastly, we look at the proportion of workers with some sort of time flexibility to tend to family and personal issues during working hours (see Figure 13.3). Across the EU, it seems that a majority of workers have some sort of freedom to tend to personal and family issues during working hours, although again this varies across countries. More than 80 per cent of workers in Northern European countries are able to take some time off during working

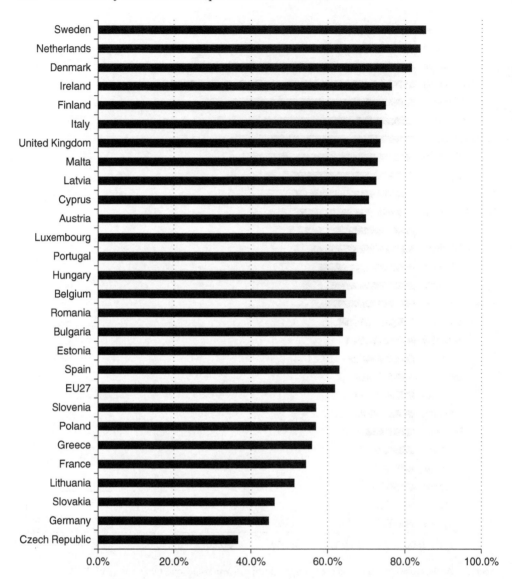

Source: Authors' own calculations based on the European Working Conditions Survey of 2010.

Figure 13.3   *Employees having access to one or two hours off work to tend to personal or family issues across 27 European Union countries, 2010 (weighted averages)*

hours to tend to personal issues. On the other hand, in the Czech Republic, Germany, and Slovakia less than half of all workers feel that they can do this. Interestingly, while some of the Southern European countries rank rather high on worker ability to take time off during working hours – for example, Italy, Malta, and Cyprus – as do some Eastern European countries, Germany and France are the most inflexible countries in allowing workers to take time off during working hours.

EXPLAINING THE CROSS-NATIONAL VARIATION IN THE USE OF WORKING TIME FLEXIBILITY: INSTITUTIONAL, INDUSTRIAL RELATIONS, AND NATIONAL ECONOMY FACTORS

A review of 16 extant studies that examine the use of working time flexibility or working time control from a cross-national perspective finds that the following national-level contextual factors are most relevant in explaining company-level provision of working time flexibility: industrial relations and power resources of unions; cultural factors including national norms on gender issues and work orientation; institutional factors such as social and family policies; national-level demand measured through the extent of women's labour market participation; and economic conditions and structures such as the affluence of the country, economic labour market condition, and the composition of the economy (Chung, 2014; Chung & Tijdens, 2013).

There are two theoretical assumptions in examining the relationship between national-level policies and provision of (additional) family-friendly policies, including flexible working time arrangements by the company. Institutional theory argues that institutions and bureaucratic systems, laws, and policies put pressure on organisations to become similar through isomorphic processes (DiMaggio & Powell, 1983). Den Dulk et al. (2013a) argue that governments put institutional pressure on organisations to develop family-friendly working time arrangements through their coercive powers. Family policy and working time regulations that enforce provision and tax incentives for such policies directly influence company behaviours in offerings. For example, government regulations on the use of flexible working time, such as the right to request flexible working time arrangements, could more directly affect whether flexible working time arrangements are provided by the company. In addition, national policy provision signals the emphasis governments put on work–life balance issues, changing the norms and public demand for companies to address. Thus, company-level working time policies are expected to be more widespread in countries where there are generous family policies (Chung, 2008; den Dulk et al., 2013a; den Dulk et al., 2012; Lyness et al., 2012).

The counter-argument to this is crowding-out theory, where national social policies programmes '"crowd out" informal caring relations and social networks' (Van Oorschot & Arts, 2005: 6). Thus, in countries with generous family policies at the national level, companies will not be willing, or may not feel a need, to provide company-level working time flexibility policies to address similar issues. In countries where there are few statutory regulations on family policies, companies use family-friendly working time policies for staff retention or for other strategic reasons (den Dulk, 2001, 2005; Ollier-Malaterre, 2009). Nevertheless, there may be no clear relationship between statutory regulations and (extra) company provision (Kassinis & Stavrou, 2013; Präg & Mills, 2014), and some argue that only when there is a very large involvement from the state can a crowding-out impact be seen (Evans, 2002).

Industrial relations at the national level also has a major influence on the choices managers or companies make in the provision of family policies and providing workers with working time flexibility arrangements. According to power resource theory, a 'contagion from the Left' (Korpi, 1989: 316) influences the way employers act in providing family-friendly benefits at the company level. In addition, in the varieties of capitalism literature (Hall & Soskice, 2001), centralised negotiating structures and platforms will help employee representatives to negotiate family-friendly benefits with employers, and also change the way employers behave in choosing their strategies for competition, taking more of a high-performance route. Among seven countries compared, those with higher collective bargaining coverage, high trade union density, and employee representatives being more positive towards work–life balance, all increased worker control over working time, including the use of flexible working time arrangements (Berg et al., 2004). Empirical studies find that collective bargaining coverage rates and union density are positively correlated with the use or provision of flexitime (Chung, 2009; Lyness et al., 2012; Präg & Mills, 2014).

There also may be cross-national variations in the use of flexible working time arrangements due to the different skills and composition of the country's labour force. Employers may feel a need to provide family-friendly working time policies to retain workers (Davis & Kalleberg, 2006; Seeleib-Kaiser & Fleckenstein, 2009), especially in countries where there is a high reliance on knowledge workers. When the economy is in distress, and there is an excess supply of labour, this may decrease workers' negotiating power in relation to flexibility geared mainly towards the employee's needs. On the other hand, when demand outstrips supply, employers may use family-friendly working time arrangements as incentives to help recruit and maintain workers (Aryee et al., 1998; Batt & Valcour, 2003; Chung, 2009; den Dulk et al., 2013a). Previous empirical evidence is not as supportive (Chung, 2009; den Dulk et al., 2013a).

The prevalence of service sectors and public sectors, which influence individual companies through the diffusion of practices generally, might enhance working time flexibility practices (Chung, 2009; Lyness et al., 2012; Präg & Mills, 2014). Countries with a higher proportion of women in the labour market might well be those where there are larger demands for family-friendly policies at the company level. The use of flexitime and other working time flexibility arrangements has been shown to be positively related to female labour market participation rates (Chung, 2009; Ortega, 2009; Präg & Mills, 2014), although others have shown that there are no significant relationships once the affluence of the country is taken into account (Lyness et al., 2012). Indeed, increased gross domestic product per capita may dampen the work ethic and work centrality in a given country, but is positively linked to the use of flexitime (den Dulk et al., 2013b; Lyness et al., 2012; Präg & Mills, 2014; Stam et al., 2013). In national cultures with higher work centrality, companies have been shown to reduce the provision of family-friendly arrangements, including flexitime, working time banking, and rights to part-time work or reduced work hours.

CONCLUSION

Flexible work time arrangements offer prospects to enhance work-role and family-role performance, balance, or harmonisation. However, examination of the ways FWAs are structured and integrated into organisational practice reveals that these are not inevitable outcomes. Along with a business case for expanding access to FWAs for employees, evidence indicates that organisations are currently not inclined to make such arrangements widely available within their workforces, and tend to offer only select options to select workers. Lacking statutory controls, both access and use in the USA remains limited and uneven. In contrast, in European Union nations, access and use is far more widespread and accepted. From an employee perspective, these findings suggest the usefulness of regulatory reins to constrain the implementation of negative flexibilities and to promote or mandate implementation of positive flexibilities. The relatively more individualised 'rights to request' processes across some EU countries, which include altering the timing of one's work schedule, appear to improve employee well-being and work performance.

ACKNOWLEDGEMENTS

Alison Earle, for providing Work–Family Community Nexus Survey data, and Barbara Wiens-Tuers and Jaeseung Kim for analysing General Social Survey data.

REFERENCES

Aryee, S., Luk, V., & Stone, R. (1998). Family-responsive variables and retention-relevant outcomes among employed parents. *Human Relations*, 51(1), 73–87.

Batt, R., & Valcour, P.M. (2003). Human resources practices as predictors of work–family outcomes and employee turnover. *Industrial Relations: A Journal of Economy and Society*, 42(2), 189–220.

Berg, P., Appelbaum, E., Bailey, T., & Kalleberg, A.L. (2004). Contesting time: International comparisons of employee control of working time. *Industrial and Labor Relations Review*, 57(3), 331–349.

Blair-Loy, M., & Wharton, A.S. (2002). Employee's use of work–family policies and the workplace social context. *Social Forces*, 80(3), 813–845.

Budd, J., & Mumford, K. (2004). Trade unions and family-friendly policies in Britain. *Industrial and Labor Relations Review*, 57(2), 204–222.

Chung, H. (2008). Provision of work–life balance arrangements in European companies: Public vs. private. In M. Keune, J. Leschke, and A. Watt (eds), *Privatisation and Marketisation of Services: Social and Economic Impacts on Employment, Labour Markets and Trade Unions*: 285–319. Brussels: ETUI-REHS.

Chung, H. (2009). *Flexibility For Whom? Working Time Flexibility Practices of European Companies*. Ridderkerk: Ridderprint.

Chung, H. (2014). Explaining the provision of flexitime in companies across Europe (in the pre- and post-crisis Europe): Role of national contexts. Working Paper 1, Work, Autonomy, Flexibility Working Papers Series. Canterbury: University of Kent.

Chung, H., & Tijdens, K. (2013). Working time flexibility components and working time regimes in Europe: Using company-level data across 21 countries. *International Journal of Human Resource Management*, 24(7), 1418–1434.

Clawson, D., & Gerstel, N. (2014). *Unequal Time: Gender, Class and Family in Employment Schedules*. New York: Russell Sage Foundation.

Cooper, R., & Baird, M. (2015). Bringing the 'right to request' flexible working arrangements to life: From policies to practices. *Employee Relations*, 37(5), 568–581.

Costa, G., Sartori, S., & Angstkerstedt, T. (2006). Influence of flexibility and variability of working hours on health and well-being. *Chronobiology International*, 23(6), 1125–1137.

Davis, A.E., & Kalleberg, A.L. (2006). Family-friendly organizations? Work and family programs in the 1990s. *Work and Occupations*, 33(2), 191–223.

den Dulk, L. (2001). *Work–Family Arrangements in Organisations: A Cross-National Study in the Netherlands, Italy, the United Kingdom and Sweden*. Amsterdam: Rozenberg Publishers.

den Dulk, L. (2005). Workplace work–family arrangements: A study and explanatory framework of differences between organizational provisions in different welfare states. In S.A.Y. Poelmans (ed.), *Work and Family: An International Research Perspective*: 211–238. Manwah, NJ: Lawrence Erlbaum Associates.

den Dulk, L., & de Ruijter, J. (2008). Managing work–life policies: Disruption versus dependency arguments. Explaining managerial attitudes towards employee utilization of work–life policies. *International Journal of Human Resource Management*, 19(7), 1222–1236. doi:10.1080/09585190802109986.

den Dulk, L., Groeneveld, S., Ollier-Malaterre, A., & Valcour, M. (2013a). National context in work–life research: A multi-level cross-national analysis of the adoption of workplace work–life arrangements in Europe. *European Management Journal*, 31(5), 478–494.

den Dulk, L., Groeneveld, S., Ollier-Malaterre, A., & Valcour, M. (2013b). National context in work–life research: A multi-level cross-national analysis of the adoption of workplace work–life arrangements in Europe. *European Management Journal*, 21(5), 478–494.

den Dulk, L., Peters, P., & Poutsma, E. (2012). Variations in adoption of workplace work–family arrangements in Europe: The influence of welfare-state regime and organizational characteristics. *International Journal of Human Resource Management*, 23(13), 2785–2808.

DiMaggio, P.J., & Powell, W.W. (1983). The iron cage revisited: Institutional isomorphism and collective rationality in organizational fields. *American Sociological Review*, 48(2), 147–160.

Eaton, S.C. (2003). If you can use them: Flexibility policies, organizational commitment, and perceived performance. *Industrial Relations*, (2), 145–167.

Evans, J.M. (2002). Work/family reconciliation, gender wage equity and occupational segregation: The role of firms and public policy. *Canadian Public Policy/Analyse de Politiques*, 28(1), 187–216.

Gerstel, N., & Clawson, D. (2001). Unions' responses to family concerns. *Social Problems*, 48(2), 277–297.

Golden, L. (2001). Flexible work schedules: What are we trading off to get them? *Monthly Labor Review*, 124(3), 50–67. Retrieved from http://www.bls.gov/opub/mlr/2001/03/art3full.pdf.

Golden, L. (2009). Flexible daily work schedules in the US jobs: Formal introductions needed? *Industrial Relations*, 48(1), 27–54.

Golden, L., Henly, J., & Lambert, S. (2013). Work schedule flexibility: A contributor to happiness? *Journal of Social Research and Policy*, 4(2), 107.

Gregory, A., & Milner, S. (2009). Trade unions and work–life balance: Changing times in France and the UK? *British Journal of Industrial Relations*, 47(1), 122–146.

Grzywacz, J., & Butler, A. (2008). Schedule flexibility and stress: Linking formal flexible arrangements and perceived flexibility to employee health. *Community, Work and Family*, 11(2), 199–214.

Grzywacz, J., & Tucker, J. (2008). Work–family experiences and physical health: A summary and critical review. *Work and Family Encyclopedia*, http://wfnetwork.bc.edu/encyclopedia_entry.php?id=6410&area=All.

Hall, P.A., & Soskice, D.W. (2001). *Varieties of Capitalism: The Institutional Foundations of Comparative Advantage*. New York: Oxford University Press.

Hayman, J.R. (2009). Flexible work arrangements: Exploring the linkages between perceived usability of flexible work schedules and work/life balance. *Community, Work and Family*, 12(3), 327–338.

Hegewisch, A. (2009). Flexible working policies: A comparative review. Manchester: Equality and Human Rights Commission.

Hegewisch, A., & Gornick, J.C. (2008). Statutory routes to workplace flexibility in cross-national perspective. Washington, DC: Washington, DC: Institute for Women's Policy Research. http://www. iwpr. org/pdf/B258workplaceflex.pdf.

Henly, J., & Lambert, S. (2014). Unpredictable work timing in retail jobs: Implications for employee work–life conflict. *Industrial and Labor Relations Review*, 67(3), 986–1016.

Henly, J., Shaefer, H.L., & Waxman, E. (2006). Nonstandard work schedules: Employer- and employee-driven flexibility in retail jobs. *Social Services Review*, 37(4), 609–634.

James, J.B., Pitt-Catsouphes, M., McNamara, T., Snow, D., & Johnson, P. (2015). The relationship of work unit pressure to satisfaction with work–family balance: A new twist on negative spillover? *Research in the Sociology of Work*, 26, 219–247.

Kassinis, G.I., & Stavrou, E.T. (2013). Non-standard work arrangements and national context. *European Management Journal*, 31(5), 464–477.

Kelliher, C. & Anderson, D. (2010). Doing more with less? Flexible working practices and the intensification of work. *Human Relations*, 63(1), 83–106.

Kelly, E. (2006). Work–family policies: The United States in international perspective. In M. Pitt-Catsouphes, E.E. Kossek, and S. Sweet (eds), *The Work and Family Handbook: Multidisciplinary Perspectives, Methods and Approaches*: 99–124. Boston, MA: Lawrence Erlbaum.

Kelly, E., Kossek, E.E., Hammer, L., et al. (2008). Getting there from here: Research on the effects of work–family initiatives on work–family conflict and business outcomes. In J. Walsh and A. Brief (eds), *The Academy of Management Annals (Volume 2)*: 305–349. New York: Academy of Management.

Korpi, W. (1989). Power, politics, and state autonomy in the development of social citizenship: Social rights during sickness in eighteen OECD countries since 1930. *American Sociological Review*, 54(3), 309–328.

Kossek, E.E., & Lautsch, B. (2012). Work–family boundary management styles in organizations: A cross level model. *Organizational Psychology Review*, 2(2), 152–171.

Kossek, E.E., Lautsch, B., & Eaton, S. (2004). Flexibility enactment theory: Flexibility type, control, and boundary management for work and family effectives. In E.E. Kossek and S. Lambert (eds), *Work and Life Integration: Organizational, Cultural and Individulas Perspectives*: 243–261. Mahwah, NJ: Lawrence Erlbaum Associates.

Kossek, E.E., Lewis, S., & Hammer, L. (2010). Work–life initiatives and organizational change: Overcoming mixed messages to move from the marging to the mainstream. *Human Relations*, 63(1), 1–17. doi:10.1 177/0018726709352385.

Lambert, S. (2008). Passing the buck: Labor flexibility practices that transfer risk onto hourly workers. *Human Relations*, 61(9), 1203–1227.

Lambert, S. (2009a). Lessons from the policy world: How the economy, work supports, and education matter for low-income workers. *Work and Occupations*, 36(1), 56–65.

Lambert, S. (ed.) (2009b). *Making a Difference for Hourly Employees*. Washington, DC: Urban Institute Press.

Lambert, S.J., Haley-Lock, A., & Henly, J.R. (2012). Schedule flexibility in hourly jobs: Unanticipated consequences and promising directions. *Community, Work and Family*, 15(3), 293–315. doi:10.1080/13668803.20 12.662803.

Liu, J., Lee, C., Hui, C., Kwan, H.K., & Wu, L.-Z. (2013). Idiosyncratic deals and employee outcomes: The mediating roles of social exchange and self-enhancement and the moderating role of individualism. *Journal of Applied Psychology*, 98(5), 832–840. doi:10.1037/a0032571.

Luce, S. (2014). *Labor Movements: Global Perspectives*. Cambridge: Polity Press.

Lyness, K.S., Gornick, J.C., Stone, P., & Grotto, A.R. (2012). It's all about control: Worker control over schedule and hours in cross-national context. *American Sociological Review*, 77(6), 1023–1049.

Meyer, J., & Rowan, B. (1977). Institutional organizations: Formal structure as myth and ceremony. *American Journal of Sociology*, 83(2), 340–363. doi:10.1086/226550.

Moen, P., Kelly, E., & Hill, R. (2011a). Does enhancing work-time control and flexibility reduce turnover? A naturally occurring experiment. *Social Problems*, 58(1), 69–98. doi:10.1525/sp.2011.58.1.69.

Moen, P., Kelly, E., Tranby, E., & Huang, Q. (2011b). Changing work, changing health: Can real work-time flexibility promote health behaviors and well-being? *Journal of Health and Social Behavior*, 52(4), 404–429.

Moen, P., Lam, J., Ammons, S., & Kelly, E.L. (2013). Time work by overworked professionals: Strategies in response to the stress of higher status. *Work and Occupations*, 40(2), 79–114. doi:10.1177/0730888413481482.

Muse, L. (2011). Flexibility implementation to a global workforce: A case study of Merck and Company, Inc. *Community, Work and Family*, 14(2), 249–256.

Muse, L., Harris, S., Giles, W., & Field, H. (2008). Work–life benefits and positive organizational behavior: Is there a connection? *Journal of Organizational Behavior*, 29(1), 171–192. doi:10.1002/job.506.

Ollier-Malaterre, A. (2009). Organizational work–life initiatives: context matters: France compared to the UK and the US. *Community, Work and Family*, 12(2), 159–178.

Ortega, J. (2009). Why do employers give discretion? Family versus performance concerns. *Industrial Relations: A Journal of Economy and Society*, 48(1), 1–26.

Pollert, A. (1988). Dismantling flexibility. *Capital and Class*, 34, 42–75.

Präg, P., & Mills, M. (2014). Family-related working schedule flexibility across Europe. Retrieved from http://ec.europa.eu/justice/gender-equality/files/documents/140502_gender_equality_workforce_ssr6_en.pdf.

Putnam, L., Myers, K., & Gailliard, B. (2013). Examining the tensions in workplace flexibility and exploring options for new directions. *Human Relations*, 67(4), 1–28. doi:10.1177/0018726713495704.

Schieman, S., & Young, M. (2010). When work interferes with life: Work–nonwork interference and the influence of work-related demands and resources. *Social Science Research*, 39(2), 246–259.

Seeleib-Kaiser, M., & Fleckenstein, T. (2009). The political economy of occupational family policies: Comparing workplaces in Britain and Germany. *British Journal of Industrial Relations*, 47(4), 741–764.

Stam, K., Verbakel, E., & De Graaf, P.M. (2013). Explaining variation in work ethic in Europe: Religious heritage rather than modernisation, the welfare state and communism. *European Societies*, 15(2), 268–289.

Stavrou, E.T., Parry, E., & Andersen, D. (2015). Non-standard work arrangements and configurations of firm and societal systems. *International Journal of Human Resource Management*, 26(19/20), 2412–2433.

Sweet, S. (2014). *The Work–Family Interface: An Introduction*. Thousand Oaks, CA: SAGE.

Sweet, S., Besen, E., Pitt-Catsouphes, M., & Golden, L. (2014). Explaining organizational variation in flexible work arrangements: Why the pattern and scale of availability matter. *Community, Work and Family*, 17(2), 115–141. doi:10.1080/13668803.2014.887553.

Sweet, S., James, J.B., & Pitt-Catsouphes, M. (2015). Successes in changing flexible work arrangement use: Managers and work-unit variation in a financial services organization. *Work and Occupations*, 43(1), 75–109.

Sweet, S., James, J.B., & Pitt-Catsouphes, M. (forthcoming). Consequences of expanding and curtailing flexible work arrangement use: A longitudinal study of team functioning.

Sweet, S., & Meiksins, P. (2017). *Changing Contours of Work: Jobs and Opportunities in the New Economy 3rd Edition*. Thousand Oaks, CA: Pine Forge Press.

Van Oorschot, W., & Arts, W. (2005). The social capital of European welfare states: The crowding out hypothesis revisited. *Journal of European Social Policy*, 15(1), 5–26.

Visser, J. (2003). Negotiated flexibility, working time and transitions in the Netherlands. In J. O'Reilly (ed.), *Regulating Working-Time Transitions in Europe*: 123–169. Cheltenham, UK and Northampton, MA, USA: Edward Elgar Publishing.

White, M., Hill, S., McGovern, P., Mills, C., & Smeaton, D. (2003). 'High-performance' management practices, working hours and work–life balance. *British Journal of Industrial Relations*, 41(2), 175–195.

Yang, S., & Zheng, L. (2011). The paradox of de-coupling: A study of flexible work program and workers' productivity. *Social Science Research*, 40(1), 299–311. doi:10.1016/j.ssresearch.2010.04.005.

Yasbek, P. (2004). The business case for firm-level work–life balance policies: A review of the literature. Retrieved from http://www.dol.govt.nz/PDFs/FirmLevelWLB.pdf.

Yerkes, M. (2009). Part-time work in the Dutch welfare state: The ideal combination of work and care? *Policy and Politics*, 37(4), 535–552.

Zeytinoglu, I., Cooke, G., & Mann, S. (2009). Flexibility: Whose choice is it anyway? *Relations Industrielles/ Industrial Relations*, 64(4), 555–574.

14. Comparative career studies: conceptual issues and empirical results

Mila Lazarova, Wolfgang Mayrhofer, Jon Briscoe,
Michael Dickmann, Douglas T. (Tim) Hall, and Emma Parry

INTRODUCTION

In this chapter, we describe the state of comparative research on individual careers and organisational career management activities. The field is in its early stages, exploring basic issues such as the application and relevance of career-related constructs across various national, institutional, or cultural contexts. Given the rather 'disjointed' state of our knowledge at this point, our objective is not so much a review of all that has been published to date but rather pointing towards examples illustrating major current research efforts and promising roads for the future.

The chapter is organised as follows. We first clarify the key concepts in research on individual careers and organisational career management. We then outline the emerging field of comparative career studies with its focus on comparative analyses of individual careers and career management activities across a broad variety of contexts. In a final step, we present insights from two large-scale comparative projects with direct relevance to career studies, one looking at individual careers and one investigating, among others, career management-related human resource management (HRM) practices.

DEFINITIONS AND BACKGROUND

Individual Careers

Much of the current research on careers is strongly influenced by the United States (US) view that focuses on the subjective dimension of careers. In that perspective, career is defined as '*the evolving sequence of a person's work experience over time*' (Arthur et al., 1989: 8). Following the steps of the Chicago school (Hughes, 1958), numerous scholars refuse to reduce careers to the paths of those benefiting from hierarchical advancements within organisations. Putting to the fore that a career mainly refers to the meanings individuals attribute to their situations, they claim that career should not been limited to a series of 'objective' promotions. Rather, in addition to vertical (up/down), it can involve horizontal or even radial movements (Schein, 1971). A career move does not need to be a positive experience, nor should it necessarily involve change in level or occupation. Plateauing should not be considered to represent experiencing a glass ceiling; for instance, many professionals grow within their occupation without experiencing any job changes. Researchers have also suggested considering as career moves even the experiences of parents shifting from one job to another in order to make a living, while their main concern is to raise their children.

In a context where careers are less linear and less predictable, the key priority becomes helping everyone to achieve professional goals and/or find a balance between professional and personal life. The very fact that individuals have personal career orientations, or anchors (Schein, 1990; Derr, 1986), strongly suggests that careers have been increasingly viewed as belonging to individuals. Beside noting that individuals are likely to hold different career orientations due to differences in competencies and personality as well as differences in cycles of their biological life and their careers, the individually driven view of careers also builds on the assumption that in new organisations individuals have more room to act as sculptors rather than as sculpture (Bell & Staw, 1989; Alvarez, 2000), even if they are not aware of that opportunity.

Both the literature dedicated to the boundaryless career (Arthur & Rousseau, 1996) and research suggesting a shift from a relational to a transactional employment relationship (Rousseau & Schalk, 2000) suggest that there is a need to break away from the tendency to restrict a career to 'a succession of related jobs, arranged in a hierarchy of prestige, through which persons move in an ordered more or less predictable sequence' (Wilensky, 1961: 523). Because of the claim that employers themselves admit that it is no longer possible for them to promise anyone an organisational career, the boundaryless career is now assumed to be prototypical rather than atypical (Arthur, 1994). From that perspective, individuals are no longer supposed to develop a specific relationship with their employer. Instead, according to the metaphors introduced by the new careers literature, they should act as 'career capitalists' (Inkson & Arthur, 2001) and develop 'intelligent careers' (Arthur et al., 1995). Careers are viewed as the result of individual decisions, while organisations are no longer described as being in charge of career management. They are just settings that offer specific experiences on which individuals must build to enhance their career capital.

We should note here that while now established, the boundaryless career perspective has been under increased criticism, even within the United States of America (USA), where it originated. Criticism has been directed at the individualistic bias inherent in the perspective, which talks about what individual actors gain but rarely discusses dangers and drawbacks for the individual, group, organisation, or larger community. Its broad relevance has also been questioned, as it applies primarily to professional workers in select industries, and so has its overly optimistic stance. The literature tends to highlight and celebrate those that benefit from boundaryless careers but largely ignores those whose job security diminishes as a result to a shift to boundaryless careers (Cadin et al., 2000; Dany, 2003; Dany et al., 2003; Guest, 2004; Mallon, 1998; Pringle & Mallon, 2003; Zeitz et al., 2009).

Organisational Career Management

Not only individuals, but employers too, are interested in managing individual careers of their employees over time. Even though individuals may feel obliged to take care of their careers by themselves, organisational career management systems (Dany, 2003) heavily influence individual careers, for example by channelling individuals into certain tracks or offering specific development programmes. Hence, both individual and organisational decisions shape careers.

Career management is one of the core elements of HRM and is usually linked to training and development as one of the major tasks of a strategic approach to HRM (see, e.g., Devanna et al., 1984) with both the HRM specialists and line manager collaborating. It comprises issues at the individual level such as personal career development (Agbenyo & Collett, 2014), support during various types of career transitions (e.g. Renn et al., 2014), or career coaching (Reid, 2016); as well as at the organisational level, for example organisational career trajectories, promotion criteria, or the existence of support programmes for specific employee groups such as high potentials or minorities.

Several main goals continue to justify employers' commitment to career management (Greenhaus et al., 2010: 382ff.). The most important rationale involves employee development to increase the human capital. This benefits both individuals and organisations, although the latter face the tension of potentially investing into human capital that will go elsewhere. Transferring employees across jobs or locations enhances their understanding of how their company operates, helps them to build important professional skills, and develops their capability to navigate new situations. From an individual standpoint, such transfers (and the resulting idiosyncratic career paths) are important vis-à-vis both internal and external employability. From an organisational standpoint, they offer greater flexibility that ultimately results in positive economic effects.

Organisational career management is also a tool in the 'war for talent' (Michaels et al., 2001; for a more critical view, see Pfeffer, 2001), in particular through offering opportunities for so-called talent, and more efficient utilisation of talent (Scullion & Collings, 2011; Sparrow et al., 2014), but it also makes organisational exits easier or helps organisations to avoid redundancies altogether. A related objective of career management is succession planning (Rothwell et al., 2005), which has retained its importance even in circumstances that make it difficult for organisations to make any firm promises regarding long-term careers. Besides contributing to achieving fit between companies' needs and their human resources, career management can also be used to influence employee attitudes and behaviour. For example, career management programmes can be used to sustain employee motivation and commitment and decrease turnover by promoting employees to higher-status positions or by assigning them to projects that increase their employability, highlight new interesting aspects of their jobs, or allow them to lead more balanced lives. By matching employees' interests and capabilities with organisational opportunities, career management programmes can help an organisation to achieve a balance between individual career needs and the company's workforce needs.

COMPARATIVE CAREER STUDIES: AN EMERGING DISCOURSE

In the field of organisation and management career studies (Gunz & Mayrhofer, forthcoming), various subfields exist which attract enough interest to establish a continuous discourse. Besides discourses such as mentoring (e.g., Chandler et al., 2011), personality and career success (e.g., Ganzach & Pazy, 2015), and organisational career development (e.g. Sampson et al., 2014), studies on international careers have also emerged as an important stream of research. This is hardly surprising. Careers do not develop in a vacuum, but within a variety of contexts. The concept of career and core career attributes are influenced by the social, economic, cultural, and institutional environment (Byars-Winston & Fouad, 2006; Inkson et al., 2007; Khapova & Korotov, 2007; Mayrhofer et al., 2007). While the importance of context and the value of investigating similarities and differences in careers and career management across national borders was recognised decades ago (e.g. Schein, 1984), research on such issues is still in its infancy. A closer look at international career studies (Tams & Arthur, 2007; Thomas & Inkson, 2007) reveals that the following discourses exist.

Oldest and most numerous are studies dealing with careers across national and cultural boundaries, that is, career paths of employees across postings in different countries or cultural regions across the globe. Here, expatriation is arguably the most developed topic. Various aspects such as adjustment when arriving in the host country (e.g., Haslberger et al., 2014) or repatriation when returning home from a foreign assignment (e.g., Kraimer et al., 2012) are well researched. More recently, a broader view of working abroad (Mayrhofer et al., 2012) has emerged, including areas such as self-initiated expatriation (e.g. Andresen et al., 2013) and migration, be it enforced or chosen (e.g. Al Ariss & Syed, 2011). This stream of research is not only part of international career studies; it also has strong roots in the literatures about international human resource management (Stahl et al., 2012; Harzing & Pinnington, 2015; Brewster et al., 2016) and international business (Cavusgil et al., 2010; Wood & Demirbag, 2012).

A second stream of research focuses on single-country indigenous careers, but either has as its implicit or explicit point of reference a global standard model against which the national situation is benchmarked, or replicates studies from other contexts, hoping for additional insight through an ad hoc comparison. For example, some researchers take the path of indigenous research and explore how careers develop and change in specific cultural and institutional settings (such as Kato & Suzuki, 2006 on careers in Japan). Others take an established framework (typically one that originates in the USA) and apply it to a new environment, discussing similarities and differences found along the way (for example, see the study on careers and changing career patterns in Russia: Khapova & Korotov, 2007).

A third stream is comparative career studies. Here, the aim is to systematically compare various aspects of careers across a variety of different contexts (Briscoe et al., 2012;). In doing so, this research stream uses various frames such as culture (Hofstede, 1980; House et al., 2004) or institutional context (Greenwood et al., 2008; Thornton et al., 2012). Examples for comparative work describing and explaining various career-related aspects of individual and organisational behaviour include career transitions (Chudzikowski et al., 2009), career success (Shen et al., 2015; Mayrhofer et al., 2016b), the design of organisational management development systems (Mabey & Gooderham, 2005; Mabey & Ramirez, 2005), models of the use of social networks in job search (Song & Werbel, 2007), and the prevalence of so-called new careers (Kelly et al., 2003).

Various assumptions and aims underlie the comparative career studies discourse. Arguably the most basic one comprises the identification of context-invariant and context-sensitive aspects, respectively, of various career constructs. Take the example of career success. Despite its central position in career studies, both indigenous and international, it is largely unclear what people mean when they talk about career success. Likewise, career research has a truncated understanding of theorising and operationalising the career success construct, limiting it to but a few dimensions such as income, hierarchical advancement, or career satisfaction. Responding to this are a number of current efforts to identify a more diverse set of core dimensions of this construct (e.g., Dries et al., 2008; Gunz & Mayrhofer, 2011; Dries, 2011; Shockley et al., 2010; Mayrhofer et al., 2016b). Putting these efforts into an explicitly comparative perspective allows one to pursue the question of the context sensitivity of the various dimensions. For example: do different national levels of economic wealth, education, or gender equality influence the relative importance of the dimensions? Are there some dimensions of career success which are quite stable regardless of contextual forces, while others react more to contextual forces? And if yes, which are these forces? Looking at careers from a comparative angle inevitably also leads to the question how the identified commonalities and differences develop over time, that is, whether the relative position of the units of analysis – usually, countries – remain stable or change.

Conceptually underlying these efforts is the debate about universalist versus contextual approaches which has quite some tradition in the comparative HRM debate (Delery & Doty, 1996; Brewster & Mayrhofer, 2015; see also Chapter 1 in this volume). The former assumes that ultimately there is a valid model of doing things, at both the individual and the organisational level, that can serve as a benchmark. For example, so-called best practices in terms of coaching or setting up succession systems exist, which lead to an optimal outcome at the individual and/or organisational level. The contextual approach emphasises that the various contextual elements which shape a situation make a 'one-size-fits-all' approach meaningless. It argues for a context-sensitive analysis, and emphasises the importance of subjective attribution of meaning and the development of practical measures which take into account the various relevant attributes of the respective situation. For example, while merit-based promotion systems might be in an abstract sense 'best' for providing incentives for individual performance, the introduction of such systems also has to take into account local idiosyncrasies such as the obligations vis-à-vis one's clan based on established local cultural norms (Saher & Mayrhofer, 2014).

In addition to identifying commonalities and differences against the backdrop of various theoretical frames, this perspective also aims at diagnosing developments over time. This raises the issue of convergence, divergence, or stasis (Mayrhofer et al., 2004; Mayrhofer, et al., 2011; see also Chapter 1 in this book). Stasis refers to an unchanged situation over time. Divergence indicates that the units of analysis move further apart over time; for example, organisations in various countries differ to a greater extent in their use of mentoring as a career development intervention; or differences in the importance of hierarchical advancement as a primary career goal for individuals increase between countries. Convergence comes in two forms. Final convergence has a common endpoint where a common model or view emerges over time, that is used across different countries; for example, a similar view of the relative importance of various aspects of career success across different countries and cultures. Directional convergence reflects changes in the same direction while leaving the relative position to each other unchanged; for example, when in all countries analysed work–life balance as an individual career goal becomes more important, while the relative differences in actual levels of work–life balance between countries remain the same. To that end, Tams and Arthur (2007) comment that while there is evidence that globalisation enhances the ability to work across nations, and leads to cultural change and some convergence, it is still premature and simplistic to confirm the inevitable arrival of widespread convergence towards Western capitalism (see also Inkson et al., 2007). These are issues that should be explored by future research, along with questions regarding whether such convergence is desirable, effective, and beneficial to all employees (Tams & Arthur, 2007).

INDIVIDUAL CAREERS: A COMPARATIVE ANGLE

Context matters in terms of how careers are seen by individuals and organisations, how they unfold, and how the institutional environment influences career patterns and mastery (Mayrhofer et al., 2007; Ng et al., 2007). It has long been argued that career studies and theory should embed the cultural context (Schein, 1984; Hartung, 2002; Tams & Arthur, 2007) in order to capture the rich diversity of career patterns and to assess the impact of influencing factors such as varying perceptions, inherent values, and diverse conceptualisations. Researchers have taken up this call and have explored a range of cultural context variables and their effect on career management (Derr & Laurent, 1989; Segalla et al., 2001). More recently, Hall & Yip (2014) have shown how it is possible to identify distinctive career cultures and climates in organisations that put their imprint on employees and their career development. While many other career writers implicitly argue that their findings are applicable across contexts – including that of different organisations, nations, and cultural areas – we advocate that it will be important to understand both the commonalities as well as the differences of careers across the world. We require more nuanced career studies that are able to explore career patterns factoring in a wide array of institutional and cultural differences.

There have been repeated calls to explore careers in different cultures and countries. In the field of international management and expatriation there has been much work to explore how individuals' careers unfold in different countries. For instance, much is known about the motivations of individuals to work abroad (Stahl et al., 2002; Dickmann & Doherty, 2008; Hippler, 2009; Doherty et al., 2011). In addition, the effects on a wide array of issues including their careers, job prospects, and marketability have been explored (Shaffer et al., 2012; Dickmann & Doherty, 2008; Suutari & Mäkelä, 2007; Jokinen, 2010). In addition, repatriation and long-term career and marketability issues have been researched (Lazarova & Cerdin, 2007; Suutari et al., forthcoming; Dickmann et al., 2016). However, these studies are concerned with international assignees (and increasingly with other forms of global working, Baruch et al., 2013) but do not normally cover the comparative perspective of individuals from different home countries working domestically. We still lack information regarding specific career concepts in different countries (Arthur et al., 1989; Boudreau et al., 2001), career patterns of different age and professional groups (Gunz & Peiperl, 2007), and country-specific career success conceptualisations (Heslin, 2005; Gunz & Heslin, 2005).

Values and behaviours at work are impacted upon by national cultural differences (Hofstede, 1996; Triandis, 1994; House et al., 2004; see Chapter 3 in this book) and have a substantial impact on careers (Gunz & Peiperl, 2007). The perspective to compare careers and career success between cultures is relatively neglected (Brown, 2002; Spokane et al., 2003), even though some work explicitly summarises the available evidence and calls for more context-sensitive research (Khapova et al., 2012).

There is a wide range of cultural models and approaches that are available in the literature (Hofstede, 2001; Trompenaars, 1994; Schwartz, 1994). All these have developed several cultural dimensions which are often the base for further research and/or criticism (McSweeney, 2002). One of the most ambitious research projects, Global Leadership and Organizational Behavior Effectiveness (GLOBE), incorporated 170 researchers in 62 countries. GLOBE investigated how leadership is viewed by cultures in all parts of the world, based on a quantitative research design that provides a broad classification of nine cultural dimensions. GLOBE gives some insights into ten culturally distinct regions and explores what leadership approaches are acceptable within these (House et al., 2004; Chhokar et al., 2007).

In order to take up the call for cross-cultural careers research, the 5C project (Cross-Cultural Collaboration on Contemporary Careers; www.5C.careers) was formed in 2004. The first stage of its research was a qualitative exploration into career transitions and career success perceptions in 11 countries spread between Europe, North and Middle America, Asia, and Africa. The results of this stage are broadly outlined in several publications (Shen et al., 2015; Briscoe et al., 2012; Chudzikowski et al., 2009), including the first edition of this *Handbook*. They confirmed that for career transitions and success, context matters; and that the historical and economic development of diverse states had an influence on perceptions of professional identity amongst the different researched populations: business school graduates, nurses, and blue-collar workers. In addition, the research argued that there were some shared trends in perceptions in all 11 countries. Job satisfaction, achievement, and job task characteristics were the key categories that influenced the meaning of career success at the aggregate level (Shen et al., 2015). Moreover, both subjective and objective career success factors were stressed in most countries (but not Japan) as one of the three most important elements (Briscoe et al., 2012). Intriguingly, at a closer look, a range of career success differences emerged that included societal and cultural factors. These findings – as well as the atmosphere, leadership, and general curiosity in the 5C group – were an impetus to broaden and deepen the research in the following stage.

Stage 2 of the 5C project included a quantitative survey across 25 countries, which examined the conceptualisation of career success in each country. Participants were asked to indicate which of seven career success dimensions were most important to them. The seven dimensions, based upon the qualitative research discussed above, were: learning and development; work–life balance; positive impact; positive work relationships; financial security; financial achievement; and entrepreneurship (Mayrhofer et al., 2016a). We now present some preliminary findings from this survey research, based upon almost 16,000 participants.

An examination of the average scores for the importance of learning and development (out of a total of 5) by country (Figure 14.1) shows that, while this dimension of career success is generally important across countries, there are some minor variations. Learning and development was seen as particularly important in Nigeria and Malawi (4.7 in each), compared to Japan (3.5), Argentina (3.7), and Korea (3.9).

Work–life balance was seen as particularly important by respondents in the USA (4.7) and Greece (4.6), compared to Argentina (3.9) and Korea (3.9) (Figure 14.2).

More variation across countries can be seen in relation to positive impact as a dimension of career success (Figure 14.3). This dimension was particularly important for

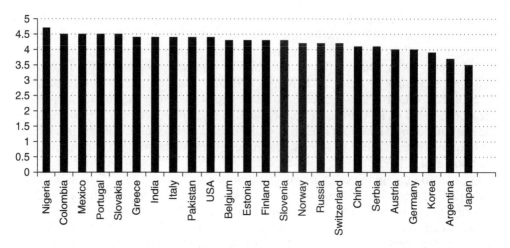

Figure 14.1   Learning and development by country

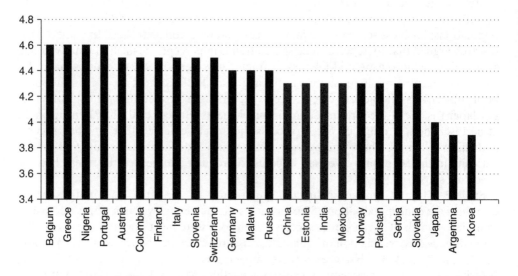

Figure 14.2   Work–life balance by country

respondents from Nigeria (4.7), Malawi (4.6) and Slovakia (4.6). Positive impact was less important in Japan (3.4) and Argentina (3.4).

Positive relationships as a dimension of career success (Figure 14.4) was particularly important to respondents in Nigeria (4.7), Malawi (4.7), Slovakia (4.6), and Slovenia (4.6), compared to Japan (3.6), Argentina (3.7), and Colombia (3.8).

Financial security (Figure 15.5) was an important dimension of career success across most countries but was particularly important in Malawi, Nigeria, Slovakia, Slovenia, and the USA (all 4.8). Financial security was less important in Japan (4.0), Argentina (4.0), and Korea (4.1).

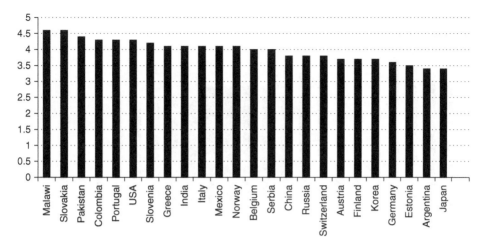

Figure 14.3   Positive impact by country

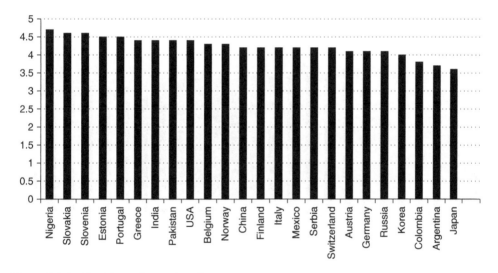

Figure 14.4   Positive relationships by country

Financial achievement was again consistently important across countries, with some slight variations (Figure 14.6). Nigeria showed the highest average level of importance in this dimension of career success (4.7) with Norway (3.1) showing the lowest level of average importance.

The career success dimension of entrepreneurship showed the most apparent variation across countries (Figure 14.7). Entrepreneurship was most important as a dimension of career success among respondents in Nigeria (4.6) and Malawi (4.2) and least important among respondents in Slovakia (1.6) and Norway (1.9).

It is clear from the figures that, while there are similarities between conceptualisations

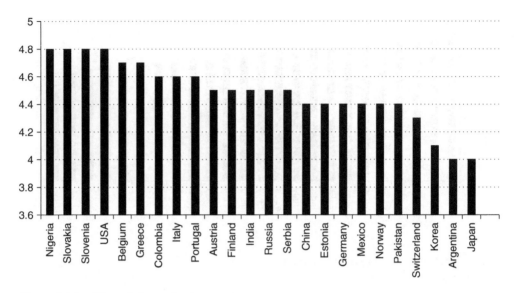

Figure 14.5   Financial security by country

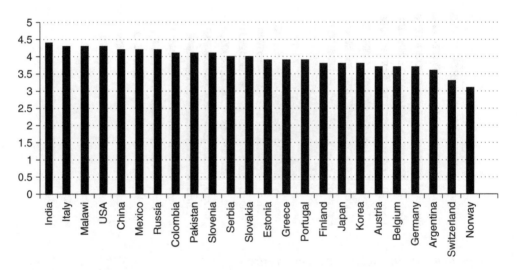

Figure 14.6   Financial achievement by country

of career success, these are not entirely consistent across counties. From this initial analysis, however, it is difficult to distinguish between what might be differences in responding (that is, do countries such as Argentina always respond in a less positive way?) or actual differences in conceptualisations of career success. This will need further analysis in future research on this data.

We also do not know from these simple analyses why differences between countries might exist or, more specifically, which aspects of national context are driving these differences. Some preliminary analysis of the 5C data (Mayrhofer et al., 2016a) suggests a

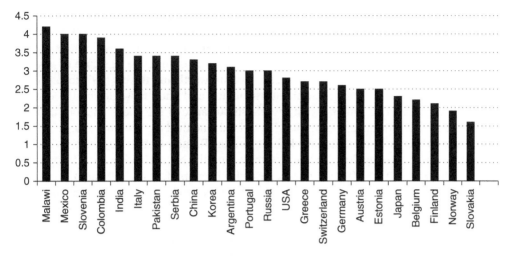

Figure 14.7   Entrepreneurship by country

number of characteristics of national context that might be responsible for these varia-tions. First, differences in conceptualisations of career success might be influenced by national culture. For example, positive impact is less important as an aspect of subjec-tive career success to participants in countries with stronger institutional collectivism (Finland, Norway), while financial achievement is less important to participants in coun-tries with stronger performance orientation (Norway, Switzerland). Second, economic characteristics of a national context might also affect attitudes towards career success. For instance, analyses showed that financial achievement is more important as an aspect of subjective career success in countries with strong income inequality (Nigeria, India, USA). However, income equality did not influence the importance of positive impact as an aspect of career success. At this early stage in the 5C research, much of the cultural influences that could be part of the explanation of the above differences remain to be explored. In addition, other contextual factors – including institutional differences – are likely to play a role (Greenwood et al., 2008; Thornton et al., 2012; Brewster et al., 2016). It is clear that much more research is needed in order to establish the precise relationships and influences between characteristics of national culture, the institutional context, and other contextual factors on careers, but the above results suggest that career concepts, in this case career success, are not necessarily consistent across national contexts.

ORGANISATIONAL CAREER MANAGEMENT: A COMPARATIVE ANGLE

Clusters of HRM

Echoing research on cultural values and clusters of countries with similar values, research in the broader area of HRM also suggests that clustering of countries can be observed, based on how national organisations tend to manage their human resources. Several ways of distinguishing between regional clusters in the context of HRM and industrial relations have been proposed. Thus, Hall and Soskice (2001) and Gooderham et al. (1999) contrast Anglo-Saxon-style free-market capitalism with capitalism varieties where there is greater state intervention. Garten (1993) shares this view and also notes the existence of government-induced market systems such as Japan. Hollingsworth and Boyer (1997) focus on the presence or absence of communitarian infrastructures and find the Anglo cultures distinct from the rest of Europe. Others emphasise the importance of the role of the state and differentiate between countries such as the UK, Ireland, and the Nordic countries in which the state has a limited role in industrial relations, and the Roman-Germanic countries such as France, Spain, Germany, Italy, Belgium, Greece, and the Netherlands where the opposite is true (Due et al., 1991: 90). Arguments have also been made for a 'Northern European' approach to HRM based around those countries where English is widely spoken and trade unions are stronger (Brewster & Larsen, 2000). One analysis of HRM practices found 'three clusters: a Latin cluster [which includes Spain, Italy, France]; a central European cluster . . . and a Nordic cluster' (Filella, 1991: 14). In addition, HRM approaches in various parts of Asia, especially in China, India, and Japan have also received more attention (see, e.g., Budhwar, 2004; the special issue of *Management Revue* (4/2007) on HRM in Asia Pacific; Sparrow & Budhwar, 1996). In other words, while there has been no universally agreed-upon way of clustering countries, there is little disagreement regarding the general idea that clusters of countries with different patterns of HRM activities exist.

Career Management

There are few sources that can be used for a comprehensive and integrated international comparison of core aspects of HRM. Arguably, Cranet (www.cranet.org), an international research network dedicated to analysing HRM developments in public and private sector organisations with more than 100 employees at the national and country-comparative level, in a trend-study since 1989, is a primary source (for an overview see Brewster et al., 2004; Parry et al., 2013). Currently, more than 45 countries are part of the network. Each country is represented by a national university which is responsible for creating a representative sample of the respective company population. For the purposes of this chapter, we examined the 2014–16 Cranet database to provide some illustrative examples of how career management-related HRM practices differ across countries. Building on the idea of country groupings, we examine country clusters, and individual countries within the clusters. We differentiate between the following groups: Anglo (including Australia, United Kingdom, United States of America), Baltic (Estonia, Latvia, Lithuania), BRIC (Brazil, Russia), Central and Eastern Europe (Croatia, Hungary, Serbia, Slovakia, Slovenia), Germanic (including Austria, Belgium, Germany, Switzerland), Mediterranean (Cyprus, France, Greece, Spain, Turkey), Nordic (Denmark, Finland, Iceland, Norway, Sweden), and Others (Indonesia, Israel, Philippines, South Africa). We look at various aspects of career management and in particular at the link between performance appraisal and career decisions, career-related action programmes for specific employee groups, and the use of career development tools.

Performance appraisal and career management
Notably, performance appraisal is widely used (74 per cent on average) to inform career decisions on an organisational scale (Figure 14.8). It is least used in South Africa, at 45 per

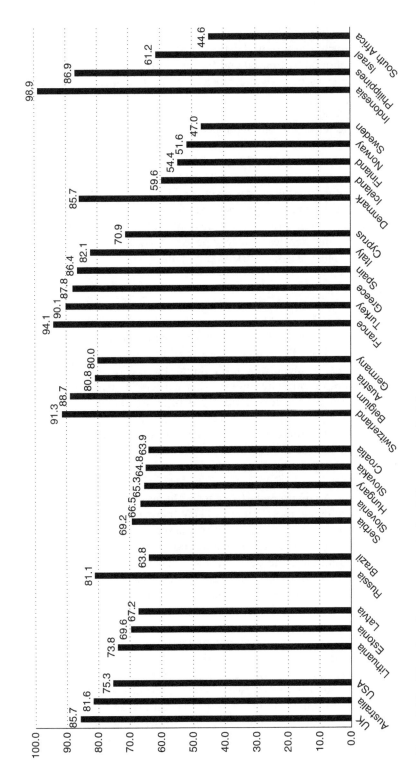

Figure 14.8   Use of performance appraisal to inform career decisions

cent; and nearly universally used (99 per cent) in Indonesia. On the whole, with the exception of Denmark, performance appraisal data are least likely to be used in career decisions in Nordic countries, followed by Central and Eastern European countries; they are more widely used in Germanic Europe, Mediterranean Europe, and Anglo-Saxon countries.

Use of formal career plans

On the other hand, fewer organisations appear to have formal career plans in place (Figure 14.9). When asked to assess on a scale from 0 to 4, with 0 indicating that no formal career plans were used in the organisations, and 4 indicating extensive use of such plans, the average value across countries was only 1.21, suggesting only minimal use. There was no country in which the average value exceeded the midpoint of the scale. Juxtaposed with the widespread use of performance appraisal data for career decisions, this finding suggests that perhaps organisations are somewhat reactive rather than proactive in managing careers. Formal career plans were least likely to be used in the Baltic states, and most likely to be used in the Philippines, Russia, Turkey, and Spain.

Career development tools

Mentoring   Mentoring appears to be more widely used than formal carer plans, although not by a substantial amount (Figure 14.10). Using the same 0 to 4 scale, the average score across counties was still 1.56. There was more variation across the countries, with relatively more consistent use of mentoring in the Baltic states, Anglo-Saxon countries, and Nordic countries, and more variability in the other clusters (highest use was reported in Russia, and lowest in Brazil). A note of caution is in order when interpreting these results. The survey question the graph represents asked managers about the use of formal mentoring programmes only. It is quite possible that mentoring was present even in countries that appear to have low scores here, but it was not reported because it was informal rather than sanctioned and managed by the company.

High-flier programmes   Again using the 0 to 4 scale, the average score was 1.24, indicating a scarce use of this development tool (Figure 14.11). While in the Nordic as well as the Baltic states organisations seem to be quite reluctant to use such programmes, organisations in other parts of Europe, in particular the Germanic and Southern European area, are more open to it. Overall, we find the highest use in Russia, Belgium, and France; with Slovakia, Latvia, and Denmark at the other end of the scale. Arguably, a more egalitarian or economically challenging context might prevent organisations from using high-flier programmes.

International work assignments   In a similar way, international work assignments do not belong to the mainstream personnel development measures used by many companies. On the contrary, the average score (0 = not used, 4 = extensively used) of 0.87 reveals that organisations are pretty cautious in this respect (Figure 14.12). While such programmes seem to be frequent in Southern Europe (with the exception of Cyprus) and, as the overall leader, in Belgium, organisations in other European countries and also the Anglo cluster (Australia, UK, USA) are clearly more reluctant to systematically use international assignments in their career management programmes. Brazil with 0.36 and Sweden with 0.48 are countries at the bottom of the list.

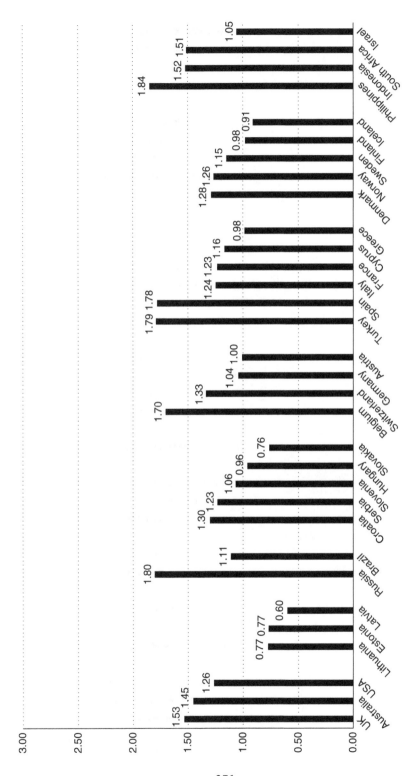

Figure 14.9   Use of formal career plans for career management

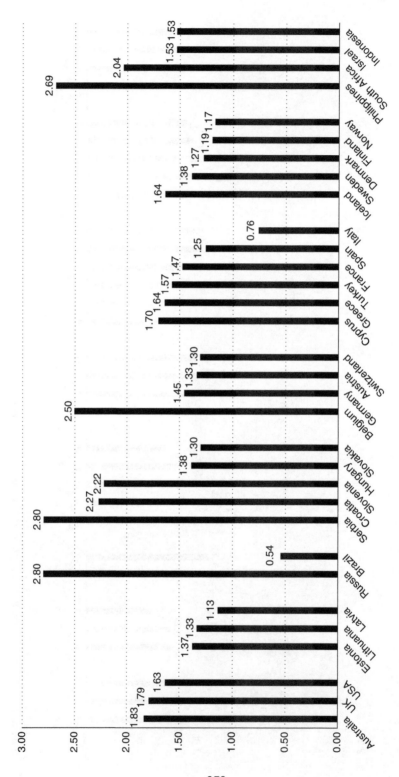

Figure 14.10 Use of mentoring for career management

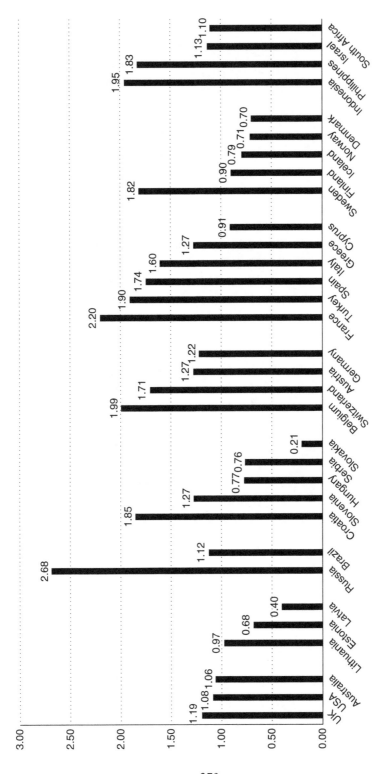

Figure 14.11   Use of high-flier programmes for career management

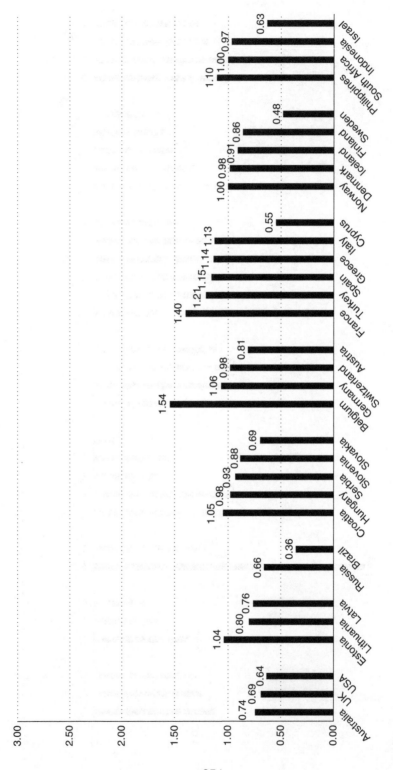

Figure 14.12 Use of international work assignments for career management

Career-related action programmes for specific groups

Women   While France and Indonesia have specific career-related action programmes for women (Figure 14.13), in most countries there is no broad effort in this area (overall average: 0.24). Indonesia, France, and the Philippines are leading, with the Baltic states, Hungary, and Slovenia coming at the bottom of this list. One major explanation for this can be the strong history that these countries have in terms of women employment. During the communist era, women were an integral part of the workforce. To be sure, this is not to say that they had equal opportunities, but taking part in the joint effort to build the future was widely expected.

Younger employees   In terms of frequency of use, career-related action programmes for younger employees constitute the bottom of the table with an average score of 0.22 (Figure 14.14). Again, the Nordic countries and the Baltic states have the lowest values here. Relatively speaking, Indonesia and, to a lesser extent, the UK, Russia, France, and the Philippines are most active in this area.

The descriptive data presented above require much more in-depth analysis in order to better understand the underlying mechanisms at work. Yet, even at this stage of analysis, at least two common threads emerge. First, both between and within the country clusters, there are different solutions to similar problems. Countries considerably vary in their use of the various HR tools related to organisational career management. This points towards cultural and institutional as well as organisational factors as potential causes for this. Second, the size and kind of differences within and between the country clusters depend on the concrete career management tools. An explanation of this requires a closer look at the role of the respective instruments within organisational HRM and their cultural and institutional fit with the national context.

CONCLUDING REMARKS

Despite the success of the US rhetoric and the individual perspective, careers are still strongly marked by contexts. Differences according to cultural and institutional factors still exist in the way companies manage careers and the way nations support economic and individual development with their economic and social policies and practices. Likewise, individuals all over the world may have different expectations toward their careers.

It is our belief that, armed with the kind of new research findings that we summarise here, it is now possible to form a profile of how effectively a nation or an organisation develops and utilitises its human resources. And, based on these improved diagnostic measures, we are better equipped to find ways to improve individual career development and organisational performance.

Nevertheless, we are convinced that more research is needed to better understand these differences, the factors that contribute to them, and the methods for improvement. On the last point we contend, in particular, that promising next steps for research would be to know more about the pros and cons of various ways of managing individual careers and establishing organisational management practices. While the literature does not yet show any conclusive evidence regarding career clusters, we believe that comparative research

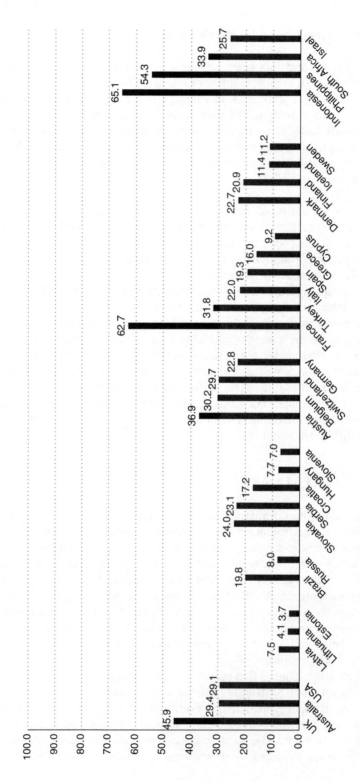

Figure 14.13   Career related action programmes for women

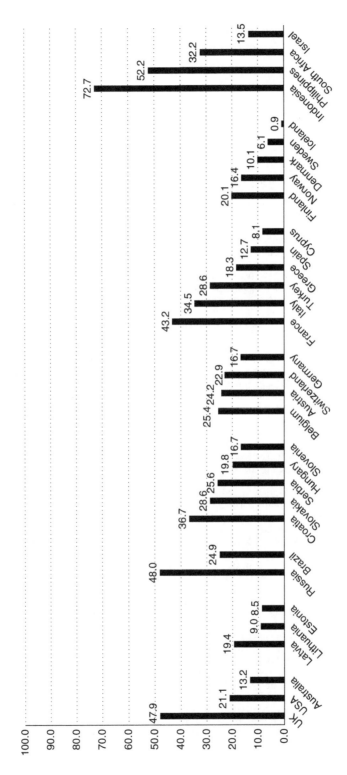

Figure 14.14 Career related action programmes for younger employees

on career would help to draw attention to commonalities and differences which have been overlooked so far, but which can be very useful to push forward our understanding of career.

REFERENCES

Agbenyo, H. & Collett, K. 2014. Career advice and guidance in a world where vocational skills matter. In G. Arulmani, A.J. Bakshi, F.T.L. Leong, and A.G. Watts (eds), *Handbook of Career Development: International Perspectives*: 255–270. New York: Springer.

Al Ariss, A. & Syed, J. 2011. Capital mobilization of skilled migrants: A relational perspective. *British Journal of Management*, 22: 286–304.

Alvarez, J.L. 2000. Theories of managerial action and their impact on the conceptualization of executive careers. In M. Peiperl, M. Arthur, R. Goffee, and T. Morris (eds), *Career Frontiers*: 127–137. Oxford: Oxford University Press.

Andresen, M., Al Ariss, A., & Walther, M. (eds). 2013. *Self-Initiated Expatriation: Individual, Organizational, and National Perspectives*. London, UK and New York, USA: Routledge.

Arthur, M.B. 1994. The boundaryless career: A new perspective for organizational inquiry. *Journal of Organizational Behavior*, 15(4): 295–306.

Arthur, M.B., Claman, P.H., & DeFillippi, R.J. 1995. Intelligent enterprise, intelligent careers. *Academy of Management Executive*, 9(4): 7–22.

Arthur, M.B., Hall, D.T., & Lawrence, B.S. 1989. Generating new directions in career theory: The case for a transdisciplinary approach. In M.B. Arthur, D.T. Hall, and B.S. Lawrence (eds), *Handbook of Career Theory*: 7–25. Cambridge: Cambridge University Press.

Arthur, M.B. & Rousseau, D.B. (eds). 1996. *The Boundaryless Career: A New Employment Principle for a New Organizational Era*. New York, USA and Oxford, UK: Oxford University Press.

Baruch, Y., Dickmann, M., Altman, Y., & Bournois, F. 2013. Exploring international work: types and dimensions of global careers. *International Journal of Human Resource Management*, 24(12): 2369–2393.

Bell, N.E. & Staw, B.M. 1989. People as sculptors versus sculpture: The role of personality and personal control. In M.B. Arthur, D.T. Hall, and B.S. Lawrence (eds), *Handbook of Career Theory*: 232–251. Cambridge: Cambridge University Press.

Boudreau, J.W., Boswell, W.R., & Judge, T.A. 2001. Effects of personality on executive career success in the United States and Europe. *Journal of Vocational Behavior*, 58(1): 53–81.

Brewster, C. & Larsen, H.H. 2000. The Northern European dimension: A distinctive environment for HRM. In C. Brewster and H.H. Larsen (eds), *Human Resource Management in Northern Europe*: 24–38. Oxford: Blackwell.

Brewster, C., Mayrhofer, W., & Morley, M. (eds). 2004. *Human Resource Management in Europe: Evidence of convergence?*. Oxford: Elsevier/Butterworth-Heinemann.

Brewster, C. & Mayrhofer, W. 2015. Comparative human resource management. In A.-W. Harzing and A. Pinnington (eds), *International Human Rescource Management* (4th edn): 45–79. London et al.: SAGE.

Brewster, C., Sparrow, P.S., Vernon, G., & Houldsworth, L. 2016. *International Human Resource Management* (4th edn). Wimbledon: CIPD.

Briscoe, J.P., Hall, D.T., & Mayrhofer, W. (eds). 2012. *Careers Around the World: Individual and Contextual Perspectives*. New York, USA and Abingdon, UK: Routledge.

Brown, D. 2002. The role of work and cultural values in occupational choice, satisfaction, and success: A theoretical statement. *Journal of Counseling and Development*, 80(Winter): 48–56.

Budhwar, P.S. (ed.). 2004. *Managing Human Resources in Asia-Pacific*. London: Routledge.

Byars-Winston, A.M. & Fouad, N.A. 2006. Metacognition and multicultural competence: Extending the culturally appropriate career counseling model. *Career Development Quarterly*, 54: 187–201.

Cadin, L., Bailly-Bender, A.-F., & de Saint Giniez, V. 2000. Exploring boundaryless careers in the French context. In M.A. Peiperl, M.B. Arthur, R. Goffee, and T. Morris (eds), *Career Frontiers: New Conceptions of Working Lives*: 228–255. Oxford: Oxford University Press.

Cavusgil, S.T., Knight, G., & Riesenberger, J. 2010. *International Business: Strategy, Management and the New Realities*. Harlow: Pearson Educational.

Chandler, D.E., Kram, K.E., & Yip, J. 2011. An ecological systems perspective on mentoring at work: A review and future prospects. *Academy of Management Annals*, 5(1): 519–570.

Chhokar, J.S., Brodbeck, F.C., & House, R.J. (eds). 2007. *Culture and Leadership Across the World: The GLOBE Book of In-Depth Studies of 25 Societies*. Mahwah, NJ, USA and London, UK: Lawrence Erlbaum Associates.

Chudzikowski, K., Demel, B., Mayrhofer, W., et al. 2009. Career transitions and their causes: A country-comparative perspective. *Journal of Occupational and Organizational Psychology*, 82: 825–849.

Dany, F. 2003. 'Free actors' and organizations: Critical remarks about the new career literature, based on French insights. *International Journal of Human Resource Management*, 14(5): 821–838.

Dany, F., Mallon, M., & Arthur, M.B. 2003. The odyssey of career and the opportunity for international comparison. *International Journal of Human Resource Management*, 14(5): 705–712.

Delery, J.E. & Doty, D.H. 1996. Modes of theorizing in strategic human resource management: Tests of universalistic, contingency, and configurational performance predictions. *Academy of Management Journal*, 39(4): 802–835.

Derr, C.B. 1986. Five definitions of career success: Implications for relationships. *Review of Applied Psychology*, 35: 415–435.

Derr, C.B. & Laurent, A. 1989. The internal and external career: A theoretical and cross-cultural perspective. In M.B. Arthur, D.T. Hall, and B.S. Lawrence (eds), *Handbook of Career Theory*: 454–476. New York: Cambridge University Press.

Devanna, M.A., Fombrun, C.J., & Tichy, N. 1984. A framework for strategic human resource management. In C.J. Fombrun, N. Tichy, and M.A. Devanna (eds), *Strategic Human Resource Management*: 11–17. New York: Wiley.

Dickmann, M. & Doherty, N. 2008. Exploring the career capital impact of international assignments within distinct organizational contexts. *British Journal of Management*, 19: 145–161.

Dickmann, M., Suutari, V., Brewster, C., et al. 2016. The career competencies of self-initiated and assigned expatriates: assessing the development of career capital over time. *International Journal of Human Resource Management*, https://doi.org/10.1080/09585192.2016.1172657.

Doherty, N., Dickmann, M., & Mills, T. 2011. Exploring the motives of company-backed and self-initiated expatriates. *International Journal of Human Resource Management*, 22(3): 595–611.

Dries, N. 2011. The meaning of career success: Avoiding reification through a closer inspection of historical, cultural, and ideological context. *Career Development International*, 16(4): 364–384.

Dries, N., Pepermans, R., & Calier, O. 2008. Career success: Constructing a multidimensional model. *Journal of Vocational Behavior*, 73(2): 254–267.

Due, J., Madsen, J.S., & Jensen, C.S. 1991. The social dimension: Convergence or diversification of IR in the Single European Market? *Industrial Relations Journal*, 22(2): 85–102.

Filella, J. 1991. Is there a Latin model in the management of human resources?. *Personnel Review*, 20(6): 14–23.

Ganzach, Y. & Pazy, A. 2015. Cognitive versus non-cognitive individual differences and the dynamics of career success. *Applied Psychology – an International Review / Psychologie Appliquee – Revue Internationale*, 64(4): 701–726.

Garten, J.E. 1993. *A Cold Peace: America, Japan and Germany and the Struggle for Supremacy*. New York: Times Books.

Gooderham, P.N., Nordhaug, O., & Ringdal, K. 1999. Institutional and rational determinants of organizational practices: Human resource management in European firms. *Administrative Sciences Quarterly*, 44(3): 507–531.

Greenhaus, J.H., Callanan, G.A., & Godshalk, V.M. 2010. *Career Management* (4th edn). Los Angeles, CA: SAGE.

Greenwood, R., Oliver, C., Sahlin, K., & Suddaby, R. (eds). 2008. *The SAGE Handbook of Organizational Institutionalism*. London: SAGE.

Guest, D.E. 2004. Flexible employment contracts, the psychological contract and employee outcomes: An analysis and review of the evidence. *International Journal of Management Reviews*, 5/6(1): 1–19.

Gunz, H. & Peiperl, M. 2007. Introduction. In H.P. Gunz and M.A. Peiperl (eds), *Handbook of Career Studies*: 1–10. London: SAGE.

Gunz, H. & Mayrhofer, W. 2011. Re-conceptualizing career success: A contextual approach. *Journal for Labour Market Research*, 43(3): 251–260.

Gunz, H. & Mayrhofer, W. forthcoming. *Rethinking Career Studies: Facilitating Conversation Across Boundaries with the Social Chronology Framework*. Cambridge: Cambridge University Press.

Gunz, H.P. & Heslin, P.A. 2005. Reconceptualizing career success. *Journal of Organizational Behavior*, 26(2): 105–111.

Hall, D.T. & Yip, J. 2014. Career cultures and climates in organizations. In B. Schneider and K.M. Barbera (eds), *The Oxford Handbook of Organizational Climate and Culture*: 215–234. Oxford: Oxford University Press.

Hall, P.A. & Soskice, D. 2001. An introduction to the varieties of capitalism. In P.A. Hall and D. Soskice (eds), *Varieties of Capitalism: The Institutional Foundations of Comparative Advantage*: 1–68. Oxford: Oxford University Press.

Hartung, P.J. 2002. Cultural context in career theory and practice: Role salience and values. *Career Development Quarterly*, 51(1): 12–25.

Harzing, A.-W. & Pinnington, A. (eds). 2015. *International Human Resource Management* (4th edn). London: SAGE.

Haslberger, A., Brewster, C., & Hippler, T. 2014. *Managing Performance Abroad: A New Model for Understanding Expatriate Adjustment*. New York, USA and London, UK: Routledge.

Heslin, P.A. 2005. Conceptualizing and evaluating career success. *Journal of Organizational Behavior*, 26(2): 113–136.

Hippler, T. 2009. Why do they go? Empirical evidence of employees' motives for seeking or accepting relocation. *International Journal of Human Resource Management*, 20(6): 1381–1401.

Hofstede, G. 1980. *Culture's Consequences: International Differences in Work-Related Values*. Newbury Park, CA: SAGE Publications.

Hofstede, G. 1996. *Culture's Consequences: International Differences in Work-Related Values*. Newbury Park, CA: SAGE.

Hofstede, G. 2001. *Culture's Consequences: Comparing Values, Behaviors, Insitutions and Organizations Across Nations* (2nd edn). London: SAGE.

Hollingsworth, J.R. & Boyer, R. (eds). 1997. *Contemporary Capitalism*. Cambridge: Cambridge University Press.

House, R.J., Hanges, P.J., Javidan, M., Dorfman, P.W., & Gupta, V. (eds). 2004. *Culture, Leadership, and Organizations: The GLOBE Study of 62 Societies*. Thousand Oaks, CA: SAGE.

Hughes, E.C. 1958. *Men and Their Work*. Glencoe, IL: Free Press.

Inkson, K. & Arthur, M. 2001. How to be a successful career capitalist. *Organizational Dynamics*, 30(1): 48–60.

Inkson, K., Khapova, S.N., & Parker, P. 2007. Careers in cross-cultural perspective. *Career Development International*, 12(1): 5–8.

Jokinen, T. 2010. Development of career capital through international assignments and its transferability to new contexts. *Thunderbird International Business Review*, 52(4): 325–336.

Kato, I. & Suzuki, R. 2006. Career 'mist,' 'hope,' and 'drift': Conceptual framework for understanding career development in Japan. *Career Development International*, 11(3): 265–276.

Kelly, A., Brannick, T., Hulpke, J., et al. 2003. Linking organisational training and development practices with new forms of career structure: A cross-national exploration. *Journal of European Industrial Training*, 27(2/3/4): 160–168.

Khapova, S.N. & Korotov, K. 2007. Dynamics of Western career attributes in the Russian context. *Career Development International*, 12(1): 68–85.

Khapova, S.N., Briscoe, J.P., & Dickmann, M. 2012. Careers in cross-cultural perspective. In J.P. Briscoe, D.T. Hall, and W. Mayrhofer (eds), *Careers Around the World*: 15–38. New York, USA and London, UK: Routledge Taylor & Francis Group.

Kraimer, M.L., Shaffer, M.A., Harrison, D.A., & Ren, H. 2012. No place like home? An identity strain perspective on repatriate turnover. *Academy of Management Journal*, 55: 399–420.

Lazarova, M.B. & Cerdin, J.L. 2007. Revisiting repatriation concerns: Organizational support versus career and contextual influences. *Journal of International Business Studies*, 38(3): 404–429.

Mabey, C. & Gooderham, P. 2005. The impact of management development on the organizational performance of European firms. *European Management Review*, 2(2): 131–142.

Mabey, C. & Ramirez, M. 2005. Does management development improve organizational productivity? A six-country analysis of European firms. *International Journal of Human Resource Management*, 16(7): 1067–1082.

Mallon, M. 1998. The portfolio career: Pushed in or pulled to it?. *Personnel Review*, 27(5): 361–377.

Mayrhofer, W., Apospori, E., Gubler, M., et al. 2016a. Views on career success across the globe: First steps towards a 'World Map Of Career Success'. Presented at the Annual Meeting of the Academy of Management 2016, Anaheim, CA, 5–9 August.

Mayrhofer, W., Brewster, C., Morley, M., & Ledolter, J. 2011. Hearing a different drummer? Convergence of human resource management in Europe – a longitudinal analysis. *Human Resource Management Review*, 21(1): 50–67.

Mayrhofer, W., Briscoe, J.P., Hall, D.T., et al. 2016b. Career success across the globe – insights from the 5C project. *Organizational Dynamics*, 45(2): 197–205.

Mayrhofer, W., Meyer, M., & Steyrer, J. 2007. Contextual issues in the study of careers. In H.P. Gunz and M.A. Peiperl (eds), *Handbook of Career Studies*: 215–240. Thousand Oaks, CA: SAGE.

Mayrhofer, W., Morley, M., & Brewster, C. 2004. Convergence, stasis, or divergence?. In C. Brewster, W. Mayrhofer, and M. Morley (eds), *Human Resource Management in Europe: Evidence of Convergence?*: 417–436. London: Elsevier/Butterworth-Heinemann.

Mayrhofer, W., Reichel, A., & Sparrow, P. 2012. Alternative forms of international working. In G.K. Stahl, I. Björkman, and S. Morris (eds), *Handbook of Research in International Human Resource Management* (2nd edn): 300–327. Cheltenham, UK and Northampton, MA, USA: Edward Elgar Publishing.

McSweeney, B. 2002. Hofstede's model of national cultural differences and their consequences: A triumph of faith – a failure of analysis. *Human Relations*, 55(1): 89–118.

Michaels, E., Handfield-Jones, H., & Axelrod, B. 2001. *The War for Talent*. Boston, MA: Harvard Business School Press.

Ng, T.W.H., Sorensen, K.L., Eby, L.T., & Feldman, D.C. 2007. Determinants of job mobility: A theoretical integration and extension. *Journal of Occupational and Organizational Psychology*, 80(3): 363–386.

Parry, E., Stavrou, E., & Lazarova, M.B. (eds). 2013. *Global Trends in Human Resource Management*. Houndsmills, UK and New York, USA: Palgrave Macmillan.

Pfeffer, J. 2001. Fighting the war for talent is hazardous to your organization's health. *Organizational Dynamics*, 29(4): 248–259.

Pringle, J.K. & Mallon, M. 2003. Challenges for the boundaryless career odyssey. *International Journal of Human Resource Management*, 14(5): 839–853.

Reid, H. 2016. *Introduction to Career Counselling and Coaching*. London: SAGE.

Renn, R.W., Steinbauer, R., Taylor, R., & Detwiler, D. 2014. School-to-work transition: Mentor career support and student career planning, job search intentions, and self-defeating job search behavior. *Journal of Vocational Behavior*, 85(3): 422–432.

Rothwell, W.J., Jackson, R.D., Knight, S.C., & Lindholm, J.E. 2005. *Career Planning and Succession Management: Developing Your Organization's Talent – for Today and Tomorrow*. Westport, CT: Praeger.

Rousseau, D.B. & Schalk, R. 2000. *Psychological Contracts in Employment: Cross-National Perspectives*. Thousand Oaks, CA: SAGE.

Saher, N. & Mayrhofer, W. 2014. The role of Vartan Bhanji in implementing HRM practices in Pakistan. *International Journal of Human Resource Management*, 25(13): 1881–1903.

Sampson, J.P., Hou, P.-C., Kronholz, J.F., et al. 2014. A content analysis of career development theory, research, and practice – 2013. *Career Development Quarterly*, 62(4): 290–326.

Schein, E.H. 1971. The individual, the organization, and the career: A conceptual scheme. *Journal of Applied Behavioral Science*, 7: 401–426.

Schein, E.H. 1984. Culture as an environmental context for careers. *Journal of Occupational Behavior*, 5(1): 71–81.

Schein, E. 1990. *Career Anchors: Discovering Your Real Values*. San Diego, CA: Pfeiffer & Company.

Schwartz, S.H. 1994. Beyond individualism/collectivism: New dimensions of values. In U. Kim, H.C. Triandis, C. Kagitçibasi, et al. (eds), *Individualism and Collectivism: Theory Application and Methods*: 85–119. Newbury Park, CA: SAGE.

Scullion, H. & Collings, D. (eds). 2011. *Global Talent Management*. London: Routledge.

Segalla, M., Sauquet, A., & Turatic, C. 2001. Symbolic vs functional recruitment: Cultural influences on employee recruitment policy. *European Management Journal*, 19(1): 32–43.

Shaffer, M.A., Kraimer, M.L., Chen, Y.-P., & Bolino, M.C. 2012. Choices, challenges, and career consequences of global work experiences: A review and future agenda. *Journal of Management*, 38(4): 1282–1327.

Shen, Y., Demel, B., Unite, J., et al. 2015. Career success across eleven countries: Implications for international human resource management. *International Journal of Human Resource Management*, 26(13): 1753–1778.

Shockley, K.M., Rodopman, O.B., Poteat, L.F., et al. 2010. Subjective career success: A measurement approach. Paper presented at the 25th SIOP Annual Conference, Atlanta, GA.

Song, L.J. & Werbel, J.D. 2007. Guanxi as impetus? Career exploration in China and the United States. *Career Development International*, 12(1): 51–67.

Sparrow, P.R. & Budhwar, P.S. 1996. HRM in the new economic environment: An empirical study of India. *Management Research News*, 19(4/5): 30–35.

Sparrow, P., Scullion, H., & Tarique, I. (eds). 2014. *Strategic Talent Management: Contemporary Issues in International Context*. Cambridge: Cambridge University Press.

Spokane, A.R., Fouad, N.A., & Swanson, J.L. 2003. Culture-centered career intervention. *Journal of Vocational Behavior*, 62(3): 453–458.

Stahl, G., Björkman, I., & Morris, S. (eds). 2012. *Handbook of Research in International Human Resource Management* (2nd edn). Cheltenham, UK and Northampton, MA, USA: Edward Elgar Publishing.

Stahl, G.K., Miller, E.L., & Tung, R.L. 2002. Toward the boundaryless career: A closer look at the expatriate career concept and the perceived implications of an international assignment. *Journal of World Business*, 37(3): 216–227.

Suutari, V., Brewster, C., Mäkelä, L., et al. Forthcoming. The effect of international work experience on the career success of expatriates: A comparison of assigned and self-initiated expatriates. *Human Resource Management*, doi 10.1002/hrm.21827.

Suutari, V. & Mäkelä, K. 2007. The career capital of managers with global careers. *Journal of Managerial Psychology*, 22(7): 628.

Tams, S. & Arthur, M. 2007. Studying careers across cultures: Distinguishing international, cross-cultural and globalization perspectives. *Career Development International*, 12(1): 86–98.

Thomas, D.C. & Inkson, K. 2007. Careers across cultures. In H.P. Gunz and M.A. Peiperl (eds), *Handbook of Career Studies*: 451–471. Thousand Oaks, CA: SAGE.

Thornton, P.H., Ocasio, W., & Lounsbury, M. 2012. *The Institutional Logics Perspective: A New Approach to Culture, Structure and Process*. Oxford: Oxford University Press.

Triandis, H.C. 1994. Cross-cultural industrial and organizational psychology. In H.C. Triandis, M.D. Dunnette, and L.M. Hough (eds), *Handbook of Industrial and Organizational Psychology* (2nd edn), Vol. 4: 103–172. Palo Alto, CA: Consulting Psychologists Press.

Trompenaars, F. 1994. *Riding the Waves of Culture: Understanding Diversity in Global Business*. Chicago, IL: Irwin.

Wilensky, H.L. 1961. Orderly careers and social participation: The impact of work history on social integration in the middle mass. *American Sociological Review*, 26: 521–539.

Wood, G. & Demirbag, M. (eds). 2012. *Handbook of Institutional Approaches to International Business*. Cheltenham, UK and Northampton, MA, USA: Edward Elgar Publishing.

Zeitz, G., Blau, G., & Fertig, J. 2009. Boundaryless careers and institutional resources. *International Journal of Human Resource Management*, 20(2): 372–398.

15. Financial participation: the nature and causes of national variation

Paul E. M. Ligthart, Andrew Pendleton, and Erik Poutsma

INTRODUCTION

In recent decades many countries have witnessed an increase in the use of employee share ownership plans and profit sharing (financial participation). By the end of the first decade of the twenty-first century, employee financial participation had come to be a typical feature of human resource management (HRM) and employment practices in large firms in some countries. In the United Kingdom (UK), for instance, nearly all firms in the FTSE 100 (the 100 largest listed firms) had at least one all-employee share ownership plan. Nevertheless, pronounced differences remain between countries in the extent and significance of financial participation. In some countries, there is extensive statutory and fiscal support for financial participation; in others there is little or none. It has become clear from several surveys and comparisons over the years (Uvalic, 1991; Vaughan-Whitehead, 1995; Poutsma, 2001; Lowitzsch, 2006) that the availability of fiscal benefits to companies and employees is an extremely important influence on the use of financial participation schemes. Efforts to promote financial participation have therefore typically called on governments to introduce or improve legislation and fiscal provisions. But a deeper question is why legislation has been more prevalent in some countries than others.

This question has not been fully addressed in the literature on financial participation, though many accounts touch on a broad set of reasons for national differences. Poole (1989) proposed that 'favourable conjunctures' of economic and political circumstances could explain the popularity or growth of financial participation in given countries. For instance, the widespread use of financial participation in the UK can be attributed to the shift of economic power from workers to firms, and the political emphasis on undermining trade unionism and promoting employer–employee cooperation in the early 1980s (when some of the current financial participation schemes were introduced by government). More recently, the concepts of 'national business systems' and 'varieties of capitalism' provide a more comprehensive and theoretically grounded way of explaining variations in the use of financial participation between countries. However, the financial participation literature has only just begun to draw on these ideas (Croucher et al., 2010).

In this chapter, we outline the main forms of financial participation and present some recent survey evidence on the incidence of financial participation in Europe and further afield. We then present a set of country profiles of financial participation, before reflecting on reasons for differences between countries in the character and incidence of financial participation.

FINANCIAL PARTICIPATION: DIVERSITY IN FORMS AND MEANING

Financial participation or 'economic democracy' is the participation of employees in enterprise profits and outcomes. In the European Union (EU), financial participation is often referred to as PEPPER – promotion of employee participation in profits and enterprise results – and a number of major inquiries have been referred to as PEPPER reports (Uvalic, 1991; Poutsma, 2001; Lowitzsch, 2006). It is often considered alongside employee participation in enterprise decision-making, usually referred to as direct participation (where individual employees participate) and indirect participation (where representatives participate on the employees' behalf). These other forms are also sometimes referred to as 'industrial democracy'.

There is a wide diversity in the characteristics of financial participation schemes around the world but policy-makers and scholars usually identify two main forms: profit-sharing and employee share ownership (Poutsma, 2001). However, the picture is complicated by the presence of hybrid arrangements: particular financial participation plans may have elements of both profit-sharing and share ownership. Each of these two main forms has a number of subtypes, which once again may be combined with others. To complicate matters further, either type of financial participation may also be combined with employee savings schemes or pension arrangements. As pension arrangements become more diverse in many countries, the relationship with financial participation has become more complex.

Profit-sharing provides a variable income component, in addition to a base or fixed wage, linked to profits or some other measure of enterprise results. Contrary to traditional bonuses linked to individual performance (such as piece rates), profit-sharing is a collective scheme applied to all or to a large group of employees. Some definitions of profit-sharing emphasise that it should be based on a formula that is used from year to year, to distinguish it from one-off or irregular bonuses awarded when the company is doing well. In practice, profit-sharing can take various forms. At the enterprise level, it can provide employees with immediate or deferred benefits; it can be paid in cash, enterprise shares, or other securities; or it can be allocated to specific funds invested for the benefit of employees. At higher levels, profit-sharing takes the form of economy-wide, sectoral or regional wage-earners' funds.

The simplest form of profit sharing is cash-based profit-sharing (CPS); in this instance, employees receive cash payments based on profits more or less at the time that the profits are determined. This form of profit sharing typically does not attract any fiscal concessions because it can be difficult to differentiate the profit shares from base wages, thereby raising tax compliance issues.

Deferred profit-sharing (DPS) is a form of deferred compensation under which the allocated profit share is held by the employer for a while, most commonly in trust, and is not immediately available to the employee. A typical scheme would release the payment to employees after about three years. A DPS scheme might allocate a percentage of profits to enterprise funds, which are then invested (either in the company, other companies, or other investment vehicles) in the name of the employee. Alternatively, the amount can be allocated to the employee's account, with a certain minimum retention period before the amount is made available. Generally, in most countries with any statutory policy on financial participation, a DPS plan must be approved by tax authorities, particularly where tax concessions to employer or employee are involved. In fact, most countries regulate plan features, such as eligibility, contribution rates, vesting, investments, and distribution.

Share-based profit-sharing consists of granting employees shares in the company based on profits or some other measure of performance. These shares are usually frozen in a fund for a certain period before employees are allowed to sell them. When shares are subject to a minimum retention period, the term 'deferred share-based profit-sharing' can be used.

There is often a close relationship between profit-sharing and asset accumulation or savings plans. The employee's profit shares may be paid into an enterprise-based savings plan for the employee. These contributions may be matched by further employer contributions. In some countries, governments give bonuses on employee contributions. There may be further tax benefits on the interest accruing from these savings. Whilst the link between profit-sharing and these savings plans has often taken a medium-term character, changes in pensions regimes have recently encouraged more long-term linkages between profit-sharing and employee savings. With the decline in state-provided and employer-provided pensions in many countries, there has been increasing attention paid to personal pensions. In some instances, profit shares can be used for contributions to pension plans.

A variant of profit-sharing is gain-sharing. Here employees share in the gains obtained from efficiency programmes and reductions in costs. These plans are seen as especially suitable for non-profit organisations, such as many of those located in the public sector. They rarely attract tax benefits because it can be difficult to demonstrate for tax compliance purposes a separation between the base wage and the gain-sharing payment.

Employee share ownership provides for employee participation in enterprise results in an indirect way, either by receiving dividends or by the appreciation of employee-owned capital, or a combination of both. Where appreciation in the market value of shares is the primary benefit, financial participation is indirectly linked to company profits.

There are also several types of employee share ownership plan. The first is the award of free shares to employees. Here there is an obvious overlap with profit-sharing schemes insofar as the distribution of shares might be financed out of profits. Alternatively, share ownership plans may provide for employees to purchase shares in the company, possibly on advantageous terms (for example, at a discount on market price). In some plans employers may match the purchases made by employees. Once again there may be a link with pensions in that the share purchases may be part of larger and wider portfolios of investments made by the employee in conjunction with their employer, as in 401(k) retirement savings plans in the United States of America (USA). Another form of share acquisition is the stock option plan. Employees may be granted the right to acquire shares at some point in the future, typically between three and ten years ahead. Although this does not necessarily lead to ownership, because the employee may simultaneously exercise the option and sell the shares, in most all-employee plans of this sort some employees will exercise the option and hold the shares. There is another potential link with savings plans in that there may be arrangements for employees to save from their salary so as to accumulate the capital necessary to exercise the option.

There is a wide diversity of taxation arrangement for employee share ownership plans depending on the kind of gains that employees make from them. Where shares are distributed freely or at a discount, employees gain an employment benefit on the value of the shares (or the discount) and hence would normally expect to pay income tax on this. Tax-advantageous schemes may waive this income tax liability (and associated social insurance charges). The growth in value of shares may be taxed at capital gains tax rates rather than income tax rates, and these are often more advantageous to the employee because of either lower marginal rates or additional tax exempt allowances. There is wide diversity between countries in the point at which tax becomes liable in employee share plans, especially those based on granting of options. Some tax at grant, some at exercise, some at sale of the shares, and some on a combination of these.

Employee share ownership can be both individual and collective. In some cases shares are held collectively for employees in a trust or foundation, and are not distributed to individual employees. In this instance, the dividends on the shares received by the trust may be distributed to employees as a profit-share. Alternatively, shares may initially be held collectively but then distributed to individual employees over time. This is typically what occurs in employee share ownership plans (ESOPs). In this form of share ownership, shares are initially passed to an employee benefits trust, financed either by loans, profits, or a gift from the company owner, before being distributed to employees. ESOPs have acquired a specific meaning in the USA, where they have grown tremendously over the last 30 years, partly as a result of favourable tax considerations for companies that establish them. From the point of view of the employee participant, there may be little difference between an ESOP and a deferred share-based profit-sharing plan, since employees receive direct ownership of shares some time after the initial allocation of shares to a collective share-owning vehicle such as a trust.

By and large, employee share ownership plans should be differentiated from workers' co-operatives and worker-managed firms. Co-operatives are usually required to abide by a set of principles including 100 per cent worker ownership and equal distribution of ownership amongst employee-owners, though it is not necessarily the case that all those employed by co-operatives are owners. The most well-known workers' co-operatives are those grouped in the Mondragon region of northern Spain. For a variety of reasons, co-operatives are often small in size and are often concentrated in certain areas of economic activity, such as those that are labour-intensive (Bonin et al., 1993). Firms with share ownership plans are often keen to differentiate themselves from co-operatives: they emphasise their 'conventional' management structures compared with what they see as worker 'interference' in management in co-operatives. This criticism of co-operatives is often unfair but it is undoubtedly the case that the small size of many co-operatives does facilitate more direct worker involvement in management. There has been a great deal of discussion about the long-term viability of worker's co-operatives in the literature (Estrin & Jones, 1992). There appears to have been a decline recently in the number of co-operatives in some economies (the USA and the UK, for instance) but they are more entrenched in some European economies such as France and Italy. It may be that co-operatives and other forms of employee ownership tend to substitute for each other.

THE INCIDENCE OF FINANCIAL PARTICIPATION AROUND THE WORLD

There are pronounced differences in the incidence and character of financial participation between countries. Unfortunately, it is difficult to make systematic comparisons because the information available on financial participation differs between countries. Generally speaking, the more prevalent and prominent financial participation is in a country, the greater the level of information about it. Relevant statistical information is not collected in many countries with low levels of financial participation because the schemes in use do not have a clear legal identity.

There are therefore not many comparative data sources that have information on the incidence and development of financial participation. There are almost no data available on African and Latin America countries, and limited data are available from Asia. The only comprehensive sources of comparative data are the Cranet HRM Surveys with organisation-level data and the European Working Conditions Surveys with employee-level data. The Cranet survey is carried out on a global scale, involving a network of more than 40 top business schools and universities, and collecting factual, representative, and comparative information. Data are collected by a postal survey of senior HRM directors from organisations with more than 100 employees in all economic sectors. The survey is conducted periodically, thereby providing longitudinal information on human resource management policies and practices.

Figure 15.1 provides an overview of the use of employee share ownership in most EU countries based on the Cranet network data of 2009. These are data of private sector organisations with more than 200 employees. Pendleton et al. (2003) used an earlier dataset of Cranet that showed that the use of schemes tends to be higher for management and professional staff, and lower for clerical staff and manual workers. However, it is important to bear in mind that those outcomes do not necessarily mean that schemes are more common for management staff than manual or clerical staff in a given workplace. They refer to the proportion of workplaces with a scheme for the particular occupational group, so the distribution of figures between occupations in a country is obviously affected by the occupational composition of workplaces. A series of tables below compare the incidence of narrow-based plans, open only to management and selected groups, and broad-based plans, where all occupational groups are eligible to participate. An important proviso is that 'broad-based' does not necessarily mean a high participation rate as eligible employees do not necessarily participate, especially when they have to contribute to schemes. We know from other sources that participation rates in share schemes are typically lower than in profit-sharing schemes.

Figure 15.1 presents the incidence of narrow-based and broad-based share ownership schemes. In general, the proportion of companies with schemes is low: on average 20 per cent for broad-based schemes and 9 per cent for narrow-based schemes. Broad-based share ownership plans are most common in Japan and Taiwan, Ireland, the UK, Slovakia, Hungary, and Australia. Mediterranean countries, such as Cyprus, the Turkish Cypriot community, Greece, and Italy, and some other Eastern European countries (Russia, Lithuania, and Estonia) and Nordic countries, such as Iceland, Sweden, and Finland, tend to have the lowest incidence. The incidence rates in the Eastern European cluster is diverse. Although some new member states of the European Union initially promoted

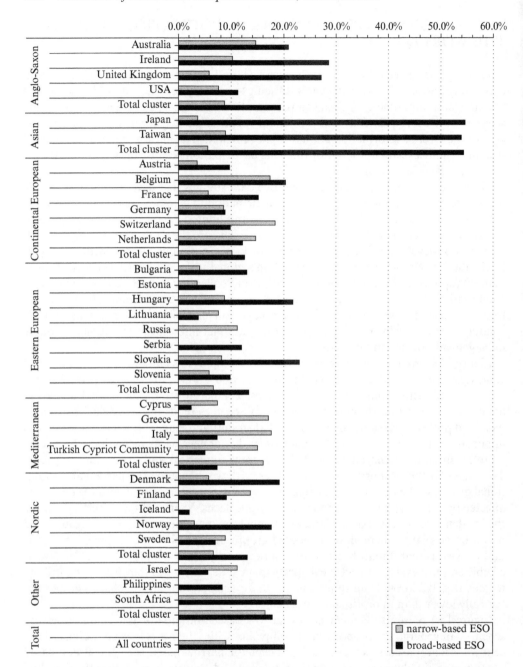

Source: Own calculations, based on Cranet data.

Figure 15.1   Incidence rate of narrow-based and broad-based employee share ownership (ESO) per country and geographical cluster (companies with >200 employees, year: 2009, total N = 3315)

employee share ownership as part of the privatisation process at transition, employee share ownership has declined in most of these countries subsequently (Hashi et al., 2006). The table also shows that the differences between countries are more pronounced for broad-based than for narrow-based schemes. This is similar to the results of the previous Cranet survey in 1999 (see Pendleton et al., 2001; Pendleton et al., 2003) where it was found that narrow-based schemes are less determined by country and institutional differences than broad-based schemes.

Incidence rates for profit-sharing are generally higher than for share schemes: on average, 26.5 per cent for broad-based and almost 10 per cent for narrow-based schemes (see Figure 15.2). As can be seen, France and Finland have more broad-based profit-sharing than any other country. This is because profit-sharing is compulsory for larger organisations in France, and Finland has a tradition of 'Personnel Funds'. Other countries with relatively high incidence of broad-based profit-sharing are Taiwan, Switzerland, Germany, the Netherlands, the USA, and Austria. Some countries where broad-based share ownership is relatively widespread have relatively little profit-sharing: the UK and Denmark are cases in point. Lower incidences are found in the Eastern European and Mediterranean cluster. Again, narrow-based profit-sharing is more evenly distributed among countries, suggesting that certain arrangements in specific countries may influence the existence of broad-based schemes.

Figure 15.3 presents the incidence rate for stock option plans. Here again, on average only a minority of companies offer these plans: 9.7 per cent broad-based and 12.5 per cent narrow-based plans. The striking difference compared to other types of share scheme and profit-sharing is that the incidence rate of narrow-based schemes is higher than broad-based schemes in most countries (with exceptions for Taiwan, the USA, the UK, Greece, Serbia, Bulgaria, and Japan). Stock options have been a typical component of remuneration policy for management, but less so for other employees. Again, we note large differences in incidence rates between countries, suggesting diversity in arrangements and country-specific determinants of the existence of schemes.

The Cranet data provide organisation-level data. One of the few sources for employee-level data is the European Working Conditions Survey (Welz & Fernández-Macías, 2007). This is a face-to-face employee-level survey conducted periodically in all EU and other European countries by the European Foundation for the Improvement of Living and Working Conditions. In most countries the survey aims to sample 1000 employees and self-employed; response rates range from around 30 to 70 per cent. The survey is primarily concerned with working and employment conditions rather than pay, so is not an ideal means for examining financial participation. Nevertheless, the survey contains useful questions on income received from profit-sharing and share ownership, and provides a welcome employee-level source of data on the incidence of financial participation.

The Working Conditions Survey gives a rather different picture to that provided by Cranet, as pointed out by Welz and Fernández-Macías (2008). They found that the use of financial participation is very low in most countries, and much lower than regularly estimated using company-based surveys: only around 12 per cent of European employees receive income from some form of profit-sharing scheme, and only 2.3 per cent from shares in the companies they work for. In only six countries (Slovakia, Slovenia, Sweden, the Netherlands, Finland, and France) does profit-sharing affect more than one-fifth of employees; and in only four (Ireland, France, Luxembourg, and Belgium) do more than

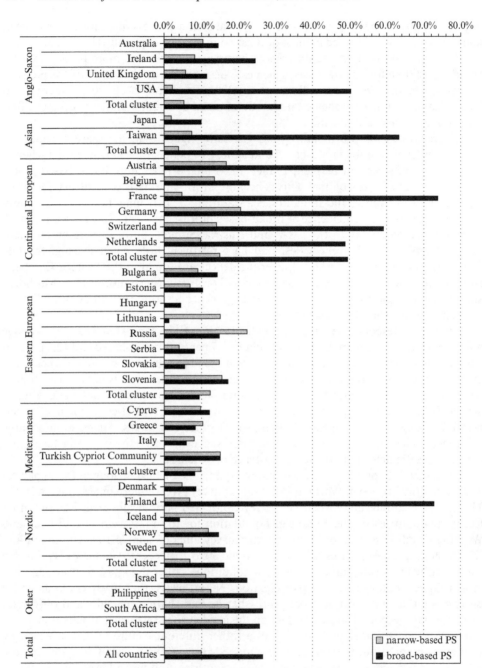

Source: Own calculations, based on Cranet data.

Figure 15.2   Incidence rate of narrow-based and broad-based profit-sharing schemes (PS) per country and geographical cluster (companies with >200 employees, year: 2009, total N = 3315)

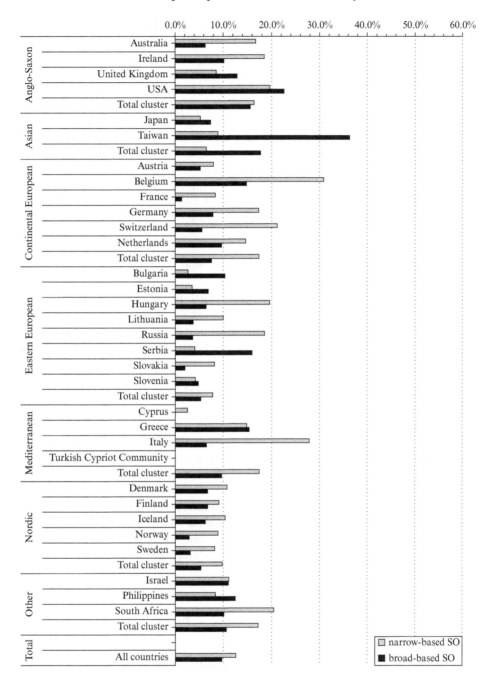

Source: Own calculations, based on Cranet data.

Figure 15.3   Incidence rate of narrow-based and broad-based stock options (SO) per country and geographical cluster (companies with >200 employees, year: 2009, total N = 3315)

5 per cent receive income from shares in their companies. Welz and Fernández-Macías (2007: 17) compared data from the surveys in 2000/2001 and 2005 and concluded that in almost all cases there was an increase in the proportion of employees receiving profits and shares as part of their remuneration. Although the levels are low, in the previous five years they have been consistently increasing in all the 15 EU member states that were in both surveys, except for the UK. They have not been increasing in most new member states.

Welz and Fernández-Macías's (2007) analysis also reveals that financial participation is very unevenly distributed among different types of companies, jobs, and individuals. Employees in managerial positions are more than four times more likely to participate in these schemes than manual workers, even after controlling for variables such as sector, establishment size, or education. Financial participation is also distributed unevenly between men and women, and between permanent and temporary workers. They conclude that the low incidence of financial participation at the level of the individual employee, and the high unevenness of its distribution, puts a question mark against it from a policy perspective. The findings suggest that concerns regarding the distributional effects of financial participation schemes (that is, that they can reinforce pre-existing inequalities in pay and earnings) are well founded.

One limitation of the Working Conditions Survey, however, is that its reference to incomes received from shares is likely to understate employee participation in share ownership plans. As the discussion of share ownership plans earlier indicated, employees may participate in share plans for some time before they receive any direct benefits from them.

FINANCIAL PARTICIPATION IN ACTION: SELECTED COUNTRIES

The previous section has provided a broad indication of the prevalence of financial participation around the world. However, to fully understand the operation of financial participation it is necessary to consider it within its national institutional context. To this end we provide short sketches of the nature of financial participation in selected countries in Europe and beyond. As will become clear, profit-sharing, share ownership, and employee savings plans can be closely intertwined. This reflects differences between countries in the history of financial participation. These country profiles also make clear that there are large differences in the national embeddedness of the phenomenon.

France

Profit-sharing is deeply entrenched in France, and is interconnected with employee savings plans and, increasingly, employee share ownership. The profit-share system was introduced by General de Gaulle in the 1960s with the intention of bridging the gap between capital and labour and promoting national unity. The main form of financial participation over the years has been profit-sharing, with two main schemes in operation.

First, deferred profit-sharing (*participation*) is compulsory in firms with more than 50 employees. Profits are shared according to a mandatory pre-set formula or one settled by collective bargaining (if more favourable than the pre-set formula). The profit share is paid into a fund and attracts tax advantages if it is held there for at least five years.

Second, cash profit-sharing (*interessement*) is a voluntary scheme. Tax benefits may be secured if the profit share is paid into a company savings scheme (*plan d'épargne d'entreprise*, PEE). PEE contributions can be supplemented by bonus payments from the company and voluntary employee contributions (up to a quarter of annual salary) (Degeorge et al., 2004; Poutsma, 2001). Most of the funds in savings plans are invested in *fonds communs de placement d'entreprise* (FCPE), which in turn invest either in a diversified fund or in the shares of the employer. This is the most typical approach to promote employee share ownership in the French system. Recent evidence indicates that nearly half of PEEs are used as a means for employee share acquisition and approximately one-quarter of employee savings are invested in company shares. Employee contributions to the PEE, including any derived from bonus payments, are exempt from taxes, whilst employer contributions can be offset against corporation tax, and social security charges are not levied.

A new tax (known as *forfait social*) was introduced recently for companies that have to pay up to 20 per cent of the bonuses that they distribute to their employees (*participation* + *interessement* + any amount paid in the PEE by the company in addition to a voluntary payment by the employee). In 2001, the Fabius Law enabled small and medium-sized enterprises (SMEs) to collaborate to provide a joint PEE. In 2003, a new savings plan, Plan d'Epargne Retraite Collectif (PERCO), was launched in which savings are frozen until retirement; these are prevented from investing more than 5 per cent of fund assets in company shares. Since 2005 it has been possible for firms to offer free shares to employees. Since the Law 2015-990 of 6 August 2015 the vesting period is limited to one year followed by a holding period decided by the Annual general Meeting (AGM) (but altogether these two periods cannot last less than two years), and these shares can be paid to the FCPE.

An important feature of *interessement* is that it can only be introduced either through a collective agreement with trade unions, with the involvement of trade union representatives at enterprise level, with the works council, or with the agreement of a two-thirds majority of the employees. Recent French legislation also gives employees a right to representation on the company's board when they hold 3 per cent or more of the company's shares. This is compulsory for companies with more than 1000 employees in France or more than 5000 employees worldwide (in France and in its foreign subsidiaries or branches).

United Kingdom

The UK has extensive arrangements for financial participation: there are a number of schemes established by statute and attracting favourable taxation arrangements. Two all-employee plans are currently in widespread use: the Save-As-You-Earn (SAYE) share option or saving plan introduced in 1984, and the Share Incentive Plan introduced in 2000. In SAYE (widely referred to as Sharesave), employees are allowed to take out options to be exercised in three or five years' time, at up to 20 per cent discount on market value at the time of grant. There is no income tax payable on the eventual sale of shares. Instead there is a capital gains tax liability, with marginal capital gains tax (CGT) rates usually being lower than the corresponding marginal income tax rate for most employees. The employee accrues the funds to exercise the options by participating in an SAYE savings plan. The Share Incentive Plan is a 'modular' plan with provision for grants of free shares, share purchases by employees, awards of matching shares to supplement employee purchases, and share awards based on the dividends accruing to employee share owners. The UK also has the Enterprise Management Incentives (EMI) plan, a set of arrangements for employees to be awarded options; and Company Share Options. Although both are aimed primarily at managers, they can be used for all-employee plans. A further scheme, Employee Shareholder Shares, provides for income tax and CGT concessions on shares awarded in return for giving up employment rights relating to unfair dismissal and statutory redundancy pay. An overview of these schemes can be found at https://www.gov.uk/tax-employee-share-schemes/overview.

Employee share ownership is firmly entrenched in the UK. In 2013/14 there were 11 460 tax-approved schemes in operation, though some companies operate more than one type of scheme (HM Revenue and Customs, 2015). This is an increase from 5160 schemes in 2000. However, this overall growth masks a decline in some schemes. The number of companies operating SAYE schemes has fallen from more than 1000 to 440. The Share Incentive Plan, introduced in 2000, grew to nearly 1000 schemes before the financial crisis of 2007 but has stabilised at around 820 companies. The source of the growth observed in the overall statistics is in the number of companies operating Enterprise Management Incentives. Nearly 10 000 companies now have EMI arrangements in place. However, the number of employees awarded EMI options in any given year is small: 20 000 in 2013/14 (https://www.gov.uk/government/collections/employee-share-schemes-statistics).

Most FTSE 100 firms have at least one all-employee plan, and they are also widespread amongst other listed firms. In recent years governments have been keen to encourage the use of share plans in unlisted companies, and the Share Incentive Plan and Enterprise Management Incentives were explicitly designed with this aim. The rationale for share ownership plans in the UK focuses very much on their favourable effects for companies, and the broader economy. It has been argued that share plans have the potential to enhance company productivity by aligning employee interests with those of the firm. There has been less attention in the UK to the potential for share ownership plans to redistribute wealth and to promote long-term savings, even though the UK has a comparatively low level of personal savings.

The UK does not currently have tax-approved arrangements to support generalised use of profit-sharing. It did have a scheme in the late 1980s and 1990s: Profit-Related Pay (PRP). Here the intention was to combat 'wage stickiness' and stimulate employment creation by providing tax benefits for wage flexibility. In PRP schemes part of employees' pay was explicitly linked to profits. To induce employees to bear this risk, the profit-related element was granted income tax concessions. This scheme was very popular indeed, with several thousand companies using it at its height. However, much of its popularity seems to have been based on the potential to operate 'cosmetic' profit-sharing, with pay flexibility being more apparent than real. Thus, tax concessions were granted in effect for pay that was fixed rather than flexible. For this reason, this scheme was abolished in 1997. However, a form of profit-sharing was introduced in 2014 for companies where a majority of the ownership is held by an Employee Ownership Trust (also newly introduced in 2014). These companies can pay bonuses to their employees each year free of income tax.

Unlike France, there is no requirement in the UK that financial participation has to be introduced with the agreement of employee representatives or employees themselves (though individual employee consent is necessary for joining a plan). Research has shown that many of those companies operating a share plan do, however, have union representation, but these representatives have little involvement in the design, implementation, or operation of the plan (Pendleton, 2005: Kalmi et al., 2006).

Germany[1]

In Germany, financial participation has been viewed primarily as a form of employee participation in productive capital and as a means to achieve a modest redistribution of wealth. The role of financial participation as a means to promote social consensus at work has received less emphasis in Germany, probably because there are alternative and well-developed institutions to achieve social dialogue and partnership such as Works Councils and employee board representation. However, with the recent spread of liberal market economy philosophies amongst top listed companies, the role of financial participation (employee share ownership in particular) as a tool to encourage employee commitment has achieved greater prominence.

Financial participation has been supported in Germany by the combination of three pieces of legislation: the Fifth Capital Formation Law, the Third Capital Participation Law, and the Income Tax Law. These provide the conditions under which employees may make regular savings and receive bonuses on these savings from the state and their employer (a profit share may be used for this). These savings may be invested in various vehicles, such as building societies, and in the employer. In the case of the latter, savings may be used to acquire employer shares, to make a loan to the employer, or to enter into a 'silent partnership' arrangement with the employer. In the latter, the participating employee receives a profit share on their invested savings but does not acquire the control rights typically held by full shareholders. This type of arrangement is typically found in private limited companies (GmbH) without a readily tradeable share capital, and has been a common form of financial participation (Carstensen et al., 1995). The Capital Formation and Capital Participation laws have restricted the eligibility of these arrangements to lower-income groups and have set out the maximum amounts that may be contributed by employers and the state. The Income Tax Law has provided for tax and social security concessions, though these have been fairly modest.

It is perhaps not surprising that the incidence of financial participation, share ownership plans especially, has not been high in Germany. The IAB Establishment Panel (www. iab.de/en/erhebungen/iab-betriebspanel.aspx), a nationally representative survey conducted regularly by the Institute for Employment Research) found that profit-sharing was used in 10 per cent of establishments in 2011 (Möller, 2013). Employee share ownership was found in just 2 per cent of establishments. With both forms, the likelihood of its use tends to grow with establishment size. Although the incidence of share ownership plans is low, participation rates are relatively high, with around half of employees on average participating. Employee loans and silent partnerships are more common than share ownership plans but, as they are predominantly used in the SME sector, their employee coverage is considerably smaller.

In 2005, an extensive public debate on financial participation developed with all of

---

[1]   We are grateful to Peter Wilke for assistance with the information on Germany.

the major political parties developing proposals to extend it. The Christian Democratic Union (CDU) proposed that financial participation should focus on the enterprise level and that tax concessions should be made more favourable. Meanwhile, the Social Democrats (SPD) favoured the creation of a 'German Fund', which would acquire shares in a range of companies, thereby spreading risk for participating employees. The outcome was the employee share ownership law of 1 April 2009. The tax concessions on acquiring employer shares have been increased, as have the size of the bonuses on savings arrangements. Nevertheless, the size of the concessions remains relatively small compared with other major European countries. The introduction of 'employee participation funds' (*Mitarbeiterbeteiligungs-Sondervermögen*) has been innovative. Employees could acquire shares in these funds, which then invest in the employing enterprise and other companies in the same sector or region. The proposed benefit for employees, compared with single-company financial participation, is that risk is diversified and the shares are readily tradeable. However, the regulations for these funds were abolished in July 2013. At the time of writing in 2016, there are no indications that this law and associated tax breaks have led to significant increase in uptake.

Australia

In Australia interest in financial participation has predominantly focused on employee share ownership rather than profit-sharing. Employee share ownership has enjoyed bipartisan support in Australia since the mid-1970s, though concrete initiatives from government have been less in evidence and have not always encouraged employee share ownership schemes. As elsewhere, part of the rationale for employee share ownership in Australia has focused on promoting an identity of interests between employees and employer. Encouragement of long-term savings has also been important, reflecting concern at low levels of personal savings until the introduction of compulsory occupational superannuation funds in the 1990s. In the 1990s and early 2000s, the Coalition Government believed that share ownership could fit with its policy of decentralisation of wage bargaining and the promotion of individualism in Australian industrial relations (Waring & Burgess, 2006). Against this, there has been a persistent anxiety in Australian politics that employee share ownership is prone to 'rorting' (that is, tax evasion and excessive extraction of benefits from companies, especially by top managers). This tension colours the nature and extent of legislative support for share ownership in Australia, and was exemplified by the legislative reforms of the Rudd Labor Government in 2009. More recently, the Coalition Government has sought to promote share ownership schemes, especially in start-ups and SMEs, with new legislation in 2015.

After the 2009 Budget, there have been two main ways in which employee share ownership is promoted. The first – the 'reduction concession' – enables employees on taxable incomes of up to AUS$180 000 to receive up to AUS$1000 of benefit in employer shares each financial year free of income and fringe benefits tax at the time of grant. Any subsequent increase or decrease in the value of the shares is treated as a taxable capital gain or loss in the financial year the shares are sold. Shares must be held for three years while still employed by the organisation and there can be no forfeiture clause. The second – the 'deferral concession' – enabled employees to defer income tax on share-based remuneration benefits for up to seven years. This concession was available for salary sacrifice share schemes involving share benefits up to AUS$5000 per annum or where there is the potential for forfeiture. This concession also applied to option-based plans. The employee became entitled to exercise these options after satisfying performance hurdles. Income tax on the benefit of the option could be deferred if there is a real risk of forfeiture. For tax benefits to be available at least 75 per cent of permanent employees of three years standing had to have a right to participate.

Although this legislation clarified the legal identity of share schemes to some extent, it had some negative aspects which led to a decline in the use of employee share ownership. A major problem was the set of criteria for securing the deferral concession. Because all-employee share option plans, and share options in start-ups, were unlikely to meet these, the taxation point for options was in effect shifted to when options were granted, rather than when employees realise value on the options. Employees could pay tax on the options even if the options subsequently became 'underwater' (that is, the price at exercise was lower than the price at grant). To counter this, the Coalition Government, with cross-party support, amended the legislation in 2015. Employees will now be able to defer tax until they exercise the options because the forfeiture requirement has been relaxed. The deferral period has also been increased to 15 years. The Government was also keen to encourage the use of share schemes amongst start-ups. If a company meets the criteria (to be unlisted, resident in Australia, be under ten years old, and have aggregate turnover of less than AUS$50 million), it can grant options or discounted shares that are free of income tax at grant or exercise. As in other countries such as the UK, capital gains tax is payable instead on disposal of the shares.

Research found that 57 per cent of listed companies had a broad-based share ownership plan in the mid-2000s and that most of these had adopted the plan since 2000. Most plans were structured to take advantage of tax exemptions, and required employees to subscribe to shares or options (or both) (Landau et al., 2009). The proportion of employees in Australia receiving shares was 5.9 per cent (Australian Bureau of Statistics, 2005; Landau et al., 2010). After 2009, it is clear that the use of share schemes declined as a result of the share plan changes, but there is no firm research evidence on the extent of the decline. As for the effects of the 2015 changes, it is too early to tell.

USA[2]

The USA has a long history of support for employee share ownership, with substantial ownership of employer shares and active public discussions of the topic dating back to the 1920s and before. The notion that ordinary workers may own their firm, or part of it, harks back to Jeffersonian ideas about broad-based ownership of property and wealth articulated by many of the other founders of the country across the political spectrum at the time (Blasi & Kruse, 2006). In the 1950s and 1960s American investment expert Louis Kelso devised what came to be known as the Employee Stock Ownership Plan (ESOP) as a means of widening the ownership of productive assets and overcoming the fundamental divide between capital and labour. Kelso attracted the support of Senator Russell Long, who was instrumental in drafting the landmark Employment Retirement Income

---

[2]   We are grateful to Joseph Blasi for his assistance in preparing this section.

Security Act (ERISA) passed in 1974. This introduced a set of tax benefits for ESOPs. In a leveraged ESOP, a corporation can borrow funds to purchase company stock and pay for the stock out of its profits while deducting the principal and interest on the loan from its corporate income for tax purposes. In a non-leveraged ESOP (similar to a stock bonus plan) a corporation contributes cash or stock to a worker trust. In both cases, workers gain stock without buying it with their savings or pledging any personal assets for the loans or contributions by the company. With these methods, Kelso overcame the barrier to regular working people buying parts of their companies. The ESOP holds employee allocations of shares in a trust.

Profit-sharing has an even longer pedigree in American history and was common from the mid-1800s and throughout the twentieth century. Sometimes cash or deferred profit-sharing was used to buy company stock. This form of employee ownership grew dramatically in the wake of ERISA but has stabilised more recently. In 2014, there were about 6900 ESOPs covering 13.4 million participants. ESOPs are mainly found in privately owned, rather than listed, companies. Very few ESOPs involve wage concessions or purchases of failing firms by workers, despite the fact that a small number of such cases have received extensive attention in the media. Most are medium-sized firms that were profitable under family ownership and were sold to the employees and professional managers. The other main forms of share scheme in the USA are broad-based stock option plans, 401(k) plans, and employee stock purchase plans (so-called '423 plans', as they meet the rules of Internal Revenue Code Section 423). Stock options are widespread in listed companies in the USA and recent estimates suggest there are approximately 3000 broad-based plans (Rosen, 2010). The 401(k) plans are self-directed defined contribution retirement plans whereby employees allocate funds to a variety of investment funds and assets. These may include employer stock. In some cases employers match employee contributions with awards of their stock. The result has been that many employees hold a substantial component of their 401(k) investments in employer shares. While the employer match in stock is not based on worker savings, the fact that much of 401(k) employee ownership is bought with worker savings makes it substantially more risky than ESOPs (Mitchell & Utkus, 2003). Finally, employee stock purchase plans, whereby employees use their wages to acquire company shares on favourable terms, are also widespread.

Data from the 2014 General Social Survey show that 22.9 million employees own stock in their company through a 401(k) plan, ESOP, direct stock grant, or similar plan, while 8.5 million hold stock options (some employees have options and own stock through other plans, so these numbers are not additive). That means that 19.5 per cent of the total workforce, but 34.9 per cent of those who work for companies that have stock, own stock through some kind of benefit plan; while 7.2 per cent of the workforce, but 13.1 per cent of those in companies with stock, hold options.

Financial participation is therefore relatively widespread in the USA. Although early discussions of employee ownership saw it as a way of spreading wealth, the development of share ownership in the USA has taken two alternative directions. One has seen share ownership plans substituting for wages. Blasi and Kruse (2006) draw attention to the decline of collective bargaining in the USA and of the notion of a constantly increasing 'fixed wage' adjusted for inflation, which was a common expectation in the decades after World War II. They suggest that some share ownership plans have increasingly substituted for an element of wages, rather than supplementing them and spreading wealth.

The 401(k) form of employee ownership funded by employee savings is an example of this type. Insofar as they form part of a shift to defined contribution pension systems they form part of a system that is characterised by increasing insecurity and risk for the worker. However, some plans, most notably those taking the ESOP form, do spread wealth, do not substitute for fixed wages, and allow many workers to accumulate meaningful capital incomes on top of fair wages (Kruse et al., 2008; Kruse et al., 2010).

NATIONAL DIFFERENCES IN FINANCIAL PARTICIPATION

The preceding discussion shows that there are clear differences in the incidence and character of financial participation plans between countries. A key question is why these differences are present. To answer this requires analysis at two levels. One concerns the presence of legislation and fiscal concessions for financial participation: more developed statutory frameworks provide greater capacity and opportunity for firms to operate financial participation schemes. The second concerns the propensity of firms to use financial participation where such arrangements are present. Clearly, the presence of legislation and tax concessions may influence firm behaviour but there are also other possible influences on corporate behaviour. These include ownership structures, trade unions and industrial relations arrangements, and broader ideological considerations. In other words, the institutional environment in which firms operate is likely to structure and influence the companies' financial participation decisions (or 'non-decisions'). But equally, the nature of the business system is likely to influence the propensity of governments to take action in this area. At the same time, government influences the nature of the business system. There is thus a highly complex set of interrelationships between actors and institutions.

Evidence to date strongly indicates that legislative and fiscal frameworks have a critical influence on the incidence and character of financial participation. By implication, they provide an opportunity for firms to use financial participation, and possibly incentives and encouragement to do so. The role of government action is well expressed in the EU proposal for a Council Recommendation by the European Commission in 1992 (Commission of the European Communities, 1992) repeated in a Commission communication in 2002:

> the development of financial participation schemes is strongly influenced by government action. Governments are primarily responsible for the creation of a legal and fiscal framework that may flavour such schemes but may also impede their introduction. This is illustrated by the finding of the PEPPER Report that in those countries where a particular type of financial participation scheme has been encouraged by government, the schemes most commonly introduced by enterprises are indeed the ones promoted through official government measures. In particular the availability of tax incentives makes a big difference. (Commission of the European Communities, 2002: 19)

Within a European context, the prevalence of financial participation in countries such as France and the United Kingdom is testament to long-standing legislation. The recent growth in financial participation in several European countries, such as Belgium and Germany, reflects recent government initiatives to promote financial participation. Government action operates in two ways. First, it can remove obstacles to the use of share plans or profit-sharing by firms. For instance, in the absence of specific government action, employee share ownership plans may be inhibited by a requirement to tax employees twice: once at the point of grant (if there is a discount) and once at the point of sale. A further impediment (mainly removed in Europe by the Prospectus Directive) is the typical requirement in securities law for a prospectus to be issued by companies whenever they offer shares for sale. Second, fiscal and social security concessions can provide an incentive for firms to implement financial participation plans.

A deeper question is why some governments have been more (or less) likely to promote financial participation through legislation. One influence is likely to be the objectives, policies, and strength of the 'social partners': trade unions and employers' associations (Pendleton & Poutsma, 2004). Left-wing union movements have tended to oppose employee share ownership on the grounds that it blurs a fundamental conflict between capital and labour. As for employers' associations, there is a tension between desires to promote cooperation and an anxiety that employee share ownership might weaken managerial control. Some employer bodies are more supportive of financial participation than others. Besides the role of specific groups, governmental action is influenced by the broader institutional environment or business system in which governments operate. For instance, in economies where there are well-developed and liquid stock markets and dispersed ownership, governments are more likely to see stock-based instruments as a viable form of employee reward. Black et al. (2007) find that the prevalence of share ownership plans in countries is associated with the extent of ownership dispersion in the listed company sector.

At a broader level still, it is noticeable that share ownership plans receive most support from governments and are most prevalent in those countries that are viewed as 'liberal market economies' in the 'varieties of capitalism' literature. In these countries it is said that exchanges between key factors, such as labour and firms, are predominantly market or transactional in character whereas in 'coordinated market economies' there is greater emphasis on relationships. Thus, in the latter, employee commitment might be secured through well-developed systems for employee involvement and representation; whereas in liberal market economics there is a greater reliance on market-based rewards such as company stock plans (Blair, 1995).

At company level, institutional isomorphism (homogenisation) in the use of employee financial participation is likely. Firms may mimic their rivals in the use of practices, they may react to coercive pressures to conform to legislation and informal rules, or they may uphold and follow certain employment practices and norms found in the business system. The existing order, however, may be disrupted by outsiders. For instance, the spread of financial participation in countries that have not been noted for extensive financial participation has been stimulated by the presence of US multinationals transferring practices common in the USA to their overseas subsidiaries (Poutsma et al., 2005).

Over recent years there have been major changes in institutions, especially in systems of collective bargaining and other elements of employment relations. In many of the more regulated and centralised national systems of collective bargaining, such as in Germany and the Scandinavian countries, there has been substantial decentralisation of collective bargaining. Alongside these changes in the processes of collective bargaining, pay systems themselves have become more individualistic (Traxler et al., 2008). Financial participation is often seen as being a key component of these trends: it is viewed as contributing to high performance and flexibility (Poutsma & de Nijs, 2003; Kaarsemaker & Poutsma, 2006).

This suggests gradual growth of the phenomenon in the near future. Despite this possible trend the differences in adoption between firms located in different national settings will probably persist, reflecting directional convergence: developments in the same direction, but not final convergence to one universal model.

CONCLUSIONS

In this chapter, we have highlighted variations between countries in the use of financial participation practices by companies. The country profiles show that corporate behaviour is influenced by a complex set of actors and institutions. Whilst legislation and tax concessions are of prime importance, industrial relations systems and ideological constraints are also highly relevant. From a comparative HRM perspective, financial participation is embedded in distinct settings. The concept of 'national business system' is useful in understanding differences in company contexts, and we have highlighted the interaction between institutions in shaping the form and adoption of financial participation. One implication of the way that firms are embedded in distinct national contexts is that financial participation practices are not universally applied. This means that multinational companies will probably need to amend any practices that they might want to transfer across their subsidiaries: even where they can operate the same practices in different settings, the operation, meaning, and results of those practices might be quite different in different contexts.

REFERENCES

Australian Bureau of Statistics. 2005. Spotlight: Employee Share Schemes. Canberra: Australian Labour Market Statistics.

Black, B., Gospel, H., & Pendleton, A. 2007. Finance, corporate governance, and the employment relationship. *Industrial Relations*, 46(3): 643–650.

Blair, M. 1995. *Ownership and Control: Rethinking Corporate Governance for the Twenty-First Century*. Washington, DC: Brookings Institution.

Blasi, J.R., & Kruse, D.L. 2006. The political economy of employee ownership in the United States: From economic democracy to industrial democracy?. *International Review of Sociology*, 16(1): 127–147.

Bonin, J., Jones, D., & Putterman, L. 1993. Theoretical and empirical studies of producer cooperatives: Will ever the twain meet?. *Journal of Economic Literature*, 31(3): 1290–1320.

Carstensen, V., Gerlach, K., & Hubler, O. 1995. Profit sharing in German firms. In F. Buttler, W. Franz, R. Schettkat, and D. Soskice (eds), *Institutional Frameworks and Labor Market Performance: Comparative Views of the US and German Economies*. London: Routledge.

Commission of the European Communities. 1992. Council Recommendation n° 92/443/EEC of 27 July 1992 concerning the promotion of participation by employed persons in profits and enterprise results (including equity participation), *Official Journal* L245(26/08/1992): 0053–0055.

Commission of the European Communities. 2002. Communication from the Commission to the council, the European Parliament, the Economic and Social Committee and the Committee of the Regions: on a Framework for the Promotion of Employee Financial participation. In Commission of the European Communities (ed.), *COM (2002) 364 final*. Brussels.

Croucher, R., Brookes, M., Wood, G., & Brewster, C. 2010. Context, strategy and financial participation: A comparative analysis. *Human Relations*, 63(6): 835–855.

Degeorge, F., Jenter, D., Moel, A., & Tufano, P. 2004. Selling company shares to reluctant employees: France Telecom's experience. *Journal of Financial Economics*, 71(1): 169–202.

Estrin, S., & Jones, D. 1992. The viability of employee-owned firms: Evidence from France. *Industrial and Labor Relations Review*, 45(2): 323–338.

Hashi, I., Lowitzsch, J., Uvalic, M., & Vaughan-Whitehead, D. 2006. PEPPER III: An overview of employee financial participation. In J. Lowitzsch (ed.), *The PEPPER II Report: Promotion of Employee Participation in Profits and Enterprise Results in the new Member and Candidate Countries of the European Union*. Berlin: Free University, Inter-University Centre at the Institute for Eastern European Studies.

HM Revenue and Customs. 2015. Employee share scheme statistics. London: HM Revenue and Customs. Available at https://www.gov.uk/government/statistics/companies-with-tax-advantaged-employee-share-schemes.

Kaarsemaker, E., & Poutsma, E. 2006. The fit of employee ownership with other human resource management practices: Theoretical and empirical suggestions regarding the existence of an ownership high-performance work system, or theory 0. *Economic and Industrial Democracy*, 27(4): 669–685.

Kalmi, P., Pendleton, A., & Poutsma, E. 2006. The relationship between financial participation and other forms of employee participation: New survey evidence from Europe. *Economic and Industrial Democracy*, 27(4): 637–667.

Kruse, D.L., Blasi, J.R., & Park, R. 2010. Shared capitalism in the US economy? Prevalence, characteristics, and employee views of financial participation in enterprises. In D.L. Kruse, R.B. Freeman, and J.R. Blasi (eds), *Shared Capitalism at Work: Employee Ownership, Profit and Gain Sharing, and Broad-based Stock Options*. Chicago, IL: University of Chicago Press.

Kruse, D.L., Freeman, R.B., & Blasi, J.R. 2008. Do workers gain by sharing? Employee outcomes under employee ownership, profit sharing, and broad-based stock options. NBER Working Paper Series, 14233.

Landau, I., Mitchell, R., O'Connell, A., Ramsay, I., & Marshall, S. 2009. Broad-based employee share owner-ship in Australian listed companies: Survey report. *Research Report*. Melbourne: University of Melbourne Law School.

Landau, I., O'Connell, A., & Ramsay, I. 2010. *Employee Share Schemes: Regulation and Policy*. Melbourne: University of Melbourne Law School.

Lowitzsch, J. 2006. *The PEPPER III Report: Promotion of Employee Participation in Profits and Enterprise Results in the New Member and Candidate Countries of the European Union*. Berlin: Free University: Inter-University Centre at the Institute for Eastern European Studies.

Mitchell, O., & Utkus, S. 2003. The role of company stock in defined contribution plans. In O. Mitchell and K. Smetters (eds), *The Pension Challenge: Risk Transfers and Retirement Income Security*. Philadelphia, PA: University of Pennsylvania Press.

Möller, I. 2013. Finanzielle Mitarbeiterbeteiligung. Noch viel Platz für Ausbau. *IAB-Forum*, 1: 48–53.

Pendleton, A. 2005. Employee share ownership, employment relationships, and corporate governance. In B. Harley, J. Hyman, and P. Thompson (eds), *Participation and Democracy at Work: Essays in Honour of Harvie Ramsay*. London: Palgrave.

Pendleton, A., & Poutsma, E. 2004. The policies and views of peak organisations towards financial participation (sythesis report). Dublin: European Foundation.

Pendleton, A., Poutsma, E., Brewster, C., & van Ommeren, J. 2001. *Employee Share Ownership and Profit Sharing in the European Union*. Dublin: Foundation for the Improvement of Living and Working Conditions.

Pendleton, A., Poutsma, E., van Ommeren, J., & Brewster, C. 2003. The incidence and determinants of employee share ownership and profit sharing in Europe. In T. Kato and J. Pliskin (eds), *The Determinants of the Incidence and the Effects of Participatory Organizations*. Amsterdam: JAI Press.

Poole, M. 1989. *The Origins of Economic Democracy: Profit-sharing and Employee-shareholding Schemes*. London: Routledge.

Poutsma, E. 2001. *Recent Trends in Employee Financial Participation in the European Union*. Luxembourg: Office for Official Publications of the European Communities.

Poutsma, E., & de Nijs, W.F. 2003. Broad-based employee financial participation in the European Union. *International Journal of Human Resource Management*, 14(6): 863–892.

Poutsma, E., Ligthart, P., & Schouteten, R. 2005. Employee share schemes in Europe. The influence of US multinationals. *Management Revue*, 16(1): 99–122.

Rosen, C. 2010. *The State of Broad-Based Equity Plans*. Berkley, CA: National Center for Employee Ownership.

Traxler, F., Brandl, B., & Glassner, V. 2008. Pattern bargaining: An investigation into its agency, context and evidence. *British Journal of Industrial Relations*, 46(1): 33–58.

Uvalic, M. 1991. The promotion of employee participation in profits and enterprise results. In Commission of the European Communities (ed.), *Social Europe, Supplement 3/91*. Luxembourg: Office for Official Publications of the European Communities.

Vaughan-Whitehead, D. 1995. *Workers' Financial Participation: East-West Experiences*. Geneva: International Labour Office.

Waring, P., & Burgess, J. 2006. WorkChoices: The privileging of individualism in Australian industrial relations. *International Journal of Employment Studies*, 14(1): 61–80.

Welz, C., & Fernández-Macías, E. 2007. *Financial Participation of Employees in the European Union: Much Ado about Nothing?*. Dublin: European Foundation for the Improvement of Living and Working Conditions.

Welz, C., & Fernández-Macías, E. 2008. Financial participation of employees in the European Union: Much ado about nothing?. *European Journal of Industrial Relations*, 14(4): 479–496.

16. Comparative perspectives on diversity and equality: the challenges of gender, sexual orientation, race, ethnicity, and religion

Gwendolyn Combs, Rana Haq, Alain Klarsfeld,
Lourdes Susaeta, and Esperanza Suarez

INTRODUCTION

An international perspective on diversity and equal treatment policies and practices has been aptly described and analysed (Klarsfeld, Combs, Susaeta, & Belizon, 2012). That research revolved around the emergence of diversity management (Cox & Blake, 1991; Cox, 1994), and how international comparisons could inform the general shift from equality to diversity and the mapping of similarities and differences in equality legislations regardless of diversity strands (these were taken generally as illustrations). This chapter builds on earlier research and takes a more focused perspective on four specific diversity strands (gender; sexual orientation; race, ethnicity, and immigration; and religion) where important developments have been unfolding in recent years, sometimes in the midst of extreme violence and challenges.

As regards gender, we see two parallel shifts: one of growing rights and participation of women in employment and the public sphere; and the other, a retraction of women's basic rights and freedoms in some parts of the world, particularly in areas that are under the control of Islamist terrorist violence and/or under the influence of fundamentalist interpretations of Islam or Judaism in Africa, Asia, and the Middle East. The chapter section on sexual orientation and lesbian, gay, bisexual, and transgender (LGBT) rights shows evidence of considerable formal advances, with the world now roughly segmented into countries where there is near equality of rights for LGBT individuals; countries where there is no such equality and where LGBT people suffer considerable discrimination, in part owing to the lack of a formal legal framework; and countries where LGBT people are not only demeaned in the society at large but are also considered as criminals from a legal perspective. Ethnic, racial, and religious diversity is growing in most parts of the world owing to mass migration movements. The contrast is growing between a reduced number of countries that attract migrants (in net flows) as a result of successfully welcoming and valuing racial, ethnic, and religious diversity (Australia, Canada, the United Kingdom, the United States of America), as opposed to a number of countries that explicitly tolerate this diversity but implicitly either refuse or demean it (France, Denmark, and Germany but for the very recent policy following the Syrian crisis), or countries where one or several of these diversity strands come under more or less severe restrictions or even threats to life (South Africa). A review of the literature is provided for each strand, highlighting the difficulties but also the possible legal advances or examples of good practice. Finally, a summary table is provided in the concluding section.

GENDER

Although our analysis focuses mostly on developed economies, the difficulties women and girls continue to face in developing regions are clear, such as reduced access to education, formal employment, and healthcare. According to the metric used, gender differences are stark. For example, one important indicator of gender differences is the maternal mortality ratio (that is, the number of women who die per 100 000 childbirths). In this respect, the range is immense, from 1 (Belarus) to 1100 (Sierra Leone). Such an index contrasts most Organisation for Economic Co-operation and Development (OECD) countries, where values are 14 or below, with Africa, where values are 200 or above in almost all countries. Latin America, the Middle East, and Asia tend to be split between countries with relatively low maternal mortality ratios (10–50) and countries with relatively high maternal mortality (100 and above). It is noticeable that among OECD countries, the United States of America (USA) stands out as having a relatively high maternal mortality ratio of 28 (United Nations Development Programme, 2016). When looking at political participation, in contrast, many African countries have a better track record than most OECD countries (United Nations Development Programme, 2016). Context also matters within a given region, such as Europe. For instance, Spain and Italy have relatively low gender pay gaps compared with other countries such as Germany and the United Kingdom (UK), but this is in part due to many women not participating in the workforce in these countries in the first place. Gender gaps change according to the metrics used (*The Economist*, 2015).

Context matters, and should guide us on how to choose relevant indicators and how to interpret performance on specific indicators. For instance, an increase in labour market participation in developed countries can be seen as an improvement in the condition of women; whereas record-high female labour market participation in most sub-Saharan African countries is in part due to restricted access to education, maternity or parental leave, and retirement schemes.

Statistics on labour force participation rates are less reliable for developing societies, partly because so many people work in the informal sectors of these economies. Available estimates, however, show the highest rates of female employment in sub-Saharan Africa, where poverty pushes nearly all men and women into some sort of market activity, and in East Asia, which includes the booming Chinese economy (United Nations Development Programme, 2016). In much of the North African and West Asian regions, by contrast, cultural values call for strict separation of male and female domains, and official male employment rates exceed female rates by more than 45 percentage points.

Having analysed the enormous differences in gender inequalities from a cross country-comparative perspective, it is therefore appropriate to identify the main areas of focus in the current literature debate. 'Glass ceilings', 'glass doors', 'sticky floors', 'mommy tracks', and 'boardroom quotas' are topics relevant both to the developing and developed economies' contexts.

The glass ceiling metaphor has been used to describe invisible systemic barriers (Davies-Netzley, 1998). These barriers prevent large numbers of women from obtaining and securing the highest-grossing jobs in the workforce (Hesse-Biber & Carter, 2005: 77). Removing these barriers in order to increase female participation is an important component of gender equality policies, with Scandinavian countries appearing most advanced in this effort.

While the glass ceiling seems to persist, the pressure against it has noticeably amplified across the world due to a growing generation of educated, experienced, and ambitious women impatient to grow to their potential. Even though women outperform men in education and higher education, they still face significant shortfalls in the labour market. In 26 European countries, by 2008 women's employment constituted at least 45 per cent of the labour force, and the overall gender employment gap for the European Union's 27 member countries narrowed from 23 per cent for 20–64-year-olds in 1998, to 15.1 per cent in 2008. However, the labour market remains gendered, and problems regarding the biased implementation of human resource management (HRM) policies persist (Smith, 2010).

Various authors (e.g., Albrecht et al., 2003; Cotter et al., 2004; Huffman et al., 2008) discuss the mechanisms through which the glass ceiling is formed: discrimination, educational choice, life cycle explanations, cohort effects. These mechanisms were found to negatively affect women's career development, leading to a 'frozen pipeline', where there is a scarcity of women eligible for promotion.

Based on data mainly from the OECD, *The Economist*'s (2015) 'glass ceiling index' compares nine indicators across 26 countries: the number of men and women respectively with tertiary education; female labour force participation; the male–female wage gap; the proportion of women in senior jobs; net childcare costs relative to the average wage; paid maternity leave; share of Graduate Management Admission Test (GMAT) candidates; women in parliament; and share of women on company boards. New Zealand scores high on all the indicators. Finland does best on education; Finland has the highest female labour force participation rate; and Spain has one of the smallest wage gaps, at 8.6 per cent. We must bear in mind that the OECD-based 'glass ceiling index' does not do justice to its manifestation in many developing countries, where the major issues facing women are access to education, formal employment, and decent work in the context of unchanged gender roles in the domestic sphere and poor healthcare provisions, in particular for mothers (Addati et al., 2014; Floro & Moeurs, 2009; United Nations Development Programme, 2016).

Self-selection and HRM recruiting policies can also reinforce the glass ceiling. Similarly qualified men and women apply to different kinds of jobs based on the effects of their gender role beliefs. Factors influencing applications are: work–life balance, identification, and the expectation of a successful application. For example, women are less likely to apply for finance jobs. They also do not apply as much as men to consulting jobs, due to the perception of a lack of work–life balance (Barbulescu & Bidwell, 2013). Therefore, even if policies are in place, they cannot be effective if they do not result in countering such perceptions.

An alternative explanation for the glass ceiling experienced by females is disproportionate sorting of men and women across high-paying versus low-paying firms: the 'glass door' effect (Pendakur & Woodcock, 2010). The glass door effect also exists further on in professional development due to the limited external hiring of women for top positions (Chamberlain, 2015). However, research has found that companies in service industries tend to have greater representation of women in top management (Capelli & Hamori, 2004; Hillman et al., 2007, Goodman et al., 2003), and points to other promising signs (Helfat et al., 2006). In companies with female executives, women were younger, had less company tenure, and less tenure in their current positions than their male counterparts. This suggests that companies were aggressively hiring and promoting women into the top executive ranks.

Differences are observed in the extent of government involvement. Among 'economically advanced' nations, the Anglo-Saxon countries tend to have less public policy regarding gender equality than Scandinavian countries and Quebec, where policies supporting women's participation are typically stronger. Henrekson and Stenkula (2009: 241) show that negative consequences (in terms of career progression) may occur in countries such as Sweden, Denmark, Finland, Iceland, and Norway, where the state offers large subsidies to parental leave and grants employees statutory rights to stay at home for an extended period (Booth, 2007). Disentangling the effects of subsidized parental leave and of childcare on women's progression is therefore a difficult research question.

Other than childcare, extensive research has acknowledged the relevance of mentoring and networking (e.g., Metz, 2005), as well as differences in networking success for men and women (e.g., Baert et al., 2015; Lyness & Thompson, 2000; Van Emmerik et al., 2006). Overall, academic research indicates that managers continue to see women as less promotable, performing more poorly, and having inferior 'job fit' because they identify women as facing greater levels of family–work conflicts than men (Duehr & Bono, 2006; Meyerson & Fletcher, 2000).

Future research will provide a better understanding of the impact that family–work conflict bias and other forms of subtle disadvantage have on the promotion of women (Hoobler et al., 2009). On a positive note, Hensvik (2014) has recently found that female managers are better informed about other women's productivity. It could also be, however, that talented female workers may choose to enter women-led firms because they anticipate better career opportunities and no wage differences with men. Providing a better understanding of these sorting patterns is therefore important for future research.

The term 'sticky floor' describes an employment pattern that keeps a certain group of workers at the bottom of the job scale. Confirmation for the existence of sticky floors has been found in countries such as Australia (Johnston & Lee, 2012), Italy (Filippin & Ichino, 2005), Spain (Gradin & del Rio, 2009), Thailand (Fang & Sakellariou, 2011), and the USA (Baker, 2003). However, it is unclear whether sticky floors result from gender differences in human capital, preferences, and behaviours on the employee's side, or from preferences (and unequal treatment) on the employer's side (Arulampalam et al., 2007; Bertrand et al., 2014; Christofides et al., 2013; Dinovitzer et al., 2009). Efforts to 'masculinize' bottom female jobs may reverse this imbalance in the future.

However complex the occupational segregation causes are, evidence suggests that being a mother causes disadvantage in the workplace. Research found a motherhood penalty in Australia, Canada, the UK, the USA, Germany, Finland, and Sweden (Harkness & Waldfogel, 2003), and in Austria, Germany, Italy, Luxembourg, the Netherlands, Canada, Belgium, France, and Sweden (Misra et al., 2005). In many developing countries, motherhood will translate into segregation of women into low-paid, home-based and informal jobs, and maternity and parental leave provisions are either unavailable or poorly enforced (Addati et al., 2014; Floro & Moeurs, 2009). The motherhood penalty appears to have remained stable over time (Avellar & Smock, 2003). Career pauses or decelerations are likely to have long-term effects on subsequent career success. A partial mitigation of this effect may be accomplished through delay of the professional career – that is, postponement of retirement – and changing perceptions regarding the 'right' age to be considered a promotable person.

'Mommy track jobs', 'on-ramping jobs', and 'opting out' are discussed in Kalleberg (2008). The 'mommy track' refers to the diminishing opportunities of women in the workforce once they become mothers. On-ramping is the process of re-entering the workforce after taking a career break. It is paired with the term 'off-ramping', or exiting the workforce for a temporary career break. Lommerud et al. (2015) investigate whether self-fulfilling expectations may lead to higher hiring or promotion standards for women, and discover the existence of discriminatory outcomes where women are less likely to be placed in fast-track jobs. Reversing the self-fulfilling expectations is a key to promote gender equality.

There is a debate about what types of public policy could potentially end such discrimi-nation, and among them increasing female presence in boards through quotas is making progress. Traditionally, women have not successfully achieved equal representation on corporate boards, a concern that has attracted significant practitioner, policy, and schol-arly interest (Catalyst, 2013; *The Economist*, 2011a, 2011b; Pande & Ford, 2011; European Commission, 2012; Torchia et al., 2011). As stated in Terjesen et al. (2015: 34) in their study of 67 countries, females comprise only 10.3 per cent of board directorships, with some of the lowest rates in Morocco (0 per cent), Japan (0.9 per cent), and Chile (2.4 per cent); and some of the highest in Norway (42 per cent), Sweden (28 per cent), Finland (27.2 per cent), and France (22 per cent).

Across 11 territories (that is, Belgium, Finland, France, Germany, Iceland, Israel, Italy, Kenya, Norway, Spain, Quebec), recently enacted legislation generally consists of a set gender quota (usually 33–50 per cent), time period (often 3–5 years), and strong penal-ties for non-compliance (for example, in Spain, any board appointment that violates the quota is considered legally invalid; in Norway, companies are dissolved). The Norwegian government was the first to establish a 40 per cent female quota in 2003. Spain established a 40 per cent female quota in 2007. Nine other countries and regions now have quota legislation (Belgium, Finland, France, Germany, Iceland, Israel, Italy, Kenya, Quebec).

Another 15 countries (Australia, Austria, Denmark, Germany, Ireland, Luxemburg, Malawi, Malaysia, the Netherlands, Nigeria, Poland, South Africa, Sweden, the UK, the USA) have not gone as far as positive discrimination, but require companies to report gender diversity recruitment efforts and board gender and diversity composition, under a 'comply or explain' principle ('encouraged voluntarism' as per the typology presented in Klarsfeld et al., 2012). Other countries such as Indonesia, Japan, and Mexico have limited or non-existent legislation. Terjesen et al. (2015) suggest that quotas tied to strong sanc-tions do tend to elicit better representation of women in the boardroom. Whether this will impact upon HRM policies and women at large is still unclear (Nelson et al., 2016).

SEXUAL ORIENTATION

In this section we offer a comparative examination of the discrimination experienced by LGBT (lesbian, gay, bisexual, transgender) individuals in several countries. It is to be noted that LGBT people still face negative legal discrimination (from no access to marriage, up to the death penalty in extreme cases) in most countries of the world. However, great strides have been made in, for example, same-sex marriage, which was non-existent 12 years ago, and is now legal in 16 countries. However, comparably less pro-gress has been made in providing formalized overarching protections for LGBT equality in the workplace.

Globally, LGBT individuals are more likely than heterosexual persons to report life and work experiences of discrimination. The non-dominant position of LGBT sexual orientations can negatively impact upon success in both family and work (Ozturk, 2011; Drydakis, 2015). Drydakis (2015) investigated sexual orientation discrimination in the United Kingdom and found that for male- or female-dominated occupations, or occupations with masculine or feminine personality traits, LGBT applicants received fewer invitations for interviews than their non-LGBT counterparts. Workplace discrimination based on sexual orientation also occurs in many European countries where discrimination and hostility towards rights for LGBT individuals is overtly displayed (Helfer & Voeten, 2014). For example, in spite of European Union (EU) legislation, several have considered proposals to criminalize homosexual activity and to outlaw public expressions of affection displayed by LGBT individuals (Helfer & Voeten, 2014). In addition to governmental actions, the socio-cultural environment in many countries also demonstrates abusive attitudes toward LGBT citizens. For example, in Turkey, family members often adopt potentially threatening and mentally abusive attitudes when homosexuality is revealed, which results in an additional stigma towards divergent sexual orientation identities (Ozturk, 2011).

In South America, persons with non-heterosexual identities experience similar challenges. Normative sexuality that is protected by social institutions, such as church, school, and family, fosters homophobia at all levels. Through a series of interviews, Barrientos et al. (2010) found that approximately 75 per cent of LGBT individuals reported experiencing ridicule, and almost 60 per cent reported experiencing insults or threats. However, the authors also observe that South American countries are slowly incorporating a more tolerant and accepting attitude toward LGBT individuals, and more unfavourable attitudes towards discrimination on the basis of sexual orientation.

Similarly, the rights of sexual minorities are also suppressed in Africa. Although South Africa is the first African country to legalize same-sex marriages and include sexual orientation protection in its Constitution (Booysen & Wishik, 2016), it is still recognized as an unsafe place for LGBT individuals to seek asylum (Angert & Parakkal, 2014). South African society and culture are a long way from accepting the letter and spirit of the law. Acts of cruelty towards LGBT individuals have occurred in other African countries such as Uganda and Nigeria (Angert & Parakkal, 2014). Finally, Massad (2002) indicates that same-sex relationships are often met with persecution and hostility, and there are no words for 'homosexuality' or 'heterosexuality' in the Quran (Amer, 2012).

Unlike South America and Africa, the USA and Canada generally display a greater tolerance and attitude of inclusion for members of the LGBT community (Eliason et al., 2011). Although LGBT individuals sometimes still experience discriminatory treatment in their daily lives, many members of the political elites in the USA and Canada have facilitated the legalization of gay marriage (Nakamura & Pope, 2013). In the USA, same-sex marriage was declared legal in June 2015 by the Supreme Court. Despite this court ruling, overarching federal-level employment protections for LGBT individuals have not been enacted. In Canada, sexual orientation has federally protected status within the Canadian constitution (Meyer, 2010).

Worldwide, the determinants of LGBT laws and policy are juxtaposed between religious doctrine and public policy and country domestic factors (Amer, 2012). Even with the constitutional determination for same-sex marriages in the USA, large factions of the religious community and members of the general public have expressed their disagreement and were provided direction by member churches. Although the general trend is tolerance towards more open expressions of sexuality among LGBT individuals and a corresponding increase in acceptance of LGBT lifestyles, there remains a silence regarding non-heterosexual orientation, even in reportedly inclusive organizations. For example, Priola et al. (2014), in a study of five Italian organizations, find that although these organizations supported marginalized population groups, LGBT employees of these organizations are met with an organizational silence regarding LGBT issues that prevents them from integrating their work and sexual identities.

It is evident that LGBT individuals encounter serious misconceptions and barriers in the job market. Workplaces might therefore take steps to prevent discrimination and actively encourage employee expressions of their LGBT identities. Teamwork is an important aspect of firm productivity and success, and happy employees and good relations between employers and employees improve job attitudes and benefit firms as a whole (Drydakis, 2015; Ozeren, 2014). LGBT studies provide insights into LGBT discrimination issues and provide solutions to strengthen the centripetal forces of employees.

Whereas previous research has largely focused on a small set of cases or on a particular region or society, future research should analyse a larger range of national contexts, detailing the complexity of legislative diffusion across many sets of nations and pieces of legislation. Another approach would be to conduct a longitudinal, qualitative assessment study of LGBT groups on a global scale.

ETHNICITY, RACE, AND MIGRATION

Concepts of race, ethnicity., and migration continue to be important as we examine and discuss issues of equality. While distinctions of the terms 'race' and 'ethnicity' give rise to much debate, the term 'race' is used to depict differences in phenotype and other characteristics that are often treated as biological differences between groups; while 'ethnicity' refers to differences in cultures, customs, traditions, and belief systems among groups (Helms & Talleyrand, 1997). Although the concept of race has been described as a socially construed phenomenon, the negative and detrimental effects of racial classification and identification are real and enduring (Alexander, 2012; Lopez, 2014). Depending on location and context, race, ethnicity, and migration may be superimposed (for example, the migrant-origin group being in turn minority or majority, oppressor or oppressed), whereas in others, race and/or ethnicity may be disconnected from the notion of migration (as in India, or Nigeria). For example, in parts of Europe minority ethnicity status often coincides with immigrant status, deprived social class status, and religious minority status (mainly Muslim). These challenges are underscored by the migrant crisis that began in 2014, plaguing much of the Middle East and sub-Saharan Africa, which has triggered an unprecedented wave of migration to European countries. Internationally, legal protection for minority ethnic groups is uneven and, when it exists, it is generally directed to natives, or nationals, rather than to migrant groups which have to face legal negative discrimination in most locations of the world.

In the USA, perceptions of racial prejudice and conflict have evolved over recent years (Bell, 2012). While in most instances racism is no longer manifested in overt behavioural actions between individuals, the demonstration of racial bias tends to be manifested in more subtle ways, and yet the consequences continue to be egregious and debilitating

(Essed, 1991; Sue et al., 2007; Reid & Foels, 2010). Racial inequality and discrimination are now expressed in a somewhat formalized 'progressive racial ideology' that negates race as an important concern. For example, in the USA the election of an African American President is suggested by some as evidence that race no longer matters in the decision-making of US citizens (Valentino & Brader, 2011). However, continuing incidents of racial profiling and killings of young African American men and women by the police, the continued charges of racial discrimination in the workplace (US Equal Employment Opportunity Commission, 2015), the stark economic and employment disparities between racial and ethnic groups (Byrd & Mirken, 2011), and the disproportionate sentencing and incarceration across racial lines (Alexander, 2012), are indicative of heightened racial and ethnic tensions. Stark labour market inequalities exist. For example, the 2013 unemployment rate for African American college graduates was 12.4 per cent, compared to 5.6 per cent for all college graduates, and 55.9 per cent of employed African American college graduates were underemployed (Jones & Schmidt, 2014). Compared to the 5.9 per cent overall rate of unemployment in the USA, overall unemployment rates for Hispanics and Latinos, and for African Americans, were 7.9 per cent and 12.4 per cent, respectively (US Bureau of Labor Statistics, 2014).

Immigration reform and large numbers of undocumented immigrants are also current issues in the USA. Based on the 2010 Census, the USA housed more than 40 million immigrants, with California, New York, Texas, Florida, and New Jersey being the top five states for immigrant residence (Camarota, 2012). In 2013 there were reportedly 11 million unauthorized immigrants living in the USA (Wolgin & Aneja, 2013). Court battles have ensued regarding the legality of provisions in state immigrant-related regulations. The highly charged discourse surrounding mechanisms to redress the migration of undocumented immigrants largely from Mexico, and the negative characterization of these immigrants, suggest racial and ethnic undertones (Johnson, 2012). Regarding issues from policing to immigration reform, race and ethnicity continue to be intertwined in economic, social, and political systems. Racial tensions, discrimination, and inequality remain contemporary issues in the USA (Lopez, 2014; Soto et al., 2011). These issues have human resource management implications in terms of organizational policies and practices, ranging from disparate treatment and access to employment, to imposed dress codes (for example, cultural-centric attire and hair styles), and prescribed language usage (for example, English-only rules) in the workplace (Bell, 2012; Brown, 2014; Dowling et al., 2012).

Similar to the USA, other countries are also challenged with social and economic inequalities affecting indigenous, racial and ethnic minority, and immigrant populations. Many European countries are faced with continued inequality, prejudice, and hostility due to strained relationships between immigrants and country citizens (Bisin et al., 2011). For example, France, the UK, and Sweden continue to struggle with allegations of inequitable treatment of persons of Northern African and Muslim backgrounds. Issues of divergent cultural norms and patterns and degree of assimilation appear to be the reasons for racial conflict. Each country has a different perspective on the level of cultural integration desired. France seeks full assimilation, while the UK and Sweden promote multiculturalism that permits a dual existence of cultural norms (Adida et al., 2014). However, political forces in Sweden are reversing the country's liberal acceptance policy for refugees and persons seeking asylum (Shapiro, 2015). In Hungary, the huge upsurge of Syrian immigrants is resulting in the establishment of camps and holding facilities with procedures perceived by some as invoking images of concentration camps (Lyman, 2015), and members of the Jobbik Party are propagating anti-Semitic and anti-immigrant views (Szakacs, 2015). Canada, while perceived as more accommodating to population group differences (Harell et al., 2011), is grappling with inequality in the economic condition of native Inuits (Shah, 2010), discrimination towards aboriginal population groups (Currie et al., 2013), and earnings disparities between European immigrants and immigrants from non-white and non-traditional countries of origin (Bejan, 2012). Research by Currie et al. (2013) indicates Canadian occurrences of racial discrimination towards urban adult aboriginals that include racial insults and taunting. More than half of the aboriginals sampled reported high levels of racism due to their ethnic background.

In the UK the comparison of labour force participation rates of blacks and minority groups to whites reveals stark inequalities. The 2011 Census reports that British whites had unemployment rates between 4 and 6 per cent, while black and most other minority ethnic groups had unemployment rates ranging from 9 to 20 per cent (Nazroo & Kapadia, 2013). Reports on the composition of workers in upper-level executive positions in organizations reveal similar representational disparities. The ratio of whites to non-whites is 88.0 per cent to 12.2 per cent in upper-level positions in the USA (US Equal Employment Opportunity Commission, 2013); ethnic minorities occupied 1 in 16 top-level positions in Great Britain in 2012 (Roland, 2014); and in Canada few visible minorities and aboriginal people are represented at the top management levels compared to their population representation (Jain et al., 2012).

Research demonstrates that both actual events of discrimination and the perception of discrimination have very negative impacts on individuals' psychological and physical well-being (Clark et al., 1999). These negative impacts include anxiety disorders, hypertension, and debilitating stress disorders. Current research streams seek to examine critically the connection between experiences of discrimination and equality on individual and group-level stress and well-being. Racism, prejudice, harassment, and discrimination create powerful stressors that impede personal and professional success for members of targeted groups (Ahmed et al., 2011; Combs & Milosevic, 2015).

Examination of relational forces that can impact upon racial and ethnic discrimination and inequalities in organizational settings include: prejudice reduction through interracial contact (Dixon et al., 2010); stigmatized identities and responses to identity threats (Toyoki & Brown, 2013); and application of implicit bias constructs to reduce bias tendencies. For example, the Dixon et al. (2010) study takes a collective action framework where the research focus is on the target group of discrimination and their perceptions of discrimination and unequal treatment on the part of a specified dominant group. South African blacks were surveyed on their perceptions of perceived in-group discrimination and racial attitudes towards whites based on the frequency and quality of interracial contact. Their findings show that the quality of contact correlates with lower levels of perceived in-group discrimination.

Employment equity is affected by discrimination in selection and workplace interactional spaces. For example, in the USA, black men with equal qualifications to white men were less likely to receive job interviews, and recently incarcerated white men fared much better than black men with no criminal record (Pager et al., 2009). Bisin et al. (2011) examined ethnic identity and employment opportunities for immigrants in Europe with origins from non-European countries. Their study, using data on 85 000 individuals from the European Social Survey, finds that a strong ethnic identity in non-EU immigrants is associated with higher probability of unemployment. The authors suggest discrimination as one of several potential reasons for this finding. Research is also examining immigrant satisfaction with their host country through a broader lens, based not on discrimination but rather on immigrant networks, social embeddedness, size and special segregation of immigrant communities, and characteristics of the country of origin (Safi, 2010).

RELIGIOUS DIVERSITY

Although research on workplace diversity is on the increase, it is largely focused on race, ethnicity, and gender, as a result of affirmative action (AA) and equal opportunity (EO) legislation, with a very limited focus on religious diversity and accommodation in the workplace. The main objective of AA and EO policies, although there is variation between the legislation and implementation within countries, is to promote a 'level playing field' by eliminating discrimination based on individual social group identities such as sex, race, age, or disability (Klarsfeld et al., 2012: 393). In addition, many countries also have a human rights code to prevent discrimination in employment based on several grounds, including religion (Ng et al., 2014). Beyond this, some countries tolerate, encourage, or even legally support religious accommodation in the workplace, which is not to be confused with religious states where the presence of one religion comes at the expense of the others. Striking the right balance between religious rights and secularism is the major challenge faced by most religiously pluralistic societies. It has been widely recognized that diversity influences how people perceive themselves and others, which in turn influences interactions in the workplace. Therefore, HRM professionals have to effectively manage the equality, inclusion, and accommodation needs of a diverse workforce (Tatli & Özbilgin, 2009). Further, there is also the need for contextualizing diversity and its implications to country-specific contexts (Klarsfeld, 2010; Klarsfeld et al., 2012, 2014) at the macro, meso, and micro levels (Syed & Ozbilgin, 2009).

The PEW Research Center (PEW, 2012) documents the percentage of the world population following the eight major religions of the world: Christianity, Islam, Hinduism, Buddhism, Folk religions (including African traditional religions, Chinese folk religions, Native American religions, and Australian Aboriginal religions), Jewish, Unaffiliated (including atheists, agnostics, or those who believe in nothing in particular), and Other (Baha'i, Jainism, Sikhism, Shinto, Taoism, Tenrikyo, Wicca, Zoroastrianism, among others); based on country data from 2500 national censuses, surveys, and population registers in more than 200 countries and territories. Notably, some of the faiths consolidated into the Folk religions and Other religions categories have millions of adherents across the world, but are not specifically measured in censuses, surveys, or other population registers.

PEW (2014) developed a Religious Diversity Index (RDI) on a ten-point scale based on the percentage of each country's population belonging to each of the eight religious groups. Findings show that the Asia-Pacific region has 'very high' religious diversity (RDI = 9.2); sub-Saharan Africa is ranked as 'high' (RDI = 5.8); Europe is ranked as 'moderate' (RDI = 4.6); followed by North America (RDI = 4.2). Latin America–Caribbean (RDI = 2.1) and the Middle East–North Africa (RDI = 1.5) are both ranked as 'low' religious diversity regions (PEW, 2014).

Interestingly, most of the religious diversity research comes from the 'moderate' RDI score regions, such as North America and Europe. However, the low religious diversity regions such as Latin America and the Middle East can be deceptive, since the differences between the various denominations within Christianity and Islam have not been further identified (PEW, 2014). Among the 232 countries and territories in this study, Singapore scored the highest at 9.0 points on the ten-point RDI, with Buddhists (34 per cent), Christians (18 per cent), Unaffiliated (16 per cent), Muslims (14 per cent), Hindus (5 per cent), Other (10 per cent), Folk religionists (2 per cent), and Jews (less than 1 per cent) (PEW, 2014).

Religious accommodation best practices come from some of the most religiously diverse countries. The religious accommodation in the workplace in North American and European countries is predominantly related to compliance with the legal requirements, particularly for Muslim employees in the USA (Mujtaba & Cavico, 2015; Middlemiss, 2015) and in Europe where the *hijab* is banned or poorly accepted, although there are also cases in Canada for other religious accommodation, such as for the Sikh turban and *kirpan*, and the Jewish *kippa* (Haq, 2015; Saint-Onge, 2015). For example, in the USA in 2015, at the end of a seven-year-long, much publicized discrimination case, Abercrombie & Fitch had to pay US$44653 to Samantha Elauf, a Muslim applicant who was denied a job because of her *hijab*, which violated their strict 'look-policy'. The Supreme Court ruled that 'the popular retail chain was legally obliged to offer accommodation to employees who wear headscarves for religious reasons – even if it is implied, rather than overtly expressed. "An employer may not make an applicant's religious practice, confirmed or otherwise, a factor in employment decisions" Justice Antonin Scalia said' (Middlemiss, 2015).

In most Asia-Pacific countries, religion is a fundamental necessity in people's day-to-day lives. Therefore, religious accommodation in the workplace is an essential everyday necessity. And while there is not much evidence in terms of formal policies or academic research on managing religious accommodation, there is a long tradition of sensitivity to religious freedom, observance, expression, and accommodation in the workplace that is widely practiced and universally expected in these countries. For example, in India, Malaysia, Indonesia, and the Philippines, it is commonplace to see religious accommodation in three key areas: respectful display of religious symbols and dress code; time off for prayers, rituals, and holidays; and sensitivity to dietary restrictions based on religious beliefs.

In India, religious displays are commonplace in decorating one's office space with idols or images of Hindu gods and goddesses. Dress symbols include Sikhs wearing turbans, married Hindu women wearing a *sindoor* (red dot or vermilion on the forehead) and *mangalsutra* (black and gold beaded necklace) as a sign of marriage, and modest dressing for women. There is also accommodation for Muslims, with prayer rooms for following their prayer schedules in the afternoon and Friday prayers, as well as flexible workweeks during the fasting month of Ramadan, and paid holidays for all major religions. Finally, religion-based food choices are respected in cafeterias by offering no beef or strictly vegetarian food for Hindus, and no pork and *halal* meat for Muslims (Sharma & Pardasani, 2015: 227).

Being a secular democratic republic, the Indian constitution specifies that every religion will be treated with equal respect. It is worth noting that different countries define secularism differently. For example, while the French concept of secularism (*laïcité*) implies a complete separation of religion (which is considered a personal and individual choice) from public spheres of activity (including work and education), the Indian idea of secularism does not demand a separation of religion from public life. (Patel, 2010: 286)

Malaysia's five major religions are Islam (60.4 per cent), Buddhism (19.2 per cent), Christianity (9.1 per cent), Hinduism (6.3 per cent), and Confucionism, Taoism and other traditional Chinese religions (2.6 per cent). Although Islam is the official religion, the Federal Constitution allows for religious freedom and the government allocates funds to provide places of religious worship such as mosques, churches, and Chinese and Indian temples (Abdullah, 2010: 15). 'In the context of Malaysian business and commerce, the government's role in its structural and operational approach of Islam Hadari substantially affects the way MNCs [multinational corporations] and government-linked corporations (GLCs) operate their businesses, such as promoting Islamic banking services and developing Halal foods hubs' (Abdullah, 2010: 19).

In Indonesia, there are six legally acknowledged religions: Islam, Christianity – Catholic, Christianity – Protestant, Hindu, Buddhism, and Kong Hu Cu (Confucianism):

> Under Indonesian Labour Law . . . the employer must provide enough time for their employees to do compulsory religious rituals without any pay reduction . . . Religious holidays in Indonesia that are acknowledged and receive an allowance are Eid al-Fitr for Muslims, Christmas for Christians, Nyepi for Hindus, Waisak (Vesak) for Buddhists and Imlek for Kong Hu Cu . . . In practice, the allowance [one month salary] is given once a year close to Eid al-Fitr to all eligible employees regardless of their religion. (Afrianty et al., 2015: 260–261)

In a study of 111 Philippines organizations it was found that, in general, no explicit policies on religious expression exist, but nonetheless the following are practiced in most organizations surveyed:

> decoration of office space for holidays, display of religious materials in the work area, time off for religious observances, consideration of different religions in planning holiday-related activities, consideration of religious needs . . . when providing food/meals, allowing religious practices in the workplace (prayers, meditations and so on), and wearing of religious messages on clothing (crucifix necklace, pro-life button and so on). (Supangco, 2015: 245)

Religious accommodation is an important current issue not only in North America and Europe but across the globe, and will foreseeably become increasingly important as the present Middle East refugee crisis results in more and more primarily Muslim refugees entering various countries and their workplaces. Given that religious fundamentalism and intolerance is on the rise in an increasingly globalized world, it is imperative that inter-religious and interfaith understanding, dialogue, and interaction is promoted for managing diversity in organizations, societies, and the world. Since management coverage and research in this area is presently rather limited, this section of the chapter has sought to contribute to that growing conversation.

CONCLUSIONS

We conclude this chapter by using the information above, the work reported in Klarsfeld (2010), Klarsfeld et al. (2014), and the typology provided by Klarsfeld et al. (2012), to summarize the extent of protection provided for gender; sexual orientation; race, ethnicity and migration; and religion in a sample of different countries (see Table 16.1). One of the major takeaways from this work is the disparity that exists regarding legal protection between and within the various diversity strands. After a period of progression tied to

Table 16.1 *Degree of 'positiveness' of legislation regarding four diversity strands, with country examples*

	Gender	LGBT	Race/ethnicity/ migration	Religion
Negative discrimination laws	e.g., Saudi Arabia	e.g., Most of the Middle East and Africa, and much of South-East Asia (e.g., Singapore)	e.g., Myanmar, Malaysia for some groups (such as Rohingya, Chinese, respectively)	e.g., religious-grounded states have provisions that hamper minority religions
Restricted equality of rights (no reporting or visibility is possible)		e.g., France and most of the EU, where statistics on sexual orientation are not allowed except for research purposes and under state scrutiny	e.g., France and most of the EU, where statistics on origin are not allowed except for research purposes and under state scrutiny	e.g., restricted secularism such as France and most of the EU, where religious expression is taboo
Equality of rights possibly encouraged by non-governmental organizations		Canada, the USA, the UK, where sexual identity may be collected on an anonymous basis	e.g., the Netherlands, where the habit remained to collect data even after the law that made it compulsory was repealed; India (public sector)	e.g., the USA, where religious freedom and visibility is foundational
Encouraged voluntarism	e.g., the UK, where private firms are encouraged (but not obliged) to define equality plans modelled on the public sector		e.g., the UK, where private firms are encouraged (but not obliged) to define equality plans modelled on the public sector; in the USA, private sector	e.g., India, the Philippines, where religious accommodation is culturally encouraged

Table 16.1   (continued)

	Gender	LGBT	Race/ethnicity/ migration	Religion
			organizations develop diversity and affirmative action plans on a voluntary basis	
Constrained process	e.g., gender equality plans in Australia and France; Canada, the USA, South Africa; public sector equality duties in the UK; 'comply or explain' board legislation in 15 countries		e.g., South Africa; the UK (public sector); Canada and the USA, for federal contractors and the public sector: in the USA, private and public sector organizations are required under Title VII of the Civil Rights Act to follow Equal Employment Opportunity practices	e.g., Canada, where religious accommodation is a legal duty; Indonesia, but only for the six officially recognized religions
Constrained outcome (positive discrimination)	e.g., gender quotas in boards (as introduced in 11 countries)		e.g., India and Malaysia, for specific targeted groups such as the Dalit, other backward classes and native Malays	

Source: Based on Klarsfeld et al. (2012: 401).

the fall in much of the negative discrimination of a legal nature encountered by women in most OECD countries starting in the 1970s, the persistence of glass ceilings and doors, of sticky floors and motherhood penalties, remains a puzzle and a challenge for the future, even in the most 'advanced' countries in the field of gender equality, not to mention obstacles faced by women in those least advanced.

Progress in rights for LGBT populations has perhaps seen the fastest growth over the last decade due to the legalization of same-sex marriage in an increasing number of countries. However, considerable challenges to equality remain for sexual orientation, particularly in parts of Asia and most of the Middle East, where homosexuality is considered a criminal offence. The pervasive persistence of economic and employment disparities continues to contribute to the complexity of inequality based on race and ethnicity for many countries across the globe. The determination of viable solutions to such problems continues to be slow. Migration waves have always been an opportunity and a challenge, but all the more so as sluggish economies and the vanishing of low-end jobs make competition with the resident population more salient. Finally, the generalization of multi-religious societies in relation to mass migrations should encourage leaders in most countries affected to seek best-practice examples in places where religious coexistence has been a lived reality for centuries, albeit a difficult one at times, in particular in South-East Asia.

REFERENCES

Abdullah, Z. 2010. Cultural diversity management in Malaysia: A perspective of communication management. In J. Syed and M. Ozbilgin (eds), *Managing Cultural Diversity in Asia: A Research Companion*: 14–38. Cheltenham, UK and Northampton, MA, USA: Edward Elgar Publishing.

Addati, L., Cassirer, N., & Gilchrist, K. 2014. *Maternity and Paternity at Work: Law and Practice across the World*. Geneva: International Labour Office.

Adida, C.L., Laitin, D.D., & Valfort, M.-A. 2014. Muslims in France: Identifying a discriminatory equilibrium. *Journal of Population Economics*, 27(4): 1039–1086.

Afrianty, T.W., Issa, T., & Burgess, J. 2015. Work-based religiosity support in Indonesia. In S. Gröschl and R. Bendl (eds), *Managing Religious Diversity at the Workplace: Lessons from Around the World*: 253–280. Farnham: Gower Applied Research.

Ahmed, S.R., Kia-Keating, M., & Tsai, K.H. 2011. A structural model of racial discrimination, acculturative stress, and cultural resources among Arab American adolescents. *American Journal of Community Psychology*, 48(3/4): 181–192.

Albrecht, J., Björklund, A., & Vroman, S. 2003. Is there a glass ceiling in Sweden?. *Journal of Labor Economics*, 21(1): 145–177.

Alexander, M. 2012. *The New Jim Crow: Mass Incarceration in the Age of Colorblindness*. New York: New Press.

Amer, S. 2012. Naming to empower: Lesbianism in the Arab Islamicate world today. *Journal of Lesbian Studies*, 16(4): 381–397.

Angert, S., & Parakkal, R. 2014. Branding LGBT rights in South Africa. Contemporary Perspectives. Retrieved from http://www2.philau.edu/collegestudies/Documents/Sara%20Angert.pdf.

Arulampalam, W., Booth, A.L., & Bryan, M.L. 2007. Is there a glass ceiling over Europe? Exploring the gender pay gap across the wage distribution. *Industrial and Labor Relations Review*, 60: 163–186.

Avellar, S., & Smock, P.J. 2003. Has the price of motherhood declined over time? A cross-cohort comparison of the motherhood wage penalty. *Journal of Marriage and Family*, 65(3): 597–607.

Baert, S., Cockx, B., Gheyle, N., & Vandamme, C. 2015. Is there less discrimination in occupations where recruitment is difficult?. *Industrial and Labor Relations Review*, 68(3): 467–500.

Baker, J.G. 2003. Glass ceilings or sticky floors? A model of high-income law graduates. *Journal of Labor Research*, 24: 695–711.

Barbulescu, R., & Bidwell, M. 2013 Do women choose different jobs from men? Mechanisms of application segregation in the market for managerial workers. *Organization Science*, 24(3): 737–756.

Barrientos, J., Silva, J., Catalan, S., Gomez, F., & Longueira, J. 2010. Discrimination and victimization: Parade for lesbian, gay, bisexual, and transgender (LGBT) pride, in Chile. *Journal of Homosexuality*, 57(6): 760–775.

Bejan, R. 2012. Smoke and mirrors: How an allegedly inclusionary strategy perpetuates an exclusionary discourse. *Canadian Ethnic Studies*, 43(3): 165–181.

Bell, M.P. 2012. *Diversity in Organizations*. Mason, OH: Thomson Southwestern.

Bertrand, S.E., Black, S.E., Jensen, S., & Lleras-Muney, A. 2014. Breaking the glass ceiling? The effect of board quotas on female labor market outcomes. IZA No. 8266, June. Norway.

Bisin, A., Patacchini, E., Verdier, T., & Zenou, Y. 2011. Ethnic identity and labour market outcomes of immigrants in Europe. *Economic Policy*, 26(65): 57–92.

Booth, A. 2007. The glass ceiling in Europe: Why are women doing badly in the labour market?. *Swedish Economic Policy Review*, 14: 121–144.

Booysen, L., & Wishik, H. 2016 A comparison of lesbian, gay, bisexual, transgender and queer rights and politics in South Africa and the USA. In A. Klarsfeld, E. Ng, L. Booysen, et al. (eds), *International and Comparative Perspectives on Equality, Diversity and Inclusion*: 171–198. Cheltenham, UK and Northampton, MA, USA: Edward Elgar Publishing.

Brown, K.R. 2014. Addressing dressing for success. *Workforce*, 93(8): 22–23.

Byrd, D., & Mirken, B. 2011. *Post Racial? Americans and Race in the Age of Obama*. Berkeley, CA: Greenlining Institute.

Camarota, S.A. 2012. Immigrants in the United States, 2010: A profile of America's foreign-born population. Center for Immigration Studies. Retrieved from http://cis.org/2012-profile-of-americas-foreign-born-population (ed.).

Capelli, P., & Hamori, M. 2004. The path to the top: Changes in the attributes and careers of corporate executives, 1980–2001. NBER Working Paper No. 10507, March.

Catalyst. 2013. *Quick Take: Women on Boards*. New York: Catalyst.

Chamberlain, A. 2015. Why is hiring taking longer? New insights from Glassdoor data. Glassdoor Research Report, June. https://research-content.glassdoor.com/app/uploads/sites/2/2015/06/GD_Report_3.pdf.

Christofides, L., Polycarpou, A., & Vrachimis, K. 2013. Gender wage gaps, 'sticky floors' and 'glass ceilings' in Europe. *Labour Economics*, 21: 86–102.

Clark, R., Anderson, N.B., Clark, V.R., & Williams, D.R. 1999. Racism as a stressor for African Americans: A biopsychosocial model. *American Psychologist*, 54(10): 805.

Combs, G.M., & Milosevic, I. 2015. Workplace discrimination and the wellbeing of minority women: Overview, prospects, and implications. In M. Connerley, and J. Wu (eds), *Handbook on the Wellbeing of Working Women*: 17–31. Quality of Work–Life Research Series. New York: Springer.

Cotter, D.A., Hermsen, J.M., & Vanneman, R. 2004. *Gender Inequality at Work*. New York: Russell Sage Foundation.

Cox, J., & Blake, S. 1991. Managing cultural diversity: Implications for organisational competitiveness. *Academy of Management Executive*, 5(3): 45–56.

Cox, T. 1994. *Cultural Diversity in Organizations: Theory, Research, and Practice*. San Francisco, CA: Berrett-Koehler.

Currie, C.L., Wild, T.C., Schopflocher, D.P., et al. 2013. Racial discrimination, post traumatic stress, and gambling problems among urban Aboriginal adults in Canada. *Journal of Gambling Studies*, 29(3): 393–341.

Davies-Netzley, S.A. 1998. Women above the glass ceiling: Perceptions on corporate mobility and strategies for success. *Gender and Society*, 12(3): 340.

Dinovitzer, R., Reichman, N., & Sterling, J. 2009. The differential valuation of women's work: A new look at the gender gap in lawyers' incomes. *Social Forces*, 88(2): 819–864.

Dixon, J., Durrheim, K., Tredoux, C., et al. 2010. A paradox of integration? Interracial contact, prejudice reduction, and perceptions of racial discrimination. *Journal of Social Issues*, 66(2): 401–416.

Dowling, J.A., Ellison, C.G., & Leal, D.L. 2012. Who doesn't value English? Debunking myths about Mexican immigrants' attitudes toward the English language. *Social Science Quarterly*, 93(2): 356–378.

Drydakis, N. 2015. Sexual orientation discrimination in the United Kingdom's labour market: A field experiment. *Human Relations*, 66(11): 1769–1796.

Duehr, E.E., & Bono, J.E. 2006. Men, women, and managers: Are stereotypes finally changing?. *Personnel Psychology*, 59: 815–846.

The Economist. 2011a. Still lonely at the top. 21 July.

The Economist. 2011b. The wrong way to promote women. 21 July.

The Economist. 2015. The glass ceiling index. http://www.economist.com/blogs/graphicdetail/2015/03/daily-chart-1, accessed 18 February 2016.

Eliason, M.J., Dibble, S.L., & Robertson, P.A. 2011. Lesbian, gay, bisexual, and transgender (LGBT) physicians' experiences in the workplace. *Journal of Homosexuality*, 58(10): 1355–1371.

Essed, P. 1991. *Understanding Everyday Racism: An Interdisciplinary Theory*. Newbury, CA: SAGE.

European Commission. 2012. Women in economic decision-making in the EU: Progress report. A Europe 2020 initiative.

Fang, Z., & Sakellariou, C. 2011. A case of sticky floors: gender wage differentials in Thailand. *Asian Economic Journal*, 25(1): 35–54.

Filippin, A., & Ichino, A. 2005. Gender wage gap in expectations and realizations. *Labour Economics*, 12(1): 125–145.

Floro, M., & Moeurs, M. 2009. *Global Trends in Women's Access to 'Decent Work'*. Geneva: ILO.

Goodman, J.S., Fields, D.L., & Blum, T.C. 2003. Cracks in the glass ceiling: In what kinds of organizations do women make it to the top?. *Group and Organization Management*, 28(4): 475–501.

Gradin, C., & del Rio, C. 2009. Gender wage differentials in Spain: A distributional approach by subpopulations. *Hacienda Pública Española*, 189: 9–46.

Haq, R. 2015. Accommodating religious diversity in the Canadian workplace: The hijab predicament in Quebec & Ontario. In S. Gröschl, & R. Bendl (eds), *Managing Religious Diversity in the Workplace: Examples from Around the World*: 31–52. Farnham: Gower Applied Research.

Harell, A., Soroka, S.N., & Iyengar, S. 2011. Attitudes toward immigration and immigrants: The impact of economic and cultural cues in the US and Canada. APSA 2011 Annual Meeting Paper.

Harkness, S., & Waldfogel, J. 2003. The family gap in pay: Evidence from seven industrialised countries. *Research in Labor Economics*, 22: 369–414.

Helfat, C., Dawn, H., & Wolfson, P. 2006. The pipeline to the top: Women and men in the top executive ranks of US corporations. *Academy of Management Perspectives*, 20(4): 42–64.

Helfer, L.R., & Voeten, E. 2014. International courts as agents of legal change: Evidence from LGBT rights in Europe. *International Organization*, 68(1): 77–110.

Helms, J.E., & Talleyrand, R.M. 1997. Race is not ethnicity. *Anerican Psychologist*, 52(11): 1246–1247.

Henrekson, M., & Stenkula, M. 2009. Why are there so few female top executives in egalitarian welfare states?. *Independent Review*, 14(2): 239–270.

Hensvik, L.E. 2014. Manager impartiality: Worker–firm matching and the gender wage gap. *Industrial and Labor Relations Review*, 67(2): 395–421.

Hesse-Biber, S.N., & Carter, G.L. 2005. *Working women in America: Split Dreams*. New York: Oxford University Press.

Hillman, A.J., Shropshire, C., & Cannella, A.A. 2007. Organizational predictors of women on corporate boards. *Academy of Management Journal*, 50(4): 941–952.

Hoobler, J.M., Wayne, S.J., & Lemmon, G. 2009. Bosses' perceptions of family–work conflict and women's promotability: Glass ceiling effects. *Academy of Management Journal*, 52(5): 939–957.

Huffman, M.L., Cohen, P.N., & Pearlman, J. 2008. Management matters? Female managers and workplace segregation, 1975–2005. Unpublished manuscript. University of North Carolina, Chapel Hill and University of California, Irvine.

Jain, H.C., Horwitz, F., & Wilkin, C.L. 2012. Employment equity in Canada and South Africa: A comparative review. *International Journal of Human Resource Management*, 23(1): 1–17.

Johnson, K.R. 2012. Immigration and civil rights: State and local efforts to regulate immigration. University of California Davis Legal Studies Research Paper No. 293. Available at SSRN: https://ssrn.com/abstract=2046328.

Johnston, D.W., & Lee, W.S. 2012. Climbing the job ladder: New evidence of gender inequity. *Industrial Relations: A Journal of Economy and Society*, 51(1): 129–151.

Jones, J., & Schmidt, J. 2014. A college degree is not a guarantee. Retrieved from http://www.cepr.net/documents/black-coll-grads-2014-05.pdf (accessed 28 November 2014).

Kalleberg, A.L. 2008. The mismatched worker: When people don't fit their jobs. *Academy of Management Perspectives*, 22(1): 24–40.

Klarsfeld, A. 2010. *International Handbook on Diversity Management at Work: Country Perspectives on Diversity and Equal Treatment*. Cheltenham, UK and Northampton, MA, USA: Edward Elgar Publishing.

Klarsfeld, A., Booysen, L., Ng, E., Roper, I., & Tatli, A. 2014. *International Handbook on Diversity Management at Work: Country Perspectives on Diversity and Equal Treatment* (2nd edn). Cheltenham, UK and Northampton, MA, USA: Edward Elgar Publishing.

Klarsfeld, A., Combs, G.M., Susaeta, L., & Belizon, M. 2012. International perspectives on diversity and equal treatment policies and practices. In C. Brewster and W. Mayrhofer (eds), *Handbook of Research on Comparative Human Resource Management*: 393–415. Cheltenham, UK and Northampton, MA, USA: Edward Elgar Publishing.

Lommerud, J.E., Straume, O.R., & Vagstad, S. 2015. Mommy tracks and public policy: On self-fulfilling prophecies and gender gaps in hiring and promotion. *Journal of Economic Behavior and Organization*, 116: 540–554.

Lopez, I. 2014. *Dog Whistle Politics: How Coded Racial Appeals have Reinvented Racism and Wrecked the Middle Class*. Oxford: Oxford University Press.

Lyman, R. 2015. Treatment of migrants evokes memories of Europe's darkest hour. *New York Times*, 4

September. Retrieved from http://www.nytimes.com/2015/09/05/world/treatment-of-migrants-evokes-memo ries-of-europes-darkest-hour.html.

Lyness, K.S., & Thompson, D.E. 2000. Climbing the corporate ladder: Do female and male executives follow the same route?. *Journal of Applied Psychology*, 85(1): 86–101.

Massad, J.A. 2002. Re-orienting desire: The gay international and the Arab world. *Public Culture*, 14(2): 361–385.

Metz, I. 2005. Advancing the careers of women with children. *Career Development International*, 10(3): 228–245.

Meyer, E.J. 2010. Teachers, sexual orientation, and the law in Canada: A human rights perspective. *Clearing House*, 83(3): 89–95.

Meyerson, D.E., & Fletcher, J.K. 2000. A modest manifesto for shattering the glass ceiling. *Harvard Business Review*, 78(1): 126–136.

Middlemiss, N. 2015. Abercrombie's 7-year headscarf saga finally ends. HRM-ONLINE, 24 July. Retrieved 15 August from http://www.hrmonline.ca/hr-news/abercrombies-7year-headscarf-saga-finally-ends-193552. aspx.

Misra, J., Budig, M., & Moller, S. 2005. Employment, wages, and poverty: Reconciliation policies and gender equity. Paper presented at the annual meeting of the American Sociological Association, Philadelphia, August.

Mujtaba, B.G., & Cavico, F.J. 2015. Islam in American organizations: Legal analysis and recommendations. In S. Gröschl, and R. Bendl (eds), *Managing Religious Diversity at the Workplace: Lessons from Around the World*: 73–112. Farnham: Gower Applied Research.

Nakamura, N., & Pope, M. 2013. Borders and margins: Giving voice to lesbian, gay, bisexual, and transgender immigrant experiences. *Journal of LGBT Issues in Counseling*, 7(2): 122–124.

Nazroo, J.Y., & Kapadia, D. 2013. Have ethnic inequalities in employment persisted between 1991 and 2011?. ESRC Centre on Dynamics of Ethnicity, University of Manchester for Joseph Rowntree Foundation.

Nelson, T.A., Callison, K., & Thomas, A. 2016. A comparative study of five countries with critical mass and its ambiguous impact on HRM policies. In A. Klarsfeld, E. Ng, L. Booysen, et al. (eds), *International and Comparative Perspectives on Equality, Diversity and Inclusion*: 249–302. Cheltenham, UK and Northampton, MA, USA: Edward Elgar Publishing.

Ng, E., Haq, R., & Tremblay, D.G. 2014. Twenty-one years of employment equity in Canada (1987–2008): A review. In A. Klarsfeld, L. Booysen, E. Ng, et al. (eds), *International Handbook on Diversity Management at Work: Country Perspectives on Diversity and Equal Treatment* (2nd edn): 46–67. Cheltenham, UK and Northampton, MA, USA: Edward Elgar Publishing.

Ozeren, E. 2014. Sexual orientation discrimination in the workplace: A systematic review of literature. *Procedia-Social and Behavioral Sciences*, 109: 1203–1215.

Ozturk, M.B. 2011. Sexual orientation discrimination: Exploring the experiences of lesbian, gay and bisexual employees in Turkey. *Human Relations*, 64(8): 1099–1118.

Pager, D., Western, B., & Bonikowski, B. 2009. Discrimination in a low-wage labor market: A field experiment. *American Sociological Review*, 74(5): 777–799.

Pande, R., & Ford, D. 2011. Gender quotas and female leadership: A review. Background paper for the World Development Report. Retrieved 22 August from http://scholar.harvard.edu/rpande/publications/gender-quotas-and-female-leadership-review.

Patel, T. 2010. Confronting discrimination through affirmative action in India: Playing the right music with the wrong instrument. In J. Syed and M. Ozbilgin (eds), *Managing Cultural Diversity in Asia: A Research Companion*: 278–306. Cheltenham, UK and Northampton, MA, USA: Edward Elgar Publishing.

Pendakur, K., & Woodcock, S. 2010. Glass ceilings or glass doors? Wage disparity within and between firms. *Journal of Business and Economic Statistics*, 28(1): 181–189.

PEW. 2012. Global Religious Landscape Report. Retrieved 20 August 2015 from http://www.pewforum.org/2014/04/04/global-religious-diversity/.

PEW. 2014. Global Religious Diversity Report. 4 April. Retrieved on 20 August 2015 from http://www.pewforum.org/2014/04/04/global-religious-diversity/.

Priola, V., Lasio, D., De Simone, S., & Serri, F. 2014. The sound of silence: Lesbian, gay, bisexual and transgender discrimination in 'inclusive organizations'. *British Journal of Management*, 25(3): 488–502.

Reid, L.D., & Foels, R. 2010. Cognitive complexity and the perception of subtle racism. *Basic and Applied Social Psychology*, 32(4): 291–301.

Roland, D. 2014. Britain at a point of no return in ethnic equality. *Telegraph*. Retrieved from http://www.telegraph.co.uk/finance/economics/10903754/Britain-at-point-of-no-return-for-ethnic-equality.html.

Safi, M. 2010. Immigrants' life satisfaction in Europe: Between assimilation and discrimination. *European Sociological Review*, 26(2): 159–176.

Saint-Onge, S. 2015. Accommodations in religious matters: Quebec and Canadian perspectives. In S. Gröschl and R. Bendl (eds), *Managing Religious Diversity at the Workplace: Lessons from Around the World*: 9–30. Farnham: Gower Applied Research.

Comparative perspectives on diversity and equality 321

Shah, A. 2010. Racism. *Global Issues*. Retrieved from http://www.globalissues.org/article/165/racism.
Shapiro, A. 2015. Sweden's immigrant influx unleashes a backlash. Parallels NPR. Retrieved from http:// www. npr.org.
Sharma, R.R., & Pardasani, R. 2015. Management of religious diversity by organizations in India. In S. Gröschl, and R. Bendl (eds), *Managing Religious Diversity at the Workplace: Lessons from Around the World*: 223–238. Farnham: Gower Applied Research.
Smith, M. 2010. Analysis note: The gender pay gap in the EU – What policy responses? Grenoble Ecole de Management (France). EGGE – European Network of Experts on Employment and Gender Equality issues – Fondazione Giacomo Brodolini. .
Soto, J.A., Dawson-Andoh, N.A., & BeLue, R. 2011. The relationship between perceived discrimination and generalized anxiety disorder among African Americans, Afro Caribbeans, and non-Hispanic Whites. *Journal of Anxiety Disorders*, 25(2): 258–265.
Sue, D.W., Capodilupo, C.M., Torino, G.C., et al. 2007. Racial microaggressions in everyday life: Implications for clinical practice. *American Psychologist*, 62(4): 271.
Supangco, V.T. 2015. Managing workplace diversity of religious expressions in the Philippines. In S. Gröschl and R. Bendl (eds), *Managing Religious Diversity at the Workplace: Lessons from Around the World*: 239–252. Farnham: Gower Applied Research.
Syed, J., & Ozbilgin, M.F. 2009. A relational framework for international transfer of diversity management practices. *International Journal of Human Resource Management*, 20(12): 2435–2453.
Szakacs, G. 2015. Far-right Jobbik party hurting Hungary's image: Jewish leader. Reuters. Retrieved from http:// www.reuters.com/article/2015/04/12/us-hungary-rally-idUSKBN0N30TZ20150412.
Tatli, A., & Özbilgin, M.F. 2009. Understanding diversity managers' role in organizational change: Towards a conceptual framework. *Canadian Journal of Administrative Sciences/Revue Canadienne des Sciences de l'Administration*, 26(3): 244–258.
Terjesen, S., Aguilera, R.V., & Lorenz, R. 2015. Legislating a woman's seat on the board: Institutional factors driving gender quotas for boards of directors. *Journal of Business Ethics*, 128(2): 233–251.
Torchia, M., Calabrò, A., & Huse, M. 2011. Women directors on corporate boards: From tokenism to critical mass. *Journal of Business Ethics*, 102(2): 299–317.
Toyoki, S., & Brown, A.D. 2013. Stigma, identity and power: Managing stigmatized identities through discourse. *Human Relations*, 67(6): 715–737.
United Nations Development Programme. 2016. Gender Inequality Index. http://hdr.undp.org/fr/composite/GII, accessed 11 February 2016.
US Bureau of Labor Statistics. 2014. Employment situation summary. Available at http://www.bls.gov/news.release/empsit.nr0.htm.
US Equal Employment Opportunity Commission. 2013. 2013 Job patterns for minorities and women in private industry (EEO-1). Retrieved from http://www1.eeoc.gov/eeoc/statistics/employment/jobpat-eeo1/2013/index.cfm#select_label.
US Equal Employment Opportunity Commission. 2015. Charge statistics FY 1997 through FY 2014. Retrieved From http://www.eeoc.gov/eeoc/statistics/enforcement/charges.cfm.
Valentino, N.A., & Brader, T. 2011. The sword's other edge perceptions of discrimination and racial policy opinion after Obama. *Public Opinion Quarterly*, 75(2): 201–226.
Van Emmerik, I.H., Euwema, M.C., Geschiere, M., & Schouten, M. 2006. Networking your way through the organization: gender differences in the relationship between network participation and career satisfaction. *Women in Management Review*, 21(1): 54–66.
Wolgin, P., & Aneja, A. 2013. Top reasons why immigration reform in 2013 is different than in 1986. Center for American Progress. Retrieved from http://www.americanprogress.org.

17. Organising HRM in a comparative perspective
Julia Brandl, Anna Bos-Nehles, and Ina Aust

INTRODUCTION

This chapter presents a state-of the art review of research on cross-national variation in organising human resource management (HRM) work. We suggest that practical efforts for organising HRM are based on three alternative models. We familiarise readers with how scholars have researched cross-national differences in using these models, identifying major theoretical traditions that have guided research on organising HRM work, their core concepts and research outcomes. Based on the inclusion of more recent empirical studies the updated chapter includes a new section on research in the tradition of new institutional theory and a revision of key issues and research directions.

A core characteristic of HRM work is that it cannot be fully allocated to one particular actor or unit within the organisation. Instead, HRM work involves HRM specialists, line and top management, is sometimes delegated to employees ('self-services'), performed by works councillors, or outsourced to external service providers. Organising HRM work addresses the task of assigning HRM tasks and authority to different units and enabling these units to coordinate their work with each other. The variation of roles of HRM departments across organisational settings (Brandl & Pohler, 2010; Farndale et al., 2009, 2010), the debate over devolution of HRM tasks from specialists to the line (Brandl et al., 2009; Brewster et al., 2013; Nehles et al., 2006) and beyond (Bredin & Söderlund, 2011; Keegan et al., 2012; Mol et al., 2014; Swart & Kinnie, 2014), and the heterogeneous beliefs about the appropriate ways of organising HRM (Budhwar & Sparrow, 2002; Pernkopf-Konhaeusner & Brandl, 2010), indicate that there is no one best way for assigning HRM tasks and responsibilities. But what are the possible alternatives for organising HRM work? And why do organisations employ a particular form of organisation?

In this chapter, we review how HRM scholars have explained differences and similarities in the prevalence of alternative forms of organising HRM from a cross-national perspective. Our focus on the national context builds on the premise that organisations are open systems that need to relate their structural elements to their environments in order to survive. While contextual influences relevant for organising HRM work can be found at various levels (for example, industry, organisational), the national context seems particularly relevant: first, national government initiatives such as labour legislation and regulation of labour markets have historically played a significant role in the rise of HRM departments and their relations with line managers (Baron et al., 1986; Jacoby, 2003); second, cross-national research is helpful to analyse – rather than just claim – whether national context plays a role for organising HRM, and how.

We outline three models for organising HRM work that we contrast along several core dimensions. Building on this framework, we review how five major theoretical perspectives (contingency, culture, comparative institutional, new institutional, paradox) have informed empirical research on organising HRM work cross-nationally. Finally, we discuss limitations in current analyses and how we can advance research on HRM organisation across national boundaries. When we updated the literature for the second edition of this book, we were delighted to see the increase in research on organising HRM across national settings. We found that the three basic models of organising HRM that we proposed in the first edition – that is, the classic, the neo-classic and the modern HRM organisation – continue to capture recently researched forms of organising HRM (for example, project-based organisations, multiple-employer networks). To reflect the increasing attention to institutional approaches in HRM, we now distinguish between comparative and new institutional perspectives for studying organising HRM. After reading the chapter, one should have gained an overview of major alternatives to organising HRM, and be able to acknowledge the key arguments of major theoretical perspectives, and understand their usefulness and potential in explaining cross-national differences and similarities in organising HRM work.

MODELS FOR ORGANISING HRM WORK

We differentiate three major forms for organising HRM work that we see as generic alternatives. Following Whitley's (1999) concept of work systems, we see options for organising HRM work as internally consistent alternatives for organising HRM that can be differentiated along six characteristics covering how work processes are organised and controlled, how workplace relations among actors are shaped, and what employment policies apply. Depending on the particular configuration of these characteristics, we refer to classic, neo-classic, and modern[1] ways of organising HRM work (see Table 17.1).

Table 17.1   Basic alternatives for organising HRM work

Work systems characteristics	Classic	HRM work type Neo-classic	Modern
Task fragmentation (specialisation)	High	Low	Low
HRM strategy integration and devolution	Low	high	Limited to high
Control of HRM work	High	Some	Some
Separation of HRM specialists from line managers	High	Low	Low to high
Employer commitment to in-house HRM practice	Low	Considerable	Limited
Rewards for engaging with HRM activities tied to . . .	Standardised jobs/ roles	Skills, individual performance	Skills, personal evaluation, and individual performance

Source: Adapted and extended from Whitley (1999).

[1]   The meaning of 'modern' is not 'more recent' or 'better' but it is used as an alternative to imply a systems development perspective.

Classic HRM Organisation

The classic HRM organisation has its roots in the ideas of Frederick Taylor's 'scientific management' and Max Weber's 'bureaucracy'. Based on a detailed division of labour, HRM tasks are precisely defined so that responsibilities for them can be assigned to different entities that assume distinct roles in managing people. This often means centralisation of HRM tasks (for example, developing and implementing HRM strategy, administrative tasks) in the HRM department. In contrast, the role of line managers is limited to the application of HRM rules, which requires strict supervision of subordinates. The HRM department's major role is to administer HRM processes. Core components of this role involve providing instructions to line management and checking line managers' compliance with rules and implementing HRM strategy. A further characteristic of the classic form of organising HRM work is strong control over HRM tasks by the centralised units (see Whitley, 1999: 90), which prescribe to other business units or worldwide subsidiaries what HRM tasks need to be accomplished and how to execute them. The separation of responsibilities between HR managers, HRM business partners and line management 'laymen' is associated with a segmentation of knowledge, that is, the prevalence of distinct skills in each unit. Typically, HRM department positions are staffed with highly specialised employees who are technically skilled in administering HRM processes. Since needs for mutual consultation between HRM department and line managers are limited, specialist HRM tasks can be centralised, for example, in shared service centres, and human resource information system (HRIS) and e-HRM applications be used for facilitating standardised usage (see Chapter 18 in this volume). Replacement of individual HRM specialists is fairly easy, as is externalisation of HRM tasks. The latter can range from specialised in-house units, such as 'centres of expertise', through 'business within the business' solutions, to external consultancy (Sparrow & Braun, 2008; Ulrich et al., 2008). In extreme cases, the organisation outsources all HRM tasks to external service providers. Expected role behaviour is achieved through rewards that are tied to specific roles and job descriptions. Meeting the demands of roles defined in job descriptions is the base for assessing performance. This technical and specialised nature of HRM jobs suggests the relevance of operational performance measures (for example, costs for administering payrolls).

Empirical studies suggest that the classic HRM organisation is common in practice. In Europe, Mayrhofer et al. (2011) found that HRM responsibilities have moved to the HRM specialists, providing the HRM department with more control. Also, Brewster et al. (2015) see a trend to take a more controlling role, especially when linkages with corporate strategy exist and when trade union membership is high. In the United Kingdom (UK), organisations tend to keep most HRM responsibilities centralised in the HRM department (Brewster et al., 2015; Farndale, 2005; Jones & Saundry, 2012; Larsen & Brewster, 2003). In the United States of America (USA), too, evidence of the classic HRM organisation can be found, realised by HRM focusing on administrative and legislative issues and compliance with employment regulations (Keegan et al., 2012). The strict division of labour between HRM specialists and line responsibilities causes interactions between the HRM department and line managers to be weak in classic HRM organisations, as highlighted for example by Agrawal (2010) for companies in India, and Jones and Saundry (2012) in Northern England. The focus on administrative tasks is common in organisations in Spain (Cascón-Pereira et al., 2006) as well as in Portugal (Cabral-Cardoso, 2004).

It is also widespread in Slovenia, where two out of every three HRM directors are not positioned as members of top management (Zupan & Kaše, 2005). The focus on administrative tasks has also been frequent in Africa (Taylor, 1992); however, with a more pragmatic approach that is often difficult for Western managers to understand (see Chapters 27 and 28 in this volume).

Neo-Classic HRM Organisation

The neo-classic HRM organisation has its roots in behavioural perspectives of the firm, which emphasise that factors such as bounded rationality, psychological contracts, group processes, and associated concepts characterise organisational settings and propose a higher task complexity and mutual dependence between organisational entities (Whitley, 1999: 92). Assuming that employees should receive individual attention, HRM tasks are both complex and holistic, and require different organisational units to share responsibility for conducting HRM work. Devolving HRM tasks to line managers is crucial to success as direct supervisors understand employee needs and have considerable influence on how HRM tasks are executed. But Cascón-Pereira and Valverde (2014) show that devolution can come in different forms, and thus distinguish between devolution of task implementation, devolution of decision-making power, devolution of financial power to manage budgets, and the devolution of knowledge. They found superficial levels of devolution, because the implementation of tasks is devolved, but devolution in terms of decision-making power and taking decisions regarding the budget for their services was much less common.

The neo-classic model of organising HRM assumes a mutually dependent relationship between HRM specialists, line managers, senior managers, and employees. Guest and Bos-Nehles (2013) distinguish in their model of HRM implementation between different stages in the implementation of HRM practices, and show the responsibility of HR managers, senior executives, line managers, and employees. In this model, HR managers and senior executives share the responsibility for the development and introduction of qualitatively sound HRM practices, whereas line managers are responsible for their implementation on the shopfloor (see also Bos-Nehles et al., 2013; Brewster et al., 2013; Sikora & Ferris, 2014). Senior executives act as line managers' advocates by providing expert knowledge and credibility (McDermott et al., 2015). Alongside senior executives, HR managers, and line managers, employees are important stakeholders, considering the quality of HRM implementation.

Given the need for intensive cooperation, skill requirements for HRM specialists become similar to those of top or line managers, and vice versa. This is indicated by the need for HRM departments to develop business competencies, and for line managers to elaborate HRM competencies. But HR managers also have an important task in selecting, developing, and training line managers to implement HRM practices effectively (Bos-Nehles et al., 2013). If the accomplishment of HRM tasks requires a broad range of professional skills, including technical and social competencies as well as solid business knowledge, it becomes rather difficult for companies to outsource HRM tasks or to replace individual actors. Since professional skills are crucial to success in the neo-classic HRM organisation, organisational members are rewarded for investments in the development of skills and individual performance.

The neo-classic HRM model is frequently found in organisations in Northern European countries and in Australia, where line managers are given latitude in making HRM-related choices (Brewster et al., 2015; Gollan et al., 2015). While in the Spanish context the HRM department is still in charge of most HRM domains, although supported by the line (Valverde et al., 2006), in the Dutch context we see more shared responsibility between HRM specialists and line managers (for example, in staffing and compensation decisions) but also solely line management responsibility (for example, in performance appraisal, and training and development; Keegan et al., 2012; Nehles et al., 2006). The neo-classic model is also reported in the Philippines, where Audea et al. (2005) suggest that there are high levels of adoption of HRM practices and the HRM department takes a strategic role.

Modern HRM Organisation

The modern HRM organisation assumes an ongoing contestation between competing forces in highly complex and dynamic environments. Its theoretical roots are systems development and evolutionary approaches. HRM structures are conceptualised as decentralised, flexible, informal, fluid, non-linear, and in a process of continuous change. The constant changeability of organising HRM work is reflected in 'flexible specialisation' (Whitley, 1999). HRM tasks and responsibilities are varied and wide-ranging. Since organisational boundaries are viewed as fluid, not only a wide range of organisational members, but also network partners, are involved in HRM work (Swart & Kinnie, 2014). Integration of HRM topics in strategic business planning is important, but not restricted to input by HRM specialists. The holistic view of HRM work goes along with a need for strong discretion of actors. The challenge for actors is to cope with the inconsistencies and contradictory requirements arising from the dynamic environments. Control over managing HRM work is accomplished through cultural integration. Actors need to be equipped with excellent self-management, networking, and often also with cross-cultural skills, in addition to their technical qualifications. Knowledge of HRM work is continuous within the company; that is, HRM specialists and line managers share experience and have similar skills and backgrounds. Networks and flat hierarchies characterise managing HRM tasks, lowering boundaries between actors. Under these conditions, commitment to structures and responsibilities is rather limited. Replacement of existing solutions is encouraged by, for example, a high mobility of HRM staff, but also by a limited commitment of line managers to share long-term HRM risks (for example, investment in integration of new employees). Necessary role behaviour is achieved by rewarding individual capabilities and social capital (for example, networks).

Evidence for the existence of modern forms of organising HRM work comes from research on multiple employer networks (Marchington et al., 2011) and from project-based organisations (Bredin & Söderlund, 2007, 2011; Keegan et al., 2012). Research on project teams shows a complex interplay of roles between HRM specialists, line managers, and project managers, and a diversity of practices for managing this interplay; and reveals that HRM specialists perform a monitoring role for the coordination between project and line (Keegan et al., 2012).

Having outlined three basic alternative models for organising HRM work, and illustrated settings in which HRM scholars have found elements of these models, we next look at explanations for the prevalence of these models across countries. To this end, we review theoretical perspectives that HRM scholars have used for examining cross-national developments in HRM and related empirical studies.

CONTINGENCY THEORY

Core Concepts

Breaking with the idea that 'one solution fits all', the core assumption of the contingency theory that is based on the ideas of the classic organisation theory school (e.g., Burns & Stalker, 1961; Lawrence & Lorsch, 1967) is that organisations are structured in a way that fits their external environment. Thus, a particular model of HRM work should be chosen to reflect relevant contingencies: internal factors, such as business strategy, internationalisation strategy, HRM strategy, organisation size, and life-stage; and external factors, such as industry and sector. For example, Novicevic and Harvey (2001) posit the critical role of the multinational corepration's (MNC) internationalisation strategy for the HRM function's role. They argue that pressures for consistent global strategies and flexibility demand a more powerful HRM role. Contingency theorists hold that linkages between these contingencies and structural elements are stable across countries. Cross-national research in the contingency tradition (e.g., Hickson et al., 1974) focuses on the complexity and stability of national settings to account for differences and similarities in organisational structures. Hence, explanations of differences and similarities of organising HRM, and for choosing HRM models across countries, should take into account how diverse and how dynamic national settings are.

Empirical Research in the Contingency Tradition

Empirical research has paid particular attention to the linkage between an organisation's HRM strategy and the organisation of HRM work, in particular the strategic role of HRM specialists and devolution of HRM to line managers. For instance, Bowen et al. (2002) examine whether the strategic role of the HRM department is consistent with three HRM strategies – organisational capability, differentiation, and cost leadership – proposed by Schuler and Jackson (1987) in a sample of organisations in Anglo, Asian, and Latin countries. Their study analyses whether such contingencies apply beyond the US context. They find that high HRM status in organisations in Australia, Canada, the USA, Latin America, and China is linked with the organisational capability strategy of the HRM department; in Australia, China, and Korea it is linked with a differentiation strategy; and with leadership strategy in Australia, the USA, China, and Korea. The study finds that linkages between business strategies and types of HRM organisation do vary across national settings. The neo-classic HRM organisation is found in all strategy types in Canada and China, and is not linked to a particular business strategy. Overall, Bowen et al.'s (2002) study indicates that cross-national differences in the prevalence of a neo-classic HRM organisation cannot be fully explained by the HRM strategy.

Mesner Andolšek and Štebe (2005) use a sample of European countries to examine how the extent to which HRM work is devolved to line managers varies across national settings, and test a broader set of contingency factors (including size, organisational age,

HRM strategy, sector) that may account for these differences. Consistent with Bowen et al.'s (2002) research they find limited support that contingency factors explain patterns of organising HRM across national settings.

Arguing that corporate internationalisation strategy is a critical factor in how HRM work is organised, Farndale et al. (2010) examine, in an exploratory analysis of 16 MNCs with headquarters in different countries, how corporate HRM roles vary based on how MNCs design the relationships between headquarters and subsidiaries. In line with their reasoning that corporate HRM roles depend on the extent of mutual intra-organisational reliance in these relationships, the study provides evidence that in the case of independent subsidiaries, the corporate HRM role has limited influence. With increasing dependence, the corporate HRM role also increases, focusing on HRM processes and managing knowledge. The findings suggest that the corporate internationalisation strategy is indeed an important contingency for organising HRM work. More specifically, the study suggests that independent and interdependent relationships promote modern forms of organising HRM work, whereas dependent relationships foster neo-classic forms of organising.

CULTURAL APPROACHES

Core Concepts

Cultural approaches to cross-national comparative research on HRM work assume that similarities and differences in organising HRM work between countries prevail due to collectively held values and assumptions of the individuals who operate in these settings (see Chapter 3 in this volume). Individuals carry implicit theories about organisational processes and managing organisations, which guide their valuation of alternatives and choices for implementing particular models (Guillén, 1994; Laurent, 1986). These theories are shaped by the specific societal context in which individuals are socialised (Hofstede, 1980). Managers select forms of organising HRM that correspond to their implicit theories of valued organising models. Assuming that culture shapes the meaning that organisational members attribute to models of organising, cultural approaches analyse the attitudes that organisational members have to alternative models of organising work (Inzerilli & Laurent, 1983). Hence, 'even if the structure of different organisations may appear the same on some objective dimensions the meaning of structure to the organisation members may be quite different, and this difference may be important in influencing their behavior' (Inzerilli & Laurent, 1983: 98).

Empirical Research in the Cultural Tradition

Empirical research on HRM work using culture approaches has been based on exploratory research designs, using small samples and interviews for collecting data. Budhwar and Sparrow (2002) analysed a matched sample of 48 Indian and UK firms in the manufacturing sector to compare HRM managers' understanding of two core elements of the neo-classic model for organising HRM work: strategic integration and devolution of HRM work to line management. They employ a multi-mapping methodology for assessing companies' HRM specialists' understanding of these elements and of the influence of national culture on them. The study reveals considerable cross-national differences in how HRM specialists interpret the conditions for and consequences of the neo-classic model. Indian HRM specialists conceptualise integration as a result of recent economic reforms and associate it primarily with MNCs. Devolution of HRM work to line managers is seen as a necessity of the economic liberalisation process (Budhwar & Sparrow, 2002: 618). British HRM specialists, in contrast, emphasise a larger variety of issues associated with devolution, also including dysfunctional outcomes. Given that cultural approaches see managers' implicit theories as crucial for decision-making, the study suggests cross-national differences in the use of the neo-classic model: the narrowly defined scope of strategic integration in India suggests that HRM specialists may employ this concept less widely than their British counterparts. On the other hand, Indian HRM specialists have fewer concerns with devolving HRM tasks to line managers and, therefore, may more deliberately delegate responsibility for operational HRM work than British HRM specialists.

Osland and Osland (2005) explore local considerations involved in the varying utilisation of HRM models by MNCs in Central America (see also Chapter 22 in this volume). They note considerable variation in organisational and HRM processes and their underpinning theories. They identify '*solidarismo*' as an important principle prevailing in Costa Rica, which postulates compromise and negotiation, and builds on the assumption that management and employees are interdependent. The study reveals that MNCs operating in the region involve a broad range of actors, with HRM work beyond the organisational boundaries. For instance, Osland and Osland report partnerships between firms and universities, multi-firm forums, and note the relevance of consulting companies. These elements suggest evidence for the modern HRM model.

Pernkopf-Konhäusner and Brandl (2010) analyse cross-national patterns of views on organising HRM in a German and Russian consulting firm. They find that German employees' expectations of organising HRM are closest to the neo-classic HRM organisation model, which is exemplified by the importance given to cooperation between line managers and HRM specialists for training programmes. This view is widely shared across different groups in the firm. In contrast, in the Russian setting the views of how tasks and responsibilities should be allocated vary considerably across employees, suggesting conflicts over the appropriate HRM model.

COMPARATIVE INSTITUTIONAL THEORY

Core Concepts

Scholars within the comparative institutional tradition (Hall & Soskice, 2001; Whitley, 1999) build on the premise that existing variations between different systems of economic organisation remain and are reproduced through different social arrangements at the national level (see Chapter 2 in this volume). Whitley (1999: 19) asserts that 'nation states constitute the prevalent arena in which social and political competition is decided in industrial capitalist societies', implying that organising HRM work is shaped by the existence of national interest groups, and rules that govern their interaction and control over resources. For example, the classic HRM model is unlikely where managers share experiences or skills with the workforce, or where labour organisations (for example, unions) are incorporated into state mechanisms for regulating conflicts between interest groups. The neo-classic model is less likely where managers and workers have distinct backgrounds, or where they are mobile between firms or industries, or where owners reject long-term risks in specific firms; the neo-classic model is likely where strong industrial and craft unions have limited control over work organisations. Finally, the modern HRM model is encouraged by a strong public training system.

Empirical Research in the Comparative Institutional Tradition

Comparative institutional theory had early on informed studies on variations in organising HRM cross-nationally (Barnett et al., 1996; Tung & Havlovic, 1996), and gained increasing importance more recently (Vaiman & Brewster, 2015; Wood et al., 2014). While early research used institutional arguments as post-hoc explanations, newer research draws on explicit frameworks and has begun to test the relevance of institutional arguments in relation to alternative explanations.

Building on the business systems perspective, Wächter et al. (2006) examine the operation and roles of HRM departments of US MNC subsidiaries in Spain, the UK, Ireland, and Germany. Assuming that typical features of US HRM departments are internal functional specialisation (employment management, compensation, training, and employee relations), relatively small size and low hierarchical level, the authors explore in detailed case analyses whether and how these three characteristics vary, and how such variations may be associated with national institutional conditions. They find that national institutional factors play a minor role in determining HRM department roles, which they suggest to be largely determined by efficiency pressures and the differentiation between transactional and strategic HRM tasks. Germany is an exception to this rule because the institutional context requires relations between HRM departments and works councils. HRM departments have addressed these pressures by devolving transactional tasks to line managers and by trying to increase their strategic involvement.

Jacoby et al. (2005) analyse the role of HRM executives in the USA and Japan from a varieties of capitalism perspective to examine whether coordinated (Japan) and liberal market (USA) economies converge. Building on a survey of 229 Japanese and 149 US firms they trace changes in organising HRM work over the previous five years. They find that in both countries companies have reduced HRM department staff; however, in Japan reduction is realised by buying services from outsourced in-house units, and in the USA external service-providers are used. Responsibility devolution to line management has increased in Japan in a limited number of companies, while devolution has been widespread in the USA. The study shows that whereas the number of HRM executives who are involved strategically has increased in the USA, involvement in Japan is still higher. This study is notable because of its comprehensive analysis of recent developments in organising HRM work, showing that while organisations respond to global pressures to deregulation, their responses vary depending on national institutional traditions.

Using data from the Cranfield Network on International Human Resource Management (Cranet) organisation survey, Brewster and colleagues have tested the relevance of national business system characteristics for cross-national variations in organising HRM in a number of studies (Brewster et al., 2006; Brewster et al., 2015; Mol et al., 2014).

Brewster et al. (2006) analyse how business system characteristics are linked with the resources allocated to HRM departments. They argue that in Rhineland economies and Japan, which represent large-firm models, the transactional nature of HRM work requires larger HRM departments; whereas in countries with compartmentalised, transitional, or peripheral business system models, the emphasis on strategic HRM work suggests small HRM departments. Brewster et al. (2006) find that HRM departments are smaller in the former communist countries of Central Europe as well as in Southern Europe. In Japan, HRM departments are larger, but not in Germany. In a follow-up study, Brewster et al. (2015) examine cross-national variations in assignment of HRM responsibilities to line managers, a core element of the neo-classic HRM organisation. Testing organisational characteristics and characteristics of 11 national economies according to the varieties of capitalism model, they find that devolution to the line is most likely in coordinated market economies, and least likely in countries where the liberal market model prevails. Firm-level factors such as organisation size, role of HRM specialists, and works councils have a negative influence on devolution, which holds irrespective of the national economy. Mol et al. (2014) use the Cranet dataset to examine the relevance of firm-, industry-, and national-level factors for assigning HRM responsibility to external service providers. They report that firm-level factors are less useful for explaining variation in outsourcing than national-level factors; however, the national variations do not match existing classifications of countries according to comparative institutional approaches. Hence, the comparative tradition may not tell the full story of institutional influences on organising HRM.

NEW INSTITUTIONAL THEORY

Core Concepts

New institutional theory also assumes that organisations adopt particular forms of organising HRM because societal arrangements pressure them to do so. Unlike comparative institutional approaches, scholars in this tradition emphasise a varying role of national traditions for adopting particular organisation models, and the decreasing influence of national arrangements in the long run. New institutional theory assumes the de-legitimation of national institutions as Western principles of organising work diffuse globally (Meyer et al., 2006). The proposed worldwide expansion of Western principles brings about the extension of strategic activities in organisations, and the involvement of an increasing number of people in and outside organisations in strategy-making. World cultural models of managing employees promoted by management gurus (Ulrich et al., 2008) and social movements (for example, HRM professional associations) encourage organisations to reorganise their HRM work so that they match world cultural models. Differences between countries are explained through their different exposure to global models of organising. Even if organisations lack the resources for implementing world cultural models, they still may have ambitions to do so. Organisations hide possible discrepancies between goals and realisation of implementing HRM models in order to maintain trust.

Empirical Research in the New Institutional Theory Tradition

Longitudinal research designs are most suitable to capture the diffusion of Western principles and their manifestation in HRM organisation, but scholars also use cross-national comparisons to show national patterns and variations in local adaption. For instance, Jennings et al. (1995) analyse how the relationship between external and internal labour markets accounts for the emergence of professionalised HRM departments in the Pacific Rim area. Professionalisation – that is, the acknowledgement of specialised disciplinary knowledge – resembles strategic integration element in the neo-classic HRM organisation. Jennings et al. (1995) specify seven factors that foster professionalisation: existence of professional associations, prevalence of bureaucratic HRM models, prevalence of large firms, cultural support for specialisation, unionisation, state involvement, and an educated workforce.

Mayrhofer et al. (2011) use the Cranet database to examine whether the devolution of HRM tasks to line, a core element of the neo-classic HRM organisation, became more similar in the period 1992 to 2004 in 13 European countries. They report support for directional convergence – that is, a change of the devolution in the countries in the same direction – and increasing similarities over time, but find no evidence for final convergence, which provides clear support for new institutionalist arguments. Based on a survey with HRM specialists in four Asian countries, De Guzman et al. (2011) reports practitioners' ideas of ideal HRM roles. At different management levels and across national settings, these ideas hint at models of neo-classic HRM organisation. The study also reveals considerable discrepancies between these ideals and their experience in everyday work, a phenomenon known in new institutional theory as 'de-coupling'.

PARADOX THEORY

Core Concepts

Assuming that contradictory forces or 'poles' operate in organisations, paradox theory asserts that organisational success or failure depends on how organisations cope with such forces (Smith & Lewis, 2011). In contrast to theories that suggest organisations need to adjust their structure so that it is aligned with one particular context, paradox theory postulates that organisations should accept the coexistence of contradictions in HRM, and need to manage contradictions actively. For example, a common tension for organising HRM work in MNCs lies in the opposing forces for local responsiveness and global integration that occur as business internationalises (Evans, 1999). Holding that 'either/ or' solutions are likely to be ineffective, paradox theory suggests the coexistence of multiple forms of organising HRM work, as they are best represented in the modern HRM model, as a way for taking into account contradictory requirements. Paradox theory has just started to inform HRM research, and issues of organising HRM in particular (Aust et al., 2015; Aust et al., 2017, for an overview).

Empirical Research in the Paradox Tradition

A small, but growing body of literature on organising HRM work in MNCs (e.g., Chung et al., 2012; Stiles & Trevor, 2006) draws on paradox theory. Based on a comparative case study of a Dutch and a Japanese MNC in China, Stiles and Trevor (2006: 50) assess how the HRM departments of these two companies balance three types of tensions: strategic versus other HRM roles, opposing interests between management and employees, and centralising versus de-centralising HRM activities. The comparison of a Dutch and a Japanese MNC in China illustrates how the approaches to reconcile these tensions vary cross-nationally. The tension between strategic and operational HRM roles is managed in both companies by subdividing the HRM function into corporate, line, and internal consultancy units (Stiles & Trevor, 2006: 58). This indicates a coexistence of classic and neo-classic HRM work models. Apart from these similarities in structure, however, substantial differences prevail in managing the global integration of HRM activities. In the case of Philips operating in China, Stiles and Trevor (2006) find considerable efforts to manage coordination tightly between locally operating HRM units. This is realised, for example, through sharing resources for administrative HRM between the locally operating shared service centres; exchanging best practices between the division-specific HRM units responsible for consulting; executing business-specific HRM policies and programmes in the specific business divisions; and by promoting consistency between the shared service centres and HRM in the business units through a functional HRM unit.

By contrast, in the Japanese MNC in China, although HRM work is also devolved to HRM units in the business divisions, some HRM activities (for example, performance management) remain centralised in corporate HRM, which also holds wide-ranging responsibilities for implementing HRM solutions. Within this structure of minimal coordination through corporate HRM, the HRM units in the Chinese divisions operate under a highly fragmented regional structure with 'no transfer of knowledge or best practice' (Stiles & Trevor, 2006: 59). The lack of coordination of HRM work between the business divisions in China is reflected in the inconsistency of HRM practices (for example, different work conditions for same jobs). The finding that employment is considered as 'an element of the production process' (ibid.: 59) indicates that the local Chinese HRM units predominantly follow the classic HRM organisation.

Since the two firms operate in the same business and are similar in other contingency factors such as expansion strategy, Stiles and Trevor (2006) see the different solutions for organising HRM work within the Chinese subsidiaries, one being integrated and the other one fragmented, as an indicator for the relevance of country of origin for how MNCs deal with tensions in organising HRM work. This illuminates that paradox theory and comparative institutional approaches are not mutually exclusive, but complement each other. Paradox theory highlights potentially interesting foci for comparisons of organising HRM work, whereas comparative institutional approaches may explain how MNCs from particular national contexts address these foci. Therefore, we believe it is worth combining the two approaches in future studies to understand how MNCs organise their HRM work across different countries more fully.

KEY ISSUES AND FUTURE DIRECTIONS

While cross-national research on HRM organisation has increased since the first edition of this chapter and scholars have started to address some issues (for example, clarification of constructs, theory-driven research), other issues still deserve attention and new issues have come up. We highlight in this section three topics that we believe have potential to elaborate previous work.

The first topic concerns the broadening of the focus on how HRM work is organised in empirical investigations to better capture recent developments of organising HRM in practice. So far, the focus of cross-national research has mostly been on the strategic integration of HRM specialists and line managers' involvement; that is, the difference between classic and neo-classic HRM organisation. These topics are insufficient to capture the emerging modern forms of organising HRM, as exemplified by shared service centres (Ulrich et al., 2008), HRM in project-based organisations (e.g., Bredin & Söderlund, 2011; Keegan et al., 2012), or HRM work in inter-firm networks (e.g., Marchington et al., 2011; Swart & Kinnie, 2014). In order to analyse the prevalence of modern forms of organising HRM across national settings, it is necessary to extend the focus of studies beyond HRM specialists and line managers. The three basic alternatives of organising HRM that we have introduced in this chapter offer a useful device for conducting future research on this issue.

The second topic concerns the need for the complementing of macro-level by micro-level research designs. Our overview indicates that recent macro-level research has provided comprehensive data on cross-national variation in organising HRM, and has started to examine the usefulness of various theoretical frameworks (e.g., Brewster et al., 2013; Mayrhofer et al., 2011). Since findings of macro-level studies have provided mixed support for hypotheses and sometimes led to unanticipated findings, we still lack an understanding of the patterns of organising HRM work in a cross-national perspective. To address such shortcomings, future research should be devoted to combining macro- and micro-level research designs that can refine our understanding of how societal context informs organising HRM. To this end, the often deterministic understanding of context would benefit from ideas of corporate choice (Valverde et al., 2006: 631). We believe that work in the tradition of translation of management concepts (e.g., Boglind et al., 2011) is particular fruitful for analysing the local adaptation of global concepts for organising HRM. The negotiated order approach that earlier cross-national research on organising HRM has used (Barnett et al., 1996) may be useful for analysing the role of stakeholders and power for the adoption of particular forms of organising HRM. Finally, the potential of paradox theory is fruitful for analysing the challenges of organising HRM across national borders.

The third issue of need concerns the assumption that organisational decisions on adopting particular HRM organising models are generally nested within countries. Most research that seeks to contextualise how HRM is organised views the national context as a stable influencing factor. This is particularly evident in culture approaches and comparative institutional theory, two much used perspectives in contemporary cross-national HRM research. Yet, this premise makes it difficult to take into account the potentially changing influence of national factors on organisational decisions over time. To consider such possibilities, cross-national studies would benefit from being combined with a longitudinal perspective (e.g., Mayrhofer et al., 2011). New institutional theory, in particular its notion of 'world culture', can offer a useful lens for theorising the changing relevance of influence factors at the country level over time.

CONCLUSION

Managing people requires organisations to make decisions on how different units contribute to this work and coordinate their activities with each other. Recognising the growing interest in the impact of national contexts on organising HRM work, this chapter has provided an overview of comparative research on organising HRM work in a cross-national perspective. We have outlined three alternatives that companies may employ for organising HRM work – classic, neo-classic, and modern – and sketched out five theoretical perspectives that provide answers to how national settings matter for organising HRM work. Our review addressed how theoretical perspectives have been used so far and what major findings studies have produced. The literature reviewed in this chapter has strengthened our impression that the national context exerts considerable influence on how companies organise HRM work. We reasoned that future research analysing HRM work in a cross-national perspective should focus more on the following aspects: (1) expand the focus of research on modern HRM models; (2) combine macro- with micro-level study designs to improve understanding of patterns; and (3) view country level as a variable rather than as a stable influence factor on organising HRM.

REFERENCES

Agrawal, R.K. 2010. Relationship between line and human resource executives in Indian organisations. *International Journal of Indian Culture and Business Management*, 3(3): 285–306.

Audea, T., Teo, S.T., & Crawford, J. 2005. HRM professionals and their perceptions of HRM and firm performance in the Philippines. *International Journal of Human Resource Management*, 16(4): 532–552.

Aust, I., Brandl, J., & Keegan, A. 2015. State-of-the-art and future directions for HRM from a paradox perspective: Introduction to the Special Issue. *Zeitschrift für Personalforschung*, 29(3/4): 194–213.

Aust, I., Brandl, J., Keegan, A., & Lensges, M. 2017. Paradoxical tensions in the HRM context. In M.W. Lewis, W.K. Smith, A. Langley, and P. Jarzabkowski (eds), *The Oxford Handbook of Organizational Paradox*: 413–433. Oxford: Oxford University Press.

Barnett, S., Patrickson, M., & Maddern, J. 1996. Negotiating the evolution of the HR function: Practical advice from the health care sector. *Human Resource Management Journal*, 6(4): 18–37.

Baron, J.N., Dobbin, F.R., & Jennings, P.D. 1986. War and peace: The evolution of modern personnel administration in US industry. *American Journal of Sociology*, 92(2): 350–386.

Boglind, A., Hallsten, F., & Thilander, P. 2011. HR transformation and shared services: Adoption and adaptation in Swedish organisations. *Personnel Review*, 40(5): 570–588.

Bos-Nehles, A.C., Van Riemsdijk, M.J., & Kees Looise, J. 2013. Employee perceptions of line management performance: Applying the AMO theory to explain the effectiveness of line managers' HRM implementation. *Human Resource Management*, 52(6): 861–877.

Bowen, D.E., Galang, C., & Pillai, R. 2002. The role of human resource management: An exploratory study of cross-country variance. *Human Resource Management*, 41(1): 103–122.

Brandl, J., Madsen, M.T., & Madsen, H. 2009. The perceived importance of HR duties to Danish line managers. *Human Resource Management Journal*, 19(2): 194–210.

Brandl, J., & Pohler, D. 2010. The human resource department's role and conditions that affect its development: Explanations from Austrian CEOs. *Human Resource Management*, 49(6): 1025–1046.

Bredin, K., & Söderlund, J. 2007. Reconceptualising line management in project-based organisations: The case of competence coaches at Tetra Pak. *Personnel Review*, 36(5): 815–833.

Bredin, K., & Söderlund, J. 2011. The HR quadriad: A framework for the analysis of HRM in project-based organizations. *International Journal of Human Resource Management*, 22(10): 2202–2221.

Brewster, C., Brookes, M., & Gollan, P.J. 2015. The institutional antecedents of the assignment of HRM responsibilities to line managers. *Human Resource Management*, 54(4): 577–597.

Brewster, C., Gollan, P.J., & Wright, P.M. 2013. Guest editors' note: Human resource management and the line. *Human Resource Management*, 52(6): 829–838.

Brewster, C., Wood, G., Brookes, M., & Ommeren, J.V. 2006. What determines the size of the HR function? A cross-national analysis. *Human Resource Management*, 45(1): 3–21.

Budhwar, P.S., & Sparrow, P.R. 2002. Strategic HRM through the cultural looking glass: Mapping the cognition of British and Indian managers. *Organization Studies*, 23(4): 599–638.

Burns, T., & Stalker, G.M. 1961. *The Management of Innovation.* London: Tavistock.

Cabral-Cardoso, C. 2004. The evolving Portuguese model of HRM. *International Journal of Human Resource Management*, 15(6): 959–977.

Cascón-Pereira, R., & Valverde, M. 2014. HRM devolution to middle managers: Dimension identification. *BRQ Business Research Quarterly*, 17(3): 149–160.

Cascón-Pereira, R., Valverde, M., & Ryan, G. 2006. Mapping out devolution: An exploration of the realities of devolution. *Journal of European Industrial Training*, 30(2): 129–151.

Chung, C., Bozkurt, Ö., & Sparrow, P. 2012. Managing the duality of IHRM: Unravelling the strategy and perceptions of key actors in South Korean MNCs. *International Journal of Human Resource Management*, 23(11): 2333–2353.

de Guzman, G.M., Neelankavil, J.P., & Sengupta, K. 2011. Human resources roles. Ideal versus practiced: a cross-country comparison among organizations in Asia. *International Journal of Human Resource Management*, 22(13): 2665–2682.

Evans, P.A. 1999. HRM on the edge: A duality perspective. *Organization*, 6(2): 325–338.

Farndale, E. 2005. HR department professionalism: A comparison between the UK and other European countries. *International Journal of Human Resource Management*, 16(5): 660–675.

Farndale, E., Paauwe, J., & Hoeksema, L. 2009. In-sourcing HR: Shared service centres in the Netherlands. *International Journal of Human Resource Management*, 20(3): 544–561.

Farndale, E., Paauwe, J., Morris, S.S., et al. 2010. Context-bound configurations of corporate HR functions in multinational corporations. *Human Resource Management*, 49(1): 45–66.

Gollan, P.J., Kalfa, S., & Xu, Y. 2015. Strategic HRM and devolving HR to the line: Cochlear during the shift to lean manufacturing. *Asia Pacific Journal of Human Resources*, 53(2): 144–162.

Guest, D., & Bos-Nehles, A. 2013. HRM and performance: The role of effective implementation. In D. Guest, J. Paauwe, and P. Wright (eds), *HRM and Performance: Achievements and Challenges*: 79–96. Chichester: Wiley-Blackwell.

Guillén, M.F. 1994. *Models of Management: Work, Authority, and Organization in a Comparative Perspective.* Chicago, IL: University of Chicago Press.

Hall, P.A., & Soskice, D. 2001. *Varieties of Capitalism: The Institutional Foundation for Comparative Advantage.* Oxford: Oxford University Press.

Hickson, D.J., Hinings, C.R., McMillan, C.J., & Schwitter, J.P. 1974. The culture-free context of organization structure: A tri-national comparison. *Sociology*, 8(1): 59–80.

Hofstede, G. 1980. *Culture's Consequences: International Differences in Work-Related Values.* Beverly Hills, CA: SAGE.

Inzerilli, G., & Laurent, A. 1983. Managerial views of organization structure in France and the USA. *International Studies of Management and Organization*, 13(1/2): 97–118.

Jacoby, S.M. 2003. A century of human resource management. In B.E. Kaufman, R.A. Beaumont, and R.B. Helfgott (eds), *Industrial Relations to Human Resources and Beyond*: 147–171. Armonk: Sharpe.

Jacoby, S.M., Nason, E.M., & Saguchi, K. 2005. The role of the senior HR executive in Japan and the United States: Employment relations, corporate governance, and values. *Industrial Relations: A Journal of Economy and Society*, 44(2): 207–241.

Jennings, P.D., Cyr, D., & Moore, L.F. 1995. Human resource management on the Pacific Rim: An integration. In L.F. Moore, and P.D. Jennings (eds), *Human Resource Management on the Pacific Rim*: 351–379. Berlin: de Gruyter.

Jones, C., & Saundry, R. 2012. The practice of discipline: evaluating the roles and relationship between managers and HR professionals. *Human Resource Management Journal*, 22(3): 252–266.

Keegan, A., Huemann, M., & Turner, J.R. 2012. Beyond the line: Exploring the HRM responsibilities of line managers, project managers and the HRM department in four project-oriented companies in the Netherlands, Austria, the UK and the USA. *International Journal of Human Resource Management*, 23(15): 3085–3104.

Larsen, H.H., & Brewster, C. 2003. Line management responsibility for HRM: What is happening in Europe?. *Employee Relations*, 25(3): 228–244.

Laurent, A. 1986. The cross-cultural puzzle of international human resource management. *Human resource management*, 25(1): 91–102.

Lawrence, P.R., & Lorsch, J.W. 1967. *Organization and Environment: Managing Differentiation and Integration*. Boston, MA: Harvard Business School, Division of Research.

Marchington, M., Rubery, J., & Grimshaw, D. 2011. Alignment, integration, and consistency in HRM across multi-employer networks. *Human Resource Management*, 50(3): 313–339.

Mayrhofer, W., Brewster, C., Morley, M.J., & Ledolter, J. 2011. Hearing a different drummer? Convergence of human resource management in Europe – A longitudinal analysis. *Human Resource Management Review*, 21(1): 50–67.

McDermott, A.M., Fitzgerald, L., Van Gestel, N.M., & Keating, M.A. 2015. From bipartite to tripartite devolved HRM in professional service contexts: Evidence from hospitals in three countries. *Human Resource Management*, 54(5): 813–831.

Mesner Andolšek, D., & Štebe, J. 2005. Devolution or (de) centralization of HRM function in European organizations. *International Journal of Human Resource Management*, 16(3): 311–329.

Meyer, J.W., Drori, G.S., & Hwang, H. 2006. World society and the proliferation of formal organization. In G. S. Drori, J.W. Meyer, and H. Hwang (eds), *Globalization and Organization: World Society and Organizational Change*: 25–49. Oxford: Oxford University Press.

Mol, M., Brewster, C., Wood, G., & Brookes, M. 2014. How much does country matter? A cross-national comparison of HRM outsourcing decisions. In G. Wood, C. Brewster, and M. Brookes (eds), *Human Resource Management and the Institutional Perspective*: 200–220. New York, USA and London, UK: Routledge Taylor & Francis.

Nehles, A.C., van Riemsdijk, M., Kok, I., & Looise, J.K. 2006. Implementing human resource management successfully: A first-line management challenge. *Management Revue*, 17(3): 256–273.

Novicevic, M.M., & Harvey, M. 2001. The changing role of the corporate HR function in global organizations of the twenty-first century. *International Journal of Human Resource Management*, 12(8): 1251–1268.

Osland, A., & Osland, J.S. 2005. Contextualization and strategic international human resource management approaches: The case of Central America and Panama. *International Journal of Human Resource Management*, 16(12): 2218–2236.

Pernkopf-Konhaeusner, K., & Brandl, J. 2010. How should human resources be managed? From comparing models of staff development in a German and Russian professional service firm: A conventionalist approach. *European Journal of Cross-Cultural Competence and Management*, 1(4): 356–377.

Schuler, R.S., & Jackson, S.E. 1987. Linking competitive strategies with human resource management practices. *Academy of Management Executive (1987–1989)*, 1(3): 207–219.

Sikora, D.M., & Ferris, G.R. 2014. Strategic human resource practice implementation: The critical role of line management. *Human Resource Management Review*, 24(3): 271–281.

Smith, W.K., & Lewis, M.W. 2011. Toward a theory of paradox: A dynamic equilibrium model of organizing. *Academy of Management Review*, 36(2): 381–403.

Sparrow, P., & Braun, W. 2008. HR sourcing and shoring: Strategies, drivers, success factors and implications for HR. In C. Brewster, M. Dickmann, and P. Sparrow (eds), *International HRM: Contemporary Issues in Europe*: 39–66. London: Routledge.

Stiles, P., & Trevor, J. 2006. The human resource department: Roles, coordination and influence. In G.A.B. Stahl (ed.), *Handbook of Research in International Human Resource Management*: 49–67. Cheltenham, UK and Northampton, MA, USA: Edward Elgar Publishing.

Swart, J., & Kinnie, N. 2014. Reconsidering boundaries: Human resource management in a networked world. *Human Resource Management*, 53(2): 291–310.

Taylor, H. 1992. Public sector personnel management in three African countries: Current problems and possibilities. *Public Administration and Development*, 12(2): 193–207.

Tung, R.L., & Havlovic, S.J. 1996. Human resource management in transitional economies: The case of Poland and the Czech Republic. *International Journal of Human Resource Management*, 7(1): 1–19.

Ulrich, D., Younger, J., & Brockbank, W. 2008. The twenty-first-century HR organization. *Human Resource Management*, 47(4): 829–850.

Vaiman, V., & Brewster, C. 2015. How far do cultural differences explain the differences between nations? Implications for HRM. *International Journal of Human Resource Management*, 26(2): 151–164.

Valverde, M., Ryan, G., & Soler, C. 2006. Distributing HRM responsibilities: A classification of organisations. *Personnel Review*, 35(6): 618–636.

Wächter, H., Peters, R., Ferner, A., Gunnigle, P., & Quintanilla, J. 2006. The role of the international personnel function in US MNCs. In P. Almond and A. Ferner (eds), *American Multinationals in Europe: Managing Employment Relations across National Borders*: 248–269. Oxford: University of Oxford Press.

Whitley, R. 1999. *Divergent Capitalisms: The Social Structuring and Change of Business Systems*. Oxford: Oxford University Press.

Wood, G., Brewster, C., & Brookes, M. 2014. *Human Resource Management and the Institutional Perspective.* New York, London: Routledge Taylor & Francis.

Zupan, N., & Kaše, R. 2005. Strategic human resource management in European transition economies: Building a conceptual model on the case of Slovenia. *International Journal of Human Resource Management*, 16(6): 882–906.

18. The intersection between information technology and human resource management from a cross-national perspective: towards a research model

Huub J.M. Ruël and Tanya Bondarouk

INTRODUCTION

The intersection between information technology (IT) and human resource management (HRM) has resulted in a stream of research starting in the 1990s. Research on this intersection, in this chapter referred to as electronic HRM (e-HRM), has addressed questions regarding the implementation of e-HRM, the adoption of e-HRM, and the outcomes of e-HRM use. Organisations all around the world have invested in e-HRM in one way or another, be it in the use of online recruitment practices or e-recruitment, the automation of HRM administrative processes, or the implementation of a competence management-based package as a way to link HRM policies and practices with strategic goals. Annual surveys conducted by international consultancy firms (e.g., CedarCrestone's annual surveys) have shown a growth in e-HRM adoption and use year after year since the 1990s. e-HRM as a research field, as Strohmeier (2007) puts it, is relatively new and intriguing and is an innovative, lasting, and substantial development in HRM resulting in new phenomena and major changes. Scholars have worked hard to understand the phenomenon of e-HRM and its multilevel implications within and across organisations. One sign of this are the five special issues on e-HRM in international academic journals between 2004 and 2010 (*Human Resource Management*, 2004, 2008; *Journal of Managerial Psychology*, 2009; *International Journal of Human Resource Management*, 2009; *International Journal of Technology and Human Interaction*, 2010). This field has been changing so fast that, since 2011, five further special issues appeared in international journals (*German Journal of Research in Human Resource Management*, 2012; *Human Resource Management Review*, 2013; *Journal of Strategic Information Systems*, 2013; *European Journal of International Management*, 2013; and *Employee Relations*, 2014).

However, the field faces a number of major challenges, as Bondarouk (2014) highlights. The current state of the e-HRM field is characterised by its predominantly non-theoretical character and positivistic research philosophy; a broad range of different qualitative and quantitative approaches; lack of specification of levels of analysis; and patchiness of the topics covered. Strohmeier (2007) brings up an additional characteristic of the current state of the field, namely a lack of international comparative studies. This characteristic is the main stimulus for this chapter: e-HRM research needs 'to go international' in order to contribute to a full and comprehensive understanding of the phenomenon.

The goal of this chapter is to develop a model for comparative e-HRM research in an international context. In order to do so, we review the existing literature on e-HRM with the intention of presenting a picture of what exactly is known about e-HRM in different national contexts. The conclusions drawn from this review are linked to the convergence/

divergence debate in international management and business studies. From there we will start to construct a model that can help to describe, understand, and explain the differences and similarities in e-HRM between national contexts, which could be a starting point to improve our understanding of these differences and similarities.

E-HRM RESEARCH AND THE CROSS-NATIONAL FOCUS: A LITERATURE REVIEW

We depart from our earlier definition of e-HRM (Bondarouk & Ruël, 2009), but put forward a new definition, and view it as an integration of the IT and HRM fields of scholarly inquiry that focuses on all HRM content shared via IT, with the intention of making HRM processes distinctive and consistent, more efficient, and higher in quality, and which create long-term opportunities within and across organisations for targeted users.

Since the first edition of this edited volume in 2012 there has been increased attention to the history of e-HRM and human resource information systems, or HRIS (Bondarouk & Furtmueller, 2012; Marler & Fisher, 2013; van Geffen et al., 2013; Ruël & Bondarouk, 2014). Therefore, in this edition we turn immediately to the cross-cultural focus of e-HRM and refer the reader to the first edition (Ruël & Bondarouk, 2012) to know more about the e-HRM research history.

Our main questions for the literature review were: how many studies on comparative e-HRM have been published in academic journals, books, and conference proceedings? What do these studies tell us? Where are the data gathered that are used for studies on e-HRM, and what is the overall picture that emerges from these studies when it comes to convergence and divergence of e-HRM practices?

Since this literature review was part of larger project conducted in 2011, only research publications to 2010 were included in the initial analysis. In 2016 we conducted an additional 'quick scan' to investigate how many more new research publications addressing any reference to an international perspective (such as country name in the title or the abstract) were published in the period 2011–16. The results of this additional analysis is presented after the initial literature analysis.

Studies concerning e-HRM were found using three online databases (Scopus, Picarta, Web of Science) as well as scholar.google.com, and covering a large variety of disciplines, from the social sciences to engineering. Fifteen different search terms were used, including general terms such as 'e-HRM' and 'HRIS' and related terms such as 'e-recruiting' and 'virtual teams'. Citations of articles found through the databases were also utilised in order to find older literature, as suggested by Torraco (2005). Only papers in the English language were considered, as it is the largest and dominant academic language area. We applied a certain hierarchy to the publications: first, papers published in academic journals were taken into consideration, then book chapters, and finally conference papers in officially published proceedings. An overview was made of the various papers, based on the concept matrix as outlined by Webster and Watson (2002). The matrix criteria included, among other things, the main topic of the paper, the findings, the level of analysis, and the countries in which the research was performed.

Analysis of the publications allowed us to distinguish four groups related to research into e-HRM in a cross-national context: e-HRM studies with a cross-continental focus;

e-HRM studies with a cross-national focus but limited to one continent; e-HRM studies with a cross-national focus but within one company; and e-HRM studies within a specifically mentioned national context.

e-HRM Studies with a Cross-Continental Focus

The number of research publications on cross-cultural or cross-continental e-HRM is limited. Let us first briefly describe their main findings. Beulen (2008) and Rao (2009a) focused on e-HRM activities in emerging economies. The researchers were interested in the role of internet recruitment methods in companies in emerging economies in Asia, South America, and Europe. The case study performed by Beulen (2008) at global organisations' branches in Argentina, Brazil, China, India, Latvia, and Slovakia explores 'how IT supports HR work and how it contributes to their efforts in the global war for talent' (Beulen, 2008: 215). Overall, organisations were standardising their HRIS in the 'war for talent'; however, some cultural factors influenced a particular division to divert from this standardisation. This was especially true for the outsourcing division in India, which deals with large numbers of résumés. The study suggests that strategic decision-making at the corporate level will deal with the discrepancy between the need for standardisation and local needs.

Rao (2009a, 2009b) addressed in a conceptual paper the challenges of e-recruitment in the emerging economies of India and Mexico. The predominant challenges of e-recruitment in both India and Mexico are the poor telecommunication infrastructure and the importance of personal interaction because of the collectivist culture. An additional challenge in India is the large number of recruiters, while in Mexico employees fear a loss of confidentiality in submitting their details on the internet.

Williams et al. (2009) conducted a case study with project teams working in multinational corporations (MNCs). The team members originated from the United Kingdom (UK), the United States of America (USA), Germany, and Canada. The purpose was to identify the HRIS skills and knowledge in global projects. The authors presented a framework based on human capital theory. The framework included guidelines for the collection of employee details, personal attributes, employees' skills, and firm-specific attributes.

Puck et al. (2006, 2009) focused on internet recruitment and included emerging as well as developed economies. Fourteen different countries from three different continents were included in their study of the role of national culture on corporate website recruitment. In particular, they analysed the use of pre-selection and selection methods, and the use of the information function of corporate websites. Based on Hofstede's model of national culture, seven hypotheses were formulated and tested. Results showed that national cultures do affect the use of the internet in corporate website recruitment, with several implications for the companies and the job applicants as well as for the companies developing corporate website recruitment software. Power distance and individualism were negatively related to the comprehensiveness of information in corporate website recruiting. Additionally, firms in a culture with a high level of uncertainty avoidance made less integrative use of corporate website recruiting.

A study by Marler and Parry (2008) included a large number of countries, representing many regions. Based on the Cranet survey in which HRM professionals from 29 countries participated, they investigated the strategic role of e-HRM. There does not appear to be a direct linking mechanism between HRM strategy and elevating the HRM function into a strategic business partner. However, the relationship between e-HRM and strategic HRM operates indirectly through the company's HRM strategy. The study did not include cultural or national context as a control variable.

Harris et al. (2003) included the USA and Belgium in their research investigating privacy and attitudes towards internet-based selection systems. By means of a survey, four hypotheses were tested. The results showed some commonalities between the two countries as well as some cross-cultural differences; however, the relation with the cultural factors of the countries was not explored. In both countries the same amount of reluctance to submit employment-related data over the internet was observed, and higher self-rated knowledge of the internet led to less concern about employment-related data falling into the wrong hands. A main difference is that in Belgium there is a stronger belief among knowledge workers that companies have to get approval before releasing information about a candidate, while in the USA the dominant belief is the opposite.

Olivas-Luján and Florkowski (2009) investigated the diffusion of HRIS technologies across English-speaking countries. They found that diffusion is stimulated more by internal influences from the information system of potential adopters than by external influences, except for integrated HRM suites and HRM intranets. The analysis showed no differences in diffusion between countries.

AbuZaineh and Ruël (2008) explored and compared the use of e-HRM tools in SMEs in Kuwait and the Netherlands and found that the main objective in both countries was to reduce costs and time. The cultural context, especially the higher uncertainty avoidance tendency in Kuwait compared with the Netherlands, could help to explain the lag in adoption of e-HRM in Kuwaiti small and medium-sized enterprises (SMEs) compared with the Netherlands.

Overall, the number of studies with a cross-continental focus is very limited, especially those focused on finding differences and similarities between countries (Table 18.1), and is clearly skewed towards the USA and Europe. Studies with a cross-continental focus do not go beyond concluding that culture seems to be important and a possible explanatory factor for the differences between continents and countries.

Table 18.1   e-HRM studies including cross-continental data

Author	Region	Topic	Type of study
AbuZaineh and Ruël (2008)	Asia (Middle East)	e-HRM usage	Qualitative
Beulen (2008)	Asia, Europe, South America	HRIS	Qualitative
Harris et al. (2003)	Europe, North America	e-selection	Quantitative
Marler and Parry (2008)	Africa, Asia, Australia, Europe, North America, South America	e-HRM	Quantitative
Olivas-Lujan and Florkowski (2009)	Europe, North America	HRIS	Quantitative
Puck et al. (2006)	Asia, Europe, North America	e-recruitment	Quantitative
Williams et al. (2009)	Europe, North America	Virtual teams	Quantitative
Rao (2009a)	Asia, South America	e-recruitment	Literature study

Table 18.2   Cross-national, one-continent e-HRM studies

Author(s)	Region	Topic	Type of study
Beamish et al. (2002)	Europe	e-learning	Qualitative
Galanaki and Panayotopoulou (2009)	Europe	e-HRM	Qualitative
Imperatori and De Marco (2009)	Europe	e-work	Qualitative
Ruël et al. (2004)	Europe	e-HRM	Qualitative
Strohmeier and Kabst (2009)	Europe	e-HRM	Qualitative

e-HRM with a Cross-National Focus but Limited to One Continent

Another group of studies on e-HRM is cross-national in focus, though within one continent (see Table 18.2). A good example of these kinds of studies is the investigation of the adoption of e-HRM in companies in 16 different European countries performed by Galanaki and Panayotopoulou (2009). They found some links with a nation's characteristics, such as internet penetration, and the adoption of e-HRM. Their study showed a positive relationship between a company's characteristics and the level of use of e-HRM, such as company size (mostly multinationals were included), the level of the strategic orientation of the HRM function, the level of education received by employees, and the level of innovation and service quality.

Beamish et al. (2002) investigated the deployment of e-learning in the UK and European corporate organisations. The managers who participated in the study were able to identify a series of benefits from e-learning, such as cost-effectiveness, as well as barriers, usually based on cultural resistance and learner motivation. In general, managers supported the view that e-learning can have a role in strategy-led training. No attention was paid to culture as an explanatory factor. Ruël et al. (2004) explored e-HRM in large companies in the Netherlands, Luxembourg, Germany, and Belgium. They conclude that the e-HRM goals of companies are cost reduction, service quality improvement, and improving HRM's strategic focus. There is a gap between available e-HRM functionalities and its actual use; e-HRM implies a process of 'growth' in a company. Outcomes of e-HRM are a reduction of costs, an improvement of client satisfaction with HRM services, and improved quality of the communication. Cultural or national differences were not taken into account as an explanatory factor, but the study raises some interesting issues such as the role of the language of the e-HRM applications in their adoption by users in foreign subsidiaries, and the differences of communication styles between the USA and Western Europe in the case of a US-based multinational.

Imperatori and De Marco (2009) looked at the real labour transformation process related to the introduction of e-work projects in four different companies in the UK and Italy. The results confirm the alignment of the managerial discourse with organisational practices. Factors concerning the design and implementation of technology-based work systems were evaluated, such as the organisational and employer viewpoint, the organisational culture, and evaluation and monitoring phases during the project. Cultural and national differences were not included in their analysis.

Strohmeier and Kabst (2009) conducted a large-scale survey in 23 European countries and found that e-HRM is a common practice throughout Europe. Major determinants

Table 18.3   Cross-national e-HRM research within one multinational company

Author	Region	Topic	Type of study
Tixier (2004)	Europe	HRIS	Qualitative
Vaughan and MacVicar (2004)	Europe	e-learning	Quantitative

of e-HRM are size, work organisation, and HRM configuration, according to their study. Interestingly, they found cross-national differences in e-HRM adoption: Eastern European post-communist countries are ahead of Western European countries. The study was not able to conclude about convergence of adoption over time.

The overall picture that emerges from this overview of e-HRM studies with a cross-national focus but within the same continent is that all those studies are done in Europe. Hardly any of the studies aimed at revealing cross-national differences. Only Strohmeier and Kabst (2009) partly include a cross-national focus in their analysis. However, no clear theory is applied to explain the differences and similarities in e-HRM adoption.

e-HRM with a Cross-National Focus but Within One Company

Some e-HRM studies include cross-national data, but collected within one company (see Table 18.3). Beulen (2008) and Williams et al. (2009) are examples of this type of study, but, as discussed earlier, the focus of the studies was to find cross-national differences rather than to focus on the company. Other international case studies focus on establishments in European countries. An example of this kind of research is the case study of Tixier (2004) at the Rexel group in four different European countries: Belgium, England, Portugal, and Spain. She followed the implementation of HRIS and examined the influence of the local contexts on that implementation. The study included exogenous factors, industry, and country or regional characteristics of the subsidiaries. Tixier identified two distinctive HRM practices in the different subsidiaries, which she called the management staff (with a focus on quantitative manpower and conflict resolution) and the human resource management system (with a focus on the utilisation of resources to achieve organisational goals). The author concluded that HRIS could support the harmonisation of practices in a multinational company.

Vaughan and MacVicar (2004) studied the blended approach to e-learning of a large multinational banking organisation in the UK. The pre-implementation procedure and the perceptions of employees were investigated in subsidiaries in England, Northern Ireland and Scotland. A qualitative investigation showed a low awareness of e-learning among the employees, and that the attitudes of managers were diverse, ranging from being very supportive towards learning and the development of employees, to not being supportive at all. The major barrier is the time spent on learning and development, while the major benefits of e-learning are its accessibility, relevance and user-friendliness.

The overall picture that is that cross-national e-HRM research conducted within one multinational company is Western-biased, exploratory in nature, and more importantly, not explicitly contributing to the cross-national and cross-cultural body of knowledge on e-HRM.

e-HRM Studies Within a Specific National Context

In Europe, Majó (2006) investigated the condition of e-recruitment in Hungary by studying the internet sites of 50 different companies. International trends related to the diffusion of IT for recruitment purposes can be observed in Hungarian companies, yet to a minor extent and with lower intensity. Parry and Wilson (2006) concentrated their study on online recruitment in the UK. Factors influencing the adoption of e-recruitment were relative advantage, difficulties, and external compatibility for corporate websites; and relative advantage and compatibility for commercial websites. Fernándes-Sánchez et al. (2009) explored the recruitment process in Spanish firms. They noted that HRIS are being introduced steadily in Spanish firms; however, the presence of traditional information systems is still strong.

Hausdorf and Duncan (2004) investigated internet recruiting in Canada in relation to firm size. Large companies more often have their own website and use more internet recruiters, while small firms are less aware of internet recruitment. The adoption of e-HRM in large New Zealand organisations was the focus of Lau and Hooper's (2009) study, while Olivas-Luján et al. (2006) concentrated on the same topic in Mexico. In New Zealand the popularity of e-HRM is a growing phenomenon among large companies (Lau & Hooper, 2009). Olivas-Luján et al. (2006) identified several research gaps for e-HRM in Mexico. They also found that Mexican enterprises face a bigger challenge in implementing an e-HRM system as they are mainly production-oriented and thus have difficulties in justifying the investment.

Some studies were also performed in Asia. Hooi (2006) investigated the readiness for e-HRM in Malaysian small and medium-sized companies. The author found that many organisations are still utilising traditional HRM instead of e-HRM. Financial resources and expertise seem to be the main barriers to e-HRM implementation. In Taiwan, organisational support and HRIS effectiveness were greater in the case of a higher HRIS level, as measured by their use by top managers and HRM staff (Lin, 1997). Jones (2007) studied e-HRM in Kuwait. She addressed the challenges involved in implementing a management system for training and development. She highlighted the importance of skilled senior management and HRM staff. In India, successful HRIS practices included internal job positioning, e-recruitment, learning communities, and e-learning.

Among those who explicitly mentioned a national context in the title of the publication, but did not evidence any intention of linking the results to the characteristics of that particular context, we find Bondarouk and Ruël (2006) with their investigation of e-HRM in a Dutch ministry; Koopman and Batenburg (2008) focusing on employee self-service applications in the Dutch public sector; Farndale and Paauwe (2006) investigating HRM Shared Service Centres (SSCs) in Dutch organisations; and Rahim and Singh (2007) studying B2E systems in two Australian universities. The studies in this category (see Table 18.4), we observe, hardly relate their findings to the specific characteristics of the national context in which the data were collected, although this context is included in the title of their paper.

Table 18.4   e-HRM research with a specific national context

Author	Region	Topic	Type of study
Majó (2006)	Europe	e-recruitment	Qualitative/website analysis
Parry and Wilson (2006)	Europe (UK)	Online recruitment	Qualitative/ quantitative
Fernándes-Sánchez et al. (2009)	Europe	HRIS	
Hausdorf and Duncan (2004)	North America	Internet recruiting	Quantitative
Lau and Hooper (2009)	New Zealand	e-HRM adoption	Quantitative
Olivas-Luján et al. (2006)	North America	e-HRM adoption	Quantitative
Hooi (2006)	Asia (Malaysia)	e-HRM readiness	Quantitative
Lin (1997)	Asia (Taiwan)	HRIS effectiveness	Quantitative
Jones (2007)	Asia (Kuwait)	HRIS training and development	Qualitative
Bondarouk and Ruël (2006)	Europe (Netherlands)	e-HRM implementation	Qualitative
Koopman and Batenburg (2008)	Europe (Netherlands)	Employee self-service	Quantitative
Farndale and Paauwe (2006)	Europe (Netherlands)	Shared Service Centres	Quantitative
Rahim and Sigh (2007)	Asia Pacific (Australia)	Business-to-employee systems	Qualitative

Results from an Additional 'Quick Scan', 2011–16

Since the analysis above focuses on the period until 2010, it is interesting to see whether the next five years resulted in an increase in the number of publications with an international perspective. For that reason we searched for research publications in journal, books, and conference proceedings in the period 2011–16 (see Table 18.5). The key criterion for inclusion was that a geographical reference was made in the title or the abstract.

We conclude that only eight research publications with a geographical reference in the title or mentioned in the abstract were published in the 2011–16 period. This is a poor result of approximately one publication per year on average. It is our overall observation that the interest in e-HRM in general has grown since 2010, based on the number of new special issues in research journals since 2010. That makes the result of our 2011–16 'quick scan' even more disappointing. The share of the latest published research on e-HRM and HRIS referring to a geographical location in relation to research coming from the USA or Europe has most likely decreased.

Summarizing Cross-National e-HRM Studies

Truly international comparative e-HRM research is scarce, something that clearly emerges from this literature review. The comparative studies available are basically atheoretical and

Table 18.5   Results additional analysis 2011–16 HRIS publications with geographical reference

Author	Region	Topic	Type of study
Troshani et al. (2011)	Australia	HRIS adoption	Quantitative
Normalini et al. (2012)	Asia (Malaysia)	Antecedents and outcomes of HRIS use	Quantitative
Spero et al. (2011)	Africa	HRIS for health workforce	Quantitative
Razali and Vrontis (2010)	Asia (Malaysia)	Employee reactions towards HRIS implementation	Quantitative
Kundu and Kadian (2012)	Asia (India)	HRIS application in India	Quantitative
Troshani et al. (2010)	Australia	HRIS adoption	Qualitative
Kabir et al. (2013)	Asia (Bangladesh)	HRIS practices in universities	Quantitative
Iwu and Benedict (2013)	Africa	HRIS investment and economic recession	Quantitative

do not refer to cultural or national contextual aspects as an explanatory factor. Most of the e-HRM research originates from the USA and from Europe, and MNCs are the units of analysis. Small and medium-sized enterprises are underrepresented. As such, this picture can lead us to the following conclusion, however cautiously: Western-based multinationals lead the way in e-HRM adoption and use, but MNCs from non-Western regions are quickly following suit. SMEs in Western countries are lagging behind but adopting e-HRM as well. All the studies on e-HRM so far have not been suitable to conclude whether e-HRM in Western countries and non-Western countries looks similar or is developing similarly or not. In other words, no study to date has clearly addressed the basic issue underlying international comparative research, which is the convergence/divergence debate.

MANAGEMENT PRACTICES IN A COMPARATIVE PERSPECTIVE: THE CONVERGENCE/DIVERGENCE DEBATE

The main purpose of international comparative research is to identify and explain differences and similarities. This issue is referred to as the convergence/divergence debate; a debate that has been keeping researchers busy since the beginning of the twentieth century. Around that time the current debate took up Veblen's statement that developing countries have an advantage by adapting technologies that had been developed by the more mature countries (Elmslie, 1995). Nowadays, the debate on convergence/divergence is widespread in all kinds of research areas, for instance Baumol (1986) who initiated the debate on economic convergence.

Today's convergence/divergence debate in the area of organisation and management practices started in the mid-1980s, with the increase in globalisation. Economies have become more and more integrated. This integration has led to a spreading of global management structures and the adoption of similar operating techniques. Hence it can be argued that global organisations are converging (McGaughey & De Cieri, 1999). The following circumstances led to this convergence: the rise of the internet, which simplified the global communication process and data exchange; increased travelling; and the deregulation of economic activities by governments (Levitt, 2006; Doz & Prahalad, 1991). However, opponents of the convergence hypothesis state that despite the structural and technological convergence, cultural differences remain.

The debate on convergence/divergence was extended in 1993 with the 'crossvergence' perspective (Ralston et al., 1993). The results of that study showed that the managerial values of a country are often influenced by both culture and the business environment. Therefore, they suggested a third perspective, a combination of convergence and divergence: crossvergence. In 1997, Ralston et al. broadened the definition of crossvergence: 'crossvergence advocates that the combination of socio-cultural influences and business ideology influences is the driving force that precipitates the development of new and unique values systems among individuals in a society due to the dynamic interaction of these influences' (Ralston et al., 1997: 183).

McGaughey and De Cieri (1999) developed a conceptual framework based on micro-, macro-, and meso-level organisational variables and processes, which offers four different types of convergence/divergence: assimilation, integration, separation, and novelty. Assimilation takes place when an entity loses a part of its own characteristics by adopting norms from another entity. Integration is a combination of characteristics of two or more entities. Separation purposefully avoids integration of the characteristics of the other entity. Novelty does not maintain its own characteristics, nor those from the other entity. In addition to convergence and divergence, McGaughey and De Cieri (1999) introduced 'maintenance' as a third option: keeping the level of similarity or dissimilarity as a possible direction.

In 2006, Spicer offered a new view on the debate. Instead of arguing that organisational logics are converging into one model or diverging into national types, he suggested that organisational logics are transforming (Spicer, 2006). This means that when organisation logics move across space, they undergo a process of transformation. A remarkable aspect of the convergence/divergence debate is that the researchers did not try to extend each other's work; instead, it seems that they more or less ignored it.

Convergence/Divergence in HRM

In the field of IHRM, Brewster et al. (2008) examined whether there was similarity, isomorphism, or duality in the HRM policies and practices in host countries of MNCs, based on three schools of thought: global homogeneity or ethnocentricity, local isomorphism, and duality theories. They found evidence for common global practices, but the duality theories provided the best explanation.

Wöcke et al. (2007) examined the differences between HRM practices of parent MNCs and affiliates. They concluded that there are several factors that influence the need for standardisation or localisation: variation in the business model, the need to accommodate national culture, and the type and role of organisational culture in the MNC. Additionally, the evolution of a MNC leads to a higher level of standardisation of HRM practices.

Standardisation/Localisation

Linked to the convergence/divergence debate, the standardisation/localisation debate plays a role in the area of organisation and management practices (Prahalad & Doz, 1987). This debate is concentrated on the company or meso level, while convergence/ divergence is more focused on the macro level (Pudelko & Harzing, 2007). Rosenzweig and Nohria (1994) defined standardisation/localisation as: the extent to which subsidiaries of multinational companies are behaving as local firms (localisation) versus the extent to which their practices are similar to those of the headquarters (standardisation). HRM plays an important role in this debate because it deals with the management of people and is therefore seen as least likely to converge across countries. MNCs are more likely to localise practices than to export country-of-origin practices (Leat & El-Kot, 2007).

Over the years numerous studies have examined cross-cultural comparisons of HRM. Some studies examined the transfer of HRM practices, while others focused on which HRM practices and issues are relevant for a certain country (Myloni et al., 2004). Laurent (1986) argued that HRM practices represent the values of national culture, and because of this an HRM system that is successful in one culture may not be successful in another. Rosenzweig and Nahria (1994) examined what the influence of national culture is on HRM policies and practices. Schuler et al. (1993) addressed the tension between integration and differentiation between inter-unit linkages, and how to operate effectively in the local environment. Lu and Björkman (1997) examined the tension between standardisation and localisation in joint China–Western ventures using five 'classical' HRM practices.

Pudelko and Harzing (2008) extended the debate. In their study, they examined whether MNCs from different countries (Germany, Japan, and the USA) put different emphases on the extent of standardisation versus localisation of the HRM practices of their foreign subsidiaries. Based on an international survey (mostly completed by highly placed HRM managers), they concluded that the debate on standardisation and localisation needs a major extension. Their results showed that standardisation not only takes place towards the headquarters but can also take place towards global best practices, wherever they originate from. Based on these findings, they stated that in today's globalised corporate environment, ethnocentric approaches to management are no longer sustainable.

There are several factors that determine the degree of standardisation. Parry et al. (2008) mentions four reasons why companies are likely to standardise their processes: HRM practices are more likely to be transferred from the headquarters if they are regarded as superior; HRM policies and practices can be standardised in order to support their wider business strategy; ethical issues such as minimum rights and precluding child labour can lead to international standardisation of practices; and finally, knowledge transfer, quality standards, and creating an international network can lead to the standardisation of HRM practices and policies. There are numerous factors that determine the degree of standardisation, such as the relationship between the headquarters and the subsidiary, organisational culture, authority structures, market characteristics, work norms, and so on (Parry et al., 2008). Local factors that have an influence are unions, labour market, and legal and political context (Ngo et al., 1998; Brewster, 1995).

TOWARDS A MODEL FOR CROSS-NATIONAL E-HRM RESEARCH

The study of the role of technology in organisations has a long tradition. Over the years, different views on technology have developed in parallel with theoretical perspectives on organisations: Orlikowski (2008) mentions, for example: contingency theory, strategic choice models, Marxist studies, symbolic interactionist approaches, transaction-cost economics, network analyses, practice theories, and structurational models. Nowadays, technology and organisations undergo rapid and radical changes in form and function. Therefore, researchers on technology are also using the ideas of innovation, learning, and improvisation for a better understanding of the implications of new technologies on organisations (Orlikowski, 2008).

In an attempt to overcome the limitations of contingency theory in linking technology and organisational forms, a number of scholars in the mid-1980s started to use Giddens's (1984) theory of structuration (Schuessler, 2006). Barley (1986) was one of the first researchers to use structuration theory in order to study the relation between technology and organisational structure. Based on this theory, he argued that technology can be constraining and enabling. Technology was considered to be social in nature rather than a physical object. Most interestingly, and opposing a deterministic view on technology, Barley's study showed that the organisations responded differently to the implementation of the same sort of technology. He concluded that 'technologies do influence organisational structures in orderly ways, but their influence depends on the specific historical process in which they are embedded' (Barley, 1986: 107).

DeSanctis and Poole (1994) adapted structuration theory to study the interaction of groups and organisations with advanced information technologies (AITs), such as group decision support systems (GDSSs). They developed the adaptive structuration theory (AST). 'The AST examines the process from two positions: the type of structures that are provided by advanced technologies and the structures that actually emerge in human action as people interact with these technologies' (DeSanctis & Poole, 1994: 121). Or, formulated differently, AST is focused on the rules and resources of advanced technologies and how users in small groups adapt to the rules and use the resources. The adaption can lead to different outcomes even in the same context because users can act differently when utilising the same technology.

An important aspect of the AST is spirit: 'The spirit is the "official line" which the technology presents to people regarding how to act when using the system, how to interpret its features, and how to fill in gaps in procedure which are not explicitly specified' (DeSanctis & Poole, 1994: 126). Another central aspect of the AST is the concept of appropriation. Appropriation in the context of information systems in organisations refers to the process of actively selecting 'structural features' of a given system or application and incorporating them in their daily work activities. From a large set of potentially applicable features, individuals actively choose the ones they judge as most useful and easy to use, though in the way individuals interpret those features. This implies that a similar set of structural features of an information system can be used in different ways and therefore have different expected or unexpected consequences.

As mentioned earlier, the rapid and radical changes in technologies and organisations have called for new concepts, such as improvisation and emergence, for studying and understanding the use of technology in practice. With similar intentions, Orlikowski (2008) extended her view on technology as being an emergent structure, a process of enactment (to constitute or perform). This view focuses on how humans enact structures that shape their emergent and situated use of the technology during the interaction with that technology in their daily life. This means that structures are not embedded in technology, but enacted by users. There are three types of enactment: inertia – technology used to maintain the status quo; application – technology used to modify and improve (work) processes; and change – technology used to change the status quo considerably.

As the foundation of a research model, the framework of Ruël et al. (2004) was adopted in the first edition of this book (Brewster & Mayrhofer, 2012). In this chapter, we briefly outline this and then explain its convergence/divergence dimension. The basic framework (Ruël et al., 2004) distinguishes four 'phases' in e-HRM adoption in organisations. In the middle of the model are the internal agents who determine and influence the four phases. Ongoing maintenance by human action sustains the technology, and it is constituted through use. On its own, technology plays no role. Therefore, it seems legitimate to place internal agents in the middle of the model (see Figure 18.1).

The internal agents and the four phases are situated in a context. The model distinguishes six factors that play a role: competition, technological development, the state of HRM, the labour market, societal developments, and government regulation. These factors can also be referred to as conditions and consequences (Orlikowski, 2008). Conditions are subdivided into: interpretive conditions (the way that members of a community share

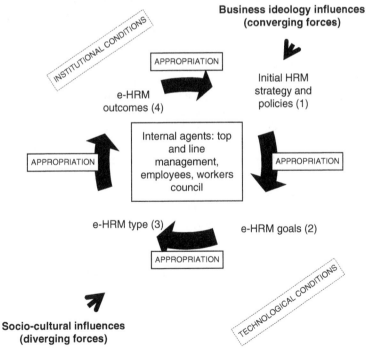

Figure 18.1   The research model

meanings and understandings to make sense about their world, including the technology they use), technological conditions (tools and data available), and institutional conditions (social structures that form part of the larger social system within which users work). Consequences are subdivided into: process consequences (execution and outcomes of users' work practices), technology consequences (technological prosperity available to users), and structure consequences (structures that users enact as part of the larger social system in which they are participating) (Orlikowski, 2008).

The first phase of the model, initial HRM strategy and policy, refers to the state of HRM in an organisation. When companies start with or invest further in e-HRM, there will be certain implicit or explicit HRM policy assumptions and practices already in use. Based on the classic work of Beer et al. (1985), three types of policies can be distinguished: bureaucratic policies, found in organisations that operate in a stable environment; market policies, found in organisations that have to respond rapidly to changes in the environment; and clan policies, found in organisations that rely heavily on delivering quality and innovation.

The second phase refers to the goals of e-HRM. Goals are selected by internal agents within the existing HRM policy context (or internal institutional properties) in which they act, but intermediated by external institutional properties such as competition and technological developments. In terms of the work of Giddens's, Orlikowski's, and DeSanctis and Poole's AST, the existing HRM policy is a set of 'structures' interpreted and applied by internal agents, in AST terms referred to as 'appropriation'. The e-HRM goals selected, whether implicitly or explicitly, are outcomes of that appropriation process.

From the e-HRM goals selected, as a third phase, an e-HRM type emerges as an outcome of deliberations by internal agents interpreting and applying e-HRM goals in day-to-day organisational practices. e-HRM types refer to a combination of selected technologies and their appropriation by internal agents. Therefore, it is not a static context with a technological application deployed in a technical sense. Rather, e-HRM types are a dynamic context, in which at a certain point in time there can be a huge gap between available technological functionalities and real use of these functionalities by internal agents. Analytically, three types of e-HRM can be distinguished: operational e-HRM, meaning that the dominant use consists of more traditional administrative services such as salary administration and record-keeping; relational E-HRM, meaning that the dominant use consists of executing HRM processes, such as recruitment, compensation, and training and development; and transformational e-HRM, meaning that the dominant use has a strategic character, such as knowledge management, strategic competence management, and organisational change. From the appropriation of e-HRM applications, e-HRM outcomes emerge, intended and unintended ones.

The fourth phase comprises the e-HRM outcomes. In general terms, the outcome can be one or a combination of the following goals: to improve the strategic orientation of HRM; to reduce costs and/or increase efficiency; and to improve the quality of HRM service for management and employees. We link the goals of e-HRM to what DeSanctis and Poole (1994) refer to as the spirit of technology. The spirit is concerned with questions such as: 'What kind of goals are being promoted by this technology?' and 'What kind of values are being supported?' (DeSanctis & Poole, 1994: 127). For example, e-HRM applications can 'contain' the spirit of 'improving client services'.

The e-HRM outcomes should not be confused with the e-HRM goals described as phase two of the model. Ruël et al. (2004) state that e-HRM is a way of carrying out HRM; it is a way of thinking about and implementing HRM strategies, policies, and practices aimed at achieving certain goals: improving the strategic role of HRM, improving the client services, and improving efficiency and administrative processes. Besides these goals, there are a number of overall HRM policy outcomes to which all e-HRM activities will be directed, implicitly or explicitly. Beer et al. (1985) distinguish the following four: (1) commitment – the trust between management and employees; (2) competence – the ability of employees to learn and perform new tasks; (3) cost effectiveness – financial competiveness; and (4) congruence – structuring the internal organisation, the reward system, and the input–output of personnel in the interests of stakeholders. The e-HRM outcomes can be considered as interpretations by internal agents, applied and reflected in an organisation's HRM policy. The types of enactments described earlier can also be seen as types of outcomes, and are added to the fourth phase of the model.

As can be seen in Figure 18.1, revising the original Ruël et al. (2004) model, we have divided the research model into two parts. One side represents the part in which institutional conditions are the dominant influential factors (phases one and four): the e-HRM system is part of a larger social system, and the social structures of the social system will influence the way the technology is designed. For example, the type of HRM policies will be influenced by the environment of the organisation. The other side represents the part in which technological conditions are the dominant influential factors (phases two and three): agents determine the goals of the technology and the type of e-HRM which eventually provides tools and data for the users. The combination of the conditions and consequences can lead to three different types of enactments (inertia, application, and change). The full research model as explained above is visualised in Figure 18.1.

CONCLUSIONS AND IMPLICATIONS FOR CROSS-NATIONAL E-HRM RESEARCH

In this chapter, we have proposed a research model for cross-national e-HRM research. The model is based on a constructivist view of the relationship between technology and organisation, adopting the lines of thought of Orlikowski (1992) and DeSanctis and Poole (1994). The model identifies four phases of e-HRM in organisations, assuming these phases analytically as separate and sequential, although empirically they are likely to be overlapping.

The research model can be used as a framework for cross-national comparative e-HRM research. It is suitable for this purpose due to its all-encompassing nature, including the main focus areas of e-HRM research (goals, implementation, adoption, outcomes, HRM transformation), and therefore allows comparison of these areas and variables across borders in an MNC context. However, as mentioned earlier, comparative international research as such does not serve much of a purpose on its own: it needs contextualisation.

The convergence/divergence debate is the relevant debate in which international comparative e-HRM research should be positioned, as it offers a relevant and rich explanatory ground for differences and similarities across national and cultural boundaries. The model proposed in this chapter is a stimulus for e-HRM studies that aim to contribute to this debate. In its current form, the model hypothesises that e-HRM in different national or cultural contexts will show predominantly converging tendencies during phase one (reigning HRM policy under which e-HRM decisions are taken in organisations) and phase two (explicitly or implicitly formulated e-HRM goals that are most likely to be chosen given the spirit of the business ideology). Diverging, socio-cultural specific tendencies will most likely appear during phase three (e-HRM types, reflecting the appropriation of e-HRM by internal agents) and phase four (e-HRM outcomes, reflecting the perceptions of internal agents regarding intended and unintended consequences of e-HRM appropriation).

The proposed model can be used for quantitative as well as qualitative research approaches and can allow different additional theoretical lenses. For quantitative studies, the model triggers research questions such as: Do converging forces have a dominant impact on how e-HRM is shaped in organisations in phases one and two? Do diverging forces have a dominant impact on how e-HRM is shaped in organisations in phases three and four? Do converging and diverging influences on the phases of e-HRM in organisations differ per national or cultural context? To what extent do different internal agents perceive converging and diverging influences differently related to different phases of e-HRM?

For qualitative studies, interesting research questions include: how do internal agents appropriate business ideological and socio-cultural features in the different phases of e-HRM? How do internal agents arrive, between each other, at decisions on how to shape e-HRM in different national or cultural contexts? How are e-HRM outcomes perceived and interpreted by internal agents in different national and cultural contexts and 'translated' into the HRM policy? How do internal agents bring about change in e-HRM in different national and cultural contexts? How do converging and diverging influences 'interact' during an e-HRM change project?

In terms of additional theoretical perspectives, researchers can adopt political, behavioural, economic, as well as cultural lenses to shape and specify their research questions. Political lenses will help to understand the role of power and how power is exercised regarding e-HRM, and how it results in converging or diverging tendencies. Behavioural lenses will contribute to revealing the role of individual actions and interpersonal interactions, and economic lenses may focus on quantifying costs and benefits of converging and diverging tendencies in shaping e-HRM in organisations. Finally, cultural lenses will help to understand how the cultural backgrounds of internal agents play a role in shaping e-HRM in organisations and how this results in either converging or diverging tendencies.

REFERENCES

AbuZaineh, T., & Ruël, H. 2008. e-HRM-user perceptions of e-HRM tools in Kuwaiti SMEs. In H. Ruël and R. Magalhaes (eds), *Proceedings of the Second International Workshop on Human Resource Information Systems*: 124–135. Barcelona: INSTICC Press.

Barley, S. 1986. Technology as an occasion for structuring: Evidence from observations of CT scanners and the social order of radiology departments. *Administrative Science Quarterly*, 31(1): 78–108.

Baumol, W. 1986. Productivity growth, convergence, and welfare: What the long-run data show. *American Economic Review*, 76(5): 1072–1085.

Beamish, N., Armistead, C., Watkinson, M., & Armfield, G. 2002. The deployment of e-learning in UK/ European corporate organisations. *European Business Journal*, 14(3): 105–115.

Beer, M., Walton, R., Spector, B., & Mills, D. 1985. *Human Resource Management: A General Manager's Perspective: Text and Cases*. New York: Free Press.

Beulen, E. 2008. The enabling role of information technology in the global war for talent: Accenture's industrialized approach. *Information Technology for Development*, 14(3): 213–224.

Bondarouk, T. 2014. *Orchestrating the e-HRM Symphony*. Enschede: Universiteit Twente.

Bondarouk, T., & Furtmueller, E. 2012. Electronic human resource management: Four decades of empirical evidence. *Best Paper Proceedings of the Academy of Management Meeting 2012*, Boston, MA, 3–7 August.

Bondarouk, T., & Ruël, H. 2006. e-HRM effectiveness in a Dutch Ministry: Results of survey and discursive exploration combined. *Proceedings of the First European Academic Workshop on e-HRM*: 1–17, Enschede, The Netherlands: University of Twente.

Bondarouk, T., & Ruël, H. 2009. Electronic human resource management: Challenges in the digital era. *International Journal of Human Resource Management*, 20(3): 505–514.

Brewster, C. 1995. Towards a 'European' model of human resource management. *Journal of International Business Studies*, 26(1): 1–21.

Brewster, C., & Mayrhofer, W. 2012. *Handbook of Research on Comparative Human Resource Management*. Cheltenham, UK and Northampton, MA, USA: Edward Elgar Publishing.

Brewster, C., Wood, G., & Brookes, M. 2008. Similarity, isomorphism or duality? Recent survey evidence on the HRM policies of MNCs. *British Journal of Management*, 19(4): 320–342.

DeSanctis, G., & Poole, M. 1994. Capturing the complexity in advanced technology use: Adaptive structuration theory. *Organization Science*, 5(2): 121–147.

Doz, Y., & Prahalad, C. 1991. Managing DMNCs: A search for a new paradigm. *Strategic Management Journal*, 12(S1): 145–164.

Elmslie, B. 1995. The convergence debate between David Hume and Josiah Tucker. *Journal of Economic Perspectives*, 9(4): 207–216.

Farndale, E., & Paauwe, J. 2006. HR shared service centres in the Netherlands: Restructuring the HR function. *Proceedings of the First European Academic Workshop on e-HRM*: 18–29, Enschede, the Netherlands: University of Twente.

Fernández-Sánchez, J.A., de Juana-Espinosa, S., & Valdés-Conca, J. 2009. Exploring the relation between the use of HRIS and their implementation in Spanish firms. In T. Torres-Coronas and M. Arias-Oliva (eds), *Encyclopedia of Human Resources Information Systems: Challenges in e-HRM: Challenges in e-HRM*, Vol. 1: 399–405. New York: Hershey.

Galanaki, E., & Panayotopoulou, L. 2009. Adoption and success of e-HRM in European firms. In T. Torres-Coronas and M. Arias-Oliva (eds), *Encyclopedia of Human Resources Information Systems: Challenges in e-HRM*, Vol. 1: 24–30. New York: Hershey.

Giddens, A. 1984. *The Constitution of Society: Outline of the Theory of Structuration*. Berkeley, CA: University of California Press.

Harris, M.M., van Hoye, G., & Lievens, F. 2003. Privacy and attitudes towards internet-based selection systems: A cross-cultural comparison. *International Journal of Selection and Assessment*, 11(2/3): 230–236.

Hausdorf, P.A., & Duncan, D. 2004. Firm size and internet recruiting in Canada: A preliminary investigation. *Journal of Small Business Management*, 42(3): 325–334.

Hooi, L.W. 2006. Implementing e-HRM: The readiness of small and medium sized manufacturing companies in Malaysia. *Asia Pacific Business Review*, 12(4): 465–485.

Imperatori, B., & De Marco, M. 2009. e-Work and labor processes transformation. In T. Bondarouk, H. Ruël, K. Guidedoni-Jourdain, and E. Oiry (eds), *Handbook of Research on E-Transformation and Human Resources Management Technologies: Organizational Outcomes and Challenges*: 34–54. New York: Hershey.

Iwu, C., & Benedict, H. 2013. Economic recession and investment on human resource information systems (HRIS): Perspectives on some South African firms. *Journal of Management Development*, 32(4): 404–418.

Jones, S. 2007. The challenges of implementing an integrated web-based software system for managing training and development in a large organization: An example from the Middle East. In H. Ruël and R. Magalhaes (eds), *Proceedings of the first International Workshop on Human Resource Information Systems*: 40–47. Funchal/Madiera, Portugal: INSTICC Press.

Kabir, R., Bhuiyan, F., & Masum, A.K.M. 2013. HRIS practices in universities: An exploratory study on the private universities in Bangladesh. *Global Journal of Human-Social Science Research*, 13(7): 1–6.

Koopman, G., & Batenburg, R. 2008. User participation and involvement in the development of HR self-service applications within the Dutch Government. In H. Ruël and R. Magalhaes (eds), *Proceedings of the second International Workshop on Human Resource Information Systems*: 16–29. Barcelona: INSTICC Press.

Kundu, S.C., & Kadian, R. 2012. Applications of HRIS in human resource management in India: A study. *European Journal of Business and Management*, 4(21): 34–41.

Lau, G., & Hooper, V. 2009. Adoption of e-HRM in large New Zealand organisations. In T. Torres-Coronas and M. Arias-Oliva (eds), *Encyclopedia of Human Resources Information Systems: Challenges in e-HRM*, Vol. 1: 31–41. New York: Hershey.

Laurent, A. 1986. The cross-cultural puzzle of international human resource management. *Human Resource Management*, 25(1): 91–102.

Leat, M., & El-Kot, G. 2007. HRM practices in Egypt: The influence of national context?. *International Journal of Human Resource Management*, 18(1): 147–158.

Levitt, T. 2006. What business are you in? Classic advice from Theodore Levitt. *Harvard Business Review*, 84(10): 126–137.

Lin, C.Y.Y. 1997. Human resource information systems: Implementation in Taiwan. *Research and Practice in Human Resource Management*, 5(1): 57–72.

Lu, Y., & Björkman, I. 1997. HRM practices in China–Western joint ventures: MNC standardization versus localization. *International Journal of Human Resource Management*, 8(5): 614–628.

Majó, Z. 2006. Development of web-based human resource management: Corporate practice of e-recruitment in Hungary. *Proceedings of the First European Academic Workshop on e-HRM*: 64–75. Enschede, the Netherlands: University of Twente.

Marler, J.H., & Fisher, S.H. 2013. An evidence-based review of e-HRM and strategic human resource management. *Human Resource Management Review*, 23(1): 18–36.

Marler, J.H., & Parry, E. 2008. Which comes first e-HRM or SHRM?. *Proceedings of the second International Workshop on Human Resource Information Systems*: 40–50. Barcelona, Spain: INSTICC Press.

McGaughey, S., & De Cieri, H. 1999. Reassessment of convergence and divergence dynamics: Implications for international HRM. *International Journal of Human Resource Management*, 10(2): 235–250.

Myloni, B., Harzing, A.-W., & Mirza, H. 2004. Human resource management in Greece: Have the colours of culture faded away?. *International Journal of Cross Cultural Management*, 4(1): 59–76.

Ngo, H.-Y., Turban, D., Lau, C.M., & Lui, S.-Y. 1998. Human resource practices and firm performance of multinational corporations: Influences of country origin. *International Journal of Human Resource Management*, 9(4): 632–652.

Normalini, M.K., Ramayah, T., & Kurnia, S. 2012. Antecedents and outcomes of human resource information system (HRIS) use. *International Journal of Productivity and Performance Management*, 61(6): 603–623.

Olivas-Luján, M.R., & Florkowski, G.W. 2009. The diffusion of HRITs across English-speaking countries. In T. Torres-Coronas and M. Arias-Oliva (eds), *Encyclopedia of Human Resources Information Systems: Challenges in e-HRM*, Vol. 1: 242–247. New York: Hershey.

Olivas-Luján, M.R., Ramirez, J., & Zapata Cantú, L. 2006. e-HRM in Mexico – towards a research agenda. *Proceedings of the First European Academic Workshop on E-HRM*: 113–124. Enschede, the Netherlands: University of Twente.

Orlikowski, W. 1992. The duality of technology: Rethinking the concept of technology in organizations. *Organization Science*, 3(3): 398–427.

Orlikowski, W. 2008. Using technology and constituting structures: A practice lens for studying technology in organizations. In M. Ackerman, C. Halverson, T. Erickson, and W. Kellog (eds), *Resources, Co-evolution and Artifacts in Theory in CSCW*: 255–305. London: Springer-Verlag.

Parry, E., Dickmann, M., & Morley, M. 2008. North American MNCs and their HR policies in liberal and coordinated market economies. *International Journal of Human Resource Management*, 19(11): 2024–2040.

Parry, E., & Wilson, H. 2006. Online recruitment within the UK: A model of the factors affecting its adoption. *Proceedings of the First European Academic Workshop on e-HRM*: 133–145. Enschede, the Netherlands: University of Twente.

Prahalad, C., & Doz, Y. 1987. *The Multinational Mission: Balancing Local Demands and Global Vision*. New York: Free Press.

Puck, J., Holtbrügge, D., & Mohr, A. 2006. Applicant information and selection strategies in corporate web site recruiting: The role of national culture. *Proceedings of the First European Academic Workshop on e-HRM*: 154–164. Enschede, the Netherlands: University of Twente.

Puck, J., Holtbrügge, D., & Mohr, A. 2009. Applicant information and selection strategies in corporate web site recruiting: The role of national culture. In T. Bandarouk, H. Ruël, K. Guidedoni-Jourdain, and E. Oiry (eds), *Handbook of Research on E-Transformation and Human Resources Management Technologies: Organizational Outcomes and Challenges*: 187–201. New York: Hershey.

Pudelko, M., & Harzing, A.-W. 2007. Country-of-origin, localization, or dominance effect? An empirical investigation of HRM practices in foreign subsidiaries. *Human Resource Management*, 46(4): 535–559.

Pudelko, M., & Harzing, A.-W. 2008. The golden triangle for MNCs: Standardization towards headquarters practices, standardization towards global best practices and localization. *Organizational Dynamics*, 37(4): 394–404.

Rahim, M., & Singh, M. 2007. Understanding benefits and impediments of b2e e-business systems adoption: Experiences of two large Australian universities. *Journal of Internet Commerce*, 6(2): 3–17.

Ralston, D., Gustafson, D., Cheung, F., & Terpstra, R. 1993. Differences in managerial values: A study of US, Hong Kong and PRC managers. *Journal of International Business Studies*, 24(2): 249–275.

Ralston, D., Holt, D., Terpstra, R., & Kai-Cheng, Y. 1997. The impact of natural culture and economic ideology on managerial work values: A study of the United States, Russia, Japan, and China. *Journal of International Business Studies*, 28(1): 177–207.

Rao, P. 2009a. e-Recruitment in emerging economies. In T. Torres-Coronas and M. Arias-Oliva (eds), *Encyclopedia of Human Resources Information Systems: Challenges in e-HRM*, Vol. 1: 357–362. New York: Hershey.

Rao, P. 2009b. The role of national culture on e-recruitment in India and Mexico. In T. Bondarouk, H. Ruël, K. Guidedoni-Jourdain, and E. Oiry (eds), *Handbook of Research on E-Transformation and Human Resources Management Technologies: Organizational Outcomes and Challenges*: 218–230. New York: Hershey.

Razali, M.Z., & Vrontis, D. 2010. The reactions of employees toward the implementation of human resources information systems (HRIS) as a planned change program: A case study in Malaysia. *Journal of Transnational Management*, 15(3): 229–245.

Rosenzweig, P., & Nohria, N. 1994. Influences on HRM practices in multinational corporations. *Journal of International Business Studies*, 25(2): 229–251.

Ruël, H., & Bondarouk, T. 2012. A cross-national perspective on the intersection between information technology and HRM. In C. Brewster, and W. Mayrhofer (eds), *Handbook of Research On Comparative Human Resource Management*: 416–446. Cheltenham, UK and Northampton, MA, USA: Edward Elgar Publishing.

Ruël, H., & Bondarouk, T. 2014. E-HRM research and practice: Facing the challenges ahead. In F. Martinez-López (ed.), *Handbook of Strategic e-Business Management*: 589–604. Berlin: Springer-Verlag.

Ruël, H., Bondarouk, T., & Looise, J.K. 2004. E-HRM: Innovation or irritation. An explorative empirical study in five large companies on web-based HRM. *Management Revue*, 15(3): 364–380.

Schuessler, E. 2006. Implementing E-HRM. A structurational approach to investigating technological and organisational change. Paper presented at the First European Academic Workshop on Electronic Human Resource Management. Netherlands: University of Twente.

Schuler, R.S., Dowling, P.J., & De Cieri, H. 1993. An integrative framework of strategic international human resource management. *Journal of Management*, 19(2): 419–459.

Spero, J.C., McQuide, P.A., & Matte, R. 2011. Tracking and monitoring the health workforce: A new human resources information system (HRIS) in Uganda. *Human Resources for Health*, 9(6), doi: 10.1186/1478-4491-9-6.

Spicer, A. 2006. Beyond the convergence–divergence debate: The role of spatial scales in transforming organizational logic. *Organizational Studies*, 27(10): 1467–1483.

Strohmeier, S. 2007. Research in e-HRM: Review and implications. *Human Resource Management Review*, 17(1): 19–37.

Strohmeier, S., & Kabst, R. 2009. Organizational adoption of e-HRM in Europe: An empirical exploration of major adoption factors. *Journal of Managerial Psychology*, 24(6): 482–501.

Tixier, J. 2004. Does the evolution of the human resources practices imply the implementation of an information system? For a contextualism of practices. *International Journal of Human Resources Development and Management*, 4(4): 414–430.

Torraco, R.J. 2005. Writing integrative literature reviews: Guidelines and examples. *Human Resource Development Review*, 4(3): 356–367.

Troshani, I., Jerram, C., & Gerrard, M. 2010. Exploring the organizational adoption of human resources information systems (HRIS) in the Australian public sector. *Proceedings of the 21st Australasian Conference on Information Systems (ACIS2010)*: 1–3. December. Brisbane, Australia.

Troshani, I., Jerram, C., & Rao Hill, S. 2011. Exploring the public sector adoption of HRIS. *Industrial Management and Data Systems*, 111(3): 470–488.

van Geffen, C., Ruël, H., & Bondarouk, T. 2013. E-HRM in MNCs: What can be learned from a review of the IS literature?. *European Journal of International Management*, 7(4): 373–393.

Vaughan, K., & MacVicar, A. 2004. Employees' pre-implementation attitudes and perceptions to e-Learning: A banking case study analysis. *Journal of European Industrial Training*, 28(5): 400–413.

Webster, J., & Watson, R.T. 2002. Analyzing the past to prepare for the future: Writing a literature review. *MIS Quaterly*, 26(2): xiii–xxiii.

Williams, H., Tansley, C., & Foster, C. 2009. HRIS project teams skills and knowledge: A human capital analysis. In T. Bondarouk, H. Ruël, K. Guidedoni-Jourdain, and E. Oiry (eds), *Handbook of Research on E-Transformation and Human Resources Management Technologies: Organizational Outcomes and Challenges*: 135–152. New York: Hershey.

Wöcke, A., Bendixen, M., & Rijamampianina, R. 2007. Building flexibility into multi-national human resource strategy: A study of four South African multi-national enterprises. *International Journal of Human Resource Management*, 18(5): 829–844.

19. Sustainable HRM: a comparative and international perspective

Ina Aust, Michael Muller-Camen, and Erik Poutsma

INTRODUCTION

This chapter introduces a new domain in comparative research: sustainable human resource management (HRM). In the recent past, in particular, there has been a growing interest in sustainable HRM in practice and in academia. In practice, sustainable HRM has become relevant for those organisations that develop and implement corporate sustainability and corporate social responsibility (CSR) strategies, and that recognise that people and how they are managed are a key success factor in institutionalising sustainability and CSR practices (see, for example, Unilever's Sustainable Living Plan; Unilever, 2016). These organisations also increasingly recognise that their credibility and legitimacy can be undermined if sustainability refers to economic and ecological issues, but not to people management issues (SHRM, 2011). While the concepts of corporate sustainability and CSR have diverse origins in the literature (Ehnert, 2009), these terms have been used synonymously in recent years in corporate practice – especially in European multinational corporations (MNCs) – and in this chapter we adapt to this discourse about CSR.

In academia, a growing number of journal articles, special issues, books, and edited volumes on sustainable HRM have emerged from different disciplinary and theoretical perspectives (for an overview, see Ehnert et al., 2014). This literature has in common that it addresses critical global and local ecological, societal, and human sustainability issues that are currently under-represented in mainstream HRM research. Amongst these issues are the role of HRM in designing, implementing, and reporting on CSR strategies (Ehnert et al., 2016; Taylor et al., 2012); greening issues in HRM (Renwick et al., 2016); and the search for new answers to challenges from broader societal and economic developments such as, for example, demographic developments and ageing workforces (Muller-Camen et al., 2011), work intensification and an increasing number of work-related psychological illnesses including depression, burnout, disengagement (Docherty et al., 2009), or work flexibilisation, employability, and career management (De Vos & Van der Heijden, 2015; Peters & Lam, 2015).

In addition, a growing global trend towards externalisation in labour relations through outsourcing and labour contracting (the 'race to the bottom') emphasises the relevance of sustainable HRM in a global context (Pinnington et al., 2007; Cotton, 2015) and shows that meeting current and prospective employee needs and interests has to be taken seriously (Cooke & He, 2010; Aguilera et al., 2007). Given the growing interest of boards of directors in sustainability and CSR issues, it is suggested that HRM could improve its standing if these debates were not left to sustainability and CSR functions only, but that HRM should take a more active role in designing and implementing corporate sustainability and CSR strategies (Cohen et al., 2012; Ehnert et al., 2014) and that the HRM function would hence be taken more seriously.

The aim of this chapter is to explore existing literature on sustainable HRM from a comparative and international perspective. We start by defining the notion of sustainable HRM. Next, we focus on international differences by proposing first steps towards a comparative conceptual framework and by using the issue of multinational corporations and human rights as an example of how our framework can be applied. We then highlight emerging country models of sustainable HRM, before concluding our chapter with implications for future research.

WHAT IS SUSTAINABLE HRM?

Currently there are different conceptualisations and empirical accounts of the concept of sustainable HRM. A number of overlapping concepts are present in the literature, such as ethical HRM (Mason & Simmons, 2011; Greenwood, 2013), green HRM (Jackson et al., 2011), and socially responsible HRM (Shen, 2011). Ethical HRM focuses on debates on whether HRM practices and conceptualisations are (un)ethical (Greenwood, 2013). Green HRM addresses the role of HRM in environmental management and in 'greening' organisations through HRM practices. While socially responsible (international) HRM deals with the voluntary and required societal obligations of business organisations, the understanding of sustainable HRM focuses on applying the sustainability idea to all HRM tasks and functions (Ehnert, 2009), also on the contribution of HRM to the ecological, economic, social, and human sustainability of the business organisation.

The definition of sustainable HRM we adopt for this chapter is based on Ehnert et al. (2016: 90), for whom '[s]ustainable HRM can be defined as the adoption of HRM strategies and practices that enable the achievement of financial, social and ecological goals, with an impact inside and outside of the organisation and over a long-term time horizon while controlling for unintended side effects and negative feedback'. Sustainable HRM can be considered as an extension of strategic HRM (Ehnert, 2009), which has been defined as 'the pattern of planned Human Resource deployments and activities intended to enable the firm to achieve its goals' (Wright & McMahan, 1992: 298). Sustainable HRM adds two aspects to strategic HRM. First, that sustainable HRM – unlike strategic HRM – recognises 'multiple, potentially contradictory, economic, ecological and social goals such as human sustainability or ecological sustainability' (Ehnert, 2009: 3), in particular, when going beyond the business case (Hahn & Figge, 2011). Second, sustainable HRM – also unlike strategic HRM – acknowledges the impact of HRM activities on an organisation's human, social, and natural environments and the need to control negative side effects and feedback of this impact, as well as to invest in long-term resource reproduction (Ehnert et al., 2016).

As this goes beyond basic assumptions in strategic HRM, most of its advocates (Ehnert et al., 2014; Kramar, 2014; Taylor et al., 2012) imply that sustainable HRM is a new paradigm replacing strategic HRM. In recent years, research on sustainable HRM has become increasingly diverse and has addressed several 'old' HRM problems from a new sustainability lens (Ehnert & Harry, 2012; Ehnert et al., 2014). However, calls in this literature for more international and comparative research have yet to be answered (for an exception, see Ehnert et al., 2016).

INTERNATIONAL DIFFERENCES: TOWARDS A COMPARATIVE CONCEPTUAL FRAMEWORK

Given that sustainable HRM is a new concept, international comparisons are still rare. In this paragraph we attempt to highlight a number of perspectives in order to develop a framework for future research. How organisations behave towards their multiple stakeholders, including employees, by and large depends on the institutional context in which they operate (Campbell, 2007). Prior research on national context influences on HRM is, in contrast, extensive and has produced a contextual approach (Paauwe & Boselie, 2007), which argues that HRM practices are affected by the specifics of the institutional and cultural context of a country (Brewster & Mayrhofer, 2012). The impact of the context on sustainable HRM policies and practices, however, has received limited attention, and only recently have comparative studies started emerging in the area of CSR (Williams & Aguilera, 2008; Gjølberg, 2009). In comparative research two perspectives are used to explain country variation and diversity in HRM: the culturalist and the institutionalist perspective (see Chapter 3 by Reiche et al. and Chapter 2 by Wood et al. in this volume). In this chapter, we focus on the institutionalist perspective, given the call for more focus on institutional theory explaining CSR developments (Brammer et al., 2012). It is also a more comprehensive approach since it emphasises the embeddedness of sustainable HRM in supranational and national institutional environments, including institutions such as intergovernmental organisations, the state, regulatory institutions, interest groups, public opinion, and norms. The institutional perspective also emphasises the topic of governance.

According to this perspective, organisational responses to stakeholder expectations are constrained and enabled by regulative, normative, and cognitive institutions (North, 1991; Campbell, 2007), such as regulatory structures, governmental agencies, laws, courts, professions, interest groups, and public opinion (Oliver, 1997). Compared to sustainable HRM, empirical research on the institutional-level predictors of CSR is rather extensive and has offered evidence to support the impact of stakeholder and institutional pressures on organisational engagement in CSR. Aguinis and Glavas (2012) grouped the CSR-related studies on institutional level pressures into four broad categories: institutional and stakeholder pressures (for example, shareholder activism, media pressure, and so on); regulations and standards; third party evaluations (for example, environmental and social ratings); and context (such as country context and socio-cultural environment).

A critical issue regarding this perspective of institutional pressures is that it does not fully capture the dynamics of sustainable HRM in a global context. At the macro country level, cross-national variation of sustainable HRM may not only relate to institutional pressures. At the meso organisation level, firms may also have strategic imperatives that influence the engagement or disengagement with sustainable HRM, that is, taking an internal actor agency perspective, organisational actors may decide on a corporate strategy which may or may not align with external institutional forces. More specifically, voluntary engagement with sustainable HRM may relate to the business case that it serves. It may attract employees to the company, or it could serve as a retention device for talented people. Much of the general CSR market-oriented competitive approach has been critiqued for the focus on efficiency and profitability, that is, for its focus on shareholder support (e.g., Hahn & Figge, 2011). The business-centred approach may have rather limited value. The argument that engagement in sustainable HRM is just another way to improve efficiency and profit maximisation may not be able to explain fully why organisations engage in and disengage from sustainable HRM (see also Orlitzky, 2008).

In contrast, organisations may react differently to different institutional pressures. This perspective assumes that rational actors strive for the maximum realisation of their goals, but that increasingly institutional pressures are taken into account as being part of rational actors' choice frames (Oliver, 1997). In the context of fiercer global competition, for example, present-day employers need to strive for additional goals beyond short-term economic gain. Reputation, status in society, and harmonious employment relations, for instance, play an increasingly important role in the decision-making processes. Taking this pluralist perspective, sustainable HRM policies and practices are considered to contribute to organisations' goals, as these may contribute to the social legitimacy of companies by improving employees' work–life balance, improving health and safety, reducing absenteeism and turnover rates, improving employee identification and commitment, and influencing subsequent outcomes such as productivity and profitability.

Emergent research suggests that there are important differences in sustainable HRM between countries due to institutional pressures and the strategic reaction of organisations. In this regard Matten and Moon's (2008) distinction between implicit and explicit CSR is useful. They argue that in Anglo-Saxon countries explicit CSR is dominant, which means that corporations usually do not practice CSR, but rather focus on promoting those initiatives that fit CSR goals. In contrast, corporations in Rhineland Europe have followed implicit CSR for decades. This means that their business practices are to a large extent in line with CSR, but until recently they did not actively present themselves as sustainable organisations. For HRM this could mean that the explicit, hard, non-union version of HRM dominant in Anglo-Saxon countries is less compatible with sustainable HRM than the pluralist German HRM model (Muller, 1999), which is also common in many other European countries. Thus, existing regional models of HRM can be evaluated according to the extent to which they comply with demands for more sustainable HRM practices.

A related theme is that this view on implicit and explicit sustainable HRM measures of corporations suggests that voluntary, 'explicit' sustainable HRM and institutionalised 'implicit' sustainable HRM may act as substitutes for each other (Jackson & Apostolakou, 2010). In other words, an organisation may not need to develop explicit sustainable HRM, since policies already reflect implicit guidelines. However, the opposite may also be true, to the extent that institutions may empower stakeholders, enabling them to put additional pressure on corporations requiring legitimacy and compliance. For example, trade unions in countries with supporting institutions may be in a stronger position to pressure companies to adopt better labour standards or adopt programmes for diversity and vulnerable groups, mirroring the institutional environment. Empirical accounts of these substitution and mirror hypotheses, however, are limited.

Moving beyond the implicit and explicit divide, and the possibility of substitution or mirroring, comparative research could also focus on how different varieties of capitalism

(Hall & Soskice, 2001) influence sustainable HRM and what mechanisms – that is, institutional complementarities – channel this influence. For instance, how is shareholder-oriented corporate governance linked to voluntary market-oriented competitive forms of sustainable HRM? How are stakeholder-driven forms of corporate governance or other forms of governance linked to forms of sustainable HRM? This line of argumentation suggests that corporatist forms of social solidarity have a strong influence on the emergence of sustainable HRM. Kinderman (2012) proposed such an analysis for the broader issue of CSR but it can also be applied to sustainable HRM; at least for its legitimacy-oriented perspective. This approach also addresses the question of recent changes in corporate governance in nation states. Does the recent move of countries towards more liberal or shareholder-oriented forms of governance also lead companies towards adopting more market-oriented and competitive forms of sustainable HRM, instead of stakeholder-driven HRM?

A last theme in our framework consists of sustainable HRM practice and policies in multinational or transnational companies, and how these practices and policies are influenced by transnational and global institutions. Recent critical events and disasters in the supply chain have boosted institutionalisation of sustainable HRM in different forms. Global (semi-)private and public regulations, standards, or self-commitment such as the Global Compact and the Global Reporting Initiative (GRI) have emerged. The main question in this area is how these institutions function and how and to what extent MNCs comply with these standards. A critical issue is that powerful transnational MNCs may put pressure on nation state governments to focus on business-friendly regulations (Banerjee, 2007) which, in fact, may institutionalise less sustainable HRM practices and policies. In summary, the above conceptual reasoning is presented in Figure 19.1.

In the following sections, we provide examples of research related to two of the issues raised above. First, we examine how sustainable HRM is developed in MNCs and enforced by the global institutionalisation of sustainable HRM. Second, we discuss country variations in institutional pressures for sustainable HRM and the response strategies of organisations.

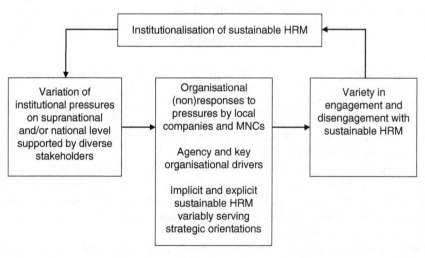

Figure 19.1   Institutional approach to sustainable HRM in an international context

MNC, SUSTAINABLE HRM, AND TRANSFER OF HRM POLICIES AND PRACTICES

The international HRM literature suggests that MNCs transfer HRM policies and practices between countries. This could also apply to sustainable HRM practices. One example is diversity management (see also Chapter 16 in this volume), which according to CSR reports is the most popular sustainable HRM policy (Hartog et al., 2008). This management concept was developed in the 1990s in the United States of America (USA) and one of the main transfer mechanisms to the rest of the world were MNCs (Ferner et al., 2005). Still in the early 2000s, diversity management remained uncommon in Europe, and met some resistance not only in more coordinated market economies such as Germany and Spain, but also in the liberal market economy of the United Kingdom (UK) (Ferner et al., 2006). Another example is vocational training (see also Chapter 10 in this volume). Dickmann (2003) described how German companies in the UK tried to establish vocational training systems in their UK subsidiaries. Finally, another example refers to the transfer of sustainability reporting practices in MNCs following the Global Reporting Initiative (GRI) guidelines (see Ehnert et al., 2016). Two categories in the GRI guidelines are related to sustainable HRM, the 'labour practices and decent work' (LA) category and the 'human rights' (HR) category. By applying the GRI guidelines, MNCs contribute to the institutionalisation of global transfer of sustainable HRM practices; however, sometimes by disregarding local sustainable HRM practices.

For example, MNCs from developed economies are accused of exploiting workforces in developing economies by using low-road HRM practices: low standards of health and safety, poor pay, long working hours, suppression of labour organisations, and more (Chan & Ross, 2003; Bolton et al., 2012). However, there is also a literature suggesting that the HRM practices of the subsidiaries of MNCs in developing economies are often superior to those of indigenous companies. In particular, MNCs often pay higher wages, offer more training, and have higher health and safety standards than local firms.

Whereas most international HRM literature has focused to date on HRM within the MNC, some scholars have started looking at the supply chain (Fisher et al., 2010). In contrast to HRM, there is a developed literature on social relations in global supply chains in industrial relations (see, e.g., Croucher & Cotton, 2011). The sustainability and CSR discourses suggest that it is not only ethical but also economically rational for MNCs to control labour and ecological standards in their supply chains. With regard to labour standards, human rights are a major concern. Building on earlier works that connected HRM and human rights within the context of sustainable HRM (Cohen et al., 2012), Muller-Camen and Elsik (2015) suggest that HRM practices in the supply chain should become a concern for the field of international HRM. Auditing, training, and communication can ensure that suppliers implement basic labour standards that do not violate human rights.

In the following section, we discuss insights from emergent country-level models of sustainable (or unsustainable) HRM, describing examples from the USA, continental Europe, Japan, as well as China and other emerging economies. We specifically look at different institutional pressures.

EMERGENT COUNTRY-LEVEL MODELS OF SUSTAINABLE HRM

Sustainable HRM in the USA

According to Taylor and Lewis (2014) and Pfeffer (2010), sustainable HRM in the USA is characterised by a focus on the environmental dimension of CSR and a neglect of human sustainability issues. This is explained by the strong financial performance and shareholder orientation of North American HRM research and practice, which can have negative impacts for employees. In this regard Taylor and Lewis (2014) also point to the importance of managerial autonomy and the predominance of a unitarist employee relations philosophy dominant in the USA. This has resulted in a strong non-union strategy being followed by most employers. Pfeffer's (2010) argument focuses on employee health and well-being. He suggests that limited provision of health insurance, widespread compulsory redundancies, extensive work hours, inequality, and poor job design are causing stress and ill-health in the workforce.

Although US corporations may generally neglect the human dimension of CSR, at least two important elements of sustainable HRM strategies originate from the USA. One of them is diversity management, which today forms an important part of the sustainable HRM strategies in global corporations. Compared to MNCs from other countries such as Germany, USA MNCs appear to put a strong emphasis on promoting diversity. Not only is an extensive range of diversity dimensions such as gender, ethnicity, sexual orientation, and veteran status covered, but diversity staff functions, diversity strategies, and even diverse supplier policies exist (Hanappi-Egger et al., 2015). Another increasingly widespread instrument in sustainable HRM is employee volunteering (Caligiuri et al., 2013). Corporations support the voluntary activities of their employees in social or environmental projects with free time and/or financial resources (Cohen et al., 2012). Whereas some years ago only US corporations pointed to such activities in their sustainability or CSR reports, today employee volunteering is also becoming increasingly popular elsewhere.

Sustainable HRM in Continental Europe

Starting with Brewster (1993) and Sparrow and Hiltrop (1994), the notion of 'European HRM' has been developed. This usually refers to HRM in continental Western and Northern Europe, which is assumed to be characterised by a focus on stakeholders (rather than shareholders), a strong influence of the state, strict labour laws, a more long-term perspective, as well as the importance of consultation and collective bargaining (Mayrhofer et al., 2012). Given this context, Ehnert et al. (2014: 340) suggest that: 'European HRM can and should take a leading role in developing and implementing sustainability strategies and practices in organisations and also in making HRM systems themselves sustainable'. To some extent this is already taking place. For example, Muller (1999), using the example of Germany, showed how modern HRM practices developed in the non-union US context can be applied in the pluralist German context where there are influential works councils at the company level and many large corporations are covered by industry-wide collective bargaining. Rather than being a constraint on managerial autonomy, these institutions can exert pressure towards more sustainable HRM practices. In particular, they require management not to neglect equity, employee well-being, and development.

A particular challenge in most of Europe relates to demographics: declining birth rates in countries such as Germany have led to a significant increase in the percentage of older workers in the workplace. As organisations tend to focus on young and healthy workers, this constitutes a challenge for maintaining the human resource base. One answer is age management. Most large German companies, for example, have started to develop age management strategies, using a combination of health management, work organisation, and HR development policies that aim to keep employees productive in the workplace until old age (Schröder et al., 2014). Overall, however, the efforts in European organisa-tions to develop and implement sustainable HRM practices are usually limited to the present workforce; future workforces are not systematically being taken into account (Ehnert, 2009). What is also missing from the sustainable HRM literature is a greater focus on employees external to the organisation, such as a focus on human rights in sustainable supply chains.

Sustainable HRM in Japan

Influenced by the values of Confucianism and Buddhism and the emergence of a welfare corporatist system after World War II, a Japanese model of HRM developed that was characterised by stable employment, seniority, low wage differentials, and a paternalistic style of management (Debroux et al., 2012). In some ways this has been a model for sustainable HRM in Japan. Since the 1990s when Japan started to experience serious eco-nomic problems, this Japanese model of HRM has changed. Many Japanese corporations started to implement a more financial performance-based version of HRM to cope with growing labour costs. According to Debroux et al. (2012), this has had negative impacts on social capital, which has led to decreased collaboration and less altruistic behaviour. Moreover, atypical workers, often employed in smaller firms in the supply chain, and in particular women, have never been included in the Japanese model of HRM. Similar to most Asian organisations, there are still few foreigners and women in managerial posi-tions (Debroux, 2014). One reason for the underutilisation of women's talent are work habits that are still characterised by long working hours and short holidays, which make it difficult to maintain a work–life balance (Debroux, 2014). In the aftermath of the nuclear disaster at Fukushima, CSR and also sustainable HRM related to ecological issues are receiving growing attention in Japan. However, the implications of these developments for HRM are currently under-researched.

Sustainable HRM in China

The implementation of CSR in China has been influenced by economic globalisation and China's accession to the World Trade Organization (WTO) (Wang, 2005). Subsequently, China has been facing mounting pressure to take sustainability issues seriously, especially regarding environmental and labour standards. The country's poor reputation in labour standards creates risks for corporate brands, and sales to ethically concerned markets and investors. As a response to global institutional pressures, the Chinese government has shown a growing interest in engaging companies in social and environmental policies. Existing studies in China focus primarily on labour standards in the supply chain (Chan & Ross, 2003). These studies show that CSR activities were introduced into China in the mid-1990s, when MNCs, under pressure from anti-sweatshop activities abroad, started to impose supplier codes of conduct on the Chinese textile and apparel industry and began auditing them (Chan & Ross, 2003). Firms reacted to these pressures, but Cooke and He (2010) revealed that firms in the textile and apparel industry tend to adopt a business case approach to CSR, focusing on the market rather than their employees. The study also showed that, according to the managers there, legal compliance remains the main source of pressure, while ethical concerns and voluntary activities are limited.

Emerging and Developing Economies

According to regional comparative perspectives of HRM (Brewster & Mayrhofer, 2012), HRM in emerging markets is characterised by insecure, low-paid employment, poor working conditions, little investment in training, and hostility to trade unions (see, for example, Davila & Elvira, 2012 on Latin America; and Bischoff & Wood, 2012 on HRM in Africa). Nevertheless, there are some exceptions. In their review of Latin American HRM models, Davila and Elvira (2012) present examples of companies that invest in employees, cooperate with trade unions, and have become centres for community development. Within Latin America, Brazil has a progressive reputation in CSR and environmental sustainability. CSR was introduced to Brazil in 1998 and has since been adopted by hundreds of firms (Wehling et al., 2009). Several institutional pressures account for this development. Brazilians expect firms to be involved in CSR. The Ethos Institute has developed Indicators of Social Responsibility that are used to evaluate company performance in Brazil. Given Brazil's pressing social issues, many CSR programmes are poverty-related. In the recent past, Petrobras won an award for CSR programmes that involve stakeholder dialogue with poor communities and a partner organisation devoted to sustainability (ibid: 181). The more progressive role of Brazil was also an explanation for the fact that German MNCs could transfer sustainability values to Brazilian subsidiaries, as the study of Wehling et al. (2009) showed. However, the recent corruption scandal of Petrobas, where directors developed funds to line their own pockets, also reflects the relative instability of CSR initiatives in the Brazilian context.

Emerging market models of sustainable HRM demonstrate that approaches that simultaneously address ecological, economic, societal, and human sustainability issues are still exceptions in practice and in research today. Further research in this area is required that focuses on international differences driven by institutional and cultural contexts.

CONCLUSIONS

Overall, we argue that there is no single emergent universal model of sustainable HRM. Instead, different institutional environments lead to the emergence of different models. However, some of these are more conducive to demands for increasing attention to environmental, social, and human sustainability of HRM. In this chapter, we have started to highlight potential questions and areas for future research from a sustainable HRM perspective. Particularly, we would like to emphasise the following aspects as being of paramount relevance for future research on comparative sustainable HRM:

- Comparative research can be a valuable source for answers to the main research questions of sustainable HRM. In particular, our framework suggests focusing on questions related to the response strategies of organisations towards varied institutional pressures.
- Research should take into account country-specific models of sustainable HRM, highlighting institutional complementarities and related response strategies.
- Research should focus on the institutionalisation of sustainable HRM on local and global levels.
- Research should consider the role of MNCs and their reactions to institutionalisation and institutional pressures in those contexts in which they operate.

In conclusion, we need more research on country and regional models of sustainable HRM from other areas than the limited set that is developing currently. For example, a focus on research in India or Africa would be particularly welcomed, since sustainability and sustainable development should play a major role in these regions, also for the MNCs operating there.

REFERENCES

Aguilera, R.V., Rupp, D., Williams, C.A., & Ganapathi, J. 2007. Putting the S back in corporate social responsibility: A multilevel theory of social change in organizations. *Academy of Management Review*, 32(3): 836–863.

Aguinis, H., & Glavas, A. 2012. What we know and don't know about corporate social responsibility: A review and research agenda. *Journal of Management*, 38(4): 932–968.

Banerjee, S.B. 2007. *Corporate Social Responsibility: The Good, the Bad and the Ugly*. Cheltenham, UK and Northampton, MA, USA: Edward Elgar Publishing.

Bischoff, C., & Wood, G. 2012. The practice of HRM in Africa in comparative perspective. In C. Brewster and W. Mayrhofer (eds), *Handbook of Research on Comparative Human Resource Management*: 494–511. Cheltenham, UK and Northampton, MA, USA: Edward Elgar Publishing.

Bolton, S., Houlihan, M., & Laaser, K. 2012. Contingent work and its contradictions: Towards a moral economy framework. *Journal of Business Ethics*, 111(1): 121–132.

Brammer, S., Jackson, G., & Matten, D. 2012. Corporate social responsibility and institutional theory: New perspectives on private governance. *Socio-Economic Review*, 10(1): 3–28.

Brewster, C. 1993. Developing a 'European' model of human resource management. *International Journal of Human Resource Management*, 4(4): 765–784.

Brewster, C., & Mayrhofer, W. 2012. Comparative human resource management: An introduction. In C. Brewster and W. Mayrhofer (eds), *Handbook of Research on Comparative Human Resource Management*: 1–26. Cheltenham, UK and Northampton, MA, USA: Edward Elgar Publishing.

Caligiuri, P., Mencin, A., & Jiang, K. 2013. Win–win–win: The influence of company–sponsored volunteerism programs on employees, NGOs, and business units. *Personnel Psychology*, 66(4): 825–860.

Campbell, J.L. 2007. Why would corporations behave in socially responsible ways? An institutional theory of corporate social responsibility. *Academy of Management Review*, 32(3): 946–967.

Chan, A., & Ross, R. 2003. Racing to the bottom: International trade without a social clause. *Third World Quarterly*, 24(6): 1011–1028.

Cohen, E., Taylor, S., & Muller-Camen, M. 2012. HRM's role in corporate social and environmental sustainability. Alexandria, VA: SHRM. https://www.shrm.org/about/foundation/products/documents/4-12%20csr%20report%20final%20for%20web.pdf.

Cooke, F.L., & He, Q. 2010. Corporate social responsibility and HRM in China: A study of textile and apparel enterprises. *Asia Pacific Business Review*, 16(3): 355–376.

Cotton, E. 2015. Transnational regulation of temporary agency work compromised partnership between private employment agencies and global union federations. *Work, Employment and Society*, 29(1): 137–153.

Croucher, R., & Cotton, E. 2011. *Global Unions, Global Business: Global Union Federations and International Business*. London: Libri Publishing.

Davila, A., & Elvira, M.M. 2012. Latin American HRM models. In C. Brewster and W. Mayrhofer (eds), *Handbook of Research on Comparative Human Resource Management*: 478–493. Cheltenham, UK and Northampton, MA, USA: Edward Elgar Publishing.

De Vos, A., & Van der Heijden, B.I.J.M. 2015. *Handbook of Research on Sustainable Careers*. Cheltenham, UK and Northampton, MA, USA: Edward Elgar Publishing.

Debroux, P. 2014. Sustainable HRM in East and Southeast Asia. In I. Ehnert, W. Harry, and K.J. Zink (eds), *Sustainability and Human Resource Management*: 315–338. Berlin & Heidelberg: Springer.

Debroux, P., Harry, W., Hayashi, S., et al. 2012. Japan, Korea and Taiwan: Issues and trends in human resource management. In C. Brewster and W. Mayrhofer (eds), *Handbook of Research on Comparative Human Resource Management*: 620–643. Cheltenham, UK and Northampton, MA, USA: Edward Elgar Publishing.

Dickmann, M. 2003. Implementing German HRM abroad: Desired, feasible, successful?. *International Journal of Human Resource Management*, 14(2): 265–283.

Docherty, P., Kira, M., & Shani, A.B.R. 2009. *Creating Sustainable Work Systems: Developing Social Sustainability*. London: Routledge.

Ehnert, I. 2009. *Sustainable Human Resource Management: A Conceptual and Exploratory Analysis from a Paradox Perspective*. Contributions to Management Science series. Heidelberg: Physica-Springer.

Ehnert, I., & Harry, W. 2012. Recent developments and future prospects on sustainable human resource management: Introduction to the special issue. *Management Revue*, 23(3): 221–238.

Ehnert, I., Harry, W., & Brewster, C. 2014. Sustainable HRM in Europe diverse contexts and multiple bottom lines. In I. Ehnert, W. Harry, and K.J. Zink (eds), *Sustainability and Human Resource Management*: 339–358. Berlin & Heidelberg: Springer.

Ehnert, I., Parsa, S., Roper, I., Wagner, M., & Muller-Camen, M. 2016. Reporting on sustainability and HRM: A comparative study of sustainability reporting practices by the world's largest companies. *International Journal of Human Resource Management*, 27(1): 88–108.

Ferner, A., Almond, P., & Colling, T. 2005. Institutional theory and the cross-national transfer of employment policy: The case of 'workforce diversity' in US multinationals. *Journal of International Business Studies*, 36(3): 304–321.

Ferner, A., Morley, M., Muller-Camen, M., & Lourdes, S. 2006. Workforce diversity policies. In P. Almond and A. Ferner (eds), *American Multinationals in Europe: Managing Employment Relations across International Borders*: 146–171. Oxford: Oxford University Press.

Fisher, S.L., Graham, M.E., Vachon, S., & Vereecke, A. 2010. Don't miss the boat: Research on HRM and supply chains. *Human Resource Management*, 49(5): 813–828.

Gjølberg, M. 2009. Measuring the immeasurable?: Constructing an index of CSR practices and CSR performance in 20 countries. *Scandinavian Journal of Management*, 25(1): 10–22.

Greenwood, M.R. 2013. Ethical analyses of HRM: A review and research agenda. *Journal of Business Ethics*, 114(2): 355-366. DOI 310.1007/s10551-10012-11354-y.

Hahn, T., & Figge, F. 2011. Beyond the bounded instrumentality in current corporate sustainability research: Toward an inclusive notion of profitability. *Journal of Business Ethics*, 104(3): 325–345.

Hall, P.A., & Soskice, D. 2001. *Varieties of Capitalism: The Institutional Foundations of Comparative Advantage*. Oxford: Oxford University Press.

Hanappi-Egger, E., Müller-Camen, M., & Schuhbeck, V. 2015. Kontextualisierung von Diversitätsmanagement: Ein Vergleich zwischen den USA und Deutschland. In E. Hanappi-Egger and R. Bendl (eds), *Diversität, Diversifizierung, (Ent)Solidarisierung in der Organisationsforschung: eine Standortbestimmung im deutschen Sprachraum*: 149–167. Weisbaden: Springer.

Hartog, M., Morton, C., & Muller-Camen, M. 2008. Corporate social responsibility and sustainable HRM. In M. Muller-Camen, R. Croucher, and S. Leigh (eds), *Human Resource Management: A Case Study Approach*: 467–488. London: CIPD.

Jackson, G., & Apostolakou, A. 2010. Corporate social responsibility in Western Europe: An institutional mirror or substitute? *Journal of Business Ethics*, 94(3): 371–394.

Jackson, S.E., Renwick, D.W.S., Jabbour, C.J.C., & Muller-Camen, M. 2011. State-of-the-art and future directions for green human resource management: Introduction to the special issue. *German Journal of Human Resource Management: Zeitschrift für Personalforschung*, 25(2): 99–116.

Kinderman, D. 2012. 'Free us up so we can be responsible!' The co-evolution of corporate social responsibility and neo-liberalism in the UK, 1977–2010. *Socio-Economic Review*, 10(1): 29–57.

Kramar, R. 2014. Beyond strategic human resource management: Is sustainable human resource management the next approach?. *International Journal of Human Resource Management*, 25(8): 1069–1089.

Mason, C., & Simmons, J. 2011. Forward looking or looking unaffordable? Utilising academic perspectives on corporate social responsibility to assess the factors influencing its adoption by business. *Business Ethics: A European Review*, 20(2): 159–176.

Matten, D., & Moon, J. 2008. 'Implicit' and 'explicit' CSR: A conceptual framework for a comparative understanding of corporate social responsibility. *Academy of Management Review*, 33(2): 404–424.

Mayrhofer, W., Sparrow, P., & Brewster, C. 2012. European human resource management: A contextualized stakeholder perspective. In C. Brewster and W. Mayrhofer (eds), *Handbook of Research on Comparative Human Resource Management*: 528–549. Cheltenham, UK and Northampton, MA, USA: Edward Elgar Publishing.

Muller, M. 1999. Unitarism, pluralism, and human resource management in Germany. *Management International Review*, 39(3): 125–144.

Muller-Camen, M., Croucher, R., Flynn, M., & Schröder, H. 2011. National institutions and employers' age management practices in Britain and Germany: 'Path dependence' and option exploration. *Human Relations*, 64(4): 507–530.

Muller-Camen, M., & Elsik, W. 2015. IHRM's role in managing ethics and CSR globally. In D.G. Collings, G. Wood, and P. Caligiuri (eds), *The Routledge Companion to International Human Resource Management*: 552–561. London, UK & New York, USA: Routledge.

North, D.C. 1991. Institutions. *Journal of Economic Perspectives*, 5(1): 97–112.

Oliver, C. 1997. Sustainable competitive advantage: Combining institutional and resource-based views. *Strategic Management Journal*, 18(9): 697–713.

Orlitzky, M. 2008. Corporate social performance and financial performance: a research synthesis. In A. Crane, A. McWilliams, D. Matten, J. Moon, and D.S. Siegel (eds), *The Oxford Handbook of Corporate Social Responsibility*: 113–136. Oxford: Oxford University Press.

Paauwe, J., & Boselie, P. 2007. HRM and societal embeddedness. In P. Boxall, J. Purcell, and P. Wright (eds), *The Oxford Handbook of Human Resource Management*: 166–184. Oxford: Oxford University Press.

Peters, P., & Lam, W. 2015. Can employability do the trick? Revealing paradoxical tensions and responses in the process of adopting innovative employability enhancing policies and practices in organizations. *German Journal of Human Resource Management: Zeitschrift für Personalforschung*, 29(3/4): 235–258.

Pfeffer, J. 2010. Building sustainable organizations: The human factor. *Academy of Management Perspectives*, 24(1): 34–45.

Pinnington, A., Macklin, R., & Campbell, T. 2007. Introduction: Ethical human resource management. In A. Pinnington, R. Macklin, and T. Campbell (eds), *Human Resource Management: Ethics and Employment*: 1–20. Oxford: Oxford University Press.

Renwick, D.W.S., Jabbour, C.J.C., Muller-Camen, M., Redman, T., & Wilkinson, A. 2016. Contemporary developments in Green (environmental) HRM scholarship (editorial of SI Green HRM). *International Journal of Human Resource Management*, 27(2): 114–128.

Schröder, H., Muller-Camen, M., & Flynn, M. 2014. The management of an ageing workforce: Organisational policies in Germany and Britain. *Human Resource Management Journal*, 24(4): 394–409.

Shen, J. 2011. Developing the concept of socially responsible international human resource management. *The International Journal of Human Resource Management*, 22(6): 1351–1363.

SHRM. 2011. Advancing sustainability: HR's role. A research report by the Society for Human Resource Management, BSR and Aurosoorya. Available at http://www.shrm.org/Research/SurveyFindings/Articles/Documents/11-0066_AdvSustainHR_FNL_FULL.pdf.

Sparrow, P., & Hiltrop, J.M. 1994. *European Human Resource Management in Transition*. Hempel Hempstead: Prentice Hall.

Taylor, S., & Lewis, C. 2014. Sustainable HRM in the US. In I. Ehnert, W. Harry, and K.J. Zink (eds), *Sustainability and Human Resource Management*: 297–314. Berlin & Heidelberg: Springer.

Taylor, S., Osland, J., & Egri, C.P. 2012. Guest editors'introduction: Introduction to HRM's role in sustainability: Systems, strategies, and practices. *Human Resource Management*, 51(6): 789–798.

Unilever. 2016. The Unilever Sustainable Living Plan. Retrieved 14 April 2016 from https://www.unilever.com/sustainable-living/the-sustainable-living-plan/.

Wang, C. 2005. The current situation and countermeasures of Chinese enterprises' social responsibilities. *Journal of Yanan University*, 27(5): 72–73.

Wehling, C., Guanipa Hernandez, A., Osland, J., et al. 2009. An exploratory study of the role of HRM and the transfer of German MNC sustainability values to Brazil. *European Journal of International Management*, 3(2): 176–198.

Williams, C.A., & Aguilera, R.V. 2008. Corporate social responsibility in a comparative perspective. In A. Crane, A. McWilliams, et al. (eds), *The Oxford Handbook of Corporate Social Responsibility*: 452–472. New York: Oxford University Press.

Wright, P.M., & McMahan, G.C. 1992. Theoretical perspectives for strategic human resource management. *Journal of Management*, 18(2): 295–320.

PART III

REGIONAL PERSPECTIVES

20. HRM practice and scholarship in North America
Susan E. Jackson, Andrea Kim, and Randall S. Schuler

INTRODUCTION

Human resource management (HRM) in the United States of America (USA) and Canada, referred to here as the North American perspective, has undergone dramatic change during the past 30 years.[1] While there are some differences in HRM policies and practices between the USA and Canada, the North American approach reflects the liberal market economies found in both countries (Hall & Soskice, 2001) as well as the penetration of US multinationals into the Canadian economy (Parry et al., 2008; Dickmann & Muller-Camen, 2006). In our coverage of North American HRM practices and scholarship, we make no attempt to compare and contrast the North American HRM scene to other regions or countries. We note, however, that comparative studies have described North American HRM practices as characterized by: using an individualized approach to handling employment relations and communication; relying on sophisticated selection techniques; using individualized, performance-based rewards; emphasizing training and development for the purpose of human capital accumulation; showing strong concern with diversity management; and adopting a rather ethnocentric approach to managing international operations in the belief that North American HRM practices reflect a 'one best way' (Parry et al., 2008; Fenton-O'Creevy et al., 2008). The North American approach to HRM research and practice is also characterized by a strong interest in the strategic role of effective HRM. As executives in large North American firms increasingly expect HRM professionals to be business partners who help to shape strategic decisions, both the practice of HRM and its study within academia have evolved (for detailed reviews of this evolution, see Jackson et al., 2014; Kaufman, 2014). Increasingly, HRM professionals are now viewed as 'human capital' asset experts whose efforts are directed at creating competitive advantages for the firm (Barney & Wright, 1998; Schuler & Jackson, 2007; Wright et al., 2014).

In this chapter, we focus on the current state of North American HRM practice and scholarship in larger public and private sector organizations, while recognizing that these will continue to evolve and change in response to dynamic business conditions. After providing a broad overview of the current state of HRM practice in North America, we focus more specifically on three issues for HRM scholars and professionals that have important implications for managing employees in North American firms – the burgeoning freelance economy, achieving gender balance among the managerial tier of organizations, and heightened corporate transparency – and review scholarship that addresses these trends.

---

[1] A geographic definition of North America would include the countries of Central America. These, however, are covered in Chapter 22 in this volume.

THE CURRENT STATE OF HRM PRACTICE IN NORTH AMERICA

For the past two decades, North American HRM professionals and scholars alike have emphasized 'strategic HRM', which is the term used broadly to signal the view that HRM activities should contribute to business effectiveness. Included under the broad umbrella of strategic HRM activities are the development and articulation of an HRM philosophy, the design of HRM policies that reflect the firm's overarching philosophy, as well as the implementation and evaluation of specific HRM practices (for example, planning, recruitment, training, and compensation). The strategic HRM approach typically implies that improved firm performance is a major objective. While firm performance is often equated with financial performance, there is increasing recognition that organizational success requires balancing the diverse concerns of stakeholders. In addition to meeting the financial objectives of owners and investors, the concerns of communities, customers, employees, and strategic partners must all be taken into account. Strategic HRM also recognizes that effective HRM must contemplate a firm's unique context; that is, its specific organizational characteristics and conditions in its external environment. Recently, Jackson et al. (2014) presented an integrative framework that summarizes the many elements comprising the evolving meaning of strategic HRM, shown in Figure 20.1. The authors referred to this framework as 'aspirational' in recognition of the fact that neither HRM professionals nor HRM scholars have fully incorporated all aspects of the framework into their ongoing work.

Integrated HRM Systems

Integration and coherence among a firm's many HRM activities are hallmarks of a well-designed HRM system, but alignment among HRM activities (which include policies, practices, and processes) is not sufficient. The set of HRM activities also should be aligned with the many elements of an organization's internal and external environments.

In North America, the practice of HRM has long been shaped by legal regulations, which provide to employees a variety of rights and protections against unfair and unsafe employment practices.[2] Monitoring the legal and regulatory environment to ensure that a firm's HRM practices comply with legal requirements has long been a primary role for North American HRM professionals. Recent laws and regulations concerning health care insurance; the rights of lesbian, gay, bisexual, and transgender (LGBT) employees; and changes in minimum pay levels, are particularly salient. In addition, HRM professionals have traditionally been responsible for monitoring competitors' pay practices to ensure the external equity of their pay practices for the same jobs and labor. Today, concerns about the growing pay gap between executives and employees are attracting greater attention. And because an organization's planning for future recruitment, staffing, and development is affected by supply and demand in the external labor market, HRM professionals generally monitor and interpret labor market conditions. Today, the structure of employment relationships means that such monitoring is increasingly done

---

[2]   Readers should compare the more limited extent of employment legislation in the USA, for example, with other countries and regions represented in this volume.

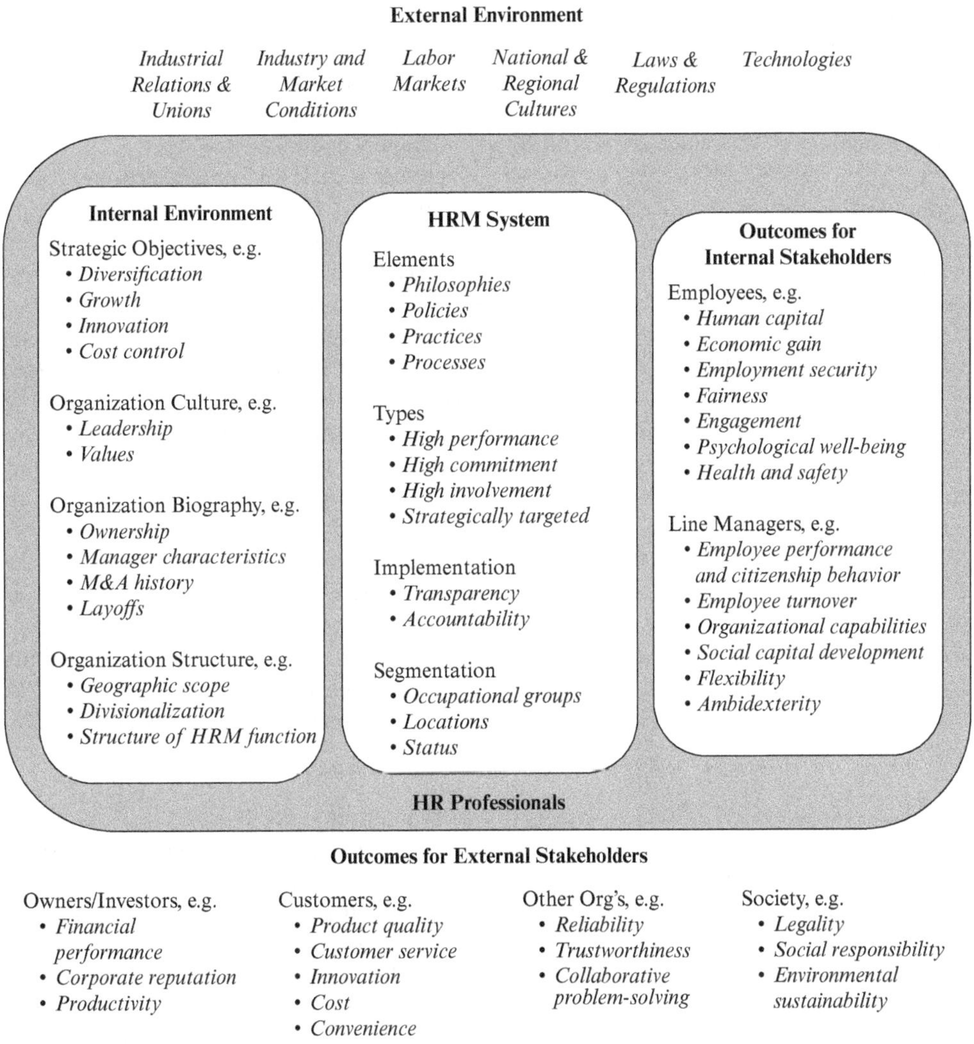

External Environment

| *Industrial Relations & Unions* | *Industry and Market Conditions* | *Labor Markets* | *National & Regional Cultures* | *Laws & Regulations* | *Technologies* |

Internal Environment

Strategic Objectives, e.g.
- *Diversification*
- *Growth*
- *Innovation*
- *Cost control*

Organization Culture, e.g.
- *Leadership*
- *Values*

Organization Biography, e.g.
- *Ownership*
- *Manager characteristics*
- *M&A history*
- *Layoffs*

Organization Structure, e.g.
- *Geographic scope*
- *Divisionalization*
- *Structure of HRM function*

HRM System

Elements
- *Philosophies*
- *Policies*
- *Practices*
- *Processes*

Types
- *High performance*
- *High commitment*
- *High involvement*
- *Strategically targeted*

Implementation
- *Transparency*
- *Accountability*

Segmentation
- *Occupational groups*
- *Locations*
- *Status*

Outcomes for Internal Stakeholders

Employees, e.g.
- *Human capital*
- *Economic gain*
- *Employment security*
- *Fairness*
- *Engagement*
- *Psychological well-being*
- *Health and safety*

Line Managers, e.g.
- *Employee performance and citizenship behavior*
- *Employee turnover*
- *Organizational capabilities*
- *Social capital development*
- *Flexibility*
- *Ambidexterity*

HR Professionals

Outcomes for External Stakeholders

Owners/Investors, e.g.
- *Financial performance*
- *Corporate reputation*
- *Productivity*

Customers, e.g.
- *Product quality*
- *Customer service*
- *Innovation*
- *Cost*
- *Convenience*

Other Org's, e.g.
- *Reliability*
- *Trustworthiness*
- *Collaborative problem-solving*

Society, e.g.
- *Legality*
- *Social responsibility*
- *Environmental sustainability*

Source: Jackson et al. (2014: 3).

Figure 20.1   Aspirational framework for strategic HRM

on a global scale for many large North American firms, rather than focused mostly on local conditions.

Demonstrating the Effectiveness of HRM

Assessments of the 'effectiveness' of an organization's HRM practices were traditionally made using technical criteria established by the profession (for example, validity and reliability) and embodied in legal regulations. Then, beginning in the 1990s, HRM professionals were increasingly called on to demonstrate the strategic effectiveness of HRM practices in monetary terms. Heavy reliance on monetary criteria continues today, although non-monetary criteria are now also gaining attention.

Using monetary effectiveness criteria to satisfy managers and investors

Thirty years ago, efforts to demonstrate the effectiveness of HRM practices in monetary terms usually employed utility analysis (e.g., Schmidt et al., 1979) or cost accounting (e.g., Cascio, 2000). Regardless of the technical merits of such approaches, they have not been widely adopted by North American firms. Instead, HRM professionals face growing pressure to demonstrate the effectiveness of HRM practices using business-relevant metrics. Thus, HRM consultants offer a variety of more sophisticated measures that estimate the economic value added (EVA) or return-on-investment (ROI) for HRM activities (see Becker et al., 2001; Fitz-Enz, 2000). Such metrics focus on costs and benefits, reflecting great deference to the financial interests of shareholders and other owners.

This narrow approach to assessing HRM effectiveness is slowly beginning to change, however, as organizations better understand the underlying drivers of long-term organizational success. For example, using the logic of balanced scorecards and strategy maps (Kaplan & Norton, 1996), firms began developing sophisticated models of how HRM practices can contribute to achieving strategic objectives (Rucci et al., 1998; Becker et al., 2001). Such efforts are becoming prominent as the volume of data available to firms expands. Looking ahead, we anticipate that North American firms will continue to develop business-related approaches to evaluating the effectiveness of their HRM systems. Today, such efforts are broadly covered by the emerging new labels of 'big data' and 'analytics' (see Phillips & Phillips, 2014).

Using non-monetary effectiveness criteria to satisfy multiple stakeholders

A more complete assessment of HRM effectiveness evaluates the effects of an HRM system on the organization's broad array of multiple stakeholders (Colakoglu et al., 2006; Hyland & Jackson, 2006). Certainly, the organization itself is a primary stakeholder, so it is appropriate to assess the impact of the HRM system against objectives such as improving productivity, maximizing profitability, and ensuring the organization's long-term survival. Many employers also recognize that total quality, innovation, and customer service goals cannot be met unless employees are willing to strive for these goals on the organization's behalf. Thus, top management is recognizing employee feelings about the organization (e.g., commitment, satisfaction, engagement) as relevant indicators of HRM effectiveness (Boudreau, 2003; Macey & Schneider, 2008). Numerous studies have revealed that well-designed HRM practices are associated with positive employee outcomes including job satisfaction, positive relationships with managers, employee development, and employee safety (Jiang et al., 2012).

Some organizations also evaluate HRM effectiveness against its consequences for customers. An effective HRM system should influence the quality and variety of products available to customers, the price at which products can be profitably sold, the service customers receive, and so on. As the US economy evolved toward services, customers' expectations have been incorporated into job descriptions, their preferences have influenced criteria used to select new employees, and their input is often sought to assess employee performance (White & Schneider, 2003).

Other stakeholders impacted by an organization's HRM system have received much less attention from the North American HRM community. Suppliers (see Fu et al., 2013; Lengnick-Hall et al., 2013; Schuler & MacMillan, 1984) and strategic alliance partners involved in cooperative alliances formed to address shared research and development needs or joint ventures that provide access to new markets have been acknowledged as important stakeholders (Fjeldstad et al., 2012; Gulati et al., 2012), but to date little systematic knowledge has been developed concerning HRM systems that span beyond one organization's boundaries.

HRM SCHOLARSHIP

During the past two decades, North American HRM scholars have invested heavily in research that investigates the relationship between how organizations manage their human resources and their success in effectively implementing business strategies and achieving economic success. Often referred to as 'strategic HRM', this branch of North American research addresses several specific issues, but the unifying theme is generally that these studies examine the antecedents and outcomes associated with HRM systems. That is, rather than studying specific policies and practices, strategic HRM considers an organization's entire set of HRM policies and practices. More specifically, strategic HRM scholarship is 'the study of HRM systems (and/or subsystems) and their interrelationships with other elements comprising an organizational system, including the organization's external and internal environments, the multiple players who enact HRM systems, and the multiple stakeholders who evaluate the organization's effectiveness and determine its long-term survival' (Jackson et al., 2014: 2). Readers interested in the various streams of research comprising HRM are referred to Kaše et al. (2014).

A major conceptual development in strategic HRM research is to differentiate between studies focusing on: (1) the direct effects of HRM practices and/or systems on relevant outcomes; and (2) studies focusing on various contingencies that impact the use and effectiveness of HRM practices. Many early strategic HRM scholars examined the impact of individual HRM activities in search of 'best practices' that positively influence various outcomes. Strategic HRM scholars shifted to consideration of HRM practice 'bundles', arguing that a key element of research in this field is to focus on the entire HRM system. That is, HRM practices are assumed to operate in concert with each other. As noted by MacDuffie (1995: 198), 'an HR bundle or system must be integrated with complementary bundles of practices from core business functions'. When properly aligned, several practices together may reinforce each other; when mismatched, they may work against each other and interfere with performance. Alternatively, some practices may serve as substitutes for other practices.

Several empirical studies have shown that firms using bundles of so-called high performance HRM practices outperformed firms that used only a few of these practices (Becker & Huselid, 1998). Recent reviews of the accumulated evidence have been provided by Batt and Banerjee (2012) and Jiang et al. (2012). However, as critics have pointed out, there has been some inconsistency in the specific practices that various authors consider to be among the preferred practices, making it difficult to draw general conclusions about which practices qualify as 'best practices' (see Becker & Gerhart, 1996). In order to continue moving forward with this line of research, more theory-driven research may be needed. The challenge is to trace the causal chain that explains how specific bundles of HRM practices influence intermediate outcomes such as motivation, productivity, turnover, and how those outcomes, in turn, can influence specific indicators of financial performance.

One approach to clarifying the role of HRM bundles in shaping organizational performance is to look at HRM systems designed to target particular outcomes. Thus, some scholars have described specific HRM systems that are likely to help an organization to achieve specific strategic objectives, such as network-building (Collins & Clark, 2003), customer service (Chuang & Liao, 2010), occupational safety (Zacharatos et al., 2005), and knowledge-intensive teamwork (Chuang et al., 2016; Jackson et al., 2006). Presumably, HRM systems with specific targets more clearly communicate the organization's strategic focus, aligning employee attitudes and behaviors with organizational goals. Going forward, research that identifies the key elements of targeted HRM systems may prove more useful to managers charged with achieving specific strategic objectives, compared to so-called high-performance HRM system. And it is interesting to note that this recent line of research better reflects the earliest descriptions of strategic HRM, which adopted a contingency perspective (e.g., Miles & Snow, 1984; Schuler & Jackson, 1987) and assumed that managers adopt strategies to compete in the specific environments they face.

IDENTIFYING THREE CURRENT ISSUES OF CONCERN TO HRM SCHOLARS AND PROFESSIONALS

Our review of the most recent HRM research conducted in North America shows that there is a growing body of research that is directly relevant to the HRM issues that managers and HRM professionals say are most important for their organizations. To illustrate how the concerns of managers are intersecting with the topics being addressed by HRM research, we turn next to a discussion of three issues that are current concerns to HRM professionals and scholars, focusing on research conducted during the past decade. To identify concerns of interest to a broad population of HRM professionals, we sought evidence from the business literature, paying particular attention to recent surveys of managers and executives. This search process identified several HRM-related issues that repeatedly rose to the top of the list of the most pressing issues for North American managers, as follows: (1) the burgeoning freelance economy; (2) achieving gender balance among the managerial tier of organizations; and (3) heightened corporate transparency. Below, we briefly describe these issues, and the relevant HRM research recently conducted and published in North America.

Burgeoning Freelance Economy

Recent labor statistics have highlighted the growing numbers of employees working as free agents or freelancers in North America. The term 'freelancer' is generally used to denote a person with a short-term employment arrangement and typically includes temporary workers, independent contractors, and moonlighters. The number of freelancing workers has been estimated to be approximately one-third of the total employed workforce in the

USA and Canada, and this segment of the workforce has been projected to exceed 40 percent by 2020 (Freelancers Union & Elance-oDesk, 2014; Schawbel, 2014). In general, people under 35 years of age are more likely to work as freelancers, so some of the issues associated with freelance work are confounded with age-related issues. Nevertheless, free-lance arrangements are sufficiently widespread that they are viewed as a long-term trend that increasingly affects workers across the entire age spectrum.

For employers, the growing number of freelance workers can be attributed to the increased flexibility and efficiency of such arrangements. Research indicates that North American employers find the use of low-skilled freelance employees has significant economic value. Thus, for example, unionized workplaces tend to benefit from the use of non-standard temporary work arrangements (i.e., employees commonly referred to as 'temps' and 'contractors') in the USA (Chen & Brudney, 2009), because their employment provides a way for employers to avoid or reduce the costs and rigidity associated with the collectively bargained agreements that constrain their treatment of 'permanent' or traditional employees. Supplementing an organization's core standard workforce with flexible contingent employees with non-standard arrangements is especially appealing as a means for North American employers to reduce labor costs for jobs that are highly standardized and for which performance evaluation can be reliably formalized. Thus, somewhat surprisingly, the fairly bureaucratic and heavily unionized American public sector tends to rely more on freelance employees than do private sector employers (Chen & Brudney, 2009). Canadian and US call centers are another sector where non-traditional employment contracts are common. Such jobs can be readily monitored and controlled, which reduces the risk to employers while also maximizing efficiency and labor productivity (Kwon & van Jaarsveld, 2013).

The effectiveness of freelancers is well established for low-skill jobs that are highly routinized, but such jobs are an increasingly small sector of the North American economy. Thus, scholars have begun to investigate the conditions under which freelancers are effective in jobs that are not easily routinized because they are performed under conditions of greater ambiguity and/or for work that requires greater interdependence with other employees. Thus, recent relevant research has investigated the characteristics of freelancing workers, their relationships and interaction with standard workers, and their impact on psychological and behavioral outcomes of standard workers in the North American organizations.

The psychological traits of freelancers

In order to motivate freelancing workers, it is important to understand why they decide to step out of standard employment relations and how they are psychologically linked to the employing organization. In the case of North American information technology (IT) professionals, it appears that some workers become freelancers after negative experiences in previous jobs (e.g., being terminated unexpectedly), while others enjoy the prestige of being affiliated with a highly visible, reputable organization that would not otherwise hire them (Bidwell & Briscoe, 2009). In the USA, IT professionals working as freelancers tend to identify with their employers based on perceptions of organizational characteristics such as distinctiveness and prestige, and their social relationships with the organization, including how much they trust management, and attraction to their colleagues (George & Chattopadhyay, 2005). For freelance workers in the Canadian financial industry, research has revealed that affective commitment and positive relationships with standard employees are more likely to be found when the free agents experience feelings of support from supervisors and standard employees, leading to a greater sense of being an 'insider' who is equally valued by the employing organization (Lapalme et al., 2009).

How freelance work affects standard employees

Although employers typically expect economic benefits to accrue from the use of freelance workers, research using data from North American organizations reveals some negative consequences of freelance work arrangements for standard workers. For example, the use of non-standard employees has been associated with increased voluntary turnover intentions and behaviors among group members with standard contracts working in US financial firms (Broschak & Davis-Blake, 2006) and full-time permanent employees of US and Canadian call centers (Kwon & van Jaarsveld, 2013). Also, a study of Canadian firms found that the organizational objective of reducing labor costs by using freelancers could be undermined by increased withdrawal behaviors among standard employees (Way et al., 2010).

HRM practices for managing the mix of freelancers and standard employees

Given the interpersonal dynamics that arise in organizations with a mix of freelancers and standard workers, HRM professionals are interested in identifying HRM practices that can reduce the potential outcomes associated with mixing employees working under different contractual arrangements. Recent North American research suggests that among the effective practices to be considered are investing in the socialization of freelancers, promoting the involvement and engagement of both standard and freelance workers, and communicating the organization's reasons for hiring freelancers. Evidence that such practices can be effective includes a study that found a positive effect of providing new temporary employees with employee development opportunities on their intention to remain, job satisfaction, and organizational commitment; and these outcomes appeared to be explained by reductions in the amount of role conflict and ambiguity the workers experienced (Slattery et al., 2008). In another study, the positive relationship between the use of freelancers and the voluntary turnover rate of full-time employees was found to be weaker in US and Canadian call centers that adopted a high-involvement approach to managing employees (Kwon & van Jaarsveld, 2013).

Gender Parity

Over the past several years, gender-based differences in employment experiences and outcomes have been a topic of persistent concern among HRM professionals and employees in North American organizations (Catalyst, 2013a, 2013b), as is true in many other regions (for a review of this topic worldwide, see Chapter 16 in this volume; see also Kulik & Metz, 2017). Drawing particular attention in recent years has been the slow pace of change at the top of organizations, where female executives remain relatively rare. Indeed, throughout all ranks, differences between females and males are evident for a variety of outcomes.

In addition to their near absence in jobs at the top of organizations, differences in pay and promotion have been well documented. A recent meta-analytic review (Joshi et al.,

2015) of 30 years of empirical research located more than 90 studies that reported gender data for performance evaluations and rewards. The analysis revealed substantial gender-based differences in rewards, but only small differences in performance evaluations. Summarizing their findings, the authors concluded: 'Across all research settings, sex differences in organizational rewards were almost fourteen times larger than sex differences in performance evaluation.' Furthermore, differences in performance did not account for the differences in rewards received, providing strong evidence that the observed differences in men's and women's earnings are likely not due to differences in merit. Although the gender gap in pay has narrowed over time, females continue to earn less than their male counterparts in many occupations, with the greatest pay gaps in high-paying jobs (e.g., financial managers and software developers; CNN Money, 2014). Also, the proportions of female chief executive officers (CEOs) and board members in large companies in the USA remain discouraging low at less than 5 percent and 20 percent, respectively, as of April 2015 (Catalyst, 2015).

While North American female workers have been suffering from unfavorable gender-based differences in terms of pay and promotion, research has consistently supported the performance-enhancing effects of having more women in positions of power. For instance, over the past decade, S&P 500 firms with greater female representation on the top management team were correlated with better performance (i.e., Tobin's q) than those with lower female representation (Dezsö & Ross, 2012). In Canada, firms with higher female representation in top management teams benefited from continuous stock market returns (Francoeur et al., 2008). US organizations with more female board members have stronger corporate social responsibility ratings and in turn enjoy more positive corporate reputations (Bear et al., 2010). The benefits of greater gender parity may be particular evident in the USA where gender parity is relatively greater and shareholder protections are relatively stronger as compared to other countries (Post & Byron, 2015).

Despite the positive outcomes associated with greater gender parity, in US organizations positions of power continue to be filled disproportionately by men (Blau & Devaro, 2007). Although the performance of female workers is evaluated slightly higher than that of male workers, males are promoted more than females (Roth et al., 2012). In the USA, sometimes females are promoted to CEOs in struggling firms but replaced by white males if firm performance decreases during their tenure (Cook & Glass, 2014). Understanding the reasons for observed gender differences in promotion rates and career achievement has long been of interest to HRM scholars, and there is no evidence that interest in this topic is waning. Two approaches to understanding the dynamics that explain gender differences at work are those that focus on (perceived) psychological traits, and those that focus on organizational contexts. Both approaches continue to be represented in the North American scholarship.

Psychological traits of female workers in power positions

Spurred by evidence which seems to show that having more women in top management is associated with improved firm performance, some scholars have sought to explain that relationship. One line of work seeks to determine the psychological differences between men and women. For example, one study found that female managers were better at understanding their colleagues, and as a consequence they received better performance ratings from their supervisors, and their subordinates reported being more satisfied

(Byron, 2007). That is, women appear to have greater emotional intelligence and they are able to use this managerial competency to gain positive performance evaluations. Gender differences in ethical judgments have also been suggested as an explanation for why having more women in top management is associated with organizational effectiveness. Thus, for example, a study of female marketing professionals in US firms found that female marketers demonstrated better ethical judgment than male marketers (Lund, 2007). In a somewhat similar vein, female CEOs in the USA tend to follow more conservative accounting practices, characterized by greater risk aversion and ethical sensitivity (Ho et al., 2015). These ethical leadership characteristics may account for the enhanced corporate social responsibility performance of female-led firms.

Organizational contexts pertinent to female leadership

Given that men and women in managerial roles appear to exhibit somewhat different behaviors, on average, it is possible that their behaviors fit better (i.e., are more effective) in some contexts rather than others. A few studies are beginning to identify some of the organizational contexts in which female leadership is more likely to be realized. For example, gender demographics appear to play an important role. In US firms, a pipeline of potential future female leaders is more likely to be found where the number of female managers is greater, because lower-level jobs are more likely to be filled by women when they are better represented at higher ranks (Cohen & Broschak, 2013). This finding implies that female leaders give more opportunities for female employees, who can be developed to be the next leaders through mentoring. Similarly, a study of one large American firm found that the pay gap between men and women was smaller in units that had more women managers (Joshi et al., 2006). Presumably, female managers helped to create a context in which effective women were recognized and rewarded on par with their male peers.

To summarize, the issue of gender parity in the workplace continues to draw attention among North American managers, employees, and scholars. Many decades after American and Canadian laws were passed to reduce unfair sex discrimination at work, some progress has been made. Yet true parity remains elusive. The optimistic view is that organizations increasingly realize the value of women and the potential benefits of treating them well for the organization and its stakeholders. Thus, many major firms in North America are searching for so-called best practices for diversity management. According to a recent report by the Conference Board (Bustamante et al., 2015), current trends and their desired effects include:

- introducing behavioral and cognitive training interventions designed to address unconscious bias with the hope that these will reduce the negative consequences of unconscious bias for talent management decisions;
- examining the linkages between innovation and gender (as well as other types of diversity) by introducing activities such as innovation jams, ideation summits, and roundtables, with the hope of generating innovations that address business challenges and thereby demonstrate the value of the differing perspectives of men and women;
- using analytics to measure more rigorously progress in achieving gender parity goals, the impact of such progress, and the financial returns it brings, thereby align-

ing these activities with the data-driven culture that pervades most other areas of business activity; and

- including men in the gender diversity agenda rather than treating it as a women's issue that can be solved by focusing on just on women, with the hope of creating engaging men in developing and implementing solutions to gender-parity concerns.

Whether such efforts will be effective remains to be seen, but the evidence from past HRM research suggests that some of these popular approaches might not be the most effective. For example, evidence of the effectiveness of diversity awareness training programs, which are typically conducted over the course of one or two days, suggests that such training is not very effective in creating attitudinal and behavior changes. Based on a review of 20 studies conducted in organizational settings, Kulik and Roberson (2008) concluded that diversity awareness training results in improvements in overall attitudes toward diversity, but attitudes toward specific demographic groups (e.g., defined by ethnicity, gender, age) appear to be more resistant to change and may even be at risk of a backlash effect.

Likewise, efforts to use analytics to measure the financial returns associated with improving gender parity may backfire. While a few studies have found a positive association between having more women at the top of organizations and firm performance, the causality is not clear. Studies that have examined the relationship between gender diversity and performance at the level of teams and smaller business units have found weak associations at best (see Jackson et al., 2003). Unless other organizational practices also change, to create a positive diversity climate or otherwise ensure the success of women, their increased numbers may not result in improved financial performance. And in some contexts, increasing the representation of women might increase conflict, reduce feelings of loyalty, and increase employee turnover (see discussions by Joshi et al., 2015; Chung et al., 2015; Kochan et al., 2003). Thus, if improved financial performance is the criterion used to decide whether to make an investment in creating gender parity, it is possible that some firms will conclude that the investment is not 'worthwhile'. Some evidence (e.g., Chung et al., 2015) indicates that changes in the gender mix of an organization's workforce is more likely to result in positive outcomes (or, at least, not result in negative outcomes) in organizations where diverse employees feel that all members of the organization are integrated into the social life of the organization practices (Mor Barak et al., 1998). What is not yet well understood, however, is how HRM practices can be used to create a positive diversity climate.

By collaborating with organizations as they experiment with well-intentioned interventions, such as becoming more data-driven to show the benefits of including women or using activities such as innovation jams and ideation summits to leverage gender differences, HRM scholars could contribute to improving our knowledge about gender issues in the workplace and perhaps also speed up the process of eventually achieving full gender parity. Of particular value would be collaborations to rigorously evaluate the effectiveness of the new interventions being promoted by consulting firms. Such evaluation studies may yield unexpected results. For example, when Kalev et al. (2006) sought to determine whether diversity initiatives improved outcomes such as diversity among top executives or firm performance using from 708 private sector establishments, they concluded that diversity practices aimed at reducing managerial bias (e.g., diversity training) were the least effective in increasing the proportion of women, while practices aimed at reducing social isolation (e.g., mentoring) were modestly effective and practices aimed at increasing accountability for meeting diversity goals were the most effective.

Heightened Corporate Transparency

Compared to the topics discussed above, concerns about corporate transparency are relatively recent in North America, having risen in prominence as technology makes information increasingly easy to access and distribute, both legitimately and through actions of questionable legitimacy. Company executives and employees alike can be affected by the revealing of data that are routinely collected and stored through electronic means, and thus increasingly discoverable.

A wide variety of issues are covered by the broad umbrella of heightened corporate transparency, a few of which are especially relevant to HRM professionals. A report by Forbes about the top workplace trends for the year 2015 concluded that transparency will become increasingly important because younger generations of employees will demand it.

The USA and Canada both have federal privacy laws that give individuals the right to verify information collected about them and used by federal agencies (not private employers) in employment decisions. (A comparison of privacy laws in the USA and Europe is provided by Determann and Sprague, 2011.) What many North American employees do not understand is that employers have substantial rights, too. For example, most electronic documents can be considered business records, which employers may be obligated to preserve (Roberts, 2007; Smith, 2007). Personal e-mails sent on a company computer; e-mail messages typed on a company computer but never sent; personal Web searches conducted on a company computer; personal instant or text messages sent to friends from a company computer; and text entered into a Word document that the employee later deleted – all can be treated as business records (Zeidner, 2007).

The prevalence of self-disclosure using social media tools suggests that awareness of privacy issues and views about privacy versus transparency are evolving as technology changes the availability of so many types of information, including both work-related behaviors and personal activities. As employees increasingly conduct work on their own personal devices and conduct personal business on company devices, the line between work and the rest of life is being blurred, and one consequence is that employers can increasingly learn about many aspects of their employees' personal lives (Wan et al., 2015). The consequences of such changes for all aspects of HRM are anticipated but largely unknown. For example, a report by the consulting company Deloitte on human capital trends in 2015 concluded that changes in employees' attitudes about privacy and transparency are raising new questions about who 'owns' HRM data. According to their survey of employees, about 24 percent of companies make the data they collect about employees completely transparent by sharing it with the employees (Bersin et al., 2015). In fact, 'one in four respondents to our survey said that their employers now give employees full transparency into the data they collect' (ibid.: 81). That statistic means that the vast majority of employers do not fully disclose the data they collect. Perhaps employees can take some comfort from evidence showing that HRM professionals consider it unethical to gather employees' personal information if it is not work-related (Kaupins et al., 2012), but given that IT often simply captures everything, the potential for privacy breaches is high and such breaches are perhaps unavoidable.

Despite some prior interest in workplace privacy issues among North American HRM scholars (e.g., Eddy et al., 1999; Lane, 2004; Saton & Network, 2000), this topic has not received much attention in recent years. Given the monumental change in IT and its implications for transparency and privacy, we anticipate that future HRM research will reflect the growing importance of the many issues involved.

Something Important is Missing: Climate Change and Environmental Degradation[3]

In reviewing the current issues of HRM professionals and scholars in North America, we were surprised by the absence of attention paid to a major topic that garners considerable attention from the general public in the region, namely: the rising awareness of the long-term implications of climate change and environmental degradation (Jackson, 2012a, 2012b, 2012c).

Respect and reverence toward the natural environment are evident in many religions and ancient cultural traditions worldwide, yet consideration of the environmental effects of economic development and expansion is fairly recent. By the end of the nineteenth century, American politicians began taking actions to safeguard pristine landscapes, but it was nearly a century later that governments began to pass regulations designed to safeguard the water and air that sustains daily life.

Amongst scientists, there is widespread agreement that the earth's climate changed substantially during the past 150 years, and continues to do so at an accelerating rate. But for businesses in North America, the voices of investors are more influential, and recently, investors have begun pressuring companies to improve their environmental performance as part of a broader desire to encourage businesses to balance their drive for profitability with a concern for social responsibility and sustainable development. The development of financial tools such as the Dow Jones Sustainability Indexes, which identify environmentally responsible companies in a variety of regions and industry sectors, attest to this important trend.

Surveys of executives worldwide show that environmental issues such as climate change, energy efficiency, biodiversity, and pollution are recognized as important business issues that present both threats and opportunities (see McKinsey & Company, 2010, 2011), and a growing body of empirical evidence supports the assertion that improving environmental performance can be profitable for firms (see Ambec & Lanoie, 2012). Regardless of the specific strategic approach used by firms, attending to environmental sustainability requires the active involvement of HRM professionals. While it seems obvious that HRM professionals and scholars should be engaged in helping firms to transform their businesses to improve environmental sustainability, within North America the HRM community is mostly unengaged.

The potential avenues for HRM engagement around environmental sustainability issues are numerous and have been described in detail elsewhere (see Jackson & Seo, 2010; Jackson et al., 2012; Ehnert & Harry, 2012; Ehnert et al., 2012; Jackson et al., 2011; Ren,

---

[3]   See also Chapter 19 in this volume.

Tang & Jackson, *in press*). Here we very briefly note a few of the opportunities for HRM professionals and scholars to become more engaged in efforts to build more sustainable businesses.

Recruitment and selection

Opinion polls conducted in the USA indicate that many job applicants pay attention to the environmental reputation of companies and use such information when deciding where to seek employment (see Stringer, 2009). Recruiting practices can support effective environmental management by attracting job applicants who understand the company's environmental concerns and share its environmental values, and selection practices can help to ensure that the organization hires job applicants who are knowledgeable and care about environmental sustainability. An understanding of individual predispositions associated with positive attitudes and behaviors related to environmental sustainability may also provide useful guidance for recruiting and selecting employees who are likely to perform well in such positions (Bauer et al., 2012).

Training

As a general rule, when managers determine that organizational change is necessary, training is among the first areas for HRM involvement. This general pattern appears to be true for organizations embarking on environmental initiatives (Jabbour et al., 2010). Training to improve employee awareness of the organization's environmental goals and business strategy may be especially important for an organization that is undergoing a major change in its business strategy, a major transformation of the company culture, or entering into relationships with new supply chain partners (Teixeira, Jabbour, deSousa Jabbour, Latan, & de Oliveira, 2016). For employees whose job behaviors and performance directly impact the environment, training may be required to develop their technical knowledge and skills. For example, employees directly involved in the disposal of raw materials may require training around regulatory requirements and technical standards to ensure compliance.

Leadership identification and development

The important influence of leaders and supervisors on the behavior of employees is well established, and their influence on their subordinates' environmentally friendly work behaviors is no exception (see Kim et al., 2017; Van Velsor & Quinn, 2012). Indeed, some evidence suggests that leader behavior can function as a substitute for effective HRM systems (Chuang et al., 2016). Research that provides new insights into the processes through which leaders can promote the development of pro-environment attitudes is beginning to appear in the North American literature (see Kim et al., 2017; Robertson & Barling, 2013), and we anticipate that this will continue to be a fruitful area of work in the future.

Metrics

The measures used to assess job performance provide a strong signal that tells employees which aspects of their performance are of true importance to their employer. Effective performance metrics provide valuable feedback and support continuous improvement. Without performance metrics that capture various aspects of environmental activity –

such as metrics to monitor resource use and reuse, waste, pollution, emissions, and energy efficiency – employers cannot make significant progress toward improving the organization's environmental performance. Nevertheless, many companies that say their business strategy incorporates environmental sustainability issues also acknowledge that there is little accountability for environmental performance among top executives. Likewise, advancing our understanding of how management practices influence environmental outcomes requires developing new metrics to assess the use of so-called 'Green HRM systems' (see Tang, Chen, Jiang, Paillé & Jia, in press, for an example).

Compensation, rewards, and recognition

For managers and executives, offering monetary bonuses and other rewards for achieving environmental goals can be a powerful way to focus attention and invigorate efforts to achieve the goals. The effectiveness of such pay practices is suggested by a longitudinal study of 469 US firms operating in high-polluting industries. The results revealed that firms with good environmental performance paid their CEOs more, and basing pay on long-term company results was associated with more successful pollution prevention (Berrone & Gomez-Mejia, 2009).

Greening the company culture

If environmental sustainability is taken seriously by employees, it will be evident in the company culture, as it is at 3M. Surveys of HRM professionals in North America reveal that only a few are playing active roles as business partners in companies striving to achieve environmental sustainability (Schmit et al., 2012). How does one get started? With so many possibilities, deciding what to do may be the most difficult task. Certainly, decisions about what specific activities an HRM professional should attempt to promote and pursue must reflect the unique circumstances they face. There is no 'one best way' to move forward. However, for those who are motivated to become more actively involved in achieving environmental sustainability, adopting a strategic HRM perspective may be best. A strategic perspective ensures that HRM practices are aligned with business objectives and recognizes the legitimate interests of all major shareholders, including governments, investors, consumers, local communities, and members of the workforce.

CONCLUSION

HRM in North America is evolving rapidly as firms focus on the new strategic challenges of the twenty-first century. Incrementally, HRM issues are recognized as integral elements in strategy implementation. With the objective of providing an overview of HRM in North America, we have briefly commented on a few major developments, including the importance of analyzing and interpreting the impact of context and responding to the concerns of multiple stakeholders. Then, we discussed in detail a few current issues that are attracting the attention of North American HRM professionals and scholars today, while also pointing to one ignored, yet important topic.

While we have focused on the HRM scene in North America, we acknowledge that the dynamics of the global economy and labor markets increasingly shape HRM in North America. These dynamics are so powerful that drawing a distinction between domestic and international HRM may become an obsolete exercise. Almost all large North American firms have operations and/or strategic partners located in other countries. To the extent that large firms set the norms and standards for workforce management, small- and medium-sized firms are also influenced by the increasing global economy within North America. Thus, for HRM professionals and scholars, the pressing challenge now is to develop contextualized and dynamic frameworks for understanding and effectively managing human resources in organizations that span the globe and compete in an increasingly integrated economic system.

REFERENCES

Ambec, S., & Lanoie, P. 2012. The strategic importance of environmental sustainability. In S.E. Jackson, D. Ones, and S. Dilchert (eds), *Managing Human Resources for Environmental Sustainability*: 21–23. San Francisco, CA: Jossey-Bass.

Barney, J.B., & Wright, P. 1998. On becoming a strategic partner. The role of human resources in gaining competitive advantage. *Human Resource Management*, 37: 31–46.

Batt, R., & Banerjee, M. 2012. The scope and trajectory of strategic HR research: Evidence from American and British journals. *International Journal of Human Resource Management*, 23(9): 1739–1762.

Bauer, T.N., Erdogan, B., & Taylor, S. 2012. Creating and maintaining environmentally sustainable organizations: Recruitment and on-boarding. In S.E. Jackson, D. Ones, and S. Dilchert (eds), *Managing Human Resources for Environmental Sustainability*: 222–240. San Francisco, CA: Jossey-Bass.

Bear, S., Rahman, N., & Post, C. 2010. The impact of board diversity and gender composition on corporate social responsibility and firm reputation. *Journal of Business Ethics*, 97: 207–221.

Becker, B., & Gerhart, B. 1996. The impact of human resource management on organizational performance: Progress and prospects. *Academy of Management Journal*, 39: 779–801.

Becker, B., & Huselid, M. 1998. High performance work systems and firm performance: A synthesis of research and managerial implications. *Research in Personnel and Human Resource Management*, 16: 53–101.

Becker, B., Huselid, M., & Ulrich, D. 2001. *The HR Scorecard: Linking People, Strategy, and Performance*. Boston, MA: Harvard Business School Press.

Berrone, P., & Gomez-Mejia, L. 2009. Environmental performance and executive compensation: An integrated agency-institutional perspective. *Academy of Management Journal*, 52: 103–126.

Bersin, J., Agarwal, D., Pelster, B., & Schwartz, J. 2015. *Global Human Capital Trends 2015*. New York, USA and London, UK: Routledge.

Bidwell, M.J., & Briscoe, F. 2009. Who contracts? Determinants of the decision to work as an independent contractor among information technology workers. *Academy of Management Journal*, 52: 1148–1168.

Blau, F.D., & Devaro, J. 2007. New evidence on gender differences in promotion rates: An empirical analysis of a sample of new hires. *Industrial Relations*, 46: 511–549.

Boudreau, J.W. 2003. Strategic knowledge measurement and management. In S.E. Jackson, M.A. Hitt, and A.S. DeNisi (eds), *Managing Knowledge for Sustained Competitive Advantage*: 360–398. San Francisco, CA: Jossey-Bass.

Broschak, J.P., & Davis-Blake, A. 2006. Mixing standard work and nonstandard deals: The consequences of heterogeneity in employment arrangements. *Academy of Management Journal*, 49: 371–393.

Bustamante, J., Stabley, J., Ray, R., & Mitchell, C. 2015. The evolution of D&I management: Current trends in an era of globalization. The Conference Board. Accessed 3 September 2015, at https://www.conference-board.org/publications/publicationdetail.cfm?publicationid=2901.

Byron, K. 2007. Male and female managers' ability to 'read' emotions: Relationships with supervisor's performance ratings and subordinates' satisfaction ratings. *Journal of Occupational and Organizational Psychology*, 80: 713–733.

Cascio, W.F. 2000. *Costing Human Resources*. Mason, OH: South-Western College.

Catalyst. 2013a. Catalyst census: Fortune 500 women board directors. Catalyst Knowledge Center. Accessed 3 September 2015, at http://www.catalyst.org/knowledge/2013-catalyst-census-fortune-500-women-board-directors.

Catalyst. 2013b. Catalyst census: Fortune 500 women executive officers and top earners. Catalyst Knowledge Center. Accessed 3 September 2015, at http://www.catalyst.org/knowledge/2013-catalyst-census-fortune-500-women-executive-officers-and-top-earners.

Catalyst. 2015. Women in S&P 500 Companies. Retrieved from: http://www.catalyst.org/knowledge/women-sp-50 0-companies.

Chen, C.A., & Brudney, J.L. 2009. A cross-sector comparison of using non-standard workers: Explaining use and impacts on the employment relationship. *Administration and Society*, 41: 313–339.

Chuang, C.-H., Jackson, S.E., & Jiang, Y. 2016. Can knowledge-intensive teamwork be managed? Examining the roles of HRM systems, leadership, and tacit knowledge. *Journal of Management*, 42(2): 524–554.

Chuang, C.-H., & Liao, H. 2010. Strategic human resource management in service context: Taking care of business by taking care of employees and customers. *Personnel Psychology*, 63: 153–196.

Chung, Y., Liao, H., Jackson, S.E., et al. 2015. Cracking but not breaking: Joint effects of faultline strength and diversity climate on loyal behavior. *Academy of Management Journal*, 58(5): 1495–1515.

CNN Money. 2014. 5 big trends shaking up the job market. Retrieved from: http://money.cnn.com/2014/09/04/news/economy/5-big-job-market-trends/.

Cohen, L.E., & Broschak, J.P. 2013. Whose jobs are these? The impact of the proportion of female managers on the number of new management jobs filled by women versus men. *Administrative Science Quarterly*, 58: 509–541.

Colakoglu, S., Lepak, D.P., & Hong, Y. 2006. Measuring HRM effectiveness: Considering multiple stakeholders in a global context. *Human Resource Management Review*, 16(2): 209–218.

Collins, C.J., & Clark, K.D. 2003. Strategic human resource practices, top management team social networks, and firm performance: The role of human resource practices in creating organizational competitive advantage. *Academy of Management Journal*, 46(6): 740–751.

Cook, A., & Glass, C. 2014. Above the glass ceiling: When are women and racial/ethnic minorities promoted to CEO? *Strategic Management Journal*, 35(7): 1080–1089.

Determann, L., & Sprague, R. 2011. Intrusive monitoring: Employee privacy expectations are reasonable in Europe, destroyed in the United States. *Berkeley Technology Law Journal*, 26(2): 979–1036.

Dezsö, C.L., & Ross, D.G. 2012. Does female representation in top management improve firm performance? A panel data investigation. *Strategic Management Journal*, 33(9): 1072–1089.

Dickmann, M., & Muller-Camen, M. 2006. A typology of international human resource management strategies and processes. *International Human Resource Management Journal*, 17: 580–601.

Eddy, E., Stone, D., & Stone-Romero, E. 1999. The effects of information management policies on reactions to human resource information systems: An integration of privacy and procedural justice perspectives. *Personnel Psychology*, 52: 335–358.

Ehnert, I., & Harry, W. 2012. Recent developments and future prospects on sustainable human resource management: Introduction to the special issue. *Management Revue*, 23(3): 221–238.

Ehnert, I., Harry, W., & Zink, K.J. 2012. *Sustainability and Human Resource Management: Developing Sustainable Business Organizations*. New York: Springer.

Fenton-O'Creevy, M., Gooderham, P., & Nordhaug, O. 2008. Human resource management in US subsidiaries in Europe and Australia: Centralisation or autonomy? *Journal of International Business Studies*, 39(1): 151–166.

Fitz-Enz, J. 2000. *The ROI of Human Capital*. New York: Amacom.

Fjeldstad, Ø.D., Snow, C.C., Miles, R.E., & Lettl, C. 2012. The architecture of collaboration. *Strategic Management Journal*, 33(6): 734–750.

Francoeur, C., Labelle, R., & Sinclair-Desgagné, B. 2008. Gender diversity in corporate governance and top management. *Journal of Business Ethics*, 81(1): 83–95.

Freelancers Union & Elance-oDesk. 2014. Freelancing in America: A national survey of the new workforce.

Fu, N., Flood, P.C., Bosak, J., Morris, T., & O'Regan, P. 2013. Exploring the performance effect of HPWS on professional service supply chain management. *Supply Chain Management: An International Journal*, 18(3): 292–307.

George, E., & Chattopadhyay, P. 2005. One foot in each camp: The dual identification of contract workers. *Administrative Science Quarterly*, 50(1): 68–99.

Gulati, R., Wohlgezogen, F., & Zhelyazkov, P. 2012. The two facets of collaboration: Cooperation and coordination in strategic alliances. *Academy of Management Annals*, 6(1): 1–53.

Hall, P., & Soskice, D. 2001. *Varieties of Capitalism: The Institutional Foundation for Comparative Advantage*. Oxford: Oxford University Press.

Ho, S.S., Li, A.Y., Tam, K., & Zhang, F. 2015. CEO gender, ethical leadership, and accounting conservatism. *Journal of Business Ethics*, 127(2): 351–370.

Hyland, M.A., & Jackson, S.E. 2006. A multiple stakeholder perspective: Implications for measuring work–family outcomes. In M. Pitt-Catsouphes, E.E. Kossek, and S. Sweet (eds), *The Work and Family Handbook: Multi-disciplinary Perspectives and Approaches*: 527–549. Mahwah. NJ: Lawrence Erlbaum.

Jabbour, C.J.C., Santos, F.C.A., & Nagano, M.S. 2010. Contributions of HRM throughout the stages of environmental management: Methodological triangulation applied to companies in Brazil. *International Journal of Human Resource Management*, 21(7): 1049–1089.

Jackson, S.E. 2012a. Building empirical foundations to inform the future practice of environmental sustainability. In S.E. Jackson, D. Ones, and S. Dilchert (eds), *Managing Human Resources for Environmental Sustainability*: 416–432. San Francisco, CA: Jossey-Bass.

Jackson, S.E. 2012b. Melding industrial–organizational scholarship and practice for environmental sustainability. *Industrial and Organizational Psychology*, 5(4): 477–480.

Jackson, S.E. 2012c. Portrait of a slow revolution toward environmental sustainability. In S.E. Jackson, D. Ones, and S. Dilchert (eds), *Managing Human Resources for Environmental Sustainability*: 3–20. San Francisco, CA: Jossey-Bass.

Jackson, S.E., Chuang, J., Harden, E., & Jiang, Y. 2006. Toward developing human resource management systems for knowledge-intensive teamwork. In J. Martocchio (ed.), *Research in Personnel and Human Resource Management*, Vol. 25: 27–70. Oxford: Elsevier.

Jackson, S.E., Joshi, A., & Erhardt, N.L. 2003. Recent research on team and organizational diversity: SWOT analysis and implications. *Journal of Management*, 29(6): 801–830.

Jackson, S.E., Ones, D.S., & Dilchert, S. 2012. *Managing Human Resources for Environmental Sustainability*. San Francisco, CA: Jossey-Bass.

Jackson, S.E., Renwick, D.W., Jabbour, C.J., & Muller-Camen, M. 2011. State-of-the-art and future directions for green human resource management: Introduction to the special issue. *German Journal of Human Resource Management*, 25(2): 99–116.

Jackson, S.E., Schuler, R.S., & Jiang, K. 2014. An aspirational framework for strategic human resource management. *Academy of Management Annals*, 8(1): 1–56.

Jackson, S.E., & Seo, J. 2010. The greening of strategic HRM scholarship. *Organization Management Journal*, 7(4): 278–290.

Jiang, K., Lepak, D.P., Hu, J., & Baer, J.C. 2012. How does human resource management influence organizational outcomes? A meta-analytic investigation of mediating mechanisms. *Academy of Management Journal*, 55(6): 1264–1294.

Joshi, A., Liao, H., & Jackson, S.E. 2006. Cross-level effects of workplace diversity on sales performance and pay. *Academy of Management Journal*, 49(3): 459–481.

Joshi, A., Son, J., & Roh, H. 2015. When can women close the gap? A meta-analytic test of sex differences in performance and rewards. *Academy of Management Journal*, 58(5): 1516–1545.

Kalev, A., Kelly, E., & Dobbin, F. 2006. Best practices or best guesses? Assessing the efficacy of corporate affirmative action and diversity policies. *American Sociological Review*, 71(4): 589–617.

Kaplan, R.S., & Norton, D.P. 1996. *Translating Strategy into Action, The Balanced Scorecard*. Boston, MA: Harvard Business School Press.

Kaše, R., Paauwe, J., & Batistič, S. 2014. In the eyes of Janus: The intellectual structure of HRM–performance debate and its future prospects. *Journal of Organizational Effectiveness*, 1: 56–76.

Kaufman, B.E. 2014. The historical development of American HRM broadly viewed. *Human Resource Management Review*, 24(3): 196–218.

Kaupins, G., Reed, D., Coco, M., & Little, A. 2012. Human resource professional ethical perceptions of organizational online monitoring. *International Journal of Business and Public Administration*, 9: 1–14.

Kim, A., Kim, Y., Han, K., Jackson, S.E., & Ployhart, R.E. 2017. Multilevel influences on voluntary workplace green behavior individual differences, leader behavior, and coworker advocacy. *Journal of Management*, 43(5), 1335–1358.

Kochan, T., Bezrukova, K., Ely, R., et al. 2003. The effects of diversity on business performance: Report of the diversity research network. *Human Resource Management*, 42(1): 3–21.

Kulik, C.T., & Metz, I. 2017. Women at the top: Will more women in senior roles impact organizational outcomes? In M.A. Hitt, S.E. Jackson, S. Carmona, et al. (eds), *The Oxford Handbook of Strategy Implementation: Managing Strategic Resources*: 239–282. Oxford: Oxford University Press.

Kulik, C.T., & Roberson, L. 2008. Diversity initiative effectiveness: What organizations can (and cannot) expect from diversity recruitment, diversity training, and formal mentoring programs. In A.P. Brief (ed.), *Diversity at Work*: 265–317. Cambridge: Cambridge University Press.

Kwon, H., & van Jaarsveld, D. 2013. It's all in the mix: Determinants and consequences of workforce blending in call centres. *Human Relations*, 66(8): 1075–1100.

Lane, F.S. 2004. *The Naked Employee*. New York: AMACOM.

Lapalme, M.-E., Stamper, C.L., Semard, G., & Tremblay, M. 2009. Bringing the outside in: Can external workers experience insider status?. *Journal of Organizational Behavior*, 30: 919–940.

Lengnick-Hall, M.L., Lengnick-Hall, C.A., & Rigsbee, C.M. 2013. Strategic human resource management and supply chain orientation. *Human Resource Management Review*, 23(4): 366–377.

Lund, D.B. 2007. Gender differences in ethics judgment of marketing professionals in the United States. *Journal of Business Ethics*, 77(4): 501–515.

MacDuffie, J.P. 1995. Human resource bundles and manufacturing performance: Organizational logic and flexible production systems in the world auto industry. *Industrial and Labor Relations Review*, 48(2): 197–221.

Macey, W.H., & Schneider, B. 2008. The meaning of employee engagement. *Industrial and Organizational Psychology*, 1(1): 3–30.

McKinsey & Company. 2010. The next environmental issue for business: McKinsey Global Survey results. *McKinsey Quarterly*, April. www.mckinseyquarterly.com.

McKinsey & Company. 2011. The business of sustainability: McKinsey Global Survey results. *McKinsey Quarterly*, October. www.mckinseyquarterly.com.

Miles, R.E., & Snow, C.C. 1984. Designing strategic human resources systems. *Organizational Dynamics*, 13(1): 36–52.

Mor Barak, M.E., Cherin, D.A., & Berkman, S. 1998. Organizational and personal dimensions in diversity climate ethnic and gender differences in employee perceptions. *Journal of Applied Behavioral Science*, 34(1): 82–104.

Parry, E., Dickmann, M., & Morley, M. 2008. North American MNCs and their HR policies in liberal and coordinated market economies. *International Journal of Human Resource Management*, 19(11): 2024–2040.

Phillips, P.P., & Phillips, J.J. 2014. *Making Human Capital Analytics Work: Measuring the ROI of Human Capital Processes and Outcomes*. New York: McGraw-Hill.

Post, C., & Byron, K. 2015. Women on boards and firm financial performance: A meta-analysis. *Academy of Management Journal*, 58(5): 1546–1571.

Ren, S., Tang, G., & Jackson, S.E. in press. Green human resource management research in emergence: A review and future directions. *Asia Pacific Journal of Management*. Doi: 10.1007/s10490-017-9532-1

Renwick, D.W., Jabbour, C.J., Muller-Camen, M., Redman, T., & Wilkinson, A. 2016. Contemporary developments in Green (environmental) HRM scholarship. *The International Journal of Human Resource Management*, 27(2): 114–128.

Roberts, B. 2007. Avoiding the perils of electronic data. *HR Magazine*, 52(1): 72.

Robertson, J.L., & Barling, J. 2013. Greening organizations through leaders' influence on employees' pro-environmental behaviors. *Journal of Organizational Behavior*, 34(2): 176–194.

Roth, P.L., Purvis, K.L., & Bobko, P. 2012. A meta-analysis of gender group differences for measures of job performance in field studies. *Journal of Management*, 38(2): 719–739.

Rucci, A.J., Kirn, S.P., & Quinn, R.T. 1998. The employee–customer–profit chain at Sears. *Harvard Business Review*, 76: 82–98.

Saton, D., & Network, W. 2000. *Workplace Privacy: Real Answers and Practical Solutions*. Toronto: Thompson.

Schawbel, D. 2014. 10 workplace trends for 2015. *Forbes*, 14 October. Retrieved from: http://www.forbes.com/sites/danschawbel/2014/10/29/the-top-10-workplace-trends-for-2015/.

Schmidt, F.L., Hunter, J.E., McKenzie, R.C., & Muldrow, T.W. 1979. Impact of valid selection procedures on work-force productivity. *Journal of Applied Psychology*, 64: 609–626.

Schmit, M.J., Fegley, S., Esen, E., Schramm, J., & Tomassetti, A. 2012. Human resource management efforts for environmental sustainability: A survey of organizations. In S.E. Jackson, S. Dilchert, & D.S. Ones (eds), *Managing Human Resources for Environmental Sustainability*: 61–79. San Francisco, CA: Jossey-Bass.

Schuler, R.S., & Jackson, S.E. 1987. Linking competitive strategies with human resource management practices. *Academy of Management Executive*, 1(3): 207–219.

Schuler, R.S., & Jackson, S.E. 2007. *Strategic Human Resource Management: A Reader*. London: Blackwell.

Schuler, R.S., & MacMillan, I.C. 1984. Gaining competitive advantage through human resource management practices. *Human Resource Management*, 23(3): 241–255.

Slattery, J.P., Selvarajan, T., & Anderson, J.E. 2008. The influences of new employee development practices upon role stressors and work-related attitudes of temporary employees. *International Journal of Human Resource Management*, 19(12): 2268–2293.

Smith, A. 2007. Federal rules define duty to preserve work e-mails. *HR Magazine*, 27: 36.

Stringer, L. 2009. *The Green Workplace: Sustainable Strategies that Benefit Employees, the Environment, and the Bottom Line*. New York: Palgrave Macmillan.

Tang, G., Chen, Y., Jiang, Y., Paillé, P., & Jia, J. in press. Green human resource management practices: scale development and validity. *Asia Pacific Journal of Human Resources*. DOI: 10.1111/1744-7941.12147.

Teixeira, A.A., Jabbour, C.J.C., de Sousa Jabbour, A.B.L., Latan, H., & de Oliveira, J.H.C. 2016. Green training and green supply chain management: evidence from Brazilian firms. *Journal of Cleaner Production*, 116: 170–176.

Van Velsor, E., & Quinn, L. 2012. Leadership and environmental sustainability. In S.E. Jackson, D. Ones, & S. Dilchert (eds), *Managing Human Resources for Environmental Sustainability*: 241–262. San Francisco, CA: Jossey-Bass.

Wan, M., Shaffer, M., Francesco, A.M., Joplin, J.R., Lau, T., & Cheung, E. 2015. Cross-domain communication technology, work–family interface and life satisfaction, Presentation made at the annual conference of the Academy of Management. Vancouver, British Columbia, Canada.

Way, S.A., Lepak, D.P., Fay, C.H., & Thacker, J.W. 2010. Contingent workers' impact on standard employee withdrawal behaviors: Does what you use them for matter?. *Human Resource Management*, 49(1): 109–138.

White, S., & Schneider, B. 2003. *Service quality*. Mahwah, NJ: Lawrence Erlbaum.
Wright, P.M., Coff, R., & Moliterno, T.P. 2014. Strategic human capital crossing the great divide. *Journal of Management*, 40(2): 353–370.
Zacharatos, A., Barling, J., & Iverson, R.D. 2005. High-performance work systems and occupational safety. *Journal of Applied Psychology*, 90(1): 77–93.
Zeidner, R. 2007. Employees don't 'get' electronic storage. *HR Magazine*, January: 36.

21. Revisiting the Latin American HRM model
Anabella Davila and Marta M. Elvira

INTRODUCTION

In the first edition of this book we presented a Latin American model of human resources management (HRM) using the stakeholder perspective (Davila & Elvira, 2012). We acknowledged that HRM practices differ across countries, organisations, and industries in Latin America, and assumed that traditional models of management and organisation would offer only partial explanations for HRM complexity in this region where contextual elements challenge the use of a single disciplinary approach. Then, we took a broader perspective and explored how the changes in economic, political, and social elements in the region affect organisational HRM systems. Based also on our earlier work (Elvira & Davila, 2005a; Davila & Elvira, 2009), we identified key contextual elements that were absent in traditional HRM research in Latin America, including the role of the enterprise as a social institution, the value of the individual within society, and the pragmatic character of public policies. Ultimately, we used the stakeholder perspective to identify the key stakeholders involved in employment relationships and determine how HRM systems were configured around such stakeholders.

While traditionally the stakeholder perspective focuses on stakeholder attribute salience relative to the focal organisation (Mitchell et al., 1997), some stakeholders may lack resources to defend their interests and thus may be ignored by business organisations (Tavis, 1994). Even if firms ignore the potential effects of such stakeholders' claims or their legitimate role in society, they are affected in their ability to meet objectives. We refer to these stakeholders as 'silent' because even if invisible to the organisation–stakeholder network they are part of the socio-economic sector. From this perspective, we have examined how effective HRM systems met the diverse demands of various stakeholders in Latin America such as employees, unions, and relevant community members.

In this chapter, we revisit and develop arguments supporting the three pillars upon which we built the stakeholder HRM model, namely: (1) investment in employees: salary and benefits levels as well as education, training, and development; (2) efforts to operate within a cooperative labour relations framework; and (3) corporate social responsibility (CSR) practices centred on the community. These three pillars emerged after a thorough analysis of in-depth qualitative case studies of business organisations operating in the region (Davila & Elvira, 2009). Our initial argument was that firms play a key role as social institutions (Elvira & Davila, 2005b), and their environment includes stakeholders seeking social integration regardless of their legitimacy or power. We concluded that HRM practices appear to perform best when including multiple stakeholders, both powerful and silent ones.

Our second argument relies on the aspirational egalitarian mentality of the Latin American society. While Latin Americans aspire to fair social conditions, they have experienced high levels of income and education inequality since the early industrialisation period (Williamson, 2010), relying on hierarchical economic and social structures that shape organisations and HRM models (Friel, 2011). Currently, employees are starting to ask for a voice in the structure of employment relationships (e.g., Andonova et al., 2009). Moreover, other relevant stakeholders affected by employee–organisation–community relationships have a voice in granting corporations a social licence to operate (e.g., Osland et al., 2009).

Seeking to mitigate the impact of social hierarchies in business organisations and economic systems, Latin Americans have developed intricate social networks composed of compact and homogenous social groups. From an HRM viewpoint, one can understand the role of social relationships as mechanisms that help bureaucratic HRM practices take a more egalitarian orientation (Davila & Elvira, 2015). Thus, in our 2012 HRM model we proposed that HRM practices that promote inclusive, horizontal relationships between organisations and stakeholders – instead of hierarchical relationships of subordination – describe a more comprehensive stakeholder HRM model. Consequently, HRM systems would be most effective when strengthening the horizontal organisation–stakeholder relationship that facilitates social inclusion of diverse Latin American groups.

To illustrate the validity of this theoretical approach, here we analyse the needs and demands of stakeholders involved in the employment relationship and the role of HRM in Latin America. Seeking evidence for the model just presented, we performed a systematic analysis of ten Latin American multinational corporations' (LAT-MNCs) annual and sustainability reports, focusing on the employee- and community-relations sections.

Below we first take the stakeholder perspective and present a stakeholder-centred HRM model for Latin America. Next, we identify LAT-MNCs' silent stakeholders and the approaches that firms take to interact with them as described in annual reports. Then, we discuss: (1) the strategies LAT-MNCs list as promoting employee involvement with the local community in their role as social institutions; and (2) the HRM practices that link employees with their proximal community to foster social inclusion. We close by distilling new insights to strengthen the stakeholder HRM model for Latin America.

THE STAKEHOLDER PERSPECTIVE

Research on the stakeholder perspective of the organisation has focused on two central questions: (1) who key stakeholders are; and (2) how organisations interact with them. The stakeholder perspective has been used to describe organisations and the various interests of internal or external corporate constituencies, as well as the specific connections between an organisation and salient individuals or groups of stakeholders relative to performance from a strategic viewpoint (Clarkson, 1995). The stakeholder logic has also served to interpret the purpose of a corporation regarding its moral obligations, with a strong emphasis on ethics and CSR (Clarkson, 1995; Donaldson & Preston, 1995; Freeman, 1984). Thus, a stakeholder is commonly defined as 'any group or individual who can affect or is affected by the achievement of the organisation's objectives' (Freeman, 1984: 46). The constellation of organisational stakeholders can be defined broadly to include even governmental agencies, universities or vocational schools, or media. This contrasts with a narrow view of organisational stakeholders that considers mostly individuals or groups close to the organisation such as customers, suppliers, employees, or neighbour communities (Freeman, 1984).

A strategic stakeholder approach tends to follow the narrow view and include only those groups that provide resources for the firm or to whom the firm offers products or services. Under this view the salience of various stakeholders is central to stakeholder management. Thus, stakeholder attributes such as power, legitimacy, or urgency (Mitchell et al., 1997) potentially influence firm executives' values, perceptions, and actions towards defining how to satisfy stakeholders demands (Agle et al., 1999).

The importance given to identifying who the stakeholders are and what their interests, needs, or demands are suggests that stakeholder theory is overly concerned with potential conflict emerging from diverse views on resource dependency or control issues (Frooman, 1999). Therefore, searching for strategies that avoid or mitigate such conflicts turns researchers' attention toward the organisation–stakeholder relationship.

How organisations relate to or interact with stakeholders is another substantive concern for work in this perspective. Researchers tend to grant either to the organisation (Donaldson & Preston, 1995; Mitchell et al., 1997) or to the stakeholder (Frooman, 1999) centrality in the relationship according to the level of resource dependency the actors possess. However, granting centrality to the organisation or to the stakeholder derives from the same principle: that the interaction established is a hierarchical relationship. Moreover, the relationship translates into a hierarchy because the entity in power only follows its interests and seeks to satisfy its demands.

Other studies emphasise stakeholders' alliances with different stakeholders to set rules targeting organisational membership, governance, or monitoring of target organisations (Fransen & Kolk, 2007). Further, stakeholders become key players when directly contributing to the economic functioning of a business. Therefore, focusing on stakeholder centrality presents an unequal hierarchical relationship towards the focal organisation.

In general, we surmise that research on organisation–stakeholder relationships takes an instrumental view of stakeholder management, whether from the firm or the stakeholder's standpoint. That is, a stakeholder is defined as such when possessing something that the organisation needs or vice versa. While this managerial approach has produced valuable findings, we argue that there exist more than instrumental goals to stakeholder management. The salience of specific stakeholders might depend on factors beyond managerial value preferences, resource dependency, or contractual actions.

An international view of this theory could provide further insights on which stakeholders matter and how and why they interact with organisations. Here we focus on the Latin American region through the lens of HRM and related CSR practices.

STAKEHOLDER MANAGEMENT IN LATIN AMERICA AND HRM

Our Latin American stakeholder-centred HRM model from 2012 built on Brewster's (1999: 215) contextual paradigm 'of what is contextually unique and why' in international HRM. This view acknowledges that different constituencies (such as societies, governments, or regions) can affect strategic human resources management (SHRM) practices, not just firms. Yet for HRM, the inclusion of multiple constituencies in the management of the employment relationships might mean conflicting or contrasting interests and demands, difficult to satisfy simultaneously. This seems to fit the reality of HRM in Latin America, where employees, organised labour, managers, and other stakeholders often have differing interests and, therefore, demands or expectations; perhaps more so than in other world regions, due to the late development of labour institutions (Elvira & Davila, 2005b; Davila & Elvira, 2012).

In addition, various constituents base their interests and demands in the social contract developed through regular interactions and on assumptions about what an employment relationship ought to be like (Kochan, 1999). In Latin America, economic opening and political adjustments have influenced expectations for the social contract in terms of demands for employment security, reduced inequality, and requirements to trust employers.

Therefore, the contextual and social contract approaches help to frame our reasoning: HRM structures are built around the needs of both powerful and silent stakeholders and thus serve as mechanisms through which organisations act as social institutions. Still, firms need to not only cater to multiple constituencies through the employment relationship, but also strengthen the horizontal relationship with stakeholders to facilitate their social inclusion via HRM and CSR practices.

For example, indigenous groups' demands often turn into valid and long-term relationships that originally lacked such legitimacy. Take the mining industry, where few firms have understood the needs and demands of the community around their operations. Such is the case of Newmont, a United States mining company operating in Peru with a long history of tensions with its surrounding community. Gifford and Kestler (2008) document how this poor and vulnerable community, lacking government protection, demanded benefits beyond the provision of jobs or health services in order to address employee productivity problems. An honest effort to improve the company's relationship with the community allowed Newmont to acquire an in-depth knowledge of their deprivation. Advised by a team of social scientists, the company learned that the shortage of health services could serve as a starting point to earn local legitimacy for the 'silent' stakeholders. Thus Newmont partnered with community groups to understand and identify their needs, and leveraged its existing social infrastructure. The analysis of key stakeholders, health infrastructure, health workforce, and other community health issues revealed a whole spectrum of needs beyond medical problems or healthcare services. The company's approach illustrates the social embeddedness capability of successful MNCs when operating in emerging markets, which includes developing relationships with non-traditional partners, co-inventing custom solutions, and building local capacity (London & Hart, 2004). Based on this case, Gifford and Kestler (2008) encourage firms to develop a social embeddedness capability to obtain local legitimacy. We do too, while also suggesting the value of building horizontal relationships with silent stakeholders.

Newmont's example in Peru illustrates that in Latin America, diverse stakeholders coexist with organisations and desire to achieve social integration, contributing to countries' development efforts. Relative to other world regions, Latin America suffers widespread scarcity of reliable institutions, which makes people place greater trust in firms. In fact, considering the macroeconomic environment could help us understand that the role that business organisations play in economic growth includes social inclusion. The World Economic Forum (WEF) recently released the Inclusive Growth and Development Report 2015, which identifies a wide range of policy options to drive socially inclusive economic growth (WEF, 2015). The report analyses 112 economies along seven dimensions, called pillars:

1. Education and skills development: access, quality, equity.
2. Employment and labour compensation: productive employment, wage and non-wage labour compensation.
3. Asset-building and entrepreneurship: small business ownership, home and financial asset ownership.
4. Financial intermediation of real economy investment: financial system inclusion, intermediation of business investment.
5. Corruption and rents: business and political ethics, concentration of rents.
6. Basic services and infrastructure: basic infrastructure, health-related services and infrastructure.
7. Fiscal transfers: tax code, social protection.

The report notes that all countries offer opportunities to make economic growth more socially inclusive without dampening incentives to work, save, and invest. Countries are divided into four groups, to enable meaningful comparisons: advanced, upper-middle income, lower-middle income, and lower-income. Most Latin American countries are considered in the upper-middle income level except for Bolivia, the Dominican Republic, El Salvador, Guatemala, Honduras, Nicaragua, and Paraguay, which fall in the lower-middle income level. Country indicators are based on a scale of 1–7 (1 = not well at all; 7 = extremely well). The Latin American countries that scored high on specific pillars within their income level group are: Panama 4.87 in employment; Chile 4.21 in asset-building; Uruguay 4.23 and Chile 4.13 in corruption and rents; Costa Rica 5.63, Uruguay 5.62, Chile 5.62 in basic services; Panama 4.20 and Costa Rica 4.03 in fiscal transfers.

The rest of the countries within the upper-middle income level underperformed in all pillars. Importantly, none of the Latin American countries scored high in the education pillar. Countries in the lower-middle income level that performed high within their group are: Guatemala 4.36 in education; Honduras 3.79 and Nicaragua 3.70 in asset-building; Honduras 3.42 in financial intermediation. This group of countries underperformed in the rest of the pillars.

We interpret the performance of Latin American countries in this report as evidence that very few institutions perform well, and even then they do so only in specific countries, especially if we compare these countries to others in their income group. The report's framework also advocates the need for incentives to the private sector rather than direct transfers through the public sector. One may ask to what extent business organisations should consider stakeholders that have been marginalised by economic development systems and, therefore, lack socio-political representation. In the case of Latin America, if local public government institutions are incapable of or unwilling to represent some segments of society, those segments are largely dependent upon the decisions and actions of firms for their well-being (Tavis, 1994). Companies that understand their role in their employees' welfare channel their actions through an HRM philosophy that includes ways of treating and valuing people. For instance, Grupo ALFA, a Mexican multinational conglomerate, defines its HRM philosophy as a promoter of opportunities for its employees, their families, and its surrounding community's development (Alfa, 2013).

In Latin America, some social groups present unique characteristics because of historical and cultural reasons that currently demand social inclusion. The concept of social inclusion originally aimed to redress the exclusion of people who were not part of the social security welfare system. Nowadays, social inclusion is used in both the economic and the social sense. In business organisations, social inclusion studies revolve around the quality of employment that translates into decent salaries, respect for labour rights, union representation, and other related issues (Carrillo & Gomis, 2014). Typically, inclusion refers not only to employees but also to their families and immediate community. In our view, stakeholder management in Latin America grants a leading role to HRM when defining policies that benefit employees and their relevant in-group members for social inclusion (Elvira & Davila, 2005b).

WEF (2015) data indicate that inequality often starts in the labour market. According to the report, inequality – in terms of wage distribution and job losses – fell considerably in Argentina (2003–12) and Brazil (2001–12), where changes in the distribution of wages and paid employment accounted for 87 per cent and 72 per cent of the change, respectively. These outcomes suggest that labour policies should include regulation for minimum wages and collective bargaining, besides employment and social protection benefits. The WEF report highlights that Argentina provides relatively good basic services such as healthcare and sanitation, despite the need to improve their quality and coverage. Similarly, in terms of educational services, access to quality education is tied to students' socio-economic backgrounds; that is, only students from middle and upper classes have access to quality education. This fact contributes to deepening social inequality in this country. Moreover, Argentina needs to reduce unemployment, particularly among youth (WEF, 2015). Additionally, Brazil's unemployment is lower than in many other countries in the region, although the informal sector remains large. Brazil continues to depend on cash transfer programmes for social protection. Access to and quality of education are also important areas of improvement from the viewpoint of social equality. Finally, to grow more sustainably and inclusively, Brazil needs to improve its infrastructure and basic services such as healthcare (WEF, 2015).

Besides re-examining who key stakeholders are, it matters to know what both stakeholders and organisations care about in Latin America. To illustrate the arguments, we use the same cases as in our 2012 stakeholder HRM model, because there is still scant research on HRM in the region. First, respect for property rights is a key factor in rural Colombia, where the conflict-ridden environment has severely damaged all economic activity. Property rights helped to centre HRM policies that provide protection and guarantee peace in the communities where companies operate (Andonova et al., 2009). Two agribusiness companies, Hacienda Gavilanes and Indupalma, worked closely with workers to develop a co-operative ownership model aligning workers' interests with the organisations' objectives. HRM practices that work effectively in this environment include extensive technical and administrative training for employees (now co-owners in the co-operative) and, specifically, education in workers' rights and personal development. In this context, designing a socially responsible corporate strategy to satisfy indigenous stakeholders' needs fell short, requiring also the sharing of control rights and ownership-related privileges with employees.

These illustrations suggest that the role of HRM departments is crucial when national and local institutions fail to enforce basic property rights, or to provide protection and security. In such circumstances employment conflicts tend to escalate into wider social, political, and economic clashes. Therefore, attending to the broad employment relationship becomes much more important than has traditionally been recognised in HRM research.

Considering the evidence just discussed, we observe that organisations and stakeholders in Latin America tend to interact not so much on the basis of a strict dependency relationship, or contributing principle of their accountability in providing resources and knowledge for businesses, but on a social contract infused by trust (or lacking it). Naturally, an exchange system based on social relationships reaches a limit for member participation or integration. In particular, in Latin America, social groups are closed and tied to long-term kin relationships, potentially seeking self-interested group behaviour and, in the long run, possibly corrupting the system and its values.

In sum, to approach the Latin America HRM model from a stakeholder management perspective one should understand not only business organisations' role in the socio-economic arena, but also how well HRM practices satisfy the interests of those groups that lack specific attributes to be generally considered as stakeholders. We have identified those stakeholders as 'silent' because of their lack of salience attributes, but we consider them relevant for granting organisations local legitimacy or the social licence to operate. In the rest of the chapter, we present firm-level data to validate this model, describe the methodology used to analyse such data, and explain the findings and conclusions.

METHODOLOGY

To help identify silent stakeholders we reviewed the sustainability annual reports of ten LAT-MNCs. We used the 2013 *AmericaEconomía* ranking of the largest companies in the region and selected privately owned companies that publish their sustainability report. We left out state-owned companies because our purpose is to explore HRM systems in companies facing similar challenges when dealing with economic and social institutions, while state-owned companies present different HRM challenges.

We used company sustainability reports because they have become a legitimacy activity to comply with international standards of transparency and accountability before diverse stakeholders. Sustainability reports include a section on HRM and community development, following the guidelines of the Global Reporting Initiative (GRI). The GRI is an international independent organisation that seeks to help businesses, governments, and other organisations understand and communicate the impact of business on critical sustainability issues such as climate change, human rights, corruption, and many other issues. Since 1997, when GRI emerged, companies have voluntarily adopted its framework to elaborate on their sustainability. The GRI framework is revised periodically by corporate representatives, non-governmental organisations (NGOs), labour groups, and members of society at large. Descriptive data on the selected companies appear listed in Table 21.1.

After systematically reading the community section in these annual reports, we developed three analytical criteria for categorising silent stakeholders. First, silent stakeholders should be reported by the organisation but not linked to its supply chain. This criterion follows from the argument that silent stakeholders are groups without a legitimate voice before the organisation, and lack visibility within the stakeholder network.

Table 21.1 Description of the corporate sustainability reports

Company	Country	Year	Main industrial sector	Type of report analysed[*]	No. countries	No. geographic zones	Direct employees	Global Reporting Initiative
ALFA	Mexico	2011	Chemicals; Food; Auto-parts	Sustainability	50	8	57000	Yes
America Movil	Mexico	2012	Telecommunications	Sustainability	15	8	158719	Yes
CEMEX	Mexico	2013	Cement	Annual	11	5	43000	N/A
GRUMA	Mexico	2013	Food	Annual	17	6	19000	Yes
Grupo BIMBO	Mexico	2013	Food	Annual	16	5	125000	Yes
Grupo JBS-FRIBOI	Brazil	2012	Food	Sustainability	30	7	142142	Yes
IMPSA	Argentina	2010–12	Energy	Sustainability	35	7	6156	Yes
LATAM	Chile	2013	Airline	Sustainability	19	6	52000	Yes
ODEBRECHT	Brazil	2013	Construction	Annual	14	6	175031	No
TENARIS	Argentina	2013	Steel	Annual	8	2	16800	N/A

400

Second, silent stakeholders ought to be related to the organisation through any initiative in which employees were reported as actively involved. This analytical criterion derives from the fact that HRM supports the organisation's social institution role partly through employee involvement in their immediate community. Third, we categorised a stakeholder as silent when evidence suggested that the organisation's actions targeted the development or welfare of the specific group. Here we assumed that organisations aware of their role as social institutions would develop HRM policies and practices benefiting relevant members of the community. We did not consider actions targeting natural resources or environmental conservation strategies, which are important topics for HRM but beyond the scope of our chapter.

Having gathered the raw information, we then classified all the actions and initiatives reported by companies as targeting different stakeholders and identified the themes that emerged across firms. We present these findings below.

HRM SYSTEMS THAT SHAPE ORGANISATIONS AS SOCIAL INSTITUTIONS

HRM systems that contribute to organisations' role as social institutions include not only extended benefits for employees' families, but also initiatives that involve employees in the company's social strategy and programmes that target the human development of specific stakeholders. We define such human development dimensions following the United Nations Development Programme (UNDP): health, education, and living standards. Stakeholders that appear repeatedly in all reports include local youth, employees' families, local community, small and medium-sized enterprises (SMEs), and indigenous people.

Clearly LAT-MNCs care for the children in the communities where they work. Seven LAT-MNCs reported programmes oriented to children's development in three main areas: basic education, culture, and sports. One representative example is Chilean LAN (the airline). In Ecuador, LAN organises a version of Caring for my Destination, developed with volunteers of the company on Tourism Day, and the Toqué el Cielo con Lan (I Touch the Sky with LAN) project (LAN Kids), which seeks to familiarise children with aviation through their first flight to a tourist attraction in their city of destination. Similarly, the company has two programmes in Peru: Chicos que Sueñan (Kids that Dream) and Chicos que VueLAN (Kids that FlyLAN), offering lectures to foster awareness and understanding of the environment.

We also observe firms offering direct benefits for employees' families, including scholarships for employees' children (for example, Mexican Grupo ALFA, a diversified conglomerate), health insurance for employees' families (for example, Brazilian ODEBRECHT, construction and petrochemicals), and work–family balance programmes (for example, Mexican GRUMA, food).

The initiatives that target members of the local community consist mostly of educational programmes either for job training or for self-employment in which employees participate as volunteers. For example, Argentinian energy firm IMPSA offers open academic training programmes to the entire community in which it is located. LAT-MNCs also report active participation in helping to rescue and rebuild community infrastructure after natural disasters. The Argentinian TENARIS (steel), for instance, offers specific support to communities hit by natural disasters or catastrophes. Similarly, the Mexican Grupo BIMBO (bakery) has the Grupo Bimbo Fund, a volunteer programme for natural disasters. The Mexican America Movil (telecommunications) offers free communications during times of disaster. Interestingly, through joint intervention in cases of natural disaster, LAT-MNCs have developed alliances among themselves. Take the example of Red SumaRSE, an initiative of citizens and corporations in Mexico and in Panama. It started in Mexico, helping the communities most hit by Hurricane Alex in 2010. Today, this initiative runs programmes oriented to rebuilding the social structure and developing a civic mindset in those marginalised communities. It also addresses family integration, economic development opportunities, citizenship, image, identity and culture, recovery of public spaces, inter-sectorial communication, and protection of the environment. Among the partners in this initiative we find the Mexican conglomerate Grupo ALFA.

Companies' relationships with nearby SMEs are also frequently mentioned in the community section of sustainability reports. Remember that we only considered SMEs unrelated to the company's supply chain and focused on initiatives that listed SMEs as members of the local community. Latin America's entrepreneurial activity has been well documented in the literature (Acs & Amorós, 2008; Amorós et al., 2013). These studies lead to two major conclusions. First, entrepreneurship is often related to lack of employment, which in turn depends on the economic stability of each country. When a country is economically stable, entrepreneurial activity diminishes because individuals prefer to obtain a formal job, and vice versa (Acs & Amorós, 2008). Second, entrepreneurial activity has a different meaning in the rural and urban areas. In Chile, rural entrepreneurs complain about difficulties accessing financial resources, yet perceive high market dynamism. Surprisingly, these entrepreneurs view government programmes as supporting entrepreneurship, though the Chilean government apparently has not promoted many regional policies (Amorós et al., 2013).

The instability of SMEs and the limited success of public policies addressing entrepreneurs' needs is an opportunity for LAT-MNCs to promote entrepreneurial activity. For instance, Grupo ALFA, assisted by resources from the Mexican Development Bank (NAFINSA), helps to finance SME development. In Brazil, ODEBRECHT offers a programme for budding entrepreneurs. Grupo BIMBO promotes: (1) RED, A. C., an alliance of Mexican companies committed to the country's development, where BIMBO develops and provides ongoing business workshops; and (2) From Entrepreneur to Entrepreneur, a programme that brings members of the business community to share experiences, connect with other companies, and do business together. BIMBO also participates in an Alliance with ProEmpleo Productivo Foundation, which offers training and consulting services to entrepreneurs, and has helped more than 300 entrepreneurs to start up or grow their businesses. Thus, these data suggest that supporting entrepreneurship activity is also part of the role of LAT-MNCs as social institutions.

Another theme emerging from those reports concerns the native communities reported as living around a company. LAT-MNCs relate to these groups mainly in three general forms: building infrastructure; provision of health services; and connecting through foundations or charity institutions. The most prominent activity of these is building infrastructures. TENARIS (Argentina) partners financially with bridge-builder movements in rural communities. America Movil (Mexico) provides equipment for Infocenters in Ecuador, a digital inclusiveness project of the Telecommunications Ministry. In Nicaragua the company installed infrastructure to offer educational, news, and entertainment programming to 12 rural municipalities. The Mexican Grupo BIMBO offers the programme Reforestemos México (Reforest Mexico) which, aided by a large number of volunteers, works with forestry firms to sustainably manage woodlands, and supports the development of individuals and communities that work on productive projects.

In addition, LAT-MNCs relate with indigenous groups through the provision of health services such as the Programme Cirugía Extramuros (Extramural Surgery) Organ and Tissue Donation and Transplant Programme financed by America Movil. Finally, LAT-MNCs use foundations (for example, Grupo ALFA) or charity organisations (for example, LAN or GRUMA) to channel their help to native communities.

Based on the data retrieved from the annual reports related to our emerging criteria for identifying organisations' silent stakeholders and the substantial volume of organisations' social programmes that target those stakeholders, we offer:

Proposition 1: HRM systems that support organisations in their role as social institutions are more likely to affect silent stakeholders identified as being from the following groups: local youth, employees' families, local community, SMEs and indigenous people.

LAT-MNCs' sustainability reports persistently emphasise the active role of organisations in the promotion and implementation of social strategies that affect education, health, and living standards of the communities in which they operate. The sharing of company knowledge and employee volunteers for firms' social strategies leads us to the following proposition:

Proposition 2: HRM systems that support organisations in their role as social institutions are more likely to have HR practices that provide for human development of organisations' silent but relevant stakeholders.

HRM SYSTEMS THAT PROMOTE HORIZONTAL ORGANISATION–STAKEHOLDERS RELATIONSHIPS

Best HRM practices in Latin America, and other emergent economies, often promote horizontal organisation–stakeholders relationships based on the principle of social inclusion (Andonova et al., 2009; Leguizamon et al., 2009; Osland et al., 2009). A number of such practices link employees with their proximal community. Training and development aiming to develop employee leadership skills is the most recurrent practice reported. In particular, leadership development programmes target young leaders (for example, Grupo ALFA), global leaders (for example, TENARIS), and coaching programmes (for example, CEMEX). However, only two LAT-MNCs emphasise values and human rights in the content of their leadership development programmes (Grupo BIMBO and ODEBRECHT).

Close inspection of the sustainability reports suggests the existence of both internally and externally oriented horizontal organisation–stakeholders relationships. To start, organisations promote an internal egalitarian social structure through diverse HRM practices that aim to engage employees. For example, ODEBRECHT outlines its Communities of Knowledge Programme that disseminates the knowledge generated throughout the company to all parts of the organisation. CEMEX uses an Engagement Survey to measure employees' levels of engagement across its global operations, and explores how the workplace environment enables employees to perform their jobs to the best of their ability. LAN and ODEBRECHT have a policy of hiring local individuals for managerial positions and as staff employees. Grupo ALFA brands itself as a 'Family-Responsible Company' offering initiatives such as flexible working hours, alternative working schedules, adjustments for pre- and post-maternity leave, breastfeeding rooms, and parental leave. GRUMA describes its work environment as one where employees 'trust their leaders, are proud of what they do and like the people they work with'.

Additionally, the studied organisations report community engagement practices seeking to link their employees with their immediate community with the objective of improving social inclusion. CEMEX reports a Stakeholder Outreach Teams programme in which teams of employees plan activities that engage community members and develop a quarterly Stakeholder Outreach Report. All projects must be aligned with one of the following key categories: biodiversity; community outreach; hosting tours; and education for employees, retirees, customers, and vendors. Also in Mexico, Grupo ALFA conducts socio-economic surveys to determine each community's needs before defining its social strategy. The Argentinian IMPSA reports ties to universities and colleges to improve labour placement and create shared knowledge. Finally, all the LAT-MNCs analysed have well-established volunteer programmes that link employees with the local community.

Evidence from our LAT-MNCs sample points to elements in HRM systems that facilitate the social inclusion of silent stakeholders through horizontal organisation–stakeholders relationships. This suggests the following:

Proposition 3: HRM systems that promote horizontal organisation–stakeholders relationships would be most effective when including extensive employee participation in awareness of social inclusion.

Proposition 4: HRM systems that promote horizontal organisation–stakeholders relationships would be most effective when combining both internal and external orientations.

CONCLUSION

HRM practices in Latin America are largely understood by using a stakeholder management approach. Taking a social perspective on the organisation–stakeholders relationship highlights: (1) the silence of some stakeholders due to Latin American organisations' role in individual, family, and community development; and (2) the HRM practices that organisations implement to reach not only salient but also silent stakeholders might be unique to this region. In this context, the organisation–stakeholder relationship is based on trust and respect for the social contract, taking on a horizontal character of social inclusion, versus a hierarchical, power-centred relationship with the organisation.

The stakeholder model of HRM presented here contributes to existing research from the theoretical and empirical standpoints. In particular, our model is consistent with recent calls for research on HRM practices and their role in social development. Specifically, the multi-stakeholder perspective on HRM outlined by Beer et al. (2015) challenges the narrow view of traditional HRM focused on the individual and their contribution to the economic performance of organisations. Although this view has helped design HRM practices based on the organisation's economic logic, it is limited by the absence of context and HRM's multiple constituencies. Moreover, HRM research has overlooked the impact of this function on society's well-being, in part because of the challenges associated with measuring HRM performance in this arena. Therefore, these authors also call for qualitative research to shed light on the link between HRM policies and practices and their various outcomes, and specifically propose using a multi-stakeholder perspective to guide future research.

Our overview on HRM practices depicts a set of companies catering to diverse stakeholders who seek social integration yet often hold relatively low legitimacy or power. Interestingly, top-performing companies are perceived simultaneously as leading economic and social development and as satisfying self-interested demands. The cases also illustrate how stakeholder management strategies are grounded in local and country-driven needs rather than universal corporate social responsible objectives.

Developing common evaluation criteria for a general HRM model applicable to Latin America implies that all stakeholders have similar needs or demands. However, given the diversity among and within stakeholder groups we are inclined toward recognising these differences through a contextual approach in this specific region (Brewster, 1999). In particular, from the company data studied, we identified as silent stakeholders the following groups: local youth, employees' families, local community, SMEs, and indigenous people.

Based on the pillars of our original stakeholder HRM model, we first argue that HRM systems support organisations as social institutions. The exploratory analysis of LAT-MNCs reports reveals some basic elements that could define what it means for a company to perform the role of social institution in Latin America when considering silent stakeholders. Those include looking after children's development; providing direct benefits to employees' families; offering educational programmes either for job training or for self-employment to the members of the local community, in which employees participate; supporting entrepreneurial activity; and providing health services to indigenous people.

The second pillar upon which our 2012 HRM model is based refers to the promotion of horizontal organisation–stakeholders relationships that facilitate social inclusion. The companies studied report several strategies that promote this type of relationship, including: employee training and development for awareness of social inclusion; internal and externally oriented horizontal organisation–stakeholders relationships; and volunteer programmes that link employees with the local community.

Our analysis of selected stakeholders serves as the foundation for an inductive model of HRM in Latin America that enriches both stakeholder management theory and HRM systems work. Such a model would first consider salient as well as silent stakeholders and their primary needs and demands, distinguishing among diverse stakeholder groups and within the same group, and consequently describe HRM policies and practices as a bridge between a company, its employees, and their communities.

For managers wishing to design successful HRM systems, our stakeholder approach offers valuable guidance regarding identification of relevant social stakeholders, providing for their human development, promoting horizontal relationships with employee involvement, and including both internal and external orientations.

In sum, the evidence presented here strengthens our earlier model by presenting and discussing the arguments that support the three pillars upon which we built the stakeholder HRM model, namely: (1) investment in employees: salary and benefits levels as well as education, training, and development; (2) efforts to operate within a cooperative labour relations framework; and (3) community-centred CSR practices.

ACKNOWLEDGEMENTS

The authors would like to thank the editors of this volume and Tatiana Kostova for their helpful comments on earlier versions of this chapter.

REFERENCES

Acs, Z.J., & Amorós, J.E. 2008. Entrepreneurship and competitiveness dynamics in Latin America. *Small Business Economics*, 31(3): 305–322.

Agle, B.R., Mitchell, R.K., & Sonnenfeld, J.A. 1999. Who matters to CEOs? An investigation of stakeholder attributes and salience, corporate performance, and CEO values. *Academy of Management Journal*, 42(5): 507–525.

Alfa. 2013 Social Responsibility Report. Retrieved 15 June 2015 from: http://www.alfa.com.mx/down/ALFA_Rsoc13_i.pdf

Amorós, J.E., Felzensztein, C., & Gimmon, E. 2013. Entrepreneurial opportunities in peripheral versus core regions in Chile. *Small Business Economics*, 40(1): 119–139.

Andonova, V., Gutierrez, R., & Avella, L.F. 2009. The strategic importance of close employment relations in conflict-ridden environments. Three cases from Colombia. In A. Davila and M.M. Elvira (eds), *Best HRM Practices in Latin America*: 25–36. Oxford: Routledge.

Beer, M., Boselie, P., & Brewster, C. 2015. Back to the future: Implications for the field of HRM of the multistakeholder perspective proposed 30 years ago. *Human Resource Management*, 54(3): 427–438.

Brewster, C. 1999. Different paradigms in strategic HRM: Questions raised by comparative research. In P.M. Wright, L.D. Dyer, J.W. Boudreau, and G.T. Milkovich (eds), *Strategic Human Resource Management in the Twenty First Century: Research in Personnel and Human Resource Management*, Supplement 4: 213–238. Stamford, CT: JAI Press.

Carrillo, J., & Gomis, R. 2014. Empresas multinacionales en México: innovación con inclusión social?. Santiago, Chile: CIEPLAN. Retrieved 9 August 2015 from: http://www.cieplan.org/media/publicaciones/archivos/348/Empresas_multinacionales_en_Mexico__innovacion_con_inclusion_social_.pdf.

Clarkson, M.B.E. 1995. A stakeholder framework for analyzing and evaluating corporate social responsibility. *Academy of Management Review*, 20(1): 92–117.

Davila, A., & Elvira, M. 2009. Theoretical approaches to best HRM in Latin America. In A. Davila and M. Elvira (eds), *Best HRM Practices in Latin America*: 180–188. Oxford: Routledge.

Davila, A., & Elvira, M. 2015. Human resources management in a kinship society: The case of Latin America. In F. Horwitz, & P. Budhwar (eds), *Handbook of Human Resource Management in Emerging Markets*: 372–392. Cheltenham, UK and Northampton, MA, USA: Edward Elgar Publishing.

Davila, A., & Elvira, M.M. 2012. Latin American HRM models. In C. Brewster and W. Mayrhofer (eds), *Handbook of Research on Comparative Human Resource Management*: 478–493. Cheltenham, UK and Northampton, MA, USA: Edward Elgar Publishing.

Donaldson, T., & Preston, L. 1995. The stakeholder theory of the corporation: Concepts, evidence, and implications. *Academy of Management Review*, 20(1): 85–91.

Elvira, M.M., & Davila, A. 2005a. Emergent directions for human resource management research in Latin America. *International Journal of Human Resource Management*, 16(12): 2265–2282.

Elvira, M.M., & Davila, A. 2005b. Emergent directions for human resource management research in Latin America. *International Journal of Human Resources Management*, 16(12): 2265–2282.

Fransen, L.W., & Kolk, A. 2007. Global rule-setting for business: A critical analysis of multi-stakeholder standards. *Organization*, 14(5): 667–684.

Freeman, R.E. 1984. *Strategic Management: A Stakeholder Approach*. Boston, MA: Pitman.

Friel, D. 2011. Forging a comparative institutional advantage in Argentina: Implications for theory and praxis. *Human Relations*, 64(4): 553–572.

Frooman, J. 1999. Stakeholder influence strategies. *Academy of Management Review*, 24(2): 191–205.

Gifford, B., & Kestler, A. 2008. Toward a theory of local legitimacy by MNEs in developing nations: Newmont mining and health sustainable development in Peru. *Journal of International Management*, 14(4): 340–352.

Kochan, T. 1999. Beyond myopia: Human resources and the changing social contract. In P.M. Wright, L.D. Dyer, J.W. Boudreau, and G.T. Milkovich (eds), *Strategic Human Resource Management in the Twenty First Century: Research in Personnel and Human Resource Management*, Supplement 4. Stamford, CT: JAI Press.

Leguizamon, F.A., Ickis, J.C., & Ogliastri, E. 2009. Human resource practices and business performance: Grupo San Nicolás. In A. Davila and M. Elvira (eds), *Best HRM Practices in Latin America*: 85–96. Oxford: Routledge.

London, T., & Hart, S.L. 2004. Reinventing strategies for emerging markets: Beyond the transnational model. *Journal of International Business Studies*, 35(5): 350–370.

Mitchell, R.K., Agle, B.R., & Wood, D.J. 1997. Toward a theory of stakeholder identification and salience: Defining the principle of who and what really counts. *Academy of Management Review*, 22(4): 853–886.

Osland, A., Osland, J.S., Tanure, B., & Gabrish, R. 2009. Stakeholder management: The case of Aracruz Celulose in Brazil. In A. Davila and M. Elvira (eds), *Best HRM Practices in Latin America*: 10–24. Oxford: Routledge.

Tavis, L. 1994. Bifurcated development and multinational corporate responsibility. In W.M. Hoffman, J.B. Kamm, R.E. Frederick, and E.S. Petry (eds), *Emerging Global Business Ethics*: 255–274. Westport, CT: Quorum Books.

Williamson, J.G. 2010. Five centuries of Latin American income inequality. *Revista de Historia Económica / Journal of Iberian and Latin American Economic History (Second Series)*, 28(2): 227–252.

World Economic Forum (WEF). 2015. The Inclusive Growth and Development Report 2015. Retrieved 19 September 2015 from: http://www3.weforum.org/docs/Media/WEF_Inclusive_Growth.pdf.

22. HRM in Mexico, Central America, and the Caribbean

Sergio M. Madero-Gómez and Miguel R. Olivas-Luján

INTRODUCTION

Uncovering research in human resources management (HRM) in Mexico, Central America, and the Caribbean requires passing a number of barriers, but it is a highly rewarding experience when we realise that this area of the world is ripe for systematic work that can help HRM professionals, workers, companies, and society at large. HRM research in this region is conducted by both domestic and international organisations, with academic and non-academic purposes. Publications dealing with HRM in these countries can more easily be found in English, but a growing body of knowledge is being published in Spanish, as one should expect of increasingly competitive economies such as Costa Rica, Mexico, Panama, and Puerto Rico (World Economic Forum, 2014), whose mainstream language is Spanish. This chapter describes recent research within these limits, with the double-pronged intention of describing and proposing HRM research that will advance the state of the science in an area identified as the second most important emerging region in the world (Vassolo et al., 2011).

This chapter is structured in three main sections. We begin by depicting the geographic scope of our study using macroeconomic, social, and other indicators appropriate to better understand the context in which HRM operates in the area, including the presence of professional HRM associations. Next, we explain the frameworks that guided our search for and extraction of information from published sources. In the final section, we offer the most important lessons we derived from this investigation, in an effort to influence future work on HRM in Mexico, Central America, and the Caribbean.

GEOGRAPHIC SCOPE

In the first edition of this *Handbook*, Brewster and Mayrhofer (2012) use the metaphor of a telescope to illustrate how the levels of analysis can be higher or finer with respect to the differences under study; in a similar manner, countries and geographic regions may be included in broader or narrower comparative studies of HRM. In the first decade of the current century, Elvira and Davila (2005b) led the charge in documenting the various ways in which HRM is enacted in the American landmass in countries as far North as Mexico or as far South as Chile, with their books on HRM in Latin America (Elvira & Davila, 2005a; Davila & Elvira, 2009) and special issues of the *International Journal of Human Resource Management* (2005) and the *International Journal of Manpower* (2007). Recent studies suggest that it is time to take a more granular view of the status of HRM and related themes (Lenartowicz & Johnson, 2003; Olivas-Luján et al., 2009;

Ruiz-Gutierrez et al., 2012; Vassolo et al., 2011) so that finer-grained descriptions can be offered to practitioners, researchers, and other parties with an interest in this research stream. Thus, in this chapter we focus our attention on the following countries: Belize, Costa Rica, Cuba, the Dominican Republic, El Salvador, Guatemala, Haiti, Honduras, Jamaica, Mexico, Nicaragua, Panama, and Puerto Rico. They lie roughly south of the United States of America (USA) and north and north-west of Colombia, connecting Central and South America. HRM in South America is covered in Chapter 23 in this volume.

National Descriptors

In addition to the geographic location, several other reasons support this choice of countries. Among the motivations are the region's proximity to the USA – a leading national economy in the world – and the common historic, social, religious, and cultural factors of the different countries that constitute the region, which indicate more commonalities than differences. From an economic perspective, most of these countries hold double-digit figures for gross domestic product (GDP) per capita (in thousands of purchase parity power, PPP, dollars), which grants them the World Bank (2015) classification as 'middle income' economies (see Table 22.1). Puerto Rico (which has held 'unincorporated territory of the USA' status since the end of the nineteenth century) is classified as 'high income' in spite of its double-digit unemployment rate and other factors. Among the countries in our study, only Haiti is in the 'low income' category.

Of course, large differences exist, as Table 22.1 also shows. Perhaps the most obvious outlier is Mexico, whose population is at least eight times larger than Guatemala's – the second most populated nation in our study; and its economy is 20 times larger than that of the Dominican Republic, the second-largest in terms of GDP as of 2014 estimates (Central Intelligence Agency, 2015); in fact, Mexico's GDP was 3.24 times that of all other nations in this group combined in 2014. Another measure of industrialisation, carbon dioxide production, shows that Mexico produced almost 17 times more than Puerto Rico, the second-ranked country in this indicator (Central Intelligence Agency, 2015). The Mexican labour force is almost 175 per cent greater than that of all other countries in our study combined (International Labour Organization, 2013), its unemployment rate among the lowest, and its labour force participation rate within the 60 per cent range (World Bank, 2015). In spite of its size, Mexico's labour market appears rather tight, with a 4.8 per cent unemployment rate that strongly masks underemployment, informal, and other forms of precarious employment conditions (Olivas-Luján & González Chávez, 2006).

At the other end of the spectrum, Belize's characteristics show the smallest population (less than 15 per cent of Jamaica's, the second smallest), GDP (less than 20 per cent that of Haiti, which has more than 23 times Belize's population), labour force, and carbon dioxide production; but one of the highest unemployment rates (14.4 per cent, which is very close to those of Jamaica, Puerto Rico, and the Dominican Republic). Haiti's unemployment (40.6 per cent in 2010) and GDP per capita (a dismal $1800 in PPP) are symptomatic of its severe poverty. Extending the telescope metaphor to the planets in the solar system, we might consider Mexico as analogous to Jupiter (the largest); and Belize or Haiti (the smallest, depending on the indicator chosen) akin to Pluto or Mercury; with

Table 22.1   Countries in the study: selected demographic characteristics

Countries (language if not Spanish; 2-letter code)	Population (in 000s)[a]	GDP (US$ bn)[a]	GDP per capita[a] ($000s, PPP)	Labour force (m, 2014 est.)[b]	Labour participation rate[c]	Unemployment[b]	CO$_2$ (in m Mt, 2012 est.)[a]
Mexico (MX)	121 737	$1 283.00	17.9	52.900	60.5	4.8	453.80
Guatemala (GT)	14 919	60.42	7.5	4.576	60.1	3.0	13.07
Cuba (CU)	11 031	77.15	10.2	5.092	76.1	8.5	25.99
Dominican Republic (DO)	10 479	64.08	13.0	4.996	64.2	15.0	20.80
Haiti (French; HT)	10 110	8.71	1.8	4.810	n/a	40.6 (2010)	2.09
Honduras (HN)	8747	19.51	4.7	3.579	59.9	4.5	10.33
El Salvador (SV)	6141	25.44	8.0	2.752	63.2	5.9	6.38
Nicaragua (NI)	5908	11.71	4.7	2.953	72.3	4.8	5.29
Costa Rica (CR)	4814	48.14	14.9	2.257	60.1	8.5	7.29
Panama (PA)	3657	43.78	19.5	1.563	63.5	4.8	16.23
Puerto Rico (PR)	3598	61.46[d]	28.5[d]	1.139	41.6	13.7	26.81
Jamaica (English; JM)	2950	13.79	8.6	1.311	62.7	15.3	12.75
Belize (English; BZ)	437	1.69	8.2	0.121	n/a	14.4	0.68

Notes:
Data for most recent year available.
a   CIA (2015).
b   ILO (2013).
c   World Bank (2015).
d   2013 (est.).
Spanish is the predominant language in these countries, except as noted in parenthesis.
Costa Rican population does not include Nicaraguans living there.
ILO data are 2012–14, whichever is more recent. Unemployment data from ILO or CIA, ILO preferred when available.

Guatemala, Cuba, Dominican Republic, Haiti, Honduras, El Salvador, Nicaragua, Costa Rica, Panama, Puerto Rico, and Jamaica in between.

Even though Spanish is the predominant language for most of these nations, English is principally spoken in Jamaica and Belize, and French in Haiti, as a direct result of the European nation – Spain, United Kingdom or France – that colonised each of these countries for longest during the sixteenth to nineteenth centuries. In a similar train of thought, Catholicism is the most widespread religion in the area, although other Christian denominations are present to varying degrees, as are other religions, including native and syncretic belief systems such as Santería, Vodou, and others. Judaism, Islam, Orthodox Christianity, atheism, and agnosticism can also be found, though less frequently than in other latitudes.

These historical and national-level descriptors set the stage for a societal environment in which the HRM literature has documented work-related values and other characteristics that, within reasonable limits, raise expectations of organisational policies and practices that are likely to be more prevalent or acceptable. To illustrate, high power distance, low individualism, medium to high masculinity, high uncertainty avoidance, and low long-term orientation (Hofstede, 2015) tend to be exhibited by most of these countries. These popular descriptors of national culture set the expectation that organisational hierarchies and respect for authority will be very powerful (high power distance); that employees will have self-construals that are strongly related to their co-workers, their families, and other members of their in-groups (low individualism); that rules and regulations (sometimes in the form of exhaustive labour regulations, company manuals, job descriptions, and so on) will be widespread, even if not rigidly enforced (high uncertainty avoidance); and that planning horizons will be more pragmatic and span shorter times than those from future-oriented cultures (low long-term orientation). Any practitioner or researcher with some experience in these countries will probably agree with these generalisations, but the globalised, increasingly interdependent world in which we live guarantees that there will be exceptions (for example, self-managed teams in Mexico in the 1990s were expected to face culture-based conflict, but their successful use is now well documented by Nicholls et al., 1999 and Gómez, 2004). Documenting both confirming and exceptional preferences and practices in a systematic manner is the only way to make the discipline more professional, evidence-based, and useful to all (Rousseau & Barends, 2011).

Professionalisation of HRM

As a profession, HRM is well established in many of the countries of this area; we have included the most salient professional organisations in this region in Table 22.2. Seven of the countries in our study have professional associations affiliated with the World Federation of People Management Associations (WFPMA) based on geographic and socio-cultural factors. Costa Rica's ACGRH (Asociación Costarricense de Gestores de Recursos Humanos), Dominican Republic's ADOARH (Asociación Dominicana de Recursos Humanos), Guatemala's AGH (Asociación Guatemalteca de Profesionales de Gestión Humana), Nicaragua's AERHNIC (Asociación de Ejecutivos de Recursos Humanos de Nicaragua), and Panama's ANREH (Asociación Nacional de Profesionales de Recursos Humanos de Panamá), along with other professional associations from South American countries (Argentina, Bolivia, Brazil, Chile, Colombia, Ecuador, Paraguay,

Table 22.2   HRM professional associations in the region

Country	Name of the professional organisation Acronym, website or internet presence; area served	Membership
Costa Rica	Asociación Costarricense de Gestores de Recursos Humanos* ACGRH, www.acgrh.net	355
Dominican Republic	Asociación Dominicana de Administradores de Gestión Humana* ADOARH, www.adoarh.org	320
El Salvador	Asociación de Líderes del Talento Humano de El Salvador ALTHES, Facebook page	130
Guatemala	Asociación Guatemalteca de Profesionales de Gestión Humana* AGH, www.agh.gt/web plus Facebook page	187
Haiti	Societé Haïtienne de Management des Ressources Humaines SHAMARH, shamarh.com plus Facebook	n/a
Jamaica	The Human Resource Management Association of Jamaica HRMAJ, hrmaj.org	n/a
Mexico	Asociación Mexicana de Dirección de Recursos Humanos* AMEDIRH, amedirh.com.mx; Mexico city, country	2587 (or 800 firms)
	Confederación Mexicana de Recursos Humanos COMARI, none; Mexico city, Guadalajara	767
	ARIOAC Asociación de Recursos Humanos ARIOAC, arioac.com; Guadalajara	n/a
	ERIAC Capital Humano ERIAC, Facebook page; Monterrey	200+
Nicaragua	Asociación de Ejecutivos de Recursos Humanos de Nicaragua* AERHNIC, aerhnic.org	250
Panama	Asociación Nacional de Profesionales de Recursos Humanos de Panamá* ANREH, anrehpanama.org	151
Puerto Rico	SHRM Puerto Rico* (through US-based SHRM) SHRMPR, shrmpr.org	1300+

Notes:
Data from the focal association, WFPMA, or SHRM websites or reports. Information valid as of mid- to late 2016. We were unable to identify professional HRM associations in Belize, Cuba, and Honduras.
Members of the World Federation of Personnel Management Associations (WFPMA) are identified with an asterisk.

Peru, Uruguay, and Venezuela), are part of FIDAGH (Federación Interamericana de Asociaciones de Gestión Humana, or Interamerican Federation of People Management Associations). Mexico's AMEDIRH (Asociación Mexicana de Dirección de Recursos Humanos) as well as SHRM PR (Society for Human Resource Management, Puerto Rico chapter) by virtue of its affiliation with the USA-based SHRM, are part of NAHRMA, the North American HRM Association.

In addition to these professional organisations that have worldwide links, we are aware of others in El Salvador (ALTHES, Asociación de Líderes del Talento Humano de El Salvador), Haiti (SHAMARH, Societé Haïtienne de Management des Ressources Humaines), Jamaica (HRMAJ, Human Resource Management Association of Jamaica); and of three other large HRM associations in Mexico: COMARI (Confederación Mexicana de Recursos Humanos), ARIOAC Asociación de Recursos Humanos (formerly Asociación de Relaciones Industriales de Oriente, A.C.), and ERIAC Capital Humano (formerly Ejecutivos de Relaciones Industriales, A.C.) that have varying degrees of organisational activity, some including recurring meetings, conferences, certifications, large events, internet presence, and so on. We are also aware that, at least in Mexico, there are more HRM associations of professionals in some of the industrialised cities (for example, Saltillo, Veracruz, Tijuana), but the four largest and more influential are included in the table. We would expect a similar situation in other countries from this region. Their activities assist HRM practitioners in their constant quest to increase their positive influence and status within and outside organisations.

The USA-based SHRM, the largest practitioner organisation in North America, carried out a comparative survey of HRM professionalism in 23 different countries, including the Dominican Republic and Mexico (the other countries in this study were not part of SHRM's investigation). In the Dominican Republic, ADOARH cooperated with SHRM (2004a) while in Mexico AMEDIRH, COMARI, ARIOAC Asociación de Recursos Humanos, and ERIAC Capital Humano assisted in the study (SHRM, 2004b). The reports document that HRM is a profession with an identifiable body of knowledge, societal recognition, and defined credentials, which are characteristics expected of a mature profession from the perspective of sociological models.

There are other signs that HRM is achieving professional status in these countries. HRM-related education, in the form of university-level degrees (*licenciaturas* or bachelors' degrees, as well as graduate degrees including *maestrías* and even *doctorados*) can be found in many institutions of higher learning in Mexico, Puerto Rico, and other countries in the study. Labour legislation that regulates unionisation, collective bargaining, occupational safety, anti-discrimination, pensions, and diverse forms of compensation and social security are a virtual guarantee that knowledgeable individuals will be increasingly required by businesses and other types of organisations (governmental, non-governmental, for-profit, non-profit, and so on) that can no longer afford to manage these issues in a casual manner. Industrial psychology, industrial relations, organisational development, and labour law are among the concentration areas taught throughout the region that are aimed, explicitly and intentionally, at HR managers for domestic and international companies. In fact, the increasingly open economies in most of these countries – even Cuba has re-established its diplomatic relations with the USA – create stronger pressures to professionalise the management of workers through multinational organisations both within the area and outside it. The rise of *multilatinas* (multinational companies emerging from Latin America), particularly from Mexico, has required those companies (for example, CEMEX, Nemak, Telmex, FEMSA, Gruma, Grupo Bimbo, Grupo Modelo) that have entered international markets to standardise, adjust, and professionalise all their business operations, in particular those related to their human resource management (Santiso, 2008; Madero & Olivas-Luján, 2014).

RESEARCH FRAMEWORKS AND METHOD

Even if incipient, the literature on HRM in Mexico, Central America, and the Caribbean needs to be classified using conceptual frameworks to identify both what is known and where the gaps are. To this end, we used two major classifications: a cultural perspective to comparative HRM, as described by Reiche et al. (2012), complemented by an inferential view based upon our findings. Based on a systematic review of the literature, our adaptation of this cultural perspective starts with: (1) general descriptions of HRM; followed by the well-known HRM subfunctions that include: (2) recruitment and selection; (3) compensation and benefits; (4) performance management; and (5) training and development. Our classification of the extant literature led us to identify three more groups: (6) unions, labour relations, reforms and related; (7) *maquiladoras* (also known as 'in-bond' or 'twin' plants) and their like; and (8) special topics (including international, equity and justice, and values). Box 22.1 summarises our findings. In this section, we first explain the search strategy we used to identify the studies and then we show the HRM areas that these studies cover.

We carefully classified each of the studies in accordance with their main subject area. In the cases where more than one area was covered (for example, some studies might focus on selection and recruitment, our second category, in *maquilas*, our seventh category; or on how training and development, category five, are different in unionised plants, the sixth category) we assigned the study to the grouping for which it appeared to make a more focused contribution, in terms of the publication's content, the keywords or the abstract, the sample, or some other relevant characteristic if necessary. We admit that other researchers might have categorised some of the studies in a different manner, but we believe that our classification keeps simplicity and diligence levels high.

Method

As indicated above, HRM research dealing with the countries in our study is predominantly found in English and Spanish. For that reason, in addition to the well-known databases in English such as EBSCO, ProQuest, and Emerald, we looked for articles on EBSCO Fuente Académica, Infolatina, Prisma, and Redalyc. We also paid particular attention to business or management research journals that, being based in Spain or Latin America, attract contributions from authors who prefer to write in the Spanish language, including *Innovar* (Colombia), *Cuadernos de Economía y Dirección de Empresas* (Colombia), *Cuadernos de Administración, Academia Revista Latinoamericana de Administración* (Colombia), *Universia Business Review* (Spain), *ESIC-Market* (bilingual, based in Spain), *Contaduría y Administración* (Mexico), and *Management Research: Journal of the Iberoamerican Academy of Management* (English). The Google Scholar site (scholar.google.com) was also used frequently to find the full text of each article that seemed to fit our search.

We used the following keywords to find articles published in the 25 years from 1990: human resource management (HRM), employee recruitment, employee selection, training, professional development, career development, compensation management, performance appraisal, performance management, turnover, education, cultural values, bullying, mobbing, social psychology, unions, expatriate management. With respect to location, we used 'Latin America' and 'Central America' as broad terms that might include countries within the geographic scope of our study, and the names of our 13 countries more specifically: Belize, Costa Rica, Cuba, Dominican Republic, El Salvador, Guatemala, Haiti, Honduras, Jamaica, Mexico, Nicaragua, Panama, and Puerto Rico. We also inspected the bibliography of the studies we found, looking for other studies within the scope of our project that did not appear in the computer searches (misclassifications due to automation are unfortunately not rare). In keeping to the scope of our chapter,

BOX 22.1   HRM LITERATURE ON THE CARIBBEAN, CENTRAL AMERICA, AND MEXICO

HR topic; Reference, language of publication (if not English) and description of study with country code(s) as follows: BZ, Belize; CR, Costa Rica; CU, Cuba; DO, Dominican Republic; SV, El Salvador; GT, Guatemala; HT, Haiti; HN, Honduras; JM, Jamaica; MX, Mexico; NI, Nicaragua; PA, Panama; PR, Puerto Rico. Countries in square brackets are not disaggregated in the focal study.

1. HR in general or specific practices aggregated
      Alhama Belamaric (2003) – Spanish; HR indices and considerations for CU
      Arias-Galicia (2005) – overview of HRM in MX
      Arias & Heredia (2009) – Spanish; textbook on HRM used in MX
      Bonache et al. (2012) – [CR, SV, GT, HN, MX, NI, PA, PR], HRM models
      Cunha & Cunha (2004) – overview of HRM in CU
      Cunh et al. (2007) – a sense-making view of 'best firms' from CU
      Elvira & Davila (2005a) – Spanish; HRM overview with examples from CR, MX
      Elvira & Davila (2005b, 2005c) – HRM and culture with examples from MX
      Germán Pérez (2001) – public management comparative analysis for CU, DO, JM, PR
      Gómez & Sanchez (2005) – HR practices that foster social capital in MX
      Hernández Darias et al. (2011) – Spanish; HRD national efforts in CU
      Klingner & Pallavicini (2002) – public HRM examples from CR, CU, DO, HN, JM, MX
      Leguizamon et al. (2009) – Grupo San Nicolás case from SV
      Martinez (2003, 2005) – paternalism and its effects in MX
      Osland & Osland (2005a, 2005b) – HRM overview in CR, SV, GT, HN, NI, PA
      Rao (2014) – HR practices of 'Great Place to Work' winners in MX
      Schuler et al. (1996) – a culture-informed view of HRM in MX
      SHRM – status of the HRM profession in DO (SHRM, 2004a) and MX (SHRM, 2004b)
      Stephens & Greer (1995) – cultural differences comparing MX to the USA
      Zevallos (2006) – Spanish; problems for SMEs in CR, SV and PA

2. Recruitment and selection
      Curiel Sandoval (2013) – Spanish; new laws for outsourcing in MX
      Daspro (2009b, 2009a) – recruitment ads in MX by MNCs v. local firms
      Godínez Rivera & Zarazúa Vilchis (2012) – Spanish; designing best job ads in MX
      Linnehan & Blau (2003) – turnover predictors in a MX *maquiladora*
      Madero (2009) – Spanish; factors attracting potential employees in MX
      Posthuma et al. (2014) – comparison of job interviews in MX and other countries
      Rao (2009) – executive staffing in USA-MX joint ventures
      Zarazúa Vilchis (2013) – Spanish; selection by competencies in MX

3. Compensation and benefits
      Fairris et al. (2008) – normative effects of minimum wages in MX
      García et al. (2009) – pay satisfaction in MX *maquiladoras*
      Madero – Spanish; factors attracting employees (Madero, 2010b) and the HR perspective (Madero, 2010a) in MX
      Madero & Peña (2012) – Spanish; HR processes and benefits in MX
      Madero & Trevinyo (2011) – Spanish; compensation for Generation Y in MX family firms
      Madero et al. (2012) – Spanish; family firms in MX
      Masuda et al. (2012) – flex work effects in [PR]
      Miller et al. (2001) – *maquiladora* pay and turnover in MX
      Sánchez-Marín et al. (2010) – compensation in family firms comparing MX to Spain

4. Performance management
    Arellano-Gault (2012) – government agencies in MX
    Davila & Elvira (2007, 2009) – performance appraisals in MX
    Flores Zambada & Madero Gómez (2010) – Spanish; performance and relationship quality
    for promotability in MX
    Gómez (2004) – use of self-managed work teams in MX
    Selvarajan & Cloninger (2012) – type of appraisal and outcomes in MX
    Valdés-Padrón et al. (2015) – Spanish; making appraisals more quantitative in CU

5. Training and development
    Blunch & Castro (2007) – effects of ISO 9000 in training for HN, NI
    Dooley et al. (2004) – evaluation tools for training in CR
    Drost et al. (2002) – T&D in MX, [CR, GT, NI, PA and Venezuela]
    Felix Rodriguez et al. (2011) – IT certifications in PR
    Grosse (2004) – English language needs for executives in/from MX
    Kovács et al. (2012) – skills for logisticians in HT
    Littrell & Barba (2013) – leadership preferences in MX
    Nicholls et al. (1999) – self-managed teams in MX
    Ollivier Fierro (2015) – training and technology in MX *maquilas*
    Padilla Rodriguez & Armellini (2013) – corporate e-learning in MX
    Villar et al. (2013) – a T&D country overview for MX

6. Unions, labour relations, reforms, and related
    Borgeaud Garciandía (2007) – Spanish; unions and *maquilas* in NI
    Díaz-González (2010) – Spanish; unionisation in CR
    Fairris – unionisation decline (Fairris & Levine, 2004), wages (Fairris, 2003), and other effects
    (Fairris, 2006) in MX
    Kaplan (2009) – labour reforms' effects in SV, GT, HN, MX, NI and PA
    Mendoza (2010) – Spanish; labour markets and policies in MX (northern states)
    Olivas-Luján & González Chávez (2006) – French; international trade and employment in MX
    Posthuma et al. (2000) – labour and employment law comparison MX and USA
    Ramírez Sánchez (2011) – MX, Monterrey's 'white' unions
    Sánchez Díaz (2014) – Spanish; MX, unions in the social sciences

7. *Maquiladoras* and related
    Borgeaud-Garciandía & Lautier (2009) – Spanish; *maquilas* and domestic work in NI
    Borgeaud-Garciandía (2009) – Spanish; *maquila* work and family life for women in NI
    Borgeaud-Garciandía (2010) – French; *maquilas* in the political discourse in NI
    Butler & Teagarden (1993) – *maquilas,* safety, environment in MX
    Castilla Ramos & Labrecque (2009) – Spanish; special issue of *maquilas* in CR, GT, HN, MX
    and NI
    Castilla Ramos & Torres Góngora (2009) – Spanish; worker experiences in three plants in
    Yucatán, MX
    Goldín (2009) – Spanish; *maquilas* in GT gave hope in the 1990s; in 2008 there is burnout
    Gowan et al. (1996) – *maquilas'* corporate philanthropy in MX
    Guadarrama Olivera (2009) – Spanish; work trajectories for women in CR *maquilas*
    Jun et al. (2004) – *maquilas* barriers to TQM implementation in MX
    Martinez & Ricks (1989) – MX, parent company influence in HR
    Nabor (2009) – Spanish; *maquiladora* women workers and migration in Puebla, MX
    Paik & Teagarden (1995) – MX, *maquilas,* parent country effects
    Pelled & Hill – MX, work values, commitment (Pelled & Hill, 1997a), participative management
    (Pelled & Hill, 1997b) in *maquilas*
    Pelled et al. – MX, relational demography (Pelled & Xin, 1998), demography and conflict
    (Pelled et al., 2001) in *maquilas*

Peña (2000) – MX retention in *maquiladoras*
Pine (2009) – Spanish; emancipation and problems faced by women in HN *maquiladoras*
Teagarden et al. (1991) – MX, HRM practices in *maquiladoras*

8. Special topics: internationalisation, equity and justice issues, and values
Internationalisation:
    Carrillo & Gomis (2011) – Spanish; comparing MNCs and MX firms
    De Forest (1994) – business culture in MX
    Drost & Von Glinow (1998) – leadership behaviors in MX
    Edmond (2002) – expatriate adjustment in MX
    Fernández Cueto & Sánchez (2011) – expatriate performance in DO
    Madero & Olivas-Luján (2014) – Spanish; MX, CEMEX expatriates case
    Olivas-Luján et al. (2007) – HRM information technologies in MX
    Ramirez & Zapata-Cantú (2009) – HR systems in a Danish company in MX
Equity and justice issues:
    Davila & Pagán (1999) – gender pay gaps in CR and SV
    Fairris (2002) – efficiency and cumulative motion disorders in MX
    Hotchkiss & Moore (1996) – gender pay gaps in JM
    Olivas-Luján et al. (2009) – values and attitudes toward women in MX
    Osland et al. (1998) – female managerial styles in CR and NI
    Peek et al. (2007) – comparison of sexual harassment in MX, the USA and Canada
    Power et al. (2013) – workplace bullying acceptability in Latino [MX] v. other countries
    Ramirez et al. (2015a) – how 'narcoterrorism' has influenced HRM systems in MX
    Ramirez et al. (2015b) – psychological contracts in high-risk environments in MX
Values:
    Mujtaba et al. (2009) – values and other national comparisons in BZ
    Ruiz-Gutierrez et al. (2012) – work values and family characteristics in MX v. other nations.

we did not include articles dealing with Latin America in broad terms without offering some empirical evidence from at least one of the countries in our study. We also decided not to include purely conceptual studies that did not have at least some substantiation from field observations; while we consider those texts to be quite valuable and worthy of further study, we believe this decision makes the chapter (and hence, this *Handbook*) more relevant to practitioners and other stakeholders with more immediate and pragmatic needs for this knowledge. Our search revealed 111 studies dealing with HRM in one or more of the 13 countries within our geographic area. The studies are listed in Box 22.1, subdivided into eight major themes.

(1) General Descriptions of HRM

Within this group, we explored scholarly publications describing the HRM landscape in general terms. Many studies included some empirical evidence (26 out of 111, or 23.4 per cent); five of them were published in Spanish. We focus further here on these 26 studies. As one might expect, based on the size of the country and its economy, within this category Mexico is the nation upon which the largest number of published studies focused, with 16 (61.5 per cent). Another factor that likely contributed to the attention Mexico received at the end of the past century and beginning of the current one was the economic integration brought about by the North American Free Trade Agreement

(NAFTA) between Canada, Mexico, and the USA. Anticipation of the start of NAFTA in 1994 and its obvious regional implications motivated increased attention in the form of a significant number of studies.

(2)   Recruitment and Selection

In this subfield, the landscape is totally dominated by Mexico. We found no studies on recruitment and selection in any other country.

(3)   Compensation and Benefits

Within this theme, in addition to nine studies that had a focus on Mexico (90 per cent), we found one that included Puerto Rico (Masuda et al., 2012).

(4)   Performance Management

This is the category for which we found the least number of studies, with seven. As in previous categories, Mexico received more attention (six studies, or 85.7 per cent).

(5)   Training and Development

This is a subfield that we could call more 'balanced' in the sense that studies dealing with Mexico were closer to one-half: seven (of 11) deal with Mexico. Most of these articles were published in English.

(6)   Unions, Labour Relations, Labour Reform, Markets, and Related

Within this subfield, we located nine studies focused on seven countries. Several of these studies were published in Spanish.

(7)   Maquiladoras

Maquiladoras or *maquilas*, also known as 'twin plants' or 'in-bond plants', have captured scholarly attention for at least 40 years. As an outgrowth of cooperation between Mexico (and other countries in our area) and the USA (though companies from other countries, particularly those interested in accessing the USA market also established *maquilas*) to strengthen each other's economies, or as a tool for exploitation of cheap labour, these labour-intensive organisations have been investigated from various scholarly perspectives. Mexican *maquiladoras* have received more attention than those from other countries, in spite of the large proportion of employment they have held within these other countries; Castilla Ramos and Labrecque (2009) report that *maquiladoras* have reached 25 to 30 per cent of formal employment in Central America. In addition to the studies mentioned above and in the following section, our search found 20 studies: 14 of them focused on Mexico, four on Nicaragua, and two studies including Costa Rica, Guatemala, and Honduras; eight of the studies we found were published in Spanish, one in French.

(8)   Special Topics: Internationalisation, Equity and Justice, and Values

This category does not deal with traditional HRM issues, but with 'people management' topics that are under-researched in our region; for this reason, we decided to create three subcategories instead of reviewing each country as we did in the case of previous categories. The first subcategory deals with internationalisation issues such as those facing multinational corporations (MNCs). The emerging theme of 'multilatinas', or MNCs whose country of origin is in Latin America, and their strategies, implementations, and problems can be found in a large proportion of these studies. We believe that this is a stream that is quite likely to grow, as Latin American businesses continue to learn and realise that markets beyond their frontiers may have a need for their products and services.

Our equity and justice subcategory included eight studies dealing mostly with gender issues, but our recommendation is to go beyond this stage. It is evident that studies on gender differences and discrimination already exist in this region; the next stage would be to study how sexual minorities – including, but not limited to gay, lesbian, bisexual, transsexual and others that have close to meaningless legal protection in most of these countries – are affected, and what HRM practitioners can do, and in fact do, to go beyond mere compliance with existing laws. Regardless of existing legal protection, the workplace should be free from interference from non-work-related preferences. HRM research is required denouncing suboptimal (sometimes inhuman) situations and offering solutions that make employment a context in which people can grow personally and contribute to their families and their communities. This region might in fact benefit from research that uncovers classism, skin colour, and other types that are rarely contemplated in the extant literature and have traditionally been dismissed in the region as 'problems of developed countries'.

Our last subcategory deals with values. Many of the studies above used Hofstede's (2015) well-known work-related values paradigm. Other paradigms mentioned with less frequency include the Global Leadership and Organizational Behavior Effectiveness (GLOBE) programme study of 62 societies (House et al., 2004) or Rokeach's (1973) work. Studying the explanatory power of these competing paradigms might enhance our understanding and design of HRM practices in diverse settings. Our concluding thoughts based on this mapping of the HRM field in Mexico, Central America, and the Caribbean now follow.

LESSONS LEARNED AND RECOMMENDATIONS

More Research Needed, at all Levels

In a review of cross-cultural and cross-national HRM studies, Arvey et al. (1991) distinguished three levels of sophistication. Level 1 is 'descriptive and comparative', in which basic descriptions of practices, variables, procedures, and other relevant characteristics are quantified and compared across cultures or nations. Level 2 deals with 'relationship analyses', which seek to identify moderators of independent/dependent variables and how culture may affect the strength of such relationships. 'Etic' (also referred to as universalistic) and 'emic' (particularistic) approaches to culture would seem to be the backdrops for

Level 2 and Level 1 research, respectively, according to Arvey et al.'s (1991: 370) study. The third level is titled 'meta-theory, research, analyses, and questions' and they describe it as 'represented by broad theory-oriented questions and examination'. They seem to suggest that this research is the most sophisticated, crossing levels of analyses and academic domains, including 'political science, economics and sociology', in search of theories that may more strongly enhance both scholarly understanding and practical application. A quarter of a century later, we concur with their appreciation that 'Level 3 research efforts are almost non-existent in the HRM literature' (ibid.: 399), albeit we now apply those words to the state of the HRM discipline in Mexico, Central America, and the Caribbean.

Arvey et al. (1991: 399) also, however, called for 'more specific descriptive information . . . across a *wide* range of nationalities and cultures', not just for theoretical work, and we concur with this as well. Our review of HRM research for our area reveals that many nations may currently be considered blank slates in need of systematic analyses at all three levels of research sophistication in all areas of HRM. To illustrate, the fact that we could find more HRM studies including Cuba than Guatemala, in spite of the fact that the latter's population is about 35 per cent larger than the former's, is distressing; perhaps even more distressing is that we found fewer studies dealing with Puerto Rico than with Costa Rica, Cuba, El Salvador, Guatemala, Honduras, Nicaragua, or Panama, in spite of Puerto Rico's economic and geographic importance.

Time to Study the Effects of Crossing Borders

Even in the face of decreasing border permeability (at least from a legal perspective), population flows are not likely to decrease, creating a growing need for describing and assessing the effectiveness of HRM practices for individuals who cross national borders. We can already see some emerging signs of such research in the USA, as in the case of a recent special issue on Hispanics and Latin Americans at the workplace published by the *Journal of Managerial Psychology* (*JMP*). To illustrate, Offerman et al. (2014) have described how the use of more than one language in the USA can be challenging for speakers of both the local and the incoming language. Arévalo-Flechas et al. (2014) also found how care-givers with Hispanic origins carry a measurably higher psychological burden, and show lower general health, and social and physical function, than their non-Hispanic counterparts. Beutell and Schneer (2014) found that Hispanic men and women differ in statistically significant ways with respect to work–family conflict, family interfering with work and synergy, in ways largely consistent with the cultural expectations regarding gender roles, suggesting that ethnicity and gender can have strong interactions predicting depression, job satisfaction, and life satisfaction. Guerrero and Posthuma (2014) provide an overview of how the increasing flows of workers between the USA, Mexico, and nations from Central America and the Caribbean – as well as international mobility across other regions – guarantee that job-related outcomes affected by perceptions will continue to confront practitioners, investigators, policy-makers, and many other stakeholders of comparative HRM research.

Apart from the *JMP* special issue, Canales et al. (2009) described how construction language courses for USA supervisors and Hispanic workers can increase confidence and ability to communicate. Pagán and Dávila (1996) measured how Mexican Americans' wages in the USA were negatively affected after the Immigration Reform and Control Act (IRCA) of 1986 was enacted. The need for this type of research seems to be even more extreme in the case of undocumented foreign-born employees in the USA, as Luksyte et al.'s (2014) study on the well-being of foreign-born, Hispanic workers exemplifies; they found that the lack of legal documentation as well as a lower English proficiency are powerful, negative influences on this group. We have little doubt that similar statements can be made about other workers and in other geographic locations.

We have made a conscious attempt to avoid the temptation to criticise methodologies and other aspects dealing with the rigour and quality of the research we found; finding imperfections is much easier than building from what so far has been documented. Of course, larger samples, theoretical frameworks, and more longitudinal designs with multiple sources of data are needed to publish in the most influential HRM journals. However, if the objective were not as much to publish in the 'A journals' as to benefit its stakeholders, to truly be effective and impactful, HRM research dealing with Mexico, Central America, and the Caribbean needs to be translated into Spanish, the most prevalent language for the area. By documenting in this chapter the languages in which our sources were published, we believe we can conclude in more than tentative terms that using English only would have made this review quite incomplete. The need to include publications in Spanish (and often even French) when investigating HRM (and many other themes) in this region is reaching crucial importance.

The scarcity of scholarly publications in HRM and other organisational sciences in the region poses a large threat to the dissemination of knowledge that has the potential to change organisational practices and working lives for the best. This chapter provides an overview of research in the field that may be of help for researchers intending to make much needed contributions.

ACKNOWLEDGEMENTS

Authorship order is alphabetical, as both authors contributed to this chapter in equivalent ways. The second author gratefully acknowledges a research support grant and a course release from Clarion University of Pennsylvania's College of Business Administration & Information Sciences, that were instrumental to develop this chapter. Collegial comments from Dianna Stone and Terri Lituchi helped us to improve this chapter; any errors or omissions are of course our own.

REFERENCES

Alhama Belamaric, R. 2003. Medición del impacto de la gestión de recursos humanos en Cuba. Retrieved from http://www.gestiopolis.com/medicion-del-impacto-de-la-gestion-de-recursos-humanos-en-cuba/.
Arellano-Gault, D. 2012. The evaluation of performance in the Mexican Federal Government: A study of the monitoring agencies' modernization process. *Public Administration Review*, 72(1): 135–142.
Arévalo-Flechas, L.C., Acton, G., Escamilla, M.I., et al. 2014. Latino Alzheimer's caregivers: What is important to them? *Journal of Managerial Psychology*, 29(6): 661–684.
Arias, F., & Heredia, V. 2009. *Administración de Recursos Humanos para el Alto Desempeño* (6th edn). México: Editorial Trillas.
Arias-Galicia, L.F. 2005. Human resource management in Mexico. In M.M. Elvira and A. Davila (eds), *Managing Human Resources in Latin America: An Agenda for International Leaders*: 179–190. Abingdon: Routledge.

Arvey, R.D., Bhagat, R.S., & Salas, E. 1991. Cross-cultural and cross-national issues in personnel and human resources management: Where do we go from here?. *Research in Personnel and Human Resources Management*, 9: 367–407.

Beutell, N.J., & Schneer, J.A. 2014. Work–family conflict and synergy among Hispanics. *Journal of Managerial Psychology*, 29(6): 705–735.

Blunch, N.H., & Castro, P. 2007. Enterprise-level training in developing countries: Do international standards matter?. *International Journal of Training and Development*, 11(4): 314–324.

Bonache, J., Trullen, J., & Sanchez, J.I. 2012. Managing cross-cultural differences: Testing human resource models in Latin America. *Journal of Business Research*, 65(12): 1773–1781.

Borgeaud-Garciandía, N. 2007. Qué será de los sindicatos en las maquilas de Nicaragua? Pregunta abierta. *El Cotidiano – Revista de la Realidad Mexicana*, 142(1): 64–73.

Borgeaud-Garciandía, N. 2009. Dominación laboral y vida privada de las obreras de maquilas textiles en Nicaragua. *TRACE (Travaux et Recherches dans les Amériques du Centre)*, 55: 76–89. Retrieved from http://trace.revues.org/758.

Borgeaud-Garciandía, N. 2010. Entre construction juridique et discours dominant: les maquilas et le Nicaragua postrévolutionnaire. *Nuevo Mundo Mundos Nuevos*, 55: 76–89. Retrieved from http://nuevomundo.revues.org/58418.

Borgeaud-Garciandía, N., & Lautier, B. 2009. La personalización de la relación de dominación laboral: las obreras de las maquilas y las empleadas domésticas en América Latina. *Revista Mexicana de Sociología*, 76(1): 89–113.

Brewster, C., & Mayrhofer, W. 2012. Comparative human resource management: An introduction. In C. Brewster and W. Mayrhofer (eds), *Handbook of Research on Comparative Human Resource Management*: 1–23. Cheltenham, UK and Northampton, MA, USA: Edward Elgar Publishing.

Butler, M.C., & Teagarden, M.B. 1993. Strategic management of worker health, safety, and environmental issues in Mexico's Maquiladora industry. *Human Resource Management*, 32(4): 479–503.

Canales, A.R., Arbelaez, M., Vasquez, E., et al. 2009. Exploring training needs and development of construction language courses for American supervisors and Hispanic craft workers. *Journal of Construction Engineering and Management*, 135(5): 387–396.

Carrillo, J., & Gomis, R. 2011. Un estudio sobre prácticas de empleo en firmas multinacionales en México: Un primer mapeo. *Frontera Norte*, 23(46): 35–60.

Castilla Ramos, B., & Labrecque, M.F. 2009. Trabajo y género en las maquiladoras –Prólogo. *TRACE (Travaux et Recherches dans les Amériques du Centre)*, 55: 3–15. Retrieved from http://trace.revues.org/742.

Castilla Ramos, B., & Torres Góngora, B. 2009. Del hogar a la fábrica: trabajadoras de las empresas transnacionales en Yucatán, México. *TRACE (Travaux et Recherches dans les Amériques du Centre)*, 55: 31–52. Retrieved from http://trace.revues.org/796.

Central Intelligence Agency (CIA). 2015. *The World Factbook*. Retrieved from https://www.cia.gov/library/publications/the-world-factbook.

Cunha, M.P., & Cunha, R.C. 2004. The dialectics of human resource management in Cuba. *International Journal of Human Resource Management*, 15(7): 1280–1292.

Cunha, M.P., Cunha, R.C., & Rego, A. 2007. Toward a cross-cultural theory of 'exemplary organizations': Evidence from Cuba. *Thunderbird International Business Review*, 49(5): 545–565.

Curiel Sandoval, V.A. 2013. La reforma a la Ley Federal del Trabajo en materia de subcontratación en México. *Alegatos-Revista Jurídica de la Universidad Autónoma Metropolitana*, 83: 213–236.

Daspro, E. 2009a. An analysis of US multinationals' recruitment practices in Mexico. *Journal of Business Ethics*, 87(1): 221–232.

Daspro, E. 2009b. A cross-cultural comparison of multinational firms' recruitment practices in Mexico and the United States. *Latin American Business Review*, 10(1): 1–19.

Davila, A., & Elvira, M. 2007. Psychological contracts and performance management in Mexico. *International Journal of Manpower*, 28(5): 384–402.

Davila, A., & Elvira, M. 2009. Performance management in knowledge-intensive firms. In A. Davila and M. Elvira (eds), *Best Human Resource Management Practices in Latin America*: 113–127. Abingdon: Routledge.

Davila, A., & Pagán, J.A. 1999. Gender pay and occupational-attainment gaps in Costa Rica and El Salvador: A relative comparison of the late 1980s. *Review of Development Economics*, 3(2): 215–230.

De Forest, M. 1994. Thinking of a plant in Mexico?. *Academy of Management Executive*, 8(1): 33–40.

Díaz-González, J.A. 2010. Propuesta de periodización y desarrollo del sindicalismo en Costa Rica (1932–1998). *Revista de Ciencias Sociales*, 128–129: 137–157.

Dooley, K.E., Lindner, J.R., Dooley, L.M., & Alagaraja, M. 2004. Behaviorally anchored competencies: evaluation tool for training via distance. *Human Resource Development International*, 7(3): 315–332.

Drost, E.A., Frayne, C.A., Lowe, K.B., & Geringer, J.M. 2002. Benchmarking training and development practices: a multi-country comparative analysis. *Human Resource Management*, 41(1): 67–86.

Drost, E.A., & Von Glinow, M.A. 1998. Leadership behavior in Mexico: Etic philosophies/emic practices. *Research in International Business and International Relations*, 7: 3–28.

Edmond, S. 2002. Exploring the success of expatriates of US multinational firms in Mexico. *International Trade Journal*, 16(3): 233–255.

Elvira, M., & Davila, A. 2005a. Cultura y administración de recursos humanos en América Latina. *Universia Business Review*, 1(5): 28–45.

Elvira, M., & Davila, A. 2005b. Culture and human resource management research in Latin America. In M.M. Elvira and A. Davila (eds), *Managing Human Resources in Latin America: An Agenda for International Leaders*: 3–24. Abingdon: Routledge.

Elvira, M., & Davila, A. 2005c. Emergent directions for human resource management research in Latin America. *International Journal of Human Resource Management*, 16(12): 2265–2282.

Fairris, D. 2002. Es mayor la eficiencia productiva en los procesos de trabajo transformados?. *Región y Sociedad*, 14(23): 43–67.

Fairris, D. 2003. Unions and wage inequality in Mexico. *Industrial and Labor Relations Review*, 56(3): 481–497.

Fairris, D. 2006. Union voice effects in Mexico. *British Journal of Industrial Relations*, 44(4): 781–800.

Fairris, D., & Levine, E. 2004. Declining union density in Mexico, 1984–2000. *Monthly Labor Review*, 127: 10–17.

Fairris, D., Popli, G., & Zepeda, E. 2008. Minimum wages and the wage structure in Mexico. *Review of Social Economy*, 66(2): 181–208.

Félix Rodríguez, O., Fernández, F., & Soto Torres, R. 2011. Impact of information technology certifications in Puerto Rico. *Management Research: Journal of the Iberoamerican Academy of Management*, 9(2): 137–153.

Fernández Cueto, J.E., & Sánchez, J.I. 2011. Validity of context-specific versus broad individual differences in international assignments. *Revista de Psicología del Trabajo y de las Organizaciones*, 27(1): 5–15.

Flores Zambada, R., & Madero Gómez, S.M. 2010. Género, sociabilidad, dependientes económicos y desempeño laboral como determinantes de promociones: Experimento con ejecutivos jóvenes. *Conciencia Tecnológica*, 39: 12–16.

García, M.F., Posthuma, R.A., Mumford, T., & Quiñones, M. 2009. The five dimensions of pay satisfaction in a maquiladora plant in Mexico. *Applied Psychology: An International Review*, 58(4): 509–519.

Germán Pérez, D. 2001. Public personnel management in the Caribbean: A comparative analysis of trends in the Dominican Republic, Cuba, Puerto Rico, Jamaica, and St Vincent and Grenada. *Public Personnel Management in the Caribbean*, 30(1): 27–35.

Godínez Rivera, M.T., & Zarazúa Vilchis, J.L. 2012. Propuesta de estructura de anuncios para el reclutamiento de personal en las Mipymes mexicanas. *Gestion y Estrategia*, 42: 67–79.

Goldín, L.R. 2009. Flexibles, cansados y desesperanzados: alta rotación entre los trabajadores de las maquilas rurales de Guatemala. *TRACE (Travaux et Recherches dans les Amériques du Centre)*, 55: 53–62. Retrieved from http://trace.revues.org/745.

Gómez, C. 2004. The influence of environmental, organizational, and HRM factors on employee behaviors in subsidiaries: A Mexican case study of organizational learning. *Journal of World Business*, 39(1): 1–11.

Gómez, C., & Sanchez, J.I. 2005. Managing HR to build social capital in Latin America within MNCs. In M.M. Elvira and A. Davila (eds), *Managing Human Resources in Latin America: An Agenda for International Leaders*: 57–74. Abingdon: Routledge.

Gowan, M., Ibarreche, S., & Lackey, C. 1996. Doing the right things in Mexico. *Academy of Management Executive*, 10: 74–81.

Grosse, C.U. 2004. English business communication needs of Mexican executives in a distance-learning class. *Business Communication Quarterly*, 67(1): 7–23.

Guadarrama Olivera, R. 2009. Trayectorias, identidades laborales y sujetos femeninos en la maquila de confección. Costa Rica, 1980–2002. *TRACE (Travaux et Recherches dans les Amériques du Centre)*, 55: 90–111. Retrieved from http://trace.revues.org/790.

Guerrero, L., & Posthuma, R. 2014. Perceptions and behaviors of Hispanic workers: a review. *Journal of Managerial Psychology*, 29(6): 616–643.

Hernández Darias, I., Fleitas Triana, S., & Salazar Fernández, D. 2011. Particularidades de la gestión de los recursos humanos en empresas cubanas. *Revista Avanzada Científica*, 14(1): 1–13. Retrieved from http://dialnet.unirioja.es/descarga/articulo/3646564.pdf.

Hofstede, G. 2015. Dimensions of national cultures. Retrieved from http://geert-hofstede.nl/dimensions-of-national-cultures.

Hotchkiss, J.L., & Moore, R.E. 1996. Gender compensation differentials in Jamaica. *Economic Development and Cultural Change*, 44(3): 657–676.

House, R.J., Hanges, P.J., Javidan, M., Dorfman, P.W., & Gupta, V. 2004. *Culture, Leadership and Organizations: The GLOBE Study of 62 Societies*. Thousand Oaks, CA: SAGE Publications.

International Journal of Human Resource Management. 2005. Special Issue, 16(12).

International Journal of Manpower. 2007. Special Issue, 28(5).

International Labour Organization (ILO). 2013. ILOSTAT Database. Retrieved from http://www.ilo.org/ilostat.

Jun, M., Cai, S., & Peterson, R. 2004. Obstacles to TQM implementation in Mexico's maquiladora industry. *Total Quality Management and Business Excellence*, 15(1): 59–72.

Kaplan, D.S. 2009. Job creation and labor reform in Latin America. *Journal of Comparative Economics*, 37(1): 91–105.

Klingner, D.E., & Pallavicini, C.V. 2002. Building public HRM capacity in Latin America and the Caribbean: What works and what doesn't. *Public Organization Review*, 2(4): 349–364.

Kovács, G., Tatham, P., & Larson, P.D. 2012. What skills are needed to be a humanitarian logistician?. *Journal of Business Logistics*, 33(3): 245–258.

Leguizamon, F.A., Ickis, J.C., & Oligastri, E. 2009. Human resource practices and business performance. In A. Davila and M. Elvira (eds), *Best Human Resource Management Practices in Latin America*: 84–96. Abingdon: Routledge.

Lenartowicz, T., & Johnson, J. P. 2003. A cross-national assessment of the values of Latin America managers: Contrasting hues or shades of gray?. *Journal of International Business Studies*, 34(3): 266–281.

Linnehan, F., & Blau, G. 2003. Testing the impact of job search and recruitment source on new hire turnover in a maquiladora. *Applied Psychology: An International Review*, 52(2): 253–271.

Littrell, R.F., & Barba, E. 2013 North and South Latin America influence of values on preferred leader behaviour in Chile and Mexico. *Journal of Management Development*, 32(6): 629–656.

Luksyte, A., Spitzmueller, C., & Rivera-Minaya, C.Y. 2014. Factors relating to wellbeing of foreign-born Hispanic workers. *Journal of Managerial Psychology*, 29(6): 685–704.

Madero, S. 2009. Factores de atracción y retención del mercado laboral, para empleados potenciales. *Economía, Gestión y Desarrollo*, 7: 131–147.

Madero, S.M. 2010a. Factores claves para el uso y diseño de un sistema de compensaciones en empresas de servicio: desde una perspectiva cualitativa y descriptiva. *Investigación Administrativa*, 104: 7–25.

Madero, S.M. 2010b. Factores relevantes del desarrollo professional y de compensaciones en la carrera laboral del trabajador. *Contaduría y Administración*, 232: 109–130.

Madero, S.M., & Olivas-Luján, M.R. 2014. Experiencias directivas y movilidad en CEMEX Asia. In O. Morales Tristán and A. Borda Reyes (eds), *Casos de Empresas Latinoamericanas en Asia*: 69–89. Mason, OH: CENGAGE Learning.

Madero, S.M., & Peña Rivera, H. 2012. Análisis de los procesos de recursos humanos y su influencia en los bonos y prestaciones. *Cuadernos de Administración*, 28(48): 25–36.

Madero, S.M., & Trevinyo-Rodríguez, R.N. 2011. Las recompensas en el trabajo dentro de la empresa familiar mexicana: desde la perspectiva de la generación Y. *Investigación Administrativa*, 107: 7–18.

Madero, S.M., Trevinyo, R.N., & Avendaño, J. 2012. Compensaciones en la empresa familiar Mexicana: sus componentes, herramientas de apoyo y criterios de efectividad. *Revista Internacional Administración & Finanzas*, 5(5): 41–56.

Martínez, P.G. 2003. Paternalism as a positive form of leader–subordinate exchange: Evidence from Mexico. *Management Research: Journal of the Iberoamerican Academy of Management*, 1(3): 227–242.

Martínez, P.G. 2005. Paternalism as a positive form of leadership in the Latin American context: Leader benevolence, decision-making control and human resource management practices. In M.M. Elvira and A. Davila (eds), *Managing Human Resources in Latin America: An Agenda for International Leaders*: 75–93. Abingdon: Routledge.

Martinez, Z.L., & Ricks, D.A. 1989. Multinational parent companies' influence over human resource decisions of affiliates: US firms in Mexico. *Journal of International Business Studies*, 20(3): 465–487.

Masuda, A.D., Poelmans, S.A., Allen, T.D., et al. 2012. Flexible work arrangements availability and their relationship with work-to-family conflict, job satisfaction, and turnover intentions: A comparison of three country clusters. *Applied Psychology: An International Review*, 61(1): 1–29.

Mendoza, J.E. 2010. El mercado laboral en la frontera norte de México: estructura y políticas de empleo. *Estudios Fronterizos*, 11(21): 9–42.

Miller, J.S., Hom, P.W., & Gomez-Mejia, L.R. 2001. The high cost of low wages: Does maquiladora compensation reduce turnover?. *Journal of International Business Studies*, 32(3): 585–595.

Mujtaba, B.G., Murphy Jr, E.F., McCartney, T., et al. 2009. Convergence and divergence of values and type A behavior patterns between developing and developed countries. *Icfai University Journal of Organizational Behavior*, 8(2): 6–34.

Nabor, E.S. 2009. Globalización, migración y trabajo en la capital del 'Blue Jeans'. *TRACE (Travaux et Recherches dans les Amériques du Centre)*, 55: 16–30. Retrieved from http://trace.revues.org/731.

Nicholls, C.E., Lane, H.W., & Brechu, M.B. 1999. Taking self-managed teams to Mexico. *Academy of Management Executive*, 13(3): 15–25.

Offermann, L.R., Matos, K., & DeGraaf, S.B. 2014. Están hablando de mí? Challenges for multilingual organizations. *Journal of Managerial Psychology*, 29(6): 644–660.

Olivas-Luján, M.R., & González Chávez, D. 2006. Influences de la mondialisation sur les indicateurs de l'emploi au Mexique. In F. Pinot de Villechenon (ed.), *La mondialisation et ses effets: nouveaux debats: Approches d'Europe et d'Amérique latine*: 59–69. Collection Changement Social. Paris: Diffusion L'Harmattan.

Olivas-Luján, M.R., Monserrat, S.I., Ruiz-Gutierrez, J.A., et al. 2009. Values and attitudes towards women in Argentina, Brazil, Colombia, and Mexico. *Employee Relations*, 31(3): 227–244.

Olivas-Luján, M.R., Ramirez, J., & Zapata-Cantu, L. 2007. e-HRM in Mexico: adapting innovations for global competitiveness. *International Journal of Manpower*, 28(5): 418–434.

Ollivier Fierro, J.Ó. 2015. Capacitación y tecnología del proceso en la industria maquiladora. *Frontera Norte*, 17(33): 7–24.

Osland, A., & Osland, J.S. 2005a. Contextualization and strategic international human resource management approaches: The case of Central America and Panama. *International Journal of Human Resource Management*, 16(12): 2218–2236.

Osland, A., & Osland, J.S. 2005b. Human resource management in Central America and Panama. In M.M. Elvira and A. Davila (eds), *Managing Human Resources in Latin America: An Agenda for International Leaders*: 129–147. Abingdon: Routledge.

Osland, J.S., Snyder, M.M., & Hunter, L. 1998. A comparative study of managerial styles among female executives in Nicaragua and Costa Rica. *International Studies of Management and Organization*, 28(2): 54–73.

Padilla Rodriguez, B.C., & Armellini, A. 2013. Interaction and effectiveness of corporate e-learning programmes. *Human Resource Development International*, 16(4): 480–489.

Pagán, J.A., & Davila, A. 1996. On-the-job training, immigration reform, and the true wages of native male workers. *Industrial Relations: A Journal of Economy and Society*, 35(1): 45–58.

Paik, Y., & Teagarden, M.B. 1995. Strategic international human resource management approaches in the maquiladora industry: A comparison of Japanese, Korean and US firms. *International Journal of Human Resource Management*, 6(3): 568–587.

Peek, L., Roxas, M., Peek, G., et al. 2007. NAFTA students' whistle-blowing perceptions: A case of sexual harassment. *Journal of Business Ethics*, 74(3): 219–231.

Pelled, L.H., & Hill, K.D. 1997a. Employee work values and organizational attachment in North Mexican maquiladoras. *International Journal of Human Resource Management*, 8(4): 495–505.

Pelled, L.H., & Hill, K.D. 1997b. Participative management in Northern Mexico: A study of maquiladoras. *International Journal of Human Resource Management*, 8(2): 197–212.

Pelled, L.H., & Xin, K.R. 1998. Birds of a feather: Leader–member demographic similarity and organizational attachment in Mexico. *Leadership Quarterly*, 8(4): 433–450.

Pelled, L.H., Xin, K.R., & Weiss, A.M. 2001. No es como mi: Relational demography and conflict in a Mexican production facility. *Journal of Occupational and Organizational Psychology*, 74(1): 63–84.

Peña, L. 2000. Retaining a Mexican labor force. *Journal of Business Ethics*, 26(2): 123–131.

Pine, A. 2009. Tú eres gallo … pero la de los huevos soy yo: Producción y género en las maquiladoras de Honduras. *TRACE (Travaux et Recherches dans les Amériques du Centre)*, 55: 63–75. Retrieved from http://trace.revues.org/751.

Posthuma, R.A., Dworkin, J., Torres, V., & Bustillos, D. 2000. Labor and employment laws in the United States and Mexico: An international comparison. *Labor Law Journal*, 51: 95–111.

Posthuma, R.A., Levashina, J., Lievens, F., et al. 2014. Comparing employment interviews in Latin America with other countries. *Journal of Business Research*, 67(5): 943–951.

Power, J.L., Brotheridge, C.M., Blenkinsopp, J., et al. 2013 Acceptability of workplace bullying: A comparative study on six continents. *Journal of Business Research*, 66(3): 374–380.

Ramirez, J., Madero, S., & Muñiz, C. 2015a. The impact of narcoterrorism on HRM systems. *International Journal of Human Resource Management*, 27(19): 2202–2232.

Ramirez, J., Vélez-Zapata, C., & Madero, S. 2015b. Building psychological contracts in security-risk environments: evidence from Colombia and Mexico. *European Journal of International Management*, 9(6): 690–711.

Ramirez, J., & Zapata-Cantú, L. 2009. HRM systems in Mexico. In A. Davila and M. Elvira (eds), *Best Human Resource Management Practices in Latin America*: 97–112. Abingdon: Routledge.

Ramírez Sánchez, M.Á. 2011. Los sindicatos blancos de Monterrey (1931–2009). *Frontera Norte*, 23(46): 177–210.

Rao, P. 2009. Executive staffing practices in US–Mexican joint ventures. In A. Davila and M. Elvira (eds), *Best Human Resource Management Practices in Latin America*: 141–156. Abingdon: Routledge.

Rao, P. 2014. A resource-based view of the' best' companies in Mexico: A multiple-case design approach. *SAM Advanced Management Journal*, 79(2): 12–25.

Reiche, B.S., Lee, Y., & Quintanilla, J. 2012. Cultural perspectives on comparative HRM. In C. Brewster and W. Mayrhofer (eds), *Handbook of Research on Comparative Human Resource Management*: 51–68. Cheltenham, UK and Northampton, MA, USA: Edward Elgar Publishing.

Rokeach, M. 1973. *The Nature of Human Values*. New York: Free Press.

Rousseau, D.M., & Barends, E.G. 2011. Becoming an evidence-based HR practitioner. *Human Resource Management Journal*, 21(3): 221–235.

Ruiz-Gutierrez, J.A., Murphy Jr, E.F., Greenwood, R.A., et al. 2012. Work, family and values in four Latin-American countries. *Management Research: Journal of the Iberoamerican Academy of Management*, 10(1): 29–42.

Sánchez Díaz, S.G. 2014. Los sindicatos ante las ciencias sociales y la antropología social en México: Antecedentes, logros y perspectivas en el siglo XXI. *Nueva Antropología: Revista de Ciencias Sociales*, 27(80): 59–82.

Sánchez-Marín, G., Carrasco-Hernández, A., & Madero-Gómez, S. 2010. La retribución de los empleados de la empresa familiar: Un análisis comparativo regional España-México. *Cuadernos de Administración*, 23(41): 37–59.

Santiso, J. 2008. La emergencia de las multilatinas. *Revista de la CEPAL*, 95: 7–30. Retrieved from http://reposi torio.cepal.org/bitstream/handle/11362/11249/095007030_es.pdf?sequence=1.

Schuler, R.S., Jackson, S.E., Jackofsky, E., & Slocum, J.W. 1996. Managing human resources in Mexico: A cultural understanding. *Business Horizons*, 39(3): 55–61.

Selvarajan, T., & Cloninger, P.A. 2012. Can performance appraisals motivate employees to improve performance? A Mexican study. *International Journal of Human Resource Management*, 23(15): 3063–3084.

Society for Human Resource Management (SHRM). 2004a. The maturing profession of human resources worldwide: Summary report for Dominican Republic. Alexandria: VA: SHRM. Retrieved from http://www. shrm.org/Research/SurveyFindings/Articles/Documents/HR%20Profession%20Dominican%20Republic%20 final.pdf.

Society for Human Resource Management (SHRM). 2004b. The maturing profession of human resources worldwide: Summary report for Mexico. Alexandria: VA: SHRM. Retrieved from http://www.shrm.org/ foreign/espanol/Documents/Mexico%20Survey%20Report.pdf.

Stephens, G.K., & Greer, C.R. 1995. Doing business in Mexico: Understanding cultural differences. *Organizational Dynamics*, 24(1): 39–55.

Teagarden, M.B., Butler, M.C., & Von Glinow, M.A. 1991. Mexico's maquiladora industry: Where strategic human resource management makes a difference. *Organizational Dynamics*, 20(3): 34–47.

Valdés-Padrón, M., Garza-Ríos, R., Pérez-Vergara, I., Gé-Varona, M., & Chávez-Vivó, A.R. 2015. Una propuesta para la evaluación del desempeño de los trabajadores apoyada en el uso de técnicas cuantitativas. *Ingeniería Industrial*, 36(1): 48–57.

Vassolo, R.S., De Castro, J.O., & Gomez-Mejia, L.R. 2011. Managing in Latin America: Common issues and a research agenda. *Academy of Management Perspectives*, 25(4): 22–36.

Villar, A.B., Llinàs-Audet, X., & Escardíbul, J.O. 2013. International Briefing 31: Training and development in Mexico. *International Journal of Training and Development*, 17(4): 310–320.

World Bank. 2015. Data. Retrieved from http://data.worldbank.org.

World Economic Forum. 2014. The Global Competitiveness Report 2014–2015. Geneva: World Economic Forum. Retrieved from http://www3.weforum.org/docs/WEF_GlobalCompetitivenessReport_2014-15.pdf.

Zarazúa Vilchis, J.L. 2013. La selección de personal por competencias. Cómo aplica en la empresa mexicana? *Gestión y Estrategia*, 43: 67–79.

Zevallos, E. 2006. Obstaculos al desarrollo de las pequeñas y medianas empresas en America Latina. *Cuadernos de Difusión*, 11(20): 75–96.

23. Comparative HRM research in South America: a call for comparative institutional approaches

Michel Hermans

INTRODUCTION

The ongoing changes and enduring contrasts in the South American[1] business context challenge our understanding of human resource management (HRM) in this region. Characterized by pendular swings between military and democratic governments and attempts to industrialize through import substitution in the period before the 1990s, most South American countries shifted to democratic stability and neoliberal economic policies in the decade before 2000. The increased presence of multinational corporations (MNCs), training of HRM professionals in the United States of America (USA) and Europe, and international collaboration among HRM associations led companies to adopt 'global best practice' approaches to HRM. However, in response to the collapse of the Argentine economy in 2001, the return of populist political regimes in countries such as Venezuela, Bolivia, and Argentina, and the recent end of an economic bonanza based on the region's commodity exports, organizations found themselves obliged to reconsider how they manage people according to the industry they operate in, their exposure to government intervention, needs for trained personnel, and increased union activism in some countries. The resulting fragmentation of the South American landscape of HRM requires researchers to develop an understanding of how organizations in this region manage people that is both contextually and historically sensitive.

In this chapter, I focus on HRM research conducted in South America and argue that insights derived from cross-cultural approaches (Hofstede, 1980, 1991; Laurent, 1986) to studying HRM could be enriched by integrating comparative institutional perspectives into organization-level research (see Chapters 2 and 3 in this volume). Cross-cultural research has been instrumental in identifying what differentiates HRM in Latin America from other regions (e.g., Elvira & Davila, 2005b) as well as explaining some intra-regional differences (e.g., Lenartowicz & Johnson, 2003; Varela et al., 2009), and it continues to yield valuable insights. Cross-cultural perspectives, however, also have some inherent limitations, leading to partial explanations of important questions, such as how and why human resource management varies within countries, across different industries, and between the political and economic cycles that mark the Latin American region. Comparative institutional approaches (e.g., Amable, 2003; Hall & Soskice, 2001; Whitley, 1999) provide useful frameworks that may help to overcome some of these limitations. They consider the formal and informal rules and regulations that govern economic

---

[1] 'South America' refers to the following countries: Argentina, Chile, Bolivia, Paraguay, Uruguay, Brazil, Peru, Ecuador, Colombia, Venezuela, French Guiana, Surinam and Guyana. Additionally, the Falkland Islands (a British Overseas Territory disputed by Argentina), the ABC islands of the Netherlands, and Trinidad and Tobago, are frequently considered to be part of South America.

activity and are based on the assumption that organizations are embedded in industries and national and sub-national institutional contexts. This historical embeddedness both creates opportunities and places constraints on managerial decisions regarding HRM. Hence, an institutional lens may help to explain why MNCs or their subsidiaries operating in Brazil may have opportunities or constraints that differ from those in Argentina or Colombia; and in turn, how those differences shape variation in the adoption of HRM practices, and their related outcomes and competitiveness in the global economy.

While the integration of comparative institutional approaches into HRM research offers a more comprehensive understanding of HRM in a global context, integrating institutional and organization-level research is difficult to achieve (Batt & Hermans, 2012). Moreover, because the comparative institutional literature has relied heavily on empirical studies in advanced economies, particularly in Europe, its premises must be examined to assess whether and how they can be adapted to the South American context. This chapter lays out opportunities and challenges for integrating comparative institutional approaches into HRM research in South America, and hopefully can serve to inform global HRM research 'from the margins' (Alcadipani & Faria, 2014; Faria, 2010).

In the following sections, I briefly review cross-cultural approaches as used in South American HRM research and present comparative institutional approaches as a complementary theoretical perspective, highlighting a stream of recent contributions that focus specifically on Latin America. I then identify how scholars can move beyond some of the biases in the comparative institutional literature and thereby advance an integrated approach to empirical HRM research in Latin America. This integration can both inform Latin American empirical research and also locate that research in the broader body of comparative institutional and HRM literature, thereby enhancing its theoretical power. Beyond identifying merits of and challenges for comparative institutional approaches for HRM research in South America, I raise a set of research questions and offer suggestions for scholars to advance an institutionally grounded approach to South American HRM research.

CROSS-CULTURAL APPROACHES IN SOUTH AMERICAN HRM RESEARCH

Cross-cultural perspectives on South American HRM research draw on the observations of many scholars that Latin American countries share historical, economic, and cultural features (e.g., Elvira & Davila, 2005b; Nicholls-Nixon et al., 2011). Some of the most salient characteristics include the colonization by Spanish and, in the case of Brazil, Portuguese *conquistadores* who made their languages and Catholic religion predominant throughout the region. Most South American countries became independent between 1810 and 1830 and were emancipated through pendular swings between democracy and military coups. Economic development depended to a large extent on the extraction of natural resources and was led by family-based elites. During the 1990s, Latin American markets were opened to global competition and witnessed a significant wave of privatization in response to earlier episodes of high inflation and debt crises.

Elvira and Davila (2005b) argued that similarities in the historical and institutional development of the region's countries have shaped a common work culture, characterized by high rankings on the power distance and collectivism dimensions. Cultural traits, such as an emphasis on social relationships and respect for authority, have behavioural consequences such as paternalistic supervisor–subordinate relationships, avoidance of public confrontation of employees with their superiors, a need for person-to-person communication, and loyalty to the in-group. Hence, Elvira and Davila (2005b: 2166) suggested that 'these characteristics rest on work values that suggest an appropriate cultural frame for understanding how Latin American organizations manage human resources'. Their concept of a 'Latin America management model' has sparked cross-cultural HRM research across the region. At the national level, researchers have addressed the impact of cultural traits on HRM in Venezuela (Gomez-Samper & Monteferrante, 2005), Peru (Sully de Luque & Arbaiza, 2005), Chile (Perez Arrau et al., 2012), and Brazil (Fischer & de Albuquerque, 2005; Tanure & Duarte, 2005). Similarly, researchers have applied cross-cultural approaches in studies of the adoption of HRM practices by subsidiaries of MNCs (Lertxundi & Landeta, 2011), the impact of national culture on organizational change (Hojman & Pérez, 2005), premises that underlie labour contracts (Rodriguez & Rios, 2007), practices aimed at enhancing safety in high-risk jobs (Perez-Floriano & Gonzalez, 2007), the management of project teams in Brazilian multinationals (Rodrigues & Sbragia, 2013), and the relationship between work, family, and values (Ruiz-Gutierrez et al., 2012).

While cross-cultural theory is not the only approach found in Latin American HRM research (e.g., Tonelli, 2003; Davila et al., 2007; Lertxundi, 2007), it is by far the dominant one, and the one most frequently used in top-tier international publications. This dominance of one perspective is problematic for a number of reasons. First, cross-cultural perspectives have received increasing criticism due to methodological problems in the measurement of constructs and the validity, generalizability, and interpretation of findings (e.g., Ailon, 2008; Gerhart & Fang, 2005; Graen, 2006; McSweeney, 2002).

Second, the reliance on region or country-level characterizations of national culture, for example, leads to a lack of sensitivity to variation at other levels of analysis and, hence, a risk of ignoring alternative explanations for the adoption of HRM practices and their outcomes. At the sub-national level, it is clear from extensive anthropological research that there is substantial within-country variation in culture based on indigenous group regional variation, or variation based on the mixing of cultures of immigrants from Europe, Africa, North America, and indigenous groups (Sanabria, 2007). Subnational regional variation also emerges from the location of dominant industries in different regions; for example, the differences in HRM emerging from the mining districts of northern Chile compared to the food processing industries in the centre and south of the country, or a large services sector in its capital. At the organizational level, managers may adopt culturally incongruent HRM practices because of the logic of production in global value chains (Edwards & Kuruvilla, 2005; Gereffi, 2005), the need for internal consistency across MNC operations (Schuler et al., 1993), public pressure in a third country for an MNC to revise its HRM practices (Locke et al., 2009), or because of MNC home-country effects in the firm's organizational logic (Almond et al., 2005).

Third, a focus on the cultural context in which organizations operate to explain distinctive features of HRM is likely to ignore the influence of other contextual political, social, and economic determinants (see also Chapter 2 in this volume). In the case of South America, studies by political scientists, sociologists, and industrial relations scholars, for example, have addressed the effects of globalization, particularly the effects of free trade agreements on wages and working conditions (e.g., Fraile, 2009), and responses of unions to globalization (e.g., Anner, 2011). Other studies have focused on compliance with employment regulation (e.g., Ronconi, 2010) and policies designed to integrate unemployed or informally employed people into the workforce (e.g., Galasso et al., 2004). Failure to integrate an analysis of how regulatory institutions, and changes in regulation, affect management decisions at the firm level limits the explanatory power of HRM research regarding variation in the adoption of HRM practices, turnover, HRM–performance linkages, and the like. Considering the close relationships between governments and unions, and high levels of union membership in a number of South American countries (Cook, 2007), employment regulation and industrial relations systems represent important boundary conditions that affect how and why organizations adopt HRM policies and, in turn, the outcomes of those policies.

HRM researchers in Latin America are increasingly aware of how cross-cultural perspectives do not fully explain their empirical findings. For example, in their study on adaptation of Brazilian expatriates Tanure et al. (2009) proposed a shift from analysing cultural distance based on Hofstede's (1980, 1991) dimensions towards a broader conceptualization of 'distance', adding administrative, geographical, and economic dimensions. Characteristics of the South American socio-economic landscape – such as weak employment law enforcement, unions as highly visible actors in the political economy, and fragmented regulatory responses to global economic integration – have important implications for HRM decisions and outcomes in the region. Thus, while cross-cultural perspectives provide an interesting point of departure, scholars of HRM in South America need to incorporate additional theoretical lenses into their research.

COMPARATIVE INSTITUTIONAL APPROACHES FOR SOUTH AMERICAN HRM RESEARCH

Bringing comparative institutional approaches (see Chapter 2 in this volume) into South American HRM research can enrich the current base of knowledge, because scholars will be able to develop a more complete analysis of the contextual determinants of HRM and to account for variation at the national, sub-national, and sectoral levels. There is much work to be done, however – and many opportunities for scholars in the field – because South America's institutional landscape as it relates to HRM strategies is under-researched and poorly understood. That is because the comparative institutional tradition emerged in Europe and has drawn its insights from advanced industrial economies (Morgan, 2011) and, more recently, from industrializing economies in Asia (e.g., Amable, 2003; Witt & Redding, 2014) and Eastern Europe (e.g., Feldmann, 2007; Whitley, 1999).

By contrast, research on South American countries and their institutions has emerged in different fields of study, and the focus of institutional analysis has not been on firm-level business strategies or HRM. For example, political scientists have focused on the role of unions in Latin American politics and the implications for labour regulation (e.g., Cook, 2007), and labour economists have analysed education and skill development systems in South America to explain wage levels (e.g., Manacorda et al., 2010). The focus in these studies on particular institutions allows for in-depth analysis of particular dimensions of labour and employment practices, but renders them less informative with regard to how institutions interact and affect decision-making at the level of the individual firm. Hence, they provide an incomplete understanding of the contextual determinants of HRM in South America.

More recent attempts to apply the varieties of capitalism (VoC) framework to Latin America (Schneider, 2008, 2009, 2013; Schneider & Soskice, 2009) provide a promising starting point for discussion. Schneider and colleagues have argued that Latin American regimes may be characterized as hierarchical market economies (HMEs). The HME variety is defined in terms of interaction among economic actors in the same spheres as the original VoC framework (Hall & Soskice, 2001). While HMEs share similarities with liberal market economies, they differ in terms of the character of the dominant corporate actors and how they relate to other actors. In Latin American economies, corporate actors such as MNCs and domestic business groups occupy dominant positions. A history of large flows of foreign direct investment (FDI), typically aimed at exploiting the region's vast natural resources but later also in manufacturing and services, helps to explain the significant presence of MNCs in Latin America. MNC subsidiaries are among the largest firms operating in the region (America Economía, 2014) and are responsible for much of the transfer of technology and technological upgrading of local supplier networks (e.g., McDermott & Corredoira, 2010; Meyer, 2004). Domestic business groups, often called *Grupos*, are conglomerates of commercially and technologically unrelated business units operating through separately owned subsidiaries. Though *Grupos* are generally considered inefficient organizational forms for developed markets, in South America they have survived frequent episodes of macroeconomic turbulence through unrelated diversification (Garrido & Peres, 1998; Khanna & Yafeh, 2007; Schneider, 2008). Closely intertwined with local and national governments, they have been able to use their ties to manage risk based on privileged information and to gain access to further diversification opportunities resulting from privatization and deregulation (e.g., Bonelli, 1998; Kosacoff, 2000; Ruiz Caro, 2002). Ownership is typically concentrated in families who have held these companies for several generations (Sargent, 2005). While mainly focused on markets within the region, a number of *Grupos* have pursued international expansion strategies (Chudnovsky et al., 1999; ECLAC, 2014). The entrance of large Latin American conglomerates into the markets of developed economies during the last decade has given rise to the term 'multilatinas' (Casanova, 2009; ECLAC, 2014). The relationships among MNCs and *Grupos*, and with other actors in the political economy, explain the hierarchical characterization of the Latin American variety of capitalism. Inter-firm relationships between MNCs and *Grupos* are generally not competitive, because of oligopolistic positions or regulation of industries. By contrast, the terms of relationships between these large firms and their smaller suppliers and distributors are typically imposed by the large firms' owners or managers, because these firms hold central positions in the organization of capital and technology.

The same hierarchical logic applies to South American labour markets, which are characterized by a high degree of regulation, low skill levels, high turnover, weak unions, and high levels of informality (Schneider & Karcher, 2010). These features give owners and managers of large firms much discretion in decisions regarding investments in employees' training and development. Similarly, they can use precarious employee protection arrangements and their relationships with governments to their benefit, to fence off unions. Building on the notion of institutional complementarity (Hall & Soskice, 2001), Schneider and Karcher (2010) identified negative complementarities in the Latin American context. They related the behaviours of economic agents that maximize their individual utility to the interaction among the principal institutional features of Latin American labour markets to explain the persistence of these features.

Several scholars have criticized the proposed HME variety of capitalism. Schrank (2009b) argued that the HME variety of capitalism ignores the Iberian roots of the region's principal economic institutions and, instead, explains the behaviour of economic actors from a North American perspective. He proposed that the lack of fiscal development, which causes inequalities in the distribution of income, is one of the principal characteristics of the Latin American region. Crouch (2012) found only weak support for the suggested patterns in the typology when focusing on employment provision and innovation, and pointed to its ahistorical approach.

Thus, there is considerable debate over how to characterize the institutional context in South American societies, and whether one model is sufficient to capture the diversity found across countries in the region. The parsimonious HME variety outlined above highlights important aspects of the region's context that HRM researchers should take into account. But much more theoretical and empirical research is needed to identify which configurations of institutions are most important in shaping firm-level approaches to managing the workforce. In this process, researchers face multiple challenges, as they need to examine the limitations found in comparative institutional theory in general, determine which of its assumptions are applicable to Latin America, and overcome limitations related to the incipient documentation of the Latin American institutional landscape. In the following sections, I identify five limitations that are relevant to Latin American HRM research, and suggest potential solutions and future research questions.

CURRENT LIMITATIONS FOR SOUTH AMERICAN HRM RESEARCH

Addressing Variation at Different Levels of Analysis

While comparative institutional approaches emphasize the effects of institutions on firm behaviour, firms are treated as black boxes and within-firm characteristics and dynamics are largely ignored. This lack of attention to differences within and across organizations in their responses to institutional pressure leads to incomplete explanations of variation in HRM practices and their outcomes. This is where HRM scholars have the expertise to complete the analysis: linking institutional rules not only to firm-level business strategies but to how they intersect with HRM strategies and the management of employees. HRM researchers, for example, have found that the characteristics of employee groups, the ease of replacing employees, and mode of contracting influence investments in human capital and the adoption of HRM practices (Lepak & Snell, 2002; Tsui et al., 1997). Likewise, observed variation in HRM practices and their outcomes may be due to line managers' and supervisors' interpretation of the practice or its suitability to the particular work situation (Khilji & Wang, 2006; Purcell & Hutchinson, 2007) and employee attributions regarding a firm's motives for adopting certain HRM practices (Nishii et al., 2008).

For researchers of HRM in Latin America, the consideration of intra-firm characteristics and dynamics is particularly relevant given the substantial differences between types of organizations. MNCs that operate in South America, and the *Grupos*, including those that have become multilatinas, are substantially different from small and medium-sized firms in terms of management practices, tenure of employees, professionalization of management, and quality of jobs. The United Nations Economic Commission for Latin America and the Caribbean (ECLAC) (ECLAC, 2013), for example, reports substantial differences in South America with respect to wages, investments in training, and working conditions between subsidiaries of MNCs and locally owned companies. Subsidiaries of MNCs pay wages that are 50 per cent higher on average, while in most countries studied MNC subsidiaries invested significantly more in training than locally owned companies.

The logic of MNC operations also has significant implications for HRM outcomes. For example, in a study of the impact of FDI on employment in Brazil, Mexico, and Argentina during the 1990–2004 period, Ernst et al. (2007) found that much investment was focused on privatizations and the acquisition of existing companies. In the cases of Argentina and Brazil, where acquisitions of existing companies dominated, the restructuring and modernization of acquired companies had negative consequences for employment. By contrast, in the case of Mexico, investment in new manufacturing facilities was associated with job creation; and the adoption of sophisticated production technologies in some *maquiladoras* (Mexican processing or assembly operations that are exempt from paying duties and tariffs on imports as long as they export their production) led to an increased demand for qualified workers and internal training programmes.

With regard to the *Grupos*, including those that have become multilatinas, HRM researchers should be aware of the concentration of ownership and the importance of family and social ties in corporate governance. Direct ownership and involvement in day-to-day management influence HRM practices. As owner-managers preserve their discretion in people management decisions, the implementation of HRM practices is likely to be conditioned by the relationships of trust between owner-managers and employees in key positions, and to reflect the beliefs of founders and their family members with regard to employee relations (Baron et al., 1996). Santiago Castro et al. (2009) studied corporate governance in Brazil, Chile, and Mexico between 2000 and 2002 and observed that on average companies had nine positions on their boards of directors, of which only one was occupied by an independent external director. Moreover, an average of 58.2 per cent of company ownership was concentrated in a dominant family and their social ties.

Family ownership may become less visible over time, especially in countries that implement institutional reforms aimed at connecting to global capital markets. For instance, research by Khanna and Rivkin (2006) questions the relevance of family ties and direct ownership as delineators of Chilean *Grupos*, as they found overlaps in ownership, interlocking directorships, and indirect ownership to be better predictors of organizational boundaries. While these findings suggest decreased influence of families over managerial decision-making within groups, the authors speculated that family and social ties may have come to pervade the Chilean economy as a whole (Khanna & Rivkin, 2006). Notwithstanding ongoing institutional reform in most South American countries, and a growing number of *Grupos* with listings on international stock exchanges, the influence of family ownership cannot be underestimated.

Families and their extended social ties are not the only kind of owners that exert influence on HRM. Cuervo-Cazurra et al. (2014) identified Brazilian oil company Petrobras, Petroleos de Venezuela, and mining conglomerate Vale from Brazil as MNCs in which managers need to take into account not only the interests of politicians, but also those of the citizens who elect politicians. Full or partial state ownership challenges the assumption, which underlies most strategic HRM research, that firms' primary goal is to maximize financial performance. Roger Agnelli (former chief executive officer of Vale from Brazil), for example, lost support from the Brazilian government because of his plans to lay off workers in Brazil while investing in operations abroad (*The Economist*, 2011). Additionally, HRM researchers are likely to find a stronger emphasis on social inclusion in selection practices, and the influence of politics in performance management and promotion decisions where state ownership occurs.

Recent progress in explaining variation in HRM practices by integrating insights from comparative institutional and organizational-level approaches offers several suggestions for HRM researchers in South America. First, successful integration of comparative institutional approaches requires the identification of which institutions are most relevant to the subject of study. As the institutional landscape of South American countries is less well documented and understood (Morgan, 2011), this implies that researchers need to conduct extensive fieldwork to identify the factors that shape HRM at each level of analysis (region, industry, firm, and so on), to understand how different levels interact, and to assess their relative importance. Second, careful research design is critical to develop a deeper understanding of the factors that condition HRM in South America. Researchers may limit samples to a particular type of firm, or study the impact of a particular institutional feature on firms that have different national origins, operate in different sectors, organize their operations differently, or have distinct ownership structures. Such a piecemeal approach requires more time and effort but will contribute to a more comprehensive understanding of HRM in the region.

Examining the State and the Strength of Institutions

Comparative institutional approaches emphasize the constraining effects of institutions on firm behaviour and managerial discretion. But individual firms may have the power to evade local regulations, avoid institutional pressures (Deeg & Jackson, 2007), or even overturn regulations and promote new ones that are supportive of their management practices (Almond & Ferner, 2006; Fenton-O'Creevy et al., 2008). Firms' power positions vis-à-vis other actors is a particular source of leverage for avoiding institutional rules.

The power of societal norms or of the state to enforce regulations varies substantially across nations. Compared to those in developed economies, individual firms in South America have considerably more power to avoid institutional pressures and state regulations. The importance of some MNCs and *Grupos* to the economy of smaller countries or regional economies allows these firms to negotiate with national, provincial, and municipal governments to obtain special conditions regarding labour, healthcare, and pension laws; financial subventions; grace periods; and the like. Moreover, the mobility of MNCs' operations places these firms in a powerful position to arbitrate institutional contexts to their advantage, while the relations between *Grupos* and government allow the former to influence and anticipate employment regulation and benefit from public support programmes.

Avoidance of institutional rules in South America is not only a result of firms' positions and strategies. Governments often lack structures, resources, and societal support that allow them to effectively enforce labour regulation (Anner, 2008; Schrank, 2009a; Ronconi, 2010, 2012). Additionally, potential bribing of labour inspectors,[2] frequent changes in health and safety regulations, special fiscal treatment of wage increases, atomized and unprofessional union structures, and lack of self-regulation enforced by employer associations provide further opportunities to shun institutional rules.

Given these differences, comparative institutional HRM researchers in South America need to assess the relative power of individual firms vis-à-vis the state in order to explain how and why they adopt one set of HRM practices or another; and in turn, variation in outcomes. The existing assumptions in the comparative institutional literature do not seem to fit well with the South American context. On the one hand, the literature assumes that in the liberal market model of the USA, a laissez-faire environment ensures that firms have a high degree of managerial discretion and strategic choice in the adoption and implementation of HRM practices. The coordinated market model, by contrast, assumes that there are dense networks of institutions – the state, employers' associations, unions, and works councils – that play a critical role in shaping HRM practices and their outcomes for employees, communities, and shareholders (e.g., Paauwe & Boselie, 2003; Brewster, 2007). The South American context shares characteristics of both models, as states, employers' organizations, and unions create institutions that shape HRM, similar to the coordinated market model. The combination of failure to enforce institutions and the avoidance strategies of individual firms, however, confers on some firms the managerial discretion that characterizes the liberal market model, while less powerful firms need to comply. Unlike the liberal and the coordinated models, some individual firms – in particular MNCs and *Grupos* – hold power positions that allow them to proactively shape institutions to their advantage, or create institutional pockets such as free trade zones, tax exemptions, or subsidies that fit their particular activities.

As a result, researchers of HRM in Latin America need to consider which mix of institutions (for example, capital, labour, product market rules) affect HRM strategies at the level of the individual firm, and whether those institutions provide a coherent or contradictory set of incentives for their activities. They also need to investigate the relative independence of the state from economic actors and its relative power to enforce regulations. Do firms simply manoeuvre to avoid institutional rules in a context of weak enforcement, or do they influence the process of rule-making itself? Lack of control and weak enforcement also imply a divergence between formal HRM policies and procedures and the HRM practices that managers actually apply. While the former may be drafted to comply 'on paper', the latter will reflect managerial discretion to the extent that the individual firm holds a position of power or is able to avoid institutional rules. Consequently, to increase the reliability of their findings, researchers need to undertake qualitative as well as quantitative data collection – especially at the workplace level – with employees to understand what they actually do, with line managers to capture their level of discretion in

---

[2]　According to Transparency International (2013), most Latin American countries have high rates of bribery of public officers. More specifically, Piore and Schrank (2008) show how the design of labour inspection systems in most Latin American countries opens a door to the bribing of lower-level inspectors.

the implementation of HRM practices, and with union representatives or other external sources.

Examining Formal and Informal Sector Practices

The comparative capitalisms literature focuses on the interactions between economic actors in a political economy, typically at the national level (Morgan, 2011). Again reflecting its origins in developed economies, this literature focuses on the formal sector; that is, labour markets that are regulated by formal national laws. Most South American countries, however, have highly segmented labour markets in which a major portion of the population works in the informal economy with little or no regulatory oversight. Schneider and Soskice (2009) argued that informal labour markets complement formal labour in Latin America. Likewise, Schneider and Karcher (2010) observed that companies operating in the formal sector often rely on informal sector suppliers and distributors as a means of creating a more flexible workforce that can be adjusted according to the economic cycle.

South American HRM research is typically conducted in the formal sector, without consideration of its connection with the informal sector. This is problematic because the informal sector in most South American countries is large, and the rules governing labour are different than those in the formal economy. In countries such as Bolivia or Paraguay, the informal economy is estimated to represent up to 70 per cent of gross domestic product (Vuletin, 2008). Moreover, research on social enterprise suggests that organizations that operate in South America's formal economy frequently act in the informal economy through foundations, company volunteer programmes, or charitable organizations (Ogliastri et al., 2006). Such initiatives are generally related to HRM initiatives and have effects on outcomes relevant to HRM research, such as commitment to the employer.

Due to the size of the informal sector and the possible blurring of boundaries between the formal and informal sectors, HRM scholars need to take into account whether the existence of the informal sector influences the HRM strategies and practices of firms in the formal sector. Studies that focus on the formal sector alone clearly produce findings that are less generalizable than findings obtained in developed economies where the formal sector is dominant. In particular, researchers need to avoid proposing broad notions of country-specific HRM models when their data collection is limited to MNCs, multilatinas, or *Grupos*.

Moreover, failure to acknowledge differences between the formal and informal sectors may lead scholars to simply apply the assumptions used in formal sector research to the informal economy. HRM research, for example, suggests that employers may improve organizational performance by investing in human resource practices that enhance the human capital in their firms (Combs et al., 2006; Wright et al., 2005). By contrast, in the South American informal sector, investments in training or information-sharing may lead to employee-initiated litigation. Courts have frequently ruled that by making such investments the employer acknowledges the existence of an employment relationship that should be formalized. As a result, the employer is required to make social security contributions and may have to pay penalties.

Also, the size of the informal sector in South American countries suggests that considerable variation exists within informal labour markets. Contrary to Schneider and

Soskice's (2009: 34) characterization of the informal workforce as having 'low or very low educational attainment' and being in 'badly-paid, insecure jobs with no possibility of training', Beneria (2001) and Maloney (2004) found that informal employment may represent a valid option for workers with higher skill levels. For example, commission-based stock trading and the offshoring of translation work and software development to freelancers in South America via websites, such as freelancer.com, provide informal but well-paid employment opportunities to skilled workers.

Finally, in many South American countries, the collective entitlements associated with formal employment do not necessarily provide the same security as privately acquired insurance and care arrangements. In a review of social security pensions and healthcare insurance reforms, Mesa-Lago (2008) related changing state regulation, controlled competition, and a lack of administrative efficiency to deficiencies in the sufficiency and quality of social security in South America, and observed limitations to the free choice of providers in many countries.

In sum, although informal and formal employment are closely intertwined in South America, HRM researchers need to acknowledge each type's particularities, be specific in their sample descriptions, and explain how and why their interconnections make a difference for HRM policies and practices. Formal employment diminished during the 1990s because of structural reform, market deregulation, and reductions of public employment due to budget cuts and privatization programmes (Pérez Sainz, 2000) and is only slowly returning to previous levels (ECLAC-ILO, 2013). Ignoring the characteristics of informal sector employment is likely to lead to biased research findings and a lack of understanding of the complexities of human resource management in South America.

Accounting for the Impact of Institutional Change on HRM

Comparative institutional research has been criticized for its inability to explain institutional change. Whereas researchers historically explained change in institutional arrangements as the result of crises or exogenous shocks, after which institutional actors reaccommodate (Hall & Taylor, 1996), more recent frameworks suggest that institutional change often occurs via incremental actions as a result of competition among the actors (Jackson & Deeg, 2006). Researchers increasingly acknowledge agency by individual actors in the definition and adoption of organizational structures and practices (e.g., Crouch, 2005; Streeck & Thelen, 2005). While these contributions represent theoretical progress, empirical support regarding the relative importance of different mechanisms of change is still thin.

The South American region features institutional change of both types. On the one hand, changes in the region fit the description of exogenous shocks rather well. Sudden changes in government resulting from military coups, foreign interventionism, and waves of democratization have been accompanied by radical shifts in economic policy and employment regulation. In less than a century, South American economies have shifted from being extractive export economies, to promoting industrialization through import substitution in the 1950s, to adopting neoliberal recipes for integration into the world economy in the 1980s and 1990s. During the 2000s, most South American countries have returned to higher levels of state intervention, combining exports of commodities to developed economies with intra-regional trade of industrial goods (UNCTAD, 2011).

At each stage, these dramatic shifts in economic development policy have created very different sets of institutional resources and constraints for firms operating in the region.

On the other hand, more gradual changes have also affected firms and how they manage their employees. Since the 1990s, MNCs have significantly increased their participation in South American economies (ECLAC, 2013), and numerous *Grupos* have pursued international expansion themselves and have become multilatinas (Casanova, 2009). South America is also increasingly integrated into global financial markets. Firms that have their origin in the region have obtained listings on stock exchanges in the USA, the United Kingdom, and within the region. MNCs, particularly from Spain, have listed Latin American subsidiaries on local and international stock exchanges, and sovereign wealth and private equity funds increasingly provide financing for business ventures in South America (Jiménez & Manuelito, 2011). Technological upgrading has become necessary for firms that produce for international markets, particularly those that are part of international value chains (e.g., McDermott & Corredoira, 2010). In many cases, the importance of MNCs in the transfer of technology has diminished as a result of local firms' access to capital markets and international technology vendors. Finally, despite a sharp educational divide, a small but growing segment of internationally trained professionals contributes to the adoption of global standards in production technologies and management practices.

In South America, institutional arrangements and firms' capabilities and resources continue to evolve as a result of the combination of exogenous shocks and more gradual changes in the region's political economy. In contrast to the stability and deep legacy of dense, interlocking institutions found in continental Europe, the assumption that institutions are stable or slow to change is questionable for South America. Rather, the continuous feedback loops between fragmented, evolving institutions and employment systems create a confusing landscape in which firms may experiment with a wide range of HRM practices while evading or ignoring formal institutional rules altogether.

This set of circumstances raises a number of research questions. For example, to what extent do the rules and regulations governing product, capital, and labour markets provide a coherent set of incentives for firms and their adoption of HRM policies? Which institutions are more stable and influential than others? How do firms cope with ongoing changes in market rules? What costs and benefits do they experience from institutional instability? In order to understand why firms adopt particular management practices, and in turn how they affect performance outcomes, scholars of HRM in Latin America need to carefully examine the changing institutional landscape in which firms operate and how that intersects with their HRM strategies. They need to offer qualitative, 'thick' descriptions, because our current knowledge of these processes is undeveloped. Likewise, our understanding of HRM in Latin America would benefit from longitudinal studies in which changes in HRM practices and their outcomes are related to changes in the institutional context.

Defining Organizational Performance

Comparative institutional perspectives suggest that managerial discretion is constrained by institutional rules to which organizations respond by adopting structures and practices that 'fit' the institutional context in which they operate. Consequently, researchers have focused primarily on explaining variation in firm behaviour and have paid less attention to performance outcomes. While the literature does offer the idea that countries have different 'comparative institutional advantages', enabling firms in each country to 'produce some kinds of goods more efficiently' than others (Hall & Soskice, 2001: 37), comparative institutional approaches are not specifically concerned with organizational performance. By contrast, linkages between HRM and performance outcomes – including employee behaviours and operational and financial performance – are the primary focus of HRM research (Batt & Banerjee, 2012).

Examining performance measures in Latin America-focused HRM research requires researchers to overcome several obstacles. First, the use of productivity measures such as sales per employee, or financial measures such as profitability, requires comparable accounting practices. Locally operating companies do not necessarily rely on the standards of generally accepted accounting principles (GAAP), and transfer pricing practices in MNCs may make local tax systems more relevant in determining profit than the organization's actual performance (Edwards & Kuruvilla, 2005). Second, Elvira and Davila (2005a) posited that in addition to their role in economic development, companies that operate in Latin America also play a role in social development. The implication for evaluations of performance is that the interests of stakeholders such as employees' families, local communities, and indigenous groups are juxtaposed to the financial outcomes associated with shareholder value creation. Davila and Elvira (2012) provide several examples of HRM departments that assume responsibilities related to enforcement of property rights, and providing protection and social security when national or local institutions fail.

This raises a series of questions for HRM researchers to pursue. How much variation, for example, exists in what firms define as the relevant performance goals that they seek? When performance goals conflict – between cost efficiencies, profitability, and social welfare or employment stability goals – how do firms manage those trade-offs? What role do laws and institutional norms play in shaping firm performance goals and how do these differ cross-nationally? To the extent that South American HRM departments do take into consideration the interests of a broad set of stakeholders, then failure to take this into account may lead to incomplete or biased findings. Researchers who transfer the North American interpretation of performance as exclusively shareholder value creation to the Latin American context may find that HRM–performance linkages are less evident. Cascio (2012) provided general indications to overcome the problems related to the equivalence of measures across contexts and measurement error in international HRM research. More specifically, researchers of HRM in South America need to describe what the performance construct entails for the organizations comprised in their samples, or rely on subjective measures of performance that may be transferred across contexts (e.g., Wall et al., 2004).

CONCLUSION

As South America's relevance to and interconnection with the world economy continues to grow, researchers and practitioners increasingly press for a more comprehensive understanding of HRM in the region. The adoption of cross-cultural approaches has yielded valuable insights. As Gelfand et al. (2006: 1225) stated: 'The importance of cross-cultural research cannot be underestimated; cross-cultural research is critical to ... helping organizations manage cultural differences as they continue to globalize'. At the same time, scholars are increasingly becoming aware of the inherent limitations of cross-cultural approaches and the need for alternative theoretical frameworks, ones that move beyond a 'Latin America management model' or country-level HRM profiles. Comparative institutional approaches identify specific contextual factors that condition managerial decision-making. They include product, labour, and capital market regulation; the relative enforcement capacity of the state; financing structures; education and training systems; inter-firm networks; and interaction patterns between actors in the political economy that shape the adoption of HRM practices and their outcomes.

The comparative institutional literature owes much of its development to the study of labour market institutions, in particular skill formation systems and industrial relations systems. However, different research questions, theory, and methodology pose challenges to the integration of comparative institutional perspectives into HRM research (Batt & Hermans, 2012), which in the case of South American HRM research are exacerbated by the lack of documentation of the region's institutional landscape (Morgan, 2011). Hence, the main contribution of this chapter is its identification of five issues that are common to comparative institutional approaches and that are particularly relevant to HRM research in the South American context. First, the widely divergent characteristics of organizations that operate in South America are associated with considerable varia-tion in approaches to HRM and suggest that the notion of a 'Latin America manage-ment model' may only be useful to distinguish the region from other regions. Second, in South America, institutional resources and constraints do not affect firms in a uniform fashion because firms vary substantially in their power and political influence and ability to affect rule-making as well as their ability to evade rules. Third, because of their origin in developed economies and their focus at the national level of analysis, comparative institutional approaches often fail to acknowledge the distinct institutional logic of the informal sector. Fourth, the frequency of changes in the political economy of South America poses a challenge to comparative institutional approaches to HRM research. Fifth, explaining organizational performance is a central focus of HRM research but not comparative institutional theory.

The South American region offers a wealth of opportunities for HRM research that scholars increasingly exploit. While insights derived from cross-cultural studies continue to enhance our understanding of HRM in the region, incorporating alternative theoreti-cal lenses to account for the effects of contextual determinants of HRM and its outcomes offers a promising avenue for future research. This type of integration involves considera-tion of the institutions that differentiate the South American region from other regions, and countries or sectors of economic activity within the region, while accounting for the characteristics of organizations and the strategies of their decision-makers over time. Contributions in this direction will not only inform the fields of international, compara-tive, and strategic HRM 'from the margins' (Alcadipani & Faria, 2014; Faria, 2010), but they will also support practitioners with responsibility for HRM in South America in their day-to-day decision-making.

REFERENCES

Ailon, G. 2008. Mirror, mirror on the wall: Culture's consequences in a value test of its own design. *Academy of Management Review*, 33(4): 885–904.

Alcadipani, R., & Faria, A. 2014. Fighting Latin American marginality in 'international' business. *Critical Perspectives on International Business*, 10: 86–99.

Almond, P., Edwards, T., Colling, T., et al. 2005. Unraveling home and host country effects: An investigation of the HR policies of an American multinational in four European countries. *Industrial Relations: A Journal of Economy and Society*, 44(2): 276–306.

Almond, P., & Ferner, A. 2006. *American Multinationals in Europe: Managing Employment Relations Across National Borders*. Oxford: Oxford University Press.

Amable, B. 2003. *The Diversity of Modern Capitalism*. Oxford: Oxford University Press.

America Economía. 2014. Ranking de las 500 mayores empresas de América Latina 2014. Retrieved from: http://rankings.americaeconomia.com/las-500-mayores-empresas-de-latinoamerica-2014/ranking-500-latam-451-500/.

Anner, M. 2008. Meeting the challenges of industrial restructuring: Labor reform and enforcement in Latin America. *Latin American Politics and Society*, 50(2): 33–65.

Anner, M.S. 2011. *Solidarity Transformed: Labor Responses to Globalization and Crisis in Latin America*. Ithaca, NY: Cornell University Press.

Baron, J.N., Burton, M.D., & Hannan, M.T. 1996. The road taken: Origins and evolution of employment systems in emerging companies. *Industrial and Corporate Change*, 5(2): 239–275.

Batt, R., & Banerjee, M. 2012. The scope and trajectory of strategic HR research: Evidence from American and British journals. *International Journal of Human Resource Management*, 23(9): 1739–1762.

Batt, R., & Hermans, M. 2012. Global human resource management: Bridging strategic and institutional perspectives. In J.J. Martocchio, A. Joshi, & H. Liao (eds), *Research in Personnel and Human Resources Management*: 1–52. Bingley: Emerald Group Publishing.

Benería, L. 2001. Shifting the risk: New employment patterns, informalization, and women's work. *International Journal of Politics, Culture, and Society*, 15(1): 27–53.

Bonelli, R. 1998. Las estrategias de los grandes grupos económicos brasileños. In W. Peres (ed.), *Grandes empresas y grupos indstriales Latinoamericanos*: 218–284. Mexico: DF: Siglo XXI Editores.

Brewster, C. 2007. Comparative HRM: European views and perspectives. *International Journal of Human Resource Management*, 18(5): 769–787.

Casanova, L. 2009. *Global Latinas: Emerging Multinationals from Latin America*. Basingstoke: Palgrave Macmillan.

Cascio, W.F. 2012. Methodological issues in international HR management research. *International Journal of Human Resource Management*, 23(12): 2532–2545.

Chudnovsky, D., Kosacoff, B., & López, A. 1999. *Las multinacionales latinoamericanas: sus estrategias en un mundo globalizado*. Buenos Aires: Fondo de Cultura Económica.

Combs, J., Liu, Y., Hall, A., & Ketchen, D. 2006. How much do high-performance work practices matter? A meta-analysis of their effects on organizational performance. *Personnel Psychology*, 59: 501–528.

Cook, M.L. 2007. *The Politics of Labor Reform in Latin America: Between Flexibility and Rights*. University Park, PA: Pennsylvania State University Press.

Crouch, C. 2005. *Capitalist Diversity and Change: Recombinant Governance and Institutional Entrepreneurs* Oxford, UK and New York, USA: Oxford University Press.

Crouch, C. 2012. National varieties of labour market exposure. In G. Morgan and R. Whitley (eds), *Capitalisms and Capitalism in the Twenty-First Century*: 90–117. New York: Oxford University Press.

Cuervo-Cazurra, A., Inkpen, A., Musacchio, A., & Ramaswamy, K. 2014. Governments as owners: State-owned multinational companies. *Journal of International Business Studies*, 45(8): 919–942.

Davila, A., & Elvira, M.M. 2012. Latin American HRM models. In C. Brewster and W. Mayrhofer (eds), *Handbook of Research on Comparative Human Resource Management*: 478–493. Cheltenham, UK and Northampton, MA, USA: Edward Elgar Publishing.

Davila, A., Elvira, M.M., Perez-Floriano, L.R., & Gonzalez, J.A. 2007. Risk, safety and culture in Brazil and Argentina: The case of TransInc Corporation. *International Journal of Manpower*, 28(5): 403–417.

Deeg, R., & Jackson, G. 2007. Towards a more dynamic theory of capitalist variety. *Socio-Economic Review*, 5(1): 149–179.

ECLAC. 2013. *Foreign Direct Investment in Latin America and the Caribbean*. Santiago de Chile: United Nations Publications.

ECLAC. 2014. *Foreign Direct Investment in Latin America and the Caribbean*. Santiago de Chile: United Nations Publications.

ECLAC-ILO. 2013. *The Employment Situation in Latin America and the Caribbean*. Santiago de Chile: United Nations Publications.

The Economist. 2011. Vale dumps its boss: Roger and out. 1 April. Retrieved from http://www.economist.com/blogs/schumpeter/2011/04/vale_dumps_its_boss.

Edwards, T., & Kuruvilla, S. 2005. International HRM: National business systems, organizational politics and the international division of labour in MNCs. *International Journal of Human Resource Management*, 16(1): 1–21.

Elvira, M.M., & Davila, A. 2005a. Emergent directions for human resource management research in Latin America. *International Journal of Human Resource Management*, 16(12): 2265–2282.

Elvira, M.M., & Davila, A. 2005b. Special research issue on human resource management in Latin America. *International Journal of Human Resource Management*, 16(12): 2164–2172.

Ernst, C., Berg, J., & Auer, P. 2007. Retos en materia de empleo y respuestas de política en Argentina, Brasil y México. *Revista de la CEPAL*(91): 95–110.

Faria, A. 2010. To, from and beyond the margins. *Management Research: Journal of the Iberoamerican Academy of Management*, 8(3): 221–233.

Feldmann, M. 2007. The origins of varieties of capitalism: Lessons from post-socialist transition in Estonia and Slovenia. In B. Hancke, M. Rhodes, and M. Thatcher (eds), *Beyond Varieties of Capitalism*: 328–350. New York: Oxford University Press.

Fenton-O'Creevy, M., Gooderham, P., & Nordhaug, O. 2008. Human resource management in US subsidiaries in Europe and Australia: Centralisation or autonomy?. *Journal of International Business Studies*, 39(1): 151–166.

Fischer, A.L., & de Albuquerque, L.G. 2005. Trends of the human resources management model in Brazilian companies: A forecast according to opinion leaders from the area. *International Journal of Human Resource Management*, 16(7): 1211–1227.

Fraile, L. 2009. Lessons from Latin America's neo-liberal experiment: An overview of labour and social policies since the 1980s. *International Labour Review*, 148(3): 215–233.

Galasso, E., Ravallion, M., & Salvia, A. 2004. Assisting the transition from workfare to work: A randomized experiment. *Industrial and Labor Relations Review*, 58(1): 128–142.

Garrido, C., & Peres, W. 1998. Las grandes empresas y grupos latinoamericanos en los anos noventa. In W. Peres (ed.), *Grandes empresas y grupos indstriales Latinoamericanos*: 13–80. Mexico DF: Siglo XXI Editores.

Gelfand, M.J., Nishii, L.H., & Raver, J.L. 2006. On the nature and importance of cultural tightness–looseness. *Journal of Applied Psychology*, 91(6): 1225–1244.

Gereffi, G. 2005. The global economy: Organization, governance and development. In R. Swedborg (ed.), *The Handbook of Economic Sociology*: 160–182. Princeton, NJ: Princeton University Press and Russell Sage Foundation.

Gerhart, B., & Fang, M. 2005. National culture and human resource management: Assumptions and evidence. *International Journal of Human Resource Management*, 16(6): 971–986.

Gomez-Samper, H., & Monteferrante, P. 2005. Managing people in Venezuela: Where are we headed?. *International Journal of Human Resource Management*, 16(12): 2254–2264.

Graen, G.B. 2006. In the eye of the beholder: Cross-cultural lesson in leadership from project GLOBE. A response viewed from the third culture bonding (TCB) model of cross-cultural leadership. *Academy of Management Perspectives*, 20(4): 95–101.

Hall, P., & Soskice, D. 2001. *Varieties of Capitalism: The Institutional Foundation of Comparative Advantage*. New York: Oxford University Press.

Hall, P.A., & Taylor, R.C. 1996. Political science and the three new institutionalisms. *Political Studies*, 44(5): 936–957.

Hofstede, G. 1980. *Culture's Consequences: International Differences in Work-Related Values*. Beverly Hills, CA: SAGE.

Hofstede, G. 1991. *Cultures and Organizations: Software of the Mind*. London: McGraw-Hill.

Hojman, D.E., & Pérez, G. 2005. Cultura nacional y cultura organizacional en tiempos de cambio: la experiencia chilena. *Academia. Revista Latinoamericana de Administración*, 35: 87–105.

Jackson, G., & Deeg, R. 2006. How many varieties of capitalism? Comparing the comparative institutional analyses of capitalist diversity. MPIfG Discussion Paper, Max-Planck-Institut für Gesellschaftsforschung, Köln, 06(2).

Jiménez, L.F., & Manuelito, S. 2011. Latin America: Financial systems and financing of investment. *CEPAL Review*, (103): 45–71.

Khanna, T., & Rivkin, J.W. 2006. Interorganizational ties and business group boundaries: Evidence from an emerging economy. *Organization Science*, 17(3): 333–352.

Khanna, T., & Yafeh, Y. 2007. Business groups in emerging markets: Paragons or parasites?. *Journal of Economic Literature*, 45: 331–372.

Khilji, S.E., & Wang, X. 2006. 'Intended'and 'implemented' HRM: The missing linchpin in strategic human resource management research. *International Journal of Human Resource Management*, 17(7): 1171–1189.

Kosacoff, B. 2000. *Corporate Strategies under Structural Adjustment in Argentina: Responses by Industrial Firms to a New Set of Uncertainties.* Basingstoke and London: Macmillan Press.

Laurent, A. 1986. The cross-cultural puzzle of international human resource management. *Human Resource Management*, 25(1): 91–102.

Lenartowicz, T., & Johnson, J.P. 2003. A cross-national assessment of the values of Latin America managers: Contrasting hues or shades of gray?. *Journal of International Business Studies*, 34: 266–294.

Lepak, D.P., & Snell, S.A. 2002. Examining the human resource architecture: The relationships among human capital, employment, and human resource configurations. *Journal of Management*, 28(4): 517–543.

Lertxundi, A. 2007. Transfer of HRM practices to subsidiaries: Importance of the efficiency of the HRM system. *Management Research: Journal of the Iberoamerican Academy of Management*, 6(1): 63–73.

Lertxundi, A., & Landeta, J. 2011. The moderating effect of cultural context in the relation between HPWS and performance: an exploratory study in Spanish multinational companies. *International Journal of Human Resource Management*, 22(18): 3949–3967.

Locke, R., Amengual, M., & Mangla, A. 2009. Virtue out of necessity? Compliance, commitment, and the improvement of labor conditions in global supply chains. *Politics and Society*, 37(3): 319–351.

Maloney, W.F. 2004. Informality revisited. *World Development*, 32(7): 1159–1178.

Manacorda, M., Sánchez-Páramo, C., & Schady, N. 2010. Changes in returns to education in Latin America: The role of demand and supply of skills. *Industrial and Labor Relations Review*, 63(2): 307–326.

McDermott, G.A., & Corredoira, R.A. 2010. Network composition, collaborative ties, and upgrading in emerging-market firms: Lessons from the Argentine autoparts sector. *Journal of International Business Studies*, 41(2): 308–329.

McSweeney, B. 2002. Hofstede's model of national cultural differences and their consequences: A triumph of faith-a failure of analysis. *Human Relations*, 55(1): 89–118.

Mesa-Lago, C. 2008. *Reassembling Social Security: A Survey of Pensions and Health Care Reforms in Latin America.* Oxford: Oxford University Press and Pan-American Health Organization.

Meyer, K.E. 2004. Perspectives on multinational enterprises in emerging economies. *Journal of International Business Studies*, 35(4): 259–276.

Morgan, G. 2011. Comparative capitalisms: A framework for the analysis of emerging and developing economies. *International Studies of Management and Organization*, 41(1): 12–34.

Nicholls-Nixon, C.L., Castilla, J.A.D., Garcia, J.S., & Pesquera, M.R. 2011. Latin America management research: Review, synthesis, and extension. *Journal of Management*, 37(4): 1178–1227.

Nishii, L.H., Lepak, D.P., & Schneider, B. 2008. Employee attributions of the 'why' of HR practices: Their effects on employee attitudes and behaviors, and customer satisfaction. *Personnel Psychology*, 61(3): 503–545.

Ogliastri, E., Gutierrez, R., Reficco, E., & Austin, J. 2006. *Effective Management of Social Enterprises: Lessons from Businesses and Civil Society Organizations in Iberoamerica.* Cambridge, MA: Harvard University Press.

Paauwe, J., & Boselie, P. 2003. Challenging 'strategic HRM' and the relevance of the institutional setting. *Human Resource Management Journal*, 13(3): 56–70.

Perez Arrau, G., Eades, E., & Wilson, J. 2012. Managing human resources in the Latin American context: The case of Chile. *International Journal of Human Resource Management*, 23(15): 3133–3150.

Perez-Floriano, L.R., & Gonzalez, J.A. 2007. Risk, safety and culture in Brazil and Argentina: The case of TransInc Corporation. *International Journal of Manpower*, 28: 403–417.

Pérez Sainz, J.P. 2000. Labor market transformation in Latin America during the 1990s: Some analytical remarks. Working Paper, FLACSO, Costa Rica.

Piore, M.J., & Schrank, A. 2008. Toward managed flexibility: The revival of labour inspection in the Latin world. *International Labour Review*, 147(1): 1–23.

Purcell, J., & Hutchinson, S. 2007. Front-line managers as agents in the HRM–performance causal chain: Theory, analysis and evidence. *Human Resource Management Journal*, 17(1): 3–20.

Rodrigues, I., & Sbragia, R. 2013. The cultural challenges of managing global project teams: A study of Brazilian multinationals. *Journal of Technology Management and Innovation*, 8: 38–52.

Rodriguez, D., & Rios, R. 2007. Latent premises of labor contracts: Paternalism and productivity. Two cases from the banking industry in Chile. *International Journal of Manpower*, 28(5): 354–368.

Ronconi, L. 2010. Enforcement and compliance with labor regulations in Argentina. *Industrial and Labor Relations Review*, 63(4): 719–736.

Ronconi, L. 2012. Globalization, domestic institutions, and enforcement of labor law: Evidence from Latin America. *Industrial Relations: A Journal of Economy and Society*, 51(1): 89–105.

Ruiz Caro, A. 2002. El proceso de privatizaciones en el Perú durante el período 1991–2002. Documento 22, Santiago de Chile: Instituto Latinoamericano y del Caribe de Planificación Económica y Social – ILPES.

Ruiz-Gutierrez, J.A., Murphy Jr, E.F., Greenwood, R.A., et al. 2012. Work, family and values in four Latin-American countries. *Management Research: Journal of the Iberoamerican Academy of Management*, 10(1): 29–42.

Sanabria, H. 2007. *The Anthropology of Latin America and the Caribbean.* Boston, MA: Pearson Allyn & Bacon.

Santiago Castro, M., Brown, C.J., & Báez-Díaz, A. 2009. Prácticas de gobierno corporativo en América Latina. *Academia. Revista Latinoamericana de Administración*, 43: 26–40.

Sargent, J. 2005. Large firms and business groups in Latin America: Towards a theory based, contextually relevant research agenda. *Latin American Business Review*, 6(2): 39–66.

Schneider, B.R. 2008. *Competing Capitalisms: Liberal, Coordinated, Network and Hierarchical Varieties.* Evanston, IL: Northwestern University.

Schneider, B.R. 2009. Hierarchical market economies and varieties of capitalism in Latin America. *Journal of Latin American Studies*, 41(03): 553–575.

Schneider, B.R. 2013. *Hierarchical Capitalism in Latin America.* New York: Cambridge University Press.

Schneider, B.R., & Karcher, S. 2010. Complementarities and continuities in the political economy of labour markets in Latin America. *Socio-Economic Review*, 8(4): 623–651.

Schneider, B.R., & Soskice, D. 2009. Inequality in developed countries and Latin America: coordinated, liberal and hierarchical systems. *Economy and Society*, 38(1): 17–52.

Schrank, A. 2009a. Professionalization and probity in a patrimonial state: Labor inspectors in the Dominican Republic. *Latin American Politics and Society*, 51(2): 91–115.

Schrank, A. 2009b. Understanding Latin American political economy: Varieties of capitalism or fiscal sociology?. *Economy and Society*, 38(1): 53–61.

Schuler, R.S., Dowling, P.J., & Cieri, H.D. 1993. An integrative framework of strategic international human resource management. *International Journal of Human Resource Management*, 4(4): 717–764.

Streeck, W., & Thelen, K. 2005. *Beyond Continuity: Institutional Change in Advanced Political Economies.* Oxford: Oxford University Press.

Sully de Luque, M.F., & Arbaiza, L.A. 2005. The complexity of managing human resources in Peru. *International Journal of Human Resource Management*, 16(12): 2237–2253.

Tanure, B., Barcellos, E.P., & Fleury, M.T.L. 2009. Psychic distance and the challenges of expatriation from Brazil. *International Journal of Human Resource Management*, 20(5): 1039–1055.

Tanure, B., & Duarte, R.G. 2005. Leveraging competitiveness upon national cultural traits: The management of people in Brazilian companies. *International Journal of Human Resource Management*, 16(12): 2201–2217.

Tonelli, M.J. 2003. Produção Acadêmica em Recursos Humanos no Brasil: 1991–2000. *RAE – Revista de Administração de Empresas*, 43: 105–122.

Transparency International. 2013. *Global Corruption Barometer.* Berlin: Transparency International.

Tsui, A.S., Pearce, J.L., Porter, L.W., & Tripoli, A.M. 1997. Alternative approaches to the employee–organization relationship: Does investment in employees pay off? *Academy of Management Journal*, 40(5): 1089–1121.

UNCTAD. 2011. *World Investment Report 2011: Non-Equity Modes of International Production and Investment.* New York: United Nations.

Varela, O.E., Esqueda, S., & Perez, O. 2009. Birds of a feather? A test of cultural homogeneity among a sample of Latin American countries. *Management Research: Journal of the Iberoamerican Academy of Management*, 7(1): 49–59.

Vuletin, G. 2008. Measuring the informal economy in Latin America and the Caribbean. IMF Working Paper. Washington, DC: International Monetary Fund.

Wall, T.D., Michie, J., Patterson, M., et al. 2004. On the validity of subjective measures of company performance. *Personnel Psychology*, 57(1): 95–118.

Whitley, R. 1999. *Divergent Capitalisms: The Social Structuring and Change of Business Systems.* Oxford: Oxford University Press.

Witt, A.M., & Redding, G. 2014. *The Oxford Handbook of Asian Business Systems.* Oxford: Oxford University Press.

Wright, P.M., Gardner, T.M., Moynihan, L.M., & Allen, M.R. 2005. The relationship between HR practices and firm performance: Examining causal order. *Personnel Psychology*, 58(2): 409–446.

24. HRM in Western Europe: differences without, differences within

Chris Brewster, Wolfgang Mayrhofer, and Paul Sparrow

INTRODUCTION

This chapter introduces and explores human resource management (HRM) in Western Europe (Central and Eastern Europe are covered in Chapter 25 of this volume). We first address what it is that distinguishes HRM in Western Europe from that in other parts of the world. We explain the nature of HRM in Western Europe by highlighting the importance of six factors in particular: a unique political, social, and economic landscape; a stakeholder-centred approach; the heightened role of the state; the importance of social welfare; complex patterns of ownership; traditions of employee involvement and employee representation. Then the chapter successively examines some of the differences within Europe using an ever-tighter focus. We examine differences between a variety of proposed clusters of European countries, exploring in turn categorisations based on HRM practices, cultural differences, social welfare groupings, and institutional factors such as legislation and politics, and theories of synthetic comparative capitalisms. Finally, we move to discussion about HRM in Western Europe beyond consideration of country clusters. Despite taking a Western European frame, there remain differences between individual European countries, geographical differences within certain countries at regional level, and also now emerging institutional arrangements in the context of the changing economic geography of West European firms.

The chapter makes it clear that given the enormous diversity within Europe, it is not an easy task to distinguish HRM in Western Europe from that in other parts of the world whilst simultaneously recognising the myriad variations within the continent. We have elsewhere (Brewster, 1995; Brewster & Mayrhofer, 2011) used a telescope analogy. The focus can be adjusted to show more or less detail, either looking for a broader picture or seeking a close-up. As with a telescope, neither the broader picture nor the close-up is incorrect or inaccurate, it is just that each shows different kinds of detail and allows different kinds of conclusions to be drawn. Thus, what looks broadly similar in the big picture may on closer inspection reveal significant variations, and what looks to be wholly distinct to an insider may to an outsider look like minor variations on a common theme. Within this analogy, we first turn to the 'big picture' and look at Western Europe's specific characteristics and their relevance for HRM.

WESTERN EUROPE: A SPECIFIC CONTEXT FOR HRM

Western Europe shares a number of features with other developed country or regions, what have been called the WEIRD countries (Henrich et al., 2010), denoting the Western, educated, industrialised, rich, democratic states, where most HRM research has been conducted and which have dominated economic and international business research for many years (Ebenau, 2015). These developed European countries are usually located in regions covering different climate zones, and their wealth has come partly from exploiting their natural resources. They are more or less well established, have long histories and, with some notable exceptions, have had established systems of government that have worked in broadly the same way for many years. They tend to be regions where the native population is not self-reproducing, so that any future population growth will come mainly from immigration. Of course, these countries' wealth varies, but as a broad generalisation, they are amongst the richest countries in the world. Partly as a result, these are regions with working and more or less effective institutions – social security systems, educational possibilities with literate populations, and good health systems – though these systems are generally under pressure from a political consensus that sees the government role as needing to be reduced.

For most of the world, these common features are unusual (see other chapters in this book covering, for example, the Indian subcontinent and South-East Asia). Many countries in the world have only comparatively recently established their borders, as is the case for the Central and Eastern European countries, for example; are much poorer; have no established, or only recently established, systems of government or have contested systems where the contest is about the type of system that the country should have rather than who should control it; have in recent memory been exploited by other countries; have few literate people in the population; have rapidly growing populations and/or extensive emigration; and have no or weak social security or health systems. The lines of connection and causation between these factors are much debated, but the effect is to establish a very different context for HRM.

However, apart from the distinction between the WEIRD and other regions and countries, there are also a number of significant features within the WEIRD countries that distinguish the context of HRM in Western Europe specifically from those found in North America or Japan. Amongst features that will impact upon HRM we note particularly a unique political, social, and economic landscape; a stakeholder, rather than shareholder, approach to business; the role of the state as a key stakeholder, and a provider of social welfare, and as an employer; patterns of ownership; and the role of employee representation for that particular group of stakeholders. Though none of these elements is unique, and all of them are found in other regions, the combination of all these factors in Europe leads to a conceptual distinction and specific consequences for HRM. We discuss each of these in turn.

Unique Political, Social, and Economic Landscape

The Council of Europe covers 47 nation states; 28 of those states are members of the European Union (EU), with half a dozen others connected with it, which means that they have agreed to accept continent-wide legislation, even if their governments may not have voted for it. Other states are wanting to join and, as of 2017, the United Kingdom (UK) is committed to leaving the EU. Whilst these states have much in common, Europe is heterogeneous: out of roughly 7000 indigenous languages worldwide, about 225 are spoken across Europe; just the countries in membership of the EU have more than 60 indigenous regional or minority language communities, and the EU itself has 23 official languages. This was understood as an issue in the earliest days of comparative study of European HRM. For Bournois (1992) it made more sense to talk about HRM in Europe rather than European HRM, as every European country had a different historical and legal inheritance, and writers such as Lawrence (1992) argued that HRM as a concept had been grafted onto policy and practice debates in Europe, rather than having taken root.

Covering roughly the same area as the United States of America (USA), a centuries-old and often belligerent relationship between European countries creates a tradition of tension and rivalry as well as cooperation, particularly between the large European states such as the UK, France, Spain, Germany, and Italy, but strongly felt in many of the smaller ones too. Some of the states are centralised and have coherent governmental systems (UK, France) but in some of the larger countries (Spain, Germany) there are significant linguistic, religious, and cultural regional variations. These can be found within some of the smaller countries also, home to different ethnic groups, for example the Walloons and the Flemish in Belgium, and Hungarian minorities in Slovakia and Romania. Tensions between these within-state groupings are epitomised by relatively recent conflicts in Northern Ireland, Cyprus, Central and Eastern Europe, and the Basque region. World Bank Data from 2015 show that economically, countries with a comparatively high gross domestic product (GDP) per person such as France (US$39,631) or the UK (US$41,458) are a stark contrast to countries such as Greece (US$20,270) or Portugal (US$20,470).

Despite this heterogeneity, there is much that is shared. Again, from the beginnings of the field, distinctive characteristics were considered to be more restricted employer autonomy, less stress on market processes, less emphasis on the individual and more on the group, more emphasis on workers rather than managers, an increased role of social partners, and higher levels of government intervention in support of many areas of HRM (Pieper, 1990b; Guest, 1990; Ferner & Hyman, 1992; Hofstede, 1993).

In Western Europe the EU – the world's largest political entity and common market – plays a dominant role, with all Western European countries being either part of it or closely linked to it. The EU's 'four freedoms' – of movement of goods, persons, services, and capital – are a good example of this, although some of these pillars, in particular the free movement of persons, have recently been politically contested. These four freedoms have had a substantial impact on the economy of these countries and therefore indirectly on the management of people within organisations in Western Europe, and we return to this issue below, but the EU's 'cornerstones' have direct implications for HRM too. For example, the free movement of persons creates ample options for labour market mobility and affects HRM directly, especially in areas such as recruitment, career planning, and compensation. The EU also makes deliberate efforts to invest in the human capital available for organisations through programmes that support the exchange of people within Europe and create informal networks of understanding and contacts, for example through programmes such as Erasmus+, targeting education and training across Europe.

Importance of a Stakeholder-Centred Approach

The notion of HRM was invented in the USA, replacing personnel administration and personnel management both as a concept and as a label. The first books on the subject were published in the USA in the 1980s, and one of these seminal texts by Beer et al. (1984)

had a 'map of the HRM territory' that included contextual factors (or 'situational factors' as they termed them) and provided a key role for different stakeholders. However, even from the early days, HRM research in the USA was characterised by a strong emphasis on the interests of the owners of the business, following the other major text produced at the same time (Fombrun et al., 1984). The assumption here was that the purpose of HRM is to improve the operation of the organisation, with the ultimate aim of increasing organisational performance, as judged by its impact on the organisation's declared corporate strategy, its profits, customers, or its shareholders (see, e.g., Huselid, 1995; Ulrich, 1989; Becker & Gerhart, 1996; Becker et al., 1997). The legal pre-eminence of shareholders and owners in the USA may be a myth (Stout, 2012), but it is a powerful one.

Much of this was copied in HRM research in Europe, but here there was also a strong focus on a range of other stakeholders beyond the interests of shareholders. This reflected the stronger role of stakeholders in practice. In Europe many constitutions and many legal systems, certainly those within the EU, give significant rights in businesses to a range of other stakeholders (Beer et al., 2015). Again, from the earliest mapping of similarities and differences between European countries, Brewster and Hegewisch (1993: 3) concluded:

> regional patterns can be discerned . . . [and] it is clear from a global perspective [that] Europe has a coherence of its own, and a distinctiveness from other major blocs . . . found in, for example, decentralisation and devolvement, pay flexibility, the attention paid to training and development, in industrial relations and employee communications and the growth of flexible working patterns and perhaps most of all in the development of a social policy by Europe's unique supra-national level of government, the European Community.

As a result, Western Europeans were at the forefront of criticism of the rhetoric of HRM (for critical views see, for instance, Guest, 1990; Legge, 2005). In Western Europe the academic field of human resource management tended to develop from the field of industrial relations. As trade union membership and influence declined in many countries over the past quarter of a century (Katz & Darbishire, 2000; Rigby et al., 2004), academics in those disciplines tended to turn towards the management side of the topic and to embrace HRM. One effect, as noted in Chapter 1 in this volume, has been that the industrial relations tradition of assumptions of national embeddedness and awareness of national differences was transferred to human resource management, leading in turn to the development of work on comparative HRM.

The stakeholder debate bundles and conceptualises this view (Beer et al., 2015). Instead of purely looking at shareholders' interests, the stakeholder view acknowledges the greater array of actors within and outside the organisation that are of relevance for survival as well as for economic success. Stakeholders have an interest in the organisation, ranging from keeping the organisation up and running to having an ethically 'clean' entity or showing good corporate citizenship. Agency theory (for an overview, see Eisenhardt, 1989) already acknowledges two groups with potentially conflicting interests: owners (shareholders) and managers. A further enlargement identifies additional groups which have a legitimate stake in the organisation, for example, employees, customers, trade unions, creditors, non-governmental organisations, and governments. The basic argument of the stakeholder approach (Freeman et al., 2010; for a European angle, see Bonnafous-Boucher & Pesqueux, 2005) is that such groups have a collective interest in the organisation; for example, regarding decisions about employment, keeping the environment clean, or acting as a good corporate citizen in the local environment.

In Western Europe there are political debates and controversies about these concepts, though rarely couched as explicitly as here, but by and large the stakeholder concept is strong. In HRM the stakeholder approach is widespread, even if it takes different forms in different countries. Going beyond owners and managers, HRM has to take into account many other groups: not only employees and their representative bodies such as works councils or trade unions (see below) but also, for example, the local community, environmental pressure groups, political parties, or the government. As a consequence, the strategic and goal orientation of HRM in Europe has a different, more diverse, focus. Hardly surprisingly, the partly conflicting interests of various stakeholders – for example, management, trade unions, works councils, local politicians – make goal planning and achievement a tricky business.

Role of the State

Compared to the USA, the state in Europe plays a crucial role in relation to HRM and the conditions under which it operates. Arguably, the density of regulations with regard to a broad variety of work-related topics such as pay levels, working hours, labour protection, co-determination, and social security are markedly different on the opposite sides of the Atlantic. Hence, the verdict by Pieper nearly three decades ago still seems to remain an accurate assessment: 'The major difference between HRM in the US and in Western Europe is the degree to which [HRM] is influenced and determined by State regulations. Companies have a narrower scope of choice in regard to personnel management than in the United States' (Pieper, 1990a: 8).

While in the USA 'freeing business from outside interference' is arguably a broadly approved objective, this is contested in most countries in Europe. True, over the past decades, deregulation has increased. For example, '[in] the period from the mid 1980s until 2005 the German labour market was characterised by continual deregulation' (Walwei, 2015: 13). Yet, this occurred alongside some tendencies for re-regulation such as the introduction of minimum wages in Germany.

Overall, in Western Europe, governments – and in particular the EU as a supranational institution – heavily influence what goes on within organisations. This relates not only to labour law and activities in research and development, for example, through the various framework programmes of the EU, but also to the various initiatives directly related to the labour market and the qualification profile of employees. For example, the Erasmus+ Programme supports 'efforts to efficiently use the potential of Europe's talent and social assets in a lifelong learning perspective, linking support to formal, non-formal and informal learning throughout the education, training and youth fields' (European Commission, 2016: 7).

For HRM, this not only points towards a heightened sensitivity required when operating within such a context in order not to violate the respective regulations, but it also provides some leverage for HRM activities. For example, the initiatives related to vocational education and training, and the opportunities for joint collaboration between academic institutions and practitioners, adds to the potential effectiveness of an organisation's HRM by tapping into resources going beyond the organisation itself.

Social Welfare

The five decades to 2010 saw a continuous increase in the amount of public social expenditure as a percentage of GDP in all the Organisation for Economic Co-operation and Development (OECD) countries, though this may be changing. By and large, the amount has nearly tripled since 1960. Relatively speaking, EU countries spend about 50 per cent more on social issues than the USA. In concrete figures, the proportion rose in the USA from about 7 per cent in 1960 to close to 20 per cent in 2014; for EU-21 countries (the 21 member states of the European Union before the accessions of May 2004) the respective figures are 10 per cent and 30 per cent. For comparison, Japan since the mid-1990s has been somewhere between the USA and the EU, after starting from about 4 per cent in 1960 (OECD, 2014).

A closer look reveals, however, that there are quite substantial differences even within Western Europe. This not only refers to the amount of spending on social welfare, where at the one end one can find countries such as France, Finland, Belgium, and Denmark which spend more than 30 per cent of their GDP as public social expenditure, while Switzerland and Ireland are close to 20 per cent (Adema et al., 2014). It also shows that there are fundamental differences in terms of the basic approaches. Following the welfare state typology of Esping-Andersen (1990) and later works in this tradition, one can differentiate between four regimes of welfare based on the respective interplay between public and private social security institutions and the degree of 'de-commodification' and stratification (Onaran & Bösch, 2010): the social democratic (Sweden, Denmark, Finland and Norway); the conservative (Germany, France, Austria, Belgium, Italy, Netherlands, and Luxembourg), the liberal (United Kingdom, Ireland, and USA), and the southern (for example, Greece, Italy, Spain, and Portugal).

For HRM in Western Europe, these differences compared to other regions of the triad and within Europe are of great importance. Different levels of availability of support in areas such as old age, incapacity-related benefits, health, family, active labour market programmes, unemployment, and housing – typical areas that social expenditure goes to – influence what type of leeway HRM has in terms of employment policies, incentive structures, or employer branding, to name just a few.

Patterns of Ownership

Patterns of ownership also reveal some unique characteristics across Western Europe. As can be seen from Figure 24.1, in Europe, government and non-financial organisations and organisations representing householders continue to maintain a significant share of the ownership of businesses.

In Western Europe there are a lot of small businesses, whilst in Southern Europe there are a lot of family-owned or family-run businesses. Notably, Western Europe also has a much bigger public sector, especially but not just in the Nordic countries, and a far larger publicly owned sector than any other non-communist or developed world region. This creates complex patterns of ownership. For example, 'privately owned' Lufthansa is mainly owned by the German state, the German railways, and German banks; and some of these firms in turn have a significant state shareholding. Terminology is important here, so for example stock market companies are known as 'publicly owned enterprises'. Plus there is the role of the state in supporting even more typical private companies in a variety of ways.

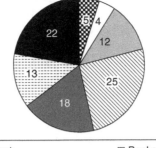

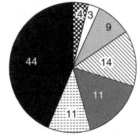

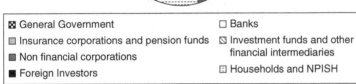

Source: Davydof et al. (2013).

Figure 24.1   The ownership structure of EU listed corporations in 2011

However, a number of trends are making it less easy to understand ownership patterns. The International Monetary Fund (IMF) notes, for example, that there is increasing use by governments of market mechanisms and private sector provision of public services, and with greater use of private sector management techniques in the public sector, or private sector provision of public goods: 'Boundary problems within the public sector are just as acute as those between the public and private sectors, mainly because of ambiguities in distinguishing "market" from "nonmarket" activities' (Lienert, 2009: 1).

As questions are being raised about ownership of the functions that are carried out, and about who controls these functions, the implication is that comparative analysis needs to capture questions about ownership and networks. Corporate ownership and control cannot be studied without reference to the economic context in which they have developed. The recent banking crises in Italy and Germany signal some of the complexities in unravelling complex patterns of ownership. For example, the 2016 crisis at Deutsche Bank and subsequent monitoring revealed that, as of June 2017 using NASDAQ data, over 17 per cent of Deutsche Bank was owned by 244 other institutions, with leading holders including Goldman Sachs Group, Vanguard Group, Norges Bank, JP Morgan Chase, HSBC Holdings, and Credit Agricole SA. Influence had moved to a group of Anglo-American investment bankers a decade earlier. In 2016 the IMF estimated that Deutsche Bank's $75 trillion exposure to future derivatives is 20 times greater than German GDP, whilst European Central Bank data compiled by Bloomberg showed that Germany has the largest volume of deposits in the EU (€3.37 trillion, compared to €2.22 trillion in France and €1.64 trillion in Italy), largely as a result of its export surpluses. In turn there is a web of cross-holdings and lending across more than 1400 savings and co-operative banks. It is the relative health of this distributed network, and not the apparent ownership, that impacts upon patterns of saving. The top five German banks own only 31 per cent of total banking assets in Germany; compared to the more centralised ownership pattern in, for example, the Netherlands, where the top five banks own 85 per cent of Dutch banking assets. Yet, in the Italian banking crisis, a different pattern of ownership is being revealed. Unicredit, for example, owns Hypovereinsbank, which is Germany's fourth- or fifth-largest bank. Banca Nazionale del Lavoro, Italy's eighth-largest lender, is owned by BNP Paribas, France's biggest bank; while Cariparma, the country's eleventh-largest lender, is owned by France's Credit Agricole. However, banking debt in Italy is widely held by individual savers, rather than institutional investors as seen in other European banking systems.

These patterns of ownership have indirect and also direct effects on HRM. Indirectly, business objectives and strategies are likely to be different for different owners. Thus, government ownership might include objectives of acting as an exemplar in employment policies or focusing on social value; bank ownership may preference long-term survival over short-term gains; and private sector ownership is more likely to be focused on immediate profits and dividends. Directly, a focus on the short term is likely to lead to pressure to extract value: a reduction in training, an increase in redundancies, and increased pressure of work. This is a typical pattern for private equity investments from the UK, in direct contrast to French private equity investments which seem to focus on increasing value rather than extracting it (Guery et al., 2017). These different patterns of ownership will have direct and indirect influences on HRM. Thus, extracting value from a company means staff job losses, holding down of salaries, and reduction or avoidance of training. Increasing the value of the company means the opposite: hiring in good-quality staff on decent salaries and investing in them. And there are different patterns of HRM in the public sector and in not-for-profit organisations.

Employee Involvement and Employee Representation

Paauwe and Boselie (2007) point towards the influence of legislation and the government in Europe. This is especially visible with regard to employees' rights, their involvement in organisational decision-making, and employee representation. Various legal regulations contained in labour law, arguably in particular the role of the trade unions and various forms of co-determination, make Europe a unique context for HRM. At the country level, in many Western European countries the rights for employees to be involved, and the centrality of trade unions for crucial organisational decisions such as terminating people's employment or closing factories, go far beyond the North American model.

For example, in the German-language countries, co-determination is comparatively strong and legally regulated. Therefore, it is not only works councils and trade unions that play a role at the organisational level. Under specific circumstances, employee representatives are part of the supervisory board and have a strong vote when appointing a member of the board of directors who is responsible for labour issues within the company. In countries such as the Netherlands, Denmark, and most famously, Germany, organisations are required to have two-tier management boards, with employees having the right to be represented on the more senior supervisory board. In European Union countries the law requires the establishment of employee representation committees in all organisations except the smallest. These arrangements give considerable (legally backed) power to the employee representatives.

Trade unions (for a broader view, see Chapter 11 in this volume) usually have a comparatively strong position in Europe. Independent trade unions have a strong tradition, and while country differences certainly exist, the degree of unionisation in Western Europe is considerable when compared to other OECD countries and to the USA and Japan (see Figure 24.2). Trade union membership in the Nordic countries is so high that most managers are also members of the union movement. The consequence is that the unions'

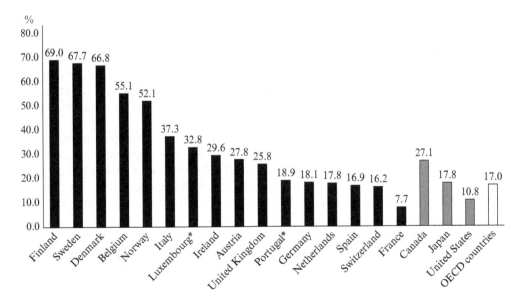

Source: OECD.STAT 2016.

Figure 24.2   Trade union density in Western Europe, 2013

views are taken into account at an early stage and the unions, understanding this, try to operate cooperatively with the employers.

Beyond the national level, the European Union has brought about considerable change not only through its Social Charter, but also with regard to creating supranational units providing the legal basis for the involvement of employees in organisational decisions. A prominent example is the introduction of European Works Councils in 1996, and the adoption of the EU Directive on the European Company (Societas Europaea, SE) five years later which, among others, also includes some regulations for establishing a Works Council at the European level. 'Both bodies for the transnational information and consultation of employees draw upon the same basic model, namely, giving information and consultation rights on transnational issues to elected employee representatives' (De Spiegelaere & Jagodzinski, 2015: 8). After a steady growth since their introduction, close to 1086 European Works Councils and SE Works Councils were operating in 2015 (see Figure 24.3).

This European model is under some challenge, particularly from the European Courts, which have tended to privilege individual rights above collective ones (Brewster et al., forthcoming), and from the more right-wing politicians who now form the government in many EU countries (Currie & Teague, 2016). Nevertheless, in comparison to most other parts of the world there is in Western Europe a broadly shared understanding that businesses need to be controlled, and to treat their employees in a socially responsible way. Consequently, key questions in HRM are about communication and consultation with the workforce. Employee representation, or 'voice' (Hirschman, 1970), may take individual or collective forms. The collective forms include both union-centred and non-union mechanisms. In Western Europe, these tend to be complementary (Brewster et al., 2007b). There is now clear evidence that organisations across the Continent are increasing the amount of communication and consultation in which they involve those employees (Mayrhofer et al., 2004; Mayrhofer et al., 2011) with the European North stronger in this area. The EU's Works Council Directive and the desire of organisations to use as many communications channels as possible has ensured that although there has been a growth in the use of individual channels of communication, the collective channels are still widely used amongst larger employers at least.

These contextual specifics with regard to the involvement of employees and their representatives provide a challenge in particular to managers and organisations used to the North American model of organisations and HRM. In contrast to the implicit assumption that the state has the responsibility, by and large, to create a context which supports managerial autonomy as much as possible, the European situation is different. For HRM, this creates a situation where it is good business logic and not a violation of some kind of strategic HRM prerequisite to invest in legal compliance, and to follow a more long-term course of action with good relationships to stakeholders besides shareholders, such as local communities, trade unions, and work councils. The business requirement of legitimacy (Palazzo & Scherer, 2006; Kostova et al., 2008) means that effective HRM involves adapting to these logics.

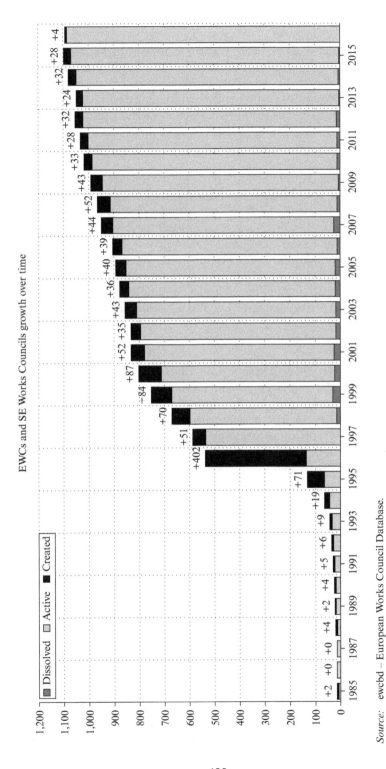

EWCs and SE Works Councils growth over time

Source: ewcbd – European Works Council Database.

Figure 24.3   Development of European Works Councils and SE Works Councils

COUNTRY CLUSTERS

Having explained the nature of HRM in Western Europe by highlighting the importance of a range of factors, we now discuss the question of country clusters within Western Europe. A number of approaches have been proposed to reduce the heterogeneity within Western Europe analytically. We briefly explore in turn the categorisations based on HRM practices, cultural differences, and institutional factors such as legislation and politics and how these have been connected through theories of synthetic comparative capitalisms.

HRM Practices

The generalisations made so far have not been able to avoid noting that there are many variations within Europe. At the level of organisational practices, in particular of HRM practices, there are a number of efforts to group European countries according to the way they conduct HRM. Thus researchers have distinguished HRM in Northern Europe from that found in Southern Europe (Apospori et al., 2008; Brewster & Larsen, 2000). They have also linked differences in HRM to major cultural groupings within Europe (see Chapter 3 in this volume), finding 'three clusters: a Latin cluster [which includes Spain, Italy, France]; a central European cluster . . . and a Nordic cluster' (Filella, 1991: 14).

Cultural Categories

Indeed, various cultural concepts have the aim of clustering similar countries together. Their basic argument, by and large, is quite similar. Assuming the national culture has certain characteristics, they try to classify countries according to these characteristics and then group them together. For HRM, culture is a major contextual factor (see Chapter 3 in this volume). Three main approaches have gained some foothold in the management literature and offer conceptual frames and empirical results relevant for comparative HRM studies. We will briefly characterise them and list the respective European countries covered by them.

Hofstede sees national culture as the collective programming of the mind which differentiates members of various groups or categories. He originally identified four dimensions of national culture (Hofstede, 1980): power distance, individualism versus collectivism, masculinity versus femininity, and uncertainty avoidance. Later work (Hofstede et al., 2010) added two further dimensions, that is, long-term orientation versus short-term orientation, and indulgence versus restraint. Based on the original model and referring to Western Europe, one can differentiate between four cultural clusters (Cole, 2004: 130):

- Anglo: UK, Ireland.
- Germanic: Austria, Germany, Switzerland.
- Latin (more developed): Belgium, France, Italy, Spain.
- Latin (less developed): Portugal.
- Nordic: Denmark, Finland, Norway, Sweden – and the Netherlands.

Schwartz (2006: 138f.) views culture as 'as the rich complex of meanings, beliefs, practices, symbols, norms, and values prevalent among people in a society . . . [that] express shared conceptions of what is good and desirable in the culture'. He differentiates between seven basic culture orientations grouped in three bipolar pairings indicating the basic approaches a culture takes: autonomy (intellectual, affective) versus embeddedness; egalitarianism versus hierarchy; and harmony versus mastery. Looking at Western Europe, Schwartz differentiates between two clusters (with a third, categorised rather differently):

- West European I, emphasising egalitarianism: Belgium, Finland, Germany, Italy, Norway, Sweden, Spain, Switzerland.
- West European II, emphasising intellectual autonomy: Austria, Denmark, Greece, France, Netherlands, Portugal.
- English-speaking: UK, Ireland.

The GLOBE study (House et al., 2004) focuses on leadership behaviour and expectations. House et al. view culture as consisting of cultural practices (that is, how things are), and cultural values (that is, how things should be), and differentiate between nine cultural attributes or dimensions (Javidan et al., 2006: 69f.): performance orientation, assertiveness, future orientation, humane orientation, institutional collectivism, in-group collectivism, gender egalitarianism, power distance, and uncertainty avoidance. With regard to Western Europe, the Global Leadership and Organizational Behavior Effectiveness (GLOBE) project results point towards four culture clusters (Chhokar et al., 2007: 13, see also Koopman et al., 1999):

- Nordic: Denmark, Finland, Sweden.
- Germanic: Austria, Germany, Netherlands, Switzerland (German-speaking).
- Anglo: UK, Ireland.
- Latin Europe: France, Italy, Portugal, Spain, Switzerland (French and Italian-speaking).

Overall, there are broad similarities between the way in which the different authorities cluster the European countries, and as we now show, these to some extent mirror the institutional analyses.

Institutional Elements

Other researchers have used the institutional literature (see Chapter 2 in this volume; and Brewster et al., 2007a; Farndale et al., 2008; Goergen et al., 2009b; Tregaskis & Brewster, 2006) to cluster the UK and Ireland, the Nordic countries, and the central continental European countries, sometimes separating out the flexicurity countries of Denmark and the Netherlands, and the Mediterranean countries.

Amongst the many different institutional aspects, researchers have used the Esping-Andersen categorisation of welfare system, as we have noted above. Others have concentrated on differences in legal systems, using La Porta and colleagues' categorisation (La Porta et al., 1997, 2000; Botero et al., 2004). In HRM terms the categorisation has shown some limited relationship with practice, for example for financial participation (Croucher et al., 2010) and downsizing (Goergen et al., 2013), except that the Scandinavian category is found at one extreme rather than in between the civil and common law models. There have also been attempts to relate certain HRM practices to politics or to political systems, but these have generally been less successful.

The 'comparative capitalisms' literature (see Chapter 2 in this volume; Jackson & Deeg, 2008) attempts to encompass many of these institutional difference in one synthetic theory. It has paid special attention to Western Europe. The influential varieties of capitalism literature (Hall & Soskice, 2001) attempts to explain why some countries did not follow the economically successful model of the US economy as espoused by the International Monetary Fund but were nonetheless successful. They identify complementarities, the way that the system worked coherently, as an explanator and outline a variety of forms of capitalism.

The typical Anglo-Saxon liberal market economies (LMEs), such as the UK and Ireland, do follow the US model to some extent, and are strong in terms of property owner rights, have a focus on competition, and government's role in business is clearly limited. The Rhineland-based coordinated market economies (CMEs) such as Germany, and to a lesser extent countries such as the Netherlands and the Nordic countries, provide rights for a wider group of stakeholders, emphasise cooperation between firms and between firms and government, and develop longer-term relationships both beyond and within the firm. Other analyses (Amable, 2003; Whitley, 1999) separate out a subset of the CMEs as the social democratic economies (SDEs) comprising the Scandinavian or, more properly, Nordic economies. Their distinguishing features include weaker employment protection than in CMEs, a stronger state role in continuous skills development, excellent social welfare systems, a high importance of collective bargaining due to the strong presence of unions, and high education levels. These authorities have also identified the Southern European or 'Mediterranean' version of capitalism with a tradition of family ownership, of centralisation, but no active employment policy, with protection of core jobs and high levels of general regulation for large organisations, but with exemptions or lack of enforcement for smaller ones, leading to a substantial dualism. General job protection is weak and law enforcement is uneven.

Whitely (1999) sees a direct connection between arrangements in the economy and those within organisations. Within organisations, economies will be distinguished by their degree of interdependence between workers and their employers and by delegation from management to workers. Thus, when it comes to HRM, LMEs are distinguished by limited interdependence – it is easier to hire and fire, and turnover rates are higher; and CMEs and the Nordic and Mediterranean economies by greater interdependence, with longer tenure (Croucher et al., 2012). This greater interdependence in turn makes it more advantageous for both firms and employees to invest in training and development: the pay-off time will be longer (Goergen et al., 2009a; Goergen et al., 2012). Delegation to employees to increase work autonomy will be lower in the LMEs and higher in the CMEs and the SDEs (Brewster et al., 2007a).

HRM IN DIFFERENT COUNTRIES, REGIONS WITHIN COUNTRIES, AND SECTOR-DRIVEN ECONOMIC GEOGRAPHIES

In this final section, we highlight three added complexities beyond the existence of country clusters when examining HRM in Western Europe. There are continuing and notable differences between each country, there are regional patterns within any one country, and indeed now we also see coordination of HRM in the context of sector clusters driven by new economic geographies, and not just clusters of countries.

Although we do not have space to go into detail, we note here that, partly as a result of these specialisations, even within the clusters, whichever category of clusters one chooses, each country remains distinct. Thus, for example, there are distinct differences between two LME states, the UK and the Republic of Ireland; and between the CME states of Germany and the Netherlands; and with countries such as France, for example, not fitting neatly into any categorisation.

The UK and Ireland are both LMEs; until just over a century ago they were part of the same country, and Ireland has historically tended to follow much UK legislation; both countries have implemented EU requirements. But there are significant distinctions between them. Ireland is dominated by religion more than the UK and has a narrower view of individual rights. It is part of the eurozone, whilst the UK has retained the pound as its currency. The UK is a much larger and more internationally interdependent economy. Ireland is largely dependent on foreign multinational enterprises, and these are a significant proportion of the far fewer large businesses in Ireland. The distinction between these larger organisations and the rest in areas such as HRM is substantial. Some trade unions operate across both countries, and in general it appears that membership remains higher in Ireland than in the UK. Given the interlinking of business and politics in small countries it is no surprise to find that both unions and employers have a more direct influence on government in the Republic than they do in the UK. France remains difficult to categorise. It is noticeably somewhat absent from the analyses of comparative capitalisms by Hall and Soskice (2001), and even from the analysis by the French academic Amable (2003).

HRM within Regions

We do not want to move on from these internal variations within Western Europe without noting the regional differences within states. Again, we do not have room to go into detail, but in some countries in Europe different regions are notably distinct. This has been, to a large extent, ignored by the cultural and institutional literature, but there are signs that this is changing (Almond, 2011). In some of these countries – some of the smaller states such as Austria, Ireland, Luxembourg, Norway, and Portugal, for example – the internal differences may feel significant to the locals, especially where there are linguistic differences, but in general HRM operates similarly more or less nationwide. The same is true for some of the larger states, such as Italy and the UK, although here somewhat different legislation and history in some of the Italian islands and in the Northern Irish region of the UK can impact upon employment issues. Some of the most obvious regional differences are found in some of the larger states, in Germany and Spain. Here, different traditions and history, and differences in language and religion, have led to a form of federal government in which the state plays a different role in the different territories, legislation varies, and historical traditions of investment, ownership, trade unionism, and community play a significant role in developing differing forms of HRM. These might be less significant between the regions than are the differences between the country as a whole and other countries, but using a closer lens they still have an effect. There are similar arrangements too in some of the smaller states, such as Belgium and Switzerland, where regional differences in language, culture, religion, and history have led to rather separate communities operating through a federal structure and having patterns of HRM that are rather different.

HRM within Sector-Driven Economic Geographies

Finally, another issue that is becoming important for European HRM researchers, given the extent of business and social changes that now seem to be taking place, is to understand the extent to which regional issues become determined by underlying patterns of industrial behaviour. Increasing awareness of the comparative capitalisms perspective is directing the attention of researchers to the interplay between the various institutional arrangements that exist, and the shape of economic developments. Will European HRM be impacted upon by changes taking place in important transnational and intra-EU sectors, such as automobiles, financial services, pharmaceuticals, research and development, and education? Are these industrial networks any more, or any less, powerful now in shaping the industrial environment compared to the early 1990s, when the Single European Market (SEM) was first being created? This raises questions about the academic boundaries that might guide future study of comparative HRM, because study of these developments has brought together academics from areas such as regional innovation systems, economic geography, institutional economics, and evolutionary geography. All of these disciplines are trying to better understand the interplay between European institutional arrangements and the subsequent industrial characteristics. Given the relatively similar factor endowments of countries within the EU, new trade and economic geography theories have become of interest to researchers wishing to explain the changing industrial structure, patterns of production and specialisation, and labour market structure of the EU.

The debates have some bearing on comparative analysis of HRM in Europe. They originally took place at the time of the creation of the SEM, and have been renewed more recently since the global financial crisis that began in 2008. Their application ranges from making predictions about the characteristics of the industries expected to become geographically concentrated, and the characteristics of the countries where such industries locate, to examining the changing shape of industrial sectors such as automobiles within the EU, patterns of innovation and smart specialisation, the impacts of the global financial crisis, and the potential impact of trade agreements between the EU and other economies such as China and Japan.

There was a major debate during the period when the SEM was being created about how the economic and industrial space of Europe would develop: would it be along inter- or intra-industry lines? The issue was debated in the early days of the European Economic Community but hidden away in the various policy reports: there was a fear that some institutional features of labour markets would give certain countries an unfair competitive advantage. The International Labour Organization (ILO) examined the impact of European integration on the development of national labour markets in 2000 (Raines, 2000). The debate drew upon on two competing theories of trade prevalent at the time. This old debate has implications for the new debates because, as noted at the time:

> Depending on the theoretical approach advocated, the integration of trade and factor markets can have either reinforcing or diverging impacts on labour market structures. The combined processes of greater capital and labour movements and the removal of trade restrictions on trade have been predicted to lead to the development and sustaining of national competitive advantage. (Raines, 2000: 14)

The first, and at the time dominant model, was the Heckscher–Ohlin–Samuelson (HOS) theory. It is based on differences in natural endowments between countries and regions, and makes neoclassical assumptions of free trade. When factors of production and consumers are scattered across regions, neoclassical theory envisages a geographically dispersed structure of industrial production, such that individual regions specialise in production of goods where they hold a comparative advantage, driven by levels of productivity. It considers that trade and labour market effects are linked together through the impact of factors such as labour costs and the spread of homogenous products. It was assumed that, without integration of labour markets and free movement of labour (an efficiency factor), increasing economic integration through freer trade would lead to the emergence of distinctive national comparative advantages, as defined by relative factor endowments. Inter-industry trade involves exchanges between countries that link complementary industries, such as steel and automobiles. Trade, competitive advantage, and specialisation reflect the possession of different economic resources and lead to trade in different products. In essence, countries begin to specialise in different economic niches; and appropriately harmonised rules and practices, including free movement of labour, might improve the process of labour reallocation and lead to even faster trade growth.

A second outcome, the growth of intra-industry trade, was used to question neoclassical assumptions and informed competing theory, relatively new at the time of the creation of the SEM. Economic geographers used theories of economic agglomeration. These assume the starting point to be imperfect competition, and argue that firms locate in an economic centre because other firms have already located there (Krugman, 1991). This then fuels a cumulative causation process, with the arrival of new firms to a location making the site more and more attractive to other firms. There are two developments from this:

1. Growth in intra-industry trade (on the basis of more subtle forms of specialisation). Intra-industry trade involves two-way international trade flows within a single industry; for example, advanced manufacturing. More of the same types of products get exported and imported between countries, with countries specialising in the production of different varieties of the same commodity, resulting in highly specialised components and subassemblies being exchanged between affiliated firms in different countries. The downstream industry forms the market for upstream firms (Amiti, 1998, 1999).
2. A process of industrial agglomeration. Krugman (1991) argued that greater labour market integration would therefore lead to greater divergence of labour market conditions, not convergence.

Under the second scenario, the ILO's prognosis was prophetic:

> agglomerations of economic activity . . . in individual countries, [are] determined by absolute rather than comparative advantage. With respect to labour market effects, this can lead to an

entrenched differential in factor prices between countries, arising from differing, and in some cases, widening productivity of production factors between countries, [resulting in] increasing divergence in key labour market factors, with respect to unemployment rates, wage levels and productivity differences. The emergence of growth nodes could lead to self-reinforcing comparative advantages arising from a combination of economies of scale, better research and technical development and lower market costs. In this scenario, trade and factor flows do not act as substitutes: as higher rates of return will continue to accrue to both sets of factors in the country with absolute advantage, the latter will act as a magnet on both labour and capital. Where such flows are stymied by various barriers, economic growth prospects in the lagging countries are likely to worsen, potentially resulting in a 'vicious' spiral of economic decline which would have the perverse effect of reinforcing labour market stratification during a period of trade integration. (Raines, 2000: 7)

Hindsight is a great thing, and as such the ILO concluded that we would only know which theory was correct in the fullness of time, many years ahead. The report noted that, given the above, the single currency created greater strains in those labour markets that would have to deal with the differential impact of 'asymmetric shocks'; the global financial crisis was such a shock.

However, when it examined the issue soon after, it considered that on balance the evidence at the time supported the competing agglomeration models of trade specialisation (Raines, 2000). Successive studies had shown that there had been little inter-industry specialisation within the European Community: for example, for the EC-6 countries between 1958 and 1977 (Balassa & Bauwens, 1988), for the EC-9 between 1970 and 1987 (Greenaway, 1987), and for the EC-12 during the period of completing the single market (CEC, 1996).

Up until 1990, the evidence from trade measures and sectoral employment data showed that EU industry became increasingly localised in the 1980s, with increasing-returns industries becoming strongly concentrated at the economic core of the EU, with only low levels of intra-industry trade across countries. High-tech industries were also strongly localised, but showed no centre–periphery gradient. The main potential for future specialisation was in sectors that had high levels of intra-industry trade but were sensitive to labour costs, with employment in these industries shifting toward the EU periphery (Brulhart, 1998). By 1994, OECD data showed that within the EU an average of 64 per cent of trade in manufactures was categorised as intra-industry. By 1998 there was evidence of increased specialisation in EU countries based on country Gini coefficients, and increasing geographical concentration, with 17 out of 27 industries showing a larger proportion of an industry's output becoming concentrated in a smaller number of countries (Amiti, 1998). Prior to monetary union, the conclusion was:

> As the EU moves towards a monetary union, it can be expected that the geographic concentration of industries will increase further, in line with developments so far, and paralleling United States experience (Krugman, 1991). This, in turn, would raise the likelihood of asymmetric shocks affecting EMU [Economic and Monetary Union] member countries, thereby raising difficulties of adjustment in the absence of nominal exchange-rate instruments. (Amiti, 1998: 53)

The conclusion by the ILO in 2000 was that what had happened until then had been a process of intra-industry specialisation (Raines, 2000), with European companies focusing on producing unique, differentiated products, creating increasing returns which became concentrated near the core of the market, and levels of intra-industry trade between the core and the periphery vanishing. Trade flows had increased faster between similar industries within member states, rather than either inter-industrial trade, or trade with non-Community partners. Aiginger and Davies (2004) analysed patterns of manufacturing from 1985 to 2002 and found that increasing inter-industry specialisation had taken place, but had been masked by faster growth in the smaller European countries, with the net result that industries appeared to be less geographically concentrated. The subsequent enlargement of the EU in 2004 reinforced this process.

More recently, Stehrer and Stöllinger (2015) have examined production integration, global value chains, and structural change, and found a growing concentration of European industrial production. Europe's manufacturing activity is becoming increasingly concentrated in a Central European (CE) core, which the IMF also refers to as the German–Central European supply chain. This CE manufacturing core is dominated by Germany and in addition comprises Austria and the four Visegrád countries (the Czech Republic, Slovakia, Hungary, and Poland). Botta (2014) similarly examined productive and technological asymmetries on the convergence or divergence between central and peripheral economies in the eurozone. There have also been examinations of the likely impact of the Europe 2020 Strategy and EU Cohesion Strategy, which now use the language of 'smart specialisation' to explain the capacity of a regional economic system to generate new specialities and more knowledge-intensive and higher added-value activities through the local concentration and agglomeration of resources and competences in these domains (McCann & Ortega-Argilés, 2015; Sörvik & Kleibrink, 2015).

CONCLUSIONS: THE STUDY OF HRM IN WESTERN EUROPE

In conclusion, early attempts to distinguish European versions of HRM (Brewster & Bournois, 1991; Thurley & Wirdenius, 1991) have led on to a considerable literature drawing on cultural and institutional theories and, on rare occasions, combining them. European academics have taken a lead in critiquing the concept and the rhetoric of HRM as it has come to us from the USA (Brewster & Cerdin, 2017; Delbridge et al., 2011; Legge, 2005), and studies of HRM in Europe generally tend to take a more critical view of the topic and to be more prepared to cover the negative side of HRM than is common elsewhere. Studies of organisations (not 'firms': European researchers include public sector and not-for-profit organisations), and their objectives and strategies will not necessarily assume the management's interests to be 'good' for the organisation, or its employees, or for society (Beer et al., 2015). There are many recent examples where this is manifestly not the case. Furthermore, European researchers in HRM are more likely not to assume that the interests of everyone in the organisation will be the same, or to have any expectation that an organisation will have a strategy that people within the organisation will support. The balancing of such different interests (between employees, unions, and management, or within the management team) are not seen as a topic to be delegated to industrial relations studies: in Europe the unions are salient enough to be a crucial topic in HRM.

Analysing the management of people as a contributor to firm performance is as common in Europe as it is in the USA, but commentators in Western Europe are more likely to analyse critically the way human resources are managed, to challenge the declared corporate strategy, and to ask whether it might have deleterious consequences for individual well-being within the organisation (Van De Voorde et al., 2012), for the long-term health of the organisation, and for the community and country within which the organisation operates.

Further, Western European academic studies are less focused on the policies of a small number of 'leading edge' major multinationals and are more likely to study the practices of smaller businesses (Wilkinson, 1999; Stavrou-Costea & Manson, 2006; Harney & Dundon, 2006; Messersmith & Wales, 2013; Verreynne et al., 2013), public sector organisations (Kim et al., 2013; Leisink & Bach, 2014; Leisink & Steijn, 2009), and third sector organisations (Brewster & Cerdin, 2017) and local workplaces. Here, the objective is less likely to be about making profit than about understanding the impact of the practices on the various stakeholders involved. Overall, in Western Europe, HRM as a concept is a more contested notion than it is elsewhere.

The notion of 'European HRM' – or perhaps more properly Western European HRM – as a conceptually distinct approach emerged, arguably as a reaction to the hegemony of US conceptions of HRM (see, e.g., Brewster, 1993; Sparrow & Hiltrop, 1994; Brewster et al., 2000). The specifics of this concept do not relate to the core tasks and basic function of HRM. Of course, supplying organisations with the right number of people with the right qualifications at a specified time and location is a characteristic of HRM in every setting. However, there are arguments about how this can and should be done, and what 'right' means in this context. Specifically, in the discussion about European HRM some of the basic assumptions behind the US version of HRM are questioned, and it is argued that they are not applicable or are only partly applicable in Europe. We argue that foundations of a distinctive European approach lie in its approach to stakeholders rather than shareholders (Beer et al., 2015). In addition, and combined with the importance of the unique context, four additional elements are cornerstones for the emerging conceptual stance in HRM: the role of the state; a belief that people have rights in and to their jobs; an acceptance that consultation is proper; and a more critical and less managerialist agenda going beyond the mere HRM–organisational performance link.

Overall, we look forward to further research on HRM in Western Europe. Given the record so far, it seems likely that the wider and more critical approach adopted in this region is likely to lead to a better understanding of HRM in general.

REFERENCES

Adema, W., Fron, P., & Ladaique, M. 2014. How much do OECD countries spend on social protection and how redistributive are their tax/benefit systems?. *International Social Security Review*, 67(1): 1–25.

Aiginger, K., & Davies, S.W. 2004. Industrial specialisation and geographic concentration: Two sides of the same coin? Not for the European Union. *Journal of Applied Economics*, 7(2): 231–248.

Almond, P. 2011. The sub-national embeddedness of international HRM. *Human Relations*, 64(4): 531–551.

Amable, B. 2003. *The Diversity of Modern Capitalism*. Oxford: Oxford University Press.

Amiti, M. 1998. New trade theories and industrial location in the EU: A survey of evidence. *Oxford Review of Economic Policy*, 14(2): 45–53.

Amiti, M. 1999. Specialization patterns in Europe. *Review of World Economics*, 135(4): 573–593.

Apospori, E., Nikandrou, I., Brewster, C., & Papalexandris, N. 2008. HRM and organizational performance in Northern and Southern Europe. *International Journal of Human Resource Management*, 19(7): 1187–1207.

Balassa, B., & Bauwens, L. 1988. The determinants of intra-European trade in manufactured goods. *European Economic Review*, 32(7): 1421–1437.

Becker, B., & Gerhart, B. 1996. The impact of human resource management on organizational performance: Progress and prospects. *Academy of Management Journal*, 39(4): 779–801.

Becker, B., Huselid, M., Pickus, P., & Spratt, M. 1997. HR as a source of shareholder value: Research and recommendations. *Human Resource Management Journal*, 36(1): 39–47.

Beer, M., Boselie, P., & Brewster, C. 2015. Back to the future: Implications for the field of HRM of the multi-stakeholder perspective proposed 30 years ago. *Human Resource Management*, 54(3): 427–438.

Beer, M., Spector, B., Lawrence, R., Quinn, M.D., & Walton, E. 1984. *Managing Human Assets: The Groundbreaking Harvard Business School Program*. New York: Free Press.

Bonnafous-Boucher, M., & Pesqueux, Y. (eds). 2005. *Stakeholder Theory: A European Perspective*. Basingstoke: Palgrave Macmillan.

Botero, J.C., Djankov, S., La Porta, R., Lopez-de-Silanes, F., & Shleifer, A. 2004. The regulation of labor. *Quarterly Journal of Economics*, 119(4): 1339–1382.

Botta, A. 2014. Structural asymmetries at the roots of the eurozone crisis: What's new for industrial policy in the EU?. *PSL Quaterly Review*, 67(269): 169–216.

Bournois, F. 1992. *La gestion des cadres en Europe*. Paris: Editions Liaisons.

Brewster, C. 1993. Developing a 'European' model of human resource management. *International Journal of Human Resource Management*, 4(4): 765–784.

Brewster, C. 1995. Towards a 'European' model of human resource management. *Journal of International Business Studies*, 26(1): 1–21.

Brewster, C., & Bournois, F. 1991. Human resource management: A European perspective. *Personnel Review*, 20(6): 4–13.

Brewster, C., Brookes, M., Croucher, R., & Wood, G. 2007a. Collective and individual voice: Convergence in Europe?. *International Journal of Human Resource Management*, 18(7): 1246–1262.

Brewster, C., & Cerdin, J.L. 2017. *Human Resource Management in Mission Driven Organizations*. New York: Palgrave.

Brewster, C., Croucher, R., & Prosser, T. forthcoming. Employee voice and participation: The European perspective. In P. Holand & J. Teicher (eds), *Employee Voice at Work*. Springer.

Brewster, C., & Hegewisch, A. 1993. A continent of diversity: Personnel management in Europe. *Personnel Management*, January: 36–40.

Brewster, C., & Larsen, H.H. (eds). 2000. *Human Resource Management in Northern Europe*. Oxford: Blackwell.

Brewster, C., & Mayrhofer, W. 2011. Comparative HRM: The debates and the evidence. In G.T. Wood and D.G. Collings (eds), *Human Resource Management: A Critical Introduction*: 278–295. London: Routledge.

Brewster, C., Mayrhofer, W., & Morley, M. 2000. The concept of strategic European human resource management. In C. Brewster, W. Mayrhofer, and M. Morley (eds), *New Challenges for European Human Resource Management*: 3–33. London: Macmillan.

Brewster, C., Wood., G., Croucher, R., & Brookes, M. 2007b. Are Works Councils and joint consultative committees a threat to trade unions? A comparative analysis. *Economic and Industrial Democracy*, 28(1): 53–81.

Brulhart, M. 1998. Trading places: Industrial specialization in the European Union. *Journal of Common Market Studies*, 36(3): 319–346.

CEC. 1996. Economic evaluation of the internal market. *European Economy, Reports and Studies*. Brussels: Commission of the European Communities.

Chhokar, J.S., Brodbeck, F.C., & House, R.J. 2007. Introduction. In J.S. Chhokar, F.C. Brodbeck, and R.J. House (eds), *Culture and Leadership Across the World: The GLOBE Book of In-Depth Studies of 25 Societies*: 1–16. Mahwah, NJ, USA and London, UK: Lawrence Erlbaum Associates.

Cole, G.A. 2004. *Management Theory and Practice* (4th edn). London: South Western Cengage Learning.

Croucher, R., Brookes, M., Wood, G., & Brewster, C. 2010. Context, strategy and financial participation: A comparative analysis. *Human Relations*, 63(6): 835–855.

Croucher, R., Wood, G., Brewster, C., & Brookes, M. 2012. Employee turnover, HRM and institutional contexts. *Economic and Industrial Democracy*, 33(4): 605–620.

Currie, D., & Teague, P. 2016. How does European integration influence employment relations?. In M. Dickmann, C. Brewster, and P. Sparrow (eds), *International Human Resource Management: Contemporary Issues in Europe* (3rd edn): 21–48. London: Routledge.

Davydoff, D., Fano, D., & Qin, L. 2013. Who owns the European Economy? Evolution of the ownership of EU-listed compagnies between 1970 and 2012. Paris: Observatoire De L'Epargne Européene, INSEAD OEE Data Services.

De Spiegelaere, S. & Jagodzinski, R. 2015. European Works Councils and SE Works Councils in 2015. Facts and figures. Brussels: European Trade Union Institute.

Delbridge, R., Hauptmeier, M., & Sengupta, S. 2011. Beyond the enterprise: Broadening the horizons of international HRM. *Human Relations*, 64(4): 483–505.

Ebenau, M. 2015. Directions and debates in the globalization of comparative capitalisms research. In

M. Ebenau, I. Bruff, and C. May (eds), *New Directions in Comparative Capitalisms Research: Critical and Global Perspectives*: 45–61. Basingstoke: Palgrave Macmillan.

Eisenhardt, K. 1989. Agency theory: An assessment and review. *Academy of Management Review*, 14(1): 57–74.

Esping-Andersen, G. 1990. *The Three Worlds of Welfare Capitalism*. Princeton, NJ: Princeton University Press.

European Commission. 2016. Erasmus+ Programme Guide. Accessed 7 December 2017 at http://ec.europa.eu/programmes/erasmus-plus/sites/erasmusplus2/files/files/resources/erasmus-plus-programme-guide_en.pdf.

Farndale, E., Brewster, C., & Poutsma, E. 2008. Coordinated vs. liberal market HRM: The impact of institutionalization on multinational firms. *International Journal of Human Resource Management*, 19(11): 2004–2023.

Ferner, A., & Hyman, R. 1992. *Industrial Relations in the New Europe*. Oxford: Blackwell Business.

Filella, J. 1991. Is there a Latin model in the management of human resources?. *Personnel Review*, 20(6): 14–23.

Fombrun, C.J., Tichy, N.M., & DeVanna, M.A. 1984. *Strategic Human Resource Management*. New York: John Wiley & Sons.

Freeman, R.E., Harrison, J.S., Wicks, A.C., et al. (eds). 2010. *Stakeholder Theory: The State of the Art*. Cambridge: Cambridge University Press.

Goergen, M., Brewster, C., & Wood, G. 2009a. Corporate governance and training. *Journal of Industrial Relations*, 51(4): 461–489.

Goergen, M., Brewster, C., & Wood, G. 2009b. Corporate governance regimes and employment relations in Europe. *Relations industrielles/Industrial Relations*, 64(4): 620–640.

Goergen, M., Brewster, C., & Wood, G.T. 2013. The effects of the national setting on employment practice: The case of downsizing. *International Business Review*, 22(6): 1051–1067.

Goergen, M., Brewster, C., Wood, G., & Wilkinson, A. 2012. Varieties of capitalism and investments in human capital. *Industrial Relations*, 51(2): 501–527.

Greenaway, D. 1987. Intra-industry trade, intra-firm trade and European integration: Evidence, gains and policy aspects. *Journal of Common Market Studies*, 26(2): 153–172.

Guery, L., Stévenot, A., Brewster, C., & Wood, G. 2017. The impact of private equity on employment: The consequences of fund country of origin – new evidence from France. *Industrial Relations*, 56(4): 723–750.

Guest, D. 1990. Human resource management and the American dream. *Journal of Management Studies*, 27(4): 377–397.

Hall, P., & Soskice, D. 2001. *Varieties of Capitalism: The Institutional Foundations of Comparative Advantage*. New York: Oxford University Press.

Harney, B., & Dundon, T. 2006. Capturing complexity: Developing an integrated approach to analysing HRM in SMEs. *Human Resource Management Journal*, 16(1): 48–73.

Henrich, J., Heine, S.J., & Norenzayan, A. 2010. The weirdest people in the world?. *Behavioral and Brain Sciences*, 33(2/3): 61–135.

Hirschman, A.O. 1970. *Exit, Voice, and Loyalty: Response to Decline in Firms, Organizations, and States*. Cambridge, MA: Harvard University Press.

Hofstede, G. 1980. *Culture's Consequences: International Differences in Work-Related Values*. Newbury Park, CA: SAGE Publications.

Hofstede, G. 1993. Intercultural conflict and synergy in Europe: Management in Western Europe. In D.J. Hickson (ed.), *Society, Culture and Organization in Twelve Nations*: 1–8. New York: de Gruyter.

Hofstede, G.H., Hofstede, G.J., & Minkov, M. 2010. *Cultures and Organizations. Software of the Mind: Intercultural Cooperation and Its Importance for Survival* (3rd edn). New York: McGraw-Hill.

House, R.J., Hanges, P.J., Javidan, M., Dorfman, P.W., & Gupta, V. (eds). 2004. *Culture, Leadership and Organisations: The GLOBE Study of 62 Societies*. London: SAGE.

Huselid, M.A. 1995. The impact of human resource management practices on turnover, productivity, and corporate financial performance. *Academy of Management Journal*, 38(3): 635–672.

Jackson, G., & Deeg, R. 2008. Comparing capitalisms: Understanding institutional diversity and its implications for international business. *Journal of International Business Studies*, 39(4): 540–561.

Javidan, M., Dorfman, P.W., De Luque, M.S., & House, R.J. 2006. In the eye of the beholder: Cross cultural lessons in leadership from Project GLOBE. *Academy of Management Perspectives*, 20(1): 67–90.

Katz, H.C., & Darbishire, O. 2000. *Converging Divergences: Worldwide Changes in Employment Systems*. Ithaca, NY: ILR Press.

Kim, S., Vandenabeele, W., Wright, B.E., et al. 2013. Investigating the structure and meaning of public service motivation across populations: Developing an international instrument and addressing issues of measurement invariance. *Journal of Public Administration Research and Theory*, 23(1): 79–102.

Koopman, P.L., Den Hartog, D.N., Konrad, E., et al. 1999. National culture and leadership profiles in Europe: Some results from the GLOBE study. *European Journal of Work and Organizational Psychology*, 8(4): 503–520.

Kostova, T., Roth, K., & Dacin, M.T. 2008. Institutional theory in the study of multinational corporations: A critique and new directions. *Academy of Management Review*, 33(4): 994–1006.

Krugman, P.R. 1991. *Geography and Trade*. Cambridge, MA: MIT Press.

La Porta, R., Lopez-de-Silanes, F., Shleifer, A., & Vishny, R. 1997. Legal determinants of external finance. *Journal of Finance*, 52(3): 1131–1150.

La Porta, R., Lopez-de-Silanes, F., Shleifer, A., & Vishny, R. 2000. Investor protection and corporate governance. *Journal of Financial Economics*, 58(1): 3–27.

Lawrence, P. 1992. Management development in Europe: A study in cultural contrast. *Human Resource Management Journal*, 3(1): 11–23.

Legge, K. 2005. *Human Resource Management: Rhetorics and Realities*. Basingstoke: Palgrave Macmillan.

Leisink, P.L.M., & Bach, S. 2014. Economic crisis and municipal public service employment: Comparing developments in seven EU member states. *Transfer: European Review of Labour and Research*, 20(3): 327–342.

Leisink, P.L.M., & Steijn, B. 2009. Public service motivation and job performance of public sector employees in the Netherlands. *International Review of Administrative Sciences*, 75(1): 35–52.

Lienert, I. 2009. *Where does the public sector end and the private sector begin?* IMF Working Paper, 09/122, Fiscal Affairs Department, International Monetary Fund.

Mayrhofer, W., Brewster, C., Morley, M., & Ledolter, J. 2011. Hearing a different drummer? Convergence of human resource management in Europe – A longitudinal analysis. *Human Resource Management Review*, 21(1): 50–67.

Mayrhofer, W., Morley, M., & Brewster, C. 2004. Convergence, stasis, or divergence? In C. Brewster, W. Mayrhofer, and M. Morley (eds), *Human Resource Management in Europe: Evidence of Convergence?*: 417–436. London: Elsevier/Butterworth-Heinemann.

McCann, P., & Ortega-Argilés, R. 2015. Smart specialization, regional growth and applications to European Union cohesion policy. *Regional Studies*, 49(8): 1291–1302.

Messersmith, J., & Wales, W. 2013. Entrepreneurial orientation and performance in young firms: The role of human resource management. *International Small Business Journal*, 31(2): 115–136.

OECD. 2014. Social expenditure update: Social spending is falling in some countries, but in many others it remains at historically high levels, *Insights from the OECD Social Expenditure database (SOCX)*, November.

Onaran, Ö., & Bösch, V. 2010. The effect of globalization on the distribution of taxes and social expenditures in Europe: Do welfare state regimes matter? *Discussion Papers SFB International Tax Coordination*, Vol. 40. Vienna: WU Vienna University of Economics and Business.

Paauwe, J., & Boselie, P. 2007. HRM and societal embeddedness. In P. Boxall, J. Purcell, and P. Wright (eds), *The Oxford Handbook of Human Resource Management*: 166–184. Oxford: Oxford University Press.

Palazzo, G., & Scherer, A.G. 2006. Corporate legitimacy as deliberation: A communicative framework. *Journal of Business Ethics*, 66(1): 71–88.

Pieper, R. 1990a. Introduction. In R. Pieper (ed.), *Human Resource Management: An International Comparison*: 1–26. Berlin: de Gruyter.

Pieper, R. (ed.). 1990b. *Human Resource Management: An International Comparison*. Berlin: de Gruyter.

Raines, P. 2000. *The Impact of European Integration on the Development of National Labour Markets*. Geneva: International Labour Office.

Rigby, M., Smith, R., & Brewster, C. 2004. The changing impact and strength of the labor movement in Europe. In G. Wood and M. Harcourt (eds), *Trade Unions and Democracy: Strategies and Perspectives*: 132–158. Manchester: Manchester University Press.

Schwartz, S.H. 2006. A theory of cultural value orientations: Explication and applications. *Comparative Sociology*, 5(2/3): 137–182.

Sörvik, J., & Kleibrink, A. 2015. Mapping innovation priorities and specialisation patterns in Europe. S3 Working Paper Series no. 08/2015. Seville: European Commission Joint Research Centre.

Sparrow, P.R., & Hiltrop, J.M. 1994. *European Human Resource Management in Transition*. London: Prentice Hall.

Stavrou-Costea, E., & Manson, B. 2006. HRM in small and medium enterprises: Typical, but typically ignored. In H.H. Larsen and W. Mayrhofer (eds), *Managing Human Resources in Europe: A Thematic Approach*: 107–130. London: Routledge.

Stehrer, R., & Stöllinger, R. 2015. *The Central European manufacturing core: What is driving regional production sharing?* Forschungsschwerpunkt Internationale Wirtschaft Research Reports 2014/15-02. FIW: Vienna Institute for International Economic Studies.

Stout, L. 2012. *The Shareholder Value Myth: How Putting Shareholders First Harms Investors, Corporations and the General Public*. San Francisco, CA: Barrett-Koehler.

Thurley, K., & Wirdenius, H. 1991. Will management become 'European'?: Strategic choice for organizations. *European Management Journal*, 9(2): 127–134.

Tregaskis, O., & Brewster, C. 2006. Converging or diverging? A comparative analysis of trends in contingent employment practice in Europe over a decade. *Journal of International Business Studies*, 37(1): 111–126.

Ulrich, D. 1989. Tie the corporate knot: Gaining complete customer commitment. *Sloan Management Review*, Summer: 19–28.

Van De Voorde, K., Paauwe, J., & Van Veldhoven, M.J.P.M. 2012. Employee well-being and the HRM–organizational performance relationship: A review of quantitative studies. *International Journal of Management Reviews*, 14(4): 391–407.

Verreynne, M.-L., Parker, P., & Wilson, M. 2013. Employment systems in small firms: A multilevel analysis. *International Small Business Journal*, 31(4): 405–431.

Walwei, U. 2015. Von der Deregulierung zur Re-Regulierung: Trendwende im Arbeitsrecht und ihre Konsequenzen für den Arbeitsmarkt / From deregulation to re-regulation: A turn around in German labour law and its possible implications. *Industrielle Beziehungen*, 22(1): 13–32.

Whitley, R. 1999. *Divergent Capitalisms: The Social Structuring and Change of Business Systems.* Oxford: Oxford University Press.

Wilkinson, A. 1999. Employment relations in SMEs. *Employee Relations*, 21(3): 206–217.

25. HRM in the transition states of Central and Eastern Europe and the former Soviet Union

Michael J. Morley, Dana Minbaeva, and Snejina Michailova

INTRODUCTION

Against the backdrop of ancient cultures, a socialist legacy and eventual institutional atrophy, many of the societies of Central and Eastern Europe (CEE) and the former Soviet Union (FSU) have pursued aggressive development trajectories since the early 1990s, though, as has become apparent, with divergent outcomes (Morley et al., 2009). This geographic territory is not historically well documented in the human resource management (HRM) literature. Several analyses have called attention to the lack of knowledge of HRM in CEE, along with its uneven coverage, with some countries such as Hungary, Poland, Slovenia, and Russia being the focus of considerably more attention than others (Dirani et al., 2015; Jankowicz, 1998; Kaše & Zupan, 2005; Morley et al., 2016; Zupan & Kaše, 2005). Michailova et al. (2009: 7) note that 'a closer review of the literature reveals most studies to be rather general, fragmented and subordinate to the Western European studies'. They also note that if the notion of 'European HRM' was developed in reaction to the hegemony of United States (US) conceptions of HRM, further systematic analyses in CEE are needed in light of the transitions experienced by these economies.

CEE countries have different endowments (Berend, 1996) and show significant variations in preferred approaches to HRM as a result of distinct cultural and developmental trajectories (Brewster & Bennett, 2010; Kohont & Brewster, 2014; Morley et al., 2009; Woldu & Budhwar, 2011). Dirani et al. (2015: 358), for example, call attention to Hungary and the Czech Republic, which were historically more integrated into the Western economic and political system than most other countries in CEE. They note that some, such as Poland and Hungary, were able to retain elements of private enterprise during Soviet occupation, which inevitably resulted in a different point of departure for the transition journey than their CEE neighbours. They stand in contrast to Romania, for example, now a member of the European Union (EU), but which 'followed a hard road from Communism to a functioning market economy' because of how detached it was from Western European intellectual, cultural, and economic trends (Dalton & Druker, 2012: 588).

Beyond historical heterogeneity under communism, an additional distinguishing factor since the transition arises in relation to the securing of foreign direct investment (FDI) in many of the CEE economies and the emergence of multinational corporations (MNCs). There is little doubt that the role of MNCs in reshaping the characteristics of the labour market and HRM practice has been significant, most especially in terms of the securing of foreign capital, the arrival of expatriate managers, and the emergence of mimetic pressures to adopt new practices (Festing & Sahakiants, 2013; Horwitz, 2011; Morley et al., 2016; Poór et al., 2014).

As a result of these and related developments, Lane (2007) argues that transition econo-mies can be divided into three categories: middle, low, and very low income. The former (including, for example, Hungary and Slovakia) are closest to continental European capi-talism, reflecting the pressures associated with joining the EU and the need to form insti-tutional arrangements that are complementary to their closest developed trading partners. Others, such as Bulgaria and Romania, are less developed and have moved closer to liberal market type arrangements (see also Bandelj, 2009; Buchen, 2007; Crowley, 2005). The very low income category includes countries such as Belarus and Ukraine. Meyer & Peng (2016: 4) note that the geographic entity of CEE as a territory may not now be as theoreti-cally meaningful as it was in earlier years. This can be accounted for by both the diver-gence of countries in the region during transition, and the convergence of some countries in the region with others outside; something which is especially evident among some of those CEE countries that joined the EU. Membership occurred for an initial cohort of eight CEE countries (the Czech Republic, Estonia, Hungary, Latvia, Lithuania, Poland, Slovakia, and Slovenia) in 2004 and subsequently for Bulgaria and Romania in 2007, with Croatia becoming the newest member state in 2013. This development has reduced their level of uniqueness as the process of reorienting politics and institutions intermeshes with altered economic dynamics. Conversely, in the case of Russia, it has also been argued that it is now difficult to locate it straightforwardly within a CEE research frame, given the uniqueness of its situation (Dirani et al., 2015; Meyer & Peng, 2016).

An important question that has emerged in analyses of CEE HRM is the extent to which 'Western' theories and 'best practices' can be applied to the region, or whether there is evidence of a unique or hybrid approach to HRM emerging. This is a question that deserves attention, given the potential significance of many of these economies. In attempting to explore it and landscape developments in HRM in CEE, scholars do not have easy access to a mapping of existing research. In this chapter, we seek to provide such a mapping and identify under-researched issues for future investigation. We reviewed (mainly) empirical studies examining HRM in CEE and FSU countries. We conducted article title, abstract, and introduction searches in the most influential international HRM journals (Caligiuri, 1999; Hoobler & Brown Johnson, 2004). We supplemented this search with additional journals in situations where the focus of the research was on specific practices neglected in previous research (for example, outsourcing in Smith et al., 2006), where the research offered a focus on a country not well covered heretofore (for example, Serbia in Milikić et al., 2008; Romania in Dalton & Druker, 2012), or where the research offered the possibility of particular insight because of the unique research methods employed (e.g., Gurkov, 2002). We organise the results of our search around whether the studies examined build knowledge underscored by the basic nomothetic assumptions of the universalistic approach, or provide more idiographic, contextual knowledge linked with institutional idiosyncrasies.

NOMOTHETIC INFORMED ENQUIRY ON HRM IN CEE AND FSU

It was only after the fall of the socialist regimes throughout CEE and the FSU that HRM, as we have come to understand it, started taking hold in management thinking (Morley et al., 2009). In the transition economies context, the Soviet model of management was centralised with a strong emphasis on rules. The people management function followed a similar pattern, with a heavy emphasis on departmentalisation, centralisation, and rule-making. While there is evidence of significant variation in personnel and HRM practices within CEE and FSU countries (Erutku & Vallee, 1997), the transformation that has occurred has essentially been a move from a unitarist to a more pluralist system.

Under socialism, the HRM function mainly performed administrative, ideological, and social roles. Letiche (1998) noted that the 'personnel office' limited itself to administrating payroll and rarely engaged in selection, organisational problem-solving and conflict resolution, training, appraisal and evaluation. Writing in the Russian context, Gurkov and Zelenova (2009) noted that in a large enterprise often there could be up to five units responsible for personnel matters, with the local Communist Party committee often having the final say in promotions. This fragmented approach, they noted, resulted in the absence of clearly articulated HRM strategy. Many of these functions were prerogatives of line management, and were a means of earning and exchanging favours (for example, *blat* in Russia; Ledeneva, 1998) or promoting the longer-term interests of their own network (for example, *clanism* in Kazakhstan; Minbaeva & Muratbekova-Touron, 2013). This was not conducive to the growth of more sophisticated, value-adding activities, with the result that there was always going to be significant ground to be made up if they were going to be able to sustain a developmental trajectory (Garavan et al., 1998; Sakowski et al., 2015). However, recent work by Holden & Vaiman (2013) suggests that CEE domestic organisations continue to employ mainly centralised and administrative HRM practices, and continue to neglect more strategic aspects. They note that although the need to move from purely administrative towards strategic HRM has already emerged, there is still little evidence that this shift has materialised (Holden & Vaiman, 2013: 134). In the Russian case, Latukha (2015: 1057) accounts for this by a lack of competencies which limits HRM specialists in their roles, something which may be linked to the 'relatively young age of Russian business culture and education system'.

Where it has taken hold, the emergence of the modern conception of HRM in CEE can be traced to the broader development of the sustainable, competitive market economy, operating in an era of globalisation, and the desire to achieve a closer alignment between strategy and HRM, and more recently in evaluating the impact of HRM on organisation performance. Our search revealed a tranche of studies in this genre in CEE and the FSU which, at their core, explore aspects of the HRM–performance question in several of the transition economies. From early in the transition process, the performance question, albeit in different guises, has formed a central policy agenda and an important aspect of academic enquiry with the emergence and institutionalisation of new approaches to workforce management being bound up in the economic transition process.

Nomothetic-led research in CEE and the FSU has been tackling the performance question in at least three distinguishable ways. First, some have focused on analysing the characteristics, attitudes, and values of the specialist charged with people management, along with the fundamental architecture of the specialist function that they lead. In one interpretation, this work can be seen to be trying to unravel the extent to which there has been a break with the past as a result of the transition, or as part of it; or conversely the extent to which there remains an underlying attitudinal continuity with the earlier command system. Second, a great deal of work has sought to examine the state of HRM and its contribution to business in CEE and the FSU, testing the receptivity of local indigenous firms to particular HRM tools that did not previously form part of the professional toolkit. Third, several research teams have focused on MNC subsidiaries that have been established in host locations in CEE and the FSU, and the systems they employ. We shall attend to all three approaches below.

The Attitudinal Legacy and the Architectural Shift

Milikić et al. (2008) examine Serbian companies and characterise them as having only recently established formal HRM departments, many of which still perform relatively limited functions, notably mostly administrative tasks required under the Serbian Labour Code. Lack of competences among HRM professionals represented an underlying problem. Several factors were thought to account for this, including a long tradition of performing rather old-style administration, a lack of appropriate education and development programmes, a preponderance of lawyers and clerical staff within the function, and a belief among managers that the main role of the specialist department is to ensure legal compliance. This last factor is consistent with findings from other transition economies where, for example, the underlying managerial mindset presents an important determinant of divergence in HRM practices, especially in terms of the absence of a deeper strategic involvement of the HRM function (Minbaeva et al., 2007; Zupan & Kaše, 2005). Reflecting on the overall extent of change, Milikić et al. (2008) conclude that their findings are relatively congruent with the 'crossvergence' hypothesis reflecting aspects of change, as part of the transition process, side by side with elements of continuity vested in existing values and traditions which are not likely to be jettisoned in the short term.

The attitudinal and structural legacy of communism and its capacity to act as a constraint on significant change is also tracked by Gurkov (2002). He draws upon longitudinal data from among surveys of Russian chief executive officers between 1998 and 2000 and concludes that despite the drive towards some modern instruments of HRM, most innovations are implemented on a trial and error basis, often without reference to international practices. Gurkov and Zelenova (2009) point to HRM systems being unsystematic, with a general underlying concern to simply mimic what other players are doing. Reflecting on the situation in the intervening years, they note that after the fall of the central planning system and the significant rise in new HRM challenges, the lack of appropriately qualified professionals meant that HRM departments did not appear well positioned to play a key strategic role (Gurkov & Zelenova, 2009).

One possible response to this dilemma has been the option of considering outsourcing HRM activity to specialists better equipped to deliver the services required. Smith et al. (2006) examined this issue in the Russian context in the initial stages of transition. They note that many believe the cost of outsourcing is prohibitive, which acts as a significant deterrent. In addition, it was observed that often the actual identification of purely outsourcable tasks or activities is not as straightforward as it might seem. From an attitudinal perspective, the low incidence of outsourcing could be linked to an underlying belief that fundamentally it causes a loss of control. However, against the backdrop of transition developments in Russia, Smith et al. (2006) postulate that outsourcing will likely grow, with a particular shift to more strategic, priority areas.

Karoliny et al. (2009) present evidence on HRM developments in Bulgaria, the Czech

Republic, Estonia, Hungary, Slovakia, and Slovenia. They identify a number of developments that appear to characterise contemporary HRM in this part of CEE. In the area of staffing, they find that managerial selection relies heavily on internal resources, with internal labour markets being highly significant in the filling of these positions. Interestingly, in the area of performance appraisal, they find that it is used the least often in the case of manual workers, despite the fact that before the start of transition this tool (or rather its predecessor, referred to as *attestatsiya*) was almost exclusively used to evaluate the performance of this staff category. With regard to compensation, they find that local establishments have the strongest role in determining basic pay. Finally, in terms of a pluralism shift, they highlight that establishment-level union figures and the relative power and influence of unions have dropped sharply. Many of these developments, they suggest, stem from market pressures to develop an underlying competitiveness and to emerge as an attractive host location for MNCs' FDI, which in turn become conduits for the dissemination of particular HRM practices. In this sense they can be seen to be relatively 'culture-free', with underlying economic and developmental exigencies determining the path of these countries. On the other hand, it is argued that it would be a mistake simply to consider them as completely permissive, receptive economic regimes. They are beset by the constraints of several old institutional factors and ideational legacies that have explanatory power in accounting for commonalities and differences. It is precisely the interplay between the old and the new dynamics that, the authors suggest, draw attention to both the path dependent feature of changes and the path creation phases of it.

Ideational and structural legacies also represent an important thread in research on HRM in Slovenia. Zupan and Kaše (2005) concentrate on the issue of the emergence of a more strategic orientation. The period between 1996 and 1998 is viewed as being unsuccessful in developing the architecture of the HRM function as strategically important. Drawing upon survey data, the authors observe the prevalence of conservative or administrative models, but with the emergence of some professional and strategic HRM models, the latter mostly being observed in those companies competing in international markets and subsidiaries of foreign multinationals. New, more flexible forms of employment did not appear to be commonplace. While a deal of training appeared to be taking place, its effectiveness was rarely measured, with little or no evidence of systematic evaluation of such interventions taking place. This led to the question of whether this training was making any contribution to preparing these companies for the challenges of the future. In terms of the overall function, Zupan and Kaše (2005) characterise it as having relatively low power, with HRM specialists often having a dearth of core competencies necessary to bring the function more centre stage. The result was a function which was best regarded as administrative, playing an often marginal role in business activity, and not well positioned to impact upon, or be seen to impact upon, business performance. The architectural shift demanded in response to the competitive, post-communist landscape was less than anticipated.

Andreeva et al. (2014) focus on preferred approaches and practices in Russian MNCs. They note that in the conventional Soviet model, because HRM departments mainly handled personnel administration and recordkeeping, there was a lack of a strategic focus by the HRM function at organisational level. Drawing on data gathered among the headquarters of Russian MNCs, they suggest that in the contemporaneous context Russian MNCs use the West as a source of best practices, but the extent and the depth of this varies significantly 'among the various segments of post socialist capitalism' (Andreeva et al., 2014: 978). Here they find that the degree to which these Western HRM practices are used depends on the company's embeddedness in the socialist employment relations system, with the degree of adoption being lowest in state-owned companies. They also note that MNCs differ in their choice of approaches depending on the target country of their international expansion and are more likely to seek to spread their own practices in developing FSU countries, but employ a mix of global best practices and local HRM practices in developed and in non-CIS countries.

Lucas et al. (2004) in their analysis of the transition in Slovakia found that there had been a move away from the traditional rigid socialist type of personnel management, but it had not been fully replaced by what could be described as a systematic approach. Of particular note, they did observe the emergence of performance-related pay and more diversified remuneration systems, along with a greater emphasis on recruitment, selection, and training. However, provision of training was not satisfactory, given the competitive challenges being faced, and there was an absence of a strategic approach to HRM. Interventions designed to enhance employee satisfaction and engagement in the workplace such as job rotation, enrichment, and enlargement had been introduced, but they were at best sporadic.

Skuza et al. (2013) landscape aspects of development in Poland, focusing on the nature and the extent of contemporary talent management practices in evidence. In common with several other contributors, they too note the historical skills deficit among Polish managers, with few being provided with opportunities to acquire appropriate management skills such as delegation skills, team skills, and planning and change management skills, resulting in a competency deficit. Pointing to an underlying ideational legacy from the communist era, the authors also note that managers sometimes did not see a need for their own self-development, despite lacking fundamental competencies necessary in the post socialist era. One result was that many managers experienced a sense of isolation during the transition process, especially middle managers. Drawing on the work of Kozminski (2008: 188), they note that waves of privatisation and direct implementation of management techniques imported from the West did not solve these issues. Polish management practice faced the problem of a constant interplay between deeply rooted 'survival patterns' developed under communism, and superficial values 'hastily imported from the West'. As a result, they argue that talent management (TM) is in the infancy stage of development, with the result that there 'is an increasing need to recruit, develop and retain high value-added talented employees who have above average abilities and commitment and will be able to lead Polish companies and enhance their competitiveness' (Skuza et al., 2013: 465).

Buck et al. (2003), in their analysis of developments in Ukraine, explore the relations between governance, HRM strategies, and performance, and the extent to which HRM policies are changing, or remain wedded to historical institutional influences. In their work they develop and dimensionalise three bundles of HRM strategies, namely a traditional social welfare model, a cost minimisation model, and a human resource investment model. This analysis in the Ukrainian context corroborates Fey and Björkman's (2001) study in Russia in that the implementation of the HRM investment bundle is again seen to be positively related to firm performance. This study goes behind strategic choice and finds that the degree of insider ownership is positively and significantly associated with this strategy, and is negatively associated with cost-cutting strategies and downsizing. Buck et al. (2003) find no significant relationship between the pursuit of the traditional social welfare model and performance. Cost-cutting HRM strategies, in turn, are associated with weaker firm performance.

Receptivity to New Tools and Techniques

Welsh et al. (1993) study the extent to which the use of US-based behavioural theories and techniques might be helpful in meeting the performance challenges facing HRM in Russia. They examined the impact of such approaches on factory workers in a textile plant in Russia. The findings confirmed that extrinsic rewards and behavioural management interventions have a positive impact on performance. However, the institutionalisation and impact of participative management as an approach to enhancing performance proved more challenging. The participative intervention seemed to have a counterproductive effect on the Russian workers' performance. The authors argue that the failure of the participative intervention does not indicate so much that this approach just will not work across cultures, but rather that historical and cultural values and norms characterising the host context need to be recognised and overcome for such a relative sophisticated technique to work effectively (Welsh et al., 1993: 75). In a study of the role of participation and empowerment in Russia, Michailova (2002), too, concluded that these HRM techniques had a counterproductive effect in that context in the late 1990s and the beginning of the 2000s. She emphasised that one-man authority, anti-individualism and dependence, tightly coupled hierarchies, lack of knowledge-sharing, and double-bind situations are important dominating factors that act against the logic of participation, and if foreign managers were to be respected by Russian managers and employees, they had to utilise alternative HRM instruments.

Shekshnia (1998) focuses on the performance question through a chronicling of the characteristics of firms that could be adjudged to have successful HRM in Russia as a result of embracing new tools and new approaches. Several features were identified that could be seen to have some explanatory power. First, concerted efforts were made to directly link business objectives, strategy, and people management practices. The establishing of a HRM strategy designed to support business objectives was a chief concern. HRM was taken seriously, something that was reflected in the level of investment in bringing about and institutionalising HRM practices. On the whole, it was observed that firms that pursued imported practices, most often introduced with Russian nationals acting as the drivers and custodians, were more successful than those that favoured remaining with the conventional domestic approach. Fey et al. (1999: 69) similarly concluded that successful companies tend to use Western 'high-performance' HRM practices but adjusted them to fit with the Russian environment. The key challenge is in trying to understand what adjustments are needed.

Western companies often tend to react negatively to existing knowledge and HRM practices that have been institutionalised in socialist times, and so they tend to implement knowledge and practices that counter the existing ones (Björkman et al., 2007; Michailova, 2000), an approach that has not worked particularly well. Peiper and Estrin (1998), in an analysis of the emerging situation in Poland, Hungary, the Czech Republic, Slovenia, Romania, and Russia, report developments in three major areas. First, they observed a modernisation of practices and tools in the areas of recruitment and training, with accompanying altered skill and work patterns. They also observed a tightness in the talent pool, with consequential skill shortages and salary and benefit adjustments; and they examined the role of expatriate managers working in these transition economies and the shift from employing expatriates to relying on locals. Despite differences between countries in reform and economic performance, the authors found these particular changes to be surprisingly common across the countries studied.

Holden & Vaiman (2013), in their account of talent management in the Russian context, point to a wariness towards this Western approach. Their analysis points to the persistence of 'Soviet mental software' coupled with an ongoing 'institutional void' which, together, serve to give short shrift to this Western framework, something which leads them to characterise talent management in Russia as dysfunctional. Of particular interest in the context of our argument here concerning receptivity to new tools and techniques, Holden and Vaiman (2013) note that, paradoxically, the operations of Western firms in Russia actually add to the dysfunction, whereby their distinctly foreign forms of TM are operating in parallel with practices in Russian firms with their tendency not to delegate and empower people, along with the actions of the Russian state to use 'negative selection' to recruit bureaucrats and enforcers tasked with preventing Russian businesses from entering any preserve that the authorities deem undesirable and a potential threat to their authority. In part, at least, they highlight how Western corporate practices and philosophies are resisted both on seemingly pragmatic grounds because 'that kind of thing won't work here', and on perhaps less overt, but nonetheless influential self-protective intellectual grounds whereby 'you foreigners simply cannot understand our problems' (Holden & Vaiman, 2013: 141). It has, however, been noted that the receptivity of local firms to Western HRM tools varies in terms of their in-country location, especially in geographically large countries such as Russia. Certain regions attract higher levels of FDI (Broadman & Recanatini, 2003), with such companies having a spillover effect and growing skill supply and demand in the largest urban regions, resulting in a larger number of local organisations practicing advanced Western-style HRM practices such as rigorous recruitment and selection processes, career management, and succession planning. The probability that a high number of organisations located in more rural parts of Russia adopt such practices is found to be significantly lower.

Multinational Company Subsidiaries and the Limits to Transfer

A third very prominent theme in nomothetic-led enquiry on HRM in CEE and the FSU relates to the experience of foreign MNC subsidiaries established in these locations, and the extent to which these economies represent liberal regimes, allowing for the adoption of foreign policies and practices. Poór et al. (2014) note that the ratio of people employed by MNCs is significantly higher in the transitional economy countries than in most Western countries, making them powerful, if 'ambiguous' (Cooke et al., 2011: 371), actors in the region. Given the power and economic dominance of MNCs, it is not surprising that there has been significant debate in recent years as to whether they act as 'nation-less organisations' (Ohmae, 1990) vis-à-vis the extent to which they 'are embedded in larger and wider societal collectivities' (Sorge, 2004: 118) and thus must organise their activities in the context of the multiple institutional environments in which they operate. Indeed it has been argued that globalisation is redefining the role of the nation state in managing the economic fortunes of nations (Boyer & Drache, 1996) and, further, that MNCs may also play a part in constructing the environment in which they operate (Williams & Geppert, 2004). There are few locations in which this could be truer than in the transition economies, which, as latecomers to internationalisation, have pursued the attraction of mobile FDI as a fundamental plank of their economic policy transition agenda. While FDI flows have traditionally been concentrated in developed countries, recent years have heralded a shift in location of such investments toward new destinations, including CEE and the former Soviet Union (Dibben et al., 2011).

Meardi (2006) argued that due to their weakly organised industrial relations systems, many of these economies provide a permissive environment allowing multinational companies to unilaterally implement their home HRM strategies. Any opposition that does arise is informal employee resistance aimed at trying to limit employer freedom. Similarly, McCann and Schwartz (2006) point to efforts towards the establishment of the most benign environment possible for the expansion of capital, entailing the augmentation of managerial prerogative and 'low-road' employment practices. In their analysis, emerging forms of management are tending towards the subordination of the work systems to a neoliberal form of world capitalism.

Weinstein and Obloj (2002) draw upon data from 303 state-owned, domestic private and foreign-owned subsidiaries located in Poland to test how strategic and environmental variables are related to the diffusion and adoption of HRM innovations. In this analysis they argue that in many instances theoretical models of HRM, developed to describe the experiences of advanced industrial democracies, are useful in understanding the early experiences of countries in transition from a planned to a market economy. The underlying concerns to achieve economic efficiency, the desire to match the preferred HRM approach to the overall business strategy, and surrounding competitive pressures, in combination, contribute to the decision to introduce new HRM policies, practices, and approaches. Their analysis revealed that the predominant mechanisms by which HRM innovations diffuse are a combination of the free flow of management personnel from foreign to domestic firms, the benchmarking of competitors' management practices, the influence of HRM consultants, and the rise of Western management education availability in the transition economy.

Taylor and Walley (2002) examine emerging HRM practices in Croatia. They draw on 21 diverse company case study experiences in this country to review emerging HRM practices and assess the relevance of Western management models. The results suggest that subsidiaries of MNCs are leading the way towards the advancement of more sophisticated HRM practices and are acting as innovators in this regard. Young Croatian managers broadly welcomed new HRM practices and identified with most of the broad objectives and philosophy of HRM. In contrast to the emergence, diffusion, and institutionalisation of new-style practices among MNC subsidiaries, the authors also point to evidence that suggests what they describe as the 'hijacking' of HRM amongst some Croatian companies by old-style traditional forces in an attempt to maintain the status quo, representing what might be classified as a strong ideational legacy.

Björkman et al. (2007) found that employees in Russian-based MNC subsidiaries received considerably more training[1] than employees in US and Finnish subsidiaries. They also found that MNCs operating in Russia use performance-based compensation and performance-based appraisal systems to a greater extent than units located in the USA, and that they also pay more attention to merit in promotion decision-making. This, the authors suggest, may be on the basis that MNCs react against what is seen as a negative heritage from the Soviet period, or what we have earlier referred to as an underlying ideational legacy, by implementing practices that counter what has been traditional in the Russian context. Similarly, Minbaeva et al. (2007) describe how in promotion decisions HR managers of foreign subsidiaries in Kazakhstan rated personality and professionalism higher than the seniority that would normally be important, given the Kazakh culture which emphasises respect for age. In addition to the ideational legacy, this could be explained by the fact that foreign subsidiaries usually attract younger employees (in the sample of Minbaeva et al., 2007, the average age of the workforce in the studied organisation was 35.5 years). Regardless, the authors argue that certain local-cultural conditions will necessitate the significant adaptation of such context-specific HRM practices as performance appraisal. Although some form of performance appraisal is practised in foreign subsidiaries, the 360-degree feedback favoured in some Western organisations is not in use due to local socio-cultural conditions. This is in line with the previous research indicating that multi-source feedback requires low power distance (Fletcher & Perry, 2001).

In a series of earlier investigations (Fey & Björkman, 2001; Fey et al., 2000) on Russia, strong support for the existence of a positive relationship between HRM practices and the performance of Russian subsidiaries of Western corporations was unearthed. The evidence appeared largely consistent with results obtained in studies of the HRM–firm performance link conducted in other geographies. However, the results pointed to the necessity to pursue different HRM bundles for managerial and non-managerial employees because, while a focus on collective responsibility and group-based bonuses appeared to work well for non-managerial employees, a stronger focus on individual responsibility-taking and rewards based on individual performance was more effective for the managerial category. Further differential configurations for managerial and non-managerial employees were also in evidence. The provision of non-technical training and high salaries were found to be positively associated with HRM outcomes for managers, while job security was a strong predictor of HRM outcomes for non-managerial employees. In addition, there was a direct positive relationship between managerial promotions based on merit and firm performance in the Russian context.

Recently, research focused on acquisitions has identified two contextual moderators as potentially affecting the adaptation of the HRM practices employed in foreign subsidiaries located in transition economies, compared to their sister subsidiaries in Western, more advanced economics. The first is the attractiveness of the acquiring firm vis-à-vis the acquired firm (Minbaeva & Muratbekova-Touron, 2011). This factor could be linked to the degree of economic development of the acquirer's country of origin but may also

---

[1]   In many cases foreign investors are obliged to provide training for local employees by the host country legislation (for example, laws around inward FDI). For example, the government of the Republic of Kazakhstan implemented a workforce nationalisation policy, which included the required investment of 1 per cent of operating capital to be allocated to training of the national workforce.

be related to the stereotypes of the acquirers formed historically and shared by the local employees (see also Koveshnikov, 2011). This is especially the case for acquisitions taking place along the developing–developing country axis (as opposed to developed-to-developed and developed-to-developing; see Lacombe et al., 2007).

Another factor is the state of local HRM development at the time of acquisition. At the beginning of the transition, all companies acquired by foreign MNCs were being acquired for the first time. As Uhlenbruck (2004) explains, given their recent establishment and limited resources, the subsidiaries in transition economies were unlikely to take significant initiatives and hence passively followed the acquirer. For example, in Kazakhstan, the underdeveloped state of local HRM coupled with the necessity to satisfy individual physiological needs proved to be favourable conditions for the uptake of aspects of North American HRM (Minbaeva et al., 2007). Over time, when the subsidiaries experience second or third consecutive acquisitions, their market and managerial capabilities have evolved, they have experienced how to deal with the foreign acquirers and, most probably, they have developed certain expectations with regard to the acquirer's behaviour during the post-acquisition stage. The later entrants are dealing with not only more dynamic but also more institutionalised labour markets. Over the 1990s, the need for rapid structural adjustment of the transitional economies after the introduction of economic and social reforms was reflected in profound amendments to national employment protection legislation at the start of economic and social reforms. Still, in the majority of countries in transition, the labour laws were not a primary concern of policy-makers. For example, in Kazakhstan, despite the rapid growth of the economy the Labour Law of the 1970s (pre-transition) was replaced only in 2001. Labour regulations in Russia and Slovenia are still regarded as strict compared to Hungary and Poland, which are amongst the most flexible for regular employment.

IDIOGRAPHIC ACCOUNTS OF HRM IN CEE AND THE FSU

The relative size, importance, and performance of the CEE states differs enormously (McCann & Schwartz, 2006), which impacts upon the nature of HRM, as does their cultural fabric, the combination of which may be 'self-reinforcing mechanisms which have produced and enhanced a specific path' for each of the CEE countries (Festing & Sahakiants, 2013: 374). Distinct developmental trajectories, coupled with differentiated levels of development and unique cultural tenets, cause issues to be viewed differently and things to be done differently in these different countries, and lead to differences in the way HRM is conceptualised, institutionalised, and practiced (Brewster et al., 2010). Obvious country-specific differences are omnipresent, which may be accounted for by the path dependent nature of change and by significant ideational legacies, many of which are not easily jettisoned (Morley, 2004). In this sense, CEE countries since 1989 have represented a form of test laboratory for HRM, which is central to the strategic directions and competitive advantage of the firms operating there (Taylor & Walley, 2002). Perhaps because of their heterogeneity, and distinct developmental trajectories since the transition process commenced in the late 1980s, they have proven the object of much academic enquiry in the contextual or more idiographic tradition, in addition to the nomothetic investigations outlined above. In contrast to the studies rooted within the universalist paradigm presented earlier, those anchored in contextualism provide a different kind of evidence on the state of HRM in the transition economies and what is distinct and different about it. Referred as an exercise in 'landscaping' (Morley et al., 2009), in the HRM field it often involves a focus on understanding what is different between and within approaches to HRM in various contexts and what the antecedents of those differences are. These studies stress the importance of focusing on national differences in understanding HRM in specific countries. Thus this approach to researching HRM explores the importance of such factors as culture, ownership structures, labour markets, the role of the state, and trade union organisation as aspects of the subject rather than external influences upon it. The scope of HRM goes beyond the organisation.

Mills (1998) explores the emerging paradigms of HRM in the Czech Republic. Here the emphasis is on linking the external environment to the organisation through the advancing of a stakeholder analysis and appropriate HRM models. In furthering the contextual debate, it is argued that the influence of external stakeholders will shape a paradigm characterised by government intervention and an insider model of corporate governance. Tung and Havlovic (1996) also explore macro-environmental variables (political-economic and socio-cultural) that have a major bearing on a firm's HRM practices and policies. In their evaluation of the transition process in both the Czech Republic and Poland, they note that despite the fact that these countries operated under the communist model for nearly four decades, their HRM policies and practices have already evolved down quite different paths in their transition to free-market economies. In particular, the authors suggest that each country seem to be wedded to a framework that is more consistent with its socio-cultural heritage and its stage of economic development and transition to a free-market economy. They note that, most likely because of its closer link with Western Europe, its higher level of industrialisation, and more robust economy, the Czech Republic has tended to exhibit characteristics that are more in line with those of the industrialised West.

Minbaeva et al. (2007) examine the development of HRM in Kazakhstan and establish the extent to which practices and policies were reflective of their countries of origin, older-style Soviet or post-Soviet practices, or an emerging Kazakhstan model and approach to HRM. The analysis points to an emerging model of HRM and employee relations practices as a hybrid of old-style Soviet practices and Western European and USA approaches. The reasons for the emergence of a new HRM style are: (1) increasing government regulation of employment practices (new labour law; profound amendments to national employment protection legislation); (2) changes in individual preferences (that is, the shift from group-oriented values to individualism) driven by an increase in the strength of certain individual 'needs' (usually those which emphasise status and achievement; that corresponds to an existing cultural emphasis on status, albeit often other than financial); and (3) availability and quality of human capital (that is, a highly competitive and very dynamic labour market, at least in central cities).

Soulsby and Clark (2006), employing a case study approach, explore changing patterns of employment in post-socialist organisations in CEE, and seek to develop a 'ground-up' mode of explanation of unemployment dynamics which starts with the examination of the real decision-making practices and processes of socially embedded enterprise managers. Through this approach, they advance an alternative theoretical framework to the dominant 'top-down' macroeconomic and institutional views that have been so significant in many of the investigations of the post-socialist economies. The authors argue that in order to understand economic outcomes more fully, researchers need to adopt a theoretical approach that combines the sociological reasoning of institutionalism with micro-processual arguments that theorise employment and unemployment as outcomes of everyday social construction; enterprise restructuring has not been a uniform or mono-causal process, emphasising once again the significance of contextual influences on transition process outcomes.

Woldu et al. (2006) in a comparative analysis examined the cultural value orientation of employees (managers and non-managers) working in three categories of organisations (professional, technical, and local services) in India, Poland, Russia, and the USA. Referring to Russia, they observed that the traditional collective and hierarchical value system of Russian managers was seen to be diminishing. In the managerial subsample of their dataset from both Poland and Russia, they found that the national cultural differences between the countries were modest, but the differences reappeared on a significant number of cultural dimensions when they compared their respective non-managerial-level respondents. On balance, they suggested that employees who work for similar organisations in relatively similar positions show a degree of cultural convergence in value orientations. Tixier (1995) observed the evolution in styles of management and the reduction of cultural differences between those involved, through an examination of the operation, dynamics, and intermingling of culturally mixed management teams with executives from France, Romania, and Bulgaria, among others. The acquiring of new or distinctive values and behaviours among local managers and employees in CEE was also observed by Cyr and Schneider (1996). Data were collected through interviews, questionnaires, and field observation in East–West joint ventures (JVs) located in Poland, Hungary, and the Czech Republic. In particular, the authors sought to integrate strategic aspects of HRM, international joint ventures (IJVs) and transition economies, and to investigate how HRM policy and practice contributes to the accomplishment of the ventures' strategic objectives in the transition economy context. The findings pointed to several conditions necessary to encourage employee performance, satisfaction, and learning in IJVs in transition contexts, including the sharing of responsibility between local and foreign managers, an emphasis on how to develop a new corporate culture that focuses on quality and results, the value of a training effort in contributing to the acquiring of new values and skills, and the structuring and institutionalisation of a rewards system that provides incentives for new behaviour.

Mihailova (2015) examined the outcomes of learning through IJVs for local parent firms in Russia. The empirical evidence presented suggests that learning through IJVs can become a source for the acquisition of and integration of advanced knowledge, which is necessary for their capability upgrading and long-term development. Mihailova also highlights that knowledge-sharing in the IJV context 'allows for more informed decisions regarding the extent and nature of cooperation which will be beneficial for Western [firms'] competitiveness in Russia and elsewhere' (Mihailova, 2015: 231). Dixon et al. (2014) explore attempts to introduce Western-style HRM processes and systems into two Russian oil companies, one of which was an IJV with a Western MNC and the other a wholly owned Russian company. In particular they noted that in the IJV the drive towards the implementation of Western practices was counteracted to a significant degree by Russian *spetfifika*, the particular and idiosyncratic Russian ways of thinking and doing things. In contrast, they observed that Western practices were absorbed at a faster pace in the more authoritarian wholly owned Russian company. Lupina-Wegener (2013) also focused on the issue of integration, in this instance of HRM among subsidiary mergers and acquisitions in Poland. In particular, insights are generated into the challenges of integrating the subsidiaries of Western MNCs in Poland and the potential problems that can arise between local and foreign managers. The qualitative data gathered revealed a number of key findings. Of note, the HRM function was mainly limited to administrative tasks and rarely played a strategic role in the pre-merger integration phase. The evidence also suggested that the success of HRM integration may be at stake in situations where HRM had low power in the subsidiary and where the investor demonstrated low multiculturalism.

CONCLUSIONS

The 'transition' from state socialism in CEE and the FSU has been judged to be one of the most significant economic and social processes in recent history (McCann & Schwartz, 2006), underscored by complex political, economic, and social dynamics. Early in the transition process, it was realised that there was a basic need for effective HRM systems in the post-socialist economies (Kovach, 1994), as these countries sought new beginnings.

In terms of what typifies the research to date, a number of characteristics are discernible. First of all, the dominant universal and contextual paradigms have inspired a great deal of nomothetic and idiographic-led enquiry, predominantly concerned with examining the core tenets of HRM in this post-socialist period and the evidence for a new epoch. Inevitably, the HRM issues in the region that have been examined are inexorably bound up in the economic transition and the phenomenal transformations that have taken place in the region, and the HRM–performance question has proven significant. At the functional level, there have been studies concerned with specific HRM practices such as training and development, selection and recruitment, performance management, and compensation issues. Some have also explored HRM issues at the strategic level, while other studies have probed into both HRM strategies and functions. MNC subsidiaries locating in the region have proven especially important as both a context for and the object of enquiry. In addition, and arising from the diversity of geographical and cultural coverage in the region and the dearth of much previous contextual knowledge in the literature, a considerable amount of the prior research has extensively utilised case studies. At a more macro level a number of studies present general, within-country descriptions of HRM, while others have engaged in comparative analysis.

On the whole, though, it is plausible to conclude that our knowledge bank of specialised and systematic research dedicated to HRM in CEE, while growing, remains circumscribed, most especially relative to the body of international business literature (Cooke et al., 2011). There have been a small number of journal special issues – among them, for example, Jankowicz (1998), Pocztowski (2008), Brewster et al. (2010), and Cooke et al. (2011) – which have focused on a limited number of countries. Valuable as these thematic special issues have been in further advancing our understanding of HRM in CEE, it is evident that further independent and systematic analyses into the HRM issues in these countries are needed. The results of the efforts to date have, in combination, given us insights into important aspects of transition dynamics, but there remain several gaps in our knowledge on HRM in the region. The state of theorising is limited and few conceptual frameworks with explanatory power exist. As Brewster (2007: 84) notes: 'In many areas of comparative HRM we lack adequate theory to explain the complexity of the differences between the meaning, policies and practices of HRM in different countries'. The overall dearth of theory has knock-on consequences for the overall empirical effort and how we might rate it. The number of studies to date is limited, and much of the work, whether of necessity or otherwise, is exploratory in nature. As a consequence, if we are to fully chart the landscape of HRM in this region, move beyond mere description, and provide a springboard for more complete and nuanced empirical accounts dealing with important research questions, we have more to do.

REFERENCES

Andreeva, T., Festing, M., Minbaeva, D.B., & Muratbekova-Touron, M. 2014. The Janus faces of IHRM in Russian MNEs. *Human Resource Management*, 53(6): 967–986.

Bandelj, N. 2009. The global economy as instituted process: The case of central and Eastern Europe. *American Sociological Review*, 74(1): 128–149.

Berend, T.I. 1996. *Central and Eastern Europe, 1944–1993: Detour from the Periphery to the Periphery.* Cambridge: Cambridge University Press.

Björkman, I., Fey, C.F., & Park, H.J. 2007. Institutional theory and MNC subsidiary HRM practices: Evidence from a three-country study. *Journal of International Business Studies*, 38(3): 430–446.

Boyer, R., & Drache, D. 1996. *States against Markets: The Limits of Globalization.* London: Routledge.

Brewster, C. 2007. Comparative HRM: European views and perspectives. *International Journal of Human Resource Management*, 18(5): 769–787.

Brewster, C., & Bennett, C. 2010. Perceptions of business cultures in Eastern Europe and their implications for international HRM. *International Journal of Human Resource Management*, 21(14): 2568–2588.

Brewster, C., Morley, M., & Buciuniene, I. 2010. The reality of human resource management in Central and Eastern Europe. *Baltic Journal of Management*, 5(2): 145–155.

Broadman, H., & Recanatini, F. 2003. Is Russia restructuring?. *Journal of Corporate Ownership and Control*, 1: 21–32.

Buchen, C. 2007. Estonia and Slovenia as Antipodes. In D. Lane and M. Myant (eds), *Varieties of Capitalism in Post-Communist Countries*: 65–89. London: Palgrave.

Buck, T., Filatotchev, I., Demina, N., & Wright, M. 2003. Insider ownership, human resource strategies and performance in a transition economy. *Journal of International Business Studies*, 34(6): 530–549.

Caligiuri, P.M. 1999. The ranking of scholarly journals in international human resource management. *International Journal of Human Resource Management*, 10(3): 515–519.

Cooke, F.L., Wood, G., Psychogios, A.G., & Szamosi, L.T. 2011. HRM in emergent market economies: Evidence and implications from Europe. *Human Resource Management Journal*, 21(4): 368–378.

Crowley, S. 2005. Welfare capitalism after communism: Labor weakness and post-communist social policies. In L. Hanley, B. Ruble, and J. Tulchin (eds), *Becoming Global and the New Poverty of Cities*: 139–164. Washington DC: Woodrow Wilson Center Press.

Cyr, D.J., & Schneider, S.C. 1996. Implications for learning: Human resource management in East–West joint ventures. *Organization Studies*, 17(2): 207–226.

Dalton, K., & Druker, J. 2012. Transferring HR concepts and practices within multi-national corporations in Romania: The management experience. *European Management Journal*, 30(6): 588–602.

Dibben, P., Wood, G., Le, H., & Williams, C.C. 2011. MNCs in Central, Southern and Central Europe and the former Soviet Union: Investment decisions and the regulation of employment. *Human Resource Management Journal*, 21(4): 379–394.

Dirani, K.M., Ardichvili, A., Cseh, M., & Zavyalova, E. 2015. Human resource management in Russia, Central and Eastern Europe. In F. Horwitz and P. Budhwar (eds), *Handbook of Human Resource Management in Emerging Markets*: 357–371: Cheltenham, UK and Northampton, MA, USA: Edward Elgar Publishing.

Dixon, S.E., Day, M., & Brewster, C. 2014. Changing HRM systems in two Russian oil companies: Western hegemony or Russian *spetsifika*?. *International Journal of Human Resource Management*, 25(22): 3134–3156.

Erutku, C., & Vallee, L. 1997. Business start-ups in today's Poland: Who and how?. *Entrepreneurship and Regional Development*, 9(2): 113–126.

Festing, M., & Sahakiants, I. 2013. Path-dependent evolution of compensation systems in Central and Eastern Europe: A case study of multinational corporation subsidiaries in the Czech Republic, Poland and Hungary. *European Management Journal*, 31(4): 373–389.

Fey, C., & Björkman, I. 2001. The effect of human resource management practices on MNC subsidiary performance in Russia. *Journal of International Business Studies*, 32(1): 59–75.

Fey, C., Björkman, I., & Pavlovskaya, A. 2000. The effect of human resource management practices on firm performance in Russia. *International Journal of Human Resource Management*, 11(1): 1–18.

Fey, C., Engström, P., & Björkman, I. 1999. Doing business in Russia: Effective human resource management practices for foreign firms in Russia. *Organizational Dynamics*, 28(2): 69-80.

Fletcher, C., & Perry, E. 2001. Performance appraisal and feedback: A consideration of national culture and a review of contemporary research and future trends. In N. Anderson, D. Ones, H. Kepir-Sinangil, and C. Viswesvaran (eds), *Handbook of Industrial, Work and Organizational Psychology*, Vol. 1: 127–145. London: SAGE Publications.

Garavan, T., Morley, M., Heraty, N., Lucewicz, J., & Suchodolski, A. 1998. Managing human resources in a post-command economy: Personnel administration or strategic HRM. *Personnel Review*, 27(3): 200–212.

Gurkov, I. 2002. Innovations and legacies in Russian human resource management practices: Surveys of 700 chief executive officers. *Post-Communist Economies*, 14(1): 137–144.

Gurkov, I., & Zelenova, O. 2009. Human resource management in Russia. In M. Morley, N. Heraty, and S. Michailova (eds), *Managing Human Resources in Central and Eastern Europe*: 278–312. London: Routledge.

Holden, N., & Vaiman, V. 2013. Talent management in Russia: Not so much war for talent as wariness of talent. *Critical Perspectives on International Business*, 9(1/2): 129–146.

Hoobler, J.M., & Brown Johnson, N. 2004. An analysis of current human resource management publications. *Personnel Review*, 33(6): 665–676.

Horwitz, F.M. 2011. Future HRM challenges for multinational firms in Eastern and Central Europe. *Human Resource Management Journal*, 21(4): 432–443.

Jankowicz, A. 1998. Issues in human resource management in central Europe. *Personnel Review*, 27(3): 169-176.

Karoliny, Z., Farkas, F., & Poór, J. 2009. In focus. Hungarian and Central Eastern European characteristics of human resource management: An international comparative survey. *Journal for East European Management Studies*, 14(1): 9–47.

Kase, R., & Zupan, N. 2005. Human resource management and firm performance in downsizing: Evidence from Slovenian manufacturing companies. *Economic and Business Review for Central and South-Eastern Europe*, 7(3): 239–262.

Kohont, A., & Brewster, C. 2014. The roles and competencies of HR managers in Slovenian multinational companies. *Baltic Journal of Management*, 9(3): 294–313.

Kovach, R.C. 1994. Matching assumptions to environment in the transfer of management. *International Studies of Management and Organization*, 24(4): 83–99.

Koveshnikov, A. 2011. The effects of cultural stereotypes on decision-making processes in Western MNCs in Russia. Conference paper, Academy of International Business. Rio de Janeiro, Brazil.

Kozminski, A.K. 2008. *Management in Transition*. Warsaw: Difin.

Lacombe, B.M.B., Tonelli, M.J., & Caldas, M.P. 2007. IHRM in developing countries: Does the functionalist vs. critical debate make sense South of the Equator? Paper presented at the EGOS Conference, Sub-theme 33: Critical Approaches to HRM.

Lane, D. 2007. Post-state socialism: A diversity of capitalisms?. In D. Lane and M. Myant (eds), *Varieties of Capitalism in Post-Communist Countries*: 13–39. London: Palgrave.

Latukha, M. 2015. Talent management in Russian companies: Domestic challenges and international experience. *International Journal of Human Resource Management*, 26(8): 1051–1075.

Ledeneva, A. 1998. *Russia's Economy of Favours: Blat, Networking and Informal Exchange*. Cambridge: Cambridge University Press.

Letiche, H. 1998. Transition and human resources in Slovakia. *Personnel Review*, 27(3): 213–226.

Lucas, R., Marinova, M., Kucerova, J., & Vetrokova, M. 2004. HRM practice in emerging economies: A long way to go in the Slovak hotel industry?. *International Journal of Human Resource Management*, 15(7): 1262–1279.

Lupina-Wegener, A.A. 2013. Human resource integration in subsidiary mergers and acquisitions: Evidence from Poland. *Journal of Organizational Change Management*, 26(2): 286–304.

McCann, L., & Schwartz, G. 2006. Terms and conditions apply: Management restructuring and the global integration of post-socialist societies. *International Journal of Human Resource Management*, 17(8): 1339–1352.

Meardi, G. 2006. Multinationals' heaven? Uncovering and understanding worker responses to multinational companies in post-communist Central Europe. *International Journal of Human Resource Management*, 17(8): 1366–1378.

Meyer, K.E., & Peng, M.W. 2016. Theoretical foundations of emerging economy business research. *Journal of International Business Studies*, 47(1): 3–22.

Michailova, S. 2000. Contrasts in culture: Russian and Western perspectives on organizational change. *Academy of Management Executive*, 14(4): 99–112.

Michailova, S. 2002. When common sense becomes uncommon: Participation and empowerment in Russian companies with Western participation. *Journal of World Business*, 37(3): 180–187.

Michailova, S., Heraty, N., & Morley, M. 2009. Studying human resource management in the international context: The case of Central and Eastern Europe. In M. Morley, N. Heraty, and S. Michailova (eds), *Managing Human Resources in Central and Eastern Europe*: 1–24. London: Routledge.

Mihailova, I. 2015. Outcomes of learning through JVs for local parent firms in transition economies: Evidence from Russia. *Journal of World Business*, 50(1): 220–233.

Milikić, B., Janićijević, N., & Petković, M. 2008. HRM in transition economies: The case of Serbia. *South East European Journal of Economics and Business*, 3(2): 75–88.

Mills, A. 1998. Contextual influences on human resource management in the Czech Republic. *Personnel Review*, 27(3): 177–199.

Minbaeva, D.B., Hutchings, K., & Thomson, S.B. 2007. Hybrid human resource management in post-Soviet Kazakhstan. *European Journal of International Management*, 1(4): 350–371.

Minbaeva, D.B., & Muratbekova-Touron, M. 2011. Experience of Canadian and Chinese acquisitions in Kazakhstan. *International Journal of Human Resource Management*, 22(14): 2946–2964.

Minbaeva, D.B., & Muratbekova-Touron, M. 2013. Clanism: Definition and implications for human resource management. *Management International Review*, 53(1): 109–139.

Morley, M. 2004. Contemporary debates in European human resource management: Context and content. *Human Resource Management Review*, 14(4): 353–364.

Morley, M., Heraty, N., & Michailova, S. 2009. *Managing Human Resources in Central and Eastern Europe*. London: Routledge.

Morley, M., Slavic, A., Poór, J., & Berber, N. 2016. Training practices and organisational performance: A comparative analysis of domestic and international market oriented organisations in Central & Eastern Europe. *Journal for East European Management Studies*, 21(3): 1–27.

Ohmae, K. 1990. *The Borderless World: Power and Strategy in the Interlinked Economy*. New York: Harper.

Peiper, M., & Estrin, S. 1998. Managerial markets in transition in Central and Eastern Europe: A field study and implications. *International Journal of Human Resource Management*, 9(1): 58–78.

Pocztowski, A. 2008. From the editor. *Human Resource Management*, 60(1): 7–9.

Poór, J., Karoliny, Z., Dobrai, K., et al. 2014. Factors influencing human resource management solutions at subsidiaries of multinational companies in Central and Eastern Europe. *Journal of East-West Business*, 20(2): 93–119.

Sakowski, K., Vadi, M., & Meriküll, J. 2015. Formalisation of organisational structure as a subject of path dependency: An example from Central and Eastern Europe. *Post-Communist Economies*, 27(1): 76–90.

Shekshnia, S. 1998. Western multinationals' human resource practices in Russia. *European Management Journal*, 16(4): 460–465.

Skuza, A., Scullion, H., & McDonnell, A. 2013. An analysis of the talent management challenges in a post-communist country: The case of Poland. *International Journal of Human Resource Management*, 24(3): 453–470.

Smith, P., Vozikis, G.S., & Varaksina, L. 2006. Outsourcing human resource management: A comparison of Russian and US practices. *Journal of Labor Research*, 27(3): 305–321.

Sorge, A. 2004 Cross national differences in human resources and organisations. In A.W.K. Harzing, and J. v. Ruysseveldt (eds), *International Human Resource Management*. London: SAGE Publications.

Soulsby, A., & Clark, E. 2006. Changing patterns of employment in post-socialist organizations in Central and Eastern Europe: management action in a transitional context. *International Journal of Human Resource Management*, 17(8): 1396–1410.

Taylor, D., & Walley, E.E. 2002. Hijacking the holy grail? Emerging HR practices in Croatia. *European Business Review*, 14(4): 294–298.

Tixier, M. 1995. Trends in international business thought and literature. Mixed management teams: How West European businesses approach Central and Eastern Europe. *International Executive*, 37(6): 631–643.

Tung, R.L., & Havlovic, S.J. 1996. Human resource management in transitional economies: The case of Poland and the Czech Republic. *International Journal of Human Resource Management*, 7(1): 1–19.

Uhlenbruck, K. 2004. Developing acquired foreign subsidiaries: The experience of MNEs in transition economies. *Journal of International Business Studies*, 35(2): 109–123.

Weinstein, M., & Obloj, K. 2002. Strategic and environmental determinants of HRM innovations in post-socialist Poland. *International Journal of Human Resource Management*, 13(4): 642–659.

Welsh, D.H., Luthans, F., & Sommer, S.M. 1993. Managing Russian factory workers: The impact of US-based behavioral and participative techniques. *Academy of Management Journal*, 35(1): 58–79.

Williams, K., & Geppert, M. 2004. Employment relations in the socio-political construction of transnational social spaces by multinational companies and their subsidiaries in Germany and the UK. Paper presented at

International Conference on Multinationals and the International Diffusion of Organizational Forms and Practices: Convergence and Divergence in the Global Economy, IESE. Barcelona, 15–18 July.

Woldu, H., Budhwar, P., & Parkes, C. 2006. A cross-national comparison of cultural value orientations of Indian, Polish, Russian and American employees. *International Journal of Human Resource Management*, 17(6): 1076–1094.

Woldu, H., & Budhwar, P.S. 2011. Cultural value orientations of the former communist countries: A gender-based analysis. *International Journal of Human Resource Management*, 22(07): 1365–1386.

Zupan, N., & Kaše, R. 2005. Strategic human resource management in European transition economies: Building a conceptual model on the case of Slovenia. *International Journal of Human Resource Management*, 16(6): 882–906.

26. HRM in the Middle East
Pawan Budhwar and Kamel Mellahi

INTRODUCTION

This chapter provides an overview regarding the scenario of human resource management (HRM) in the Middle East. In order to put things in context, it is important to consider the major socio-political, economic, and security-related developments that have taken place in the region and which are still unfolding. Many of these are an outcome of the Gulf War of 1993 and particularly of the developments taking place since late 2010. These include the beginning of the Arab Spring, a revolutionary wave of demonstrations and protests challenging the established political elite in Tunisia, Egypt, Libya, Syria, and Yemen. Such developments have implications for the management of human resources (HR) in firms operating in the region. In particular, they resulted in major displacement of people from the region.

Considering both the geographical vastness of the Middle East and the scarcity of reliable information on many countries of the region, and in order to put things into perspective, we initially describe the Middle East context and then present an analysis of relevant literature related to the developments in the field of HRM specific to the region. In doing so, we point out the main factors influencing HRM in the region, any emerging HRM models and approaches relevant to it, and conclude by highlighting the main challenges for HRM in the Middle East and an indicative way forward.

To start with, it is important to clarify the kind of terminologies used to denote the region. The literature highlights the interchangeable use of terms such as: the Middle East, Near East, Middle East–North Africa (MENA), South-West Asia, Greater Middle East, Levant, Arabian peninsula, or the Arab World in a very general sense (that is, it is applied to a group of nations existing in the region) by both academics and policy-makers (*Encyclopaedia Britannica*, 2015). However, it is important to acknowledge that despite some commonalities, each nation in the region has its own historical developments, an independent set of socio-economic components which differ from one another in content, arising inevitably from the interplay of social relations unique to themselves. Hence, it would be sensible to look at the HRM phenomena as part and parcel of the distinctive political, socio-economic, cultural, and institutional system of a given country in the region (Budhwar & Debrah, 2009). This is further complicated by the fact that countries in the Middle East region are at different stages of industrialisation, economic and political development, and are impacted upon differently by the above-mentioned developments.

Given the developments in HRM in most countries in the region (see Budhwar & Mellahi, 2006, 2007, 2016; Budhwar & Varma, 2012), it is important to define HRM in the broadest sense. This is sensible as several HRM approaches can exist within firms in different countries, each of which depend (along with a number of other factors, such as different institutions, national culture, and national policies) on a number of distinct 'internal labour markets' and approaches to human capital management (Boxall, 1995; Budhwar & Sparrow, 2002; Iles et al., 2012). Within each labour market, HRM incorporates a range of sub-functions and practices, which include systems for workforce governance, work organisation, staffing, and development and reward systems (Begin, 1992). Further, given the dominance of Islam in the region, HRM systems are strongly governed by its principles (Branine & Pollard, 2010). For this chapter, HRM is concerned with the management of all employment relationships in the firm, incorporating the management of managers as well as non-management labour.

THE MIDDLE EAST CONTEXT

As indicated, the term 'Middle East' is loosely defined and perhaps refers to a cultural area with no precise borders. There are different versions of what should be included under the Middle East region. In the broadest sense, it is the geographic region where Europe, Africa, and Asia meet. Sometimes it is referred to as an area with its centre in the eastern Mediterranean basin. The most limited version of the region includes only Syria, Lebanon, Israel, Palestine, and Jordan. Another version also includes Cyprus, Turkey, Iraq, and Egypt; while a further broader version of the Middle East includes Iran, Kuwait, Saudi Arabia, Bahrain, Qatar, the United Arab Emirates (UAE), Oman, and Yemen. Further, in some cases, the Middle East region is extended to include countries in North Africa with clear connections to Islam. Given that we have a separate chapter on North Africa in this volume (Chapter 27), these countries are excluded from this chapter.

Islam is the main religion of the Middle East with approximately 95 per cent of the total population following it (with a rough divide of 85 per cent Sunnis and 15 per cent Shias). Apart from Islam, the Middle East is also the birthplace of Judaism and Christianity. Turks and Arabs are its largest population groups, followed by Kurds and Jews. The dominant languages are Arabic, Turkish, Persian, Kurdish, English, French, and Hebrew (Answers. com, 2015). With approximately 65 per cent of the world's known oil reserves, the Middle East has occupied a position of primary strategic importance since World War II. Initially, in the 1950s, it exhibited one of the lowest levels of economic development in the world. However, in the 1960s and 1970s many countries in the region experienced strong economic growth mainly due to the discovery of oil. Still, in the 1990s the gross domestic product growth per worker in the region was roughly 1 per cent per annum (almost half the rate of other developing countries), and there has been a regular decline in total factor productivity (World Bank, 2009). Growth in the region was expected to be flat at roughly 2.2 per cent in 2015. The sharp fall in oil prices since June 2014 is a specific challenge for many of the oil-exporting countries of the region in the form of severe security challenges (such as Iraq and Yemen) or limited economic cushioning (for example, for Iran and Iraq). For oil-importing countries in the region, the fall in oil prices is partly offset by the spillover effects from the fragile economic environment in the region (World Bank, 2015).

A variety of factors are responsible for the slow economic development in the Middle East (apart from the above-mentioned recent developments). These range from structural imbalances to the so-called 'curse of natural resource abundance' (overdominance of the oil sector), underdeveloped financial markets, deficient political systems and political reforms, lack of privatisation, slow integration into the global economy, dominant public sectors, growing unemployment, lack of creation of skills, strong inclination of many locals to work only in public sector firms and only in managerial positions, underutilisation of skilled women, government systems (such as traditional sheikhdoms, absolute monarchies, military or autocratic regimes) in the region, and conditions of war and conflict (for details see Abdalla, 2015; Abed, 2003; Budhwar & Mellahi, 2006; 2016; Iles et al., 2012; Kuran, 2004; Looney, 2003; Matherly & Al Nahyan, 2015; Shaban et al., 1995; Sidani et al., 2015; Yousef, 2004).

Nevertheless, the continuous rise in oil prices between 2004 and 2008 helped the oil-rich countries of the region to grow phenomenally (World Bank, 2009). The non-oil-producing countries (such as Lebanon and Egypt) also experienced improved growth over the years; however, due to the 2008 global economic crisis and then the above-mentioned political turmoil, economic growth in the region has been substantially affected. Indeed, serious concerns over security impact upon the forecasts for both kinds of economies in the region (World Bank, 2015). Such concerns have serious implications for foreign direct investment in the region, especially in the non-oil-producing economies, which tend to rely heavily on sectors such as tourism, agriculture, and merchandise exports. Also, due to serious concerns over security, a large number of multinationals have pulled out of the disturbed parts of the Middle East, leaving a significant vacuum for economic growth. Such developments have many socio-economic and HRM implications, such as dealing with increasing unemployment and human capital management (Goby et al., 2015; Matherly & Al Nahyan, 2015; Singh & Sharma, 2015).

Most countries in the Middle East are now emphasising the development of their human resources, talent management, and organisational development (Mellahi & Budhwar, 2006; Kolachi & Akan, 2014; Singh & Sharma, 2015; Soltani & Liao, 2010). The countries with rich oil resources in the region have been making serious efforts to reduce their dependence on them and to develop other sectors, which need skilled human resources (Manafi & Subramaniam, 2015; Obeidat et al., 2014). Similarly, the non-oil-producing countries tend to rely on an efficient human resources bank for sustained economic growth. Most countries in the region still tend to rely on a foreign workforce and, given the rapidly increasing indigenous population and unemployment in the region, there is an increased emphasis on the development of 'locals' and reducing the number of 'foreigners' from the workforce, for example by Saudi Arabia, the UAE, and Oman (Forstenlechner, 2010; Goby et al., 2015; Matherly & Al Nahyan, 2015). Indeed, issues related to the creation of the right kind of employable skills in the region and to changing the mindset of locals to work in private sector and lower-level positions, are proving to be a major challenge. Such developments have serious implications for the HRM function in the region, in particular related to its role towards improving organisational performance (de Waal & Sultan, 2012; Iles et al., 2012; Mellahi & Budhwar, 2006; Mohamed et al., 2015; Zaitouni et al., 2011).

DEVELOPMENTS IN HRM IN THE MIDDLE EAST

Based on the above presentation, we can see that literature related to the field of HRM for many countries in the region, especially those that are politically stable (for example, the UAE, Oman, and Saudi Arabia) is now evolving rapidly. Nevertheless, there remain few works that can provide an overview of HRM in the region. Budhwar and Mellahi (2006, 2007) created a couple of useful volumes on HRM-related issues in a number of Middle East countries. Since then, articles have been published on various aspects of HRM (summarised below) and Afiouni et al. (2014) guest edited a special issue of the *International Journal of HRM* on 'HRM in the Middle East: Towards a Greater Understanding'. In this section, we initially summarise the main HRM-related works in the region and then present the key messages emerging from them.

Various scholars have attempted to provide a country-specific HRM overview: see, for example, on Iran, the works of Namazie and Tayeb (2006), Namazie and Frame (2007), Soltani and Liao (2010), and Manafi and Subramaniam (2015); on Oman, Al-Hamadi and Budhwar (2006), Al-Hamadi et al. (2007), Khan (2011), Katou et al. (2010), and Khan et al. (2015); on the UAE, Suliman (2006), Omair (2010), and Singh and Sharma (2015); on Kuwait, Ali and Al-Kazemi (2006) and Zaitouni et al. (2011); on Saudi Arabia, Mellahi and Wood (2004), Mellahi (2006), and Tlaiss and Elamin (2015); on Qatar, Abdalla (2006); on Jordan, Branine and Analoui (2006), Altarawneh and Aldehayyat (2011), and Syed et al. (2014); and on Kuwait, Zaitouni et al. (2011). These scholars present the nature and emerging patterns of HRM and related systems along with their key determinants in the respective countries.

Also, depending on the economic development of a given country in the region, studies covering specific aspects of HRM have been conducted. These include the effects of regulations on HRM in the Saudi Arabia private sector by Mellahi (2007), on employment policy in Kuwait by Al-Enezi (2002), and on the impact of HRM on organisational commitment in the banking sector in Kuwait (Zaitouni et al., 2011); human resource development (HRD) in Oman by Budhwar et al. (2002), talent management strategies in the UAE (Singh & Sharma, 2015), management and international business issues in Jordan by El-Said and Becker (2003), and strategic HRM in Jordan (Altarawneh & Aldehayyat, 2011). There have also been studies of the impact of cultural value orientations on preferences for HRM by Aycan et al. (2007), the challenges for employment in the Arab region by Shaban et al. (1995); on HRM and innovation in the Iranian electronic industry (Manafi & Subramaniam, 2015), on career development in Oman (Khan et al., 2015), and on general management in the Arab Middle East by Weir (2000).

There are a number of emerging studies that examine women in management-related issues in the Middle East countries (Metcalfe, 2006, for Bahrain, Jordan, and Oman; Metle, 2002, for Kuwait; Tlaiss, 2015 and Abdalla, 2015 for career success/ facilitator and barriers for women in the Arab context; Metcalfe, 2008 for women in management in the Middle East; Sidani et al., 2015 for female leadership advantage and leadership deficit; and Marmenout & Lirio, 2014 for female talent retention in the Gulf). There are also publications that debate the transfer of HRM from overseas to the region (Al-Husan & James, 2009, for Jordan). Although not an exhaustive list of all the different studies in the region, this is certainly a good indicator of the kind of HRM-related analysis being carried out.

A thorough analysis of this extant literature highlights the emergence of a number of key HRM-related themes. Perhaps the dominant theme is the one that highlights the influence of Arab culture and values on its management systems (Al-Faleh, 1987; Ali, 2010; Ali & Al-Shakis, 1985; Bakhtari, 1995; Branine & Pollard, 2010; Elsayed-Elkhouly & Buda, 1997; Hunt & At-Twaijri, 1996; Mellahi, 2003; Yasin, 1996). A number of scholars (Tayeb, 1997; Ali, 1992, 2004, 2010; Robertson et al., 2001) highlight the immense impact of Islamic values, Islamic work ethics, and Islamic principles on the management of human resources in the Islamic countries of the region (Ahmad, 1976; Branine & Pollard, 2010; Budhwar & Fadzil, 2000; Mellahi & Budhwar, 2006; Rosen, 2002). As expected, due to socio-cultural similarities, a number of countries (such as Kuwait and Qatar) tend to be similar in various aspects of cultural value orientations, being high on group orientation, strong on hierarchical structures, high on masculinity, strongly following the Arab traditions, and low on future orientation (Kabasakal & Bodur, 2002). In the Turkish context, Yucelt (1984) found that managers in traditional public sector organisations tend to lean toward a benevolent-authoritarian system and less toward a participative style.

Mellahi and Budhwar (2006) report a strong impact of high power distance on managers' perceptions about the delegation of authority to lower levels of employees and interaction with them, in countries such as Kuwait and Saudi Arabia. As a result of this, managers in such countries practise centralised decision-making processes, are less willing to delegate responsibility, and discourage active employee participation. In such circumstances with socio-cultural and traditional set-ups, loyalty to one's family and friends is expected to override loyalty to organisational procedures, and this often results in the use of inequitable criteria in recruitment, promotion, and compensation. Ali (2010), Ali and Al-Kazemi (2006), and Mellahi (2006) further highlight the influence of Islamic values: the principle of *shura* – that is, consultation, social harmony, and respect – is manifest in consensus decision-making styles, with respect for authority and age, and concern for the well-being of employees and society at large, in countries such as Kuwait and Saudi Arabia. Ali and Al-Kazemi (2006) reveal that several ideal Islamic values such as equity and fairness are often not adhered to in practice. This explains the widespread adoption of some HRM practices in the Middle East that are not compatible with Islamic values, such as the use of nepotism in recruitment and compensation, known as *wasta*, in the Gulf Cooperation Council (GCC) countries.

Due to significant differences (sociological, economic, legal, political, and so on) between the Middle East and other parts of the world (the 'West', in particular), foreign elements of management tend, at best, not to be conducive to the development of sound management practices in the region (Ali, 1995; Ali & Camp, 1995; Neal & Finlay, 2008; Yavas, 1998; Khan, 2011). An analysis by Saleh and Kleiner (2005) indicates that if United States companies want to be successful in the Middle East, they should develop an understanding of the local culture, politics, and people of the region. Similarly, Hill et al. (1998) highlight the problems of transferring technology designed and produced in developed countries to the Arab region. As technologies are culturally biased in favour of developed countries, this creates cultural and social obstacles when transferring them to developing countries. Research by Goby et al. (2015) highlights the usefulness of the creation of a positive diversity climate based on Arab cultural traditions in managing the diverse workforce (comprising both locals and expatriates) in the region.

A related theme clearly evident in the literature is that of human resource development where issues are related to the impact of Arab management styles on the effectiveness of cross-cultural negotiations and organisational development activities in the region (Ali, 1996; Kolachi & Akan, 2014), along with the relationship between management education and its impact on managerial effectiveness (Analoui & Hosseini, 2001; Ali &

Camp, 1995; Atiyyah, 1996; Anastos et al., 1980), and the need for and mechanisms of management development in the Arab world (Agnala, 1997; Al-Rasheed & Al-Qwasmeh, 2003; Budhwar et al., 2002).

Atiyyah (1991, 1996) emphasises the usefulness of cultural training and acculturation in the adjustment of expatriates to the region. Matherly and Al Nahyan (2015) propose the need for effective governance of national–expatriate knowledge transfer to build competitiveness; and Goby et al. (2015) highlight the need for the development and practise of interpersonal communication and a diversity climate framework in order to facilitate workforce localisation in countries that have an expatriate majority workforce, such as the UAE. Al-Rajhi et al. (2006) reveal the challenges for HRM in the region regarding the adjustment of impatriates. Contributions from Elmuti and Kathawala (1991), Marriot (1986), and Rodriquez and Scurry (2014) further confirm the need for foreign firms and employees to be strongly responsive and adaptive to local requirements in order to be successful in the Middle East context. Syed et al. (2014) examine the views of local Jordanians towards expatriate managers. This is important given the significant cultural diversity of the foreign workforce in the Middle East, where it is crucial for managers to recognise, understand, and acknowledge the cultural differences of subordinates and accordingly adopt a relevant leadership style. Given the high power distance nature of most Middle East nations, an employee-orientated, paternalistic approach tends to be more successful than others (Al-Rasheed, 2001; Badawy, 1980; Enshassi & Burgess, 1991; Zaitouni et al., 2011).

In the absence of awareness, an outsider might believe that there are strong similarities between nations of the Middle East. However, there remains considerable variation across countries in the Middle East that these cultural factors cannot explain. It is now well established in the literature that the management of human resources in a given context is influenced by a combination of national factors (such as the above-mentioned cultural and institutional factors), different contingent variables (such as the size, age, and nature of an organisation), and the kinds of policies and strategies an organisation pursues (Budhwar & Sparrow, 2002; Budhwar & Debrah, 2009). Many such factors and variables are shaping the HRM function in the Middle East region as well. The rest of this section further highlights the main determinants of the HRM policies and practices of the Middle East.

Over the past couple of decades, countries such as Iran and Jordan have been actively pursuing the process of privatisation (Mellahi & Budhwar, 2006). These countries are also pursuing liberalisation of their economic systems, as a result of which the central government control over HRM practices has been greatly reduced. Such developments have serious implications for the HRM systems of these countries, including job security in the public sector (which is now eroding fast), and downsizing and closure of poorly performing firms.

A number of countries in the region have also been actively pursuing localisation programmes (with an emphasis on offering jobs to locals and reducing the dependence on foreign nationals). This has implications for talent management (Singh & Sharma, 2015), interpersonal communication and diversity management (Goby et al., 2015), management of workplace quotas (Matherly & Al Nahyan, 2015), leadership behaviour of national and expatriate managers (Bealer & Bhanugopan, 2014), and barriers to such localisation programmes (Al-Waqfi & Forstenlechner, 2014). The variation in

HRM practices based on the size, nature and ownership of the firm (private, public, or multinational) is also evident from an analysis of HRM in countries such as Iran, Kuwait, and Saudi Arabia. Large private sector organisations tend to pay higher salaries than public sector organisations, but job security is low in private sector firms as compared to public sector organisations. In GCC countries (that is, Oman, the UAE, Kuwait, Saudi Arabia, and Qatar), however, public sector organisations pay higher salaries than most private sector organisations and job security is still relatively high in the public sector (Mellahi & Budhwar, 2006). Iles et al. (2012) highlight the challenges for effective human resource management in the public sector in the Middle East where the impact of *wasta* is strong.

There is also evidence that in many Middle Eastern countries (such as Oman, the UAE, Saudi Arabia, and Iran) the respective national governments are emphasising the development of human resources and accordingly giving organisations freedom in HRM matters, although within the legal framework. In this regard, the role of HRD in organisational development is being highlighted (Kolachi & Akan, 2014). The names and nature of traditional personnel departments are also changing to emphasise the development of effective HRM systems to help firms compete at home and abroad. However, in the absence of skilled HRM professionals in most Middle Eastern countries, HRM managers have been muddling through, often relying on trial and error, to cope with the impact of market liberalisation and severe international competition. In order to cover such skill gaps many countries such as the UAE, Oman, Jordan, Kuwait, Saudi Arabia, and Iran are investing heavily in the development of their human resources. A number of inherent problems with these countries, including a lack of a vocation-based education system, the supply and demand imbalance, negative perception of locals working in the private sector or in lower positions, and the lack of participation of women in the main workforce, are proving to be the main bottlenecks (Heeti & Brock, 1997; Rugh, 2002; Shaw, 2002; Mellahi, 2006; Abdalla, 2015; Sidani et al., 2015). Further, the strong emphasis of the above-mentioned localisation programmes pursued by many countries in the region is not helping either the private sector or multinational firms to achieve rationalisation of their HRM systems (Ahmad, 2004; Rees et al., 2007; Al-Waqfi & Forstenlechner, 2014).

Based on the above analysis, it can be concluded that there is now an emerging literature on different aspects of HRM systems in the Middle East, although our knowledge remains both limited and patchy, as a result of which it is difficult to draw a conclusive and comprehensive picture of the scene. We cannot confidently say whether there is such a thing as a 'Middle Eastern HRM model', that is, a single HRM model with distinct Middle Eastern characteristics (Khan, 2011). Perhaps due to a number of reasons related to diversity within the region (including historical contexts, institutional, geographical, cultural, political, legal, social, development stage of nations, support of relevant agencies, national wealth, poverty, national priorities, issues related to terrorism, the role of unions, reliance on foreign labour, increasing security related issues, and global recessionary conditions), it seems that organisations in the Middle East use a whole range of different HRM policies and practices, and that the professionalisation of HRM functions is at different stages in different countries.

CHALLENGES FOR THE FUTURE OF HRM IN THE MIDDLE EAST

Based on the above we can say that HRM policies and practices throughout the Middle East are changing, both in terms of the contexts within which they operate, and in terms of the HRM function. There is emerging evidence about major HRM-related changes in the region. A number of forces contribute in this regard, such as changes in the business environment, globalisation, increased interest in the region due to ongoing conflicts, and economic developments. For example, de Waal and Sultan (2012) highlight a move towards individualisation in HRM policies such as rewards and promotion and high-performance-based HRM systems in the Middle East. These scholars also indicate the efforts being made in most Middle Eastern countries for firms to move away from relationship-based practices and to use more performance-based criteria in recruitment, selection, rewards, and promotion (Mellahi & Budhwar, 2006; Zaitouni et al., 2011). In order to make such changes widespread and to reap their real benefits, there are massive challenges for the HRM function in the region. The first is to convince all concerned about the need to bring such changes. The second is to ensure that these changes take place both quickly and effectively. One of the major hurdles in this regard is changing the mindset of top managers whose beliefs are embedded in old routines and old ways of doing things (Mellahi, 2003). Emerging research evidence (Khan et al., 2015) suggests that, for example, involving employees in career development decision-making process, and increasing transparency and fairness, can create a win–win situation.

Related to changing the mindset of top managers, the creation of a more strategic image and status of the HRM function in the region is another major challenge. Mellahi and Budhwar (2006) conclude that the HRM function in most Middle Eastern countries suffers from low status and is often relegated to a 'common sense' function that, according to top management, does not require professional skills. To a great extent this is an outcome of the poor development of HRM managers, who are not fully capable and ready to manage change and meet current and future challenges. Given some of the inherent problems within the Middle East, such as increasing unemployment, deficiency of employable skills in the available job candidates, pressure to survive, the right size of firms during the difficulties, and reducing over-reliance on the oil economy, it is high time that the HRM function in the region was given the freedom to make the required changes and accordingly make useful contributions towards organisation performance, as has happened in many other parts of the world. In this regard, there is a need not only to overhaul the educational and vocational courses and training provided by different institutions in the region, but also to be open and receptive to adopting more of the successful systems of other parts of the world (with the required modifications), as is happening in many emerging markets, resulting in 'crossvergence' of HRM systems (Budhwar & Debrah, 2009). Reinforcing this, a recent analysis by Deloitte (2015), based on the views of 3000 HRM and business leaders related to human capital trends and challenges, also adds the need to focus on: (1) learning and development to meet the talent-related challenge; (2) reinventing HRM to make it a true partner to the business; (3) development of leaders suitable to be efficient in the present-day context; and (4) development of an organisational culture to encourage employee engagement.

In order to achieve some of these changes, it is important to move away from the inequitable relationship-based HRM policies such as *wasta*, towards a competence- or merit-based approach (Iles et al., 2012). This is now becoming a serious issue, given the aggressive localisation programmes pursued by many countries of the region. Simultaneously, firms in the region are being pushed into global economic integration in order to survive and flourish (Afiouni et al., 2014). The absence of skilled local human resources, and open discrimination against overseas skilled employees, might result in serious skill gaps in the region, which will have massive economic implications when many nations in the region are making serious attempts to move into new sectors and reduce their over-reliance on oil-related products. The HRM function in the region has serious tasks at hand to determine how such a transition (towards localisation) can take place, and also to ensure that talent is not pushed out of the region, haphazardly creating skills gaps and increasing the cost of attracting, acquiring, and retaining talent. In such conditions the emphasis on talent management (Singh & Sharma, 2015), diversity management (Goby et al., 2015), and on HRD, career, and organisational development (Khan et al., 2015), becomes critical.

This is further aggravated by the problems created by both high unemployment levels and rapidly increasing populations in most Middle Eastern countries (Harry, 2007). In future times this may be a major destabilising factor for economic development in the region. Indeed many governments of different countries in the Middle East, along with the private sector, are trying to develop schemes whereby the government contributes towards the cost of training locals, to encourage private sector firms to recruit more local workers (this is happening, for example, in Saudi Arabia, Oman, and the UAE). Dealing with such major issues not only poses major challenges to national governments but also has serious implications for HRM functions (Afiouni et al., 2014).

Given the 'infancy' stage of HRM in the region, there is a need for more research to develop a clear view of the key factors that shape the HRM function and determine its performance. But this raises another set of challenges, including: in the absence of an established research culture, how can researchers conduct meaningful research? Also, given the socio-cultural context of the Middle East and the emerging evidence about the need to adopt and modify Western HRM practices in the region, one needs to be careful of adopting Western HRM constructs, items, measures, and methodologies to conduct investigations in the region. As reported above, some work has been conducted in the past on Arab and Islamic work values and management styles and systems. This can be further developed specifically for the HRM function. In particular, future research should seek to identify and classify the unique region-specific aspects of national culture and other variables, political institutions, and other possible external factors that influence HRM in the Middle East.

In addition, there is a need for both HRM practitioners and researchers to work on issues related to diversity management, female leadership advantage, psychological contracts, HRM and performance, trust and employee engagement, emerging dominant HRM approaches and systems of the Middle East, the kind of internal labour markets suitable for firms operating in the region, tackling nepotism and corruption, ensuring a robust legal framework that works properly to safeguard both local and overseas employees, the creation of relevant employment relations, and how to encourage sharing of evidence-led best practices available with certain case companies in the Middle East. The emphasis should be on further highlighting successful indigenous HRM practices as well as practices developed elsewhere that can be adopted in the region (for example, high-performance work systems, innovative work practices, and specific participatory work practices that are successful in high-power-distance societies).

Dealing with these challenges will never be easy, as they require macro-level changes at the country level and also a change of mindset at the individual level. These are deeply rooted in the socio-cultural milieu of the region. This is even more difficult given the existence of the uncertain business environment in the region. It is important to acknowledge that conducting HRM research in most parts of the Middle East is and will continue to be a challenging task in an environment where access to reliable data and organisations is very demanding. However, analyses like this one, and indeed others, help us to identify the factors that shape and reshape HRM in the Middle East, and perhaps to understand better the mechanisms by which they do so, and guide us in what we need to do in future.

REFERENCES

Abdalla, I.A. 2006. Human resource management in Qatar. In P.S. Budhwar and K. Mellahi (eds), *Managing Human Resources in the Middle East*: 121–144. London: Routledge.

Abdalla, I.A. 2015. Career facilitators and barriers of Arab women senior executives. *International Journal of Business and Management*, 10(8): 218–232.

Abed, G.T. 2003. Unfulfilled promise. *Finance and Development*, 40(1): 10–14.

Afiouni, F., Ruël, H., & Schuler, R.S. 2014. HRM in the Middle East: Toward a greater understanding. *International Journal of Human Resource Management*, 25(2): 133–143.

Agnala, A.A. 1997. Management development in the Arab World. *Human Resource Management International Digest*, 5(5): 38–41.

Ahmad, K. 1976. *Islam: Its Meaning and Message*. London: Islamic Council of Europe.

Ahmad, M. 2004. When does final means final?. *Arab News*, 4 November.

Al-Enezi, A. 2002. Kuwait's employment policy: Its formulation, implications, and challenges. *International Journal of Public Administration*, 25(7): 885–900.

Al-Faleh, M. 1987. Cultural influences on Arab management development: A case study of Jordan. *Journal of Management Development*, 6(3): 19–33.

Al-Hamadi, A.B., & Budhwar, P. 2006. HRM in Oman. In P.S. Budhwar and K. Mellahi (eds), *Managing Human Resources in the Middle East*: 40–58. London: Routledge.

Al-Hamadi, A.B., Budhwar, P.S., & Shipton, H. 2007. Managing human resources in the Sultanate of Oman. *International Journal of Human Resource Management*, 18(1): 100–113.

Al-Husan, F.B., & James, P. 2009. Multinationals and the process of post-entry HRM reform: Evidence from three Jordanian case studies. *European Management Journal*, 27(2): 142–154.

Al-Rajhi, I., Altman, Y., Metcalfe, B., & Roussel, J. 2006. Managing impatriate adjustment as a core human resource management challenge. *Human Resource Planning*, 29(4): 15–24.

Al-Rasheed, A.M. 2001. Features of traditional Arab management and organization in the Jordan business environment. *Journal of Transnational Management Development*, 6(1/2): 27–53.

Al-Rasheed, A.M., & Al-Qwasmeh, F.M. 2003. The role of the strategic partner in the management development process: Jordan Telecom as a case study. *International Journal of Commerce and Management*, 13(2): 144–175.

Al-Waqfi, M.A., & Forstenlechner, I. 2014. Barriers to Emiratization: The role of policy design and institutional environment in determining the effectiveness of Emiratization. *International Journal of Human Resource Management*, 25(2): 167–189.

Ali, A. 1992. Islamic work ethic in Arabia. *Journal of Psychology*, 126(5): 507–519.

Ali, A. 1995. Cultural discontinuity and Arab management thought. *International Studies of Management and Organization*, 25(3): 7–30.

Ali, A. 1996. Organizational development in the Arab World. *Journal of Management Development*, 15(5): 4–21.

Ali, A. 2004. *Islamic Perspectives on Management and Organization*. Cheltenham, UK and Northampton, MA, USA: Edward Elgar Publishing.

Ali, A. 2010. Islamic challenges to HR in modern organizations. *Personnel Review*, 39(6): 692–711.

Ali, A., & Al-Kazemi, A. 2006. Human resource management in Kuwait. In P.S. Budhwar and K. Mellahi (eds), *Managing Human Resources in the Middle East*: 79–96. London: Routledge.

Ali, A., & Al-Shakis, M. 1985. Managerial value systems for working in Saudi Arabia: An empirical investigation. *Group and Organization Studies*, 10(2): 135–151.

Ali, A., & Camp, R.C. 1995. Teaching management in the Arab World: Confronting illusions. *International Journal of Educational Management*, 9(2): 10–17.

Altarawneh, I., & Aldehayyat, J.S. 2011. Strategic human resources management (SHRM) in Jordanian hotels. *International Journal of Business and Management*, 6(10): 242–255.

Analoui, F., & Hosseini, M.H. 2001. Management education and increased managerial effectiveness: The case of business managers in Iran. *Journal of Management Development*, 20(9): 785–794.

Anastos, D., Bedos, A., & Seaman, B. 1980. The development of modern management practices in Saudi Arabia. *Columbia Journal of World Business*, 15(2): 81–92.

Answers.com. 2015. http://www.answers.com/Q/What_languages_are_spoken_in_the_Middle_East.

Atiyyah, H.S. 1991. Effectiveness of management training in Arab countries. *Journal of Management Development*, 10(7): 22–29.

Atiyyah, H.S. 1996. Expatriate acculturation in Arab Gulf countries. *Journal of Management Development*, 15(5): 37–47.

Aycan, Z., Al-Hamadi, A.B., Davis, A., & Budhwar, P. 2007. Cultural orientations and preferences for HRM policies and practices: The case of Oman. *International Journal of Human Resource Management*, 18(1): 11–32.

Badawy, M.K. 1980. Styles of Mideastern managers. *California Management Review*, 22(3): 51–58.

Bakhtari, H. 1995. Cultural effects on management style: A comparative study of American and Middle Eastern management styles. *International Studies of Management and Organization*, 25(3): 97–118.

Bealer, D., & Bhanugopan, R. 2014. Transactional and transformational leadership behaviour of expatriate and national managers in the UAE: A cross-cultural comparative analysis. *International Journal of Human Resource Management*, 25(2): 293–316.

Begin, J.P. 1992. Comparative human resource management (HRM): A systems perspective. *International Journal of Human Resource Management*, 3(3): 379–408.

Boxall, P.F. 1995. Building the theory of comparative HRM. *Human Resource Management Journal*, 5(5): 5–17.

Branine, M., & Analoui, F. 2006. Human resource management in Jordan. In P.S. Budhwar and K. Mellahi (eds), *Managing Human Resources in the Middle East*: 145–159. London: Routledge.

Branine, M., & Pollard, D. 2010. Human resource management with Islamic management principles: A dialectic for a reverse diffusion in management. *Personnel Review*, 39(6): 712–727.

Budhwar, P.S., Al-Yahmadi, S., & Debrah, Y. 2002. Human resource development in the Sultanate of Oman. *International Journal of Training and Development*, 6(3): 198–215.

Budhwar, P.S., & Debrah, Y. 2009. Future research on human resource management systems in Asia. *Asia Pacific Journal of Management*, 26(2): 197–218.

Budhwar, P.S., & Fadzil, K. 2000. Globalization, economic crisis and employment practices: Lessons from a large Malaysian Islamic institution. *Asia Pacific Business Review*, 7(1): 171–198.

Budhwar, P.S., & Mellahi, K. 2006. Introduction: HRM in the Middle-East context. In P.S. Budhwar and K. Mellahi (eds), *Managing Human Resources in the Middle East*: 1–19. London: Routledge.

Budhwar, P.S., & Mellahi, K. 2007. *International Journal of Human Resource Management*, 18(1), Special Issue: Human Resource Management in the Middle East.

Budhwar, P.S., & Mellahi, K. 2016. *Handbook of Human Resource Management in the Middle East*. Cheltenham, UK and Northampton, MA, USA: Edward Elgar Publishing.

Budhwar, P.S., & Sparrow, P. 2002. An integrative framework for understanding cross-national human resource management practices. *Human Resource Management Review*, 12(3): 377–403.

Budhwar, P.S., & Varma, A. 2012. Human resource management in the Indian subcontinent. In C. Brewster and W. Mayrhofer (eds), *Handbook of Research on Comparative Human Resource Management*: 576–597. Cheltenham, UK and Northampton, MA, USA: Edward Elgar Publishing.

de Waal, A., & Sultan, S. 2012. Applicability of the high performance organization framework in the Middle East. *Education, Business and Society: Contemporary Middle Eastern Issues*, 5(3): 213–223.

Deloitte. 2015. Deloitte: Middle East organizations facing human capital trends and challenges. http://www.bq-magazine.com/economy/employment-economy/2015/06/hr-challenges-in-the-middle-east (accessed 10 October 2015).

El-Said, H., & Becker, K. 2003. *Management and International Business Issues in Jordan*. London: International Business Press.

Elmuti, D., & Kathawala, Y. 1991. An investigation of the human resources management practices of Japanese subsidiaries in the Arabian Gulf region. *Journal of Applied Business Research*, 7(2): 82–88.

Elsayed-Elkhouly, S., & Buda, R. 1997. A cross-cultural comparison of value systems of Egyptians, Americans, Africans and Arab executives. *International Journal of Commerce and Management*, 7(3/4): 102–119.

Encyclopaedia Britannica. 2015. Middle East. http://www.britannica.com/place/Middle-East.

Enshassi, A., & Burgess, R. 1991. Managerial effectiveness and the style of management in the Middle East: An empirical analysis. *Construction Management and Economics*, 9(1): 79–92.

Forstenlechner, I. 2010. Expats and citizens: Managing diverse teams in the Middle East. *Team Performance Management: An International Journal*, 16(5/6): 237–241.

Goby, V.P., Nickerson, C., & David, E. 2015. Interpersonal communication and diversity climate: Promoting workforce localization in the UAE. *International Journal of Organizational Analysis*, 23(3): 364–377.

Harry, W. 2007. Employment creation and localization: The crucial human resource issues for the GCC. *International Journal of Human Resource Management*, 18(1): 132–146.

Heeti, A.G.A., & Brock, C. 1997. Vocational education and development: Key issues, with special reference to the Arab world. *International Journal of Educational Development*, 17(4): 373–389.

Hill, C.E., Loch, K.D., Straub, D.W., & El-Sheshai, K. 1998. A qualitative assessment of Arab culture and information technology transfer. *Journal of Global Information Management*, 6(3): 29–38.

Hunt, D.M., & At-Twaijri, M.I. 1996. Values and the Saudi manager: An empirical investigation. *Journal of Management Development*, 15(5): 48–55.

Iles, P., Almhedie, A., & Baruch, Y. 2012. Managing HR in the Middle East: Challenges in the public sector. *Public Personnel Management*, 41(3): 465–492.

Kabasakal, H., & Bodur, M. 2002. Arabic cluster: A bridge between East and West. *Journal of World Business*, 37(1): 40–54.

Katou, A., Budwhar, P.S., Woldu, H., & Al-Hamadi, A.B. 2010. Influence of ethical beliefs, national culture and institutions on preferences for HRM in Oman. *Personnel Review*, 39(6): 728–745.

Khan, S.A. 2011. Convergence, divergence or middle of the path: HRM model for Oman. *Journal of Management Policy and Practice*, 12(1): 76–87.

Khan, S.A., Rajasekar, J., & Al-Asfour, A. 2015. Organizational career development practices: Learning from an Oman company. *International Journal of Business and Management*, 10(9): 88–98.

Kolachi, N., & Akan, O. 2014. HRD role in organizational development (A case of corporate thinking at ETISALAT, UAE). *International Business Research*, 7(8): 160–167.

Kuran, T. 2004. Why the Middle East is economically underdeveloped: Historical mechanisms of institutional stagnation. *Journal of Economic Perspectives*, 18(3): 71–90.

Looney, R. 2003. The Gulf Cooperation Council's cautious approach to economic integration. *Journal of Economic Cooperation*, 24(2): 137–160.

Manafi, M., & Subramaniam, I.D. 2015. Relationship between human resources management practices, transformational leadership and knowledge sharing on innovation in Iranian electronic industry. *Asian Social Science*, 11(10): 358–385.

Marmenout, K., & Lirio, P. 2014. Local female talent retention in the Gulf: Emirati women bending with the wind. *International Journal of Human Resource Management*, 25(2): 144–166.

Marriott, R.G. 1986. Ads require sensitivity to Arab culture. *Religion, Marketing News*, 20(9): 3–5.

Matherly, L., & Al Nahyan, S.S. 2015. Workplace quotas: Building competitiveness through effective governance of national-expatriate knowledge transfer and development of sustainable human capital. *International Journal of Organizational Analysis*, 23(3): 456–471.

Mellahi, K. 2003. National culture and management practices: The case of GCCs. In M. Tayeb (ed.), *International Management: Theory and Practices*: 87–105. London: Prentice-Hall.

Mellahi, K. 2006. Human resource management in Saui Arabia. In P.S. Budhwar and K. Mellahi (eds), *Managing Human Resources in the Middle East*: 97–120. London: Routledge.

Mellahi, K. 2007. The effect of regulations on HRM: Private sector firms in Saudi Arabia. *International Journal of Human Resource Management*, 18(1): 85–99.

Mellahi, K., & Budhwar, P.S. 2006. HRM challenges in the Middle East: Agenda for future research and policy. In P.S. Budhwar and K. Mellahi (eds), *Managing Human Resources in the Middle East*: 291–301. London: Routledge.

Mellahi, K., & Wood, G. 2004. Human resource management in Saudi Arabia. In P.S. Budhwar and K. Mellahi (eds), *Managing Human Resources in the Middle East*: 135–151. London: Routledge.

Metcalfe, B. 2006. Exploring cultural dimensions of gender and management in the Middle East. *Thunderbird International Business Review*, 48(1): 93–107.

Metcalfe, B.D. 2008. Women, management and globalization in the Middle East. *Journal of Business Ethics*, 83(1): 85–100.

Metle, M.K. 2002. The influence of traditional culture on attitudes towards work among Kuwaiti women employees in the public sector. *Women in Management Review*, 17(6): 245–261.

Mohamed, M.I., Mutalib, M.A., Abdulaziz, A.M., Ibrahim, M., & Habtoor, N.A.S. 2015. A review of HRM practices and labor productivity: Evidence from Libyan oil companies. *Asian Social Science*, 11(9): 215–225.

Namazie, P., & Frame, P. 2007. Developments in human resource management in Iran. *International Journal of Human Resource Management*, 18(1): 159–171.

Namazie, P., & Tayeb, M. 2006. Human resource management in Iran. In P.S. Budhwar and K. Mellahi (eds), *Managing Human Resources in the Middle East*: 20–39. London: Routledge.

Neal, M., & Finlay, J.L. 2008. American hegemony and business education in the Arab World. *Journal of Management Education*, 32(1): 38–49.

Obeidat, B.Y., Masa'deh, R., Moh'd, T., & Abdallah, A.B. 2014. The relationships among human resource management practices, organizational commitment, and knowledge management processes: A structural equation modeling approach. *International Journal of Business and Management*, 9(3): 9–26.

Omair, K. 2010. Typology of career development for Arab women managers in the United Arab Emirates. *Career Development International*, 15(2): 121–143.

Rees, C.J., Mamman, A., & Braik, A.B. 2007. Emiratization as a strategic HRM change initiative: Case study evidence from a UAE petroleum company. *International Journal of Human Resource Management*, 18(1): 33–53.

Robertson, C., Al-Habib, M., Al-Khatib, J., & Lanoue, D. 2001. Beliefs about work in the Middle East and the convergence versus divergence of values. *Journal of World Business*, 36(13): 223–235.

Rodriguez, J.K., & Scurry, T. 2014. Career capital development of self-initiated expatriates in Qatar: Cosmopolitan globetrotters, experts and outsiders. *International Journal of Human Resource Management*, 25(2): 190–211.

Rosen, L. 2002. *The Culture of Islam: Changing Aspects of Contemporary Muslim Life*. Chicago, IL: University of Chicago Press.

Rugh, W.A. 2002. Education in Saudi Arabia: Choices and constraints. *Middle East Policy*, 9(2): 40–55.

Saleh, S., & Kleiner, B.H. 2005. Issues and concerns facing American companies in the Middle East. *Management Research News*, 28(2/3): 56–62.

Shaban, R.A., Assaad, R., & Al-Qudsi, S. 1995. The challenge of unemployment in the Arab region. *International Labour Review*, 134: 65–82.

Shaw, K.E. 2002. Education and technological capability building in the Gulf. *International Journal of Technology and Design Education*, 12(1): 77–91.

Sidani, Y.M., Konrad, A., & Karam, C.M. 2015. From female leadership advantage to female leadership deficit: A developing country perspective. *Career Development International*, 20(3): 273–292.

Singh, A., & Sharma, J. 2015. Strategies for talent management: A study of select organizations in the UAE. *International Journal of Organizational Analysis*, 23(3): 337–347.

Soltani, E., & Liao, Y.-Y. 2010. Training interventions: Fulfilling managerial ends or proliferating invaluable means for employees? Some evidence from Iran. *European Business Review*, 22(2): 128–152.

Suliman, A.M.T. 2006. Human resource management in the United Arab Emirates. In P.S. Budhwar and K. Mellahi (eds), *Managing Human Resources in the Middle East*: 59–78. London: Routledge.

Syed, J., Hazboun, N.G., & Murray, P.A. 2014. What locals want: Jordanian employees' views on expatriate managers. *International Journal of Human Resource Management*, 25(2): 212–233.

Tayeb, M. 1997. Islamic revival in Asia and human resource management. *Employee Relations*, 19(4): 352–364.

Tlaiss, H.A. 2015. Neither-nor: Career success of women in an Arab Middle Eastern context. *Employee Relations*, 37(5): 525–546.

Tlaiss, H.A., & Elamin, A.M. 2015. Exploring organizational trust and organizational justice among junior and middle managers in Saudi Arabia: Trust in immediate supervisor as a mediator. *Journal of Management Development*, 34(9): 1042–1060.

Weir, D.T.H. 2000. Management in the Arab Middle East. In M. Tayeb (ed.), *International Business, Theories, Policies and Practices*: 501–510. Upper Saddle River, NJ: Pearson Education.

World Bank. 2009. *Global Economic Prospects 2009: Middle East and North Africa Regional Outlook*. Washington, DC: World Bank.

World Bank. 2015. *Global Economic Prospects*. http://www.worldbank.org/en/publication/global-economic-prospects/regional-outlooks/Global-Economic-Prospects-June-2015-Middle-East-and-North-Africa-analysis.

Yasin, M. 1996. Entrepreneurial effectiveness and achievement in Arab culture. *Journal of Business Research*, 35(1): 69–77.

Yavas, U. 1998. The efficacy of US business education in the transfer of management technology: The case of Saudi Arabia. *Journal of Education for Business*, 74(1): 50–53.

Yousef, T.M. 2004. Development, growth and policy reform in the Middle East and North Africa since 1950. *Journal of Economic Perspectives*, 18(3): 91–115.

Yucelt, U. 1984. Management styles in the Middle East: A case example. *Management Decision*, 22(5): 24–35.

Zaitouni, M., Sawalha, N.N., & El Sharif, A. 2011. The impact of human resource management practices on organizational commitment in the banking sector in Kuwait. *International Journal of Business and Management*, 6(6): 108–123.

27. HRM in Northern Africa

David B. Zoogah, Elham Kamal Metwally, and Tarek Tantoush

INTRODUCTION

There is a growing interest in developing countries because of their potential to increase return on investment, access to increased markets, and diversification gains (Chironga et al., 2011; Hoskisson et al., 2013; Hoskisson et al., 2000). Some of those countries are in Northern Africa where there is limited knowledge of human resources management processes, and how firms perform. In this chapter we examine human resource management (HRM) in five Northern African countries: Algeria, Egypt, Libya, Morocco, and Tunisia. We first briefly discuss institutional and geographic factors underlying HRM in these countries. In the next section we discuss cases studies of HRM in four companies in Algeria, Egypt, Libya, and Tunisia. We conclude by discussing theoretical and practical implications for human resources management.

BACKGROUND

In order to understand human capital systems in North Africa, it is important to understand the background of the countries. As shown in Table 27.1, there are a number of similarities and differences. First, the countries share a number of characteristics. The major common characteristics include geography, religion, and social upheaval. They are all situated in the desert region, which suggests that agroforestry as an engine of industrialization and potential source of employment is limited. Africa faces the curse of geography because of the persistent problems caused by malaria – affecting fertility, population growth, saving and investment, worker productivity, absenteeism, premature mortality, and medical costs – that undermine economic development (Collier, 2007; Collier & Gunning, 1999; Sachs & Malaney, 2002; Sachs & Warner, 1997; Zoogah & Mburu, 2015). Second, the dominant religion in North Africa is Islam. Religion is a core component of culture, which influences the cognitive, affective, and behavioural tendencies of individuals (Hofstede, 2001), and is manifested in the management discipline through the Protestant work ethic (Furnham, 1982); Islam also influences work practices in North Africa. Third, all the countries are bordered by the Mediterranean Sea. In other words, they are closer to Europe than other African countries. That proximity, and resulting ease of travel, suggests that management best practices in Europe can easily be transferred to those countries. Lastly, they have all recently experienced uprisings (that is, the Arab Spring) between 2010 and 2012. Because the uprisings were in part due to lack of opportunities and jobs, it seems probable that human resources practices, particularly staffing, may indirectly have been a contributory factor.

Table 27.1 Socio-demographic statistics of North African countries

Factor	Algeria	Egypt	Libya	Morocco	Tunisia
Colonizer	France	UK	Italy	France	France
Years since independence	53	93	64	59	59
Religion	Islam	Islam	Islam	Islam	Islam
Upheaval voice (2011–13)	No uprising	Major uprising	Major uprising	Minor uprising	Major uprising
Tribal diversity	0.32	0.16	0.15	0.48	0.04
Cultural diversity	0.24	0.00	0.13	0.36	0.03
Population***	39 208 194	82 056 378	6 201 521	33 008 150	10 886 500
Ease of Doing Business (2013) rank***	147	113	188	68	56
Overall Mo Ibrahim index**	52.86	57.70	44.49	57.02	62.70
Global Competitive Index (GCI) rank**	87	94		73	40
Manufacturing, value added (% of GDP)***		15.65		15.44	16.97
Human Development Index (HDI)**	0.71	0.66	0.73	0.59	0.71
Labour force, female (% of total labour force)***	17.21	24.24	28.57	26.96	26.85
Labour force, total***	12 431 290	27 742 106	2 319 098	12 026 239	3 979 518
Labour skill level*†	36.8	30.6		30.9	
Labour Market Efficiency (ACR, 2014) rank	144	142	137	122	

Notes: *** 2013 World Bank Indicators; ** 2012 Africa Development Indicators; * 2007 Data; † percentage of firms identifying this as a major constraint; ACR = Africa Competitiveness Ranking.

However, the countries differ with regard to historical, institutional, governance, business environment, competitiveness, human development, and population factors. Egypt has twice the population of Algeria and Morocco, eight times that of Tunisia, and about 13 times the population of Libya. Three countries – Algeria, Morocco, and Tunisia – are former colonies of France; while two – Egypt and Libya – are former colonies of the United Kingdom (UK) and Italy, respectively. Human resources management systems may be related to their respective colonizers because of economic and administrative legacies and continued ties in the post-independence era (Hinnebusch, 1981; Jack et al., 2011). They also differ in number of years since independence, ranging from Egypt (93 years) to Algeria as the most recent (53 years). Culturally, the countries differ with regard to ethnic and tribal diversity, and cultural distance between ethnic groups (Fearon, 2003). There seems to be no cultural distance within Egypt and Tunisia, but there is limited distance in Algeria and Morocco (Branine, 2001). Another area of difference is governance. According to the Mo Ibrahim index, an annual assessment of the quality of governance in African countries, Tunisia had the highest score (62.70) in 2012, and Libya had the lowest (44.49). Because the index includes human development, it relates to human resources management systems. According to the United Nations Development Programme (UNDP), countries differ in the extent to which they focus on people and capabilities. To gauge these differences, the Human Development Index (HDI) was created, a summary measure of average achievement in key dimensions of human development: (1) a long and healthy life; (2) being knowledgeable; and (3) a decent standard of living. It is a geometric mean of normalized indices for each of the three dimensions. The HDI indicates that Algeria, Libya, and Tunisia are very similar. Morocco has the lowest index.

With regard to capital market systems, Tunisia was ranked highest in the Global Competitiveness Index (GCI) (ranked 40 with a score of 4.47) and Egypt was the lowest (ranked 94, score of 3.88). The degree to which companies in a country can flexibly manage their workforce and quickly hire and fire employees (that is, labour market efficiency) (Schwab & Porter, 2008) also indicates that in 2014, Morocco had the highest score (3.84). It suggests that cooperation in labour–employer relations, flexibility of wage determination, rigidity of employment, hiring and firing practices of companies, redundancy costs, pay and productivity, reliance on professional management, brain drain, and female participation in the labour force, were relatively better than in other North African countries such as Algeria, which had the lowest rank of 144 and a score of 2.79. The Ease of Doing Business index shows that in 2013 Tunisia was the most business-friendly place (ranked 56) and Libya was the least business-friendly (ranked 188).

The labour market and labour force statistics also show differences, albeit not widely. Like other African countries, North African economies are undergirded by tribal and cultural structures. The ethnic fractualisation index (Fearon, 2003) suggests that Tunisia is the most homogeneous, while Morocco is relatively more diverse, followed by Algeria. There seems to be hardly any difference in ethnic diversity between Libya and Egypt. Cultural diversity, which refers to the heterogeneity of values, beliefs, and behavioural norms in a country (Fearon, 2003), is lowest in Egypt, followed by Tunisia and Libya. Algeria and Morocco seem to have the same level of cultural diversity. With regard to population, Egypt is the most populous; it has about ten times the population of Libya. However, it is not easy to conduct business in Egypt. According to the World Bank (2013) Ease of Doing Business index, Egypt ranks 113. Libya is much lower down, ranking 188 out of 192. Tunisia seems to have the most business-friendly environment; it has the highest ranking in the Ease of Doing Business in North Africa. The Global Competitiveness Index (GCI) seems also to show a similar pattern. The contribution of manufacturing to gross domestic product is higher in Tunisia than the other countries.

These attributes show potential similarities and differences in human resources management in North Africa. As we discuss in greater detail below, we can see that the countries with a Francophone background adopt more French practices of managing human resources, while those with Anglophone and Italian backgrounds adopt more English and Italian practices. The cultural practices – shared values, beliefs, and behavioural norms, as well as language, rituals, assumptions, and worldviews in the countries – may also affect the orientation of employers toward human resources management.

HUMAN RESOURCES MANAGEMENT

Historical Views

The demographics show that Northern Africa is characterized by countries with different historical backgrounds. Those with francophone backgrounds – Algeria, Morocco, and Tunisia – share the administrative systems of France. They use French labour and HRM systems (Bouzguenda, 2013; Dufour & Frimousse, 2007). Egypt, which has an anglophone background, uses UK personnel management systems, while Libya, a former colony of Italy, to a certain extent adopts a combination of Italian and UK systems owing to the era of the British military administration over Libya, resulting from the World War II defeat of the Italian and German forces in North Africa. During the colonial period, Morocco, Algeria, and Tunisia faced discrimination in terms of labour legislation. Employees were hired under a special 'overseas labour law' which enabled employers to hire and fire with no consequences (Mana, 2005). However, the French trade unions put strong pressure on the colonial authorities for the recognition of certain rights for Moroccan and Algerian workers. Despite this pressure, French employers seldom applied all the legal rights. After independence for North African countries (Tunisia and Morocco in 1956, and Algeria in 1962), efforts focused mainly on rebuilding the state and its basic institutions. The major objective was to establish vital public services (electricity, railways, water, and so on) to stimulate national economic growth (creation of jobs, distribution of the wages, and so on) and to maintain as much as possible the colonial administrative structure bequeathed by the departure of French civil servants. In Algeria, the March 1963 Law required self-management of factories. It also called for involvement of workers in factory administration. However, high unemployment resulted in job seekers emigrating to France, the former colonizer, which needed more workers.

After independence, private companies in North African countries largely benefited from situations of quasi monopoly. As a consequence, their HRM policies were codified and inspired by the HRM policy in the public sector. In Algeria, the 1970s were marked by the state's desire to build the economy, and a major focus on the development of heavy industry. Governments invested extensively in the creation of large powerful national companies. Concomitantly, the HRM function, which was primarily driven by the state, focused on the professional aspects (recruitment, pay, promotion, participation) and other social aspects (housing, transport, medicine, holidays, and so on).

At the end of the 1980s, the HRM function was modernized and incorporated with a certain number of management tools and methods. As a result the quality of management improved dramatically. The economic crisis of Algeria which was caused by the fall in oil income led to high unemployment and reduced investments, all of which resulted in the social explosion of October 1988, and the questioning of the political system (Dali, 1996). One major outcome of that uprising was that the Algerian state granted greater autonomy and freedom to companies, and abolished the law of the General Status of the Worker which had been inspired by communist ideology. Thereafter, the state no longer intervened directly in the economical decision-making process, and simply determined the limits that firms had to respect. Zghal (2003) observed that the industrial sector in Tunisia was essentially made up of small and medium-sized companies whose priority was primarily financial; HRM was of little importance and was very rarely strategic. According to Zghal (2000), Tunisian companies had no precise rules, no recruitment systems that relied on application, and tended to adopt paternalist models based on relations of equality and dignity.

In Morocco, the authorities engaged a process of 'social recasting' via a new industrial legislation to encourage companies to reconsider their HRM practices and also encourage trade unions to adopt a more participative and less conflictual attitude. Moreover, from the middle of the 1980s, a device was implemented by the state to encourage companies to provide training for their personnel, with possibilities of funding these costs, in order to push the Moroccan companies to reconsider their HRM practices. According to much of the research done during the 1990s, HRM in North Africa still appeared basic and unsuited to the requirements of competition, which requires an efficient workforce. Generally, it comes close to Taylor's (1911) conception of scientific management, which distinguishes between the conceptual knowledge expected of top managers and the practical knowledge expected of operatives. There seems to be a problem with the authoritative management style and weak internal communication of organizations. However, the firms most at risk from the international competition started to benchmark their competitors, especially European firms, to identify and adapt their best practices in order to stay competitive. Within the constraints of the environment these firms adapted to develop more strategic HRM policies. Moreover the countries of the western basin of the Mediterranean Sea have benefited from a renewal of the management cadre, with managers graduated from universities or business schools, sometimes foreign, who have all learned 'Western' management principles. These two phenomena created a convergence of HRM practices between European companies and their North African counterparts (Frimousse, 2006).

Especially in North African firms, economic and social relations are interlinked, and they are often accompanied by a form of fatalism. Marchesnay et al. (2006) link this behaviour to a theosophical vision of life which conforms to the Koran. These countries share Arabo-Muslim elements with high tolerance for ambiguity and uncertainty which is linked to a strong belief in destiny (*maktoub*; it is written or prescribed). The social link is omnipresent in North African firms. Informal networks often based on regional affinities dominate companies. Employees have a strong emotional link with their superiors. The traditional economy, which is characterized by 'eye in the eye and hand in the hand' (Braudel, 1980), tends to be preferred over other forms.

As a result, the development of HRM systems in Northern Africa is not homogeneous. The heterogeneity of HRM is also complicated by the Islamic practices of the countries and African traditional systems.[1] Countries in Northern Africa mix Judeo-Christian traditions of their colonizers with Islamic and African traditional cultural practices. Islam, African traditional religion, and Christianity have different socialization and human relations orientations (Hofstede, 1994), which suggests a high degree of divergence in HRM practices. Islam is a religion that has its epicentre in the Middle East. It has a belief system that encompasses social, work, economic, and political orientations (Ali, 2011). It involves veneration of God through the Prophet Mohammed. African traditional religion is less known but also involves veneration of God through ancestors. Although mainly in Africa, this religion used to dominate the entire continent until the intrusion of Islam and Christianity in the twelfth and thirteenth centuries, respectively. Christianity, arguably the most popular, involves the veneration of God through Jesus Christ. The protestant work ethic is a concept that has come into management from Christianity (Weber, 2002). These three religions have existed in North Africa for centuries, and as a result they influence not only social interactions but also work practices and systems. While Islam adopts dogmatic socialization practices and adherence to the prescriptions of religion, African traditional religions seem more liberal by tolerating grafted religious practices. Christianity uses Judaic and Western values. Interactions (for example, marriage) with outgroup members tend to be limited in Islamic practices, but open in African traditional religion and Christianity. Consequently, it seems unclear how HRM influences the effectiveness of organizations in North Africa.

Case Studies

In this section, we analyse HRM practices in specific companies in Egypt, Algeria, Tunisia, and Libya (Table 27.2). In each company, we describe the background and mission, and then the HRM practices and challenges. We focus on four companies in these countries. Three are telecommunication companies, two of which were originally founded by Orascom Telecom: Mobinil in Egypt and Djezzy in Algeria. The third one, Tunisiana (now known as Ooredoo), is in Tunisia. The fourth company, LPC, is based in Libya. Although these cases are major employers, and as such not typical of organizations in each country, they are the most dominant parastatals and as a result not only typify but also lead HRM practices in the respective countries. While some companies adopt the HRM practices out of institutional diffusion processes (through the spread of Western practices to Africa), others are often motivated by governmental influences. For example, firing employees for poor performance seems anathema because of governmental demand for provision of employment to citizens.

We begin with Mobinil Global Telecom Holding, an Egyptian telecommunications company. Mobinil was founded in 1998 by Orascom Telecom and owned by the Sawiris brothers Onsi and Naguib. The company operates in the Middle East, Asia, Africa, and

---

[1] It must be noted that the religious practices occurred as a result of the early *jihads* of Mohammed and his followers which forced traditional African tribes in Northern Africa to convert from traditional African religious practices to Islamic practices (El Hamel, 2013).

Table 27.2   A comparison of the strengths and weaknesses of the case studies

	Strengths	Weaknesses
Mobinil Egypt	Very strong determined dedicated administrative and technical management that has been highly trained by local and international experts in telecom training. Large and strong network of its own workers, sharing of knowledge and information with the new learning teams. HR department's training and innovation of teams, especially the marketing ones, are always up to date and above customer expectations to overcome the strong competition. HR department's objectives are aligned to the mission and vision of Mobinil, contributing to the fulfilment of individual and corporate goals. HR strategy is to recruit and retain good and professional employees.	Development plans are tied to the performance process, thus little training is provided to the low-performing employees, which eventually leads to demotion of performance in a vicious circle. Such challenges have not been seen in Djezzy or Tunisiana.
Djezzy	Employees are part of Djezzy's declared mission: 'We exist to . . . enrich our customers' lives through accessible communication services; ensure our shareholders' returns with the highest yields; expand our employees' horizons with exceptional growth opportunities; enable our communities' development and prosperity by always giving back.' Skilled workforce and team. Talented and loyal employees who are the key to business success constantly participate in training programmes to build their skills and develop their careers. Since its launch, Djezzy offered nearly 50 000 training opportunities. Stimulating work environment, engagement, transparency, and good compensation schemes.	The role of the HR department does not go beyond the administration of files and record-keeping of employees through complicated bureaucratic procedures. The terms and conditions of employment are completely regulated by government decrees, and like Egypt, the governance of the state has an effect on companies' HRM issues. The process of recruitment and selection in Algeria is merely a bureaucratic and administrative formality and is neither systematic nor objective, and like Egypt, Algeria suffers from behaviours such as nepotism. Much of this is believed to be a result of the French colonial legacies, and it is evident that it is also due to underdevelopment. Training and development of the employees is always seen as a cost but not an investment. Selection for training made on the basis of a training needs analysis or after a performance appraisal.

Table 27.2   (continued)

	Strengths	Weaknesses
	Djezzy meets its employees on a regular basis to exchange ideas, and communicate vision and strategies. To confirm its employer brand position, corporate citizenship, and interest in human capital, Djezzy was the official partner of the Talents and Employment exhibition, where representatives from the HR Department promoted HRM policies.	The change of ownership in the company, and resulting changes in the management, require high skills to avoid cognitive misalignment between new employees and the organization's rules and regulations.
Tunisiana	Skilled labour force. A very strong marketing team that constantly launches innovative and simple products, along with good quality. It is managed in a way that maintains it leadership role in the market, despite the high competition from other operators. Employees innovate more in team skills and creativity as one of Tunisiana's challenges is keeping up with the continuous offers provided by its competitors, especially Orange Telecom which always has a good offer, if not better than that of Tunisiana.	Political unrest, and associated instability, have implications for both the economy and society. Like most developing countries, bureaucracies are complicated, and the state has autonomy over the terms and conditions of employment, hindering the efficiency of HRM. Little, if any, recognition is given to the importance of training and development of human resources. Administrative and financial corruption exist. Customer service is not efficient enough to deal with the negative customer feedback, and with a large market share, many customers are dissatisfied. Tunisiana needs to hire more labour, which is challenging with the increasing labour costs.
LPC	Quasi-monopoly. As a former state parastatal, it has inherited the infrastructure of the old company. Government support. As a national institution, the LPC will be backed by the government. Opportunity for partnership. The status of the company can be leveraged to establish alliances with foreign competitors.	'Public ownership' culture: the company's Post Offices are regarded as 'governmental', rather than commercial offices. Weak position in partnerships. It is unable to withstand foreign competitors operating in the Libyan market. The instability and general security situation of the country following the 17 February revolution. Cultural institutions – tribalism, regionalism, provincialism, etc. – which constrain performance.

Canada, with headquarters in Cairo, Egypt.[2] Orascom's ability to function and operate in more than one continent (11 countries) indicates its managerial and operational efficiency as well as its ability to withstand country-specific challenges. Orascom is a mobile service provider in most of those countries as well as a subsidiary contractor of many telecom companies in other countries.[3] In some countries, the company operates with a different name, structure, and management, which enables us to compare how it succeeds despite locational and linguistic barriers. The three subsidiaries are Mobinil, Djezzy, and Tunisiana.

Mobinil is the first telecommunication network company in Egypt. It started operations in 1998 and is a market leader, covering about 30 million customers. It is owned by two large multinational organizations that are very successful: the Sawiris Orascom Enterprise and France Telecom. Mobinil's vision is to 'become the preferred communication services provider in Egypt', and its mission is 'providing the best customer experience, being a desired employer, creating value for our shareholders and proudly contributing to the development of our country',[4] suggesting a drive for excellence. Consequently, it has focused on dedicated administrative and technical management that have been highly trained by local and international experts in telecom training. The marketing and technological capabilities of the company enable it to beat competitors in price and services. Mobinil's culture is characterized by friendliness, dynamism, and a humane environment, with simple guidelines to assist employees in achieving operational excellence. In addition to a strong emphasis on data analytics which enables it to achieve customer retention goals, the company emphasizes use of teams, information-sharing across departments, and automatic reminders for performance management. In order to overcome competition from Vodafone and Etisalat, Mobinil relies on the HRM practices of training, performance management, hiring, and compensation to maximize the potential of the teams.

The company ensures that the human resources department's vision to 'strive to be a great place to work driven by passion, innovation and pride in the Mobinil brand', and mission to 'provide the best work environment for our people through attracting, developing and retaining talent, promoting an open culture based on equal opportunity, empowerment, innovation, diversity and transparency, and rewarding high performance that enables Mobinil to achieve its objectives and exceed its customers' expectations', are aligned to the mission and vision of the company, thereby enabling it to fulfil operational and strategic goals. Mobinil's HRM strategy is to recruit and retain good and professional employees. Compared to its competitors, the compensation and benefits seem generous. They include medical insurance and on-site doctors for employees and their dependents, continuous training and development, stipends for cell phones, transportation allowances, on-site food courts, special rebates at major shopping and entertainment outlets across Egypt, matchless prices for international trips, life insurance, and pension plans.[5]

Djezzy was established in 2002 and became the market leader for telecommunications in Algeria within less than a year. The company's market dominance was made possible

---

[2]   Global Telecom website, http://www.gtelecom.com/web/guest/founder, accessed 20 May 2015.
[3]   Ibid.
[4]   Mobinil website, www.mobinil.com, accessed 23 June 2015.
[5]   Ibid.

by the introduction of a range of prepaid and postpaid voice and data telecommunications services. Djezzy became part of VimpelCom group in 2011 after the merger between OTH and VimpelCom groups. Djezzy has a 65 per cent market share and coverage of 90 per cent of the population. Djezzy's vision 'to harness our networks to provide millions of connected customers with solutions that empower their personal and professional lives', and mission, 'we exist to . . . enrich our customers' lives through accessible communication services; ensure our shareholders' returns with the highest yields; expand our employees' horizons with exceptional growth opportunities; enable our communities' development and prosperity by always giving back', seem a little different from those of Mobinil in Egypt.

Djezzy relies on a skilled workforce and teams to run its operations. The company prefers very experienced and skilled employees who can facilitate the achievement of annual sales, publicity, and service targets. This strategy has enabled Djezzy to have a competitive advantage as the largest telecom operator in Algeria, defined by the number of the enrolled subscribers. Even though it is a strategic move to use small business units, the company is handicapped because those units are not big enough to handle the market growth prospects or effectively manage the large amount of subscribers; it needs bigger business units to sustain its competitive advantage. There is the risk of a reduced customer base due to overload on the business units. A second challenge is that of ownership in the company which is associated with changes in management and concomitant effects such as career uncertainty. Other challenges include growing competition, the tax structure, government regulations, and differences in exchange rates. The tax structure is not properly defined and constantly changes, which affects planning and forecasting. It also limits the ability of the company to manage its local and foreign transactions due to currency fluctuations. The changes in tax structures also affect material and labour costs.[6] There are unfair rules and regulations of the government, which affect operations and performance. In response to these challenges, and to increase its customer base, Djezzy devises competitive intelligence mechanisms aimed to enable it to maintain its market leadership position. Nevertheless, the African environment, where there are many opportunities, suggests that Djezzy can expand to neighbouring countries to offer advanced technological and communication network services. It may do so through strategic alliances, or acquisitions and mergers.

The dynamics of the Algerian environment and the leadership position of Djezzy as well as the nature of the telecommunication industry, which functions on value-addition, mean that the company must seek a continuous supply of skills and new technologies. As a result, it views talented and loyal employees and the HRM function as central to its success. It constantly seeks the growth and development of employees' talents, and invests in training the workforce so that they can adjust to the continuously changing market demands. It also offers a stimulating work environment and promotes engagement, transparency, career development opportunities, and good compensation schemes. For example, since its launch, the company has offered nearly 50 000 training opportunities abound at local and international, levels. Thus, the company remains a benchmark in the field. It also offers internships and other opportunities to high-talent candidates. In

---

[6] 'Djezzy – SWOT Analysis. Strength, W., Opportunities, Threats for over 40,000+ Companies and Industries'. http://swot.advisorgate.com/swot-d/11721-swot-analysis-djezzy.html, accessed 30 May 2015.

addition, Djezzy has regular companywide fora where employees exchanges ideas with leadership on how to sustain or improve the company's market dominance. Employees seem to like these fora because of the opportunity to develop a clear understanding of the company's strategy and future, as well as the challenges.

In order to maintain its position as the best employer and corporate citizen, and its interest in human capital, Djezzy officially sponsored the eleventh 'Talents and Employment' exhibition, which took place on 9–10 May 2015 at the Palace of Culture Moufdi Zakaria in Algiers. The company's stand offered candidates the opportunity to interact with the recruitment team and other representatives of the human resources department. The latter used the occasion to outline the human resource management policy of the company and to highlight the company's involvement in workforce development and job creation. As part of its corporate social responsibility (CSR) initiative, Djezzy encouraged its employees to participate in a volunteer day at the Palm Beach nursery to improve the living conditions of children awaiting adoption. The employees repainted the nursery walls, under the supervision of a specialist, and subsequently decorated it with the help of students of Algiers. Recognition certificates were awarded to participants for their involvement by the executive vice-president, Vincenzo Nesci.[7]

Tunisiana, the first privately owned telecommunication company in Tunisia, was formed on 11 May 2002. It is one of the country's leading mobile service providers. Formerly named Orascom Telecom Tunisia, the company's vision of 'enriching people's lives as a leading communications company', and mission 'to develop and implement sound procurement practices and provide quality service through teamwork and communication with all our suppliers and contactors', are similar to those of Mobinil of Egypt and Djezzy of Algeria.

With regards to its internal strengths, Tunisiana has a skilled labour force, and power in the domestic market. Like Djezzy, Tunisiana is also competing with two other telecom operators in the market, the biggest of these having the largest number of subscribers. Tunisiana covers about 40 per cent of the Tunisian territory and serves about 70 per cent of the population. The company has a very strong marketing team that constantly launches innovative and simple products, which contributes to its large share of the population in its network. Tunisiana is still the leading operator in Tunisia, and has the ability to add landline service to its mobile service. The company also uses current technologies such as 3G services, and supplies phones and tablets at affordable prices. Further, it maintains its leadership role in the market, despite the high competition from other operators, and recovered from the crisis of the 2011 revolution faster than its competitors by adapting to the new country situation, and the economic policies that were changed by the government to support employment growth in the nation.

One major weakness, however, is poor customer service. There seem to be inefficiencies that could, given continued dissatisfaction of customers, erode its share of the market. Another weakness is a recent corporate scandal which diminished its reputation as a good company. In addition to these weaknesses, the company faces the challenge of staving off offers from its competitors, especially Orange Telecom. It has to deal with negative

---

[7]   Djezzy website, http://www.djezzy.com/, accessed 27 June 2015.

customer feedback as well as hire or train customer service agents to help overcome the increasing dissatisfaction of its customers. Of course, hiring will increase the labour costs, but in the long run it will help the company.

In handling those difficulties, Tunisiana uses innovative and creative marketing strategies and teams. For example, the company formulates marketing plans and programmes to attract more customers, and to reduce the impact of competitors' offers by centralizing customers' needs in all of its products and services. It also targets youth through TV ads, billboards, and events; and creates bonds with its clients by hosting events such as the Jazz at Carthage festival every year. Through training and development Tunisiana's HRM department has made sure the marketing team is creative and skilful enough to adjust to any kind of changes in the market, especially since the revolution.

Libya Post Company (LPC) is a public company, a fully owned subsidiary of the conglomerate Libyan Post, Telecommunications & Information Technology Holding Company (LPTIC), which owns all the publicly owned companies operating in the post and telecommunications sector in Libya. It was set up in 2009 as a new, independently run concern following the dissolution of the General Post, Telecom Company of Libya (GPTCOL). LPC's total assets amount to 1 458 550 LYD. In 2014 the company's financial performance included a deficit of 108 360 320 LYD with 6 217 555 LYD in revenue and 114 577 875 LYD in expenditure (LPC, 2014). It may well be deemed a failing company from a purely commercial point of view. Even though the company might be failing from a purely commercial point of view, it is still propped up by the government because it is deemed important for the nation. In other words, it is treated as a state-owned enterprise that has to offer service to all citizens regardless of its performance. In that regard, it stands out as distinguished from so many public companies that have dominated the economic scene during the Gaddafi era.

LPS is the 'national company for postal and financial services, providing best services for customers . . . supporting the Libyan economy through utilisation of state-of-the-art technology . . . renovation of services to the highest levels of quality, and the creation of a competitive postal, financial and telecom market' (LPC, 2015B: 3). It seeks to provide 'comprehensive, nationwide, country-inclusive postal services . . . characterized with sustainability and diversification and meet the aspirations of its customers' (LPC, 2015b: 3).

The company faces a number of internal and external environmental challenges, the major internal ones being: (1) lack of standard guidelines for postal services; (2) antiquated infrastructure and information system; (3) poor marketing and promotion; (4) lack of corporate identity; (5) deficiency in employees with appropriate skill levels; and (6) a dominating culture of indifference and lack of innovation and initiative. External challenges include: (1) dominance of the societal 'public ownership' culture (that is, the company's Post Offices are regarded as 'governmental'); (2) an unprotected domestic express mail market; (3) instability in the country following the 17 February 2011 revolution; and (4) tribalism, regionalism, provincialism, and city and tribal divides.[8] These affect not only the organization's operations but also its human resource management function.

---

[8]   This may appear to be a nationwide or external environment problem, but it is equally an internal environment challenge for LPC as its geographical presence covers the whole of Libya. Problems experienced in any one of the six postal zones are always reflected inside the company and end up as political issues for senior management to resolve.

Human resources management in LPC is characterized by a profusion of personnel, and deficiency in the quality of the workforce. According to a 'Progress report on activities' submitted by the board of directors (LPC, 2015a: 16), the term 'surplus' applied to employees indicates that 55 per cent of the total workforce of LPC are not needed; only 45 per cent of the employees on the payroll contribute to the value-adding services of the company. The 'surplus' occurred because of receivership, which compelled LPC to assume a largely 'unmotivated', 'aging', 'low-skilled', and less qualified workforce. According to the company's statistics (LPC, 2015c), 43 per cent of the employees are between 49 and 58 years old, whereas 37 per cent are between 39 and 48 years of age. In addition, 23 per cent of the employees are school leavers with only primary school education (that is, six years of compulsory school education), 37 per cent have preparatory school qualifications (that is, 6 + 3 years of compulsory school education), 15 per cent have secondary school diplomas, and only 3 per cent hold university degrees. Clearly, the human capital base of the company seems low.

To address the human resource management challenges, LPC's HRM strategy is developed as an integral element of the corporate strategy. The five main strategic objectives of LPC (2015b) for the five years to 2020 include the following:

1. Securing the provision of quality, all-inclusive postal services throughout the country at competitive prices.[9]
2. Transformation of LPC from a loss-making firm to a high-growth competitor and investor.
3. Redirection of the activities of LPC towards new, promising, high-value-added areas to improve the competitiveness of the company.
4. Contribution to the national effort aimed at narrowing the 'digital gap' through the national e-government programme, e-Libya, to facilitate networked electronic administrative development and service provision throughout the country as well as with the rest of the world.
5. Leadership in human resources development through rehabilitation, training, and development.

The last objective clearly indicates the central position of HRM strategy in revitalizing LPC. HR managers are expected to implement the HRM strategy by establishing a number of projects including 'human resources rehabilitation and development' and 'development of work rules and regulations' projects. According to LPC, the rehabilitation and development programme for 2015 involved a number of activities. First, the 2015 comprehensive training plan offering 1309 training opportunities, 689 of which were carried over from the 2014 training plan, was budgeted at a total of 881 520 LYD. The 2015 plan was devised based on a thorough training needs assessment exercise, which took into account the specific skill needs of the employees, particularly information and communication technology (ICT) skills, and the ambitious strategic 'transformation' projects since 2012. Second, managers were required to devise a plan for second-in-line manage-

---

[9]   This may appear strange for a postal operator, and to declared this as a strategic objective would not be all that significant, if not for the instability and insecurity in the country brought about by the factional fighting since 2014, following the 17 February 2011 revolution.

ment leaders' assessment and development. Third, they were to devise a training plan for 2016 that focuses on evaluation of the actual implementation of the 2015 training plan; implementation of a training needs assessment for 2016; design of the 2016 training plan, and presentation of the 2016 training plan to the board of directors for approval. Fourth, HR managers were to evaluate the healthcare programme in terms of how it progressed in 2014 with a comprehensive evaluation of the insurance company providing the healthcare coverage for all employees (and their families) of LPC, and appraise any issues that arise and anticipated challenges.

In sum, LPC, a state-owned enterprise, is striving to compete as a private company but is burdened by governmental influences and requirements. Even though there is recognition of the significant role HRM can play in enhancing the company's situation, societal and governmental practices such as poor information systems, lack of transparency, bad communication, and lack of efficient resources, as well as administrative and financial corruption, limit the ability of the organization and its departments to achieve the transformative goals they desire. The HRM department is facing that situation. The poor management of human resources manifests itself in an inability to control and eliminate unacceptable and uncompetitive acts; prevalence of negligence and favouritism; emphasis on centralized (rather than participative) decision-making; and the introduction of complex and bureaucratic procedures which exacerbate the inefficiencies the company expects to eliminate.

Summary

The companies in these cases share a number of common characteristics. First, they are all in North Africa and therefore are bound by the context – that is, the cultural, socio-political, and economic institutions – of those countries. Given that the external environment of organizations influences HRM practices (Jackson & Schuler, 1995), regulative, normative, and cognitive systems of those countries thus influence the HRM of the organizations. Second, apart from LPC, three of the companies originate from Orascom. However, as independent entities in different countries, they have devised different strategies to gain competitive advantage. The challenges they face are similar with regard to the regional context of North Africa, but their experiences are different. Egypt and Tunisia had revolutions in 2011, where the citizens revolted against dictatorship and corruption, and sought social justice, which entailed ending unfair distribution of income and wealth, and provision of equal and fair opportunities of employment (see Table 27.1 for country comparisons). Algeria did not really go through a revolution; only a series of protests for about a year. Unlike the other countries, Algeria did not experience a lot of changes in the controlling party and government, and monetary and fiscal policies, and many other areas of the country continued unchanged. LPC is a private holding that emerged from the telecommunications industry.

The four companies also lack effective HRM systems and seem to suffer from other organizational malaise, for example centralization, lack of effective decision-making, corruption, nepotism, bribery, and manipulation. Organizations in North Africa are burdened by bureaucratic legislation. The terms and conditions of employment are completely regulated by government decrees which limit the flexibility of human resource management departments. As a result, it seems unlikely that any of the companies can compete with similar companies in advanced economies like the United States of America or the United Kingdom. Even though Mobinil is better than many other organizations in terms of training, bureaucratic procedures, funded resources, and administrative and financial corruption, the company is still comparatively ineffective or 'developing'. In Djezzy and Tunisiana, development plans are tied to the performance process but limited training is provided to the low-performing employees, which eventually leads to demotion of performance. In other words, the employees seem to be left to their own fate. In Libya, as in many less developed countries, management practice is characterized by poor governance, lack of transparency, complexity of procedures, personalization of management performance and work conduct, and administrative and financial corruption (Yunus, 2004).

There are a number of things that other companies, particularly those interested in North Africa, can learn from these cases. First, the cases in Egypt and Algeria suggest that the training practices and innovative use of teams by HR functions can help the organizations overcome strong competition. Second, the routine of meeting with employees on a regular basis to exchange ideas, and communicate vision and strategies, creates a shared vision that enhances commitment to the organization. Some of the companies responded strategically to 'interference' from government regulations or 'instructions' which could undermine effective employee management and efficiency. Third, companies may devise policies or strategies to counteract the excessive favoritism and nepotism observed in some of the companies. Of course, favoritism and nepotism occur in other companies too, and throughout Africa in general. Even though the frequency and conspicuity of the acts might seem unethical by Western standards and therefore unworthy of emulation, they are not perceived negatively as people expect the group to look after or protect them.

The approaches of the companies to succession planning and managing changes of ownership may be mimicked by others. North Africa in general has experienced significant changes since the Arab Spring and those changes are currently affecting companies. In Libya, for example, there is growing chaos in the country which negatively affects the cohesiveness of workers. Further, it is important to know that the practice of HRM in Libya is predominantly taking place within the boundaries of public sector organizations, and this has been the case for more than 40 years. As a result, it is strongly flavoured with a public sector culture. In addition, private sector organizations such as LPC are struggling to develop an appropriate model of HRM that is relevant to their needs and will help their mission of setting out and realizing competitive management objectives as required by their respective business environments.

Could some of these companies act as benchmarks? Mobinil in Egypt and Djezzy in Algeria can serve as role models for other companies. As a market leader in the telecommunications industry in Egypt, Mobinil's best practices – training and development and innovative use of teams, particularly for marketing its products and services – are not only always up to date and above customer expectations to overcome the strong competition, but can be adopted by other companies that are intent on overtaking the industry leader. Mobinil's determined and dedicated administrative and technical management, who are highly trained by local and international experts in telecoms, might also be emulated by other companies. The HRM strategy of recruiting only good and professional employees seems to contrast with the practices of other companies, and therefore might be adopted.

The practices that enabled Djezzy, a young company that became a market leader for telecommunications in Algeria in less than a year, can be emulated. The systems, processes, and practices that it established to reach and maintain its position as the best employer and corporate citizen can be adopted. For example, as part of its corporate social responsibility initiative, Djezzy established a programme that involved voluntary participation to improve the living conditions of children awaiting adoption at a nursery. The company has also offered nearly 50 000 training opportunities, and facilitated a stimulating work environment that involves engagement and transparency, as well as good compensation schemes. Finally, there is Djezzy's programme of regular company meetings to enables employees and employers to exchange ideas and share strategies. This horizontal leadership (a system of leadership in which executives 'come down' to the level of the subordinates) might benefit other companies.

These practices contrast with LPC. It does not stand out as the most qualified among public sector organizations to serve as a role model. It has financial problems, and at the moment its operations are declining in a high-growth industry. Nevertheless, other companies might learn 'what not to do' rather than 'what to do' from LPC.

In that regard, the cases are of great relevance to other organizations and firms in those countries. They share the same demographic and cultural attributes as well as industry (HRM) practices. They may thus encounter the same challenges and performance problems as the companies in these cases.

DISCUSSION

The increasing rise of Africa has drawn the interest of practitioners and academics to the management of organizations in African countries because of the role of not only management but also human resources in economic development (Dia, 1996). In this chapter we review HRM in Northern Africa. Northern Africa differs from other regions of Africa in one major way: it is characterized by a strong Arabic or Islamic culture. That culture seems to supersede the colonial influence. It is also a strong influence in organizations, and especially on HRM. It interacts with political and economic influences to impact upon not only interactions within organizations (for example, performance evaluation) but also entry and post-entry human resource processes. Thus, the dynamics of culture and politics seem to be the major challenge for HRM in North Africa.

Effective empirical studies are more likely to be achieved if foreigners collaborate with local scholars who understand the nuances of the Arabic culture. Such collaborations will unearth the true effects of HRM policies and practices. They will also help to isolate universal HRM practices from those that are unique to North Africa. Such findings will help foreign multinationals to adapt effectively in the region. Another area of interest is the degree to which HR managers balance the worlds of Africa. As Zoogah et al. (2015) indicate, African scholarship involves two major contextual worlds: Africa and non-Africa. In North Africa, a third world – the Islamic world – is an equally powerful influence, as we have indicated above. HR managers are likely to pivot on one to address the audiences of the others.

Furthermore, it will be meaningful to study the companies we have identified in this chapter in greater detail. Since they are major large companies in their respective countries, empirical studies exploring the perceptions of employees about their HRM and other functional practices will be insightful for international HRM scholarship. Such studies are particularly significant given the changes that have been experienced in North Africa. Research exploring the degree to which HRM practices exist, in whole or part, and the extant structure might yield some insight for international management.

Lastly, it will be very insightful for studies to develop context-specific theories based on North Africa. Such theories might be helpful in understanding, explaining, and predicting the decisions and behaviours of not only HRM managers, but also other functional managers and executives. As Zoogah & Nkomo (2011) observed, theories that are uniquely African are lacking. In conclusion, we have reviewed HRM in North Africa by examining the macro context as a background (Schuler & Jackson, 1987). We hope future research will extend these efforts empirically.

REFERENCES

Ali, M.M. 2011. *The Religion of Islam*. Dublin, OH: Ahmadiyya Anjuman Ishaat Islam.

Bouzguenda, K. 2013. Towards a global framework of recruitment practices: The effect of culture applied to Tunisian context. *European Journal of Business and Management*, 5(7): 2222–2839.

Branine, M. 2001. Human resource management in Algeria. In P.S. Budhwar and Y. Debrah (eds), *Human Resource Management in Developing Countries*: 155–173. London: Routledge.

Braudel, F. 1980. Will capitalism survive?. *Wilson Quarterly (1976–)*, 4(2): 108–116.

Chironga, M., Leke, A., Lund, S., & van Wamelen, A. 2011, May. Cracking the next growth market: Africa. *Harvard Business Review*, 89(5): 117–122.

Collier, P. 2007. Africa's economic growth: Opportunities and constraints. *African Development Review*, 19(1): 6–25.

Collier, P., & Gunning, J.W. 1999. Explaining African economic performance. *Journal of Economic Literature*, 37(1): 64–111.

Dali, A. 1996. La GRH en Algérie: Analyse critique. *Revue de l'ALGRH*, 10: 73–81.

Dia, M. 1996. *Africa's Management in the 1990s and Beyond*. Washington, DC: World Bank Publications.

Dufour, L., & Frimousse, S. 2007. Divergences and similarities in the evolution of the human resources function in the western part of the Mediterranean sea. *Tinerilor Economist (The Young Economists Journal)*, 1(8): 64–74.

El Hamel, C. 2013. *Black Morocco: A History of Slavery, Race, and Islam*. Cambridge, UK and New York, USA: Cambridge University Press.

Fearon, J. 2003. Ethnic and cultural diversity by country. *Journal of Economic Growth*, 8(2): 195–222.

Frimousse, S. 2006. Internationalisation des entreprises et hybridation des pratiques de gestion des ressources humaines: le cas du Maghreb. Thèse de Doctorat en Sciences de Gestion, IAE de Corse.

Furnham, A. 1982. The Protestant work ethic and attitudes towards unemployment. *Journal of Occupational Psychology*, 55(4): 277–285.

Hinnebusch, R.A. 1981. Egypt under Sadat: Elites, power structure, and political change in a post-populist state. University of California. http://www.jstor.org/stable/800057.

Hofstede, G. 1994. *Values Survey Module 1994 Manual*. Maastricht: Institute for Research on Intercultural Cooperation.

Hofstede, G. 2001. *Culture's Consequences*. Thousand Oaks, CA: SAGE.

Hoskisson, R., Eden, L., Lau, C.M., & Wright, M. 2000. Strategy in emerging economies. *Academy of Management Journal*, 43(3): 249–267.

Hoskisson, R., Wright, M., Filatotchev, I., & Peng, M. 2013. Emerging multinationals from mid-range economies: The influence of institutions and factor markets. *Journal of Management Studies*, 50(7): 1295–1321.

Jack, G., Westwood, R., Srinivas, N., & Sardar, Z. 2011. Deepening, broadening and re-asserting a postcolonial interrogative space in organization studies. *Organization*, 18(3): 275–302.

Jackson, S.E., & Schuler, R.S. 1995. Understanding human resource management in the context of organizations and their environments. *Annual Review of Psychology*, 46: 237–264.

LPC. 2014. The LPC Annual Budget for 2015. Unpublished. Tripoli.

LPC. 2015a. Progress Report, (submitted by the board of directors), 1 January. Unpublished. Tripoli.

LPC. 2015b. The LPC 2014 Annual Report, submitted 4 April. Unpublished. Tripoli.

LPC. 2015c. Strategic directions for the development of Libya Post Company 2015–2020. Unpublished. Tripoli.

Mana, A. 2005. L'introduction du droit du travail en Algérie. http://www.sciencespo.fr/ecole-de-droit/sites/ sciencespo.fr.ecole-de-droit/files/M%C3%A9mo%20Alg%C3%A9rie.pdf. Accessed 10 June 2016.

Marchesnay, M., Kammoun, S.C., & Karray, H.E. 2006. Y-a-t-il un entrepreneuriat méditerranéen?. *Revue Française de Gestion*, 32(1): 66–76.

Sachs, J.D., & Malaney, P. 2002. The economic and social burden of malaria. *Nature*, 415: 680–685.

Sachs, J.D., & Warner, A.M. 1997. Sources of slow growth in African economies. *Journal of African Economies*, 6(3): 335–376.

Schuler, R.S., & Jackson, S.E. 1987. Linking competitive strategies with human resource management practices. *Academy of Management Executive*, 1(3): 207–219.

Schwab, K., & Porter, M.E. 2008. *The Global Competitiveness Report 2008–2009*. Geneva: World Economic Forum.

Taylor, F. 1911. *The Principles of Scientific Management*. New York: Harper & Brothers.

Weber, M. 2002. *The Protestant Ethic and the Spirit of Capitalism: And Other Writings*. New York: Penguin Books.

World Bank. 2013. *Doing Business 2014: Understanding Regulations for Small and Medium-Size Enterprises*. Washington, DC: World Bank Publications.

Yunus, M. 2004. Development, progress, and administrative reformation in developing countries. *Economics and Political Sciences Journal of Al Fateh (Tripoli) University*, 2: 110–120.

Zghal, R. 2000. *Gestion des Ressources Humaines: les bases de la gestion prévisionnelle et de la gestion stratégique*. Tunis: Centre de Publication Universitaire.

Zghal, R. 2003. Culture et gestion: Gestion de l'harmonie ou gestion des paradoxes?. *Gestion*, 28(2): 26–32.

Zoogah, D.B., & Mburu, H. 2015. Are firms in developing countries in spider webs or iron cages? Geographic traps and firm performance. *Thunderbird International Business Review*, 57(6): 481–503.

Zoogah, D.B., & Nkomo, S. 2011. Review of African management research. In T. Lituchy, B.J. Punnet, and B. Puplampu (eds), *Management in Africa: Macro and microperspectives*: 25–37. New York: Routledge.

Zoogah, D.B., Zoogah, R.B., & Dalaba-Roohi, F. 2015. Riding the tide: Management in Africa and the role of high-impact research. *Africa Journal of Management*, 1(1): 27–53.

28. HRM in sub-Saharan Africa: comparative perspectives
Christine Bischoff and Geoffrey Wood

INTRODUCTION

There is a growing body of research on human resource management (HRM) in sub-Saharan Africa. Whilst much of the early literature concentrated on Southern Africa from a rather narrow psychological perspective that focused more on processes than contexts and real outcomes, through the 1990s and 2000s a growing body of HRM research in Africa paid much greater attention to contextual circumstances, drawing on both earlier industrial relations research and broader work on African societies and the firm. Most recently, attention has shifted to the relationship between institutions and HRM practice, drawing on the literature on comparative capitalism and rational hierarchical accounts.

HRM RESEARCH IN SUB-SAHARAN AFRICA

Much of the early work that explicitly dealt with HRM (and, indeed, personnel management) in Africa was concentrated in southern Africa, above all, South Africa, where the greatest number of large firms were located. Informed by a narrow psychological perspective, that was often completely dismissive of any alternative approach to understanding firm practices, it tended to follow on the standard preoccupations of motivation, processes, and systems (Swanepoel et al., 2008: 42; for an example, see Trever-Roberts, 1976). The task of managing people – and understanding people management – was seen as the preserve of practitioner-specialists, with strong groundings in psychology. This approach completely ignored the collective dimensions of work and employment relations or, indeed, the racial dimensions of work organisation central to apartheid South Africa, and that had been echoed across colonial-era Africa (Swanepoel et al., 2008). This did not mean that all South African industrial psychology was reactionary, closed or, indeed, wilfully stupid. The statutory Council for Scientific and Industrial Research (CSIR) had an industrial psychology wing, the National Institute for Personnel Research, that in the 1950s had already acquired a reputation for 'dangerous' open-mindedness. Most notably, in 1956 its director, S. Biesheuvel, wrote an influential critique of individualised and technicist approaches to managing people, arguing that it was (apartheid) laws and restrictions that led to low productivity. In response to such clear and forward thinking, the government set up a rival research body, the Human Sciences Research Council. Dominated by Afrikaans theologians, much of the early research it sponsored on people management was comfortably bigoted and intellectually feeble.

Parallel to all this was the somewhat fragmented body of continent-wide research on industrial relations in Africa. Roberts's (1964) account was an attempt to consolidate this.

Again, from the 1970s onwards, mostly concentrated in South Africa, but with smaller parallel bodies of work in many African countries a body of radical work sought to describe, analyse, and explain the emergence and rise of organised labour, and its relationship with liberation struggles and/or post-independence states (Wood & Brewster, 2007). In recent years, this literature has broadened to encompass HRM issues; articles on Africa in journals such as *Employee Relations* and the *International Journal of Human Resource Management* often draw on this tradition.

CROSS-CULTURAL APPROACHES TO UNDERSTANDING HRM IN SUB-SAHARAN AFRICA

A particularly influential way of understanding people management in Africa has been from a cross-cultural perspective (Jackson, 2002; Karsten & Illa, 2005; Swartz & Davies, 1997). Many of these accounts, influenced by the work of Hofstede (1991), see variations as in line with distinct cultural communities that are shared across clusters of nations within specific regions, which may be defined against a general standard. Culture is seen as a given: countries may develop their social capital, but it is not possible to depart from established ways of doing things (Fukuyama, 1995). Spector et al. (2002) argue that in dealing with HRM issues the impact of cultural variations on beliefs about participation and control need to be taken into account: it would be inappropriate to simply impose Western models on non-Western contexts.

Studies on HRM in Africa have focused on the communitarian dimension in African culture, the challenges this poses for organisations, and the extent to which this may be harnessed to promote optimal HRM, and wider organisational outcomes (Msila, 2015). For example, Gbadamosi (2003) argues that a systematic and human orientation, and a tendency to view practice in relation to an ideal, are culturally embedded values shared by many African managers. This would suggest the need to develop a broader HRM management philosophy based on African values (Msila, 2015; Gbadamosi, 2003: 279).

Swartz and Davis (1997: 290–291) argue that central dimensions of such a philosophy could incorporate the notion of *ubuntu*, solidarity, or brotherhood amongst the historically disadvantaged, the persistence of both positive and negative spirits in organisational life, the need to take account of persistent fears, the ongoing evolution of organisation and the assumption that, in the absence of collective support, any initiative will fail (cf. Karsten & Illa, 2005; Msila, 2015). Two caveats are in order. First, any cultural dimension incorporates internal contradictions (Swartz & Davies, 1997: 293). Second, the above-mentioned dimensions may not be applicable in all – or even most – African contexts (Swartz & Davies, 1997: 294): cultural diversity can be encountered at a range of levels (Horwitz & Kelliher, 2015).

A limitation of such approaches is that given assumptions of the persistence of distinct cultural traditions, poor economic performance within specific regions may be blamed on cultural shortcomings, which are not easily resolved. Making assumptions as to which cultures are functional or dysfunctional in relation to specific organisational forms and types of economic activity may, at worst, descend into racism. It discounts the possibility that firms – and countries – may radically reinvent themselves; examples of the latter would be Botswana's transformation from a poor backwater to a developed nation or, conversely, the descent of Ivory Coast from prosperity to civil conflict. Indeed, Anakwe et al. (2000) argue that there is a pressing need for research that recognises the common aspects in many cultures, despite superficial differences. Similarly, Karsten & Ghebregiorgis (2006: 145) note that it is simply wrong to conclude that Western HRM practices cannot be adopted in Africa on account of allegedly insurmountable cultural differences.

An alternative way of exploring the impact of culture on HRM has been to focus on the effects of the myths different groupings hold about each other. For example, Jackson (2002) points to the effects of negative stereotypes on HRM in theory and practice. Even if based on false premises, myths and stereotypes mould decision-making and values in organisations, and inform approaches to communication (Hansen, 2003). Indeed, individuals entrusted with human resource development tend to frame their interventions in terms of how they view the local cultural setting. Whatever their origins – in fact, fiction, or in the distant past – myths influence expectations of behaviour (Hansen, 2003). Within organisations, 'myths' become a means by which groups of individuals may impart meaning to activities; the nature of group formation, in turn, will reflect existing cleavages, on ethnicity, occupation, gender or skill lines within the organisation. Based on a comparative study, involving interviews with German, United States (US), and Ivorian managers, Hansen (2003: 25) found that non-Ivorian nationals working in Ivory Coast tended to make claims as to the 'sabotaging' effects of the local culture, steeped with clan loyalties and nepotism. In contrast, Ivorian managers felt that they were forced to micromanage, as they were likely to be blamed for any shortcomings on the behalf of their subordinates; this contributed to feelings of a loss of control.

INSTITUTIONAL APPROACHES: RATIONAL HIERARCHICAL APPROACHES

Originating in the economics literature, this tradition locates the relative fortunes of firms according to the extent to which institutional arrangements are able to secure private property rights. Herbst (2000) argues that African states are generally weak, reflecting thin and uneven population densities and, hence, state capabilities. Colonial powers tended to concentrate their activities on the coastlines, and on extracting natural resources; moreover, in most of Africa, the colonial period was relatively brief. This has led to poor private property rights, weak law enforcement capabilities, and low levels of development. Given this, modern employment relations affect only a small minority of the economically active system, since the majority of the working-age population are outside the formal employment system; hence, it could be argued that, at best, HRM is a peripheral activity in Africa.

In an influential critique, Acemoglu et al. (2000) argue that within colonies with large European settlements, most notably in southern and east Africa, colonial authorities engaged in serious institution-building in order to serve the interests of colonialists. The resulting 'mini-Europes' performed far better than the west African authorities, where institutional arrangements were largely exploitative, geared towards exploiting labour value and natural resources (Acemoglu et al., 2000). This tradition has continued into post-colonial Africa. In general, southern and east Africa has been more stable and prosperous than west Africa, with larger industrial and commercial agricultural sectors.

In turn, this has made for not necessarily better HRM, but at least more sites in which it can take place.

Recent critics of Acemoglu et al. (2000) argue that the process of state formation in eastern and southern Africa was rather more complex (Dibben et al., 2013). Parallel to institutions set up to guarantee property rights and the rule of law for the colonists were others designed to repress the indigenous population and facilitate arbitrary expropriation in the interests of settlers. In the post-colonial period, parallel institutional arrangements have persisted. This has made for very uneven and politicised law enforcement, with security forces that can operate outside the law with impunity. Although Zimbabwe and Swaziland represent extreme examples of this, the 2012 Marikana massacre of striking miners in South Africa is another example of the malign consequences of a heavily militarised and incompetent police force, and its willingness to act on behalf of economically powerful interests. Although Marikana may have represented an exception rather than a general rule, it highlighted the persistence of deep racial divisions and injustice both within and beyond the workplace. In short, the practice of people management often remains bound up with past legacies, and involves not just the operation of quotidian HRM systems, but also coping with the challenges posed by structural issues within the wider political economy.

INSTITUTIONAL APPROACHES: HRM IN THE SUB-SAHARAN AFRICAN BUSINESS SYSTEM

An alternative approach to understanding HRM in Africa has been through the use of business systems theory. Originally developed by Whitley (1999), business systems theory identifies three defining features of national business systems: variations in ownership coordination, in non-ownership coordination, and in employment relations. Whitley (1999) originally identified six archetypes (or clusters of countries) associated with particular practices, encompassing the economies of the developed world. Using business systems theory, a further archetype has been identified by Wood and Frynas (2006), the segmented business system, based on the experience of east Africa; however, this archetype is useful to understanding the practice of HRM across sub-Saharan Africa. The segmented business systems' key characteristics are summarised in Table 28.1, which are contrasted with two archetypes from the developed world. The segmented business system has many distinct characteristics. It does not represent a hybrid form of the business systems encountered in the developed world (Wood & Frynas, 2006). Whilst the segmented business system may be functional in terms of the concerns of elites, it has proven dysfunctional as a basis for sustainable growth (ibid.) (see Table 28.1).

A key aspect of HRM in such economies is an underlying dualism. On the one hand, there are relatively large organisations, such as subsidiaries of foreign multinational corporations (MNCs) and many in the public sector, characterised by formalism in systems and procedures. This may include a degree of pluralism in employment relations, including collective bargaining. On the other hand, there are smaller and/or family-owned firms, which make up the bulk of the indigenous private sector (Baruch & Clancy, 2000: 794). Such firms are mostly unitarist in HRM orientation, with decision-making being concentrated in the hands of managers, with employees being firmly subordinated (Wood &

Table 28.1   The segmented business system versus two successful business systems

Characteristics	Segmented business system	Compartmentalised (typical of Anglo-Saxon countries)	Highly coordinated (typical of Japan)
Ownership coordination			
Owner control	Direct/mixed	Market	Alliance
Ownership integration of production chains	Mixed	High	Some
Ownership integration of sectors	Low	High	Limited
Non-ownership coordination			
Alliance coordination of production chains	Marketers and end-users dominate production chains.	Low	High
Collaboration between competitors	Highly adversarial competition in informal sector; tendency to oligopolistic relations in export-orientated sectors.	Low	High
Alliance coordination of sectors	Deep variation in practices between sectors.	Low	Some
Employment relations			
Employer–employee interdependence	Some	Low	High
Delegation to employees	Low	Low	Considerable
Source	Authors	Whitley (1999)	Whitley (1999)

Frynas, 2006). Whilst job security is likely to be poor, and state regulation weak, employ-ers may be drawn into informal peasant-based networks of support, with employees being granted informal loans or handouts in the case of financial setbacks, or special occasions such as weddings and funerals (Hyden, 1983). Recruitment is likely to be informal and to centre on the use of existing staff to find new employees from amongst their friends and relatives (Wood & Frynas, 2006).

What both areas of economic activity are likely to have in common is a durable pater-nalism, with hierarchical lines of authority, and clear divisions of labour; if unions are present, the latter are likely to be in a relatively weak position, owing to high levels of unemployment (Wood & Frynas, 2006). MNCs may be under some pressure from lobby groups in their country of origin to uphold basic labour standards, although evidence would suggest that, in most cases, cost concerns will take priority (Mellahi & Wood, 2003).

What many sub-Saharan African countries have in common is that unions have a relatively narrow social base. The bulk of the working-age population are employed in agriculture and the informal sector, with unions being confined to manufacturing, public services, and in some cases, mining (Manda et al., 2001). During the 1960s and 1970s, when most tropical African states were under one party or military rule, unions were firmly subordinated to the government (Tordoff, 1984). With a general move back towards multi-partyism across the continent in the late 1980s and early 1990s, most national union movements regained their autonomy, but faced the challenges of coping with large-scale job losses as a result of ruinous neoliberal reforms. Whilst unions had more room to express alternative political views, their bargaining position was weakened as a result of the evaporation of large components of their constituency (Bracking, 2003; ILO, 1997); they had regained some power, and arguably lost much more at the same time. Moreover, as Williams (1994: 222) notes, the marketisation of social services raised the cost of the reproduction of labour power at the same time as real wages stagnated or declined. Faced with a loss of formal bargaining power, in many cases the only protests open to workers entailed a return to informal mechanisms of resistance, ranging from deliberately low productivity to sabotage or the theft of company resources (cf. Cohen, 1980).

The increased importance of informal livelihoods opened up further challenges for unions. Across the continent, unions have generally failed to organise informal or semi-formal sector workers, reflecting hard-line employer attitudes (often prompted by the very marginal nature of the enterprise itself) and the high attrition rate amongst such enterprises. Moreover, the general lack of union success in organising such workers could reflect an inability to take account of the specific needs posed by the sector, and an inattention to gender issues: many areas of informal sector work are dominated by women (Anonymous, 1999).

Wood and Frynas (2006) summarise the nature of employment relations in segmented business systems as presented in Table 28.2, drawing on Whitley's (1999) classification of the defining features of work and employment relations.

Wood and Frynas (2006) conclude that HRM in segmented business systems is characterised by authoritarian management, weak communication, and a tendency to over-rely on low-cost, unskilled labour. Such strategies are likely to result in low productivity, and poor quality control, locking firms into the 'sweatshop trap'. Firms are simply not able to move beyond low-cost, low-value-added activity: should they significantly reinvest in plant or staff skills, competitors that do not will use the opportunity to exploit their own short-term cost advantages (Wood & Frynas, 2006).

In an extensive study of Mozambican industrial relations, Webster et al. (2006) found that the practice of HRM in Mozambique followed a distinct, path dependent trajectory, as suggested by business systems theory. They argued that Mozambican employment relations could not be simply dismissed as yet another manifestation of an emerging global '*Bleak House*' model characterised by full-scale labour repression. Rather, Mozambican

Table 28.2   Employment relations in segmented business systems

Employment relations	Export and state sectors	Indigenous sector
Employer–employee interdependence	Low	Some
Delegation to employees	Low	Low

Source: Wood & Frynas (2006).

work and employment relations represented a manifestation of path dependency, reflecting the opportunities and distortions posed by national institutional realities. But what form did such work and employment relations assume? They found that a consistent strand stretching back to the colonial era was that of 'durable informalism'. A survey of employers found that many openly admitted to breaking collective agreements and making widespread use of redundancies; there is also much evidence that Mozambican employment law is often 'honoured in the breach rather than the observance'. However, employment relations is also characterised by direct and personal contact between managers and employees; the use of informal recruitment and selection techniques, giving preferential access to the relatives and friends of existing staff; and the extension of informal credit mechanisms. Hence, the resulting model is more paternalist (albeit of the authoritarian variety) than an anonymous '*Bleak House*' model would imply (Webster et al., 2006).

Based on a comparative survey of Nigerian organisations, Okpara and Wynn (2008) found that the focus of HRM managers tended to be primarily on training and development, the latter in part due to limitations in the wider training system. At the same time, this led to other key areas of the HRM function, ranging from compensation and benefits to health and safety, being neglected. Moreover, a wide range of external pressures – ranging from wider political instability to the demands placed by extended kin-based networks – often precluded managers from operating effectively. Again, Nigerian HRM tended to follow a path dependent trajectory, which had many common features with that of Mozambique and, indeed, many other states across the continent.

More recent extensions and developments to business systems theory argue that firms will modify and experiment with old ways of doing things, and try new ways as well (Morgan, 2007). This means that whilst HRM in sub-Saharan African countries remains path dependent, some adjustments to practices will take place at firm, regional, sectoral, and national levels; what defines HRM in Africa may be still evolving on an episodic and uneven basis.

DIFFERENCES AND SIMILARITIES ACROSS THE CONTINENT

Both cross-cultural and institutional accounts have highlighted similarities in regions, and in countries with similar historical experiences. Does this mean that HRM is similar across the continent? Two edited collections on industrial relations practice in different countries across the continent – Wood and Brewster's (2007) edited work, *Industrial Relations in Africa*, and a special issue of the journal *Employee Relations* (Wood, 2008) – as well as Kamoche's (2011) 'Contemporary developments in the management of human resources in Africa', bring together detailed country studies, mostly by scholars working at African universities across the continent. A few themes emerge from this work. First, it is evident that in many sub-Saharan African Anglophone countries – such as Kenya, Uganda, Zambia, and Malawi – 'labour rights that were lost during the one party era(s) were recovered' after democratisation (Dzimbiri, 2007). This has led to a return to freedom of union organising and the expansion of the individual rights of employees. At the same time, what can only be described as 'vandalistic' Structural Adjustment policies imposed by the International Monetary Fund (IMF) led to the wholesale destruction of jobs, greatly weakening the bargaining power of employees. Such policies also weakened the capacity of the state to enforce the law. This pattern of job destruction and the weakening of state capacity was similarly encountered in many Francophone and Lusophone states. However, what sets the latter apart are differences in legal traditions (Croucher, 2007: 204). Both Francophone and Lusophone countries have civil law legal traditions, which tend to circumscribe owner rights and give employees more clearly delineated rights under the law. However, any advantage this accords has, in most cases, been more than offset by political authoritarianism and, again, the destruction of much economic activity by predatory Structural Adjustment (Croucher, 2007; Essaaidi, 2007). Other differences imposed reflect the specific political traditions of countries. For example, in Eritrea a tradition of civil involvement in economic reconstruction has made for hybrid patterns involving both cooperation and authoritarianism (Ghebregiorgis & Karsten, 2007). In Uganda, the depredations of the Amin and Obote II dictatorships have posed particularly severe challenges in terms of institution rebuilding (Kiringa, 2007).

Two sub-Saharan African states represent particularly exceptional cases. South Africa is by far Africa's largest economy. An excellent infrastructure and a large industrial sector have both weathered neoliberal reforms. Unions, mostly organised under the umbrella of the Congress of South African Trade Unions (COSATU), are the strongest on the continent, and are supported by a generally labour-friendly body of labour law. However, once more, the bargaining position of organised labour has been greatly undercut by very high levels of unemployment, as much as 45 per cent in some estimates. Mass immigration from across tropical Africa and China, and to a lesser extent from South Asia and Eastern Europe, have provided the country with new skills and entrepreneurial capabilities; however, intense competition for jobs has led to periodic outbreaks of xenophobic riots. COSATU has historically been aligned to South Africa's ruling party, the African National Congress (ANC), although in recent years this relationship has soured. However, whilst there have been periodic attempts to develop new radical alternatives, they have faced difficulties in securing internal unity and developing coherent alternative political programmes.

Nigeria is by far Africa's most populous country. Oil revenues have not contributed to sustainable development but, rather, to a predatory elite and personalised politics. Within such a context, unions remain weak and vulnerable to political currents. Despite democratisation, the political system remains unstable and inconsistent, greatly reducing the chances for 'normal' industrial relations (Fajana, 2007: 160–161).

Finally, across sub-Saharan Africa, there is the issue of corruption. Hyden (1983) ascribed corruption to pre-modern forces, with extended peasant-based networks of support interpenetrating the state and commercial activity. Whilst providing a means for survival, this may also serve as a basis for corruption. This, and similar accounts of the failure of the state, concluded that modernisation would gradually weaken such ties. Given the role of the state in supporting corrupt networks, neoliberals within the IMF concluded that the simplest remedy would be to do away with the state as a site of corruption (Hoogvelt, 2005). In practice, the resultant policy prescriptions weakened the capacity of the state to enforce social order and provide basic services. Forced and over-hasty privatisations simply led to state assets being handed over to well-connected elites, worsening endemic corruption. In addition, there have been numerous corruption scandals implicating foreign companies; for example, the activities of the British arms firm, BAE, in South Africa and Tanzania. A peculiar lopsided morality invariably leads to local politicians shouldering the blame, with the briber being left free to continue its activities across the continent.

What does all this mean for the practice of HRM? First, flows of corruptly obtained monies to tax havens has meant that less money is available for local investment; this means that local firms often face difficulties of chronic undercapitalisation. Second, a culture of corruption can easily contaminate large areas of social life, increasing transaction costs in any exchange relationship.

HRM IN PRACTICE: EMERGING TRENDS AND ISSUES

In view of the above, a number of key issues emerge. First, whilst many sub-Saharan African countries have extensive bodies of labour law – of either the common or civil law variety – evidence points to uneven enforcement, reflecting both limitations in government capacity and a lack of political will (Wood & Brewster, 2007). Eronda (2004) argues that, in practice, the law is often ambiguous. This reflects the unwillingness – and inability – of national governments to protect either their citizens or local firms in the face of global competition (Greider, 1997).

Second, owing to similar capacity shortfalls, it is likely that, faced with intense adversarial competition, firms will find it hard to adopt longer-term policies that require reinvestment in plant or people. To put it another way, firms cannot afford to move much beyond labour repression. Third, and despite this, African HRM is less simply a '*Bleak House*' model than, often, an autocratic and often low-wage, low-skill model ameliorated by a kind of paternalism that incorporates conceptions of personal and family-based ties, rights, and obligations (Ovadje & Ankomah, 2001; Wood & Brewster, 2007). The overwhelming managerial focus is likely to be on control, emphasising tested processes and hierarchies, founded on pre-colonial notions of chieftainship (Beugr, 2002) and/or colonial despotism (Jackson, 2002). Low wages may be offset through ad hoc financial assistance, and the willingness of firms to countenance wage adjustments in response to unexpected increases in living or transport costs (Beugr, 2002). However, it is likely that older male managers may play a patriarchal role, women are likely to be marginalised, and informal recruitment will be along the lines of existing patronage mechanisms, excluding outsiders (Ovadje & Ankomah, 2001: 183–185).

Fourth, what bargaining power unions had is likely to have been undercut by the large-scale job losses that have universally accompanied destructive structural adjustment policies (Hyman, 2003). Fifth, risk aversion and close supervision, and a concentration of decision-making at the centre, may make for low productivity and morale (Jackson, 2002). This is compounded by imbalances in knowledge as to the potential and challenges of specific HRM situations, in turn reflecting limits in skills, knowledge, and existing enquiry (Kamoche, 2011).

Sixth, training tends to be informal and on the job, linked to the notion of a 'community concept of management', with employment not being seen so much as a formal, fixed contract, but rather as part of a set of reciprocal informal obligations (Eronda, 2004: 6; Beugr, 2002). As many firms have been forced to focus on cost rather than quality and, in the export sector, on primary products, the need for training may in any event be constrained (Jackson, 2002). The limited resources most firms have at their disposal mean that it would be difficult for them to invest in formal training systems even if they wanted to (ibid.).

Seventh, as Harvey (2002) notes, critical to understanding HRM in Africa is that not only laws but also formal rules are often ignored or bent, reflecting both limitations in the state, and the constrained nature of civil society (Webster & Wood, 2005). In part, this may allow firms a greater degree of room for manoeuvre than would otherwise be the case. At the same time, this is likely to make for lower levels of systemic trust, given the greater difficulty in enforcing both implicit and explicit contracts; in turn, this will raise transaction costs relating to the operationalisation of the employment contract, and reduce overall organisational effectiveness (Marsden, 1999).

What this body of literature has in common is the view that many existing practices have translated into poor outcomes (Kamoche, 2011, 2002; Wood & Frynas, 2006; Budhwar & Debrah, 2001; Mellahi & Wood, 2003). This would represent, at least in part, a product of the limited capacity of many sub-Saharan African states both to support the development of human resources and to enforce existing labour laws. Uneven growth (reflecting volatile primary commodity prices) and poor terms of trade, and often inappropriate and misdirected foreign aid, have worsened things. Poor outcomes also represent the product of the embeddedness of authoritarianism and patriarchy both within and the beyond the workplace. In turn, this would make it difficult to introduce and maintain advanced HRM paradigms (Hyden, 1983; Kamoche, 2002).

Finally, there is the role of international organisations to be considered. Kamoche (2011) rather optimistically suggest that foreign firms have a vital role to play in developing human capital and diffusing knowledge. However, while they may 'have a responsibility to act responsibly' (Kamoche, 2011: 2), many clearly do not. A lack of commitment to a specific locale other than as a supply of cheap raw materials, cheap labour, or a market for low-cost goods is too often the norm. Whilst it could be argued that political instability may deter many MNCs from greater investment in people and communities across much of Africa, this instability is itself at least partially a product of unequal terms of trade and an inability to move to higher-value-added production paradigms. Contrary to Kamoche (2011), we would suggest that a greater problem than a lack of ideas and skills is a lack of willingness by international players to systematically commit to developing them. Too often private and non-private international organisations are excessively short-termist in their orientation, with little attention being given to sustainability. The global financial crisis that began in 2008 appears to have worsened such tendencies, and has resulted in greatly reduced inward capital flows across the continent.

An important counter-development has been significant inflows of foreign direct investment from China. Since 2009, China has been investing in South Africa, acquiring mines and vineyards, and moving into infrastructure, construction, and car manufacturing sectors. Whilst there has been much controversy over the labour standards deployed by Chinese-owned firms in the region, the developing China–South African ties will present an opportunity (Jackson et al., 2013).

An emerging body of research on Chinese MNEs in Africa provides the foundation for the development of new theoretical approaches on the institutional and cultural dynamics of HRM across national boundaries (Cooke, 2014). A novel feature of Chinese investment, particularly to South Africa's northern neighbours, has been a tendency to import skilled and semi-skilled labour from China in place of local hires; this has both challenged existing work and employment relations paradigms and raised questions as to the long-term sustainability of such investments (Mohan & Power, 2008).

WAYS FORWARD?

Recent studies have pointed to the internal limitations within organisations, and the need for more effective use of non-financial incentives, particularly given widespread limitations in organisational resources (Mathauer & Imhoff, 2006). Whilst financial incentives are important, failings in even basic internal organisational communication may prove severely counterproductive. Trans-Africa research has revealed (as with studies elsewhere) that imparting dignity in working life, and a recognition of the worth of employees' vocations, can be highly effective HRM interventions.

Brigaldino (1996: 438) notes that a lack of access to capital (itself a product of low savings rates), poor terms of trade, and weak infrastructure mitigate heavily against the competitiveness of firms and nations in sub-Saharan Africa: no matter how effective management is, an adverse external context makes it very difficult for firms to succeed. Gender imbalances also play a role: the greater the divide between men and women in human resource indicators, the lower the national gross domestic product (Brigaldino, 1996: 439). Sustainable industrialisation depends on indigenous capabilities, including the development of human capital and infrastructure.

This focus on practical issues and constraints is echoed by Anakwe et al. (2000), who argue that the main factors moulding HRM policy within the organisation are socio-economic, rather than perceived cultural variations. At the same time, it is necessary to take a critical approach towards the former: it has become commonplace for politicians and those in the conservative community to mouth platitudes about 'good governance' or 'bridging the digital divide', when it is necessary to take account of the long time horizons needed, and the need to devote resources to incrementally developing sustainability (Helleiner, 2002). And the solutions prescribed – totally open regimes regarding foreign investment, open markets, and minimal state intervention – have time and again proven ineffective in promoting the competitiveness of firms based in poor regions of the world.

Karsten and Ghebregiorgis (2006: 145) argue that although the view that great cultural differences preclude the adoption of Western-type HRM practices is incorrect, the successful diffusion of new paradigms depends in part on adaption in the light of local social, cultural, and economic circumstances. Their research drawing on the Eritrean experience pointed to a greater degree of local expertise than might have been presumed by incoming Western organisations; in other words, there was a real risk of ignoring local capabilities. Similarly, Kamoche (1997) argues that the internal capabilities of African organisations are often discounted, when there is a real need to move beyond 'dependency' approaches. Indeed, the diverse nature of workforces within many African organisations can be a real source of competitive advantage, owing to the wide range of life experiences and perspectives.

A caveat is in order here: as noted earlier, there is considerable diversity within Africa. For example, research by Karsten and Ghebregiorgis (2006) points to a relatively high degree of consultation and workplace egalitarianism within Eritrean organisations.

Hence, it would be simply wrong to conclude that all sub-Saharan African workplaces are authoritarian environments. Institutions may mould strategic choices, but real alternatives remain even in unpromising circumstances, even if most firms seek to remain with tried and trusted tools and techniques (Harvey et al., 2002).

SOUTH AFRICAN EXCEPTIONALISM?

As noted above, studies on HRM and its relationship to the wider social context in South Africa should be seen as falling into a distinct category, on account of the country's very much more developed economy and supporting infrastructure. Two relevant strands of literature are worth exploring in more detail here.

The first strand explores the economic effects of South Africa's political transformation, and the firm level implications thereof (see, e.g., Carmody, 2002; Smith & Wood, 1998). Such studies highlight the extent to which the phased reduction of protective tariffs and associated subsidies has forced firms to become more competitive, necessitating more sophisticated HRM policies; relatively strong unions made outright labour repression an unviable option in many cases. Under apartheid, many firms relied on cheap and, in many respects, coerced labour. In the post-apartheid era, firms have often been forced to use labour more intelligently (although large islands of labour repression may be found on the rural periphery), with a stronger emphasis on skills development and the adoption of more capital-intensive production paradigms (Wood & Sela, 2000; Smith & Wood, 1998). Wood and Els (2000) found that organisations were gradually moving towards more sophisticated HRM strategies, involving team working, quality circles, and a greater investment in people. At the same time, the take-up of new production paradigms was uneven. Moreover, the adoption of 'modern' HRM systems has gone hand-in-hand with wholesale job-shedding (Smith & Wood, 1998; Wood & Els, 2000). In turn, this has both weakened the position of organised labour, and contributed to the expansion of an underclass locked in poorly paid and insecure informal sector work (Webster, 2004).

A second focus in the literature relating to HRM in South Africa has been affirmative action and the Black Economic Empowerment policy. Currently, inequity in the South African labour market is the result of past statutory discrimination in the workplace, as well as interventions by the colonial and apartheid regimes in other policy realms (see Buhlungu et al., 2008). Labour markets in the South African context are complex and were historically segmented along the lines of race, gender, class, and geography; and to date still are, despite a vastly different political, social, and economic regime since 1994. Certain pieces of legislation have been enacted in an attempt to reconfigure both the formal and informal characteristics of labour market functioning; that is, they seek to eliminate unfair discrimination in terms of access to workplace resources such as employment itself, promotions, training, and workplace benefits, as well as eliminating prejudice, intolerance, and discrimination within the workplace (Buhlungu et al., 2008).

The Black Economic Empowerment Commission members state that, due to South Africa's colonial and apartheid policies, the development of black human capital in the country has been severely stunted. The most heinous crime of all was the deliberate neglect of the country's majority population, and this was propped up by the delivery of inferior education during this period. The continued imbalance in the attainment of skills presents a formidable challenge to the possibility of equitable growth. South Africa is in a crisis, as the country does not as yet possess the human capital required to attain sustained, high levels of economic growth at a time when global competitiveness is not simply based on the mass production of standardised goods, cheap raw material inputs, and low-skill, low-wage labour (Black Economic Empowerment Commission, 2004).

As Buhlungu et al. (2008) note, the quality of labour supplies is at least partially dependent on education. There have been considerable improvements in schooling, with the percentage of people with no schooling having almost halved from 1996, to 10 per cent in 2007. Across the board, there has been a general increase in access to schooling, although women and blacks are still proportionately under-represented, especially at tertiary level.

Such work points to abiding inequality on racial lines, the over-representation of white males in management, and potential policy options. In turn, this inequality represents both a product of past injustices and present imbalances in training, and skills shortfalls (Horwitz et al., 2002; Horwitz et al., 2003). Horwitz et al. argue that diversity management is closely related to human resources development (HRD), and has 'hard' (recruitment, planning, performance awards) and 'soft' (awareness-raising) dimensions.

Currently the challenge in South Africa remains to design and implement an integrated HRD strategy. This will aid the country to plan its HRD requirements for the twenty-first century in the face of formidable obstacles identified in its educational system, but also in the face of one more worrying factor: the HIV/AIDS pandemic. This poses a threat and promises to significantly derail the attempts to substantially increase the country's human capital. According to Statistics South Africa (2015), the estimated overall HIV prevalence rate is approximately 11.2 per cent of the total South African population. The total number of people living with HIV was estimated at approximately 6.19 million in 2015. Life expectancies that incorporate the impact of AIDS (AIM model) life expectancy at birth declined in South Africa between 2002 and 2005. By 2015, life expectancy at birth was estimated at 60.6 years for males and 64.3 years for females (and 65.2 for males and 72.7 for females without HIV/AIDS) (Statistics South Africa, 2015).

RESEARCH ON HRM IN SUB-SAHARAN AFRICA: UNDER-REPRESENTED AND MARGINALISED?

African writing on work and employment relations issues in sub-Saharan Africa is under-represented in major international journals (Wood & Dibben, 2006); there is a similar underexposure of topics relating to HRM in Africa in such journals (De Cieri et al., 2007). Indeed, Ozbilgin (2004) goes so far as to conclude that, based on a general lack of coverage in terms of both printed articles and the composition of journal editorial boards, Africa represents a 'blind spot' in studying about HRM, particularly when South Africa is removed from the equation. Based on an extensive survey of academic journals in the subfield of industrial relations, Wood and Dibben (2006) found that not only was the number of papers published on Africa-related topics disproportionately small, but it was gradually declining. This reflects both the limited resources available to African scholars and the marginalisation of Africa in wider debates. However, they found no relationship between African-based authorship and the quality of journal outlet in terms of various journal rankings: African scholars were not ghettoised to the lowest-ranked journals (Wood & Dibben, 2006), suggesting that the research coming out of Africa is often of good quality. Encouragingly, African scholars are reasonably well represented in two established journals, the *International Journal of Human Resource Management* and *Employee Relations*. Finally, as Kamoche (1997) notes, much of the literature on HRM in Africa has focused on the concerns and needs of MNCs, rather than the needs of organisations and individuals based in Africa.

CONCLUSION

There is much diversity across the African continent. On the one hand, the HRM systems found in the automotive sector and many other export-orientated industries in South Africa are highly sophisticated and, in some instances, represent examples of global best practice. On the other hand, much people management continues to be authoritarian, and often steps outside legal regulation. Informal extended personal networks of support often pervade workplaces, imparting a flexibility and paternalism that sometimes ameliorates the worst consequences of the poor bargaining position sub-Saharan African workers find themselves in. Optimistic accounts have sought to highlight the extent to which the communitarian features present in many African cultures might promote more inclusive, productive, and compassionate workplaces (Msila, 2015). However, HRM is ultimately founded on the employment contract. Most sub-Saharan African workers are engaged in the informal sector, very small enterprises, and/or peasant agriculture, and have at best implicit contracts of employment. Structural Adjustment programmes in the 1980s and 1990s led to many sub-Saharan African nations reverting to an over-reliance on primary commodities. In the absence of developmental states, it can be argued that HRM will remain confined to relatively small – and in some instances, diminishing – islands of modern commercial and industrial activity (including agribusiness and non-artisanal mining).

REFERENCES

Acemoglu, D., Johnson, S., & Robinson, J.A. 2000. The colonial origins of comparative development. *American Economic Review*, 91(5): 1370–1401.

Anakwe, U.P., Igbaria, M., & Anandarajan, M. 2000. Management practices across cultures: Role of support in technology usage. *Journal of International Business Studies*, 31(4): 653–666.

Anonymous. 1999. Gender and informal sector. *International Labour Review*, 138(3): 340.

Baruch, Y., & Clancy, P. 2000. Managing AIDS in Africa: HRM challenges in Tanzania. *International Journal of Human Resource Management*, 11(4): 789–806.

Beugr, C.D. 2002. Understanding organizational justice and its impact on managing employees: An African perspective. *International Journal of Human Resource Management*, 13(7): 1091–1104.

Black Economic Empowerment Commission. 2004. Report of the Commission. Pretoria.

Bracking, S. 2003. Regulating capital in accumulation: Negotiating the imperial 'frontier'. *Review of African Political Economy*, 30(95): 11–32.

Brigaldino, G. 1996. Africa's economic renewal under the spell of globalisation. *Review of African Political Economy*, 23(69): 437–442.

Budhwar, P., & Debrah, Y.A. 2001. *Human Resource Management in Developing Countries*. London: Routledge.

Buhlungu, S., Bezuidenhout, A., Lewins, K., & Bischoff, C. 2008. Tracking progress on the implementation and impact of the employment equity act since its inception. Sociology of Work Unit, University of the Witwatersrand.

Carmody, P. 2002. Between globalisation and (post) Apartheid: The political economy of restructuring in South Africa. *Journal of Southern African Studies*, 28(2): 255–275.

Cohen, R. 1980. Resistance and hidden forms of consciousness amongst African workers. *Review of African Political Economy*, 7(19): 8–22.

Cooke, F.L. 2014. Chinese multinational firms in Asia and Africa: Relationships with institutional actors and patterns of HRM practices. *Human Resource Management*, 53(6): 877–896.

Croucher, R. 2007. Industrial Relations in Francophone Africa: the case of Niger. In G. Wood and C. Brewster (eds), *Industrial Relations in Africa*: 198–206. London: Palgrave.

De Cieri, H., Cox, J.W., & Fenwick, M. 2007. A review of international human resource management: Integration, interrogation, imitation. *International Journal of Management Reviews*, 9(4): 281–302.

Dibben, P., Wood, G., & Klerck, G. 2013. The limits of transnational solidarity: The Congress of South African Trade Unions and the Swaziland and Zimbabwean crises. *Labor History*, 54(5): 527–539.

Dzimbiri, L. 2007. Industrial relations in Malawi. In G. Wood and C. Brewster (eds), *Industrial Relations in Africa*: 53–65. London: Palgrave.

Eronda, E. 2004. Effective management: A key factor in sustainable development in sub-Saharan African economies. Working paper. Hempstead, NY: Frank G. Zarb School of Business, Hofstra University.

Essaaidi, M. 2007. Industrial relations in an emerging Morocco. In G. Wood and C. Brewster (eds), *Industrial Relations in Africa*: 137–146. London: Palgrave.

Fajana, S. 2007. The development of industrial relations in Nigeria: 1900–2006. In G. Wood and C. Brewster (eds), *Industrial Relations in Africa*: 147–161. London: Palgrave.

Fukuyama, F. 1995. *Trust: Social Virtues and the Creation of Prosperity*. New York: Free Press.

Gbadamosi, G. 2003. HRM and the commitment rhetoric: Challenges for Africa. *Management Decision*, 41(3): 274–280.

Ghebregiorgis, F., & Karsten, L. 2007. The dynamics of industrial relations in Eritrea: 1991–2006. In G. Wood and C. Brewster (eds), *Industrial Relations in Africa*: 17–27. London: Palgrave.

Greider, W. 1997. *One World, Ready or Not*. Harmondsworth: Penguin.

Hansen, C.D. 2003. Cultural myths in stories about human resource development: Analysing the cross-cultural transfer of American models to Germany and the Côte d'Ivoire. *International Journal of Training and Development*, 7(1): 16–30.

Harvey, M. 2002. Human resource management in Africa: Alice's Adventures in Wonderland. *International Journal of Human Resource Management*, 13(7): 1119–1145.

Harvey, M., Myers, M., & Novicevic, M.M. 2002. The role of MNCs in balancing the human capital books between African and developed countries. *International Journal of Human Resource Management*, 13(7): 1060–1076.

Helleiner, G. 2002. Marginalization or participation: African in today's global political economy. *Canadian Journal of Africa Studies*, 36(3): 531–550.

Herbst, J. 2000. *States and Power in Africa*. Princeton, NJ: Princeton University Press.

Hofstede, G. 1991. *Cultures and Organizations: Software of the Mind*. London: McGraw-Hill.

Hoogvelt, A. 2005. Postmodern intervention and human rights: Report of the Commission for Africa. *Review of African Political Economy*, 32(106): 595–599.

Horwitz, F.M., Bowmaker-Falconer, A., & Searll, P. 2003. Human resource development and managing diversity in South Africa. *International Journal of Manpower*, 17(4/5): 134–151.

Horwitz, F.M., Browning, V., Jain, H., & Steenkamp, A.J. 2002. Human resource practices and discrimination in South Africa: Overcoming the Apartheid legacy. *International Journal of Human Resource Management*, 13(7): 1105–1118.

Horwitz, F., & Kelliher, C. 2015. Towards a theoretical model of work organisation in emerging markets. International Employment and Labour Relations Association (ILERA) World Congress. Cape Town, South Africa, 7–11 September.

Hyden, G. 1983. *No Shortcuts to Progress*. London: Heinemann.

Hyman, R. 2003. An emerging agenda for trade unions. Labournet. www.labournet.de/diskussion/gewerkschaft/hyman.html.

ILO. 1997. Press kit: World Employment Relations Report 1996–7. Geneva.

Jackson, T. 2002. Reframing human resource management in Africa: A cross-cultural perspective. *International Journal of Human Resource Management*, 13(7): 998–1018.

Jackson, T., Louw, L., & Zhao, S. 2013. China in sub-Saharan Africa: Implications for HRM policy and practice at organizational level. *International Journal of Human Resource Management*, 24(13): 2512–2533.

Kamoche, K. 1997. Managing human resources in Africa: Strategic, organizational and epistemological issues. *International Business Review*, 6(5): 537–558.

Kamoche, K. 2002. Introduction: Human resource management in Africa. *International Journal of Human Resource Management*, 13(7): 993–997.

Kamoche, K. 2011. Contemporary developments in the management of human resources in Africa. *Journal of World Business*, 46(1): 1–4.

Karsten, L., & Ghebregiorgis, F. 2006. Human resource management practices in Eritrea: Challenges and prospects. *Employee Relations*, 28(2): 144–163.

Karsten, L., & Illa, H. 2005. Ubuntu: A key African management concept. *Journal of Managerial Psychology*, 20(7): 607–620.

Kiringa, J. 2007. Contemporary issues in industrial relations: Uganda. In G. Wood and C. Brewster (eds), *Industrial Relations in Africa*. London: Palgrave.

Manda, D.K., Bigsten, A., & Mwabu, G. 2001. Trade union membership and earnings in Kenyan manufacturing firms. In W. P. i. E. 50 (ed.), *Goteborg*: 1693–1704. Goteborg University.

Marsden, D. 1999. *A Theory of Employment Systems*. Oxford: Oxford University Press.

Mathauer, I., & Imhoff, I. 2006. Health worker motivation in Africa: The role of non-financial incentives and human resource management tools. *Human Resources and Health*, 4(24): 1–17.

Mellahi, K., & Wood, G.T. 2003. From kinship to trust: changing recruitment practices in unstable political contexts: The case of Algeria. *International Journal of Cross Cultural Management*, 3(3): 393–405.

Mohan, G., & Power, M. 2008. New African choices? The politics of Chinese engagement. *Review of African Political Economy*, 35(115): 23–42.

Morgan, G. 2007. National business systems research: Process and prospects. *Scandinavian Journal of Management*, 23(2): 127–145.

Msila, V. 2015. *Ubuntu – Shaping the Current Workplace with (African) Wisdom*. Randburg: Knowles.

Okpara, J.O., & Wynn, P. 2008. Human resource management practices in a transition economy: Challenges and prospects. *Management Research News*, 31(1): 57–76.

Ovadje, F., & Ankomah, A. 2001. Human resource management in Nigeria. In P. Budhwar and Y. Debrah (eds), *Human Resource Management in Developing Countries*: 174–189. London: Routledge.

Ozbilgin, M. 2004. International human resource management. *Personnel Review*, 33(2): 205–221.

Roberts, B. 1964. *Labour in the Tropical Territories of the Commonwealth*. London: G. Bell.

Smith, M.R., & Wood, G.T. 1998. The end of Apartheid and the organisation of work in manufacturing plants in South Africa's Eastern Cape province. *Work, Employment and Society*, 12(3): 479–495.

Spector, P.E., Cooper, C.L., Sanchez, J.I., et al.. 2002. Locus of control and well-being at work: How generalizable are Western findings?. *Academy of Management Journal*, 45(2): 453–466.

Statistics South Africa. 2015. Mid-year population estimates. Statistical Release PO 302.

Swanepoel, B., Erasmus, B., & Schenk, H. 2008. *South African Human Resource Management: Theory and Practice*. Cape Town: Juta.

Swartz, E., & Davies, R. 1997. Ubuntu – the spirit of African transformation management: A review. *Leadership and Organization Development Journal*, 18(6): 290–294.

Tordoff, W. 1984. *Government and Politics in Africa*. London: Macmillan.

Trever-Roberts, T. 1976. *A Systems Approach to Personnel Management*. Alice: Lovedale Press.

Webster, E. 2004. New forms of work and the representational gap: a Durban case study. In G. Wood and M. Harcourt (eds), *Trade Unions and Democracy*: 105–131. Manchester: Manchester University Press.

Webster, E., & Wood, G. 2005. Human resource management practice and institutional constraints. *Employee Relations*, 27(4): 369–385.

Webster, E., Wood, G., & Brookes, M. 2006. International homogenization or the persistence of national practices? The remaking of industrial relations in Mozambique. *Relations Industrielles/Industrial Relations*, 61(2): 247–270.

Whitley, R. 1999. *Divergent Capitalisms: The Social Structuring and Change of Business Systems*. Oxford: Oxford University Press.

Williams, G. 1994. Why structural adjustment is necessary and why it doesn't work. *Review of African Political Economy*, 21(60): 214–225.

Wood, G. 2008. Introduction: Employment relations in Africa. *Employee Relations*, 30(4): 329–332.

Wood, G., & Brewster, C. 2007. Introduction: comprehending industrial relations in Africa. In G. Wood and C. Brewster (eds), *Industrial Relations in Africa*: 1–14. London: Palgrave.

Wood, G., & Dibben, P. 2006. Coverage of African related studies in international journals: Greater exposure for 'public intellectuals' in sociology and industrial relations?. *African Sociological Review*, 10(1): 180–192.

Wood, G., & Els, C. 2000. The making and remaking of HRM: The practice of managing people in the Eastern Cape Province, South Africa. *International Journal of Human Resource Management*, 11(1): 112–125.

Wood, G., & Frynas, J.G. 2006. The institutional basis of economic failure: anatomy of the segmented business system. *Socio-Economic Review*, 4(2): 239–277.

Wood, G., & Sela, R. 2000. Making human resource development work. *Human Resource Development International*, 3(4): 451–464.

29. HRM in the Indian subcontinent
Pawan Budhwar, Arup Varma, and Manjusha Hirekhan

INTRODUCTION

In this chapter we provide an overview of the nature, pattern and determinants of human resource management (HRM) functions in the Indian subcontinent. Given the acknowledged usefulness of the need to examine HRM in a given context in order to conduct a meaningful analysis (Schuler et al., 2002; Budhwar & Debrah, 2009), the next section presents the geographical and socio-economic context of the Indian subcontinent. This is followed by an analysis of the existing HRM literature for the region. The analysis highlights the core aspects of the HRM function in the main countries of the subcontinent. Finally, we present the key challenges facing the HRM function the region and avenues for future research.

THE INDIAN SUBCONTINENT CONTEXT

The Indian subcontinent is a peninsula that extends towards the south from the rest of Asia like an enormous arrowhead. It is called a subcontinent because of its distinct landmass and also because it is not large enough to be considered as a continent. The Himalayas in the north and east, and the Arabian Sea, Indian Ocean, and the Bay of Bengal to the south, bound the Indian subcontinent (Ganeri, 2005). It includes the countries of India, Bangladesh, Pakistan, Sri Lanka, Nepal, and Bhutan (when the Maldives and Afghanistan are also included, then the more commonly used term is South Asia). Despite an impressive economic growth, the region scores very low on the Human Development Index (including nutrition, education, and health), and the gap between rich and poor is increasing. The section of society that most benefits from the economic growth is the booming middle class. The subcontinent is not a homogenous region and a lot of variation exists between its countries in terms of religion and culture (Islam dominating in Pakistan and Bangladesh; Hinduism in India and Nepal; and Buddhism in Sri Lanka and Bhutan), political systems, forms of government, political stability, the law and order situation in the region, and industrial growth.

Like most developing parts of the world, the countries of the Indian subcontinent also pursued a state-regulated economic system after their independence, which hindered innovation and strong economic growth. The main economic development in the region was initiated from the 1980s onward, when the markets of Sri Lanka, and later on India, Pakistan, and Bangladesh, were deregulated and opened to foreign investors (Budhwar & Varma, 2011a; Chandrakumara & Budhwar, 2005; Khilji, 2004a). Nevertheless, a strong development of the social sector, such as education and health, in Sri Lanka from the 1970s onward in comparison to other countries in the region is clearly responsible for its high performance on most human development indicators. Economic growth in the region is due to specific sectors in each of the countries. For example, in both Bangladesh and Sri Lanka it is due to the garment industry; in India it was initially because of the software sector, and then information technology enabled services (ITeS) and business process outsourcing (BPO) along with a few other emerging sectors such as pharmaceuticals. In Nepal and Bhutan it is perhaps due to the tourism industry (for more details, see Reddy, 2006).

In order to enhance intra-regional economic cooperation, in 2004 the national governments in the region outlined a plan to create a South Asian Free Trade Area (SAFTA) by 2016. The intention behind the initiative was to create a South Asian Customs Union and eventually a South Asian Economic Union, similar to the European Union. To a great extent the success of such ambitions depends on how countries in the region deal with internal strife, conflicts, terrorism, and natural disasters. The Indian subcontinent, with the exception of Bhutan, has suffered from widespread armed conflict, including the civil war in Sri Lanka; continued conflicts between certain factions of society within Pakistan; the significant intrusion of the Taliban in north-west Pakistan in 2009–10 and the continuing fragile and volatile situation since then, with an undeclared war going on; Kashmir and militancy-related conflict between India and Pakistan; the increasing terrorist attacks in both India and Pakistan; and the increasing conflict between government and Maoist rebels in Nepal. The subcontinent has also suffered regular natural disasters such as earthquakes; yearly monsoon-related floods in parts of Bangladesh; irregular floods in both India and Pakistan; and the 2015 earthquake in Nepal.

For the past seven decades or so, there has been a regular movement of people both within and outside the region, which seriously impacts upon its economies and has implications for HRM, especially with issues such as recruitment and retention (Ramaswamy, 2003; Budhwar & Varma, 2011b). Both legal and illegal migration from Nepal and Bangladesh to India has been substantial. This mainly involves low-wage and unskilled migrants. On the other hand, there has been large emigration of semi-skilled and skilled migrants from India and Pakistan, initially to the Middle East, followed by many low-skilled workers to the Gulf states (Reddy, 2006); and then of highly skilled migrants from India to North America and Western Europe. Similarly, in the 1980s many unskilled and semi-skilled migrants from Bangladesh and Pakistan went to Western Europe. From Sri Lanka, the migration has been mainly due to the internal war, which began in the 1980s and lasted until 2009; and also to many female domestic workers moving to West Asia for economic reasons. Furthermore, a significant number of students migrate from the Indian subcontinent, initially to study overseas both in the West (mainly North America and the United Kingdom) and the East (primarily to Australia, Singapore, Hong Kong, and New Zealand), and many of them try to stay there; many succeed in doing so (see Baruch et al., 2007). Those who come back (still a significant number) are trained in the Western-established ways of management education, which they try to implement and practice on their return. Similarly, management schools in the Indian subcontinent adopt a similar syllabus to those in the United States of America and the United Kingdom (UK), which also results in the creation of a Western managerial mindset. This is useful for foreign firms wanting to practise familiar global HRM policies, but creates a challenge in terms of working with local employees (Budhwar, 2012).

Such movement of people results in skills shortages and has serious implications for human resource development (HRD). On the other hand, remittances from migrants from the region working in West Asia, North America, and Western Europe make a significant contribution to the economies of India, Pakistan, Bangladesh, Nepal, and Sri Lanka, making it the leading recipient region of foreign remittances in the world. Apart from skills shortages, the region also suffers from a serious imbalance between rich and poor, a significant proportion of the population living below the poverty line, high levels of corruption affecting businesses, population pressure, poor infrastructure, less effective economic reforms, political instability, internal national security issues, and increasing competition from East Asian countries. Despite these problems, the region has a lot to offer to businesses in the global context, such as India's contributions in the above-mentioned sectors, and India becoming the highest gross domestic product (GDP) growth economy in the world (overtaking China in 2015–16). Along with other factors, the effective and efficient management of human resources can play a significant role in the economic development of the region (Budhwar, 2004; Budhwar & Singh, 2007; Debrah et al., 2000; Ramaswamy, 2003; Varma & Budhwar, 2014).

DEVELOPMENTS IN HRM IN THE INDIAN SUBCONTINENT

In comparison to many other parts of the world, there is little literature on HRM in the Indian subcontinent (though it is rapidly increasing for India). Given the variation in the economic developments in different countries of the region, an analysis of the existing literature indicates that the majority on HRM is from India, followed by Sri Lanka and Pakistan, with even less on the other countries of the subcontinent. Perhaps a sensible way of analysing the HRM-related scenario in the region would be to look at the kind of work being published in the field, and the key messages emerging from it, and then to propose a possible way forward for the HRM function in the region. In order to draw any meaningful HRM comparisons between the countries of the region, where possible an attempt is made to highlight the historical developments in the field of HRM, key determinants of HRM, and sector- and ownership-based HRM variations in each of the countries of the subcontinent.

At this stage of analysis, it is important to note that the information used in this chapter about the above-mentioned topics and issues is mostly based on, and is relevant for, the organised sector in the subcontinent – which is small, and on which only scant research evidence is available. The unorganised or the informal sector is large in countries such as India, and hardly any information is available, but it is still relatively more in comparison to other subcontinent countries. For example, the total workforce of India is more than 400 million, out of which nearly 90 per cent or more are engaged in the activities of the unorganised sector (including the so-called informal sector), with only the remaining 10 per cent of the workforce being in the organised sector (for other related data for India, see Datt & Sundram, 2014).

Also, like most parts of the world, the small and medium-sized enterprises (SMEs) in the subcontinent contribute significantly to the region's economic growth. Research clearly highlights significant differences in the pattern of HRM systems between SMEs and medium and large-scale industries. The evidence used in this chapter is mainly based on the latter, as information is not available on the former. In India, there is no legal or policy concept of SME or medium enterprise. The popular concept is the small-scale industry (SSI) sector; this is different from the SME sector in other countries. Thus, apart from SSI, the concept of 'tiny unit' (having an investment of less than 1 million rupees (£1 = 90 rupees approximately, February 2018) is also important to note, for these units are an important part of the informal sector in India. A considerable part of the Indian workforce works in this sector. A large proportion of tiny enterprises are own-account manufacturing enterprises (OAMEs). An OAME in India is defined as one which does not hire any worker on a regular basis and does not maintain any accounts. In addition to OAMEs, India's informal manufacturing sector consists of non-directory manufacturing enterprises (NDMEs) and directory manufacturing enterprises (DMEs). The former category employs less than six hired workers; the latter more than six hired workers (Datt & Sundram, 2014).

The HRM systems of both the SME/SSI and OAME in comparison to medium and large units are very different. In fact, the former do not have an HRM department, a dedicated HRM manager, nor formal HRM policies. They tend to recruit only locals from where they are based, and have a range of informal, unstructured, and highly indigenous work systems, with significant regional differences (for details, see Saini & Budhwar, 2008; Budhwar & Varma, 2011a). It is safe to assume the existence of a similar situation and nature of work for similar units in other Indian subcontinent countries.

HRM in India

The existing literature on the organised sector confirms that formalised personnel functions in Indian organisations have existed for many decades (Saini & Budhwar, 2014). Their origin can be traced back to the colonial 1920s with the concern for labour welfare in Indian factories. The Trade Union Act of 1926 gave formal recognition to workers' unions. Similarly, the recommendations of the Royal Commission on Labour gave rise to the appointment of labour officers in 1932, and the Factories Act of 1948 laid down the duties and qualifications of labour welfare officers. These developments all formed the foundations for the Personnel Function in India and seem to parallel the initial developments of the British Personnel Function (Budhwar & Bhatnagar, 2009). Provisions similar to those provided by Cadbury in the UK were initially provided by J.R.D. Tata (one of the most prominent entrepreneurial figures of India) in the early 1920s in India (Saini & Budhwar, 2014).

In the early 1950s, two HRM-related professional bodies were set up in India: the Indian Institute of Personnel Management (IIPM) formed in Calcutta and the National Institute of Labour Management (NILM) in Bombay. During the 1960s, the personnel function began to expand beyond its welfare origins, with the three areas of labour welfare, industrial relations and personnel administration developing as the constituent roles for the emerging profession. In the 1970s, the thrust of the personnel function shifted towards the need for greater organisational 'efficiency', and by the 1980s personnel professionals began to talk about new concepts such HRM and HRD. The two professional bodies of the IIPM and NILM were merged in 1980 to form the National Institute of Personnel Management (NIPM), based in Bombay. The status of the personnel function in India has therefore changed over the years (Saini & Budhwar, 2014). However, at present it is changing at an even more rapid pace, mainly due to the pressures created by the liberalisation of economic policies initiated in 1991. To summarise, looking at the evolution and developments of the Indian HRM function we can say that its status has changed from that of 'clerical' in the 1920s–1930s, to 'administrative' in the 1940s–1960s, to 'managerial' in the 1970s–1980s, to that of 'executive' in the 1990s, and towards 'strategic partner' in the 2000s and onwards. Accordingly, its emphasis has changed from statutory, welfare, paternalism to regulatory conformance to human resource development and how it can help to improve organisational performance (for more details, see Budhwar & Varma, 2011b).

Within these developmental phases, certainly the increased emphasis on HRD in the 1990s has been the dominant topic in the broad area of the personnel function. To a great extent, this was an outcome of the pressures created by foreign firms following the deregulation of the Indian economy to significantly move the contribution of Indian firms' HRM functions towards organisational performance (Saini & Budhwar, 2014). In fact, in the late 1990s in India, 'HRD' became a more often-used term to denote the personnel function than 'HRM' (Budhwar & Varma, 2011b). HRD in India has been seen as a continuous process to ensure the planned development of employee competencies and capabilities, the motivation and exploitation of internal capabilities for organisational development purposes, and the pursuit of dynamism and effectiveness (Saini & Budhwar, 2014). It also emphasised the provision of tools and techniques to the line managers who encourage its philosophy.

The changes in response to the pressure created by economic reforms on the traditional Indian personnel management system are now clearly noticeable in the way organisations are managed in India, especially in the modern and organised sectors (software, IT, BPO) and those that are managed professionally (Budhwar et al., 2006a; Budhwar et al., 2006b; Budhwar et al., 2009). This also applies to the majority of the foreign firms operating in India (Björkman & Budhwar, 2007). In most of such organisations, the HRM function is seen as well structured and rationalised. Indian organisations operating in this way are still in a minority, but their numbers are certainly on the increase. Since the traditional Indian HRM system was developed over a long time period, understandably, it will take some time to change. However, the symptoms of change are quite prominent as HRM is playing a noticeable role in bringing about changes in Indian organisations, and more and more Indian organisations are now creating a separate HRM or HRD department. Accordingly, there has been a significant increase in the level of training and development of employees (Saini & Budhwar, 2014). There are also indications of a movement towards performance-related pay and promotions (Budhwar & Varma, 2011b). Indeed, such developments have already matured in the modern industrial sectors such as business process outsourcing (Budhwar & Varma, 2011a).

Similarly, in comparison to the public sector, the internal work culture of private enterprises now places greater emphasis on an internal locus of control, future orientation in planning, participation in decision-making, effective motivation techniques, and obligation towards others in the work context (Saini & Budhwar, 2014). The existing research evidence also reveals the significant influence of different contingent variables such as age, size, and sector, and indeed national factors such as national culture and institutions, on the HRM systems of Indian firms (Budhwar & Bhatnagar, 2009). Overall, it would be appropriate to say that the HRM function in India is in a phase of rapid transition. A collective effort is now required from both practitioners and researchers to support each other and share the ongoing developments in the field with

Table 29.1   HRM research in India

Theme	Authors
Evolution of the HRM function	Balasubramanian (1994, 1995), Saini & Budhwar (2014)
HRM and the line manager's role	Budhwar & Sparrow (1997), Bamel et al. (2011), Azmi and Mushtaq (2015)
Unions, industrial relations, employee relations, grievance management, and the new economic environment	Sharma (1992), Sodhi (1994), Seth (1996), Venakata Ratnam (1998), Budhwar (2003), Cooke & Saini (2015)
Factors determining HRM and work behaviour	Budhwar & Sparrow (1997), Bhatnagar (2007), Lakshman (2014), Gupta & Singh (2014), Saini & Budhwar (2014)
HRM in MNCs operating in India, and Western HRM in India	Amba-Rao (1994), Budhwar & Khatri (2001), Björkman & Budhwar (2007), Björkman et al. (2008), Venakata Ratnam (1998), Lange et al. (2010), Budhwar (2012)
HRM, culture, and firm performance	Budhwar & Sparrow (1997), Agarwala (2003), Singh (2003), Chand & Katou (2007), Chand (2010), Nigam et al. (2011), Azmi (2011)
Talent management and learning	Bhatnagar & Sharma (2005), Bhatnagar (2007)
HRM and innovation	Som (2008, 2012), Jain et al. (2012), Bhatnagar (2014), Khandwalla (2014), Srinivasan & Chandwani (2014)
Comparative HRM: public versus private sector and HRM in SMEs	Bordia & Blau (1998), Saini & Budhwar (2008), Haq (2012), Budhwar & Boyne (2004), Murthy (2014)
HRM and business process outsourcing	Budhwar et al. (2006a), Budhwar et al. (2006b), Budhwar (2009), Sengupta & Gupta (2012)
Training and HRD	Rao et al. (1994), Sparrow & Budhwar (1997), Yadapadithaya (2000), Lakkoju (2014), Jain (2015)
Cross-national comparative HRM	Kuruvilla (1996), Budhwar & Sparrow (1997, 2002)
HRM, engagement, work–life balance, and retention	Guchait & Cho (2010), Rajadhyaksha (2012), Biswas et al. (2013), Agarwala et al. (2014), Kurian & Naik (2014), Kulkarni & Rodrigues (2014), Umamaheswari & Krishnan (2015), Pathak (2015), Sankar (2015)

different audiences. The emerging evidence also suggests that researchers are pursuing investigations on a variety of HRM-related topics in India. Table 29.1 provides a summary.

Also, a number of researchers have examined various aspects of organisational behaviour and organisational dynamics (see, e.g., Aryee et al., 2002, 2004; Kakar, 1971; Sahay & Walsham, 1997) and the influence of national culture on Indian HRM (Sharma, 1984; Budhwar & Sparrow, 2002). With a rapid increase in the number of expatriates moving to India, some scholars have initiated investigations related to their adjustment (e.g., Kim & Tung, 2013; Thite et al., 2009; Varma et al., 2006). These examples give a clear indication of the kind of HRM issues explored in the Indian setting. However, it is important to note that this is not an exhaustive list of works published on India (for details, see Budhwar & Bhatnagar, 2009; Saini & Budhwar, 2014).

HRM in Pakistan and Bangladesh

Both Pakistan and Bangladesh, being part of India prior to separation in 1947 (during Partition, India was divided into India and Pakistan; with Bangladesh as part of Pakistan, called Eastern Pakistan, until 1971, when it became independent), they also inherited a number of management systems from the UK. Hence, we can expect a number of similarities in the nature of HRM systems of the three countries, especially during the decades of the 1950s–1970s. Nevertheless, due to the variations in economic growth of the three countries, along with the growing importance of certain institutions in them contributing to both uniqueness and differences over the past few decades, we can see differences regarding both the development and the nature of the HRM function in these countries, with certain sectors and industries in India having more developed HRM functions (at least in professionally run firms), followed by Pakistan and Bangladesh. For both these countries there is scant HRM literature available.

Both Pakistan and Bangladesh are predominantly Muslim countries (approximately 96 per cent and 87 per cent of the population, respectively, following Islam), with a very high density of population (Pakistan and Bangladesh being the sixth and seventh most populous countries in the world), high illiteracy and unemployment rates, and having agriculture as the dominating sector contributing towards both GDP and employment. For Pakistan, the initial work by Khilji (2002, 2003, 2004a, 2004b; Khilji & Wang, 2006) was most comprehensive. She has researched and written on various aspects of people management in Pakistan, including the evolution of HRM functions, factors determining HRM policies and practices, comparative HRM in local and foreign firms, HRM and firms' performance, and the challenges facing the HRM function in Pakistan.

Khilji (2004a: 110–111) presents a comprehensive analysis of the impact of the main national factors on various aspects of HRM in Pakistan. Under the factor of national culture she highlights how the social and hierarchical set-up of the Pakistani society, marked by high power-distance, having a strong inheritance of UK class systems and influences of the American management systems, impacts on most spheres of HRM including recruitment, rewards, appraisals (who knows whom), decision-making (more centralised), and training. Similarly, she highlights how the competitive business environment is impacting on an increased emphasis on training; and how national instability and political uncertainly are contributing to a lack of trust amongst the key actors of the employment system. Trade unions (as in India) seem to have had a significant influence on HRM in Pakistan (on such issues as termination, dismissals, and health and safety). The impact of Islam in the workplace is also evident in Pakistan (Khilji, 2004a; Syed, 2008). For example, prayer rooms, extended lunch breaks on Fridays, and less working time during the fasting months, are provided in most organisations. Pakistan has a unique business and institutional set-up, characterised by an increasing impact of Islamic principles on work systems; increasing levels of 'red tape'; strong relationship- and caste-based social set-ups; corruption and discontentment in society at large due to poor economic growth; economic and national security-related instability; and scarcity of resources to share with the rapidly increasing population. These all have a significant impact on HRM in Pakistan.

Multinational corporations (MNCs) are required to modify their HRM practices to suit this context (Khilji, 2003) through, for example, the provision of flexible working to support employees for Friday prayers and during the fasting months, and a more localised approach to HRM practices (for example, word-of-mouth and referral-based recruitment). It is important to realise the complex dynamic within which foreign firms operate in developing countries like Pakistan. On the one hand, they directly employ staff from the host country for which they adopt a mixture of global HRM policies and local context-specific practices (recruitment, motivation, communications, and talent retention, for example). On the other hand, MNCs tend to rely on local SMEs for the supply of goods and services, SMEs that often resort to questionable practices such as employment of child labour, and violation of labour standards such as denial of minimum wage and other minimum-work conditions. Overall, the status of HRM in Pakistan is still low in comparison to other functions. This is evident from the absence of an established HRM professional body or many business schools offering HRM degrees in Pakistan (Khilji, 2004a).

Lately, some other HRM-related investigations have also emerged. For example, Qadeer et al. (2011) compared 31 aspects of HRM in public and private higher education institutes (HEIs) of Pakistan. Their analysis highlights emerging HRM patterns related to the emergence of HRM departments, HRM strategy integration, development and organisational policies, monitoring of training effectiveness, and communication. Despite similarities in these two sectors on a majority of factors, they differ significantly along factors such as development, evident HRM strategies, and translation of HRM strategies into work programmes. Traditional approaches to HRM and cultural forces impacting upon HRM are more visible. Saher and Mayrhofer (2014) acknowledged through their case study of a privatised hospital that traditional societal norms exist alongside Western HRM concepts in an ambiguous manner, and that has an effect at the individual, organisational, and societal levels. They analysed *Vartan Bhanji* (VB), a traditional notion constituting and leading local social networks, offering a 'blended situation' which is key for organisational performance and individual well-being and performance. VB shapes the meaning and management of social networks in Pakistan. Chaudhry (2013) analysed the uptake of distinctly Anglo-Saxon protean and boundaryless careers in two United States subsidiaries operating in Pakistan, and revealed that these contemporary career types often coexist with (rather than replace) traditional careers. 'New' careers that are evident in Pakistan are individualised employment contracts, self-management, and increasing employability external to the organisation. Khan et al. (2013) explored the level and extent to which HRM practices are formally used in the labour-intensive garment industry in Pakistan. This study supported the notion that, as in most developing countries, non-HRM staff in an informal style have implemented HRM, concluding that SMEs in Pakistan must move towards formal HRM practices system.

The available literature on Bangladesh is primarily on the management of the public sector and on governance issues. Zafarullah (2006) analysed new tools and practices in public governance in both Pakistan and Bangladesh. Sarker (2005, 2006) explored the factors influencing the success and failure of new public management initiatives in Bangladesh and Singapore. Zafarullah and Rahman (2008) blame successive governments for politicising administrative services in Bangladesh. They also point to the significant contribution of corruption and nepotism towards inefficiency, and the failure of the state machinery in formulating and implementing sound policies. Similarly, Zafarullah (2006) highlighted the need for better relationships between governance and socio-economic outcomes; and accountability, transparency, and participation as important ingredients for effective management developments in a developing country like Bangladesh. Due to the economic, social, and cultural positions of women in that society, perhaps a clear difference is evident when it comes to the movement of females to higher positions in Pakistan and Bangladesh (Andaleeb, 2004; Aston, 2008; Lucy et al., 2008) and India (Budhwar & Varma, 2011b) where, perhaps due to religious institutional constraints, there are less females in key positions in the former.

Recent research focuses on the impact of HRM systems and practices on financial and market performance in the public and private banking and manufacturing sectors in Bangladesh. Bhuiyan et al. (2015) demonstrate that there is a direct and positive relationship between human resource information system (HRIS) applications and the firm's financial results. Absar et al. (2012) verified the positive impact of HRM practices on the market performance of the manufacturing sector in Bangladesh.

HRM in Sri Lanka, Nepal, and Bhutan

According to the World Bank (2006), Sri Lanka was one of the first developing countries to understand the importance of investing in human resources and promoting gender equality. As a result, it has a fairly well-developed human resource base and has achieved human development outcomes more consistent with those of higher-income countries: for example, on indices such as the Human Development Index (0.665), literacy rate (92 per cent), pupils completing primary school (97 per cent), and life expectancy (71 years), Sri Lanka stands higher than all other nations in South Asia. Foreign investors have noted that the Sri Lankan labour force is highly trainable.

Recent developments in the field of HRM bear witness to the fact that both the Sri Lankan government and private sector organisations have recognised the importance of HRM's role in the nation's growth and in achieving a sustainable competitive advantage in the global marketplace. There are several examples:

- The formation of a Human Resource and Education (HR&E) Sub Committee (June 1999) by the Ceylon Chamber of Commerce in order to bridge the country's human resource development gap, with the collaboration of private sector organisations and Sri Lankan universities.
- The formation of the Association of HR Professionals (AHRP), having recognised the pivotal role that HRM plays in the present global and regional environment, in order to give due recognition to HRM, which will benefit the professionals as well as the whole country, to share knowledge and experience among HRM managers, and to establish strategic alliances with other institutions in order to carry out research projects on HRM in collaboration with academic institutions.
- The establishment of the Commercial Mediation Centre (CMC) of Sri Lanka by an Act of Parliament in order to act as a viable alternative to litigation when dealing with business disputes and conflicts, besides helping the parties to save face and continue their existing employment relationships (for more details, see Chandrakumara & Budhwar, 2005).

The existing literature reveals an increasing number of HRM research investigations being pursued in the Sri Lankan context. For example, Lee and Reade (2015) investigated the societal context, ethnic homophily perceptions, as an emergent IHRM challenge in developing economies such as Sri Lanka. They define ethnic homophily perceptions at the workplace as employees' assessment that colleagues prefer working with ethnically similar others. A survey of 550 managers revealed that employees' sensitivity to ethnic conflict is positively related to ethnic homophily perceptions, and also that workgroup ethnic diversity (WED) and quality of work relationships (QWR) can play a key role as potential tools to manage this challenge by reducing perceptions of ethnic homophily.

Jayawardana et al. (2013) examined performance evaluation outcomes, job satisfaction, and turnover intentions for middle managers in the garment sector in Sri Lanka. Their study with 155 middle-, high- and low-performing managers demonstrated that job involvement plays a substantial role in the relationship between perceived organisational support, social exchange, and economic exchange. This suggests that human resource managers need to focus on the factors that influence job involvement. An in-depth interview-based study by Fernando and Cohen (2013) on highly skilled women in public and private sector organisations in Colombo explored the organisational constraints that women perceive to impact upon their home–work harmonisation. In comparison with other neighbours from South Asian countries such as India, Sri Lankan women's socio-cultural and educational position is more favourable (Malhotra & DeGraff, 1997), though there are serious barriers to women's advancement in Sri Lankan organisations as well. This study contributes to the existing literature on Sri Lanka by helping to understand how work–life balance is experienced as a paradox; how the impact of organisational constraints is related to women's career stage; and how they manage these constraints, which impacts upon their home–work dynamics.

Wickramasinghe and Zoyza (2011) looked at a range of factors at managerial competency level that form firm-level capabilities in a Sri Lankan telecommunication service provider. In the globalised business setting, many firms operating in Sri Lanka are adopting a technology-driven HRM environment. The implementation of web-based HRM systems as a form of innovation is relatively new, and there is very little empirical evidence on its effect on the employee end-users, particularly in an emerging economy that has a reputation for IT sourcing. Wickramasinghe (2010) investigated the employee perceptions towards web-based electronic HRM systems in 30 Sri Lankan firms with such systems, as a stand-alone automation serving employees' HRM needs. Their findings suggest that the level of complexity of the system is moderated and significantly correlates with system usage. The study by Chandrakumara and Sparrow (2003) highlights the nature of work and people management practices in Sri Lanka. The analysis is based on the responses of chief executive officers (CEOs) and HRM managers of both local and foreign-invested manufacturing companies. The main aspects of work and people management practices include the existence of a moderate-level HRM planning and empowering system; performance-based rewards systems with business-driven training; functional perspectives on job–person fit; and job- and behaviour-related competence and rewards. A closer analysis highlights differences between domestic and foreign firms (either fully owned MNCs or joint ventures). For example, in comparison to domestic firms, foreign firms tend to adopt a more structured, formal, and rationalised approach to all the above-mentioned HRM practices.

Akuratiyagamage (2005, 2006) examined issues related to management development in different ownership firms in Sri Lanka. She found similarity of management development practices across the three forms of firm ownership: local, foreign, and joint ventures. Along the same lines, Mamman et al. (2006) looked at the managerial perceptions towards the role of the HRM function in the development of organisational strategy processes in Sri Lankan organisations. Their results reveal no significant differences between local and foreign firms. Wickramasinghe and Jayabandu (2007) examine issues related to 'flexitime' such as employees' attitudes towards it, their level of satisfaction with it, various hindrances in the adoption of flexitime, and the extent to which flexitime can be used effectively to attract and retain employees. Their findings reveal that flexitime allows employees autonomy to harmonise work and non-work demands, and enables them to balance work–life commitments. It is also evident that large companies offer more flexitime initiatives in comparison to small firms. Further, employees see flexitime as an important feature to have in their future workplaces. Not surprisingly, those employees who have not experienced flexitime are not yet convinced about its benefits. Chandrakumara (2007) provides empirical evidence on the impact of HRM fit on citizenship and task performance of employees, in seven manufacturing companies and a survey of 433 employees and managers in Sri Lanka. His findings confirm the thesis of a positive relationship between HRM fit and performance; more for citizenship performance than for task performance.

Chandrakumara and Sparrow (2004) found a significant impact of meaning and values of work orientation as an element of national culture in predicting HRM policy-practice design choices. Their investigations reveal that the four dominant clusters of HRM design choices (that is, planned and open career and empowering system; qualifications- and performance-based reward system; generic functional perspectives of job–person fit; and job-related competence and rewards) are influenced by eight factors of meaning and values and work orientations (that is, individual growth or humanistic beliefs-oriented work norms; organisation- and position-oriented work ethics and beliefs; status- and security-oriented upward striving; extrinsic value orientation; external work locus of control; work centrality; working defined as a burden and constraint; and work defined as a social responsibility and contribution). Wickramasinghe (2006) investigated the validity of training objectives in the Sri Lankan context. In another analysis, she found that in the private sector companies place greater weighting on the external labour market in recruitment, and the use of objective criteria in selection (Wickramasinghe & Jayabandu, 2007). Further, she found an important role for interviews, written examinations, psychometric tests, and assessment centres within the selection methods.

This evidence reveals the existence of a more professional approach to HRM in the Sri Lankan context. A comparative analysis of the Indian subcontinent countries highlights Sri Lanka (along with India) as a more attractive place for investors. Some of the main factors in this regard include its position as a regional trading hub; a provider of strategic access to South Asian markets (through bilateral free trade agreements); the presence of a highly literate and cost-competitive labour force; the existence of an open economy; the presence of free trade zones and industrial parks; the existence of a reliable infrastructure; and a relatively high quality of life (Chandrakumara & Budhwar, 2005). Nevertheless, Sri Lanka has had its own share of internal disturbances over recent decades, led by the Liberation Tigers of Tamil Eelam (LTTE).

Lately, some scholars have also initiated research on HRM-related issues in Nepal. Gautam (2015) interviewed 105 publicly listed companies in Nepal to explore the extent of strategic integration between business strategy and HRM policies. Results revealed that high-performing organisations were also high in strategic integration with HRM policies. Interestingly, half of the selected organisations in Nepal were doing business without having a business strategy, and only one-quarter of them had formulated a clear HRM strategy to support that business strategy. This also supports the need to invest more in HRM to improve organisational performance in Nepal. Adhikari and Mueller (2004) provide a good summary of the scene of HRM in Nepal and the significant impact of the business environment, national culture, and national institutions on Nepali HRM. Gautam et al. (2005) examine the constructs of organisational citizenship behaviour and organisational commitment in the Nepalese context. Further, Gautam and Davis (2007) investigate the constructs of strategic integration of HRM in terms of the corporate strategies and devolvement of responsibility for HRM to line managers, in 26 commercial banks and insurance companies operating in Nepal. The results indicate a relatively higher level of integration of HRM into the corporate strategy, in comparison to devolvement of responsibility for HRM to the line. The partial level of devolvement is more out of necessity in the absence of a strong HRM function. Such investigations are useful in revealing that Western HRM constructs are making inroads into more developed aspects of Nepalese business. They also highlight how the socio-economic and cultural context of the nation is influential in shaping the devolvement of HRM mechanisms in Nepal, and the extent to which a real transfer of Western constructs is possible in such a context (also see Pant et al., 1996). The existing literature highlights a scarcity of managerial skills in Bhutan and there is an absence of any reliable HRM-related literature (McWeeney, 1998; Rice, 2004).

Overview

A few conclusions can be drawn from the above analysis. First, there is a scarcity of HRM research on the Indian subcontinent (though emerging strongly in the Indian context). Second, there is very little evidence regarding the kind of methodologies that might be suitable for conducting useful research in the region. At present many of the above-mentioned researchers have adopted Western constructs and measures to examine HRM in the region, and have found some interesting results. Given the heterogeneity of the countries within the region and their obvious differences from the West, and knowing the limitations regarding the applicability of Western constructs and measures elsewhere, it is important to further develop more region-specific instruments and to conduct investigations using these (Budhwar & Debrah, 2009; Pant et al., 1996).

Third, there is little HRM research evidence for SMEs in the region. They recruit a significant proportion of the population, contribute to the economic growth of the region, and also strongly support MNCs operating in the region. SMEs employ a range of indigenous work and management practices, which reveal the nature of the society, which perhaps is not reflected in the above presentation. Indigenous systems are characterised by unique internal labour markets based on social connections, a high level of power distance, informality, and lack of rationalisation.

Fourth, all countries of the Indian subcontinent, apart from Bhutan, regularly experience serious disturbance from terrorists, banned groups, or unsupportive local political parties. This significantly disturbs business in general and has implications for HRM. Lastly, in order to reveal the region- and context-specific nature of HRM policies and practices, there is a strong need to identify the main aspects of indigenous management systems relevant to each country of the subcontinent, and also the main factors and variables which might be determining them.

CHALLENGES FOR HRM AND THE WAY FORWARD IN THE INDIAN SUBCONTINENT

The economic liberalisation being pursued by most countries in the Indian subcontinent, along with many related attractions for foreign investors such as availability of cheap and talented human resources, offer immense opportunities for businesses on the one hand, but on the other hand there are issues related to instability, security, uncertainty, corruption, nepotism, lack of enough skilled human resources, and so on. These pose massive challenges for overseas firms to enter the Indian subcontinent markets and flourish there. Given the evolutionary phase of the HRM function in many of the countries in the region, and the economic developments in dynamic business circumstances, there are massive challenges facing the HRM function of firms operating in the region.

It is clear that HRM systems in these countries are now rapidly evolving and are in a state of flux: the traditional mechanisms of managing human resources in the present dynamic business era are being challenged, though still strongly prevalent in SMEs; the validity of established Western or Eastern management systems in the Indian subcontinent is questionable; the establishment of 'best-practice' models to suit the subcontinent context is still emerging and will take a while to become reliable; and the pace of change is phenomenal (especially in India), as a result of which it is difficult to pinpoint the dominant and perhaps more successful ways of managing human resources in the subcontinent.

In such circumstances, perhaps the main challenge before the HRM function in the Indian subcontinent is to change the traditional mindset of top decision-makers and make them realise the useful contribution HRM can make towards achieving organisational objectives. This is certainly happening in countries such as India and Sri Lanka, and in large firms and MNCs in Pakistan. The way forward for other countries is perhaps to learn from these countries and companies and to initiate HRM-related initiatives in the form of new academic programmes, and development of HRM professional bodies, and to amend their dated labour legislation which is creating difficulties in bringing about the required changes. Apart from updating of the legislation, there is a strong need to strengthen its implementation. Corruption of different types (such as personal preferences and favours at work based on social connections) is perhaps the main hindrance in this regard.

Perhaps one of the changes needed for places like India is the downsizing of organisations in order to tackle the problem of surplus labour, especially in public sector organisations. Both the existing legislation and the existence of pressure groups (in the form of unions, and vested interests of politicians and other leaders) resist such changes and create a massive challenge for the HRM function to tackle such difficult issues. The experience of China and also a few cases in India suggest that it will only happen with the help of visionary decision-making, and pressure created by private and foreign firms on public sector firms to reform, rationalise, and professionalise their HRM systems.

The analysis also highlights the important influence of social contacts, the caste to which one belongs, one's financial position and political affiliation, for most HRM practices (also see Budhwar & Khatri, 2001; Saini & Budhwar, 2014) in the region. This aspect not only restricts optimum use of talent, but frequently simply ignores it, which results in nepotism and corruption at the workplace. This poses a major challenge for the HRM function in the subcontinent (indeed, in many other developing countries around the world as well) to stay efficient and effective. It is interesting to note that many organisations in India are now successfully pursuing a formal, structured, rationalised, and professional approach to HRM in some sectors within the traditional set-up. It is now evident that most foreign firms and firms operating in the business process outsourcing sector in India are able to pursue such modern HRM systems (Budhwar et al., 2006a; Budhwar et al., 2006b; Budhwar et al., 2009). To a great extent, the demands of the sector make this possible (in the BPO sector, most performance indicators are quantifiable and most systems are based on objective indices). A number of firms are now rapidly learning from such successful examples and are modifying their HRM systems. It is believed that growing competition, along with increased awareness about the benefits of such systems, will encourage other firms to adopt such systems. However, it is also clear that such developments will vary significantly between countries of the region, which may vary in terms of their economic development, stability, growth of professional management institutes, and the will of top decision-makers.

In the new sectors such as BPO, software, and IT, and also in foreign firms, employees in the Indian subcontinent are experiencing a move away from traditional employment practices and established internal labour markets, which might constitute a violation of their traditional psychological contracts (Budhwar & Varma, 2011b). Thus, the challenge for HRM managers is how to deal with the outcome of employees' responses to the perceived violation of the psychological contract, such as reduced effort or output, and reduced contributions in the form of loyalty and commitment (DeNisi & Griffin, 2001). We might assume that it is in the new sectors where problems relating to psychological contract and job stress are now becoming prominent. For example, in the case of India, a majority of call centre employees after a while discover the 'dark side' of the 'rosy picture' and then their level of morale declines considerably. This often results in high attrition. To a great extent, the lack of talent development initiatives and the lack of clear career structure are held responsible for this (Budhwar et al., 2006a). Such emerging trends pose challenges to HRM managers regarding their recruitment and retention policies and practices (Kuruvilla & Ranganathan, 2010).

Yet another challenge for HRM managers is the issue of diversity management, especially related to gender, caste, and religious diversity. The cultural constraints in the region (especially in Muslim countries) regarding the acceptance of females into the workforce, and certainly in key positions, are a massive challenge. It is evident that there are glass ceiling problems in subcontinental organisations. Perhaps it would be useful to learn from the successful examples of the BPO sector in India, which not only has about a 50 per cent female workforce, but also pushed the Indian government to amend its Factories Act, under which females were not allowed to work on night shifts. However, this will be a major problem in Muslim countries where there is evidence that female students are not even allowed to attend schools.

Nevertheless, it seems that the status of the personnel function in many sectors in India and Sri Lanka has improved over the last two decades or so. The number of personnel specialists moving to the position of CEO has increased over the last few years (Saini & Budhwar, 2014). Along with this move, the way forward is the adoption of a more strategic approach to HRM. To pursue such an agenda it is important that the foundations of the HRM function are sound. Perhaps this agenda is already on the move, and is being put in practice in many Indian organisations (Agarwala, 2003; Singh, 2003; Budhwar & Varma, 2011b). This also seems to be happening in Pakistan, but the momentum is repeatedly disturbed by either an internal security threat or a natural disaster. In other countries this is certainly is not the case.

A further challenge is in the form of how best to manage the 'new employee': the expatriate in the Indian subcontinent context. In countries such as India, the numbers of expatriates (self-initiated or others) are now increasing rapidly. Given the unique context of the subcontinent, it does not have established approaches for managing expatriates. Perhaps this should be seen not only as a challenge, but also as an opportunity to learn and accordingly improve management systems in the region.

Another challenge revolves around the quality of HRM research in the Indian subcontinent context. It seems that too much of the research effort has been limited to simplistic comparisons; correlational analyses providing no insight into underlying processes; and skewed, idiosyncratic sampling. There is, then, a strong need to increase both the rigour and the relevance of HRM research efforts in the Indian subcontinent context. The focus of research should also be to develop constructs that can help to study local and global issues, and enable the development and validation of new constructs so as to get deeper into issues that are more relevant to the region.

To summarise, the challenges facing HRM in the Indian subcontinent are clearly complex and daunting. The majority of these challenges have emerged due to the changes in the economic environment. In particular, globalisation and international competitiveness have brought to the fore the need for organisations to adopt appropriate HRM practices in their quest for competitive advantage. In this globalised era, competitive pressures have laid bare the limitations of the traditional models of management in all the countries of the region. Clearly, there is some indication that HRM is undergoing transformation in the region, but it is unclear what the outcome of this transformation will be. Indications from India, at least, are that a move towards a more professional approach to HRM is evolving in certain sectors. However, it is too early to see a clear model or approach emerging. Possibly, a hybrid system (based on a mixture of both traditional Asian characteristics and the Western rationalised system) will emerge. However, it is important that any HRM system that emerges in the subcontinent should be context-based.

REFERENCES

Absar, N., Nimalathasan, B., & Mahmood, M. 2012. HRM–market performance relationship: Evidence from Bangladeshi organizations. *South Asian Journal of Global Business Research*, 1(2): 238–255.

Adhikari, D.R., & Mueller, M. 2004. Human resource management in Nepal. In P. Budhwar and Y. Debra (eds), *Human Resource Management in Developing Countries*: 91–101. London: Routledge.

Agarwala, T. 2003. Innovative human resource practices and organizational commitment: An empirical investigation. *International Journal of Human Resource Management*, 14(2): 175–197.

Agarwala, T., Arizkuren-Eleta, A., Del Castillo, E., Muniz-Ferrer, M., & Gartzia, L. 2014. Influence of managerial support on work–life conflict and organizational commitment: An international comparison for India, Peru and Spain. *International Journal of Human Resource Management*, 25(10): 1460–1483.

Akuratiyagamage, V.M. 2005. Identification of management development needs: A comparison across companies of different ownership–foreign, joint venture and local in Sri Lanka. *International Journal of Human Resource Management*, 16(8): 1512–1528.

Akuratiyagamage, V.M. 2006. Management development practices: Empirical evidence from Sri Lanka. *International Journal of Human Resource Management*, 17(9): 1606–1624.

Amba-Rao, S.C. 1994. US HRM principles: Cross-country comparisons and two case applications in India. *International Journal of Human Resource Management*, 5(3): 755–778.

Andaleeb, S.S. 2004. Participation in the workplace: Gender perspectives from Bangladesh. *Women in Management Review*, 19(1): 52–64.

Aryee, S., Budhwar, P.S., & Chen, Z.X. 2002. Trust as a mediator of the relationship between organizational justice and work outcomes: Test of a social exchange model. *Journal of Organizational Behavior*, 23(3): 267–285.

Aryee, S., Chen, Z.X., & Budhwar, P.S. 2004. Exchange fairness and employee performance: An examination of the relationship between organizational politics and procedural justice. *Organizational Behavior and Human Decision Processes*, 94(1): 1–14.

Aston, J. 2008. Why Bangladeshi and Pakistani women face cultural and practical barriers to work. *People Management*, 14(1): 46.

Azmi, F.T. 2011. Strategic human resource management and its linkage with HRM effectiveness and organizational performance: evidence from India. *International Journal of Human Resource Management*, 22(18): 3888–3912.

Azmi, F.T., & Mushtaq, S. 2015. Role of line managers in human resource management: Empirical evidence from India. *International Journal of Human Resource Management*, 26(5): 616–639.

Balasubramanian, A. 1994. Evolution of personnel function in India: A re-examination, Part I. *Management and Labour Studies*, 19(4): 196–210.

Balasubramanian, A. 1995. Evolution of personnel function in India: A re-examination, Part II. *Management and Labour Studies*, 20(1): 5–14.

Bamel, U.K., Rangnekar, S., & Rastogi, R. 2011. Managerial effectiveness in Indian organisations: Reexamining an instrument in an Indian context. *Research and Practice in Human Resource Management*, 19(1): 69.

Baruch, Y., Budhwar, P.S., & Khatri, N. 2007. Brain drain: Inclination to stay abroad after studies. *Journal of World Business*, 42(1): 99–112.

Bhatnagar, J. 2007. Predictors of organizational commitment in India: Strategic HR roles, organizational learning capability and psychological empowerment. *International Journal of Human Resource Management*, 18(10): 1782–1797.

Bhatnagar, J. 2014. Mediator analysis in the management of innovation in Indian knowledge workers: The role of perceived supervisor support, psychological contract, reward and recognition and turnover intention. *International Journal of Human Resource Management*, 25(10): 1395–1416.

Bhatnagar, J., & Sharma, A. 2005. The Indian perspective of strategic HR roles and organizational learning capability. *International Journal of Human Resource Management*, 16(9): 1711–1739.

Bhuiyan, F., Rahman, M.M., & Gani, M.O. 2015. Impact of human resource information system on firm financial performance. *International Journal of Business and Management*, 10(10): 171.

Biswas, S., Varma, A., & Ramaswami, A. 2013. Linking distributive and procedural justice to employee engagement through social exchange: A field study in India. *International Journal of Human Resource Management*, 24(8): 1570–1587.

Björkman, I., & Budhwar, P. 2007. When in Rome . . .? Human resource management and the performance of foreign firms operating in India. *Employee Relations*, 29(6): 595–610.

Björkman, I., Budhwar, P., Smale, A., & Sumelius, J. 2008. Human resource management in foreign-owned subsidiaries: China versus India. *International Journal of Human Resource Management*, 19(5): 964–978.

Bordia, P., & Blau, G. 1998. Pay referent comparison and pay level satisfaction in private versus public sector organizations in India. *International Journal of Human Resource Management*, 9(1): 155–167.

Budhwar, P. 2003. Employment relations in India. *Employee Relations*, 25(2): 132–148.

Budhwar, P. 2004. Introduction: HRM in the Asia-Pacific context. In P. Budhwar (ed.), *Managing Human Resources in Asia-Pacific*: 1–15. London: Routledge.

Budhwar, P. 2009. HRM in the Indian context. In P. Budhwar and J. Bhatnagar (eds), *Changing Face of People Management in India*: 3–19. London: Routledge.

Budhwar, P. 2012. Management of human resources in foreign firms operating in India: The role of HR in country-specific headquarters. *International Journal of Human Resource Management*, 23(12): 2514–2531.

Budhwar, P., & Bhatnagar, J. 2009. *Changing Face of People Management in India*. London: Routledge.

Budhwar, P., & Boyne, G. 2004. Human resource management in the Indian public and private sectors: An empirical comparison. *International Journal of Human Resource Management*, 15(2): 346–370.

Budhwar, P., & Debrah, Y.A. 2009. Future research on human resource management systems in Asia. *Asia Pacific Journal of Management*, 26(2): 197–218.

Budhwar, P., & Khatri, N. 2001. HRM in context applicability of HRM models in India. *International Journal of Cross Cultural Management*, 1(3): 333–356.

Budhwar, P., Luthar, H.K., & Bhatnagar, J. 2006a. Dynamics of HRM systems in BPOs operating in India. *Journal of Labor Research*, 27(3): 339–360.

Budhwar, P., & Singh, V. 2007. Introduction: People management in the Indian sub-continent. *Employee Relations*, 29(6): 545–553.

Budhwar, P., & Sparrow, P. 1997. Evaluating levels of strategic integration and devolvement of human resource management in India. *International Journal of Human Resource Management*, 8(4): 476–494.

Budhwar, P., & Sparrow, P.R. 2002. Strategic HRM through the cultural looking glass: Mapping the cognition of British and Indian managers. *Organization Studies*, 23(4): 599–638.

Budhwar, P., & Varma, A. 2011a. *Doing Business in India*. London: Routledge.

Budhwar, P., & Varma, A. 2011b. Emerging HR management trends in India and the way forward. *Organizational Dynamics*, 40(4): 317–325.

Budhwar, P., Varma, A., Malhotra, N., & Mukherjee, A. 2009. Insights into the Indian call centre industry: Can internal marketing help tackle high employee turnover?. *Journal of Services Marketing*, 23(5): 351–362.

Budhwar, P., Varma, A., Singh, V., & Dhar, R. 2006b. HRM systems of Indian call centres: An exploratory study. *International Journal of Human Resource Management*, 17(5): 881–897.

Chand, M. 2010. The impact of HRM practices on service quality, customer satisfaction and performance in the Indian hotel industry. *International Journal of Human Resource Management*, 21(4): 551–566.

Chand, M., & Katou, A.A. 2007. The impact of HRM practices on organisational performance in the Indian hotel industry. *Employee Relations*, 29(6): 576–594.

Chandrakumara, A. 2007. Does HRM fit really matter to citizenship and task performance? Sri Lankan manufacturing sector experience. *Employee Relations*, 29(6): 595–610.

Chandrakumara, A., & Budhwar, P.S. 2005. Doing business in Sri Lanka. *Thunderbird International Business Review*, 47(1): 95–120.

Chandrakumara, A., & Sparrow, P. 2003 The impact of work and values orientations on HRM policies and practices in domestic and foreign invested companies in Sri Lanka, Paper presented at the 7th Annual Conference of the *International Journal of Human Resources Management*. Limerick, Ireland.

Chandrakumara, A., & Sparrow, P. 2004. Work orientation as an element of national culture and its impact on HRM policy-practice design choices: Lessons from Sri Lanka. *International Journal of Manpower*, 25(6): 564–589.

Chaudhry, S. 2013. Managerial career development in a developing host-country context: A study of American multinationals in Pakistan. *International Journal of Human Resource Management*, 24(3): 558–578.

Cooke, F.L., & Saini, D.S. 2015. From legalism to strategic HRM in India? Grievance management in transition. *Asia Pacific Journal of Management*, 32(3): 619–643.

Datt, R., & Sundram, K.P.M. 2014. *Indian Economy*. New Delhi: S. Chand & Company.

Debrah, Y.A., McGovern, I., & Budhwar, P. 2000. Complementarity or competition: The development of human resources in a South-East Asian growth triangle: Indonesia, Malaysia and Singapore. *International Journal of Human Resource Management*, 11(2): 314–335.

DeNisi, A.S., & Griffin, R.W. 2001. *Human Resource Management*. Boston, MA: Houghton Mifflin.

Fernando, W.D.A., & Cohen, L. 2013. The rhetoric and reality of home–work harmonization: A study of highly skilled Sri Lankan women from public and private sector organizations. *International Journal of Human Resource Management*, 24(15): 2876–2893.

Ganeri, A. 2005. *Indian Subcontinent*. Mankato, MN: Black Rabbit Books.

Gautam, D.K. 2015. Strategic integration of HRM for organizational performance: Nepalese reality. *South Asian Journal of Global Business Research*, 4(1): 110–128.

Gautam, D.K., & Davis, A.J. 2007. Integration and devolvement of human resource practices in Nepal. *Employee Relations*, 29(6): 711–726.

Gautam, T., Van Dick, R., Wagner, U., & Upadhyay, N. 2005. Organizational citizenship behavior and organizational commitment in Nepal. *Asian Journal of Social Psychology*, 8(3): 305–314.

Guchait, P., & Cho, S. 2010. The impact of human resource management practices on intention to leave of employees in the service industry in India: The mediating role of organizational commitment. *International Journal of Human Resource Management*, 21(8): 1228–1247.

Gupta, V., & Singh, S. 2014. Psychological capital as a mediator of the relationship between leadership and creative performance behaviors: Empirical evidence from the Indian R&D sector. *International Journal of Human Resource Management*, 25(10): 1373–1394.

Haq, R. 2012. The managing diversity mindset in public versus private organizations in India. *International Journal of Human Resource Management*, 23(5): 892–914.

Jain, H., Mathew, M., & Bedi, A. 2012. HRM innovations by Indian and foreign MNCs operating in India: A survey of HR professionals. *International Journal of Human Resource Management*, 23(5): 1006–1018.

Jain, S. 2015. Cost-effectiveness of training programmes in insurance sector of India. *Management Dynamics in the Knowledge Economy*, 3(3): 533–551.

Jayawardana, A.K., O'Donnell, M., & Jayakody, J. 2013. Job involvement and performance among middle managers in Sri Lanka. *International Journal of Human Resource Management*, 24(21): 4008–4025.

Kakar, S. 1971. Authority patterns and subordinate behavior in Indian organizations. *Administrative Science Quarterly*, 16(3): 298–307.

Khan, S.H., Syed, N.A., & Asim, M. 2013. Human resource management practices in SMEs: An exploratory study. *Global Management Journal for Academic and Corporate Studies*, 3(1): 78.

Khandwalla, P. 2014. Designing a creative and innovative India. *International Journal of Human Resource Management*, 25(10): 1417–1433.

Khilji, S.E. 2002. Modes of convergence and divergence: An integrative view of multinational practices in Pakistan. *International Journal of Human Resource Management*, 13(2): 232–253.

Khilji, S.E. 2003. To adapt or not to adapt? Exploring the role of national culture in HRM. *International Journal of Cross Cultural Management*, 3(1): 121–144.

Khilji, S.E. 2004a. Human resource management in Pakistan. In P. Budhwar, and Y. Debra (eds), *Human Resource Management in Developing Countries*: 102–120. London: Routledge.

Khilji, S.E. 2004b. Whither tradition? Evidence of generational differences in HR satisfaction from Pakistan. *International Journal of Cross Cultural Management*, 4(2): 141–156.

Khilji, S.E., & Wang, X. 2006. 'Intended' and 'implemented' HRM: The missing linchpin in strategic human resource management research. *International Journal of Human Resource Management*, 17(7): 1171–1189.

Kim, H.-D., & Tung, R.L. 2013. Opportunities and challenges for expatriates in emerging markets: An exploratory study of Korean expatriates in India. *International Journal of Human Resource Management*, 24(5): 1029–1050.

Kulkarni, M., & Rodrigues, C. 2014. Engagement with disability: Analysis of annual reports of Indian organizations. *International Journal of Human Resource Management*, 25(11): 1547–1566.

Kurian, S., & Naik, G. 2014. Sustainable compensation practices in SME's: An empirical study of machine tool companies in India. *International Journal of Entrepreneurship and Business Environment Perspectives*, 3(4): 1292.

Kuruvilla, S. 1996. Linkages between industrialization strategies and industrial relations/human resource policies: Singapore, Malaysia, the Philippines, and India. *Industrial and Labor Relations Review*, 49(4): 635–657.

Kuruvilla, S., & Ranganathan, A. 2010. Globalisation and outsourcing: confronting new human resource challenges in India's business process outsourcing industry. *Industrial Relations Journal*, 41(2): 136–153.

Lakkoju, S. 2014. An empirical analysis of managerial and non-managerial HRD climate perceptions in SBI and KVB through internal and external comparison: a case study conducted in Andhra Pradesh. *Decision*, 41(1): 51–72.

Lakshman, C. 2014. Leveraging human capital through performance management process: The role of leadership in the USA, France and India. *International Journal of Human Resource Management*, 25(10): 1351–1372.

Lange, T., Pacheco, G., & Shrotryia, V.K. 2010. Culture, industrialisation and multiple domains of employees' job satisfaction: a case for HR strategy redesign in India. *International Journal of Human Resource Management*, 21(13): 2438–2451.

Lee, H.-J., & Reade, C. 2015. Ethnic homophily perceptions as an emergent IHRM challenge: Evidence from firms operating in Sri Lanka during the ethnic conflict. *International Journal of Human Resource Management*, 26(13): 1645–1664.

Lucy, D.M., Ghosh, J., & Kujawa, E. 2008. Empowering women's leadership: A case study of Bangladeshi microcredit business. *SAM Advanced Management Journal*, 73(4): 31–40.

Malhotra, A., & DeGraff, D.S. 1997. Entry versus success in the labor force: Young women's employment in Sri Lanka. *World Development*, 25(3): 379–394.

Mamman, A., Akuratiyagamage, V.W., & Rees, C.J. 2006. Managerial perceptions of the role of the human resource function in Sri Lanka: A comparative study of local, foreign-owned and joint-venture companies. *International Journal of Human Resource Management*, 17(12): 2009–2020.

McWeeney, M. 1998. Management accountancy in Bhutan. *Management Accounting*, 76(10): 60–61.

Murthy, C.S.R. 2014. HRD practices in small and medium enterprises in India. *International Journal of Entrepreneurship & Business Environment Perspectives*, 3(3): 1201.

Nigam, A.K., Nongmaithem, S., Sharma, S., & Tripathi, N. 2011. The impact of strategic human resource management on the performance of firms in India: A study of service sector firms. *Journal of Indian Business Research*, 3(3): 148–167.

Pant, D.P., Allinson, C.W., & Hayes, J. 1996. Transferring the Western model of project organisation to a bureaucratic culture: The case of Nepal. *International Journal of Project Management*, 14(1): 53–57.

Pathak, A.A. 2015. Zen room enhances the workplace for NobelTek's women employees . . . and helps the company to retain valuable female talent. *Human Resource Management International Digest*, 23(7): 15–17.

Qadeer, F., Rehman, R., Ahmad, M., & Shafique, M. 2011. Does ownership of higher education institute influence its HRM patterns? The case of Pakistan. *International Journal of Business and Management*, 6(10): 230–241.

Rajadhyaksha, U. 2012. Work–life balance in South East Asia: The Indian experience. *South Asian Journal of Global Business Research*, 1(1): 108–127.

Ramaswamy, K.V. 2003. *Globalization and Industrial Labor Markets in South Asia: Some Aspects in a Less Integrated Region*. East-West Center, Honolulu: University of Hawaii Press.

Rao, T.V., Silveria, D.M., Shrivastava, C.M., & Vidyasagar, R. 1994. *HRD in the New Economic Environment*. New Delhi: Tata McGraw-Hill Publishing Company.

Reddy, C.M. 2006. *Globalization and Human Development in South Asia. South Asia 2006: Europa Regional Surveys of the World*. London: Routledge.

Rice, M. 2004. Bhutan gets with the program. *Intheblack*, 74(9): 13.

Sahay, S., & Walsham, G. 1997. Social structure and managerial agency in India. *Organization Studies*, 18(3): 415–444.

Saher, N., & Mayrhofer, W. 2014. The role of Vartan Bhanji in implementing HRM practices in Pakistan. *International Journal of Human Resource Management*, 25(13): 1881–1903.

Saini, D.S., & Budhwar, P.S. 2008. Managing the human resource in Indian SMEs: The role of indigenous realities in organizational working. *Journal of World Business*, 43(4): 417–434.

Saini, D., & Budhwar, P. 2014. Human resource management in India. In A. Varma and P. Budhwar (eds), *Managing Human Resources in Asia-Pacific*: 126–149. London: Routledge.

Sankar, M. 2015. Impact of hygiene factors on employee retention: Experimental study on paper industry. *New England Journal of Medicine, Indian Journal of Management Science*, 5(1): 58–61.

Sarker, A.E. 2005. New public management, service provision and non-governmental organizations in Bangladesh. *Public Organization Review*, 5(3): 249–271.

Sarker, A.E. 2006. New public management in developing countries: An analysis of success and failure with particular reference to Singapore and Bangladesh. *International Journal of Public Sector Management*, 19(2): 180–203.

Schuler, R.S., Budhwar, P.S., & Florkowski, G.W. 2002. International human resource management: Review and critique. *International Journal of Management Reviews*, 4(1): 41–70.

Sengupta, S., & Gupta, A. 2012. Exploring the dimensions of attrition in Indian BPOs. *International Journal of Human Resource Management*, 23(6): 1259–1288.

Seth, N.R. 1996. We, the trade unions. *Indian Journal of Industrial Relations*, 32(1): 1–20.

Sharma, B.R. 1992. *Managerialism Unionism: Issues in Perspective*. New Delhi: Shri Ram Centre for Industrial Relations and Human Resources.

Sharma, I. 1984. The culture context of Indian managers. *Management and Labour Studies*, 9(2): 72–80.

Singh, K. 2003. Strategic HR orientation and firm performance in India. *International Journal of Human Resource Management*, 14(4): 530–543.

Sodhi, J.S. 1994. Emerging trends in industrial relations and human resource management in Indian industry. *Indian Journal of Industrial Relations*, 30(1): 19–37.

Som, A. 2008. Innovative human resource management and corporate performance in the context of economic liberalization in India. *International Journal of Human Resource Management*, 19(7): 1278–1297.

Som, A. 2012. Organizational response through innovative HRM and re-design: A comparative study from France and India. *International Journal of Human Resource Management*, 23(5): 952–976.

Sparrow, P.R., & Budhwar, P.S. 1997. Competition and change: Mapping the Indian HRM recipe against worldwide patterns. *Journal of World Business*, 32(3): 224–242.

Srinivasan, V., & Chandwani, R. 2014. HRM innovations in rapid growth contexts: The healthcare sector in India. *International Journal of Human Resource Management*, 25(10): 1505–1525.

Syed, J. 2008. Pakistani model of diversity management: Rediscovering Jinnah's vision. *International Journal of Sociology and Social Policy*, 28(3/4): 100–113.

Thite, M., Srinivasan, V., Harvey, M., & Valk, R. 2009. Expatriates of host-country origin: 'coming home to test the waters'. *International Journal of Human Resource Management*, 20(2): 269–285.

Umamaheswari, S., & Krishnan, J. 2015. Retention factors and their relative significance in ceramic manufacturing industries in India. *Asian Social Science*, 11(13): 260.

Varma, A., & Budhwar, P. 2014. *Managing Human Resources in Asia-Pacific*. London: Routledge.

Varma, A., Toh, S.M., & Budhwar, P. 2006. A new perspective on the female expatriate experience: The role of host country national categorization. *Journal of World Business*, 41(2): 112–120.

Venakata Ratnam, C.S. 1998. Multinational companies in India. *International Journal of Human Resource Management*, 9(4): 567–589.

Wickramasinghe, V. 2006. Staffing practices in the private sector in Sri Lanka. *Career Development International*, 12(2): 108–128.

Wickramasinghe, V. 2010. Employee perceptions towards web-based human resource management systems in Sri Lanka. *International Journal of Human Resource Management*, 21(10): 1617–1630.

Wickramasinghe, V., & De Zoyza, N. 2011. Managerial competency requirements that enhance organisational competences: A study of a Sri Lankan telecom organisation. *International Journal of Human Resource Management*, 22(14): 2981–3000.

Wickramasinghe, V., & Jayabandu, S. 2007. Towards workplace flexibility: Flexitime arrangements in Sri Lanka. *Employee Relations*, 29(6): 554–575.

World Bank. 2006. Sri Lanka: Strengthening social protection. Available at: http://siteresources.worldbank.org/INTSOUTHASIA/Resources/Strengthening_Social_Protection.pdf.

Yadapadithaya, P. 2000. International briefing 5: Training and development in India. *International Journal of Training and Development*, 4(1): 79–89.

Zafarullah, H. 2006. Shaping public management for governance and development: The cases of Pakistan and Bangladesh. *International Journal of Organization Theory and Behavior*, 9(3): 352–378.

Zafarullah, H., & Rahman, R. 2008. The impaired state: Assessing state capacity and governance in Bangladesh. *International Journal of Public Sector Management*, 21(7): 739–752.

30. HRM and Asian socialist economies in transition: China, Vietnam, and North Korea

Ngan Collins, Ying Zhu, and Malcolm Warner

INTRODUCTION

In East Asia, there are three so-called 'socialist' nations, namely the People's Republic of China (PRC) (henceforth referred to as China), the Socialist Republic of Vietnam (SRV) (Vietnam), and the Democratic People's Republic of Korea (DPRK) (North Korea). These three countries have experienced very different and dramatic political, economic, and social changes since the end of World War II, against a historical background of many centuries of upheavals.

China, the most populous of the three by far, which after 1949 became the People's Republic of China under the leadership of Mao Ze-dong, embarked on its economic reforms and 'Open Door' policy in the late 1970s under the aegis of Deng Xiao-ping and has become one of the largest players in the global economy, as well as an influential political power in international affairs. Vietnam, led by Ho Chi Minh in its revolutionary struggles, was founded as a Marxist-Leninist regime in 1945 in the North and later leaders unveiled a relatively moderate reform agenda labeled as '*Doi moi*' a little later than China in 1986, as its route to economic renovation, under the guiding hand of Nguyen Van-Linh. Today, Vietnam has emerged as one of the leading economies among the Association of Southeast Asian Nations (ASEAN) group in South-East Asia. Both China and Vietnam claim their economies to be 'socialist market economies'. However, North Korea, founded as a socialist republic in 1948, had adopted a rather slow and cautious strategy regarding reform and still follows their former 'Great Leader' Chairman Kim Il-sung's initial approach with its characteristics of 'top-down' planning and political self-reliance. Great stress was placed on 'going our own way' (*urisik*). Although he was succeeded by his son Kim Jong-il in 1994, who in turn was followed by his grandson, Kim Jong-un in 2011, this model still prevails there *gross modo*. The regime started to learn from its 'socialist brothers' of China and Vietnam rather late in the day, and its economic reform initiatives have not to date been very successful.

In this chapter, we aim to illustrate the tasks and processes of economic reform and development in these countries, their changing political, ideological, and economic systems, and the impact of reform on the changing relationship between government, market, and firms, as well as the influence on management in general and on human resource management (HRM) in particular. In order to achieve these goals, we develop the following structure within this chapter. The next section reviews the economic transition and management changes. Then in the following sections we provide background information regarding the reforms in general, and reforming people-management system in particular; we illustrate the employment relations (ER) and industrial relations (IR) systems in the three countries; we explore the pattern of transformation of HRM policies and practices at enterprise level, and we examine the changing relationship and interaction between government and enterprises. We conclude the chapter by highlighting the implications for socialist economies in transition.

ECONOMIC TRANSITION AND MANAGEMENT CHANGES

China and Vietnam have a number of similarities in terms of their economic, political, and social systems, as well as their people-management models, although this is very much less the case with North Korea (Nankervis et al., 2012). China and Vietnam constitute the main subjects of this chapter as they have undergone decades of transformation into so-called 'transitional' economies, but we also make some limited comparisons with the less reformed third economy in the group. As neighbouring countries, the main two have somewhat comparable histories and cultures and share a background of Confucian values. These traditional values of harmony and collectivism, which were introduced into Vietnam through Chinese emperors since 111 BC (Warner, 2005) still remain as key social values even in modern Vietnamese, as well as in Chinese societies, both on the mainland and amongst overseas Chinese. The two Koreas, North and South, also have a shared Confucian heritage going back centuries (Flake, 2002: 4579ff). Since the late 1970s in the experience of China, and in the 1980s in the case of Vietnam, both countries claim to have transformed themselves into 'socialist market economies' (Collins, 2009; Lin, 2011; Nolan, 1993). However, North Korea has been seen, by contrast, as the last bastion of 'Stalinism' (Lankov, 2006, 2013). The fundamental cause of these reforms was that both Chinese and Vietnamese governments realized that the traditional system of running a country was no longer adequate for maintaining economic and political stability. Furthermore, economic reform was essential to the state's and Party's survival in a global economy. Through such economic transition, the respective governments aimed to attract foreign capital and bring in up-to-date technology to achieve the goal of building a 'socialist' nation with a modernized and industrialized economy, hence the 'Open Door' (*kaifang*) and 'Four Modernizations' (*sige xiandaihua*) policies in the PRC in the years after 1978 (Child, 1994; Lin, 2011; Warner, 2014).

As China became inexorably linked to the international economy and increasingly faces the challenges of globalization, for example, its enterprises and their managers not only have to adapt to external market pressures, international norms, and so on, but at the same time have respond to internal institutional ones (see Williamson & Yin, 2014). The tension between these factors, external as well as internal, provides an arena in which managers as well as workers now have to cope, perform, and survive. The government's goal of reform in transitional economies is to ensure that those economic benefits help to reduce political instability and to retain the state's power (McGregor, 2010).

Economic transition in the two main cases we consider, China and Vietnam, is unlike the process that took place in Eastern Europe (see Warner, 2005). There was no immediate blueprint at hand for China to learn for its economic reform approach, therefore gradualism was chosen for this reform, as its leadership described the reform process in China as 'crossing the river by feeling for the stones' (*mo zhe shitou guohe*) (see Vogel, 2011; Wong, 2014). As in the PRC, the reform process in Vietnam unfolded gradually, and largely in the economic sphere. There was little accompanying reform in the political system, as indeed is still the case. Both countries refer to their economies as transferring from a 'planned socialist economy' to a 'socialist market economy' (see Lin, 2011). The Communist Party remains, accordingly, the only political organization in all three countries, and holds authority to decide on policies affecting the nation (see McGregor, 2010).

Both governments, in China and Vietnam, clearly stated that the characteristic of these processes was to be pragmatic as well as gradualist, beginning with microeconomic reform, then to be followed by macroeconomic reform, but with only limited political reform. They have been assessed as following a 'third way' (Fahey, 1997), separate from the 'shock therapy' or 'big bang' approaches on the one hand, and the traditional top-down planning system on the other. The North Korean economy, however, was stuck with the Soviet model. Labour management was also consonant with this model (Kim, 2003; Kim & Lee, 2005, 2006). The economy remains, to this day, in spite of minor changes, a highly authoritarian state-planned entity (Lankov, 2013). The contrast with the South Korean economy, management, and polity is sharply defined, as can be seen by looking at the two neighbouring but highly differentiated systems (Rowley & Warner, 2014).

Chung (2003) suggests that North Korea, because it is a 'latecomer', may now be more able to choose a more advantageous path to development: 'To this end, North Korea needs to adapt a pragmatic economic policy similar to China's "White Cat, Black Cat Theory", which places priority on economic utility' (Lankov, 2013: 102). Much depends on China acting as a broker in efforts to resolve the nuclear issue and create security and stability in the peninsula, as a Rand Corporation working paper has argued (see Wolf & Levin, 2008). Yet, the regime is still stuck in a time-warp, as many media reports have vividly shown; few academic empirical studies are available, compared with South Korea.

Given that many similarities between the two transitional economies of China and Vietnam exist, there is still a difference between their reforms, in that during the pre-reform period, state-owned enterprises (SOEs) in China were more developed and operated on a larger scale than in Vietnam (Fforde & De Vylder, 1996). The Chinese government administers a huge population of 1.3 billion people and has always been firm in its leadership, so that its reform policies have been seen as very determined and decisive. It is even prepared to employ its military forces internally to enforce its objectives, as it did in 1989; yet stayed on the sidelines in Hong Kong SAR in 2014, when mass street protests took place. On the other hand, the Vietnamese government, ruling a smaller country with 93 million people, may be less willing to resort to violence against dissent because it leads what was a divided country and its authority is weaker, so it needs to be more cautious in its guidance of this process. With a long history of involvement in external and civil wars, Vietnam's economy has depended heavily on foreign aid, especially from the former Soviet Union and China. During the economic reforms, the prominent role of foreign investment in Vietnam has been even more prominent than in China. In addition, economic reform in China arguably occurred several years before Vietnam, therefore the former was a step further along the road to introducing market forces. In the early days of *Doi moi*, Vietnam often looked over its shoulder at the Chinese experience, when it put its reforming processes into place (Edwards & Phan, 2012). However, since the late 2000s, political conflicts between countries over the 'China Sea issue' and the prospect of opening the domestic market to ASEAN products and investments in 2018 have made Vietnam start to turn away from China's model and look for an alternative path for its economic development. By contrast, North Korea appears to be last in line for economic reform (Lankov, 2013).

Table 30.1   Country Profiles, 2014*

	China	Vietnam	North Korea
Area	9.5 m. sq km	0.3 m. sq km	0.1 m. sq km
Population	1.3 bn.	93 m.	24.8 m.
Population growth rate	0.44%	1.0%	0.5%
Infant mortality rate	14.79 %	18.99%	24.5%
Life expectancy (years)	75.1	72.9	69.81
Male	73.1	70.4	65.9
Female	77.4	75.65	73.85
Literacy	95.1%	93.4%	99%
Male	97.5%	95.4%	99%
Female	92.7%	91.4%	99%
GDP 2013 est. (PPP, (purchasing power parity)	$13.039 tr.	$358.9 bn.	$40 bn.
GDP 2013 est. (at official exchange rate)	$9.33 tr.	$66.4 bn.	$28 bn.
GDP per capita 2013 est. (PPP)	$9800	$4000	$1800
GDP composition 2012 est.			
Agriculture	33.6%	48.0%	23.4%
Industry	30.3%	21.0%	47.2%
Services	36.1%	31.0%	29.4%
Labour force	797.6 m.	52.95 m.	12.6 m.

Note: Most figures are estimates for 2013, although some are for the latest year available.

Source: CIA (2014), UNDP (2014).

Economic reforms have achieved great success in the more advanced reforming countries, namely China and Vietnam (see Table 30.1). China has become an 'economic super-power'; its economy is ranked second in the world after the United States of America (USA) and its gross domestic product (GDP) has grown dramatically since 1978. In Vietnam, income per head about tripled from the early days and the Vietnamese standard of living increased markedly. Both economies have been amongst the top two fastest-growing economies in Asia, although China's is now slowing down after growing at close to 10 per cent per annum for three decades. Living standards for most of their populations have improved greatly in recent years. The unevenness of development between urban and rural areas, however, has mitigated the benefits. The urban population, so far, has done better than those in rural areas. As the economic reform process has brought in wealth for many social groups, there has been the birth of a 'new middle class' in the main urban centres such as in Beijing, Guangzhou, and Shanghai, as well as in Hanoi and Ho Chi Minh City; but much less so in Pyongyang. Furthermore, there has been a large increase in income inequality between different groups of earners. The income gaps between different groups of Chinese and Vietnamese societies have become much bigger since the pre-reform days, with the Gini coefficient arguably almost tripling. Together with these new economic phenomena brought in by the reforms, there has been a shift of societal culture, as well as ideology. Even though the general culture of these societies is based in collectivism and harmony, as mentioned earlier, there has been a rise of individualism and competitiveness within the societies, especially among the young generation (Warner, 2014). Less, however, is known about North Korea, with much lower incomes per head than in the other two economies, although a thin 'new rich' stratum has emerged since limited reforms were introduced in 2002. Even so, North Koreans are said to be 40 times poorer than their South Korean cousins and score less favourably on five other indices (Khan, 2014).

Table 30.1 provides an overview of the three countries' profiles. It is obvious that China is the giant among the group in terms of area, population, GDP level, size of the labour force, and so on. But interestingly, those three so-called 'socialist' economies have relatively lower rates of infant mortality, longer life expectancy, and higher rates of literacy compared with other developing countries with a similar level of per capita income. China has a much higher GDP level, as well as GDP per capita level based on the calculation of purchasing power parity (PPP), compared with Vietnam and even more so with North Korea. In terms of the composition of GDP, China has had relatively a lower proportion derived from agriculture, with a higher proportion from industry and services. Vietnam stood second to China in these proportions, and North Korea ranked third. In addition, China generated a huge trade surplus, but both Vietnam and North Korea experienced trade deficits in recent years. All in all, however, North Korea lags far behind the other two. Indeed:

> Though the North Korean model in the above context has a number of aspects similar to those found in the Chinese and former Soviet Union models, it is still fundamentally distinct. There are also traces of the South Korean and Japanese systems to be found, but, in the final analysis, North Korea's unique system has created a society that challenges our understanding of 'normal' societies as well as our common sense. (Bertelsmann Stiftung, 2008: 1)

Socialism in the DPRK is often referred to as an expression of its own *juch'e* nationalism, rather than Marxist-Leninism, as a case of exceptionalism. Reform measures (*kaeson chochi*) in economic policy (see Choi, 2011) have, in turn, involved only lip-service to the market (*jangsi*), and a degree of 'marketization from the bottom', although it is not clear whether this step has amounted to much (see Choi & Lecy, 2012: 4).

BACKGROUND

Background in China

Under the former command economy model in China in the period 1949–78, its state-owned enterprises (SOEs) implemented a form of personnel management (*renshi guanli*) to administer their employees. It was a template partly borrowed from their Soviet counterparts (Cooke, 2005; Kaple, 1994; Warner, 1995). The enterprise-based employment system, known as the 'iron rice bowl' (*tie fan wan*) had been *de rigueur* in the SOE sector (Bian, 2005) and possibly even a paternalistic hangover from pre-communist times and the Japanese Occupation (Warner, 1995). It was characterized by what were called the 'three old irons' (*jiu santi*), that is, the pillars of life-time employment (the 'iron rice bowl', *tie fan wan*), centrally administered wages (the 'iron wage', *tie gongzi*), and ministry-based appointment and promotion of managerial staff (the 'iron chair', *tie jiaoyi*) (Ng & Warner, 1998). Since Deng's economic reforms were introduced in the 1980s, this enterprise-based system of lifetime employment and 'cradle-to-grave' mini-welfare state (*xiao shehui*) has been gradually cut back. In 1986, for example, the authorities experimented with the introduction of labour contracts for new workers (see Korzec, 1992). In 1992, another important step was the 'three personnel reforms' (*san gaige*); this inaugrated labour contracts, performance-linked rewards systems, and contributory social insurance (Warner, 1995). *Pari pasu*, access to healthcare eventually became less and less equitable. By this time, the system had already become a hybrid, mixing what remained of the old one with the newer features (Warner, 2008b). The new démarche was to be known as *renli ziyuan guanli*, quite literally meaning 'labour force resources management', having the same characters in Chinese as in Japanese, being used as a synonym for (what is in effect in many cases) recognizable HRM and 'with Chinese characteristics' (Lamond & Zheng, 2010; Warner, 2014).

Another step forward was the Labour Law of 1994, implemented in 1995, which put the emerging labour market at its heart, and legalized individual contracts (*geren hetong*) as well as collective contracts (*jiti hetong*) and the like (see Brown, 2010). The All-China Federation of Trade Unions (ACFTU, Zhonghua quanguo zonggong hui), with its now more than 275 million members, 15 industrial unions, and 2.75 million local branches, greatly influenced the legislation (Warner, 2008a, 1996, 2014; Warner & Ng, 1999), although many adherents exist only 'on paper'.

The implementation of these new legal steps led to what might be described as discernible industrial relations or employee relations, which became known as labour relations (*laodong guanxi*) in Chinese parlance (see Taylor et al., 2003). Nonetheless, there is currently no right to strike in the Chinese Constitution; this was removed in 1982. There have, however, recently been many openly 'wildcat' labour disputes and unofficial labour protests, even strikes, most about unpaid wages and pensions, downsizing or factory closures, even suicides, including the recurrent discontent at Apple's main subcontractor, the Taiwanese-owned Foxconn, amongst others (*China Labour Bulletin*, 2014; SACOM, 2014; Zhu et al., 2011). Officially recognized disputes can be sent to arbitration and many hundreds of thousands have been dealt with since the 1994 Labour Law was enacted; the new 2007 follow-up legislation may have further helped to contain grievances. So, notionally at least, the system appears to be preserving the 'social peace', but even so strikes are increasing in frequency, especially in areas such as the Shenzhen Special Economic Zone, for instance.

The Labour Contract Law in 2007 had extended worker protection further in 2007 (*The Economist, 2007*). The new law makes it mandatory for employers to offer written contracts to workers, restricts the use of temporary labour, and makes it harder to lay off employees (Brown, 2010). Workers also gained the right to form enterprise-level unions. Such changes were opposed by many foreign-invested corporations. Additionally, a new Labour Dispute, Mediation and Arbitration Law was added (see Zhu et al., 2011). In recent years, under the new central government leadership of President Xi Jin-ping and Premier Li Ke-qiang, who came to office in 2013, a greater emphasis has been placed on transparency, 'clean' governance (with strong anti-corruption campaigns), and grass-roots participation, encouraging the young 'new generation' of workers to participate at the workplace (Zhu et al., 2015). Further labour legislation to improve workplace harmony is in the pipeline. This new démarche is likely to have multiple implications for HRM in China today.

Background in Vietnam

In 1986, Vietnam formally endorsed its economic reform process, known as *Doi moi*. The adoption of changes to Vietnam's economic system accompanies and is in part a response to globalization, as in the Chinese case. 'Human resources management' in Vietnamese is *quan ly nguon nhan luc*. The introduction and adoption stages of the new HRM, to replace the old personnel management system, have followed the economic reform process in order to ensure that competitive advantage may be gained through organizational-level management reforms (Collins, 2005, 2009; Collins et al., 2013). The old permanent jobs system (*bien che*), the so-called jobs-for-life in the SOEs, were reformed at the time. HRM, training, and performance became more closely linked (Cox & Warner, 2013; Nguyen et al., 2011). Leadership self-development policies, as well as management education and training programmes in both China and Vietnam, fit for the reform era, are now in place (Ren et al., 2014).

With the economy in a serious downturn after a long period of war, economic reform was necessary for Vietnam's survival. The government at that time realized that the economy could not depend solely on traditional capital sources for its development. In addition, a number of factors prompted the government to recognize the importance of external relations to its economic well-being. The collapse of socialist regimes in the Soviet Union and former socialist countries in Eastern Europe left Vietnam isolated economically and politically. Popular demonstrations and strikes in the Mekong Delta region had also reminded the authorities how economic problems could result in political instability. In reality, *Doi moi* originated in Vietnam as a strategic compromise to maintain the power of the Communist regime. Throughout the transition, the Vietnamese government aimed to attract foreign capital and bring in up-to-date technology to provide the foundation for achieving its goal of building a 'socialist nation' with a modernized and industrialized economy, as in the case of its more populous neighbour (Warner, 2013).

However, the *Doi moi* policy gave Vietnam the chance to join with the international community after a long period of isolation. The economic restructuring led to changes in government policy and enterprise-level management practices regarding labour and human resources. Changes also occurred in the trade union structure, in the Vietnam General Confederation of Labour (VGCL, Tong lien doan lao dong Viet Nam) with around 8.5 million members in 117 000 affiliates; the only union body allowed, as in China. It should be noted, however, that union density appears to be much lower in Vietnam than in China, even if the official membership numbers are regarded quite sceptically.

The SOEs were given greater autonomy, a new union charter was drawn up, employment contract systems were introduced, and a Labour Law was implemented in 1990, with a recent revision in 2013. An employment contract (*hop dong lao dong*) is now required for both foreign and Vietnamese workers. Reforms were also made to a number of foci of working life, such as wages and working hours. These steps can be seen as the interaction between political-economic reform in society and human resources transformation at enterprise level. Vietnam's Master Plan for 2015–20 seeks to focus on the reform of the public administration system through the reform of HRM, including development of skills and competencies of its public servants, and moving toward a new performance-based system replacing the seniority- and position-based one (*Viet Nam News*, 2013).

Background in North Korea

The people-management template in North Korea was originally derived from the Soviet one, now defunct, and the Chinese state-owned enterprise 'iron rice bowl' (*tie fan wan*) model, now on the wane (Warner, 2014). Insofar as it has undertaken a very limited degree of reform, this nation lags far behind both China and Vietnam in this respect. The original post-war management mode was called the Taean system, introduced in the 1960s after experiments in the Taean Heavy Equipment Plant near the capital, Pyongyang, and named after it. It was allegedly modelled on Maoist Chinese practice, as a Brookings Institution visiting fellow (Mansourov, 2003: 1) put it:

> During the socialist construction in the 1960s and 1970s, protected by the Chinese military umbrella, the DPRK's leadership tended to follow the CCP's [Chinese Communist Party] ideological lead and copied Chinese methods of labour mobilization, e.g., the *Ch'ollima* ('Flying Horse') movement modeled after the Maoist Great Leap Forward and the *Soktojon* ('speed battle'). North Korea also adopted some Chinese-like forms of organization of industrial and agricultural production processes known as the *Taean* system. Even after Deng Xiaoping launched economic reforms in China in 1978, *Kim Il Sung* attempted to imitate the Chinese example by introducing the Joint Venture Law and a new self-accounting system in the mid-1980s. But, that is where emulation stopped.

The Taean system entailed on-site collegial management control of the enterprise by the Party officials, and limited autonomy for top managers, and has lasted for many decades. Executives had very few rights to hire and fire. But the system was phased out in the controversial, limited reforms of 2002, with results as yet to be seen. But this system had more than just symbolic meaning, as it had been the flagship policy of the late 'Great Leader'. It signalled that the primacy of politics over economics might possibly be coming to an end; but this was not to be, as we shall see below. The human resource development system of North Korea has been described by one source (Cho, 2006) as being in need of a significant degree of modernization.

Wages and living standards still remained very low in the DPRK; experts estimated the rewards ran to around US$2 per month per worker. Kim (2003) reported that state enterprise employees earned between 2000 to 3000 won per month, and 800 won of this went on rice, with a month's salary needed to buy meat for a meal. Due to the economy almost imploding in the late 1990s, many North Koreans have been close to starvation or have actually died from lack of sustenance. An estimated 10 per cent of the population died then during a prolonged famine, as the economy was mired in its inertia (Chung, 2003). The outside world, including the USA, sent food aid as the rationing system did not work; today, many survive due to the opening up of limited private market activity, as official salaries pay so little (Lankov, 2014). Migrants, however, still illegally pour across the Yalu River into the PRC, driven by hunger and deprivation; if caught, the penalties for them are harsh, including imprisonment for innocent family members.

The new regime of Kim Jong-un, however, since 2011 has introduced a number of cosmetic reforms, including allegedly encouraging a limited degree of market latitude, encouragement for small businesses, more autonomy for enterprise directors, greater flexibility in rewards for employees, and so on (Foster-Carter, 2012; Lankov, 2014; Park, 2014); and has extended the number of Special Economic Zones and industrial parks, with Chinese and South Korean foreign direct investment (FDI) principally (NCNK, 2014; NKEW, 2013). It has also recently set up a new Western-style business school with 500 students in the Pyongyang University of Science and Technology, funded by US and South Korean Christian charities, as an older Swiss-financed one in the capital, set up in 2004, had closed in 2011 (BBC, 2014). Again, the regime has also has been using the Singapore-registered private training company, Choson Exchange since 2007 (Mundy, 2014).

The Kaesong Industrial Complex (KIC), located 10 miles north of the border, was launched in June 2004; the North Korean authorities planned to employ 750 000 workers by 2012 but had only around 50 000 on-site at that date. It is run by a South Korean Committee on a 50-year lease, with Hyundai in the lead. Due to lack of foreign investment and technological and management know-how, as well as ongoing tension between North and South (the park was closed in 2013 for a long period and the North Korean workers sent home), the KIC's aspirations are still only partially fulfilled and the reforms are still in their early stages across the country.

Employment Relations, Industrial Relations, and HRM Systems in Transition

Since the transitional period of the economies in China and Vietnam, many new institutions underlying their ER systems were gradually established and fused with a new pattern of relations. These changes influenced the IR and HRM policies at national level. The establishing of a Foreign Investment Law launched the birth of multi-sector economies, where the emergence of non-state sectors included wholly owned enterprises (WOEs) and domestic private enterprises (DPEs) alongside the older state-owned enterprises (SOEs), particularly in China (Warner, 2005). The introduction of a Labour Code was also necessary, to become the basic legal framework for many important policy reforms at macro level, such as the experimentation with an individual labour contract system in 1986 in China, and in 1993 in Vietnam (Warner, 2013). This element was the beginning of the end of a 'life-time employment' system in these socialist planned economies, particularly characterized by the 'iron rice-bowl' (*tie fan wan*) system in the PRC. The wage system liberalization has in turn given SOEs full control over establishing reformed wage and payment methods. The relationship between the Party and union in the new environments has also undergone significant changes. During the pre-reform period, trade unions in both China and Vietnam were known to represent the workers' interests 'on paper' but were simultaneously in effect surrogates for Party control; now they may have somewhat more leeway (Lee et al., 2016).

Economic reform since 1978 in China has also encouraged trade unions in part to pursue sectoral interests among the enterprises but the contradiction of 'dual functioning' unions has prevented them from achieving their potential as an alternative centre of power at a national level; a similar process unfolded in Vietnam, if a little later (Warner, 2013).

Relations in the workplace have been relatively more dynamic in Vietnam, at least since the late 2000s. There have been increasing numbers of industrial strikes in DPEs and foreign enterprises (Chi & van den Broek, 2013) which have put strong pressure on the government to seek an alternative approach in union practices. To do so, the VGCL has sent its delegations to visit and study the experience of trade unions in leading indus-trialized countries such as Australia, Germany, and Japan. The amended Trade Unions Law in 2012, supported by the International Labour Organization (ILO), has given more autonomy to enterprise unions, has redefined their roles in resolving labour conflicts through mediation, and involved them in managing social security funds (Collins et al., 2013). According to the ILO:

> The new law has important new provisions, including mandatory social dialogue mechanism at workplaces, stronger role of collective bargaining, rights of upper-level trade unions to represent workers, improved rights of workers to establish unions and engage in trade union activities, and strengthened role of the Government in promoting collective bargaining and engaging in dispute settlement. (ILO, 2014: 1)

Little has shifted in North Korea in this respect. Since there has been some attempt to develop Special Economic Zones, as noted above, in concert with its southern compatriots and the PRC, there has also been a corresponding effort to codify its labour laws, at least in these locations, although this has been on a limited scale; workers are not paid directly by the foreign partners but by a joint venture (JV) or a state agency, and with substantial deductions. Managers have recently been promised more decision-making autonomy in the New Economic Management System in Our Style policy implemented in 2012, with the state allegedly relinquishing management power to factory enterprises and farms (Park, 2014). Hundreds of students and government officials and economic cadres have also been sent abroad in recent years, many to China to study its economic reforms, and a few to the West and Japan (Han & Jung, 2013). But results have been unimpressive thus far, as the Party still retains control of the economy, labour supply and mobility, as well as appointments, promotions, and job assignments, for example. Organized labour, such as it is, may in turn hinder attempts at personnel reforms, as it is argued that North Korean workers 'have little to lose' (Han & Jung, 2013: 103). In this respect, an unreformed North Korea remains where China was prior to 1978, and in a contextual framework where recognizable HRM is as yet hardly applicable.

THE ENTERPRISE LEVEL: HRM PRACTICES IN TRANSITION

The authors of this chapter have conducted a series of empirical research studies with colleagues on the transformation of people-management systems in both China and Vietnam during the period of the economic reforms. Their research has been largely at enterprise level and mainly focused on the relationships between differences in HRM practices, using various criteria, namely type of ownership, location, market orienta-tion, labour intensiveness, and workforce size. So far, the empirical research in China has had some significant general implications. Regarding the changes of HRM in SOEs, Benson and Zhu's (1999) research identified three models of transition: first, a minimal-ist approach, where organizations have made little attempt to adopt a HRM approach; second, a transitional stage between the old and the new forms of people-management; third, an innovative attempt to adopt the HRM paradigm. The fact is that liberalization of the economy and the introduction of foreign investment have created the opportunity for Chinese domestic enterprises to adopt some of the widely used Western and Japanese

HRM practices. The SOEs that are involved in JVs or contracting arrangements with foreign companies are more likely to have adopted the 'new' HRM. Therefore, globalization, more business-oriented beliefs, and a stronger customer-oriented strategy are crucial determinants of whether enterprises engage in HRM practices (Warner, 2011).

The study of Ding et al. (2002), in turn, showed that multinational corporations (MNCs) and some joint ventures both adopted more international, standardized HRM policies and practices in the Chinese case. In contrast, SOEs at that time remained more conservative regarding changes to their 'iron rice bowl' (*tie fan wan*) policies. In addition, township and village enterprises (TVEs) and other DPEs had much more autonomy in their people-management compared with SOEs.

Overall, the major changes started in the mid-1980s when the 'labour contract system' (*laodong hetong*) was introduced in the PRC (Warner & Ng, 1999). Three important aspects are associated with the introduction of the labour contract system; first, adopting individual labour contracts with a fixed term (one to five years) to replace the old 'lifetime' employment system; second, individual contracts (*geren hetong*) were supplemented by collective contracts (*jiti hetong*) in the mid-1990s; and that, third, provided an opportunity for trade unions to be involved in signing such collective contracts at firm level and setting up a 'framework agreement' for the myriad individual contracts in the enterprise (Warner & Ng, 1999). It must be made clear, however, that this contract is not fully equivalent to Western-style collective bargaining, as there are no independent unions as such (Warner, 2014). But times are changing and new practices are emerging. In addition, there is increasing autonomy of management, with the rights to hire and fire, performance evaluation, decision-making on performance standards and ways of conducting evaluations, performance-related matters such as pay and promotion, and so on (Lee et al., 2016).

Since China joined the World Trade Organization (WTO) in 2002, it has added an international dimension to its complex domestic ER and HRM systems (Zhu & Warner, 2004). Vietnam joined the WTO in 2007 but North Korea is as yet outside the fold. There has also been increasing pressure from international governing bodies, such as the ILO and international trade unions such as the International Confederation of Free Trade Unions (ICFTU), with regard to the issues of labour rights, the role of unions and labour standards, as well as broader, more controversial concerns about human rights, social protection, and political reform in China, as well as in Vietnam and, especially, North Korea.

The empirical study of Zhu and Warner (2004) regarding firms' response towards WTO accession identifies that an increasing number of firms have an active response through innovative strategies and new HRM practices. Enterprises with foreign ownership, those that have transformed from SOEs to joint stock companies (JSCs), those that are located in the coastal region, those that have weaker links with the traditional state planning system, those that have experienced modern management systems and internationalization, and those in high-value-added sectors and the new economy, are more likely to have proactive HRM responses (Warner, 2014).

In recent years, many Chinese companies, including SOEs, JVs, and DPEs, have all tried to implement a certain package of so-called 'strategic HRM' with the emphasis on high-performance work systems (HPWS) (Min et al., 2017). One of the most recent research studies (Zhu et al., 2015) found some interesting phenomena regarding this démarche. First, there is a contradiction between the high intention of participation among 'new generation' employees and the less encouraging participation opportunities in the workplace. Some basic functions of rational suggestions schemes and autonomous work teams are widely adopted but there is less action in the areas of democratic participation in decision-making and supervision, marked by the lack of involvement of the Workers' Congress (*zhigong daibiao dahui*) and the collective negotiation (*jiti xieshang*) mechanism. This observation demonstrates that the participatory structures in these Chinese enterprises are very narrow and most of the participatory types are relatively low on the ladder. However, the new generation of employees of these enterprises have a high intention to participate and want to be seen as active citizens within their organizations. Second, there is a positive relationship between new generation employee participation and their satisfaction. All the dimensions indicate that participation in management, supervision, and decision-making positively influences the level of employee satisfaction, and this follows the greater participation in management and lesser participation in decision-making and supervision. Third, the participation intention of new generation employees positively moderates the relationship between employee participation in decision-making and job satisfaction, with less effect on participation in management or supervision and job satisfaction (Zhu et al., 2015).

Clearly, at this time, there is no homogeneous model of HRM in Chinese enterprises, or indeed in Vietnamese ones. Individual enterprises are reforming their HRM systems differently, on the basis of their existing conditions and the impact of the economic reforms. Many of our investigations to date in China have shown a variety of forms, depending whether firms are in the state or private sector, indigenous or foreign-owned, JV or otherwise (Warner, 2011, 2014; Zhu et al., 2008, for example). In addition, relevant empirical research projects on Vietnam have been of great interest, and include those of Collins (2009), Collins et al. (2013), Thang and Quang (2005), Thang et al. (2007), Zhu (2002, 2005), and Zhu and Verstraeten (2013).

Zhu's (2002) work examined a number of organizations with different ownership types in Vietnam in Ho Chi Minh City, which has a more market-oriented economic environment than Hanoi. Three key variables – ownership, size, and market orientation – were used to test the transformation of HRM in Vietnam. The research finds that there are variations of HRM practices between different ownership forms, and JVs and MNCs normally use more advanced technology and more international standards of HRM policies than local organizations. However, there is a tendency for localization of MNCs' behaviour among the cases. In addition, the reformed and equitized SOEs as JSCs have transformed the old SOEs' practices into more formalized HRM practices compared with other SOEs. Another interesting finding is that the adoption of HRM is not only related to ownership, but also associated with sector (high-tech versus labour-intensive), size (large versus small) and market orientation (export versus domestic orientation), as in China (Ding et al., 2002). Generally speaking, high-tech, large, and export-oriented organizations have been more likely to adopt more formal HRM practices.

Based on these findings, Zhu (2005) introduces the notions of numerically flexible strategies and functionally flexible strategies in order to illustrate the changes in people-management in recent years, in particular since the Asian financial crisis of 1997. The data suggest that labour flexibility strategies were not fully adopted by the sample companies. Political, cultural, legal, and economic factors make labour flexibility in Vietnam different from that in other countries. For instance, companies are not able to adjust the number of regular employees, due to the constraints of legislation. In addition, Vietnamese cultural traditions that place great emphasis on organizational and personal commitment, as well as on harmonious working environments, prevent the full deployment of functional flexibility (Zhu, 2005).

Thang and Quang's (2005) research, in turn, examined Vietnamese HRM practices in five areas: the functions of HRM departments, recruitment and selection, training and development, performance appraisal, and compensation. Overall, foreign-invested enterprises are somewhat more likely to be developed in HRM practices than SOEs, which is consistent with the argument made by institutional theory about social entities seeking approval for organizational performance, and using HRM to gain legitimacy (Jackson & Schuler, 1999).

Collins (2009) study has been seen as the first in-depth research into Vietnam's HRM which has developed a model to explain current practices in Vietnamese enterprises. The study has provided a better understanding of the HRM practices among different ownership system (SOEs, DPEs, JVs, and WOEs) by generating models of HRM practices in each ownership system in order to provide guidelines for future researchers. The author argued that the HRM practices in contemporary transitional economies cannot be separated from their historical and social-political context, because ER reform is one of the elements in the process of economic transformation. The context is reflected in the differences in ER and HRM between national and enterprise levels and between different ownership types (Collins, 2009).

A good understanding of the historical background and socio-political and economic system is necessary to explain existing ER systems and HRM practices within the economic transformation context. This is because a combination of social-political, cultural, and enterprise-related factors has an influence on the way in which enterprises have adopted a new HRM model in, say, China or Vietnam (Warner, 2013).

Another investigation (Collins et al., 2011) examines the challenges of complex labour management relations in the new economic, political, and social environment in Vietnam. The study explores changing labour management relations by investigating the evolution of labour relations policy and practice since Vietnam began its economic reform. The study concludes that the mismatch between political and economic structures has been unresolved, and consequently there is to date no clear indication of which model or approach will be adopted, or which direction of trade union activities would work for Vietnam. However, it might be inferred that Vietnam, as many other Asian countries, is most likely to continue with a 'soft' convergence (Warner, 2000) approach to labour management relations, even with the omnipresence of globalization in their developing economies (Cox & Warner, 2013).

Collins et al. (2013) studied the key impacts of institutional reform of SOEs on changes in HRM practices. They concluded that strategic choices, such as the 'Western' model of HRM, were seen as the track for the companies to become modern organizations. The SOEs studied embarked on privatization and restructuring as responses to increased market competition. By the introduction of 'best practices' instigated by management, the Vietnamese SOEs suffered union fragmentation and an overformalization of roles in the system, indicating a lack of real skills in dealing with IR issues (Collins, 2009).

There are number of important results arising from these studies showing the interrelationships between the economic transition processes and governments' and enterprises' interests during the reforms in both China and Vietnam. Research on HRM in North

Korea, however, has remained problematic and there are few comparable studies. The reason for this stems from the very nature of North Korea's closed and secretive regime (Eberstadt, 1999; Lankov, 2006, 2013).

Interaction between Economic Reform Process, Governments, and Enterprises

The interaction between governments and enterprises since the economic reforms in China and Vietnam has been more complex than previously seen, because government policies no longer solely determine enterprises' HRM practices. The interests of enterprises and of the state are no longer the same, because the former's interests have changed with market reform, yet the state's desire for dominance over the economic and political systems remains largely unchanged (McGregor, 2010).

The role of the state in the reform process remains strong and the Party still retains the reins of power. As mentioned earlier, the role of the state is resolutely to maintain political stability, rather than just improve the economy as in avowedly capitalist countries. This consideration is the reason for promoting different economic policies on different time-lines or applying different policies for different regions and for different type of business ownership. This fact also helps to explain the determining factors behind two further characteristics, namely the correlation of HRM practices with location and with ownership type (Zhu et al., 2008).

Even the state wants to gain economic development advantages for political purposes; it also needs strong support from the grassroots, involving enterprises as well as workers. Therefore, the state–enterprise relationship is typified by a desire to find a compromise between these frequently conflicting interests. This ability to compromise is responsible for the HRM practices being broadly in line with government policy. In other words, the HRM functions encouraged by government policy are generally applied in areas such as training and development. It also promotes the 'unitarist' model of trade unions. In contrast, some HRM functions such as building a corporate culture or individual wage determination are not yet widely applied (Lee et al., 2016).

GOVERNMENTAL PERSPECTIVES

From its own perspective, the state sometimes feels the need to compromise with enterprises, mainly due to its desire to minimize discontent and promote economic growth. It has succeeded in that insofar as economic development in both China and Vietnam has encouraged the nations to support their socialist governments. Due to this pragmatic approach, when the government recognizes that a policy is not working well, it tries to act quickly to adjust the policy to minimize enterprises' grievances. When firms have needed more flexibility in recruiting and training workers, the government has boosted reforms in these areas to give the enterprises more freedom (Cox & Warner, 2013).

In addition, enterprise leaders have been allowed to gain a great deal more power and freedom during the 'Open Door' and *Doi moi* periods, as in China and Vietnam (Warner, 2013), but very much less so in North Korea. Firms are now free to manage their own affairs and are less strictly supervised than before the reforms in these first two transitional economies. Enterprise leadership now has greater scope to attain business targets and also has the authority to achieve individual goals made possible by their leadership position. Sometimes it appeared that the new leaderships may have shifted towards perhaps more control over SOEs at the macro level, at the same time promoting more entrepreneurial activities based on market competition at the micro level. In China, the government allowed the establishment of private banks as a complement to the SOE banking system. By 2015, Vietnam had become more welcoming to more preferential financial policies, such as promoting the stock market, and some banks are even involved in managing the government retirement funds, the government's most secure investment. In North Korea, more Special Economic Zones and industrial parks, as we mentioned earlier, have been planned, aiming to attract more foreign direct investment (Park, 2014).

ENTERPRISE PERSPECTIVES

From the enterprises' point of view, in China and Vietnam firms are more likely to comply fully with government policy and even compromise their economic interests – if and when the cultural or ideological values embodied in the policy match their own beliefs. This is clearly the case with the view of many enterprises on the role of trade unions. The historical background of these trade unions has been linked to the history of the Communist Party: in fighting against 'capitalist exploitation' in China, 'Western domination' in Vietnam, and 'resisting imperialism' in North Korea. The unions therefore, on paper at least, share the state's view vis-à-vis the role of a socialist government in protecting working class interests from 'capitalist exploitation' (Warner, 2008a). Even in the new business environment, union leaders' ideological beliefs remain the same, so the ACFTU in China and the VGCL in Vietnam see no need to replace the traditional union model and are happy to cooperate with the government. In addition, most managers, even in many MNCs, have found that the 'socialist' union structure serves business well in terms of maintaining harmony and minimizing conflict and bargaining at the workplace. This, in turn, makes the labour force easier to control. They therefore support this type of union structure and role, and the result of this is that the structure has endured in both China's and Vietnam's enterprises (Warner & Zhu, 2010; Zhu & Verstraeten, 2013).

Less is known about the role unions play in North Korea, although they played an integral part in the post-1950s factory-management model, known as the Taean system, described earlier. The trade union representation in North Korea is largely token, via a Leninist top-down 'transmission-belt' model, through the General Federation of Trade Unions of Korea (GFTUK), with 1.5 million members, mainly workers over the age of 30, employed in one of nine industries: metal and chemical; power and coal; commerce and light industry; machine building; forestry; fisheries; transportation; logistics (post); and education, culture, and public health. A recent report noted that:

> North Korea is one of the few nations in the world that still refuses to join the International Labour Organization (ILO). Forced labour is essentially the norm in the country, and workers are systematically denied freedom of association and the right to organize and bargain collectively. The government firmly controls the only authorized trade union organization, the GFTUK. (Human Rights Watch, 2014: 1)

It is not possible to confirm or disconfirm the above set of observations, as outside independent researchers cannot freely visit the country. Reports on worker's rights in the country as a whole, and on the Kaesong Industrial Complex, have been highly critical (Human Rights Watch, 2006, 2014).

Conversely, most enterprises in China and Vietnam, especially domestic ones, choose to retain the traditional HRM model for wage determination and labour–management relations. Not only does moving to a more 'Western' HRM approach for these functions not fit in with the government's principle of socialism, it goes against enterprise management's cultural values of collectivism in decision-making and harmony and could be harmful to their business by threatening the peace of the working environment. Individual bargaining in both countries is held to create a sense of jealousy between employees and thus have a negative impact on business. Even so, 'collective consultation' (*jiti xieshang*) is now *de rigueur* in the PRC and has received a boost from the most recent Labour Contract Law noted above, with compulsory collective bargaining possibly on the cards; in Vietnam, the labour contract is mainly a document which is used to enforce the responsibilities of employers and employees (Collins, 2009; Collins et al., 2013; Zhu & Fahey, 1999).

The government's emphasis on reducing workplace conflict in the workplace in both China and Vietnam is supported by the high value that enterprise management and workers still place on harmony and collectivism. Since 2006, the Chinese government policy has been to achieve the so-called 'harmonious society' (*hexie shehui*). The philosophy behind this démarche was an attempt by the former Chinese dual leadership of ex-President Hu Jin-tao and ex-Premier Wen Jia-bao to rectify perceived inequities in the economy and society, particularly wealth and income inequalities. It may in turn have an influence on how Chinese enterprises implement their HRM policies. The Party leaders, both those prior to 2013 and after, have become increasingly aware of emergent social tensions arising from the less egalitarian implications of their economic policies; consequently, they want to consolidate social harmony, appeasing the 'losers' somewhat, without penalizing the 'winners' too much (Warner, 2014).

Collective bargaining in China may soon become compulsory in the light of widespread strikes, which have grown in recent years. A recent report noted:

> On April 14, 2014, the MHRSS [Ministry of Human Resources and Social Security] released a Notice that, by the end of 2015, the collective contract regime must cover 80 per cent of the employers in China; and state-owned companies and *Fortune* 500 companies are expected to put collective contracts in place. This initiative is known as the 'Breakthrough Program'. While the Notice does not have a direct effect on employers, our expectation is that it will accelerate the trend towards compulsory rules in all provinces. (Seyfarth Shaw, 2014: 1)

To interpret national differences, current practices in each socialist system cannot be separated from history. A reason for the frequent ideological match between the state and enterprises is that it too is linked to the historical background of enterprise leaders in all three countries. Most local managers in China and Vietnam for many years came from SOE backgrounds, including those leading DPEs, JVs, and even some WOEs. This residual background and experience have strongly influenced their mindsets and the way they operate their current enterprises, although this may be changing as a new breed of managers have emerged from MBA courses in the last decade. China now, for example, has Asia's number one business school, the China–Europe International Business School, located in Shanghai. Both China and Vietnam today have a wide range of well-established business schools and MBA programmes (see Warner, 2014).

THE NATURE OF ECONOMIC TRANSITION: NEGOTIATION PROCESS BETWEEN GOVERNMENTS AND ENTERPRISES

The compromise between the state and business in the Asian socialist economies is made easier by both government ministries and enterprises leaving many HRM policies vague. Whilst this may partly be unintentional, some policies are purposely ambiguous. Needing to find a way of resolving the conflict between satisfying the political demands of the state and operating profitably in a global market environment, enterprises take advantage of the vagueness to find loopholes in the laws which suit their commercial interests. By doing so, they can often find a way to comply with government policy while still maximizing their competitiveness. For some dimensions, enterprises also take advantage of the state's inability to enforce their policies, by avoiding implementation of policies with which they disagree (Collins et al., 2013).

However, enterprises vary in the extent to which they seek to exploit loopholes or avoid implementation of government policy to maximize their commercial interests. Their doing so is dependent on two factors: their willingness to find ways around the policies, and their ability to exploit them. These in turn are dependent on their relative cultural and/ or ideological differentiation from government and their freedom from strict enforcement of government regulations. The combination of these two factors can be used to explain one of the most significant findings of the previous research of the present authors: the correlation between HRM, ownership type, and enterprise location (Zhu et al., 2008).

The foreign-influenced JVs and WOEs, in the cases we studied in both China and Vietnam, practise more HRM functions than more domestic-influenced DPEs and SOEs, principally due to the cultural and ideological gap between these enterprises and the governments. The gap serves the purpose of increasing their commitment to practising the HRM model and reducing their willingness to compromise with government policy. Consequently, they more commonly look for loopholes, or ways of avoiding government policies which prohibit or discourage practices of some HRM functions. Of the local enterprises, DPEs practise more Western-style HRM functions than SOEs and DPEs, as they are subject to less government control and are more driven by market forces.

The relation between location and practices of HRM functions can partly be explained by similar reasoning. Our research regarding the locational factor's influence on the people-management systems indicated that coastally located enterprises in China are more likely to implement formal HRM practices. The evidence suggests that enterprises located in the developed coastal region are under more pressure to innovate in order to be able to compete and survive, and adopting a formal HRM system appears to be part of their strategy for achieving this goal. However, enterprises located in the inland areas, remote from competition and the influence of globalization, are less concerned about formal HRM practices (Zhu & Warner, 2005).

In Vietnam, cities such as Ho Chi Minh City and Hanoi are also more amenable to new ideas and approaches, such as implementing the HRM model. When the government introduces a new policy, it often does not introduce the policy evenly across the country.

In some areas, the large cities are used to experiments with the new reform policy before it is implemented nationally. Sometimes these policies are not well designed and need testing before they are embedded in these locations, as they are still vague and open to interpretation. With their background making them more open to the new practices, the enterprises in such big cities can take advantage of laxer controls to choose models and find loopholes in the policies to bring greater profits to their business. The policy experiments conducted are indications of state–enterprise interaction in general. For any given policy, the state and enterprises engage in a form of indirect negotiation over a policy which each side can accept. In this process, the state introduces the policy as a trial (either overtly or by implication) and leaves it vague enough for enterprises to take some individual initiative to deal with the policy in the way that suits them best. The state observes how enterprises deal with the policy and adjusts it accordingly through tightening the regulations or, more commonly, through further compromise. Although the process of change is undoubtedly gradual, these findings indicate that economic transition, and particularly the HRM reform, in China and Vietnam is neither bottom-up nor top-down and as such does not match the transition theories posited by previous studies (Zhu, 2005; Cooke, 2012).

Examples of this experiment and adjustment approach can be found in the new employment policies introduced in China and Vietnam. Throughout the process the governments learned and adjusted their policies with the hope of satisfying both business interests and their own interests. Such was the case with the introduction of the Labour Codes in the two nations around two decades ago, as a key part of employment policy. This was the first time the governments had established such an important legal framework and they did not have much experience in this area. They looked to the ILO for guidance. As with many other policies, they were continually in the process of studying and improving the codes. Now that they have had time to trial the codes, they have amended them, following feedback from the business community. As mentioned above, political interests and ideology meant that some aspects of the codes were detrimental to businesses. However, the amended codes formalized a number of issues that reflected enterprise demands. All business sectors, including foreign-invested enterprises, can now freely recruit from the labour market. This step is a great relief for foreign-invested enterprises, because until the amended codes arrived, in both countries, they still needed to recruit through government labour agencies, which took a long time, was more expensive, and offered fewer choices, and in many cases the applicants did not fulfil the job requirements, particularly managers. The lack of fit between higher education and job market remains problematic (Ren et al., 2011). In addition, e-HRM is now relatively common in both China and Vietnam.

The state in both countries acknowledges that policy reforms are necessary but does not give the interests of enterprises top priority when forming new policies. They take other factors into consideration, of which the most important are budgetary constraints and their own political role. The policies are only suitable to the enterprises' interests if those interests coincide with or are similar to the state's interests.

Policies relating to the reform process and HRM implementation occur mainly along the lines intended by the state in China and Vietnam (Warner et al., 2005). However, because enterprises operate in a rapidly changing market-oriented environment, policies are introduced only after there is already a clear demand for them. This criterion necessitates that the enterprises addresses the situation before the state recognises it and is able to introduce new policies. While awaiting the new policies, the enterprises continue to implement the old policies, but only in a way which serves their own interests. If it is not politically expedient, then the state's amended policies may only partially satisfy business requests, leading to enterprises continuing to not fully implement the policies as intended, and a new cycle of negotiation between enterprises and the governments (Collins, 2009).

The enterprises in such transitional societies bend the policies to suit their circumstances or find a way of getting around the policies without upsetting the state. Their activities continue to be contrary to the state's objectives until they develop to a level where they can no longer be tolerated. At that time, the state introduces new policies to deal with the undesirable activities. Naturally, the motivation for introducing the new policies remains the protection of the state's own interests. Consequently, the reform of HRM in both China's and Vietnam's enterprises can now take place semi-independently of the state, and enterprises' actual implementation of new models never completely corresponds with the state's policies (Akhtar & Renyong, 2014).

The interaction between differences in the self-interests of the 'market-socialist' governments and the enterprises shows that any study of the transformation of HRM in transitional economies such as China and Vietnam cannot be isolated from changes at the macro level and in the business environment. Reform to HRM in these countries is a process of integration between a number of key actors. In other words, the practices and reform of HRM in enterprises cannot be separated from the surrounding environment. Enterprises' HRM strategies first need to fit in with their business strategies and, second, need to be well integrated with overall government policy, ideology, and cultural norms (Zhao & Du, 2012).

There is a strong interaction between three main forces responsible for determining the reform process and HRM practices, particularly in China and Vietnam. These are, in turn: first, the interrelation of the transition process; second, government interests in supporting the new practices for its political purposes; and third, the demands of business operation in enterprises. None of the three forces can be considered separately or understood in isolation. We know much less about North Korea, and perhaps one day it too will be open to Western scholars to conduct empirical research there.

CONCLUDING REMARKS

The reform of the economies in general and people-management in particular in China and Vietnam, when compared side by side, presents a fascinating two-way, interactive relationship of national state political interests and wider business activities (Warner, 2013). In this reform process, the various forces are continually negotiating a compromise to their sometimes conflicting interests. At the enterprise level, the extent to which functions of HRM are adopted depends on the relative strengths of the communist and nationalist ideological contexts and political influences on the one hand, and market economic influences on the other. These differences provide a unique context to HRM practices in China and Vietnam (Collins et al., 2013). Less interaction has been noted in North Korea where, with a new and very young leader, the state still just imposes change in policy (Lankov, 2013).

Within this context, a decade and a half into the new millennium, enterprises' overall HRM practices have changed from a traditional 'socialist' model to a new model combining aspects of some socialist, traditional, and HRM approaches in varying degrees, the so-called hybridization process (Warner, 2008b; Warner, 2014; Zhu et al., 2015), at least during reform in China and Vietnam, although only a minor shift had been seen in North Korea by 2016. The actors in the so-called transitional economies still share some common goals and, in some cases, a shared culture and ideology with the government, but there also remain significant differences between government and business interests, which are likely to grow in the coming years.

ACKNOWLEDGEMENT

We must thank Professor Vince Edwards and many others, as well as the publisher's anonymous reviewers, for advice and help in editing the final text.

REFERENCES

Akhtar, S.H., & Renyong, H. 2014. Assessment of human resource management environment in China: Past, present and future. *European Journal of Business and Management*, 6(36): 25–35.

BBC. 2014. Inside North Korea's Western-funded university. BBC News, 3 February. Accessed 14 December 2014 at www.bbc.co.uk/news/world-asia-25945931.

Benson, J., & Zhu, Y. 1999. Markets, firms and workers: The transformation of HRM in Chinese state-owned enterprises. *Human Resource Management Journal*, 9(4): 58–74.

Bertelsmann Stiftung. 2008. North Korea Country Report. Accessed 22 March 2008 at http://www.bertelsmann-transformation-index.de/114.0.html?L=0.

Bian, M.L. 2005. *The Making of the State Enterprise System in Modern China: The Dynamics of Institutional Change*. Cambridge, MA: Harvard University Press.

Brown, R.C. 2010. *Understanding Labor and Employment Law in China*. Cambridge: Cambridge University Press.

Chi, D.Q., & van den Broek, D. 2013. Wildcat strikes: A catalyst for union reform in Vietnam?. *Journal of Industrial Relations*, 55(5): 783–799.

Child, J. 1994. *Management in China During the Age of Reform*. Cambridge: Cambridge University Press.

China Labour Bulletin. 2014. Equal times: The rise of China's workers movement. 14 October. Accessed 1 January 2015 at http://www.clb.org.hk/en/content/equal-timesthe-rise-chinas-workers-movement.

Cho, J.A. 2006. *North Korea's Human Resource Development System*. Seoul: Korea Institute for National Unification.

Choi, C. 2011. Political and institutional origins of market development in North Korea: Focusing on state-society relations. PhD thesis, Syracuse University. Accessed 2 November 2014 at http://gradworks.umi.com/34/54/3454356.html.

Choi, C., & Lecy, J.D. 2012. A semantic network analysis of changes in North Korea's economic policy. *Governance: An International Journal of Policy*, 25(4): 589–616.

Chung, Y.H. 2003. The prospects for economic reform in North Korea and the direction of its economic development. *Vantage Point*, 26(5): 43–53.

CIA. 2014. *CIA World Factbook*. Accessed on 12 June 2015 at https://www.cia.gov/library/publications/the-world-factbook/.

Collins, N. 2005. Economic reform (*doi moi*) and unemployment in Vietnam. In Y. Zhu and J. Benson (eds), *Unemployment in Asia*: 176–193. London, UK and New York, USA: Routledge.

Collins, N. 2009. *Economic Reform and Employment Relations in Vietnam*. London, UK and New York, USA: Routledge.

Collins, N., Nankervis, A., Sitalaksmi, S., & Warner, M. 2011. Labour–management relationships in transitional economies: Convergence or divergence in Vietnam and Indonesia?. *Asia Pacific Business Review*, 17(3): 361–377.

Collins, N., Sitalaksmi, S., & Lansbury, R. 2013. Transforming employment relations in Vietnam and Indonesia: Case studies of state-owned enterprises. *Asia Pacific Journal of Human Resources*, 51(2): 131–151.

Cooke, F.L. 2005. Employment relations in a small commercial business in China. *Industrial Relations Journal*, 36(1): 19–37.

Cooke, F.L. 2012. *Human Resource Management in China: New Trends and Practices*. London, UK and New York, USA: Routledge.

Cox, A., & Warner, M. 2013. Whither 'training and development' in Vietnam? Learning from United States and Japanese MNCs' practice. *Asia Pacific Journal of Human Resources*, Special Issue: HRM in Vietnam, 51(2): 175–192.

Ding, D., Goodall, K., & Warner, M. 2002. The impact of economic reform on the role of trade unions in Chinese enterprises. *International Journal of Human Resource Management*, 13: 431–449.

Eberstadt, N. 1999. *The End of North Korea*. Washington, DC: American Enterprise Institute.

The Economist. 2007. Red flag. 28 July, p. 74.

Edwards, V., & Phan, A. 2012. *Managers and Management in Vietnam: 25 Years of Economic Renovation (Doi Moi)*. London, UK and New York, USA: Routledge.

Fahey, S. 1997. Vietnam and the third way: The natural of socio-economic transition. *Journal of Economic and Social Geography*, 88(5): 469–480.

Fforde, A., & De Vylder, S. 1996. *From Plan to Market: The Economic Transition in Vietnam*. Boulder, CO: Westview Press.

Flake, G. 2002. Management in North Korea. In M. Warner (ed.), *The International Encyclopedia of Business and Management* (2nd edn), Vol. 5: 4759–4766. London: Thomson.

Foster-Carter, A. 2012. Is North Korea opening? What might that mean?. 38 North. Accessed 29 December 2014 at http://38north.org/2012/02/afostercarter022912/.

Han, J.-w., & Jung, T.-h. (eds). 2013. *Understanding North Korea: Indigenous Perspectives*. Lanham, MD: Lexington Books.

Human Rights Watch. 2006. Report on North Korea: Workers' rights. Accessed 23 November 2014 at http://www.hrw.org/legacy/backgrounder/asia/korea1006/index.htm.

Human Rights Watch. 2014. North Korea. Country summary. Human Rights Watch. Accessed 1 January 2015 at http://www.hrw.org/sites/default/files/related_material/northkorea_7.pdf.

ILO. 2014. Trade Union Law now available in English. Geneva: International Labour Organization. Accessed 21 November 2014 at http://www.ilo.org/hanoi/Informationresources/Publicinformation/WCMS_218125/lang--en/index.htm.

Jackson, S.E., & Schuler, R.S. 1999. Understanding human resource management in the context of organizations and their environments. In R.S. Schuler and S.E. Jackson (eds), *Strategic Human Resource Management*: 4–28. London: Blackwell.

Kaple, D. 1994. *Dream of a Red Factory: The Legacy of High Stalinism in China*. Oxford, UK and New York, USA: Oxford University Press.

Khan, M. 2014. Six charts that show how North Korea became the most miserable place on earth. *Daily Telegraph*, 15 December. Accessed 15 December 2014 at http://www.telegraph.co.uk/news/worldnews/asia/northkorea/11260650/Six-charts-that-show-how-North-Korea-became-the-most-miserable-place-on-earth.html.

Kim, K.S. 2003. *Labour and Human Resources in North Korea*. Seoul: Seoul National University Press.

Kim, K.S., & Lee, D.M. 2005. The characteristics of work groups in the factories of North Korea. *Korean Journal of Management and Economics*, 32: 141–165.

Kim, K.S., & Lee, D.M. 2006. The contingency, structure, function, and effectiveness of working groups in the factories of North Korea. *Korean Journal of Human Resource Management*, 30: 159–181.

Korzec, M. 1992. *Labour and the Failure of Reform in China*. London, UK and New York, USA: Routledge.

Lamond, D., & Zheng, C.L. 2010. HRM research in China: Looking back and looking forward. *Journal of Chinese Human Resources Management*, 1(1): 6–16.

Lankov, A. 2006. The natural death of North Korean Stalinism. *Asia Policy*, 1(1): 95–121.

Lankov, A. 2013. *The Real North Korea: Life and Politics in the Failed Stalinist Utopia*. London, UK and New York, USA: Oxford University Press.

Lankov, A. 2014. How much money do North Koreans make?. NK News.Org. Accessed 10 October 2014 at http://www.nknews.org/2014/03/how-much-money-do-north-koreans-make/.

Lee, C.-H., Brown, W., & Wen, X. 2016. What sort of collective bargaining is emerging in China?. *British Journal of Industrial Relations*, 54(1): 214–236.

Lin, J.Y. 2011. *Demystifying the Chinese Economy*. Cambridge: Cambridge University Press.

Mansourov, A. 2003. Giving lip service with an attitude: North Korea's China debate. Brookings Institute. Accessed 8 April 2008 at http://www.brookings.edu/articles/2003/12china_mansourov.aspx.

McGregor, R. 2010. *The Party: The Secret World of China's Communist Rulers*. New York, USA: Harper, and London, UK: Allen Lane.

Min, M., Bambacas, M., & Zhu, Y. 2017. *Strategic Human Resource Management in China: A Multiple Perspective*. London, UK and New York, USA: Routledge.

Mundy, S. 2014. North Korea's business guide. *Financial Times*, 23 July. Accessed 12 November 2014 at http://www.ft.com/cms/s/0/9a6c1ee2-1192-11e4-a17a-00144feabdc0.html#axzz3NZXiL5xE.

Nankervis, A., Cooke, F.L., Chatterjee, S., & Warner, M. 2012. *New Models of Human Resource Management in China and India*. London, UK and New York, USA: Routledge.

NCNK. 2014. Special Economic Zones in the DPRK. National Committee on North Korea. Accessed 14

December 2014 at http://www.ncnk.org/resources/briefing-papers/all-briefing-papers/special-economic-zones-in-the-dprk.

Ng, S.H., & Warner, M. 1998. *China's Trade Unions and Management*. Basingstoke, UK: Macmillan, and New York, USA: St. Martin's Press.

Nguyen, T.N., Truong, Q., & Buyens, D. 2011. Training and firm performance in economies in transition: A comparison between Vietnam and China. *Asia Pacific Business Review*, 17(1): 103–119.

NKEW. 2013. DPRK's 'economic research' focuses on regional economic development zones. North Korean Economy Watch. Accessed 22 December 2014 at http://www.nkeconwatch.com/category/civil-society/art/domestic-publication/economic-research-journal/.

Nolan, P. 1993. *China's Rise, Russia's Fall*. Basingstoke, UK: Macmillan, and New York, USA: St Martins Press.

Park, H.J. 2014. North Korea's new economic management system. Korea Focus. Accessed 14 December 2014 at www.koreafocus.or.kr.

Ren, S., Collins, N., & Zhu, Y. 2014. Leadership self-development in China and Vietnam. *Asia Pacific Journal of Human Resources*, 52(1): 42–59.

Ren, S., Zhu, Y., & Warner, M. 2011. Human resources, higher education reform and employment opportunities for university graduates in the People's Republic of China. *International Journal of Human Resource Management*, 22(16): 3429–3446.

Rowley, C., & Warner, M. (eds). 2014. *Management in South Korea Revisited*. London, UK and New York, USA: Routledge.

SACOM. 2014. The lives of i-slaves – Students and Scholars against Corporate Misbehaviour. Hong Kong: SAR. Accessed 2 December 2014 at http://sacom.hk/islave-6-harsher-than-harsher/.

Seyfarth Shaw. 2014. China employment law alert: Employers prepare for compulsory collective bargaining. Accessed 29 December 2014 at http://www.seyfarth.com/publications/ChinaAlert051914.

Taylor, B.W.K., Chang, K., & Li, Q. 2003. *Industrial Relations in China*. Cheltenham, UK and Northampton, MA, USA: Edward Elgar Publishing.

Thang, L.C., & Quang, T. 2005. Antecedents and consequences of dimensions of human resource management practices in Vietnam. *International Journal of Human Resource Management*, 16(10): 1830–1846.

Thang, L.C., Rowley, C., Quang, T., & Warner, M. 2007. To what extent can management practices be transferred between countries? The case of human resource management in Vietnam. *Journal of World Business*, 42(1): 113–127.

UNDP. 2014. *Human Development Report*. Accessed 19 June 2015 at http://hdr.undp.org/en/content/human-development-report-2014.

Viet Nam News. 2013. People need a voice in reform, say experts. 7 January. Accessed 12 November 2013 at http://vietnamnews.vn/opinion/in-the-spotlight/234904/people-need-a-voice-in-reform-say-experts.html.

Vogel, E.F. 2011. *Deng Xiaoping and the Transformation of China*. Cambridge, MA: Harvard University Press.

Warner, M. 1995. *The Management of Human Resources in Chinese Industry*. Basingstoke, UK: Macmillan, and New York, USA: St Martin's Press.

Warner, M. 1996. Economic reforms, industrial relations and human resources in the People's Republic of China: An overview. *Industrial Relations Journal*, 27(3): 195–210.

Warner, M. 2000. Introduction: The Asia-Pacific HRM model revisited. *International Journal of Human Resource Management*, 11(2): 171–182.

Warner, M. (ed.). 2005. *Human Resource Management in China Revisited*. London, UK and New York, USA: Routledge.

Warner, M. 2008a. Trade unions in China: Towards the harmonious society. In J. Benson and Y. Zhu (eds), *Trade Unions in Asia*. London, UK and New York, USA: Routledge.

Warner, M. (ed.). 2008b. *Human Resource Management 'with Chinese Characteristics'*. London, UK and New York, USA: Routledge.

Warner, M. (ed.). 2011. *Confucian HRM in Greater China: Theory and Practice*. London, UK and New York, USA: Routledge.

Warner, M. 2013. Comparing human resource management in China and Vietnam: An overview. *Human Systems Management*, 32(4): 217–229.

Warner, M. 2014. *Understanding Management in China: Past, Present and Future*. London, UK and New York, USA: Routledge.

Warner, M., Edwards, V., Polonsky, G., Pucko, D., & Zhu, Y. 2005. *Management in Transitional Economies: From the Berlin Wall to the Great Wall of China*. London: RoutledgeCurzon.

Warner, M., & Ng, S.H. 1999. Collective contracts in Chinese enterprises: A new brand of collective bargaining under 'market socialism'?. *British Journal of Industrial Relations*, 37(2): 295–314.

Warner, M., & Zhu, Y. 2010. Labour–management relations in the People's Republic of China: Whither the 'harmonious society'?. *Asia Pacific Business Review*, 16(3): 267–281.

Williamson, P.J., & Yin, E. 2014. Accelerated innovation: The new challenge from China. *MIT Sloan Management Review*, 55(4): 1–8.

Wolf, C., & Levin, N.D. 2008. *Modernizing the North Korean System: Objectives, Method, and Application.* Santa Monica, CA: Rand Corporation.

Wong, J. 2014. *The Political Economy of Deng's Nanxun: Breakthrough in China's Reform and Development.* Singapore: World Scientific.

Zhao, S., & Du, J. 2012. Thirty-two years of development of human resource management in China: Review and prospects. *Human Resource Management Review*, 22(3): 179–188.

Zhu, Y. 2002. Economic reform and human resource management in Vietnam. *Asia Pacific Business Review*, 8(3): 115–134.

Zhu, Y. 2005. The Asian crisis and the implications for human resource management in Vietnam. *International Journal of Human Resource Management*, 16(7): 1262–1277.

Zhu, Y., Collins, N., Webber, M., & Benson, J. 2008. New forms of ownership and human resource practices in Vietnam. *Human Resource Management*, 47(1): 157–175.

Zhu, Y., & Fahey, S. 1999. The impact of economic reform on industrial labour relations in China and Vietnam. *Post-Communist Economies*, 11: 173–192.

Zhu, Y., & Verstraeten, M. 2013. Human resource management practices with Vietnamese characteristics: A study of managers' responses. *Asia Pacific Journal of Human Resources*, 51(2): 152–174.

Zhu, Y., & Warner, M. 2004. Changing patterns of human resource management in contemporary China. *Industrial Relations Journal*, 35(4): 311–328.

Zhu, Y., & Warner, M. 2005. Changing Chinese employment relations since WTO accession. *Personnel Review*, 34: 354–369.

Zhu, Y., Warner, M., & Feng, T. 2011. Employment relations 'with Chinese characteristics': The role of trade unions in China. *International Labour Review*, 150(1/2): 127–143.

Zhu, Y., Xie, Y.H., Warner, M., & Guo, Y.X. 2015. Employee participation and the influence on job satisfaction of the 'new generation' of Chinese employees. *International Journal of Human Resource Management*, 26(19): 2395–2411.

31. Japan, South Korea, and Taiwan: issues and trends in HRM

Philippe Debroux, Wes Harry, Shigeaki Hayashi,
Heh Jason Huang, Keith Jackson, and Toru Kiyomiya

INTRODUCTION

The three countries discussed in this chapter, although very different in ethnic and cultural backgrounds, share some common factors. The three are at the periphery of the Asian landmass; South Korea on a peninsula, and the other two in groups of islands. These countries had a shared history, at least for a time, when Korea and Taiwan (then Formosa) were occupied by Japan. During the second half of the twentieth century the three countries successfully embraced capitalism, with government support and under the influence of the United States of America (USA), and in so doing recovered fairly rapidly from the devastation of the Pacific War; in contrast to their neighbours in North Korea and the People's Republic of China which in the 1940s adopted the Communist economic model.

In this chapter for the second edition of the *Handbook* we have added sections on diversity. Each of the three states has an overwhelmingly dominant ethnic group. Although the indigenous people of Taiwan and Japan (mostly Ainu and Ryukyuans) are important elements of the population and are treated as citizens with the advantages and disadvantages that this entails, no special support is given to them despite discrimination suffered by these groups.

The largest group of the population suffering discrimination throughout this area of East Asia (and globally) are females. Governments are trying, or appearing to try, to reduce the difficulties faced by women in the workplace and to make better use of the potential offered by this half of humanity. Significant elements of the other half of humanity fear that improved opportunities for women will mean greater competition for men, who are already finding that employment security is reduced by agency and contingent work and temporary work.

In this sensitive area of diversity management Magoshi and Chang (2009) debate the issues neglected in North American and European studies when they examine the Japanese and Korean approaches to age, disability, and capability as well as gender, ethnicity, and nationality. The matter of diversity in capability is a particularly interesting element of the discussion because every society has people who are more or less capable of performing needed work tasks. By considering what can be done in the workplace for those with lower abilities we see a display of elements of the Confucius heritage of East Asia. Meanwhile these three societies are experiencing a shift in jobs from male citizens who would previously have aimed for secure employment, to males in temporary, agency, and contingent roles, and to foreigners (as jobs are exported to cheaper locations), as well as to part-time, predominantly female, employment in the service and retail sectors. Some of these major shifts in employment patterns, and challenges for the less able to fit into the post-industrial economy, are starting to be experienced in the USA and the European Union with repercussions being felt in the political arena. The solutions, some wise and some not so wise, being tried on the periphery of East Asia may offer useful lessons for societies of post-industrial Western nations.

Although outsiders push for greater migration into these states, this is strongly resisted as the strength of a homogeneous society is seen as being much more important than concerns about ageing populations. As we discuss below, the levels of unemployment, while low by European and South Asian norms, create a fear that bringing more foreigners in will lead to greater insecurity of employment for the host population. In addition there is an expectation that innovations in technology will overcome potential problems of an ageing population, thus reducing the need to import foreign workers.

As we are concentrating on the HRM aspects of these countries we have omitted many aspects of the general business environment (for the reader who wishes to understand the background we recommend Tselichtchev & Debroux, 2009); however, we cannot completely ignore major political, social, and commercial issues which have important impacts on HRM in the region. In particular the continued increase in the economic power of the People's Republic of China and its more recent projection of military power beyond its shores has consequences for organisations and institutions in East Asia.

JAPAN

Background to HRM Issues

The traditional Japanese human resource management (HRM) system is composed of a bundle of practices, policies and institutions that emerged gradually in the post-World War II period and found its full equilibrium at the end of the 1960s. It is based on an internal labour market logic leading to selective once-a-year recruitment of new graduates; extensive company training and education; low wage differentials and periodic pay raises; internal promotion based on multi-pronged evaluations; flexible job assignments and small-group activities; employment security until the age of mandatory retirement; enterprise unions grouping all regular blue- and white-collar workers and joint labour–management consultations mechanisms; and a sharp dichotomy in treatment between regular and non-regular workers. The cohort-based personnel management is complemented with other practices such as late promotion, and the centralisation of control over personnel decisions within HRM departments (Matanle, 2003).

Those practices and policies incorporate elements of the pre-war social and business system such as the living wage concept, the company-centred welfare policy, and the low wage differential. They also find their philosophical underpinning, related for example to shop-floor training, blue- and white-collar egalitarianism, and work ethics, in diverse religious and philosophical influences – Buddhism, Shintoism, Confucianism, Christianity, and Marxism – that have played a role in the emergence of Japan's modern social and business state (Hirschmeyer & Yui, 2006).

Challenges to the HRM System

Until the beginning of the 1990s, the HRM system was able to keep its tenets of economic and social stability while retaining its dynamics and consistency. However, since the 1990s core elements, especially those related to the internal labour market, have been challenged to the point that they have forced companies to rethink practices, policies, and the very philosophy of the system. The self-sustained and self-contained HRM system, whose consistency had been considered instrumental in the competitiveness of the Japanese economy, is claimed to be inappropriate in globalised markets (Schaede, 2008) and unsustainable in the ageing Japanese society.

The shift towards shareholder value-driven corporate governance during the last two decades puts companies under pressure to deliver increased financial returns. This explains the shorter-term emphasis and more selective use of training programmes (Nakata & Miyazaki, 2011). At the same time regulatory changes have tended to facilitate market-driven initiatives in the labour market, for instance relative to the use of non-regular workers (Sueki, 2012). Companies now attempt to boost competitiveness through organisational capabilities that are based on different types of monetary and non-monetary motivational tools (capital-related incentives, explicit fast tracks for the best performers, annualisation schemes, and so on) and more effective control of the wage curves (Sasajima, 2012).

Companies gradually recognise that the unconditional availability of male regular workers and the reward given for long working hours and dedication cannot remain the key sources of competitive strength and motivation. This is leading to the introduction of new recruitment, appraisal, and reward systems, linked to new work patterns privileging speed of reaction, knowledge cross-fertilisation, and risk-taking (Hentschel & Haghirian, 2010). Some companies are now putting into place HRM practices that attempt to reconcile efficiency and optimal use of human capital through work–life balance policies for all types of employees (Debroux, 2013).

Companies are coming to terms with the fact that if a certain level of consistency can (must) be achieved in order to maintain sustainable competitive advantage, the new emerging HRM system may clash with the very elements that they want to retain. As a result, the HRM system is unlikely ever to be in the same lasting state of incrementally evolving equilibrium as the previous one. With more heterogeneous stakeholder relations and a more heterogeneous workforce, as well as external market and technology forces, it is bound to be inherently more unstable and changing.

Recruitment and Selection

The traditional career is based on the Lazear (1979) theory, where employees are put in long-term competition with a stable set of peers and rewards come in the second part of their career. That does not suit the career aspirations of the mobile young Japanese and foreign elite. High-skilled and specialist workers are employed on temporary contracts for specific tasks and projects, and semi-skilled workers replace regular workers for routine jobs. However, for the time being, the differences in treatment offered to the regular and non-regular workers are creating distortions in aspects of recruitment, job design, training, and job assignment that impede the optimisation of non-regular workforce talent (Jones & Urasawa, 2011).

Around 61 per cent of current salaried workers are regular employees and about 39 per cent are non-regular employees of different categories (Ministry of Health, Labour and Welfare, MHLW, 2014), making Japan the Organisation for Economic Co-operation and Development (OECD) country with the highest level of temporary employment. The trend towards non-regular employment is likely to continue, but it has to be in a system offering more flexibility to the two parties and a wider career choice with good conditions, that is, a decent wage, access to training, the possibility to shift status, and access to welfare and pension benefits (OECD, 2015).

Non-regular jobs are seldom the springboard to secure a regular job. In Europe, 40–60 per cent of fixed-term employees transition to regular status within three years of contract work. In Japan, the five-year transition rate is around 25 per cent, and a further 30 per cent wish to become regular employees but are denied the opportunity (OECD, 2015).

Although the external labour market for managerial positions is wider than previously, it remains difficult to land an equivalent job in the same industry. This creates 'trapped' middle-aged employees whose expectations of career are low and who are difficult to motivate (Debroux, 2013).

Employee Relations

Management motivates employees to accumulate firm-specific skills that enhance productivity. Because higher productivity can lead to labour redundancy, workers have little incentive to cooperate in productivity improvement without the implicit understanding that they will keep their job until retirement and that their efforts will translate into periodic pay raises and promotion (Nitta, 2009).

In the absence of legal enforcement of job guarantees, the introduction in large companies of joint labour–management committees to facilitate information-sharing and prior consultations on important personnel matters was instrumental in the HRM stability and dynamics. Labour unions are organised and bargain at company level although they also belong to industrial federations and to an umbrella confederation. During business downturns, one of their key roles was always to discuss with management workforce redeployment through internal and external transfers, and to negotiate early retirement schemes. Thus, they became an enforcement mechanism for productivity improvement that ensured employment was secure. In this respect they were instrumental in building mutual trust between labour and management (Nitta, 2009).

Workers with marketable skills do not need the unions and the individualisation of contractual relations makes collective bargaining less relevant, especially in the now dominant service economy. Since the 1990s trade union activities have concentrated on job security of their members rather than wage increases. They also now attempt to defend the interest of the non-regular employees, in view of their growing number and importance (Song, 2014).

Training and Development

The strong emphasis on learning in Japan can be traced to the traditional concept and purpose of learning in Japanese culture. Originating from the scholarship and ideals of the Bushido code, learning has been directed at practical applications, that is, building the embedded nature of knowledge through practice (Miyamoto & Grainger, 2007). In Zen Buddhism, which is at the origin of Bushido, basic human qualities such as trust, simplicity, feeling, and understanding of the self are at work. They are presented as features emotionally grounded in the minds and hearts of the average people and not only in the minds of enlightened elites. They are expected to be useful in day-to-day private and business life and to appear in the values of organisations. The sense of responsibility, loyalty, commitment, work ethics, and discipline of the workforce coming from that heritage is reflected in Japanese products and services, and in workplace practices (Dore, 1973). In this line of thought HRM practices create continuity of moral principle. For example, spiritual principles are embodied in '5S' activities – *seiri* (storing), *seiton* (straightening), *seiso* (cleanliness), *seiketsu* (sanitary care), and *shitsuke* (sustaining discipline) – involved in daily work life (Hayashi, 2011).

Nowadays, a shift towards outsourcing and formalisation of training activities can be observed, away from the emphasis on on-the-job training. Automation destroyed many production and service-related jobs, or deskilled them, meaning that non-regular workers can perform them at lower cost and with less need for training (Hirano, 2011). Conversely, other jobs are created that require higher levels of skill and knowledge that can only be acquired through off-the-job learning (general education and specialist courses), combined with acquisition of an official qualification (Sueki, 2012). Under profit pressure, companies have become reluctant to invest in the human resources of research and development (R&D) and production when short-term returns cannot be expected. Japanese companies still place importance on employee development, but they reduce the range of in-house expertise, and outsource a growing array of knowledge and experience. This is reflected in the decline of training budgets over the last two decades (Sueki, 2012).

Reward and Performance

In recent years many companies have adopted a performance-based or merit-based system that more closely links wages to actual performance in a given job, without assuming automatically that acquisition of skills leads to higher performance. Companies are not shifting towards a purely job-related system but rather towards role-based systems utilising the competency model. This allows companies to keep job rotation, but with more precise information about the skill level for families of jobs corresponding to specific competency profiles that can be used during the whole career all over the organisation (Sueki, 2012).

In adopting relative evaluation systems using rigid forced distribution rules, along with quantitative benchmarks for evaluation, companies ran into problems of short-termist 'gaming' of the systems. Contrary to the expectations of increased risk-taking, this often led to a reluctance to challenge and to difficulties in goal-setting, because of the monetary and career-related risks (Hayashi, 2011). Employees were motivated to spend more time on easily measured tasks than those more difficult to monitor and to protect their own arena of job responsibilities, to the point that overall efficiency suffered (Nakamura, 2006).

Japanese companies have not renounced the pay-for-performance system but they are evolving toward a system that mixes objective and subjective performance indicators.

Outcome and process are taken into account in performance and the management by objectives (MBO) schemes separate the reward and the training and development objectives. Special incentives are devised to reward the long-term perspective for some types of jobs such as R&D, and for nurturing subordinates (Sueki, 2012). Many Japanese companies still want to keep the long-term learning perspective that comes from socialisation in the early career stages. Seniority and acquisition of skills remain key elements of the pay system for young employees. Individual performance is increasingly taken into account but wage differentials remain low and wider differences related to individual performance mainly come from bonus variation (Sueki, 2012).

For the highest-performing employees, fairness now means the opportunity to optimise talent and to be rewarded according to actual performance. Long-term acquisition of firm-specific skills is less important than before in many sectors and types of tasks. Acquisition of competencies related to problem-solving, learning, and speed are more important for many tasks than competencies based on experience, time, and verbal abilities. Thus, companies lower the upper wage level for each grade, try to eliminate the sub-par performers before they reach the top of each ladder and band, and impose earlier and more stringent caps on the wages of the senior employees. Since the 1980s many of them have a wage policy according to which the regular raising of wages stops at the age of mandatory retirement from managerial positions, very often set at 55 years old. This is done so as not to impede the career development of the younger generations of managers, and to minimise the cost of the ageing workforce. In fact, companies want to prevent a drift of wage cost from the earliest possible stage of the career, all the more because of regulatory changes forcing companies to keep all regular employees who so wish to stay on the payroll until 65 years old. The negative impact it could have on wage cost explains why companies prefer to create larger bonus differentials where the performance element is higher, while controlling wages at the earliest possible career stage (Sueki, 2012).

Diversity Management

Optimising female and older workers, as well as getting away from the rigid division between regular and non-regular employment, are considered necessary steps in the ageing Japanese society. Societal norms regarding the roles of women in society are changing and women are being given more opportunities to make a career (Kawaguchi, 2013). However, the burden of household duties coupled with the high level of time and energy required from regular employees makes it difficult for most of them to have a career on a par with male employees. In a skill-driven system no significant progress can be expected as long as women are not given the opportunity of developing their skills on an equal opportunity basis. Currently, around 40 per cent of companies have no female managers above the level of section chief. The ratios are particularly low in large companies, precisely those driven by the skill-grading system and the internal labour market logic (OECD, 2015).

Therefore, the limited regular status option is probably the most realistic option for the majority of female (and older) employees. It gives them more job flexibility in terms of scope of duties, location, and working time, while retaining the advantages of regular employment, for example, access to fringe benefits, pension, and training. A growing number of companies utilise this system and some of them plan to extend it to male workers as well. However, the regulatory distinctions between regular employees and limited regular employees are still unclear. This makes many companies reluctant to move forward while they are not sure that they will be able to manage the two types of employees in a cost-effective and flexible manner, while avoiding legal hassles.

Likely Future Trends

There is no easy way to fundamentally alter Japan's HRM systems. Building from the pre-war practices and concepts of labour–management relations, the post-war system was constructed during a process that lasted several decades and the current transformation follows the same gradual and zigzagging path. Coping with an ageing trend of immense scale, Japan cannot afford to neglect and waste the talent of any human resources. Attempts are now made to integrate women, foreigners, and older workers but the very characteristics of those categories of workers require deep changes in corporate culture and, thus, impact upon all HRM functions. Female labour can only be optimised in a work–life balance-driven HRM system; foreigners cannot be attracted if the modes of recruitment and career development are not transformed. But adoption of new practices that satisfy the needs of those categories of workers require a rethinking of the uniform wage system and the shift towards more contingent organisational commitment. Older workers are likely to become key human resources but their integration up to and beyond age 65 requires drastic changes in the wage system that will have an impact on wage curves starting from the younger segments of the workforce, and this imposes a rethinking of the training and development system.

Uncertainty around career progression and employment stability has a negative impact on the motivation of many regular workers. Younger workers are increasingly reluctant to accept punishing work schedules and regimes in the expectation that as they rise in the organisation their interests and aspirations will be protected (Hayashi, 2011). Workplace stress, leading to occupational mental health issues and higher levels of suicide, and declining trust in the legitimacy of management, is widely observed (Sugimoto, 2010). Many young Japanese people who find regular work in their chosen field may discover that their jobs offer few training and career development opportunities due to their company's cost-cutting efforts (Hayashi, 2011). In line with the policy promoted by the public authorities, what can be expected is the emergence of new institutional arrangements being gradually devised to provide greater work flexibility. It is only when those arrangements are linked with career development and reward legitimised by both management and workers that they may induce significant change.

REPUBLIC OF KOREA[1]

Background to HRM Issues

Korea has seen the permeation of Confucian values to every part of society for many centuries. Although Korean culture has been changing since the Korean War, this

---

[1]   For the purposes of this chapter we use 'Korea' to mean the Republic of Korea, which is also known as South Korea.

Confucian heritage remained strong during the last few decades of the twentieth century. The Confucian and collective-minded South Korean companies organised themselves around principles of respect for order and hierarchy on the one hand, and on the other, benevolence and paternalism (Miles et al., 2008).

The giant multisectoral *chaebols* provided opportunities to improve standards of living, albeit not equally for all categories of workers. Women's economic activities were reduced to ancillary production work and unpaid labour at home. During the whole period from the 1950s to the 1990s, production workers had to work long hours for low wages. The *chaebols* offered a long-term job guarantee for their permanent workers; female and temporary workers had no guarantees. Wages, salaries, and promotion were largely based on seniority. Up until the 1990s, under regulatory and social constraints, large companies rearranged work and cut back on bonus and dividends rather than dismissing any permanent workforce. The internal labour market principle was used less in South Korean small and medium-sized enterprises (SMEs) than in their Japanese equivalents. High labour mobility between firms was always the norm in Korea among the majority of the workforce (Hwang, 2006).

When South Korea joined the World Trade Organization (WTO) companies could no longer depend on government protection. After the Asian financial crisis of the mid-1990s, the International Monetary Fund pressured for a more hands-off and market-driven public policy on labour issues. Long-term job guarantees had to be curtailed and more flexible wage-setting policies had to be adopted. Companies transferred work to lower-labour-cost countries and restructured HRM at home.

The government is encouraging companies to innovate, particularly in future automobiles, drones, wearable devices, and intelligent robots (*Korea JoongAng Daily*, 2016). The shift toward knowledge-related industries requires HRM strategies attuned to the needs of knowledge workers in terms of autonomy and involvement in management, fair recognition of their contribution, and prioritisation of work–life balance. Optimising their talents and creating synergetic effects requires an environment with high levels of cooperation and coordination.

The *chaebols* have the best access to tangible and intangible assets, giving them an edge in attracting top talent (Tselichtchev & Debroux, 2009), while non-permanent workers, who amount to about half of all employees (Hemmert, 2009), have declining connections to and reward from work. This is also seen in the declining respect for the *chaebols*, their owners and senior management, as scandals and abuse of power meet greater resistance from workers, the media, and politicians (*The Economist*, 2015). A different work organisation and legal contract expertise are being introduced to treat fairly and motivate employees working with different status and under different pay systems. Dismissal of workers is easier than before, though companies try to avoid straightforward retrenchment. They devise short-term contracts, outplacement, and retraining schemes for their laid-off workers.

Recruitment and Selection

The South Korean external labour market is expanding, with growing job mobility, but recruitment of new graduates, as in Japan, remains at the centre of HRM policy. Companies are aware of the need for more diversity so they recruit more broadly, beyond the renowned universities, and put more emphasis on specific skills, abilities, and attitudes. Korean people have always been individual achievers, in contrast to most Japanese and Taiwanese. This tendency has grown further since the 1990s. Employees are becoming more individualistic and more willing to take charge of their own careers. Companies now put emphasis on job content, career opportunities, and material reward. Many companies have a signing-on bonus system and an explicit fast track for the most talented. But South Koreans are also worried about their career prospects. Companies cannot promise a long-term stable career with regular promotion to the majority of their employees. Instead, they have to offer something else: for example, training, assuring employability, or creating an attractive work environment.

Cultivation of relationships with universities is important for firms to have access to the best students, especially in natural sciences. Large companies have high expectations concerning the qualifications of the new recruits. The recruitment of permanent employees is increasingly formalised, with the use of internal tests and assessment centres. Recruitment of some types of non-permanent employees involved in routine jobs is more casual. However, companies also have strict selection criteria for those whose individual or group performance may directly impact upon company performance.

Reward and Performance

Performance-related pay (PRP) and promotion systems have been adopted in many large companies, although stock options and profit-sharing schemes are not widespread. Annualised remuneration schemes with salary based on individual performance or ability are popular.

MBO and competency frameworks are also being adopted in relation to remuneration, although they are mainly utilised for development purposes. South Korean companies still seem to have difficulties mixing appraisal and reward flexibility with the internal market logic (Hwang, 2006). PRP systems motivate employees on the fast track, but companies are said to often end up creating a culture of narrow individualism and short-termism (Miles et al., 2008). In many companies the employees are not strongly involved in the development of the new systems, raising issues of equity and fairness of the reward frameworks and procedures. The most successful companies adopt evaluation systems mixing appraisal and reward of individual and group performance. It remains difficult to create wage and salary differentials.

Only about 15 per cent of the total of business sector employees work in large companies. The majority are employed in SMEs with less than 300 employees. Although wages and salaries in large *chaebol*-related firms have increased significantly since the 1990s and working conditions have improved, this is not the case in the SMEs. Wages and salaries remain much lower, and working conditions have not improved much during the last decade. Most South Korean SMEs are still concentrated in low-profit sectors in the domestic market (Hwang, 2006) despite the increase of export-oriented ventures.

Training and Development

Traditional respect and esteem is attached to educational attainment, and efforts for self-improvement are pervasive across society. Driven by the necessity of upgrading manpower productivity and the requirement of knowledge industries, companies devote substantial resources to training. Large companies often have well-equipped learning facilities (Hemmert, 2009). For the core workers, training is linked to the promotion of values such as trust, credibility, excellence, and responsibility. The use of foreign nationals as trainers has increased: for languages, but also for technical and management skill transfers and cultural familiarity (Kim & Bae, 2004).

Foreign trainers are invited but companies also send trainees to overseas subsidiaries or to academic and business-related programmes. Many companies are active in university–business partnerships in South Korea and abroad. Organisations finance research projects, giving opportunities to their employees to work in different environments.

Employment Relations

A tripartite system of employment relations has existed at the state level since the 1990s but at company level the bargaining autonomy of the two parties has gradually replaced state regulations. Multiple unions are now allowed in each workplace. Mediation provided by the Labour Relations Commission is compulsory before starting any industrial action. Companies with more than 30 full-time employees must set up a labour–management consultation council (Dessler & Tan, 2009). The tripartite system does not yet operate optimally: at company level, employee participation through formal mechanisms is still limited. Unions have problems penetrating the new industries and attracting young workers. There are doubts about the benefits of a confrontational trade union strategy among their members. The position of the state is ambiguous: it has imposed affirmative action in favour of female workers on large companies, while pushing for better working conditions of the non-core workers. But the state is criticised for keeping restrictions on the rights of freedom of association, collective bargaining, and strikes.

Meanwhile trust has been lost in the management or regulation of many large and powerful organisations due to a series of scandals in South Korean companies, such as in Air Korea where the president's privileged daughter (see many references to 'Nut Rage') ordered crew operating an aircraft to obey her orders; or the example of the ferry owners who added features to a ferry which made it unstable, leading to great loss of life (BBC, 2015). Even apart from these scandals, the power of major corporations is increasingly challenged (*The Economist*, 2015).

Diversity Management

Korea has one of the lowest fertility rates in the world. It does not face imminent problems of labour shortage, but thinks about immigration in a longer-term perspective. It is a very culturally and racially homogeneous country where, as in most of East Asia, large-scale immigration is discouraged. Foreigners account for 2 per cent of the current population and the number is unlikely to increase significantly (CIA, 2016).

About 4 per cent of the resident population are from other ethnic groups, mostly from nearby countries such as the Philippines and China, with a particularly large representation (of various ethnicities) from the USA. Hence attention to diversity tends to be focused on gender and, to a lesser extent, age. Around 60 per cent of 25–64-year-old females in Korea are in paid work and this is despite families having few children (the average Korean woman has 1.25 children). The cause of the low participation in paid employment is poor work practices and discrimination against women, especially married women. Various government initiatives, and international employers, have attempted to address the obstacles put in the way of females, but with limited success. HRM professionals are as likely as line managers to be unwilling to advance the cause of those disadvantaged groups, especially when the traditional breadwinners or patriarchs of the family face uncertainty of employment as Korea faces the challenges of a more competitive economic environment (Magoshi & Chang, 2009).

Likely Future Trends

Contingent convergence of HRM practices with world standards is likely to continue in terms of appraisal and reward systems. Continuation of recruitment of contingent (temporary, agency, and despatch) types of human resources can also be expected. But there is a need to question what cultural changes are likely to arise from these policy changes, in terms of contributing to sustainable social and economic growth pattern. Sharp differences between categories of employees continue. This creates a loss of a sense of community and trust in society. Any solution necessarily supposes the involvement of private business. Yet, the *chaebols* are still expected by government and society at large to fulfil social responsibilities while there is increasing mistrust of their ability to meet these responsibilities.

A remaining negative point is the low integration of female labour, especially of highly qualified women. In this respect, despite progress in some companies, Korea is still an outlier, similar to Japan, among developed countries. Significant changes cannot be expected in the short term.

TAIWAN

Background to HRM Issues

While Taiwan has become an important source for a variety of products and services in the global markets, it has faced keen competition from other developed and developing countries, not least from mainland China. Companies on the island have to demonstrate their dynamic capabilities to maintain agility, flexibility, and self-renewal, while learning to meet new commercial developments. HRM's history as a major profession in Taiwan is not long, but Taiwanese firms have increasingly recognised and emphasised HRM's importance in meeting their objectives. As winning the 'talent war' has become a critical issue for survival (especially when the proportion of young people is declining), many well-trained HRM professionals have moved from foreign-invested companies to local firms. This movement has accelerated the diffusion of HRM knowledge and practices within the Taiwanese business society. Nevertheless, some leading universities such as the National Sun Yat-Sen University and National Central University established academic institutes of HRM back in the 1990s.

Confucianism is the main value system in Taiwan, as in Korea. This value system strongly emphasises education, diligence, frugality, family obligation, and patriarchal orientation. In Taiwanese business organisations, decision-making is very often guided by family influence, especially in long-established organisations. The employees' attachment and loyalty towards their organisations is very important, while management feels that companies should do as much as possible to look after the welfare of their employees. However, the external environment changed dramatically in the first decade of the twenty-first century and the influence of traditional values seems to be declining. For example, in July 2001, Acer (Taiwan's best-known company) undertook a reorganisation which involved a massive lay-off to cut 7 per cent of its Taiwan-based workforce (*Economic Daily News*, 2001). This action by Acer was a radical change in business philosophy for the company and a shock to most of the population of Taiwan. While the overall deterioration of the employment situation has slowed, unemployment among the middle-aged and older workers (aged between 45 and 64) has continued to worsen. Involuntary job losses among this age group have particular importance because they are often the main breadwinners in the household.

Some of the Western concepts and practices, such as merit pay, MBO, performance appraisal, and so on, were introduced into Taiwan and have been emulated by Taiwanese companies. However, many companies find difficulties in reconciling the cultural differences when transplanting such Western management practices.

In recent years, the increasingly deep involvement of Taiwan in mainland China's economy has been a key development for HRM. As economic exchange across the Strait became routine, labourers in Taiwan began to lose their jobs to cheaper labour on the mainland, in the People's Republic of China (PRC). As a result, the government has campaigned to attract highly skilled labour to high-tech and service industries (where qualifications and capability can be leveraged) targeted to be Taiwan's future competitive stronghold. However, even highly skilled technical jobs may be lost to mainland Chinese, as we will discuss.

The loss of jobs to the PRC, often driven by major Taiwanese investors such as Hon Hai Precision Industry (generally known as Foxconn), highlights an issue of identity among the people of Taiwan. For centuries, Taiwan has been faced with identity conflicts. A survey on political attitudes in Taiwan conducted annually over the past 24 years by National Chengchi University's Election Study Center (*Taipei Times*, 2015) shows that the number of respondents identifying themselves as Taiwanese exceeded 50 per cent for the first time in 2009, and it has continued to rise since, reaching 60 per cent in 2015, about twice as high as the percentage of those saying they are 'Taiwanese and Chinese'. Only 3.5 per cent identified themselves as 'Chinese'. Some of the consequences of the feeling of separateness are shown in the January 2016 election of Ms Tsai Ing-wen of the Democratic Progressive Party as President, gaining an overall majority in the Legislative Yuan. This election result has led to strains in the relationship between Taiwan and the PRC despite, from 2014 onwards, representatives of China and Taiwan exchanging representative offices. The direct linkages eventually led to the meeting between President Xi Jinping of China and President Ma Ying-jeou of Taiwan in Singapore on 7 November 2015. This historic summit reflected a long-term expanding cooperation. These important changes have had a lasting impact on HRM issues in Taiwan.

Recruitment and Selection

Prior to the emergence of the internet as a means of finding applicants, and candidates finding career opportunities, job seekers in Taiwan relied on newspapers for jobs. Newspaper employment advertisements are very expensive and did not necessarily attract the most suitable candidates. Thanks to the internet, companies seeking recruits can now find, for a relatively low cost, a wide range of job-bank services, such as the provision of regular updates regarding qualified applicants, recruitment of high-level or specialised applicants, and offers to provide outsourced and temporary employees.

Recruiting at university campuses is common, especially for entry-level managerial and professional positions. For middle- and senior-level positions, headhunting has become increasingly popular. In almost all recruitment relationships in Taiwan, personal networking is important for job seekers. A cross-national comparison of personnel selection practices showed that Taiwan and Japan were the only two countries where firms listed 'a person's ability to get along well with others already working here' as one of the three most important criteria for selection (Huo et al., 2002). It is noteworthy that Taiwanese tend to be more accustomed to a paternalistic culture. While assertiveness is generally a desired trait in the West, it is much less so in Taiwan society.

The key factor facilitating the transformation of Taiwan's high-tech industrial development is the availability of sufficient numbers of talented candidates. The pace of development toward high-tech industrial production cannot be met by the corresponding adjustment of human resource training within the rigid education system. Thus, university graduates had difficulty finding suitable jobs, while industries also have problems hiring the right staff. For example, despite many efforts by the government, a survey of 100 multinational corporations (MNCs) in Taiwan showed a serious deficiency of staff with information, communication, and technology (ICT) skills (Hu et al., 2007).

With the increased development and deployment of HRM techniques Taiwan has moved, to an extent, to more systematic methods of selecting and recruiting employees. Hsu and Leat (2000) found that some, but certainly not all, decision-making was shared between HRM and line management, but that the cultural sensitivity of recruitment and selection practices meant that even foreign-owned companies adjusted their systems to meet Taiwanese requirements, especially in relying upon networks, social standing, and educational background.

Training and Development

Over the past two decades, Taiwan has expanded its higher education at an unprecedented pace, admitting students from more diverse backgrounds rather than limiting education to the elites. Moreover, since the mid-1990s Taiwan's birth rate has been declining and its society is ageing. Many private higher education institutions (HEIs), especially in more remote areas, have found themselves confronted with a serious shortage of student recruits, and many HEIs have encountered operational difficulties arising from this shortage. It is expected, as in Japan, that more universities – up to one-third of the total – will likely face forced closures or mergers after 2016 (Chen, 2010). To offset the declining birth rate by increasing the numbers of international students, the government set up awards and programmes for HEIs to promote internationalisation by encouraging foreign students, promoting international exchange, and enhancing university competitiveness internationally. In 2012, the total number of international students reached 43 957.

As continuing technological advancement (and competition from other countries in the region) moved the Taiwanese economic structure from a labour-intensive to a more technology-intensive and/or capital-intensive marketplace, companies gradually began to realise that they could not compete in world markets without maintaining competent human capital. Consequently, companies have become more willing to invest in people. Generally speaking, Taiwan employers are more pragmatic and emphasise skills training. The investment in people has led to the highest-performing companies allocating an average of 3.3 per cent of payroll costs to training and development (Fei, 1990).

In a study of the high-technology firms, which Taiwan aims to develop further, Lin (1996) found that training and development was usually recommended by supervisors (rather than HRM professionals), was usually on-the-job training, and that Taiwanese and Japanese-owned firms in Taiwan emphasised employee development much more than USA-owned enterprises; in fact she found that US companies were characterised by a focus on short-term profit rather than the stability and growth favoured by Taiwanese organisations. Lin (1996) also found that foreign firms, which did not understand the Taiwanese desire for long-term career development and harmonious working relationships, experienced severe problems in attracting and retaining the most talented candidates in the labour market.

Reward and Performance

Taiwan has implemented a minimum wage system since 1984. The minimum wage, also known as the basic wage, is the lowest hourly or monthly remuneration that employers may legally pay to workers. Taiwan regularly raises the monthly minimum.

Bonuses are a significant part of compensation, the most important being the Chinese New Year bonus paid in late January or February. Bonuses range from one to six months' salary, and are given by both local and foreign firms. In addition, there is also a separate bonus known as the 'earnings distribution', a form of profit-sharing (see Chapter 15 in this volume). Public companies are required to distribute a percentage of their profits to their employees as a 'share in success' bonus. Since 2008, the earnings distribution bonus has been stated in company accounts as an expense rather than an earnings distribution. This new regulation has affected companies, especially high-tech ones, which relied on this bonus as an incentive compensation scheme to motivate and retain excellent employees. Previously, some high-tech companies in Taiwan had granted huge bonuses to their employees by giving shares instead of a cash distribution. At the same time, as pointed out by the *Asian Wall Street Journal* (2002), investors raised concerns about the adverse impact of this accounting treatment.

Salter et al. (2006) found that compared to their US counterparts, Taiwanese employers, even with a merit pay system, tend to reward most workers (including failing employees) in order to promote group harmony. TSMC, the world's biggest contract chipmaker, planned a performance management and development (PMD) system that would lead to the 5 per cent of its workers with the lowest performance evaluation scores being dismissed. It experienced serious problems: Chairman Morris Chang apologised in May

2009 for the company's mishandling of PMD, saying that TSMC would invite all of its 800 laid-off workers back to work (*Taipei Times*, 2009a).

Employee Relations

Low-wage workers tend to be temporary or part-time workers, whose work usually does not require a high level of skills, who are easily replaced, or whose work can be moved to another location with little effort. In recent years, Taiwanese enterprises have increasingly been hiring temporary workers from manpower dispatching agencies, as they can save labour expenses and enhance flexibility. There are now more than 539 000 dispatched workers in Taiwan (out of a workforce of 10.3 million, or three times as many as when this chapter was published in the first edition), who are employed, in name, by manpower dispatching agencies, but actually work for enterprises that pay the agencies directly. Dispatched workers are paid much less than regular workers, although they undertake almost the same job duties. What is worrying about the downside of the practice is that the government Ministry of Labour Affairs plans, in 2016, to revise the Labour Standards Law to block some high-risk or highly specialised businesses from hiring dispatched workers – such businesses include healthcare, security, aviation, navigation, public transportation drivers, and mining – and to limit the percentage of dispatched workers to a maximum of 3 per cent for each company.

The Labour Standards Act (LSA) adopted in 1984 is the basic labour law in Taiwan. The LSA regulates every aspect of the employment relationship, including minimum wage, overtime pay, work hours, work rules, labour contracts, leave of absence, women workers and child workers, retirement age and pensions, compensation for occupational accidents, and labour–management negotiations. Since December 1998, the law has been extended to cover all employer–employee relationships, with very few exceptions. From 1 January 2001, the maximum number of work hours is 44 regular hours per week, and no more than 84 hours every two weeks.

The Taiwan Labour Insurance Act (LIA) guarantees retirement, disability, death, and unemployment benefits to Taiwanese workers. The insurance is funded by a combination of contributions from employees, employers, and the government. The Act was amended in 2004. Since then, instead of a lump sum payment upon retirement, annuity payments have been required. Under the LIA, all companies with at least five employees are required to participate. Foreign employees in Taiwan are also covered by the Labour Insurance Act.

Taiwan has updated its occupational safety and health regulations, effective 3 July 2014, to expand the law's coverage to all workers, including the self-employed, and this must be observed by all employers in all industries. The law gives workers the right to evacuate and take shelter in the case of emergencies. The law was also amended to guard against the poor health outcomes of 'excessive overwork'. It requires that employers have preventive measures in place against mental and ergonomic stress-induced ailments or injuries in the workplace.

In Taiwan, many categories of workers, including teachers and doctors, are not allowed to form a labour union. Collective agreements are still rare, and it is hard to hold a legal strike. In the case of labour problems and conflicts, the Labour Union Law and the Law on Settlement of Labour Disputes stipulate general procedures for reaching an employer–workers agreement. Failing an agreement, a long procedure must be followed prior to calling a strike. Workers may approach the government authorities in the event of a violation of their rights or in the event of labour disputes. In 2008 (according to the Council of Labor Affairs) there were 24 540 events of this type which involved 65 274 people (*Taipei Times*, 2009b).

Diversity Management

The Employment Services Act (ESA) of 1992 guarantees equal job opportunities and access to employment services, with the objective of balancing the manpower supply and demand, efficiently using human resources, and establishing an employment information network. To protect workers' rights during times of economic slowdown, the ESA stipulates that the central government should encourage management, labour unions, and workers in negotiating working hour reductions, wage adjustments, and in-service training to avoid lay-offs. Under the ESA, employment discrimination evaluation committees have been established throughout the country. These committees, formed by government, labour, management representatives, scholars, and experts, aim to ensure equal employment opportunities.

However, despite the election of the first female President in the election of January 2016, women in Taiwan have a long way to go to achieve equality with men. Similarly, young men in contingency and temporary work will rarely achieve the job security held by older men. The ageing workforce, which is typical in Taiwanese organisations, should give opportunities for the young and for women, but employers seek to avoid government (and in the case of international employers, head office) endeavours to support diversity in the workplace. Retiring men are replaced by temporary workers, or jobs are subcontracted to small firms that can escape regulations applying to larger companies.

Likely Future Trends

Taiwan is an export-dependent economy subject to the rises and falls in global trade that eventually affect the inflow and outflow of human resources at various levels. Many foreign workers want jobs in Taiwan because of its relatively high minimum wages. The number of foreign workers reached 374 000 in July 2008 before the financial turmoil, but has continued to grow in the past few years to reach 513 570 in 2015. In the meantime, however, more and more Taiwanese work in mainland China, with Boyce (2016) claiming that at least 200 000 Taiwanese live and work in Shanghai alone. There are particular opportunities for mid-career-level professionals in the companies that expand to China. Expatriation to China is often seen as a shortcut to promotion for these lower-level managers.

As stated, despite recent tensions, the ties between China and Taiwan have improved dramatically in recent years. A noteworthy change in policy is that the Taiwan Ministry of Education (MOE) has decided to recognise diplomas conferred by 41 prestigious universities in China. This policy change had been under heated debate for years, not only because education and credentials are regarded as the most instrumental means for upward mobility in Chinese society (Huang & Cullen, 2001), but also because education plays an important role in the formation of national identity – a sensitive issue in Taiwan and the PRC.

Despite protests from critics, the MOE is intending to allow mainland Chinese graduate students to pursue master's degree courses at Taiwan's public universities, while local private universities will be permitted to enrol college students from China, not least because of a shortage of local student numbers. It is believed that a shift in policies will also encourage even more Taiwanese students to seek their higher education in China. Those Taiwanese who had previously received diplomas from PRC universities (estimated to be more than 18 000) can now seek accreditation and find attractive jobs in Taiwan. Taiwan is well placed when competing with foreign countries in trade with China, due to a common language and cultural similarities. If Taiwan succeeds in improving economic cooperation with China, this will have a major impact on HRM on both sides of the Taiwan Strait. It could be argued that the mainland will have much learning to gain from Taiwan's HRM practices.

The second decade of the twenty-first century continues to be challenging for Taiwan, and is a pivotal point for change in Taiwan's development of human resources as well as for its economy. Taiwan signed an economic cooperation framework agreement (ECFA) with mainland China in June 2010. However, Taiwan is increasing its efforts to seal free trade agreements (FTAs) with other countries on the ground that, now that an ECFA has been signed, other countries will be more willing to sign FTAs with Taiwan because PRC opposition will be less.

FINAL OVERVIEW

In the discussion of HRM in Japan, South Korea, and Taiwan we have seen how these countries are meeting the demands of changing economic circumstances and coping with the social consequences of declining certainty and predictability in business and finance. The rise of the PRC's power and influence has serious implications for each of these three countries, not least in their ability to make best use of their human resources. The importation of Western methods of managing human resources as a means of tackling these changes has led to the reduced use of seniority systems for promotion and the introduction of individual performance management, greater use of temporary workers, and a widening gap between the large and small companies. Many individual workers and smaller firms have been badly hit by competition from China and South-East Asia, where the larger companies have outsourced production.

Each country is facing severe problems on the status, access to social security, pension, and social support of the 'atypical' workers who have suffered most from cost-cutting and outsourcing production. These atypical workers (who have become increasingly typical since the first edition of this book) miss out on training, career development, and the protection of HRM policies that are given to regular workers. Among the atypical workers in traditional organisations are female workers, who are seen as temporary workers (with little more security than agency and dispatch workers). From societies' viewpoint, particularly where the available citizen workforce is declining, the neglect of the human capital present in the female population is a great waste of human resources.

It is possible, however, that among those whom outsiders consider the 'typical' workers, less obvious but just as damaging changes are taking place. The motivation of these typical workers has been severely damaged by the uncertainty around career progression and employment stability. Younger workers are increasingly reluctant to accept punishing work schedules and regimes in the expectation that, as they rise in the organisation, their interests and aspirations will be protected. The disillusionment now felt by the employees in many Japanese, South Korean, and Taiwanese organisations is likely to lead to issues around quality of output, cover-up of malpractice, workplace stress (leading to higher rates of psychological problems and higher levels of suicide), and declining trust in established powers and order within societies. The complacency and closeness between companies and regulators shown in such incidents as the Korean ferry MV *Sewol* disaster (see various BBC reports, 2015), concern over work practices such as those of Foxconn (Barboza & Duhigg, 2012), and the apparent malpractices of top management in accounting scandals such as that of Toshiba (*Japan Times*, 2015), are all symbols of what needs to be improved in workplaces within these three countries, despite them being far in advance of many other places in east Asia.

The 'working together' which was such a strength for these organisations may have been severely damaged by the introduction of Western management techniques which focused on the individual and the short term at the cost of the group, society, and long-term prosperity. The homogeneity within the communities and organisations which enabled malpractices to be hidden also provides incentives to work together for the apparent greater good, so giving more long-term strength to the societies and states which offer a different model to that of diversity and individualism encouraged in much of the post-industrial regions. It will be interesting to see how these different models and prosper/not prosper in by time the next edition of this book is written.

Endnote

The authors undertook the writing of this chapter as a collaborative effort, applying and sharing knowledge together. In the process it is hoped that we introduce the reader to greater understanding of the changes in the means of managing human resources in these countries. Those of the authors who were raised outside Asia have lived in the region for several decades between them, bringing more than transient knowledge to this chapter. Meanwhile those whose heritage is entirely in East Asia have shared their deep understanding with the reader in the hope of fostering greater understanding of these fascinating, complex countries.

REFERENCES

Asian Wall Street Journal. 2002. 18 July, p. 1.
Barboza, D., & Duhigg, C. 2012. China plant again faces labor issues on iPhones. *New York Times*, p. B1.
BBC. 2015. Sewol ferry: S. Korea court gives captain life sentence for murder. http://www.bbc.com/news/world-asia-32492263 accessed 30/01/2016.
Boyce, J. 2016. Shanghai surprise. *American Chamber of Commerce Taipei Cover Story*, January: 3.
Chen, D.S. 2010. Higher Education in Taiwan: The crisis of rapid expansion. www.isa-sociology.org/universities-in-crisis. Accessed 21 January 2016.
CIA. 2016. Korea factsheet. www.cia.gov/library/publications/the-world-factbook/geos/ks.html. Accessed 15 February.

Debroux, P. 2013. Human resource management in Japan. In A. Varma and P. Budhwar (eds), *Managing Human Resources in Asia-Pacific*: 105–128. London: Routledge.

Dessler, G., & Tan, C.-H. 2009. *Human Resource management, An Asian Perspective*. Singapore: Pearson Education.

Dore, R. 1973. *British Factory – Japanese Factory*. London: Allen & Unwin.

Economic Daily News. 2001. Acer announces second layoff in last month due to PC slowdown. 5 March, p. 5.

The Economist. 2015. The family-run behemoth secures a fiercely contested in-house merger. 17 July, p. 61.

Fei, T.Y. 1990. Training as a long term planning. *Management Magazine*, 194: 168–171.

Hayashi, S. 2011. Human resource management in Japan. In C. Brewster and W. Mayrhofer (eds), *Handbook on Comparative Human Resource Management*. Cheltenham, UK and Northampton, MA, USA: Edward Elgar Publishing.

Hemmert, M. 2009. Management in Korea. In H. Hasegawa and C. Noronha (eds), *Asian Business and Management, Theory, Practice and Perspectives*: 241–255. London: Palgrave.

Hentschel, B., & Haghirian, P. 2010. Nonaka revisited: Can Japanese companies sustain their knowledge management processes in the 21st century?. In P. Haghirian (ed.), *Innovation and Change in Japanese Management*: 199–220. Basingstoke: Palgrave Macmillan.

Hirano, M. 2011. Diversification of employment categories in Japanese firms and its functionality. In R. Bebenroth and T. Kanai (eds), *Challenges of Human Resources in Japan*. Abingdon: Routledge.

Hirschmeyer, J., & Yui, T. 2006. *Development of Japanese Business*: Taylor & Francis.

Hsu, Y.-R., & Leat, M. 2000. A study of HRM and recruitment and selection policies and practices in Taiwan. *International Journal of Human Resource Management*, 11(2): 413–435.

Hu, M.-C., Zheng, C., & Lamond, D. 2007. Recruitment and retention of ICT skills among MNCs in Taiwan. *Chinese Management Studies*, 1(2): 78–92.

Huang, H.J., & Cullen, J.B. 2001. Labour flexibility and related HRM practices: A study of large Taiwanese manufacturers. *Canadian Journal of Administrative Sciences/Revue Canadienne des Sciences de l'Administration*, 18(1): 33–39.

Huo, Y.P., Huang, H.J., & Napier, N.K. 2002. Divergence or convergence: A cross-national comparison of personnel selection practices. *Human Resource Management*, 41(1): 31–44.

Hwang, S.-K. 2006. Wage structure and skill development in Korea. Korea Labour Institute.

Japan Times. 2015. Pressure to show a profit led to Toshiba's accounting scandal. http://www.japantimes.co.jp/news/2015/09/18/business/corporate-business/pressure-to-show-a-profit-led-to-toshibas-accounting-scandal/#.VqxkKFk3Njl. Accessed 30 January 2016.

Jones, R.S., & Urasawa, S. 2011. Labour market reforms in Japan to improve growth and equity. Economics Department Working Papers No. 889. Paris: OECD.

Kawaguchi, A. 2013. Equal Employment Opportunity Act and work–life balance: Do work–family balance policies contribute to achieving gender equality?. *Japan Labour Review*, 10(2): 35–56.

Kim, D.-O., & Bae, J. 2004. *Employment Relations and HRM in South Korea*. Aldershot: Ashgate.

Korea JoongAng Daily. 2016. More red tape cut for President. 19 January, p. 1.

Lazear, E.P. 1979. Why is there mandatory retirement?. *Journal of Political Economy*, 81(6): 1261–1284.

Lin, C.Y. 1996. Training and development practices in Taiwan: A comparison of Taiwanese, American and Japanese firms. *Asia Pacific Journal of Human Resources*, 34(1): 26–43.

Magoshi, E., & Chang, E. 2009. Diversity management and the effects on employees' organizational commitment: Evidence from Japan and Korea. *Journal of World Business*, 44(1): 31–40.

Matanle, P. 2003. *Japanese Capitalism and Modernity in a Global Era: Re-fabricating Lifetime Employment Relations*. London, UK and New York, USA: Routledge-Curzon.

Miles, L., Kirkbride, J., & Howells, G. 2008. The significance of cultural norms in the evolution of Korean HRM practices. *International Journal of Law and Management*, 50(1): 33–46.

Ministry of Health, Labour and Welfare (MHLW). 2014. White Paper on the Labor Economy. Tokyo.

Miyamoto, T., & Grainger, R. 2007. Management in Japan: Contemporary issues. In S. Chatterjee and A. Nankervis (eds), *Asian Management in Transition*. Basingstoke: Palgrave Macmillan.

Nakamura, K. 2006. *Seika Shugi no Jijitsu*. Tokyo: Toyo Keizai Shinposha.

Nakata, Y., & Miyazaki, S. 2011. Have Japanese engineers changed?. In H. Miyoshi and Y. Nakata (eds), *Have Japanese Firms Changed?*. Basingstoke: Palgrave Macmillan.

Nitta, M. 2009. *Nihonteki Koyo System*. Tokyo: Nakanishiya Shuppan.

OECD. 2015. *Economic Survey of Japan*. Paris: OECD.

Salter, S.B., Brody, R.G., & Lin, S. 2006. Merit pay, responsibility, and national values: A US–Taiwan comparison. *Journal of International Accounting Research*, 5(2): 63–79.

Sasajima, Y. 2012. Nihon no Chingin Seido: Kako, Genzai soshite Mirai. *Meiji Gakuin Daigaku*, 145(1): Tokyo.

Schaede, U. 2008. *Choose and Focus: Japan's Business Strategies for the 21st Century*. Ithaca, NY: Cornell University Press.

Song, J. 2014. *Inequality in the Workplace: Labour Market Reform in Japan and Korea*. Ithaca, NY, USA and London, UK: Cornell University Press.

Sueki, N. 2012. *21 Seiki Nihon no chinginzo wo egaku*. Tokyo: Nihon Seisansei Honbu.

Sugimoto, Y. 2010. *An Introduction to Japanese Society*. Cambridge: Cambridge University Press.

Taipei Times. 2009a. Chairman Morris Chang apology. 25 May, p. 12.

Taipei Times. 2009b. Council of Labor Affairs (CLA), 24 August.

Taipei Times. 2015. www.taipeitimes.com/News/front/archives/2015/01/26/2003610092. Accessed 30 January 2016.

Tselichtchev, I., & Debroux, P. 2009. *Asia's Turning Point*. Singapore: John Wiley & Sons.

32. Comparative HRM research in Indonesia, Malaysia, and the Philippines

Vivien T. Supangco and Jessica A. Los Baños

INTRODUCTION

Over the last half-century there has been an increasing integration of economies driven by trade, business, and economic activity across borders, entailing movement of people, capital, and other resources, and enabled by phenomenal advances in telecommunications and air transportation. As companies in both advanced and developing economies scan the globe for opportunities to gain superior competitive advantage, Asia is a logical target as it is the largest and most populous continent in the world.

Amidst challenges of globalising operations, the management of human resources holds the key to the success of international firms (Bao & Analoui, 2011). Research has consistently shown that the effectiveness of human resource management (HRM) practices depends on the context or the fit between HRM practices and the host countries (Fey et al., 2009). Comparative human resource management research is important, as it looks at how human resources are managed in different countries and complements research on how firms operating in different countries manage their human resources (Boxall, 1995).

Given the importance of Asia as an attractive region for locating subsidiaries, not only because of lower labour and other costs but also because of its market potential, more studies are needed to understand HRM in this region. Asia can be divided into East Asia, South-East Asia, South Asia, Central Asia, and West Asia, with divergent cultures and economic development statuses. As the continent is far from homogenous, it is instructive to focus on sub-regions, especially those that have received little attention in HRM research to date.

In this chapter, we focus on HRM studies in the part of South-East Asia that includes Indonesia, Malaysia, and the Philippines. These are three countries with a shared history and a shared ethnic lineage, the Malays. These countries have been dubbed the 'tiger cubs' of Asia, and we are only beginning to take notice of them. Thus, to better understand HRM practices in these countries, we examine what comparative studies have been conducted regarding HRM here.

HISTORICAL BACKGROUND

The present Indonesians and Malays (of Malaysia) and Filipinos are a product of evolution and migration, and form an ethnic group (Jocano, 1975). They belonged to the same population sharing a common cultural orientation (Agoncillo, 2012), and share the same experience of being colonised, albeit by different colonisers. Indonesia was colonised by the Portuguese and the Dutch, Malaysia by the British, and the Philippines by the Spaniards and later by the United States of America (USA).

In 1963, the heads of the three countries, Tunku Abdul Rahman (Federation of Malaya), Diosdado Macapagal (Philippines), and Sukarno (Indonesia) signed the Manila Declaration, which laid down principles of equal rights and self-determination, fraternal relations, and the need to fight colonialism and build a new and better world. These principles were intended to guide the three countries in dealing with each other. The Manila Declaration, also known as the Maphilindo (Malaysia, Philippines, and Indonesia), was short-lived. In an issue over whether or not Sabah (North Borneo) and Sarawak should join the Federation of Malaysia, in 1963, along with Malaysia and Singapore, the guidelines in Maphilindo indicated that a plebiscite under the auspices of the United Nations (UN) Secretariat be conducted to determine the desires of the peoples of these two nations. While the result indicated positive votes from these nations, Indonesia and the Philippines objected, citing pressures from the United Kingdom. So the Philippines and Indonesia severed diplomatic ties with Malaysia (Agoncillo, 2012).

Soon after, diplomatic ties were re-established with Malaysia and the Philippines, and between Malaysia and Indonesia. The Association of Southeast Asian Nations (ASEAN) was established in 1967 in order to address socio-economic and cultural challenges confronting the region. The initial members of ASEAN were Indonesia, Malaysia, the Philippines, Singapore, and Thailand. Current membership in ASEAN has increased to include Brunei, Cambodia, Laos, Myanmar, and Vietnam (Agoncillo, 2012).

In 2003, leaders agreed to establish an economic community to position ASEAN as a competitive, prosperous, and stable region even as it pursues goals of equitable economic development and reduced poverty and other forms of socio-economic inequity. At the end of 2015, the ASEAN Economic Community (AEC) was formally established (ASEAN, 2015). Within the ASEAN region, members have easier access to resources, including human resources. This will have a significant impact on HRM as human capital mobility will increase, and with it the challenges to quality and standards of skills, as well as the challenges of managing a diverse workforce. In addition, firms that cater only to the domestic market will have to contend with more competition.

METHODOLOGY

Before we discuss the studies conducted on comparative HRM involving Indonesia, Malaysia, and the Philippines, we provide a brief discussion on what we mean by HRM, comparative HRM, and international HRM. It is important to identify how we approach the review of what has been written on comparative HRM inasmuch as the approach utilised determines how comparative and international HRM are defined and what articles are ultimately reviewed (Dowling, 1999).

International HRM is concerned with ways in which a firm manages its human resources across different subsidiaries. In other words, the focal point is the firm and its attendant international HRM issues (Boxall, 1995). On the other hand, comparative HRM focuses on the differences and similarities in the ways organisations in different countries manage human resources (Boxall, 1995; Brewster, 2006). Further, if comparative HRM is to contribute to theory-building, research should go beyond description: it is ultimately concerned with explanation that leads to a better understanding of important social and economic outcomes (Boxall, 1995).

Most studies that review articles on comparative HRM (Clark et al., 1999b; Clark et al., 1999a; Baruch, 2001; Ozbilgin, 2004) use as a starting point articles published in top HRM journals (as identified in the study by Caligiuri, 1999), and specify a period under study. Such studies have revealed the surge of research in the area of comparative and international HRM since 1993 (Clark et al., 1999b; Clark et al., 1999a). Moreover, these studies reveal that memberships of editorial boards (Ozbilgin, 2004) and authorships of articles (Clark et al., 1999b; Clark et al., 1999a; Baruch, 2001; Gonzalez et al., 2001) mostly come from Anglo-Saxon countries. Moreover, editorial boards consider the quality of articles on international management published in journals outside these countries to be doubtful (Boyacigiller & Adler, 1991).

Given this landscape, we pursue our review of comparative HRM research involving Indonesia, Malaysia, and the Philippines by looking at articles on HRM in their broadest sense, that is, covering any HRM functional areas such as work design, recruitment, training, compensation, performance management, and industrial relations, among others. We scanned articles that pertain to HRM which involved two or more countries regardless of publication date. In the context of globalisation, we paid particular attention to studies that address the global–local question, whether international firms adapt to local conditions, or whether local firms imitate the practices of multinational companies (Edwards & Kuruvilla, 2005). The main criterion, however, for including an article in this chapter is the approach to comparative or international HRM research used. An article is included in the review if it discusses the HRM of Indonesia, Malaysia, and the Philippines, using any of the following approaches: comparative; a combination of comparative and international; and comparing multinational corporations (MNCs) with any of the focal countries as the base.

In order to structure our review, we examined the types of articles written and looked at the major factors used in describing and analysing the situations in each country. In our presentation, we divided the articles into qualitative and quantitative. For the qualitative articles, we further categorised the articles in terms of the dominant environmental context used in the presentation and analyses. These environmental contexts include political, legal, economic, social including cultural, and technological (Aguilar, 1967). For quantitative articles, we categorised them in terms of the HRM practice areas that are studied. The groupings include recruitment and selection, training and development, performance management and compensation, industrial relations, and an 'others' category.

Comparative HRM articles that focus on Asia mostly deal with the more progressive economies such as China (Bao & Analoui, 2011; Smale et al., 2012; Wang-Cowham, 2008), Hong Kong and Singapore (Paik et al., 1996), South Korea (Bae et al., 2011), Taiwan (Sauers et al., 2009), and Thailand (Bartlett et al., 2002). To complement these, the articles included in this chapter may not be exhaustive but they give us a glimpse of the comparative HRM research that covers Indonesia, Malaysia, and the Philippines.

There are several articles that explore the HRM of specific countries. We include these articles to reinforce the scant studies of a comparative nature covering Indonesia, Malaysia, and the Philippines. We first describe the articles and find some patterns, commonalities, and differences within each country and across the three countries. Selected articles specific to Indonesia include Bennington & Habir (2003), Caraway (2004), Habir and Larasati (1999), Los Baños & Utama (2013), and Mamman & Somantri (2014). Selected articles specific to Malaysia include Azmi (2015), Ling & Nasurdin (2010), Man (2012), and Suan and Nasurdin (2014). Selected articles specific to the Philippines include Amante (1997), Selmer & de Leon (2001) and Supangco (2004, 2006, 2012).

QUALITATIVE STUDIES

One of the most important contextual factors in HRM is the legal, regulatory, and standards environment. This environment is composed of local laws as well as labour standards set by a body such as the International Labour Organization (ILO). Ratification of a labour convention signifies a member country's commitment to standards by applying them to national laws and practice (ILO, 1996–2016). The implication of applying a convention to each nation's laws is that it paves the way for the convergence of legal frameworks of HRM among member countries, including Indonesia, Malaysia, and the Philippines (ASETUC, 2013).

Most countries in ASEAN, including Indonesia, Malaysia, and the Philippines, have laws that prohibit the discrimination of employment based on sex. There is, however, a need to improve the implementation of these laws as many women in these countries – with the exception of the Philippines – still experience vertical job segregation as well as occupational segregation, which lead to wage discrimination (ASETUC, 2013). In contrast, despite no country in the ASEAN having ratified the convention on workers with family responsibilities as well as maternity protection, most ASEAN organisations do have policies on work–life balance as well as shared family responsibilities. In addition, most ASEAN countries also have systems of maternity protection, and while they vary in scope, they are similar in the sense that employers provide paid maternity leave (ASETUC, 2013).

Six ASEAN countries including Indonesia, Malaysia, and the Philippines ratified the UN Convention on the Rights of Persons with Disabilities in 2012 (ASETUC, 2013). With such ratification, these countries have established national laws addressing the concerns of persons with disabilities. In another area, Indonesia, Malaysia, and the Philippines have laws that recognise the right to form unions as a basic right, and organisations exercise social dialogues especially during times when industrial peace is challenged (ASETUC, 2013).

In addition to the legal-political environment, the economic context of an organisation also influences the management of its human resources. However, economic and legal-political factors are closely interrelated and mutually reinforcing. A country's choice of how it wants to compete in the world market significantly influences its framework of industrial relations (IR) and HRM (Kuruvilla, 1996a; Kuruvilla, 1996b; Yoon, 2009).

National policies are important for firms to compete in the global economy. Industrial peace was seen as the way to rapid industrialisation during the decades of the 1960s to the 1980s (Yoon, 2009). Low labour costs held the key to competing in the early stage of export-oriented industrialisation, and in attracting foreign investment (Kuruvilla, 1996a). But as globalisation grew, countries in Asia faced intense competition, to which firms responded by being flexible in both costs and numbers. These developments were facilitated by legislation in support of labour market flexibility, resulting in non-regular forms of employment, thereby eroding the traditional basis of trade union and collective bargaining at the enterprise level (Yoon, 2009).

Moreover, in order to attract foreign investment, the labour movement must be able to resolve labour issues promptly. As the industrialisation strategy moves on to a higher-value-added export orientation, increased skills and labour productivity become important, where labour does not resist the introduction of new technology. It also requires firms to develop the flexibility needed to respond to the changing nature of a global marketplace. Such flexibility should allow firms to change labour force numbers and compensation as well as work assignments (Kuruvilla, 1996a). These dynamics also impact upon HRM at the firm level (Kuruvilla, 1996b).

Thus when Malaysia and the Philippines pursued primarily export-oriented industrialisation (EOI), the logical response was to contain wages. There were even moves to curtail union initiatives. When Malaysia transitioned to secondary export-oriented industrialisation, the response was to develop skills and productivity coupled with workplace flexibility. It is apparent that changes in industrialisation strategies influenced changes in IR and HRM policies. The two countries tended to adopt more repressive IR policies, although the dynamics and causes differed (Kuruvilla, 1996a). In Malaysia, the change to more repressive IR policies was gradual and was seen as a means to attract foreign investment. In the Philippines, repressive IR policies were resorted to in order to maintain low labour costs (Kuruvilla, 1996a). At the firm level, import substitution industry sectors – those that produce consumer capital such as automobiles, intermediate goods like petrochemicals, and capital goods such as machinery, which lessen dependence on imports and conserve foreign exchange (Kuruvilla, 1996a) – in Malaysia and the Philippines have IR/HRM policies that are passive and paternalistic compared to firms in the export-oriented sector that have IR/HRM policies that are dynamic and flexible (Kuruvilla, 1996b).

Thus IR in East Asia including Indonesia, Malaysia, and the Philippines has experienced tremendous changes, whereby the relative stability of the 1960s to 1980s has been supplanted with conflicts starting in the early 1990s. Nevertheless, enterprise bargaining still persists in Indonesia, Malaysia, and the Philippines. This is because of government imposition of enterprise unionism in the case of Malaysia; and in the case of Indonesia and the Philippines, because of the fragmented structure of unionism, which renders the union incapable of engaging in collective bargaining beyond the enterprise level (Yoon, 2009).

QUANTITATIVE STUDIES

Most comparative HRM articles adopting a quantitative methodology focus on specific HRM practices. Thus, to provide structure here, we categorise the articles according to the HRM practices examined.

Recruitment

One stream of research in comparative HRM is the comparison of practices in local organisations with those in MNCs operating in a particular country. Japan, being a developed country in Asia, has considerable investments in other countries in Asia, such as Malaysia and the Philippines, so many studies are devoted to comparing local HRM practices with Japanese HRM practices (Amante, 1993; Hooi, 2008).

Japan is known to utilise the internal labour market. New hires come straight from college, without work experience, are further trained and developed, provided with information to equip them for participation in decision-making, and are provided with decent welfare facilities. These practices result in teamwork, and healthy labour–management relations, which is reinforced by an enterprise-based union and long-term employment (Amante, 1993; Hooi, 2008; see also Chapter 31 in this volume). Although also in Asia, it appears that Japanese recruitment practices are not readily transferrable to Malaysia or the Philippines (Hooi, 2008; Amante, 1993). In the absence of an internal labour market, recruitment is triggered by a vacancy, thus employees are hired at any level in the organisation (Hooi, 2008). Work experience becomes critical in hiring employees at levels higher than the entry level, such that training becomes less important, especially for skills that are commonly available in the market. On the other hand, internalisation of labour markets in the Philippines is hindered by minimum wage legislation that tends to emphasise job-based structures, and which leads employees to move in search of higher wages, thus resulting in high turnover rates. Moreover, there is the tendency to settle work relations issues through the legal system rather than internally (Amante, 1993).

Training and Development

A study of training practices of MNCs in six Asian countries, including Indonesia, Malaysia, and the Philippines, showed that MNCs invest a significant amount in training, particularly in the services sector (Zheng et al., 2007). For example, the percentage of non-Asian-owned MNCs that spend more than USD$1000 per employee per year on training is higher compared to that of Asian-owned MNCs. Larger firms are also known to provide more training compared to smaller firms.

Moreover, a comparative study of management development practices of MNCs and domestic firms in the Philippines, using the resource-based view of the firm and institutional theory as frameworks of analysis, showed that investment in management development was higher in MNCs. From the perspective of institutional theory, MNCs are conspicuous in the community, and that pressures them to ensure the legitimacy of their actions (Di Maggio & Powell, 1983; Deephouse, 1996). However, it is management development, whether measured in terms of investment or comprehensiveness of training programmes, and not a firm's multinational status, that influences perceived organisational performance (Supangco, 2003). This finding provides support for the resource-based view of the firm, where a firm gains competitive advantage when it is able to transform its resources into being more valuable, rare, inimitable, and non-substitutable (Barney, 1991).

Compensation

One of the functions that supports the retention effort is compensation. A compensation system must be able to attract, motivate, and retain employees in an organisation. A study of compensation practices across ten countries, including Indonesia, focused on nine practices (Lowe et al., 2002). These practices include incentive pay, benefits relative to total compensation package, pay based on group or organisational performance, long-term versus short-term performance-based pay, seniority-based pay, incentive pay relative to total compensation, level of benefits, future orientation of the pay system, and job performance as a basis in pay raises. Countries in the Americas showed more gaps between practice and the ideal situation, while the Asian countries had at most three practices with large difference scores. Narrowing the gap in these practices is one way to increase performance, satisfaction, and retention (Lowe et al., 2002).

Another study, which covered four countries – Australia, Hong Kong, Indonesia, and Malaysia – explored employee preferences for the criteria used in compensation systems (Mamman et al., 1996). The criteria included 'length of service, educational qualification, skill, market rate, performance, inflation, responsibility, special demands on the job and collective bargaining' (Mamman et al., 1996: 110). Results of the study revealed that employees across the four countries preferred multiple criteria for inclusion in a pay system. Indonesians and Malaysians had almost the same ranking in five of the nine items. To the Indonesians and Malaysians, responsibility was the most important factor in determining pay. Their rankings of educational qualification, length of service, and collective bargaining were higher than the rankings made by Australian employees (Mamman et al., 1996).

HRM Systems

Employee retention is one of the challenges of organisations in order to remain competitive in the long run. Retention starts with recruitment and selection, attracting the right people and selecting the best person for the job. Once hired, the organisation continues to provide the employee with the proper environment, remuneration, and other support for the employee to stay engaged and committed, and to remain in the organisation. All these require that, in addition to recruitment, all the other HRM systems are in place and are congruent with each other. A study of MNCs in the service sector in Indonesia, Malaysia, and the Philippines provides support for the linkages between HRM practices, retention, and service delivery (Zheng, 2009). Compared to Asian MNCs, non-Asian MNCs rely more on the internet, job fairs, and headhunters in recruiting applicants. They also send employees to training off-site, and make use of apprenticeship and traineeship programmes as part of the recruitment process (Zheng, 2009).

Role of the HR Department

In addition to a body of work focusing on HRM practices, some comparative studies explore the roles of the HR department (Bowen et al., 2002; de Guzman et al., 2011), and the transferability of Western, particularly US and Canadian, HRM practices (Galang, 2004).

In a study involving ten countries including Indonesia, the status of the HR department is influenced by organisational capability, particularly in Anglo-Saxon countries; while in Asian countries, HRM status is related to a differentiation strategy (Bowen et al., 2002). Thus there is support for aligning HRM practices with organisational strategy. In a study of HRM roles based on Ulrich's (1997) typology, differences between the actual and ideal scores of the various roles were computed (de Guzman et al., 2011). Respondents perceived themselves as better than ideal in the administrative role. However, although they perceived themselves lower than ideal in the strategic partner role, the difference between actual and ideal was not statistically significant. Moreover, a comparison of scores among countries covered (India, Indonesia, Malaysia, and Philippines) revealed that Indonesians see themselves performing best in the administrative role, while the reverse is true for the strategic partner role. Malaysia and India have similar high difference scores in the strategic partner role, while the Philippines and India have similar low difference scores for the administrative role (de Guzman et al., 2011).

In contrast, a study on the transferability of Western practices in the USA and Canada to other countries was conducted in the Philippines in 1998 as part of a larger study that sought to address the questions of prevalence and effectiveness of HRM practices, and the contingencies that influence HRM practices, among others (Galang, 2004). The study found that most HRM practices prescribed in Western management are also practiced in the Philippines. The HR department in the Philippines enjoys higher status than in the USA and Canada. Across all three countries, the status of the HR department there showed a positive correlation with the most number of HRM practices. The Philippines also had the highest number of practices that were correlated with performance. Across the three countries, and in terms of functional area, the highest number of practices that correlated with performance were in training. The results did not come as a surprise to the authors inasmuch as the Philippines management education is adapted from the US, and because textbooks are written by US authors, practices are heavily influenced by the US.

COUNTRY-SPECIFIC STUDIES

While there is a dearth of studies in comparative HRM covering Indonesia, Malaysia, and the Philippines, we find several country-specific studies, some of which we present here. We look at these country-specific studies and determine patterns within and across countries to enhance our understanding of comparative HRM.

Indonesia

This section discusses studies that are focused on Indonesia. We present qualitative studies first, which provide the context of HRM in Indonesia. These are followed by a study that looked into the roles of HRM in Indonesia.

Social justice is a very important aspect of the Indonesian culture, which affects institutions and influences practices including HRM (Los Banos & Utama, 2013). After obtaining independence from the Dutch in 1945, President Sukarno introduced a political philosophy, the Pancasila, which provides the foundation of Indonesia's legal system. Its fifth pillar, the *Keadilan Sosial bagi Seluruh Rakyat Indonesia*, translates to 'social justice for the whole people of Indonesia', encourages the protection of the weaker sector of society as part of the endeavour to achieve an equitable allocation of resources. Social justice requires that individuals, society, and the country as a whole, aim for a fair distribution of burdens and blessings according to individual capacity to contribute to achieve social solidarity (Los Banos & Utama, 2013). For example, while job opportunities are open to all, only those who have the necessary qualifications are encouraged to apply, because social justice is compromised when performance is not delivered.

Moreover, noting the dearth of HRM research relating to Indonesia, Bennington and Habir (2003) sought to contribute to narrowing the gap. Their study explores the factors that affect HRM in Indonesia: business context, demography, legal and industrial relations context, and general conditions of employment. The study also discusses issues in core HRM functions, MNC HRM practice, the role of HR managers, and an overview of current challenges for HRM in Indonesia. While the study is more than a decade old, some observations may still apply. For example, Indonesia is composed of diverse ethnic groups, which presents a challenge to HRM. In addition, while there may be regulations to protect workers, implementation remains problematic. Problems in implementation are also found in apparent discrimination against women in the form of lower wages and benefits. Thus HRM faces considerable challenges stemming from religious and ethnic tension, labour legislations, and economic pressures for efficiency, even as HR managers play various roles, depending on factors such as organisation size, industry sector, and type of ownership of the business (Bennington & Habir, 2003).

Labour reform in Indonesia is atypical of labour reforms in developing countries, as shown in a study by Caraway (2004). In this study, variables such as the power of the labour movement, ordering of reforms, partisan links, and the strength of employer organisations, identified in comparative studies of labour reform in developing countries, are not able to explain labour reform success in Indonesia. The study's two basic findings relevant to the legal aspects of HRM in Indonesia are interesting. First, as Indonesian workers already enjoy some of the highest protection in all of Asia, it was difficult to take away or reduce the protections during the process of reform. Second, Indonesian law favours the weaker party (labour organisations), thus making it easy in negotiations for the weaker party to defend their position during reform negotiations.

To answer the question, 'What roles do HR managers play in organisations in Indonesia?', Mamman and Somantri (2014), sought to address how HRM practitioners see the role they play in organisations, compared to how line managers see these roles. The study also determined whether or not culture affects the roles played by HR managers. Using Conner and Ulrich's (1996) 'model of HRM roles', the authors conducted a random survey of 140 HR practitioners, and senior and line managers from a parent company and its six subsidiaries. HR practitioners surveyed practiced all four roles, where the role performed most was the 'change agent' while the least-performed was the 'employee champion'. There are differences in how the different groups of managers perceived HRM roles. Senior managers saw HR managers as playing a more strategic role, while line managers perceived them to play more of an administrative role. Despite theorising that, inasmuch as Indonesia is a collective culture and therefore the 'employee champion' role should be more dominant, results showed that this was in fact the least-performed amongst the four roles, suggesting that bureaucratic rationalism and a labour relations system skewed against workers may have been more significant in influencing HR practitioners' roles.

The above selected articles present varied interests that collectively provide us with a comprehensive overview of HRM in Indonesia. It operates within a context of laws designed to be pro-worker. We note that the labour relations system in Indonesia is statutorily pro-worker, consistent with the notion of social justice as one of the five pillars of the Pancasila. This is highlighted with the passage of Act Number 13 Year 2003 concerning manpower. However, implementation is weak. In addition, due to its demographic, ethnic, and cultural diversity, HRM in Indonesia faces enormous challenges.

Malaysia

Three of the selected studies on HRM in Malaysia use surveys exploring the relationship between HRM practices and outcomes such as performance (Azmi, 2015), work engagement (Suan & Nasurdin, 2014), and innovation (Ling & Nasurdin, 2010). The HRM practices studied include Islamic recruitment, training, career development, compensation and rewards, and performance management (Azmi, 2015); service training, service rewards, performance appraisal, and information-sharing (Suan & Nasurdin, 2014); and recruitment, training, career management, performance appraisal, and reward systems (Ling & Nasurdin, 2010). Performance appraisal was shown to be positively related with work engagement (Suan & Nasurdin, 2014) and administrative innovation (Ling & Nasurdin, 2010). In addition, the three studies share a common finding that training is positively related with the different outcomes, providing positive feedback to Malaysian government efforts to enhance human resource development (HRD) embodied in its Malaysia Vision 2020. As Malaysia shifted its industrialisation strategy from low-cost labour towards skilled labour, it recognised the need to develop its human resources to achieve Vision 2020. The government intensified its effort in HRD where it embarked on joint programmes with industry, public research and development institutions, and universities (Man, 2012). In facilitating development of human resources, Malaysia looked to Japan as its role model. With the Look East policy in the 1980s, the government under Prime Minister Tun Dato' Seri Dr Mahathir Bin Mohammad encouraged organisations to implement Japanese management policies. The essence of Japanese-style management to be emulated included education, the industrial system, and management of human resources (Man, 2012). Thus Japanese MNCs have become the benchmark when comparing HRM practices of local Malaysian organisations.

In summary, the selected articles on HRM in Malaysia point to the relationships between HRM practices with varied measures of performance. The articles all reveal the significant relationship between training, including Islamic training practices, and the varied measures of performance. These results are in keeping with a national policy of intensifying HRD at the national level in support of Vision 2020.

Philippines

Two qualitative studies on HRM in the Philippines deal with determining the distinguishing elements of HRM there (Selmer & De Leon, 2001; Amante, 1997). The three quantitative studies included in this section examine strategic HRM. One explored the involvement of the HR department in strategic decision-making (Supangco, 2004), another in corporate governance (Supangco, 2006), and a third provides an overview of strategic HRM practices in selected organisations in the Philippines (Supangco, 2012).

The motivation of the study by Selmer and de Leon (2001) was based on two factors: the Philippines' exclusion from a comparative HRM study across Asia (Bae et al., 1998), and the inadequacy of any literature on HRM in the Philippines in international academic journals. Selmer and de Leon's (2001) analyses are based on secondary data using culture, economics, and globalisation as the contextual frameworks. Due to the Philippines' exposure to the Americans, when it was a colony of the USA from 1898 to 1946, much of its law is patterned on American laws (Pangalangan, 2010). Philippines HRM is guided by a Labour Code (Selmer & De Leon, 2001; Amante, 1997). Although Filipino managers and workers in general may seem Westernised, the Filipino culture permeates HRM. While Filipinos like to work in groups, this is not translated into organisational commitment, thus limiting the transferability of Japanese-style management to the Philippines (Tomita, 1983, in Selmer & De Leon, 2001). The non-transferability of Japanese-style management was also reported in Amante (1993). Moreover, Filipinos value positive interpersonal relationships, reciprocity, and a sense of shame. Thus there is a tendency to avoid conflict, and in any feedback or confrontation, losing face should be avoided. Cited in Selmer and de Leon (2001) is Amante's (1993, 1997) finding that although formal requirements such as police clearance, certificate of employment, and diplomas are required in recruitment, personal connections in the organisation increase one's chances of getting a job. However, this finding is not corroborated in Galang's (2004) study, which showed that hiring based on criteria of proven work experience in a similar job was among the top five practices, whereas using the right connections as a criterion in hiring ranked among the bottom five practices.

In contrast, Amante (1997) studied seven organisations and identified the divergence and convergence of HRM practices. HRM is identified as a set of practices that developed from the West, emphasising a strategic approach to HRM with an emphasis on HRD. On the other hand, IR was basically seen as concerned with adherence to labour standards amidst adversarial labour relations. Given adverse economic pressures experienced by the Philippines in the 1980s and 1990s, HRM was thus considered a means of achieving innovation in managing human resources, the goal of which was to have a multiskilled workforce and organisational flexibility in terms of number of employees, and in wage determination. At the national level, the emphasis of both the government and employers on HRD converged. This was seen as leverage in achieving non-adversarial and voluntary modes of handling labour relations. At the enterprise level, Labour–Management Councils (LMCs) provide one venue for the convergence of HRM strategies, especially since these LMCs accommodate cultural values.

A study of strategic HRM practices in selected organisations in the Philippines (Supangco, 2012) provides an overview of HRM practices. The objectives of the study were to describe strategic HRM in selected Philippine organisations and to compare results of the 2003 and 2008 Cranet surveys (for Cranet, see Brewster et al., 2004; Parry et al., 2013). In order to identify which practices to include in the analyses, the author synthesised the meanings of strategic HRM. As a process, strategic HRM involves a long-term outlook with active involvement in the activities of the board, specifically being involved in strategic formulation from the beginning of the process. As a set of activities, strategic HRM involves those that are high-value-adding, enabled by computerised HR information system (HRIS), and external providers to undertake low-value-adding activities. Given this conception of strategic HRM, practices in the Philippines took on a strategic approach where formal strategic planning took place; however, the HR department was not yet involved in strategy formulation from the outset. In addition, companies had not yet fully utilised the outsourcing of non-value-adding HRM activities. However, organisations use an HRIS for payroll, benefits, attendance, and personal records. Some

HRM practices did not change between the two survey periods (2003 and 2008), such as training and compensation, although utilisation of HRIS has increased.

An earlier work by Supangco (2004) explored the relationship between the HR department's involvement in strategy formulation and its consequences, employing three perspectives, namely: the resource based-view of the firm, institutional theory, and power. Results show that involving the HR department in strategy formulation is not always translated into competitive advantage. However, should involving the HR department be important to an organisation in gaining legitimacy, involvement is realised when the proper structure is in place, that is, when the HR head sits on the board. In addition, the study found that organisational age is not a deterrent to the adoption of the practice of involving HR specialists in strategy formulation.

In addition to exploring the HR department's involvement in strategic decision-making, a study (Supangco, 2006) looked into the role of the HR department in corporate governance. In modern corporations where ownership and control are separate, a distinction is made between governance and management: that is, the board takes charge of governance while the managers take care of the company's business (Tricker, 1994). The goal of organisations is thus to ensure that managers and employees work with the organisation's best interests in mind. One way is to align HRM systems with internal corporate governance and external regulatory objectives (Pyne & McDonald, 2001). Thus this study (Supangco, 2006) looked into the relationship between the involvement of the HR department in formulating corporate governance mechanisms and the quality of their implementation, and the former's relationship with performance. In addition, the study also determined the relationship between the quality of implementation and performance. This study was informed by agency theory, institutional theory, and the resource-based view of the firm. The results showed that quality of implementation was positively related with performance. While involvement of the HR department in formulating governance mechanisms was not related to performance, the involvement of the HR department was realised, however, in its impact on the quality of implementation.

In summary, the studies of HRM in the Philippines have focused on addressing the question of a Filipino HRM style and establishing the relationship of HRM with various outcome variables. However, researchers in search of that distinctive Filipino HRM realise that it is rather complex. Although Western HRM practices are generally transferable into the Philippines (Galang, 2004), Japanese HRM found several obstacles to its practice (Amante, 1993; Tomita, 1983, in Selmer & De Leon, 2001). Long years of exposure to the US educational system and jurisprudence, among others, have been found more than geography to impact on transferability of practices. However, beyond the seemingly pervasive Western HRM practices, local cultural values permeate how these practices are actually implemented. Thus foreign companies find the need to adapt their practices to local conditions (Selmer & De Leon, 2001). On the other hand, the growing interest in strategic HRM and its relationship with performance grew out of the increasing involvement of HR managers in more strategic pursuits. The positive relationship between HRM involvement in strategic decision-making and quality of implementation of governance mechanism builds the case for involving HRM in strategic pursuits, reinforcing its new-found role in helping the organisation to achieve its goals. Indeed the HR department in the Philippines has gained new recognition, and its status is even higher than that in the USA and Canada (2004).

Insights from Country-Specific Studies

The influences of legal, political, economic, and cultural factors in the environments of Indonesia, Malaysia, and the Philippines have been shown to affect HRM in these countries. The impact of globalisation on local HRM practices and outcomes, however, depends on the underlying culture of openness of each country to international influences, as well as on the legal, economic, and institutional contexts. The brief summaries of the different country-specific studies chosen for this chapter present us with an interesting glimpse of where comparative HRM research might want to investigate in the future.

Indonesia, unlike Malaysia and the Philippines, has a centric approach to developing its HR capital. Its HRM strategies and practices are anchored on the concept of social justice, a unique Indonesian philosophy that values the common good for the unity of the country. As noted by Habir and Lasarati (1999), Indonesian management in general is traditional and hierarchically oriented. This management approach will likely remain dominant even as Indonesia increasingly opens its market to foreign investors.

Malaysia and the Philippines are more open to foreign HRM influences. However, we see some differences as well as similarities in approaches and outcomes. While Malaysia also relies on government-directed HRD strategies similarly to Indonesia, we find Malaysia more adept at benchmarking and looking towards other countries as role models. Indeed Malaysia's Look East policy reflects its readiness to benchmark practices with Asian neighbours, particularly Japan.

The Philippines, on the other hand, does not have a formal policy on benchmarking with any country, but its exposure to US jurisprudence and the US educational system, among others, make it more open to Western practices but not to Japanese practices. In contrast, despite Malaysia's explicit policy to emulate Japanese HRM practices, the country has not been too successful at this (Hooi, 2008). We contend that adoption of any HRM style, and the Japanese-style HRM in particular, is not as simple as adopting disparate HRM practices. It requires adopting a system within a framework of organising work. For example, an internal labour market is not just a collection of HRM practices, but rather is influenced by the competing goals of the organisation, such as flexibility and predictability, and the constraints faced by the organisation, such as technology, steady supply of labour, and wage and labour legislation, among others (Osterman, 1987).

On the other hand, interests shown in several studies on the role of HR departments, and the relationship between HRM and performance, reflect a common concern among the three countries of the economic pressures affecting organisations in these countries. Providing evidence of the relationship between HRM and outcome variables builds an economic case for recognising HRM as an important unit in the organisation, and provides legitimacy to the HR department and its practices.

CONCLUSION

Despite comparative HRM in Asia's tendency to focus on the larger economies of China, Taiwan, Hong Kong, and Singapore, although underrepresented, this chapter has identified several studies published since 1993 that tackle HRM in the Indonesia, Malaysia, and the Philippines.

The qualitative studies largely cover industrial relations. The authors use political and economic contexts in comparing and explaining the directions of country policies and changes that have taken place. We did not find any comparative HRM articles that use technological influences, for example, to explain similarities and differences of HRM in the three countries. This is a gap that needs to be addressed, given that technological changes, particularly in information and telecommunication technology, have propelled globalisation and have influenced the ways in which and where work is done.

Quantitative studies have explored HRM practices (recruitment, training and development, compensation) and roles of HR departments. The articles also used varying approaches to comparative HRM research, namely comparative between countries, comparing MNCs across countries, and comparing MNCs with the host country.

Only a small number of studies explained why these countries were chosen for analysis. It appears that in most studies the choice of countries was based on convenience. One needs to provide the logic for choosing countries under study – for example, whether or not the authors want to include countries that are similar or different in certain attributes – and how such a design addresses the research question. Clear criteria and logic of choice of countries are critical in understanding the complexities of HRM across countries (Wang & Sun, 2012).

In addition, most studies deal with presenting similarities or differences without explaining them, or without presenting the assumptions of the HRM systems being compared. While some authors explain differences, they do so *post hoc* or as an afterthought. Thus concepts, relationships, and explanations remain untested (Clark et al., 1999b). Only a few studies specified the frameworks and theories used in their analyses. These included contingency theory, cultural dimensions, institutional theory, and the resource-based view of the firm.

There is therefore a substantial research gap in comparative HRM research covering emerging economies such as Indonesia, Malaysia, and the Philippines. In addition, studies are needed that clearly specify the logic behind the choice of countries, clarifying assumptions behind the HRM systems being compared; and studies that define a priori the frameworks of analyses, so that no concepts and variables are omitted. This should lead to a better understanding of differences and similarities of HRM systems and practices.

REFERENCES

Agoncillo, T. 2012. *History of the Filipino People*. Quezon City: C&E Publishing.

Aguilar, F. 1967. *Scanning the Business Environment*. New York: Macmillan.

Amante, M. 1993. Tensions in industrial democracy and human resource management: A case study of Japanese enterprises in the Philippines. *International Journal of Human Resource Management*, 4(1): 129–158.

Amante, M. 1997. Converging and diverging trends in HRM: The Philippine 'Halo-Halo'approach. *Asia Pacific Business Review*, 3(4): 111–132.

ASEAN. 2015. ASEAN Integration Report 2015. Accessed 31 May 2016 at http://www.asean.org/wp-content/uploads/images/2015/November/media-summary-ABIS/ASEAN%20Integration%20Report%202015.pdf.

ASETUC. 2013. Labor laws and practices in ASEAN: A comparative study on gender, employment of persons with disabilities, youth employment and social dialogue, Vol 2. Accessed 8 April 2016 at http://library.fes.de/pdf-files/bueros/singapur/10627.pdf.

Azmi, I.A.G. 2015. Islamic human resource practices and organizational performance. *Journal of Islamic Accounting and Business Research*, 6(1): 2–18.

Bae, J., Chen, S.-J., & Lawler, J.J. 1998. Variations in human resource management in Asian countries: MNC home-country and host-country effects. *International Journal of Human Resource Management*, 9(4): 653–670.

Bae, J., Chen, S.-J., & Rowley, C. 2011. From a paternalistic model towards what? HRM trends in Korea and Taiwan. *Personnel Review*, 40(6): 700–722.

Bao, C., & Analoui, F. 2011. An exploration of the impact of strategic international human resource management on firm performance: The case of foreign MNCs in China. *International Journal of Management and Information Systems*, 15(4): 1–40.

Barney, J. 1991. Firm resources and sustained competitive advantage. *Journal of Management*, 17(1): 99–120.

Bartlett, K.R., Lawler, J.J., Bae, J., Chen, S.J., & Wan, D. 2002. Differences in international human resource development among indigenous firms and multinational affiliates in East and Southeast Asia. *Human Resource Development Quarterly*, 13(4): 383–405.

Baruch, Y. 2001. Global or North American? A geographical based comparative analysis of publications in top management journals. *International Journal of Cross Cultural Management*, 1(1): 131–147.

Bennington, L., & Habir, A.D. 2003. Human resource management in Indonesia. *Human Resource Management Review*, 13(3): 373–392.

Bowen, D.E., Galang, C., & Pillai, R. 2002. The role of human resource management: An exploratory study of cross-country variance. *Human Resource Management*, 41(1): 103–122.

Boxall, P. 1995. Building the theory of comparative HRM. *Human Resource Management Journal*, 5(5): 5–17.

Boyacigiller, N., & Adler, N. 1991. The parochial dinosaur: The organisational sciences in a global context. *Academy of Management Review*, 16: 262–290.

Brewster, C. 2006. Comparing HRM policies and practices across geographical borders. In G. Stahl and I. Björkman (eds), *Handbook of Research in International Human Resource Management*: 68–90. Cheltenham, UK and Northampton, MA, USA: Edward Elgar Publishing.

Brewster, C., Mayrhofer, W., & Morley, M. (eds) 2004. *Human Resource Management in Europe: Evidence of Convergence?*. Oxford: Elsevier/Butterworth-Heinemann.

Caligiuri, P.M. 1999. The ranking of scholarly journals in international human resource management. *International Journal of Human Resource Management*, 10(3): 515–519.

Caraway, T.L. 2004. Protective repression, international pressure, and institutional design: Explaining labor reform in Indonesia. *Studies in Comparative International Development*, 39(3): 28–49.

Clark, T., Gospel, H., & Montgomery, J. 1999a. Running on the spot? A review of twenty years of research on the management of human resources in comparative and international perspective. *International Journal of Human Resource Management*, 10(3): 520–544.

Clark, T., Grant, D., & Heijltjes, M. 1999b. Researching comparative and international human resource management: Key challenges and contributions. *International Studies of Management & Organization*, 29(4): 6–23.

Conner, J., & Ulrich, D. 1996. Human resource roles: Creating value, not rhetoric HR. *Human Resource Planning*, 19(3): 38–49.

De Guzman, G.M., Neelankavil, J.P., & Sengupta, K. 2011. Human resources roles: Ideal versus practiced. A cross-country comparison among organizations in Asia. *International Journal of Human Resource Management*, 22(13): 2665–2682.

Deephouse, D.L. 1996. Does isomorphism legitimate?. *Academy of Management Journal*, 39(4): 1024–1039.

Di Maggio, P., & Powell, W. 1983. The iron cage revisited: Institutional isomorphism and collective rationality in organisational fields. *American Sociological Review*, 48: 147–160.

Dowling, P.J. 1999. Completing the puzzle: Issues in the development of the field of international human resource management. *Management International Review*, 39(3): 27–43.

Edwards, T., & Kuruvilla, S. 2005. International HRM: National business systems, organizational politics and the international division of labour in MNCs. *International Journal of Human Resource Management*, 16(1): 1–21.

Fey, C.F., Morgulis-Yakushev, S., Park, H.J., & Björkman, I. 2009. Opening the black box of the relationship between HRM practices and firm performance: A comparison of MNE subsidiaries in the USA, Finland, and Russia. *Journal of International Business Studies*, 40: 690–712.

Galang, M.C. 2004. The transferability question: comparing HRM practices in the Philippines with the US and Canada. *International Journal of Human Resource Management*, 15(7): 1207–1233.

Gonzalez, A., Jose, F., Castro, C., Bueno, C., Carlos, J., Gonzalez, G., & Luis, J. 2001. Dominant approaches in the field of management. *International Journal of Organisational Analysis*, 9(4): 327–353.

Habir, A.D., & Larasati, A.B. 1999. Human resource management as competitive advantage in the new millennium: An Indonesian perspective. *International journal of Manpower*, 20(8): 548–563.

Hooi, L. 2008. The adoption of Japanese recruitment practices in Malaysia. *International Journal of Manpower*, 29(4): 362–378.

ILO. 1996–2016. Conventions and recommendations. Accessed 26 July 2016 at http://www.ilo.org/global/standards/introduction-to-international-labour-standards/conventions-and-recommendations/lang--en/index.htm.

Jocano, F.L. 1975. *Philippine Prehistory: An Anthropological Overview of the Beginnings of Filipino Society and Culture*. Quezon City: Philippine Center for Advanced Studies, University of the Philippines.

Kuruvilla, S. 1996a. Linkages between industrialization strategies and industrial relations/human resource policies: Singapore, Malaysia, the Philippines, and India. *Industrial and Labor Relations Review*, 49(4): 635–657.

Kuruvilla, S. 1996b. National industrialisation strategies and their influence on patterns of HR practices. *Human Resource Management Journal*, 6(3): 22–41.

Ling, T.C., & Nasurdin, A.M. 2010. Human resource management practices and organizational innovation: An empirical study in Malaysia. *Journal of Applied Business Research*, 26(4): 105–115.

Los Banos, J., & Utama, G.I. 2013. Social justice in consumer protection: The Indonesian framework. *Malaysian Journal of Law and Society*, 17: 45–54.

Lowe, K.B., Milliman, J., De Cieri, H., & Dowling, P.J. 2002. International compensation practices: A ten-country comparative analysis. *Human Resource Management*, 41(1): 45–66.

Mamman, A., & Somantri, Y. 2014. What role do HR practitioners play in developing countries: An exploratory study in an Indonesian organization undergoing major transformation. *International Journal of Human Resource Management*, 25(11): 1567–1591.

Mamman, A., Sulaiman, M., & Fadel, A. 1996. Attitudes to pay systems: An exploratory study within and across cultures. *International Journal of Human Resource Management*, 7(1): 101–121.

Man, M.M.K. 2012. Malaysia human resource development (HRD) needs: Challenges and suggestions. *International Journal of Management and Innovation*, 4(2): 41–53.

Osterman, P. 1987. Choice of employment systems in internal labor markets. *Industrial Relations*, 26(1): 46–67.

Ozbilgin, M. 2004. 'International' human resource management: Academic parochialism in editorial boards of the 'top' 22 journals on international human resource management. *Personnel Review*, 33(2): 205–221.

Paik, Y., Vance, C.M., & Stage, H.D. 1996. The extent of divergence in human resource practice across three Chinese national cultures: Hong Kong, Taiwan and Singapore. *Human Resource Management Journal*, 6(2): 20–31.

Pangalangan, R.C. 2010. Religion and the secular state: National report for the Philippines. In W.C. Durham and J.M. Torron (eds), *Religion and the Secular State: Interim National Reports*: 559–571. Accessed 21 January 2013 at https://www.iclrs.org/content/blurb/files/Philippines%20wide.pdf.

Parry, E., Stavrou, E., & Lazarova, M.B. (eds). 2013. *Global Trends in Human Resource Management*. Houndsmills, UK and New York, USA: Palgrave Macmillan.

Pyne, V., & McDonald, O. 2001. *The Competent Company in the New Millennium*. London: PricewaterhouseCoopers.

Sauers, D.A., Lin, S.C., Kennedy, J., & Schrenkler, J. 2009. A comparison of the performance appraisal practices of US multinational subsidiaries with parent company and local Taiwanese practices. *Management Research News*, 32(3): 286–296.

Selmer, J., & De Leon, C. 2001. Pinoy-style HRM: Human resource management in the Philippines. *Asia Pacific Business Review*, 8(1): 127–144.

Smale, A., Björkman, I., & Sumelius, J. 2012. HRM integration mechanism usage in MNC subsidiaries in China. *Personnel Review*, 41(2): 180–199.

Suan, C., & Nasurdin, A. 2014. An empirical investigation into the influence of human resource management practices on work engagement: The case of customer-contact employees in Malaysia. *International Journal of Culture, Tourism and Hospitality Research*, 8(3): 345–360.

Supangco, V.T. 2003. Management development in multinational and domestic organizations: The Philippine experience. *Asia Pacific Management Review*, 9(4): 339–353.

Supangco, V.T. 2004. HR in strategic decision-making in selected Philippine organizations. *Philippine Management Review*, 11(91–100).

Supangco, V.T. 2006. HR involvement in corporate governance. *Philippine Management Review*, 13(2): 101–116.

Supangco, V.T. 2012. Strategic HR practices in some organizations in the Philippines. *Philippine Management Review*, 19: 35–48.

Tomita, T. 1983. Responses to Japanese affiliated enterprises. *Philippine Economic Journal*, 22(1): 52–81.

Tricker, R.I. 1994. *International Corporate Governance: Text, Readings and Cases*. New York: Prentice Hall.

Ulrich, D. 1997. *Human Resource Champions: The Next Agenda for Adding Value and Delivering Results*. Boston, MA: Harvard Business School Press.

Wang, G.G., & Sun, J.Y. 2012. Toward a framework for comparative HRD research. *European Journal of Training and Development*, 36(8): 791–808.

Wang-Cowham, C. 2008. HR structure and HR knowledge transfer between subsidiaries in China. *Learning Organization*, 15(1): 26–44.

Yoon, Y. 2009. A comparative study on industrial and collective bargaining in East Asian countries. Working Paper Number 8, ILO. Accessed 28 April 2015 at http://www.ilo.org/wcmsp5/groups/public/---ed_dialogue/---dialogue/documents/publication/wcms_158351.pdf.

Zheng, C. 2009. Keeping talents for advancing service firms in Asia. *Journal of Service Management*, 20(5): 482–502.

Zheng, C., Hyland, P., & Soosay, C. 2007. Training practices of multinational companies in Asia. *Journal of European Industrial Training*, 31(6): 472–494.

33. Styles of HRM in Australia and New Zealand
Peter Boxall, Hugh Bainbridge, and Stephen Frenkel

INTRODUCTION

In this chapter we compare and contrast human resource management (HRM) models in Australia and New Zealand, locating our discussion within their respective societal contexts. Both countries are liberal-market economies but there are important differences that continue to influence HRM practice. Size is critical, both in relation to the economy and regarding constituent firms. With few exceptions (e.g., Barry & Wailes, 2004), comparative studies of HRM and industrial relations in Australia and New Zealand are relatively scarce and this makes the task of comparative analysis difficult. Consequently, we focus on features of HRM that have been regarded as most significant in each country. In New Zealand we explore the small-business characteristics of HRM and the less formal and relatively empowering ways in which workers are managed. In Australia, where organisations are typically larger, we extend our discussion to include HRM in medium-sized and larger firms. We complement this analysis by discussing HRM trends in both countries before reaching our conclusions.

THE CONTEXT OF HRM IN AUSTRALIA AND NEW ZEALAND

In this section we address the question: What are the main historical, geographical, economic, and socio-political features influencing HRM in the two countries? Australia and New Zealand, located some 2000 kilometres apart in the south-western Pacific, share much in common and are increasingly integrated in terms of their economic activities. Colonised by the British during the maritime expansion of European influence in the Pacific in the eighteenth and nineteenth centuries, they are Anglophone societies with small ratios of people to space. New Zealand, with a population in 2015 of 4.69 million people,[1] is slightly larger geographically than the densely populated United Kingdom (UK), while Australia, with 23.9 million people,[2] is closer in territorial size to the much more populous United States of America (USA).

The two countries were, however, colonised in different ways. In New Zealand, the British Crown signed a treaty with the Maori chiefs in 1840, the Treaty of Waitangi. The Treaty did not prevent war erupting in New Zealand in the mid-nineteenth century. but it has enabled a major programme of settling historical grievances over land sales and confiscations, and has provided the constitutional basis for an evolving bicultural partnership between Maori – who comprise around 15 per cent of the population

---

[1]   http://www.stats.govt.nz/, accessed 6 November 2015.
[2]   http://www.abs.gov.au/ausstats/abs@.nsf/Web+Pages/Population+Clock?opendocument, accessed 6 November 2015.

(Statistics New Zealand, 2013) – and other New Zealanders. Both English and Maori are official languages in New Zealand. In Australia, the indigenous people – Aborigines and Torres Strait Islanders – suffered social and legal discrimination over many years. Their numbers were reduced by disease and organised violence, so that they currently comprise 3 per cent of Australia's population (Australian Bureau of Statistics, ABS, 2013a). Since 1967 these groups have had the vote, and some legal redress in regard to land rights was conferred on them in 1988. However, this has not substantially altered their experience of poverty and social discrimination. Thus, the life expectancy at birth for indigenous Australians born in the period 2010–12 is estimated to be 10.6 years less for men, and 9.5 years less for women, than that for non-indigenous Australians (ABS, 2013a).

An important similarity between New Zealand and Australia is that the workforce of both is now very heterogeneous in regard to country of origin. Some 25 per cent of the New Zealand population in 2013 was born outside the country, the corresponding figure for Australia being 28 per cent (ABS, 2013b; Statistics New Zealand, 2014). Both countries have historically attracted large numbers of migrants from Europe. While the UK and Ireland have been the primary source, Australia is home to a more diverse European population than New Zealand, which has attracted a much higher proportion of Polynesian migrants. In the past 30 years migrants from China and other Asian countries have become increasingly important. According to the Organisation for Economic Co-operation and Development (OECD, 2014a), in 2011, Australia had the third-highest proportion of overseas-born residents of all OECD countries.

Like the UK and the USA, Australia and New Zealand are developed economies with First World infrastructures. New Zealand, characterised by higher rainfall levels and a more mountainous terrain, is dominated by its food-processing industries (dairy, meat, horticulture, wine, and fish) and tourism. Australia is much the larger economy with a gross domestic product (GDP) in 2015 of US$1454 billion compared with US$188 billion in New Zealand (World Bank, 2015). Australia also has a higher GDP per capita ($44 407) than New Zealand ($32 847) (OECD, 2014a). It has substantial rural, manufacturing, and tourism sectors but, critically for its productivity performance and overall living standards, has internationally significant mining industries with high capital intensity. Both countries also share a feature of most advanced societies: a large service sector. This is reflected in the share of employment across sectors in Australia (agricultural, 3.3 per cent; industrial, 20.9 per cent; service, 76.3 per cent) and New Zealand (agricultural, 7.0 per cent; industrial, 20.7 per cent; service, 72.0 per cent) (OECD, 2014c).

The Australia–New Zealand Closer Economic Relations Trade Agreement (ANZCERTA, or the CER Agreement) continues to foster a high level of economic and regulatory integration. The extent of trans-Tasman trade was recently summarised by the Australian Government's Department of Foreign Affairs and Trade (DFAT) (2015) as follows:

ANZCERTA has underpinned a strong growth in trade across the Tasman with an average 8.9 per cent annual growth in New Zealand's exports to Australia and 7.5 per cent annual growth in Australia's exports to New Zealand (1983–2006). New Zealand is currently Australia's sixth largest trading partner, ninth largest source of foreign investment and third most important destination for Australian investment abroad.

The liberalisation of trade and capital flows between the two countries has naturally had greater consequences for New Zealand, given Australia's much larger economic size and higher rate of saving and investment. Many New Zealand enterprises, including almost the entire banking sector and large parts of the retail sector, are now Australian owned. Approximately 16 per cent of New Zealand employees work in organisations that are majority foreign owned (Ministry of Economic Development, 2015). Both countries are characterised by shareholder capitalism, although the New Zealand sharemarket is much the smaller. There are many more corporate headquarters located in Australia than in New Zealand, although people in both societies feel subject to 'foreign control' exerted by firms in the world's largest economies.

Australia and New Zealand share an Anglo-American democratic and legal tradition with strong property rights. As in the UK, the judiciary (the court system) is independent of the executive (elected government). A noteworthy difference is that government in New Zealand is less layered, less bureaucratic, and more amenable to fast-paced reform. New Zealand has two layers of government: the national parliament and local authorities (city and district councils), whereas Australia includes an intermediate state government tier. Another difference is that Australia has an upper house as part of the legislature, whereas New Zealand does not.

The two countries have similar forms of education, vocational training, and occupational registration, making transfer across the Tasman Sea for educational and work purposes relatively straightforward. The Trans-Tasman Mutual Recognition Arrangement (TTMRA) facilitates movement in those occupations requiring some form of licensing: a person registered to practice in Australia can typically practise in an equivalent occupation in New Zealand, and vice versa. Ease of movement of labour across the Tasman has enabled firms in each of the Australian states to treat New Zealand workers as part of their recruitment pool, as they do with workers from other Australian states. Promotion opportunities, managerial careers, and money wages are all typically higher in Australia than in New Zealand.

Working hours in both countries – which average around 43 hours per week for full-time workers – are slightly lower than the Organisation for Economic Co-operation and Development (OECD) average (OECD, 2014a). The proportion of people working part-time in Australia in 2012 (25 per cent) was the fifth-highest in the OECD, higher than in New Zealand (22 per cent), which is also above the OECD average of 16.9 per cent (OECD, 2014c).[3] Of the full-time employees in Australia, nearly three in ten (29 per cent) would like to reduce their working hours. This issue is particularly acute among professionals and managers who work longer hours and who claim to have the least control over this aspect of their work life (van Wanrooy et al., 2008: 58–61, 78). In New Zealand, those in professional occupations report the highest levels of work intensity (Le Fevre et al., 2015).

---

[3]   Women workers (around 46 per cent of the workforce) in Australia are much more likely to work part-time than men. In 2012 nearly 38 per cent of female workers worked part-time, compared to close to 13 per cent of men (OECD, 2014c). In the 2013 New Zealand Census, women made up 70 per cent of the people working part-time and 41 per cent of those working full-time (http://www.stats.govt.nz/Census/2013-census/profile-and-summary-reports/quickstats-work-unpaid/work_and_labour_force_status.aspx, accessed 6 November 2015). The OECD averages are 26 per cent and 9 per cent for women and men, respectively (OECD, 2014c). For assessments of job quality for Australian and New Zealand versus other OECD nations, see OECD (2014b).

Although there is an ongoing debate in the New Zealand (NZ) media over whether real income and work–life balance are better in Australia, there has typically been much greater skilled migration from New Zealand to Australia than the reverse. In the 2012/13 financial year, 52 012 people left New Zealand for Australia as permanent and long-term arrivals, while 16 104 migrated the other way (Department of Immigration and Border Protection (DFAT) (2015). In the international labour market, of course, both countries are small and suffer from an international 'diaspora' of skilled workers seeking greater opportunities. It is estimated that around 0.5 million New Zealanders (one in nine) live outside the country, while around 1 million (one in 20) Australians are living abroad (New Zealand Treasury, 2004; Senate Legal and Constitutional References Committee, 2005).

In both countries, the ten or so years prior to the onset of the Global Financial Crisis in 2008 were years in which employers had great difficulty recruiting. From a peak of nearly 11 per cent in late 1992, unemployment in Australia and New Zealand declined almost continuously from the mid-1990s to slightly over 4 per cent in 2008, before increasing to 6.2 per cent in Australia and 6 per cent in New Zealand in 2015.[4] Despite immigration into Australia accounting for the largest contribution to population growth in recent years (OECD, 2014c), and skill-stream migrants comprising over 40 per cent of recent settler arrivals (ABS, 2010), skill shortages have consistently been reported by employer groups as a significant barrier to investment in Australia, a constraint likely to increase with the ageing of the population. Similar concerns have been articulated in New Zealand (BusinessNZ, 2014). New Zealand (eighth) and Australia (twelfth) ranked towards the top in a recent survey of 40 000 employers exploring the degree of difficulty employers faced in filling jobs due to a lack of suitable candidates (ManpowerGroup, 2013). However, compared to 2007, there is some evidence that skill shortages in Australia have eased in recent years (Department of Employment, 2014).

Besides the extent to which they operate as a common market for skilled labour, Australia and New Zealand fit within the more liberal, Anglo-American model of labour market regulation (Freeman et al., 2007). Employer–employee relations are substantially decentralised: employment contracting typically takes place at enterprise, workplace, or individual levels. While both countries established state-controlled systems of compulsory arbitration at the turn of the twentieth century, these modes of labour regulation have been disestablished and replaced with the more typical forms seen in the Anglophone world (Barry & Wailes, 2004; Freeman et al., 2007). Laws on union recognition, collective bargaining, health and safety in employment, minimum employment conditions, and equal employment opportunity are important in this pattern, but there is significantly less labour market regulation than in the coordinated market economies of some continental European countries. At times, the role of unions has been challenged (for example, in New Zealand in the early 1990s; and in Australia between 1995 and 2007 and again in 2013–15 when the country was governed by a conservative Federal administration) but union recognition and collective bargaining remain important social norms in both societies and those who challenge them face major political risks.[5] Union membership

---

[4]   http://www.abs.gov.au/ausstats/abs@.nsf/mf/6202.0, accessed 6 November 2015; http://www.stats.govt. nz/, accessed 6 November 2015.

[5]   Industrial relations was a key election issue in the 2007 Australian general election. The successful Labor Party translated its pledges into practice by passing the Fair Work Act 2008, which reintroduced collective

and participation has, however, been declining and may have reached a crisis point. In the 1980–2013 period, trade union density dropped in Australia from 49 per cent to 17 per cent, while in New Zealand the corresponding figures are 69 per cent and 19 per cent (OECD, 2015). Thus, unions currently cover less than one in five employees, with much higher density in the public sector than in the private (Boxall et al., 2007a).[6]

STYLES OF HRM IN NEW ZEALAND

A comparative analysis of HRM styles needs to focus on overall patterns in the management of work and people. We adopt an approach in this section and the next which is based on identifying a country's dominant models of HRM and analysing their implications for its workplace outcomes (Boxall, 1995). In doing so, it helps to look at models for managing managers and then at models for managing the non-managerial workforce.

Boxall and Gilbert's (2007) typology of company styles in the management of managers is a framework which examines how such factors as organisational size and socio-cultural differences affect the ways firms try to recruit, develop, reward, and extract value from managers. The typology traverses five major styles: 'elite', 'elite-development', 'emergent', 'emergent-development', and 'transnational-hybrid'. In the 'elite' model, managerial talent is identified early, based on social status or membership of an elite cadre, as in the French *Grande École* system. Those who successfully come through this defining group are channelled into a career path that gives significant responsibility from the outset. In the 'elite-development' model, characteristic of Germany and Japan, the managerial pool is also identified early but those recruited are put through an intense and structured development programme, which ultimately involves a competitive tournament based on performance against certain criteria for advancing to senior management ranks. The 'emergent' model is characteristic of small firms almost everywhere which outgrow family resources and need to turn to external labour markets for managers. The 'emergent-development' model is the implicit model of medium-sized to large Anglo-American firms. In the most prestigious firms, there are often attempts to recruit 'the cream' from elite educational institutions, but experienced managers are also recruited to various levels from the external labour market, and the identification of managerial potential is based more on demonstrated performance than on elite background. The 'transnational-hybrid' model is characteristic of multinational firms with a global governance structure of some kind and a need to manage the tension between global strategy and local adaptation in HRM. While corporate headquarters may seek to impose one style, such firms may, within their global operations, have elements of all the other types.

Unsurprisingly, Gilbert and Boxall's (2009) empirical study of major New Zealand

---

bargaining, and restored some of the rights that had been withdrawn from unions and workers under the previous government's legislation, whose objective was to increase the power of employers, promote individual 'bargaining', and facilitate flexible employment contracts (Peetz, 2006).

[6] There is some evidence that Australians may be more favourably disposed to unions than New Zealanders. According to a 2005 survey, 65 per cent of Australian respondents agreed with the statement: 'Without trade unions, the working conditions of employees would be much worse than they are', while 55 per cent also agreed that 'Trade unions are very important for the job security of employees'. Corresponding figures for the New Zealand respondents were 51 per cent and 41 per cent, respectively (van Wanrooy et al., 2008).

companies suggests that the management of managers in New Zealand typically falls into the emergent pattern: New Zealand companies are heavily dependent on recruiting the managerial talent they need from the external labour market. Leaders of firms complain of talent shortages and feel they are at a major disadvantage in recruiting and retaining managers of sufficient calibre. This inevitably affects the ability of New Zealand companies to perform in the international environment and constrains their rate of growth. It is not all bleak, however. New Zealand's smaller, less bureaucratic companies can be more flexible in how they deploy individuals across functions, can provide greater autonomy in how individuals do their work, and often offer individuals earlier responsibility and escalated career development. However, the degree of managerial responsibility and professional development is naturally limited in a country with no indigenous companies listed in the Fortune Global 500.[7] The more international, more extensive and more highly paid managerial and professional jobs are to be found in places such as the UK, the USA, and Australia. Only a few large NZ firms have developed the kind of internal labour markets and management development structures seen in the world's largest corporations.

What is true of dominant styles of HRM for the management of managers is true more generally in terms of managing the non-managerial NZ workforce. There are, of course, large private sector firms and public sector organisations with traditions of formal, bureaucratic HRM of the kind seen in large US or UK firms. In the largest NZ organisations, one does see such practices as formal job analysis, specialised work organisation, and formal systems of recruitment, performance appraisal, and internal development. In these organisations, such practices are often evolved within a framework of collective bargaining and joint consultation (Boxall, 1997). However, the dominant model of HRM for the New Zealand operating workforce reflects the fact that the average enterprise is a small to medium-sized company. Compared with Australia, the USA, and the UK, a smaller percentage of NZ workers are employed in firms with at least 100 employees (45 per cent in NZ, compared with 64 per cent in the USA, and 60 per cent in the UK) (Mills & Timmins, 2004).[8]

Models of HRM in New Zealand therefore tend towards the less formal styles typical of small firms (Boxall & Purcell, 2016). Small employers do not adopt the HRM planning, job analysis, and career development procedures of the large and multinational employers, and rely heavily on the external labour market for relevant skills (Marchington et al., 2003). This is illustrated by the fact that NZ firms are heavy users of recruitment agencies (Dakin & Smith, 1995). An active recruitment consultancy industry is not surprising, given the fact that some 55 per cent of employment in NZ occurs in firms with less than 100 employees, which generally do not employ HRM specialists in-house. Small employers are also less able to afford large training budgets. Most employee development takes place on the job, through coaching and mentoring (Macky & Johnson, 2000).

As with managerial labour, employers have long expressed a high degree of concern over skill shortages (Westacott, 2011, May 6). An added twist is that literacy and numeracy

---

[7]   Australia, by contrast, has eight companies in the Global Fortune 500 (see http://fortune.com/global500/, accessed 12 March 2015).

[8]   A comparable figure for Australia is not readily available. However, a very small number of firms (<1 per cent) employ 200 or more employees. These companies employ a relatively large proportion of the workforce, perhaps as much as one-third.

are seen as major problems at the lower end of the labour market (Bita, 2015, May 28). In an international study of adult literacy reported by the OECD (2000), New Zealand ranked seventh among 22 OECD nations, with very similar average levels of prose literacy as Canada and Australia but behind the leaders in Northern Europe (Sweden, Finland, Norway, and the Netherlands). While the performance of the average adult seems good, the distribution includes 40 per cent of NZ adults whose prose literacy is 'very poor' or 'weak'. New Zealand's position is lower in terms of adult numeracy ('quantitative literacy'), ranking fifteenth among the OECD nations in this study. Some 50 per cent of adults are 'very poor' or 'weak' in numerical ability. Given high levels of employment in New Zealand, there is no doubt that the literacy and numeracy problem among less skilled workers is a constraint on workplace productivity growth (New Zealand Treasury, 2008). While the overall level of skills in New Zealand is consistent with a developed economy, that group of workers in the NZ workplace who have difficulty reading, writing, or apply-ing mathematical logic is less likely to participate effectively in teamwork, contribute to innovation, or show the skills needed for quality improvement. This inevitably affects workplace performance and individual career development.

This brief sketch emphasises the small-business character of HRM in New Zealand but does not tell us how NZ workers perceive the way they are managed. Recent studies of employee perceptions of, and responses to, management practices help us to build a more rounded picture of employer strategies and behaviour. Surveys of employee responses to work practices (Boxall & Macky, 2014; Macky & Boxall, 2007, 2008b), which are based on large national samples of employees (around 1000), measure worker well-being and examine the extent to which workers can exercise influence on the job, feel well informed, consider themselves well rewarded, and experience good training opportunities. While some workers report high levels of work intensification and stress, the surveys reveal a workforce that, on average, perceives high levels of job influence and reports healthy levels of well-being. The overall picture is one of 'a fairly egalitarian workplace in terms of allowing individuals, of varying skill levels, to exert control over decisions in their day-to-day work' (Macky & Boxall, 2008a: 13).

These surveys confirm the picture of high levels of employee influence and job satisfac-tion, and a generally consultative management style, found in the New Zealand Worker Representation and Participation Survey (NZWRPS) (Boxall et al., 2007b; Haynes et al., 2005). In that study, also based on a large-scale survey of NZ workers, nine out of ten workers said that they were satisfied with their job, eight out of ten said that they trusted their employer, and 85 per cent agreed that relations between employees and management were good. In this respect, they rated relationships between management and workers nearly 20 per cent better than US workers, and 15 per cent better than UK workers (Diamond & Freeman, 2002; Freeman & Rogers, 1999).

There are, of course, nuances in this picture (Boxall & Macky, 2014; Macky & Boxall, 2008a, 2008b). There is evidence of both 'low-road' (work-intensifying) and 'high-road' (high-skill or empowering) production strategies, and a range of employee experiences across different contexts. For example, employees in the private sector feel better rewarded for their performance than public sector workers and also perceive themselves as having better chances of promotion within the organisation. Professionals, technicians, and asso-ciate professionals in the private sector feel much better informed than their public sector counterparts. Employees in larger firms see themselves as having a better internal labour market. Those in unionised firms perceive better opportunities for training and development but report higher levels of stress and work–life imbalance (Macky & Boxall, 2009).

Overall, then, the evidence suggests that HRM in New Zealand workplaces is typically based on an informal, relatively empowering and consultative management style. This is not surprising given that the average workplace size is small and direct communications between employee and employer are much more possible than in the large bureaucracies seen in much bigger countries. Within this general context, a range of contingent variables produce a nuanced set of models of HRM and worker experiences, as is observed everywhere: such variables include employer industry and production strategies, organisational size, unionisation, and employee occupation, among others. In terms of workplace outcomes, the most important issues facing employers are concerned with skill shortages and mismatches, at both managerial and operating levels, and their impact on productivity and enterprise growth.

STYLES OF HRM IN AUSTRALIA

In Australia there is a somewhat different profile of enterprise size. By 'size' we are referring to firms in three categories: small companies (5–19 employees), medium-sized (20–199 employees), and large (200+ employees). In 2014, there were approximately 273 000 actively trading businesses with five or more employees. Of that total, 78 per cent had 5–19, 20 per cent had 20–199, and 1 per cent had 200 or more employees (ABS, 2014c). Nearly 30 per cent of employees were employed in large enterprises, and 23 per cent in medium-sized enterprises. In short, while medium-sized and large enterprises account for a very small proportion of the total, these businesses employ a fairly large proportion of total employees, almost 80 per cent of whom are employed on permanent or fixed-term contracts rather than on a casual basis. This proportion is similar for small, medium-sized and large businesses. Approximately 70 per cent of employees work full-time, with little variation across business size (ABS, 2014a).

Enterprise size is the most important variable accounting for different styles of management in Australia. Smaller enterprises are able to manage employees informally and individually. This is more difficult in larger firms, where bureaucratic rules facilitate predictability, and collective terms and conditions reduce transaction costs associated with individual contract discussions or bargaining while also fostering equitable treatment between employees doing similar work. Rules and collective arrangements require formalisation and create work for specialist HR managers, who are concerned with implementing them consistently. In what follows we summarise what is known about Australian HRM styles, relating these to size of enterprise.

Small Enterprises: Individualised Informalism

Approaches to employee management in small Australian organisations have many similarities with their New Zealand counterparts. Australian small businesses focus primarily on selling goods or services in the immediate area, town, or city in which the business is located (ABS, 2014b). They are generally located at a single site, and open only on weekdays during standard business hours (Australian Workplace Relations Study, AWRS, 2015).

Small businesses are typically characterised by informal approaches to employee management. Minimum pay and working conditions are determined by awards (negotiated and/or arbitrated by tribunals on a sector basis). Above these minima, employers informally determine or consult with individual employees. Small businesses are almost twice as likely as large (45 per cent versus 25 per cent) to prefer informal or undocumented approaches to flexible work arrangements. This informal approach is also reflected in the emphasis on individual, one-on-one methods of communication with the workforce (AWRS, 2015). Small firm employers often argue that they are not in position to offer employees much above the minimum pay and conditions. For example, less than a quarter of these employers offer employees the ability to buy extra annual leave, cash out annual leave or take leave without pay, select their own roster or shifts, use job-sharing, work from home, or use paid parental leave. Only a third offer flexible use of personal sick, unpaid, or compassionate leave (for example, to care for other people who are sick), while two-thirds offer flexible work hours (for example, to enable employees to deal with non-work issues) (ABS, 2014b). Finally, small firms tend to value experience rather than formal education in determining position in the company hierarchy (AWRS, 2015).

Medium-Sized Enterprises: Structured Informality

Medium-sized Australian businesses are equally likely to be located at a single site as at multiple sites. Regarding opening hours, they are equally likely to be open on weekdays and seven days a week. Two-thirds are open only during standard business hours, with the remainder implementing shift work arrangements (AWRS, 2015). These firms use more formalised approaches to employee management compared with small businesses. This is evident in the structuring of working hours. For example, the majority offer flexible work hours, and flexible use of personal sick, unpaid, or compassionate leave (ABS, 2014b). Similar to small businesses, sector-level awards[9] determine minimum pay and conditions, with informal discussion on an individual basis supplementing this arrangement (AWRS, 2015). Most medium-sized firms have insufficient resources to employ a dedicated HR manager who might introduce more advanced, formalised employee management techniques. Nevertheless, the level of formality is greater than for small enterprises. For example, a little less than three in ten offer the ability to buy extra annual leave, cash out annual leave, or take leave without pay, to select rosters or shifts, use job-sharing, work from home, or use paid parental leave. Regarding communication with employees, medium-sized firms combine collective information-sharing via workplace and team meetings with one-on-one discussions with employees. This differs from small enterprises where a greater reliance is placed on the latter method (AWRS, 2015).

Large Enterprises: Specialised Formality

Larger Australian firms are typically located at multiple sites, open seven days a week, and use shift work arrangements (AWRS, 2015). A third of large businesses sell goods

---

[9]   An award sets out the minimum wages and conditions to which an employee is entitled. In Australia, an award is a ruling of Fair Work Australia or a state industrial relations commission granting all wage earners in one industry or occupation the same minimum conditions of employment and wages.

or services in overseas markets, compared to small (9 per cent) or medium-sized (15 per cent) businesses (ABS, 2014b). Large enterprises favour formal procedures for employee management. Thus, employee pay and conditions, decided at the enterprise level, often via negotiation with unions, are formalised in written, legally binding agreements, while managers and supervisors receive pay and conditions that are determined by management, mainly via individual consultation between management and employees. These too are formalised as legally binding documents. Enterprise agreements are twice (compared to medium-sized businesses) and seven times (compared to small businesses) as likely to be the main method of pay determination in large Australian enterprises (AWRS, 2015). Such agreements typically offer flexible work hours and the flexible use of personal sick, unpaid, or compassionate leave. The majority of agreements also provide workers with the opportunity to buy extra annual leave, cash out annual leave, or take leave without pay, to work from home, and take paid parental leave. Nevertheless, only a minority of agreements offer the ability to use job-sharing arrangements or for workers to select their own roster or shifts (ABS, 2014b). Large enterprises are three times as likely as their small counterparts to have introduced a formal salary structure (25 per cent versus 8 per cent) or a job grading or classification system. These organisations rely on multiple methods to communicate with their workforce but are distinguished from small and medium-sized enterprises by their greater reliance on employee representatives and union delegates (AWRS, 2015).

The greater complexity and formalisation of employee management requires HR managers. These specialists are employed in almost all large organisations. In many enterprises the HRM function is represented at senior executive team level, where HR managers play a strategic role in enterprise planning and decision-making. This activity is more likely than in medium-sized firms where HRM has a more operational, administrative emphasis. The bureaucratic, formal style applies most strongly to large enterprises that have overseas operations or are foreign owned.

TRENDS IN AUSTRALIAN AND NZ HRM

We now turn to notable trends in HRM in Australia and New Zealand.

The Changing Face of HRM

HRM in both countries is becoming more professionalised. The educational qualifications of entrants into specialist HRM roles has increased over time. According to a survey of practising members of the Australian Human Resource Institute (AHRI), which mainly reflects employees in larger firms and consultants, the percentage of entrants with a university degree increased from 23 per cent to 46 per cent between 1995 and 2005. A recent survey of relatively large firms reported that 80 per cent of HR managers had three or more years of tertiary education (Dainty, 2011), very close to the 81.7 per cent reported in a recent survey of NZ HRM specialists (Xia & Boxall, 2013). The skills of Australian HRM professionals have been linked to performance of a strategic HRM role (Dainty, 2011). Additional evidence suggests that HRM is increasingly being viewed as a legitimate career path in its own right. University graduates are entering the HRM function as a starting point to their HRM career, rather than through clerical positions or functional areas such as marketing and sales (Dowling & Fisher, 1997; Sheehan et al., 2006). In 2005, one-third of specialist managers commenced work in the HRM function (Sheehan et al., 2006) and the number of direct entrants into a HRM career path has continued to grow since then. This, however, means that HRM specialists are less likely to have experience in a line management role, which can undermine their credibility with other managers, and can also limit their prospects of advancement to general management (Xia & Boxall, 2013).

The HRM function has traditionally been an occupational area with a high level of female representation. While recent data underline that this remains the case (72 per cent female; AHRI, 2014), women are increasingly occupying more senior roles within HRM departments (Kramar, 2012). The nature of HR work is also changing. An increasing amount of the HR work is being undertaken with the use of human resource information systems (HRIS). This shift has reshaped the management of employee records and pay, and has more broadly influenced how work is performed in the areas of recruitment and selection, training, scheduling, performance management, career management, and succession planning (Kramar, 2012). The work of Australian HRM managers is also becoming more integrated into strategic planning and implementation processes (Brown et al., 2009; Dainty, 2011; Sheehan & De Cieri, 2012). Kramar and Steane (2012) report high expectations among HR professionals that HR departments will increasingly be charged with developing human capital as a business strategic imperative. Moreover, HR executives and specialists are placing greater emphasis on the use of metrics to demonstrate how HR specialists add value to the business (Kramar & Steane, 2012). The greater weight placed on strategic concerns and the exercise of influence is consistent with research demonstrating the connection between Australian HR executives' involvement in strategic decision-making and organisational performance (Sheehan et al., 2016).

The character of HRM in Australia and New Zealand is also being shaped by the transfer of responsibilities that were traditionally performed by HRM specialists to line managers. There has been a substantial transfer of a range of operational HRM activities to line managers in recent years. HR managers are tending to concentrate on specialist areas such as industrial relations, workers' compensation, human resource planning, and remuneration and benefits; while line managers have been leading in operational areas such as coaching, performance management, and promotion decisions (Kulik & Bainbridge, 2006). There is evidence that Australian line managers are generally satisfied with the performance of their HRM departments (Teo & Rodwell, 2007). Furthermore, Teo and Rodwell (2007) found that the extent to which operational HRM activities are devolved to line managers is positively related to the HRM department's level of influence as perceived by senior managers. However, devolution does present challenges. A key issue is that HR and line managers often view the process in different ways. In general, HR managers perceive devolution as having positive organisational consequences. However, line managers are generally more sceptical. Line managers express concern over insufficient training in HRM, while HR managers are more inclined to state that employee satisfaction has increased and to want to continue the process so that they can focus on 'strategic issues' (Kulik & Bainbridge, 2006). There is a danger that some employee management responsibilities 'fall between the cracks'. This occurs when HR and line managers view particular employee management responsibilities as the responsibility of the other party and fail to resolve this tension satisfactorily. Establishing effective partnerships is increasingly recognised as important (Frenkel et al., 2012). This is likely to require greater understanding of business issues on the part of HRM specialists (Xia & Boxall, 2013), improved HRM skills on the part of line managers (Townsend, 2013), refined line manager job descriptions that include a clear statement of people management responsibilities, and performance appraisals that promote accountability by incorporating an assessment of people management effectiveness (Bainbridge, 2015b).

HRM in an Era of Increasing Workforce Diversity

Skill shortages, low unemployment, and pressure for more equitable treatment by diverse groups in Australia and New Zealand have encouraged management to seek entrants to particular jobs from segments that have not traditionally been the focus of recruitment and retention initiatives. Specialised workforce practices are now increasingly prevalent that are designed to address the specific needs of women, different ethnicities, the mature-aged, people with disabilities, and the family and friends who care for them. Employer groups, such as the NZ EEO Trust, are increasingly concerned with initiatives and processes that will help to create a positive climate for diversity in workplaces (Houkamau & Boxall, 2011).

In relation to women, the Australian Workplace Gender Equality Act 2012 requires non-public sector employers with 100 or more employees to submit an annual report to the Australian Workplace Gender Equality Agency (WGEA) on six gender equality indicators: workforce composition, composition of governing bodies, remuneration, flexible working arrangements, consultation with employees, and harassment and discrimination. Reports are now annually submitted on behalf of more than 11000 employers and 3.9 million employees, representing a third of Australia's total labour force (WGEA, 2014). Data based on these reports indicate that women's average total remuneration is 25 per cent less than men's. This gap is most evident in financial and insurance services. Despite this, only a quarter of employers had conducted an analysis to check for potential pay equity issues. Few organisations had set a target to increase the number of directorships held by women, despite women holding a minority of directorships and chairing roles. Half of employers consulted with employees in relation to gender equality matters. Such consultation was generally in the form of exit interviews or surveys. Almost all employers had a policy or strategy on prevention of sex-based harassment and discrimination, and a grievance process for addressing harassment. Three-quarters of Australian organisations provided sexual harassment training to managers (WGEA, 2014). However, this training appears to be less extensive than in the USA, where 90 per cent of organisations provide sexual harassment training (Dolezalek, 2005). This gap may stem from US organisations' greater access to supportive resources and the greater use of HRM policies that reinforce pro-training behaviours in managers (Bainbridge et al., 2018).

There is also increasing interest in practices designed to accommodate the needs of mature-aged individuals, people with disabilities, and people with a range of non-work responsibilities such as those who provide unpaid care for family members and friends. These initiatives occur against a background of government initiatives and legislative changes that have extended employment protections and provided incentives for inclusion of groups with historically low levels of workforce participation. Successive governments

have focused on enhancing the employment outcomes of a range of 'high-priority' segments of the population including ethnic minorities, people with disabilities and those
family members and friends who provide care for them, single parents, new parents, and
mature-age workers.

A major challenge for both countries is the ageing of the population. This issue has
been addressed by successive Australian governments which have sought to reduce the
incentives for early retirement. These government policies are consequential because they
influence employer views about the importance of mature-aged individuals as either job
candidates or employees. Workforce ageing is coming to be viewed as a significant issue
by management. However, questions remain as to the extent to which this interest has
translated into HRM practices that address the needs of mature-aged people (Oakman
& Wells, 2016). A recent survey suggests that attitudes towards these workers are more
positive regarding hiring than retraining practices, and that supportive practices are more
prevalent in public sector and larger organisations in Australia (Taylor et al., 2013).

With respect to non-work responsibilities, there remains a significant gap between
the prevalence of workplace policies that address the needs of employees who provide
childcare versus informal care (for example, for a person with disabilities or who is
elderly) (Bainbridge & Broady, 2017). This gap is also reflected at a societal level via a
distinct media portrayal of the workplace support available to each group (Bainbridge,
2015a). General policies for supporting non-work responsibilities such as flexible working
arrangements exist in about half of Australian organisations, but few have a broader
strategy for flexible working arrangements. While half of reporting enterprises provide
primary carer's leave in addition to the Federal Government's paid parental leave scheme,
only a third provide such leave to a secondary carer (WGEA, 2014). In New Zealand,
research suggests that family-friendly employment practices are well established across
all types of organisation (Houkamau & Boxall, 2011). Interestingly, while the incidence
of formal diversity policies (of various kinds) is greater in the public sector, employees
rate the actual climate for diversity more highly in the private sector. New Zealand private
sector organisations, as noted above, are smaller and responses to changing workforce
needs can be more rapidly implemented in them.

Employer Reputation and Treatment of Employees

A tight labour market has increased incentives for Australian and New Zealand organisations to promote their workplace as a desirable destination to potential employees while
simultaneously seeking to improve the engagement of current employees. These efforts
are important in an environment in which issues such as work intensification and work–
life imbalance can be expected to lead to disaffection and lower commitment (Boxall &
Macky, 2014). A survey conducted by van Wanrooy et al. (2008: 60) found that 18 per
cent of Australian managers strongly agreed, and a further 39 per cent agreed, that 'more
and more is expected of me for the same amount of pay', very close to the 17 per cent
and 37 per cent of other employees answering the same question. Both groups feel under
increased pressure at work.

Anecdotally, it seems that employee engagement surveys have become widespread
among the larger employers as managers try to bring better measurement of employee
attitudes into their reporting systems. Access to these surveys remains in the hands of

employers, but there are studies which help us to assess attitudes across the Antipodean economies. In relation to job satisfaction, AWRS (2015) provides data concerning employees' satisfaction with their job overall, and also for seven aspects of their job. The highest levels of satisfaction were reported in relation to having flexibility to balance work and non-work commitments, and in relation to having the freedom to decide how to do their work. Overall, employees were least satisfied with their total pay. Interestingly, greater satisfaction was reported across all dimensions by female compared with male employees. Female employees were most satisfied with the flexibility to balance work and non-work commitments, while male employees were most satisfied with having the freedom to decide how to do their own work (AWRS, 2015).

Along with engagement surveys, practices that help to improve management responsiveness to workforce needs are relatively prevalent. In a large-scale survey in Australian workplaces conducted by Teicher et al. (2007), 83 per cent of employees reported an open-door policy to discuss problems with management, and 60 per cent reported the presence of regular staff meetings. Joint consultative committees were claimed to exist in half the workplaces surveyed. Almost 80 per cent of respondents in non-union workplaces with consultative committees reported them to be effective. This is similar to findings regarding consultative practices and committees in New Zealand (Teicher et al., 2007: 139). As in New Zealand, these data suggest that employee relations is now conducted in a more consultative way despite the fact that union pressure is lower (Haynes et al., 2005). Van Wanrooy et al. (2008: 32) confirm this impression in their finding that 74 per cent of employees in 2008 perceived management to consult with employees over issues affecting them; up from 71 per cent in 2007. In addition, close to 70 per cent of employees in 2008 agreed or strongly agreed with the statement that 'managers at my workplace can be trusted to tell things the way they are' (the equivalent figure in New Zealand, as noted above, is eight out of ten). Finally, in terms of fair treatment, over three-quarters of respondents agreed that 'I feel employees are treated fairly at my workplace'.

In sum, there are signs that Australian and New Zealand employers have tried to adapt to the tighter labour markets of the last decade by adopting a more consultative, responsive style of HRM, an approach that helps to facilitate a better understanding of employee aspirations and better retention of valued employees. Their ability to meet the needs of an increasingly diverse and complex workforce will remain a key issue, but there are signs of progress.

CONCLUSIONS

What, then, are the characteristics of HRM in Australia and New Zealand? The evidence presented above suggests that Australia and New Zealand fit the liberal-market pattern of HRM and employment relations typical of Canada, the USA, and the UK, rather than the more coordinated economies of Northern Europe. Labour market regulation has been through controversial periods in both countries, but both seem to have settled into a decentralised pattern of employment contracting which preserves trade unionism and collective bargaining, although at a much reduced level than under the auspices of previously more centralised systems in which arbitration was a major feature. In New Zealand, small-business styles of HRM dominate: people are managed in relatively informal and empowering ways, which most employees find appealing. However, internal career development opportunities for skilled workers are fewer than in Australia, making New Zealand more vulnerable to employee mobility on the international labour market. The larger average size of Australian firms brings about both a higher level of bureaucracy, but also more career development opportunities than in New Zealand.

The ongoing challenge is for management to address the implications of the key issues and emerging trends that characterise HRM in this region. Building capable workforces, retaining talented workers with international options, managing diversity, and enhancing employee engagement, are key concerns. How senior managers ensure that HRM–line management partnerships are adequately resourced and promote high-quality employee relations will be critical. This includes how well they integrate HRM into strategic planning and reporting. Organisations in which managers prove themselves to be high-quality employers will have a greater chance of success in the competitive product, labour, and financial markets they encounter.

REFERENCES

ABS. 2010. Australian demographic statistics, December 2009. Catalogue No. 3101.0. Canberra: ABS.
ABS. 2013a. Estimates of Aboriginal and Torres Strait Islander Australians, June 2011. Catalogue No. 3238.0.55.001. Canberra: ABS.
ABS. 2013b. Migration, Australia. Catalogue No. 3412.0. Canberra: ABS.
ABS. 2014a. Employee earnings, benefits and trade union membership, Australia, August 2013. Catalogue No. 6310.0. Canberra: ABS.
ABS. 2014b. Selected characteristics of Australian business, 2012–13. Catalogue No. 8167.0. Canberra: ABS.
ABS. 2014c. Counts of Australian businesses, including entries and exits, Jun 2010 to Jun 2014. Catalogue No. 8165.0. Canberra: ABS.
Australian Human Resources Institute (AHRI). 2014. 2014 Annual Report. Retrieved from https://www.ahri.com.au/__data/assets/pdf_file/0019/47116/Annual_report_2014_low.pdf.
AWRS. 2015. First findings report. Retrieved from https://www.fwc.gov.au/first-findings-report/about-report.
Bainbridge, H.T.J. 2015a. Carers in the news: Examining the media's portrayal of individuals who care for people with and without disabilities. Paper presented at the Carers NSW 2015 Biennial Conference, Sydney, Australia.
Bainbridge, H.T.J. 2015b. Devolving people management to the line: How different rationales for devolution influence people management effectiveness. *Personnel Review*, 44(6): 847–865.
Bainbridge, H.T.J., & Broady, T.R. 2017. Caregiving responsibilities for a child, spouse or parent: The impact of care recipient independence on employee well-being. *Journal of Vocational Behavior*, 101: 57–76.
Bainbridge, H.T.J., Perry, E., & Kulik, C.T. 2018. Sexual harassment training: Explaining differences in Australian and US approaches. *Asia Pacific Journal of Human Resources*, 56: 124–147.
Barry, M., & Wailes, N. 2004. Contrasting systems? 100 years of arbitration in Australia and New Zealand. *Journal of Industrial Relations*, 46(4): 430–447.
Bita, N. 2015, 28 May. Skills shortage to worsen. Retrieved from http://www.theaustralian.com.au/national-affairs/education/skills-shortage-to-worsen/story-fn59nlz9-1227371842658.
Boxall, P. 1995. Building the theory of comparative HRM. *Human Resource Management Journal*, 5(5): 5–17.
Boxall, P. 1997. Models of employment and labour productivity in New Zealand: An interpretation of change since the Employment Contracts Act. *New Zealand Journal of Employment Relations*, 22(1): 22–36.
Boxall, P., & Gilbert, J. 2007. The management of managers: A review and conceptual framework. *International Journal of Management Reviews*, 9(2): 1–21.
Boxall, P., Haynes, P., & Freeman, R.B. 2007a. Conclusion: What workers say in the Anglo-American world. In R.B. Freeman, P. Boxall, and P. Haynes (eds), *What Workers Say: Employee Voice in the Anglo-American Workplace*: 206–220. Ithaca, NY: Cornell University Press.
Boxall, P., Haynes, P., & Macky, K. 2007b. Employee voice and voicelessness in New Zealand. In R.B. Freeman, P. Boxall, and P. Haynes (eds), *What Workers Say: Employee Voice in the Anglo-American Workplace*: 145–165. Ithaca, NY: Cornell University Press.
Boxall, P., & Macky, K. 2014. High-involvement work processes, work intensification and employee well-being. *Work, Employment and Society*, 28(6): 963–984.

Boxall, P., & Purcell, J. 2016. *Strategy and Human Resource Management* (4th edn). London: Palgrave.

Brown, M., Metz, I., Cregan, C., & Kulik, C.T. 2009. Irreconcilable differences? Strategic human resource management and employee well-being. *Asia Pacific Journal of Human Resources*, 47(3): 270–294.

BusinessNZ. 2014. Business manifesto 2014. Retrieved from http://www.businessnz.org.nz/__data/assets/pdf_file/0005/85424/Business-Manifesto-2014.pdf.

Dainty, P. 2011. The strategic HR role: Do Australian HR professionals have the required skills?. *Asia Pacific Journal of Human Resources*, 49(1): 55–70.

Dakin, S., & Smith, M. 1995. Staffing. In P. Boxall (ed.), *The Challenge of Human Resource Management: Directions and Debates in New Zealand*: 112–149. Auckland: Addison Wesley Longman.

Department of Employment. 2014. Skill shortages Australia, 2014. Retrieved from https://docs.employment.gov.au/system/files/doc/other/skillshortagesaustralia_0.pdf.

DFAT. 2015. Australia-New Zealand Closer Economic Relations Trade Agreement. Retrieved from http://www.dfat.gov.au/trade/agreements/anzcerta/Pages/australia-new-zealand-closer-economic-relations-trade-agreement.aspx.

Diamond, W., & Freeman, R.B. 2002. What workers want from workplace organisations: A report to the TUC's promoting trade unionism task group. London: Trades Union Congress.

Dolezalek, H. 2005. 2005 industry report. *Training*, 41(12): 14–28.

Dowling, P.J., & Fisher, C. 1997. The Australian HR professional: A 1995 profile. *Asia Pacific Journal of Human Resources*, 35(1): 1–20.

Freeman, R.B., Boxall, P., & Haynes, P. 2007. Introduction: The Anglo-American economies and employee voice. In R.B. Freeman, P. Boxall, and P. Haynes (eds), *What Workers Say: Employee Voice in the Anglo-American Workplace*: 1–24. Ithaca, NY: Cornell University Press.

Freeman, R.B., & Rogers, J. 1999. *What Workers Want*. Ithaca, NY: ILR Press.

Frenkel, S.J., Sanders, K., & Bednall, T. 2012. Employee perceptions of management relations as influences on job satisfaction and quit intentions. *Asia Pacific Journal of Management*, 30(1): 7–29.

Gilbert, J., & Boxall, P. 2009. The management of managers: Challenges in a small economy. *Journal of European Industrial Training*, 33(4): 323–340.

Haynes, P., Boxall, P., & Macky, K. 2005. Non-union voice and the effectiveness of joint consultation in New Zealand. *Economic and Industrial Democracy*, 26(2): 229–256.

Houkamau, C., & Boxall, P. 2011. The incidence and impacts of diversity management: A survey of New Zealand employees. *Asia Pacific Journal of Human Resources*, 49(4): 440–460.

Kramar, R. 2012. Trends in Australian human resource management: What next?. *Asia Pacific Journal of Human Resources*, 50(2): 133–150.

Kramar, R., & Steane, P. 2012. Emerging HRM skills in Australia. *Asia Pacific Journal of Business Administration*, 4(2): 139–157.

Kulik, C.T., & Bainbridge, H.T.J. 2006. HR and the line: The distribution of HR activities in Australian organisations. *Asia Pacific Journal of Human Resources*, 44(2): 240–256.

Le Fevre, M., Boxall, P., & Macky, K. 2015. Which workers are more vulnerable to work intensification? An analysis of two national surveys. *International Journal of Manpower*, 36(6): 966–983.

Macky, K., & Boxall, P. 2007. The relationship between high-performance work practices and employee attitudes: An investigation of additive and interaction effects. *International Journal of Human Resource Management*, 18(4): 537–567.

Macky, K., & Boxall, P. 2008a. Employee experiences of high-performance work systems: An analysis of sectoral, occupational, organisational and employee variables. *New Zealand Journal of Employment Relations*, 33(1): 1–18.

Macky, K., & Boxall, P. 2008b. High-involvement work processes, work intensification and employee well-being: A study of New Zealand worker experiences. *Asia Pacific Journal of Human Resources*, 46(1): 38–55.

Macky, K., & Boxall, P. 2009. Employee well-being and union membership. *New Zealand Journal of Employment Relations*, 34(3): 14–25.

Macky, K., & Johnson, G. 2000. *The Strategic Management of Human Resources*. Auckland: McGraw-Hill.

ManpowerGroup. 2013. 2013 Talent Shortage Survey. Retrieved from http://www.manpower.com.au/documents/White-Papers/2013_Talent_Shortage_Survey_Results_Global_rs.pdf.

Marchington, M., Carroll, M., & Boxall, P. 2003. Labour scarcity and the survival of small firms: A resource-based view of the road haulage industry. *Human Resource Management Journal*, 13(4): 3–22.

Mills, D., & Timmins, J. 2004. Firm dynamics in New Zealand: A comparative analysis with OECD countries. New Zealand Treasury Working Paper 04/11. Wellington: New Zealand Treasury.

Ministry of Economic Development. 2015. Employment in firms with 50% or more foreign ownership, 2013. Retrieved from http://www.mbie.govt.nz/info-services/business/business-growth-agenda/regions/regional-economic-activity-report-charts/Chart-24.pdf/view?searchterm=foreign%20ownership.

New Zealand Treasury. 2004. New Zealand's diaspora and overseas-born population. New Zealand Treasury

Working Paper 04/13. Retrieved from http://www.treasury.govt.nz/publications/research-policy/wp/2004/04-13/twp04-13.pdf.

New Zealand Treasury. 2008. Working smarter: Driving productivity growth through skills. New Zealand Treasury Productivity Paper 08/06. Retrieved from http://www.treasury.govt.nz/publications/research-policy/tprp/08-06.

Oakman, J., & Wells, Y. 2016. Working longer: What is the relationship between person–environment fit and retirement intentions?. *Asia Pacific Journal of Human Resources*, 54: 207–229.

OECD. 2000. *Literacy in the Information Age*. Paris: OECD.

OECD. 2014a. *OECD Factbook 2014*. Paris: OECD.

OECD. 2014b. *OECD Employment Outlook 2014*. Paris: OECD.

OECD. 2014c. *OECD Labour Force Statistics 2013*. Paris: OECD.

OECD. 2015. Stat extracts: trade union density. Retrieved from http://stats.oecd.org/Index.aspx?DataSetCode=UN_DEN#.

Peetz, D. 2006. *Brave New Workplace: How Individual Contracts Are Changing Our Lives*. Sydney: Allen & Unwin.

Senate Legal and Constitutional References Committee. 2005. They still call Australia home: Inquiry into Australian expatriates. Canberra: Department of the Senate, Parliament House.

Sheehan, C., & De Cieri, H. 2012. Charting the strategic trajectory of the Australian HR professional. *Asia Pacific Journal of Human Resources*, 50(2): 151–168.

Sheehan, C., De Cieri, H., & Cooper, B.K. 2016. The impact of HR political skill in the HRM and organisational performance relationship. *Australian Journal of Management*, 41: 161–181.

Sheehan, C., Holland, P., & De Cieri, H. 2006. Current developments in HRM in Australian organisations. *Asia Pacific Journal of Human Resources*, 44(2): 132–152.

Statistics New Zealand. 2013. 2013 Census quickstats about Māori. Retrieved from http://www.stats.govt.nz/~/media/Statistics/Census/2013%20Census/profile-and-summary-reports/quickstats-about-maori/qs-maori.pdf.

Statistics New Zealand. 2014. 2013 Census quickstats about culture and identity. Retrieved from http://www.stats.govt.nz/Census/2013-census/profile-and-summary-reports/quickstats-culture-identity.aspx.

Taylor, P., McLoughlin, C., Brooke, E., Di Biase, T., & Steinberg, M. 2013. Managing older workers during a period of tight labour supply. *Ageing and Society*, 33(1): 16–43.

Teicher, J., Holland, P., Pyman, A., & Cooper, B. 2007. Australian workers: Finding their voice. In R. Freeman, P. Boxall, and P. Haynes (eds), *What Workers Say: Employee Voice in the Anglo-American Workplace*: 125–144. Ithaca, NY: Cornell University Press.

Teo, S.T.T., & Rodwell, J.J. 2007. To be strategic in the new public sector, HR must remember its operational activities. *Human Resource Management*, 46(2): 265–284.

Townsend, K. 2013. To what extent do line managers play a role in modern industrial relations?. *Asia Pacific Journal of Human Resources*, 51(4): 421–436.

Van Wanrooy, B., Jakubauskas, M., Buchanan, J., Wilson, S., & Scalmer, S. 2008. Working lives: Statistics and stories. Retrieved from http://www.australiaatwork.org.au/assets/2.%20Australia%20at%20Work%20W2%20Working%20Lives.pdf.

WGEA. 2014. Australia's gender equality scorecard. Retrieved from https://www.wgea.gov.au/sites/default/files/2013-14_summary_report_website.pdf.

Westacott, J. 2011, 6 May. Essential skills in short supply. Retrieved from http://www.bca.com.au/newsroom/essential-skills-in-short-supply.

World Bank. 2015. World Development Indicators database. World Bank, 1 July. Retrieved from http://databank.worldbank.org/data/download/GDP.pdf.

Xia, Y., & Boxall, P. 2013. Attitudes to continuing professional development: A study of New Zealand human resource specialists. *New Zealand Journal of Human Resource Management*, 13(1): 36–47.

PART IV

CONCLUSIONS

34. Future avenues for comparative human resource management
Wolfgang Mayrhofer, Chris Brewster, and Elaine Farndale

THE STATUS QUO REVISITED

The contributions in this *Handbook* convincingly show that comparative human resource management (CHRM) has gained momentum and developed into a discourse of its own, with a firmly established place within the rubric of HRM. Of course, as this *Handbook* shows too, CHRM is not monolithic: it has developed several sub-discourses, depending on the chosen area of investigation and the respective theoretical, methodological, and empirical stance. Using the telescope analogy of varying in-depth foci on the field itself (Brewster, 1995), zooming out reveals the broader picture that CHRM, as part of HRM, is located at the intersection of many other disciplines. These disciplines have also invited or required a comparative angle as part of their own identity. Their research discourses, often much broader than HRM, have traditionally had a comparative angle built into them. We believe there is value in taking a closer look at neighbouring scientific endeavours to make future efforts in CHRM even more fruitful. Leaving aside research streams that use 'comparative' in a different meaning – for example, comparative effectiveness research (Rogers, 2014) – and the broad discussions of comparative methodology (e.g., Hantrais, 2009; Kenworthy & Hicks, 2008; Liamputtong, 2010; van de Vijver et al., 2008), we still face a substantial list of relevant discourses with a built-in comparative angle.

Industrial relations, a sister discipline to CHRM, has always been rooted in national institutions and systems and hence has a long-standing and well-developed tradition of comparing various facets of industrial relations across nation states (Frege & Kelly, 2013; Blanpain, 2010; Blanpain et al., 2009; Blanpain et al., 2008; Bamber et al., 2004; Bean, 1985; Bennett & Fawcett, 1985; Schappi, 1984). This includes issues such as patterns of the employment relationship (Casale, 2011), the role of employee representative bodies such as trade unions and works councils (Blanpain et al., 2007), and the relationship between industrial relations and wages as well as pay equity (Grimshaw, 2013; Rönnmar, 2008). Indeed, the relationship between industrial relations and HRM (Kaufman, 2010; Guest, 1987) is itself contextual: the rise of studies in HRM has meant that, perhaps more in some European countries than was the case in the United States of America (USA), researchers trained in industrial relations have switched allegiance to HRM. The effect has been that the industrial relations tradition of awareness of national differences has been to an extent transferred to HRM, supporting the work in CHRM.

Similarly, cross-cultural studies, which focus on generic characteristics of national or group culture and compare various cultures to find commonalities and differences (Esmer & Pettersson, 2007; Halman et al., 2008; Hofstede, 1980; Hofstede et al., 2010; Minkov, 2011), have obvious ramifications for CHRM. They consider issues that are close to or part of HRM: organization and work (Bhagat & Steers, 2009), management in specific regions of the world such as East Asia (Warner, 2013), leadership (Chhokar et al., 2007; Moran et al., 2011), ageing and the life course (Lynch & Danely, 2013), knowledge management (Del Giudice et al., 2012), learning (Li, 2012), decision-making (Schmorrow & Nicholson, 2011), and negotiation (Brett, 2007).

From a different theoretical angle, comparative studies in economics originate from the early comparisons of capitalism and socialism (Montias et al., 1993; also Loucks & Hoot, 1938 who include communism, fascism, and cooperation). After the collapse of the Soviet Union, such studies currently deal with differing models of capitalism (Amable, 2003; Hall & Soskice, 2001; Jackson & Deeg, 2008; Whitley, 1999) and their manifestations in various countries as a result of systematic and tremendous differences in the institutions relevant for political action, securing property rights, allocating credit, or resolving disputes (Djankov et al., 2003). One stream considers, for example, the transition paths of formerly socialist economies, or alternative paths among developing economies (Rosser & Rosser, 2004).

Linked to such institutional studies, the field of international business addresses issues related to the management and impact of multinational corporations (MNCs). The major impact of MNCs for CHRM lies in their possible desire to, and possible ability to, standardize HRM practices across their operations in different countries. They may not want to, preferring to take advantage of particular labour markets because of their particular skills in areas such as information technology, or in terms of cheap labour (Rugman & Verbeke, 2001). And if they do, cultural and, much more significantly, institutional constraints mean that they will never be able to standardize completely. HRM remains the most 'local' of management practices, just as it was decades ago (Rosenzweig & Nohria, 1994). The field of the international transfer of knowledge (Minbaeva et al., 2014) comes very close to HRM. The question that this raises is whether such knowledge transfer is reducing cross-national differences in HRM. As we see in Chapter 1 of this *Handbook*, the evidence is equivocal but seems to indicate that it is safe to say that national differences remain over time, although countries and country groups as a whole change over time in various aspects of HRM.

Not typically seen as quite so close to CHRM, but still relevant, the subject of comparative sociology (Armer & Marsh, 1982) analyses various relational aspects of a global world in transition, going beyond the long-standing division between capitalist, state socialist, and underdeveloped countries (Crow, 1997) and using a systematic set of comparative approaches (Dogan, 2009). Cross-cultural psychology looks at the effects of culture on a great variety of psychological phenomena, including motivation and cognition (van de Vijver et al., 2011; Keith, 2011; Sorrentino & Yamaguchi, 2008). Studies in anthropology (Boas & Benedict, 1938; Kroeber, 1923; Wulf, 2013) implicitly or explicitly have a comparative angle and analyse the universal questions of mankind: how we know who we are; why, exactly, the world is how it is; or what it means to be alone as individuals in different cultural and national settings (Astuti et al., 2007).

Beyond these adjacent fields, a number of other well-established and HRM-related research discourses have developed a comparative angle within their areas of interest. Table 34.1 gives an overview of major areas.

Each of these fields of national comparative research has obvious overlaps with and messages for CHRM, and we could continue this listing. Already, however, it shows that there is the potential for a greater synergy between disciplines and the possibility of

Table 34.1   Comparative discourses related to HRM

Label	Core focus	Examples
Comparative social policy research	Goes beyond the predominantly inward-looking domestic preoccupation of social policy within the boundaries of the state by using a more integrated, international and outward approach to analysis	Kennett (2013)
Comparative media systems research	Unearths commonalities and differences in national media systems and their influencing factors both in Western countries and beyond	Hallin & Mancini (2012), Volkmer (2012)
Comparative communications research	Explores communication within the realm of at least two macro units such as countries or markets in order to understand the phenomenon more deeply and work towards more robust conclusions	Esser & Hanitzsch (2012)
Comparative education	Analyses issues such as mass elementary education or national systems of education from a country-comparative angle, including developments in the technological, societal, and economic arena and, among others, aiming to inform relevant policy makers	Noah & Eckstein (1969), Crossley et al. (2007), Cowen & Kazamias (2009)
Comparative law; comparative employment law	Deals with the broad variety of fields covered by legal regulations such as family law, legal systems, or commercial law from a primarily country-comparative angle	Butler et al. (2011), Örücü & Nelken (2007), Blanpain et al. (2007), Botero et al. (2004)
Comparative politics	Looks at subfields such as political economy, political sociology, area studies, or international relations, examining issues such as government formation, contours, dynamics, and ideologies of the nation state, the role of policy programmes and patronage for running a political party, as well as emerging areas such as terrorism and electoral corruption	Landman & Robinson (2009), Lebow & Lichbach (2007), Boix & Stokes (2007)
Comparative public management research	Covers the differential impact of public administration theory on different contexts in different parts of the world	Holzer & Kasymova (2012), Vries et al. (2008)
Comparative social and cultural geography	Not only focuses on geographic ideas and traditions, but also allows for comparison between countries	Kitchin (2007)

considerable cross-learning. Amidst this variety, there is at least one underlying common thread running through these areas of scholarly endeavour: the conviction that fields of social science are inevitably required to emphasize contextual variety. 'There is no such thing as comparative chemistry or contextual physics. In the natural sciences, the chain of causality is everywhere identical . . . On the contrary, the social sciences, because of the diversity and idiosyncrasy of human societies, are contextual and relativistic' (Dogan, 2009: 13). Or, as Pascal half-despairingly, half-jokingly remarked: '*Vérité au deçà des Pyrénées, erreur au delà*'[1] (Pascal, 1671: Chapter 25, p. 74).

There is a lesson in these scientific discourses for both HRM and CHRM. In HRM's original models, in particular the model by Beer et al. (1984), context was built in as an essential element of the whole architecture, and in this respect HRM from the beginning was highly contextual. This has always been a small but significant part of the HRM discourse (see, e.g., Begin, 1992; Lam, 1994; Boxall, 1995; Brewster, 1995; Jackson & Schuler, 1995; Budhwar & Debrah, 2001; Lowe et al., 2002; Psychogios & Wood, 2010). However, looking at the bulk of empirical research in HRM and the highly cited papers in this area, this contextual anchoring has to a large extent been lost. The attempts to explore high-performance work systems or to link HRM to organizational performance have favoured a 'one size fits all' way of thinking. More broadly, the strong and, as we have argued continuously, disproportionate influence of US thinking in academia in general,[2] and HRM in particular, with its strong focus on national samples, has by and large led to an impoverishment and sometimes blatant ignoring of the contextual component of HRM (Beer et al., 2015). This has harmed the overall progress of the field (Brewster et al., 2016a). An integral problem has been that the unique advantages of a comparative angle have largely not yet been realized in HRM.

Five major advantages of a comparative angle on HRM can be identified (Esser & Hanitzsch, 2013):

- First, a comparative angle is crucial to generalizing findings and interpretations from mono-contextual studies. Comparative analyses help to determine the extent to which such findings and interpretations are valid beyond the original context. The more research finds similar results across a variety of contextual settings, the more confident we can be in terms of looking at a generalizable phenomenon; in addition, comparative studies will determine which findings are specific to certain cases and not generalizable beyond them.
- Second, comparative analyses help us to be cautious in terms of stretching our arguments based on mono-contextual studies too far, thus overgeneralizing findings or working on implicit assumptions not necessarily shared by other cultures. Take, for example, the implicit assumption that compensation systems or selection criteria should be merit-based: in countries where individual merit is just one, and perhaps not the most important, of several criteria for selection, assessment, or promotion, HRM has to take into account other potential criteria such as teamwork, family bonding, and past obligations.
- Third, a comparative angle is something of an antidote against an unjustified dominant paradigm built on implicit assumptions that one's own context is 'normal' and all deviations from that are aberrations that have to be updated. In this sense the comparative lens serves as a corrective.
- Fourth, a comparative angle strengthens the development of an international

---

[1] 'Truth on this side of the Pyrenees, error on the other side'.
[2] The Academy of Management still frequently uses 'international' to mean 'non-USA'.

community of scholars not only supporting the exchange of ideas, but also offering scholars from countries or regions less visible in the international arena the opportunity of taking part in the discourse. Comparative efforts can have a strong developmental and egalitarian subtext.

- Fifth and finally, a comparative view helps to reduce the blind spot vis-à-vis one's own country by showing alternative solutions to similar problems, thus broadening the view of researchers and showing ways out of seeming dead ends.

From this, we argue, it follows that comparative HRM has a unique and non-substitutable place in the HRM discourse. It both advances and challenges existing HRM wisdom through the specifics of the comparative angle.

WHERE WE CAN GO FROM HERE

The Need for Intensifying Comparative Research

Comparative HRM research is more complex and more difficult than research looking at one country or focusing solely on the practices of MNCs, but is at least equally exciting and informative. As the world becomes more global, so must our research. Empirically, a rich, if somewhat daunting, research agenda exists since there are many countries in the world about which we still have little information; and in many cases the information we have is stereotyped, inadequate, or non-comparable. At this point in our knowledge we still need the deep but narrow understanding of meaning and process that can be provided by detailed comparative case studies; the wide but shallow evidential base that large-scale surveys can bring; and access to secondary data provided by governments and international organizations for further analysis and exploration. In addition, if our evidence about and understanding of national differences remains a gap in our research, there is a chasm in our knowledge of developments in HRM over time that can only be filled by longitudinal research designs.

The need for more and better CHRM research also connects to the formidable task of understanding HRM practice in MNCs (Brewster et al., 2016b): if an organization covers more than just a few countries, even the experts at the centre, usually the headquarters, cannot know the details of HRM expectations and common practice in each local context. They are highly dependent on the information they obtain from their expatriate managers and the (usually local) HRM practitioners in each country – and they may have different agendas and understandings. The fact that most organizations manage to cope with this complexity at all is perhaps more noteworthy than that there are times when they make mistakes. CHRM can contribute to better HRM practice by providing and improving the information base that HRM practitioners rely on when deciding on operational HRM practices as well as strategic issues.

Similar issues apply within supply chains: popular reports suggest that these are sometimes used as ways of MNCs 'distancing' themselves and their governance structures from brutal, unpleasant, and occasionally murderous practices in 'cheap labour' contexts. We need more internationally comparative studies of the work aspects of corporate social responsibility, and more research on HRM in supply chains and the impact of the non-HRM management practice and requirements on HRM in poorer countries. Working together with practitioners in organizations operating across national and cultural borders, as well as with international professional HRM organizations, increases the potential impact of CHRM as it leads research and theory-building towards practically relevant issues, especially when new phenomena appear that are first detected by people involved in HRM practice rather than from academia.

Comparative HRM exposes significant differences in the way the concept of HRM is understood, managed, and implemented in different countries. For researchers and for organisations operating internationally this raises crucial theoretical, methodological, and empirical issues. Based on developments in the broader societal and economic context, recent literature in comparative HRM, and current trends in the academic HRM debate, we identify two core areas in which further progress is especially needed and where, therefore, there is ample scope for comparative HRM analysis to develop: first, conceptual issues revolving around potential areas of interest, available theory and data, as well as the object of research itself; and second, issues of research methodology in a comparative setting. For each area, we outline the main ideas, felicitously under three further subheadings for each area, and illustrate them with a few examples (see also Budhwar & Debrah, 2001; Larsen & Mayrhofer, 2006; Brewster, 2007; Mayrhofer, 2007; Mayrhofer & Reichel, 2009; Al Ariss & Sidani, 2016). We then conclude with a discussion of the political game of how to strengthen one's position within the scientific communities.

Core Area 1: Conceptual Issues

Within the conceptual issues that CHRM will have to deal with in the future, we consider three as of immediate relevance: further clarifying the object of CHRM research; concentrating on fruitful research themes; and using more and better theory.

Clarifying the object of research

HRM research in general has difficulties agreeing about its 'object'. While there is some consensus on core functions of HRM such as recruitment and selection, training and development or compensation, there is a great variety of views on what HRM 'actually' is (see, for example, the different basic approaches pointed out by Legge, 2005). Scanning through the research literature reveals that what is observed when HRM is the focus of interest varies widely. There are a number of reasons for this. First, all scientific disciplines have debates about what does or does not fall within their scope, and encompass a variety of definitions of their construct. HRM is still a relatively young field of scholarly activity and so the problem is exacerbated.

Second, business practice has a large influence on HRM and there is a need to connect to the language and thinking of practitioners. Since the influence of management consultancies and 'gurus' is on being up-to-date and fashionable, HRM tends to adopt similar approaches. For example, the current discussions about human capital management or talent management are in part a response to the rhetoric used in practitioner circles about personnel being the most valuable asset. In many cases, this trendy terminology confuses the issue and adds in extra 'jangle fallacies' (Molloy & Ployhart, 2012) rather than clarifying the subject of study.

Third, being a young branch sometimes leads to clear leaps in the understanding of the field. For example, while it was quite controversial in the 1980s and 1990s whether the change from 'personnel' to 'human resource management' constituted more than a change in terminology, in hindsight it marks such a leap. Fourth, and maybe most important, what HRM 'really' is inevitably varies across time and space. Even if one agrees on some basic functions of HRM, the actual context matters considerably. For example, it is easy to see that our understanding of the way people are and should be managed clearly has to be different in different circumstances, such as in as situations of labour surplus versus labour shortage, dictatorship versus democracy, centrally planned versus free market economy and, perhaps most relevantly, a shareholder-based economy like that of the USA versus a stakeholder-based economy as in Northern Europe.

All this creates major problems for comparative HRM research. Crucial questions emerge if there is, at best, moderate agreement about core aspects of HRM; if there is little agreement about how to operationalize HRM; and worst of all, if HRM is a moving target constantly changing its shape due to the sometimes rapid development of our understanding and the differences between various contexts. How can we compare what might be decisively different in national contexts in a snapshot or cross-sectional analysis? How do we cope with progress in our understanding of HRM in longitudinal research where the research object changes due to different practices and concepts? What does this mean for cumulative research that requires a certain amount of joint understanding and established views? While there are currently few answers to such questions, these issues constitute crucial aspects for the future development of the field.

Fruitful research themes

Much of the early CHRM analysis was originally descriptive, simply recording similarities and differences. Many of the early CHRM texts reported single-country studies, showing that they were different from the accepted models in the USA. However, the fascination of 'here are we different, here alike' has slowly, but surely, faded in favour of attempts to understand HRM in different contexts, at least for those world regions such as Europe, North America, Australasia, and Japan where a substantial literature has emerged and is available in the global scientific discourse. To be sure, there remains a need for basic description of HRM policies and practices in regions of the world (or parts of them) such as Latin America, sub-Saharan Africa, and parts of Asia where either little is known or where the locally available knowledge is not fed into the global scientific discourse (for exceptions, of course, see the relevant chapters in this volume). It is important that such research takes an emic perspective, seeking to identify empirical practice, whatever it may be; rather than a sterile etic perspective, seeking to check whether US-style practices exist in these countries.

Basically, fruitful research themes can come from two, hopefully connected, points of departure. First, they can come from the existing scientific discourse. Based on what has been done to date, we can identify promising themes that support rigorous components of extant research and increase the potential for cumulative work. Examples for future research based on such a view include an analysis of basic national HRM indicators and their development over time in different parts of Europe, including those states in the European Union (EU) and those outside; the use of institutional theories to define organizational fields and the application of these fields as measures for comparison, for example between MNCs and indigenous companies; or setting up a longitudinal cohort study with an organizational panel and/or using existing panel data.

Second, themes can emerge from practical problems in the world of work, emphasizing the relevance component. Potentially, this type of research has greater societal effects and may in some cases allow access to specific types of grant money linked to themes deemed important by policy-makers, practitioner foundations, or science managers. Examples include the effect on HRM of European integration (or perhaps, given 'Brexit', reductions in integration), economic performance at the national and organizational level, integration of refugees from abroad, becoming a knowledge society, and sustainability. Further study of the HRM developments in the ex-communist states in Europe would be valuable, as would studies of the consequences of changing demographics and different patterns of opening up national labour markets at individual, organizational, and national levels. Other prominent themes drawn from practice developments include sustainability, inequality, and corporate social responsibility as it applies to HRM (Ehnert, 2009; Jackson & Seo, 2010; Jackson et al., 2011; Ehnert & Harry, 2012; Strauss & Connerley, 2003; Watson, 2004). CHRM research can connect to these themes, for example by comparing how legal regulations in various countries influence the integration of sustainability themes into HRM policies and practices; analysing across countries the link between different degrees of societal inequality; and examining the different ways organisations communicate with their employees and what type of 'voice' employees have.

More and better theory
Introducing more and better-elaborated theory is a continuous call in organisation research. We introduce a note of caution here. We note, but explore no further here, that the meaning of 'theory' is unclear and contentious. More significantly, in line with Wright (2015) in one of his typically perceptive contributions, we believe that such calls are often a lazy substitute for genuine critique; risk privileging what is 'new' over what is 'true'; stem from a misunderstanding of 'proper science' (Beer et al., 2015) where in fact replications of 'established fact' are published frequently, building up a picture of the boundaries of extant theory; and that contribution may be more important than theory development. We identify an additional problem with these calls for 'better theory' in that in practice they are often demands to apply etic understanding of ideas developed in countries such as the USA to substantially different contexts. It can be a form of 'labour restriction' preventing scholars from publishing emic research in the top journals.

Even with this caution, however, better and more realistic theory will benefit HRM and particularly CHRM. Our specific comparative angle requires theoretical perspectives that explicitly take into account the time perspective and a developmental perspective, that is, how current differences between units of analysis – most often countries – will develop over time. For example, the institutional theorists point to crucial varieties at the macro level (e.g., Hall & Soskice, 2001; Amable, 2003; Whitley, 1999) that lead to distinct differences at the meso or micro level such as in organizations or HRM. CHRM analyses have used such theories (see, e.g., Croucher et al., 2012; Goergen et al., 2009), but these theories in turn have been criticized as being incapable of dealing with change (Deeg & Jackson, 2007), and attempts have been made to address the notion of change and development within the basic theory (Thelen, 2014). There is scope for considerably more work here, bridging the analyses at national level and the firm-level evidence on the internal relationships between managements and employees (Whitley, 1992), to enhance both.

In a similar vein, one can argue for a stronger emphasis on a hybridization perspective. Arguably, both the cultural and the institutional perspectives have value as explicators of country differences, and both are needed to fully understand policy differences and differences in HRM practice across countries. Both perspectives are aware of the importance of the other. The cultural specialists often use institutional differences as examples of the importance of culture, arguing that clear elements of culture have an effect on organizational structures, and hence on HRM (Maurice, 1989). Equally, the institutional literature often includes reference to informal institutions (Dikova et al., 2010; Slangen & Beugelsdijk, 2010) or soft institutions (North, 1990), which come close to cultural explanations; they argue that cultures are part of the institutions (Berry et al., 2010), or they discuss issues of legitimacy (Suchman, 1995), which in its manifestation as the perceptions of the public and society (Aerts & Cormier, 2009) appears to be a cultural artefact.

It seems that exclusively cross-cultural or exclusively institutional analysis may miss key elements impacting upon HRM. Culture by its nature is less tangible and, to some extent, organizations can manage culture. They can, for example, deliberately recruit people who are at the edges of the normal distribution curve of that country: loud, confident Malaysians, or aggressive, self-aggrandizing Swedes. There is much less they can do about institutions. True, in countries with weak institutions or following a political or military coup, a powerful international bank, for example, may be able to have a significant influence on the emerging institutions, and all large businesses will lobby government for changes. By and large, however, organizations have to deal with the institutions they find in the country. So cultural differences may be important in setting the framework for national institutions, but it is institutional differences that will matter to MNCs. Where the institutions are silent about particular HRM practices, where there are no regulations or constraints, then cultures may explain significant differences between home and host country; otherwise institutional analyses are more powerful for organizational-level research (Vaiman & Brewster, 2015).

Other theoretical concepts are still in their infancy in CHRM, but may also be promising. For example, convention theory (*économie des conventions*; Dupuy et al., 1989) argues that in situations of human action and coordination, actors use conventions to justify appreciation or criticism of objects and persons (Boltanski & Thévenot, 1991a; Boltanski & Thévenot, 1991b [2006]), thus reducing uncertainty (Diaz-Bone & Salais, 2011) and coordinating their interactions with others in order to achieve a common goal (Salais & Storper, 1993; Storper & Salais, 1997). Also called 'orders of worth', these conventions are higher-order principles or interpretative schemes; stem from major philosophical ideas; and, it is argued, cover six ideal-types: market, industrial, domestic, civic, inspired, and fame. They are an application of 'the taxonomy of cultural repertoires that present different justifications of worth to understand how people disagree, compromise, and conclude agreements' (Thornton et al., 2012: 34). This theoretical approach can help CHRM in analysing the extent to which existing HRM configurations, and policies and practices, at the organisational and national level are a result of negotiating between different orders of worth; or how crucial individual and collective actors – for example, chief executive officers, HRM directors, and key national organisations – in different national contexts, handle existing conflicts between various orders of worth.

Clearly, there is still more theoretical work to do. In particular, this includes further understanding mechanisms for translating contextual conditions into organizational and individual action. This targets the interplay between various layers of internal and external context and the HRM chain; that is, HRM strategies, policies, and practices, as well as the respective outcomes at various levels ranging from the individual to the society (Paauwe, 2004). Likewise, this can help in explaining the long-term development of country differences and their effects on HRM.

Core Area 2: Empirical Issues

Empirically, too, we see three themes that are especially important for progress in the field: making better use of existing datasets; exploiting new developments in terms of analytical methods; and the practical issues surrounding international research teams conducting comparative studies.

Better use of existing datasets

Much of current CHRM research is small scale, rather ad hoc, heavily constrained in terms of resources, and limited to a comparatively small number of units of analysis, typically countries. This is no surprise, since setting up one's own database is difficult if it goes beyond a 'convenience sample' such as students. In CHRM research, a lack of local contacts in different countries that are interested and have the capacity and resources for data-gathering and analysis is a serious problem. This is particularly true in countries almost absent from the international discourse, and where local researchers often simply have no resources to carry out any serious research.

A much too rarely used alternative to creating one's own pool of data is the exploitation of publicly available databases offering comparative data. The past decades have seen a surge in the number of large datasets available for comparative management research. This includes both national and international comparative surveys to which basically every academic, under certain conditions, has access. Examples abound and include, but are not limited to:

- Organisation for Economic Co-operation and Development (OECD) databases: for example, the World Indicators of Skills for Employment (WISE) database about skills and work.
- International Monetary Fund (IMF) databases: for example, the Coordinated Direct Investment Survey (CDIS).
- International Labour Organization (ILO) databases: for example, country-specific labour force surveys.
- The World Value Survey (WVS).
- Regional databases: for example, the European Work Condition Survey; European Union Statistics on Income and Living Conditions (EU-SILC); open data by the government of the USA, such as Education Demographic and Geographic Estimates.

At the country level, datasets such as the German IAB Establishment Panel, a longitudinal representative employer survey of employment parameters at individual establishments (www.iab.de/en/erhebungen/iab-betriebspanel.aspx), or various surveys accessible through the UK Data Service (www.ukdataservice.ac.uk) funded by the Economic and

Social Research Council (ESRC), the major United Kingdom funding agency, can be the starting point for a comparative angle. While such sources have been used in other research arenas, they have not been systematically exploited for CHRM.

In addition, the dramatic increase in the availability of digitalized data creates a potentially rich source for analyses. For example, the availability of text on the web allows access to real-life data in an unobtrusive way. Company homepages contain information about how employees are seen; websites specialize on characterizing and rating current and past employers (for example, www.glassdoor.com); new social networks allow a fresh look at how people deal with organizations and vice versa. In combination with methods in qualitative data analysis allowing the processing of large amounts of text, now available as a result of increased computing power (e.g., Alexa & Zuell, 2000; Tausczik & Pennebaker, 2010; Hopkins & King, 2010), these opportunities become even more promising.

Advances in methods

Comparative HRM is affected by three major constraints typical for research conducted across national and/or cultural boundaries. First, when using theoretical frameworks in empirical research across national and cultural boundaries, some difficulties are usually acknowledged. Yet, the debate seems more or less closed, building on the emerging tacit assumption behind much of current work: 'Let's assume it's universal and works well enough, somehow'.

Second, there is the problem of making sense of the local environment in a comparative setting. This affects the design of the studies as well as the interpretation of the results. In CHRM, there has been a positive move away from 'safari research' (Peterson, 2001) with single researchers going to 'exotic' places marvelling at the local customs, towards culturally mixed research teams. These can operate on single projects or can be large-scale global research networks pooling both local expertise and global insight. Examples of the latter include Cranet (www.cranet.org), with a focus on HRM policies and practices, or 5C (www.5C.careers), a collaboration investigating contemporary careers across the globe.

Third, the use of established analytical methods across national and cultural boundaries is a long-standing issue. In the objective paradigm with its focus on questionnaire-based data-gathering, this is widely debated and 'quasi-solutions' are offered. For example, several translation–retranslation techniques supporting a preferably identical meaning of the questions are standard touchstones within these approaches. There is less discussion of the interpretative paradigm, though. Methods linked to the analysis of texts, for example, depend heavily on sufficient insight into the respective language (Björkman & Piekkari, 2009). Yet, in culturally mixed teams doing interpretative analysis, a number of tricky issues evolve that cannot easily be solved, and where little established advice is available. The following example, from a qualitative country and culture comparative study on careers (Briscoe et al., 2012b) conducted by an international academic research collaboration, illustrates this:

> Beyond classical translation problems a number of difficulties arose in a multi-lingual comparative research setting. There are potential losses of richness of the interview data due to a different number and degree of language changes and translation when collecting and interpreting data. There might be no change from the original language, for example, when US members of the

team look at South African transcribed interviews conducted in English, since they can use the same language although even then interpretations inevitably will vary due to subtleties of the respective language and different mindset. However, when Austrian researchers look at the US data they are filtering their understanding through one language change; and when Malaysian members of the team look at core categories formulated in English based on an interview conducted in Spanish there are two such changes. Each change leads to a loss of nuance, difficulties in consulting the original interview texts, which sometimes is practically impossible for non-native speakers, e.g. Japanese transcripts for non-Japanese speakers, or a lack of density when discussing texts in culturally mixed interpretation groups or struggling for coding categories and interpretations. There is no easy solution for this. It is certain that suggestions about how to handle these problems properly are unlikely to come solely or even primarily from within comparative HRM. Rather, this provides a fruitful task for the discourses specialising on various methodologies within the interpretative paradigm.

Fourth, the past two decades have brought significant advances in terms of analyses across different levels of social complexity. For CHRM, this is especially significant since often you have the situation that you want to account for the influence of, for example, a level 2 variable such as country or organization on a level 1 variable, for example organizations in various countries or individuals in various organizations. For such a situation, various forms of multilevel models have emerged which, under certain conditions, allow for rigorous statistical analysis across levels (for a cautionary note see, for example, Bryan & Jenkins, 2016; Schmidt-Catran & Fairbrother, 2016). CHRM can greatly profit from these advances since they allow a more profound analysis. While this also puts new requirements on data collection, the overall effects seem to be positive.

Managing international research teams

The current 'gold standard' in CHRM research is a collaborative effort with research team members coming from the different countries and cultures analysed. Inevitably, then, the problem of forming and maintaining culturally mixed research teams emerges. Currently, a lot of verbal and considerable material support exists for cross-border efforts from policy-makers and grant agencies. For example, Horizon 2020 as the eighth phase of the Framework Programmes for Research and Technological Development (FP8) not only supports collaboration within the European Union, but under specific circumstances can also include researchers from countries outside Europe. In addition, the background of junior researchers is changing. Increasingly now, they are themselves bi- or multicultural and/or often have substantial experience in working in culturally mixed teams from the student level on. Beyond that, a number of high-ranking academic associations such as the European Group for Organization Studies (EGOS) or the Academy of Management (AOM) regularly offer workshops supporting the collaboration of young academics from different countries. All this leads to a favourable overall climate for comparative research efforts.

Beyond formation, however, the continuous management of long-standing research teams across national and cultural boundaries is potentially difficult (Briscoe et al., 2012a; Brewster et al., 2011; Mayrhofer, 1998). Long-standing teams are often quite diverse in terms of time spent in the academic system and preferences for scientific work. Hence, team members often have very different resources available, which leads to varying contributions, raising questions of relative fairness and sharing of the work load. Beyond that, they often have different objectives for their academic work; for example, heavily practitioner oriented versus clearly science oriented. This leads to sometimes fruitful, sometimes dysfunctional, tensions within the research team when it comes to crucial debates about the future course of work. Over time, roles of key researchers change, too. Besides a certain amount of 'normal' fluctuation, with some individuals dropping out and others joining the team, there is also a change in the roles of those staying in the research team, due to factors such as seniority, priorities, personal life circumstances, or acceptance within the team. Particular problems arise when the founder of the network retires or moves on, and only a few networks survive this change. Within the academic environment, where notions of equality are widespread and scepticism towards formal relations prevails, keeping a long-standing research team viable across national and cultural borders is not easy.

Working together with 'strangers' incentivized primarily by the prospect of a grant resulting from external incentive structures is a relatively recent phenomenon. National as well as international grant agencies sometimes require the inclusion of different countries to show a geographical spread. In order to gain access to such funds, teams are sometimes partly formed around criteria that go beyond technical knowledge and established personal relationships. They may include academics with poor technical expertise and/or social fit who are recruited because the funding agencies want a representative of such a country and there is no one else at hand; or who have a primary interest in being part of a project with international grant money that increases their status in their home academic system. This leads to a number of potential pitfalls such as different (explicit or implicit) interests and agendas when joining the research project. For example, scientific interest or interest in building networks may be subordinated to the financial and prestige incentives. Such 'research mercenaries' or 'funding vultures' usually have immediate negative effects on the research team itself, since their interest and capacity vanish once the money is gone, or sometimes even as soon as the money is granted. In addition, this also leads to an increasing commercialization and functionalization of collaborative research.

When grant money alone becomes the major driver for establishing an international research team, it is more than likely that interpersonal learning will be limited, and the interest and the capacity for comparative work will fade once the monetary source is exhausted. This also can lead to biases in the work of a larger consortium because of uneven input by the members of the network. Unless these trends are countered, what one might expect to see in the future is the increasing emergence of 'business-like' research networks driven less by interest in the topic and joint views about how to tackle problems, and more by the interest in getting financed. For CHRM, then, the availability of grant money built on the requirement of international teams is both an opportunity and a threat for the further development of the field.

CLOSING REMARKS

Like every other scientific discourse, CHRM is embedded in a broader context. Among others, this context consists of the various scientific disciplines not only struggling to uncover more of the truth, but also competing for monetary and non-monetary resources enabling future research. They are also, perhaps inevitably, struggling for the attention of fellow researchers in neighbouring disciplines and of the general public. In the current global context, with its many voices, this requires substantial visibility which seems to call for a consistent and attractive brand. To turn CHRM into such a brand, at least three steps seem essential.

First, it is important to develop a shared understanding of CHRM as one of the umbrellas under which researchers rally, providing the backdrop against which comparative HRM analyses are conducted. As a concept and as a label, however, CHRM can serve the purpose of common ground. This includes a moratorium on trendy or creative interpretations of what CHRM 'really' is all about and what components it includes. At least for the time being, exploiting what already exists in terms of frameworks and definitions seems to be a good approach to create the basis for cumulative research efforts.

Second, the mere fact of flagging comparative studies as such would be a step forward. Many significant contributions in the field – whether deliberately or not – fail to use 'comparative HRM' as a label signifying their work. In building a recognisable brand, an established label and its consistent use is crucial.

Third, in the long run, CHRM as a field in its own right can only survive if it becomes attractive for good – and ideally good young – researchers. A major step towards that is an increase in the visibility of CHRM in top journals. This would signal that the topic is substantial enough to get published in top journals; which, again, is a prerequisite for getting excellent people interested.

Clearly, the field of comparative HRM has travelled a long way in a short time, but there is much that remains to be explored. We look forward, with excitement, to further developments over future years.

REFERENCES

Aerts, W., & Cormier, D. 2009. Media legitimacy and corporate environmental communication. *Accounting, Organizations and Society*, 34(1): 1–27.

Al Ariss, A., & Sidani, Y. 2016. Comparative international human resource management: Future research directions. *Human Resource Management Review*, 26(4): 352–358.

Alexa, M., & Zuell, C. 2000. Text analysis software: commonalities, differences and limitations: The results of a review. *Quantity and Quality*, 34: 99–321.

Amable, B. 2003. *The Diversity of Modern Capitalism*. Oxford: Oxford University Press.

Armer, J.M., & Marsh, R.M. (eds). 1982. *Comparative Sociological Research in the 1960s and 1970s*. Leiden: Brill.

Astuti, R., Parry, J.P., & Stafford, C. (eds). 2007. *Questions of Anthropology*. Oxford: Berg.

Bamber, G., Lansbury, R.D., & Wailes, N. (eds). 2004. *International and Comparative Employment Relations: Globalisation and the Developed Market Economies* (4th edn). London: SAGE Publications.

Bean, R. 1985. *Comparative Industrial Relations: An Introduction to Cross-National Perspectives*. New York: St Martin's Press.

Beer, M., Boselie, P., & Brewster, C. 2015. Back to the future: Implications for the field of HRM of the multi-stakeholder perspective proposed 30 years ago. *Human Resource Management*, 54(3): 427–438.

Beer, M., Spector, B., Lawrence, P.R., Quinn Mills, D., & Walton, R.E. 1984. *Managing Human Assets: The Groundbreaking Harvard Business School Program*. New York: Free Press.

Begin, J.P. 1992. Comparative human resource management (HRM): A systems perspective. *International Journal of Human Resource Management*, 3(3): 379–408.

Bennett, J.D., & Fawcett, J. 1985. *Industrial Relations: An International and Comparative Bibliography*. London: Mansell.

Berry, H., Guillén, M.F., & Zhou, N. 2010. An institutional approach to cross-national distance. *Journal of International Business Studies*, 41: 1460–1480.

Bhagat, R.S., & Steers, R.M. (eds). 2009. *Cambridge Handbook of Culture, Organizations, and Work*. Cambridge: Cambridge University Press.

Björkman, A., & Piekkari, R. 2009. Language and subsidiary control: An empirical test. *Journal of International Management*, 15(1): 105–117.

Blanpain, R. (ed.). 2010. *Comparative Labour Law and Industrial Relations in Industrialized Market Economies* (10th edn). Austin, TX: Wolters Kluwer Law & Business.

Blanpain, R., Bisom-Rapp, S., Corbett, W.R., et al. (eds). 2007. *The Global Workplace: International and Comparative Employment Law-Cases and Materials*. Cambridge: Cambridge University Press.

Blanpain, R., Bromwich, W., Rymkevich, O., et al. (eds). 2009. *The Modernization of Labour Law and Industrial Relations in a Comparative Perspective*. Austin, TX: Wolters Kluwer Law & Business.

Blanpain, R., Dickens, L., & Andersen, S.K. (eds). 2008. *Challenges in European Employment Relations: Employment Regulation; Trade Union Organization; Equality, Flexicurity, Training and New Approaches to Pay*. Austin, TX: Wolters Kluwer Law & Business.

Blanpain, R., Ōuchi, S., & Araki, T. (eds). 2007. *Decentralizing Industrial Relations and the Role of Labour Unions and Employee Representatives*. The Hague: Kluwer Law International.

Boas, F., & Benedict, R. 1938. *General Anthropology*. Boston, MA: D.C. Heath & Company.

Boix, C., & Stokes, S.C. (eds). 2007. *The Oxford Handbook of Comparative Politics*. Oxford: Oxford University Press.

Boltanski, L., & Thévenot, L. 1991a. *De la Justification: Les Économies de la Grandeur*. Paris: Gallimard.

Boltanski, L., & Thévenot, L. 1991b [2006]. *On Justification.: Economies of Worth*. Princeton, NJ: Princeton University Press.

Botero, J.C., Djankov, S., La Porta, R., Lopez-de-Salanes, F., & Shleifer, A. 2004. The regulation of labor. *Quarterly Journal of Economics*, 119(4): 1339–1382.

Boxall, P.F. 1995. Building the theory of comparative HRM. *Human Resource Management Journal*, 5(5): 5–17.

Brett, J.M. 2007. *Negotiating Globally: How to Negotiate Deals, Resolve Disputes, and Make Decisions Across Cultural Boundaries* (2nd edn). San Francisco, CA: Jossey-Bass.

Brewster, C. 1995. Towards a 'European' model of human resource management. *Journal of International Business Studies*, 26(1): 1–21.

Brewster, C. 2007. Comparative HRM: European views and perspectives. *International Journal of Human Resource Management*, 18(5): 769–787.

Brewster, C., Gooderham, P.N., & Mayrhofer, W. 2016a. Human resource management: The promise, the performance, the consequences. *Journal of Organizational Effectiveness: People and Performance*, 3(2): 181–190.

Brewster, C., Mayrhofer, W., & Reichel, A. 2011. Riding the tiger? Going along with Cranet for two decades – A relational perspective. *Human Resource Management Review*, 21(1): 5–15.

Brewster, C., Mayrhofer, W., & Smale, A. 2016b. Crossing the streams: HRM in multinational enterprises and comparative HRM. *Human Resource Management Review*, 26(4): 285–297.

Briscoe, J.P., Chudzikowski, K., Demel, B., et al. 2012a. The 5C Project: Our story and our research. In J.P. Briscoe, D.T. Hall, & W. Mayrhofer (eds), *Careers Around the World*: 39–56. New York, USA and London, UK: Routledge Taylor & Francis Group.

Briscoe, J.P., Hall, D.T., & Mayrhofer, W. (eds). 2012b. *Careers Around the World: Individual and Contextual Perspectives*. New York, USA and Abingdon, UK: Routledge.

Bryan, M.L., & Jenkins, S.P. 2016. Multilevel modelling of country effects: A cautionary tale. *European Sociological Review*, 32(1): 3–22.

Budhwar, P.S., & Debrah, Y. 2001. Rethinking comparative and cross-national human resource management research. *International Journal of Human Resource Management*, 12(3): 497–515.

Butler, W.E., Kresin, O.V., & Shemshuchenko, I.S. 2011. *Foundations of Comparative Law: Methods and Typologies*. London: Wildy, Simmonds & Hill.

Casale, G. (ed.). 2011. *The Employment Relationship: A Comparative Overview*. Oxford: Hart.

Chhokar, J.S., Brodbeck, F.C., & House, R.J. (eds). 2007. *Culture and Leadership Across the World: The GLOBE Book of In-Depth Studies of 25 Societies*. Mahwah, NJ, USA and London, UK: Lawrence Erlbaum Associates.

Cowen, R., & Kazamias, A.M. (eds). 2009. *International Handbook of Comparative Education. Part 1*. Dordecht: Springer.

Crossley, M., Broadfoot, P., & Schweisfurth, M. (eds). 2007. *Changing Educational Contexts, Issues and Identities: 40 Years of Comparative Education*. London: Routledge.

Croucher, R., Wood, G., Brewster, C., & Brookes, M. 2012. Employee turnover, HRM and institutional contexts *Economic and Industrial Democracy*, 33(4): 605–620.

Crow, G. 1997. *Comparative Sociology and Social Theory: Beyond the Three Worlds*. Basingstoke: Macmillan Press.

Deeg, R., & Jackson, G. 2007. Towards a more dynamic theory of capitalist variety. *Socio-Economic Review*, 5(1): 149–179.

Del Giudice, M., Carayannis, E.G., & Della Peruta, M.R. 2012. *Cross-Cultural Knowledge Management: Fostering Innovation and Collaboration Inside the Multicultural Enterprise*. New York: Springer.

Diaz-Bone, R., & Salais, R. 2011. Economics of convention and the history of economies: Towards a transdisciplinary approach in economic history. *Historical Social Research*, 36(4): 7–39.

Dikova, D., Sahib, P.R., & van Witteloostuijn, A. 2010. Cross-border acquistion abandonment and completion: The effect of institutional differences and organizational learning in the international business service industry, 1981–2001. *Journal of International Business Studies*, 41(2): 223–245.

Djankov, S., Glaeser, E., La Porta, R., Lopez-de-Silanes, F., & Shleifer, A. 2003. The new comparative economics. *Journal of Comparative Economics*, 31(4): 595–619.

Dogan, M. 2009. Strategies in Comparative Sociology. In M. Sasaki (ed.), *New Frontiers in Comparative Sociology*: 13–44. Leiden, Netherlands and Boston, MA, USA: Brill.

Dupuy, J.P., Eymard-Duvernay, F., Favereau, O., Orléan, A., Salais, R., & Thévenot, L. 1989. Introduction. *Revue économique*, 40(2): 141–145.

Ehnert, I. 2009. *Sustainable Human Resource Management: A Conceptual and Exploratory Analysis from a Paradox Perspective*. Heidelberg: Physica-Verlag.

Ehnert, I., & Harry, W. 2012. Recent developments and future prospects on sustainable human resource management: Introduction to the Special Issue. *Management Revue*, 23(3): 221–238.

Esmer, Y.R., & Pettersson, T. (eds). 2007. *Measuring and Mapping Cultures: 25 Years of Comparative Value Surveys*. Leiden: Brill.

Esser, F., & Hanitzsch, T. (eds). 2012. *Handbook of Comparative Communication Research*. New York: Routledge.

Esser, F., & Hanitzsch, T. 2013. On the why and how of comparative inquiry in communication studies. In F. Esser and T. Hanitzsch (eds), *Handbook of Communication Research*: 3–22. New York: Routledge.

Frege, C.M., & Kelly, J.E. (eds). 2013. *Comparative Employment Relations in the Global Economy*. London: Routledge.

Goergen, M., Brewster, C., & Wood, G. 2009. Corporate governance regimes and employment relations in Europe. *Relations industrielles/Industrial Relations*, 64(4): 620–640.

Grimshaw, D. (ed.). 2013. *Minimum Wages, Pay Equity and Comparative Industrial Relations*. New York: Routledge.

Guest, D.E. 1987. Human resource management and industrial relations. *Journal of Management Studies*, 24(5): 503–521.

Hall, P.A., & Soskice, D. (eds). 2001. *Varieties of Capitalism: The Institutional Foundations of Comparative Advantage*. Oxford: Oxford University Press.

Hallin, D.C., & Mancini, P. (eds). 2012. *Comparing Media Systems beyond the Western World*. Cambridge: Cambridge University Press.

Halman, L., Inglehart, R., Díez-Mendrano, J., et al. (eds). 2008. *Changing Values and Beliefs in 85 Countries: Trends from the Values Surveys from 1981 to 2004*. Leiden, Netherlands and Boston, MA, USA: Brill.

Hantrais, L. 2009. *International Comparative Research: Theory, Methods and Practice*. Basingstoke: Palgrave Macmillan.

Hofstede, G. 1980. *Culture's Consequences: International Differences in Work-Related Values*. Newbury Park, CA: SAGE Publications.

Hofstede, G.H., Hofstede, G.J., & Minkov, M. 2010. *Cultures and Organizations. Software of the Mind: Intercultural Cooperation and its Importance for Survival* (3rd edn). New York: McGraw-Hill.

Holzer, M., & Kasymova, J. 2012. Restating the relevanace of comparative public administration. *Public Administration Review*, 72(1): 162–164.

Hopkins, D., & King, G. 2010. A method of automated nonparametric content analysis for social science. *American Journal of Political Science*, 54: 229–247.

Jackson, G., & Deeg, R. 2008. Comparing capitalisms: Understanding institutional diversity and its implications for international business. *Journal of International Business Studies*, 39(4): 540–561.

Jackson, S.E., Renwick, D.W.S., Jabbour, C.J.C., & Muller-Camen, M. 2011. State-of-the-art and future directions for green human resource management. *Zeitschrift für Personalforschung*, 25(2): 99–116.

Jackson, S.E., & Schuler, R.S. 1995. Understanding human resource management in the context of organizations and their environments. *Annual Review of Psychology*, 46: 237–264.

Jackson, S.E., & Seo, J. 2010. The greening of strategic HRM scholarship. *Organization Management Journal*, 7(4): 278–290.

Kaufman, B.E. 2010. The theoretical foundation of industrial relations and its implications for labor economics and human resource management. *Industrial and Labor Relations Review*, 64(1): 74–108.

Keith, K.D. (ed.). 2011. *Cross-Cultural Psychology: Contemporary Themes and Perspectives*. Chichester: Wiley-Blackwell.

Kennett, P. (ed.). 2013. *A Handbook of Comparative Social Policy* (2nd edn). Cheltenham, UK and Northampton, MA, USA: Edward Elgar Publishing.

Kenworthy, L., & Hicks, A. (eds). 2008. *Method and Substance in Macrocomparative Analysis*. Basingstoke, UK and New York, USA: Palgrave Macmillan.

Kitchin, R. 2007. *Mapping Worlds: International Perspectives on Social and Cultural Geographies.* London: Routledge.

Kroeber, A.L. 1923. *Anthropology.* New York: Harcourt, Brace & Company.

Lam, A. 1994. The utilisation of human resources: A comparative study of British and Japanese engineers in electronics industries. *Human Resource Management Journal,* 4(3): 22–40.

Landman, T., & Robinson, N. (eds). 2009. *The SAGE Handbook of Comparative Politics.* Los Angeles, CA: SAGE.

Larsen, H.H., & Mayrhofer, W. 2006. European HRM: On the road again. In H.H. Larsen and W. Mayrhofer (eds), *Managing Human Resources in Europe: A Thematic Approach:* 259–270. London: Routledge.

Lebow, R.N., & Lichbach, M.I. (eds). 2007. *Theory and Evidence in Comparative Politics and International Relations.* New York: Palgrave Macmillan.

Legge, K. 2005. *Human Resource Management: Rhetorics and Realities.* Basingstoke: Palgrave Macmillan.

Li, J. 2012. *Cultural Foundations of Learning: East and West.* Cambridge: Cambridge University Press.

Liamputtong, P. 2010. *Performing Qualitative Cross-Cultural Research.* Cambridge: Cambridge University Press.

Loucks, W.N., & Hoot, J.W. 1938. *Comparative Economic Systems: Capitalism, Socialism, Communism, Fascism, Cooperation.* New York: Harper & Brothers.

Lowe, K.B., Milliman, J., De Cieri, H., & Dowling, P.J. 2002. International compensation practices: A ten-country comparative analysis. *Human Resource Management,* 41(1): 45–66.

Lynch, C., & Danely, J. (eds). 2013. *Transitions and Transformations: Cultural Perspectives on Aging and the Life Course.* New York: Berghahn.

Maurice, M. 1989. Méthode comparative et analyse sociétale: les implications théoriques des comparaisons internationales. *Sociologie du travail,* 31(2): 175–191.

Mayrhofer, W. 1998. Between market, bureaucracy, and clan – coordination and control mechanisms in the Cranfield Network on European Human Resource Management (Cranet-E). *Journal of Managerial Psychology,* 13(3/4): 241–258.

Mayrhofer, W. 2007. European comparative management research: Towards a research agenda. *European Journal of International Management,* 1(3): 191–205.

Mayrhofer, W., & Reichel, A. 2009. Comparative analysis of HR. In P.R. Sparrow (ed.), *Handbook of International Human Resource Management: Integrating People, Process, and Context:* 41–62. Chichester: Wiley.

Minbaeva, D., Pedersen, T., Björkman, I., et al. 2014. MNC knowledge transfer, subsidiary absorptive capacity and HRM. *Journal of International Business Studies,* 45(1): 38–51.

Minkov, M. 2011. *Cultural Differences in a Globalizing World.* Bingley: Emerald.

Molloy, J.C., & Ployhart, R.E. 2012. Construct clarity: Multidisciplinary considerations and an illustration using human capital. *Human Resource Management Review,* 22(2): 152–156.

Montias, J.M., Ben-Ner, A., & Neuberger, E. 1993. *Comparative Economics.* Chur: Harwood Academic Publishers.

Moran, R.T., Harris, P.R., & Moran, S.V. 2011. *Managing Cultural Differences: Global Leadership Strategies for Cross-Cultural Business Success* (8th edn). Oxford: Butterworth-Heinemann.

Noah, H.J., & Eckstein, M.A. 1969. *Toward a Science of Comparative Education.* New York: Macmillan.

North, D.C. 1990. *Institutions, Institutional Change and Economic Performance.* Cambridge: Cambridge University Press.

Örücü, E., & Nelken, D. 2007. *Comparative Law: A Handbook.* Oxford: Hart.

Paauwe, J. 2004. *HRM and Performance: Achieving Long Term Viability.* Oxford: Oxford University Press.

Pascal, B. 1671. *Pensées de M. Pascal sur la religion et sur quelques autres sujets* (3rd edn). Paris: Guillaume Desprez.

Peterson, M.F. 2001. International collaboration in organizational behavior research. *Journal of Organizational Behavior,* 22: 59–81.

Psychogios, A., & Wood, G.T. 2010. Human resource management in comparative perspective: Alternative institutional perspectives and empirical reality. *International Journal of Human Resource Management,* 21(4): 2614–2630.

Rogers, M.A.M. 2014. *Comparative Effectiveness Research.* New York: Oxford University Press.

Rönnmar, M. (ed.). 2008. *EU Industrial Relations v. National Industrial Relations: Comparative and Interdisciplinary Perspectives.* Austin, TX: Wolters Kluwer Law & Business.

Rosenzweig, P.M., & Nohria, N. 1994. Influences on human resource management practices in multinational corporations. *Journal of International Business Studies,* 25(2): 229–251.

Rosser, J.B., & Rosser, M.V. 2004. *Comparative Economics in a Transforming World Economy* (2nd edn). Cambridge, MA: MIT Press.

Rugman, A.M., & Verbeke, A. 2001. Subsidiary-specific advantages in multinational enterprises. *Strategic Management Journal,* 22(3): 237–250.

Salais, R., & Storper, M. 1993. *Les Mondes du Production: Enquête sur l'Identité Économique de la France*. Paris: EHESS.

Schappi, J.V. (ed.). 1984. Comparative industrial relations: A Trans-Atlantic dialogue. *Proceedings of the First Oxford University/BNA Symposium*, Merton College, University of Oxford, 3–17 August 1983. Oxford: Bureau of National Affairs, Oxford University, Dept. of External Studies.

Schmidt-Catran, A.W., & Fairbrother, M. 2016. The random effects in multilevel models: Getting them wrong and getting them right. *European Sociological Review*, 32(1): 23–38.

Schmorrow, D., & Nicholson, D. (eds). 2011. *Advances in Cross-Cultural Decision Making*. Boca Raton, FL: CRC Press.

Slangen, A.H.L., & Beugelsdijk, S. 2010. The impact of instituional hazards on foreign multinational activity: A contingency perspective. *Journal of International Business Studies*, 41: 980–1057.

Sorrentino, R.M., & Yamaguchi, S. (eds). 2008. *Handbook of Motivation and Cognition across Cultures*. San Diego, CA: Academic.

Storper, M., & Salais, R. 1997. *Worlds of Production*. Cambridge, MA, USA and London, UK: Harvard University Press.

Strauss, J.P., & Connerley, M.L. 2003. Demographics, personality, contact, and universal-diverse orientation: An exploratory analysis. *Human Resource Management*, 42(2): 159–174.

Suchman, M.C. 1995. Managing legitimacy: Strategic and institutional approaches. *Academy of Management Review*, 20(3): 571–610.

Tausczik, Y.R., & Pennebaker, J.W. 2010. The psychological meaning of words: LIWC and computerized text analysis methods. *Journal of Language and Social Psychology*, 29(1): 24–54.

Thelen, K. 2014. *Varieties of Liberalization and the New Politics of Social Solidarity*. Cambridge: Cambridge University Press.

Thornton, P.H., Ocasio, W., & Lounsbury, M. 2012. *The Institutional Logics Perspective: A New Approach to Culture, Structure and Process*. Oxford: Oxford University Press.

Vaiman, V., & Brewster, C. 2015. How far do cultural differences explain the differences between nations? Implications for HRM. *International Journal of Human Resource Management*, 26(2): 151–164.

Van de Vijver, F.J.R., Chasiotis, A., & Breugelmans, S.M. (eds). 2011. *Fundamental Questions in Cross-Cultural Psychology*. Cambridge: Cambridge University Press.

Van de Vijver, F.J.R., Hemert, D.A.v., & Poortinga, Y.H. (eds). 2008. *Multilevel Analysis of Individuals and Cultures*. New York: Lawrence Erlbaum Associates.

Volkmer, I. (ed.). 2012. *Handbook of Global Media Research*. Hoboken, NJ: Wiley-Blackwell.

Vries, M.S.d., Reddy, P.S., & Haque, M.S. (eds). 2008. *Improving Local Government: Outcomes of Comparative Research*. Basingstoke: Palgrave Macmillan.

Warner, M. (ed.). 2013. *Managing across Diverse Cultures in East Asia: Issues and Challenges in a Changing Globalized World*. London: Routledge.

Watson, T. 2004. HRM and critical social science analysis. *Journal of Management Studies*, 41(3): 447–467.

Whitley, R. 1992. Societies, firms and markets: The social structuring of business systems. In R. Whitley (ed.), *European Business Systems: Firms and Markets in Their National Contexts*: 5–45. London: SAGE.

Whitley, R. 1999. *Divergent Capitalisms: The Social Structuring and Change of Business Systems*. Oxford: Oxford University Press.

Wright, P.M. 2015. Rethinking 'contribution'. *Journal of Management*, 41(3): 765–768.

Wulf, C. 2013. *Anthropology: A Continental Perspective*. Chicago, IL: University of Chicago Press.

Index

Please note: HRM refers to Human Resource Management; CHRM refers to Comparative Human Resource Management; IHRM refers to International Human Resource Management; SIHRM refers to Strategic International Human Resource Management